EIGHT EDITION

Social
Problems
A Down-to-Earth Approach

James M. Henslin
Southern Illinois University, Edwardsville

Boston   New York   San Francisco
Mexico City   Montreal   Toronto   London   Madrid   Munich   Paris
Hong Kong   Singapore   Tokyo   Cape Town   Sydney

> For those yet to enter this scene not of their own making—
> may they live in a better world.

Executive Editor: Jeff Lasser
Associate Editor: Deb Hanlon
Series Editorial Assistant: Lauren Houlihan
Senior Marketing Manager: Kelly May
Editorial Production Service: Dusty Friedman (Nesbitt Graphics, Inc.)
Composition Buyer: Linda Cox
Manufacturing Buyer: Megan Cochran
Electronic Composition: Nesbitt Graphics, Inc.
Interior Design: Carol Somberg
Photo Researcher: Kate Cebik
Cover Administrator: Linda Knowles

For related titles and support materials, visit our online catalog at www.ablongman.com.

Copyright © 2008, 2006, 2003, 2000, 1996, 1994, 1990 by James M. Henslin.
Copyright © 1983 by James M. Henslin and Donald W. Light

All rights reserved. No part of the material protected by this copyright notice may be reproduced or utilized in any form or by any means, electronic or mechanical, including photocopying, recording, or by any information storage and retrieval system, without written permission from the copyright owner, James M. Henslin.

To obtain permission(s) to use material from this work, please submit a written request to the copyright holder, henslin@aol.com.

Between the time website information is gathered and then published, it is not unusual for some sites to have closed. Also, the transcription of URLs can result in typographical errors. The publisher would appreciate notification where these errors occur so that they may be corrected in subsequent editions.

ISBN 13: 978-0-205-50804-4   ISBN 10: 0-205-50804-9

Library of Congress Cataloging-in-Publication Data

Henslin, James M.
   Social problems : a down-to-earth approach / James M. Henslin. — 8th ed.
      p. cm.
   Includes bibliographical references and index.
   ISBN 978-0-205-50804-4 (alk. paper)
   1. Social problems. 2. Deviant behavior. 3. Equality. 4. Social change. 5. Symbolic interactionism.
   6. Functionalism (Social sciences) 7. United States—Social conditions—1980- I. Title.

   HM585.H45 2008
   361.1—dc22
                                    2007010844

Printed in the United States of America
10 9 8 7 6 5 4 3 2 RRD-OH 11 10 09 08

Credits appear on page 1, which constitutes an extension of the copyright page.

BRIEF CONTENTS

PART IV SOCIAL CHANGE AND MEGAPROBLEMS

CONTENTS

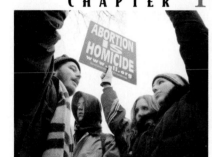

CHAPTER 7 Economic Problems: Wealth and Poverty 208

PART II Norm Violations in Social Context

CHAPTER 4 Alcohol and Other Drugs   **84**

CHAPTER 10 **Medical Care: Physical and Mental Illness**   318

PART IV Social Change and Megaproblems

CHAPTER **11** **The Changing Family**   **362**

CHAPTER **12** **Urban Problems**   **398**

CHAPTER 13 Population and Food   434

CHAPTER **14** **The Environmental Crisis** **472**

BOXED FEATURES

A Global Glimpse

A Global Glimpse

"WHAT'S A POOR FARMER TO DO?" HEROIN SUPPLIES FOREVER

Life is tough in Afghanistan, even outside the war-torn cities. Farmers barely eke out a living; their mud huts lack both electricity and running water.

Were it not for the poppies, they might not even have enough food for their children.

The lush poppy fields of the Afghan countryside bring the cash that allows farmers to survive, sometimes even enough to build a small house.

Why does Afghanistan produce three-fourths or more of the world's opium? First, growing poppies is a centuries-old custom. It's a part of the culture—the taken-for-granted, routine, normal part of life—of Afghan farmers. One of them, Ahmad Jan, said, "We will not abandon poppy cultivation until the end of this world." He thought about what he'd said for a moment, and then added, "if the government gives us something in return, we might stop" (Gall 2006).

Second, the farmers face a dilemma. For survival a mechanic must have machines to fix, or a teacher must have students to teach. And farmers must have crops to grow. In some places in Afghanistan, the land is salty, because it was reclaimed from the desert. Little grows on it, except the hardy poppy plant. Because there is so little rainfall, the farmers have to pump water for irrigation from wells about 300 feet deep. No one would survive growing wheat or melons.

Third, even the farmers who are lucky enough to have more productive land must confront the political situation. The central government of Afghanistan remains weak, and its control over the countryside is fragile. Here, tribal chiefs and private armies are still in control (Scherer 2003). If these local rulers tell farmers to grow poppies, how can they refuse?

In some areas, the Taliban is in control. The U.S. invasion after September 11 drove this political and religious group out of power in the cities, but it lives on in the more remote regions. For the Taliban, the poppy crop is a cash cow, and it even distributes leaflets ordering farmers to grow poppy. The Taliban takes opium production so seriously that its leaders provide armed protection for drug convoys and will battle government troops that dare to interfere with the drug smuggling (Gall 2006).

Even so, at the urging—and with the healthy payments—of Western nations, the central and regional governments do send out soldiers and police to eradicate poppy fields. But the police and soldiers are poor, and it doesn't take much to bribe them into either skipping some farmer's land or leaving part of the crop.

When one group of farmers had their poppy fields destroyed, they figured that this was the cost of having a new government that was bringing them peace. When they learned that the farmers in a neighboring village had bribed the police to not destroy their crops, they felt indignant. "What kind of government is this?" they asked. When Alam, one of these farmers, was interviewed, he said, "Of course I will plant poppy! And if our neighbors give bribes to the police again, then we'll just give bribes that are three times as high. We understand the system now." (Aizenman 2005)

Despite these obstacles, the West remains determined to get rid of the poppy fields. Western governments continue to pump hundreds of millions of dollars into Afghanistan.

Not only do they try to eradicate the crop, but they also try to train farmers to grow fruit trees and plant vineyards instead of poppy fields. In a culture where the government is thought of as an illegitimate force, officials fight a losing battle. One farmer said that he does go along with the Western-financed program to grow alternative crops, but only to a certain extent. If he doesn't grow poppy on at least some of his land, the other villagers will accuse him of working for the government.

And how the West's plans can backfire! When the British government, which is leading the international efforts to combat Afghan drugs, offered farmers money to destroy their poppy crops, the word spread quickly. Many farmers rushed home to plant more poppies. Why not, since the British government was going to guarantee the price? When the British cash didn't arrive, the farmers harvested their poppies, giving the drug dealers a boom crop to turn into heroin (North 2004).

FOR YOUR CONSIDERATION

Why is it unlikely that the poppy fields of Afghanistan will be eradicated? In addition to the scenario just outlined, keep yet another factor in mind: The situation is like a balloon. Squeeze one end, and the balloon expands on the other end. If eradication programs reduce crops in one area, crops increase in another region—or even in an adjacent country. Given what you have read here, what solutions would you suggest to stop heroin? Or would you support the legalization of heroin? Or something else entirely?

Issues in Social Problems

Issues in Social Problems

WHAT DOES DAY CARE COST A COMPANY?

Suppose that you are the president of Union Bank in Monterey, California. Some of your employees have asked you to provide a day care center. You would like to do so, but you can't spend stockholders' money on day care simply because you think it is a nice idea. You are accountable for the performance of your stock, and you have to know the bottom line.

"Find out what it would cost us to have a day care center," the manager told Sandra Burud, a social science researcher. At first, determining costs may sound fairly easy. You simply add the cost of the facilities and personnel, and you have the answer. But what you want to know is the net cost. After all, day care is supposed to benefit the company. Will the benefits be greater or less than the cost? How much in either direction?

Now the problem becomes difficult. How can you accurately estimate changes that the day care center will make in employee turnover? This, in turn, will change interview costs, hiring bonuses, and job advertisements. Then, too, you have to try to measure the productive time that will be lost while an employee is on maternity leave or is job hunting, while a job goes unfilled, or while a new employee is learning the ropes. Employee turnover is costly: Merck Pharmaceuticals has determined that during their first fourteen months on the job new employees cost the company five months of work. Some costs are impossible to measure, such as poor morale and loss of reputation with the community if a lot of employees quit. In fact, Burud decided that she couldn't put numbers on these variables and had to skip them.

In the midst of such uncertainties, Union Bank decided to go ahead and open a day care center. This cost the bank $105,000. Then Burud compared 87 employees who used the center with a control group of 105 employees who didn't use the center. She found that employee turnover among the center's users was 2 percent; among the control group, it was 10 percent. Employees who used the center were also absent an average of two days a year less than the control group. Their maternity leaves were also one week shorter. The bottom line? After subtracting its costs of running the day care center, the bank saved $232,000.

Should you, the president, have your bank open a day care center? Now, that is an easy decision.

Such companies as Marriott Hotels have paid attention to the bottom-line results of corporate day care and have opened their own centers. Other companies, such as Levi Strauss and AT&T, subsidize employees' child care.

Based on Solomon 1988; Shellenbarger 1994.

Technology and Social Problems

Technology and Social Problems
HOW TO GET PAID TO POLLUTE: CORPORATE WELFARE AND BIG WELFARE BUCKS

Welfare is one of the most controversial topics in the United States. It arouses the ire of wealthy and middle-class Americans, who view the poor who collect welfare as parasites. But have you heard about *corporate welfare*?

Corporate welfare refers to handouts given to corporations. A state may reduce a company's taxes if it will locate within the state or remain if it has threatened to leave. A state may even provide land and factories at bargain prices. The reason: jobs.

Corporate welfare even goes to companies that foul the land, water, and air. Borden Chemicals in Louisiana has buried hazardous wastes without a permit and released clouds of hazardous chemicals so thick that to protect drivers, the police have sometimes had to shut down the highway that runs near the plant. Borden even contaminated the groundwater beneath its plant, threatening the aquifer that provides drinking water for residents of Louisiana and Texas.

Near Baton Rouge, Louisiana.

to help get started was Shell Oil Company, which had $140 million slashed from its taxes (Bartlett and Steele 1998). Then there were a few other mom-and-pop operations: International Paper, Dow Chemical, Union Carbide, Boise Cascade, Georgia Pacific, and another tiny one called Procter & Gamble.

Of course, you can always improve welfare programs. Can you imagine what a welfare program would be like if the recipients of welfare got the chance to design them? You can be certain

Thinking Critically About Social Problems

THINKING CRITICALLY About Social Problems
CAN A PLANE RIDE CHANGE YOUR RACE?

According to common sense, the title of this box is nonsense—our racial classifications represent biological differences. Sociologists, in contrast, stress that what we call races are *social* classifications, not biological categories.

Sociologists point out that our "race" depends more on the society in which we live than on our biological characteristics. For example, the racial categories that are common in the United States are merely one of *numerous* ways by which people around the world classify physical appearances. Although groups around the world use different categories, each group assumes that its categories are natural, merely a logical response to visible physical differences.

To better understand this essential sociological point—that race is more social than it is biological—consider this: In the United States, children who are born to the same parents are all of the same race. I am sure that you are thinking, "What could be more natural?" This is the common view of Americans. But in Brazil, children who are born to the same parents can be of different races—if their appearances differ. "What could be more natural?" assume Brazilians.

Consider how Americans usually classify a child who has a "black" mother and a "white" father. Why do they usually say that the child is "black"? Wouldn't it be equally logical to classify the child as "white"? Similarly, if a child's grandmother is "black" but all her other ancestors are "white," the child is often considered "black." Yet she has much more "white blood" than "black blood." Why, then, is she considered "black"? Certainly not because of biology. Rather, such thinking is a legacy of slavery. Before the Civil War, numerous children were born whose fathers were white slave masters and whose mothers were black slaves. In an attempt to preserve the "purity" of

What "race" are this mother and her daughter?

their "race," whites classified anyone with even a "drop of black blood" as "not white."

Race is so social—and fluid—that even a plane ride can change a person's race. In the city of Salvador in Brazil, people classify one another by the color of their skin and eyes, the breadth of their nose and lips, and the color and curliness of their hair. They use at least seven terms for what we call white and black. Consider again a U.S. child who has one "white" and one "black" parent. Although she is "black" in the United States, if she flies to Brazil, she will belong to one of their several "whiter" categories (Fish 1995).

On the flight just mentioned, did the girl's "race" actually change? Our common sense revolts at this, I know, but it actually did. We want to argue that because her biological characteristics remain unchanged, her race remains unchanged. This is because we think of race as biological, *when race is actually a label we use to describe perceived biological characteristics.* Simply put, the race we "are" depends on where we are—on who is doing the classifying.

"Racial" classifications are so fluid, not fixed, that you can see change occurring even now. In the United States, we recently began to use the term "multiracial." This new category indicates changing thought about race, a change picked up by the new classification on U.S. census forms, "two or more races."

FOR YOUR CONSIDERATION
How would you explain to "Joe Six-Pack" the sociological point that race is more a social classification than a biological one? Can you come up with any arguments to refute this view? How do you think our racial-ethnic categories will change in the future?

Spotlight on Social Research

Spotlight on Social Research
STUDYING VIOLENCE AMONG "THE LIONS"

When she was a graduate student at the University of Chicago, RUTH HOROWITZ *(now Professor of Sociology at New York University) did a participant observation study of young people in a Chicano community in Chicago. Her purpose was not to understand violence, but to understand poverty. She wanted to see how the explanations of poverty that sociologists had developed matched what she observed in "real life."*

Two major explanations of poverty did apply. Violence had been part of the culture they had learned, and a lack of opportunities did contribute to a sense of being left out. But there was more to it. Actual violence depended on how the "Lions" defined a particular situation. As sociologists phrase this: Violence was situational and constructed interactionally.

these women went on to college; others became pregnant and married. The life experience of siblings varied, too; some went to school and became white-collar workers, while others ran afoul of the legal system and went to prison.

When I first began my research, the "Lions" were 15 to 17 years old, had guns, and did a lot of fighting. Some had after-school jobs and dressed in tuxedos for *quinceaneras* and weddings. In the streets, these same young men had developed a reputation for being tougher than other gangs. They would even seek opportunities to challenge others. At home and during most parties, in contrast, they were polite and conformed to strict rules of etiquette.

For seven years, I did participant observation with these youths. When I returned after a three-year absence, many of the "Lions" were still hanging out together, but quite a few were working, had married, and had children. A few of the gang members attended college, and others remained in the street. One had been killed in a drug deal gone wrong. A major change was their relationship to violence. Instead of provoking incidents, now they responded only when someone challenged their reputations.

The two models of poverty did apply. Violence had

Two major explanations of poverty and the social structure of poverty. According to the culture of poverty, poor people have different values than the middle class, and this is why they act as they do. According to the social structural perspective, the poor act as they do because, unlike middle-class people, they do not have the same opportunities to attend good schools or to obtain good jobs. Consequently, the poor turn to illegal opportunities, and crime becomes part of their life.

One afternoon, a month after I met the "Lions" gang and shook hands with all of them in the park, several 16-year-old young women introduced themselves. They asked me several questions about myself, and they were able to give me a definition of sociology. They told me about school and their trips around the city. Several of

It is a pleasure to see this text go into its eighth edition, and to welcome Allyn and Bacon as its publisher. Doing the revisions for this edition was a demanding task, but it was also enormously gratifying. I have tried to analyze the latest research and the social trends that give direction to social problems. I trust that your students will react positively to this text, that it will be a source of provocative discussions of the major issues that face the country, and that the ideas presented here can become a foundation for students for viewing social life.

As in earlier editions, I have kept the focus on both theory and research. Adopters have commented that they appreciate how consistently I apply sociological theories to social problems, and that the theories are presented clearly, making them easy for students to understand. In addition, I have expanded the emphasis on the *social* nature of social problems—how objective concerns are essential in developing a social problem. This theoretical framing is especially significant for students. As the students go through life, the specific facts of social problems are going to change, but from this course they can take with them a sociological framework for interpreting the changing conditions of society.

Spotlight on Social Research

This edition maintains the feature called *Spotlight on Social Research*. In this feature, researchers on social problems share with students a sort of insider's perspective. The researchers explain how they became interested in a particular social problem and how they did their research. As they do so, they take students "into the field" with them, letting students look over their shoulders as they face and solve problems in doing research.

The authors of this boxed feature are:

Phyllis Moen: Discovering that the elderly are "young people who got old," Chapter 2

Edward Laumann: Studying human sexuality—and the stigma that comes from this research, Chapter 3

James A. Inciardi: Learning about prescription drug abuse in the club culture of Miami, Chapter 4

Ruth Horowitz: Getting an insider's perspective on Chicano gangs, Chapter 5

William Chambliss: Discussing his personal journey into sociology, Chapter 6

Herbert Gans: Doing research on the exploitation of people in poverty, Chapter 7

Nazli Kibria: Studying the identity problems of Asian Americans, Chapter 8

Rafael Ezekiel: Studying neo-Nazis and Klans, Chapter 8

Kirsten Dellinger: Exploring the meanings of sexual harassment, Chapter 9

William Cockerham: Solving a medical mystery, Deaths in Russia, Chapter 10

Kathleen Ferraro: Gaining an insider's view of intimate violence, Chapter 11

Eli Anderson: Doing research in the inner city, Chapter 12

Carl Haub: Doing research on population and food, Chapter 13

Robert Gottlieb: Discovering changing meanings of the environment, Chapter 14

Morten Ender: Studying the military as an "embedded" sociologist, Chapter 15

Scope and Coverage of the Eighth Edition

Social Problems is an enjoyable course to teach, and many students find it to be the most exciting course in sociology. Certainly the topics are fascinating, ranging from such controversial matters as prostitution and pornography to such deeply embedded problems as racism, poverty, and gender. Some of the issues are intensely personal, such as abortion, suicide, and being the victim of violent crime; others, such as war and the loss of jobs, center on global stratification and the globalization of capitalism. All are significant, but especially vital for our present and for our future are the changing relationships of power among the nation-states of the world.

For students, the benefits of this course are similarly wide-ranging. Not only do they gain a sociological understanding of social problems, but also they are able to explore—and evaluate—their own opinions about specific social problems. As the course progresses, they are also able to attain greater awareness of the social forces that shape their orientations to social problems and their perspectives on social life. The ideas in this book, then, can penetrate students' thinking and give shape to their views of the world.

The Sociological Task: The Goal of Objectivity

This process of insight and self-discovery—so essential to good sociology and to good teaching—is one of the most rewarding aspects of teaching Social Problems. But teaching this class presents a special challenge, for it requires objectivity in the midst of deep controversy. In this text, I have tried to present both sides of issues fairly and objectively. I have no hidden agenda, no axes to grind. I know, of course, that it is impossible to achieve total objectivity, no matter how ardently it may be desired or pursued, but I think that objectivity should be the hallmark of Social Problems, and I have tried to attain it. The most obvious example is found in Chapter 1, where I use abortion as the substantive issue to illustrate basic sociological principles. Beginning with this topic jump-starts the course, placing us squarely in the midst of one of the most debated and heated issues in U.S. society. It also brings deep-seated attitudes to the surface. Used creatively, this approach allows us to illustrate the social origin of ideas, which is so essential to understanding social problems.

If I have been successful in my efforts, both students and instructors who are on the extreme opposite ends of this issue—those who favor abortion on demand and those who oppose abortion under any circumstances—should feel that their position is represented fairly. They also will likely feel that I have somehow represented the other side too favorably. To check whether I succeeded in attaining objectivity in this controversial matter, I sent this first chapter to national officers of both pro-choice and right to life organizations and asked for their comments. *Both sides* responded that I had been "trapped" into being too fair to the other side. I also asked my classes, after they had read the chapter, where they thought I stood on abortion. I was astonished—and pleased—when half replied that I was pro-choice and half that I was right to life.

The goal of this text, then, is to present objectively the major research findings on social problems, to explain their theoretical interpretations, and to describe clearly the underlying assumptions and implications of competing points of view. In endeavoring to reach this goal, I have strived to present the best of the sociology of social problems and to introduce competing views fairly. To again use Chapter 1 as an illustration: I use the terms *proabortion* and *antiabortion,* which, though far from perfect, are more neutrally descriptive than those preferred by proponents of either position—*prochoice* and *freedom of choice,* on one hand, and *prolife* and *right to life* on the other. While not everyone will be happy with my choice of terms—and they certainly cannot do justice to the many nuances and positions inherent in both sides of this crucial issue—I feel that they are the more neutral and objective labels.

If I have been successful, readers should find themselves content when they encounter views with which they are in agreement and uncomfortable as they confront those with which they disagree. This should hold true for readers of all persuasions, whether "radical," "liberal," "conservative"—or any other label currently in fashion. It should also make for an exciting class.

Incorporating Theory into the Text

For students, the word theory is often a frightening term. This is because they find theories to be vague, abstract, and difficult to understand. This is far from necessary.

Theories can be easy to understand—even enjoyable—*if* they are presented in the right way. Students and instructors alike have reacted favorably to the ways in which sociological theories are presented in this text. One of the main reasons for this favorable reaction is because I embed the theories in clarifying contexts. For example, when I introduce the three basic theories in Chapter 2—symbolic interaction theory, functional theory, and conflict theory—I make them concrete by applying each to problems that the elderly confront. This puts a face on the theories.

In the following chapters, I consistently apply these theories to *each* social problem. This approach helps give students a cohesive understanding of what otherwise might appear to be a disparate collection of problematic events and issues. The effect is cumulative, for each new chapter allows students to broaden their understanding of these perspectives. As one reviewer said, most texts in social problems simply mention theory in an initial chapter and then dispense with it thereafter, whereas this text follows through with the "theoretical promise" of its introductory chapters. The single exception to applying each theory to each social problem is Chapter 3. Because I treat three social problems in this chapter, and because at this point students are becoming familiar with these theories, it is more effective to apply a single theory in greater detail to each of these social problems.

Chapter Organization and Features

A major impediment to learning is the seemingly whimsical way in which authors of textbooks present social problems. In the typical case, the analysis is jumbled—the order differs markedly from one chapter to the next, with no regularity of structure. To overcome this, I utilize a consistent structure within the chapters. This gives students a "road map" to guide them through each social problem, letting them know what to expect in each chapter. After the first three chapters, I use the following framework to analyze each social problem:

Opening Vignette Intended to arouse student interest in the social problem and to stimulate the desire to read more, this brief opening story presents essential elements of the social problem.

The Problem in Sociological Perspective By presenting a broad sociological background, we set the stage for understanding the social problem.

The Scope of the Problem This section presents basic data on the extent or severity of the problem. It allows students to grasp the problem's wider ramifications.

Looking at the Problem Theoretically Here I present a theoretical analysis of the problem or some major aspect of it. I consistently begin on the more personal level, with symbolic interaction theory, move from there to functional theory, and conclude with the perspective of conflict theory.

Research Findings Discussed here are both current and classic sociological studies—and, where relevant, studies from other academic disciplines as well. To allow students to become more familiar with primary research, I present many sociological studies in detail. In addition, the feature written by researchers themselves, *Spotlight on Research,* helps students understand how the researcher's personal background leads to interest in a social problem and how research on social problems is actually done.

Social Policy This section focuses on actions that have been taken or could be taken to try to solve the social problem. I often spell out the assumptions on which these policies are based and the dilemmas that they create.

The Future of the Problem Because students want to know what lies ahead of them in life, I conclude with an overview of the direction that the problem is likely to take, given what we now know about the problem's dimensions and trends.

Summary and Review To reinforce what the students are learning, I provide a succinct point-by-point summary of the main ideas in the chapter. Students also find this summary helpful for review purposes, especially in preparing for tests. Some students also find it useful as a preview of the chapter, reading the summary before they read the chapter.

Key Terms When a term first appears in the text, it is set in bold type and is defined in context. Key terms are also listed and defined at the end of each chapter.

Thinking Critically About the Chapter At the end of each chapter are several questions designed to help students evaluate what they have read. These questions also lend themselves well for stimulating class discussions.

New in This Edition

To analyze social problems is to be on the cutting edge of society. Since social problems are ever changing, taking different forms as they wind their way through society or as various groups react to them, this new edition has numerous new topics. Here are some of them:

- "alcopops" and the increase in drinking by women
- merging birth rates of African American and white women, Figure 13-11
- the world's first licensed brothel for female clients
- cannabis dependence
- cesarean deliveries as a social issue among feminists.
- child support payments, Figure 7-9
- circumcised women and their support for circumcision, Figure 9-1
- living arrangements of the elderly, Figure 11-12
- environment: moral issues of the environment—and global solutions
- faith-based social programs
- news analysis about the coming collapse of the world's fishing grounds
- gangs: global aspects of urban youth
- genetically modified foods and the transatlantic quarrel
- honor killings
- immigrants and culture conflict in France
- London bus bombings
- Madrid train bombings
- meth addiction
- migration: global upheaval and the demographic transition
  - murder and rape, new international statistics from UN
  - Native Americans and forced, off-reservation boarding schools
  - online child pornography
  - public housing, new experiment on low-rise, mixed-income housing
  - race-ethnicity: level of education, from grade school to the doctorate, Table 8-3
  - race-ethnicity: Michigan constitution, banning racial-ethnic (and gender) preferences
  - rape in Islamic countries, why the reported rates are so low
  - rape, its decrease in the United States
  - recidivism, new study of 272,000 former prisoners
  - robots to care for residents of nursing homes in Japan
  - Russia's membership in the WTO
  - sexual slavery in prisons
  - terrorism: Gadhafi, renouncing terrorism for Libya
  - white-collar crime: Sara Lee and listeria deaths
  - women legislators: percentage across the nation, Figure 9-3

I have also included these new boxes for this edition:

CHAPTER 2

Spotlight on Social Research: Studying Young People Who Became Old

Keeping references up to date is critical to a revision; all new references are printed in blue in the end-of-book bibliography.

Suggestions for Using This Text

Authors of social problems texts, as well as those who teach this course, must decide whether they want to begin with the more "micro" or the more "macro" problems. Each approach is popular, and each has much to commend it. In my own teaching, I prefer to begin at the micro level. I begin by focusing on problems of personal concern to students—issues about which they are already curious and have questions they want answered. In my experience, this approach provides a compelling context for helping students become familiar with the sociological perspective and sociological theory. From there, I move to an examination of broader social problems, those whose more apparent connections to global events often make them seem more remote to students.

This is nothing more than a preference, and it is as equally logical to begin with problems that involve large-scale social change and then to wrap up the course with a focus on more individualistic problems. Instructors who wish to begin with the more macro problems can simply move Part II of this text to the end of their course. Nothing else will be affected.

Because this book is written for students, I have resisted the urge to insert qualifying footnotes, the kind that read: "A fuller amplification of this position would include reference to the works of so-and-so," or "This theoretical position is really much more complex than I can describe here, but because of lack of space. . . ." Such qualifiers are directed to a professional audience, and though they might serve to fend off some potential attack on the work, such "disclaimers" do not benefit students.

Invitation for You to Respond

This text flows from years of teaching the basic course in social problems. Especially formative have been the reactions of my students, who questioned and reconsidered their views of social problems. This text also incorporates feedback that instructors have graciously shared. I have designed the book to help make your course more successful—so it would both challenge students' thinking and make the sociological perspective clear and readily understandable. As we all know, results count, however, not intentions. What matters, then, is how this text actually works in your classroom. Consequently, I would greatly appreciate your feedback—whether positive or negative. Because your reactions are based on your own classroom experience, I will find them useful. My e-mail address is *Henslin@aol.com*

Acknowledgments

Finally, as is the custom in prefatory rituals, I want to acknowledge the contributions of others to this book. My heartfelt appreciation goes to Jeff Lasser, who succeeded in transferring this book to Allyn & Bacon from its previous publisher; to Jenn Albanese, who provided research materials; to Joan Pendleton, for editing; to Kate Cebik, for photo research; to Judy Fiske, who oversaw production; and to Dusty Friedman, who coordinated the production process. I also want to thank Kelly May for her expertise and Carol Somberg for our new design.

Reviewers of the seventh edition:

Sandra Emory, *Pensacola Junior College*

Michael W. Flota, *Daytona Beach Community College*

Victor M. Kogan, *Saint Martin's University*

Mark Miller, *East Texas Baptist University*

Daniel M. Roddick, *Rio Hondo College*

Annette M. Schwabe, *Florida State University*

Reviewers of previous editions:

Gary Burbridge, *Grand Rapids Community College*

Carole A. Campbell, *California State University—Long Beach*

Cheryl Childers, *Washburn University*

Susan Claxton, *Floyd College*

Al Cook, *Trinity Valley Community College*

David D. Friedrichs, *University of Scranton*

Michele Gigliotti, *Broward Community College*

Rosalind Gottfried, *San Joaquin Delta College*

Charles Hall, *Purdue University*

Carl M. Hand, *Valdosta State University*

Rosa Haritos, *University of North Carolina at Chapel Hill*

Rachel Ivie, *South Plains College*

Cardell Jacobson, *Brigham Young University*

Joseph F. Jones, *Portland State University*

Victor M. Kogan, *Saint Martin's College*

Muketiwa Wilbrod Madzura, *Normandale Community College*

Paul Magee, *North Lake College*

Marguerite Marin, *Gonzaga University*

John Mitrano, *Central Connecticut State University*

Sharon Erickson Nepstad, *University of Colorado—Boulder*

Kevin R. Ousley, *East Carolina University*

Dennis L. Peck, *The University of Alabama*

Richard P. Rettig, *University of Central Oklahoma*

Barbara L. Richardson, *Eastern Michigan University*

Edwin Rosenberg, *Appalachian State University*

James P. Sikora, *Illinois Wesleyan University*

K. S. Thompson, *Northern Michigan University*

Richard T. Vick, *Idaho State University*

Finally, my heartfelt best wishes to both instructors and students. I hope that this text provides understanding and insight into the major problems facing our country, many of which have global ramifications—and all of which have an impact on our own lives.

May our children live in a better world!

James M. Henslin, Professor Emeritus
Department of Sociology
Southern Illinois University, Edwardsville

I welcome your correspondence. E-mail is the best way to reach me: henslin@aol.com

A NOTE FROM THE PUBLISHER ON SUPPLEMENTS

Instructor's Supplements

Instructor's Manual

For each chapter in the text, the Instructor's Manual provides a list of key changes to the new edition, chapter summaries and outlines, learning objectives, key terms and people, classroom activities, discussion topics, recommended films, Web sites, and additional references. Adopters can request a print copy or download the electronic file by logging in to our Instructor Resource Center, at **www.ablongman.com/irc**.

Test Bank

The test bank contains approximately 1500 questions per chapter including multiple choice, true/false, short answer, essay, and open-book formats. All questions are labeled and scaled according to Bloom's Taxonomy. Adopters can request a print copy or download the electronic file by logging in to our Instructor Resource Center, at www.ablongman.com/irc.

Computerized Test Bank

The printed Test Bank is also available through Allyn and Bacon's computerized testing system. This fully networkable test-generating software is available on a multiplatform CD-ROM for Windows and Macintosh. The user-friendly interface allows you to view, edit, and add questions, transfer questions to tests, and print tests in a variety of fonts. Search and sort features allow you to locate questions quickly and to arrange them in whatever order you prefer. Adopters can request a copy on CD or download the electronic file by logging in to our Instructor Resource Center, at www.ablongman.com/irc.

PowerPoint™ Presentation

These PowerPoint slides feature lecture outlines for every chapter and corresponding artwork from the text. PowerPoint software is not required, as a PowerPoint viewer is included. Available on request at no additional cost to adopters. Available online from our Instructor Resource Center, at www.ablongman.com/irc.

The Sociology Digital Media Archive IV

This CD-ROM contains hundreds of graphs, charts, and maps that you can use to build PowerPoint slides to supplement your lectures and illustrate key sociological concepts. If you have full multimedia capability, you can use the DMA's video segments and links to sociology Web sites. Available on request to adopters.

Allyn and Bacon/ABC News Sociology Videos

If you like to use news footage and documentary-style programs to illustrate sociological themes, this series of videos contain programs from *Nightline, World News Tonight,* and *20/20.*

Each video has an accompanying User's Guide (available electronically). Available titles are *Poverty and Stratification, Race and Ethnicity, Gender, Deviance,* and *Aging.* Videocassettes are available on request to adopters.

The Video Professor: Applying Lessons in Sociology to Classic and Modern Films

ANTHONY W. ZUMPETTA, WEST CHESTER UNIVERSITY

This manual describes hundreds of commercially available videos that represent nineteen of the most important topics in introductory sociology textbooks. Each topic lists a number of movies, along with specific assignments and suggestions for class use. Adopters can request a print copy or download the electronic file by logging in to our Instructor Resource Center.

InterWrite PRS (Personal Response System)

Assess your students' progress with the Personal Response System—an easy-to-use wireless polling system that enables you to pose questions, record results, and display those results instantly in your classroom. Designed by teachers, for teachers, PRS is easy to integrate into your lectures:

- Each student uses a cell-phone-sized transmitter that they bring to class.
- You ask multiple-choice, numerical-answer, or matching questions during class; students simply click their answer into their transmitter.
- A classroom receiver (portable or mounted) connected to your computer tabulates all answers and displays them graphically in class.
- Results can be recorded for grading, attendance, or simply used as a discussion point.

Our partnership with PRS allows us to offer student rebate cards bundled with any Allyn & Bacon / Longman text. The rebate card is a direct value of $20.00 and can be redeemed with the purchase of a new PRS student transmitter. In addition, institutions that order 40 or more new textbook + rebate card bundles will receive the classroom receiver—a $250 value—software and support at no additional cost. Contact your Allyn & Bacon / Longman representative or visit http://www.ablongman.com/prs for more information.

Student Supplements

Study Guide

The Study Guide includes exercises, key terms, and lecture outlines that correspond to the PowerPoint presentation for this text. Practice test with 25 multiple-choice questions per chapter help students prepare for quizzes and exams. Packaged on request at no additional cost with this text.

Social Problems: Seeing the Social Context. Readings to Accompany : *Social Problems: A Down-to-Earth Approach*

JAMES M. HENSLIN

This brief reader contains one reading for each chapter of the text, chosen and introduced by James M. Henslin. The reader can be purchased separately at full price or packaged with this text for an additional $5 net to the bookstore. An Instructor's Manual for the reader is available electronically from our Instructor Resource Center, www.ablongman.com/irc.

Online Course Management
New! MySocKit

MySocKit is a book-specific online resource available on request with a MySocKit access code card packaged with the text. MySocLab for *Social Problems* 8/e features:

- Practice Tests for every chapter.
- Flash Cards for reviewing key terms and concepts.
- Video activities based on interviews with leading sociologists and streaming video footage from sources such as *Frontline*.
- Audio activities based on interviews and stories from the National Public Radio archives.
- "Sociology in the News"—recent articles from the *New York Times,* updated every 30 days.
- "Writing About Sociology"—a set of tutorials on topics such as working with sources, documentation style, outlining, formatting written assignments, avoiding plagiarism.
- Research Navigator—a searchable online database of full-text articles from hundreds of scholarly journals, plus popular newspapers and magazines such as the *New York Times* and *Newsweek.*

Additional Supplements

Research Navigator™

(ACCESS CODE REQUIRED)
This online research database is available at no additional cost to students when the text is packaged with a MySocLab Access Code Card, or the *Research Navigator Guide* for Sociology (see below). Searchable by keyword, it gives your students access to thousands of full-text articles from scholarly social science journals and popular magazines and newspapers included in the *ContentSelect Research Database,* as well as a one-year archive of *New York Times* articles.

ResearchNavigator.com Guide: Sociology

JOSEPH E. JACOBY, BOWLING GREEN STATE UNIVERSITY
This updated booklet includes tips, resources, and URLs to aid students conducting research on Pearson Education's research Web site, www.researchnavigator.com. The guide contains a student access code for the Research Navigator database, offering students unlimited access to a collection of more than 25,000 discipline specific articles from top-tier academic publications and peer-reviewed journals, as well as the *New York Times* and popular news publications. The guide introduces students to the basics of the Internet and the World Wide Web, and includes tips for searching for articles on the site, and a list of journals useful for research in their discipline. Also included are hundreds of web resources for the discipline, as well as information on how to correctly cite research. The guide is available packaged with new copies of the text.

Building Bridges: The Allyn and Bacon Guide to Service Learning

DORIS HAMNER
This manual offers practical advice for students who must complete a service-learning project as part of their required course work. Packaged on request at no additional cost with this text.

Careers in Sociology, Third Edition

W. RICHARD STEPHENS, EASTERN NAZARENE COLLEGE
This supplement explains how sociology can help students prepare for careers in such fields as law, gerontology, social work, business, and computers. It also examines how sociologists enter the field. Packaged on request at no additional cost with this text.

PHOTO CREDITS

Chapter 1: p. 2: © Jason Reed/Reuters/Corbis; p. 7: Amit Bhargava/ Corbis; p. 8: John Watney/Photo Researchers, Inc.; p. 13: © Matthew Cavanaugh/epa/Corbis; p. 17, left, © A. Ramey/PhotoEdit Inc.; p. 17, right, © Laima Druskis/Photo Researchers, Inc.; **Chapter 2:** p. 24: David Young-Wolff/PhotoEdit Inc.; p. 27: Reuters/Mian Khursheed/Landov; p. 29: Courtesy of Phyllis Moen; p. 31: A. Ramey/PhotoEdit Inc.; p. 33: AP Images/HO; p. 35, left, © Gary Salter/zefa/Corbis; p. 35, right, Blend Images/Alamy Royalty Free; p. 37: Yoshikazu Tsuno/AFP/Getty Images; p. 39: Jacob A Riis/Getty Images; p. 40: Brown Brothers p. 41: Pauline Lubens/Detroit Free Press Inc.; p. 44, left, © Josef Polleross/The Image Works; p. 44: right, Getty Images; p. 45: Mario Ruiz/Time Life Pictures/ Getty Images; **Chapter 3:** p. 48: © Edward Holub/Corbis; p. 53: Emily Baron/Sipa/GayBridge; p. 54: Spencer Platt/Getty Images; p. 55: © 2002 Marilyn Humphries/The Image Works; p. 57: Courtesy of Edward O. Laumann; p. 58: A. Ramey/PhotoEdit. Inc.; p. 61: The Bridgeman Art Library/Getty Images; p. 63: James M. Henslin; p. 64: Paul Simcock/The Image Bank/Getty Images; p. 66: Chung Sung-Jun/Getty Images; p. 68: © ND/Roger-Viollet/The Image Works; p. 69: Reuters/Paul Vreeker /Landov; p. 71: Frederic Neema/Gamma; p. 72: Rhoda Sidney/PhotoEdit, Inc.; p. 78: Mark Mellett/Stock Boston; p. 79: © Creasource/Corbis; p. 80: David McNew/Getty Image; p. 81: © National Pictures/Topham/The Image Works; p. 82: © various images GmbH & Co.KG/Alamy; **Chapter 4:** p. 84: David Young-Wolff/PhotoEdit, Inc.; p. 86: The Art Archive; p. 87, left, Getty Images Royalty Free; p. 87, right, Tony Freeman/PhotoEdit, Inc.; p. 91: © Bettmann/Corbis; p. 93: UPI Photo/Terry Schmitt/Landov; p. 94: George A. Hirliman Productions Inc./20th Century Fox/Photofest; p. 98: Courtesy of James A. Inciardi; p. 103: National Archives and Records Administration; p. 104: ©SSPL/The Image Works; p. 108: © Richard Levine/Alamy; p. 110, T: Owen Franken/Corbis/Bettmann; p. 110, B: Justin Sutcliffe/Polaris; p. 112: Ted Thai/Time Life Pictures/Getty Images; p. 113: Reuters/Str/Landov; p. 114: © Morton Beebe/Corbis; p. 115: Courtesy of Faces of Meth; p. 118: Levine Heidi/Sipa; p. 121: © The Courier-Journal; p. 123: Reuters/Tomas Bravo/Landov; p. 125: AP Images/Gary Kazanjian; **Chapter 5:** p. 130: Karen Moskowitz/Stone/Getty Images; p. 134: Alain Daussin/Photographer's Choice/Getty Images; p. 140: Courtesy of Ruth Horowitz; p. 142: Getty Images Royalty Free; p. 148: Deborah Davis/PhotoEdit, Inc.; p. 153: © Jeff Greenberg/The Image Works; p, 157: James M. Henslin; p. 160: © Houston Chronicle; **Chapter 6:** p. 164: © Bob Daemmrich/The Image Works; p. 168: A. Ramey/PhotoEdit, Inc; p. 169: AP Images/Post-Crescent, Mike DeSisti; p. 176: Parker & Hart/Creators Syndicate; p. 177: A. Ramey/PhotoEdit, Inc.; p. 178: Courtesy of William Cambliss; p. 182: Bryan Smith/ZUMA Press/ Newscom; p. 185: Carolyn Cole/Los Angeles Times Syndicate; p. 188: Tony Freeman/PhotoEdit, Inc.; p. 189: AP Images; p. 191: Interfoto USA/Sipa; p. 192: The Cartoon Bank/© The New Yorker Collection; p. 194: STR/ AFP/Getty Images; p. 196: Mike Simons/AFP/Getty Images; p. 199: A. Ramey/PhotoEdit, Inc.; p. 200: © Tony Kurdzuk/Star Ledger/Corbis; p. 201: © John Eastcott and Yva Momatiuk/Photo Researchers, Inc.; p. 203: © Bob Daemmrich/The Image Works; **Chapter 7:** p. 208: AP Images/Adam Nadel; p. 210, left, Brunei Department of Information via Getty Images; p. 210, right, Reuters/Rupak De Chowdhuri; p. 216: Park Street/PhotoEdit, Inc.; p. 221: © Noah Addis/Star Ledger/Corbis; p. 222: Courtesy of Herbert J. Gans; p. 223: David R. Frazier/Photo Researchers, Inc.; p. 225: Ebby May/Taxi/ Getty Images; p. 228: © Peter Turnley/Corbis; p. 229: © Margot Granitsas/ The Image Works; p. 234: James M. Henslin; p. 237: Original Artwork: Painting by Moses Soyer, Photo by MPI/Getty Images; p. 240: Stephen Chernin/Getty Images; **Chapter 8:** p. 244: AP Images/LM Otero; p. 248: The Granger Collection; p. 249: American Philosophical Society; p. 250: David Young-Wolff/PhotoEdit, Inc.; p. 252: Jim Cummins/Corbis; p. 254: Corbis Royalty Free; p. 255: Nazli Kibria; p. 256: William Thomas Cain/ Getty Images; p. 260: Courtesy of Rafael S. Ezekiel; p. 266: © Corbis; p. 267: Jill Johnson/KRP Photos/Newscom; p. 270: © Andrew Holbrooke/Corbis; p. 271: A. Ramey/PhotoEdit, Inc.; p. 272: © US National Archives/Roger-Viollet/The Image Works; p. 275: © Bettmann/Corbis; **Chapter 9:** p. 284:

© Bob Daemmrich/The Image Works; p. 287: Frederick M. Brown/Getty Images; p. 291: Kambou Sia/AFP/Getty Images; p. 293: Dan Bosler/ Photographer's Choices/Getty Images; p. 296: Courtesy of Steven Goldberg; p. 297: Courtesy of Cynthia Fuchs Epstein; p. 301: Dennis Van Tine/Landov; p. 303: Bill Aron/PhotoEdit, Inc.; p. 305: AP Images/Ed Betz; p. 309: Ezra Shaw/Getty Images; p. 311: © Tibor Bognar/Corbis; p. 312: Courtesy of Kirsten Dellinger; p. 313: Peter McBride/Aurora Photos; **Chapter 10:** p. 318: © Stockbyte Platinum/Alamy Royalty Free; p. 321: Reuters/Anthony P. Bolante /Landov; p. 322: © P. Ward/OSF/Animals Animals; p. 324: ONC/Wenn Photos/Newscom; p. 326, left, Mark Richards/PhotoEdit, Inc.; p. 326, right, © Tom Stewart/Corbis; p. 331: Darren McCollester/Newsmakers; p. 332: AP Image/Jacqueline Larma; p. 337: AP Images; p. 341: © Alex Hofford/epa/Corbis; p. 346, left, © Robin Nelson/PhotoEdit, Inc.; p. 346, right, CBS/Tony Esparza /Landov; p. 348: © David Bacon/The Image Works; p. 352: Aaron St. Clair/Splash News/Newscom; p. 353: AP Images/ Lauren Greenfield/VII; p. 355: William C. Cockerham; p. 356: STR/AFP/ Getty Images; p. 359: AP Images/Richard Sheinwald; **Chapter 11:** p. 362: Digital Vision/Getty Royalty Free; p. 364: © Lauren Goodsmith/The Image Works; p. 366: Bob Daemmrich/PhotoEdit Inc.; p. 371: © Peter Blakely/ Corbis Saba; p. 372: Richard B.Levine/Frances M. Roberts; p. 374: Reuters/Sukree Sukplang; p. 379: © SSPL/The Image Works; p. 383Courtesy of Kathleen Ferraro; p. 385: Jeff Greenberg/PhotoEdit, Inc.; p. 387: Pool/ Getty Images; p. 391: Adam Smith/Taxi/Getty Images; p. 396: Mark Richards/PhotoEdit, Inc.; **Chapter 12:** p. 398: © John Nordell/The Image Works; p. 404: © Sean Sprague/The Image Works; p. 406: Courtesy of Professor Elijah Anderson; p. 412: Angel Franco/The New York Times; p. 413: Tim Boyle/Getty Images; p. 415: © Journal-Courier/Steve Warmowski/ The Image Works; p. 417: © Jerome Sessini/In Visu/Corbis; p. 419, left, © Bettmann/Corbis; p. 419, right, © R. Duyos/Sun Sentinel/Corbis Sygma; p. 422: © Lee Snider/The Image Works; p. 429: © Lee Snider/The Image Works; p. 430: Chris Hondros/Newsmakers/Getty Images; p. 432, T: A. Ramey/PhotoEdit, Inc.; p. 432, B: Studio Daniel Libeskind; **Chapter 13:** p. 434: © Andrew Holbrooke/The Image Works; p. 439: © Karin Retief/Trace Images/Images Works; p. 440: Courtesy of Carl Haub; p. 444: Photo by Paula Bronstein/Getty Images; p. 446: Gabriel Jecan/Corbis/Bettmann; p. 450, left, © Finbarr O'Reilly/Reuters/Corbis; p. 450, right, AP Images/Eau Claire Leader-Telegram, Steve Kinderman; p. 452: © DPA/The Image Works; p. 455: Jack Kurtz/The Image Works; p. 458: Davis Barber/PhotoEdit, Inc.; p. 462: David Butow/Corbis/Bettmann; p. 466: Rhoda Sidney/PhotoEdit Inc.; p. 468: Christophe Simon/AFP/Getty Images; p. 469: Johner Images/Getty Images Royalty Free; **Chapter 14:** p. 472: © Julio Etchart/The Image Works; p. 474: Warren Morgan/Corbis/Bettmann; p. 476: China Photos/Getty Images; p. 478, left, Phil Gilham/Getty Images; p. 478, right, AP Images/ Denis Farrell; p. 479: © Corbis; p. 482: Sam Kittner/National Geographic/ Getty Images; p. 483: Alvaro De Levia/Liaison/Getty Images; p. 486: © Zoriah/ The Image Works; p. 493, left, © Jeff Greenberg/The Image Works; p. 493, right, © Rachel Epstein/The Image Works; p. 495: James M. Henslin; p. 497: AP Images/Walter Astrada; p. 500: © James Marshall/The Image Works; p. 503, left, Copyright © 1996 by Paul R. Ehrlich and Anne H. Ehrlich. Reproduced by permission of Island Press, Washington, D.C.; p. 503, right, Copyright © (1999) by Transaction Publishers. Reprinted by permission of the publisher.; p. 505: © Oxford Picture Library/Alamy; p. 507: © Tony Savino/The Image Works; p. 510: Scott Eells/The New York Times; p. 512: Courtesy Robert Gottlieb; p. 513: SVven Nackstrand/AFP/Getty Images; **Chapter 15:** p. 516: © Manuel H. de LeÛn/epa/Corbis; p. 519: © Topham/The Image Works; p. 524: © Mary Evans Picture Library/The Image Works; p. 527: Courtesy of Morten Ender; p. 531: © Archivo Iconografico, S.A./Corbis; p. 532: Corbis/Bettmann; p. 535: © Hulton-Deutsch Collection/Corbis; p. 539: © Thomas White/Reuters/Corbis; p. 541: © David Turnley/Corbis; p. 545: Rob Elliott/AFP/Getty Images; p. 548: James M. Henslin; p. 549: © Monika Graff/The Image Works; p. 553: © Chris Fitzgerald/The Image Works.

1

How Sociologists View Social Problems: The Abortion Dilemma

"But you don't understand! It's *not* a baby!" Lisa shouted once again. She felt desperate, at her wit's end. The argument with her grandmother seemed to have gone on forever.

With tears in her eyes, her grandmother said, "You don't know what you're doing, Lisa. You're taking the life of an innocent baby!"

"You're wrong! There's only one life involved here—mine!" replied Lisa. "It's *my* body and *my* life. I've worked too hard for that manager's job to let this pregnancy ruin everything."

"But Lisa, you have a new responsibility—to the baby."

> ## "But you don't understand! It's *not* a baby!"

"Don't judge my life by your standards. You never wanted a career. All you ever wanted was to raise a family."

"That's not the point," her grandmother pressed. "You're carrying a baby, and now you want to kill it."

"How can you talk like that? This is just a medical procedure—like when you had your gallstones taken out."

"I can't believe my own granddaughter is saying that butchering a baby is like taking out gallstones!"

Lisa and her grandmother looked at each other, knowing they were worlds apart. They both began to cry inside.

The Sociological Imagination

L ike Lisa and her grandmother, when we have problems, we usually see them in highly personal—and often emotional—terms. Our perspective is limited primarily to our immediate situation, and without a sociological imagination we fail to see the broader context in which our problems arise. Because we seldom connect our personal lives with the larger social context, like Lisa and her grandmother, we tend to blame ourselves and one another for our troubles.

What Is the Sociological Imagination?

The term **sociological imagination** refers to looking at people's behavior and attitudes in the context of the social forces that shape them. C. Wright Mills, the sociologist who developed this concept, emphasized that changes in society influence our lives profoundly. As with Lisa and her grandmother, we get caught on various sides of social issues. Until 1973, legal abortions were not available in the United States. At that time, too, almost everyone thought of abortion as a despicable act. When the law changed, however, and doctors were allowed to perform abortions, many people's attitudes changed. The *sociological imagination,* then, is an emphasis on how the larger events swirling around us influence how we think, feel, and act.

APPLYING THE SOCIOLOGICAL IMAGINATION TO PERSONAL TROUBLES. The historical forces that are changing our society also have an impact on our own lives. As you know, a major trend in global capitalism is to export jobs to countries where workers earn just a dollar or two a day. This global force is not something abstract, but, instead, something that changes our lives. Some of the impact is positive; the reduced labor costs, for example, lower what we pay for our clothing and cars. Some of it is negative, however, especially for the workers who lose their jobs and, after months of looking for work, end up with jobs that pay half of what they were earning. Mills used the term **personal troubles** to refer to things like this, to how the large-scale events of history bring trouble to people's lives. With all the publicity given to moving jobs overseas, "everyone" knows that this particular large-scale event causes a loss of jobs here. In most cases of personal troubles, however, we get so caught up in what is bothering us that we are unaware of how they are related to larger social forces.

To better understand this connection between personal troubles and larger social forces, let's apply the sociological imagination to Lisa and her grandmother. Lisa's values reflect developments in our society that were not part of her grandmother's consciousness when she grew up. Lisa's views have been shaped by the women's movement, which stresses that each woman has the right to make choices and to exercise judgment about her own body. From this perspective, which has become part of Lisa's outlook on the world, a woman has the right to terminate her pregnancy. Abortion is simply one way that she controls her body. In the extreme, proponents of this view state that a woman's right in this area is absolute. For example, she can choose to have an abortion at any point in her pregnancy, even if she is nine months along—without informing her husband if she is married or her parents if she is a minor.

The sociological imagination also sensitizes us to the social forces that shaped Lisa's grandmother's point of view. When she was growing up, abortion was not only illegal but also considered so shameful that people did not even talk openly about it. *Every* woman was expected to become a mother, and almost all girls grew up with marriage and motherhood as their *foremost* goal in life. Careers and advanced education were secondary to a woman becoming a wife and mother. Marriage and motherhood were a woman's destiny, her fulfillment in life. Without this, she was incomplete, not a full woman. Like Lisa's grandmother, almost everyone also agreed that abortion was murder. Within this context, any woman who had an abortion had to keep her crime a secret. Some women who had abortions, frightened out of their wits, were taken to their destination blindfolded in a taxi. They endured kitchen-table surgery that carried a high risk of postoperative infection and death.

Yet neither Lisa nor her grandmother sees this finely woven net that has been cast over them, turning their lives upside down. Instead, the impact of social change hits them on a personal level: This is where they feel it, in their intimate and everyday lives. It affects what they think and feel and what they do—and, as in the opening vignette, how they relate to one another.

In contrast, the sociological imagination (also called the **sociological perspective**) invites us to look at our lives afresh. The sociological imagination asks us to understand how the social context shapes or influences our ideas, attitudes, behaviors, and even our emotions. The social context encompasses historical periods and very broad events, such as the era in which we grow up, war, terrorism, and other historical turmoil. It also includes our *social locations*—the broad but narrower factors that also influence our lives profoundly, such as our gender, race-ethnicity, religion, and social class. Then there are the smaller *social locations* in which we find ourselves, such as our age and health, our jobs and associates. Finally, there is the intimate level, our relationships with people who are close to us: our parents and siblings, our friends and children, our wife, husband, or lover. Together, these many levels combine to make up the social context that shapes the way we look at life.

THE SIGNIFICANCE OF SOCIAL LOCATION. Table 1-1 illustrates how significant social location is in influencing whether a woman has an abortion. From this table, you can see the difference that age, race-ethnicity, marital status, and length of pregnancy make. Look at age: This table shows that half (519 of 1,000) of girls under the age of 15 who get pregnant have an abortion. Those who are the next most likely to have abortions are other teenagers and women in their early 20s. The rate of abortion keeps dropping with age until women reach their 40s, when it increases sharply. Now look at the influence of race-ethnicity. As you can see from this table, African American women are *twice* as likely to have abortions than are white women. The most striking difference, however—which cuts across age and race-ethnicity—is marital status: Unmarried women are *six* times more likely than married women to obtain an abortion.

TABLE 1-1   Who Has Abortions?

ABORTIONS	NUMBER OF ABORTIONS	PERCENT OF ALL ABORTIONS	ABORTIONS PER 1,000 BIRTHS[1]	PERCENTAGE OF PREGNANCIES THAT END IN ABORTION
Age				
Under 15	8,000	1%	519	52%
15–19	225,000	17%	341	34%
20–24	434,000	33%	298	30%
25–29	295,000	23%	219	22%
30–34	194,000	15%	171	17%
35–39	109,000	8%	195	20%
40 and over	38,000	3%	276	28%
Race/Ethnicity				
White	723,000	56%	186	19%
Black and other[2]	579,000	44%	407	41%
Marital Status				
Married	238,000	18%	80	8%
Unmarried	1,065,000	82%	456	46%
Weeks of Gestation				
Less than 9	772,000	59%	NA[3]	NA
9–10	251,000	19%	NA	NA
11–12	132,000	10%	NA	NA
13 or more	147,000	11%	NA	NA
Number of Prior Abortions				
None	700,000	54%	NA	NA
1	349,000	27%	NA	NA
2 or more	254,000	19%	NA	NA

[1] The source calls this the abortion ratio, formulating it from the "number of abortions per 1,000 abortions and live births."
[2] This is the rather strange classification used in the source.
[3] Not Available or Not Applicable

Source: By the author. Based on *Statistical Abstract* 2006:Table 94.

Suppose, then, that you are a woman in her late 20s. Can you see how much more likely you would be to have an abortion if you were single than if you were married? Similarly, suppose that you are an unmarried white teenager, and you get pregnant. Can you see how much less likely you would be to have an abortion than if you were an African American teenager who got pregnant?

I don't want you to think that using the sociological imagination makes people seem like little robots. If you are of a certain race-ethnicity and age, for example, it does *not* mean that you will do a certain thing, such as have or not have an abortion. The sociological imagination or perspective does not mean this at all. Rather, it means that people who experience certain locations in society are exposed to influences that are different from the influences on people who occupy other corners of life. These influences make a difference in people's attitudes and behaviors, but in any individual case, you never know in advance the consequences of those influences. Within this context, then, you cannot tell for certain whether some particular individual will have an abortion. But—and this is important—as Table 1-1 makes apparent, we tend to make up our minds along predictable, well-traveled social avenues.

IN SUM Sociologists stress the need to use the sociological imagination to understand social problems and personal troubles. The sociological perspective helps make us aware of how the social context—from our historical era to our smaller social locations—influences

our ideas, behaviors, and personal troubles. Just as with Lisa and her grandmother, this context also shapes *our* views of what is or is not a social problem and of what should be done about it. Let's look more closely at how this shaping occurs.

What Is a Social Problem?

Because the focus of this text is on social problems, it is important to understand clearly what social problems are. As you will see, social problems have two essential elements.

The Characteristics of Social Problems

TWO ESSENTIAL ELEMENTS. A **social problem** is some aspect of society that people are concerned about and would like changed. Social problems have *two* key components. The first is an **objective condition,** some aspect of society that can be measured or experienced. With abortion, this objective condition includes whether abortions are legal, who obtains them, and under what circumstances. The second key component of a social problem is **subjective concern,** the concern that a significant number of people (or a number of significant people) have about the objective condition. Subjective concern about abortion includes some people's distress that any woman must give birth to an unwanted child. It also includes other people's distress that any woman would terminate the life of her unborn child. To see how subjective concerns about abortion differ in another part of the world, see the Global Glimpse box on the next page.

SOCIAL PROBLEMS ARE DYNAMIC. As society changes, so do these two essential elements: objective conditions and subjective concerns. In other words, social problems are dynamic. As I mentioned, abortion was illegal in the United States until 1973. In that year, the U.S. Supreme Court made a landmark decision known as *Roe v. Wade,* by which the Court legalized abortion. Before this decision, the social problem of abortion was quite unlike what it is today. The primary *objective condition* was the illegality of abortion. The *subjective concerns* centered on women who wanted abortions but could not get them, as well as on the conditions under which illegal abortions took place: With most abortions performed by untrained people, many women died from botched, underground surgeries. As growing numbers of people became concerned, they worked to change the law. Their success transformed the problem: Large numbers of people became upset that abortion had become legal. Convinced that abortion is murder, these people began their own campaigns to make their subjective concerns known and to change the law. Those who favor legal abortion oppose each step these people take. We'll look more closely at this process in a moment, but at this point I simply want you to see how social problem are dynamic, how they take shape as groups react to one another.

SOCIAL PROBLEMS ARE RELATIVE. As you can see from the example of abortion, what people consider to be a social problem depends on their values. *A social problem for some is often a solution for others.* While some were pleased with the *Roe v. Wade* decision of 1973, others found it a disaster. Obviously, mugging is not a social problem for muggers. Nor do Boeing and other corporations that profit from arming the world consider the billions of dollars spent on weapons to be a social problem. In the same way, nuclear power is not a social problem for the corporations that use it to generate electricity. From the Issues in Social Problems box on page 8 and from Table 1-2, you can see that how people define abortion leads to contrasting views of this social problem.

COMPETING VIEWS. Since we live in a pluralistic world of competing, contrasting, and conflictive groups, our society is filled with competing, contrasting, and conflictive views of life. This certainly makes life interesting, but in such a dynamic world, whose definition of a social problem wins? The answer centers on **power,** the ability to get your way despite obstacles. After abortion became legal in 1973, most observers assumed that the social problem was over—the opponents of abortion had lost, and they would quietly fade

A Global Glimpse
ONLY FEMALES ELIGIBLE: SEX-SELECTION ABORTION IN INDIA

"May you be the mother of a hundred sons" is the toast made to brides in India, where the birth of a son brings shouts of rejoicing, but the birth of a daughter brings tears of sadness.

Why? A son continues the family name, preserves wealth and property within the family, takes care of aged parents (the elderly have no Social Security), and performs the parents' funeral rites. Hinduism even teaches that a sonless man cannot achieve salvation.

A daughter, in contrast, is a liability. Men want to marry only virgins, and the parents of a daughter bear the burden of having to be constantly on guard to protect her virginity. For their daughter to marry, the parents must also pay a dowry to her husband. A common saying in India reflects the female's low status: "To bring up a daughter is like watering a neighbor's plant."

This cultural context sets the stage for female infanticide, killing newborn girl babies, a practice that has been common in India for thousands of years. Using diagnostic techniques (amniocentesis and ultrasound) to reveal the sex of the fetus, many Indians have replaced female infanticide with gender-selective abortion. If prenatal tests reveal that the fetus is female, they abort it. Some clinics even put up billboards that proclaim, "Invest Rs.500 now, save Rs.50,000 later." This means that by paying Rs.500 (500 Indian rupees) to abort a female, a family can save a future dowry of 50,000 rupees.

Even though their husbands and other relatives urge them to have an abortion, some women who are pregnant with a female fetus resist. Since these abortions are profitable, medical personnel try to sell reluctant women on the idea. To overcome their resistance, one clinic has hit on an ingenious technique: Nurses reach under the counter where they keep the preserved fetuses of twin girls. When a woman sees these bottled fetuses, the horror of double vigilance and two dowries is often sufficient to convince her to have an abortion.

National newspapers headlined the events in one clinic: A *male* fetus had been unintentionally aborted. This sparked protests, and the Indian legislature passed a law forbidding doctors to tell would-be parents the sex of their fetuses. Physicians who violate the law can be sent to prison and banned from their profession.

Going unenforced, however, this law has had little or no effect. An eminent physician has even stated publicly: "The need for a male child is an economic need in our society, and our feminists who are raising such hue and cry about female feticide should realize that it is better to get rid of an unwanted child than to make it suffer all its life."

What do you think? In answering this, try to put yourself in the position of Indians in poverty.

Based on Kusum 1993; Holman 1994; Raghunathan 2003.

---

away. As you know, this assumption was naive. Feelings were so strong that groups which had been hostile to one another for centuries, such as Roman Catholics and Baptists, began to work together to oppose abortion. Shocked at what they considered the killing of babies, they took to the streets and to the courts, fighting pitched battles over this issue that lies at the heart of social divisions in U.S. society.

A NOTE ON TERMS. Before we go further in our analysis of abortion as a social problem, we need to pause to consider the matter of terms. Definitions and terms are always significant, but especially so when we deal with highly sensitive issues such as abortion. The terms *prochoice* and *prolife,* chosen by advocates on each side on this social problem, represent attitudes and positions which sometimes provoke strong emotional response. As you may have noticed as you read the box on the relativity of social problems, I use the terms *antiabortion* and *proabortion.* Although these terms, purposely chosen and intended to be neutral, are not entirely satisfactory, I shall use the term *antiabortion* to refer to those who oppose the legal right to abortion and *proabortion* to refer to those who favor this legal right. As I discuss in the Preface, *neither side* on the abortion issue prefers these terms. (For detailed background, see pages xviii–ix). If I have succeeded in my intentions in this chapter, even if readers do not like this choice of terms, both those who favor the legal right to abortion and those who oppose it will feel that I have presented their side fairly.

Issues in Social Problems
A PROBLEM FOR SOME IS A SOLUTION FOR OTHERS: THE RELATIVITY OF SOCIAL PROBLEMS

To be socialized means to learn ways of looking at the world. As we participate in groups—from our family and friends to groups at school and work—their perspectives tend to become part of how we view life. Among the other perspectives that we learn is a way of viewing the objective conditions of social problems.

The meanings that objective conditions have for us are not written in stone. The views that we currently have arose from our experiences with particular groups and our exposure to certain ideas. Experiences with different groups, or encounters with different ideas and information, can similarly change our position on a social problem. We might think that the subjective concerns we have now are the only right and reasonable way of viewing some objective condition. But just as we arrived at our subjective concerns through our social locations, so our views can change if our journey takes us in a different direction. In short, our views, or subjective concerns, are relative to our experiences.

This relativity is illustrated in the social problem of abortion. The central issue is how people define the status of the unborn. Is the fetus a human being, as the antiabortionists believe, or only a potential human, as the proabortionists believe?

Let's look at the two main opposing views.

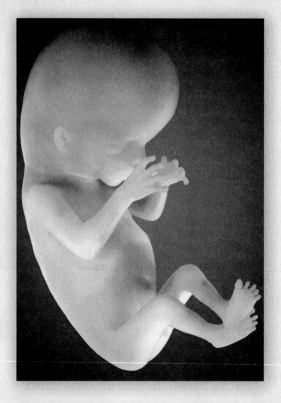

How people define the unborn is the essence of their position on abortion. That which is pictured here is about eleven weeks' gestation. To describe it, those on one side of the abortion controversy use terms such as fetus and "product of conception," while those on the other side call it a baby.

THE FETUS IS NOT A HUMAN BEING

This is the position of most people who believe that abortion is a woman's right. "The fetus is a potential person that looks increasingly human as it develops" (NARAL Pro-Choice America). It follows, then, that abortion is not killing but merely a medical procedure. It is the woman's right to have an abortion for whatever reason she expresses—from financial pressures to health problems—and for the purpose of attaining her goals, whether those be to limit family size, to finish school, to win a promotion at work, or to fulfill any other plans that she might have. The state, therefore, should permit abortion on demand.

WHAT DO YOU THINK?

THE FETUS IS A HUMAN BEING

This is the position of most people who oppose abortion. It follows, then, that abortion is murder, the killing of unborn babies. To simply want an abortion cannot justify murdering a baby. We need to protect and nourish these babies, not kill them. Women have no right to abortion, for it is not just their bodies that are involved but also the lives of other humans—their children. The exception is when another human life, the mother's, lies in the balance. The state has no business legalizing murder, and abortion should be illegal.

WHAT DO YOU THINK?

TABLE 1-2 How Definitions of Abortion Affect People's Views

WHO DOES THE DEFINING?	WHAT ABORTION IS	WHAT IS ABORTED	THE WOMAN	THE RESULTING VIEWS	
				The Act of Abortion	The One Who Performs the Abortion
People Who Favor Abortion	A woman's right	Fetus	Independent individual	A service to women	Skilled technician
People Who Oppose Abortion	Murder	Baby	Mother	Killing a baby	Murderer
People Who Do Abortions	Part of my work	Fetus	Client	A medical procedure	Professional

Source: Modified from Roe 1989.

The Natural History of Social Problems: Four Stages

Sociologists have found that social problems go through four stages, which they call *the natural history of a social problem.* Let's continue with the example of abortion to see how this process occurs. To do this, it is important to set the background for understanding abortion in the United States. Before 1970, abortion was illegal in all 50 U.S. states. Although several states had liberalized their abortion laws, they still kept abortion illegal except for special circumstances, such as when pregnancy endangered the mother's life. Then in 1970, in an unprecedented move, Hawaii legalized abortion. Hawaii's law defined abortion as a private, noncriminal act.

What made Hawaii receptive to such radical change? Three background factors are significant (Steinhoff and Diamond 1977). First, more than three-quarters of the population lived on the island of Oahu. Here, they had a tradition of personally knowing their politicians and participating in public hearings. Second, two-income families had become common, and half of the women over age 16 worked. Finally, an epidemic of German measles hit Hawaii in 1964 and 1965. During this time, many obstetricians aborted fetuses to prevent them from being born with deformities. This was a turning point for Hawaiian physicians, and the rate of abortion never fell back to its pre-1964 level.

Now that we've set this brief background, we can trace the natural history of abortion. Let's look at how it developed in Hawaii, as well as in the United States as a whole. As we do so, you will see that social problems go through four stages.

The First Stage: Defining the Problem, the Emergence of Leaders, and Beginning to Organize

DEFINING THE PROBLEM. As you have just seen, for a social problem to come into being, people have to become upset about some objective condition. This involves a shift in outlook, a questioning of something that had been taken for granted. This change in perspective can come about in several ways. For example, if values change, an old, established pattern will no longer look the same. This is what happened with abortion. The 1960s brought extensive, wrenching social change to the United States. Young people—primarily teenagers and those in their 20s—challenged long-established values. Amidst political uproar, accompanied by widespread demonstrations, many new values were adopted. The women's movement was part of this challenge to established ideas. As this movement gained followers, more and more women felt that they should not have to become criminals to terminate a pregnancy. They became convinced that they had the *right* to legal abortions.

THE EMERGENCE OF LEADERS. As people discussed their concerns about abortion being illegal, leaders emerged who helped to crystallize the issues. In Hawaii, Vincent Yano, a Roman Catholic state senator and the father of ten, argued that if abortion were a sin, it would be better to have no abortion law than to have one that allowed it under certain circumstances (Steinhoff and Diamond 1977). This reasoning allowed Yano to maintain his religious opposition to abortion while favoring the repeal of Hawaii's law against abortion.

ORGANIZING AROUND THE ISSUE. Another leader emerged: Joan Hayes, a former Washington lobbyist. She felt that simply to liberalize the laws against abortion would be to duck what she saw as the major issue: the right of a woman to choose whether to have a baby. Hayes understood the use of power—and the value of arousing a concerned public. She invited leaders in medicine, business, labor, politics, religion, and the media to a citizens' seminar on abortion sponsored by the American Association of University Women.

The Second Stage: Crafting an Official Response

The stages of a social problem don't have neat ending and beginning points. Their edges are blurry, and they overlap. In this case, between 1967 and 1968, legislators had introduced several bills to soften Hawaii's law against abortion. These bills, which would have broadened the circumstances under which abortion would be legal, were actually attempts to redefine abortion. Thus, the stages of defining the social problem and officially responding to it were intertwined.

The turning point came when Senator Yano announced that he would support the repeal of the abortion law. This stimulated other official responses as organizations—from the Chamber of Commerce to the Roman Catholic Church—endorsed or rejected the repeal. Public forums and legislative hearings were held, generating huge amounts of publicity. This publicity served as a vital bridge between the public at large and the advocates of repeal. As Hawaiians became keenly aware of the abortion issue, polls showed that most wanted to repeal the law against abortion. In 1970, Hawaii did just that.

The Third Stage: Reacting to the Official Response

As sometimes happens, the official response to a social problem becomes defined as a social problem. This is what happened with abortion, especially after 1973, when the U.S. Supreme Court concurred with the Hawaiian legislation and struck down all state laws that prohibited abortion. Indignant about what they saw as murder, antiabortion groups picketed and used political pressure to try to sway public opinion and turn legislative defeat into victory.

Besides inspiring new opposition, official response also can change the definition of the social problem that is held by those who promoted the reform in the first place. In this case, proabortion groups noted that despite their Supreme Court victory, most counties did not offer abortions, and many women who wanted abortions could not obtain them. Consequently, they began to promote abortion clinics to make abortion more readily accessible.

Figure 1-1 shows the success of these efforts. In 1973, the first year of legal abortion, 745,000 abortions were performed. This number climbed quickly to one million, then to a million and a half, where it reached a plateau. From 1979 to 1994, the total ran between 1,500,000 and 1,600,000 each year, but beginning in 1995 the number began to drop. It now is about 1,300,000 a year. Figure 1-2 presents another overview of abortion. From this figure, you can see that the abortion ratio climbed sharply, plateaued for about 10 years, and then dropped. Today, for every 100 live births there are 32 abortions.

FIGURE 1-1 Number of Abortions and Live Births

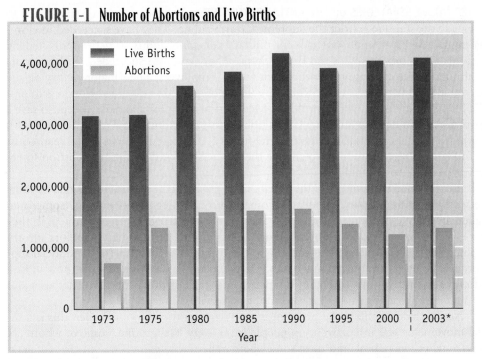

Source: By the author. Based on *Statistical Abstract of the United States* 2007:Table 93. This is the latest year listed in the 2007 source.

FIGURE 1-2 Number of Abortions per 100 Live Births

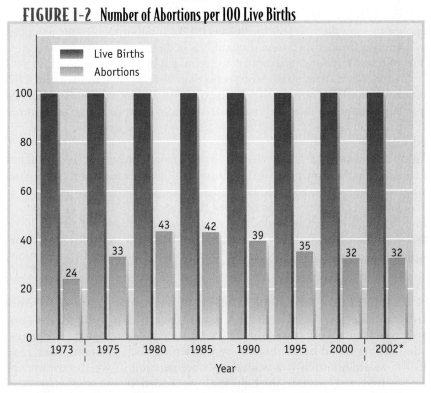

Source: By the author. Based on *Statistical Abstract of the United States* 1988:Tables 81, 103; 2007:Table 93. This is the latest year listed in the 2007 source.

The Fourth Stage: Developing Alternative Strategies

The millions of abortions after the Supreme Court's ruling led to a pitched battle that still rages. Let's look at some of the alternative strategies developed by the pro- and antiabortion groups.

ALTERNATIVE STRATEGIES OF THE ANTIABORTIONISTS. Antiabortion groups have tried to persuade the states to restrict the Supreme Court's ruling. They have succeeded in eliminating federal funding of abortions for military personnel and their dependents, federal prisoners, and workers with the Peace Corps. They have also succeeded in eliminating health insurance coverage of abortions for federal employees. Their major victory on the federal level took place in 1976, when opponents of abortion persuaded Congress to pass the Hyde Amendment, which prohibits Medicaid funding for abortions except to save a woman's life. When the Supreme Court upheld this amendment in 1980 (Lewis 1988), the number of abortions paid for by federal funds plummeted from 300,000 a year to just 17. Despite repeated attempts to change the Hyde Amendment, the antiabortion forces have succeeded in retaining it.

A highly effective strategy of the antiabortion groups is the establishment of a national network of "crisis pregnancy centers." Women who call "pregnancy hotlines" (sometimes called life lines or birth lines) are offered free pregnancy testing. When they accept it, they are directed to counselors who encourage them to give birth. The counselors inform women about fetal development and talk to them about the financial help and social support available to them during pregnancy. They also advise the women about how to find adoptive parents or how to obtain financial support after the birth. Some activists also operate maternity homes and provide adoption services.

Neither side on this social problem is a single, organized group. Rather, this is a social movement, and it has swept up people from every background, some of whom are moderate, others radical, and most somewhere in between.

The moderates choose moderate alternative strategies. They call their friends, run newspaper ads, and write their representatives. Those in between picket abortion clinics. In the years after *Roe v. Wade,* some took their cue from the civil rights movement of the 1950s and practiced passive resistance. Lying immobile in front of abortion clinics, they allowed the police to carry them to jail. In the late 1980s, antiabortion groups practiced massive nonviolent civil disobedience, and thousands of demonstrators were arrested. This social movement grew so large and its members so active that by 1990 more abortion protesters had been arrested than the number of people who were arrested in the entire civil rights movement (Allen 1988; Lacayo 1991; Kirkpatrick 1992). Since then, with the U.S. Supreme Court upholding state laws that restrict demonstrations at clinics and the homes of clinic staff (Walsh and Goldstein 2000), protesters have become less active, and arrests have dropped.

Radical activists, in contrast, lean toward radical methods. They have thrown blood on abortion clinics, pulled the plug on abortion machines, jammed locks with superglue, set off stink bombs, and telephoned women at night with recordings of babies screaming. Radical activists also have burned and bombed abortion clinics. In the town in which I taught, Edwardsville, Illinois, a group kidnapped a physician and threatened his life if he did not shut down his abortion clinics. Radical activists have shot and killed seven abortion doctors, acts that have been condemned by both proabortionists and antiabortionists alike.

ALTERNATIVE STRATEGIES OF THE PROABORTIONISTS. Proabortion groups, too, have developed alternative strategies. Their counterattack has taken three primary forms: campaigning for proabortion politicians, lobbying lawmakers to vote against restrictive legislation, and seeking broad-based support by publicizing their position. They have stressed a dual message: Abortion is a woman's private decision in which government should not be involved, and "without the right to choose abortion, any other guarantees of liberty have little meaning for women" (Michelman 1988). The proabortion forces have recruited women who had abortions when it was back-alley business to alert the public to what it would be like if the right to abortion were taken away. Their message: rich women flying to countries where abortion is legal, poor women victimized by unqualified underground abortionists, and thousands of women dying from illegal abortions.

Much of the proabortionists' strategy has been limited to fighting rearguard actions, to trying to prevent the antiabortionists from chipping away at *Roe* by getting states to restrict abortion rights. In a preemptive move, proabortionists have succeeded in getting

California and five other states to codify *Roe,* that is, to guarantee abortion rights in their states if *Roe* is overturned (Solomon 2006).

MAKING MUTUAL ACCUSATIONS. Part of the alternative strategy of each side is to point the finger at the other. As it promotes its own point of view, each side paints the other as grotesque, uncaring, and evil. Proabortionists accuse antiabortionists of being concerned about fetuses but not about pregnant women. They also point to the killing of physicians as evidence of hypocrisy—people who say they stand for life kill others. For their part, antiabortionists accuse proabortionists of suppressing information about the health risks of abortion—and of murdering helpless, innocent, unborn children.

THE CONTROVERSY CONTINUES: THE SUPREME COURT AFTER *ROE.* As each side knows so well, the U.S. Supreme Court remains the final arbiter of abortion. Short of a constitutional amendment, if either side on this issue succeeds in getting a state, or even Congress, to pass some law, the Supreme Court decides whether that law is constitutional. Consequently, a primary alternative strategy of both proabortionists and antiabortionists is to try to influence the president's choice of Supreme Court nominees and how the Senate votes on them. For the past couple of decades, U.S. presidents have taken strong positions on abortion and have proposed nominees for the Supreme Court that reflect their position. We can expect this stacking of the Court to continue.

The eight men and one woman who serve for life on the U.S. Supreme Court determine the constitutionality of the laws passed by the states and the U.S. Congress. Because their interpretations of the U.S. Constitution are biased by their political and personal views, their rulings on matters concerning abortion are uncertain.

Three Supreme Court decisions since the 1973 *Roe v. Wade* decision are especially significant. The first is *Webster v. Reproductive Services.* In 1989, by a vote of 5–4, the Supreme Court ruled that

1. States have no obligation to finance abortion: They can prohibit the use of public funds for abortions and abortion counseling, and they can ban abortions at public hospitals.
2. States have a compelling interest to protect fetal life: Before doctors can abort a fetus that is 20 weeks or over, they must perform tests to determine its viability (capacity to live outside the uterus).

The second significant decision is *Casey v. Planned Parenthood.* In 1992, by a vote of 6 to 3, the Supreme Court upheld a Pennsylvania law requiring that a woman under age 18 obtain the consent of at least one parent, that a 24-hour waiting period between confirming a pregnancy and having an abortion be enforced, and that the woman be given materials describing the fetus, as well as a list of agencies offering adoption services and alternatives to abortion. By a 5–4 vote, however, the Court also ruled that a wife has no obligation to inform her husband of her intention to have an abortion. *Casey* allows states to pass laws that restrict abortion—unless such laws impose an "undue burden" on a woman's ability to have an abortion.

A third significant legal decision occurred in 1993, this time in favor of the proabortion forces. In that year, they won a major victory when Congress passed the Freedom of Access to Clinic Entrances Act. This law requires picketers and other demonstrators to remain 300 feet away from the entrances to abortion clinics. If demonstrators don't, they face up to three years in prison. The Supreme Court has ruled that this Act does not violate freedom of speech. This significant victory for the proabortion side practically eliminated the picketing of abortion clinics.

NO MIDDLE GROUND. Neither the proabortionists nor the antiabortionists can be satisfied, as there is no middle ground. Both sides consider their alternative strategies as only nibbling at the edges of the problem. Each seeks total victory. The antiabortion groups advocate a constitutional amendment that would define human life as beginning at conception and abortion as murder. In almost a mirror image, the proabortion groups want Congress to pass a Freedom of Choice Act that would remove all state restrictions on abortion.

The activists in this ongoing social problem illustrate how interest groups develop alternative strategies as they line up on opposing sides of a social issue. In the case of abortion, the final results are still unclear—and perhaps they never will be final. On both sides are highly motivated people. Each side considers the other unreasonable. Each is rationally and emotionally dedicated to its view of morality: One talks about killing babies, the other about forcing women to bear unwanted children, even those conceived from incest and rape. With no middle ground to bridge the chasm, there is no end in sight to this bitter, determined struggle.

The Role of Sociology in Social Problems

Sociology as a Tool for Breaking Through Emotions and Defenses

One of the primary characteristics of humans is that we think of our world in personal and moral terms. In the chapter's opening vignette, for example, Lisa may think that her grandmother is narrow-minded, and her grandmother may wonder how Lisa acquired such casual morals. We all put up defenses to protect our self-concept, and most of us are convinced that our views—and what we feel and what we do—are right, that it is others who are wrong. Obviously, such self-protective attitudes and defenses are major obstacles when it comes to understanding social problems. Let's see how sociology can help.

FIVE CONTRIBUTIONS OF SOCIOLOGY TO UNDERSTANDING SOCIAL PROBLEMS. Sociology, the study of social behavior, helps us to see past the passions that surround a social problem. There are five ways by which sociology can penetrate such emotions and defenses to yield a better understanding of social problems.

1. *Sociologists can measure objective conditions.* For abortion, sociologists can gather information on the number of abortions performed in clinics and hospitals and on how the states vary in their access to abortions. They can also determine why women have or do not have abortions, how women adjust to their decision to abort or to bear a child, and how their husbands or boyfriends react.

2. Sociologists can *measure subjective concerns;* that is, they can determine people's attitudes and views about social problems (Becker 1966). Such information is useful in evaluating potential policies. To establish sound public policy involves much more than measuring public opinion, of course, but accurate measurements can guide policy makers. Table 1-3, which summarizes Americans' attitudes about the legality of abortion, provides an example of how sociologists measure subjective concerns. Note how people's attitudes are related to their gender, race-ethnicity, age, education, income, politics, and place of residence.

3. *Sociologists can apply the sociological imagination;* that is, they can place social problems into their broad social context. For example, abortion is related to people's attitudes about sexuality and sex roles. Abortion is also related to profound differences of opinion about privacy, what human life is, when life begins and ends, the role of the medical profession in terminating life, and the role of religious institutions in a pluralistic society. It is also related to ideas about individual freedom versus responsibility to the group, desirable standards of living and parenting, and what is and is not moral (Lerner et al. 1990).

4. *Sociologists can identify different ways to intervene in a social problem.* They can suggest potential social policies: courses of action for public and private agencies, educational programs, public awareness campaigns, and legal changes to address a social problem.

5. *Sociologists can evaluate likely consequences of social policies* (Becker 1966). For example, sociologists can estimate how a proposed social policy on abortion will affect the birth rate, population growth, crime rate, and expenditures for welfare and education.

TABLE 1-3 Should Abortion Be Legal or Illegal?

This question was asked of a representative sample of Americans:
"Do you think abortions should be legal under any circumstances, legal only under certain circumstances, or illegal in all circumstances?"

	ALWAYS LEGAL	LEGAL UNDER CERTAIN CIRCUMSTANCES	NEVER LEGAL
National	24%	56%	19%
Sex			
Male	19%	62%	18%
Female	28%	51%	20%
Race			
White	24%	58%	17%
Nonwhite	23%	50%	25%
Black	25%	42%	31%
Age			
18–29 years	29%	50%	21%
30–49 years	24%	56%	19%
50–64 years	22%	60%	17%
50 years and older	21%	59%	19%
65 years and older	19%	58%	22%
Education			
College postgraduate	36%	55%	9%
College graduate	30%	61%	9%
Some college	28%	53%	17%
High school graduate or less	14%	58%	27%
Income			
$75,000 and over	33%	56%	10%
$50,000–$74,999	26%	54%	20%
$30,000–$49,999	24%	56%	20%
$20,000–$29,999	16%	65%	19%
Under $20,000	13%	54%	33%
Community			
Urban area	30%	52%	17%
Suburban area	24%	57%	18%
Rural area	16%	59%	24%
Region			
East	29%	54%	16%
Midwest	19%	62%	17%
South	16%	58%	24%
West	35%	49%	16%
Politics			
Republican	12%	65%	23%
Democrat	35%	47%	17%
Independent	23%	58%	17%

Note: Because of rounding, rows do not always add to 100%.

Source: Table 2.101 of *Sourcebook of Criminal Justice Statistics*, 2005.

These five tasks are much more easily listed than performed. Although sociologists gather extensive information on social problems, making accurate predictions from those data is difficult. People often change their behaviors, which can throw off the best predictions of social scientists. Sociology, however, is especially useful for clarifying issues in social problems. Clarification, of course, requires facts. This, in turn, leads to the question of how sociologists get dependable information. Why don't they simply depend on common sense?

Sociology and Common Sense

All of us have "gut feelings" about the world. Based on our experiences, we "just know" that some things are true and others are not. We use **common sense,** the ideas common to our society (or to some group within our society), to make sense out of our experiences in life. Our commonsense interpretations also give us ideas about social problems. As a result, we all develop opinions about what causes a social problem, and we all have ideas about what should be done to solve it.

COMMON SENSE NOT ENOUGH. Because the impressions on which common sense is based may not be correct, common sense is not adequate for deciding how we should address a social problem. To see why, let's see how common sense holds up when it comes to abortion. Commonsense views about abortion include the ideas that abortion is a last resort, that women who get abortions do not know how to use contraceptives, and, certainly, that women who get abortions did not want to get pregnant.

Although these commonsense ideas appear obvious, they are *all* false. More accurately stated, they aren't always true. For example, abortion is not always a last resort. In Russia, abortion is a major means of birth control, and the average Russian woman used to have six abortions in her lifetime (Yablonsky 1981; Eberstadt 1988). Although the rate of abortion has decreased, there are still more abortions than births in Russia (Deschner and Cohen 2003; Greenall 2003).

Nor is it true that women who have abortions don't know how to use contraceptives. Sociologist Kristin Luker (1975), who studied an abortion clinic in California, found that many women had not used contraceptives, even though they knew how to use them and did not want to get pregnant. They avoided contraceptives because they interfered with intimacy, were expensive, were disapproved of by their boyfriends, or caused adverse side effects. Some even avoided contraceptives to protect their self-concept. If they used contraceptives, they would think of themselves as "available" or sexually promiscuous. Without contraceptives, they could view sex as something that "just happened." Luker's study shows that some women take chances—and they get pregnant and have abortions.

Sociologist Leon Dash (1990), who studied pregnancy among teenagers in Washington, D.C., found that the third commonsense idea is also not necessarily true. Contrary to a middle-class perspective, many poor, young, unmarried teenagers get pregnant because they *want* to. Some want children so that, as they said, "I can have something to hold onto, that I can call my own." Some boyfriends also urge their girlfriends to get pregnant. This, they say, will make them "feel like a man." And, as Luker discovered, some women get pregnant to test their boyfriend's commitment. As many of these women found out, however, their relationship turned out to be short-term. After it soured, the young women decided that they didn't want to bear a child after all, and they found abortion to be a way out of their situation.

PRINCIPLES UNDERLYING SOCIOLOGICAL RESEARCH. From Luker's and Dash's research, we can see that our commonsense ideas may not be correct. But what allows sociological research to give us the understandings that we need to deal with social problems? Three basic characteristics of sociological research help to accomplish this:

1. Rather than basing their conclusions on personal experience, hunches, assumptions, or opinions, sociologists *use scientific methods* to provide objective, systematic research.
2. Sociologists *do not base their conclusions on emotions or personal values.* To do so would obscure their perspective and prevent them from seeing things objectively. Even if sociologists discover things that contradict their own values, they are obligated ethically to report those findings.
3. Sociologists *use the sociological imagination.* To discover the underlying causes of social problems, sociologists interpret them within the framework of the larger picture. In contrast, as we saw with Lisa and her grandmother, people's common sense leads them to perceive matters on a personal level, rather than in the context of larger social patterns.

That sociologists can do objective research does not mean that sociology has all the answers. Sociologists can suggest which consequences may result if some particular social

With each side of the controversy over abortion firmly committed to its cause, deeply entrenched in its views, and strongly convinced of its morality, this social issue seems to be eternally renewed.

policy is followed, but they have no expertise for determining which social policy *should* be followed. Social policy is based on values, on the outcomes that people want to see. *Because sociology cannot determine that one set of values is superior to another, it provides no basis for making value decisions.* In short, from sociology we can estimate likely outcomes of specific social policies, but we cannot determine which social policy should be chosen. We'll come back to this in a moment, but first let's look at how sociologists do their research.

Methods for Studying Social Problems

To investigate social problems, sociologists choose from several **methods** (ways of doing research). Which method they choose depends on two things: the questions they want to investigate and what is practical. First, they must determine what they want to find out about a social problem, for *different goals require different methods.* Suppose, for example, that you want to find out how people form their ideas about abortion. This calls for a different method of research than if you want to compare the abortion rates of high-school dropouts and college-educated women. Second, not everything a researcher would like to do is practical. A sociologist might like to interview huge numbers of people or to conduct large-scale experiments, but limitations of money and time, or of ethics in the case of experiments, can make such methods impractical.

Let's review the methods that sociologists use to study social problems. We shall first distinguish how sociologists design their studies, then describe how they gather their information.

FOUR BASIC RESEARCH DESIGNS. Most studies fall into one of four **research designs:** case studies, surveys, experiments, and field studies. Let's look at each.

Case studies ▪ The **case study** is used to gather in-depth information on some specific situation. As the name implies, the researcher focuses on one *case*—an individual, an event, or even an organization such as an abortion clinic or a crisis pregnancy center. Let's suppose that you want in-depth information about how women experience abortion. You might want to know what emotions they undergo as they wrestle with the decision to give birth or to have an abortion, whom they talk to about it, even how they feel during the abortion and how they adjust afterward. A case study could provide this type of detail.

Surveys ▪ As you can see, though, while the case study provides rich detail, it has a drawback. If you focus on just one woman, how can you know if her experiences are similar to those of other women who have abortions? The **survey** overcomes this limitation. In a survey, you focus on a **sample** of the group you want to study. (Sociologists use the term **population** to refer to your target group.) Samples are intended to represent the entire group that you are studying. Done correctly, surveys allow you to **generalize** what you find—that is, you are able to apply your findings to people who are part of the group but who are not in your sample.

The best sample is a **random sample.** This is a sample in which everyone in your population has an equal chance of being included in your study. When researchers do national surveys, whether on attitudes toward abortion or anything else, they need to get information from only about 2,000 people. Yet, random samples are so powerful that these surveys represent accurately the opinions of 300,000,000 Americans.

Experiments ■ Another research method is the **experiment.** If you were to use this method, you would divide people who have certain characteristics (such as Latinas between the ages of 18 and 21 with two years of college) into two groups. You would expose half of them to some experience. These people are called the **experimental group.** You would do this to see how their reactions differ from those of the other half, who do not have this experience (the **control group**). How the experimental group responds is thought to be generalizable to people who share their characteristics.

Experiments are rare in the study of social problems, partly because ethics do not allow us to create problems for people. For example, to study how women adjust to abortion, you cannot use random samples to order some pregnant women to give birth and others to have abortions. However, you can use experiments in more limited ways. For example, if you want to learn how some type of information affects people's attitudes toward abortion, you could measure a group's attitudes, have a random half of that group learn that information (such as reading a report or listening to a woman talk about her abortion), and then measure the attitudes of both halves of the group.

Field studies ■ In **field studies** (or **participant observation**), researchers go into a setting that they want to learn more about. (This is called "going into the field.") For example, Magda Denes (1976) wanted to know what an abortion clinic was like—for the women and the staff—so she obtained permission to be present and observe what took place. The result was a moving book, *In Necessity and Sorrow.* Denes believes that women should be able to choose abortion, but in the abortion clinic she found sadness everywhere. She describes picking up fetuses from the trash barrel, their little arms broken, cut, and bleeding. A doctor tells her how the fetus stops moving about half an hour after he injects the saline solution, but the women rarely mention this change within them. A single woman talks about her affair with a married man who does not know that she is having an abortion. No other research method could obtain information like this.

Because each method (or research design) has its strengths and weaknesses, sociologists often use more than one. Luker and Denes, for example, each studied women in a single abortion clinic. Their studies could be followed up with surveys of women from many abortion clinics.

FOUR METHODS FOR GATHERING INFORMATION. After choosing a research design, you must decide how to gather your information. Four basic techniques are available: interviews, questionnaires, documents, and observations.

Interviews ■ If you use an **interview,** you will ask people questions on the topics that you want to explore. You can choose from two types of interviews. If you use a **structured interview,** you will ask everyone the same questions (for example, "What is your relationship to the man who made you pregnant?"). If you use an **unstructured interview,** you will let people talk in depth about their experiences; you will, however, make certain that everyone covers specific areas (contraceptive history, family relations, the reasons for the abortion, and so on). Look at the Thinking Critically box on the next page. To learn how women interpret their abortion, I used unstructured interviews. The women could talk about their experiences in any way they wanted, and I never knew where that would lead. Structured interviews would not have tapped such in-depth feelings and perspectives.

Questionnaires ■ If you were to use the second technique, **questionnaires,** you would ask people to answer written questions. Your questions can be either *open ended*

THINKING CRITICALLY About Social Problems

COPING WITH GUILT AFTER AN ABORTION

Having an abortion solves the immediate problem of an unwanted pregnancy, but it also creates new problems. One is how to define the abortion. For those who view the fetus as nonhuman, this can be relatively simple. For those who view the fetus as a human, however (as well as for those with mixed views, which appears to characterize most women), the situation is more complicated.

How do women cope? While abortions were still illegal (1971), I interviewed twenty-two college women who had abortions. These women used four major techniques to help them cope:

1. Some women think of abortion as *the lesser of two evils*. They view abortion as preferable to having a child and ruining their own life or the lives of people they love; as preferable to shifting the responsibility for rearing the child onto others; or as preferable to resenting the child for having been born. One woman said:

   > We saved ourselves and a child and very numerous other people from a lot of hurt because of this. And besides that, it was the only thing I could do—the only thing that I wanted to do, let's put it that way.

2. Some women look at abortion as a *positive good* in and of itself:

   > (My mom) thought it'd be the best thing. . . . After my mom told me, I started to talk to my girlfriend,

and she decided it would probably be the best thing for me, too. . . . I told (my boyfriend). . . . He thought that would be the best thing. . . . I always told myself that, you know, I'd probably get one if I didn't get married, 'cause to me that would be the best thing for me.

3. Some women see themselves as having *no responsibility because they had no choice*:

   > He (boyfriend) insisted that I do this. I was against it. . . . I knew that I didn't want to . . . but when you have someone saying, "Well, this is what I want you to do"—and he didn't want to get married, and he wouldn't let me just have the child like I wanted to do—so I really didn't have a whole lot of choices. You know what I mean?

4. Some women think in terms of *a future pregnancy that will replace the "pregnancy-abortion"*:

   > The mistake is past, if it was a mistake. At any rate, we can do nothing about it now. Now we have to look to the future. In another year John and I will hopefully have the start of our own family. Thoughts of being a mother have entered my mind frequently since the abortion. I really look forward to that day!

(people answer in their own words) or *closed ended* (people choose from a list of prepared answers). An open-ended question might be "What is your relationship to the man who made you pregnant?" The woman would state the relationship in her own words. A closed-ended form of this question would ask the person to check an item on a list, such as husband, boyfriend, casual acquaintance, other. It is easier to compare answers to closed-ended questions, but open-ended questions tap a richer world, eliciting comments and even topics that you might not anticipate.

Documents ■ Written sources or records, called **documents,** can also provide valuable data about social problems. You might examine official records. Kristin Luker, for example, analyzed the records of 500 women who came to the abortion clinic that she studied. Or you might look at more informal records, such as journals, blogs, and letters. These documents can reveal people's attitudes and provide insight into how they cope with troubles.

Observation ■ The fourth technique, **observation,** is just what the term implies: To use it, you observe what is occurring in some setting. You watch and listen to what is taking place and record or take notes on people's conversations or the statements they make. You might use a tape recorder, but if recording will interfere with what people are doing, you will take notes instead, either while something occurs or afterward. If you use *overt* observation, you will identify yourself as a researcher, but if you use *covert* observation, the people in the setting will be unaware that you are studying them.

Sociologists often combine these methods. For example, in her study of the abortion clinic Luker used three of these methods: observation, interviews, and documents. Not only did she observe women and abortion providers in the clinic, but she also interviewed women who were having abortions, and she examined the clinic's records on its patients.

STRIVING FOR ACCURACY AND OBJECTIVITY. When doing research, it is essential to strive for objectivity. You must be on guard against producing biased data. For example, it is obvious that if you were to ask a woman "What is your opinion about killing babies by abortion?" your study would be biased in an antiabortion direction. No one—whether proabortion or antiabortion—favors killing babies. This sort of question would not constitute scientific research. Nor would this question, which would bias answers in the other direction: "What is your opinion on forcing a woman to have a baby when she wants an abortion?"

You can see, then, that scientific studies require objectivity. Compare the biased questions that I just mentioned with these. Here is a neutral closed-ended question: "Do you favor or oppose abortion?" Here is a neutral open-ended question: "What is your opinion about abortion?" For either of these questions, you might specify the trimester being considered. Can you see that these questions are neutral, that they don't tilt answers in any direction? If you ask questions like these, your own opinions about abortion, whatever they might be, will not interfere with your research.

Like everyone else, those of us who are sociologists get our ideas and opinions from the groups with which we associate and the ideas to which we are exposed. No matter how we dislike it, this means that we have biases. Fortunately, we have a safeguard that helps to prevent our biases from contaminating our research on social problems. This is the publication of our findings. In our articles and books, we include details on the methods we use. Other sociologists examine these publications in detail, eager to point out any flaws they can find, including bias.

To help you better understand how sociologists do their research, I asked several researchers to share their experiences with us. The result is a feature in this text called *Spotlight on Social Research*. For an overview of this feature, see the box on the next page.

Should Sociologists Take Sides?

THE PROBLEM OF DETERMINING MORALITY. These research methods allow us to gather objective information on social problems, but they do *not* reveal what attitude or social policy is "correct." This takes us back to the issue I mentioned earlier, that of sociology not having the capacity to specify that one value is superior to another. Abortion, for example, is interwoven with thorny philosophical and religious issues concerning "great questions": life, death, morality, freedom, responsibility, and ultimate existence. Sociologists can study people's ideas about such topics, but sociology has no way to judge whether those ideas are right or wrong, much less to determine the ultimate meaning that may underlie such issues.

To take a position on a social problem is to take sides—and because sociology is not equipped to make judgments about values and morality, sociology cannot tell us what side to take. Even so, the question of taking sides on social problems is debated hotly among sociologists, for, like other thoughtful people, sociologists have their own concerns and ideas about social problems.

The issue is clear-cut. Should sociologists, because they are scientists, forget their own subjective concerns and strive to remain dispassionate, detached, and value-free? If so, they would merely report the facts and not take sides on the social issues that affect our society. Or should they use their professional authority to promote the side of an issue that they see as right? For example, should they try to help the "oppressed," the "down and out," the poor, and others who are on the receiving end of social problems?

THE DEBATE AMONG SOCIOLOGISTS. Those who champion neutrality stress the position that sociologists enjoy no superior vantage point from which to make moral judgments. Sociologists do have knowledge and skills to offer, they say, but not morality. In their study of social problems, sociologists can indicate the potential consequences of different social

Spotlight on Social Research: An Overview of This Feature

Sociologists do a lot of research on social problems. In fact, this is one of their favorite areas of study. As we review the major social problems in this text, you will be introduced to both classic research and the most recent research findings.

To acquaint you with some of these researchers, ten of the chapters have a boxed feature titled **Spotlight on Social Research.** Each box features a researcher who has studied a particular social problem. These boxes are unique, for the researchers themselves have written them.

The research that you will read about in *Spotlight on Social Research* is incredibly varied. With these researchers, you will visit a youth gang in Chicago, a bar in Chicago's inner city where gangsters hang out, and neo-Nazis in Detroit. You'll even be present at a Klan rally. In a study of workers at two magazines, you will learn how views of sexual harassment differ from one work setting to another. You will also learn how one sociologist became so inter-

"That's the worst set of opinions I've heard in my entire life."

Sociologists strive for objectivity and accuracy in their research. To attain this goal, they must put away their personal opinions or biases.

ested in military matters that he went to Iraq. One researcher recounts how his picking beans in the fields of Washington led to a lifetime of doing research on crime. Another researcher shares how her own abuse at the hands of her husband while she was yet a student motivated her to do research on intimate violence.

As these researchers reflect on their studies, they pull back the curtains to let you look behind the scenes. This lets you see how research is actually conducted. To help provide a broader context to appreciate their research, I open each box by sharing a little about the researcher's background and how the researcher became interested in a particular social problem.

I think that you'll enjoy *Spotlight on Social Research*. The "inside" information that these researchers share gives a unique flavor to this text. From these reports, you will learn things about research that are not available anywhere else. I am grateful to these researchers for taking time out of their research and teaching to share their experiences with us. It was a pleasure corresponding with them and gaining insight into their work.

---

policies, but they should not promote any particular policy or solution. To do so would be to hide a moral or value position under the guise of sociology.

On the other side of this issue are sociologists who are convinced that they have a moral obligation to take a stand. "If sociology is not useful for helping to reform society," they ask, "of what value is it?" They stress that sociologists are in a strategic position to relate the surface manifestations of a social problem (such as poverty) to deeper social causes (such as the control of a country's resources by the wealthy and powerful). They say that sociologists should do their research objectively—and always side with those who are being hurt and exploited. Those on the extreme end of this side of this debate also say that sociologists have a moral obligation to make the oppressed aware of their condition and to organize them to do battle against those who oppress them.

UNCOVERING VALUES. To make the issues in this debate clearer, we need to make more evident that values are hidden in all proposed solutions to a social problem. To do this, let's turn away from things that most of us agree on, such as the desirability of eliminating poverty and oppression, and consider controversial matters. What if a group of sociologists were to study unmarried pregnant teenagers and conclude that they all should have abortions? Arguments can be made for and against this position, of course, but should sociologists promote such a point of view? Or consider an even more extreme case. What if sociologists, after analyzing the soaring costs of Social Security and Medicare, became convinced that the solution to this severe problem would be to euthanize the physically and mentally handicapped? Or what if their conclusion was that all people, after celebrating their 80th birthday, should be "put to sleep" by means of painless drugs? Would professional activity on behalf of such proposed social policies be appropriate?

No sociologist is going to support such positions, but I think you get the point. Whenever someone takes a position on a social problem and advocates one solution or another, values of some sort underlie that person's views. Should sociologists, then, *as sociologists,* advocate or promote solutions to social problems?

TAKING SIDES: DIVISIONS AND AGREEMENT. This question of taking sides as *professionals* divided U.S. sociology during the Vietnam War—and it has done so again with Gulf War II. Some sociologists are convinced that professional associations such as the Society for the Study of Social Problems should make public antiwar pronouncements; others, in contrast, feel just as strongly that such a position is out of order. Although wars come and go and issues change, this broad cleavage among sociologists remains. Some say that sociologists should work toward changing society in order to help the less powerful; others are just as convinced that sociology's proper role is only to investigate and report objectively. They say that if sociologists want to take sides on any issue, they should do so as *private citizens,* not as sociologists.

This debate keeps sociologists sensitive to the boundaries between objectivity and partisanship. Although there is little room for middle ground, most sociologists attempt to resolve this dilemma by separating the evidence on social problems from their own values and opinions. What they observe and measure, they attempt to report dispassionately and to analyze as accurately as possible. They try to be explicit when they move from neutral description to a value position.

Despite their disagreements about taking sides on social problems, sociologists agree that they are in a unique position to study social problems and that they should produce thorough and objective studies. Sociologists do possess the tools to do such research, and their studies can be valuable for both the public and policy makers.

A PERSONAL NOTE. As the author of this book, I sincerely hope that the coming chapters help you to acquire a sociological imagination that will allow you to work toward creative solutions for the pressing social problems we face. Sociologists can provide facts on objective conditions, sensitize you to the broader context that nourishes social problems, and suggest the likely consequences of intervention. Your decisions about what should be done about a social problem, however, will have to be made according to *your* values.

SUMMARY AND REVIEW

1. Sociologists use what is called the *sociological imagination* (or perspective) to view the social problems that affect people's lives. This means that they look at how social locations shape people's behavior and attitudes.

2. A *social problem* is some aspect of society that people are concerned about and would like changed. It consists of *objective conditions,* things that are measurable, and *subjective concerns,* the feelings and attitudes that people have about those conditions. Social problems are relative—one group's solution may be another group's problem.

3. Social problems go through a *natural history* of four stages that often overlap: defining the problem, crafting an official response, reacting to the official response, and pursuing alternative strategies.

4. Sociologists are able to make five contributions to the study of social problems: They can help determine the extent of a social problem, clarify people's attitudes toward social problems, apply the sociological imagination to social problems, identify potential social

policies for dealing with social problems, and evaluate likely consequences of those policies.

5. The sociological understanding of a social problem differs from a commonsense understanding because the sociological perspective is not based on emotions or personal values. Instead, sociologists examine how social problems affect people, view the causes of social problems as located in society rather than in individuals, and use scientific methods to gather information about social problems.

6. To study social problems, sociologists use four major *research designs: surveys, case studies, experiments,* and *field studies.* Sociologists gather information in four basic ways: *interviews, questionnaires, documents,* and *observations.* These methods are often used in combination.

7. Because social problems can be viewed from so many vantage points, sociologists disagree on whether they should choose sides as professionals. They do agree, however, that sociological studies must provide objective, accurate, and verifiable data.

KEY TERMS

Case study, 17
Common sense, 16
Control group, 18
Documents, 19
Experiment, 18
Experimental group, 18
Field study (or Participant observation), 18
Generalize, 18
Interview, 18

Methods (Research methods or **Methodology),** 17
Objective condition, 6
Observation, 19
Participant observation (or Field study), 18
Personal trouble, 4
Population, 18
Power, 6
Questionnaire, 19
Random sample, 18

Research design, 17
Sample, 17
Social problem, 6
Sociological imagination (or sociological perspective), 3
Sociological perspective, 4
Sociology, 14
Structured interview, 18
Subjective concern, 6
Survey, 17
Unstructured interview, 18

FOR REFERENCE

Contexts. Published by the American Sociological Association, this magazine summarizes sociological research in an informal and informative manner. Many topics are covered, not just social problems.

Social Problems. Official journal of the Society for the Study of Social Problems, the organization for sociologists and other social scientists who are concerned about social

problems. Available in most college libraries, the journal presents research and theorizing on social problems.

Mother Jones. A magazine with radical and muckraking reporting that covers controversial aspects of social problems.

The Public Interest. A journal whose less-sensational coverage balances the approach of *Mother Jones.*

THINKING CRITICALLY ABOUT CHAPTER 1

1. Select a social problem and apply the sociological imagination to it.
   - What makes this situation a social problem? (Explain how it matches the definition of a social problem outlined in this chapter.)
   - What are the values of the people who are involved in this social problem? (Be sure to look at *both* sides of the problem, not just the one that matches your ideas of what is right or wrong.)
   - What social forces shaped the parties' points of view?

   - What objective conditions changed to bring this problem to the surface?

2. Who do you think is winning the battle between the proabortion and antiabortion activists? Why? Use the court decisions cited in this chapter to support your answer.

3. Select a social problem. Which research methods do you think would be most appropriate for studying this social problem? Why?

4. Do you think that sociologists have a responsibility to take sides on social problems? Why or why not?

Interpreting
Social Problems: Aging

In 1928, Charles Hart, who was working on his Ph.D. in anthropology, did fieldwork with the Tiwi, a preliterate people who live on an island off the northern coast of Australia. Because the Tiwi are uncomfortable around people who do not belong to a clan, they assigned Hart to the bird (Jabijabui) clan and told him that a particular woman was his mother. Hart described the woman as "toothless, almost blind, withered," and added that she was "physically quite revolting and mentally rather senile." He then described this remarkable event:

> How seriously they took my presence in their kinship system is something I never will be sure about. . . . However, toward the end of my time on the islands an incident occurred that surprised me because it suggested that some of them had been taking my presence in the kinship system much more seriously than I had thought. I was approached by a group of about eight or nine senior men. . . . They were the senior members of the Jabijabui clan and they had decided among themselves that the time had come to get rid of the decrepit old woman who had first called me son and whom I now called mother. . . . As I knew, they said, it was Tiwi custom, when an old woman became too feeble to look after herself, to "cover her up." This could only be done by her sons and her brothers and all of them had to agree beforehand, since once it

The Tiwi . . . sometimes got rid of their ancient and decrepit females.

was done they did not want any dissension among the brothers or clansmen, as that might lead to a feud. My "mother" was now completely blind, she was constantly falling over logs or into fires, and they, her senior clansmen, were in agreement that she would be better out of the way. Did I agree?

> I already knew about "covering up." The Tiwi, like many other hunting and gathering peoples, sometimes got rid of their ancient and decrepit females. The method was to dig a hole in the ground in some lonely place, put the old woman in the hole and fill it in with earth until only her head was showing. Everybody went away for a day or two and then went back to the hole to discover to their great surprise, that the old woman was dead, having been too feeble to raise her arms from the earth. Nobody had "killed" her; her death in Tiwi eyes was a natural one. She had been alive when her relatives last saw her. I had never seen it done, though I knew it was the custom, so I asked my brothers if it was necessary for me to attend the "covering up."

> They said no and they would do it, but only after they had my agreement. Of course I agreed, and a week or two later we heard in our camp that my "mother" was dead, and we all wailed and put on the trimmings of mourning.

C. W. M. Hart in Hart and Pilling 1979:125–126.

I don't know about you, but I was shocked when I read Hart's account. He did not see any moral issue in agreeing that the old woman should be "covered up." His only concern was whether he would have to watch the woman die. In our society, too, some people feel that the elderly have outlived their social usefulness and that we should devise our own forms of "covering up." "Why spend precious resources (all that money) on people who have only a few years—or just a few months—more to live?" goes their reasoning.

"Wouldn't we be better off having some way to usher them off the stage of life—with dignity, of course?"

Such opinions elicit a wide range of reactions. Some agree that the frail elderly are a burden and that society is better off without them. This kind of thinking sends chills down the spine of others. If such programs of euthanasia were ever initiated, who would be put in charge of deciding which old people are "socially valuable" and which ones are not? Some fear that the frail elderly might simply be the first targets, to be followed by others whom some officials decide are "useless"—or at least of "less value" and, for the good of the general society, in need of being "covered up."

Although few human groups choose "covering up" as their solution, every society must deal with the problem of people who grow old and frail. You may have noted that the Tiwi "cover up" only old women. This is an extreme example of the discrimination against females that is common throughout the world. This topic is so significant that we shall spend all of Chapter 9 discussing issues of gender. In this present chapter, in which we consider how theories help us to understand social life, we shall explore the social problem of the elderly.

Sociological Theories and Social Problems

As sociologists do research on social problems, they uncover a lot of "facts." If you have just a jumble of "facts," however, how can you understand what they mean? To make sense of those "facts," you have to put them in some order, so you can see how they are related to one another. To do this, sociologists use theories. A **theory** explains how two or more concepts (or "facts"), such as age and suicide, are related. A *theory*, then, gives us a framework for organizing facts, and in so doing it provides a way of interpreting social life.

In this chapter, we shall look at the three main theories that sociologists use—symbolic interactionism, functionalism, and conflict theory. Before we begin, you may want to look at an overview of these theories, which are summarized in Table 2-1 below. Because each theory focuses on some particular "slice" of a social problem, each provides a different

TABLE 2-1   A Summary of Sociological Theories

	SYMBOLIC INTERACTIONISM	FUNCTIONALISM	CONFLICT THEORY
What is society?	People's patterns of behavior; always changing	A social system composed of parts that work together to benefit the whole	Groups competing with one another within the same social system
What are the key terms?	Symbols Interaction Communication Meanings Definitions	Structure Function System Equilibrium Goals	Competition Conflict Special Interests Power Exploitation
What is a social problem?	Whatever a group decides is a social problem is a social problem for that group	The failure of some part to fulfill its function, which interferes with the smooth functioning of the system	The natural and inevitable outcome as interest groups compete for scarce or limited resources
How does something become a social problem?	One set of definitions becomes accepted; competing views are rejected	Some part of the system fails, usually because of rapid social change	Authority and power are used by the powerful to exploit weaker groups

Source: By the author.

perspective on the problem. As you study these theories, keep in mind that each theory is like a spotlight shining onto a dark area: It illuminates only a particular part of that area. Taken together, these theories throw much more light on problems that we want to understand.

Symbolic Interactionism and Social Problems

Introducing Symbolic Interactionism

THE SIGNIFICANCE OF CULTURE. **Symbolic interactionism** is the sociological theory that focuses on the symbols that people use to make sense out of life. Old age, for example, is a symbol, and, like other symbols, it has no constant meaning. Its meaning even differs from one culture to another. When we first see someone advanced in years, for example, we classify him or her as an "old person." As we look at this person, we tend to see the characteristics that our culture assigns to this symbol—wrinkled, weak, unstylish, over the hill. Because we internalize the symbols that dominate our culture, many elderly also see themselves in such terms. In contrast, someone from a culture in which old age symbolizes wisdom or power or privilege tends to perceive an old person in a different light—and so does that elderly person.

This brings us to the essence of the symbolic interactionist perspective: We all see the world through **symbols,** things to which we attach meaning and that we use to communicate with one another. Symbolic interactionists study how symbols, such as the terms we use to classify people, give us our view of the world. As we use the symbols that our culture provides to communicate with one another, we share and reinforce the ways we look at life. The images on television, the printed and spoken word, our body language, our gestures, our tone of voice, our clothing, even our hairstyles—all are symbols by which we communicate views of life. And our views of life include what we consider to be social problems.

THE SIGNIFICANCE OF HISTORICAL CHANGE. Biologically, old age creeps up on us all. As the years pass, we feel our bodies gradually age. Sociologically, however, old age comes suddenly—at retirement, with the first Social Security check, or upon admittance to a nursing home. Our images of old age are largely unpleasant. We use phrases such as old and sick, old and crabby, old and dependent, old and useless. Take your pick. None is pleasant.

Yet during an earlier period of the United States, "old" meant something quite different. Back then—and strange to our ears—the idea of "old" summoned images of wisdom, generosity, even graciousness and beauty. Why did earlier generations have ideas of old age so startlingly different from ours? To find out, Andrew Achenbaum (1978) traced the history of old age in the United States. He found that 200 years ago people placed a high value on the elderly because most people died young. With so few people reaching old age, those who did were admired for their accomplishment. The younger also perceived the elderly as having accumulated valuable knowledge about life. At this time, people also placed a higher value on being actively involved in work, and to quit working simply because of age was considered foolish. Because the elderly were more skilled at their jobs—this was before machinery displaced individual skills—younger workers looked up to them.

How did such a fundamental shift occur in the meaning of old age? We can trace this change back to the late 1800s, an era

As symbolic interactionists stress, our age does not contain built-in meanings. Although the emphasis in this chapter is on the cultural meanings of old age, we can reverse this and look at the cultural meanings of young age. The 5-year-old girl standing in the left foreground of this photo is to be a bride, in an exchange arranged by Pakistani families in Abbakhel.

that saw major advances in public health, especially improvements in sanitation. As a result, many more people reached old age, and no longer was being elderly a distinction. During this time, ideas about work were changing, too. With the invention of machine-driven tools and the development of mass production techniques, work was becoming "deskilled." No longer did it take years of apprenticeship under highly skilled workers to learn how to do a job. The new machines were social levelers; they made the younger workers just as knowledgeable and productive as the older ones. As the elderly lost the uniqueness that had brought them respect, their social value declined. Old age began to suggest uselessness rather than usefulness, foolishness rather than wisdom. In short, being old was no longer an asset but a liability.

Because symbols change, so do social problems. Earlier in our history, when most people died young, some people survived the odds and reached advanced age. At that time, if they had problems because of their age, those problems were matters for them or their family to handle. They were no one else's responsibility. Old age was a *personal* problem, not a *social* problem. Today, in contrast, with so many people reaching old age, we perceive elderly people as a group. We tend to lump them together, and we consider social action (laws and policies) to be appropriate for solving their problems. A major transition had occurred, and *what was once a personal problem had become a social problem.*

IN SUM From our brief review of what it meant to be elderly during an earlier period in the United States, we can see that as society changes, so do its symbols. Because the term *social problem* is also a symbol, what people consider to be a social problem also changes from one historical period to another. The elderly, for example, don't think of the aged in the same way as younger people do, one of the topics of the Spotlight on Research box by Phyllis Moen on the next page. *From the perspective of symbolic interactionism, then, social problems are whatever people in a society define as social problems.* What we now take for granted, we may later see as a problem, and what we now see as a problem, we may later take for granted.

The Development of Symbolic Interactionism

Symbols are so essential for what we are and for what we become that they could be the essence that separates us from the rest of life on this planet. Symbols allow us to think about other people and objects, even when they are not present. We also symbolize our own self (that is, we think about our self in a certain way, such as young, attractive, and personable).

How we symbolize others and our self influences our behavior. For example, as we saw in Chapter 1, some women risk unwanted pregnancies because the use of contraceptives would conflict with their self-image. Although the specifics differ, all of us make choices on the basis of what is comfortable for our self-images—from the clothing we wear and the type of car we drive to the music we listen to and the type of career we aspire to.

COOLEY AND THE LOOKING-GLASS SELF. To such insights, Charles Horton Cooley (1864–1929) added this principle: By interacting with others, *people come to view themselves as they think others perceive them.* He summarized this principle in the following couplet:

Each to each a looking-glass
Reflects the other that doth pass.

Cooley said that our interactions with others create a **looking-glass self.** By this, he meant that our self has three elements: (1) how we think we appear to others, (2) how we think others feel about what they perceive, and (3) how we feel about this reflected image. According to Cooley, our self-esteem depends on our looking-glass self. It is the same with the elderly. If a society reflects negative images to its old people, the elderly tend to think of themselves negatively.

Spotlight on Research

STUDYING YOUNG PEOPLE WHO BECAME OLD

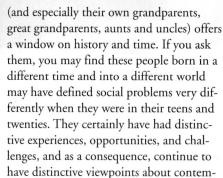

PHYLLIS MOEN, *Professor of Sociology at the University of Minnesota, does research on the problems and challenges people face as they advance through the life course. Much of her research focuses on the careers and working lives of people who are approaching retirement age.*

Gerontologists are scholars who study older people. I became a gerontologist by the back door. I started out (and continue to be) a life-course sociologist, interested in people's pathways through work and family roles and relationships, and how these are shaped by gender and social policy.

When I was a young professor at Cornell University, I found out that one of my colleagues (Robin M. Williams, Jr.) had, many years previously (in the 1950s), interviewed a random sample of young women in Elmira, New York. This is the only project he had never completed, and Robin regretted over the years never having followed through on it. One of my graduate students, Donna Dempster-McClain, and I got together to study his 1950s data and were fascinated by the differences in women's lives then from our own. Donna and I got the bright idea of reinterviewing these women 30 years later, and reinterviewing their (now adult) daughters as well. We thought this a wonderful opportunity to document the ways tremendous social changes in gender roles touched women's lives across the generations. With the help of graduate students, other committed researchers, and a grant from the National Institute on Aging, we found almost all of these women and reinterviewed them and their daughters, capturing their remarkable life histories from the 1950s through the 1980s. What we knew cognitively but hadn't counted on emotionally was that these young mothers in the 1950s had, three decades later, aged. And that is how I got into studying older people!

Because my focus has been on lives and not any one age group, my perspective is not on people as ever being "old." I always encourage students to capture the life histories of the older people in their lives, to see the remarkable ways they have come to be the people they are today. Students who do so often find that interviewing earlier cohorts (and especially their own grandparents, great grandparents, aunts and uncles) offers a window on history and time. If you ask them, you may find these people born in a different time and into a different world may have defined social problems very differently when they were in their teens and twenties. They certainly have had distinctive experiences, opportunities, and challenges, and as a consequence, continue to have distinctive viewpoints about contemporary social issues. Asking about the timing of people's trajectories and transitions in education, paid work, and family life helps to reveal the "person" behind the stereotypes and myths about older people. The interviewee may be in his or her 60s, 70s, or 80s, but still see themselves as the same person they were years ago—the kid attending school, the employee starting a job, part of a couple buying the first house and raising a family—in what seems to them like only yesterday.

I continue to study differences in life pathways by cohort and gender, especially as people move from their career jobs to what are traditionally thought of as the retirement years.

My research breaks the myths and stereotypes about retirement as the gateway to being "old." I find that most older workers and retirees in their 60s and early 70s *want* to work—whether for pay or as a volunteer, but not full-time! Boomers can look forward to unparalleled health and longevity as they age, along with potential "second acts:" opportunities for flexible new careers, whether as paid employees or as unpaid volunteers. The large babyboom cohort confronts this transition in a climate of uncertainty and ambiguity, where career jobs and pensions often disappear in the face of globalization, mergers and downsizing.

And, for the first time in history, women are also retiring in unprecedented numbers. Couples often face two retirements: his and hers. My research shows that couples may live together longer "retired" than they did prior to retirement. But they seldom plan for retirement, beyond thinking about the age or date they will retire. It is the same way many young people plan for the wedding but not the years of married life. And yet the retirees I interview typically say they should have planned for life in retirement: how they will spend the ten, twenty, or thirty years of healthy, "youthful" living they can now look forward to.

MEAD AND TAKING THE ROLE OF THE OTHER. Another sociologist of Cooley's era, George Herbert Mead (1863–1931), focused on the role of symbols in social life. Symbols are so important, he said, that without them we couldn't even have social life, for it is symbols that allow us to have goals, to plan, to evaluate, even to know what love is. He concluded that even our self-concept, which evolves during childhood, is based on symbols. One of the major means by which we develop our self-concept is learning to **take the role of the other.** That is, as children we gradually become capable of putting ourselves in someone else's shoes, able to empathize with how that person feels and thinks and to anticipate how he or she will act. After this, we learn to take the role of people in general—which Mead called the **generalized other.**

To illustrate these terms, consider baseball, one of Mead's favorite examples. Suppose that after an exhausting, but exhilarating, season, your team has made it to the playoffs for the state championship. Now, in the final game of the series, it is the bottom of the ninth inning. There are two outs, the bases are loaded, the score is tied, and you are at bat. You feel intense pressure, unlike anything you've experienced before. It is all up to you. This will be your moment of glory—or of defeat. At this point, you probably won't *take the role of the other*, but you could. That is, you do understand some of the pressures that the pitcher feels as he or she winds up. And you probably do sense a heightened awareness of *the generalized other* at this point, of how others in general—your teammates, the opposing team, your family, and the fans—will feel if you strike out or get a hit.

THE SOCIAL CONSTRUCTION OF REALITY. As we go through life, we all try to make sense out of what happens to us or, as the symbolic interactionists phrase it, each of us is involved in the **social construction of reality.** As we reflect on our experiences, we have a choice of symbols (or definitions, or meanings) that our culture provides to apply to them. To choose one set of symbols yields one way of interpreting what happens to us, while to choose another set gives our experiences a different meaning.

The implications of this concept are profound. It means that reality does not come with built-in meanings, but, rather, that we construct our realities as we apply symbols to our experiences. To help understand this idea, let's apply it to the question of when "old age" begins. Did you know that the answer is rooted more in *social* experiences than in biology? Certainly, there is nothing magical about turning 65—or any other age—that automatically makes someone "old." Yet the 65th birthday has become a marker of old age. Why? Strangely, it is rooted in nineteenth-century German politics. At that time Otto von Bismarck (1815–1898), the architect of the German empire, was fighting a political movement known as socialism. In order to weaken the appeal of socialism to Germans, Bismarck pioneered the idea of social security payments to older people. But at what age should such payments begin? To force some of his generals out of power, Bismarck chose 65 as the mandatory retirement age. Bismarck's political decision has given us a symbol that significantly affects how we perceive age.

To help make the social construction of reality clearer, think about the family of a Japanese officer who has fallen on his sword after losing a battle. His family uses the symbols that their culture provides, those of honor and duty, to understand why he took his life. Now think about Americans who have just learned that their sister has committed suicide: As they try to figure out why she took her life, they, too, use symbols that their culture provides. These symbols, in contrast, emphasize the responsibility of friends and family, and they end up asking such questions as "Am *I* to blame for not picking up on hints of suicide?" "Should *I* feel guilty?" "What could *I* have done differently?" In each instance, that of the Japanese and the Americans, the survivors use the symbols of their culture to socially construct reality. In each instance, too, that reality is different because the symbols that the culture provides are different. To catch a glimpse of Americans as they work out answers to the "why" of suicide, see the Issues in Social Problems box on the next page.

IN SUM To socially construct reality is a part of everyday life. We all try to make sense of what happens to us—whether this means figuring out why we received an A or an F on our last test, why we were promoted or fired at work, or even why we like or dislike some television program or video game. In short, *the events of life do not come with built-in meanings, and we all use the symbols provided by our culture to make sense out of life.* Symbolic interactionists call this process *the social construction of reality.*

Issues in Social Problems

MAKING SENSE OF SUICIDE: THE SOCIAL CONSTRUCTION OF REALITY

Some of the most difficult research I have done was to interview the friends and family of people who had committed suicide. Their wrenching emotional turmoil created similar effects in me. The interviews yielded rich data, however, and here are some things I found concerning suicide and the social construction of reality.

After someone commits suicide, people who were close to that person try to make sense out of what happened. As their shock wears off, they mentally relive events associated with the dead person. They begin to interpret these events in light of the suicide. As they do so, the events take on new meaning. Survivors almost always ask why the individual took his or her life. As they explore this "why," they confront the horrifying possibility that they themselves could have been part of the reason. They then face this burning issue: "If I had done something different, maybe he (she) would still be alive."

This search for meaning and for cause leads survivors to reconstruct the past, which can be a tortured process. Listen to this father of a 25-year-old who shot himself with a handgun. You can hear the questions that plague him as he reconstructs events in his search for satisfactory answers regarding his son's death:

> I've wondered where it began if it was suicide. Was it in grade school? Or college? Or was it all this girl? Could I have done something different? Or wouldn't it have helped? Wondering which is right and which is wrong. . . . I think this thing or that thing could have been done to change the course of events. But you just don't know. I even thought, "If we hadn't moved from St. Louis to Crestview years ago."

To interpret what happens to us in life, we all use symbols to socially construct reality. When it comes to death by suicide, our culture does not offer satisfactory symbols. This leaves people perplexed as they search for meaning.

Contrast suicide with death from disease. When people die from a disease, family members don't face this type of challenge to the self. Seldom does the symbol *disease* trigger the question "Could I have done something different?" This symbol points to causes beyond us—to germs and chances in life and other factors usually beyond a person's control. The symbol *suicide*, in contrast, denies us this more comfortable interpretation of causation.

The cultural symbols of *normal* and *not normal* also come into play. *Normal* points to causes beyond us. When the label *suicide* is attached to a death, however, we are denied this category, too. Our culture defines suicide as *not normal*. This forces us into a search for the meaning of suicide, which can bring severe challenges to the self. Listen to this survivor as he explains why he can't use the symbol *normal*:

> If he'd been driving and killed in a car wreck—that's an everyday thing. But this was special, and there had to be something wrong—whether with me or the family—if a car wreck, a normal way people die—and his personality—figured he'd never do something like that, and couldn't really believe he could have done it. It's an unusual way, and is evidently caused by something or other—some kind of a problem.

Our culture offers many symbols to help people adjust to the death of loved ones. Among them is "God's will." This symbol, if it can be used, moves causation clearly beyond the survivors of the deceased, allowing easier acceptance of the event. If God called the individual home, the survivors certainly bear no responsibility for the death. The family members of a suicide, however, are denied this category, too. Listen to this woman as she struggles with the meaning of her husband's death:

> Well, I would have felt in my own mind that God had called him from the earth and that He had a reason for calling him, and that we could have accepted it as Christians that it was the will of God, and that we could feel in our hearts that God, in his tenderness, had taken him up with him. I can't feel that this was the will of God.

From these examples, you can see that culture provides symbols (labels, categories, concepts, words, terms) that people use to interpret the events of their life. By looking at how the survivors of suicide search for meaning, we can observe *the social construction of reality* as it occurs. We can see that the usual symbols offered by our culture are denied these people, plunging them into uncertainty, a search for meaning that usually ends in despair.

These examples can make us more aware of how *we* use our culture's symbols to provide meaning for *our* experiences. You can see that if our culture provided different symbols, we would interpret our experiences differently. The *social construction of reality*, sometimes difficult to understand, is an ordinary part of our everyday lives.

Based on Henslin 1970.

Applying Symbolic Interactionism to Social Problems

THE SOCIAL CONSTRUCTION OF SOCIAL PROBLEMS. In Chapter 1, we discussed how some groups consider an objective condition of society to be a social problem, while others do not. This embodies the symbolic interactionist perspective. Social problems are not like stones lying along the roadside, independent of whoever observes them or picks them up. Rather, from among all the objective conditions in society, people pick some out and define them as problems.

The elderly provide a good example. As we have seen, they do not automatically constitute a social problem. The status of the elderly depends on how people view them. The aged can be admired and respected—or regarded as worthless. Just as the meaning of being old once made a major shift in U.S. society, so it could again. If the elderly grow wealthier and more powerful, for example, then more positive features of social life will be associated with old age, and the elderly will receive greater respect. They might even be admired, but for certain they would no longer be considered a social problem. In short, social problems are socially constructed, and what is considered a social problem changes over time.

As emphasized in the Issues in Social Problems box on suicide (page 31), symbolic interactionists stress the significance of **labeling.** This simply means that people categorize things—that they put tags on other people or on events and then act accordingly. For example, the label "old age" is sometimes used to explain health problems. Medical professionals may write off an elderly woman's mental or physical problems as being due to her age (perhaps labeling her "senile"). This label (or symbol) lets them feel comfortable about not treating her or about giving her placebos (fake medicine). They may think, "What else can you expect from such an old woman?" In many cases, medical treatment could alleviate problems that are written off as "that's-the-way-old-people-are." For example, using the labels "malnutrition" and "Alzheimer's disease" to account for someone's memory loss and confusion implies the need to search for physiological causes and treatment. In contrast, the labels "old" and "senile" usually do not imply such a search. Labels, then, affect how we perceive and react to problems.

Symbolic Interactionism and Social Problems: A Summary

IN SUM Symbolic interactionists stress that social problems are socially constructed; that is, people decide to place the label *social problem* on some objective condition. If they don't place the label on that objective condition, it is not a social problem. If they do, it is. To understand social problems, then, we must focus on how objective conditions become socially constructed into social problems. Symbolic interactionists also stress that to understand any social problem, we must take into account what that problem means to the people who are involved in it.

Functionalism and Social Problems

Introducing Functionalism

The second major theory that sociologists use to interpret social problems is **functionalism** (or **functional analysis**). Functionalists compare society to a self-adjusting machine that is composed of many parts. Each part of a machine has a *function*. When a part is working properly, it fulfills that function, and the machine hums along. Functionalists also use the analogy of an animal. An animal has many organs, and when an organ is working properly, it contributes to the well-being of the animal. Like a machine or animal, society is also composed of many parts. Each of society's parts also has a function. When a part is working properly, it contributes to the well-being (stability or equilibrium) of society. When a part is not working properly, it hurts the well-being of society.

To see how one part of society helps other parts, consider health care and Social Security, two social services designed to help the elderly. Of the vast sums spent on health care for the elderly, some goes into medical research. The discoveries by medical researchers help not only the elderly but also children and adults of all ages. Similarly, not only do the 36 million retired and disabled workers who collect Social Security benefit from this program but so do the 64,000 people who work for this federal agency (*Statistical Abstract* 2006:Tables 483, 537). Their families also benefit. The spending of these vast sums, in turn, helps businesses across the nation. In other words, functionalists stress how each part of society contributes to the well-being of other parts of society.

To see how the functionalist perspective applies to social problems, think of society as a single machine with many parts. When each part does its job, the machine runs smoothly. If some part fails, however, the whole machine can suffer. Functionalists call these failures **dysfunctions.** If a dysfunction creates instability or disequilibrium in society, it is a social problem. *From the functionalist perspective, then, a social problem is the failure of some part of society, which then interferes with society's smooth functioning.* Of the many components of the social problem of the aged, consider red tape and nursing homes. When the aged try to get help, they face complicated bureaucratic rules and regulations called red tape. Although not intended to, this red tape interferes with the distribution of resources to the elderly. Another problem is "rip-off" nursing homes: Money that is intended to go to the most dependent among the elderly goes instead into the pockets of unscrupulous operators.

The Development of Functionalism

AUGUSTE COMTE: SOCIETY AS ORGANISM. Functionalism has its roots in the origins of sociology (Turner 1978). Auguste Comte (1798–1857), who is called the founder of sociology, developed his ideas during the social upheaval that followed the French Revolution. Comte concluded that society is like an animal: Just as an animal has tissues and organs that are interrelated and function together, so does society. For a society to function smoothly, its parts must be in balance.

HERBERT SPENCER: SOCIETY AS STRUCTURE. Herbert Spencer (1820–1903) built on these ideas. He emphasized that the parts of society work together in a **structure** (a system, or whole). Just as each part of an animal, taken together, forms the animal's structure (or whole), so each part of society, taken together, forms its structure. Each part also makes some contribution to the structure, which Spencer called its **function.** Because the parts are interrelated, a change in one part affects other parts.

EMILE DURKHEIM: NORMAL AND ABNORMAL STATES. Later in the nineteenth century, Emile Durkheim (1858–1917) built on the idea that a society is composed of parts that perform functions. When society's parts perform their functions, he said, society is in a "normal" state. If society's parts do not fulfill their functions, society is in an "abnormal" or "pathological" state. To understand society, we need to look at both **structure**—how the parts of a society are related to one another—and **function**—how each part contributes to society.

ROBERT MERTON: FUNCTIONS AND DYSFUNCTIONS. The final functionalist I shall mention is Robert Merton (1910–2003). Merton defined *functions* as the beneficial consequences of people's actions. Functions help a social system to survive (to maintain stability or equilibrium). Functions can be either manifest or latent. A **manifest function** is an action that is *intended* to help some part of the system. For example, Social Security is intended to make life better for the elderly. Improving life for the aged, then, is a *manifest*

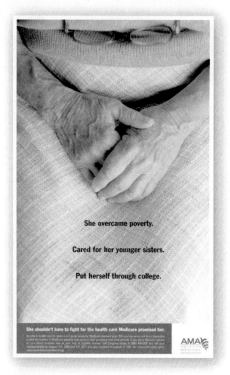

She overcame poverty.

Cared for her younger sisters.

Put herself through college.

She shouldn't have to fight for the health care Medicare promised her.

Functionalists analyze functions and dysfunctions of human actions. One of the latent (unintended) functions of some medical research has been to enable more people to live into old age. This, in turn, has both functions (positive consequences) and dysfunctions (negative consequences) for other parts of society.

function of Social Security. As Merton emphasized, our actions also have **latent functions.** These are consequences that also help a system to adjust, but they are *not intended* for that purpose. For example, the salaries paid to the 64,000 employees of the Social Security Administration help to stabilize our economy. Because this beneficial consequence of Social Security is not intended, however, it is a *latent* function.

Merton (1968) stressed that human actions also have dysfunctions. These are consequences that disrupt a system's stability, making it more difficult to survive. If a part fails to meet its functions, it contributes to society's maladjustment and is part of a social problem.

Because the consequences of people's actions that disrupt a system's equilibrium usually are unintended, Merton called them **latent dysfunctions.** For example, the Social Security Administration has thousands of rules, written in incredible detail, designed to anticipate every potential situation. If the 64,000 employees of this agency were to follow each procedure exactly, the resulting red tape would interfere with their ability to serve the elderly. The rules are not intended to have this effect, however, so they are *latent* dysfunctions.

IN SUM   Although these theorists had different emphases, they have this in common: They sensitize us to think in terms of *systems*, to see whatever we are studying as part of a larger unit. Functionalists emphasize that when we examine one part of a system, we must look at how it is related to other parts. As we do so, we analyze that part's functions or dysfunctions. Let's apply these terms of functionalism to the social problem of aging.

Applying Functionalism to Social Problems

From the functionalist perspective, *society* is a social system composed of interconnected parts that function together. When those parts work well, each contributes to the equilibrium of society. Equilibrium simply means that society's parts are balanced, that they have made an adjustment to one another. A *social problem*, then, is a condition in which the parts of society are not working well together. There is an imbalance of some sort.

SOCIAL PROBLEMS AS A RESULT OF CHANGE. A major source of social problems is social change, for change disrupts the adjustment of society's parts, forcing those parts to make new adjustments. We already have seen how social change caused a shift in the meaning of old age. When machine production made many of the elderly's skills outdated, the elderly came to be seen as a dependent group that needed to be taken care of. From the functionalist perspective, a change in one part of society (in this case, production) changed an interrelated part of society (elderly workers), and a new social problem arose.

FUNCTIONS. Now let's see how *functions* applies to this social problem. Society needs to pass its positions of responsibility (jobs) from one group (the elderly) to another group (younger people). To entice the elderly to leave their positions, dangled before them are Social Security and private pensions. In exchange for these benefits, the elderly transfer their jobs to younger people. In this view, called **disengagement theory,** the elderly get paid for not working and, in return, the younger people take over their jobs (Cumming and Henry 1961; Cockerham 1991). This trade-off is functional for society, for both old and young benefit from the exchange. From the functionalist perspective, this is an example of how society is a self-regulating machine that makes the adjustments necessary to keep it humming along.

Even nursing homes, despite their negative publicity, are functional: They have helped society adjust to social change. Care of the elderly used to fall primarily upon women's shoulders. Because women worked at home and few people made it to old age, this was not a general problem. But then two forces clashed: More women began to work outside the home and life expectancy started to jump. The result was more frail elderly who needed care and fewer women available to care for them. Nursing homes were developed to

Stereotypes of the elderly are inadequate. There are many types of elderly people. In general, people carry into their older years the habits and lifestyles they developed during their younger years.

replace these women, and today 4.5 percent of Americans over the age of 65 live in nursing homes (*Statistical Abstract* 2006:Tables 11, 68). This is the total at any one time. Over the years 37 percent of all 65-year-olds need such long-term care (Kemper et al. 2006). Most of these residents are *not* typical of older people: Most are ill, very old, or have no family. Again, the machine has adjusted to change.

As they analyze social problems, functionalists also look for *latent* functions, such as those revealed in interviews with the adult children of the residents of a nursing home. For about half of these adult children, caring for a frail parent who had health problems had been such a burden that it had strained their affection for their parent. After they placed their parent in the nursing home, the love that had been obscured by duty gradually recovered. As one 57-year-old daughter reported: "My mother demanded rather than earned respect and love. We had a poor past relationship—a love/hate relationship. Now I can do for her because I want to. I can finally love her because I want to" (Smith and Bengston 1979:441). Because it was not intended, restored love is a *latent* function of this nursing home.

DYSFUNCTIONS. Functionalists also study *dysfunctions.* Unlike the nursing home in this study, which was middle class and well run, few nursing homes are pleasant places. Some analysts refer to nursing homes as "houses of death" or "human junkyards." Many stink of urine, and it is depressing to see so many sad people clustered together. After being admitted to a nursing home, most elderly people *decline* physically and mentally. A chief reason is the dehumanized way they are treated: segregated from the outside world, denied privacy, and placed under rigid controls. Many nursing homes control their residents chemically, giving them psychotropic drugs such as Thorazine and Prozac (Gurvich and Cunningham 2000). These "chemical straitjackets" keep elderly patients quiet, but they also can reduce them to an empty shell of their former selves. This particular dysfunction, elderly people being abandoned in abusive nursing homes, is concentrated among the poor elderly who have no close family and friends.

Research on nursing homes shows that abuse is common (Harris and Benson 2006). Sociologists Karl Pillemer and David Moore (1989) surveyed nursing homes in New Hampshire. Thirty-one percent of the staff reported that during the past year they had seen physical abuse—patients being pushed, grabbed, shoved, pinched, kicked, or slapped. Eighty-one percent said they had seen psychological abuse—patients being cursed, insulted, yelled at, or threatened. When asked if they themselves had abused patients, 10 percent admitted that they had physically abused them, and 40 percent admitted to psychological abuse. The most abusive staff members were those who were thinking about quitting their jobs and those who thought of patients as being childlike.

Another dysfunction of nursing homes is neglect, such as ignoring patients or not giving medications on time. Some neglect comes from conscientious workers who are assigned so many responsibilities that they can't keep up with them all. Other neglect is purposeful, coming from workers who don't care about their patients or who even take pleasure in harming them. Here is an example of atrocious neglect:

> A nursing home patient was sent to the hospital for the treatment of a bedsore. The hospital staff treated the condition and gave the nursing home instructions on how to keep the wound clean and dressed. Several days later, family members noticed an odor and seepage from the wound and asked that the patient be returned to the hospital. The hospital staff looked at the bandage and saw that it had not been changed as they instructed. When the bandage was removed, insects crawled and flew out of the wound. (Harris and Benson 2006:87)

With the public painfully aware of abuse in nursing homes, to decide whether or not to place an elderly family member in a nursing home can be agonizing. Even though an aged parent may be too sick to be cared for at home, to place a parent in a nursing home is viewed by many as a callous denial of love and duty. Nursing homes don't have to be abusive places, however. To see how two major units of society, the government and the family, can work together to provide high-quality care for the elderly, see the Global Glimpse box on the next page.

Functionalism and Social Problems: A Summary

IN SUM   Table 2-2 presents an overview of functionalism. As you look at this table, begin with the column marked *Action*. This column refers to actions that have taken place in the social system. The examples in this table refer to business, government, medicine, and the family, but we could include the other social institutions. The column headed *Manifest Function* refers to the intended beneficial consequence of the action. The column headed *Latent Function* refers to a beneficial consequence of the action that was not

TABLE 2-2 Old Age: A Functionalist Overview

RELATED PARTS OF THE SOCIAL SYSTEM[1]	ACTION	MANIFEST FUNCTION	LATENT FUNCTION	LATENT DYSFUNCTION
Economic (business)	Pension and retirement benefits	Provide income and leisure time for the aged	Jobs for younger workers	Displacement of the elderly; loss of self-esteem; loss of purpose
Political (government)	Social Security payments	Stable income for the aged; dignity in old age	Employment for 64,000 people by the Social Security Administration	Inadequate income; many recipients live on the edge of poverty
Medical	Technological developments; gerontological specialties	Longer lives for the population	A larger proportion of the elderly in the population	The Social Security system becomes much more expensive
	Medicare and Medicaid	Provide good health care for the elderly	Financing bonanza for the medical profession	"Rip-off" nursing homes
Family	Grown children live apart from their parents	Independence of both younger and older generations	Institutionalized care for the elderly; greater mobility of younger workers	Isolation of elderly parents; loneliness and despair

[1]As used here, "parts" of the social system are social institutions.
Source: By the author.

A Global Glimpse
THE COMING TIDAL WAVE: JAPAN'S ELDERLY

With one of the world's lowest birth rates, Japan's population is aging faster than that of any other nation. In 1950, only 66 Japanese turned 100. Now it is 1,700 a year. To see how rapidly Japan's population of elderly is growing, look at Table 2-3. In just a few years, one of every four Japanese will be age 65 or older.

Think about the implications of such a large percentage of elderly. What will happen to Japan's health care services? About half of the Japanese elderly will be age 75 and over. More than 1 million of them are expected to be bedridden. Another million are likely to be senile. By the year 2020, Japan's medical bill is likely to run six times higher than it is now. How will Japan be able to meet the health needs of this coming tidal wave of elderly?

This question must be placed within the context of Japanese culture, specifically, the obligations of one generation to another. The Japanese believe that because parents took care of their children, the children are obligated to care for their parents. Unlike in the United States, *most* aged Japanese live with their adult children. As the number of elderly mushrooms, will the Japanese family be able to carry on its traditional caregiving and protective roles?

With a shortage of younger workers, Japan is turning to robots for help. Shown here is Hello Kitty Robo, designed to replace receptionists of hotels, hospitals, and other businesses. One form of this robot, the ifbot, will be used in nursing homes.

TABLE 2-3	Japan's Population Age 65 and Older			
1950	1970	1990	2000	2020
4%	7%	12%	16%	24%

Because Europe faces similar problems, Japanese leaders decided that they could learn from Europe's system. But when Japanese observers saw Europe's lower work ethic, higher taxes, and lower savings—all leading to a declining ability to compete in global markets—the Japanese decided to work out their own plan. One goal is to reduce inequality among the aged. With this goal in mind, the government has begun to unify the country's pension systems and has increased spending for social security. To care for the elderly who have no families and those who are the sickest, the government is building nursing homes. To improve the quality of life for the healthy elderly, the government is financing 10,000 day service centers. These will be available to the poor and rich alike. The government will also provide transportation to physiotherapy centers and offer free testing for the early detection of cancer and heart disease. The government has also created a new position called "home helper." After passing a government examination, 100,000 specialists will help the elderly at home.

Japan's low birth rate amidst a surging older population has led to the search for alternative workers to care for the elderly. In an Orwellian twist, a Japanese company has come with an unusual answer—robots. These robots, called Hello Kitty Robo, are able to transmit both messages and images. To keep residents of nursing homes mentally active, the robots will ask riddles and quiz residents on math problems. They will also chat with residents and ask about their health.

These services and facilities are not intended to replace the family's care for the elderly, but, rather, to supplement it. They are meant to strengthen, not crowd out the family.

Gnawing at these ambitious plans, however, is a disturbing economic reality. For over a decade, Japan has been in the midst of a depression. Only now is the country coming out of it. With huge federal deficits, some of these plans will have to be shelved. Regardless of economic conditions or whether the society is ready, the tidal wave of elderly is on its way. It will arrive on schedule.

Based on Freed 1994; Nishio 1994; Otten 1995; Mackellar and Horlacher 2000; "Hello Kitty Robot . . . " 2006.

---

intended. The last column, *Latent Dysfunction,* refers to an unintended harmful consequence of the action.

Remember that functionalists assume that society is like a well-oiled, self-adjusting machine. They examine how the parts of that machine (society, or the social system) are interrelated, analyzing how those parts adjust to one another. As society undergoes change, a social problem arises when some part or parts of society do not adjust to the change and are not functioning properly.

Conflict Theory and Social Problems

Introducing Conflict Theory

"We couldn't disagree more," reply conflict theorists to the functionalist position. The parts of society do not work together harmoniously. If you look below the surface, you will see that society's parts are competing with one another for scarce resources. There are only so many resources to go around, and the competition for them is so severe that conflict is barely kept in check. Whether they recognize it or not, the elderly, for example, are competing with younger people for available resources. If the competition heats up, open conflict between the young and the elderly could erupt, throwing society into turmoil. In short, the guiding principle of social life is disequilibrium and conflict, not equilibrium and harmony, as the functionalists say.

From the conflict perspective, social problems are the natural and inevitable outcome of social struggle. No matter what a social problem may look like on its surface, at its essence lies a conflict for limited resources between the more and less powerful. As the more powerful exploit society's resources and oppress the less powerful, they create such social problems as poverty and discrimination. As those who are exploited react to their oppression, still other social problems emerge: street crime, escapist drug abuse, suicide, homicide, riots, revolution, terrorism. To study social problems, we need to penetrate their surface manifestations and expose their basic, underlying conflict.

The Development of Conflict Theory

KARL MARX: CAPITALISM AND CONFLICT. Karl Marx (1818–1883), the founder of **conflict theory,** witnessed the Industrial Revolution that transformed Europe. Cities mushroomed as peasants left the land to seek work. The new industrialists put the peasants—and their children—to work at near-starvation wages. As poverty and exploitation grew, political unrest followed, and upheaval swept across Europe.

Shocked by the suffering and inhumanity that he saw, Marx concluded that the hallmark of history is a struggle for power. In this struggle, some group always holds the top position, and, inevitably, it oppresses those groups under it. Marx also concluded that a major turning point in this historical struggle occurred when **capitalism** became dominant in the Western world—that is, when a small group of people gained control over the means of production and made profit their goal. As machinery replaced workers' tools, the **capitalists** (owners of the capital, factories, and equipment) gained an exploitive advantage.

Because tens of thousands of peasants had crowded into the cities in a desperate search for work, the capitalists, who owned the means of production, were able to impose miserable working conditions. They paid workers little and fired them at will. The capitalists at this time also controlled the politicians. When workers rebelled, they could count on the police to use violence to bring them under control. When the capitalists made concessions to workers, these were not signs of cooperation but, rather, strategic devices to control workers and weaken their political solidarity. The day of reckoning will finally come, said Marx, quite pointedly, and it will be bloody. The workers will overthrow their oppressors and will establish a classless society in which the goal will be not profits for the few but, rather, the good of the many.

In Marx's time, workers were at the mercy of their bosses. Workers lacked what many take for granted today—a minimum wage, eight-hour workdays, five-day workweeks, paid vacations, medical benefits, sick leave, unemployment compensation, pensions, Social Security, even the right to strike. Conflict theorists remind us that such benefits came about not because of the generous hearts of the rich but because workers fought for them—sometimes to the death.

It is difficult for us to grasp what conditions were like for workers in early capitalism. With the daily wage the equivalent of a loaf or two of bread, workers could not afford what we would call homes. The luckier ones slept 20 to a room, acquaintances and entire families sprawled out on the floor. The less fortunate ones, as in this photo, made do with even less. It was conditions like this that motivated Karl Marx to do his research.

GEORG SIMMEL: SUBORDINATES AND SUPERORDINATES. Some sociologists have extended conflict theory far beyond workers and capitalists. Sociologist Georg Simmel (1858–1918), for example, compared the relationships of people who occupy higher positions (superordinates) with those who are in lower positions (subordinates). Simmel noted that a main concern of superordinates is to protect their positions of privilege. Because subordinates possess some power, however, the more powerful must take them into consideration as they make these decisions (Coser 1977). Consequently, superordinate–subordinate relationships are marked not by one-way naked power but by exchange. If employers want to lower the benefits of a pension plan, for example, they must get unions to agree. In return, the workers will insist on a trade-off, such as increased job security.

Conflict, noted Simmel, also has positive features. For example, when the members of a group confront an external threat, they tend to pull together. Similarly, if several groups face a common enemy, they tend to become more cohesive (Giddens 1969; Turner 1978). In times of war, for instance, antagonistic groups often shelve their differences in order to work together for the good of the nation. Workers might give up their right to strike, as U.S. workers did during World War II. In return, employers might agree to binding arbitration of all disputes. To prevent sabotage at U.S. docks during World War II, the U.S. Justice Department even asked Lucky Luciano, who headed the Mafia at the time, to spy on dock workers. Hoping to gain U.S. citizenship, Luciano did so. (After the war, Luciano was deported.)

LEWIS COSER: CONFLICT IN SOCIAL NETWORKS. Sociologist Lewis Coser (1913–2003) analyzed why conflict is especially likely to develop among people who have close relationships. He pointed out that whether we refer to bosses and workers or to a husband and wife, each is part of a balance of power, responsibilities, and rewards. Through some system of negotiation or the imposition of power, the members have developed a relationship, one that is precariously balanced. Actions by either party, such as making new decisions—which are necessary to adjust to changing times—can upset the balances that people in the same network have worked out.

Applying Conflict Theory to Social Problems

THE SOCIAL CONFLICT UNDERLYING SOCIAL SECURITY. As we apply the conflict perspective to the elderly, let's see how Social Security came about. In this drama, the three major players are elderly workers, younger workers, and employers. A fourth, Congress, also appears. From this perspective, Congress represents the interests of the employers.

From the point of view of conflict theory, old people became a social problem when those in power found it advantageous to push them aside. When the Industrial Revolution spread across the United States, old people turned out to be a nuisance to the owners of big business. Not only did these older workers earn more than younger workers, but also they were not as docile. As the new machinery of the Industrial Revolution "deskilled" work, younger workers became as productive as the older workers, and the owners fired many of the elderly. This thrust most of the elderly into poverty, because in those days there was no unemployment compensation and Social Security. As a result, during the 1920s, *two-thirds* of all Americans over 65 could not support themselves (Holtzman 1963; Hudson 1978). In short, industrialization transformed the elderly from a productive and respected group to a deprived and disgraced group.

Then the Great Depression struck, bringing even more suffering to millions of elderly. In 1930, in the midst of national despair, Francis Everett Townsend, a physician, spearheaded a social movement to rally the elderly into a political force. He soon had one-third of all Americans over 65 enrolled in his Townsend Clubs. Feeling their power, the elderly demanded benefits from the government (Holtzman 1963). Townsend's plan was for the federal government to impose a national sales tax of 2 percent to provide $200 a month for every person over 65. This is the equivalent of about $2,200 a month today. Townsend argued that the elderly's increased spending would generate new businesses and lift the nation out of the depression.

By 1934, the Townsend Clubs had gathered hundreds of thousands of signatures on petitions, and the Townsend Plan went before Congress. This was an election year, and

The U.S. elderly, who today are a potent political force, were not a political group until Dr. Francis Everett Townsend (shown here) organized them in the 1930s. Townsend, a retired physician, gained national prominence when in the midst of the Great Depression he proposed a $200 a month pension plan for all the nation's elderly. Potential revolutionaries ("commies," as they were called) were arousing people all over the country, and Townsend, too, frightened politicians. Townsend also spear-headed campaigns against congressional members who objected to his plan.

Congress felt vulnerable to a grassroots revolt by old people. But Congress was caught in a bind: The Townsend Plan called for a high monthly pension during a period of unprecedented unemployment when the country was strapped for money. Many also feared that if younger people knew that the government was going to give them a pension when they were old, it would sap their incentive to work and save (Schottland 1963). Congress looked for a way to reject the Townsend Plan without angering the elderly by appearing to oppose old-age pensions. Seeing the political opportunity, President Franklin Roosevelt announced his own, more modest Social Security plan in June 1934. Relieved at this way out of its bind, Congress embraced Roosevelt's proposal.

Although the Townsend Clubs did not get their plan passed, they did force Congress to pass Social Security. The clubs then fought to improve Social Security. Benefits were not scheduled to begin until 1942, which would leave millions of workers without support. As the Great Depression lingered, dragging even more old people into poverty, the clubs stepped up their political pressure. As a result, Congress voted to begin paying Social Security benefits in 1940 and to increase the amounts paid to the destitute elderly (called old-age assistance grants).

IN SUM When conflict theorists analyze a social problem, they look for conflict among competing interest groups. In this example, they emphasize that today's Social Security benefits did not come from generous hearts in Congress, but from the political power of the elderly, who had banded together to push their own interests. To appease the elderly and avoid a political crisis, Congress gave in, but granted as little as it thought it could get by with. Only when the elderly stepped up the pressure did Congress increase benefits—and that reluctantly. The elderly, however, paid dearly for their benefits: They were removed from the workforce—for Congress set a mandatory retirement age of 65. This, in turn, gave employers the goal they wanted: a younger, less costly, and more compliant workforce.

Conflict Theory and Social Problems: A Summary

CONFLICT AND SOCIAL PROBLEMS. At the root of each social problem lies conflict over the distribution of power and privilege. This means that social problems are inevitable, for it is inevitable that groups will come in conflict with one another as they try to maintain or to gain control over power and privilege. Most conflict is limited—not a battle to the death, but a fairly orderly, focused affair. Retired Americans, for example, have not fought bloody battles in the streets, but they have formed political lobbies to compete for resources with other groups. Understanding that power and privilege lie at the root of social problems helps analysts to penetrate the surface and to pinpoint what any particular social problem is all about.

TWO TYPES OF SOCIAL PROBLEMS. From the conflict perspective, social problems come in two forms. One is the trouble experienced by people who are exploited by the powerful. The other is the trouble experienced by the powerful when the exploited resist, rebel, or even appeal to higher values. Although their resources are limited, the exploited do find ways to resist. Some go on hunger strikes or campaign for political office. Others take up arms against those in power. As we saw with the Townsend movement, the elderly—a group weak in and of itself—were able to seize the initiative during a troubled period and force a change to improve their circumstances.

IN SUMMARY

As you can see, each of the three theoretical perspectives provides a unique interpretation of social life. By focusing on different aspects of a social problem, each paints a different picture of that problem. In the coming chapters, we will apply these three theoretical perspectives to the social problems that we analyze. To conclude this chapter, let's look at the probable future of the social problem of the elderly.

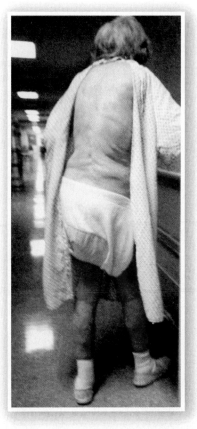

As the number of elderly increase, so do the costs of their health care. Cost is only one issue. Another is the quality of care, including the need to treat the elderly with respect. As is evident from the photo of this woman, in some medical settings even basic dignity is stripped from the elderly.

The Future of the Problem: The Pendulum Swings

Changing Objective Conditions and Subjective Concerns

Images of poor, ill, neglected grandparents have been used to promote programs for elderly Americans. But such images are no longer broadly accurate. Economic growth and the expansion of federal programs have reduced the poverty rate for the aged to the point that it is now *below* the nation's average. To get an idea of how tremendously poverty among the aged has dropped, consider this: In 1970, 25 percent of the elderly were poor, but today just 10 percent are (*Statistical Abstract* 1990:Table 746; 2006:Table 696).

This turnaround is so remarkable that some people think that the elderly are now receiving more than their fair share—an attitude that reflects a fundamental shift in the subjective concerns of this social problem. This shift takes several forms. One is the idea that the decline of poverty among the elderly has come at the cost of other groups. Figure 2-1 shows the objective conditions concerning age and poverty. Note how poverty among the elderly has declined and how poverty among children has fluctuated. The reduction in poverty among the elderly has not caused anyone else to move into poverty.

This change in subjective concerns—the belief that the elderly are demanding, and getting, more than their fair share of society's resources—often centers on the costs of health care. Look at Figure 2-2. You can see how the costs of Medicare and Medicaid have soared. These costs have zoomed past the wildest projections of earlier years. Another subjective concern is the cost of Social Security. In 1950, Social Security payments ran $784 million, but today they run $493 billion. Analysts are alarmed when they see that the current payout is more than *600 times* the amount paid in 1950 (*Statistical Abstract* 1998 and 2006:Table 538).

Despite the rapid run-up in the costs of Social Security, Medicare, and Medicaid, there is no sign that these costs will level off. Today, about one in eight Americans is age 65 or over. Figure 2-3 on page 44 shows how the percentage of U.S. elderly will grow over the next decades. In about 20 years or so, one in five Americans will be elderly. This growth will hit Social Security and health care hard.

FIGURE 2-1   The Poverty Rates of Children and the Elderly

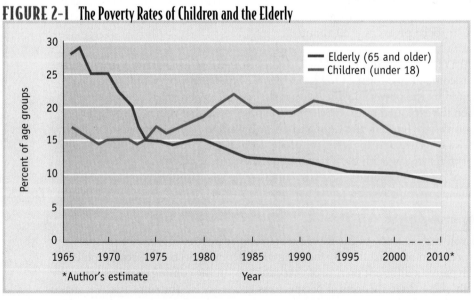

Source: Congressional Research Services; Statistical Abstract 1994:Tables 728, 731; 2006:Table 693.

FIGURE 2-2 Health Care Costs for the Elderly (and Disabled)

Medicare funds are provided to the elderly and disabled by the federal government. Medicaid is intended for the needy and is financed by federal, state, and local governments. Although these two programs began at modest levels, their costs have soared.

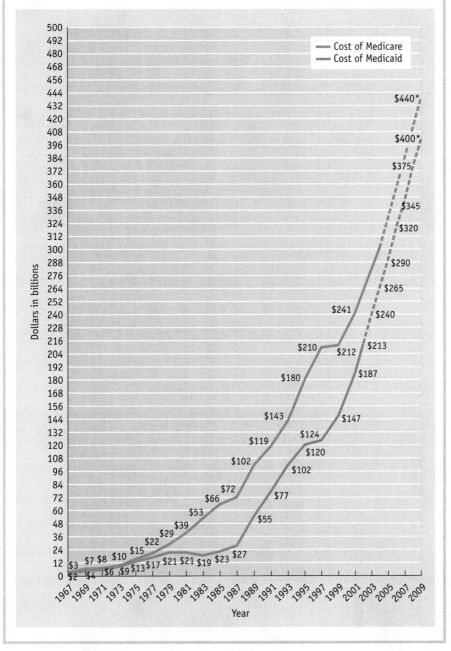

* The author's estimate.

Source: Statistical Abstract 1992:Table 147; 1994:Table 159; 1997:Tables 164, 165; 2006:Tables 133, 136.

The Emerging Struggle

"Congress has caved in and has given too many benefits to old people." So goes a chorus of complaints, based on fears that the growing numbers of elderly—who are more likely to vote than are younger people—have been able to manipulate Congress. With this observation, some want to trim Social Security, Medicare, and other programs for

FIGURE 2-3 The Graying of America

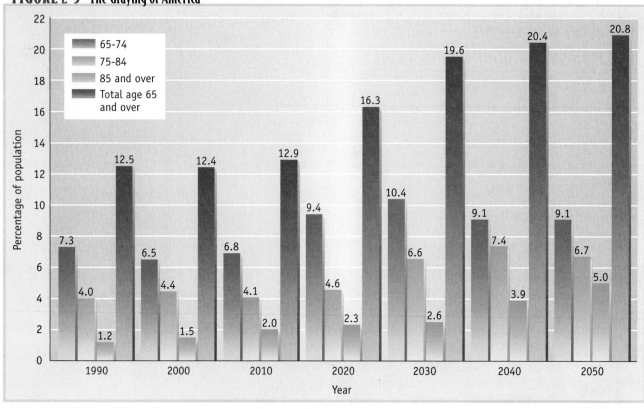

Legend:
- 65-74
- 75-84
- 85 and over
- Total age 65 and over

Y-axis: Percentage of population
X-axis: Year

1990: 7.3, 4.0, 1.2, 12.5
2000: 6.5, 4.4, 1.5, 12.4
2010: 6.8, 4.1, 2.0, 12.9
2020: 9.4, 4.6, 2.3, 16.3
2030: 10.4, 6.6, 2.6, 19.6
2040: 9.1, 7.4, 3.9, 20.4
2050: 9.1, 6.7, 5.0, 20.8

Source: Statistical Abstract 2003:Tables 11, 12; 2006:Table 12.

Apparently there are two dominant images of the elderly: the poor and the wealthy. Certainly there are some of each among the elderly, but, in general, the elderly are neither poor nor wealthy. With the implementation of social programs, especially Social Security, the poverty rate of the elderly is less than that of the nation as a whole.

the elderly. These benefits, they say, go beyond the nation's ability to pay. As a result of these complaints, some reductions have been made. Social Security income, for example, used to be tax free, but it is now taxable. Despite such measures, as you saw from Figure 2-2, costs continue to escalate.

To protect their gains, older Americans have organized a powerful political lobby. This group, AARP (formerly the American Association of Retired Persons), boasts 35 million members and a staff of 1,200. For politicians, whose foremost goal appears to be to get reelected, it is difficult to ignore such numbers. Could a battle between younger people and the elderly be on its way? Consider the activities of the Gray Panthers, whose position is summarized in the Issues in Social Problems box below.

Some form of conflict does seem inevitable, for the interests of younger and older groups are on a collision course. There are two major problems. The first is that the money a worker "contributes" to Social Security is not put into the worker's own account. Instead, the money that is collected from workers across the nation is paid out to retired workers—a sort of chain-letter arrangement by which the younger support the older. The second problem is that the proportion of workers who collect Social Security benefits is growing,

Issues in Social Problems
THE GRAY PANTHERS

WHO WE ARE

We are a group of people—old and young—drawn together by deeply felt common concerns for human liberation and social change. The old and young live outside the mainstream of society. **Ageism**—discrimination against persons on the basis of chronological age—deprives both groups of power and influence.

Besides being a movement of older and younger persons, as Gray Panthers we consider ourselves distinctive in the following ways:

We are against ageism that forces any group to live roles that are defined purely on the basis of age. We view aging as a total life process in which the individual develops from birth to death. Therefore, we are concerned about the needs of all age groups and ageism directed at any age group.

We have a strong sense of militancy. Our concern is not only for education and services, but also for effective nonviolent action with an awareness of timing and urgency.

We advocate a radical approach to social change by attacking those forces that corrupt our institutions, attitudes, and values, such as materialism, racism, sexism, paternalism, militarism, and extreme nationalism.

Over the years, the elderly have become more politically astute in their lobbying. They have influenced political decisions by both threatening bloc votes and by manipulating images of poverty and the elderly.

WHAT WE WANT

1. To develop a new and positive self-awareness in our culture that can regard the total life span as a continuing process in maturity and fulfillment.
2. To strive for new options for lifestyles for older and younger people that will challenge the present paternalism in our institutions and culture, and to help eliminate the poverty and powerlessness in which most older and younger people are forced to live, and to change society's destructive attitudes about aging.
3. To make responsible use of our freedom to bring about social change, to develop a list of priorities among social issues, and to struggle nonviolently for social change that will bring greater human freedom, justice, dignity, and peace.
4. To build a new power base in our society uniting presently disenfranchised and oppressed groups, realizing the common qualities and concerns of age and youth working in coalition with other movements with similar goals and principles.
5. To reinforce and support each other in our quest for liberation and to celebrate our shared humanity.

Reprinted by permission of The Gray Panthers.

but the proportion of people who are working—those who pay for these benefits out of their wages—is shrinking. We are seeing a major shift in the **dependency ratio,** the number of workers compared with the number of Social Security recipients. Presently, just under five working-age Americans pay Social Security taxes to support each person collecting Social Security. In about a generation, this ratio will drop to about 3 to 1 (Melloan 1994; *Statistical Abstract* 2006:Tables 535, 537).

A third problem is the so-called Social Security Trust Fund, which is supposed to prevent an intergenerational showdown. The problem is that there is no fund, and you can't trust it. The U.S. government has collected $1 trillion more in Social Security taxes than it has paid to retirees. Supposedly, this huge excess has been placed into a trust fund, reserved for future generations. The "fund," however, exists in name only. Its billions of dollars disappear into thin air. Just as fast as they come in, the federal government "borrows" them and spends them on whatever it desires (Henslin 2007). The day of reckoning between the generations can't be far off.

To close this chapter, let's see what different pictures emerge when we apply the three sociological perspectives to the struggle between the generations.

THINKING CRITICALLY About Social Problems

APPLYING THE THEORIES: UNDERSTANDING THE INTERGENERATIONAL BATTLE

Theories often appear vague and abstract. To help overcome this obstacle, as I introduced each theory in this chapter I applied it to the social problem of aging in U.S. society. Because these theories will be used throughout this text, it is important to understand them. Let's apply these three perspectives to the potential battle between the generations—the cutting edge of this social problem of aging and something that, in one way or another, you are likely to experience personally. Each theory yields a unique picture of a social problem, allowing us to compare their different interpretations.

Symbolic Interactionism: Symbols are the essence of social life, including social problems. We use symbols to interpret the events we experience in life. If we were to use different symbols, we would understand our experiences differently. Just as the meaning of old age shifted during industrialization, so this symbol is shifting again. Today's elderly have grown more affluent, and they are choosing new lifestyles: Their condos, motor homes, and vacations in exotic destinations make their new affluence highly visible. As a consequence, people's ideas of the elderly are changing. Out of the struggle that is shaping up between the generations will come a new set of symbols, one that will guide how we think about and act toward old people.

Functionalism: Younger workers and the elderly are two major parts within the same social system. Because each part must work together if society is to function smoothly, these parts must also fit together well. If one of them absorbs too much of a society's resources, it creates an imbalance between these parts. Whenever an imbalance occurs, the parts must adjust in order for the larger unit (in this case, society) to attain equilibrium. Just as giving more resources to the elderly during the past two generations was an adjustment, so now, if those resources have become disproportionate, it will require another adjustment. Although the adjustment will be difficult, both the younger workers and the elderly are essential parts of society. The final result will be a harmonious balance between them.

Conflict Theory: Of course, there is a battle shaping up. Like other groups within society, the older and younger are marked by unequal power and privilege. Like other groups, each will struggle for its own interests. The AARP will push its own agenda, striving for greater advantage and as many resources as it can grab for itself. The concern of the elderly will be their own interests, regardless of how their gains may affect younger people. For their part, younger people will do the same, pursuing their own interests to the exclusion of other groups. Whenever one group gains a larger share of society's limited resources, others will resent those gains. The coming struggle between the generations is likely to be fierce, and the group with more power will win. Regardless of the outcome of this current competition for resources, conflict will continue in future generations.

SUMMARY AND REVIEW

1. The frameworks that sociologists use to interpret their research findings are called *theories*. To interpret social problems, sociologists use three major theories: *symbolic interactionism, functionalism,* and *conflict theory.* Each theory provides a different interpretation of society and of social problems. No one theory is "right." Rather, taken together, these perspectives give us a more complete picture of the whole.

2. *Symbolic interactionists* view social problems not as objective conditions but as views that are collectively held about some matter; that is, if people view something as a social problem, it is a social problem. As people's views (or definitions or symbols) change, so do their ideas about social problems.

3. *Functionalists* see society as a self-correcting, orderly system, much like a well-oiled machine. Its parts work in harmony to bring the whole into equilibrium. Each part performs a function (hence, the term *functional* analysis) that contributes to the system's well-being. When a part is functioning imperfectly, however, it creates problems for the system. Those dysfunctions are called social problems.

4. *Conflict theorists* view social problems as a natural outcome of unequal power arrangements. Those in power try to preserve the social order and their own privileged position within it. They take the needs of other groups into consideration only when it is in their own interest to do so. As they exploit others, the powerful create social problems, such as poverty and discrimination. Other social problems, such as revolution, crime, suicide, and drug abuse, represent reactions of the oppressed to their exploitation.

KEY TERMS

Ageism, 45
Capitalism, 38
Capitalists, 38
Conflict theory, 38
Dependency ratio, 46
Disengagement theory, 34
Dysfunction, 33
Function, 33

Functionalism, 32
Generalized other, 30
Labeling, 32
Latent dysfunctions, 34
Latent functions, 34
Looking-glass self, 28
Manifest function, 33

(The) Social construction of reality, 30
Structure, 33
Symbol, 27
Symbolic interactionism, 27
Taking the role of the other, 30
Theory, 26

THINKING CRITICALLY ABOUT CHAPTER 2

1. Of the three theories identified in this chapter, which one do you think does the best job of explaining social problems? Why?

2. Select a social problem other than aging:
   - How would symbolic interactionists explain this problem?
   - How would functionalists explain the problem?
   - How would conflict theorists explain the problem?

3. What do you think are the biggest problems that we are likely to face regarding the "graying of America" (the aging of the U.S. population)? Select a social problem other than aging:
   - Why do you feel your solutions might work?
   - What might prevent your solutions from working?

CHAPTER 3

Human Sexual Behavior

The issue of same-sex marriage divides Americans. For example, here are some reactions to the Massachusetts Supreme Court's ruling in 2004 that marriage between people of the same sex did not violate that state's constitution:

A state representative lamented: "From the Bay State to the Gay State. Massachusetts will be forever known as the birthplace of homosexual marriage." He added, "I had hoped that people of common sense, who understand what nature and marriage is all about, would prevent this from happening." He then sponsored an amendment to the state constitution that would ban same-sex marriages. That amendment failed. Others are being proposed.

On the other side was a lawyer who had argued before the state supreme court that same-sex couples had the constitutional right to marry. His reaction: "I hope what people see is that there are very committed couples from all walks of life in Massachusetts who, in some cases, have been waiting decades to take legal responsibility for one another. This case has always been about real people and real families."

> # The issue of same-sex marriage divides Americans.

The court's decision was offensive to people from many faiths. The archbishop of Boston said, "The creation of a right to same-sex marriage in the end will not strengthen the institution of marriage within our society but only weaken it, as marriage becomes only one lifestyle choice among many others."

Even the President of the United States weighed in, saying, "Marriage is a sacred institution between a man and a woman. [The Massachusetts] decision . . . violates this important principle. I will work with congressional leaders and others to do what is legally necessary to defend the sanctity of marriage."

Across the nation, same-sex marriage has become a common theme in gay pride marches and parades.

Activists on both sides have proposed state and federal legislation that would either limit marriage to a union between a man and a woman or would allow marriage between people of the same sex.

Based on Bayles 2004; Davey 2004; Healy 2004; Weitzstein 2004; LeBlanc 2007.

Objective Conditions and Subjective Concerns

Determining what is and is not a social problem when it comes to human sexuality takes us to those principles that I stressed in the first chapter of this text. You will recall from our discussion that objective conditions alone are not adequate to make something a social problem. Also essential are subjective concerns: A lot of people must dislike the objective condition and want to see it changed. This principle applies to all the topics we discuss in this book, including those that we review in this chapter. If we had only objective conditions—people who have sexual preference for members of their own sex, for example—we would have no social problem.

Some people who have no difficulty applying this principle to discrimination against women or minority groups or to the dominance of small nations by international corporations get upset when sociologists say that homosexuality is a social problem. What they fail to realize is that sociologists are not making a judgment about homosexuality. Rather, as illustrated by same-sex marriage, sociologists are simply pointing out that homosexuality fits the definition of social problems perfectly—there is an objective condition that upsets large numbers of people who want to do something about it. As you read this chapter, then, keep in mind that to say that homosexuality is a social problem says *nothing* about whether homosexuality is desirable or undesirable, only that large numbers of people are upset about it.

It is the same with prostitution and pornography. When sociologists say that these sexual behaviors are social problems, they are not making a value judgment. They are applying the essence of social problems—objective conditions (the existence of prostitution and pornography) are accompanied by subjective concerns (people's negative reactions). When it comes to prostitution and pornography, however, the reaction to sociological objectivity often goes in the opposite direction: People sometimes get upset when they realize that sociologists are *not* saying that prostitution and pornography are bad, that they are analyzing them without making value judgments.

Our job in this chapter is to examine three human activities that are mired in controversy, more so, perhaps, than any social problem other than abortion. As we do so, it is important to stress a sociological principle that is fundamental to this chapter: As much as we might like it otherwise, *sex is never only a personal matter*. All societies control or channel human sexual behavior, primarily through the social institution of marriage and family, which is fundamental for shaping people's ideas of right and wrong. As is evident from the issue of same-sex marriage, challenges to people's established ideas of marriage and family are not taken lightly.

Because many people view the topics of this chapter in moral terms, it is also important to stress another point made in the first chapter: Sociology has no tools to make moral judgments. Sociology, in contrast, is well-equipped to report on attitudes and social controversy—the concerns that make contemporary life so exciting. To help us understand the three social problems that make up this chapter, we will apply one of the three theories to each topic. We shall apply conflict theory to homosexuality, view prostitution through the lens of functionalism, and use symbolic interactionism to analyze pornography. As usual, we shall present both the scientific evidence and the controversies that surround these behaviors.

Homosexuality

Let's begin by looking at what researchers have to say about the issues on people's minds when they talk about homosexuality. Despite strong social norms and early and continued socialization into heterosexuality, how do people become homosexuals? How many people are homosexuals? Do some heterosexuals have sex with people of their own gender? With changing norms, how much opposition is there to homosexuality today?

Background: Getting the Larger Picture

HOMOSEXUAL BEHAVIOR VERSUS HOMOSEXUALITY. To place matters in perspective, we need to see the larger picture. Attitudes toward **homosexual behavior**—sexual *relations* between people of the same sex—vary widely around the world. To Westerners, the attitudes and behavior of the Sambia and the Keraki of New Guinea are startling. The Sambia believe that boys do not grow into men naturally, that they will remain small and weak if they do not swallow semen. To ensure that they turn into men, all Sambian boys have oral sex with the men of the tribe. The homosexual behavior of the Keraki occurs during their puberty rites, which are kept secret from females. At this time, the older boys and the unmarried men have anal intercourse with the younger boys. During the next year's puberty ceremonies, the same thing happens. After that, until these boys marry (a woman), they, too, sodomize the younger boys (Ford and Beach 1972). For both the Sambia and the Keraki, homosexual behaviors are considered a passage to "masculinization." Both Sambian and Keraki boys go on to a heterosexual life; they marry women and become fathers (Gilmore 1990).

Attitudes also vary toward **homosexuality,** the sexual *preference* for people of one's own sex, but here cross-cultural attitudes are more consistent. No society in the world considers exclusive, or even predominant, homosexuality in adulthood to be the norm. From a functionalist viewpoint, the primary reason is the family's role in human societies. To perpetuate the human group, adults are expected to become parents, and all societies build the family around some form of mother, father, and children. General homosexuality would upset this biologically based arrangement.

ATTITUDES IN THE UNITED STATES. In recent years, Americans have grown more tolerant toward homosexuality. This tolerance is reflected in the changing attitudes of college freshmen. Look at Figure 3-1, which is based on national samples that represent accurately the attitudes of all U.S. college freshmen. As you can see, their attitudes held fairly constant until 1990, after which they made a sharp shift toward greater tolerance. As you can also see, the attitudes of the women have been consistently more favorable than those of the men. Despite this change, of all freshmen across the United States, one of four or five women and about two of five men still want homosexual relations to be illegal.

Let's move beyond college freshmen to get a broader picture of U.S. attitudes. The survey results shown in Table 3-1 are also from a well-chosen national sample. From this table, you can see that 52 percent of Americans think that homosexual relations between consenting adults should be legal, and 43 percent want homosexual relations—even between consenting adults—to be illegal. The information from this table allows you to sketch a profile of those who are most likely to support the legalization of homosexual relations: college-educated younger white women who live in a Western city or the suburbs, who make over $75,000 a year, and who are Democrats or Independents. Those most

FIGURE 3-1 What Do College Freshmen Say About Homosexual Relationships Being Illegal?

The percentage of U.S. college students who agree with this statement: "It is important to have laws prohibiting homosexual relationships."

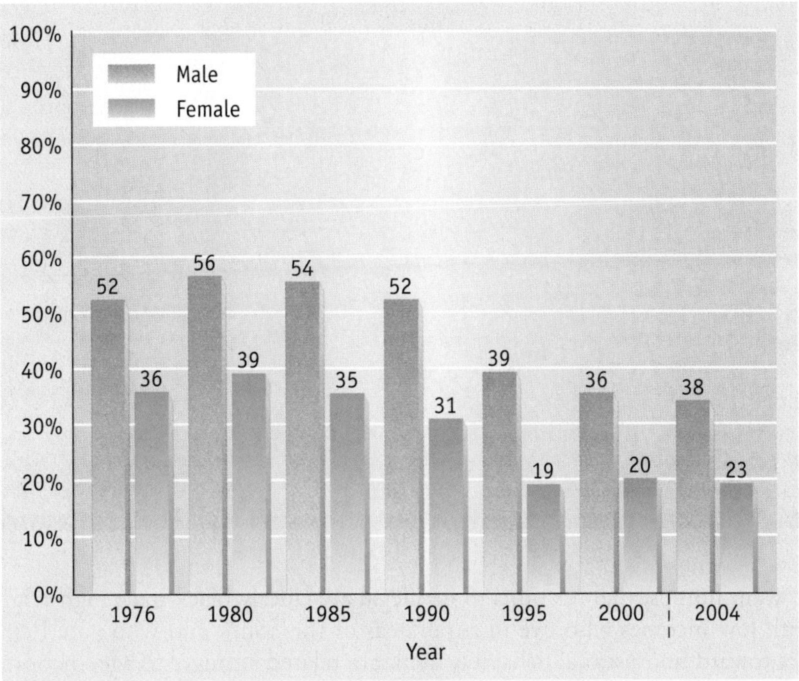

Source: Sourcebook of Criminal Justice Statistics 2005:Table 2.94.

TABLE 3-1 Attitudes Toward the Legality of Homosexual Relations

Question: "Do you think homosexual relations between consenting adults should or should not be legal?"

	LEGAL	NOT LEGAL	NO OPINION
National	52%	43%	5%
Sex			
Female	55%	41%	4%
Male	50%	45%	5%
Race–Ethnicity[1]			
White	55%	41%	4%
Black	36%	59%	5%
Age			
18 to 29 years	59%	41%	0%
30 to 49 years	58%	34%	8%
50 to 64 years	52%	46%	2%
50 years and older	45%	51%	4%
65 years and older	35%	57%	8%
Education			
College postgraduate	68%	28%	4%
College graduate	71%	24%	5%
Some college	58%	37%	5%
High school graduate or less	37%	58%	5%
Income			
Under $20,000	39%	58%	3%
$20,000 to $29,999	47%	45%	8%
$30,000 to $49,999	54%	43%	3%
$50,000 to $74,999	53%	42%	5%
$75,000 and over	65%	30%	5%
Urban/Rural			
Urban area	56%	38%	6%
Suburban area	55%	40%	5%
Rural area	42%	55%	3%
Region			
West	63%	33%	4%
East	58%	35%	7%
Midwest	56%	41%	3%
South	40%	56%	4%
Politics			
Independent	56%	38%	6%
Democrat	59%	37%	4%
Republican	43%	53%	4%

[1] Only these two groups are listed in the source, other than an even more amorphous category, "Nonwhite."

Source: *Sourcebook of Criminal Justice Statistics* 2005:Table 2.99.

likely to want homosexual relations to be illegal are elderly black male high school graduates with low incomes who live in rural areas of the South and who vote Republican. Attitudes toward homosexual behavior, then, are related strongly to age, income, education, race–ethnicity, geography, and politics. The attitudes of men and women across the nation follow the same pattern as those of college freshmen: Women are more likely to favor the legality of homosexual relations.

HOMOSEXUALS AND THE LAW. The social institutions of U.S. society have presumed the norm of **heterosexuality,** the sexual preference for persons of the opposite sex. For example, until 1960, *in all states,* even private, consensual sexual acts between adults of the same sex were illegal. In 2003, twelve states still had these laws on their books, but in that year, in *Lawrence et al. v. Texas,* the U.S. Supreme Court struck down the Texas law that made such sex illegal (Liptak 2005). This decision applies to all states.

Over the years, homosexuals have been the victims of violence because of their sexual orientation. Until recently, however, there was no way of knowing the extent of their victimization. This changed in 1990 when Congress passed the *Hate Crime Statistics Act,* which authorized the FBI to collect data on "crimes that manifest evidence of prejudice based on race, religion, ethnicity, and sexual orientation." Later, disability and national origin were added to this list. **Hate crimes** are not distinct crimes but, rather, are ordinary crimes such as assault that are motivated by dislike or hatred of the victim's characteristics. In this instance, the victim is chosen because he or she is a homosexual. Each year, about 1,500 homosexuals are the victims of hate crimes (*Statistical Abstract* 2006:Table 305). The actual total is larger, because not all victims file reports and not all police agencies report these data to the FBI.

Owing to the activities of gay liberation groups and the American Civil Liberties Union, as well as by changing attitudes, homosexuals face less discrimination than they used to. The Civil Service Commission used to deny federal employment to homosexuals, but no longer. Similarly, such multinational giants as AT&T, GM, Ford, and IBM no longer discriminate against homosexuals in hiring or promotion. San Francisco even purposely recruits homosexuals to be members of its police force. Homosexuals used to be easy targets of politicians who wanted to ingratiate themselves with voters and further their own political ambitions. Today, a politician who verbally attacked homosexuals would likely be facing the end of a political career.

Despite such changes, discrimination against homosexuals persists, especially in hiring and promotion at small businesses. Some groups openly discriminate. For example, the FBI and CIA will not hire known homosexuals. Although the Defense Department follows a "Don't Ask, Don't Tell" policy, soldiers who are discovered to be homosexual are discharged from the military. The Supreme Court has upheld this policy.

You are now familiar with the two dimensions of social problems; objective conditions and subjective concerns. As symbolic interactionists stress, subjective concerns are matters of definition—how people view something. What symbols do you see in this photo that the demonstrators are using with the goal of changing subjective concerns?

To understand homosexual–heterosexual relations better, let's look at them through the lens of conflict theory.

Homosexuality Viewed Theoretically: Applying Conflict Theory

In reaction to the discrimination they experienced, homosexuals found that politics was the best way to forge social change. *Coming out of the closet*—that is, publicly asserting a homosexual identity—they marched in public demonstrations, campaigning for legal reform and demanding more social rights. Beginning with local campaigns in cities such as San Francisco and New York, homosexuals made an impact on national politics. As a result, some politicians actively court the homosexual vote, and unlike in the recent past, no politicians with serious ambitions can make them a target of hostility.

As homosexuals have publicized their demands, homosexuality has become a political and social issue. The promotion of homosexuality as an alternative lifestyle has generated intense opposition, becoming a hot issue in schools and in work settings. Conflict is inevitable when opposing groups jockey for position. One demands greater power, and the other resists that demand. Out of conflict can come a shift in power alignments and a reevaluation of ideas, attitudes, and positions. A common solution to keeping the peace is for competing groups to make trade-offs, each giving up something that it desires. Truces, however, are often uneasy, especially when they involve groups whose values are antithetical. In these instances, conflict eventually resurfaces. All it takes is for one side to try to shift the terms of the uneasy and often unspoken alignment.

Research on Homosexuality

THE KINSEY RESEARCH. Let's turn to an overview of sociological studies of homosexuality. Alfred Kinsey and his associates included homosexuality in their pathbreaking study, *Sexual Behavior in the Human Male* (1948). To understand the Kinsey findings of more than a half century ago, keep in mind the distinction between homosexual behavior and homosexuality. Based on case histories of about 5,300 males, Kinsey found that 37 percent of U.S. males have at least one sexual experience with a same-sex partner that results

Gay Pride days offer homosexuals the opportunity both to protest and to affirm their identity and views. Demonstrations, as with this parade in Manhattan, New York, arouse both support and opposition.

in orgasm. Such experiences, however, do not make people homosexuals. As Kinsey pointed out, most of these homosexual behaviors are a form of experimentation, and almost all of these males go on to live heterosexual lives. Kinsey also concluded that about 4 percent of U.S. males are exclusively homosexual throughout life.

Kinsey's findings shocked the U.S. public and unleashed a storm of criticism in the academic community. The primary problem is that Kinsey used a biased sample, and there is no scientific way to generalize from his findings. Kinsey recruited some subjects from prisons and reform schools, whose inmates hardly represent the general population. He also interviewed only whites, and the percentage of men from the lower class was too high (Himmelhoch and Fava 1955). Consequently, researchers no longer trust Kinsey's findings.

THE LAUMANN RESEARCH. In contrast, a team of researchers headed by sociologist Edward Laumann has done accurate research on U.S. sexual behavior (1994). Because Laumann interviewed a representative sample of the U.S. population, we can generalize his findings to the entire U.S. population. As you can see from Figure 3-2, Laumann found that during the preceding five years, 2.2 percent of U.S. women and 4.1 percent of U.S. men had had sex with a same-sex partner. If the time period is extended to include all the years of their lives, these totals increase to 3.8 percent of the women and 7.1 percent of the men. This is a far cry from Kinsey's 37 percent for men.

As Figure 3-2 also shows, 1.4 percent of U.S. women and 2.8 percent of U.S. men identify themselves as homosexuals. These percentages are almost identical to those who reported that they had sex with a same-sex partner during the preceding year (1.3 percent of the women and 2.7 percent of the men). Even these figures may be slightly high, as the Laumann researchers counted as homosexuals people who identify themselves as bisexuals.

In the Spotlight on Social Research box on page 57, Laumann explains why he did his research and the opposition that he had to overcome to do it.

Laumann's sampling technique is excellent, and this research gives us data from which we can generalize to the U.S. population. What it is missing, though, is qualitative data, which allow us to analyze people's interactions and understand their perspectives. Qualitative data help us to see how people put their worlds together—that concept we discussed in Chapter 2, the social construction of reality.

Although homosexuals have made great strides in gaining acceptance in most areas of society, discrimination remains, most notably in the military. These students at Harvard Law School are protesting their school allowing the U.S. military to recruit on campus.

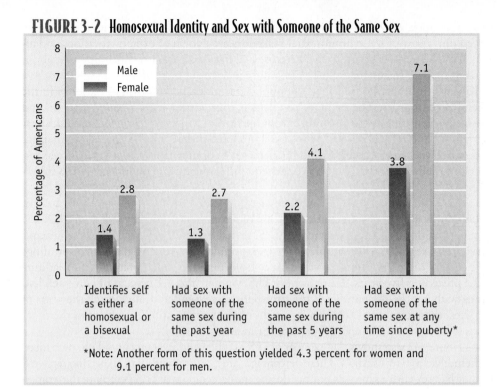

FIGURE 3-2 Homosexual Identity and Sex with Someone of the Same Sex

Source: Laumann et al. 1994:293–296.

THE HUMPHREYS RESEARCH. To get qualitative data on homosexual behavior, sociologist Laud Humphreys devised an ingenious but widely criticized method. Knowing that some male homosexuals have impersonal sex in public restrooms ("tearooms," in the homosexual vernacular), Humphreys (1970/1975) began hanging around these restrooms. Taking the role of "watch queen," the one who gives warning when strangers approach, he observed what went on in this setting. Humphreys reported that these men use a system of gestures to initiate sex at the urinal and then move to a toilet stall for fellatio (oral sex). Their quick, anonymous sex usually occurs without the exchange of a single word. Another sociologist, Edward Delph (1978), confirmed the silence that surrounds these sexual encounters.

Humphreys also found that 38 percent of the men he observed having "tearoom" sex were married. He wanted to know why these married men engaged in homosexual behavior, and he decided to interview them. He found that the men identified themselves as heterosexuals, but they were frustrated sexually with their wives. Having sex in a "tearoom" did not threaten their emotional commitment to their wives, for it required neither socializing nor any other kind of relationship. This kind of sex was also convenient, often a fast stop on their way home from work. In essence, the "tearooms" functioned as free houses of prostitution, places where the men could obtain quick, oral sex at no charge and with no emotional entanglements. Sociologists Jay Corzine and Richard Kirby (1977) found similar homosexual behavior at truck stops: Heterosexual truckers have sex with homosexuals who search out partners at highway rest areas.

You may have wondered how Humphreys knew that 38 percent of the men he observed having sex in restrooms were married. What he did was to write down these men's license plate numbers and then trace their home addresses. With the cooperation of his professors, who were conducting a health survey, he had these men added to their sample. Humphreys then interviewed the men in their homes, supposedly for the purpose of the medical study. For this deception, Humphreys was criticized severely, both by other sociologists and even by the public. At first Humphreys vigorously defended himself, but in the second edition of his book (1975) he agreed that he should have identified himself as a researcher.

Spotlight on Social Research
STUDYING SEX IN AMERICA

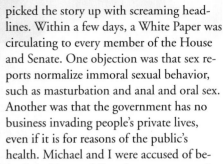

EDWARD LAUMANN, *Dean of the Social Science Division at the University of Chicago, has done research on health, politics, power, status, and sex. Although he has pioneered theoretical work in how people form, maintain, and dissolve relationships, it is his research on sex that has received the most attention.*

In the 1980s, when we were in the midst of an AIDS epidemic so vicious that the number of people with this disease was doubling every 10 months, I organized a workshop on AIDS and Society. As I listened to the presentations, I became convinced that there would be no magic bullet to stop this epidemic through immunization. To contain the spread of AIDS, people would have to change their behavior. Robert Michael, an economic demographer, and I concluded that we needed a national sex survey to document the sex practices of Americans. With this information, we could design ways to persuade people to take defensive measures.

Research into human sexual behavior is often considered "illegitimate," even by many social scientists. Despite this disapproval, we wanted the University of Chicago to pool its strengths in survey and sample design to conduct this national survey. John Gagnon, a sexologist, joined our research team. When the National Institutes of Health announced a search for research proposals to combat AIDS, we submitted our design for a national sex survey. We won that competition.

When *Science* magazine reported that our proposal was under review at the White House's Office of Management and the Budget, the *Washington Times* picked the story up with screaming headlines. Within a few days, a White Paper was circulating to every member of the House and Senate. One objection was that sex reports normalize immoral sexual behavior, such as masturbation and anal and oral sex. Another was that the government has no business invading people's private lives, even if it is for reasons of the public's health. Michael and I were accused of being fronts for a cabal of homophiles who were attempting to legitimize gay sex.

Although the Senate Appropriations Committee recommended that our survey be funded, the House Appropriations Committee disagreed. For two years, we lobbied Congressional staffers, Senators, and Representatives for their support in funding the research, but with few results. Then Senator Jesse Helms submitted an amendment to an appropriations bill that transferred the funding that had been intended for our sex survey to a "say no to sex" campaign. The Senate voted 66 to 34 in favor of the amendment, giving me the dubious distinction of having Congress trying to stop my research.

With government funding cut off, we turned to private foundations. The Robert Wood Johnson, Henry Kaiser, Rockefeller, and McArthur foundations agreed to fund our research. To share the results of our survey with the scientific community, we wrote *The Social Organization of Sexuality.* This is a technical book, and as some have noted, it took the University of Chicago to take the fun out of sex.

We felt strongly that the public needed to know what we had discovered, and we wanted to have a hand in framing the public's understanding, not leave it to others. To do this, we arranged for Gina Kolata, a *New York Times* reporter who specializes in science and health news, to write a companion volume, *Sex in America.*

SITUATIONAL HOMOSEXUAL BEHAVIOR: THE PRISON. Certain places, such as prisons and boarding schools, are often the site of **situational homosexual behavior.** This term refers to homosexual behavior by people who, if members of the opposite sex were available, would be involved in heterosexual relations. To better understand situational homosexual behavior, let's look at a study of inmates in the state prison at Soledad, California. Sociologist George Kirkham (1971) found that the participants identified themselves as "queens," "punks," and "wolves."

The men used "queen" to refer to an inmate who prefers male sexual partners. The queen, then, does not engage in situational homosexual behavior, for, in prison or out, "she" prefers male partners. To attract fellow prisoners, the queen exaggerates aspects of female sexuality. She may adopt a feminine nickname ("Peaches," "Dee-Dee"), tear the back pockets from tight prison denims to make them more form-fitting, use cosmetics made from medical and food supplies, and wear jewelry produced in hobby shops. The

The term *situational homosexual behavior* refers to sexual behavior between people of the same sex that is induced by the situation. Typical examples are same-sex boarding schools and prisons, such as this one in Maricopa County Jail, Arizona.

queen lets her hair grow as long as the guards allow and shows an exaggerated "swish" as she walks.

When they first enter prison, most men find queens despicable. As the months pass, however, and as the femininity of the queens evokes their memory and longing for women, some change their mind and have sex with queens. Even though they are heterosexual, some of these men enter into long-term relationships with queens. Some of these relationships resemble marriage, with emotional ties and the expectation of sexual fidelity. The relationships are brittle, though, for most queens are promiscuous. Some queens become the victims of prison pimps, who force them to prostitute themselves or even sell them to other pimps.

Next to the "rat," or informer, the "punk" has the least social status among prisoners. There are two types: "canteen punks," those who exchange sex for candy, cigarettes, money, or personal favors, and "pressure punks," those who give sex to other men because of beatings or threats of violence. The other prisoners despise punks: canteen punks because they sacrifice their manhood to obtain goods or services, and pressure punks because they show weakness in the face of threats and violence.

How do men become pressure punks? Some are beaten and gang raped and then forced into this status for the rest of their prison term. Others are tricked into it. Some "fish" (new inmates), unacquainted with prison ways, accept cigarettes, money, or help of some sort from an experienced inmate. Others are the victims of rigged gambling games. In either case, if the fish cannot pay when the experienced inmate demands settlement of the debt, he is told that he must give sex as payment. At this point, the fish has only two choices—to submit or to fight. A fish who submits is marked as a punk from then on and must continue to provide sex for the rest of his prison term.

In some prisons, especially those in Texas, any homosexual who is unfortunate enough to be incarcerated is claimed by a gang. This individual is gang raped and forced into being a sex slave during his entire time in prison. He is rented out or sold, as the gang desires. In some prisons, gangs allocate homosexuals among themselves; if one gang already has "its" sex slave when another homosexual is admitted to the prison, another gang claims that individual (Liptak 2004).

The prisoners' view of the "wolf" is different. Although the wolf has sex with punks, he does not lose his status as a "man." To remain a "man" and still engage in sex with other men, he presents an image of exaggerated toughness. Because force and rape match the manly image that prisoners hold, the more violence that surrounds the wolf's sexual acts, the more he is seen as masculine. The wolf must also keep his sexual acts emotionless and impersonal. Some wolves "own" punks and prostitute them for cigarettes, drugs, or other favors.

FORMING A HOMOSEXUAL IDENTITY: SIX STAGES. For heterosexual men in prison, punks serve as substitutes for women, and after they leave prison, these men have sex with women. Once more, this reminds us of the distinction made earlier between homosexuality and homosexual behavior. But what do we know about the causes of homosexuality—the *sexual preference* for someone of one's own sex?

Despite many theories and thousands of studies, we do not know the answer. At this point, we cannot rule out the possibility that genetics in some form—such as DNA markers or the organization of the brain—underlie human sexual orientation. It is the same with the prenatal environment, such as uterine sex hormones (which can be related to the number of sons a woman has given birth to) (Rahman 2005; Blanchard et al. 2006). Researchers, however, have found no chemical, biological, or even psychological differences that distinguish homosexuals and heterosexuals (Hooker 1957; Masters and Johnson 1979; Hamer et al. 1993; LeVay 1993; Laumann et al. 1994). Because of this, sociologists do not view homosexuality as the result of genetics or the prenatal environment, nor do they consider homosexuality to be due to certain types of family relations, such as an aloof, "weak" father and a close, "dominant" mother.

For reasons currently unknown, then, some people feel erotic desires for members of their own sex. Erotic desires are insufficient for people to label themselves as homosexual, however, for many people who experience such desires identify themselves as heterosexuals (Laumann et al. 1994). How, then, do people develop an *identity* as homosexual? Sociologist Vivienne Cass (1979) found that this transition centers on self-labeling. Using case studies and symbolic interactionism, Cass identified six stages in this process:

1. **Identity confusion** Finding his or her feelings or behaviors at odds with heterosexual orientations, the individual becomes confused and upset. He or she asks, "Who am I?" and replies, *"My behavior or feelings could be called homosexual."*
2. **Identity comparison** The individual begins to feel "different," as though he or she does not belong. He or she makes the first tentative commitment to a homosexual identity by saying, *"I may be a homosexual."*
3. **Identity tolerance** The individual's self-image continues to change as he or she identifies less with heterosexuality and more with homosexuality. The conclusion at this point is, *"I probably am a homosexual."*
4. **Identity acceptance** The individual moves from tolerating a homosexual self-image to accepting a homosexual identity. After increasing contact with others who define themselves as homosexual, he or she concludes, *"I am a homosexual."*
5. **Identity pride** The individual thinks of homosexuality as good and heterosexuality as bad. He or she makes a strong commitment to a homosexual group, which generates a firm sense of group identity. The individual may become politically active and concludes, *"I am a homosexual and proud of it."*
6. **Identity synthesis** The individual decides that the "them and us" view is inappropriate. He or she begins to feel quite similar to some heterosexuals—and quite different from some homosexuals. Although homosexuality remains essential to the individual's identity, it becomes merely one aspect of the self. The individual may say, *"I am a homosexual—but I am also a lot of other things in life."*

SEXUAL IDENTITIES ARE NOT FIXED. Like other symbolic interactionists, Cass stresses that people construct their own self-images. In this case, individuals who have begun to interpret their feelings and behavior in terms of homosexuality may stop at any stage. Some may even move back toward a heterosexual identity. For example, in stage 1 when people consider the possibility that their behavior *could* be called homosexual, some stop the behavior. Others continue it, but define it as situational rather than as part of their sexual orientation. People in the third stage may feel positive about "probably" being homosexual and eagerly move to the fourth stage—or they may dislike this probability and move away from a homosexual identity. In metaphorical terms, people who have begun the journey to homosexuality can continue it to the last station or they can get off at any station along the way. Some even get off at a station called "Return to Heterosexuality" (Bell et al. 1981).

When people are in the process of acquiring a sexual identity, they try to confirm that identity. They often do this by associating with others who reinforce their budding identity. People who feel that they are heterosexual associate with heterosexuals and do "heterosexual things." Similarly, people who feel that they are homosexual associate with homosexuals and do "homosexual things." Both are confirming their developing identities. The heterosexual and homosexual worlds overlap, of course, and the point at which they cross can present a challenge to fragile, developing identities.

Although our sexual identity may be tenuous during childhood, over time it becomes more firmly rooted. By the time we are adults, we seldom question it. Not everyone's sexual identity is this firm, however, and some homosexuals and heterosexuals are plagued by doubts about who they "really" are. As sociologist Rose Weitz (1991) found, AIDS poses a special challenge to homosexuals whose sexual identity sits uneasily. For some in her sample, getting AIDS became a catalyst that stimulated them to embrace a homosexual identity. For others, AIDS was the motivation to reaffirm social norms that condemn homosexual activities. Asking their families, churches, and God to accept their apologies and to forgive them, they asserted a "new self." Some even insisted that this was their "real self" all along.

IN SUM According to symbolic interactionism, identities, including our sexual identity, do not come with our birth. Instead, we are born with an undirected sexual potential that our experiences channel into a homosexual or heterosexual direction. A heterosexual or homosexual identity does not unfold automatically from within—like an acorn that can become only an oak tree. Rather, sexual preferences are learned, and people acquire sexual identities to match.

Differences Between Male and Female Homosexuals

What differences have researchers found between male and female homosexuals? (The term for female homosexuals, **lesbian,** apparently first referred to the Greek island of Lesbos, home of the poet Sappho, who wrote lyric poetry celebrating the love of woman for woman.)

INCIDENCE AND NUMBER OF SEXUAL PARTNERS. You already have seen that homosexuality is more common among males than females, a finding that is supported by all researchers who have reported on this matter. Let's see what other differences researchers have found. Some of the most significant are that lesbians are more likely to seek lasting relationships, place a premium on emotional commitment and mutual fidelity, and shun the bar scene (Wolf 1979; Lowenstein 1980; Peplau and Amaro 1982). Indeed, although most male homosexuals have "cruised" (sought impersonal sex with strangers), fewer than 20 percent of lesbians have done so. As a result, lesbians tend to have fewer sexual partners than do male homosexuals.

Psychologist Alan Bell and sociologist Martin Weinberg (1978) interviewed about 1,500 homosexuals. They found that almost half of the white and one-third of the African American homosexual males had at least 500 different sexual partners. About 28 percent of the white sample had more than 1,000 different partners. Although their sample is large, it is not representative of homosexuals, because their research focused heavily on bars and steam baths. In these settings, people are looking for sex, so the sample is skewed toward people who have many sexual partners. We need balancing studies of homosexuals who are committed to a partner, or, even better, national samples. Bell and Weinberg's findings do, however, support other studies that indicate extensive promiscuity among male homosexuals.

Why do male and female homosexuals show such substantial differences? Symbolic interactionists would argue that socialization is the chief reason. Girls are more likely to learn to associate sex with emotional relationships; and like their heterosexual counterparts, lesbians tend to conform to this gender expectation. Similarly, boys tend to learn to separate sex from affection, to validate their self-images by how much sex they have and the number of partners they have it with, and to see fidelity as a restriction on their independence and their pursuit of sexual satisfaction. In short, male and female homosexuals reflect the broad-based gender expectations of our culture.

AIDS AND RISKY SEX. When AIDS first appeared, it meant a death sentence. As shock and fear shook the homosexual community, men reduced their number of sexual partners. After a cocktail of drugs to treat AIDS was developed, deaths plummeted, and it became apparent that people who were infected with HIV (the virus that causes AIDS) could live long lives. As health concerns dropped, many male homosexuals turned again to risky sex (Public Health 2002). Bath houses, where anonymous sex is the norm, were shunned when AIDS meant death, but they are again busy places as men engage in unprotected sex with strangers (Elwoood et al. 2003). Similarly, "cruising" and other forms of anonymous sex have again increased. So has the rate of AIDS among male homosexuals.

IN SUM As stressed in Chapter 1, no social problem has only objective conditions. Like other social problems, homosexuality is a social problem because of subjective concerns. The two major concerns of heterosexuals are that it is immoral for people of the same sex to have sex with one another and that homosexuality poses a threat to the family. Americans, however, are divided on this issue, and some view homosexuality as a permissible alternative lifestyle. Like other social problems, homosexuality draws its share of extremists. Those on one side argue that homosexuals should be punished with legal and social sanctions, whereas extremists on the other side argue that homosexuality should be encouraged among our youth.

Prostitution

Background: Getting the Larger Picture

It is no accident that **prostitution,** the renting of one's body for sexual purposes, has been called "the world's oldest profession." Accounts of prostitution by both females and males reach back to the beginnings of recorded history. It exists in one form or another almost everywhere.

With the exception of small tribal groups, prostitution exists in all cultures. This painting from the 1600s, artist unknown, is titled, "A Mughal Prince Receiving a Lady of the Night." The Mughal empire included today's India and Afghanistan.

ATTITUDES TOWARD PROSTITUTION. Around the world, attitudes toward prostitution vary immensely. The ancient inhabitants of the Mediterranean area, Asia Minor, West Africa, and southern India held an attitude that is startling to contemporary Westerners (Henriques 1966). There, prostitution was part of religion, taking place in the temple as a type of service to their gods. In one form of **temple prostitution,** every woman was required to perform an act of prostitution before she was allowed to marry. In another, a woman was dedicated to the gods of the temple as a sacred prostitute—either for a specific time or, more commonly, for life. On a visit to India, I was surprised to find that in some villages temple prostitution still exists.

In ancient Greece, high-class prostitutes, called *hetairae,* were respected. Their portraits and statues were placed "in the temples and other public buildings by the side of meritorious generals and statesmen" (Henriques 1966:64).

Today, in many Latin countries prostitution is seen as a necessary evil—something that keeps hot-blooded men away from pure, innocent girls and women. Although many Mexicans, Italians, and South Americans may consider prostitution disgusting, they are also convinced that prostitution protects the virtue of their own wives and daughters.

The attitudes of Americans toward the legalization of prostitution are shown in Table 3-2 on the next page. This research reveals interesting profiles. Those most likely to favor legal prostitution are white male college graduates with high incomes who live in the West.

Those least likely to favor legal prostitution are black female high school graduates with low incomes who live in the Midwest. A surprise is that people who are between the ages of 50 to 64, usually a very conservative group, are the most likely to favor the legalization of prostitution.

PROSTITUTION TODAY. With prostitution flourishing in the United States, researchers have tried to determine how many prostitutes there are. Given the subterranean nature of prostitutes' activities, this has proven to be a challenge. Using sampling techniques, researchers estimate that there are 23 prostitutes per 100,000 Americans. This comes to a total of 69,000 prostitutes in the United States (Pottêrat et al. 1990; Brewer et al. 2000). Researchers estimate that the average prostitute has 694 customers a year. Some prostitutes, however, those who work in crack houses, have over 5,000 customers a year. The average prostitute apparently works for 5 years. If so, she has about 3,500 customers during this time (Brewer et al. 2000). If this seems high, we should note that prostitutes in Nairobi report even more clients: One reports six a day for 23 years, a total of about 50,000 clients (Cowley 2006).

The only place in the United States where prostitution is legal is Nevada, where prostitutes are licensed to sell sex. Prostitution is not legal in five of Nevada's counties, though, including the urban counties where Reno, Las Vegas, and Lake Tahoe are located. Officials

---

TABLE 3-2 Attitudes Toward the Legalization of Prostitution

Question: "In your opinion, should prostitution involving adults aged 18 years of age and older be legal or illegal in your state?"

	LEGAL	ILLEGAL	DON'T KNOW/REFUSED
National	26%	70%	4%
Sex			
Male	32%	63%	5%
Female	21%	77%	2%
Race/Ethnicity*			
White	27%	70%	3%
Black	20%	79%	1%
Age			
18 to 29 years	25%	74%	1%
30 to 49 years	28%	68%	4%
50 to 64 years	32%	65%	3%
65 years and older	18%	77%	5%
Education			
College graduate	28%	69%	3%
High school	21%	76%	3%
Income			
$50,000 and over	33%	64%	3%
$30,000 to $49,999	26%	70%	4%
$20,000 to $29,999	27%	71%	2%
Under $20,000	18%	80%	2%
Region			
East	28%	68%	4%
Midwest	20%	78%	2%
South	24%	75%	1%
West	34%	58%	8%

*Only these two groups are listed in the source.
Source: Sourcebook of Criminal Justice Statistics 1997:Table 2–99. Table dropped in later editions.

in these counties believe that legal prostitution might drive away "family-type" gamblers. Illegal prostitution also thrives in Nevada, as evidenced by police files on thousands of prostitutes who have been arrested in Las Vegas—and by the photo on this page.

Prostitutes have kept up with the times. Even though the elaborately furnished "whorehouse" of bygone days is indeed bygone, massage parlors, call girls, and escort services have taken its place. Under cover of a legitimate service, "massage parlors" offer sex for sale. So do escort services: For a set fee a client arranges a date and privately negotiates the inclusion of sexual services. In Spain, "masseuses" make house calls. Their newspaper and magazine ads mention their qualifications, such as "19 years old, blue eyes, and just arrived from Germany." Local newspapers in Florida and several other states also carry such ads.

Another variation is corporate prostitution, in which a corporation hires prostitutes for its customers. A New York telephone company, for example, held what its executives called "pervert" conventions, weeklong, raucous sessions during which prostitutes provided sex for the company's suppliers (Carnevale 1990). In the Issues in Social Problems box on pages 64–65, one of my students explains how she became a corporate prostitute.

In short, prostitution, which changes along with other aspects of society, serves social functions—from playing a role in religious rituals to giving some corporations a competitive edge. In the following section, we shall examine the social functions of prostitution in more detail.

Although illegal, prostitution is practiced fairly openly in some areas. This card was thrust into my hand as I was walking on The Strip in Las Vegas–even though I was walking hand-in-hand with my wife.

Prostitution Viewed Theoretically: Applying Functionalism

THE SOCIAL FUNCTIONS OF PROSTITUTION. On the most obvious level, prostitution flourishes because it satisfies sexual needs that are not met elsewhere. This, of course, is precisely why prostitution can never be eliminated. In a classic article, sociologist Kingsley Davis (1937, 1966) concluded that prostitutes provide a sexual outlet for men who

1. Have difficulty establishing sexual relationships (such as disfigured or shy men or those with handicaps)
2. Cannot find long-term partners (such as travelers and sailors)
3. Have a broken relationship (such as the separated or divorced)
4. Want sexual gratification that they can't get from their wives or girlfriends

Other researchers (Freund et al. 1991; Gemme 1993; Monto 2004) have noted that prostitutes also provide a sexual outlet for men who

5. Want quick sex without attachment
6. Are sexually dissatisfied in marriage
7. Want to have sex with someone who has a specific body type, age, or race–ethnicity.

An eighth reason goes beyond sex. Sociologist Elizabeth Bernstein (2001), who studied the motivations of customers of prostitutes, found that some men find emotional satisfaction with prostitutes. They feel that they "connect" with the prostitute. Some are even convinced that the prostitute from whom they are buying sex has special feelings for them.

THE FUNCTIONALIST CONCLUSION: PROSTITUTION AS A WAY OF CONTROLLING SEXUAL BEHAVIOR. Although most of these observations may seem obvious, the conclusion that functionalists draw from them is not. By meeting such needs, they say, prostitution functions as *a form of social control* over sexual behavior. By this, they mean that prostitution channels sexual desires away from unwilling women to women who, for a price, are willing to satisfy those desires. For example, some people (whom prostitutes call "kinkies," "weirdos," and "freaks") achieve sexual gratification by inflicting pain on others (**sadists**) or by having others inflict pain on them (**masochists**). Some customers enjoy being sexually humiliated, being told by the prostitute that they are no good or being ordered to do

Issues in Social Problems
ME, A PROSTITUTE?

As illustrated by what my student wrote in this box, college students who are prostitutes don't stand out from college students who work at legitimate jobs.

Many women learn to be prostitutes only gradually, going through a step-by-step process similar to the one recounted here. This account, written by one of my students who wishes to remain anonymous, has been set according to the original paper, including typos and misspellings.

I am a average looking blond with blue eyes. I am a female of twenty years of age. My mother is a elementary school teacher with a doctorit degree. My father is the head of instramentation for a large oil company. He write books, makes movies and teaches around the world. I have one sibbling. She is 10 years old. My parents are very old fashioned. they are strickt with both my sister and I. We are Hard-Shell-Baptist, and attend church no-matter-what. They've instilled wonderful values in me. We live in the country on a farm (pleasure, we don't grow things). Our home is large and because both of my parents work we have a maid that comes three days a week to clean. I've always had to work around the house. Cooking meals, cleaning and doing farm chores such as, feeding the horses and cows, have always been a part of my dayly routine. Yet, there's never been anything I've ever done without. Anything that could be bought was automatically mine, just for the asking. Our entire family is close. We visit one another frequently and have get-togethers regularly.

I am from a family with an average annual income of over $100,000.00. My parents have never neglected me. No one has ever abused me. I've caused my share of trouble, but it was all jouvenile, never anything against the law of the state. I've never been a misfit. I was one of the "cool" kids. I was in with the "popular" crowd. I was in Student Government and Peer Leadership in High School. I was elected Snow Queen my junior year. I never had any problems with guys. There was always plenty around my house. I just could never get attached to guys my age, they came and they went . . . no big deal! I had a taste for older men even then.

When I was seventeen, I met a guy who was twenty-two. He was exciting and fun. He was my first love. He was also the first guy I'd ever had sex with. Kinky wouldn't even begin to explain him. We went out for about a year and a half. Through him I met Jesse. A gorgeous Spaniard, queer as a three dollar bill, but one of the nicest people you'll ever meet. Jesse is a "BIG" record promoter for a famous record corporation. We've been friends since the day we met. We call each other all the time and "dish" on guys.

I called Jesse up one day and asked if he'd get me tickets to go to a concert I wanted to see. He said sure as he had a million times before. Only this time he too had a request. He said, "I'm in a bit of a bind. I need someone to pick up a client and show him around town Friday!" "Cool!" I said. Jesse went on to explain, "You'll be given

humiliating things. Others combine the sex act with fantasy role playing; they may wear costumes or ask the prostitute to do so. Some even wear diapers, while others have sex in coffins (Hall 1972; Millett 1973; Prus and Irini 1988).

These, however, are the unusual customers of prostitutes. Most clients (called "johns" or "tricks") are regular Joe Six-Packs—married, middle-aged men (Wells 1970; Freund et al. 1991; Monto 2004). Why do married men patronize prostitutes? Perhaps the two most common reasons are that they find their wives sexually unreceptive, or they desire sexual variety that their wives are unwilling to provide—especially "frenching" (fellatio, or oral sex), apparently the act most requested of prostitutes (Melody 1969; Heyl 1979; Gemme 1993).

Functionalists, then, see prostitution as a means of controlling or channeling sexual behavior. Prostitutes meet the needs of the sexually unattached and of those who want

$200.00 to buy him dinner, go dancing, or whatever else he may want to do . . . what's left is yours to keep." "Wow, thats great," I exclaimed! I thought to myself, what could be better, a date in which we can do anything, the sky's the limit . . . you get payed for playing!!! What could possibly be better than that?

I made about $70. I had a wonderful time and so did the client. I told Jesse I loved being a escort and to fix me up as often as he liked. I was assigned many men after that. I'd say a good 75% wanted to finish off their evenings with sex. Some even would get quite insistent. I asked Jesse what to do. Jesse said do what you want to do, guys will offer you their own money (as a write off to their own company as entertainment). To sleep with me, I thought. He said, "Do what you want to do, if you want the money, go for it! If you don't keep standing firm!" I told Jesse I couldn't do it. So, he began to filter my dates more so and more so. He was always careful not to set me up with the weirdo's or the real wild party hardy guys. I mostly got the married with three kids and a dog type from then on.

I worked at the pace of picking up $20–$100 per date, for about three months; about 60 guys total. Then I met with a client from Europe for the second time. He was a very attractive man of 40. His black hair was salted with a whitened silver. He was a family man. Though, as was the story with many of the men I escorted, he was having alot of problems with his wife. While sitting at a bar he whispered in my ear, "Would you please consider being with me tonight?" Knowing I'd turned him down the last time he was in town, he reached into his pocket for inspiration. $500.00 in crisp $100.00 bills he waved out like a fan and placed on the table. I looked at him and shook my head "No" I said. He put his hand on my arm and said, "How much do I have to offer you, $600, $700?" At this point I was getting pissed! In order to control my temper I flew off to the restroom in a rage. I remember standing at the sink, looking into the mirror, and thinking who in the hell does this man think he is!! I don't need his money! But still that much money, for sex?! . . . how could it be? I went back to the table with thousands of thoughts running through my mind. He looked at me and said, "I'm sorry if I upset you, but, I'm willing to give you all the money I have with me, $1000 dollars. Hows that sound?" My initial thought was to slap the crap out of him, however, the things I could do with $1000 cash. I agreed and it wasn't hard. No commitments, no future to worry about, and no love to get in the way of habitions. I went home that night with 10 crisp $100 dollar bills and two $20's left over from the date, in my coat pocket. There's nothing to it. I can spend $100 on myself and stick the rest in a savings account. It's no biggy!

I told Jesse about it. I told him I couldn't believe how easy or how much money I made. He laughed and asked me if I had plans of ever doing this again. I said sure, it's no problem. He started throughing me that "kind" of clients. I made over $10,000 in the 4 months to follow. Enough to buy me a new car. I never have made $1000 in a evening again but, it became a game to me. How high can you raise the bid? How much will it take to make this man make an offer straight up? How much teasing can you get buy with, without having him drop his attention?

I've worked more than 2 yrs. I've totally mellowed out of the games. If it looks good to me, and if I find the man attractive I'll do it. I've become very secure financially. I have multiple CD's, bonds and ect. I have three savings accounts and alot of money tied up in the stock market. My only regrets are I have to keep it a complete secret from everyone. My parents, who mean more to me than the world, my family, and even my dearest friends. I miss out on the average everyday social life of a college student. I have to lie to practically everyone I meet. But, nowhere will I find a job in which I can save as much money for my future. Or for that matter when I get out of college and get a respectable job in advertising, make that kind of money. But, my life will be back to a "normal" one. One in which I can be proud of, one which I can share with my friends and family, one in which I can make a "honest" living.

sexual acts that are not otherwise readily available to them. Prostitutes also provide access to sexual variety in a nonemotional and fleeting relationship. Furthermore, unlike dates, prostitutes do not threaten the male ego—it is unlikely that the john will be "turned down."

Functionalists stress that when people demand a service that is not supplied by legitimate sources, a subterranean source will develop to meet the need. The underground channeling of illegitimate services to clients, called a **black market,** is built on **symbiosis** (a mutually beneficial relationship). Those who purchase a service, those who provide it, and, often, those who are supposed to suppress it benefit from the illegal service. The clients of prostitutes purchase the sex they want; prostitutes work with a minimum of legal hassles (even calling their occasional fines the price of "licensing"); pimps and criminal organizations earn untaxed income; and for a price, police who are "on the take" look the other way.

THE FEMINIST PERSPECTIVE: CONFLICT. The conflict perspective, as usual, contrasts sharply with that of the functionalists. Taking the conflict perspective, feminists point out that prostitution is just one of the many ways that men exploit and degrade women. Some men use prostitutes as objects for their own pleasure. Other men (pimps, police "on the take") exploit prostitutes for profit. The Global Glimpse box below explores the sexual exploitation of women in the Least Industrialized Nations.

Research on Prostitution

TYPES OF PROSTITUTES. Besides masseuses and corporate prostitutes, already mentioned, what kinds of prostitutes are there? Let's do a quick overview.

Call girls, the elite of the prostitutes, can be selective in choosing their customers. Building a steady, repeat business, they usually meet their customers at their own place or at the client's (Lucas 2005). To keep up with appointments, they use cell phones, pagers, fax machines, and e-mail. To meet clients' continuous demand for variety, some groups of call girls fly from city to city, where new customers await them (Campo-Flores 2002).

A Global Glimpse
THE PATRIOTIC PROSTITUTE

A new wrinkle in the history of prostitution is the "patriotic prostitute." Patriotic prostitutes are young women who are encouraged by their government to prostitute themselves to help the country's economy. Patriotic prostitution is part of global stratification, the division of the world's countries into "have" and "have-not" nations. Some have-nots, or Least Industrialized Nations, view their women as a cash crop, encouraging prostitution as a way to accumulate capital for investment or to help pay interest on their national debt. A notorious example is Thailand, where in a country of 30 million females, between a half million and a million are prostitutes. About 20,000 are under the age of 15.

In some countries, government officials encourage prostitution by telling young women that they are performing a service to their country. In South Korea, officials issue identification cards to prostitutes, which serve as hotel passes. In orientation sessions, they tell these young women, "Your carnal conversations with foreign tourists do not prostitute either yourself or the nation, but express your heroic patriotism."

With such an official blessing, "sex tourism" has become a global growth industry. Travel agencies in Germany advertise "trips to Thailand with erotic pleasures included in the price."

Now that South Korea has become a prosperous nation, officials are trying to reduce prostitution. To protest the new laws, these prostitutes have put on traditional funeral robes.

Japan Air Lines hands out brochures that advertise the "charming attractions" of Kisaeng girls, advising men to fly JAL for "a night spent with a consummate Kisaeng girl dressed in a gorgeous Korean blouse and skirt."

The advertising, showing beautiful young women with "come hither" smiles, fails to mention the miserable slavery that underlies sex tourism. Many of the prostitutes were sold as children. Some are held in bondage while they pay off their families' debts. Some are even locked up to keep them from running away.

The enticing ads also leave out AIDS. In Nairobi, where about 10,000 prostitutes serve this thriving industry, perhaps half are infected with AIDS. Nor is the destruction of children mentioned. Although customers pay more for young girls and boys, especially for those who are advertised as virgins or "clean," the children are vulnerable to infection from lesions and injuries during intercourse. When they become too sick to service clients—or their disease becomes too noticeable—the children are thrown into the streets like so much rubbish.

Based on Gay 1985; Shaw 1987; Hornblower 1993; Beddoe et al. 2001; Leuchtag 2004.

Convention prostitutes, as the name implies, are women who specialize in conventions. Posing as secretaries or sales agents, they roam hotel lobbies, display rooms, and cocktail parties. Some develop opinions about which professionals spend the most money, and they try to concentrate on their conventions. In the symbiotic manner referred to earlier, the organizers of a convention may make arrangements for prostitutes to be available.

Apartment prostitutes rent an apartment and set up a business at which they work set hours. Some apartment prostitutes are married women who attempt to match their apartment hours to their husband's working hours. A husband who is ignorant of his wife's activities is likely to think that she has a regular job.

Stag party workers serve as topless waitresses or put on strip shows at stag parties—that is, parties for men only. They arrange to meet customers after the party or, sometimes, in a side room during the party.

Hotel prostitutes work out of a hotel and share their fees with the bell captain, desk clerk, or bellboys who steer johns to them (Reichert and Frey 1985; Prus and Irini 1988). Because this "added service" attracts male guests, some hotels provide their room free or at a cut rate.

House prostitutes work in a house of prostitution, or "whorehouse." This form of prostitution still exists, but it has declined. During the 1800s and early 1900s, almost all large U.S. cities and many small ones had brothels, which were located in an area known as the "red light district." A red bulb shining from a window or house front informed passersby of what went on behind those closed doors.

Barbara Heyl, a sociologist who studied house prostitutes, reported that the women gather in the living room, the john looks them over and makes his selection, and the woman then takes the john to a bedroom. The manager of the house (the "madam") keeps from 50 to 60 percent of the prostitutes' earnings. It is one of the tasks of house prostitutes to try to persuade their johns to spend more than they intend. Heyl (1979:120) found that this is especially difficult for the novice, "because the woman must learn to discuss sexual acts, whereas in her previous experience, sexual behavior and preferences had been negotiated non-verbally."

Bar girls, also known as "B-girls," wait in a bar for customers. Some pay or "tip" the bartender for being able to use the bar as their headquarters. Others hustle drinks (are friendly to bar patrons to get them to buy overpriced drinks), receiving a set fee for each drink they sell.

Streetwalkers have the lowest status among prostitutes. They also are the most frequently arrested. They are visible to the public, as they "work the street" in view of police and customers. In some U.S. cities, streetwalkers are aggressive, hailing passing cars and opening the doors of cars that have stopped at traffic lights. Many are drug addicts who are also involved in larceny.

Another type of prostitute is known as a *parking lot lizard.* These prostitutes frequent truck stops, moving from one truck to another in search of clients.

Male prostitutes who service women are known as "gigolos." In 1980, sociologist Ed Sagarin concluded that this "is an infrequent behavior, for which there is little demand and probably more folklore than reality." Since then, sexual norms have changed, and apparently it is more common for women to pay men for sex (Sanchez Taylor 2001). "Beach boys" in Bali even report that they prefer Japanese women as clients, saying that they are more generous than others (Beddoe et al. 2001).

As a sign of changing times, Heidi Fleiss, who became famous after she was arrested in Hollywood for running a high-priced call girl operation that catered to wealthy men, including movie stars, decided to open a brothel in Nevada that would cater to women customers. Her plans were to hire twenty men to work as prostitutes. They would charge $250 an hour, split this fee with Fleiss, but keep their tips. She quickly received 1,000 applications (Friess 2005). As Fleiss said, "Women make more money these days, and let's face it, it's hard to meet someone." She added, "And then you've got the situation with the old husband leaving his wife for the younger girl, and the lady sitting at home crying. Well, now she has a place to go, and say, 'Right back at you, buddy, and on your credit card'" (Friess 2005). Nevada authorities were not happy with these plans, though, and as

Prostitution has flourished in places where men have outnumbered women, such as the "Old West." Pictured here is a prostitute from the late 1800s. It is not her clothing, but the cigarette, that indicates her status.

of this writing, Heidi's Stud Farm, designed to be the world's first licensed brothel catering exclusively to female clients, remains unlicensed (Gorman 2005).

BECOMING A PROSTITUTE. Researchers focus on prostitutes who are the most easily accessible—which means that they do research primarily on the poor and those who have been arrested. (Those who get arrested also tend to be poor.) Prostitutes who come from higher social class backgrounds, such as my student featured in the Issues in Social Problems box on pages 64–65, engage in forms of prostitution that make them less accessible to the police—and to sociologists. Keeping in mind this biased sampling of prostitutes, let's see why women become prostitutes.

The simplest answer to why someone becomes a prostitute is money—to make as much of it as easily as possible. This is an oversimplification, however, for running through the accounts that prostitutes give of their early home life are themes of emotional deprivation and sexual abuse (James and Meyerding 1977; Davis 1978; Williams and Kornblum 1985; Hodgson 1997). Sociologist Robert Gemme (1993), who interviewed Montreal street prostitutes, found that before they became prostitutes one-third had been raped and about half had been sexually abused. Sociologist James Hodgson (1997) found that money was not the motivation for young prostitutes (ages 10 to 15). Instead, they were "in love" with a pimp, who, after seducing them, insisted they "turn tricks" to help out.

From the conflict perspective, this pattern of abuse is significant. Abused as children, most often by men, these women become locked into a way of life in which they continue to be victimized by men—by pimps who exploit their bodies for profit and by "johns" who exploit them for sexual pleasure.

We have to keep in mind, however, that because of their accessibility, researchers have focused almost invariably on streetwalkers. The themes of abuse and emotional deprivation do seem to characterize these women, but these themes are less likely to appear when it comes to more privileged prostitutes. Call girls, for example, refer more to choice than constraint when they explain why they became prostitutes (Lucas 2005). Their stories are more in line with how people choose other occupations. It is likely, too, that the backgrounds of these women reflect less abuse and deprivation. To know if this is true, however, we need to be able to compare the backgrounds of call girls not only with those of streetwalkers but also with those of women from the classes from which different types of prostitutes are drawn. We have no such data.

THREE STAGES IN BECOMING A PROSTITUTE. As you saw in the box "Me, a Prostitute?" on pages 64–65, becoming a prostitute can be a gradual process. Nanette Davis, a symbolic interactionist documented how this occurs. Interviewing prostitutes in three correctional institutions in Minnesota, she discovered that prostitutes go through three stages.

1. In the first stage, they *drift* from casual sex to their first act of prostitution. During their "drift," the women faced a series of forks in the road, where the choices they made channeled them toward prostitution (James and Davis 1982). Circumstances that led to their drifting included broken homes, dropping out of school, pregnancy, drug use, a juvenile record, and having sex at a young age. On average, these women first had sex when they were 13 (the youngest was age 7, the oldest 18). For about four years, the girls engaged in casual sex and then drifted to selling sex. One of Davis' informants described it this way:

   I was going to school and I wanted to go to this dance the night after. I needed new clothes. I went out at ten o'clock and home at twelve. I had three tricks the first time, and fifteen dollars (about $40 in today's money) for every trick. (Davis 1978:206)

2. Davis calls the second stage *transitional deviance*. During this stage, which lasts an average of six months, girls experience **role ambivalence;** that is, they are not sure whether they want to be a prostitute. They feel both attracted to and repulsed by prostitution. To help overcome their ambivalence, many girls try to **normalize** their acts;

This photo from Amsterdam, Holland illustrates how attitudes toward prostitution vary around the world. The woman in the chair is waiting for customers who, walking along the street, do "window shopping." When I tried to take a photo of the prostitutes in Amsterdam's red light district, two prostitutes rushed out of the building, shouting something in what I assumed was Dutch. One threw her shoe at me. I retreated. I was later told that had they caught me they would have thrown both me and my camera into the canal.

that is, they try to think of what they are doing as normal. For example, although they sell sex, they may call it something else. As one girl said:

> I'm a person who likes to walk. There's nothing wrong with picking somebody up while you're walking. I always like walking around at night, and girls will be tempted. Girls like the offer. They like to see what a guy is going to say. (Davis 1978:203–209)

To "normalize" selling sex is to turn the deviance into a normal act. In effect, this girl is saying, "I'm just doing a normal thing, walking. It's the guy who makes the offer. If a girl is tempted—well, that's only natural, too."

3. Davis calls the third stage *professionalization.* During this stage, the girls no longer tell themselves that their behavior is normal, and they come to think of themselves as prostitutes. At this point, they begin to build their lives around this identity. They also defend their involvement in prostitution. Some sound as though they have read the functionalist perspective—they claim that they help wives by giving their husbands a sexual outlet that reduces marital tensions. Others, such as a madam who wrote a book about her life, say that prostitutes help to prevent rape. Note how closely this madam's statement resembles the analysis of the functionalists:

> As to my claim about performing a useful social service, every lusty, tourist-jammed town like San Francisco needs safety valves and outlets for its males. Shut down a town and the rape rate soars higher than an astronaut. (Stanford 1968:206–207)

From a symbolic interactionist framework, prostitutes eventually come full circle. They begin by defining their activities as normal, denying that they are prostituting themselves. Then, in this last stage, they again use normalization, acknowledging their prostitution but defining it as beneficial.

AGE OF PROSTITUTES. To see how young some prostitutes are—as well as how old—look at Table 3-3 on the next page. The involvement of children in commercial sex is what especially upsets people. We shall return to this topic in the section on child pornography.

TABLE 3-3 Arrests for Prostitution and Commercialized Sex, by Age

AGE	PERCENT	NUMBER
Under 18	1.9%	1,204
Under 10	—	11
10–12	—	10
13–14	0.2%	142
15–17	1.7%	1,041
18–24	24.4%	15,320
25–34	28.7%	17,977
35–44	29.6%	18,564
45–54	12.2%	7,620
55–64	2.4%	1,527
65 and older	0.7%	456
Total arrested:		62,663

Note: The source does not list prostitution separately, but includes it in a category called prostitution and commercialized vice. Consequently, the totals include a large proportion (20 percent) of males (Table 39 of the *UCR*).

Source: By the author. Based on *Uniform Crime Reports* 2006:Table 38.

THE PIMP AND THE PROSTITUTE. Why would a woman rent her body, gamble on not being hurt by sadists, even risk death by AIDS, and then turn the money she makes over to a man? Let's see how the three sociological perspectives help explain this.

Functionalists emphasize the services that pimps provide. Presumably, pimps locate customers, try to screen out sadists, and bail the woman out of jail if she is arrested. In actuality, however, pimps are more likely to make the woman chase up her own customers, to be unconcerned if she is beaten by a john, and to be unavailable when she is arrested (Hodgson 1997). For this reason, we have to move beyond functionalism for an explanation.

Conflict theorists would provide a different answer. Simply put, pimps have the power. They, not the prostitutes, control the streets. To control women, they use their greater physical strength, and they are ruthless. Consider what a former prostitute said:

> I saw a girl walk into a bar and hand the pimp a $100 bill. He took it and burned it in her face and turned around and knocked her down on the floor and kicked her and said, "I told you, bitch, $200. I want $200, not $100." Now she's gotta go out again and make not another hundred, but two hundred. (Millett 1973:134)

This answer, however, is incomplete. A lot more is taking place than brute power. To get a more in-depth view, let's look at the insights provided by symbolic interactionists, who attempt to attain a "view from within." We need to begin by asking what pimps mean to prostitutes. To understand this, the typical background of prostitutes, which we discussed earlier, is significant. Being victimized as children makes these women dependent emotionally, and pimps are experts at playing on their insecurities and fears. Many offer a sense of belonging, affection, and tenderness. Some hold out the hope of marriage, children, even a home in the suburbs after they have saved enough money from the woman's earnings. Pimps, however, are exploiters, and a pimp may be making the same promises to several women. He may tell each that she is the special woman in his life, cautioning her not to tell the others so the two of them can use the earnings of the other women to fulfill their plans.

Pimps, however, are unconcerned about the welfare of their women, except as it affects their earnings. To them, the women are mere money machines, objects to be used or abused at will. The pimp's real interest is in the prestige he gets from other street males. His status depends on the number of women he controls in his "stable"; on how aloof he can remain from women while still making them bend to his will; and on his personal grooming, jewelry, cars, leisure, and free-spending ways (Milner and Milner 1972; Williamson and Cluse-Tolar 2002).

Symbolic interactionists stress that to understand people we need to grasp their definitions of the situation. We need to see how their norms influence their behavior—just as our norms influence what we do. When we take an insider's view, the world looks like a different place—and it is. And this is precisely the point: to see from within in order to understand human behavior—especially when it contradicts our own standards and experiences.

HOMOSEXUAL PROSTITUTION. Before we consider why prostitution is a social problem, let's turn to the selling and buying of sexual acts between people of the same sex. Homosexual prostitution often takes place in areas known as "meat racks," public settings such as street corners, parks, and bars. A study in Rome found that some homosexual prostitutes have 1,500 sexual partners a year (Gattari et al. 1992). A study in Chicago by sociologist David Luckenbill (1986) found that male prostitutes have a hierarchy that parallels that of their female counterparts. At the top are escort prostitutes, those who work for modeling or dating agencies. At the bottom are street hustlers, and at the middle level are bar hustlers. The charge per trick goes up with each level.

Sociologist David Pittman (1971) studied a house of male prostitution (for males) in St. Louis. To recruit male prostitutes, the "madam" (a man) advertises for male models.

When young men apply, he explains why he really wants to hire them. He photographs those who take the job, putting their photographs in a catalog of nude "models" that customers view. With youth being so highly prized and customers insisting on a continuous supply of fresh bodies, these male prostitutes face intense pressure. Many turn to stimulant drugs, become depressed, and drink heavily. Their sexual performance flags, they lose customers, and are fired.

In a classic study from the 1960s, sociologist Albert Reiss, Jr. (1961) found that teenagers who were paid by homosexuals to receive oral sex managed to maintain a heterosexual identity. As you can imagine, this required an intricate balancing act. The boys accomplished this by (1) allowing no emotional involvement with the adult fellator, (2) making money the only purpose of the act (not sexual gratification, which they reserved for females), (3) tolerating no sexual act other than receiving fellatio, (4) never seeing a homosexual socially, and (5) openly having a girlfriend.

Prostitution by boys has become more open since Reiss studied it and probably more common as well (Cates and Markley 1992; Beddoe et al. 2001). Many of the boys are runaways from lower-class or welfare families. Some prostitute themselves to survive, others simply to have extra money. In some countries, such as Thailand, young boys are forced into prostitution. Many see the apparent increase in boy prostitution as a social problem in and of itself. A related problem is AIDS among homosexual prostitutes.

Prostitution by teenage boys has become more open since sociologists first studied it in the 1950s. In some urban areas known as "meat racks," boy prostitutes gather in search of customers.

PROSTITUTION AS A SOCIAL PROBLEM. Why does prostitution arouse subjective concerns? Morality is the primary reason (Brace 1880:123–131). For some, morality is an issue because prostitution involves sexual behavior between people who are not married to one another. Others perceive prostitution as immoral because the sex is sold—that for a price prostitutes engage in sexual acts. A second concern is that prostitution exploits women's bodies, degrades their spirit, and subjugates them to men. A third concern is that prostitution ruins "good" neighborhoods, depressing property values by bringing in unsavory characters and illegal activities such as drug dealing. A fourth concern is that prostitution is a crime. Victimless or not, prostitution is illegal, and this makes it part of a larger social problem. A fifth concern is that profits from prostitution feed organized crime. A sixth is that these profits are also used to corrupt police and judges, uniting these "enforcers of morality" with pimps, madams, and organized criminals. Another subjective concern is that prostitutes spread disease. AIDS has given this concern special urgency. There is also a concern about aesthetics—the disgust that people feel when they see used condoms and tissues left in public places, including schoolyards. In summary, subjective concerns about prostitution center on morality, exploitation, property values, criminality, corruption of officials, the transmission of disease, and aesthetics.

Let's now turn to another sexual behavior that has become widespread but that also arouses subjective concerns.

Pornography

Background: Getting the Larger Picture

DEFINING PORNOGRAPHY. Originally, pornography referred to writings by prostitutes or to descriptions of the life of prostitutes. (*Porna* is Greek for "prostitute.") For our purposes, we can define **pornography** as writings, pictures, or objects of a sexual nature that people object to as being filthy or immoral.

Materials intended to cause sexual excitement go far back in history. Pornography abounded in the Roman Empire, as shown by excavations of the Mediterranean resort city of Pompeii, which was destroyed by an eruption of Mount Vesuvius in A.D. 79. There, archaeologists uncovered brothels decorated with mosaics of men and women engaging

Sex sells, and, with changing sexual norms, pornography has proliferated in the United States. With pornography offensive to most Americans, however, it is subject to more rigorous controls than other businesses. One form of social control used by many city officials is to segregate pornographic outlets, limiting them to specified areas of the city.

in a variety of sexual acts. The *Kama Sutra,* an Indian religious book dating from the eighth century after Christ, which is explicit about sex, includes suggestions on how prostitutes can please their customers (Henriques 1966).

Deciding what is pornographic is difficult, for like beauty, pornography lies in the eye of the beholder. For example, are nude statues pornographic? Some think so, while others say they merely illustrate the beauty of the human body. Are movies that depict sexual intercourse pornographic? More would probably say they are. How about movies or photos that depict oral sex? A larger number would probably say yes. Or those that depict anal intercourse? The number who think so would probably increase even more. How about movies that show sex between adults and children or between humans and animals? At this point, the rate of agreement that these are pornographic would increase sharply.

On one matter, almost everyone agrees—pornography, whatever it is, should be restricted. As shown in Table 3-4 on the next page, 56 percent of Americans think that the sale of pornography to teenagers should be banned, and another 38 percent would outlaw pornography altogether—a total of 94 percent who favor legal restrictions. Attitudes toward censorship follow broad social avenues. Those most likely to want to ban pornography for everyone are women, whites, those with only a high school education, older people, and Protestants. Those least likely to want pornography to be illegal for everyone are men, African Americans, college graduates, younger people, and Jews.

THE PORNIFYING OF AMERICA. From its beginnings as an underground cottage industry, pornography has grown into an open and aggressive multibillion-dollar-a-year business. Behind today's pornography lies an extensive network of people who profit from it: writers, publishers, actors, and filmmakers; owners of bookstores, video stores, and theaters; corner newsstands and supermarket chains; and banks and financiers. HBO and Time Warner profit from selling pornographic movies, as do Holiday Inn, Marriott, Hyatt, Hilton, Sheraton, and other hotels that offer pay-per-view pornography to their guests. To the extent that people subscribe to Internet Service Providers in order to gain access to pornography, even AOL and CompuServe get their share. Like politics, pornography makes strange bedfellows.

TABLE 3-4 Attitudes About the Distribution of Pornography

	SHOULD BE ILLEGAL FOR EVERYONE				SHOULD BE ILLEGAL ONLY FOR PEOPLE UNDER 18				SHOULD BE LEGAL FOR EVERYONE			
	1980	1990	2000	2002[1]	1980	1990	2000	2002	1980	1990	2000	2002
National	40%	41%	36%	38%	51%	52%	60%	56%	6%	6%	3%	5%
Sex												
Male	31%	33%	24%	31%	60%	59%	72%	62%	8%	6%	3%	7%
Female	47%	47%	45%	43%	45%	47%	51%	52%	5%	5%	3%	4%
Race/Ethnicity[2]												
White	41%	42%	36%	39%	52%	51%	60%	56%	6%	5%	3%	5%
African American	35%	34%	34%	32%	51%	57%	59%	60%	10%	7%	5%	6%
Education												
College	31%	36%	31%	34%	59%	57%	65%	61%	8%	7%	3%	4%
High School	42%	44%	41%	40%	52%	51%	55%	52%	5%	5%	3%	8%
Age												
18–20	12%	17%	18%	29%	79%	65%	77%	59%	9%	13%	4%	12%
21–29	23%	29%	17%	17%	69%	67%	78%	75%	7%	3%	4%	8%
30–49	32%	36%	29%	32%	60%	60%	68%	64%	7%	4%	2%	4%
50 and over	40%	53%	52%	54%	50%	36%	43%	40%	8%	8%	4%	6%
Religion												
Protestant	45%	46%	44%	46%	48%	48%	53%	50%	5%	5%	2%	4%
Catholic	40%	39%	31%	34%	52%	56%	66%	61%	6%	4%	2%	4%
Jew	25%	25%	20%	19%	10%	59%	53%	79%	75%	20%	5%	2%
None	8%	22%	16%	21%	74%	66%	76%	68%	15%	9%	7%	11%

[1] Latest year available.

[2] Only these two groups are given in the sources; African American is listed as Black/other.

Source: Sourcebook of Criminal Justice Statistics 1992:Table 2–98; 2003:Table 2–97.

Pornography has become so common that we can say that the United States has become pornified. The basic reason is technology. The Internet allows people to pursue pornography privately, without risking their reputations by being seen in a porn shop in a seedy part of town. About one in four Internet users access adult sites, where they spend an average of 74 minutes a month (Paul 2005). This does *not* count time spent visiting amateur sites. About 70 percent of 18–24-year-old men visit a pornographic site in a typical month.

Pornography Viewed Theoretically: Applying Symbolic Interactionism

ROTH V. U.S. The controversy about what is and is not pornography—and what should be done about it—has bedeviled the courts. In 1957, the U.S. Supreme Court tried to define pornography for the nation. In *Roth v. U.S.,* the Court ruled that materials are pornographic or obscene when

1. "Taken as a whole," the "dominant theme" appeals to "prurient interest" in sex.
2. The material affronts "contemporary community standards."
3. The material is "utterly without redeeming social value."

Instead of settling anything, however, the key terms of the *Roth* decision (placed in quotes above) added fuel to the fire. *Prurient,* for example, means "lewd or impure." But the use of such a word solves nothing—it simply takes you back to the issue of what pornography is in the first place—for what is lewd or impure to one person is not to another. The guidelines, which were supposed to clear up matters, merely muddied the waters. If the terms were clear, they were clear only to the Court—and that is most unlikely.

As symbolic interactionists emphasize, until people put meaning into them, words are merely sounds and human acts merely behavior. If two people look at the same photo or watch the same movie or stage play, one might see nudity or sexual intercourse as the expression of art and love, while the other perceives the filth of pornography. What, then, does the Court's phrase "redeeming social value" mean? Where does it leave us if I decide that the sexual content of a book or movie has "redeeming social value," but you do not?

And so the war of symbols goes on. Some claim that certain materials violate "contemporary community standards," whereas others say that those same materials reflect community standards. Still others say there are no community standards! The Internet, developed after the *Roth* decision, has complicated the matter even more. Do people who exchange sexually explicit photos on the Internet form a "community," and should it be their values by which we judge something as pornographic or not? Or does "community" refer to the place where the materials were produced? Or where they were downloaded?

CALIFORNIA V. MILLER. As you can see, the *Roth* decision didn't clarify a thing. Its ambiguities, however, made it difficult for prosecutors to obtain convictions for pornography. In 1973, in *California v. Miller*, the Court tried to remove these ambiguities. It kept the dominant "prurient" theme, said that "contemporary community standards" meant the local community, and, giving up on trying to figure out what it had meant by "redeeming social value," simply dropped the term (Lewis and Peoples 1978:1071).

Like the *Roth* decision, the *Miller* decision settled nothing. What is or is not pornographic still remained in the eye of the beholder. In some communities, the depiction of sexual acts symbolized filth and depravity to significant numbers of people (or to a number of influential people), and pornography was either banned or restricted to outlets in designated areas. In other communities, those same depictions were viewed differently, and not only images but also live presentations of those acts were allowed. With such inconsistencies, the matter was brought again before the Supreme Court. In 1976 (*Young v. American Mini Theaters*) and 1986 (*Renton v. Playtime Theatres*), the Court took a middle ground, ruling that it was constitutional to restrict the location of adult movie theaters (Sitomer 1986).

A QUESTION OF "TASTE." Social class is significant in helping to determine people's perceptions of acts as pornographic or not. This became evident in a later Court ruling that some nudity, such as that in theater productions and art, is permissible because it is "tasteful." In contrast, other forms of nudity, such as striptease dancing, are not "tasteful." They are "low-art," if "art" at all, and not allowable (Heins 1991). The question of "taste," of course, simply takes us back to the original question of what pornography is, for whose "taste" determines this? As conflict theorists would point out, it is not surprising that Supreme Court justices decide that their own class-based preferences for nudity are not pornographic, but those of the lower classes are.

CHILD PORNOGRAPHY. When it comes to depicting sex with children, hardly anyone finds "community standards" an adequate defense. Magazines that depicted children in sex acts with adults or with other children used to be easily accessible, although, like depictions of humans having sex with animals today, they were "under-the-counter" or "back room" items. Some of the children were as young as 3 or 4, but most buyers of these magazines seemed to prefer prepubescents between the ages of 8 and 10. These publications bore such titles as *Lollitots* and *Moppets* (Dubar 1980).

As states passed laws against child pornography and as judges grew willing to impose prison sentences for possessing these materials, such magazines and movies practically disappeared. Child pornography, however, did not disappear. It just went underground, resurfacing on the Internet. There, people who are stimulated by sex with children "meet" in chat rooms, where they share stories of their exploits, real or imagined. They also buy, sell, and exchange files of children who have been bribed, tricked, or forced into sex acts. The photos, movies, and streaming videos are illegal, but with the Web sites located

Technology and Social Problems

"NOW TAKE OFF YOUR . . . ": LIVE EXHIBITIONS BY CHILDREN ON WEBCAMS

When Justin was 13, he felt scrawny and didn't have many friends. He bought a Web camera and, projecting his image on his own Web site, waited for responses from other teenagers. Those responses never came. But responses from men did.

The men told Justin just what he needed to hear. He was handsome and intelligent. They asked Justin if he would take off his shirt so they could check him out a little more. They even offered him $50 and opened a PayPal account for him so he could collect the money instantly. "Why not?" thought Justin. "I sit at the pool without a shirt for nothing." When Justin took off his shirt, the men complimented him on his physique.

Justin began to look forward to these online chats. Eventually, the men asked him to pose in his shorts. After a while, they asked him to let them see him take them off.

So began Justin's secret life. Each request went only a little farther than the last one, so none of them seemed like a big deal.

As the requests escalated, Justin ended up showing an erection for the men, then masturbating before the camera, and having sex.

Justin had become a cyberporn star or, as they are known in the vernacular of those who watch these teenagers, a camwhore. As Justin's popularity grew, he opened his own pay-for-view site, charging subscribers $45 a month. He also offered private shows, charging up to $300, depending on what the men wanted him to do on streaming video.

Justin's parents didn't catch on. They thought that their son, in his bedroom, was doing his homework.

Teenaged girls have also found the Webcam to be an easy way to supplement their allowances. They, too, operate pay-for-view Web sites, with their Webcams beaming their images around the world. The instant messages pour in: I would like to see you in jeans with a belt, in a miniskirt with your feet bare, in pantyhose, with bare legs, with a lacy bra, in red panties, wearing nothing . . .

Based on Eichenwald 2005; Brockman 2006.

FOR YOUR CONSIDERATION

Justin, and those like him, are not forced to do anything. They decide to show their bodies, or to engage in sex acts, for a fee. Why should this be considered part of a social problem?

---

throughout the world, the use of passwords and encryption, and some sites requiring newcomers to be introduced by members, law enforcement agents find it difficult to track them down (Ruethling 2006). In the Technology and Social Problems box above, we explore the evolution of child pornography on the Internet.

It may get even harder to stop child porn. In 2002, in *Ashcroft v. Free Speech Coalition*, the U.S. Supreme Court ruled that it is legal to possess virtual child pornography—that is, computer-generated images of children in sex acts. Because no real child is involved, the Court concluded, there is no victim. This ruling handicaps law enforcement officials, because the improved quality of virtual images makes it difficult to tell the fake from the real thing. As a U.S. customs official said, "We're going to be forced to prove that every picture is of a real child" (Sager et al. 2002).

With perceptions and values varying so widely, it is impossible to pin down what pornography is. Cable operators, for example, try not to cross the line between "acceptable adult programming" and pornography. But where is this line, since showing vaginal penetration, anal sex, oral sex, and group sex is considered acceptable in some markets (Paul 2005)?

Controversy and Research on Pornography

THE NATIONAL COMMISSION ON OBSCENITY AND PORNOGRAPHY. Like other social problems, pornography is not only a controversial issue but also an emotional one. A common fear is that pornography corrupts people, that it destroys their morals, perverts their sense of sexuality, and even encourages men to rape. In the 1960s, Americans were so concerned that President Johnson appointed a National Commission on Obscenity and Pornography. In 1970, the commission concluded that pornography affects some people more than others—that it stimulates the young more than the old, the college-educated more than the less educated, the religiously inactive more than the religiously active, and the sexually experienced more than the sexually inexperienced. Unlike Kinsey (1953), who reported that erotic material arouses males considerably more than females, the commission found that women and men are about equally aroused by watching pornography (Schmidt and Sigusch 1970).

THE MEESE COMMISSION. These conclusions were rather innocuous. They didn't point the finger at pornography as being seriously harmful to society. As pornography proliferated, however, so did subjective concerns, and in the 1980s President Reagan asked the attorney general to appoint another commission to study the effects of pornography. This group, the Meese Commission (1986), concluded that pornography poses a serious threat to women:

> The clinical and experimental evidence supports the conclusion that there is a causal relationship between exposure to sexually violent materials and an increase in aggressive behavior directed towards women. . . . (p. 39)

An increase in pornography, said the Commission, "will cause an increase in the level of sexual violence directed at women."

The commission's more specific findings (McManus 1986) include these:

1. Of 411 sex offenders, the average had 336 victims.
2. Rape increases where pornography laws are liberalized.
3. Rapists are much more likely than nonoffenders to have been exposed as children to hard-core pornography.
4. Pornography makes rape seem "legitimate."
5. States with higher sales of pornography have higher rates of rape.
6. Males exposed to pornography that features sexual violence become desensitized and see rape victims as "less injured and less worthy."

The Meese commission (1986:39) also concluded that "common-sense" makes it evident that violent pornography causes sex crimes. As illustrated in Chapter 1, not everything evident to our "common sense" is right. If all we need is common sense, we wouldn't need science, and science requires evidence. It is precisely this jump from the evidence (the frequency of pornography among sex offenders) to the conclusion (pornography causes sex crimes) that critics attacked when the commission published its report. Critics said that because the commission was predisposed to see pornography as evil and as the cause of crime, it misinterpreted the evidence and ignored studies that contradicted its preconceptions (Baron 1987; Brannigan 1987; Linz, Donnerstein, and Penrod 1987).

A QUESTION OF CAUSE AND EFFECT. Because neither the Meese Commission's report nor its rebuttals give us final answers, we are left with the thorny question, Does pornography *cause* sex crimes? Or are sex criminals, such as rapists and child molesters, just more likely to use pornography? Or is it possible that violent pornography, even child pornography, satisfies deviant sexual urges and *decreases* attacks against women and children? Researchers have been able to document only **correlations** (two or more things occurring together). For example, although sex offenders tend to use more pornography than do nonoffenders, not all sex criminals do so. In addition, many noncriminals use pornography. Scientific proof (objective, consistent, verifiable) of a causal relationship, then, remains elusive, and these questions remain unanswered.

Some analysts point out that sex crimes against children in Denmark dropped after that country's lawmakers made hard-core pornography legal in 1965 (Kutchinsky 1973). It is possible that some men who want to have sex with children find it more appealing to masturbate to pornographic images than to face the threat of prison if they indulge their fantasies with real children. Some child molesters may not even prefer children, taking them as substitutes because they are unable to relate sexually to adults. For these people, too, pornographic images may provide a substitute.

When Japan allowed hard-core pornography during the 1980s and 1990s, there, too, the number of rapes dropped (Diamond and Uchiyama 1999). It is the same in the United States. Although pornography—including that depicting violence against women—has become more common, rape has become less common. The rate of rape in the United States increased until the early 1990s, but since then dropped 25 percent (*Statistical Abstract of the United States* 2006:Table 293). It is difficult to determine cause and effect, but one thing seems clear: If pornography is proven to *increase* sexual attacks, there will be an outcry to get rid of it, but if it actually *reduces* sexual attacks, there is not likely to be an outcry to increase it.

The matter of cause and effect is seldom simple, but it is made all the more difficult because pornography has different effects on different people. Some researchers have found that pornography that shows violence against women tends to trigger sexual aggression against women among angry, aggressive men (Malamuth et al. 2000), while it does not have these effects on more relaxed, "laid back" men. There certainly are problems with such categorizing of men, and even if these categores are valid, the findings are preliminary, and we need more research to determine whether this is so.

SCIENCE VS. SOCIAL ACTION. This is science at work. When research is published, it enters what we might call the "court" of science, where it is judged by a jury of critical scientific peers. As researchers report their findings, other researchers meticulously examine their studies. They challenge the data and repeat the study or reanalyze the original data and publish their own conclusions. This critical process exposes researchers' biases. The conclusions that emerge and knowledge that builds either replace or confirm our commonsense notions about social problems.

Some people find this rigorous and exacting process too slow. Convinced that severe consequences are at stake, they feel a pressing need to take a stand now. And based on their ideas about what is right and wrong and what they find offensive, they do take a stand.

For example, many people are upset about how pornography portrays women. They are convinced that pornography teaches men to view women as "pieces of meat" and that it teaches women to devalue their own selves. Whether pornography causes sex crimes is not the point, they insist. Even if it does not, the degrading portrayal of women is another way that women are debased and victimized in society. This is reason enough for pornography—at least the type that shows violence against females—to be banned. As discussed in the Thinking Critically About Social Problems box on the next page, resistance to pornography, though strongly rooted, has lost to the porn industry.

SAFETY VALVE OR TRIGGER? There is no doubt that pornography does influence people. To think otherwise would be absurd. A generation ago, sociologists Donal MacNamara and Edward Sagarin (1977:205) made this point:

> To say that pornography cannot influence a person is to contend that books and the printed word, graphics, art, and slogans cannot move people and cause changes in their thoughts and hence their actions.

The question, then, is not whether pornography influences people but, rather, *how.* Is the **safety valve theory** of pornography right? That is, do some types of pornography protect women and children from rape and other sexual violence by providing the private release of sexual fantasies? If so, this type of pornography should be encouraged. Or is the **trigger theory** of pornography right? That is, do some types of pornography trigger sexual offenses by stimulating sexual appetites, often for deviance and violence? If so, these types of pornography should be banned.

Unfortunately, researchers have been unable to settle this question. Until they can—and if they can—social activists will continue to struggle for what they see as a better social world. No matter which side of the issue they are on, however, they will be acting on their subjective concerns, not on irrefutable evidence.

THINKING CRITICALLY About Social Problems

THE PORNIFYING OF AMERICA: CRUSHING RESISTANCE AND CO-OPTING FEMINISTS

Pornography is big business, but to find a market for the many magazines, millions of photographs, and thousands of pornographic movies produced each year required changed attitudes. To get Americans to change their attitudes, deep-seated resistance to pornography had to be overcome.

First, there were the religious people who viewed pornography as a moral issue. They looked at the portrayal of sexual acts as sinful and the proliferation of pornography as a sign of the growing depravity of U.S. culture. These people put up a stiff resistance, but as pornography became common, they capitulated to changing times. They eventually came to view further resistance as labor wasted on a lost cause. Occasionally, a religious leader will still bemoan pornography, but he or she is preaching to the choir—some of whom rush home to their private collections of favorite sex acts.

There were also the feminists. Feminists didn't take the same moral route, as they didn't want to be seen as aligned with those they considered religious fanatics. But they, too, found something morally objectionable to pornography. Pornography exploits women, they said. Not only are women shown as a bunch of body parts to be used at the pleasure of men, but also many women who work in the porn industry suffer sexual and emotional abuse. On top of this, they are underpaid. Feminists who took this route rallied for better working conditions and health standards for those they labeled as sex workers. Feminists who publicized this position found that other feminists called them "feminazis" and "prudes." The porn industry was delighted by this division among such a usually outspoken group. Their resistance, too, was crushed into silence.

The victory for the porn industry has been so complete that to criticize pornography has become "uncool, unsexy, and reactionary" (Paul 2005). The porn industry has even been able to turn things upside down. Pornography is now often viewed as part of women's freedom, not their oppression. Women's magazines discuss pornography from the perspective of equal opportunity for women—how women can introduce pornography into their sex lives, how pornography gives them the chance to get "in touch" with their sexuality (Paul 2005). These articles, too, have become part of the porn industry, a way for another group to make money from porn.

Demonstrations against pornography seem to have lessened. For the most part, opponents seem to have resigned themselves to what they see as inevitable social change. Certain aspects of pornography, especially the depiction of children, however, still arouse protest.

Social Policy

Now that homosexual acts in private between consenting adults are no longer illegal, the issue that remains centers on developing social policy to protect homosexuals from discrimination and to make certain that they have equality before the law. When it comes to prostitution and pornography, we still face issues of criminal acts. Let's look at these in some detail.

The Question of Making Consensual Behavior Illegal

THE MATTER OF ILLEGAL CONSENSUAL ACTS. Sociologists use the term **victimless crime** to refer to illegal acts to which the participants consent. The crime has no victim because the people agree to do something with or for one another. A man pays a woman for sex; someone sells or buys pictures of adults involved in sexual acts—both may be illegal, but they occur with the consent of the people involved.

In most crimes, someone does something against the will of someone else. There is a victim and a perpetrator. When a victim reports a crime, the police know where and when it happened and who the victim is. Without a victim, however, the police end up spending precious public resources attempting to determine that a crime occurred in the first place, and then prosecutors have difficulty in obtaining convictions because the people involved consented to what took place. Unless there is a public outcry, both the public and the police prefer that law enforcement agents pursue criminals who have victims—thieves, muggers, rapists, and murderers.

Not all prostitution and pornography involve victimless crimes, however. There can be force, threats, or less than informed consent. If there is force, it is rape, a different matter entirely. If there is less than informed consent, there is also a victim. Child pornography, for example, is not a victimless crime. The children are not of age to give their consent, and child pornography often involves the abuse of adult authority. To deal adequately with social policy, we must separate such instances from those that involve full consent.

Alternatives to Making Consensual Behavior Illegal

LEGALIZING PROSTITUTION. Let's consider prostitution. Because prostitution is a commercial transaction—a business—some argue that it should be legal. We license and tax businesses, so why should we exempt prostitution? Proponents of legalization point out that prostitution will persist and suggest that it is time for the state to regulate it. For pro and con arguments on legalizing prostitution, see the Thinking Critically box below.

THINKING CRITICALLY About Social Problems

SHOULD WE LEGALIZE PROSTITUTION?

YES

1. Prostitutes perform a service for society. They provide sex for people who otherwise cannot find sexual partners. They even help marriages by reducing sexual demands on wives.
2. To keep prostitution illegal is dysfunctional. This stigmatizes and marginalizes women who want to work as prostitutes. It also corrupts many police officers, who accept bribes to allow prostitutes to work. Some prostitution is run by organized crime, with women held in bondage. Legalizing prostitution will eliminate these problems.
3. If prostitution is declared a legal occupation, the government can regulate it. The government can license prostitutes and tax them. It can also require prostitutes to have regular medical checkups and to display a dated and signed medical certificate stating that they are free of sexually transmitted diseases.

NO

1. Prostitution is immoral, and we should not legalize immoral activities. The foundation of society is the family, and we should take steps to strengthen the family, not tear it apart by approving sex as a commercial transaction outside the family.
2. The legalization of prostitution will not stop sexually transmitted diseases. For example, the HIV virus can be transmitted before the disease shows up in blood tests. Even though prostitutes are licensed, they will spread AIDS during this interval.
3. Prostitution degrades women. To legalize prostitution is to give the state's approval to their degradation. It also would affirm class oppression: Most prostitutes come from the working class and serve as objects to satisfy the sexual desires of men from more privileged classes.

THE MATTER OF PRIVACY. Central to deciding social policy is the issue of privacy. The argument is that if adults want to have sex in private, anyone may judge the morality of the act, but why should it concern the state? It may be a sin, but it should not be a crime. But there is another side to the privacy argument—the right of *privacy from* people who are involved in sexual acts. Those who find such activities morally repugnant should not have to see them. If the law were to permit these sexual acts, it should also prohibit street solicitation by prostitutes, sex in public places, and the display of sexual acts on the covers of magazines in supermarkets and other stores.

To allow people to pay for sex *and* to make it so that unwilling people do not have to view them, some suggest **segregation**—limiting these activities to specified areas. They also would insist on preventing blatancy in even those areas. For example, if prostitutes were segregated to a certain area of the city, they could advertise for customers through ads in newspapers or by a red light in an apartment window, but they could not walk the streets. Nor could pornographic outlets show sexually explicit marquees or posters. This would allow the patrons of prostitutes and the consumers of pornography to be able to carry out their consensual activities in semiprivate, while respecting the rights of others to avoid seeing these activities.

THE MATTER OF CHILDREN. The use of children in prostitution and pornography is an entirely different matter. Almost everyone feels that children should be protected from sexual exploitation. Their position: If the purpose of the law is not to protect the least defenseless of our society, what is its purpose? As the Issues in Social Problems box below shows, private citizens can help to protect children from sexual victimization.

Issues in Social Problems

APPLYING SOCIOLOGY: TAKING BACK CHILDREN FROM THE NIGHT

Lois Lee isn't afraid to apply her sociological training to social problems. Lee did her master's thesis on the pimp–prostitute relationship and her doctoral dissertation on the social world of the prostitute. After receiving her Ph.D. in sociology from United States International University in 1981, Lee began to work with adult prostitutes. They told her, "You know, it's too late for you to help us, Lois. You've got to do something about these kids. We made a choice to be out here . . . a conscious decision. But these kids don't stand a chance."

Lee began by taking those kids, the teenagers who were prostituting themselves, into her home. In three years, she brought 250 to her home, where she lived with her husband and baby son. Lee then founded "Children of the Night," which reaches the kids by means of "a 24-hour hotline, a street outreach program, a walk-in crisis center, crisis intervention for medical or life-threatening situations, family counseling, job placement, and foster home or group placement." By providing alternatives to prostitution and petty crime, Children of the Night has helped thousands of young runaways and prostitutes to get off the streets.

Lee's work has brought her national publicity and an award from the president. She credits her success to her sociological training, especially the sensitivities it gave her "to understand and move safely through intersecting deviant worlds, to relate positively to police and caretaking agencies while retaining a critical perspective, to know which game to play in which situation."

As Lee said during a CBS interview, "I know what the street rules are, I know what the pimp game is, I know what the con games are, and it's up to me to play that game correctly. . . . It's all sociology. That's why when people call me a social worker I always correct them."

Based on Buff 1987.

The Future of the Problem

With the rapid social change that engulfs us, it is difficult to peer far into the future. Assuming that the United States does not devolve into a dictatorship, which, curtailing civil rights, could drive homosexuality, prostitution, and pornography underground, I foresee the following.

Homosexuality and the Future

Two primary issues are generating controversy. The first is the political struggle by homosexuals to be allowed legal marriage. This issue is likely to reach the U.S. Supreme Court, where the decision will be decided not according to the U.S. Constitution, which is silent on this matter, but by the politics of the justices who happen to make up the Court when the case comes before it. Obviously, then, the decision could go either way. The second issue also centers on a legal and social right: to serve as role models—to be openly homosexual and to occupy positions that mold the orientations of youth, such as public school teachers and scout leaders. The vast middle ground between those who espouse homosexuality and those who fear or despise it is likely to be occupied by those who believe that homosexuality should be discouraged but that homosexuals should not be oppressed.

Elton John, one of the world's most famous entertainers, who has given concerts in 60 countries, used to keep his sexual preference at least semi-hidden. With changing sexual norms, John has been open about his 11-year relationship with David Furnish. In many ways, homosexual relationships are mirror images of heterosexual ones. The wealthy and famous always manage to have younger partners. John is 59; Furnish is 39.

Prostitution and the Future

Perhaps the easiest forecast in the entire book is this one: The demand for the services of prostitutes will continue. There will always be sexually deprived people who want to patronize prostitutes, as well as those who want to pay for the specialized sexual services that prostitutes offer.

Although prostitution will continue to flourish, it will remain illegal in almost all areas of the United States. The police will overlook all but the most blatant acts both because they feel that they have better things to do and because many of them are convinced that sexual acts between consenting adults should be legal. Granted current trends, we are likely to see an increase in an aspect of prostitution that upsets both the public and the police, the prostitution of children. As the media give more publicity to prostituted children, subjective concerns among the public will grow. Spurred by the media, influential individuals will launch campaigns against the prostitution of children (and the exploitation of children in pornography), placing greater pressure on lawmakers. More laws will be passed. Most of them will have little effect.

Pornography and the Future

Changes in pornography are likely to be driven by two forces: technology and profits. As each new communication technology appears, pornography will be adapted to fit it. With the increased ease of producing and viewing moving images, with Webcams and DVDs, for example, more people will make their own "home porno." Because pornography is so profitable, it is likely that the mainstream media will embrace it even more. Cable television, which offers subscribers XXX options, is likely to become even more explicit, perhaps even to broadcast live sex programs. As pornography goes more mainstream, the line between pornography and art will become even more blurred. It will become increasingly difficult to distinguish between pornography and regular Hollywood films. See the Technology and Social Problems box on electronic pornography below.

Some continuing clash between the pro- and antipornography forces seems inevitable, for the values of these groups are contrary, and each desires to control the media. But pornography is now so entrenched in our society that it is likely that those who oppose pornography will limit themselves to an occasional statement decrying the fall of American values and then retreat into enclaves of people who agree with their views.

Technology and Social Problems
PORNOGRAPHY ON THE INTERNET

Pornography vividly illustrates one of the sociological prin-ciples discussed in this chapter—that people adapt their sexual behaviors to social change. It was not long after photography was invented that pornographic photography appeared. Today a major issue is pornography on the Internet.

What is the problem? Why can't people electronically exchange nude photos with one another if they want to? If that were the issue, there would be no problem. The real issue, however, is something quite different. What disturbs many people are the photos that show bondage, torture, rape, and bestiality (humans having sex with animals). Judging from the number of such sites, apparently many people derive sexual excitement from such photos. To avoid legal prosecution, pornographers locate the sites that host such materials in countries with weak laws or enforcement.

The Internet abounds with "chat rooms" (people who "meet" online to discuss some topic). No one is bothered about the chat rooms that center on Roman architecture or rap music or turtle racing. But news groups that focus on how to torture women are another matter. So are those that focus on how to seduce children—or on the delights of having sex with preschoolers.

Any call for censorship raises the hackles of civil libertarians, who see all censorship as an attack on basic freedoms. Censorship, they say, is just the first step toward a totalitarian society. The extreme among them defend the right to display and exchange photos of children who are being sexually abused. But only the extremists. Most civil libertarians appear to draw the

line at child pornography, but only reluctantly; and they don't want the line drawn any further.

Granted that such pornographic sites and related chat rooms will continue, the issue, then, is how to protect others from being exposed to them. For example, should school and public libraries be allowed to install Internet filters that screen out designated sites? One side insists that this violates the guarantee of the First Amendment's right of free speech, the other that it is only a reasonable precaution to protect children.

What do you think?

Based on Clausing 1998; Etzioni 1998; Kaplan 1998; Mendels 1998; O'Connell 1998; Locy and Biskupic 2003.

SUMMARY AND REVIEW

1. All societies attempt to channel sexual behavior in ways they consider acceptable. When the violation of sexual norms is felt to be a threat to society, especially to the family, it is considered a social problem.

2. In applying conflict theory to homosexuality, we see that fundamental tensions exist between homosexuals and heterosexuals and that their adjustment to one another is uneasy. Symbolic interactionists have analyzed how a homosexual identity is learned through interaction with others. The process by which people take on a homosexual identity appears to involve six stages: identity confusion, comparison, tolerance, acceptance, pride, and finally synthesis.

3. Through the lens of functionalism, we saw that prostitution persists because it serves social functions. From a functionalist perspective, as prostitutes service customers who are sexually dissatisfied or whose sexual desires are deviant, they relieve pressures that otherwise might be placed on people who are unwilling to participate. The three stages in becoming a prostitute are drift (drifting from casual sex into selling sex), ambivalence, and professionalization. Some young men who sell sex to men manipulate symbols to maintain heterosexual identities.

4. Most Americans agree that the distribution of pornography should be restricted. Women favor greater restrictions than do men. Deciding what is and is not pornographic has confused many, including the U.S. Supreme Court, which, in the tradition of symbolic interactionism, has ruled that what a community decides is pornographic is pornographic—for them.

5. Social scientists have been unable to determine the social effects of pornography. Feminists are concerned that, by dehumanizing women, pornography encourages men to see women as sexual objects to be manipulated and exploited. Social activists take action on the basis of their convictions, not on the basis of proof about causation.

6. *Victimless crimes* are illegal acts to which the participants consent. Prostitution and pornography are classified as victimless crimes by sociologists when adults are involved, but not when children participate, as they cannot give full consent. The suggestion that we legalize prostitution runs into huge opposition.

7. The interests of people who approve and disapprove of homosexuality, prostitution, and pornography are likely to continue to clash, but those who disapprove of them are likely to be fighting rearguard actions. It is inevitable that prostitution and pornography will adapt to technological advancements, making them more widely available than ever.

KEY TERMS

Black market, 65
Correlation, 76
Hate crimes, 53
Heterosexuality, 53
Homosexual behavior, 50
Homosexuality, 51
Lesbian, 60
Masochists, 63

Normalization (of deviance), 68
Pornography, 71
Prostitution, 61
Role ambivalence, 68
Sadists, 63
Safety valve theory (of pornography), 77

Segregation, 80
Situational homosxual behavior, 56
Symbiosis, 65
Temple prostitution, 61
Trigger theory (of pornography), 77
Victimless crime, 78

THINKING CRITICALLY ABOUT CHAPTER 3

1. This chapter began by stating that "a basic sociological principle is that sex is never only a personal matter." It goes on to explain that all societies control human sexual behavior. Why do you think this is true? What is it about sex that makes us inclined to control the sexual behavior of others? Be sure to base your explanation on group aspects of society, not on personality or individuals.

2. Do you think there should be a separate legal category called *hate crimes*? Explain. Does your answer depend on whether we refer to sexual orientation, race–ethnicity, or some other category?

3. What is your opinion of this? Child pornography is illegal, and people are arrested and put in prison for possessing it. Pictures of tortured and sexually abused women are legal.

CHAPTER 4

Alcohol and Other Drugs

Debbie! What's this?"

Seeing the familiar plastic bag, Debbie felt her face redden. Why hadn't she put it away as she always did? She swallowed, then burst out defiantly:

"My purse! You've got no business snooping in my purse!"

"I was just looking for a match—but I found a lot more! I never expected a daughter of mine to be a drug addict."

"Drug addict, huh? That's funny! Just because someone smokes grass doesn't mean she's a drug addict."

"Everybody knows marijuana is just the first step to the hard stuff, like heroin."

Mom, it's you who's hooked.

"Mom, it's you who's hooked. The first thing you do in the morning is light up a cigarette and have a cup of coffee. And after that you start popping Prozac."

"Don't you compare my medicine with your drugs. My doctor prescribes Prozac for my nerves."

"Okay, then what do you call your martinis? And I know why you dug in my purse for a match—it's because you're hooked on cigarettes."

"Don't you talk back to me, young lady. Ever since you started college you think you know it all. Just wait 'til your Dad gets home."

"Yeah, sure. Then you'll do the same thing you do every night—talk about it over a drink."

The Problem in Sociological Perspective

Just as Debbie's mother was shocked to discover that her daughter smoked marijuana, so hundreds of thousands of parents have had similar rude awakenings. Long an element of culture in the Far and Middle East, using drugs for pleasure has become common in the West: on college campuses, in the suburbs, and in the executive suite. One president of the United States even admitted to smoking marijuana—although, bringing laughter to millions, he said that he "didn't inhale."

Background of the Problem

DRUG USE IN ANCIENT SOCIETIES. Records of drug use stretch far back in history. Over 4,000 years ago, a Chinese emperor recommended marijuana for "female weakness, gout, rheumatism, malaria, beriberi, constipation and absentmindedness" (Ray and Ksir 2004). About 2,500 years ago, the famous physician Hippocrates recommended mandrake, taken with a little wine, to relieve depression and anxiety (Blum et al. 1969). And about 500 years ago, when the Spanish conquistadors landed in South America, they discovered that the natives chewed coca leaves for the stimulating effects of cocaine (DeRios and Smith 1977; Goode 1989).

DEFINING DRUG ABUSE. Just as drug use goes far back in history, so does **drug abuse**—using drugs in such a way that they harm one's health, impair one's physical or mental functioning, or interfere with one's social life. Noah, who is listed as the ninth descendant of Adam, is reported to have abused alcohol. After the flood, he planted a vineyard, made wine from its first harvest, and drank himself into a stupor (Genesis 9). What is consid-

For generations, tobacco companies worked to get Americans hooked on nicotine. This ad from the 1950s urged people to give cigarettes as a Christmas gift. Nicotine's effects are deadly, but slow, and it may take 30 years or longer for nicotine to kill. During that time, the cigarette companies make huge profits from their victims. Nicotine, although legal, kills more people than the number who die from all illegal drugs combined.

ered drug abuse, of course, depends on social norms, and you know how norms change from group to group. In one group, smoking a joint of marijuana can be considered drug abuse, whereas in another group smoking marijuana might be considered just "more of the usual."

THE SOCIAL HISTORY OF DRUGS. It is important to emphasize that *no drug is good or bad in and of itself* (Szasz 1975). Whether a drug is considered good or bad is simply a matter of social definition—how a group of people views the drug and reacts to it. And how perspectives change! You are familiar with today's dominant view of tobacco—and the health warnings on cigarette packages. But contrast today's perspective with that of the 1940s and 1950s. Back then, doctors actually used to recommend particular brands of cigarettes as good for people's health. I think you will find the ad for Chesterfields on this page, featuring a future U. S. president, rather different from today's ads.

Attempts to Deal with the Problem

THE FAILURE OF PUNISHMENT. But let's reach back a little further in tobacco's social history. When Christopher Columbus arrived on these shores, he found that Native Americans smoked tobacco, something he hadn't seen before. He took some back with him to the Old World. Europeans tried it, and smoking tobacco became common. King James I of England disliked this new habit, however, and in 1604 he wrote a pamphlet warning his subjects that tobacco was "harmful to the brain, dangerous to the lungs" (Ray and Ksir 2004). Other rulers who viewed tobacco as evil went far beyond just issuing warnings. In 1634, the czar of Russia ordered the noses of tobacco smokers slit. The rulers of China went a bit further: They had smokers' heads cut off. Turkish rulers, too, ordered smokers put to death (Goode 1989). All these anti-drug campaigns failed.

Like many people today, King James was not one to let health concerns interfere with making money. When tobacco growing became profitable, he declared its trade a royal monopoly (Ray and Ksir 2004). Today we have universities and foundations that tout their concerns about social justice but can't resist the juicy dividends that tobacco stocks pay.

Although some people will risk their neck for a good smoke, others will do the same for the beverage that may or may not be good to the last drop. After coffee was introduced in Arabia in the 1500s, Islamic religious leaders became upset that people drank coffee to help them stay awake during long vigils. Thinking that coffee was intoxicating and, therefore, prohibited by the Koran, the religious leaders ordered coffee dealers beaten across the soles of their feet. These anti-drug measures, too, failed (Brecher et al. 1972). A century later, in 1674, a group of Englishwomen wrote a pamphlet titled "The Women's Petition Against Coffee." They complained that their men were leaving "good old ale" in order to drink "base, black, thick, nasty, bitter, stinking, nauseous" coffee. Their real complaint? The coffee, they said, was making their men less active sexually (Meyer 1954).

CHANGING SOCIAL DEFINITIONS. In the United States, attitudes toward drugs have undergone major changes. I've already mentioned cigarettes, but consider this: In the 1800s, you could buy opium and morphine in drugstores, grocery stores, and general stores. If you found shopping inconvenient, you could order these drugs by mail. Opium was advertised as a cure for diarrhea, colds, fever, teething, pelvic disorders, even athlete's foot and baldness (Inciardi 1986). Opium was so common that each year U.S. mothers fed their babies about 750,000 bottles of opium-laced syrup. To smoke cigarettes or drink alcohol was far more offensive than to use opium (Isbell 1969; Duster 1970; Brecher et al. 1972).

People project their fantasies and fears onto drugs. They may initially view a drug as a holy gift, but later define that same drug as part of a social problem. This drives home

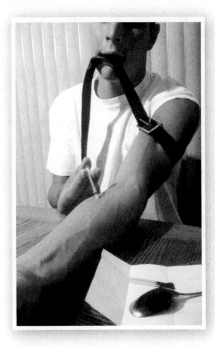

If a drug is in high demand, passing a law will not stop that demand. The law merely drives the use of the drug underground, to a black market that connects users and suppliers in an intricate, illegal relationship. Although coffee is broadly socially acceptable today, in some societies it was once an illegal drug, with severe penalties attached to its possession and consumption.

the point made in Chapter 1 about objective conditions and subjective concerns. It is not the *objective conditions* of drugs—such as whether or not they are harmful—that makes their use a social problem. Rather, it takes *subjective concerns*. As we saw with coffee and tobacco, what is considered normal drug use at one point in history may be viewed as drug abuse at another time. Just as with abortion and prostitution, drugs are a part of social controversy. As with other social problems, people acquire different views of drugs and line up on opposing sides of the issue.

IN SUM **OBJECTIVE CONDITIONS AND SUBJECTIVE CONCERNS.** *Whether a drug is considered good or bad depends not on objective conditions but on subjective concerns. Subjective concerns are not fixed, but change over time. These concerns, and the views they generate, influence how people use and abuse drugs, whether a drug will be legal or illegal, and what social policies people want to adopt* (see Table 4-1). This is the central sociological principle of drug use and abuse, one that we shall stress over and over in this chapter.

TABLE 4-1 Legal Status and Use of Drugs

	USE OF DRUGS	
	Legal Use	Illegal Use
Legal Drugs	a. Prescription b. Over the counter c. "Over the bar" and in vending machines	a. Forged prescriptions b. Black market sales of prescription drugs c. "After-hours" sales; "Underage" sales
Illegal Drugs	a. Marijuana prescribed for medical problems b. Cocaine for surgery	a. Crack, heroin, etc.
Source: By the author.		

The Scope of the Problem

The Social Problem and the Pro-Drug Orientation of U.S. Society

Debbie, in our opening vignette, is like the other 15 million Americans who smoked marijuana during the past month (*Statistical Abstract* 2006:Tables 11, 194). To Debbie, marijuana isn't a drug. It's just something that she likes to smoke with friends. It makes her feel good and is "no big deal." On her part, Debbie's mother is like most Americans—she drinks coffee, alcohol, and colas; smokes cigarettes; and ingests a variety of substances that *she* has a hard time thinking of as drugs.

Like marijuana, alcohol and nicotine are drugs. To be a drug, a substance does not have to be sold in an alley or exchanged furtively for money in a van. A **drug** is a substance that people take to produce a change in their thinking, consciousness, emotions, or bodily functions or behavior. Obviously, people take many substances to cause such changes. The essential difference among these substances *is not which ones they use, but whether a substance is socially acceptable or disapproved of.* From this comes the clash in people's perspectives, such as those of Debbie and her mother.

Humans are often born with the aid of drugs, and drugs often ease our departure from life. We use drugs for sickness and for pleasure; to relieve anxiety, queasy stomachs, and headaches; and for all sorts of other pains and discomforts. As with alcohol, we take drugs to help us be sociable. And as with cigarettes, coffee, and colas, we take them routinely, unthinkingly, and habitually. (Yes, coffee, Coke, and Pepsi contain a drug. This drug, caffeine, is addictive, and some people "just can't get going" in the morning without their "fixes.") *Far from being an anti-drug society, we are actually highly pro-drug.*

DRUG ABUSE AS A PERSONAL OR SOCIAL PROBLEM. Most of us take this kind of drug use for granted. To us, this is like eating popcorn or munching on potato chips. When drug use interferes with someone's health or how that person gets along in life, though, we begin to question it. But we consider this a *personal* problem. If large numbers of people become upset about a drug, however, and want to see something done about it, then that drug becomes part of a *social* problem. This, of course, takes us back to the main point with which we began this text: objective conditions and subjective concerns. As we consider two common drugs, nicotine and alcohol, note how much more important subjective concerns are than objective conditions.

NICOTINE AS A SOCIAL PROBLEM.

> Let's suppose that you are on your way to the airport to leave for a long-awaited vacation. You are listening to the radio and anticipating your arrival in sunny Hawaii. Suddenly, an announcer breaks into your reverie with a flash bulletin: Terrorists have hidden bombs aboard five jumbo jets scheduled for takeoff today. Each jet is going to crash. On each jet will be 200 passengers and crew, who will plummet from the skies, leaving a trail of agonizing screams as they meet their fiery destiny.
>
> The announcer pauses, then adds: "The authorities have not been able to find the bombs. Because no one knows which flights will crash, all flights will depart on schedule."
>
> What would you do? My guess is that you turn your car around and go home. Adios to Hawaii's beaches, and hello to your own backyard.

What does this have to do with nicotine? Nicotine is the addictive ingredient in tobacco. And cigarette smoking—bringing creeping emphysema and several types of cancer—kills more than 400,000 Americans each year (Surgeon General 2005). This is the equivalent of five fully loaded jets, each carrying 200 passengers and 20 crew members, crashing each and very day. The crashes continue without letup, day after day, year after year. The passengers *know* that one of the jets will crash that day; yet they climb aboard anyway, thinking that it won't be *their* jet that crashes. Obviously no one would get on a plane if this were the case. And if planes crashed like this, the government would stop the flights and fix the problem. Who in their right mind would take the risk that *their* plane would not be among those that crashed? Yet smokers do. They know that nicotine is lethal. They also know that smoking-related deaths are lingering and painful, a burden to both the victims and their families. Although smoking cuts the average smoker's life short by thirteen or fourteen years, 20 percent of Americans continue to smoke (*Statistical Abstract* 2006:Table 191). They put this deadly poison to their lips, thinking that it won't be their plane that goes down.

ALCOHOL AS A SOCIAL PROBLEM. Alcohol, too, is far more dangerous than its broad social acceptability would imply. A dramatic example is motor vehicle accidents, which kill 43,000 Americans each year. Alcohol is a factor in 40 percent of these accidents, bringing the death toll from them to 17,000—about 47 a day (*Statistical Abstract* 2006:Table 1092). To continue our analogy, this is the equivalent of two jumbo jets, each loaded with 165 passengers and crew, crashing each and every week of the year.

Alcohol abusers, their organs ravaged and decaying, become a burden to themselves and to their families. Men are more likely to suffer the consequences of this drug, for most abusers of alcohol are men—about two or three men for each woman. In addition to the many health problems and deaths that come from alcohol abuse, like nicotine, this drug costs the nation billions of dollars a year in health care and in lost productivity.

Addiction and Dependence

A serious problem with some drugs is **addiction,** or **drug dependence.** That is, people come to depend on the regular consumption of a drug to make it through the day. When people think of **drug addiction,** they are likely to think of addicts huddled in slum doorways, the dregs of society who seldom venture into daylight—unless it is to rob someone. Most people don't associate addiction with "good," middle-class neighborhoods and "solid citizens."

ADDICTION AND NICOTINE. But let's look at drug addiction a little more closely. Although most people may think of heroin as the prime example of an addictive drug, I suggest that nicotine is the better example. I remember a next-door neighbor as he stood in his backyard, a lit cigarette in his hand, describing the operation in which the surgeon removed one of his lungs. I say "remember," because soon after our conversation he died from his addiction.

A major disease that comes from smoking is emphysema. As the disease progresses, breathing becomes increasingly difficult, resulting in death from respiratory failure. You'd think that developing this disease would be enough to make smokers quit, but chest specialists report that "even during the last months of their ordeal, when they must breathe oxygen intermittently instead of air, some of them go right on alternating cigarette smoke and oxygen" (Brecher et al. 1972:216).

Another example of nicotine's addictive power is Buerger's disease:

> In this disease the blood vessels become so constricted that circulation is impaired whenever nicotine enters the bloodstream. When gangrene sets in, at first a toe or two may have to be amputated. If the person continues to smoke, the foot may have to be amputated at the ankle, then the leg at the knee, and ultimately at the hip. Somewhere along this gruesome progression gangrene may also attack the other leg. Patients are told that if they will stop smoking, this horrible march of gangrene up their legs will be curbed. Yet surgeons report that some patients vigorously puff away in their hospital beds following even a second or third amputation. (Brecher et al. 1972:216)

AVOIDING WITHDRAWAL. Why don't drug addicts just quit? Even when they know that a drug is harming them, people continue to use it to avoid **withdrawal,** the intense distress—nausea, vomiting, aches and pains, nervousness, anxiety, and depression—they feel when they abstain from the drug. Withdrawal creates **craving,** an intense desire for the missed drug. Even after someone has kicked the habit, the craving may last for months or even years. Craving is especially strong during times of emotional distress. Years after breaking the physical habit, people may still experience an occasional desire for the drug. This is referred to as **psychological dependence.** (A personal note: After I quit smoking and no longer felt craving, I would have recurring dreams that I was smoking cigarettes. These dreams were so vivid that I would awaken abruptly in the middle of the night— feeling guilty for having fallen back into the habit.)

Looking at the Problem Theoretically

Why is it legal to use drugs as lethal as alcohol and nicotine, and yet people are arrested and put in prison for using milder drugs? This question points up how subjective concerns outweigh objective conditions, how the meanings we assign to drugs go far beyond their pharmaceutical characteristics. To understand the *social* significance of drugs, let's look at drugs through our three theoretical lenses.

Symbolic Interactionism

THE TEMPERANCE MOVEMENT AND THE MEANING OF DRUGS. The meaning of a drug depends on who is considering it. A physician might perceive a drug as a tool to help patients; a drug dealer might view the same drug as a high-profit product; the police might see it as an evil substance to be stamped out; users might perceive it as the pathway to an adventure, a "high," or even a religious experience. Some users might view the drug as simply a mild diversion that they can do without, whereas others view it as an absolute necessity for getting through the day. The meaning of a drug, then, does not depend on the drug, but on how people interpret the drug.

As the Issues in Social Problems box on the next page illustrates, alcohol has been associated with Americans from the time this country began. How, then, could this beverage ever have been outlawed, as it was in 1919—a legal change that ushered in organized crime and the "speakeasies" that you may have seen in old movies?

Sociologist Joseph Gusfield (1963) analyzed how this happened. Anglo-Saxon Protestants had settled New England, and their customs and religion dominated the region. Then in the 1820s, millions of uneducated, poor immigrants poured in from Italy, Germany, and Ireland. The educated and well-to-do New England "aristocracy" found the customs of the new immigrants offensive—especially their religion (Roman Catholicism) and their practice of drinking a lot of wine, beer, and spirits. The Anglo-Saxon Protestants viewed the new immigrants as ignorant, Catholic drunkards.

To the dismay of the established immigrants, the Anglo-Saxons, the new immigrants continued to pour in. As the old immigrants gradually lost political power, they began a temperance (nondrinking) movement. They reasoned that if they couldn't control the politics of the region, they at least could control its morals. Their goal was to turn the new immigrants into clean, sober, and godly people whose customs would reflect the Anglo-Saxons' moral leadership of New England.

As a result, drinking and abstinence became two contrary symbols, identifying people as members of one of two major groups. Abstinence was associated with morality and respectability. It symbolized hard workers, people who were established and reputable. Drinking, in contrast, symbolized unreliable drifters, uneducated immigrants of questionable background. To abstain from alcohol became a requirement for anyone who strove for higher social standing.

As the United States grew more urban, secular, and Roman Catholic, Protestants saw their power and values slipping even further away. Intensifying their efforts to pass laws that upheld temperance, they rejoiced in 1919 when the Eighteenth Amendment to the Constitution was passed. Overnight, it became illegal for Americans to buy even a glass of beer. Prohibition, Gusfield says, marked the victory of middle-class, Protestant, rural

Issues in Social Problems
THE PILGRIMS, BEER, AND THANKSGIVING

The *Mayflower* had completed its historic voyage. Now the Pilgrims faced the daunting task of settling the wilderness of the New World. They found the Indians friendly enough, but the bitter winter of 1620 was something else. Samoset, a tribesman, helped them survive that first harsh winter.

But beer also helped.

When winter hit, the colonists' buildings were still unfinished. To continue to work on them, the immigrants had to brave the icy February winds as they ferried back and forth from the *Mayflower*. Life was becoming unbearable, and the colonists were falling victim to pneumonia, scurvy, and exposure.

Adding to their misery was the first beer crisis in the New World. It wasn't as though the Pilgrims lacked foresight. They were careful planners, and they had brought with them a large supply of beer. Like other Europeans of the time, they distrusted water and thought of alcohol as essential for good health. A stiff drink kept off chills and fevers, aided digestion, made work easier to bear, and warmed the body on cold nights. The Pilgrims considered nondrinkers to be "crank-brained."

But the journey across the ocean had taken longer than expected, and so had their attempt to establish a beachhead in the wilderness. They had run out of beer, and now they were forced to drink water. Seeing their plight, the captain of the *Mayflower* shared beer from the crew's supplies. He could do this only so long, however, for he had to make sure that his crew had enough beer to drink on the long voyage back to England. When these supplies ran short, he had to stop sharing.

For the Pilgrims, the situation was desperate. William Bradford, who became the governor of Plymouth, pleaded for just one "can" of beer. The captain of the *Mayflower* refused him. As the deaths mounted, however, the captain took pity on the Pilgrims. To alleviate their suffering, from his personal supplies he gave beer "for them that hath need for it," particularly the sick.

With prayers, the help of Samoset, the *Mayflower*'s captain, and beer, the Pilgrims made it through that first bleak winter. And, unlike our grade school images, during their first Thanksgiving feast, the Pilgrims drank beer—and Samoset joined their merrymaking, for by this time he, too, had developed a taste for this frothy, heart-warming liquid.

Based on Lender and Martin 1982.

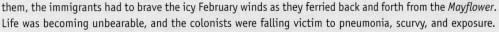

values over working-class, Roman Catholic, urban values. Like the other anti-drug laws before it, however, Prohibition was a failure. It did not stop people from using the drug of their choice. As the anti-Catholic and antiurban forces weakened, fourteen years later, in 1933, this grand experiment in drug control was repealed.

CHANGING MEANINGS OF OTHER DRUGS. It is difficult for us today to see how emotionally charged the issue of drinking a glass of beer was or how any adult could have been arrested for possessing a bottle of beer or other alcohol. This is another illustration of the significance of subjective concerns, how our understanding of any drug must center on discovering the meanings that people attach to it. For example, many people view cocaine use as immoral, but for others it represents sophistication. Contrasting meanings also surround marijuana. As long as marijuana was confined to "bohemian" or marginal groups, this drug posed no cultural threat. But in the 1960s, rebellious middle-class youth formed a subculture that was alien to their parents' world of hard work and straight living. To show their rejection of the middle-class world, they promoted marijuana and other psychedelic drugs. At that point, the meaning of marijuana changed—and a social problem was born.

Functionalism

THE SOCIAL FUNCTIONS AND DYSFUNCTIONS OF DRUGS. When functionalists study a drug, whether it be legal or illegal, they examine its functions and dysfunctions. Recreational drugs such as alcohol and marijuana "loosen" people up, or otherwise help remove tensions that interfere with sociability. These drugs are also functional for those who make money from growing, processing, distributing, and selling them. These same drugs are dysfunctional for people who abuse them. Similarly, prescription drugs are functional both for the medical profession and for the patients they serve. These drugs, too, are dysfunctional for those who abuse them—or for those who have adverse reactions to them.

A striking example of how prescription drugs are functional is their use with mental patients. In the 1950s, more than a half million Americans were locked in mental hospitals. Since then, our population has doubled, and if the rate of commitment had stayed the same, about a million Americans would be locked in asylums, instead of the 180,000 currently there (*Statistical Abstract* 2006:Table 173). But in the 1950s, psychiatrists began to prescribe mood-altering drugs (the psychopharmaceuticals), and in just a few years the number of patients confined to mental hospitals shrank by several hundred thousand. For these people, drugs were functional.

Prescription drugs are also dysfunctional. Some psychiatrists use them to put patients in "pharmacological straitjackets." Instead of trying to find out what is wrong with the patient or with the patient's social environment, the physician takes the easier road and prescribes drugs. Such drug therapy exacts a price. "Doped up" patients become befuddled and lethargic. Some suffer neurological damage.

In short, drug use is dysfunctional when it interferes with people's physical or social functioning. As we saw in the example cited earlier of Buerger's disease, nicotine addiction provides a striking example of the dysfunction of a drug. Alcohol abuse is also dysfunctional, leaving behind a trail of impaired health, poverty, broken homes, and smashed dreams. Similarly, heroin, the barbiturates, and other addictive drugs create severe problems for addicts and their families and friends.

The dysfunctions of drugs extend far beyond the individual. Although difficult to measure, these large-scale costs involve drug-related crimes, such as burglaries and muggings, that are committed in order to support addiction; unemployment; medical costs due to illness and disease; the spread of AIDS among addicts who share needles; the deaths and injuries suffered by people in automobile accidents; and the loss to society of a reservoir of human potential as people retreat into drugs.

LATENT FUNCTIONS OF DRUG CONTROL: THE EXAMPLE OF MARIJUANA. To follow the history of drugs takes us to some unexpected twists and turns. Making a drug illegal, for example, has the latent function (not its intended purpose) of strengthening the agencies that control that drug. Without these laws, some government agencies would go out of business. To protect their jobs, some bureaucrats eagerly try to define many drugs as dangerous to the public's welfare. The more drugs that are illegal, the more secure their jobs.

Marijuana provides a beautiful illustration. In 1930, Harry Anslinger was appointed to head the Treasury Department's new Bureau of Narcotics. Congress cut his budget because the country was in the midst of the Great Depression. Although marijuana was legal at this time, Anslinger saw the drug as offering an opportunity to strengthen his faltering organization (Dickson 1968). Embarking on a campaign to pass a federal law against marijuana, Anslinger became a **moral entrepreneur,** a crusading reformer who wages battle to enforce his or her idea of morality. Anslinger received support from an unexpected source, heads of the liquor industry who feared that marijuana might compete with alcohol (Rockwell 1972). With the help of this new ally, Anslinger was victorious, and Congress passed the Marijuana Tax Act in 1937. Anslinger's campaign to frighten people is recounted in the Issues in Social Problems box on the next page.

The Marijuana Tax Act has been functional for the Bureau of Narcotics, which is still going strong. This law, however, has been dysfunctional for the hundreds of thousands of Americans who have been caught in its enforcement web. When marijuana became popular with middle-class youth and it became impossible to enforce abstinence among millions of smokers, this did not stop the drug enforcers from searching out and arresting offenders. Drug use has kept them in business. This illustrates a central tenet of functional analysis: What is functional for some is dysfunctional for others.

Conflict Theory

DRUG LAWS AS A WAY TO CONTROL SOCIETY. Common sense sometimes doesn't get us very far when it comes to drugs. As discussed in the Issues in Social Problems box below, much more is involved in making a drug illegal than the harm done by that drug. We have to consider power. Some groups have the power to get laws passed to protect their interests; others don't. This takes us to the heart of the conflict perspective, that drugs are used as a political tool. If the use of a particular drug is common among some group, by making the drug illegal the authorities can unleash the police against them. In contrast, by keeping a drug legal, the state can protect favored groups that make money from a drug.

Issues in Social Problems
SOCIOLOGY AND COMMON SENSE: LEGAL AND ILLEGAL DRUGS

COMMON SENSE

1. Common sense suggests that drugs that are illegal are harmful, whereas drugs that are legal are not harmful.
2. Common sense suggests that if a legal drug turns out to be addictive and is abused, it will be made illegal.
3. Common sense suggests that if a nonnarcotic has been classified mistakenly in the law as a narcotic, it will be reclassified and treated differently.

SOCIOLOGY

1. Drugs do not become illegal (or remain legal) on the basis of the social or personal injury they do. Drugs have a social history (page 86) that affects their legal classification. Making a drug illegal is a political process. If a drug is illegal, some interest groups have managed to get their viewpoints written into law.

2. Some addictive drugs are backed by well-financed interest groups, and these drugs (such as alcohol, nicotine, Prozac, Valium, and OxyContin) remain legal.
3. Marijuana was classified improperly as a narcotic in the 1937 Marijuana Tax Act. Although knowledge of this error is common, no interest group has been powerful enough to get this classification changed.

Issues in Social Problems
MARIJUANA: ASSASSIN OF YOUTH

In his campaign to make marijuana illegal, Harry Anslinger used dramatic accounts and exaggeration. To frighten people, he wrote articles for popular magazines (Reasons 1974). In one of them, he tells this story:

> There was this young girl. . . . Her story is typical. Some time before, this girl, like others of her age who attend our high schools, had heard the whispering of a secret which has gone the rounds of American youth. It promised a new thrill, the smoking of a type of cigarette which contained a "real kick." According to the whispers, this cigarette could accomplish wonderful reactions and with no harmful aftereffects. So the adventurous girl and a group of her friends gathered in an apartment, thrilled with the idea of doing "something different" in which there was "no harm." Then a friend produced a few cigarettes of the loosely rolled "homemade" type. They were passed from one to another of the young people, each taking a few puffs.
>
> The results were weird. Some of the party went into paroxysms of laughter; every remark, no matter how silly, seemed excruciatingly funny. Others of mediocre musical ability became almost expert; the piano dinned constantly. Still others found themselves discussing weighty problems of youth with remarkable clarity. As one youngster expressed it, he "could see through stone walls." The girl danced without fatigue, and the night of unexplainable exhilaration seemed to stretch out as though it were a year long. Time, conscience, or consequences became too trivial for consideration.
>
> Other parties followed, in which inhibitions vanished, conventional barriers departed, all at the command of this strange cigarette with its ropy, resinous odor. Finally there came a gathering at a time when the girl was behind in her studies and greatly worried. With every puff of the smoke the feeling of despondency lessened. Everything was going to be all right—at last. The girl was "floating" now, a term given to marijuana intoxication. Suddenly, in the midst of laughter and dancing, she thought of her school problems. Instantly they were solved. Without hesitancy, she walked to a window and leaped to her death. Thus can marijuana "solve" one's difficulties.

Here's another story that Anslinger told.

> It was an unprovoked crime some years ago which brought the first realization that the age-old drug had gained a foothold in America. An entire family was murdered by a youthful addict in Florida. When officers arrived at the home they found the youth staggering about in a human slaughterhouse. With an ax he had killed his father, his mother, two brothers, and a sister. He seemed to be in a daze. . . . He had no recollection of having committed the multiple crime. The officers knew him ordinarily as a sane, rather quiet young man; now he was pitifully crazed. They sought the reason. The boy said he had been in the habit of smoking something which youthful friends called "muggles," a childish name for marijuana. . . .
>
> [People need to be] told that addicts may often develop a delirious rage during which they are temporarily and violently insane, that this insanity may take the form of a desire for self-destruction or a persecution complex to be satisfied only by the commission of some heinous crime. (Anslinger and Cooper 1937)

If these stories didn't convince people, Anslinger had an ace up his sleeve. He said that this killer weed—his term—made men impotent (Galliher and Walker 1977).

All things considered, it is little wonder that Anslinger's campaign resulted in Congress passing the Marijuana Tax Act in 1937.

Let's look at how drug laws have been used as a political tool. In the 1920s, the United States was in the midst of an economic boom, and workers from Mexico were valued as a source of cheap labor. Then came the Great Depression of the 1930s. With millions thrown out of work, the Mexicans came to be viewed as people who stole jobs from citizens (Galliher and Walker 1977). Marijuana use was not popular in the United States, but it was among these workers. As we saw in the box on "Marijuana: Assassin of Youth" on the facing page, the head of the Bureau of Narcotics began a campaign to label the drug favored by this unpopular group as dangerous. In one of his articles, Anslinger even referred to "a hot tamale salesman pushing his cart about town . . . peddling marijuana cigarettes." The Marijuana Tax Act of 1937 became a political tool to drive unneeded Mexican workers back across the border (Helmer 1975).

Chinese immigrants have also been on the receiving end of drug laws. In the 1800s, thousands of Chinese men came to the United States to help build the cross-country railroad. They brought opium with them, a legal drug at the time. When the railroad was completed, these workers were thrown onto the job market. This coincided with a depression and a national financial panic in 1873. Willing to work for less money than the white workers, the Chinese posed a threat, and the white workers beat, threatened, and killed them. In 1875, San Francisco and other West Coast cities began to prohibit opium dens. These laws did not target opium but, rather, the Chinese men who threatened the jobs of whites (Morgan 1978). Even the U.S. Congress got into the act. In 1887, it passed a law that prohibited the importation of opium *by the Chinese* but not by white Americans (Szasz 1975).

Conflict theorists also stress that politicians use drug laws to control what are called "the dangerous classes," those whose members are likely to rebel. When oppressed people seek refuge in addictive drugs, their anger is diverted away from rebellion. Drugs, not social change, become their passion, the goal around which their life revolves. Contrary to the impression that news reports sometimes give, that society is about to explode in a paroxysm of drug violence, from this perspective drugs such as heroin and crack stabilize society. They divert the attention and energy of the exploited away from their oppression, diluting their interest in social change. In addition, violence becomes directed toward members of their own community, not toward the ruling class. In this theoretical light, sociologist Andrew Karmen (1980) said that heroin users become "too passive when nodding and too self-absorbed when they aren't high to fight for community control over the schools, to organize tenants for a rent strike, or to march on City Hall to demand decent jobs for all who want to work." Indeed, "since narcotics pacify those who suffer most from mental and physical degradation, it's likely that some astute members of the ruling circles have decided its benefits outweigh its costs" (p. 174).

One does not have to agree that society's elite mastermind the trade in heroin and crack cocaine to see that drugs can serve the interests of the powerful. An old ploy sometimes used by groups in power to protect their position is to focus attention on some supposed threat posed by a disfavored group. This tactic diverts attention from internal problems and makes people feel that they are all in the same boat—and that they had better bail together, because the boat is leaking.

Our history provides numerous examples of how those in power have used drugs to consolidate sentiment against disfavored groups. During the 1800s, Chinese opium dens were pictured as outposts of corruption, places where evil Chinese men seduced innocent white women. By World War I the "enemy" had changed, and German pharmaceutical firms and anarchists were supposedly smuggling heroin into this country. With the outbreak of World War II, Japan was identified as the power behind the narcotics trade. Then during the Cold War of the 1950s, the Soviet secret police were fingered as the sinister heroin supplier. During the Korean War, China became the culprit. Then during the Vietnam War, North Vietnam and the National Liberation Front were named as masterminds of the narcotics trade (Karmen 1980). Today, with the Cold War over, the government seems to be looking for a new enemy supplier. Top candidates are groups they call the "war lords" of Afghanistan (for the most part, these are heads of clans who refuse to cooperate with the U. S. occupation).

Each theory contributes a unique understanding of drugs as a social problem. Symbolic interactionists stress how drugs become powerful symbols that affect social life, as was the case with alcohol and the great drug experiment known as Prohibition. Functionalists examine the functions and dysfunctions of drug use: For example, some mental patients benefit from legal mood-altering drugs, but those same drugs impair the physical or social functioning of other patients. Conflict theorists examine drugs as part of a social order in which a privileged few are in control: Because drugs have been manipulated in the past for the purpose of enhancing power and control, some think that this same process may underlie the heroin and cocaine trade today.

Research Findings: The Use and Abuse of Drugs

Before we review research findings on specific drugs, let's examine the medicalization of human problems, try to explain why people have different experiences with the same drug, and then get an overview of the drug use of U.S. students.

Medicalizing Human Problems

The King had a difficult time getting through the day—and the nights were no better. Middle age, unwelcome by almost everyone but especially dreaded by celebrities, had settled in, bringing a paunch and double chin that the Hollywood magazines ridiculed. To make matters worse, the breakup of his marriage had torn his only child from him. Throughout these ordeals, a longtime friend, Dr. George Nichopoulos, had been a great help. During the past thirty-one months he had prescribed 19,000 stimulants, depressants, and painkillers, some of which were highly addictive.

Now the King of Rock and Roll lay dead on his bathroom floor. The official report stated that Elvis Presley had died from heart disease. Other medical examiners claimed that his death could have resulted from the interaction of the many drugs in his system. Presley's body contained toxic levels of the sedative methaqualone, ten times more codeine than was needed for therapy, and low levels of ten other drugs: morphine, Demerol, and phenyltoloxamine (painkillers); amobarbital, phenobarbital, and amitriptyline (sedatives); pentobarbital (a sedative and sleep-inducer); Valmid and Placidyl (sleep-inducers); and Valium (a muscle relaxant).

At his trial for overprescribing, Dr. Nichopoulos testified that his drug plan for Presley called for drugs to reduce his appetite, drugs to stimulate his bowels, drugs to help him urinate, drugs to relieve itching, drugs to help dizziness, drugs to relieve pain, and drugs to help him relax. Dr. Nichopoulos was found not guilty.

THE APPEAL OF MEDICALIZING HUMAN PROBLEMS. Though extreme, Elvis Presley's death pinpoints one of today's major drug problems: the legal abuse of legal drugs. During the 1930s, the pharmaceutical industry began to manufacture psychoactive drugs, which have gradually swept us up in a drug revolution. Physicians now prescribe drugs for conditions that people used to assume were a normal part of life: anxiety and distress, feeling upset or uncertain, social unease, inability to concentrate, feeling "down," wrestling with perplexing problems, even sensing vague dissatisfactions or feeling as if you don't "fit in." All of these have been redefined as medical problems. If the old attitude was that we all confront problems like these and we have to develop coping skills to deal with them, today's attitude is that such situations call for drugs. Sociologists call this **medicalizing human problems**—that is, offering a medical "solution" for the problems that people confront in everyday life.

The antidepressants and anti-anxiety drugs are a case in point. Effexor, Prozac, Valium, Xanax, and Zoloft promise help in getting through the problems of everyday life. Doctors prescribe these drugs for anxiety, irritability, sleeplessness, restlessness, inability to concentrate, and even a pounding heart. Although the serenity offered by prescription drugs can be elusive, and these drugs have side effects—from forgetfulness to suicidal thoughts—they are highly profitable. Doctors make millions of dollars from scribbling the names of these drugs on little pieces of paper. Pharmacists make additional millions by counting the little pills and putting them in little bottles. Then there are the drug companies, of course, which rake in billions of dollars from these drugs. Zoloft alone brings in $3 billion a year, while Effexor snags another $2.5 billion (Herper 2006).

With so many people looking for an easy solution to life's problems (and who wouldn't want all of their problems to disappear by simply popping a pill!), medicalizing the problems of life has turned the order of medicine upside down. In many cases, no longer is it the doctors who do the prescribing but, rather, the patients. Here's how it works. Drug companies flood television and magazines with commercials for medications that you *cannot* buy over the counter. To get these drugs, you have to tell your doctor that you want that particular drug. This marketing strategy works. People see the commercials and imagine themselves living happy, carefree lives if they can just get their hands on Xanax, Prozac, or some other drug. Physicians don't want to lose business, so they write the prescriptions that their customers ask for. The doctors make money from writing—literally—millions of prescriptions. So do the pharmacists who eagerly fill them. And the drug companies laugh all the way to the bank.

The abuse of prescription drugs takes many forms, one of which is a subculture of abuse. Using "club drugs" is discussed in the Spotlight on Social Research box on the next page.

MEDICALIZING DEVIANT BEHAVIOR: PROBLEM KIDS AND REBELS. Medicalizing human problems—thinking of them not as normal aspects of everyday life, but as a matter of "sickness"—has become so common that even children's rowdy behavior is a "medical" problem. We used to say that children who disrupted their classroom were *unruly* and in need of discipline by parents and school. Now we call them *sick*—as though they have some sort of illness that medicine can cure.

There is, of course, nothing new about teachers complaining that children are difficult to teach or parents grumbling that it is difficult to control their children. What *is* new is for teachers and doctors *to turn behaviors into illnesses*. When a child's unacceptable behavior is given a name—perhaps **attention deficit-hyperactivity disorder** (ADHD, or *hyperkinesis* or *hyperactivity*)—it sounds as though the child *has* something. (The doctor or teacher looks solemnly at the alarmed parents and pronounces, "She *has* ADHD"). How frightening—and how untrue. What the child really has is a bogus "psychiatric disease" (Vatz 1994).

Just as unruly children are unacceptable to those in authority, so are political dissenters. And like teachers, politicians like to define dissenters as mentally disturbed so they can be given drugs to control their behavior. In the former Soviet Union, scholars, scientists, and artists who spoke out against oppression were jailed in medical facilities and given "drug therapy." The same thing is happening in today's China, where to criticize the government indicates a "delusion of grandeur" (Kahn 2006b). In some instances, the drugs given to "treat" the dissenter produce disorganized thinking, which, in turn, "prove" that the dissenter is "crazy."

FUNCTIONS AND DYSFUNCTIONS OF MEDICALIZING HUMAN BEHAVIOR. The functions of medicalizing disruptive behavior—whether for criticizing a government or for disrupting a classroom—are obvious. In the case of China, "drug therapy" helps authorities justify the imprisonment of dissenters. In the case of unruly children, most of the hundreds of thousands of U.S. children who take Ritalin or other drugs for their "illness" sit still longer and appear to pay attention. The drugs work so well that doctors even prescribe them for toddlers who are going through their "terrible twos" (Kalb 2000). As you can see, the drug is not really for the patient but, rather, for the political authorities, the teachers, and the parents.

There also are dysfunctions. Some schoolchildren get stuck with the label of mentally ill. For others, drugs such as Ritalin bring tics, lethargy, depression, even brain damage and cancer. There also are hallucinations, most commonly seeing or feeling snakes and worms (Harris 2006, March 23). The dysfunction for the political dissenters in China is

Spotlight on Social Research

THE MIAMI CLUB CULTURE: PRESCRIPTION DRUG ABUSE AMONG ECSTASY USERS

JAMES A. INCIARDI *is Director of the Center for Drug and Alcohol Studies at the University of Delaware. He is also a member of the International Advisory Committee of the White House Office of National Drug Control Policy. His research focuses on substance abuse, criminal justice, and public policy.*

Miami, Florida, historically a major tourist destination—and since the 1970s a national center for cocaine importation, distribution, and use—is also a major player in the U.S. club drug scene. With the restoration of Miami's art deco districts and the popularity of the South Beach area, Miami has become an international destination for partying, sexual tourism, and club drug use. To a great extent, South Beach has also become an East Coast center for the club culture—setting trends that are replicated elsewhere in the United States, western Europe, and Latin America. The Drug Enforcement Administration has identified Miami as a destination for large amounts of prescription drugs that are channeled into the illegal marketplace. One of the more recent trends has been a significant incursion of prescription drugs into the club culture, accompanied by the health consequences associated with their abuse. To "get high," about 80 percent of ecstasy users in the Miami club culture appear to be using prescription narcotics (OxyContin, Vicodin, Percocet, and morphine), "downers" (Xanax and Valium), and stimulants (Ritalin and Adderall) (Kurtz et al. 2005).

To investigate this abuse of prescription drugs, we conducted focus groups with scores of young adults from a wide variety of race/ethnic backgrounds. Although a few of the participants said that they had experimented with prescription drugs as early as their junior high years, most had recently begun to use prescription drugs to ease the "come down" from the "highs" produced by such party drugs as ecstasy, cocaine, ketamine, and methamphetamine. The demand for a "smooth landing" is so great that dealers often "package" ecstasy and methamphetamine with prescription depressants or narcotics. Antidepressants are also commonly used by ecstasy and methamphetamine users to ease withdrawal-related depression.

To achieve a "better high," prescription drugs are also used in *combination* with club drugs. Popular combinations include marijuana, Ritalin, and alcohol; prescription narcotics with methamphetamine and ecstasy; and

hydrocodone with cocaine. One respondent recalled having an "excellent" night out after having "4 Seroquels (an antischizophrenic), 3 Lillys (Olanzapine, an antipsychotic), 2 bars (2 mg Xanax pills), alcohol, marijuana and cocaine," after which he managed to successfully drive a carload of friends home. Participants also described the interchangeability of certain club and prescription drugs. To get high, some would substitute phentermine (a diet drug) for methamphetamine; to feel drunk, they would substitute GHB for painkillers and combine this with alcohol. To ease withdrawal from stimulants, they used Xanax or marijuana.

Some participants described the practice of "colon rolling," also known as "booty bumping"—dissolving prescription and other drugs and then taking the solution rectally with an eye dropper or turkey baster. Some preferred this anal route of administration because it made the drugs' effect slower and more even. Of particular note in this regard was the "Royal Flush"—a dangerous combination of methamphetamine, ecstasy, and Viagra.

The focus group participants reported extremely diverse sources for obtaining the prescription drugs they abused. These included drug dealers, on the street and in nightclubs; HIV-positive patients, who have access to prescription medications through their physicians; parents and other relatives; pharmacy employees; online pharmacies; under-the-door apartment flyers advertising telephone numbers to call; Medicaid and Medicare fraud; doctor shopping; leftover supplies following an illness or injury; visits to Mexico, South America, and the Caribbean; prescriptions intended for treatment of drug dependence or mental illness; theft from pharmacies and hospitals; friends and acquaintances; and "stealing from grandma's medicine cabinet." All participants said they had no difficulty in obtaining prescription medications, although they were often happy to take what was available without seeking out a specific drug or brand name.

Those who relocated to Miami from other cities in the United States said that the illicit prescription drug market in Miami was much easier to navigate than the market in other places they had lived, including New York and Boston. They also said that street prices in Miami were much lower than those charged by online pharmacies.

Most participants described the "high" from prescription drugs as less exciting and less euphoric than that from illicit drugs, but they perceived prescription drugs to be purer, safer, more respectable, and more legal, as well as producing fewer withdrawal symptoms.

Note: This discussion was based, in part on Kurtz, Inciardi, Surratt, and Cottler, 2005.

more obvious: the loss of freedom. For the little kids who are medicalized to help *their parents* get through the "terrible twos," we don't yet have the results. They are likely to be equally as unpleasant.

Because pills seem such a handy answer to problems that perplex us, medicalizing human problems has become a standard feature of contemporary life. If only we could find the perfect pill, our personal and social problems would disappear as we dip into the pharmacological treasury of medical miracles.

Drug Use by Students

Let's look at some of the findings of sociologists who have studied the drug use of high school and college students. We'll begin with Figure 4-1 below, which is based on a sample so good that we can generalize these findings to all U.S. eighth graders and high school sophomores and seniors. As you can see, during the past month about half of all U.S. high school seniors drank alcohol. And in the last thirty days, about three of ten got drunk.

Do you think that having plans to go to college makes a difference in whether high school seniors use drugs? If so, do you think that this makes them more or less likely to use drugs? Look at Table 4-2 on the next page. From this table, you can see that high school seniors who plan on going to four years of college use fewer drugs than those who don't have these plans. Cause and effect can be elusive, however. Although we know that college plans influence the decisions that high school seniors make, going to college is also related to social class. The higher their parents' income, the more likely that high school seniors will head off to college (Carnevale and Rose 2003). Drug use in high school, then, could be related more to social class than to people's college plans.

From Table 4-2, you can also see that underage drinking is common—as though you didn't know this. You may not have known, however, just how common marijuana smoking is among high school seniors. About 850,000 high school seniors smoked marijuana during the past month. About 230,000 went to school stoned every day—except for those who confine their *daily* marijuana smoking to the evenings. Even then, the effects would linger (Johnston et al. 2005:Tables 4-7, 4-8; *Statistical Abstract* 2006:Table 211).

FIGURE 4-1   Who Drinks Alcohol?

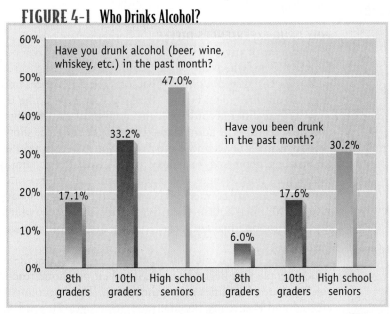

Source: By the author. Based on Johnston et al. 2006:Table 3.

TABLE 4-2 What Drugs Do High School Seniors Use? (in the last 30 days)

| | SEX | | COLLEGE PLANS | |
	M	F	None, or Less Than 4 Years	4 years
Alcohol	51.1%	45.1%	52.1%	47.0%
Been Drunk	36.0%	29.0%	34.7%	31.2%
Alcohol Daily	4.1%	1.4%	4.3%	2.2%
Cigarettes	25.3%	24.1%	36.8%	21.6%
Cigarettes Daily	15.4%	15.0%	26.9%	12.2%
Marijuana	23.0%	16.6%	24.1%	18.3%
Marijuana Daily	7.7%	3.1%	8.1%	4.5%
Amphetamines	4.6%	4.5%	6.5%	4.0%
Barbiturates (Sedatives)	3.2%	2.5%	3.9%	2.6%
Powder Cocaine	2.9%	1.7%	4.1%	1.7%
LSD	2.4%	0.8%	2.2%	1.3%
Steroids	2.1%	1.0%	2.5%	1.3%
Crack Cocaine	1.2%	0.7%	1.9%	0.7%
Crystal Meth (Ice)	1.1%	0.6%	1.8%	0.5%
Heroin	0.7%	0.2%	2.5%	1.3%

Source: By the author. Based on Johnston et al. 2005:Tables 4-7, 4-8.

Now let's look at the drug use of college students. The sample on which Table 4-3 is based is also so good that these findings apply to *all* college students across the nation. Three main findings stand out: First, you can see how college students maintain the patterns of drug use that they established in high school: Alcohol is the most commonly used drug, followed by nicotine and marijuana. The second pattern is one that shows up regularly in drug studies: Men use more illegal drugs than do women. Finally, note how college students avoid some drugs.

The Effects of Drugs

WHY DRUG EXPERIENCES DIFFER. Whether we are talking about college students or anyone else, the same drug can affect two people differently. Even when the same person takes a drug on different occasions, its effects can differ. What someone experiences from a drug depends on three main factors (Ray and Ksir 2004). The first is the *drug.* Effects differ according to the amount of the drug, its quality, and how the drug is administered (ingested, smoked, shot into the bloodstream). The second is the *individual.* Effects can differ if users are anxious, depressed, or relaxed. They also differ according to the individual's body weight and metabolism, and for reasons yet unknown, drugs affect men and women differently (Acharyya and Zhang 2003; Bell 2006). The third factor is the *setting,* which can influence the individual's expectations and, in turn, can change a drug's effects.

Use of LSD (lysergic acid diethylamide) illustrates these factors. When people first began to use LSD, their psychotic reactions and suicides made headlines across the nation. These accounts then decreased and eventually became rare. Sociologist Howard S. Becker (1967) concluded that the people who first took LSD thought that it might create panic—and they were likely to experience panic. The subculture that grew around LSD, however, changed people's

TABLE 4-3 What Drugs Do Full-Time College Students Use?

In the past 30 days

	TOTAL	MEN	WOMEN
Alcohol	68.9%	70.2%	68.0%
Cigarettes	26.7%	30.0%	24.6%
Marijuana	19.7%	23.7%	17.2%
Amphetamines	3.0%	3.2%	2.8%
Cocaine			
Powder	1.6%	2.2%	1.2%
Crack	0.3%	0.1%	0.4%
Ecstasy (MDMA)	0.7%	0.9%	0.7%
LSD	0.2%	0.4%	0.1%
Heroin[1]	0.0%	0.0%	0.0%
Daily Use			
Cigarettes	15.9%	16.6%	15.4%
Alcohol	5.0%	7.0%	3.7%
Marijuana	4.1%	5.7%	3.0%

Source: By the author. Based on Johnston et al. 2003: Tables 8-3, 8-4.
[1] Certainly there are *some* college students who have used heroin in the past 30 days, but use of this drug is so rare that it does not register in this national survey of college students.

expectations—and their experiences. When experienced users introduced LSD to their friends, they told them what to expect. When first-time users saw strange colors, walls breathing, or felt a unity with plants, their "trip guides" assured them that this was normal, that it was temporary, and that they should relax and enjoy the sensations. As a result, negative LSD experiences dropped sharply.

Expectations are especially important in regard to drugs that people use to alter their perception, to change their mood, or to make them more sociable—drugs that we shall now consider.

Research Findings: The Recreational Mood Elevators

Alcohol

> A little down? Want to feel better?
> You feel fine, but you'd like to feel even finer?
> A little uptight, and you want those problems to float away?
> Going to a party, and you want to feel more at ease?
> You want to get ride of those tensions from your college classes?

Some of these questions might sound familiar. So might the answer. When it comes to drugs taken for sociability, alcohol is America's first choice—and not just for college students. Each year, the average American drinks 25 gallons of alcoholic beverages—about 21.6 gallons of beer, 2.2 gallons of wine, and 1.3 gallons of hard liquor (*Statistical Abstract* 2006:Table 201). The average drinker accounts for about *twice* this amount, since half of adult Americans do not drink alcoholic beverages (*Statistical Abstract* 2006:Table 194). Yes, you read that right: The average drinker consumes about 50 gallons of alcohol a year.

ALCOHOL CONSUMPTION AS A SOCIAL PROBLEM. About 10 million Americans are considered **alcoholics,** people who have severe alcohol-related problems. Relatively few of them become derelicts and stand on street corners panhandling strangers. Rather, almost all—whether working or middle class—continue with their routines but have impaired social relationships. Their work and family life suffer the most.

Alcohol abuse is so common that each year between 200,000 and 300,000 Americans are treated for this problem at substance abuse centers (*Statistical Abstract* 2006:Table 193). The bill for their treatment runs several billion dollars a year, which everyone, including abstainers, must pay. If we consider reduced productivity and alcohol-related accidents, the total runs over $100 billion a year (Simon et al. 2005). Then, too, there are the costs of alcohol-related crime and social welfare. These costs make alcohol the most expensive of all drug abuse problems. Alcohol abuse also brings severe costs that we can't measure in dollars—the abuse of spouse and family, the disturbed children, and the shattered marriages.

FEMINIZING MACHO DRINKING. As noted earlier, each year about 17,000 Americans die in alcohol-related car and truck wrecks. Most of the drivers are young men, sloppy drunk. Why aren't just as many young women—or older Americans, for that matter—killed in vehicle accidents? The basic reason centers on what being a man means in our culture. Getting drunk is seen as *macho,* a way by which young men prove their budding masculinity (Snow and Cunningham 1985; Peele 1987). With driving after you've had "one too many" (or more than this) a symbol of male potency, the risk taking of driving while drunk validates young men's still-developing sense of masculinity.

My own experience as a member of U.S. culture confirms these ideas. I, too, had to prove my masculinity to my teenaged buddies by showing how much alcohol I could down in an evening. Anyone who wouldn't do so would have been marked as a weenie. I still recall the approval of my friends—as well as some of the retching that followed. I haven't got it figured out, but somehow, sitting on a bathroom floor with your head hung over a toilet is masculine.

If getting drunk were equated with femininity, we would have a lot more young women drinking to excess. Based on my observations of high school students at drinking parties, we are approaching this point in cultural change. "Femininity" apparently is being redefined in more macho terms, with getting drunk becoming a greater part of the girl's rite of passage into womanhood. If this continues, as I expect it to, we can also anticipate an increase in the deaths of young women in car wrecks.

The liquor industry has not failed to notice this increase in drinking by young women. Seizing the opportunity, the industry has targeted more of its advertising toward women and has developed "feminine" products. "Alcopops," flavored premixed drinks that resemble alcohol-spiked soda pop, have been a home run. Catering to an image of femininity, "Cocktails by Jenn" offers Lemon Drop and Blue Lagoon. Never mind that "Jenn" is actually two men, Jason and Larry. These men have found that "Jenn" sells—especially when they make their drinks pastel-colored and put them in bottles with small metal charms—a high-heeled shoe, a purse, a diamond ring, and a heart (Ball and O'Connell 2006).

HEALTH CONSEQUENCES OF DRINKING ALCOHOL. To adequately understand any social problem, we need solid research—whether or not the findings match what we want. Research on alcohol, for example, shows both positive and negative consequences for health. Let's look at the positive first. Light-to-moderate drinking—one to two drinks a day, five or six days a week—has positive health consequences. Compared with people who don't drink alcohol, light-to-moderate drinkers have only one-third as many heart attacks (Rehm et al. 2003). Some researchers have found that fourteen or more drinks a week are even better for people's health (Mukamal et al. 2006). Earlier studies reported that it was red wine that improved people's health. Although these results still hold, it seems to make no difference whether someone drinks red wine, white wine, beer, whiskey, or vodka. Regardless of the form it comes in, alcohol apparently stimulates production of the "good" cholesterol, HDL.

Although the form that alcohol comes in may be unimportant, the *pattern* of drinking is important. *Binge drinking,* having five or more drinks on the same occasion, increases the risk of sudden death from stroke and heart attacks (Rehm et al. 2003). Binge drinking is common, and within the next thirty days one-fifth of alcohol drinkers will binge-drink. Among drinkers between the ages 18 to 25, two of five will binge-drink during the next month (*Statistical Abstract* 2006:Table 194). Because binge drinking is especially prevalent on college campuses, this is a significant statistic for the readers of this text.

Heavy drinking is also harmful. Heavy drinkers are more likely to have heart attacks and problems with their endocrine, metabolic, immune, and reproductive systems. They are also more likely to come down with diabetes, epilepsy, and depression and to develop cancer of the tongue, mouth, liver, lungs, esophagus, larynx, stomach, colon, and rectum. For women, heavy drinking increases the risk of breast cancer (*Seventh Special Report* 1990; Rehm et al. 2003; Kruk and Aboul-Enein 2006).

ALCOHOL, PREGNANCY, AND CHILDBIRTH. Embedded in this social problem is another problem, the use of drugs by pregnant women. Like other drugs, alcohol enters the fetal circulatory system. Unlike the mother, however, a fetus cannot metabolize alcohol. When pregnant women drink, the alcohol becomes concentrated in the fetus' blood, raising its blood alcohol level to about *ten times* that of the mother.

The consequences of this abuse are anything but pleasant. Each year about 5,000 U.S. babies are born with a cluster of problems called **fetal alcohol syndrome.** These children are born addicted to alcohol, and for a week to six months they suffer painful withdrawal: They are irritable, their little hearts beat irregularly, and some go into convulsions. Brain damage, which reduces their intelligence and brings problems with learning, memory, speech, and coordination, means lifelong disability (Howell et al. 2006). As you would expect, fetal alcohol syndrome is concentrated among groups that have higher rates of alcoholism. Apparently the hardest hit are Native Americans, whose rate of fetal alcohol syndrome is two to three times the national average ("Congress" 1994; Carroll 2000).

After Prohibition ended, Americans celebrated their freedom to again drink openly. This particular celebration—an international beer drinking contest—took place in Los Angeles. To have the contestants lie on their backs while participating may have proved convenient—after a winner was declared, it is likely that some contestants remained in this position.

SIGNIFICANCE OF HOW PEOPLE LEARN TO DRINK. Social researchers have found that *how* one learns to drink is significant in setting the stage for having or not having alcohol-related problems. Studies of groups with low rates of alcoholism, such as Spaniards, Italians, Orthodox Jews, Greeks, Chinese, and Lebanese, indicate five keys to low-problem drinking (Hanson 1995):

- Drinking alcohol is a regular part of life.
- Alcohol is viewed as neutral—it is neither a poison nor a magic elixir.
- Drinking is not viewed as a sign of adulthood or virility.
- There is no tolerance for abusive drinking.
- Learning to drink starts early and in the home. Parents provide role models of moderate (light, social, nonabusive) drinking.

To better appreciate why these can be called conditions for "good" drinking, consider their opposites, which lead to alcohol problems.

- Drinking alcohol is considered something special.
- Alcohol is viewed as either horrible and sinful or else as a magical substance that makes the world more pleasant.
- Drinking is considered a sign of becoming an adult.
- Getting drunk is looked on favorably.
- One learns to drink through sneaky drinking outside the home.

Sound familiar? These five characteristics are an apt description of many adolescent subcultures.

BIOLOGY, SOCIOLOGY, AND ALCOHOL ADDICTION. Some research supports a biological basis for alcoholism. Sons of alcoholic fathers run a higher risk than others of becoming alcoholics (Buck 1998), and twins are more likely to have the same drinking patterns than are nontwins (Prescott 2004). As sociologists point out, however, we cannot rule out *social* reasons for these findings. Sons of alcoholic fathers, for example, may be following in the footsteps of alcoholic role models. As for twins, they grow up in environments so similar that they are likely to produce all sorts of similar behaviors. At this point, though, we can't rule out the possibility that biology makes a difference in how people's cells react to alcohol, predisposing some to alcohol abuse. The evidence that links alcoholism to genes, however, is mixed, with contradictory findings.

Nicotine

Nicotine is the second most popular recreational drug in the United States. The Surgeon General has identified smoking as "the chief, single, avoidable cause of death in our society, and the most important health issue of our time" (Smith 1986). Tobacco is so harmful that "a nonsmoker has a better chance of reaching the age of 75 than a smoker has of reaching the age of 65" (Goode 1989). The dollar cost is also high, about $28 billion a year in health care and another $43 billion in lost productivity. Yet the tobacco industry spends $10 billion a year to promote its products, mostly to convince young people that smoking is sexy and a fast road to growing up (American Lung 2003). Tobacco companies still target youth, but perhaps none so brazenly as the company featured in the Global Glimpse box below.

In the second half of the twentieth century, increasing knowledge about the health consequences of smoking—along with advertisements that targeted youth—aroused widespread subjective concerns. These concerns gave birth to a strident, powerful antismoking campaign. Among the results are no-smoking sections in restaurants and a ban on smoking in offices, on flights, on buses, in government buildings, and in some states such

A Global Glimpse
FIRST DEATH, THEN SHAG: TARGETING COLLEGE STUDENTS

Every package of cigarettes sold in the United States contains a warning from the U.S. Surgeon General. Americans know that this warning isn't true. After all, those thousands of happy, carefree young people who are smoking cigarettes in those countless ads wouldn't be happy and smiling if cigarettes really killed people.

In the 1990s, the Enlightened Tobacco Company of England skipped the ads that showed happy young people and introduced a brand called Death. They put the cigarettes in a black package emblazoned with a white skull-and-crossbones. The death logo was also stamped near the filter of each cigarette. Ads for Death were bordered in black, resembling funeral announcements.

The company's position was that the tobacco industry has the right to sell cigarettes, people have the right to smoke, and smokers should know what they are doing to their bodies. To openly advertise death, they said, is morally superior to telling half-truths, being deceptive, or giving weaselly health warnings.

But just maybe confronting smokers with death isn't good for business. Death cigarettes died a quick death. If Death didn't appeal to college students, then there must be another way. Still trying the unusual approach, another tobacco company in Great Britain introduced a brand of cigarettes called Shag (British slang for sexual intercourse). The company's slogan: "Have you had one lately?" To promote Shag, the company hands out free samples to college students, along with a wink and a free Shag condom (Murray 2004).

Death and Shag—in a twisted way, at opposite ends of life's spectrum. Fascinating and a little fun. But no matter how you look at it, smoking kills. Death from smoking isn't merciful—as it may be for those who meet their end in lethal accidents or while they sleep. Nicotine deaths are agonizing and slow—like those of people mutilated in car wrecks, who linger with intense pain for months, slowly wasting away, and when nothing but a shell of their former self remains, mercifully pass on.

as California, in bars. (Some of you will find this difficult to believe, but prior to this campaign, professors and students used to smoke in class.) Table 4-4 below shows how effective this campaign has been. As you can see, at the height of addiction, *most* men smoked, as did one of three women. The decline has been precipitous, to one of four men and one of five women. The lowest rate of smoking—among those age 65 and over—does not represent results from the antismoking campaign. Rather, by this age so many smokers have died that there aren't many smokers left alive.

Figure 4-2 on the next page also depicts the sharp decline in smoking since the height of its popularity in the 1960s. In a strange twist of logic, the tobacco industry claims credit for this decrease, saying that it is evidence of its efforts "to deter youths from smoking" ("Frequent Tobacco Use" 1992)! For another view, see the Issues in Social Problems box on targeting kids and minorities on pages 108 and 109.

With Americans smoking less, the tobacco companies face a shrinking market for their products, not an easy situation for the manufacturers of any product. Since they don't want to go out of the business of promoting death, these companies have turned to the Least Industrialized Nations to pursue easier victims. So many men in these countries already smoke, however, that all the companies can do is fight one another for the same male customers. But the women in these countries—they are another matter entirely. Because only a small proportion of the women smoke, they have become the companies' next target (Preidt 2003b; Bansal et al. 2005). The result is easy to predict. The global death toll of what is being called the *brown plague* comes to about 5 million lives a year. Most of these victims are men who live in the Least Industrialized Nations. The industry's seductive advertising is bound to entice more women in these nations to smoke, with the result that these women will make up a growing percentage of the globe's tobacco deaths.

Because the costs of caring for U.S. victims falls largely on the government in the form of higher Medicaid bills, in the 1990s the states sued the tobacco companies. In return for dropping their lawsuits, the states were awarded $209 billion from the cigarette manufacturers. This huge settlement, to be paid over 25 years, did not put a single cigarette company out of business. To cover their costs, cigarette manufacturers merely raised prices for their addicted smokers. The states are spending only about half of their award on health care. They are diverting the other half to a variety of projects, from fixing sidewalks to balancing state budgets ("GAO Delineates . . ." 2003).

TABLE 4-4 Cigarette Smoking by Sex and Age					
	1965	**1975**	**1985**	**1995**	**2003**
By Sex					
Male	52%	43%	33%	27%	24%
Female	34%	32%	28%	23%	19%
By Sex and Age					
Males					
18–24 years	54%	42%	28%	28%	26%
25–34 years	61%	51%	38%	30%	29%
35–44 years	58%	51%	38%	32%	28%
45–64 years	52%	43%	33%	27%	24%
65 and over	29%	25%	20%	15%	10%
Females					
18–24 years	38%	34%	30%	22%	22%
25–34 years	44%	39%	32%	26%	21%
35–44 years	44%	40%	32%	27%	24%
45–64 years	32%	33%	30%	24%	20%
65 and over	10%	12%	14%	12%	8%

Source: By the author. Based on *Statistical Abstract of the United States* 1994:Table 212; 1997:Table 221; 1998:Table 238; 2006:Table 190.

FIGURE 4-2 Number of Cigarettes That Americans Age 18 and Older Smoke Each Year

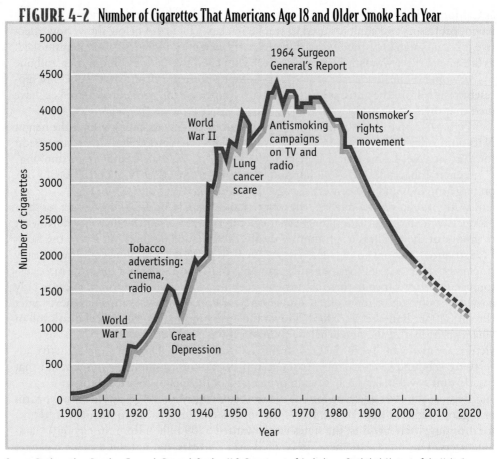

Source: By the author. Based on Economic Research Service, U.S. Department of Agriculture, *Statistical Abstract of the United States* 2006:Table 989; projection by the author.

Marijuana

The third most popular recreational drug in the United States is marijuana. Marijuana used to be an underground drug smoked furtively by a few adventurous souls. Then came the norm-bending 1960s, and with it the rebellious youth who embraced this drug. By 1979, one of three Americans age 18 to 25 smoked marijuana at least once a month. Since then, the popularity of marijuana has dropped by half, and today 17 percent of Americans of this age smoke marijuana this often (*Statistical Abstract* 1998:Table 237; 2006:Table 194).

When marijuana surged in popularity during the 1960s, government officials panicked, thinking that the country was going to hell in a handbasket. The states didn't know what to do, so they took their usual course of action and passed laws right and left. Like a schizophrenic, they jumped from one reality to another. While Nevada made the possession of even a single joint punishable by up to six years in prison, Alaska legalized the possession of marijuana for personal consumption (Goode 1989:30). Then both states decided they had made a mistake. Alaskans revoked their law, and Nevadans lightened up, making the possession of up to one ounce of marijuana punishable only by fines, with no jail time allowed.

Although marijuana has declined in overall usage, it remains a popular drug. As I mentioned earlier, about 13 million Americans smoke marijuana. Figure 4-3 on the next page summarizes marijuana use among high school and college students. You can see that marijuana use peaks during the senior year in high school, then drops slightly during the college years.

HEALTH CONSEQUENCES OF MARIJUANA USE. How does marijuana affect its users' health? Many assertions have been made—that marijuana harms the body's immune system, reduces

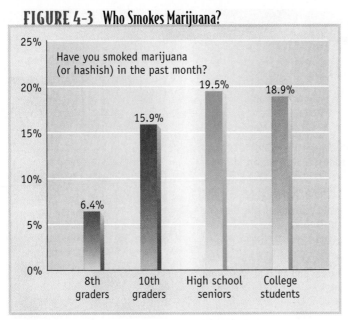

FIGURE 4-3 Who Smokes Marijuana?

Have you smoked marijuana
(or hashish) in the past month?

- 8th graders: 6.4%
- 10th graders: 15.9%
- High school seniors: 19.5%
- College students: 18.9%

Source: By the author. Based on Johnston et al. 2006:Table 2-3.

the male sex hormone testosterone, lowers fertility, damages chromosomes, and causes brain damage. Although each study was widely heralded in the mass media when it first appeared, follow-up studies have not confirmed these findings. Like smoking cigarettes, however, smoking marijuana can damage the respiratory system. An analysis of the health of a nationally representative sample of 7,000 Americans showed that marijuana smokers have more bronchitis, coughing, and wheezing (Moore et al. 2004). At this point, though, we know little about the health consequences of smoking marijuana; and, since this drug is so popular, we need good studies.

Smoking marijuana, however, impairs motor coordination and reduces consciousness of external stimuli, such as red lights or stop signs (Carroll 2000). As a consequence, people who drive after smoking marijuana are three to seven times more likely to have an accident (Ramaekers et al. 2004). Although THC, the primary psychoactive agent in marijuana, remains in the body several days after smoking, its lingering effects are not perceptible to the smoker. In one study, pilots who were tested 24 hours after they had smoked marijuana, when they no longer felt "high," showed deterioration in performing simulated landing maneuvers. Perhaps most telling is this finding: In a posthumous sample of 400 male drivers in California who had been killed in auto accidents, 37 percent had THC in their blood (Goode 1989:147). It seems safe to conclude that it is not prudent to ride or to fly with someone who has smoked marijuana.

Research findings also show positive aspects of marijuana, such as relieving glaucoma and migraine headaches. Marijuana also helps to reduce the nausea and vomiting of patients in chemotherapy. Marijuana also relieves "asthma, epilepsy, muscle spasticity, anxiety, depression, pain, reduced appetite, and withdrawal from alcohol and narcotics" (Carroll 2000). To uncover marijuana's positive and negative effects, we need further research. In today's political climate, however, such research is discouraged because of marijuana's social reputation. It also won't go down well with many if marijuana turns out to have further positive effects on health.

ADDICTION AND MARIJUANA. When smoking marijuana became popular a generation ago, alarmed parents and officials warned youth that marijuana was addictive. The smokers scoffed, saying that they could quit at any time. And they were right—or at least most of them were. Recent research, however, shows that some marijuana smokers can't quit. They become preoccupied with making certain that they are able to smoke every day, and they suffer symptoms of withdrawal when they try to stop smoking. Researchers

Issues in Social Problems
TARGETING KIDS AND MINORITIES

Let's listen to a conversation between Kent Reynolds, the CEO of a major tobacco company, and Chester Winston, director of sales.

"Chester, I want to show you something. My daughter brought this social problems text home from college. Look at this table on page 105."

"Yeah, that confirms our own studies. Our customer base is eroding. Too many people believe those lies the (expletive deleted) antismokers are telling—cancer and all that. We've got to get the kids started earlier."

"What've you got in mind?"

"Well, if we could get the kids hooked—I mean started . . . I was thinking about adding some flavor they like."

"Good idea. They've already added cherry to Skoal Long Cut. That's getting to a lot of kids. And they've been smart about it—keeping the nicotine down so the kids gradually get into it. Then they move on to Copenhagen after they're hooked—I mean, used to the taste. No one's done chocolate yet. Kids love chocolate."

"If you okay it, we can test-market Chocolate Smokeless Tobacco. And, of course, chocolate-flavored cigarettes. And we might try butterscotch and raspberry. We'll make'em all low-nicotine and low-tar."

"What about the minorities?"

"We're already loading *Ebony* with ads. My research department reported that one of eight pages of *Ebony*'s color ads go to cigarettes."

"Great. How about sponsoring cultural events, like a jazz festival?"

"Kool's already got that covered."

"Come to think of it, Parliament's already got that World Beat Concert Series, too."

"Yeah, but we're underwriting the Harlem Week Festival in New York City."

"And don't forget all the money we're using to buy—I mean, contribute—to the National Black Caucus of State Legislatures."

If this ad is not aimed at teenaged boys, who is the target? Could it be old women in nursing homes? Despite their straight-faced denial that they had ever targeted anyone under 18 (sworn before Congress on their mothers' graves), tobacco executives have agreed to no longer use ads like this.

estimate that 2 to 3 percent of marijuana smokers become addicted within two years of smoking their first joint, that at some point up to 10 percent of smokers become cannabis dependent (Roffman and Stephens 2006). We need more research, but apparently some smokers do become dependent on cannabis, or THC, the active ingredient in marijuana. If just the more conservative 2 percent total is correct, this comes to a quarter million Americans.

SOCIAL CONSEQUENCES OF MARIJUANA USE. On the negative side, researchers have found that marijuana smokers tend to receive poorer grades than those who don't smoke this drug, and they are more likely to drop out of high school (Kleinman et al. 1987; Fergusson et al. 2003). As we have seen in several instances in this text, we must approach "facts" with caution, for a look below the surface often yields a different view. A deeper look at this fact, which is true, shows that, compared with their classmates, heavy marijuana smokers are more likely to come from broken homes, to drink more alcohol, to commit more

"And the United Negro College Fund and the National Urban League are already in our budget."

"Sometimes I wonder if all this money is paying off."

"Don't worry about that! You never see any of that antismoking propaganda in *Ebony*—and that's no coincidence."

"I've never even seen a copy. But I depend on you to know these things, Chester."

"Well, the real payoff is that African American men are smoking more than the whites."

"What about the women?"

"Sorry. Despite everything we've done, they've got the lowest rate of smoking."

"We've got to do better, Chester."

"We will."

"But we've got to be careful. They're starting to blame us for blacks having higher rates of lung cancer and heart disease and stuff like that!"

"It's their soul food, Kent."

"What about Latinos?"

"Marlboro's got them pretty well covered. Remember those rodeos for Mexican Americans they sponsor in California?"

"That's right."

"And we're already buying off—I mean, contributing—all that money to the Hispanic Congressional Caucus and the National Association of Hispanic Journalists."

"How about the Native Americans, then? Maybe we're missing them."

"I think you've got something there. And the Chinese Americans, too. And then there's the Abyssinian Americans and the . . ."

"I'd like to bypass all that race and gender stuff and just target three-year-olds of every background."

"I'll get to work on that right away. I know it can be done. Ninety percent of six-year-olds used to be able to match Joe Camel with Camel cigarettes. Too bad they can't use Joe any more." (laughs)

"Maybe we can make a kid's nicotine gum—just a little nicotine in the spearmint."

"Now you're talking."

"Yeah. And how about cute cutouts of our cigarette packs for the preschools—and maybe coloring books, too!"

"We can give the kids free colors in flip-top boxes that look like our cigarette packs."

"Great idea! We can call'em Kiddie Packs. Maybe we can wrap the colors in white paper."

"Maybe we can include a play cigarette lighter, too."

That night both Kent and Chester enjoy their well-earned, peaceful sleep, dreaming of chocolate-flavored cigarettes, and butterscotch, and raspberry, and . . .

Based on Johnson 1992; Freedman 1994; Pollay 1997; *Statistical Abstract* 2006:Table 190.

delinquent acts, and to be involved in a subculture that places less value on academic achievement. In other words, we can't depend on correlations but we must always try to separate cause and effect. Marijuana can be just "one element in a large and complex picture of interrelated problems and behaviors" (Kleinman et al. 1987; White 1991).

Marijuana is also associated with an **amotivational syndrome.** Some heavy marijuana smokers become lethargic, lose their concentration, and drift away from long-range goals. The evidence for an amotivational syndrome in humans is weak, though, consisting mainly of impressions and anecdotes: "Before she smoked grass, Shirley had so many plans, but look at her now." But then there are the monkeys. It turns out that monkeys that smoke marijuana are less motivated than monkeys that don't tote joints. When researchers make monkeys work for bananas, the smoking monkeys don't stick with the task as long as the nonsmoking monkeys. (I'm not kidding you. This is a real experiment.) When researchers take away their marijuana, the monkeys' motivation returns to normal—but it takes about nine months for this to happen (Slikker 1992). This is intriguing research, and amotivation

Although the popularity of marijuana has declined, it remains a major drug of choice of young Americans. Because of legal bans on research, we know little of the health consequences of marijuana use, either positive or negative.

could be a serious consequence of heavy marijuana smoking; but, obviously, we need to do research on humans.

SUBJECTIVE REACTIONS. Marijuana certainly is an excellent example of the subjective nature of social problems. Reactions are so subjective that they range from perceiving marijuana as a threat to society to viewing it as a treatment for medical problems. Until 1937, when the Marijuana Tax Act was passed, marijuana was an ingredient in about thirty medicines (Carroll 2000). Physicians prescribed marijuana to treat a variety of conditions. If doctors did this today, they would be jailed. To possess marijuana used to be legal for anyone in every state, but now marijuana possession is subject to some type of penalty in every state. At one point in our history, an Alabama judge even sentenced a man *to death* for selling marijuana ("First Death Sentence" 1991).

Today, 13 million Americans pay thousands of illegal distributors so they can smoke marijuana, while thousands of enforcement agents are collecting pay to stop this distribution. Each year, those agents arrest 87,000 sellers of marijuana, arrest 625,000 smokers, and seize 2.5 million pounds of marijuana (*Statistical Abstract* 2006:Tables 318, 319).

Cocaine

THE SOCIAL HISTORY OF COCAINE. Cocaine, a fourth drug that is used for recreational purposes, helps us to understand that a "devil drug" can become socially respectable and that a socially respectable drug can be transformed into a social problem. Cocaine got off to a rocky start with Europeans. When the Spaniards invaded Peru in the 1500s, they conquered a people who chewed coca leaves. The Spaniards attributed the drug's effects to the devil and said that cocaine was evil.

As the text explains, drugs have social reputations that have nothing to do with their relative harm. As with cocaine, those reputations can undergo severe change. Cocaine's current status is so negative that people associated with it risk their own reputation, livelihood, and even freedom.

As more Europeans tried the drug and as physicians discovered medicinal uses for it, cocaine became popular and gained high social approval. By the late 1800s, physicians were praising cocaine, which had become a common ingredient in patent medicines. Famous people, such as Sigmund Freud, the founder of psychoanalysis, and Sir Arthur Conan Doyle, the creator of Sherlock Holmes, swore that cocaine got their creative juices going. When Angelo Mariana, a French chemist, introduced a wine that contained the coca leaf extract, the pope enjoyed the wine so much that he presented Mariana with a medal (Ray and Ksir 2004). At this time, hundreds of thousands of Americans were sipping cocaine as a "pick-me-up," for cocaine had become an ingredient in Coca-Cola, a drink that is named after the coca leaf.

Yet by 1910, cocaine had been transformed from a medicine and a "pick-me-up" into a dangerous drug, much as Dr. Jekyll became Mr. Hyde—a story, by the way, that was written in three days by Robert Louis Stevenson while he was high on cocaine (Ashley 1975). What led to the drug's downfall?

In the late 1800s, reporters began to link cocaine with the poor and with criminals. They started to say that gunmen took cocaine to get up their nerve to commit robberies (Ashley 1975). These news stories led to a public outcry, and in 1903 the Coca-Cola Company found it prudent to eliminate cocaine from its drink. Even today, however, Coca-Cola contains an extract from the coca leaf (Miller 1994). In the early 1900s, it was still legal to use cocaine in products, but it had to be listed as an ingredient. Then in 1914, the Harrison Act classified cocaine as a narcotic (an error, because cocaine is a stimulant), making it illegal to sell the drug.

THE BLACK MARKET IN COCAINE. The Harrison Act paved the way for a black market in cocaine, one that still exists almost a hundred years after the law was passed. This black market delivers cocaine effectively: About 15 percent of Americans age 12 and over—about 37 million people—have used cocaine, and about 2.5 million use this drug at least once a month (*Statistical Abstract* 2006:Tables 12, 194). As we saw in Tables 4-2 and 4-3 on page 100, in just the past month between 3 and 4 percent of all U.S. high school seniors and 2 percent of college students used cocaine. Though snorting is the preferred method of use, smoking cocaine base, called *freebasing*, is also popular.

USES OF COCAINE. Cocaine has a distinctive medical use. Surgeons apply cocaine as a local anesthetic and as a vasoconstrictor (a substance that reduces blood flow to the area to which it is applied). The drug is so effective that cocaine is the medical profession's anesthetic of choice for surgery involving the nose, throat, larynx, and lower respiratory passages. The most common use of cocaine, however, is to obtain a high—feelings of well-being, optimism, confidence, competence, and energy. Cocaine also has a reputation as an aphrodisiac; it is thought to create or heighten sexual desires, to increase sexual endurance, and to cure frigidity and impotence (Inciardi 1986:78–79).

From the coca plant can come an abundance of legal products: soap, shampoo, toothpaste, flour, tea, calcium and iron supplements, even an aid to grow hair (Forero 2006). Evo Morales, the president of Bolivia, the source of most cocaine, used to be a farmer—and he used to grow coca. He argues that the legal coca products should be accepted in the international commodities market. He wants to say yes to growing coca and no to trafficking in cocaine. "A likely situation" retort U.S. government officials, who want all coca plants eradicated.

DYSFUNCTIONS OF COCAINE. Cocaine's high is intense. Those who become addicted to cocaine report a craving so strong that "they will give up many of the things they value—money, possessions, relationships, jobs, and careers—in order to continue taking the drug" (Goode 1989:198–199). In the form of cocaine called *crack,* the pleasure is so intense it is akin to orgasm. The high, which lasts from 5 to 12 minutes, is followed by a "crash" that leaves its users irritable, depressed, nervous, or paranoid. Although crack is inexpensive, because its effects are short-lived, users find that it is costly to remain high. The desire for the intense pleasure is so great that some women rent their bodies for crack; and, as we saw in Chapter 3, a form of prostitute, the "crack whore," has emerged.

Cocaine has other dysfunctions. Among them are heart attacks, brain damage, and death (Kozel 1996; Julien 2001). The dysfunction that captures headlines and stimulates subjective concerns, though, is "crack babies." As with alcohol and nicotine, if a pregnant woman uses cocaine, it enters the fetus' system. There, the drug's concentration can equal or exceed that of the mother. The cocaine can interfere with the normal development of the heart, brain, and other organs. It can also cause the brain to bleed (Julien 2001). In an attempt to prevent "crack babies," some authorities are following the controversial social policy discussed in the Thinking Critically About Social Problems box on the next page.

CRACK COCAINE. Crack can be produced easily in a home kitchen. With huge profits at stake, illegal drug entrepreneurs ("corner crack dealers") fight for territory ("turf") and customers. As a result, violence sometimes surrounds crack—coming from those who will do anything to get the drug and from those who will do anything to make money from the drug.

Crack cocaine's social history includes racial discrimination. Following on the heels of publicity over violence associated with crack, in 1986 the U.S. Congress made selling

THINKING CRITICALLY About Social Problems

ON PREGNANCY, DRUGS, AND JAIL

Consider the following court cases.

A pregnant woman in Washington, D.C., was charged with check forgery. The usual sentence for first-time offenders is probation. When the woman tested positive for cocaine, the judge sentenced her to prison, saying; "I'm going to keep her locked up until the baby's born."

A California woman who had taken street drugs was charged with child abuse after she delivered a brain-damaged baby who died soon after birth.

An Illinois woman was charged with manslaughter when her two-day-old infant died because she had snorted cocaine during pregnancy.

In Florida, a woman was convicted of two counts of delivering drugs to a minor. The prosecution alleged that the woman had passed cocaine to her newborn child through

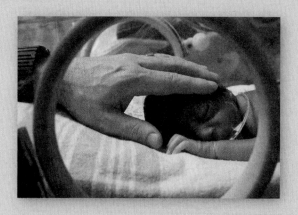

Some judges have charged women who used illegal drugs when pregnant with child abuse and delivering drugs to a minor.

the umbilical cord after the baby was delivered but before the cord was cut.

In Texas, eighteen pregnant women were charged with delivering drugs to their unborn children, using the umbilical cord as the delivery vehicle

FOR YOUR CONSIDERATION

Should judges jail a pregnant woman because she uses drugs such as cocaine that can harm her fetus? If so, because alcohol and nicotine can harm a fetus, should judges jail pregnant women who smoke cigarettes or drink alcohol? If not, what's the difference?

In 2006, a Texas Appeals Court overturned convictions of two pregnant women for transferring drugs to their fetuses. What do you think about their conviction? About their conviction being overturned?

Based on Broff 1989; Humphries et al. 1992; Pagelow 1992; Chen 2006.

---

crack a federal offense. With the new law, judges began to give longer jail and prison sentences for crack than for powder cocaine. Because powder cocaine is more likely to be used by whites and crack by African Americans (Lewis 1996; Riley 1998), blacks charged racial discrimination. After eight years of prison sentences that were handed down primarily to African American users, in *U.S. v. Ricky Davis* (1994) the U.S. District Court in Georgia declared that crack and cocaine are one and the same drug. Now sentences imposed for the use of crack can be no heavier than those imposed for the use of powder cocaine.

PRINCIPLES UNDERLYING A DRUG'S SOCIAL REPUTATION. From this brief social history of cocaine, we can see that several principles are involved in determining a drug's social reputation:

1. A drug's reputation is not based on objective conditions. It does not, for instance, derive from tests that reveal that drug A causes serious problems, drug B does not, and therefore drug A is banned and drug B permitted. If such a scientific approach characterized a drug's social history, alcohol would be banned, and marijuana would be available in grocery stores (Ashley 1975).
2. Like humans, drugs gain their reputation through the people and events with which they are associated.
3. Drugs that are associated with people or events generally considered respectable are likely to be defined as good and desirable, while drugs associated with people or events generally considered disreputable are likely to be defined as bad and undesirable.
4. The reputation or social acceptability of drugs can change.

As functionalists stress, whenever laws are passed against a drug that is in high demand, a symbiotic black market springs up to meet that demand. Although it is illegal, cocaine is in high demand; the intricate black market that serves the demand stretches across continents. Shown here are 2,400 pounds of cocaine that were shipped from Colombia to the United States. The cocaine was seized in Baltimore, Maryland.

Research Findings: The Hallucinogens

LSD

Perhaps the most famous of the hallucinogens is LSD (lysergic acid diethylamide). This drug was first synthesized in 1938 by Albert Hoffman, a Swiss chemist. Hoffman discovered that LSD was psychoactive in 1943, when he accidentally inhaled a minute dose of the drug. Here is what he says happened to him:

> Last Friday, April 16, 1943, I was forced to stop my work in the laboratory in the middle of the afternoon and to go home, as I was seized by a peculiar restlessness associated with a sensation of mild dizziness. Having reached home, I lay down and sank in a kind of drunkenness which was not unpleasant and which was characterized by extreme activity of imagination. As I lay in a dazed condition with my eyes closed (I experienced daylight as disagreeably bright) there surged upon me an uninterrupted stream of fantastic images of extraordinary plasticity and vividness and accompanied by an intense, kaleidoscope-like play of colors. This condition gradually passed off after about two hours. (Hoffman 1968:184–185)

LSD was thought to produce psychoses, and people avoided it. Then in 1960, Timothy Leary, a Harvard professor, began experimenting with LSD. After Leary was fired for violating experimental guidelines, he became a guru of the 1960s youth counterculture. Leary's message was that that everyone should take some LSD to experience changed consciousness and become nonconformist. Leary's slogan, "turn on, tune in, and drop out," struck a responsive chord with the youth of the time, and LSD use spread. This tasteless, odorless substance, an ounce of which contains 300,000 doses, reached its height of media attention in about 1967 and its peak of usage in about 1979 (Goode 1989:178–179). As we saw on Table 4-2 on page 100, about 1.5 percent of U.S. high school seniors took LSD within the past month. Although this is a small percentage, it totals about 60,000

Drugs that are acceptable in one culture can be offensive in another culture. Mescaline (from peyote buttons) and psilocybin (from mushrooms) are a part of the culture of some Native-American Mexicans. Shown here is a *huichol* (yarn painting), a standard art form among these groups. *Huicholes* reflect visions induced by these drugs.

high school seniors. The 0.2 percent of college students who used LSD in the past month equals about 30,000 students (*Statistical Abstract* 2006:Table 204).

Peyote and Mescaline

The use of peyote is an old custom on this continent, for Native Americans were using this cactus product when Cortez arrived in the 1500s. In the United States, peyote can be used legally—but only by members of the Native American Church for religious purposes (Schaefer 2004). About twenty states forbid any use of peyote (Carroll 2000). Mescaline, synthesized from peyote in 1919, produces similar visual effects. Both peyote and mescaline have had famous proponents: Havelock Ellis (1897, 1902) was enthusiastic about peyote, and Aldous Huxley (1954) sang the praises of mescaline. In the 1960s and 1970s, anthropologist Carlos Castaneda (1968, 1971, 1974) popularized the use of peyote among a cultlike following. The drug always has a die-hard group of users, with occasional recruits.

Psilocybin

The magic mushrooms of Mexico (*Psilocybe mexicana*) were also being used when Cortez arrived on these shores. Because the mushrooms were associated with pagan rituals, Cortez launched a campaign against them (as he had against peyote), driving their use underground. Not until the 1930s was it discovered that natives of southern Mexico were still using them. Their active ingredient is psilocybin, which was isolated by Albert Hoffman in 1958 and later synthesized. As with peyote, reports about the effects of this drug often contain a spiritual or religious emphasis (Ray and Ksir 2004).

PCP

PCP (phencyclidine hydrochloride), called *angel dust*, was synthesized in 1957 by Parke-Davis and sold as a painkiller. As people soon discovered, this drug also produces hallucinations. Because PCP requires little equipment to manufacture, it is often made in home laboratories. PCP affects the central nervous system, making it difficult to speak and usually producing altered body images and feelings of unreality. Some users report feeling euphoria and a sense of power, loneliness, or isolation. Others experience numbness and even feelings of dying (which is why users refer to PCP as "embalming fluid"). Higher dosages may result in loss of inhibition, disorientation, rage, convulsions, or coma (Crider 1986; Ray and Ksir 2004).

Ecstasy

Ecstasy (MDMA, methylenedioxyamphetamine), a popular party drug, gives a euphoric rush like that of cocaine combined with some of the mind-expanding effects of the psychedelics. Users report that Ecstasy relaxes them, increases empathy and feelings of intimacy, and enhances sensual experiences, such as making touching more pleasurable. Side effects for some users are mental confusion and anxiety. The main concern about this drug, though, is that it may act as a toxic substance and cause brain damage (Carroll 2000).

Research Findings: The Amphetamines, Barbiturates, and Heroin

The Amphetamines

The amphetamines—Benzedrine, Dexedrine, Methedrine, Desoxyn, Biphetamine, and Dexamyl—go by such street names as "uppers," "pep pills," "bennies," "dexies," "speed," "meth," "crystal," and "ice" (Carroll 2000). Discovered in 1887, Benzedrine became popular in the 1920s in over-the-counter inhalers intended to dilate the bronchial tubes. Later Benzedrine was available by prescription in tablet form for hyperkinesis and, in 1939, as an appetite suppressant. During World War II, the military gave amphetamines

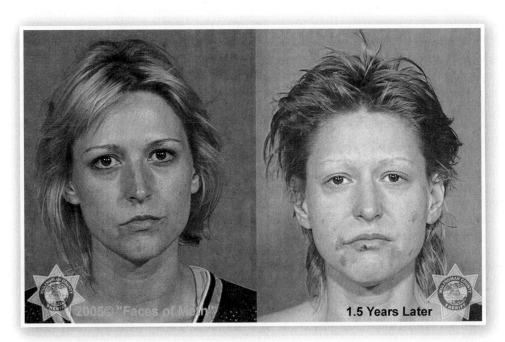

These photos are of the same person—before and after meth addiction. For some, it takes but a couple of years or less for this type of transition to occur.

to soldiers to help them stay awake. Also at this time, people began to soak the amphetamine from Benzedrine inhalers, and amphetamine abuse began.

"Speed" (methamphetamine dissolved in liquid) is used by "speed freaks," who inject the drug, sometimes every two or three hours, for "runs" of three or four days. Each injection of this kind produces a "rush" or "flash," a sudden feeling of intense pleasure, followed by moderate feelings of euphoria. Some users hallucinate, while others develop feelings of paranoia, or become hostile and aggressive—symptoms that have been called the *amphetamine psychosis* (Ray and Ksir 2004). Heavy amphetamine use is sometimes accompanied by behavioral fixations—a person repeating an activity over and over, such as counting the corn flakes in a box of cereal. Amphetamine withdrawal may bring outbursts of aggression, feelings of terror, and thoughts of suicide or homicide (Carroll 2000; Julien 2001).

"Meth" addiction has become a problem across the country. With meth easily made at home, using ordinary household items like Sudafed (pseudoephedrine, a common nonprescription cold or sinus medicine), matches, aluminum foil, and charcoal, meth labs have sprung up, especially in rural areas. Meth users experience such severe side effects—including high blood pressure and high fevers—that they have become a burden to the emergency services of hospitals (Zernike 2006). Officials are so concerned about meth addiction and meth manufacturing that the White House Office of National Drug Control Policy runs television advertisements to discourage meth use, and a provision of the Patriot Act forces states to restrict purchases of pseudoephedrine (Tierney 2006).

The Barbiturates

In 1862, Dr. A. Bayer of Munich, Germany (the Bayer of aspirin fame), combined urea with malonic acid and made a new compound, barbituric acid, from which over 2,500 drugs have been derived. Of these, phenobarbital (Luminal), amobarbital (Amytal), pentobarbital (Nembutal), and secobarbital (Seconal) are the best known. Medically, the barbiturates are used as an anesthetic and to treat anxiety, insomnia, and epilepsy. Used for nonmedical purposes, the barbiturates provide an experience similar to that of alcohol. Regular barbiturate use leads to physical dependence. Withdrawal causes nausea, anxiety, sweating, dizziness, trembling, muscular twitching, and sometimes convulsions, coma, and death. Because the risk of death is higher for those who stop "cold turkey" (abruptly), physicians usually substitute a long-lasting barbiturate and then withdraw it slowly (Ray and Ksir 2004).

Heroin

As you know, flowers acquire social reputations. Red roses become symbolic of love, for example, and black lilies of death. The social reputation of one flower became so bad that in 1901 it became illegal to import this flower. By 1942, Americans couldn't even grow this flower without getting a license from the secretary of the Treasury. U.S. officials dislike this flower so much that they even made it possible to execute someone who sells derivatives of the flower to anyone under age 18 (Ray and Ksir 2004).

What flower is this? It is the opium poppy. The derivative that is so feared and hated by some (and intensely desired by others) is heroin. The process by which opium yields heroin, illustrated on Figure 4-4 on the next page, has been simplified by Afghans, who filter the opium juice through a flour sack and dry it in the sun (Shishkin and Crawford 2006).

As you probably know, Western nations decided years ago that to stop the heroin trade, they had to go to the source and destroy the poppy fields. If you've ever wondered why there is always plenty of heroin for those who want it, despite the money spent by Western governments to eradicate the poppy fields, read the Global Glimpse box on page 118.

ADDICTION TO HEROIN. The common view is that heroin is so addictive and the withdrawal pains so severe that addicts will do anything to avoid withdrawal. Here is how novelist William Burroughs (1975:135) described his own addiction:

Junk (heroin) yields a basic formula of . . . total need. . . . Beyond a certain frequency need knows absolutely no limit or control. In the words of total need: "Wouldn't you?" Yes you would. You would lie, cheat, inform on your friends, steal, do anything to satisfy total need. Because you would be in a state of total sickness, total possession, and not in a position to act in any other way. . . . A rabid dog can't choose but bite.

This is the conventional view of heroin. When a team of sociologists headed by Bruce Johnson (1985) explored heroin addiction, however, they found something different. These researchers rented a storefront in a neighborhood in Harlem that had "the highest number of street-level heroin abusers in the country." In a different location that had similar characteristics, they rented another storefront. The two neighborhoods were so well known for heroin dealing that they drew customers from around the region. To build repeat business, some dealers even devised brand names: Tragic Magic, Black Death, and Dynamite. For two years, a research staff of former heroin users built rapport with 201 current users. From the day-to-day reports they collected from these addicts, the researchers found that many heroin users are *not* physically addicted. For a period of time, they use heroin once or twice a day, and then—without suffering withdrawal symptoms—they go for several days without the drug. Other researchers have noted that some people use heroin on an occasional basis, such as at weekend parties, without becoming addicted (Spunt 2003).

Use of heroin by U.S. soldiers in Vietnam also supports these findings. About 14 percent of the soldiers used heroin, and it was far stronger than any available back home. After the soldiers left Vietnam, were reunited with family and friends, and went back to work, the vast majority ceased using heroin. They had few, if any, noticeable physical problems. As the Assistant Secretary of Defense for Health and Environment said:

> Everything that I learned in medical school—that anyone who ever tried heroin was instantly, totally, and perpetually hooked—failed to prepare me for dealing with this situation. (Peele 1987:211)

These contradictory reports leave us with a problem to solve. Certainly William Burroughs' description of his own addiction to heroin (and similar reports by other users) is accurate. He did not make it up. Nor did Johnson and his associates make up their findings either. How can we reconcile such mixed reports? The simplest explanation seems to be that heroin is addicting to some people, but not to others. Some users of heroin do become addicts and match the stereotypical profile. Others are able to use heroin on a recreational basis.

Both, then, may be right. With the evidence we have at this point, it would be inappropriate to side with either extreme. That is, it would not match research findings to conclude that anyone can use heroin without getting addicted or that anyone who uses heroin gets addicted. We must await further research to find the key to heroin addiction.

FETAL NARCOTIC SYNDROME. As with alcohol and cocaine, pregnant women who use narcotics deliver babies that are addicted. Suffering from **fetal narcotic syndrome,** these newborns are pitiful. They have tremors and can't sleep right, and they vomit, sneeze, and frantically suck their tiny fists (*Drug Dependence in Pregnancy* 1979). They also are more likely to be born prematurely, to be underweight, and to be starting life with such a cluster of problems that they are less likely than other babies to survive (Choo et al. 2004).

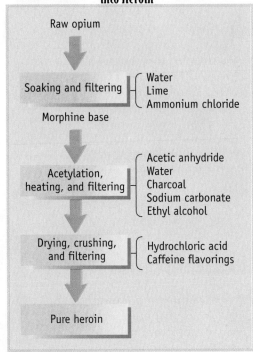

FIGURE 4-4 How Opium Is Converted into Heroin

Raw opium
↓
Soaking and filtering — Water / Lime / Ammonium chloride
↓
Morphine base
↓
Acetylation, heating, and filtering — Acetic anhydride / Water / Charcoal / Sodium carbonate / Ethyl alcohol
↓
Drying, crushing, and filtering — Hydrochloric acid / Caffeine flavorings
↓
Pure heroin

Source: By the author, based on *The Heroin Trail*, 1974, and "Opium Poppy Cultivation . . ." 2001.

A Global Glimpse
"WHAT'S A POOR FARMER TO DO?" HEROIN SUPPLIES FOREVER

Life is tough in Afghanistan, even outside the war-torn cities. Farmers barely eke out a living; their mud huts lack both electricity and running water.

Were it not for the poppies, they might not even have enough food for their children.

The lush poppy fields of the Afghan countryside bring the cash that allows farmers to survive, sometimes even enough to build a small house.

Why does Afghanistan produce three-fourths or more of the world's opium? First, growing poppies is a centuries-old custom. It's a part of the culture—the taken-for-granted, routine, normal part of life—of Afghan farmers. One of them, Ahmad Jan, said, "We will not abandon poppy cultivation until the end of this world." He thought about what he'd said for a moment, and then added, "if the government gives us something in return, we might stop" (Gall 2006).

Second, the farmers face a dilemma. For survival a mechanic must have machines to fix, or a teacher must have students to teach. And farmers must have crops to grow. In some places in Afghanistan, the land is salty, because it was reclaimed from the desert. Little grows on it, except the hardy poppy plant. Because there is so little rainfall, the farmers have to pump water for irrigation from wells about 300 feet deep. No one would survive growing wheat or melons.

Third, even the farmers who are lucky enough to have more productive land must confront the political situation. The central government of Afghanistan remains weak, and its control over the countryside is fragile. Here, tribal chiefs and private armies are still in control (Scherer 2003). If these local rulers tell farmers to grow poppies, how can they refuse?

In some areas, the Taliban is in control. The U.S. invasion after September 11 drove this political and religious group out of power in the cities, but it lives on in the more remote regions. For the Taliban, the poppy crop is a cash cow, and it even distributes leaflets ordering farmers to grow poppy. The Taliban takes opium production so seriously that its leaders provide armed protection for drug convoys and will battle government troops that dare to interfere with the drug smuggling (Gall 2006).

Even so, at the urging—and with the healthy payments—of Western nations, the central and regional governments do send out soldiers and police to eradicate poppy fields. But the police and soldiers are poor, and it doesn't take much to bribe them into either skipping some farmer's land or leaving part of the crop.

When one group of farmers had their poppy fields destroyed, they figured that this was the cost of having a new government that was bringing them peace. When they learned that the farmers in a neighboring village had bribed the police to not destroy their crops, they felt indignant. "What kind of government is this?" they asked. When Alam, one of these farmers, was interviewed, he said, "Of course I will plant poppy! And if our neighbors give bribes to the police again, then we'll just give bribes that are three times as high. We understand the system now." (Aizenman 2005)

Despite these obstacles, the West remains determined to get rid of the poppy fields. Western governments continue to pump hundreds of millions of dollars into Afghanistan. Not only do they try to eradicate the crop, but they also try to train farmers to grow fruit trees and plant vineyards instead of poppy fields. In a culture where the government is thought of as an illegitimate force, officials fight a losing battle. One farmer said that he does go along with the Western-financed program to grow alternative crops, but only to a certain extent. If he doesn't grow poppy on at least some of his land, the other villagers will accuse him of working for the government.

And how the West's plans can backfire! When the British government, which is leading the international efforts to combat Afghan drugs, offered farmers money to destroy their poppy crops, the word spread quickly. Many farmers rushed home to plant more poppies. Why not, since the British government was going to guarantee the price? When the British cash didn't arrive, the farmers harvested their poppies, giving the drug dealers a boom crop to turn into heroin (North 2004).

FOR YOUR CONSIDERATION

Why is it unlikely that the poppy fields of Afghanistan will be eradicated? In addition to the scenario just outlined, keep yet another factor in mind: The situation is like a balloon. Squeeze one end, and the balloon expands on the other end. If eradication programs reduce crops in one area, crops increase in another region—or even in an adjacent country. Given what you have read here, what solutions would you suggest to stop heroin? Or would you support the legalization of heroin? Or something else entirely?

Research Findings: Narcotics, Crime, and the Law

Heroin causes crime. It destroys people's incentive to work. It also devastates their users' health.

Everyone know that these things are true, so why even mention them?

These statements bring us, again, face to face with sociology and commonsense assumptions about social life that are not true. In this section, we are going to report on some unusual research findings.

These common assumptions about crime, health, and work seem to be supported by sociological research. Sociologists James Inciardi and Anne Pottieger (1994), who studied Miami crack users, found that the average crack user had committed 6,000 crimes in just the preceding three months!

This astronomical number comes into somewhat better focus when we learn that 98 percent of their crimes were illegal drug sales. Similarly, sociologists Bruce Johnson, Kevin Anderson, and Eric Wish (1988), who interviewed 105 drug addicts, found that during just the preceding 24 hours these men had committed 46 robberies, 18 burglaries, and 41 thefts. Seventy-five percent of the $7,771 they netted went for drugs, and 25 percent for other things such as food. The average street addict commits 150 nondrug crimes a year, about one every two or three days (Johnson et al. 1985:185).

But here is the surprise: Narcotics are *not* the cause of these crimes. Narcotics do *not* make people unproductive nor do they destroy people's health. These three beliefs are myths. Because this conclusion flies in the face of common assumptions, let's look at the research that was done on physicians who had become addicted to narcotics. The researchers found that these addicts do *not* hold up cabbies, mug pedestrians, burgle houses, or become prostitutes. Nor do they stop working. Nor does their health deteriorate (Winick 1961).

Why not? The answer is the different corner of life that physicians occupy. To obtain narcotics, physician addicts divert them from legal sources, such as hospital supplies. They do not have to scramble for money to buy narcotics. With pure drugs cheap and readily obtainable, they have no need to prey on others. In addition, they continue to work at their medical practice. This research on doctors is supported by the observations of middle-class weekend users of heroin. They, too, find no need to prey on others. They simply pay for their drug of choice from their earnings at work (Spunt 2003). *Life circumstances make the difference, not narcotic addiction.*

In and of themselves, then, the narcotics do not drive people to crime, make people stop working, or destroy people's health. Although such conditions are common among street addicts, they are not the consequence of narcotics. Jerome Jaffe (1965:292), a physician who studied physician addicts, concluded

> The addict who is able to obtain an adequate supply of the drug through legitimate channels and has adequate funds, usually dresses properly, maintains his nutrition, and is able to discharge his social and occupational obligations with reasonable efficiency. He usually remains in good health, suffers little inconvenience, and is, in general, difficult to distinguish from other persons.

This point must be underscored. Narcotics do *not* cause the things we commonly associate with them. Yet the observation that robbery, burglary, prostitution, unemployment, and poor health are associated with narcotic addicts is correct. The narcotics, however, are not the cause.

What then is the cause? It is *the laws* that make these drugs illegal. These laws create a black market, which provides a rich source of income for organized crime. Running a monopoly, the criminal underworld is able to command high prices, and *poor* addicts turn to crime to buy drugs. Spending their money on drugs, they don't eat right, and their health deteriorates. Physician addicts, in contrast, are not dependent on this black market. Middle-class users, who do use the black market in heroin, are able to afford the price.

Both the physicians and the middle-class users are able to function in a comparatively normal fashion.

These laws force most addicts to use street heroin, and with no state or federal drug agencies protecting the consumer, addicts never know what they are buying. Street heroin can be cut with substances that kill, or might not be cut enough and thereby be potent enough to kill. Users may develop allergies to the quinine commonly used to cut heroin, or even to the heroin itself, and die from acute congestion and edema of the lungs. Some users die so rapidly that the needle is still in their arm when they are found.

As we noted at the beginning of this chapter, making a drug illegal will not stop it from being available. Nor, as mentioned, does attaching severe penalties to its use or distribution. The law simply drives the transaction underground and makes a black market profitable. If tough laws are not the answer (recall the mutilation and the death penalty that once applied to tobacco use), then what is? Let's look at some alternatives.

Social Policy

The Dilemmas of Social Policy

Of all the social problems, developing adequate policies for drug use is one of the most difficult. Like abortion, this problem is surrounded by irreconcilable differences of opinion, strong emotions, prejudices, and fuzzy thinking. Complicating social policy even further are contrasting moralities, subcultural values, and vested financial and personal interests. For just one example of how difficult, perhaps impossible, it is to formulate "adequate" social policy, see the Issues in Social Problems box on the next page. For another, consider this: The health findings on alcohol suggest that we should encourage light to moderate drinking, but discourage heavy drinking. Which of our high schools and colleges—or our churches and state governments—would promote such a policy? ("Okay, class, this is why you should drink a beer or two almost every day.")

Even trying to analyze the health consequences of drugs poses a dilemma. As Oakley Ray (1998) put it:

> From a medical point of view no drug is safe. With some doses, modes of administration, and frequency of use, all drugs cause toxic effects and even death. It is equally true that at some doses, modes of administration, and frequency of use all drugs are safe. The concern here is whether a drug, used the way most people use it today, is physically harmful. From this position, alcohol and marijuana are relatively safe drugs the way most people use them. Nicotine, in contrast, is a very harmful drug, since the usual amount of cigarette smoking does increase the mortality rate.

From a medical standpoint, then, no drug is safe and all drugs are safe. Rational social policy should be built around the dimension of *social harm*. Why prohibit drugs, for example, that don't cause social harm? But how do we determine harm? *Symbolic interactionists* would want to know from whose point of view we define social harm. For example, with their worlds so different, the middle class' definition of social harm would differ considerably from that of the dispossessed of the inner city. And why should we force the perspective of one group on the other? For *functionalists,* the question would be, When do drugs interfere with people reaching their goals or when do they interfere with the welfare of society? And how do we determine this? *Conflict sociologists* might suggest something entirely different—that the so-called social harm could be a prelude to wide-scale social change that actually leads to a more just society.

THE "GET TOUGH" APPROACH. Within this morass of conflicting perspectives, U.S. officials have vacillated from one social policy to another. Currently, a *get tough* approach appears to be the dominant sentiment in the United States—passing strict laws and putting

Issues in Social Problems

JUST WHAT *CAN* YOU DO?
THE LARRY MAHONEY CASE

The school bus on which 27 people were killed by drunken driver Larry Mahoney.

"Larry Mahoney," said his friend, "wouldn't hurt anybody for the world." Another said that "since he was a little baby, he hasn't any meanness in him." Those are apt descriptions of this 34-year-old father from Kentucky. He is an all-around, pleasant, easygoing guy. How, then, could he have killed twenty-four teenagers and three adults?

It happened on a Saturday night in May. All Larry wanted was to have a good time, so he did what most of the "good old boys" of his town did: After a hard week of work at the chemical company, Larry headed for his favorite watering hole. There he met his friends, and he drank, and laughed, and drank some more. The time passed quickly, and Larry had to get home to his wife and children.

He climbed into his pickup truck and took off down the road. Things looked a little blurry, but they always did after his drinking sprees. This time, though, he didn't notice that he was going the wrong way on the interstate.

As if from nowhere, Larry saw a school bus headed toward him. Then he heard the sounds that he still can't shake—the loud crash of metal searing against metal, followed by piercing screams of agony as the bus and its passengers were engulfed in flames.

After he was charged with twenty-seven counts of murder, Larry's friends rallied to his defense. Bobby Simmons, a gas station attendant, said, "It's a terrible mistake he made. But that boy ain't no murderer." Some families held bake sales and yard sales to raise money for his bail. Lillian O'Banion, a widow in her eighties, put up the deed to her farm.

Chris Rogers, a farm worker, pinpointed the attitude in Carrollton, Kentucky, where Larry grew up and lived all his life, when he said, "Let's tell the truth about it. That could be you or me sitting in that jail. What he done ain't no different than what a lot of people in this town or anywhere else have done. To hear people on TV talk, you'd think Larry don't even feel bad about this. Let me tell you, he feels himself like he ought to be killed."

Sickened at this outpouring of support for Larry, the national president of MADD (Mothers Against Drunk Driving) said, "This was no accident. People intentionally drink, and they intentionally drive. I'm sick and tired of people sugar-coating murder."

A few miles south, on Interstate 71, where Larry Mahoney killed the twenty-four children and three adults, someone erected a white wooden cross and planted roses in the grassy median. Forty of the passengers on that church outing escaped with their lives, but they wonder why their friends had to die just because Larry Mahoney wanted a good time.

FOR YOUR CONSIDERATION

Mahoney served ten years in the Kentucky state prison at La Grange. Do you think this was just? Instead of going to prison, do you think that he should have been fined and had his driver's license revoked? Or should he have been given the death sentence, as some prosecutors demanded? What do you think would have been appropriate?

Based on Johnson 1988.

teeth in them. What is wrong with a get-tough policy? Recall the discussion at the beginning of this chapter about other societies in history. Some slit noses and cut off heads for smoking cigarettes or beat the soles of people's feet for drinking coffee. Even draconian measures don't work when people want drugs.

Back in the 1980s, President George H.W. Bush declared a "war on drugs." He ordered the Coast Guard, the Customs Service, the Border Patrol, the Immigration and Naturalization Service, and the Drug Enforcement Agency to stop illegal drugs from coming into the United States. The Pentagon even attempted to build a "fence" of radar-equipped balloons at the Mexican border (Fialka 1988). The result? Before the so-called war on drugs, a huge supply of drugs flowed into the United States. After the war on drugs, an even larger supply of drugs flowed into the United States, enough that the price of heroin dropped, and its purity increased. So much for that war.

Some just shake their heads and say that if we can't stop the drugs from coming in, at least we can lock up the dealers and users. *This is impossible*: Consider that millions of Americans use illegal drugs, from cocaine and heroin to the hallucinogens, barbiturates, and inhalants. During just the past month, about 13 million Americans smoked marijuana. How could we possibly lock up all of these people? How many dealers does it take to supply just the marijuana smokers? If each dealer has twenty-five customers, there are a half million dealers. We simply don't have enough jails and prisons to lock all of these people up.

Some would say that we should just build new prisons. Perhaps, but consider this: To build one prison cell costs about $100,000. To keep one inmate locked up for one year costs a minimum of $25,000. If we skipped the users of illicit drugs and were going to lock up just the drug dealers, where would we get the money? Assume that there are a half million dealers (and there likely are more) and all were arrested. If we put two dealers in a cell, 250,000 new cells would run $25 billion. It would then cost another $12 billion a year to keep those dealers in prison.

Lurking in back of a "lock-'em-up" approach is the assumption that to jail a dealer is to eliminate that dealer's drug deals. The reality is quite different. An arrest of a dealer is a business opportunity for would-be dealers, who are waiting eagerly in line to take over vacated territory. Get rid of one dealer, and two fight to take his or her place.

Consider also what we reviewed earlier, that get-tough policies fuel black markets. They unintentionally produce fountains of profits for those who are willing to take the risk, for both independent entrepreneurs and for organized crime. This hard reality became visible when we made drinking alcohol a criminal act. An underground network sprang up immediately to keep that drug supply going. It is no different with other drugs as we can see with the huge amounts of money flowing to dealers of marijuana, cocaine, heroin. When a drug is criminalized, people who want that drug buy it from an underground network. To get the money to buy addictive drugs, which are made expensive by the criminal laws, the poor who are addicted prey on others. These latent dysfunctions of criminalizing drugs—the bankrolling of organized crime and an increase in muggings, burglaries, thefts, prostitution, and premature deaths—are they not worse than the original problem that the laws address?

Or you might want to consider the situation in other countries and the controversial drug policy suggested in the Global Glimpse box on the next page.

WHEN "REASONABLE" BACKFIRES. With illegal drugs so popular and attitudes so divergent, how can we ever develop a reasonable social policy? As functionalists stress, we must anticipate the unintended consequences of social policy. To discourage cigarette smoking, let's suppose that we raise taxes by, say, $3 more a pack. If we did so, as intended, cigarette smoking would decline. An unintended consequence, however, would be that crime would increase—that of smuggling cigarettes from Mexico and Canada. Even more serious, though, is that such a policy could have the *opposite* effect among teenagers. It might encourage more of them to smoke. I'm sure that you think I'm exaggerating, but an increase in smoking by teenagers is just what happened when lawmakers in Canada raised cigarette taxes (Izumi 1997). The huge black market in cigarettes that sprang up made it easier for teenagers to obtain cigarettes.

A Global Glimpse

DRUGS AND DRUG VIOLENCE: WHAT SHALL WE DO?

It was a typical night at El Sol y Sombra in Uruapan, a little town in Michoacan, Mexico. Some couples were dancing to Norteño, while others were flirting. As the drinks took effect, the problems of life receded.

The reverie was abruptly broken when several men burst into the night club, waving machine guns and shooting wildly into the air. The music stopped and the revelers, their alcohol-induced escape suddenly cut short, huddled against the walls. The men threw a garbage bag onto the middle of the emptied dance floor.

Five human heads rolled out, the eyes staring ghastly into space, the blood still dripping from the freshly severed necks.

"Now that's something you don't see every day," said a bartender at El Sol y Sombra when reporters talked to him later. "Very ugly."

That's an understatement, even here in Michoacan, where drug-related violence is an almost daily occurrence. The drug dealers have become so brazen that they kill even the police. They raided one police station with grenades and bazookas. In another town, after receiving death threats, eighteen of the thirty-two policemen resigned.

The drug dealers have also killed judges and prosecutors.

No longer are the drug dealers content to threaten rival dealers, or even to kill them—or the police or reporters who are getting too close. Cutting off heads and putting them on display sends a more impressive message.

And since some people, for whatever reason, might not get the message, the dealers have begun leaving notes alongside the heads.

At El Sol y Sombra, the note said, "The family does not kill for money. It does not kill women. It does not kill innocents. It kills only those who deserve to die. Everyone should know, this is divine justice."

"The family" ("La familia") is the term this group has given itself.

At another location, this note accompanied more severed heads: "See. Hear. Shut Up. If you want to stay alive."

The nightclub in Uruapan where the heads were dumped onto the dance floor.

Not surprisingly, investigators are finding it difficult to locate anyone who has seen or heard anything.

If the drug dealers had their way, they would control Mexico. Some say they just about do so now. This, of course, is an exaggeration, but drug money and corruption go hand in hand. Throughout Mexico, corruption has overtaken both the police and politicians. According to some observers, drug corruption has reached into the presidential palace—at least in previous administrations.

In Colombia, drug dealers became so brazen in the 1990s that they assassinated three presidential candidates. Dealers are still powerful there, forging alliances with revolutionaries, paying for protection in the areas the rebels control so they can process cocaine without interruption. Despite massive antidrug efforts by the Colombian government, financed by the United States, Colombia accounts for about 80 percent of the world's cocaine—about 90 percent of the cocaine that flows into the United States.

FOR YOUR CONSIDERATION

What do you think can be done to solve this problem? The drug violence is fueled by a war over its tremendous profits. Some suggest that the most effective way to eliminate drug violence is to strike the problem at its root by making drugs legal. Removing the profits in illegal drugs would cause the problem to disappear overnight. At the same time, legalization would eliminate the thousands upon thousands of arrests for drug dealing and possession.

On the one hand, what reasons can you offer against the legalization of drugs, letting adults put whatever substances they want into their body? On the other hand, if the drugs that are now illegal were made legal, what social problems do you think this would produce?

Based on "Colombia" 2006; McKinley 2006a, 2006b; MicKinley and Lacey 2006 2006c.

Deciding Social Policy

BANNING ADVERTISING. An adequate social policy could begin by banning *all* advertising for drugs known to be harmful. Nicotine is certainly a case in point. As it now stands, when young people open magazines and newspapers, they are greeted by smiling, happy, healthy young people beckoning them to join their carefree lifestyle of pleasurable smoking. If all advertising for cigarettes and tobacco products were eliminated, this source of enticement would be removed.

DRUG EDUCATION. An adequate social policy must also include drug education that is based on scientific studies. Such a program would require that we determine *both* the beneficial and the harmful effects of drugs—and that we communicate those findings, even if they go against our biases. Our own values concerning "good" or "bad" drugs should be irrelevant. For example, if scientific evidence shows that marijuana is safer than tobacco, which appears to be the case, then, like it or not, we need to communicate that information. We cannot shy away from communicating either the good or the bad effects of marijuana just because we have a bias for or against this drug. This same principle applies to all drugs.

Drug education is a two-edged sword. On the one hand, students who are given information about drugs use drugs in greater moderation. On the other hand, giving students information piques their curiosity, and more of them use drugs (Blum et al. 1976; Levine 1986). More drug use, but in greater moderation, then, is what we can expect from formal drug education programs. I stress formal, because an informal drug education program is already at work—the one that comes from the streets and is filled with misinformation. The alternative, no formal drug education, produces two extremes: fewer people using drugs, but heavier drug use by those who do. In sum, although drug education stimulates interest in drugs, it also cuts down on their abuse. If the purpose of drug education is to decrease drug *use,* it is missing the mark; if its purpose is to decrease drug *abuse,* it is on target.

DRUG ADDICTION. We also need an adequate social policy to deal with drug addiction. Locking up addicted people fails to break addiction, for upon release most of them go back to their drugs. A successful program cannot focus on addiction as though addicts live in a social vacuum. It must take into account the background factors of an addict's life. Addiction is often part of subcultural orientations and deprivations— often poverty, unemployment, dropping out of school, hopelessness, despair, and a bleak future. To reflect the life realities of drug abusers, drug programs must take multiple approaches.

People who become drug dependent are strongly motivated to continue their drug use. With cigarettes available legally, nicotine addicts have no difficulty obtaining their drug. Tobacco is available in any community, and tobacco crops are even subsidized by the Department of Agriculture. With the average cost of supporting a nicotine habit running about $1,000 or so a year, cigarette addicts do not mug, steal, or kill to obtain their drug. In contrast, heroin and cocaine are illegal, their cost is considerably higher, and many of their users are involved in crime.

A successful drug addiction program, then, might include free or very cheap drugs. For example, heroin addicts could be prescribed heroin by physicians who would treat them as patients. As Arnold Trebach (1987:369) put it:

> The availability of prescribed heroin would mean that multitudes of addicts would be able to function as decent law-abiding citizens for the first time in years. Their health should be much improved because their drugs would be clean and measured in labeled dosages. The number of crimes they commit should drop dramatically. By implication, addicts to other narcotics, such as morphine and codeine, would also reap the same benefits. They would be eligible to receive maintenance doses of the drugs on which they are dependent. Hordes of potential crime victims would, accordingly, be denied the pleasure.

Methadone maintenance is a controversial treatment for heroin addiction. At least, it passes for treatment. Methadone maintenance simply replaces an illegal narcotic with a legal one. "Treatment" consists of merely transferring addiction from one drug to another.

Such a policy would break the addicts' dependence on the black market, remove a major source of profit for organized crime, and eliminate the need for addicts to prey on others. If the program provided only such benefits, it would be a night-and-day improvement over the present situation, but still needed would be a three-pronged attack: counseling for personal problems, practical help in seeking and maintaining employment, and clinical services for those who want to end their addiction.

Methadone maintenance helps us to understand some of the problems of developing rational social policies for dealing with drug addiction. Methadone, a synthetic narcotic that is in itself addicting, was developed by the Germans during World War II as a painkiller for wounded soldiers (Wren 1998). Today, given orally in medically supervised clinics, methadone is used to help break addiction to heroin. This transfers addiction from an illegal drug, heroin, to a legal drug, methadone.

Why transfer someone's addiction from one narcotic to another? Not needing heroin, the addicts are no longer dependent on a black market, freeing them from what they perceive as the need to commit crimes to support their expensive addiction. But if we are going to supply drugs to addicts, why not simply give them the narcotic to which they already are addicted? Obviously, the answer goes back to the social reputation of drugs with which this chapter opened. The social equation reads: The narcotic heroin is evil; the narcotic methadone is good.

The methadone maintenance program was supposed to have been backed up by counseling and jobs. For budgetary reasons, however, at most locations these elements were stripped from the program. Only the "bare bones" of the original plan are left—giving methadone to addicts. This failing alerts us to a danger of social policy: Politicians who fund a program may not see it in the same way as do the professionals who designed it. If politicians and bureaucrats scuttle essentials in order to cut costs, they dismantle the original program in all but name.

ALCOHOLICS ANONYMOUS. Alcoholics Anonymous (AA) is a successful program whose principles have been applied to other drug addictions. Cocaine Anonymous is an example of this application. The main principle of AA is that the program should be directed and staffed by people who have experienced the addiction themselves—and have overcome it. They know firsthand what the addicts are going through. Intimately familiar with the addicts' orientations, they can talk their language on a "gut level."

Alcoholics Anonymous was started in 1935 in Akron, Ohio, by two alcoholics. It is now a worldwide organization of 100,000 local groups, numbering about 2 million members in 150 countries ("AA Fact File," 2004). The essentials of Alcoholics Anonymous are summarized in what this group calls The Twelve Steps. To overcome addiction to alcohol, you must

1. Admit that you are powerless over alcohol and your life has become unmanageable.
2. Believe that a Power greater than yourself can help restore you to wholeness.
3. Make a decision to turn your will and life over to God, as you understand God.
4. Make an honest moral inventory of yourself.
5. Admit to God, yourself, and another human being exactly what you have done wrong.
6. Be ready to work with God to remove your defects of character.
7. Ask God to remove your shortcomings.
8. Make a list of every person you have harmed and be willing to make amends to them.
9. Make amends whenever possible, except where it would harm them or others.
10. Continue to take personal inventory, and promptly admit your wrongs.
11. Through prayer and meditation, seek to improve your contact with God, as you understand God, praying for knowledge of God's will for yourself and the power to carry it out.
12. Have a spiritual awakening as a result of these steps; try to carry this message to other alcoholics; and practice these principles in all your dealings with others.

To put these steps into practice, members meet weekly with others who used to have alcohol problems or who are struggling to overcome them. From their fellow members, they draw encouragement to continue their abstinence. They also carry the telephone number of "someone who has been through it." They can call this person at any hour for personal support in handling a crisis without turning to alcohol.

PRINCIPLES OF EFFECTIVE SOCIAL POLICY. To be effective, a social policy must match the subculture of its target group. A policy must be geared to the group members' age, race-ethnicity, gender, and social class, as well as to the members' values, lifestyle, and problems. This means that programs for different groups must have different emphases. For example, a program that is successful with middle-class youth will fail if it is transferred without modification to inner-city youth.

Social policies must also match general cultural values, such as the belief in individual rights. Applied to social policy, this value means the right of people to abuse their bodies with drugs they choose. Regardless of how we may feel about the abuse, it seems that people have the right to consume substances that you and I may choose not to. Another primary value in our culture is that people work productively. One reason that *some* drugs used for pleasure are viewed negatively is the fear that individuals will drop out, live off the efforts of others, and not take care of themselves or contribute to society. To address these concerns, drug programs must encourage active participation in our economic system. Encouragement by itself is mere words. To be effective, drug programs should offer an alternative lifestyle and reward conventional behavior (Faupel and Klockars 1987). This means that addicts need to be integrated into a community of people where "straight" values are dominant, including social networks that value employment and nonexploitive relationships.

Finally, if drug education is to be successful, it is essential that it be related to *the realities of the users*. Nonusers' ideas about morality and the risks of using drugs are not the same as those of users. Consider two extremes from PCP. To stress that violence is associated with PCP is not effective if the users do not see violence as a problem. Yet to emphasize a milder consequence of PCP—that it produces a foggy, forgetful condition—can be effective if that is what the users experience and fear (Feldman 1985:5). To try to impose an outside reality onto users is to ensure failure.

A POSSIBLE NATIONAL GOAL. Owing to our backgrounds, all of us have biases. We all hold strong opinions about addicts and drugs, which makes it difficult to develop sound social policy. Legislators, for example, pass laws designed to punish the "evil" of drug use, "evil" as defined from their perspective. Because we see the world from different perspectives, no social policy can satisfy everyone, and all social policies are bound to displease many. You may have found some of the policies I suggested in this chapter to be unreasonable, perhaps even ridiculous, while others see those same policies as reasonable and desirable. Despite these many differences, because ours is a drug-using society, it seems that a rational goal would be to teach people to *use* drugs sensibly and thus to decrease the amount of drug *abuse*. This principle would apply to all drugs—not just to those that match *our* ideas of "good" drugs.

The Future of the Problem

In light of the pro-drug orientation of Americans, we can expect drug use to remain high. Because drugs are subject to fads, as some drugs decrease in popularity, others will become more popular. As a young clientele rushes to the latest high, we can expect moral entrepreneurs to alarm the public, to alert them that some particular drug is a threat to dominant values, in the extreme perhaps even threatening the existence of society itself. Alarms over different drugs, then, will be sounded from time to time.

With advances in chemistry, a new generation of drugs will appear. Designed to work only on particular receptors of the brain, these drugs will be more precise in their effects. The market for these drugs will be high, because many people prefer to take drugs to cope with the rigors of modern life rather than to work on solving their problems. This ready market will stimulate the demand for drugs, putting even greater pressure on physicians to become "drug dispensers."

The social reputations of drugs will continue to influence people's lives profoundly. Some drugs will remain in disrepute, their users disgraced and stigmatized. Other drugs will maintain their social approval. Advertised in glossy magazines and in other media, their use will continue to be an accepted part of social life.

From the standpoint of functionalism, to protect their jobs and enhance their positions, we can expect drug enforcement agents to try to keep many substances illegal. To do this, they will work with legislators and government agencies to influence drug legislation and policy. In 2006, the Federal Drug Administration did just this. Although a panel of scientists had examined the evidence regarding the medical uses of marijuana and made recommendations for this drug's limited medical use, the FDA rejected the panel's findings (Harris 2006).

The refusal to take an unbiased look at the potential of the medical use of marijuana, or to fund such research, accompanied by the rigid insistence that marijuana is an evil plant that by definition can have no redeeming virtue helps keep the black market alive and profitable. This closed attitude by officials who determine social policy will continue to produce a self-fulfilling prophecy: The resulting crimes, especially the headline-producing violence, will continue to make the drug enforcement establishment seem vital for society. *Organized crime and drug enforcement agents*, then, sharing as they do a mutual interest in keeping drugs illegal, will remain partners, although reluctant symbiotic ones.

If we view ourselves as the "good" people and "them" as "evil others" in our midst (people who don't really belong in our society), then drug abusers will continue to be treated harshly. We good people can turn a blind eye to what happens to them, for the perception of their "evilness" and "strangeness" severs mutual identity, ultimately denying them even basic humanity. This perception impedes the development of adequate social policy, not only for drug abusers but also for the mentally ill and others who violate middle-class standards of behavior. From such attitudes flow totalitarianism, the curtailment of people's rights, and the treatment of others as subhumans—all for the sake of maintaining a middle-class view of the world. Lurking in the shadows of social policy, this threat needs to be brought into the light where it can be examined thoroughly.

SUMMARY AND REVIEW

1. What constitutes *drug abuse* is a matter of social definition. What is considered drug use at one time or in one society may be considered drug abuse at another time or in another society. From the historical record, we know that drug use and abuse are ancient.

2. Americans have a strong pro-drug orientation, although they consider some drugs to be disreputable and those who use them to be part of a social problem. People generally consider the particular drugs that they use to not be part of a social problem.

3. A major problem in drug abuse is *addiction*— becoming dependent on a drug so that its absence creates the stress of withdrawal. One of the most highly addicting drugs is nicotine. Heroin appears to be less addicting than previously thought.

4. Symbolic interactionists emphasize the social meanings of drugs. Prohibition, for example, has been analyzed as a symbolic crusade: As the old order lost political control, it attempted to dominate society morally by wrapping itself in abstinence (morality) and associating drunkenness (immorality) with the newcomers.

5. In examining the functions and dysfunctions of drugs, functionalists stress not just that legal drugs are functional for the medical profession, their patients, and those who manufacture and sell these drugs, but also that illegal drugs are functional for their users, manufacturers (or growers), and distributors. The dysfunctions of drugs include problems with the law and abuse that harms people physically and socially. A major latent function of illegal drugs is to support agents of social control.

6. Conflict theorists stress how the criminalization of drugs is related to power. Opium, for example, was made illegal in an attempt to overcome the economic threat that Chinese immigrants posed to white workers. Similarly, marijuana legislation was directed against the Mexican working class in the United States. Some see the heroin trade as a means of defusing revolutionary potential.

7. Pharmaceutical companies, with the cooperation of the medical profession, play a central role in getting Americans to define drugs as a *the way* to relieve the stresses of everyday life. Defining problems of living as medical matters, known as *the medicalization of human problems,* includes defining unruly children as in need of medication.

8. The same drug has different effects on different people and on the same person at different times. These differences are due to characteristics of the drug, the individual who is taking it, and the setting in which it is taken. Especially significant are the user's expectations.

9. Of all the drugs that Americans use, nicotine causes the most harm. Alcohol abuse, which destroys vital body organs, also causes *fetal alcohol syndrome.* The social setting in which people learn to drink influences their chances of becoming problem drinkers. We need more studies to determine the effects of marijuana and other drugs. Cocaine's social history illustrates how a drug's reputation depends on the people with whom it is associated.

10. Although addicting to many people, in and of themselves the narcotics do not cause crime or destroy people's work incentive or health. Street addicts deal with a black market that demands high prices and motivates them to commit predatory crimes. Street addicts buy drugs whose purity is far from guaranteed—and suffer the consequences. In contrast, physician narcotic addicts maintain normal lives because they need not deal with a black market and are able to obtain pure drugs.

11. Developing an adequate social policy is difficult because drugs arouse strong emotions and biases. At a minimum, an adequate social policy would involve drug education that presents scientific findings honestly, whether they are favorable or unfavorable to any particular drug. It would also break the addicts' dependence on a black market and provide help for their multiple problems. Alcoholics Anonymous appears to be a model recovery program.

12. We can anticipate that the future will bring new drugs from pharmaceutical companies, continuation of the symbiotic partnership between law enforcement agents and drug dealers based on their shared interests, and social policies that protect the users of favored drugs and penalize the users of those in disfavor.

KEY TERMS

Addiction, 89
Alcoholic, 101
Amotivational syndrome, 109
Attention deficit-hyperactivity disorder, 97
Craving, 89

Drug, 88
Drug abuse, 85
Drug addiction, 89
Fetal alcohol syndrome, 103
Fetal narcotic syndrome, 117

Medicalization of human problems, 96
Methadone maintenance, 125
Moral entrepreneur, 92
Psychological dependence, 90
Withdrawal, 89

1. Which perspective—symbolic interactionism, functionalism, or conflict theory—do you think best explains drug policies in the United States? Why?
2. If women can be prosecuted for child abuse for taking drugs during pregnancy, does it follow that they should also be prosecuted for failure to attend prenatal classes or for not eating properly during pregnancy? How about for smoking cigarettes? Why or why not?
3. If you had the power to decide which drugs should be legal and which should not, what criteria would you use in making your decision?

CHAPTER 5

Violence in Society: Rape and Murder

There wasn't much for teenagers to do in Littleton, Colorado. Not much happened in this quiet town of 35,000, a middle-class suburb southwest of Denver. To get attention, some of the high school kids wore black trench coats and black shirts with swastikas. They called themselves the "Trenchcoat Mafia" and threw around a few phrases in German.

"Just kids. They'll grow out of it," was the adults' typical response. "We all went through stages."

The Trenchcoat Mafia had their own table in the cafeteria and their group picture in the yearbook. The caption: "Who says we're different? Insanity's healthy. . . . Stay alive, stay different, stay crazy! Oh, and stay away from CREAM SODA!!"

Just another high school group: jocks, preps, cheerleaders, dorks, Goths, punks, and gamers. Every school has them.

The jocks despised the Trenchcoat Mafia. They threw them into lockers and called them scumbags, faggots, and inbreeds. They threw rocks and bottles at them from passing cars.

Two seniors, Eric Harris and Dylan Klebold, honors students and members of the Trenchcoat Mafia, talked about killing their classmates, especially the jocks. Eric even had his own Web page, where he named those he wanted to kill and the methods he would like to use to kill them. As a class project, Eric and Dylan made a video in which they pretended to kill the classmates

They killed twelve of their fellow students.

they didn't like. Just talk. But as the killings on *Doom*, the video game they loved, no longer satisfied, the boys hatched a plan for real killing. It was risky. Maybe they would survive, maybe not. But if not, they would go out in a blaze of glory. April 20, Hitler's birthday, would be perfect.

The carnage left Columbine High School seared into the national memory. TV viewers switched on their sets and found that a quiet Tuesday afternoon had been interrupted by stunning events. The drama was high as SWAT teams moved in and cautiously began to assess the situation. Bodies lay strewn on sidewalks. No one knew how many were dead inside the school. The nation watched transfixed as events unfolded.

As bombs went off and shots rang out, students fled in terror. Some hid in closets; others crawled under tables. Harris and Klebold went from room to room in search of victims. In the library, they found several students hiding under a table. "Do you believe in God?" asked one of the shooters. "Yes," replied Cassie Bernall. "There is no God," the gunman retorted, as he placed a gun against her head and squeezed the trigger.

Before the boys turned their guns on themselves, they killed twelve of their fellow students and one teacher. They wounded another twenty-three students.

Based on Bai 1999; Gibbs 1999.

The Problem in Sociological Perspective

Violence grabs our attention, whether we see it on the street or on television. The media are filled with accounts of violence, their audiences enraptured with the sordid details of the latest rape or murder. The more gruesome the violence, the greater the attention. In this chapter, we will examine violence from many angles. Let's begin with an overview of the sociological perspective on violence.

The Sociological Perspective on Violence

Violence, the use of force to injure people or to destroy their property, goes far beyond individual tendencies or what some might term "violent personalities." Violence involves society itself. Some societies encourage violence, whereas others discourage it. As a result, some societies have high rates of violence, and others have low rates. Sociologists, then, don't focus on personality or on individual tendencies. Rather, *the sociological question of violence is,* What is it about a society that increases or decreases the likelihood of violence? Throughout this chapter, we shall grapple with this central question.

TYPES OF VIOLENCE. Sociologists divide violence into two major types: individual violence and group violence. **Individual** (or **personal**) **violence** consists of one person physically attacking others or destroying their property. **Group** (or **collective**) **violence** consists of two or more people doing these same things. Sociologists divide group violence into three types.

1. **Situational group violence** is unplanned and spontaneous. Something in the situation stimulates or triggers the violence. An example is a brawl among hockey players.
2. **Organized group violence** is planned, but unauthorized, like the school shooting in our opening vignette or acts committed by terrorists.
3. **Institutionalized group violence** is violence carried out by agents of the government, such as an army at war or the SWAT team responding to the shootings at Columbine High School.

Rape and murder, the focus of this chapter, can take any of these forms of violence. Let's see how these types apply to rape. Rape usually takes the form of individual violence, for most victims are raped by an individual. If a rape victim is attacked by two or more men, however, it is group violence. (The common term is "gang rape.") If two or more men happen to see a woman alone and think, "Why not? We can get away with it," it is situational group violence. In contrast, if two or more men plan a rape, it is organized group violence. Finally, if there is a mass rape by soldiers after they take over a territory, it is institutionalized group violence.

The Scope of the Problem

Let's see how extensive rape and murder are. In this brief overview, we will compare the rates of rape and murder in the United States with rates in other parts of the world. First, let's distinguish between violence as a personal and as a social problem.

What Makes Violence a Social Problem?

If two people get into a fight and end up in the hospital, that is their *personal* problem. The same is true if a woman, enraged at discovering her husband with a lover, shoots them to death. And the same is true if a man rapes a woman. Although these examples involve severe, bitter violence, they portray only objective conditions. To be a *social* problem, violence must also arouse widespread subjective concerns. Many people must see the violence as reducing their quality of life and want something to be done about it.

THE SUBJECTIVE DIMENSION OF VIOLENCE. Violence has become a social problem in the United States, but it is important to note that it is not the amount of violence (an objective condition) that makes violence a social problem. Rather, *subjective concerns* about violence are widespread. Parents worry about their kids walking to school. Women feel vulnerable as they get on elevators or as they walk alone at night from their classrooms to their cars. They feel relief when they get inside their cars—after they've shut and locked their car doors. Fear of violence is not spread evenly throughout society. Table 5-1 on the next page shows that women are much more afraid than men of becoming victims of a violent crime. From this

TABLE 5-1 Are You Afraid to Walk Alone at Night?[1]

	1980 Yes	1980 No	1990 Yes	1990 No	2000 Yes	2000 No	2002[2] Yes	2002[2] No
SEX								
Male	21%	79%	19%	81%	23%	76%	19%	81%
Female	60%	39%	58%	41%	52%	47%	47%	52%
RACE-ETHNICITY[3]								
White	42%	58%	39%	60%	36%	61%	30%	70%
Black/other	52%	47%	50%	48%	45%	54%	41%	58%
AGE								
18–20 years	45%	54%	43%	5%7	40%	58%	41%	59%
21–29 years	41%	59%	33%	65%	41%	58%	30%	70%
30–49 years	39%	60%	38%	62%	36%	63%	27%	72%
50 years and over	47%	52%	48%	51%	41%	58%	37%	63%
EDUCATION								
College	42%	58%	39%	60%	38%	61%	31%	69%
High school graduate	44%	55%	41%	58%	38%	61%	34%	64%
Less than high school graduate	42%	57%	51%	48%	44%	54%	32%	67%
INCOME								
$50,000 and over	NA	NA	NA	NA	28%	71%	22%	76%
$30,000 to $49,999	NA	NA	NA	NA	34%	66%	32%	68%
$20,000 to $29,999	NA	NA	NA	NA	42%	58%	37%	62%
Under $20,000	NA	NA	NA	NA	50%	48%	41%	57%
OCCUPATION								
Professional/business	42%	58%	36%	63%	34%	65%	31%	69%
Clerical/support	53%	46%	56%	42%	54%	45%	46%	54%
Manual/service	38%	62%	38%	61%	37%	62%	26%	74%
Farming/agricultural	15%	82%	28%	72%	31%	69%	25%	75%
REGION								
Northeast	47%	53%	40%	59%	37%	62%	35%	65%
Midwest	33%	66%	36%	64%	34%	64%	23%	77%
South	44%	55%	46%	52%	42%	57%	33%	65%
West	52%	48%	41%	58%	42%	57%	38%	62%
RELIGION								
Protestant	43%	56%	43%	56%	39%	59%	31%	69%
Catholic	45%	55%	38%	61%	41%	58%	35%	65%
Jewish	50%	50%	61%	39%	36%	64%	60%	40%
None	38%	62%	32%	64%	35%	64%	30%	70%
POLITICS								
Republican	41%	57%	41%	58%	33%	66%	30%	70%
Democrat	46%	54%	47%	52%	43%	56%	39%	61%
Independent	41%	59%	35%	64%	39%	59%	28%	72%

Source: Sourcebook of Criminal Justice Statistics 2005:Table 2-37.

[1]The question that interviewers asked nationally representative samples of Americans was "Is there any area right around here—that is, within a mile—where you would be afraid to walk alone at night?"

[2]Latest year available.

[3]These two categories were used when this research was first done in the 1960s. As inadequate as these categories are, researchers still use them.

With our high rates of violence, feelings of vulnerability and fear are common. Fear is not distributed evenly throughout society, but is related to income, age, gender, and race-ethnicity. The reasons for these variables are discussed in the text.

table, you can also see that the elderly are more fearful than younger people. Note how fear recedes as income increases—largely because people with higher incomes live in "better" (read, more affluent and less violent) neighborhoods. Some of these neighborhoods are even guarded by gates and sentries.

Note that fear of violence has dropped in recent years. This is due to an accurate perception, that today's streets are safer than they used to be. Let's look at this objective dimension of violence.

THE OBJECTIVE DIMENSION OF VIOLENCE. As you can see from Figure 5-1 on the next page, violent crime in the United States has undergone remarkable changes. From the 1960s to 1991, not only did the amount of violence increase, but so did the **rate of violence,** the number of violent crimes for each 100,000 Americans. If over a ten-year period our population increases 20 percent and rape and murder also increase 20 percent, the rate would remain unchanged. There would be more rape and murder, but the increase would simply have kept pace with the larger numbers of people. One's chances of being raped or murdered would be unchanged.

As you can see from Figure 5-1, however, violent crimes did not just keep pace with the growth of the U.S. population. In just twelve years, from 1968 to 1980, the rate of violent crimes *doubled,* soaring from 300 to 600 violent crimes per 100,000 people. This means that in 1980 one's chances of being a victim of violent crime were twice what they were in 1968. If the U.S. population had not increased by a single person, there still would have been twice as many violent crimes in 1980 as there were in 1968. As you can see, the rate then dipped slightly, but again turned sharply upward, reaching its peak in 1991. From there, the rate began to drop steadily. Today's rate of murder, rape, robbery, and aggravated assault is only two-thirds of what it was in 1991. Despite this welcome decrease, the rate of violent crime remains much higher than it was in 1968.

Some people, however, perceive the United States as more dangerous than it used to be. This, too, is true. As you can see, it all depends on what years you compare. Our streets are more dangerous today than they were in 1968—but they are much safer than they were ten or fifteen years ago.

No matter how you look at it, however, we still have a *lot* of violent crime. Look at Figure 5-2 on the next page. On average, 10 women are raped every hour. This comes to 240 women every day, 1,700 a week, 7,000 a month. Every half minute someone tries to injure someone else (aggravated assault); and every half hour an American dies from these

FIGURE 5-1 The Rate of Violence

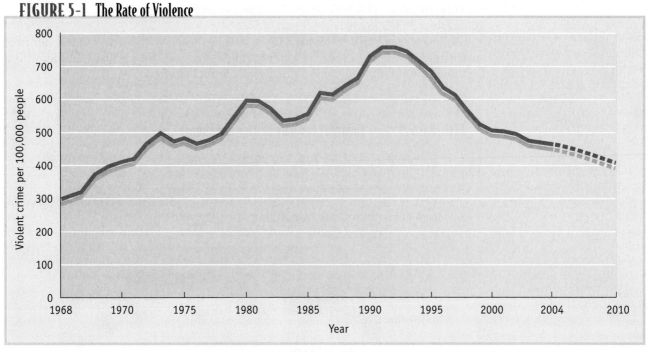

Source: By the author. Based on various editions of *FBI Uniform Crime Reports,* including 1997, 2002, and 2006.

attacks (homicide or murder). As you can see we are not talking about a fistfight here and there, an occasional rape, or isolated incidents of spouses turning on one another.

From your knowledge of U.S. society, you know that social location makes a difference in people's chances of being a victim of violence. People put this knowledge to practical use. They keep it in mind when they hunt for apartments and houses and when they choose schools for their children. But few people know that social location makes this much difference: If you live in Washington, D.C., your chances of getting murdered are forty-four times higher than if you live in Maine or South Dakota. African American males are *seven* times more likely than white males to be murdered. Similarly, African American females are more than *three* times as likely as white females to be homicide victims. Another factor is age: Those least likely to be murdered are the elderly and children through the

FIGURE 5-2 The Clock of Violence

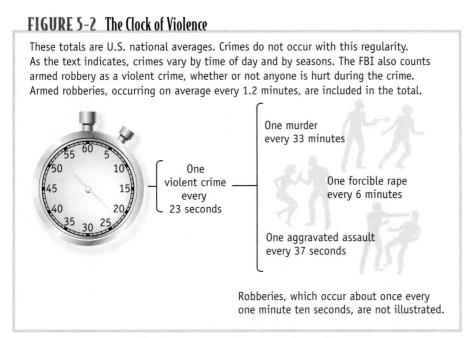

These totals are U.S. national averages. Crimes do not occur with this regularity. As the text indicates, crimes vary by time of day and by seasons. The FBI also counts armed robbery as a violent crime, whether or not anyone is hurt during the crime. Armed robberies, occurring on average every 1.2 minutes, are included in the total.

One violent crime every 23 seconds

One murder every 33 minutes

One forcible rape every 6 minutes

One aggravated assault every 37 seconds

Robberies, which occur about once every one minute ten seconds, are not illustrated.

Source: FBI Uniform Crime Reports 2006.

age of 16; those most likely to be murdered are people in their early 20s (*Statistical Abstract* 2006:Tables 293, 298, 301).

Although the United States has a lot of violence, as Figure 5-3 below shows, our rates are far from the highest in the world. From this figure, you can see that countries with a high murder rate also tend to have a high rape rate and vice versa.

FIGURE 5-3 How Countries Compare in Rape and Murder

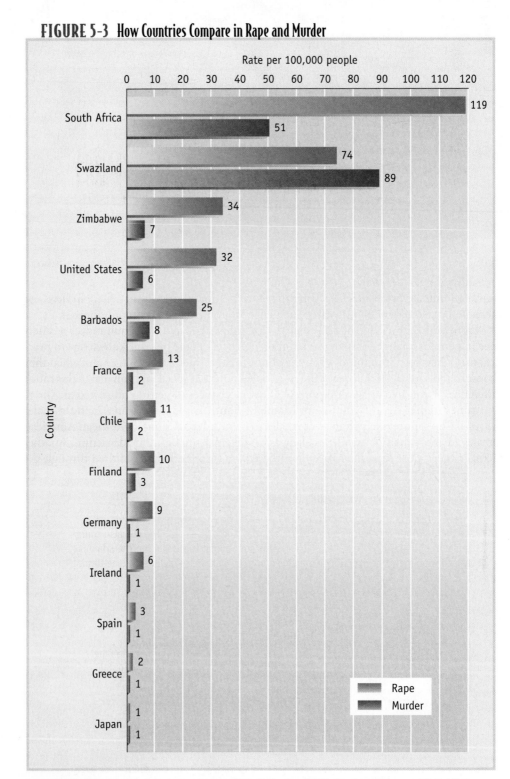

Source: By the author, based on these sources. For rape: "Cross National . . ." 2004, for all countries, except United States, which is from *Statistical Abstract of the United States* 2006:Table 302. For murder: *United Nations Surveys . . ."* 2004, for all countries, except United States, which is from *Statistical Abstract of the United States* 2006:Table 300.

Don't take the totals shown on Figure 5-3 as "facts." The way these statistics are compiled makes them subject to so much error that, at best, these numbers merely *indicate* that one country has more or less violence than another. Comparing rape, for example, is notoriously difficult for several reasons. Not only do some countries keep sloppy records, but also the definition of rape changes from one country to another. Even within the United States, not all states use the same definition. In addition, the reported rates in Islamic countries are so unreliable that I have not even included them on Figure 5-3. The official rape rates of these countries don't even come close to reality. Consider Pakistan, which reports an impossible rate of 0.04 per 100,000 people. This is 4 per million. Only a few Pakistani women report their rapes—why? If the accused is found not guilty of rape, this makes the woman automatically guilty of a crime—that of adultery if married or fornication if not married ("Cross National . . ." 2004). A Pakistani woman guilty of adultery can be stoned to death. To say the least, this is a rather strong deterrent to reporting this crime.

Let's look at the theories that social scientists have developed to explain violence.

Looking at the Problem Theoretically

Before we look at violence from the perspectives that sociology offers, let's examine some of the theories developed in other academic disciplines.

Nonsociological Theories

BIOLOGICAL EXPLANATIONS. In the 1800s, Cesare Lombroso (1835–1909), an Italian physician, treated thousands of prisoners. It struck him that they looked different from his regular patients. Lombroso (1911) concluded that violent people (and other criminals) are *atavistic;* that is, they are biological throwbacks to an earlier period when humanity was violent and primitive. His evidence was their looks: They have lower foreheads, larger ears, and receding chins.

Anthropologist Konrad Lorenz (1966) also said that evolution is the key to violence, but his explanation went like this. We humans, he said, are biologically ill-equipped for killing: We don't have claws, slashing teeth, or great strength. Because of this, we did not develop an inhibitory mechanism—as did dogs, wolves, and baboons—that stops violence when an enemy becomes submissive. Because we have a powerful intellect, however, we learned to make weapons. Our lack of a blocking mechanism and the availability of weapons produce terrible violence. In our anger or desire to dominate, we use our weapons to destroy one another. As Lionel Tiger and Robin Fox (1971:210) remarked, if baboons had hand grenades, few baboons would be left in Africa.

Others have suggested a variety of biological factors as the cause of violence—from the shape of the skull (phrenology) to hormonal imbalance and even faulty neurotransmitters (George et al. 2006). A theory that was taken seriously for a time was proposed by anthropologist Earnest Hooton (1939), who concluded that body type is the key to understanding violence: Tall, thin men, he said, tend to be the killers, and short, heavy men the rapists. A more recent biological explanation of violence is the XYY chromosome theory: Most men have an X and a Y chromosome; some men, however, have an extra Y chromosome, which supposedly propels them toward violence. Some theorists propose a Darwinian explanation. Those humans that survived prehistorical times were the violent ones, and these select few passed to their children genes that predispose us to violence. As a result, violence is part of our nature.

Psychologist John Dollard (Dollard et al. 1939/1961), who also stressed that violence is built into our nature, proposed a **frustration-aggression** theory of violence. As you know, you feel frustrated when you want something and you can't get it. Dollard conducted a series of experiments on how people whose goals are blocked relieve their frustration by striking out at others. Often we strike out in mild ways, such as telling someone off, but sometimes we strike out violently.

PSYCHOLOGICAL THEORIES. Some psychologists point to learning as the cause of violence. Following the lead of B. F. Skinner (1948, 1953, 1971), they stress that if someone is rewarded ("reinforced," as they call it), that person will tend to be violent again. The "reward" (or "reinforcement") can be any gain—consumables such as candy or food, or social symbols such as money, status, or even a smile. For a rapist, the reward can be sex and power. For a killer, the reward might be revenge, power, or satisfaction at exterminating an enemy. Other psychologists emphasize that violence is learned through **modeling,** copying another person's behavior. In a classic study, psychologists Albert Bandura and R. H. Walters (1963) found that children who see others hitting dolls or pounding on furniture tend to do the same things themselves. Children who have not seen this sort of behavior are less likely to perform it.

THE SOCIOLOGICAL APPROACH TO UNDERSTANDING VIOLENCE. Sociologists are not impressed by theories that look inside people, but they do acknowledge the value of explanations that stress factors in the environment, such as frustration-aggression and modeling. Rather than looking for violence-inducing characteristics *within* people, such as chromosomes and inhibitory mechanisms, sociologists focus on matters *outside* people. They examine how *social life* shapes and encourages—or discourages—violence. For example, in one society, violence may be channeled into approved forms, such as the social roles of warrior, boxer, or football player. Other societies, in contrast, may downplay violence and develop mechanisms to ensure that it rarely occurs.

Let's apply our three sociological perspectives to violence. In doing so, let's try to understand why males are more likely than females to be violent and why violence is higher among members of the working or lower classes.

Symbolic Interactionism

Why do people kill? Consider what a detective on the Dallas police force said back in the 1960s:

> Murders result from little ol' arguments over nothing at all. . . . Tempers flare. A fight starts, and somebody gets stabbed or shot. I've worked on cases where the principals had been arguing over a 10 cent record on a juke box, or over a dollar gambling debt from a dice game. (Mulvihill et al. 1969:230)

EDWIN SUTHERLAND: DIFFERENTIAL ASSOCIATION. People still kill over "little" things. Symbolic interactionists have developed two theories that help us to understand why. In the first, Edwin Sutherland (1947) stressed that people learn criminal behavior by interacting with others. In its simplest form, Sutherland's theory goes like this: People who associate with lawbreakers are more likely to learn to break the law than are people who associate with those who follow the law. To refer to this basic principle, Sutherland used the term **differential association**—that is, the lawbreakers and law-abiders associate with different people or groups.

Although Sutherland developed his theory to explain lawbreaking, we can apply its five basic points to violence:

1. People learn violence by interacting with others, primarily in intimate relationships.
2. People learn not only techniques for doing violence but also attitudes, motives, drives, and rationalizations about violence.
3. People use violence because they learn more attitudes (or definitions) that are favorable to using violence than they learn attitudes (or definitions) that are unfavorable to using violence. (Sutherland called this an *excess of definitions.*)
4. The most significant interactions in which people learn violence are those that take place earliest in life and those that are the most frequent, endure the longest, and are the most emotional or meaningful.

5. The mechanisms for learning violence are the same as those for learning anything else, including nonviolent or cooperative behavior.

MARVIN WOLFGANG: SUBCULTURES OF VIOLENCE. A second theory, **subcultural theory,** complements differential association. In a nutshell, this theory says that people who grow up in a subculture that approves of violent behavior have a high chance of learning to be violent. Sociologist Marvin Wolfgang wanted to know why the homicide rate was high among lower-class African American males. In a classic study (1958), Wolfgang examined the murders that occurred in Philadelphia from 1948 through 1952. He also observed police interrogations.

Wolfgang found something significant: The men he studied connected a willingness to be violent with honor and manliness. They viewed insults as challenges to their manliness, and violence as the appropriate response. Situations that others might perceive as trivial were *not* trivial to them. Anyone who backed down from a confrontation (even if it was about that dollar gambling debt in the quote from the Dallas detective) was seen as less than a real man. If he backed down, he risked being viewed as a "chicken" or a "girl"—and would be laughed at by others. With their "rep" at stake and "dissing" (insulting) common, a self-fulfilling prophecy was set in motion: The young men carried weapons for both protection and as a symbol of their manliness. As a result, violence among these men was common.

FITTING THE THEORIES TOGETHER. Differential association and subcultural theory fit together well. Subcultural theory stresses that violence is woven into the life of some groups, and differential association emphasizes that people in these groups learn that violence is a suitable response to many of the problems of life. To be "dissed" or insulted is not a trivial matter, even if it is over a minor gambling debt or a record on a jukebox. This situation puts the young man's reputation at stake, making the willingness to use violence necessary to keep a high standing among peers. Sociologist Elijah Anderson (1990, 2006) has documented how equating manliness with violence continues to be a feature of the everyday lives of African American inner-city young men. This explanation goes a long way toward explaining their high homicide rates.

Other groups also connect manliness and violence. In her participant observation of a Chicano gang, sociologist Ruth Horowitz (1983) found that these young men also equate manliness and honor with violence. In the Spotlight on Social Research on the next page, Horowitz shares insights that she gained from her research.

The situation is similar in the Mafia. Michael Franzese, a college-educated member of the Mafia, put it this way:

> If somebody were to dishonor my wife or my child, I would view it as something that I had to take into my own hands. I don't see why I have to go to the police. As a man, I would feel that it was an obligation that I had to take care of. And I would have to be prepared in my own mind to kill this guy. This is a basic principle. (Barnes and Shebar 1987)

IN SUM Based on their research, symbolic interactionists stress how "manliness" (or "masculinity") is associated with violence. As a result, we find more violence among males than females. Social class is also significant, for the working class incorporates more violence into its definitions of appropriate male behavior than do the middle and upper classes. As a result, year after year, across racial-ethnic lines and in every region of the United States, violence is more prevalent among males than females and among working-class males than males from higher social classes. Until the association between masculinity and violence is broken, you can expect these patterns to continue.

Functionalism

EMILE DURKHEIM: ASKING THE SOCIOLOGICAL QUESTION. Violence was one of the first social problems that sociologists studied. In the late 1800s, Emile Durkheim, the first

Spotlight on Social Research
STUDYING VIOLENCE AMONG "THE LIONS"

When she was a graduate student at the University of Chicago, RUTH HOROWITZ *(now Professor of Sociology at New York University) did a participant observation study of young people in a Chicano community in Chicago. Her purpose was not to understand violence, but to understand poverty. She wanted to see how the explanations of poverty that sociologists had developed matched what she observed in "real life."*

Two major explanations of poverty are the culture of poverty and the social structure of poverty. According to the culture of poverty, poor people have different values than the middle class, and this is why they act as they do. According to the social structural perspective, the poor act as they do because, unlike middle-class people, they do not have the same opportunities to attend good schools or to obtain good jobs. Consequently, the poor turn to illegal opportunities, and crime becomes part of their life.

One afternoon, a month after I met the "Lions" gang and shook hands with all of them in the park, several 16-year-old young women introduced themselves. They asked me several questions about myself, and they were able to give me a definition of sociology. They told me about school and their trips around the city. Several of

these women went on to college; others became pregnant and married. The life experience of siblings varied, too; some went to school and became white-collar workers, while others ran afoul of the legal system and went to prison.

When I first began my research, the "Lions" were 15 to 17 years old, had guns, and did a lot of fighting. Some had after-school jobs and dressed in tuxedos for *quinceaneras* and weddings. In the streets, these same young men had developed a reputation by being tougher than other gangs. They would even seek opportunities to challenge others. At home and during most parties, in contrast, they were polite and conformed to strict rules of etiquette.

For seven years, I did participant observation with these youths. When I returned after a three-year absence, many of the "Lions" were still hanging out together, but quite a few were working, had married, and had children. A few of the gang members attended college, and others remained in the street. One had been killed in a drug deal gone wrong. A major change was their relationship to violence. Instead of provoking incidents, now they responded only when someone challenged their reputations.

The two models of poverty did apply. Violence had been part of the culture they had learned, and a lack of opportunities did contribute to a sense of being left out. But there was more to it. Actual violence depended on how the "Lions" defined a particular situation. As sociologists phrase this: Violence was situational and constructed interactionally.

---

university professor to be formally identified as a sociologist, examined the murder rates in Paris and the suicide rates in several European countries (1897/1951, 1904/1938). He was struck by how stable these rates were. Year after year, the countries that had high rates of violence continued to have high rates, whereas those with low rates continued to have low rates. Durkheim found that a country's rate of violence was so consistent that he could use it to predict its future rate. He called this **normal violence**—the violence that a group normally (or usually) has.

Durkheim found this regularity to be a sociological puzzle. If murder and suicide rates represent the number of *individual* acts of killing, why doesn't a country's rate of murder and suicide fluctuate, with its rate high one year and low another? To solve this puzzle, Durkheim developed the *sociological perspective*. He concluded that the characteristics of a society regulate individual impulses and desires.

To appreciate Durkheim's conclusion, consider what life used to be like in farming communities. Children followed in their parents' footsteps and either worked in the village in which they were reared or farmed nearby land. They spent their entire lives in a village where everyone knew one another. Their close bonds restrained whatever individual impulses they might have had to lash out violently, for how they followed the community's norms affected their social standing—and they needed the community to survive.

Their close relationships (or high social integration, in Durkheim's term) kept the rate of violence low.

Now imagine that this same community is undergoing rapid social change. The society is industrializing, and the villagers are moving away to take low-paying, unskilled jobs in cities where they know few people. They live in the midst of strangers, where they face being fired by bosses who care about profits, not workers, and eviction by landlords who care more about collecting rent than about what happens to a family. Unlike the factors that promote cohesion in farming communities, these urban characteristics loosen social bonds. People feel fewer ties with one another, and the rules that used to apply no longer work. Durkheim gave the name **anomie** to such feelings of being unconnected and uprooted. Under these circumstances, no longer do impulses to violence have the constraints that they did in the village. As a result, the city is a more dangerous place.

ROBERT MERTON: STRAIN THEORY. Another functionalist, Robert Merton (1968), used anomie to explain crime in U.S. society. He developed what is called **strain theory.** Merton said that success—especially in the form of money or material goods—is a **cultural goal;** that is, this goal is held out for all Americans. Society also offers approved (or legitimate) ways to reach this goal, such as education and jobs. These are called **cultural means.** Socializing people into the cultural goal is remarkably successful, and almost all Americans learn to want money or material goods. The cultural (approved) means for reaching the goal, however, are limited. Those who find their way blocked are more likely to turn to illegitimate means, such as robbery and theft. The *strain* (or frustration and anxiety) that comes from blocked goals also motivates people to commit crimes of violence. Just as strain theory would predict, we find higher rates of violence among groups that experience higher blockage to financial success—the poor, and most minorities.

WALTER RECKLESS: CONTROL THEORY. Strain theory does not explain why some people whose goals are blocked become violent but others do not. We all face blocked goals, but few of us attack others. To answer this question, sociologist Walter Reckless (1973) developed **control theory** (also called **containment theory**). Other sociologists have expanded on these ideas (Gottfredson and Hirschi 1990; Burton et al. 1998). Reckless assumed that people have a natural tendency toward violence. He then asked what forms of social control overcome our natural inclinations. He theorized that two systems control our "pushes and pulls" toward violence. The first, *inner* controls, refers to our inner capacity to withstand pressures to be violent. The second, *outer* controls, refers to groups, such as family, friends, and the police, that divert us from violence. The likelihood that we will be violent depends on the strength of these two control systems relative to our pushes and pulls toward violence. If our control systems are weaker than the pushes and pulls, we are violent. If they are stronger, we are not.

As you can see, this theory is so vague that it explains everything—and nothing. Consider differences in groups: If women are less violent, it must be because their systems of control are stronger than their pushes and pulls toward violence. If some ethnic group is more violent than another, it must be because its systems of control are weaker than the pushes and pulls that it experiences. It is the same for individuals: If John is violent and Mary is not, then John's controls are weaker than his pushes and pulls toward violence, but Mary's are stronger. When everything is vaguely answered, then nothing is answered.

Conflict Theory

VIOLENCE IS INHERENT IN SOCIETY. We can expect violence because groups are competing with each other for highly desired but limited resources. Although conflict may be hidden beneath surface cooperation and even goodwill, the true nature of human relationships is adversarial. When this basic nature emerges, violence often is the consequence.

The major division among people in our society is social class. Despite appearances to the contrary, say conflict theorists, the social classes find themselves on opposite sides of vital issues in life. The essential division is between those who own the means of production—the factories, the machines, and the capital (investment money)—and those who work for the owners (Marx and Engels 1848/1964, 1906). The workers, who must struggle to put food on the table, pay rent, and buy clothing, are at the mercy of the owners, who make their decisions on the basis of profit, not the workers' welfare. For example, the owners can decide to close a factory and move the manufacturing or assembling process to Mexico or China. With their low pay and the threat of unemployment hovering over them, the working class, both male and female, is the most likely to strike out violently at others.

The situation is particularly tense for working-class males. Traditionally, men of all social classes assumed the role of breadwinner. This role has always been threatened by capitalism's recurring boom and bust cycle, which makes working-class men expendable pawns in the capitalists' pursuit of profits. Today, men face another threat—women who are competing for the jobs that men have traditionally held. With their position in the family threatened and their economic security flimsy, working-class men commit more violent crimes than do either working-class women or men from higher social classes. And the most exploited—those who are confined to the inner city and whose breadwinner role is practically nonexistent—have the highest rates of violence as they desperately strike out against others.

Conflict theorists also point out that if we look beneath the surface we will see that the capitalist class is actually *more* violent than the working class. Just as the wealthy own the means to produce wealth, so they control the police powers of the state, which they use to suppress riots and strikes at home and to send armies abroad to protect their markets and resources—to Vietnam, Grenada, Panama, Kuwait, Serbia, Afghanistan, Iraq, and so on. Thus, it is not violence itself but the *form* of violence that distinguishes the workers from the capitalists. The rich may not kill with their own hands, but their armies and their rape of the environment account for vastly more deaths.

As stressed throughout this text, for there to be a social problem we need not only objective conditions but also widespread subjective concerns. Suicide is ordinarily viewed as a personal problem, not a social problem. For decades, there have been educational and publicity campaigns to try to arouse the subjective concerns necessary to make suicide a social problem.

IN SUMMARY

Because violence is a universal characteristic of human societies, sociologists are interested in its causes. True to their calling, sociologists look for *social* causes. They want to know why some societies are more violent than others, as well as why some groups in the same society are more violent than others.

Symbolic interactionists stress that each group has its own ideas and norms about violence. Some groups prefer indirect ways of handling disagreements, whereas other groups consider violence an appropriate response to many situations. To solve problems, the middle and upper social classes usually turn to the legal system, which transcends personal confrontation. The lower classes, in contrast, are more likely to take matters into their own hands—and this breeds violence. Depending on the groups with which one associates (differential association), then, people have a greater or lesser chance of learning to be violent.

Functionalists emphasize that social conditions that strengthen social bonds reduce violence, and social conditions that produce *anomie* increase violence. Violence tends to be higher among groups whose access to culturally approved goals is blocked. The pushes and pulls toward violence that people experience, however, do not necessarily result in violence. The outcome depends on inner and outer controls.

Conflict theorists stress that class exploitation underlies violence. Members of the working class have high rates of violence because they face more problems in life. Seldom is their violence directed against their oppressors, however, for the capitalists control the powers of the state and use them to protect their privileged positions. Instead of targeting their oppressors, workers almost always misdirect their violence, aiming most of it against one another. Although the biased statistics produced by the state won't show this, the capitalists are more violent than are members of the working class, for their wars and destruction of the environment kill far more people.

Research Findings

As we review the research on violence, we will focus on rape and murder, the two most serious forms of violence. Because rape only recently emerged as a social problem, we pay particular attention to its natural history, especially to the role of feminists in changing our ideas about rape. (Most state laws label consensual intercourse between someone above the age of consent and someone below the age of consent **statutory rape.** Our topic is **forcible rape,** an entirely different matter, as no consent is involved.) After this, we turn our focus to murder in the United States.

Rape

The Natural History of Rape as a Social Problem

FROM A PERSONAL TO A SOCIAL PROBLEM. When I say that rape emerged only recently as a social problem, I do not mean that rape is new to the social scene. On the contrary, accounts of rape go back thousands of years to the Old Testament and Greek mythology. What is new is the perception of rape as a *social* rather than a personal problem and the understanding of rape as violence rather than passion. Let's see how this change took place.

As I have emphasized throughout this text, objective conditions are not sufficient for something to constitute a social problem. A social problem also requires subjective concerns: A significant number of people (or a number of significant people) must be upset by the objective conditions. As you know, subjective concerns about rape run throughout society. Parents teach their children not to talk to strangers. Fearful that some monster is waiting for the opportunity to snatch their children, parents escort their children to school. Afraid that strangers are lurking in the shadows—or in hallways, elevators, near their car, wherever—women live with the fear of being raped. A special concern is that their car might break down. To combat their fears, women take defensive measures, such as avoiding certain neighborhoods and carrying cell phones. Some carry guns.

RECONCEPTUALIZING RAPE: FROM PASSION TO POWER. The natural history of rape as a social problem began during the 1960s and 1970s, when Western women began to question their traditional roles, which revolved around husband, home, and children (Friedan 1963; Millett 1970). Many women began to think of themselves less as individuals who were facing unique circumstances and more as members of a social group that faced similar situations. Feminists analyzed the conditions that encourage men to be dominant and women submissive. They stressed how females are taught to be supportive of males and to have lower educational and career aspirations.

Up to this time, a traditional view of rape dominated thinking. In this view, rape is considered an act driven by a man's passion. From this perspective, rape would be a personal problem, a matter between an individual man and an individual woman. Feminists of this period took rape out of its murky background, with its unexamined assumptions of passion, and placed it in the light of sociological analysis.

Feminists pointed out how the traditional view blames women, not men, for rape. Men are thought to have an overwhelming sex drive: If they are aroused sexually, they can lose control and take a woman by force. Therefore, women must be careful not to arouse men's passions. If a man rapes a woman, it means that the woman must have acted provocatively or somehow excited the man. If not, he would not have lost control. If women would stop giving off the sexual cues that stimulate rape, the problem would go away.

"What sexual cues?" asked Dorothy Hicks, a physician who treated rape victims in Miami, Florida. "Is an 80-year-old woman or a 4-month-old baby particularly sexy?" These had been among the victims she had treated (Luy 1977).

The feminist conclusion was this: Rape is a *social* problem, not a personal problem. Rape is one of the ways by which men control women. Through rape and the fear of rape, men make women submissive and ensure their own dominance. The root of the problem, then, is the basic relationship between men and women, not women arousing men who cannot control themselves. Ultimately, they said, rape is a form of violence, not an act of passion.

This new view did not suggest that men deliberately use rape to frighten women into submissive positions. The process is much subtler. Men are taught "to associate power, dominance, strength, virility and superiority with masculinity, and submissiveness, passivity, weakness, and inferiority with femininity" (Scully 1990; Scully and Marolla 1985/2007). To equate masculinity with dominance and power teaches men that aggression is part of their sex role. By nature larger and stronger, and thus born for domination, no "real" man takes no for an answer. Besides, women say no when they don't really mean it, and, as some movies have shown, a woman's initial unwillingness may change as she is dazzled by a man's persistent sexual advances (Reynolds 1976; Finkelhor and Yllo 1985, 1989).

As you can see, the new view of rape as dominance and violence contrasts sharply with the traditional view. As these ideas were accepted, they became part of the official response to rape, and many states renamed rape **criminal sexual assault.** This new view also helps make sense of previously incomprehensible findings. Some rapists, for example, beat their victims, even those who submit or those they already have raped. Other rapists threaten their victims with death and pain and jam dirt, sticks, stones, and even shoes into their victims' vaginas.

The Social Patterns of Rape

HOW COMMON IS RAPE? According to the FBI, 72,000 U.S. women are forcibly raped each year (*FBI Uniform Crime Reports* 2006:Table 15). This is the official total, the number of women who report this crime to the police. The actual total is *three times higher.* Each year, over 200,000 U.S. women are raped.

How do we know that forcible rape is three times higher than the official statistics? Twice a year, researchers conduct what is called *The National Crime Victimization Survey.* In this survey, they interview about 90,000 Americans in 45,000 households. The researchers ask about the crimes that have happened to them and whether they reported those crimes to the police. Only 33 percent of victims report their rapes to the police (*Statistical Abstract* 2006:192).

PREDICTABLE SOCIAL PATTERNS. Here are the patterns that researchers have uncovered:

Acquaintanceship: A woman is more likely to be raped by someone she knows than by a stranger.

Place: A woman is more likely to be raped at home or at the home of a friend, relative, or neighbor than at any other place.

Time: Night is more dangerous than day, for two of three rapes occur between 6 P.M. and 6 A.M.

Season: As Figure 5-4 on the next page shows, rapes are more likely to occur in summer than in winter.

Age: Although rape victims range from babies to the elderly, the typical victim is between 12 and 24 years of age. After the age of 34, rape plummets.

Income, race-ethnicity, and geography: These women are more likely to be raped: poor women, African American women, and women who live in the South.

Weapon: About four out of five rapists use no weapon, depending instead on surprise, threats, and physical strength (*Sourcebook of Criminal Justice Statistics* 2004:Tables 3.4.2004, 3.11; *Statistical Abstract* 2006:Tables 308, 311).

Because these patterns show up year after year, sociologists conclude that rape is not the act of a few sick men from the lunatic fringe of society, but, rather, that *rape is intimately linked with our culture.* Researchers have also found that a woman's chances of being

FIGURE 5-4 Forcible Rape by Month

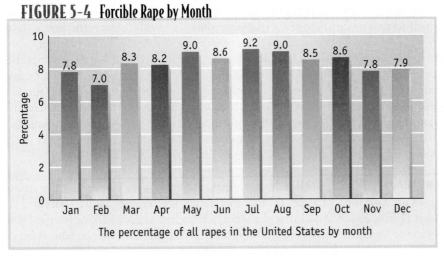

The percentage of all rapes in the United States by month

Source: By the author. Based on *FBI Uniform Crime Reports 2006:*Table 2.1.

raped vary tremendously from one state to another. Here is the extreme: Women in Alaska are six times more likely to be raped than are women in New Jersey or West Virginia. The Social Map below shows which states are the safest and which are the most dangerous.

GROUPS THAT ARE OVER-REPRESENTED. As you can conclude from these patterns, rapists are not scattered randomly throughout society. Although women can rape men or other women, rape is almost exclusively a male crime and primarily a crime of young men. Although only 7.5 percent of U.S. males are ages 17 to 21, they account for 23 percent of those who are arrested for rape (*Sourcebook* 2005:Table 4.7.2004; *Statistical Abstract* 2006:Table 11). Similar findings hold true for race-ethnicity: Only about 12 percent of the U.S. male population is African American, but African American males account for 32 percent of arrested rapists (*Sourcebook* 2005:Table 4.10.2004; *Statistical Abstract* 2006:Table 13).

FIGURE 5-5 How Safe Is Your State? Rape in the United States

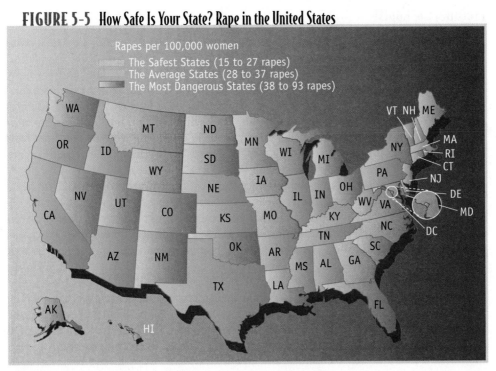

Source: By the author. Based on *Statistical Abstract of the United States* 2006:Table 295.

Why are African American men over-represented in rape statistics? For this answer, let's turn to two of our theories. First, according to *conflict theory*, the lower classes are oppressed—and, as we reviewed earlier, one reaction to oppression is violence. Compared with men from other social classes, lower-class men commit more forcible rapes. Because African Americans are over-represented in the lower social classes, they would be involved disproportionately. We can look to *functionalism*, particularly strain theory, for a second explanation. Because African American men often are blocked from legitimate avenues of attaining social status, their frustrations may lead them to turn against women inappropriately. As some have suggested, rape could be a way of establishing power in the face of socially imposed powerlessness (McNeely and Pope 1981).

INJURY, RAPE, AND RESISTANCE. Is a woman more likely to be raped if she resists or if she gives up without a struggle? In their interviews, sociologists Pauline Bart and Patricia O'Brien (1984, 1985) found that the women who had yelled, fled, or fought back were less likely to be raped. Other studies support this finding that women who resist are less likely to be raped (Kleck and Sayles 1990; Zoucha-Jensen and Coyne 1993; Ullman 1998). Apparently the more strategies that a woman uses (scratching, biting, gouging, kicking, hitting, screaming, running), the greater her chances of avoiding rape (McIntyre et al. 1979; Block and Skogan 1982).

Yet, the matter is not this simple. Although a woman who resists her attacker is less likely to be raped, she apparently is more likely to be injured. This is what sociologist Sarah Ullman (1998) found in her study of rape victims in Chicago. Her finding is supported by an earlier government study of a million rape victims (*Sourcebook* 1991:Table 3-20). In a more recent study of 203,000 victims, about half reported that fighting back helped them, and only about one-seventh said that their resistance made their situation worse (*Sourcebook* 2005:Table 3.20.2004).

How can we reconcile these findings? Not all rapists are the same. Fighting back scares some rapists away, but it enrages other attackers, causing even more injuries. In addition, some rapists want their victims to struggle, for this excites them sexually. Unfortunately, a woman who is being attacked does not know what kind of rapist she is facing, and she cannot know what the results of her resistance will be.

At this point, let's look at what kinds of rapists there are.

Profiling the Rapist

The following profiles, worked out with Linda Henslin, are based on studies of rapists who have been caught (Cohen et al. 1969; Hotchkiss 1978; Athens 1980; Hills 1980; Scully and Marolla 1985/2007). Although these profiles show that many motivations underlie rape, we do not know the proportion of rapists within each type or what other types may exist.

At some point in his life, the *woman hater* was severely hurt by a woman who was significant to him. In many cases, this woman was his mother. This hurt inflicted an emotional wound and left a hatred of women. By sexually assaulting women, this man feels a sense of personal power. By degrading his victim and sometimes brutally assaulting her sexual organs, he retaliates for his festering wound.

Although the *sadist* has no particular negative feelings toward women, he also beats his victims. He has learned to receive pleasure by hurting others, and women are merely handy outlets for him. By raping women, he combines the pleasure he receives from inflicting pain with the pleasure he receives from sex. Because he enjoys it when his victim begs, pleads, and shows fear, the sadist is likely to increase his sexual excitement by beating or torturing his victim before sexual penetration. He sometimes prolongs his pleasure by continuing to inflict pain on her during and after the rape.

For the *generally violence-prone* man, rape is just another act of violence. He sees the world as a violent affair. If he is going to get anything—and that includes sex—he must force it from others. Unlike the previous two types of rapists, his pleasure in rape is rooted in the sex rather than in the violence, and he uses only enough violence to make the woman submit. It is fine if he can accomplish the rape with threats, but if it requires injuring or killing the victim, so be it. Even though he may have abducted a total stranger, he believes that if she resists she deserves to be hurt because she is "holding out" on him.

The *revenge* rapist uses rape to get even with someone. His victim may be the person he is angry at, or she may be just a substitute for his real target. An example is a man who went to collect money that another man owed him. He thought, "I'm going to get it one way or another." When he found that the man was not home:

> I grabbed her and started beating the hell out of her. Then I committed the act. I knew what I was doing. I was mad. I could have stopped, but I didn't. I did it to get even with her and her husband. (Scully and Marolla 1985/2007)

The *political* rapist also chooses his victim as a substitute for his enemy, but, in addition, he uses the rape to make a political statement. In *Soul on Ice* (1968), Eldridge Cleaver recounts how he raped white women to "strike against the white establishment." Much of the raping done by soldiers during war is of this type. The soldiers are motivated not by hatred of women or by sadism, but by hatred of the enemy. Raping "the enemy's women" shows their contempt for the enemy and declares their own superiority.

Generally passive and submissive, the *Walter Mitty* rapist has an unrealistic image of masculinity. He uses rape to bridge the gap between the way he perceives how men ought to be and the way he perceives himself. He fantasizes that his victims enjoy being raped—for he is an excellent sex partner. Some individuals carry this fantasy one step further, calling the victim later and trying to make a date with her. The Walter Mitty rapist is unlikely to beat his victim, but he will use as much force as necessary to make her submit.

Unlike the first six types of rapists, the *opportunist* does not set out to rape. Rather, he grabs an unexpected opportunity, which often occurs during a robbery or burglary. For example, one man drove to a local supermarket to find someone to rob. The first person to come along was a pregnant woman. As he threatened her with a knife, the woman, scared out of her wits, blurted out that she would do anything if he didn't hurt her. At that point, he decided to force her to drive to a deserted area, where he raped her. He explained:

> I wasn't thinking about sex. But when she said she would do anything not to get hurt, probably because she was pregnant, I thought, "why not." (Scully and Marolla 2007)

Date rapists, also called *acquaintance rapists,* are the eighth type. Some of these rapists feel that they deserve sex because they have invested time and money in a date or sexual seduction. They are simply collecting a sexual "payoff" from their investment. Date rapists generally prefer to avoid violence. As the Issues in Social Problems box on the next page shows, contrary to common ideas, date rape consists of much more than a man being more insistent than he should. As you will see in that box, date rape also can involve many motivations other than "collecting." It is uncommon for date rapists to be reported to the police and, if reported, to be convicted (Kanin 2003).

A ninth type is the *recreational* rapist. For him, rape engenders male camaraderie, for he joins friends to participate collectively in a dangerous activity. As sociologists Diana Scully and Joseph Marolla (1985/2007) discovered in their interviews of imprisoned rapists, one man may make a date with a victim and then drive her to a predetermined location, where he and his friends rape her. One participant said that this practice had become so much a part of his group's weekend routine that they rented a house just for the purpose of recreational rape.

The last type is the *husband* rapist. Contrary to common opinion, marital rape is real rape. It is not an innocuous event involving a husband who has simply become too insistent about having sex. After interviewing wives who had been raped, sociologists David Finkelhor and Kersti Yllo (1985, 1989) concluded that this idea is a "sanitary stereotype." Marital rape can involve violence and sadism every bit as horrible as any we have discussed. Some wives are forced to flee in terror for their lives and sanity.

Issues in Social Problems
DATE (OR ACQUAINTANCE) RAPE

The public has little understanding of date rape. Some seem to think that it involves a reluctant woman who needs a "push" to go along with what she really wants. Consider these two cases:

Carol had just turned 18, and it looked as if her dreams had come true. It was only the beginning of her freshman year, and yet she had met Tom, the all-state quarterback. At Wiggins Watering Hole, the college bar, he had walked over to her table and made some crack about the English Comp professor. She had laughed, and the two had spent most of the evening talking.

When Tom asked to take her back to the dorm, Carol didn't hesitate. This was the man all the girls wanted to date! At the dorm, he said he would like to talk some more, so she signed him in. Once in the room, he began to kiss her. At first, the kisses felt good. But Tom was not about to stop with kissing. He forced her to the bed and, despite her protests, began to remove her clothing.

With his 240 pounds, and her 117, there wasn't much of a contest. Carol always wondered why she didn't cry out; she was asked this at the trial, at which Tom was found not guilty. This brutal end to her virginity also marked the end of her college career. Unable to shake the depression that followed, Carol left college and moved back with her parents. After a hearing, the university suspended Tom for a few games. Tom then resumed his life as before. He still goes to Wiggins Watering Hole.

Then there is Letitia, age 27. For her, the evening started out friendly enough. After a cozy dinner at her apartment, her boyfriend suggested that she lie down while he did the dishes. She grabbed this unexpected opportunity. As she lay in bed, though, he walked in with a butcher knife. Her formerly tender lover bound and raped her. When it was over, he fell asleep.

With convictions hard to get, some prosecutors discourage women from bringing charges of date rape. A social worker at a rape treatment center summarized the problem well when she said, "Most people are very understanding if a stranger breaks into your house with a gun and rapes you, but if you say you made a date with the rapist, they always wonder how far you went before you said no."

Obviously, most people don't know Carol and Letitia.

What can be done? Campus antirape groups—preferably composed of both women and men—offer one remedy. Lectures and workshops can introduce incoming freshmen to the reality and perils of date rape. Well-publicized prosecutions can help cut the risk, and antirape groups can encourage women to press charges and insist that prosecutors do their job. Student groups, composed of both women and men, can pressure the college administration to react strongly to date rape. As one activist said, "If there were a pattern of assaults on quarterbacks, universities would respond very quickly."

Based on Engelmayer 1983; Seligmann 1984; Taslitz 2005.

Reactions to Rape

Let's look at what happens to rape victims after their attack. We will focus first on their personal reactions and then on what some pinpoint as a social problem itself, how the criminal justice system treats rape victims.

THE TRAUMA OF RAPE. Disbelief is the first reaction of a woman who finds herself confronted by a rapist (McIntyre et al. 1979). The event is so frightening and alien that most victims report they could not believe it was actually happening. Shock quickly follows.

The trauma of rape does not end with the physical attack (Littleton and Breitkopf 2006). The woman typically finds her self-concept so wounded and her emotions in such tatters that her whole life is disrupted. Some rape victims deal with their trauma in an *expressive* style, venting their fear, anger, rage, and anxiety by crying and sobbing or by restlessness and tenseness. Others react in a *controlled* style, carefully masking their feelings behind a calm and composed exterior (Burgess and Holmstrom 1974). Investigators often expect only the expressive style, which they understand. Talking to victims who seem calm and composed can make them wonder whether a rape has actually occurred.

After a rape, life and relationships are no longer the same. Doubt, distrust, and self-blame plague rape victims. Some feel guilty for having been alone in that place at that time. Others feel that it was their fault for letting themselves get in a compromising situation. If they didn't scream and fight back, that bothers them. They feel that there must have been something—*anything*—that they could have done—or not done—that might have changed the situation. I think you get the idea of how bottomless such self-blame can be.

In addition to the nightmares, many victims become afraid—of being alone, of the dark, of walking on the street, or of doing such ordinary things as shopping and driving. Anything that reminds them of the rape can send them into anxiety and depression—and they never know what will trigger the painful memories. The victim's personal relationships may also deteriorate, for, feeling hurt and less trusting, some women feel less intimate and withdraw emotionally. To complicate matters even further, some husbands and boyfriends wonder what "really" happened, their suspicions feeding into this spiral of despair.

DEALING WITH THE LEGAL SYSTEM. At the prodding of feminists, many police departments have grown sensitive to the plight of rape victims, and they have trained women officers to do the interviewing and to collect the evidence needed to pursue a criminal case. Yet, the criminal justice system often adds to the victim's suffering (Madigan and Gamble 1991; Jordan 2001). Some police officers who arrive on the scene or at the hospital have little experience in dealing with rape victims. To conduct their investigation, they must ask for details that, by the very nature of the crime, involve sex and intimate body parts. Some officers get embarrassed, others are insensitive, and still others show disbelief. Some officers don't believe it was rape if the woman doesn't have bruises and cuts. Others suspect that the victim is using the police to "get even" with a boyfriend. Because some rape charges are bogus, this is a legitimate concern—but just when the woman needs compassion the most, when her world has been turned upside down, she can find herself the object of suspicion, which engenders hostility and embarrassment on her part.

One victim gave this account of her experience with the police:

> They rushed me down to the housing cops who asked me questions like, "Was he your boyfriend?" "Did you know him?" Here I am, hysterical. I'm 12 years old, and I don't know these things even happen to people. Anyway, they took me to the precinct after that, and there about four detectives got me in the room and asked me how long was his penis—like I was supposed to measure it. Actually, they said, "How long was the instrument?" I thought they were referring to the knife—how was I supposed to know? That I could have told them 'cause I was sure enough lookin' at the knife. (Brownmiller 1975:365)

Even if a woman is fortunate enough to be questioned by sensitive, compassionate police officers who have been trained in rape investigations, this is just the beginning of her experience in the criminal justice system. In 42 percent of the reported rapes, someone is arrested (*Sourcebook* 2005:Table 4.19.2004). The victim then faces a dilemma. If she fails to press charges, the rapist goes free—and he may well rape again. But if she prosecutes, she must relive her attack, perhaps repeatedly, as she goes over the details with the prosecuting attorney. Then she must describe everything in a public courtroom in front of her rapist, his attorney, a judge, perhaps a jury, journalists, and even curiosity seekers. Here, the defense attorney may try to blacken her character, for in some states her prior sex life can still be examined on the witness stand. Everything she says can be challenged, and because the rape was so sudden and might have occurred in darkness, any fuzziness in her account is an opportunity for the defense attorney to attack her credibility. In the courtroom, the accuser can become the accused. As one rape victim said of her experience:

> I had heard other women say that the trial is the rape. It's no exaggeration. My trial was one of the dirtiest transcripts you could read. Even though I had been warned about the defense attorney, you wouldn't believe the things he asked me to describe. It was very humiliating. I don't understand it. It was like I was the defendant and he was the plaintiff. I wasn't on trial. I don't see where I did anything wrong. I screamed, I struggled. (Brownmiller 1975:36)

Many reasons underlie this second victimization, which some call the "legal rape" of the victim. The presumption of the innocence of the accused, built into the judicial system, plays its part. If someone is accused of a crime, that person has the right to question the accuser and to present a vigorous defense. Additionally, the traditional view of rape continues to play an unexamined role in the minds of some jurors. From this perspective, men have a difficult time controlling their strong, almost overwhelming, sex drive. By their revealing clothing, some women provoke men sexually. Others are "asking for it," because they go into bars or go out alone at night. Then there are women who change their minds just before sex. When the aroused man continues with what they both had previously intended, these women cry rape. In the traditional view, women have no right to do any of these things.

HOMOSEXUAL RAPE. To be complete, I need to mention homosexual rape. Although we have concentrated on the social problem of men raping women, men also rape other men. As noted in Chapter 3, this form of rape (along with forced prostitution) is common in our prisons, with younger, weaker prisoners selected as victims. Officials and the public prefer to ignore these objective conditions. Until there is an outcry from the public or from authorities, by sociological definition we do not have a social problem. I anticipate that this will be one of the social problems of rape in the future, at which time we will look at our present attitudes as barbaric.

Murder

If Martians were to study human culture, they might find our fascination with murder bizarre. The Martians might report that murder has become a major form of entertainment, that every night Americans watch beatings, bombings, shootings, slashings, stabbings, strangulations, and other mayhem on television—with gruesome close-ups in living color. Beyond entertainment, however, behind real-life killings are real-life killers. As any mystery reader knows, to find them we must explore the who, what, when, where, and why of murder.

The Social Patterns of Murder

Let's examine the statistics so we can uncover the social patterns of murder.

THE "WHO" OF MURDER. Although most people's fears of murder center on strangers, of all violent crimes, murder is the *least* likely to be committed by a stranger. As Figure 5-6 on the next page shows, it is also the most likely to be solved. Table 5-2 on the next page shows the relationships between victims and their killers. As you can see, strangers account

FIGURE 5-6 Crimes Cleared by Arrest

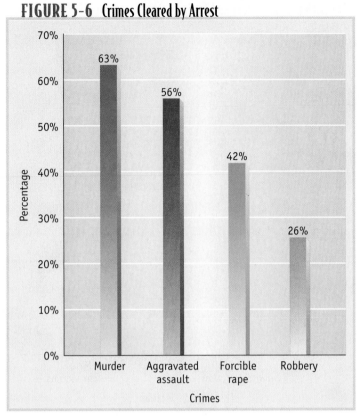

Source: By the author. Based on *Sourcebook of Criminal Justice Statistics* 2005:Table 4.19.2004.

for only about 23 percent of U.S. killings. Three out of four murder victims are killed by members of their family or by their lovers, friends, neighbors, or other acquaintances.

The "who" of U.S. murder follows the patterns of social class, sex, age, and race-ethnicity that we found when we examined the crime of rape. The poor are more likely to kill. So are younger people. Although males between the ages of 17 and 24 constitute only about 6 percent of the U.S. population, from this group come *one-third* of the killers (*FBI*

TABLE 5-2 How Are Murder Victims Related to Their Killers?

Their killers are:

Family	23.7%	Acquaintances	53.4%
Wife	7.3%	Girlfriend	5.6%
Son	2.9%	Friend	3.8%
Daughter	2.7%	Boyfriend	1.8%
Husband	1.9%	Neighbor	1.4%
Father	1.4%	Other Acquaintance	40.5%
Mother	1.5%		
Brother	1.1%	**Strangers**	22.9%
Sister	0.1%		
Other Family	3.5%		

Note: These relationships refer to cases in which the relationship between the killer and victim is known. In 44 percent of killings this relationship is unknown, either because the crime was not solved or the police did not report the relationship.

Source: By the author. Based on *FBI Uniform Crime Reports* 2006:Table 2.4.

FIGURE 5-7 Killers and Their Victims

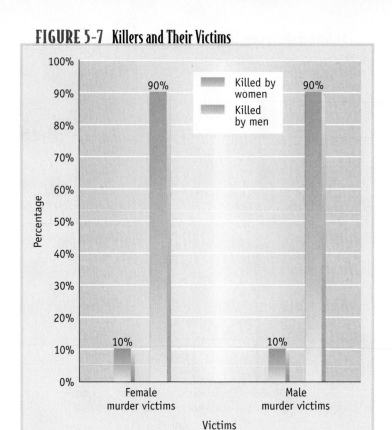

Source: By the author. Based on *FBI Uniform Crime Reports* 2006:Table 2.7.

Uniform Crime Reports 2005:Table 2.5; *Statistical Abstract* 2006:Table 11). Figure 5-7 above illustrates how much more likely males are to kill than females. Males kill 90 percent of everyone who is murdered in the United States. Although females make up 51 percent of the U.S. population, they commit only 10 percent of the murders. As you can see from Table 5-2 on the previous page, spouse murders also follow this pattern; husbands are almost four times more likely to kill their wives as wives are to kill their husbands. You can also see how much more likely boyfriends are to kill their girlfriends than girlfriends are to kill their boyfriends.

Similar startling differences mark the killings of African Americans and whites. Although African Americans make up only about 12 percent of the U.S. population, in 49 percent of the cases where the race-ethnicity of the killer is known, the murderer is an African American (*FBI Uniform Crime Reports* 2005:Table 2.7). From Table 5-3 below you can see that murder is overwhelmingly *intraracial;* 86 percent of white victims are killed by whites, and 92 percent of blacks are killed by blacks.

TABLE 5-3 Race-Ethnicity of Killers and Their Victims

		KILLERS	
		WHITE	BLACK
Victims	White	86%	14%
	Black	8%	92%

Source: By the author. Based on *FBI Uniform Crime Reports* 2006:Table 2.7.

Note: Does not include victims or killers whose race-ethnicity is unknown.

THE "WHAT" OF MURDER. Although people use a variety of weapons to commit murder, every year the number one choice of Americans is the gun. As you can see from Figure 5-8 on the next page, all other weapons take a distant second place. Guns are the favorite choice for killing for two obvious reasons: they are highly effective, and they are readily available in the United States. More subtle reasons are that men are the number one killers, and guns are identified as masculine. Significant cultural stereotypes reinforce this image. For example, our culture romanticizes cowboys and hunters, who personify the union of guns, killing, and masculinity. To settle a quarrel, then, the U.S. male is much more likely to reach for a gun than, say, a kitchen knife or a bottle of poison.

Visitors from other countries are often shocked at how many Americans own guns and how easily guns can be purchased. The debate over gun control is discussed in the text.

THE "WHEN" OF MURDER. Like rape, murder is not evenly distributed across the seasons. July and August are consistently the highest months for murder, and February the lowest (*FBI Uniform Crime Reports* 2005:Table 2.2). The FBI used to break killings down by day of the week, but they stopped doing so. When they did, they reported that nights were more dangerous than days, and weekends more dangerous than weekdays. The most dangerous time of the week is Saturday night (McGinty 2006). As sociologist Alex Thio

FIGURE 5-8 American's Choice of Murder Weapons

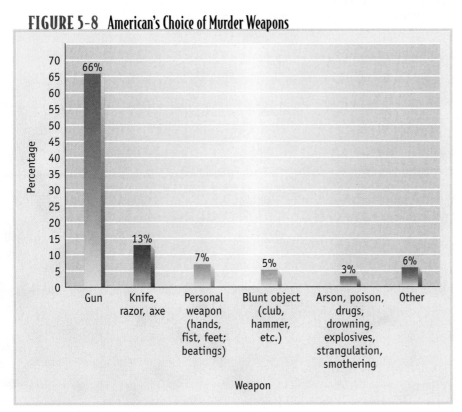

Source: By the author. Based on *FBI Uniform Crime Reports* 2006:Table 2.9.

(1978) observed back in the 1970s, this may be why cheap handguns are often referred to as "Saturday night specials."

THE "WHERE" OF MURDER. The good news is that between 1991 and 2004 the U.S. murder rate plunged 44 percent, dropping from 9.8 killings per 100,000 Americans to just 5.5 (*FBI Uniform Crime Reports* 1992, 2005). Although the U.S. murder rate has declined so sharply, as you saw on Figure 5-3 on page 136, when compared to other Western countries it remains high. As with rape, the states vary tremendously in their individual rates, and where you live vitally affects your chances of being a murder victim. As you can see from Figure 5-9 below, people in Louisiana are *thirteen* times more likely to be murdered than are people in Maine, New Hampshire, or South Dakota.

Most people think that your chances of getting murdered are greater in the city than in the country—and they are right. In large cities (those with populations over 250,000), 5.9 of every 100,000 people are murdered each year. In rural areas, the murder rate drops to 3.6 per 100,000 people. But slightly safer are the smaller cities. There, the murder rate is 3.5 per 100,000 people (*FBI Uniform Crime Reports* 2005). Table 5-4 on the next page shows how uneven the murder rate is among U.S. cities.

THE "WHY" OF MURDER. Now that we have looked at the "who," "what," "when," and "where" of murder, let's examine its "why." This is more complicated, so we will look at the "why" in more detail.

Social Bases of the Social Patterns

Why do we have the patterns that we just reviewed? As you will see, they reflect our society.

ACQUAINTANCESHIP. Most murder victims are killed by someone they know. This is because most murders are crimes of passion spurred by heated arguments. As many analysts have pointed out, we are much more likely to argue with people we know than with strangers. It is with people we know that we share money, property, and love—the things that fuel quarrels and sometimes lead to violent death.

FIGURE 5-9 The "Where" of Murder

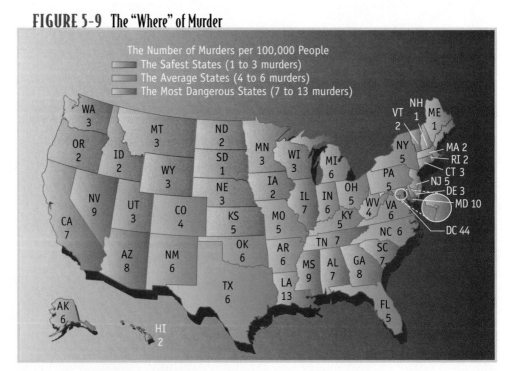

Source: By the author. Based on *FBI Uniform Crime Reports* 2003:Table 5.

TABLE 5-4 Murder: The Ten Safest and Most Dangerous U.S. Cities

SAFEST			MOST DANGEROUS		
Rank	City	Murders per 100,000 People	Rank	City	Murders per 100,000 People
1	Honolulu, HI	1.7	1	New Orleans, LA	57.7
2	Mesa, AZ	3.2	2	Washington, DC	44.0
3	San Jose, CA	3.2	3	Baltimore, MD	41.9
4	El Paso, TX	3.6	4	Detroit, MI	39.4
5	Austin, TX	4.0	5	Atlanta, GA	34.3
6	Colorado Springs, CO	4.5	6	Oakland, CA	26.8
7	Wichita, KS	4.9	7	Philadelphia, PA	23.3
8	Portland, OR	5.0	8	Chicago, IL	20.6
9	San Diego, CA	5.1	9	Miami, FL	19.4
10	Virginia Beach, VA	5.5	10	Memphis, TN	19.3

Source: By the author. Based on *Statistical Abstract of the United States* 2006:Table 296.

Note: From data reported by police officials in cities over 250,000 people.

POVERTY. Why are murderers so likely to come from the most deprived groups of society? The three sociological perspectives help us understand this pattern. *Conflict theorists,* who view the poor as oppressed people, see their high murder rates as the result of their poverty. As sociologist Elliott Currie (1985:160) put it:

> Brutal conditions breed brutal behavior. To believe otherwise requires us to argue that the experience of being confined to the mean and precarious depths of the American economy has no serious consequences for personal character or social behavior.

Because most murder victims of the killers who come from poverty are also usually poor, conflict theorists conclude that people in poverty are striking out at one another instead of at their oppressors.

Functionalists who work within strain theory point out that people feel a lot of stress when they are denied access to the approved means for attaining material success. People who feel high stress are more likely to strike out at others. Functionalists who emphasize control theory point out that the poor have weaker internal and external controls to inhibit their desires to strike out at others. For example, the poor have less to lose if they are arrested or go to jail. Compared with people from higher social classes, the poor risk less because they are unlikely to own their homes, and their jobs pay relatively little and are already insecure. Neither do the poor have reputations at stake in professional associations or in organizations such as the Chamber of Commerce.

THE MEANING BEHIND MURDER. To this, *symbolic interactionists* add that in some subcultures of the poor, police trouble actually enhances a person's reputation. Young males become more of a "man" if they are sent to "juvvie" (juvenile detention) or to jail. In some subcultures, the prison experience has become so common that young men expect to go there, just as young men in other social classes expect to go to college. Symbolic interactionists also stress that the social classes have distinct ways to resolve disputes. Middle-class people who have grievances are likely to seek legal recourse, such as lawsuits. Poor people, in contrast, not only can't afford lawyers, but also don't have the same confidence in the legal system. As a result, poor people are more likely to settle disagreements outside the law. Their direct confrontations more easily lead to heated words, physical assault, and death.

Some symbolic interactionists stress subcultural theory and differential association. In a subculture of poverty, to settle scores directly with an antagonist is a "macho" act.

People are expected to stand up to others. They are admired for doing so and looked down on if they prove themselves to be "yellow" or "chicken." This applies to both males and females. People who grow up in this subculture are likely to learn to react violently to life's problems.

To trace the path by which people became involved in murder, Lonnie Athens, a symbolic interactionist, interviewed fifty-eight prisoners. He found this general pattern: The killer found some act that the victim did intolerable. A spouse or lover might have refused sex or threatened to leave. Or someone—whether a stranger or friend—spewed insults. The killer interpreted the act as one that called for violence, often because this act threatened the killer's self-image or social standing among friends. Faced with this interpretation of the situation—intolerable conduct for which violence is the appropriate response—the individual killed.

A woman prisoner whom Athens (1980:36–37) interviewed said that a stranger at a party had accused her of cheating him of $20. The man kept insulting her and laughing at her:

> Then I told myself, "This man has got to go one way or another; I've just had enough of this (man) messing with me; I'm going to cut his dirty . . . throat." I went into my bedroom, got a $20 bill and my razor. I said to myself . . . "now he's hung himself," and I walked out of the bedroom. I went up to him with a big smile on my face. I held the $20 bill in my hand out in front of me and hid the razor in the other hand. Then I sat on his lap and said, "O.K., you're a fast dude; here's your $20 back." He said, "I'm glad that you are finally admitting it." I looked at him with a smile and said, "Let me seal it with a kiss" . . . and then I bent over like I was going to kiss him and started slicing up his throat.

KILLING AS A MANLY ACT. This last example notwithstanding, why do men kill more often than women? As we have seen, men are more likely to value violence. Men in poverty especially are likely to believe that a real man is tough—and toughness includes the willingness to be violent. One's standing in the group may depend on being known as "the kind of guy who can't be pushed around." Not to fight when insulted is cowardice, the worst quality a young man can show in certain subcultures.

As we saw earlier, among some groups killing is even associated with manliness, and spilling blood brings honor. In the Mafia, killing an enemy is a demonstration of courage: Killing is the measure of one's *capacity as a man.* There, "the more awesome and potent the victim, the more worthy and meritorious the killer" (Arlacchi 1980:113).

Symbolic interactionists stress that females are less likely to be socialized to be violent. While males learn to associate masculinity with being tough, showing bravery, and being violent when it is necessary, most females learn less-violent ways of handling loss of face. The result of this socialization into gender is that *in every society around the world* men kill at a rate several times that of women (Daly and Wilson 1988; Chernoff and Simon 2000). (To be fair, I need to point out that biological and evolutionary theorists point to this worldwide uniformity in the killing pattern as evidence for their theories of genetic inheritance.)

RACIAL-ETHNIC DIFFERENCES. Let's apply some of these social patterns to explain why African Americans kill at a higher rate than would be expected, given their proportion of the population. African Americans are more likely to be poor, and the subculture to which lower-class African American males belong identifies masculinity with the willingness to defend oneself aggressively. Functionalists would add that African Americans are socialized to strive for the cultural goal of material success, but discrimination blocks many of them from reaching that goal through legitimate means. This increases their strain, leading to a higher rate of violence, most of which is directed against people nearby. A widespread pattern of racially segregated housing helps to account for the intraracial pattern of murder, the black-on-black violence.

What about violence that crosses racial lines? To explain interracial patterns, functionalists stress the connection between race-ethnicity and money. If a burglary, robbery, or mugging results in a killing across racial lines, it is more likely to involve poor

Even with the gun control laws that have been passed in recent years, it is easier to buy weapons in the United States than in almost any country. This visitor from Europe was surprised when she saw something called "gun shops," which are unknown in her country. As you can see, she is enjoying the discovery.

African Americans robbing whites than poor whites robbing African Americans. Conflict theorists add that the oppression of African Americans by whites produces racial hatred that has many negative consequences, including deadly incidents of striking out against the dominant group. If African Americans were in the driver's seat of society and possessed vastly more wealth than whites, we would expect this pattern to be reversed.

To understand race-ethnicity and violence, we need to focus on another aspect of social class. In *The Declining Significance of Race,* William Julius Wilson (1978) analyzed how changing social events had an impact on the class divisions of African Americans. As racial barriers dropped, many African Americans joined the middle class as they were able to get more education and, with it, better jobs. Seizing their opportunity, they moved out of the ghetto and into more desirable areas of the city and suburbs. Left behind was an *underclass,* a group of people who were desperately poor and were plagued with social problems—high unemployment, single-parent households, and a lot of drug addiction, murder, robbery, and rape. As Wilson put it, this group "is increasingly isolated from mainstream patterns and norms of behavior." It is here that U.S. violence is concentrated.

TEMPORAL PATTERNS. The timing of U.S. murder also reflects broader social patterns. During weekdays, when murders are less frequent, people are working and meeting personal and family responsibilities. On weekends, when murders are more frequent, people are more likely to be socializing in public and to be drinking and using drugs more than usual. This increases the likelihood of quarrels, with the peak of violence coming on the traditional "Saturday night out." The explanation for the seasonality of murder follows similar lines. Because people are more likely to get out of the house and socialize during warm weather, murder is higher during the summer and lower during the winter. If you have ever spent time in the inner city, as I have, you are familiar with some of the "finer points" of the "summer socializing" that leads to murder: gambling, drinking, and boasting.

GEOGRAPHIC PATTERNS. Finally, the geography of murder intrigues sociologists. For more than a century, the South's murder rate has been higher than that of the rest of the country. This pattern is broadly evident in the Social Map you looked at earlier, on page 154. That the South has a higher murder rate year after year has led some researchers to conclude that there is a *southern subculture of violence*. Southerners supposedly learn more violent ways of resolving their disagreements than do people reared in other regions of the United States. More violent themes run through their music, their literature, and even their jokes. Apparently, southerners are more likely to own guns, to know how to shoot them, and to use guns during quarrels. Sociologists find these explanations suggestive, but not totally satisfactory (Doerner 1978; Huff-Corzine et al. 1986, 1991; Pridemore and Freilich 2006). We need more creative thinking to establish a more adequate explanation.

Before concluding this section, let's look at two patterns of murder that have gripped the public's attention: mass murder and serial murder.

MASS MURDER. **Mass murder** is the killing of four or more people in a single episode (Fox and Levin 2005). Examples are Richard Speck's murder of eight nursing students in Chicago one July night in 1966; Charles Whitman's killing of sixteen people in a sniper attack from a tower at the University of Texas that same year; James Huberty's shooting of twenty-one people at a McDonald's in 1984; the eighty-seven deaths caused by Julio Gonzalez, who torched the Happy Land Social Club in the Bronx in 1991 because his girlfriend was breaking up with him; George Hennard's shooting of twenty-two people at a Luby's Cafeteria in Killeen, Texas, in 1991; Colin Ferguson's 1993 shooting spree as he walked through a New York commuter train and methodically fired forty shots, an incident that left six people dead; and the school shootings that have so alarmed the public, such as the one described in our opening vignette. Only an occasional woman joins the list of mass murderers. In 1981, Priscilla Ford killed six people in Reno, Nevada, by deliberately driving her car onto a crowded sidewalk during a Thanksgiving Day parade. In Houston in 2001, Andrea Yates drowned her five small children in the family bathtub while her husband was at work.

When Timothy McVeigh blew up a federal building in Oklahoma City, Oklahoma, in 1995, 168 people died. This is the largest mass murder by a single individual in the history of the United States. (McVeigh may have been assisted by others, but, if so, only a small number of people were involved.) McVeigh's stunning number of victims was overshadowed by the events of September 11, 2001, of course, which claimed about 3,000 lives. September 11 was a special type of mass murder, for it involved many people making plans over a period of years, detailed financing, and the transportation and coordination of men from other countries. Although this act fits the definition of mass murder perfectly, it is so different from "typical" mass murder that it might be better thought of as an act of war. If we were to include war killings in this category, however, the picture would change abruptly. We will leave acts of war as a separate category.

SERIAL MURDER. **Serial murder** is the killing of several people in three or more separate events. The murders may occur over several days, weeks, or even years. The elapsed time between murders distinguishes serial killers from mass murderers. Serial killers are generally less spontaneous than mass murderers and are generally more methodical in their planning.

Because many serial killers are motivated by lust and are aroused sexually by killing, the FBI sometimes uses the term "lust murder." This type of serial killer tends to "keep souvenirs or trophies—their victims' jewelry, underwear, even body parts—to remind them of the good times they experienced while killing" (Fox and Levin 2005:44). Some serial killers, however, are more "garden variety": Motivated by greed, they rob their victims. One of the most bizarre serial killers was Jeffrey Dahmer of Milwaukee. Not only did Dahmer kill young men, but also he had sex with their dead bodies and fried and ate parts of his victims. So he wouldn't go hungry, he kept body parts in his freezer. The serial killer with the most victims appears to be Harold Shipman, a quiet, unassuming physician in

Manchester, England. From 1977 to 2000, he killed 230 to 275 of his elderly women patients, giving them lethal injections while making house calls. "Spotlight on Social Research" on the next page focuses on a teenager who became a serial killer after he came under the influence of an older person.

Almost all serial killers are men, but an occasional woman joins this list of infamy. In North Carolina in 1986, the husband of Blanche Taylor Moore was taken to the hospital with arsenic poisoning. He survived, but the police became suspicious. They exhumed six bodies, including Moore's father, her first husband, and a boyfriend. Arsenic was found in all of them. In 1987 and 1988, Dorothea Montalvo Puente, who operated a boarding house for senior citizens in Sacramento, killed seven boarders. Her motive was to collect their Social Security checks. In Missouri, from 1986 to 1989, Faye Copeland and her husband killed five transient men. Aileen Wuornos hitchhiked along Florida's freeways and killed five middle-aged men after having sex with them.

HAVE MASS AND SERIAL MURDERS BECOME MORE COMMON? Many assume that mass and serial murders are more common now than they used to be, but we do not know this. In the past, police departments had little communication with one another, and when killings occurred in different jurisdictions, it was difficult to link the killings. Today's more efficient investigative techniques make it easier for the police to conclude that a serial killer is operating in an area. Part of the perception that such killings have increased is also due to ignorance of our history: In our frontier past, serial killers went from ranch to ranch, and mass murderers wiped out entire villages of Native Americans.

Social Policy

While we could suggest many policies for dealing with offenders and their victims, the primary concern is how to prevent violence. Let's look at the potential.

Global Concerns: Preventing Violence

I suggest four social policies that can prevent violence.

First, researchers have documented that rape is higher in societies in which women are devalued (Lalumiere et al. 2005). This finding has profound implications for social policy. We can reduce rape by increasing the social value of females. To do this, we need programs that cause males to value females more highly, whether those programs are in the church, school, family, or even on television. Whatever increases men's evaluation of females will tend to reduce rape. (In this context, I invite you to review the materials in Chapter 3 on violent pornography, in which women are portrayed as cheap commodities to be brutalized and discarded.)

Second, researchers have also documented that rape is higher when the perceived cost of raping is low (Lalumiere et al. 2005). This finding also has profound implications for social policy: To reduce rape, we need social policies that increase the likelihood that rapists will be punished. Of the many possibilities, here is just one. Some men are serial rapists, who commit a large number of rapes. Some rape several times a month until they are caught—which can take years. Long sentences for repeat offenders—with little chance of parole—will prevent many women from being raped.

Third, policy makers should support research to determine how our culture creates a climate for violence. Remember the sociological question that was posed at the beginning of this chapter: What in a society increases or decreases the likelihood of violence? As indicated in my first two suggested social policies, we have some of the answers to this question. But we need more research to determine what other aspects of our culture have made our rates of violence so high. I suggest that researchers

Spotlight on Social Research

DOING RESEARCH ON A SERIAL KILLER

I researched one of the first serial killings to attract the attention of the U.S. public. In Houston, Texas, Dean Corll, with the aid of two teenaged accomplices, had tortured and killed twenty-seven boys. The 33-year-old had befriended Elmer Wayne Henley, 14, and David Brooks,15, from broken homes. Corll became their father substitute, one who molded the boys into killers. Corll had a passion for teenaged boys, and from 1971 to 1973, Henley and Brooks picked up young hitchhikers and delivered them to Corll to rape, torture, and kill. Sometimes they even brought him their own neighbors and high school classmates.

The televised reports were shocking: Corpses, one after another, were being unearthed from a rented boat storage shed in Houston. As the police worked around the clock, the reports kept coming in. All the corpses seemed to be teenagers.

I decided to go to Houston. Summer classes ended in just a few days. As soon as I taught my last class, I took off for a straight-through drive from Illinois. My budget was low (nonexistent, actually), but these were "hippie" times, and it was easy to meet a stranger and find a place to stay for a few nights.

I went to the "morgue," the newspaper office that stores its back issues. There I read systematically about the case, from the first revelation of the killings to its current coverage. The accounts included the addresses of the victims. On a city map, I marked the home of each local victim, as well as the homes of the killers. As I drove around the neighborhoods, map in hand, I saw at one of the marked homes a man painting his porch. I stopped my car, went over and introduced myself. I asked him if he were the father of one of the boys who had been killed. Although reluctant to talk about his son's death,

Elmer Wayne Henley being arrested in Houston, Texas, for the murder of Dean Corll. As detailed in this box, Henley was involved in the kidnapping, torture, and murder of dozens of boys.

he did so. His son had left the house one Saturday to go for a haircut. He never made it home. He told me bitterly that the police had refused to investigate his son's disappearance. They insisted that his son was a runaway.

Elmer Wayne Henley, one of the accused killers, was a neighborhood kid who lived just down the street.

As I drove by Henley's home, I decided to stop and try to get an interview. As I drove up, Henley's mother and grandmother were entering the house, carrying bags of groceries. I told them who I was and what I wanted. Henley's mother said that she couldn't talk to me, that her attorney had ordered her not to talk to anyone. I explained that I had driven all the way from Illinois to talk to her, and I promised that I would keep whatever she said private until after her son's trial. She agreed to be interviewed, and I went inside her home. While I was talking to her and her mother, three of Henley's friends came over. I was also able to interview them.

My interviews revealed what since has become common knowledge about serial killers: They successfully lead double lives that catch their friends and family unaware. Henley's mother swore to me that her son was a good boy and that he couldn't possibly be guilty. His high school friends stressed that Elmer couldn't be involved in homosexual rape and murder because he was interested only in girls. (To prevent contamination—one person being interviewed influencing another—I interviewed each person separately.) I conducted my interviews in Henley's bedroom, and for proof of Elmer's innocence, his friends pointed to a pair of girls' panties that were hanging in the room.

There was no question about Henley's guilt or the guilt of Brooks or Corll. (The case had come to the attention of the police when Henley killed Corll, because Corll had tried to kill him.) Henley and Brooks had methodically delivered hitchhikers and acquaintances to Corll, and the three of them had raped, tortured, and killed the boys. Henley and Brooks were sentenced to life terms in Texas prisons, where they remain today.

1. Examine less-violent cultures to determine what factors minimize violence.
2. Determine how to help Americans—especially young men—channel their aggression constructively.
3. Find ways to minimize antagonisms and increase respect between the sexes.
4. To the degree that individual violence is based on economic inequality, develop programs to provide more opportunities for the disadvantaged.

The *fourth* suggestion takes us to the center of controversy, the matter of gun control. As we saw in Figure 5-8 on page 153, most murder victims die from gunshot wounds. Proponents of gun control argue that because most murders are crimes of passion, emotional outbursts would be less lethal if guns were not so easy to get. Some propose that we could reduce the U.S. murder rate by registering all guns and licensing gun owners. Opponents argue that gun ownership is a constitutional right that should not be removed because some people abuse guns.

The two extremes of gun control illustrate why it is difficult to establish social policy concerning violence and why this debate on gun control continues without letup. On the one side are those who want to abolish gun ownership altogether. They consider gun ownership as an anachronistic custom that has "no redeeming social value." On the other side are those who argue that Americans need *more* guns. They argue that if all law-abiding citizens had guns, few rapists and killers would break into our homes—and even fewer would survive if they did. They also argue that Americans have more guns now than ever before and that most states now allow people to carry concealed handguns in public—and that the rates of both murder and rape have dropped.

Finally, we can also apply a fundamental point stressed throughout this book, that social problems do not consist only of objective conditions but also depend on subjective concerns. As sociologists Lynda Holmstrom and Ann Burgess (1989) emphasized, issues sometimes leap into prominence and then fade from sight. This is not likely to happen with murder, but it could happen with sexual violence. If we are to work toward effective solutions, we must keep this social problem before the public.

The Future of the Problem

Given our history, our rate of violence is destined to remain higher than that of most nations. From time to time, our rape and murder rates will decline, offering hope that some fundamental change is taking place, but these events will be followed by increases in rape and murder. To attain a low and permanent rate of violence will require major structural changes in our society. Without these changes, high rates of violence will be with us until our society ends—and that ending may well be a violent one.

Viewing the future through the lens of our three theoretical perspectives supports this view. *Conflict theory* indicates that tensions will remain in our society. Short of revolution (which has proven no panacea for any society), the wealthy will retain control, and discrimination will continue. Thus, the poor, especially minorities that are poor—who suffer the two-edged sword of both poverty and discrimination—will continue to show up disproportionately in the statistics on violence. The *functionalist* lens shows that violence works, not always, but often enough for it to be perpetuated: People do get revenge and other satisfactions from killing their enemies. Some rapists gain feelings of dominance, power, and sexual satisfaction through forcible rape. The *symbolic interactionist* lens focuses on violence as a cultural symbol that is held out as a means of resolving conflict. This is a potent symbol, for it combines violence, power, strength, and dominance with a sense of manliness. Violence, then, will continue, as men try to live up to this cultural image.

The *sociological* perspective on violence is essential to understanding our present and our future. Our high rate of violence cannot be laid at the doorstep of a large number of violent psychopaths. Psychopaths (or sociopaths) there are, but our social patterns of rape and murder are a product of our history and our current social structure. Into whatever future we project ourselves, without structural change that removes social inequalities, violence will remain part of our way of life. This understanding of the *social* basis of violence can become the key to changing basic relationships—and to focusing that change in a direction that decreases violence.

SUMMARY AND REVIEW

1. Sociologists analyze how violence is rooted in society. How a society is organized—its social structure—increases or decreases its amount of violence.

2. Each society has a rate of violence that, without major social change, is fairly constant over time. Sociologists call this a society's *normal violence.*

3. Biologists, anthropologists, and psychologists have theories to account for violence. The sociological response is that whatever predispositions humans have toward violence are encouraged or inhibited by the society in which they live.

4. Symbolic interactionists use two theories to explain violence. The first, *differential association,* stresses that violence is learned in association with other people. The second, *subcultural theory,* emphasizes that some groups are more approving of violence than others. People who grow up or associate with groups that approve of violence are more likely to learn violence.

5. Functionalists stress that some people become dissociated from cultural norms. Durkheim used the term *anomie* to describe this uprooting and estrangement. Anomic individuals are more likely to rape and to kill. Merton's *strain theory* suggests that violence is an alternative path that some people choose when they find the *cultural means* (such as education and jobs) to reach *cultural goals* (such as financial success) blocked. *Control* (or *containment*) *theory* suggests that the inner and outer controls of rapists and murderers

are weaker than their pushes and pulls to commit these acts.

6. Conflict theorists emphasize that the various groups that form a society compete for scarce resources. The major division is between those who own the means of production and those who do not. Those at the mercy of the owners have few resources, and they lash out violently—misdirecting their violence onto one another.

7. Feminists challenged the traditional view of rape as a personal problem, a crime of passion. Researchers now consider rape a social problem, a crime of violence rooted in the structure of relationships between men and women.

8. Rape and murder are not random acts. Related to the larger social patterns of society, they reflect patterns of class, gender, age, race-ethnicity, timing, location, and acquaintanceship.

9. To prevent violence requires restructuring those aspects of society that foster violence. Without such restructuring, high rates of violence will continue. To determine a rational basis for social policy on these emotionally charged issues requires research on the social causes of violence.

10. Research indicates that we can reduce rape through social policies that increase the value of females and increase the perceived costs of raping. Rape may fade from the public's mind as a social problem. To find workable solutions, we must keep this issue alive.

KEY TERMS

THINKING CRITICALLY ABOUT CHAPTER 5

1. What is the sociological question of violence? What materials in this chapter indicate that this is the right question to ask?

2. Which five of the profiles of rapists that are discussed on pages 146–148 do you think are the most common? Explain your choices.

3. As a social policy to reduce rape, the author suggests that we should promote programs that increase the social value of females. Why is this policy suggested, and what specific programs do you think would work?

CHAPTER 6

Crime and Criminal Justice

I was recently released from solitary confinement after being held therein for 37 months (months!). A silent system was imposed upon me and to even whisper to the man in the next cell resulted in being beaten by guards, sprayed with chemical mace, blackjacked, stomped and thrown into a strip-cell naked to sleep on a concrete floor without bedding, covering, wash basin or even toilet. The floor served as toilet and bed, and even there the silent system was enforced. . . . I have filed every writ possible against the administrative acts of brutality. The courts have all denied the petitions. Because of my refusal to let the thing die down . . . I am the most hated prisoner in (this) penitentiary, and called a "hard-core incorrigible."

> ## The floor served as toilet and bed.

Maybe I am an incorrigible. . . . I know that thieves must be punished and I don't justify stealing, even though I am a thief myself. But now I don't think I will be a thief when I am released. No, I'm not that rehabilitated. It's just that I no longer think of becoming wealthy by stealing. I now think of killing—killing those who have beaten me and treated me as if I were a dog. I hope and pray for the sake of my own soul and future life of freedom that I am able to overcome the bitterness and hatred which eats daily at my soul.

—A letter from a prisoner in a state prison, as quoted in Zimbardo (1972).

The Problem in Sociological Perspective

To understand the social problem of crime, we first need to understand what crime is.

WHAT IS CRIME? Let's look at a crime in progress:

> On a Sunday morning in July, an undercover police officer entered a supermarket on Cape Cod. He purchased two cans of Del Monte whole-kernel corn and two cans of baby carrots.
> Corn and carrots were just the beginning of the crime wave.
> The following Sunday morning, undercover officers purchased Campbell's pork and beans and Progresso chicken-noodle soup. Then it was green beans. And more carrots. (Harlan 1988)

What does selling vegetables have to do with crime? When the owner of the store stood before a judge and admitted that he had sold the canned goods, he became a convicted criminal. He had violated the Massachusetts "blue laws," which used to make it a crime to sell nonessential items on Sundays.

Your state may not have blue laws, but it does have merchandising laws. Consider the sale of alcohol. Bars and taverns have "closing hours." To sell whiskey, wine, or beer one minute before closing hour is legal; to sell them two minutes later is a crime.

These examples illustrate the essential nature of crime. **Crime** *is the violation of law.* If there is no law, there is no crime. No activity is criminal in and of itself. Although we may agree that stealing, kidnapping, and rape are immoral or harmful, only law defines them as crimes.

THE CULTURAL RELATIVITY OF CRIME. The principle that law defines crime has many implications. One is that *crime is culturally relative;* that is, because laws differ from one society to another, so does crime. Travelers are sometimes shocked by this, when they find that some behavior they take for granted at home is a crime abroad or that what is illegal at home is taken for granted elsewhere. Examples go from the sublime to the ridiculous. Although pork and alcohol are illegal in some Muslim societies, a man there may take several wives as long as he can support them. How puzzling our beer-drinking, pork chop-eating, monogamous society must seem to a Muslim!

Within the same society, behavior that is criminal at one time can later be taken for granted or even encouraged as a virtue. In China, for example, selling goods to make a profit used to be illegal. This crime, called "profiteering," was so despised that it was punishable by death, and "profiteers" were hung in the public square as an example to others. As Chinese officials gradually adopted capitalism in the 1990s, however, they decided that letting people make profits would help their economy. The change has been so thorough that now Chinese capitalists can join the Communist party.

In fact, the relativity of crime is so extreme that an act defined at one point as criminal can later be considered to be a contribution to humanity. In the early 1900s, birth control was thought to injure the family and the state, and a federal law made it illegal to send such information through the U.S. mails. Margaret Sanger broke the law and was indicted for mailing "obscene, lewd, and lascivious" materials. Today, in contrast, most people consider the same act to be a service to an overpopulated world.

MAKING ACTS CRIMINAL IS A POLITICAL PROCESS. The material we reviewed on abortion in Chapter 1 gives us another illustration of how law defines crime. Before 1973, abortion was a criminal act, and those who performed it could, and were, put in prison. After 1973, following the *Roe v. Wade* decision by the U.S. Supreme Court, abortion was not a crime. If the antiabortion groups succeed in amending the Constitution or if the Supreme Court reverses its 1973 ruling, abortion will again become a crime. This example takes us to another principle: Determining what human behavior is criminal is a **political process.** The definition of some act as illegal is the outcome of a struggle among groups that have different interests and ideologies.

These two principles—that law defines crime and that crime is the outcome of a political process—take us to significant sociological issues. They point to power. What groups in a society have the power to get their views written into the law? How do they get authorities to pass laws? Why do laws prohibit some behaviors but not others? Why do some societies punish a behavior, while others ignore—or even encourage—it? Perhaps all these questions can be summarized in this one: Whose interests do laws represent?

The Scope of the Problem

In considering crime as a social problem, we must also look at the **criminal justice system**—the agencies that respond to crime, including the police, courts, jails, and prisons. On the one hand, crime is a social problem when large numbers of people are upset about it, when they feel that crime threatens their safety, peace, or quality of life. On the other hand, the criminal justice system is a social problem if people are upset about how it fails to prevent crime, fails to rehabilitate offenders, or discriminates against some group of citizens. In this chapter, we will discuss these two intertwined parts of this social problem: crime and the criminal justice system.

Crime as a Social Problem

HOW EXTENSIVE IS CRIME? To see how extensive crime is in the United States, we use two measurements. The first is the number of crimes. Each year Americans are the victims of about 16,000 murders, 95,000 forcible rapes, and 400,000 robberies. Another 10 million

FIGURE 6-1 The U.S. Crime Rate

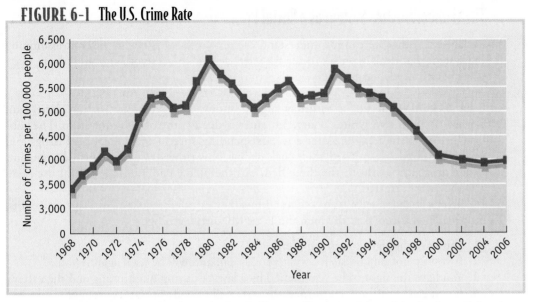

Source: By the author. Based on reports of murder-manslaughter, forcible rape, robbery, aggravated assault, burglary, larceny-theft, and automobile theft, as contained in various editions of the *FBI Uniform Crime Reports*, including *Crime in the United States* 2006:Table 1.

crimes range from aggravated assaults and automobile thefts to burglaries (*FBI Uniform Crime Reports* 2006). The second measure is the **crime rate**—the number of crimes per some unit of the population, usually per 100,000 people. Figure 6-1 shows how the U.S. crime rate climbed during the 1960s and the 1970s, reaching a sharp peak in 1980. After a choppy period, crime peaked again in 1991, and from there began a long, steep drop. We are currently in a plateau that has taken us back to the lower crime rates of 1970.

This drop in crime is welcome news, and in recent years U.S. society has become much safer. There is another side of the coin, however: Even with this huge drop, the U.S. crime rate remains one of the highest in the world. Crime in the United States is still so high that each year 4 of every 100 Americans fall victim to one of the crimes shown in Figure 6-1.

THE UNIVERSAL NATURE OF CRIME. Although many societies have lower crime rates than ours, no society is without crime. As Emile Durkheim, one of the earliest sociologists, pointed out in 1897, the very nature of crime makes it universal. Each society passes laws against behaviors that it considers a threat to its well-being. (In tribal groups, the laws are not written down, but these groups, too, regulate behavior and impose severe penalties on violators.) The behavior already exists. Passing a law does not eliminate the behavior—it just makes it illegal. When there are laws (or rules), there always will be criminals (or rule breakers). Thus, as Durkheim stressed, no society or nation can ever be free of crime.

WHY IS CRIME CONSIDERED A SOCIAL PROBLEM? As stressed in earlier chapters, the mere existence of some objective condition is not enough to make it a social problem. Subjective concerns are also necessary. People have to be upset about a situation and want something done about it. Just a few years ago, Americans considered crime to be the number one social problem facing the nation. As the crime rate dropped, so did Americans' fears of becoming a victim of violent crime. As we saw in Chapter 5 (Table 5.1, page 133), however, Americans are still concerned about their personal safety, and each urban resident knows which areas of the city to avoid. Women, who have greater concerns about becoming a crime victim, are more cautious than men and especially careful at night.

As we consider the social problem of crime, let's look first at the criminal justice system.

The Criminal Justice System as a Social Problem

Earlier, I said that we cannot understand crime as a social problem without examining the system that deals with it. To see why, let's follow the case of Buddy Hudson, Gary Carson, and Clyde Johnson.

PLEA BARGAINING. On a Saturday night, Buddy, a 19-year-old African American, teamed up with two whites, Gary, 34, and Clyde, 21, to rob a liquor store. The robbery netted them $2,590. After a week's spending spree—their dreams of drugs and women realized—they tried their luck again. This time, though, their luck ran out. When an alarm went off, the three fled, but the police had a description of the men, and they were arrested.

To ensure that the courts would not throw the case out for violating the suspects' rights, the arresting officers read the men the 1966 Miranda warning:

1. You have the right to remain silent.
2. If you do not remain silent, what you say can and will be used against you.
3. You have the right to be represented by a lawyer during questioning and thereafter.
4. If you cannot afford an attorney, the state will provide one at its expense.

The state did provide an attorney. Her advice was to say nothing—to let her talk to the prosecuting attorney, who determines what crimes suspects will be charged with. After meeting with the state's attorney, she told the men that the evidence against them was solid. They would be charged with armed robbery, resisting arrest, and assault with a deadly weapon. They could go to prison for up to 60 years. She added that she thought she could "cut a deal" and get the charges of assault and resisting arrest dropped in return for a guilty plea to armed robbery. If so, she could get them a 3-to-5 (a minimum of three years and a maximum of five years in state prison).

Social control is necessary if society is to survive. Without social control, we all would be victims of the strongest and most ruthless, facing constant extortion, injury, or death. The problem is how to make the state subject to the will of the people, to prevent it from being the agent that extorts, injures, and kills.

Knowing that there was some uncertainty on the part of the witnesses, the men figured that they could do better if they went to trial. Clyde's mother put up $20,000 to secure her son's release on bond. Unable to raise bond money, Buddy and Gary remained in jail during the nine months it took for their case to come to trial. (Nine months? See the Issues in Social Problems box on the next page.) Just before the trial, Clyde pled guilty. Both the prosecuting and defense attorneys appeared surprised when the judge suspended Clyde's sentence and placed him on probation for five years. After their trial, Buddy and Gary were found guilty of armed robbery. (The other charges were thrown out for insufficient evidence.) The judge gave Gary a 6-to-10 and sentenced Buddy to a minimum of 15 years in prison.

A reporter asked about the differences in the sentences. The judge replied, "I have to show consideration for the defendant who cops a plea. It saves the court the expense of a trial" (Gaylin 1974:188–189). He added that Clyde had a job and that to send him to prison would serve no purpose. Letting him keep his job, however, would increase his chances of staying out of trouble. When asked if the longer sentence for Buddy had anything to do with his being black, the judge, who was white, fumed and sputtered that he had no racial bias. "That," he said, "is insulting. Race has nothing to do with this case. These are just facts: Gary Carson is older, but he has fewer 'priors' (previous arrests). He doesn't need as stiff a sentence to teach him a lesson. Buddy's 'priors' tell me he's more dangerous." The judge added, "For people like you, I wish Buddy were white and Gary black." The reporter nodded, thinking that at this point, Buddy might have the same wish.

This case shows why our criminal justice system can be "more criminal than just" (Newman 1966; Gaylin 1974; Pattis 2005):

Issues in Social Problems
YOU DON'T HAVE TO BE
POOR TO GO TO JAIL—BUT IT HELPS

It isn't a crime to be poor, but poverty sure doesn't help when you're in trouble with the law. If you can't pay a fine, you go to jail.

"It's the only practical alternative," declared Woodrow Wilson, a judge in Bastrop, Louisiana. "Otherwise, some people would never be punished."

In courtrooms across the nation, defendants with ready cash pay and leave. Those without money are ushered from the courtroom to the city jail to pay their debts with days rather than dollars—or at least to wait until someone bails them out.

In rural areas especially, authorities routinely jail defendants who are unable to pay fines for minor crimes such as public drunkenness, bad checks, and speeding. They jail the poor even though this appears to violate U.S. Supreme Court rulings. Legal aid lawyers charge—irrefutably, it seems—that it is unjust to give better treatment to defendants who have money. Still, indigent defendants keep winding up in jail.

Legal aid attorneys can't patrol all the courts, and most abuses occur in small, rural communities. The attorneys try to help people who are already in jail, but that can be slow. Roger Baruch, a prisoners-aid lawyer, recalls a man who spent six months in a Georgia jail because he couldn't pay traffic fines.

Many judges and prosecutors claim not to know that such defendants are poor. "If they raised the issue, they wouldn't be put in jail," asserts an Aurora, Colorado, city attorney, "but I don't see that it's the responsibility of the court or the prosecutor to check out their ability to pay fines."

It certainly must be difficult for these officials to know whether the people who are sitting in jail for petty offenses are poor or whether they have money but have chosen to be locked up so they can save a few bucks rather than being at work or home with their families.

Some officials have tried, or at least have given the appearance of trying. In Monroe, Louisiana, about 20 miles south of Bastrop, officials hired a priest to evaluate defendants' finances. They let him go, though, because he sided with the poor too often.

Few believe that this problem ever will be solved. The practice is too deeply ingrained in the legal system.

"The so-called administration of justice is arbitrary and somewhat capricious," says Jackie Yeldell, a Bastrop attorney. "One thing is certain, though. You can be sure there aren't any wealthy persons in jail."

Based on Schmitt 1982.

1. Some of the poor spend months (even years) behind bars awaiting trial, while those with money use a bond system to buy their release.
2. Defense attorneys encourage **plea bargaining,** pleading guilty (whether or not one is guilty) in return for a lesser charge.
3. Prosecutors use the threat of mandatory minimum sentences to get guilty pleas. ("Plead guilty to this crime, to which the judge has discretion to give a shorter sentence, or I'll charge you with this other crime, which carries a longer mandatory minimum sentence which, by law, the judge must give if you are found guilty.")
4. Judges dislike "unnecessary trials" and impose harsher sentences on those who insist on a trial.
5. Factors that have nothing to do with the crime affect sentencing, such as a defendant's age, employment, and the number of previous arrests. Even when the offense is the same, those who have higher-status jobs and those who have a better employment history get more lenient sentences.

6. The *number of adult arrests,* not the seriousness of those charges, influences a sentence. Judges discount the type of charge because they know that because of plea bargaining official charges can have little to do with the actual offense.

RECIDIVISM AND REHABILITATION. If the criminal justice system seeks to rehabilitate people convicted of crime, its **recidivism rate**—the percentage of former prisoners who are rearrested—shows how inadequate such attempts are. And we should note that there really are few such attempts. Most prisoners are simply warehoused—taken off the streets until they serve their time—and then plunked back into their old neighborhoods with their old criminal buddies. They don't learn a legitimate trade in prison, and released without work skills, what do they face? Here is how one sociologist put it:

> Over two million men and women are confined to jails and prisons in the U.S. Ninety percent of them eventually return home. After having served a median prison term of 15 months, approximately 1600 inmates disgorge from state and federal prisons every single day of the week. In the greater Chicago metropolitan area alone roughly 1500 male ex-convicts return to their neighborhoods each month. They arrive home "wearing an X" on their backs, possessing meager skills of limited portability, and enjoying scanty resources on which to draw in their efforts to "make good," or live a life on the straight and narrow path of desistance. They almost always return to the same disaffected, marginalized neighborhoods in which they resided prior to incarceration but which now offer even fewer legitimate opportunities than before. The majority will stray from the path and wander into a gnarled grove of institutional failure, criminal opportunity, and the uniquely rewarding but ultimately self-defeating whorl of drug dealing and otherwise hustling street gangs. (Scott 2004)

How ineffective is our criminal justice system? It is difficult to see how this so-called system for dealing with lawbreakers could be less effective. As you can see from Figure 6-2, within just the *first year* after being released from prison, 44 percent of ex-prisoners are rearrested. Within three years of their release, this total jumps to two-thirds. During these first three years, one-half are reconvicted of crimes and land back in prison (Langan and

FIGURE 6-2

Within a year of release from prison, 44.1 percent of prisoners were rearrested; within three years, 67.5% were rearrested and about half were back in prison.

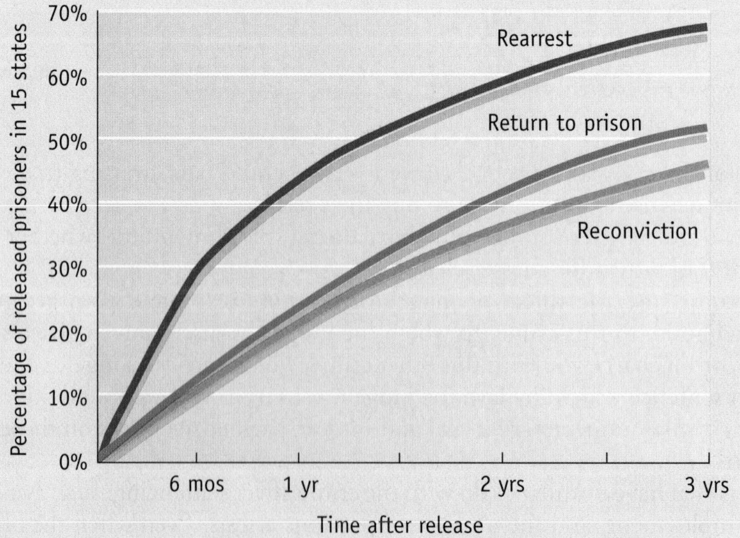

Source: Langan and Levin 2002.

Levin 2002). If these astounding statistics sound hard to believe, you should know that they are solid, based on a follow-up of 272,000 former prisoners.

You might be wondering about the crimes that these former prisoners committed after their release from prison. These statistics, too, are enlightening—and, some would say, frightening. As Table 6-1 shows, the two-thirds who were rearrested during these three years were charged with 750,000 new crimes, an average of 4 each. Over 100,000 of these charges were for violent crimes. If we add the number of crimes these individuals were charged with before they were released from prison, we find that the total comes to an astounding 4 million crimes, including 22,000 rapes and 18,000 murders.

These totals, as high as they are, are less than the actual number of crimes these individuals committed. How can we be certain of this? Simply put, few people are caught when they commit their first crime after being released from prison, and so, on average, offenders commit more crimes than they are charged with (Blumstein et al. 1988). In short, the crime rate of former prisoners is higher than their recidivism rate.

Besides the crimes they were charged with, what do we know about these former prisoners? We are missing a lot of information. The researchers didn't report important things such as their level of education or anything about their employment, aspirations, family life, or religion. The data are quite bare, but what we have are shown in Table 6-2 on the next page. From these data, we can conclude that women, whites, and older former prisoners are less likely to get in trouble with the law again. Age at release is especially interesting. You can see how the rates of rearrest, reconviction, and reincarceration decrease with age. The two main possibilities are that the older these people get, the more they learn to stay away from crime—or the older they get, the more they are able to avoid getting caught when they commit a crime. They are either smarter older criminals or more-law-abiding former criminals. (I say this with tongue only partially in cheek. We simply don't know the answer.)

Our judicial system, if it is to be judged by teaching people that crime does not pay, is a colossal failure: *The more often someone has been put in prison, the greater that person's chances of going back to prison.* How can this be? There are many reasons, of course, but for just one, recall our opening vignette: The treatment of that prisoner produced contempt and hatred, hardly the qualities we would recommend for bringing about law-abiding behavior.

To illustrate in another way how poorly our current system rehabilitates inmates, consider this: Despite being caught, convicted, and sent to prison several times, when asked, "Do you think you could do the same crime again without getting caught?" about 50 percent of inmates answer yes (Zawitz 1998).

Not only do prisons fail to rehabilitate, but they also serve as crime schools. People who have been declared unfit to live in normal society because they have committed crimes are housed together for years. One of their favorite topics of conversation is crime, and they boast to one another about all the crimes they've gotten away with. Older, more experienced prisoners also teach younger ones how to commit crimes. It is an irony, of course, that the models for younger prisoners are criminals who have failed: *All* these mentors have been caught and put in prison. This irony, however, appears to be lost on both teacher and student. Perhaps having such bad teachers is part of the reason for the high recidivism rate of former prisoners.

We will return to the issue of criminal justice, analyzing its essential role in the social problem of crime. For now, let's see what light our three theoretical lenses can throw on this social problem.

TABLE 6-1 Charges for 272,000 Offenders in the First Three Years After Their Release from Prison

Arrest Charge	Number of Arrest Charges in First 3 Years After Release
All offenses	744,480
Violent Offenses	100,531
Murder[1]	2,871
Kidnapping	2,362
Rape	2,444
Other sexual assault	3,151
Robbery	21,245
Assault	54,604
Other violent	13,854
Property offenses	208,451
Burglary	40,303
Larceny/theft	79,158
Motor vehicle theft	15,797
Arson	758
Fraud	21,360
Stolen property	21,993
Other property	29,082
Drug offenses	191,347
Possession	79,435
Trafficking	46,220
Other/unspecified	65,692
Public-order offenses	155,751
Weapons	25,647
Probation/parole violations	20,930
Traffic offenses	13,097
Driving under the influence	5,788
Other public-order	90,280
Other offenses	20,049
Unknown	68,351

[1]Murder includes nonnegligent manslaughter and negligent manslaughter.

TABLE 6-2 Recidivism of U.S. Prisoners

Within Three Years of Being Released from Prison, These Percentages of Former Prisoners Were

	REARRESTED	RECONVICTED	REINCARCERATED
All released prisoners	68%	47%	52%
Sex			
Men	68%	48%	53%
Women	58%	40%	39%
Race/Ethnicity			
White	63%	43%	50%
African American	73%	51%	54%
Latino	65%	44%	52%
Other	55%	34%	50%
Age at Release			
14–17	82%	56%	56%
18–24	75%	52%	52%
25–29	71%	50%	53%
30–34	69%	49%	55%
35–39	66%	46%	52%
40–44	58%	38%	50%
45 or older	45%	30%	41%

Source: Langan and Levin 2002:Table 8.

Looking at the Problem Theoretically

As we saw in Chapter 5, each of the three theoretical perspectives provides different insight into the problem of criminal violence. We will now use these perspectives to look at property crime and the criminal justice system. Using symbolic interactionism, we will examine the social class bias of police enforcement and learn why we must view crime statistics with caution. Then, through a functionalist perspective, we will see how crime is an adaptation to a society's core values. Finally, using conflict theory, we will examine why the law comes down hardest on the poor who have stolen little, whereas it often is lenient toward the wealthy who have stolen much.

Symbolic Interactionism

THE SAINTS AND THE ROUGHNECKS: SOCIAL CLASS AND LABELING. For two years, sociologist William Chambliss (1973/2007) observed two groups of adolescent lawbreakers in "Hanibal High School." He called one group the "saints." These were "promising young men, children of good, stable, white, upper-middle-class families, active in school affairs, good precollege students." Despite their background, however, the saints were some of the most delinquent boys in the school, "constantly occupied with truancy, drinking, wild driving, petty theft, and vandalism." Yet their teachers and families considered the boys "saints headed for success." Not one saint was ever arrested.

Chambliss also observed a second group of boys, whom he called the "roughnecks." Of the same age and race-ethnicity as the saints, and from the same high school, these boys also were delinquent, although they committed somewhat fewer criminal acts than the saints. Their teachers saw them as "roughnecks headed for serious trouble," and the police often dealt with them.

Why did the community perceive these boys so differently? Chambliss found that this was due to *social class*. As symbolic interactionists emphasize, social class vitally affects our perception and behavior. The saints came from respectable, middle-class families, the roughnecks from less-respectable, working-class families. These backgrounds led teachers and the authorities to expect good behavior from the saints but trouble from the roughnecks. And, like the rest of us, teachers and police saw what they expected to see.

The boys' social class also affected their *visibility*. The saints had automobiles, and they did their drinking and vandalism out of town. Lacking cars, the roughnecks hung around their own street corners, where their boisterous behavior drew the attention of police, confirming the idea that the community already had of them.

Social class also equipped the boys with distinct *styles of interaction*. When police or teachers questioned the saints, they were apologetic. They showed respect for authority, so highly important for winning authorities' favor. Their show of respect elicited a positive reaction from teachers and police, allowing the boys to escape school and legal problems. The roughnecks, reports Chambliss, were "almost the polar opposite." When questioned, they were hostile. Even when they put on a veneer of respect, everyone could see through it. Consequently, teachers came down hard on the roughnecks, and the police were quick to interrogate and arrest them rather than to warn them.

The saints and the roughnecks illustrate the differential association and subcultural theories introduced in Chapter 5. Unlike nondelinquent groups, both the saints and the roughnecks were immersed in vandalism and theft. Despite their similarities in delinquent behavior, however, the saints and the roughnecks were reared in subcultures that had different orientations to life. The saints learned that college was their birthright; the roughnecks did not. The saints wanted good grades; the roughnecks didn't care. The saints learned middle-class politeness, which showed in their choice of words, tone of voice, and body language; the roughnecks did not. The reactions by authorities to these subcultural differences deeply affected the boys' lives.

Chambliss' research illustrates what sociologists call *labeling,* a practice that can set people on different paths in life. The labels "saint" and "roughneck," for example, carry different expectations. They affect people's perceptions and channel behavior in different directions. All but one of the saints went to college. One became a doctor, one a lawyer, one earned a Ph.D., and the others went into management. Two of the roughnecks won athletic scholarships and went to college. They became coaches. One roughneck became a bookie. Two dropped out of high school, were convicted of separate killings, and ended up in prison. No one knows the whereabouts of the other. Although such distinctive events in life have many "causes," the boys lived up to the labels the community gave them.

POLICE DISCRETION. Sociologists Irving Piliavin and Scott Briar (1964) also observed how different styles of interaction affect outcomes with the police. Doing participant observation of the police at work, they observed these two cases:

> An 18-year-old white male was accused of statutory rape. The girl's father was prominent in local politics, and he insisted that the police take severe action. During questioning, the youth was polite and cooperative. He addressed the officers as "sir" and answered all questions. He also said that he wanted to marry the girl. The sergeant became sympathetic and decided to try to get the charges against the youth reduced or dropped.

> A 17-year-old white male was caught having sexual relations with a 15-year-old girl. When he was questioned, he answered with obvious disregard. The officers became irritated and angry. One officer accused the boy of being a "stud," interested only in sex, eating, and sleeping. He added that the young man "probably had knocked up half a dozen girls." The boy just gave back an impassive stare. The officers made out an arrest report and took him to juvenile hall.

Both young men had solid evidence against them, and the police faced political pressure to prosecute the 18-year-old. His politeness and cooperation, however, changed the officer's perception. His deference—his respect and regard for police authority—sent a powerful message that put the police on his side. The 17-year-old's demeanor, in contrast, sent a negative message and elicited negative reactions from the police.

Symbolic interactionists emphasize that the police operate within a symbolic system as they administer the law. Their ideas of "typical" people—for example, of who is "safe" and who is "dangerous"—come alive during their work. The more a suspect matches their idea of a "typical" criminal, the more likely they are to arrest that person. Using **police discretion,** deciding whether to arrest someone or to ignore a particular offense, is routine in police work.

CAUTION ABOUT CRIME STATISTICS. These examples illustrate why sociologists approach crime statistics with caution. As noted in Chapter 2, the "facts" of a social problem are not objective: Social "facts" are produced within a specific social context for a particular purpose. According to official statistics, working-class boys are much more delinquent than middle-class boys. Yet, as we have just seen, social class influences the reactions of authorities, affecting *who shows up in official statistics.* As we saw with Buddy, Gary, and Clyde, many factors other than the crime also affect how judges hand out sentences.

IN SUM Using symbols is an essential part of social life. All of us make decisions based on what things mean to us. Just as we do this in everyday life, so do the police and judges as they go about their work. As it is with us, social class, reputations, and demeanor are symbols that also influence their evaluations and decisions. The impact of police and judicial discretion can have far-reaching effects on people's lives.

Functionalism

CRIME AND A SOCIETY'S CORE VALUES. Functionalists consider crime to be a natural part of society, not an aberration. They also view many crimes as a reaction to the core values of a society. Let's see how *conformity* to cultural values can generate crime. Specifically, why back in the 1950s did sociologist Albert Cohen (1955) say that conformity to the "American way" creates crime?

To see why, let's look at what sociologists Richard Cloward and Lloyd Ohlin (1960) identified as the crucial problem of industrial societies: locating and training the most talented persons of every generation—whether born wealthy or poor—to fill the positions that require ability and diligence. Because these traits don't show up at birth, to see who has them society tries to motivate *everyone* to strive for success. Intense competition allows some of the talented to emerge as victors. "Regardless of race, sex, or social class, success can be yours" becomes the motto—a cry that motivates people to compete intensely. By making success a universal goal—one that is not limited to the privileged, as in more highly stratified societies—industrial and postindustrial societies ensure their survival.

Although almost everyone learns the goal of success, not everyone has the same access to the approved means to reach this goal. There are only a limited number of high-paying positions, for example. It is easy to see how wanting success but being cut off from the approved ways to reach it leads to strain. A summary of sociologist Robert Merton's analysis of the ways that people react to strain is presented in Table 6-3. (The *conformists* don't experience strain. They have access to approved ways to strive after success. People

TABLE 6-3 How People Match Their Goals to Their Means

Do They Feel the Strain That Leads to Anomie?	Mode of Adaptation	Cultural Goals	Institutionalized Means
No	Conformity	Accept	Accept
	Deviant Paths:		
	1. Innovation	Accept	Reject
	2. Ritualism	Reject	Accept
Yes	3. Retreatism	Reject	Reject
	4. Rebellion	Reject/Replace	Reject/Replace

who experience strain make the other four adaptations.) The *innovators* accept the cultural goals, but they substitute other means of reaching them. An example is someone who decides to pursue wealth through fraud instead of through hard work. The *ritualists* give up on the goal, but they still keep active in culturally approved ways. An example is workers who no longer hope to get ahead, but who do just enough on the job to avoid getting fired. The *retreatists* reject both the goal and the means; some, such as street addicts, retreat into drugs, others into a monastery or a convent. *Rebels* are convinced that society is corrupt and reject both the legitimate means and the goals. They also seek to replace the current social order with a new one.

Innovation is the response that interests us. This is where crime comes in. Finding the legitimate means to success blocked, and yet wanting that cultural goal, innovators turn to *illegitimate* means. Buddy, Gary, and Clyde are examples. Thus, a high proportion of crime is a response to accepting the cultural goal, or, as Cohen said, "conformity to the American way."

SOCIAL CLASS AND ILLEGITIMATE OPPORTUNITIES. Consider why the poor commit so much burglary, theft, and robbery. Functionalists stress how the poor are bombarded with messages that urge them to want material success. Television portrays vivid images of middle-class lives, suggesting that full-fledged Americans can afford the goods and services portrayed in commercials and programs. Education is one of the main approved ways of reaching the goal of success, but the middle class runs the school system. There, the children of the poor are ill prepared for the bewildering world they confront, which conflicts so sharply with their background. Their grammar and swear words, their ideas of punctuality and neatness, their lack of paper-and-pencil skills—all differ from those of middle-class students. In addition, the schools that most poor children attend are inferior to the schools that educate children from higher social classes (Kozol 1999). These barriers create higher dropout rates among working-class students, blocking them from many legitimate avenues of financial success.

Often, however, a different door opens to them, one that sociologists Richard Cloward and Lloyd Ohlin (1960) called **illegitimate opportunity structures.** These are opportunities woven into the texture of life in urban slums: robbery, burglary, drug dealing, prostitution, pimping, gambling, and other income-producing crimes or "hustles." The "hustler" or "player" becomes a model for others—glamorously successful, one of the few people in the neighborhood whose material success approximates the mainstream cultural stereotype. Such illegitimate opportunities beckon to the poor in disproportionate numbers.

The middle and upper classes are not free of crime, of course. Functionalists point out that *different* illegitimate opportunities open to them, ones that make *different forms* of crime functional. Instead of pimping, burglary, or mugging, members of the middle and upper classes commit white-collar crime—tax evasion, bribery of public officials, advertising fraud, price fixing, and securities violations. Martha Stewart is a remarkable example. She made over $1 billion the day her company, Martha Stewart Omnimedia, went public on the New York Stock Exchange. Yet, to gain a few thousand dollars, Stewart engaged in insider trading (trading stock on the basis of information gleaned from the "inside"). She was forced to resign her position as head of the company she founded, and she served a few months in a "country club" prison. To put it mildly, the opportunities for crime available to Martha Stewart were different from the opportunities for crime available to people who live in the inner city.

WHY DO ONLY SOME PEOPLE COMMIT PROPERTY CRIMES? As you know, not everyone steals and robs. With the success motif so prevalent, and with the legitimate means to success limited, why doesn't everyone who finds his or her way blocked become a criminal?

To answer this, sociologists have developed control theory, which focuses on the inner and outer controls that inhibit crime. *Inner* controls are what most of us mean by self-control. They include internalized morality, such as our ideas of right and wrong and our religious principles. They also include fears of punishment, feelings of integrity, moral beliefs, the desire to be a "good" person, and the ability to defer gratification (Hirschi 1969; Brownfield and Sorenson 1993; Schoepfer and Piquero 2006). *Outer* controls include authorities such as the police, courts, and teachers; the potential damage to one's social standing and reputation; and the reactions of one's family.

(By permission of Johnny Hart & Creators Syndicate, Inc.)

The cartoonist indicates an essential principle that is highlighted by functionalists—that crime is functional for individuals and society.

IN SUM Functionalists view property crime as *inherent* in societies that socialize people of all social classes to desire material success, while limiting the legitimate means to that success. Although society expands people's desires by holding out limitless opportunities, many people find the legitimate avenues to success blocked. Some of them turn to illegitimate means. Through a combination of inner and outer controls, however, most of us are kept in line most of the time. We will return to control theory in the section on juvenile delinquency.

Conflict Theory

Two leading U.S. aerospace companies, Hughes Electronics and Boeing Satellite Systems, were accused of illegally exporting missile technology to China. The technology allowed China to improve its delivery system for nuclear weapons, placing the United States at risk. The two companies pleaded guilty and paid fines. No executives went to jail. (Gerth 2003)

INEQUITY IN THE LEGAL SYSTEM: POWER AND SOCIAL CLASS. Have you ever wondered about such cases? By exporting technology that can make China's missiles hit U.S. cities instead of dropping harmlessly into the ocean, the top executives of Boeing and Hughes have put us all at risk. Were these executives executed for treason? Were they put in prison for the rest of their lives? Not all. They didn't spend even a single day in jail. The *companies* paid a fine out of their vast profits—and continued to chauffer the executives who committed this crime between their exclusive offices and luxurious homes. Yet we read other news reports of young men or women from the lower class who are sent to prison for stealing a $5,000 automobile.

How can we have such inequity in a legal system that is supposed to provide "law, liberty, and justice for all"? Conflict theorists, who ask such questions about crime and criminal justice, stress that every society is marked by power and inequality. The most fundamental division of a capitalist society, they say, is between those who control the means of production and those who do not. The few people who are in the buyer's seat control the means of production. Most of us must sell our labor. Those who buy labor are called *the ruling class;* those who sell their labor are called *the working class.*

The working class consists of three major groups. In the *first* are the upper-level managers and professionals. Their positions are fairly secure, and their pay is good. In return for their security and comfort, managers and professionals show high loyalty to the ruling class and give strong support to the status quo. The *second* group consists of the stable working class. Most white-collar and blue-collar workers are members of this group. They get jobs, but their work is not as stable, and the pay is less. Their jobs, however, are adequate for survival. The *third* group is made up of the marginal working class, which receives the least of society's rewards. These people have shaky jobs, and their labor is in low demand. This group includes most of the unemployed and people who are on welfare. From the marginal working class (also called the "reserve army" of the unemployed) come most burglars, muggers, armed robbers, and car thieves.

Conflict theorists emphasize that the law is not like the ideology taught in grade school—an impartial social institution that administers a code of justice shared by all. Rather, the law is controlled by the ruling class, which uses it to oppress the marginal working class and maintain their own privileges of power and wealth. Because of this, the criminal justice system does not focus on the owners of corporations and the harm they do to the public through pollution, price manipulation, or unsafe products (Coleman 1989). Instead, the police and courts monitor the marginal working class: Members of this group show little loyalty to the ruling class, and most revolutionaries come from this group. As a result, the law comes down hard on violators from the marginal working class.

Violations by owners—the ruling class that controls society—cannot be totally ignored. If their crimes were to become too flagrant, they could provoke an outcry among the working class and, ultimately, foment revolution. To prevent this, an occasional violation by the powerful is prosecuted—and given huge publicity—as was the case with Martha Stewart. This demonstration that the criminal justice system applies to all helps to stabilize society. As we saw with Hughes and Boeing—whose top executives have strong connections with powerful political figures—companies are usually only fined, and their executives go unpunished. Although the ruling class comes down hard on the property crimes of the working class, it ordinarily ensures that lesser penalties are applied to its own versions of property crime.

Except for the rare prosecutions of the wealthy, such as Martha Stewart, which are held out to the public as proof of the fairness of the judicial system, few criminals from the wealthy classes appear in court. Most go before a state or federal agency (such as the Federal Trade Commission) that has no power to imprison. The FTC, headed by people of privilege, levies token fines. Most cases of illegal sales of stocks and bonds, price fixing, restraint of trade, and so on are handled by "gentlemen overseeing gentlemen." In contrast, the property crimes of the working class are channeled into a court system that does imprison. Burglary, armed robbery, petty theft, and stealing automobiles threaten not only the sanctity of private property but also, if allowed to continue, the positions of the powerful.

IN SUM Conflict theorists stress that law enforcement is not a system of justice, but a device used by the powerful to carry out their policies and to keep themselves in power. They use the legal system to control workers, mask injustice, and stabilize society. This point comes out strongly in the Spotlight on Social Research box on the next page written by William Chambliss, a conflict theorist who has done research on criminal justice systems in different parts of the world.

Sociologists have studied urban gangs since the 1920s. They have found that some of these gangs function as substitute families. They provide security and identity and are disproportionately made up of the poor.

Research Findings

To understand crime as a social problem, we'll first review research on five types of crime: juvenile delinquency, white-collar crime, professional crime, organized crime, and political crime. Then we'll look at research on the criminal justice system.

Juvenile Delinquency

THE ORIGIN OF JUVENILE DELINQUENCY. Our twenty-first-century views of life stages make it difficult for us to grasp how differently children used to be perceived. Earlier generations did not make the distinctions between children and adults that we do. Children who broke

Spotlight on Social Research
DOING RESEARCH ON CRIMINALS

WILLIAM CHAMBLISS, *Professor of Sociology at The George Washington University in Washington, DC, became interested in criminology during his junior year in high school. That summer, he and a friend hitchhiked from Los Angeles to Walla Walla, Washington, where they worked with convicts picking peas. As Chambliss got to know the convicts, he was fascinated to discover what the bank robbers, drug dealers, burglars, and thieves were planning to do when they were released from prison—commit more crimes.*

After my experiences that summer, I knew that I wanted to be a criminologist. When I went to UCLA, I was exposed to sociology and criminology. There, I developed a passion for both that has never waned.

After college, I was drafted into the Army and sent to Korea where I spent eighteen months as a special agent with the Counter Intelligence Corps. I was exposed to an immense amount of crime. But it was the crimes of the state and of the U.S. military that most interested me. They were the most egregious, not the crimes of the petty thieves and burglars or even what today we would call "terrorists." Between the pea fields of Walla Walla and the rice paddies of South Korea, I came to ponder what a short step it is from legitimacy to crime, from interrogation to torture, and from fighting soldiers to shooting and raping civilians.

Over the years, I have done research on organized crime, economic crime, juvenile gangs, and the creation of laws in the United States. I have also studied crime abroad: in England, Sweden, Norway, Nigeria, Zambia, and Thailand. Everywhere I have gone, from the slums and drizzling rain of Seattle to the steamy heat of Nigeria, I found the same story: Some of the worst offenders are the least likely to experience the sting of the criminal justice system, while the less powerful fill the courtrooms and the prisons. This bothers me. It just isn't justice.

In one of my books, *Power, Politics and Crime* (Westview, 2001), I suggest these social policies:

1. Mandatory minimum sentences be abolished (including three-strikes laws), and, in general, the trend toward more severe punishments be reversed.
2. Crime statistics be gathered by agencies that are independent of law enforcement agencies.
3. Law enforcement agencies be put under civilian control.
4. The prosecuting attorney's office be depoliticized (removed from political influence or control).
5. Drugs be decriminalized. The primary reason for this is that the enforcement of drug laws results in systemic bias against the poor and ethnic minorities.

My journey of discovery in criminology has exposed many shortcomings in the world we live in. It has also given me an opportunity to meet and work with wonderful people, some labeled criminals, others labeled heroes. Although I sometimes wish that "I didn't know now, what I didn't know then," more often I am eternally grateful for the opportunity to explore the world of crime and crime control and to do what I can to help make it more equitable—which is its supposed purpose.

the law used to be treated the same as adults. In the 1700s, girls as young as 13 were burned to death for their crimes, and 8- and 10-year-old boys were hanged for theirs (Blackstone 1899). When society industrialized in the 1800s, it was not only the adults but also the children who worked full-time in factories and mines. Some children operated machines 14 hours a day under miserable conditions for less than the price of a loaf of bread. In the 1800s, society softened a bit, but age afforded neither an excuse for lawbreaking nor a protection from harsh penalties.

As industrialization progressed, international trade unions, founded in the 1800s, ushered in labor laws to protect children (Phelps 1939). At the same time, political and civic leaders recognized the need for an educated workforce. They also feared that the huge number of immigrants rushing into the United States were bringing" foreign values" that might change the country, and they looked at public education as a way to "Americanize" immigrants (Hellinger and Judd 1991). Mandatory education laws were passed, requiring all children to attend school, usually until they had completed the eighth grade or turned 16, whichever came first. Until this time, schooling had been voluntary, and some children went to school, but many did not.

These new laws on child labor and education represent a perceptual shift in how children were viewed. As part of this cultural transformation, teenagers came to be seen as a separate class of people. Previously, the teen years were just an age, much as ages 30 to 35 are now—there was nothing distinctive about them. As part of this perceptual shift, laws were passed that classified juveniles as a separate category in the criminal justice system (Platt 1979). This change in the law produced a new category of crime—**juvenile delinquency.** To separate children from adults, the first juvenile court was established in Illinois in 1899, which means that juvenile delinquency has been around for only a little over 100 years. Crimes by juveniles, of course, are nothing new—just the classification.

EXTENT OF JUVENILE INVOLVEMENT IN CRIME. Some juvenile delinquency consists of **status crimes,** behaviors that are crimes if juveniles commit them, but not if adults do. Examples are curfew violations, underage drinking, and running away from home. Status crimes are not the primary social problem of juvenile delinquency, for people are less concerned about them. It is the predatory crimes of violence that have most upset people and that have captured headlines.

Although 13- to 17-year-old boys make up only 3.5 percent of the U.S. population, they commit about 15 percent of the nation's **violent crimes**—murder, forcible rape, robbery, and aggravated assault. The proportion of crimes committed by this group is about *four times* greater than their proportion of the population. This group also commits about a fourth of the nation's **property crimes**—burglary, larceny, motor vehicle theft, and arson (*FBI Uniform Crime Reports* 2005:Table 39; *Statistical Abstract* 2006:Table 11). This is *seven times* greater than their proportion of the population.

Girls commit fewer crimes than boys, but they are closing the gap, which also alarms people. As you can see from Table 6-4 on the next page, girls make up an increasing percentage of juveniles arrested for both violent and property crimes. The change in what girls are arrested for is startling. While the number of boys who are arrested for violent crimes is up just 12 percent since the early 1980s, the arrests of girls for violent crimes has *doubled.* Girls used to be charged with the status crimes of underage sex and running away from home. Today, over 12,000 girls are arrested each year for murder, robbery, and aggravated assault. Another 110,000 are arrested for larceny, theft, and arson.

THE DELINQUENT CAREER. Sociologists have uncovered what they call the "delinquent career." Here are the patterns that Howard Snyder (1988) found when he studied the court records of 69,000 juvenile delinquents in Phoenix, Arizona;

1. After their first arrest, most youths (59 percent) never return to juvenile court.
2. The juveniles most likely to continue their delinquent behavior are those who are arrested a second time before age 16.

TABLE 6-4 Arrests of People Under Age 18

	NUMBER OF ARRESTS				PERCENTAGE OF ARRESTS		
	1981	2000	2004	Percent Change	1981	2000	2004
Violent Crimes[1]							
Boys	47,415	48,169	53,154	+12%	89%	82%	81%
Girls	5,825	10,686	12,149	+109%	11%	18%	19%
Totals	53,240	58,885	65,303		100%	100%	100%
Property Crimes[2]							
Boys	398,924	218,816	215,934	−46%	81%	70%	66%
Girls	95,010	94,888	110,378	+16%	19%	30%	34%
Totals	493,934	313,704	326,312		100%	100%	100%

[1]Violent crimes are murder, forcible rape, robbery, and aggravated assault

[2]Property crimes are burglary, larceny-theft, motor vehicle theft, and arson.

Source: By the author. Based on *Sourcebook of Criminal Justice Statistics* 1993:Table 35; *FBI Uniform Crime Reports* 2000:Table 37; 2005:Tables 39, 40.

3. Juveniles who are charged with a violent crime (murder, rape, robbery, or aggravated assault) are likely to have committed many crimes.
4. The younger that juveniles are when they are first charged with a violent crime, the greater the likelihood that they will be charged later with a violent crime. (Those who are first charged at age 13 are *twice* as likely to be arrested for a later violent offense as those who are first charged at age 16.)
5. The juveniles who are the *most* likely to be rearrested are those whose first charge was burglary, truancy, motor vehicle theft, or robbery (see Figure 6-3).
6. The juveniles who are the *least* likely to be rearrested are those whose first charge was underage drinking, running away, or shoplifting.
7. Girls are less likely to be rearrested than boys (29 percent versus 46 percent).

CRIME AND HIGH SCHOOL GRADUATION. You may have heard the parents of a boy who has gotten in trouble with the law say, "If only we can keep him in school, he'll have a chance. If he drops out, he's lost." Is this common observation—made by the parents of delinquent girls, too—correct? To find out, we need to compare the adult arrests of delinquents who complete high school with the adult arrests of delinquents who drop out. This is what Table 6-5 does. As you can see, by the time they are adults, delinquents who complete high school are only *half* as likely to be arrested as those who drop out of high school. The table also shows another remarkable finding: Children who are *not* delinquents who drop out of high school are *more* likely to be arrested as adults than delinquents who graduate from high school. The common observation is certainly correct.

NEUTRALIZING DEVIANCE. Juvenile delinquents know that their crimes are condemned by society, so how do they avoid guilt? In a classic study, symbolic interactionists Gresham Sykes and David Matza (1957) found that delinquents use these five **techniques of neutralization**:

1. *Denial of responsibility.* Delinquents view themselves as propelled by forces beyond their control. Their unloving parents, bad companions, or bad neighborhoods cause them to break the law. By denying responsibility, they break the link between themselves and their acts. ("I'm just a billiard ball on the pool table of life.")
2. *Denial of injury.* Delinquents admit that their acts are illegal, but deny that they hurt anyone. They call their vandalism "mischief," "pranks," or "just having a little fun." This breaks the link between them and the consequences of their acts.

FIGURE 6-3 Rearrest Based on the First Crime Juveniles Were Charged With

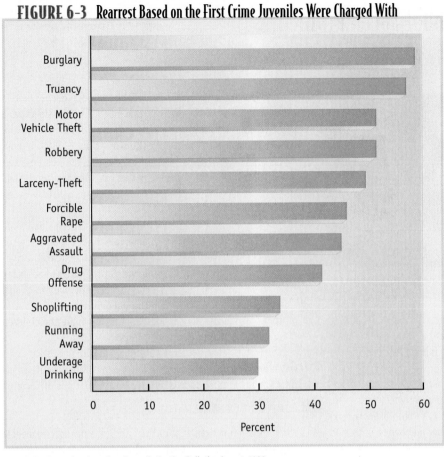

Source: By the author, based on *Juvenile Justice Bulletin*, August 1988.

3. *Denial of a victim.* If delinquents admit that they have done harm, they claim that the injury was not wrong "under the circumstances." The person they hurt was not really a victim. What they did was just a way to "get even" for some wrong. Vandalizing a school, for example, is revenge on unfair teachers; theft is retaliation against gouging storekeepers. With no victims, they can even transform themselves from wrongdoers into avengers.

4. *Condemnation of the condemners.* Delinquents also take the offensive. They call those who condemn them hypocrites and accuse the police of being brutal or "on the take." By attacking others, they deflect attention away from their own behavior.

TABLE 6-5 High School Graduation, Delinquency, and Adult Arrests

	ARRESTED AS ADULTS	
	African Americans	Whites
Delinquent in high school		
Dropped out	47%	33%
Completed high school	24%	18%
Not delinquent in high school		
Dropped out	30%	22%
Completed high school	16%	6%

Based on a longitudinal study of male Philadelphia high school students; no data for girls or other groups.
Source: By the author. Based on Rosen et al. 1991:Tables 2, 5.

THINKING CRITICALLY About Social Problems

ISLANDS IN THE STREET: URBAN GANGS IN THE UNITED STATES

For more than ten years, sociologist Martín Sánchez Jankowski (1991) did participant observation of thirty-seven African American, Chicano, Dominican, Irish, Jamaican, and Puerto Rican gangs in Boston, Los Angeles, and New York City. The gangs earned money through gambling, arson, mugging, armed robbery, and selling moonshine, drugs, guns, stolen car parts, and protection. Jankowski ate, slept, and sometimes fought with the gangs, but by mutual agreement he did not participate in drug dealing or in other illegal activities. He was seriously injured twice during the study.

Contrary to stereotypes, Jankowski did not find that the motive for joining a gang was to escape a broken home (there were as many members from intact families as from broken homes) or to seek a substitute family (the same number of boys said they were close to their families as those that said they were not). Rather, the boys joined to gain access to money, to have recreation (including girls and drugs), to maintain anonymity in committing crimes, to get protection, and to help the community. This last reason may seem surprising, but in some neighborhoods, gangs protect residents from outsiders and spearhead political change (Kontos et al. 2003). The boys also saw the gang as an alternative to the dead-end—and deadening—jobs held by their parents.

Neighborhood residents are ambivalent about gangs. On the one hand, they fear the violence. On the other hand, many adults once belonged to gangs, the gangs often provide better protection than the police, and gang members are the children of people who live in the neighborhood.

Particular gangs will come and go, but gangs will likely always remain part of the city. As functionalists point out, gangs fulfill needs of poor youth who live on the margins of society.

FOR YOUR CONSIDERATION

What are the functions that gangs fulfill (the needs they meet)? Suppose that you have been hired as an urban planner by the City of Los Angeles. How could you arrange to meet the needs that gangs fulfill in ways that minimize violence and encourage youth to follow mainstream norms?

---

5. *Appeal to higher loyalties.* Some delinquents see themselves as in the midst of role conflict, torn between two incompatible expectations. The law pulls them one way, loyalty to friends another. The friends win out. If a rival gang hurts a friend, for example, to retaliate is "more moral" than to ignore the injury.

These techniques allow delinquents to neutralize society's norms. Even if delinquents have internalized mainstream values—and not all have—these rationalizations let them commit crimes with a minimum of guilt or shame.

DELINQUENT SUBCULTURES. Some delinquents have little to neutralize. They grow up in **delinquent subcultures,** where criminal activities are taken for granted. In these subcultures, they learn norms that support crime, as well as techniques for committing burglaries, robberies, and so on. In some of these subcultures, youths even learn to rape, kill, and terrorize. Not everyone who grows up in such environments becomes delinquent, however. Why?

SOCIAL CONTROLS. For answers, let's first consider social control and then labeling theory. According to social control theory, three factors are involved: inner controls, outer controls, and the desire to commit a crime. When children grow up in the same neighborhood, the outer controls look similar. But as sociologist Joan Moore (1978) found in her classic study of three Chicano barrios (neighborhoods) in Los Angeles, the outer controls (the life situations) of youths in the same neighborhood can differ sharply. This, in turn, affects the youths' inner controls and their desire to commit criminal acts.

Moore used a variety of research techniques. She did participant observation of barrio life, interviewed residents, and also hung out with former convicts. She found that the difference begins in the family. Despite their outward similarities, families in poor neighborhoods, like families everywhere, differ in their values and what they teach their children. Some parents are more oriented toward work and education. Some stress moral responsibility. Teaching these values increases their children's inner controls and reduces their involvement in crimes (Schoepfer and Piquero 2006). These children strive to do better in school, and as teachers reward their efforts, their motivation to conform increases. For children who are reared in families where such traditional values are minimal, the criminally oriented peer group becomes more attractive. Because these children are not as oriented to work roles, gangs and crime become more enticing.

To better understand how significant outer controls are, consider extremes among families. Everyone knows that some families are rotten (in sociological terms, dysfunctional). Some parents abuse their kids sexually. Others abuse their children physically and psychologically. Abused children are likely to run away, for the streets look more appealing than what passes for a home. "On the run" these children do what they can to survive on the city's mean streets: They beg, steal, or sell their bodies. Compare such miserable situations with that of children who grow up in families where their parents love and nourish them emotionally. This commonsense assumption that home life has far-reaching effects on children's likelihood to become delinquent is supported by an abundance of sociological research. Bill McCarthy and John Hagan (1992), for example, compared homeless adolescents in Toronto with youths who were still at home. It will come as no surprise to you that the homeless youths were more likely to have been abused physically and sexually by their parents and that they were more likely to have committed crimes.

It doesn't take an exceptional home to help steer children away from delinquency, but it is more difficult for a single parent to counter the attractions of the street than it is for two parents to do so. To say this is not to detract from the efforts of single moms and dads. It is just that sociologists consistently find that children who are reared by both parents are less likely to get in trouble with the law. This is true whether or not the children's parents are married (McCurley and Snyder forthcoming). And why shouldn't two parents be more effective in guiding their children toward conformance than a single parent? There are *two* people working on this demanding task instead of just one.

LABELING AND LIFE CONSEQUENCES. Labeling theorists stress the significance of a youth being labeled a delinquent. Such labeling can be a matter of sheer luck. I know a teenager who did the same things that his buddies did, but he happened to go home early one night. While everyone else "got busted" and acquired the label "delinquent," he did not. On an even more personal note, I escaped this label, too. When I was arrested as a teenager, after spending a night in jail, for some unknown reason I never had to report to a judge or have any kind of hearing. My parents were working class, so class was not a factor. Social class, however, can be highly significant in labeling. Recall Chambliss' study of the "saints" and the "roughnecks" and how labels affected these lower- and middle-class boys differently. Being labeled a troublemaker certainly can set youths apart and cause them to continue on the path to more trouble. In some instances, labels create a cloud of suspicion that cuts an adolescent off from conforming people and activities, channeling the individual in the direction of greater deviance.

IN SUM We have reviewed how extensive crime is among adolescents and how delinquency is increasing among girls. We have seen how delinquents neutralize their crimes, how in the same neighborhood only some youths become involved in criminal acts, and how two parents are more successful than one in keeping their kids out of trouble. Social control theory, sensitizing us to differences in family structure and values and to the significance of peer groups, helps us to understand these aspects of delinquency. Labeling theory also helps to explain why some adolescents graduate from delinquency into adult crime. Social control and labeling theory also apply to crimes committed by adults, of course. Let's look at some of those crimes.

White-Collar Crime

> After flashing photos of executives from Enron and Arthur Andersen on the television monitor, Jon Stewart, the anchor of *The Daily Show*, turned to the camera and shouted: "Why aren't all of you in jail? And not like white-guy jail—jail jail. With people by the weight room going, 'Mmmmm.'" (Leaf 2004)

When corporate scandals hit the news, we learn about top executives who steal outrageous amounts of money. Occasionally, as with the bankruptcy of Enron, billions of dollars were diverted for private gain. For the most part—again, as conflict theorists say, with an occasional prosecution to illustrate that the criminal justice system is impartial—corporate criminals go unpunished. Sociologist Edwin Sutherland (1949) coined the term **white-collar crime** for crimes "committed by people of respectable and high social status in the course of their occupation."

THE COST. No one knows for sure how much white-collar crime costs the nation, but estimates place the bill at about $600 billion a year (McCain 2004), more than the cost of all street crime. Most white-collar crime never comes to the surface, but that which does can be enlightening. The most notorious example in recent years is the fraud at Enron, which cost stockholders more than $50 billion. Eleven thousand employees also suffered huge losses in their pensions. Bank robbers risk their lives for $10,000, but corporate executives manipulate computers and documents to make millions of illegal dollars for their corporations—or to rip off those same companies.

CRIMES COMMITTED TO HELP A CORPORATION. The two major types of white-collar crime are those committed by employees *on behalf of* a corporation and those committed *against* a corporation. In crimes committed *on behalf of* a corporation, employees break the law in order to benefit a business organization. Examples include car manufacturers knowingly selling dangerous automobiles, drug companies faking test data so they can keep their drugs on the market, and corporations engaging in price fixing and tax dodging.

Corporations, even major ones listed on the stock exchanges, can easily produce a criminogenic (crime-causing) culture. The corporate culture revolves around not only corporate profits but also personal achievement and recognition. Pressures to increase profits and to climb the corporate ladder, combined with the insulation of executives from the consequences of their decisions, can lead to an "ethical numbness" (Hills 1987).

Some of our most well known corporations participate in white-collar crimes, some of which result in death. In one of its factories producing Ball Park Franks, Sarah Lee stopped testing for listeria, a deadly disease. The result was the deaths of 15 people who ate their hot dogs. What was their punishment? Following the principle that white-collar criminals receive little punishment, even when the consequences of their acts are deadly, Sara Lee pled guilty to two misdemeanors and paid a fine (Mauer 2004).

The Sara Lee executives were merely careless or negligent, but corporate culture can so dominate its members that executives of major companies can even end up calculating the cold-blooded deaths of others for profit. This is illustrated by the infamous "Pinto case." The Pinto was a car manufactured by Ford in the 1970s. After three young women in Indiana burned to death when their Pinto burst into flames following a rear-end crash, the Ford Motor Company was charged with reckless homicide (Strobel 1980; Fisse and Braithwaite 1987). No executives were charged, just Ford itself. It was alleged that Ford knew that in a rear-end collision the Pinto's gas tank could rupture, spew gas, and burn passengers to death (Dowie 1977, 1979). (Never mind how a corporation can know anything. The common-sense view is that it is people in the corporation who know things, and they who make criminal decisions. Common sense and the legal system, however, often walk different paths.)

Disclosed at the trial was heart-wrenching evidence that revealed the cold-blooded malice of Ford executives. Installing a simple piece of plastic would have corrected the problem, at a cost of just $11 per car. The Ford executives faced a difficult decision—whether to pay the $11 or to sentence drivers and passengers to fiery deaths. Now, that is a difficult choice—at least it was for these executives. The memo below, revealed during the trial, shows how the executives compared what it would cost the company to make the change ("Costs") or to pay for the deaths ("Benefits," meaning the amount of benefits that would have to be paid). As you can see, the cost of installing the plastic was high ($137 million) compared to the amount of money that would have to be paid if they simply allowed people to die ($49.5 million). To save $87 million for the company, the executives decided to let 180 people burn to death. Their estimates turned out to be too low: Several hundred people burned to death, and many others were disfigured.

Ford's Internal Memo on the Pinto. Benefits and Costs Relating to Fuel Leakage Associated with the Static Rollover Test Portion of FMVSS 208

BENEFITS.

Savings: 180 burn deaths, 180 serious burn injuries, 2,100 burned vehicles.
Unit cost: $200,000 per death, $67,000 per injury, $700 per vehicle.
Total benefit: 180 × ($200,000) + 180 × ($67,000) + 2,100 × ($700) = $49.5 million.

COSTS.

Sales: 11 million cars, 1.5 million light trucks.
Unit cost: $11 per car, $11 per truck.
Total cost: 11,000,000 × ($11) + 1,500,000 × ($11) = $137 million.

Sources: Dowie 1977; Strobel 1980:286.

With the right lawyers and connections, people can get away with murder. Ford was acquitted. The company recalled its 1971–1976 Pintos for fuel tank modification and launched a publicity campaign to maintain an image of a "good" company. Ford executives claimed that the internal memo was misunderstood. They said that it "related to a proposed federal safety standard, and not to the design of the Pinto" (Fisse and Braithwaite 1987:253). Despite causing hundreds of deaths, not a single Ford executive was arrested or tried in court. They remained free, wealthy, and respected in their communities.

You might think that such a cold, homicidal act would never be repeated by a U.S. automobile company. Unfortunately, such an expectation would be wrong. In 1998, a 13-year-old boy was burned to death when the gas tank of an Oldsmobile Cutlass station wagon ruptured. When GM was sued, a memo was discovered in which GM calculated the cost to fix the problem at just $4.50 per vehicle. GM also calculated the cost of lawsuits and figured these would average just $2.40 per car. Able to save an estimated $2.10 per car, GM did not fix the problem (Boot 1998).

The Pinto and Cutlass cases confirm the perspective of the conflict theorists: The powerful can and do manipulate our legal system. They can and do escape punishment for their crimes—including in these instances what I would call serial murder. Can you possibly imagine similar results from our legal system if poor people plotted to kill a couple of hundred automobile executives? (The photo to the right illustrates the reality that underlies this example.)

CRIMES COMMITTED AGAINST A CORPORATION. The main crime *against* the corporation is employee theft, ranging from snitching company supplies to embezzling company funds.

Sociologists compute the costs of white-collar crime in dollar terms, but their analyses can make it sound as though white-collar crimes were a harmless nuisance. Perhaps most is. But some white-collar crime has horrible costs. Shown here is Patricia Anderson, who, with her four children, was burned when the gas tank of her 1979 Chevrolet Malibu exploded after a rear-end collision. One child's hand was burned off, and her ears burned to the bone. Outraged at the callousness of GM's conduct, the jury awarded these victims the staggering sum of $4.9 billion, the largest personal injury award in U.S. history. A judge later reduced the amount to $1.2 billion.

This crime also includes sabotage by disgruntled employees. To avoid tarnishing their public images with the disgrace of internal crime, most corporations deal privately with such offenders.

Stealing company secrets, such as formulas, manufacturing processes, or even marketing plans, is a form of theft. If an employee sells one company's secrets to a competitor, the matter is easily recognized as a crime. A gray area emerges, however, when a key employee goes to work for a competitor. This employee steals nothing, but is hired specifically because he or she has vital knowledge about the former employer. The employee might even be given a higher salary and bonuses because of this knowledge. Because the knowledge is inside the individual's head, and no documents are stolen, this crime is difficult to prove.

Back in the 1950s, sociologist Donald Cressey (1953) did a classic study of embezzlers. He found that employees embezzle because they have an "unsharable financial problem"—overdue taxes, children in college, sometimes gambling losses. He also found that, like juvenile delinquents, embezzlers neutralize their crime. Many consider their embezzling to be a form of borrowing—the money being simply an unauthorized loan to tide them over in their financial emergency. They will pay it back later. Some think of themselves as deserving the money because they are worth more than they are being paid or because their employer has cheated or somehow taken advantage of them: As with juvenile delinquents, the techniques of neutralization are usually effective. In this case, they let people violate the trust that their company placed in them and still consider themselves to be respectable, law-abiding citizens.

Cressey's findings are limited. Other researchers have found that not all embezzlers neutralize their crimes (Green 1993). Some just embezzle without trying to justify it (Benson 1985). Embezzlers also have many motives, not just unsharable financial problems. Some embezzle on an impulse; others are greedy (Nettler 1974). To help with ordinary family bills, some embezzle only a little, but regularly. Motives even change over the course of a long-term embezzlement. I knew an embezzler who headed a remote branch of a Spanish bank. After he embezzled a few thousand dollars for personal reasons, he saw it was so easy that he kept doing it even after he didn't need the money. When caught, his theft had amounted to millions.

The most costly crime against the corporation was the plundering of the U.S. savings and loan industry in the 1980s. The crime was so common that corporate officers across the nation looted their banks of billions of dollars. The total cost ran about $500 billion—$2,000 for every man, woman, and child in the country at that time (Kettl 1991; Newdorf 1991). Perhaps the most infamous culprit was Neil Bush, son of the then president of the United States. As an officer of Silverado, a Colorado savings and loan, Bush helped bankrupt Silverado by approving $100 million in loans to a company in which he held secret interests (Tolchin 1991a).

Future generations will suffer from this wholesale looting. The interest alone is exorbitant. At 5 percent, a year's interest on an increase of $500 billion in the national debt would run $25 billion, at 10 percent, $50 billion. Because the government does not pay its debt but merely borrows more to keep up with the compounding interest, the $500 billion now totals about $1 trillion. As the late Senator Everett Dirksen once said, "A billion here and a billion there, and pretty soon you're talking about real money."

CHANGES IN WHITE-COLLAR CRIME. Back in 1975, sociologist Rita Simon predicted that as more women worked outside the home they would become more involved in white-collar crime. This is just what happened. Like men, many women who join the corporate world are enticed by its opportunities for crime. Table 6-6 tracks this change. The largest increase is in embezzlement, a crime that women are now as likely as men to commit. As you look at this table, you might notice how the increase in white-collar crime by women parallels the rise in crime by female juveniles that we noted earlier (Table 6-4 on page 180).

SOCIAL CLASS AND PUNISHMENT. As noted in the quotation that opened this section, white-collar criminals enjoy a privileged position within the criminal justice system. Because of their social position and ability to manipulate the law, few corporate criminals are punished. Some even get away with murder, as we saw with the automobile executives.

TABLE 6-6 Arrests for White-Collar Crimes, by Sex

	1981		2000		2004	
	Male	Female	Male	Female	Male	Female
Embezzlement	70%	30%	50%	50%	50%	50%
Fraud	58%	42%	55%	45%	55%	45%
Forgery and counterfeiting	68%	32%	61%	39%	60%	40%
Fencing stolen property	88%	12%	83%	17%	81%	19%
Average	71%	29%	62%	38%	61%	39%

Note: Not all these acts meet the definition of white-collar crime as developed by Sutherland. From the categories available in the source, however, these are as close as we can come.

Source: By the author. Based on *FBI Uniform Crime Reports,* various editions, including *Crime in the United States* 2005:Table 42.

When arrested, which is seldom, white-collar criminals usually receive lenient sentences. Compared with street criminals, white-collar criminals (Carlson and Chaiken 1987) are

1. More likely to have their cases dismissed by the prosecutor (40 percent versus 26 percent)
2. Less likely to have to put up bail (13 percent versus 37 percent)
3. More likely to get probation rather than jail (54 percent versus 40 percent)
4. More likely to get shorter sentences (29 months versus 50 months)

It seems fair to conclude that this is another example of the social class bias that operates in the criminal justice system. This bias also operates *among* white-collar criminals. Even though they have committed the same crime, executives who are higher up in the company generally are charged with lesser crimes and given shorter sentences (Coleman 1989).

It is rare for executives to be convicted for their crimes and, if convicted, unusual for them to serve even a single day in prison. In a study of the 582 largest U.S. corporations, sociologist Marshall Clinard (Clinard et al. 1979; Clinard 1990) found that criminal charges had been filed against 1,553 executives. Only 56 were convicted, giving them a better than 96 percent chance of avoiding conviction if arrested. Of this small number, 40 served no time in prison. The 16 who did go to prison served a total of 597 days. Their average stay of 37 days was about what poor people serve for disorderly conduct. Another way of looking at this matter is to note that of 150,000 inmates in federal prisons, only 1,000 are white-collar criminals (Leaf 2004). Similarly, Neil Bush, the president's son who looted people's savings, had to pay a $50,000 fine—after friends of the president paid his legal fees (Tolchin 1991b; "Suit Settled" 1992). As sociologist Daniel Glaser (1978) observed, in a classic understatement, the criminal law has difficulty dealing with white-collar crime.

Professional Crime

CRIME AS WORK. **Professional criminals** are people who make their living from crime. The jewel thieves and counterfeiters—so highly romanticized in movies and books—are examples of professional criminals. So are fences—those who buy stolen goods for resale. Their activities, although illegal, are a form of work, and they pride themselves on their skills and successes.

In a classic study, Edwin Sutherland (1937) found that professional criminals organize their lives around their "work," much as people who work at legal jobs do. Professional thieves plan their work and may steal almost every day of the year—taking planned vacations and days off to celebrate birthdays, anniversaries, and some holidays. They associate with like-minded people who share their approach to life, including their values of loyalty, mutual aid, and scorn for the "straight world." They also teach one another technical skills for committing crimes and avoiding detection.

Some of the criminal activities that Sutherland studied have declined. As people switched from cash to credit cards, pickpocketing faded. It is the same with safecracking.

Technology and Social Problems
LEGOS AND MORE LEGOS: HIGH-TECH SHOPLIFTING

Shoplifting has been around as long as there have been shops. In the typical case, the shoplifter shoves some merchandise in a pocket or purse and walks away without paying for it. This is still the most common case.

But shoplifters are keeping up with the times by taking advantage of new technology. There is the bar code scam, for example. The shoplifter, if he or she can still be called that, replaces an item's bar code with the bar code of a lower-priced item. It is obviously awkward to remove an item's bar code in the store and then slap it on another item. Doing so could also draw some unwanted attention. Scammers get around this problem by buying the lower-priced item, then using scanners and computers they reproduce the bar code. They go into the store with a supply of the fake bar codes, stick them on the more expensive item, and join the other shoppers in the checkout line.

Can this scam be profitable? Consider William Swanberg, who specialized in Legos, those perennially popular children's building toys. He printed $19 bar codes from the cheap sets of Legos and inserted them on the $100 sets. He would buy ten sets at a time, all at his private 80 percent discount.

Swanberg liked Legos so much that he travelled around five Western states running his scam. He was meticulous, following an itinerary that specified his preferred "shopping" order, first Target, then Wal-Mart, followed by Toys-R-Us.

What did Swanberg do with all the Legos? He didn't have a garage or basement filled with strange creations he was working on. Rather, technology again provided the answer. He became a vendor on Bricklink.com, which specializes in Legos. (Yes, there is even a Web site for Legos people.) There, not surprisingly, Mr. Swanberg became known as a vendor with a terrific inventory. Target officials figure that Swanberg stole $200,000 worth of Legos just from their stores.

Bar-code swindlers are hard to catch, but don't get the idea that this might be a profitable side venture to honest work: Mr. Swanberg was sentenced to prison.

Based on Zimmerman 2006.

As some forms of professional crime dwindle, however, others, such as identity fraud, increase. Thieves use computers at one location to hack into computers that may be thousands of miles away, even on different continents. As you can see from the Technology and Social Problems box above, crime is keeping up with changing technology.

Although its forms change, professional crime continues to be characterized by in-group loyalty, scorn for the values of the straight world, and pride in specialized skills. One of my students found these traits to be evident among the car thieves he studied for my undergraduate course in deviance. Based on the demand for parts, the owner of the "chop shop" ordered specific cars, paying set prices according to the make and model he wanted. He and his workers used acetylene torches and other tools to disassemble the cars. They sold the fenders, motors, transmissions, seats, doors, and so on to dealers in used auto parts. The small amount of metal that was left over was hauled away by an older man who sold it for scrap. Like small business owners across the country, the owner-manager of the "chop shop" carried a great deal of responsibility. He made the decisions, paid the rent on the shop, and had to meet the weekly payroll. Unlike "straight" employers, however, he arranged for a surreptitious supply of oxygen for the acetylene torches, paid wages in cash, and did not pay taxes.

Not only did the members of the "chop shop" work together as a team, each performing a specialized function, but each also knew that they were working on stolen cars.

With their work carrying the risk of arrest, they built solidarity to increase their trust and dependence on one another. When they weren't working, the men socialized together. They drank at the same tavern (which was frequented by other professional criminals), and they visited at one another's homes. By integrating their working and social lives, they minimized the intrusion of straight values, kept close tabs on one another, and reinforced ideas about the rightness and desirability of how they made their living.

Unlike amateurs, few professional criminals are troubled by their criminality. To them, crime is simply one of many possible ways to make a living. They see themselves as businesspeople, no different from clerks who sell shoddy merchandise or surgeons who perform unnecessary operations. Theirs is just another form of "making it" in U.S. society.

Organized Crime

The professional criminals we have discussed are independent operators. In contrast, another group of professional criminals, participants in **organized crime,** work in a local organization, which, in turn, is part of a national or international network. These professional criminals not only make their living from crime, but they also belong to interconnected criminal organizations.

"Chop shops" operate all over the nation. Shown here are parts of a Jeep Cherokee that were recovered from a chop shop in Philadelphia, Pennsylvania. When my son's Jeep Cherokee was stolen, it never was found. Within a couple of days, I am sure, it, too, had been broken into its component parts, and they were on sale at several St. Louis locations.

THE MAFIA: ORIGINS AND CHARACTERISTICS. In one sense, the Mafia is a myth. The myth is that a criminal organization developed in Sicily, moved to the United States, and now controls organized crime here. The Mafia does exist, and it did originate in Sicily. As *The Godfather* series depicts, the Sicilian government was weak, and local strongmen united to protect their families and communities from bandits. After establishing a private government, they also protected their communities from other strongmen—in return for regular tribute (Anderson 1965; Blok 1974; Catanzaro 1992). As the formal government became more powerful, these men resisted, maintaining their control over areas of Sicily. After the 1860s, they became known as the **Mafia.**

The twin foundations of these private governments are the family and *omertá,* a vow of secrecy. These twin foundations are designed to ensure secrecy, solidarity, and separation from outsiders. To maintain close connections, the Mafia forges bonds through *village endogamy* (marriage between people from the same village) and *fictive kinship* (assigning obligations associated with close blood relatives to people who are not related; a godfather, for example, unites two families).

According to the Mafia myth, Sicilians introduced organized crime to the United States. New York City, however, has had organized crime for more than 150 years. It has been dominated by successive waves of ethnic immigrants—first the Irish, then the Jews, and only after that the Italians (Bell 1960). Today, no ethnic group dominates organized crime in New York City, which includes Sicilians and Italians, but also African Americans and Puerto Ricans. In their turn, Miami has Cuban organized crime, and San Francisco and Los Angeles have Japanese organized crime (Wagman 1981). Russian mobsters are the new ethnic contender, arriving on the U.S. crime scene after the breakup of the Soviet empire in 1991.

The Mafia myth, however, is valid in pinpointing an organization that is dominated by Americans of Sicilian-Italian descent, with connections across the United States and abroad. Transplanted to the United States, the various Mafias—and I emphasize the plural—continued their illegal activities among their own ethnic group. Prohibition provided the stimulus for these tightly knit organizations to expand. By the time Prohibition was repealed in 1933, the Mafias had become a power structure in major cities, especially Chicago and New York City (Sykes 1978). The Mafia developed a **bureaucracy,** a hierarchy that has specialized personnel (gunmen, runners, executives, and others), departmentalization (narcotics, prostitution, loan sharking, and gambling), and an enforcement arm to collect debts and keep profits flowing upward.

The Mafias do not make their organizational structures public, of course, but some cities appear to have the equivalent of a board of directors, a president and vice president, district managers with executive assistants, and, at the lowest level, soldiers who carry out the orders (Anderson 1965). In the Sicilian-American Mafia, about 5,000 members belong to about 24 "families" of 200 to 700 members each. These families are linked to each other by understandings and "treaties." The leaders of the most powerful families form a "commission" or "combine" to which weaker families pay deference (Cressey 1969; Riesel 1982a). Members call this structure the Mafia, or **cosa nostra** ("our thing").

Crime is the Mafias' business, and they are successful at their specializations. The Mafias flourish—despite the U.S. government's perpetual "war" against them and a series of premature obituaries trumpeted in the media. The Mafias—whether in their Sicilian, Colombian, or Russian versions—are the major importers and wholesalers of narcotics. They also run loan-sharking operations (making private, illegal loans at high rates of interest). In some areas, they control the labor unions and the construction trade (Penn 1982; Riesel 1982b; Trust 1986). The Mafias also have infiltrated many legitimate businesses, such as the garment industry of New York City. Violence remains the way the Mafias do business—despite their public relations claims to the contrary.

Why has organized crime been so successful, despite efforts of the U.S. government? We can cite the following reasons (*Organized Crime* 1976):

1. Organized crime *is* organized. The more organized Mafias have a bureaucracy with full-time specialists in many criminal pursuits.
2. Organized crime provides illegal *services in high demand* (prostitution, gambling, and loan sharking)—"victimless crimes" in which no one complains to the police.
3. Organized crime wields influence through *political corruption.*
4. Organized crime uses *violence and intimidation* against victims and its own members.

Conflict theorists add a *fifth* reason—that organized crime serves the goals of the U.S. ruling class. According to sociologist David Simon (1981), the ruling class has used organized crime to keep U.S. labor from getting too organized or becoming too "radical." During the 1920s and the 1940s, periods of great labor unrest, corporations hired gangsters to break strikes and infiltrate unions, especially among autoworkers and longshoremen. During World War II, U.S. Navy Intelligence asked Mafia boss Charles "Lucky" Luciano to protect the New York docks from sabotage. Luciano, who was directing Mafia operations from prison, cooperated. He also helped get the Sicilian Mafia to support the U.S. invasion of Sicily. As a reward, Luciano's prison sentence was commuted, and he was deported to Italy.

The allegations of Judith Campbell Exner add another dimension to the connection between the ruling class and the Mafia. Exner claimed to be one of President John F. Kennedy's lovers and also a mistress of Sam Giancana, the head of the Chicago Mafia. She reported that she carried messages between them (Kelley 1988). Supposedly, Giancana delivered votes to Kennedy in key states and, at Kennedy's request, plotted the assassination of Fidel Castro. This alleged connection has led to one of the many theories about Kennedy's assassination, that the mob assassinated Kennedy when he turned on them and directed his brother, Robert, head of the Justice Department, to pursue organized crime. Although conspiracy buffs love this theory, it is based only on allegations, and there may be no substance to it (DiEugenio 1997).

Some sociologists emphasize that organized crime threatens the well-being of the United States. The most serious problem is not gambling, prostitution, loan sharking, and so on, but the corruption of our social institutions. With their many millions of untaxed dollars, the Mafias bribe police, judges, and politicians, subverting the institutions and organizations that deal with crime. Thus violence, bribery, and other forms of corruption work their way into the social system (Cressey 1969; Teresa 1973; Gudkov 1980; Schwidrowski 1980). This leaves us with the frightening possibility that, as is the case in Russia today, much of our society could one day be controlled by organized crime.

In our often surrealistic world, mobsters sometimes imitate actors who are imitating mobsters, adopting their gestures, ways of speaking, and such. Shown here are members of *The Sopranos,* a popular television series on organized crime.

It is certain that crime will continue, and along with it various versions of organized crime. The future of the Mafias, however, at least of the Sicilian-American version, is uncertain. In recent years, this Mafia has faced stiff competition from other groups, *omertá* has been weakened, and the FBI has infiltrated the organization. With the police using powerful electronic surveillance devices and more mobsters willing to talk to avoid jail or to have their sentences reduced, the police have been able to indict and convict even top Mafia bosses. One of these bosses, John Gotti (called "the Teflon don" because he had beaten so many criminal charges), captured the public's attention. Despite his crimes, which included murder, Gotti, who died in prison, was romanticized and became a darling of the media. The Mafia appears to be in decline, but it is too soon to sound its death knell. We will have to see how this group adapts to its changing situation.

Political Crime

Some conflict theorists view almost every crime as political—an act by the ruling class to repress the working class or an act of the working class to resist that repression. I use the term **political crime** in a narrower sense—to describe crimes designed either to change or to maintain the social order. Crimes to *change the social order* include treason (the betrayal of one's country), sedition (rebellion, an attempt to overthrow the government), and such activities as resistance to the draft. A more extreme example is the blowing up of a federal building in Oklahoma City by Timothy McVeigh and his conspirators.

Crimes designed to *maintain the social order* include illegal surveillance of citizens by the FBI and illegal acts by the CIA such as assassinations and manipulation of foreign governments. Political crimes include the illegal activities of President Richard Nixon and his aides during Watergate and probably the activities of President Ronald Reagan and Lt. Col. Oliver North to support the contras of Nicaragua. Some allege that political crime also includes using drug money to finance President Bill Clinton's campaign (Reed and Cummings 1994) and the unauthorized wiretapping and interceptions of e-mail by President George W. Bush. As you can see, political crime cuts across the political spectrum and with the power that exists at high levels of government is especially difficult to prove.

Although there is no end to conspiracy theories—which flourish during political crises but vary from difficult to impossible to prove—we have ample evidence that U.S. politicians and bureaucrats do order illegal acts. In some cases, those acts become a routine part of the agency. Consider just one example: From the 1940s into the 1970s, the FBI committed thousands of burglaries and illegally opened and photographed tens of thousands of letters (Coleman 1995).

JUST WHAT IS THE PROBLEM? Political crime illustrates clearly that social problems are a matter of definition rather than a collection of objective facts. Some people see the illegal activities of those who want to change the social order as a major social problem, while they excuse the political crimes of government officials as necessary for securing the domestic order. Others view the illegal acts of government officials as a major social problem, because these acts subvert the constitutional system that the officials are sworn to uphold. For still others, all political crime, whether designed to maintain or to change the social order, is a social problem simply because it is illegal.

The Criminal Justice System

THE STING OF JUSTICE. Certain types of crime are easier to get away with than others. Least likely to be arrested are those who commit political crimes to maintain the status quo, for they are protected by the political system that they are supporting. Also running low risk are white-collar criminals who commit crimes in the name of a corporation and those at the top levels of organized crime. Respectability, wealth, power, and underlings insulate these lawbreakers. Probably the next safest are those who commit crimes against a corporation and professional criminals. The former are insulated by the corporation's desire to avoid negative publicity, while the latter are protected by skill, by a criminal subculture, and by having minimal contact with the "straight" world. Those in organized crime who run the highest risk of arrest are "soldiers" who occupy the lowest level in the organization; they are considered expendable. Juvenile delinquents and others who commit street crimes run high risks of being apprehended. Because crimes that are designed to change the political system threaten the power elite, the state focuses on these threats and is probably the most efficient in dealing with this type of crime.

ASSEMBLY-LINE JUSTICE. Keeping in mind, then, that the sting of the criminal justice system is more venomous for some than others, let's examine how this system operates. Buddy, Gary, and Clyde, whose defense attorney suggested that they plead guilty, represent in microcosm our criminal justice system. Prosecutors charge people with the most serious crimes possible and then offer to accept a guilty plea to lesser offenses. Despite their constitutional obligation to *defend* their clients, public defense attorneys usually suggest to their clients that they plead guilty (Blumberg 1967; Maynard 1984). In *most* cases, what is supposed to be a trial is simply an announcement of deals worked out in the back room (Pattis 2005).

Plea bargaining has become the standard in the U.S. criminal justice system. *In the vast majority of cases, people accused of a crime do* not *receive a trial.* On average, juries hear only *4 percent* of criminal cases (*Sourcebook of Criminal Justice Statistics* 2004:Table 5.43). Back in the 1960s, sociologist Abraham Blumberg explained that public defenders—despite their formal job description—develop "implicit understandings" about what their job *really* is—to be team players who produce "assembly-line justice" for the poor (Blumberg 1967). Today's situation remains unchanged. Of all the research that I have read on this topic, this statement has struck me as the most revealing: In urging his client to accept a jail sentence, one public defender said, "Even if you're innocent, it's a good deal" (Penn 1985).

"You look like this sketch of someone who's thinking about committing a crime."

A common perception is that bias in the criminal justice system works only against African Americans and Latinos. Sociological studies, however, indicate that this bias also favors these groups.

(© The New Yorker Collection 2000. David Sipress from cartoonbank.com. All Rights Reserved.)

The criminal justice system is also slow and inefficient. Courtrooms are jammed and their hours in session short. The snail's pace is exasperating for police officers and other witnesses who must wait hours, even days, for cases to be called. Lawyers are expensive, and those assigned to the poor are overburdened. Rules for presenting evidence are complex. For those who plead guilty, the average time between arrest and sentencing is 6 months. For those who choose a jury trial, it is twice as long, 12 months (*Sourcebook* 2004:Table 5.43). During this time, some innocent people remain locked behind bars, while some guilty people are released to commit more crimes while awaiting a distant trial.

Plea bargaining and the inefficiencies of the court system subvert the Sixth Amendment to the Constitution, which declares that "the accused shall enjoy the right to a speedy and public trial, by an impartial jury of the State and district wherein the crime shall have been committed." The poor do not receive a speedy trial. Indeed, most do not even receive a trial.

BIAS IN THE CRIMINAL JUSTICE SYSTEM. Let's discuss racial-ethnic discrimination in the criminal justice system. As you will recall, Buddy, the only African American in the trio, received the most severe sentence. The judge claimed that this was only because of Buddy's "priors." What is the answer?

The issue is complicated, and sociologists differ in their conclusions. At first glance, the judicial system certainly seems to discriminate along racial-ethnic lines, especially when it comes to African Americans. Although African Americans make up just 12 percent of the U.S. population, they make up 39 percent of jail inmates and 45 percent of inmates in prison (*Sourcebook of Criminal Justice Statistics* 2005:Tables 6.17, 6.34). From Table 6-7 below, you can see that the percentage of African Americans on death row is three and one half times greater than you would expect from their percentage in the U.S. population. No other group makes up such a disproportionate share of prisoners or death row inmates. Perhaps no statement illustrates the impact of the criminal justice system on African Americans better than this one: On any given day, one of every eight black males age 25 to 34 is locked up, and one-third of black males born today can expect to spend time in prison (Mauer 2004).

These data do *not* let us draw conclusions about bias, however, because they do not account for differences in crime among racial-ethnic groups. Sociologists have compared victimization studies (which contain no police bias) with the arrest rates of African Americans and white Americans for rape, robbery, and aggravated assault. They find that the racial-ethnic makeup that victims report closely matches arrest rates (Hindelang 1978; Shim and DeBerry 1988; *Sourcebook of Criminal Justice Statistics* 2005:Tables 42, 48).

Many sociologists, however, are convinced that the criminal justice system is biased against African Americans (Sellin 1928; Bridges and Stein 1998; Mauer 2004). Sociologists

TABLE 6-7 Prisoners on Death Row, by Race-Ethnicity

Race-Ethnicity	Number on Death Row	Percentage of Death Row Inmates	Percentage of U.S. Population	More (+) or Less (−) Than What You Would Expect from the Group's Percentage of the U.S. Population[1]
White	1,531	45.4%	68.0%	−33%
African American	1,411	41.8%	12.2%	+243%
Latino	353	10.5%	13.7%	−23%
Native American	39	1.2%	0.8%	+50%
Asian American	38	1.1%	4.0%	−72%
Claim two or more races			1.3%	
Totals	3,503	100%	100%	

[1]This total is computed by dividing the difference between the group's percentage of the U.S. population and its percentage of death row inmates by its percentage of the U.S. population.

Source: By the author. Based on *Sourcebook of Criminal Justice Statistics* 2006:Table 6.80; Henslin 2007b:Figure 12.5.

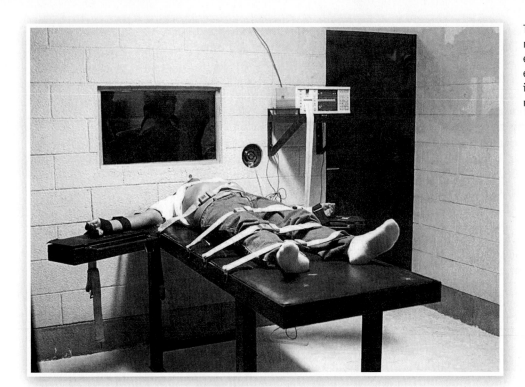

Throughout history, many methods have been used to execute prisoners. Death by electrocution was supposedly an improvement over earlier methods.

Douglas Smith and Christy Visher (1981) trained civilians to ride with the police in Missouri, New York, and Florida. After observing almost 6,000 encounters between police and citizens, they concluded that the police are more likely to arrest African American suspects. An examination of felony convictions in Florida showed that whites were more likely to have their cases dropped or to receive probation, and African Americans more likely to be convicted and to go to prison (Hale 1980). Sociologist Gary LaFree (1980), who examined the court records of a Midwestern city, found that African Americans who raped white women received more severe sentences than whites who raped white women.

Other studies show that bias works in *both* directions: Sometimes whites get more favorable treatment, but at other times minorities do. Consider these mixed findings: African Americans are given longer prison terms for rape and drugs, but whites get longer sentences for murder (Butterfield 1999). Sociologist John Tinker (1981) found that Latinos in Fresno, California, were more likely than whites to have their charges dismissed. If they were tried, however, they were more likely to go to prison. Sociologist Joan Petersilia (1983) found that minority suspects in California were more likely than whites to be released after arrest. If convicted of a felony, however, they were more likely to be given longer sentences. Petersilia, along with sociologists Stephen Klein and Susan Turner (1990), found that race did not make a difference in sentences for assault, robbery, burglary, theft, and forgery. For drug offenses, however, Latinos were more likely to be sent to prison.

Sociologists Martha Myers and Susette Talarico (1986:246) found something even more surprising in Georgia—that whites are discriminated against:

> Where blacks are a substantial minority (24–49 percent), black and white offenders bear the brunt of greater punitiveness equally. Once blacks become a numerical majority, white offenders are at a distinct disadvantage. Put concretely, they are more likely than blacks to be imprisoned.

We also find mixed results when we look at how juvenile delinquents are handled in the courts. While they wait for a judge to hear their case, whites are more likely to be sent home, and blacks are more likely to be kept in juvenile hall. When they do receive a hearing, however, African Americans are more likely to have their cases dismissed (*Sourcebook* 1998:Table 5.77; 2004:Table 5.64).

At this point, then, we cannot conclude that the courts are biased for or against minorities or for or against whites. The evidence goes both ways.

THE DEATH PENALTY. A look at **capital punishment** (the death penalty), however, shows that overwhelming racial bias once existed, especially when it came to rape. No one has been executed for rape since 1967, but between 1930 and 1967, 455 U.S. prisoners were executed for rape. Forty-eight were whites; 407 were African Americans. Donald Partington (1965), a lawyer, examined all executions for rape and attempted rape in Virginia between 1908 and 1963. Convicted of these crimes were 2,798 men (56 percent whites and 44 percent African Americans). Forty-one men were executed for rape and 13 for attempted rape. *All were African Americans. Not one of the whites was executed.*

When judges used to give the death penalty for rape, what really made the difference was the race of the attacker *and* the race of the victim. In their study of rape and the death penalty in Georgia, sociologists Marvin Wolfgang and Marc Reidel (1975) found this: The best predictor of whether a man would be sentenced to death was knowing that the victim was white and the accused black.

The death penalty was so biased that in 1972 the Supreme Court ruled in *Furman v. Georgia* that it was being applied unconstitutionally. As Table 6-8 shows, up to this point 3,896 prisoners had been executed. Fifty-three percent were African American, 46 percent white, and 1 percent Native American or Asian American. The states rewrote their laws, and in 1977 they again began to execute prisoners. As you can see, since then Table 6-8 shows 65 percent of those put to death have been white and 35 percent African American.

The death penalty apparently shows a strong gender bias: Of the 4,803 prisoners who have been executed since 1930, only 42 were women, a mere 0.9 percent. Since the death

TABLE 6-8 Prisoners Executed, by Race-Ethnicity

Year	WHITE		AFRICAN AMERICAN		NATIVE AMERICAN/ ASIAN AMERICAN		Total
	Number	Percentage	Number	Percentage	Number	Percentage	
Before the death penalty was abolished							
1930–34	371	48%	395	51%	10	1%	772
1935–39	456	51%	421	47%	14	2%	891
1940–44	276	43%	362	56%	7	1%	645
1945–49	214	33%	419	66%	6	1%	639
1950–54	201	49%	209	50%	3	1%	413
1955–59	135	44%	167	55%	2	1%	304
1960–64	90	50%	91	50%	0	0%	181
1965–69	8	80%	2	20%	0	0%	10
Totals	**1,774**	**46%**	**2,080**	**53%**	**42**	**1%**	**3,896**
Since the death penalty was reinstated							
1970–74	0	0%	0	0%	0	0%	0
1975–79	3	100%	0	0%	0	0%	3
1980–84	19	66%	10	34%	0	0%	29
1985–89	49	56%	39	44%	0	0%	88
1990–94	85	62%	50	36%	2	2%	137
1995–99	218	66%	114	34%	n/a	n/a	332
2000–04	233	68%	109	32%	n/a	n/a	220
Totals	**607**	**65%**	**320**	**35%**	**n/a**	**n/a**	**807**

Note: Because this table does not include prisoners who were executed by the federal government, the total does not agree with that in Table 6-9.
n/a—not available

Source: By the author. Based on *Sourcebook of Criminal Justice Statistics* 1998:Table 6.88; 2004:Table 6.86; *Statistical Abstract of the United States* 2006:Table 342.

FIGURE 6-4 Which States Have the Death Penalty?

Have the Death Penalty
Do Not Have the Death Penalty

Source: By the author. Based on Bonczar and Snel 2005.

penalty was restored in 1976, 810 men have been executed, but only 10 women (*Statistical Abstract* 2006:Table 342). At present, only 1.5 percent of prisoners (52) on death row are women (*Sourcebook of Criminal Justice Statistics* 2005:Table 6.83). These totals could indicate bias in favor of women, but they could also reflect the relative frequency and severity of their crimes. We need more research to see what is really occurring.

We do know that geography makes a huge difference in a person's chances of being executed. As the Social Map above shows, 37 states have the death penalty and 13 states

Federal prisons are known as the country clubs of the U.S. prison system. Alabama, in contrast, has some of the toughest prisons in the nation. As shown in this photo shot at Butler County, Ohio, to be sentenced to serve "hard labor" means exactly that.

do not. As you can see from Table 6-9, some states, especially southern ones since the death penalty was reinstated, are much more willing to order executions than are others. Texas held the record before the death penalty was abolished and does so once again. One of every three executions (36 percent) since 1977 has taken place in Texas. Texas is a huge state, though, with 23 million people living there. With its much smaller population of just 3 1/2 million and its 75 executions since 1977, a criminal is more likely to be executed in Oklahoma than in Texas.

THE PRISON EXPERIENCE. Finally, let's look at the prison experience. Unlike Clyde, Buddy and Gary had to serve time. Prison turned out to be horrible. As with the prisoner whose letter opens this chapter, Buddy and Gary were offered no rehabilitation program. They and their fellow prisoners were locked away, forgotten by society—except when a riot riveted public attention. The warden was a political appointee, awarded his supposedly easy job for party loyalty. As long as the prison remained "quiet," his job was secure. Buddy and Gary soon discovered that in return for the prisoners' cooperation in keeping the prison quiet, guards overlooked gambling, alcohol, drugs, and homosexual rape. To supplement their low salaries, guards smuggled in alcohol and drugs.

Buddy and Gary were herded about like animals, forbidden to make even simple decisions. They were told when to work, what TV programs to watch, and when to sleep. Their letters were censored, their packages rifled, and their telephone conversations recorded. They expected these things, because they were prisoners. What they did not expect was the brutality and violence of the guards. As the prisoner in the opening vignette observed, violence could result from breaking a rule or even the suspicion of having broken one. Buddy and Gary concluded that the prison recruited sadists, since that is how they saw the guards. If they had taken this social problems course, however, they might have gained a different understanding of this brutal fact of prison life. Let's see why.

THE ZIMBARDO EXPERIMENT. Philip Zimbardo, a social psychologist, conducted a fascinating experiment. Using paid volunteers, Zimbardo (1972/2007) matched 24 college students on the basis of their education, race, and parents' social class. He randomly assigned one group as guards and the other as prisoners. Without warning, one night real police cars arrived at the homes of those who had been designated prisoners. They were "arrested," fingerprinted, and taken to the basement of the psychology building at Stanford University, which had been turned into a prison. Both "guards" and "prisoners" were given appropriate uniforms.

Subject to the arbitrary control of their captors, the prisoners felt a loss of power and personal identity. The guards, in contrast, felt an increase in social power and status. They also developed strong ingroup loyalty. After several days, rumors of a prison rebellion spread. The guards reacted brutally, with about a third treating the prisoners as though they were subhuman. Things started to get out of hand, and after six days Zimbardo stopped the experiment.

Zimbardo's experiment illustrates a fundamental sociological principle: The way society is structured and the groups to which we belong provide the bases for our orientations and how we act toward others. How a prison is organized is more important in determining how guards and prisoners act than are their individual personalities. As guards work in a prison, they come to see themselves as representatives of morality and the prisoners as enemies that need to be subdued,

TABLE 6-9 Number of Prisoners Executed, by Jurisdiction, 1930–2000

State	NUMBER EXECUTED	
	Since 1930	Since 1977
U.S. total	4,803	945
Texas	633	336
Georgia	402	36
New York	329	0
California	302	10
North Carolina	297	34
Florida	229	59
South Carolina	194	32
Ohio	187	15
Virginia	186	94
Alabama	165	30
Louisiana	160	27
Mississippi	160	6
Pennsylvania	155	3
Arkansas	144	26
Oklahoma	135	75
Missouri	123	61
Kentucky	105	2
Illinois	102	12
Tennessee	94	1
New Jersey	74	0
Maryland	72	4
Arizona	60	22
Washington	51	4
Indiana	52	11
Colorado	48	1
Nevada	40	11
District of Columbia	40	0
West Virginia	40	0
Federal system	36	3
Massachusetts	27	0
Delaware	25	13
Oregon	21	2
Connecticut	21	1
Utah	19	6
Iowa	18	0
Kansas	15	0
New Mexico	9	1
Montana	8	2
Wyoming	8	1
Nebraska	7	3
Idaho	4	1
Vermont	4	0
New Hampshire	1	0
South Dakota	1	0

Source: Sourcebook of Criminal Justice Statistics 2005:Table 6.84; plus an execution in Connecticut in 2005, its first in 45 years.

rather than as people who need to be helped. The guards' goal becomes upholding authority at all costs, even if this requires brutality, which in their view is justified. Eventually, the guards can come to see prisoners as "animals" who understand nothing but violence.

Zimbardo's experiment created a stir in the scientific community. Some fellow social scientists accused Zimbardo of being cruel and irresponsible. The federal government responded with strict guidelines for research on human subjects, and it is not likely that similar experiments will be conducted again. Zimbardo's research, however, provides insight into what is wrong with our prisons, adding to our knowledge of why prisons fail to reduce crime.

If prisons are not the answer, what is?

Social Policy

What is being done to solve these twin social problems of crime and the criminal justice system? We can never eliminate crime, but to the extent that we can encourage people to follow the law or prevent people from breaking it, we can reduce the problem. Because street crime bothers Americans the most, and street crime is linked to poverty, the *best policy* would be to reduce poverty. Education is an effective way to reduce poverty because, on average, the farther that people go in school, the more they earn. In addition, as we saw, researchers have found a direct link between adult crime and dropping out of high school, so programs that help students graduate from high school and go to college or technical and trade schools would help to prevent crime.

We will, of course, always have criminals, so we need effective policies for dealing with them. There are four basic approaches: retribution, deterrence, rehabilitation, and incapacitation. Let's consider each.

RETRIBUTION. *Punishing* criminals to uphold collective values (ideas of right and wrong) and to demonstrate that criminal behavior will not be tolerated is called **retribution.** Proponents of retribution view offenders as morally responsible for their violations. They also look at the violations as having created a moral imbalance. To help restore the moral order, the punishment should fit the crime (Cohen 1940). An interesting form of retribution is *shaming,* which is discussed in the Thinking Critically box on the next page.

Restitution, making offenders compensate their victims, is a form of retribution. Restitution is an attempt to mend the broken moral order, to help even things up. If people have stolen, for example, they need to pay the money back. Restitution is practical for property crimes, when the offender can repay the victim. It is less practical for offenders who don't have jobs, although some judges require the unemployed to "work their debt off" in a variety of creative projects. Attempts to restore the "moral balance" are evident in the following attempts to "make the punishment fit the crime":

A Memphis judge invited victims to visit the thief's house and "steal" something back (Stevens 1992).

A Florida judge sentenced a white man who was convicted of harassing an interracial couple to work weekends at an African American church.

A Texas judge ordered a deadbeat who had fathered 13 children to attend Planned Parenthood meetings (Gerlin 1994).

For throwing beer bottles at a car and taunting a woman, a judge in Ohio sentenced two men to dress in women's clothing and to walk down Main Street (Leinwand 2004).

Critics emphasize how difficult it is to decide that a crime merits a particular punishment and how inconsistent judges are in making those decisions. They also note that for crimes of violence, retribution might require unusual measures, such as castration for rapists—acts that courts will likely declare unconstitutional. A California judge, for example, wanted to withhold AIDS treatment from a man who had raped two teenagers after he was released from prison for a previous rape (Farah 1995). Proponents reply that if retribution is the goal of punishment, the Constitution needs to be brought into line with the goal.

PUBLIC SHAMING AS SOCIAL POLICY

"Shame on you!"

Do you remember those horrifying words from your childhood? If your childhood was like mine, you do. The words were accompanied by an index finger that pointed directly at me, while another index finger, rubbing on top of it, seemed to send shame in my direction.

With a harsh voice or one that showed disappointment, this gesture was effective. I always felt bad when this happened. I felt even worse when I saw the looks of disgust on the faces of my parents or grandparents in response to my childish offense, whatever it may have been.

If you have read Nathaniel Hawthorne's *The Scarlet Letter,* you know about shaming. Hester Prynne, who committed adultery, a serious offense at the time, because it struck at the community's moral roots, had to wear a red A on her clothing. For life, wherever she went, she was marked as a shameful adulteress.

Some judges are bringing back this old-fashioned device. Not the scarlet A, but its equivalent.

A judge ordered thieves to wear sandwich boards that said, "I stole from this store." They had to parade back and forth outside the stores they stole from.

A Texas judge ordered a piano teacher who pleaded guilty to molesting his young students to give away his prized $12,000 piano and to not play the piano for 20 years. If you don't think this was harsh, consider the shaming that accompanied this punishment: He had to post a sign prominently on the door of his home declaring himself a child molester.

Officials in the legal system have tried numerous ways to motivate offenders to stop breaking the law. An old technique being revisited is public shaming. Convicted of shoplifting, these individuals in Nashville, Tennessee have been sentenced to display humiliating signs as they stand in front of the store they stole from.

Judges have ordered drunk drivers to put bright orange bumper stickers on their cars that say, "I am a convicted drunk driver. Report any erratic driving to the police."

The Minneapolis police department has even organized "shaming details." Prostitutes and their johns must stand handcuffed in front of citizens who let loose with "verbal stones," shouting things like "You're the reason our children aren't safe in this neighborhood!"

Kansas City tried a different approach to prostitution. "John TV" shows the mug shots of men who have been arrested for trying to buy sex and of the women who have been arrested for selling it. Their names, birth dates, and hometowns are displayed prominently.

Rosters of convicted sex offenders are available at the click of a mouse. On your computer screen, you can see the individual's photo, name, date of birth, conviction, and, in some instances, even the offender's current address and a clickable neighborhood map. While this information is supposed to be intended to alert citizens to potential danger, it certainly is a shaming device.

Does shaming work? No one knows whether it reduces lawbreaking. But shaming certainly can be powerful. A woman convicted of welfare fraud was ordered to wear a sign in public that said, "I stole food from poor people." She chose to go to jail instead.

Even if shaming doesn't work, it does satisfy a strong urge to punish, to get even. In today's eager-to-punish climate, perhaps retribution is purpose enough. And perhaps it does help to restore a moral balance.

Examples are based on Gerlin 1994 and Belluck 1998; current events 2006.

DETERRENCE. Proponents of **deterrence,** which aims to create fear by letting potential offenders know that they will be punished, view offenders as rational people who weigh the possible consequences of their actions. In this view, someone who is considering a crime will avoid it if punishment seems likely. Back in the 1970s, criminologist Ernest van den Haag (1975, 1983) proposed that we treat juveniles who commit violent crimes the same as adults ("adult crime, adult time"), abolish parole boards, and operate work programs for prisoners. With citizens demanding strong action, attempts at deterrence have become popular.

Researchers have discovered two principles: First, the longer the interval between a crime and its punishment, the less the deterrence, or fear of the punishment. This underscores the

Halfway houses, such as this one in Hoboken, NJ, refer to a supervised environment in which residents live "half way" between freedom and being locked up in an institution. Residents set and enforce their own rules for living with one another. They also have limited freedom to come and go.

need for the speedy trials, already guaranteed by the Constitution, and for swift punishment for the guilty. Second, the more uncertain the penalty, the less the deterrence. To meet this principle, some have proposed **uniform sentencing,** the same sentence for everyone convicted of the same crime.

Critics of deterrence point out that offenders are not always rational about their crimes. Many act on impulse and do not weigh the consequences of their acts. If they do, many take the chance anyway, regardless of the consequences. For example, back in the 1700s, hanging was the punishment for picking pockets in England. Hangings were public affairs, and you might think that such a severe punishment would stop this crime. Instead, when a pickpocket was being hung, other pickpockets worked the crowd. The hanging, with crowd's attention riveted on the gallows, provided them easier victims (Hibbert 1963).

"Scared Straight" was once trumpeted by the mass media as a successful program of deterrence. To scare them straight, delinquents were taken on prison tours, where inmates gave them a close-up view of prison life. Leering and shouting obscenities, they said they could hardly wait for the youths to be sent to prison so they could rape them. Those who operated the program reported that it kept 80 to 90 percent of the youths from further trouble with the law. Follow-up studies by sociologists, however, showed that the program had backfired. Criminologist James Finckenauer (1982) matched delinquents on the basis of their sex, race-ethnicity, age, and criminal acts. He then compared those who had been exposed to the "Scared Straight" program (the experimental group) with delinquents who had not been exposed to it (the control group). Within six months, 41 percent of the experimental group were again in trouble with the law, but only 11 percent of the control group.

How could such a program backfire? It sounds so good. Finckenauer suggests that the boys were impressed by the macho performance of hypermasculine, in-charge men. (Let your imagination go a little here: You've probably seen photos or TV programs that show the tattoos and muscles and threatening posture that many male convicts display.) These boys want to be powerful men, and that is how they perceived these convicts. Committing crimes after listening to these men was a way of showing their peers that their talk hadn't frightened them, that they, too, were macho and couldn't be scared.

The failure of "scared straight" does not mean that programs of deterrence cannot work. It does, however, underline the need for sociological research to find out what actually works. We cannot *assume* that a program is successful just because it sounds good, because it appeals to our common sense, or because its operators say that it works. If we are to develop sound social policy, we need solid research so we can evaluate programs. This point is underscored in the Thinking Critically box on "prison boot camps" on the next page.

REHABILITATION. The focus of **rehabilitation** is resocializing offenders, to help them become conforming citizens. A major program of rehabilitation is *probation:* Instead of going to prison, offenders stay in the community under the supervision of a probation officer. *Imprisonment* is also part of rehabilitation—if it has the goal of teaching prisoners a trade or useful skills or if it educates them with high school or college courses. Rehabilitation programs also include *parole,* releasing prisoners before they serve their full sentence, both as a reward for good behavior and as a threat (for, as in probation, if the court's rules are violated the convict goes back to prison to serve out the sentence); *furloughs,* freedom for a set time, such as a weekend, toward the end of the sentence, to let convicts adjust gradually to non-prison life; *halfway houses,* residences in which released convicts report to the authorities but supervise many aspects of their own lives, such as household tasks, drinking, drugs, and curfews; and *honor farms* for prisoners who have shown good behavior, where supervision is less stringent and convicts can learn cooperation and responsibility (Morash and Anderson 1978).

The public is fed up with failed attempts at rehabilitation. Many perceive probation as an opportunity for felons to commit more crime—and this perception is accurate. Figure 6-5

SQUEEZE YOU LIKE A GRAPE

As they step out of the police cars into the Georgia countryside, a guard shouts into their faces, "You're nothing! You're nobody! You're fools! You're maggots!"

The youths look dumbfounded. Another guard shouts, "I don't like ya. I got no use for ya, and I don't care who ya are on the streets. This is hell's half acre, and I don't give a damn if ya get tossed outta here into prison. I promise ya, ya won't last five minutes before you're somebody's wife. Do ya know what that means, tough guys?"

The offenders are ages 17 to 25. Convicted of nonviolent crimes, they were given a choice of either one to five years in prison or 90 days of prison boot camp, followed by probation.

"You have to hit a mule between the eyes with a two-by-four to get his attention," explains a guard. "And that's what we do here." Within an hour of arriving, inmates are stripped of every sign of their previous life. Guards take their cigarettes and personal possessions. Their heads are shaved, and a white prison uniform with wide blue stripes replaces their jeans and T-shirts.

Inmates may not speak without permission. All responses must begin and end with "Sir." The lights go out at 10. Television watching is limited to one hour a day—only the news and PBS—all in black and white. No visitors are allowed for the first 45 days.

Inmates do hard physical labor. Up at 5 A.M., they cut grass with scythes and dig up tree trunks with shovels and pickaxes. If an inmate talks on the work crew without permission, he must do push-ups—or take the "chair position," unsupported, of course. Repeated violations mean being handcuffed and placed in a police car. Other inmates are made to watch as the violator is taken away to prison to serve the longer sentence.

Prison boot camps, like this one in Swan Lake, Montana, are intended to provide a structure of discipline which judges feel is lacking in the offenders' lives. We have no evidence that this punishment—or any other—is effective in changing offenders into law-abiding citizens.

Mississippi opened the first boot camp in 1985. Thirty-one states followed. Seven states opened camps for women.

The warden of this Georgia camp says, "They're not going to leave here any smarter, but we can provide some structure and discipline that they've never gotten. We can't fix the sociological problems that led to crime in the first place, but we can influence what they do next."

The sociologist, of course, replies, "Let's see the statistics. We need matched groups (offenders of the same background convicted of the same crimes) who go to prison and who go to boot camp. Or else we need randomized samples. When we compare the rearrest rate of each group, we'll know if boot camps work."

It took some time, but we finally got random samples—and we now have measurements of the rearrest rates. Sociologists Jean Bottcher and Michael Ezell (2005) compared randomized samples of offenders who went through California's boot camp program with a control group of those who had not. The results are not encouraging. After seven years, there were no differences between the groups in terms of how long it took to their first arrest or how often they were arrested. Other researchers who compared the recidivism of juveniles who went through prisoner boot camps with the recidivism of juveniles who were sent to prison have found nothing consistent. In some cases the recidivism rate of the juveniles who had gone to boot camp was lower, but in other cases it was higher. As a result, some states have shut down their boot camps and are sending their young offenders to traditional prisons.

Sources: Lamar 1986; Gest 1987; *Life,* July 1988:82–83; Morash and Rucker 1990; MacKenzie and Souryal 1995; Bottcher and Michael Ezell 2005; Lohn 2005; Willing 2005.

on page 202 summarizes what happened to 79,000 felons who were given probation. Within three years, 43 percent were rearrested for a violent crime (murder, rape, robbery, or aggravated assault) or a drug offense (Langan and Cunniff 1992). Another 19 percent had violated conditions of their probation.

However, the concept of probation is not unsound, although our implementation of it is. If probation were given to felons with the most promise, if they were provided with follow-up counseling, and if trained probation officers had small caseloads, it might work. As you have seen with the "Scared Straight" and boot camp programs, however, seemingly

FIGURE 6-5   The Failure of Probation

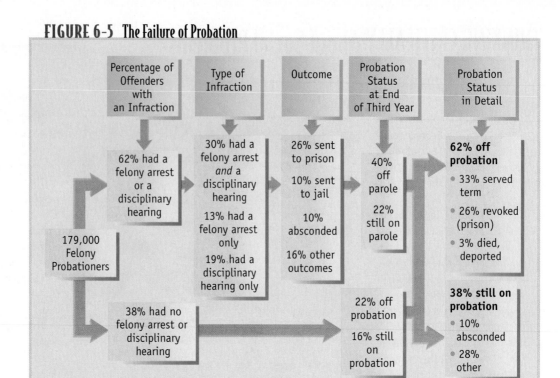

Source: Revised version of a chart in Langan and Cunniff 1992.

sound ideas can prove quite disappointing. To find out whether these ideas work in practice, we would need sociological research.

Another approach to rehabilitation is **diversion,** diverting offenders *away from* courts and jails. The goal is to keep offenders out of the criminal justice system—to shift them to community organizations or to funnel them into administrative hearings rather than to criminal trials. Diversionary programs aim to avoid stigmatizing offenders and to keep them out of the crime schools that go under the name of jails and prisons.

If rehabilitation programs were successful, almost everyone would favor them. The cost of rehabilitation would certainly be less than the price that criminals now exact from society—from the harm they cause their victims to the cost of supporting them in prison. The problem is that we do not know which rehabilitation programs work. The studies show conflicting results and do not inspire confidence.

INCAPACITATION. Consequently, the public clamors for **incapacitation,** removing offenders from circulation. The view of those who propose incapacitation is direct and to the point: Everything else has failed. We cannot change people who don't want to change, so let's get them off the streets so they can't hurt people. Some offenders commit crime after crime ("career criminals"), so let's free ourselves of recidivists. For a new form of incapacitation, see the Technology and Social Problems box on the next page.

Incapacitation has aroused considerable debate in sociology. Criminologist James Wilson (1975), who said repeatedly that incapacitation is the *only* solution that makes sense, advocated incapacitation in books, scholarly journals, and the popular media. Ernest van den Haag proposed "added incapacitation," increasing an individual's sentence each time that person is convicted of a crime. Some estimated that if everyone convicted of a serious offense were imprisoned for three years, our rate of serious crime would drop by two-thirds (Shinnar and Shinnar 1975). Others estimated that such sentencing would reduce crime by only 3 or 4 percent (Greenberg 1975; Cohen 1978). Some sociologists say that those who proposed incapacitation were right, that as we saw earlier, as judges gave out tougher sentences, the crime rate plummeted. Other sociologists, however, claim that the drop in the crime rate was due to other factors.

Technology and Social Problems
USING TECHNOLOGY TO STOP CRIME

The idea is simple. "It's expensive to keep people in prison, and not everyone who is convicted of a crime should go to prison. Yet we need to keep tabs on offenders. How can we use technology to do this?"

The ankle bracelet, simple and effective, is able to transmit an offender's location 24 hours a day. A transmitter is strapped around the offender's ankle, which transmits a signal to a central monitor. If the offender leaves home, it breaks the signal, setting off an alarm at the monitoring station.

The ankle monitor also lowers costs. To keep a juvenile in custody runs about $100 a day, but the cost for home monitoring is just $10 a day. To keep an adult in prison runs about $75 a day, but the cost to use the ankle device is just $12 a day. The costs include equipment and staff.

Some jurisdictions have even developed a pay-as-you go plan. Judges give adult clients a choice—go to jail or pay $12 a day for electronic monitoring. Not eligible are drug dealers, those who committed a violent crime, and those who used guns to commit their crime. In some Florida counties, even those accused of drunk driving have to wear this device and pay its daily cost (author's notes 2005).

The ankle monitor is also suitable for probation and parole. Software can be programmed with an offender's work schedule and location. Probation officers can park outside a workplace to pick up a signal; better yet, failure to appear at work also sets off a signal. Probation officers check to make certain that it isn't a false call, then alert the police.

Hidden within this new technology is another benefit. Because electronic monitoring frees up prison cells, it allows courts to keep violent offenders in prison longer.

Victims of stalking get a special benefit. The software can be programmed to sound an alarm if an offender comes within a specified distance of a victim's home or workplace. Workers at the monitoring station warn the victim, who can leave the area.

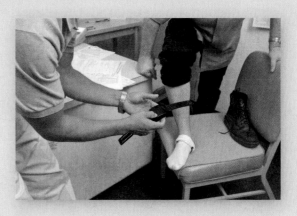

Monitoring people convicted of a crime through the Global Positioning System (GPS) has become a common way to track parolees, people awaiting sentencing, and those under house arrest. Shown here is a Texas parole officer and his client.

Future technology will soon make this tool seem primitive. Signaling devices will be implanted in felons' bodies. The implant will be connected electronically to the Global Positioning System, satellites that can track the precise location of any object. Software will be programmed with the offender's schedule—times and location of work or rehabilitation classes, even routes to and from work and restricted places in the community. If the individual deviates from the schedule, a computer will notify the police to make an arrest.

Technology is moving rapidly. We already have the capacity to insert devices in an offender's brain that can send pain if an individual deviates from scheduled activities. Soon we may be able to implant devices that will direct the individual's movements. This capacity to monitor and control people, of course, leads to the question of potential abuse by authorities. Putting such devices on felons, some fear, is merely a step toward the goal of monitoring all citizens and residents. In light of the fear of terrorism, this is a chilling possibility. Implants and the marvels of the Global Positioning System—what more could Big Brother ask to control its citizens?

Based on Campbell 1995, McGarigle 1997, "GPS Creates Global Jail" 1998, Knights 1999; fitzpatrick 2004.

THE DEBATE OVER CAPITAL PUNISHMENT. One of the most provocative issues in social policy is the death penalty. Its proponents argue that death is an appropriate punishment for heinous crimes, that it deters, and of course, that it incapacitates absolutely. Its opponents argue that killing is never justified. Its proponents say that this is almost true, but the exceptions are war, self-defense when one's life is threatened, and capital punishment. The opponents of capital punishment point out that if it did deter, then states with the death penalty would have a lower homicide rate than those without it—but they don't. In fact, the homicide rate of the states without the death penalty averages about *half* that of the states that have the death penalty (*Sociological Abstract* 2006:Table 295). This fact doesn't faze those who favor the death penalty, who reply that this fact just goes to show that the

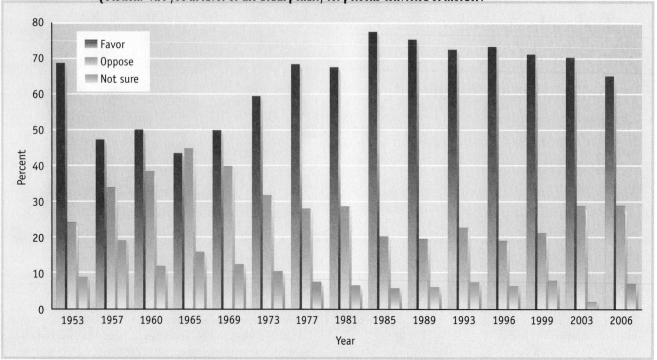

Source: By the author. Based on various editions of *Sourcebook of Criminal Justice Statistic,* including 2006:Table 2.51.

states that have the death penalty really need it. Opponents also argue that the death penalty is capricious—jurors deliberate in secrecy and indulge their prejudices in recommending death—and that judges are irrational, merciful to some but not to others. Proponents reply that in their opinion judges and juries are doing a good job under difficult circumstances. Opponents stress that innocent people have been executed: They point to the men released from death row because of DNA testing. Opponents reply that they are happy that we have DNA testing, that now we can be even more certain of the guilt of the killers we execute.

Neither side convinces the other. Nevertheless, the public demands that "something be done," and as Figure 6-6 shows, about two-thirds of Americans favor the death penalty. Figures 6-7 and 6-8 show the increase in the number of prisoners sentenced to death and the numbers who have been executed.

GOALS AND PRINCIPLES. The United States has tried a variety of approaches to solve its crime problem. With little agreement on the basic purpose for the social response to crime (prevention, retribution, deterrence, rehabilitation, or incapacitation), our solutions are piecemeal and in disarray. To have a rational social policy, we need to reform the criminal justice system. I suggest the following goals and guiding principles:

1. Clear laws based on the broadest possible consensus, rather than on the interests or moral concerns of small groups.
2. Swift justice based on legal evidence presented in adversarial proceedings. (This would require eliminating plea bargaining and lengthy delays based on legal technicalities; it would guarantee a speedy trial for all who plead not guilty and require more courts, more judges, and longer working hours for judges.)
3. More rehabilitation programs, including diversion for most first offenders who did not commit violent crimes, with the goal of integrating them into the community.
4. "Added incapacitation": Harsh penalties for violent offenders, with the penalty becoming harsher each time a person is convicted of a crime.
5. Task forces to investigate organized crime and white-collar crime (with the provision that, for a specified time such as five years after they leave a task force, members cannot accept employment from the corporations they investigated).

FIGURE 6-7 Persons Under Sentence of Death

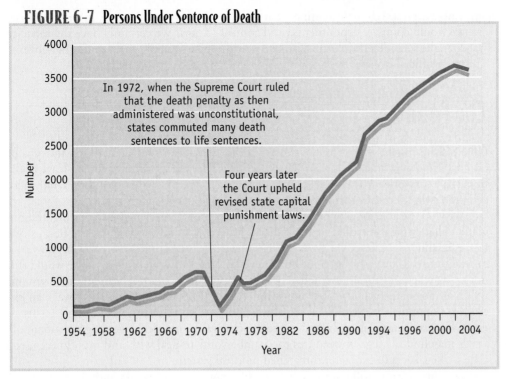

In 1972, when the Supreme Court ruled that the death penalty as then administered was unconstitutional, states commuted many death sentences to life sentences.

Four years later the Court upheld revised state capital punishment laws.

Sources: By the author. Based on Greenfield 1991; various editions of *Sourcebook of Criminal Justice Statistics; Statistical Abstract of the United States* 2006:Table 341.

6. Harsh penalties for people who are convicted of crime on behalf of a corporation, including jail for executives, the forced sale of any division found guilty of crime, and huge fines to reduce the motive of corporate profit (Liazos 1981).

7. Prison reform, including making the position of prison warden a civil service job, training prison guards rigorously and paying them well, allowing prisoners to have conjugal visits, and giving *to the nonviolent* the right to visit friends and family on the outside.

FIGURE 6-8 Persons Executed in the United States

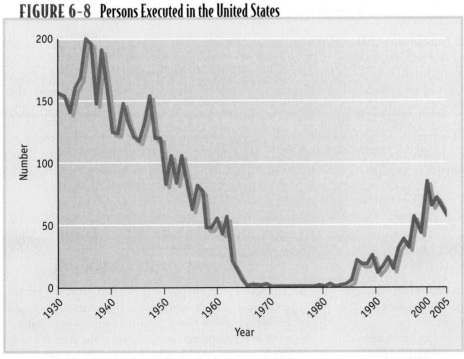

Source: By the author. Based on various editions of *Sourcebook of Criminal Justice Statistics* and *Statistical Abstract of the United States* 2007:Table 40.

8. Unbiased research to determine what works and what doesn't work. In the ideal case, we would compare experimental and control groups. We certainly have the capacity to make such determinations, but we need cooperative politicians and other government officials to approve and fund such research.

The Future of the Problem

CHANGES IN CRIME. Will crime increase or decrease? The answer depends on the type of crime. Crime by women, for example, will probably increase as more women leave traditional roles to work at paid jobs. Their opportunities for crime will increase, and, like men, they, too, will follow illegitimate opportunities.

We won't be able to tell whether white-collar crime is increasing or decreasing. If more white-collar crime is handled by the judicial system, it will *appear* to increase. Because we lack a baseline of white-collar crime from which to draw accurate comparisons, however, official statistics could show a doubling or even more in any given year, and we would still not know whether this represented an increase or just a greater use of the judicial system.

The incidence of political crime will depend on political events. If we wage an extended, unpopular war, we could relive the political protests of the 1960s and 1970s. If we do have substantial illegal acts designed to change the political system, government officials may find the legal procedures too cumbersome to deal with and may, in turn, engage in illegal acts to protect a threatened political system.

Organized crime will continue, taking different forms as social conditions change. If enforcement efforts that are directed against one part of organized crime, such as the Sicilian-American Mafia, succeed, that group will turn increasingly to legitimate businesses. The Mafia will not forsake crime, however, as illegal activities are the heart of its existence.

THE CRIMINAL JUSTICE SYSTEM. The judicial system changes slowly. I anticipate that the criminal justice system will continue to focus on street crime and that the crimes of the powerful will be largely overlooked or will be handled by civil agencies. I also anticipate an increase in a recent innovation in prisons—the hiring by states of private, for-profit businesses to build and operate prisons. Private firms now operate prisons with over 100,000 inmates (Harrison and Beck 2006:Table 3). This change is superficial, however, merely a switch in who is operating a prison. It does not affect the basic system.

NEED FOR FUNDAMENTAL CHANGE. If we ever get serious about preventing the poor from being recruited to street crime, we must open the doors to legitimate ways of achieving success. This means that we must provide access to quality education and training for good jobs. If the private sector doesn't create enough jobs for everyone who wants to work, then the government needs to create jobs—and, to be successful for this purpose, the jobs must pay a living wage. This is fundamental, as people who have a high investment in the social system commit fewer street crimes. To change the social system in ways that open opportunities and reduce poverty is a radical proposal; but, unfortunately, we are not likely to undertake such radical change, and crime will remain a serious social problem.

SUMMARY AND REVIEW

1. Whether an act is a *crime* depends on the law, which, in turn, depends on power relationships in society.
2. Crime is universal, because all societies make rules against acts they consider undesirable. Laws turn these acts into crimes. Because laws differ, crime differs from one society to another and in the same society over time.

3. The social problem of crime has two parts: the crimes committed and the criminal justice system. Crime is a problem because people are upset about the threat to their lives, property, and well-being; the criminal justice system is a problem because people are upset about its failures and want something done about it.

4. Chambliss' study of the "saints" and the "roughnecks" illustrates how social class affects the perception and reactions of authorities, as well as how crime statistics are distorted.

5. Functionalists note that property crimes represent conformity to the goal of success but rejection of the approved means of achieving success. Just as some people have more access to legitimate opportunities, others have more access to *illegitimate opportunities*.

6. Conflict theorists regard the criminal justice system as a tool that the ruling class uses to mask injustice, control workers, and stabilize the social system. Law enforcement is a means that the elite use to maintain their dominance.

7. *Juvenile delinquents* use five major *neutralization techniques* to deflect society's norms: denial of responsibility, denial of injury, denial of a victim, condemning the condemners, and an appeal to higher loyalty.

8. *White-collar crime* is extensive but underreported. Corporations usually insulate white-collar criminals from the law, especially when the crimes benefit the corporation.

9. *Professional criminals* are people who make their living from crime. They have high in-group loyalty, scorn the "straight" world, and take pride in their specialized skills.

10. *Organized crime* is best represented by the Mafia, whose use of violence within a highly developed bureaucracy lies at the heart of its success.

11. *Political crime,* illegal activities intended to change the political system or to maintain it, ebbs and flows as political conditions change.

12. The criminal justice system fails to deliver justice because of overcrowded courts, *plea bargaining,* a team-player system that subverts public defense attorneys, possible racial-ethnic bias, and prisons that foster hostility and hatred.

13. Because our criminal justice system has no unifying philosophy with which to establish and evaluate social response to crime, our policies of social control are in disarray.

14. Social change—including the role of women, social policies toward crime, and economic and political events—will influence the direction of crime in the future.

15. To get at the root of this problem requires reform of the criminal justice system and a basic overhaul of our social institutions, especially changes that open more opportunities to the poor.

KEY TERMS

Bureaucracy, 189
Capital punishment, 195
Cosa nostra, 190
Crime, 165
Crime rate, 167
Criminal justice system, 166
Delinquent subculture, 182
Deterrence, 199
Diversion, 202
Illegitimate opportunity structure, 175

Incapacitation, 202
Juvenile delinquency, 179
Mafia, 189
Organized crime, 189
Plea bargaining, 169
Police discretion, 174
Political crime, 191
Political process, 166
Professional criminals, 187
Property crime, 179

Recidivism rate, 170
Rehabilitation, 200
Restitution, 198
Retribution, 198
Status crimes, 179
Techniques of neutralization, 180
Uniform sentencing, 200
Violent crimes, 179
White-collar crime, 184

THINKING CRITICALLY ABOUT CHAPTER 6

1. Which of the three theoretical perspectives (symbolic interactionism, functionalism, or conflict theory) do you think does the best job of explaining the causes of crime? Why?

2. Which of the three perspectives (symbolic interactionism, functionalism, or conflict theory) do you think does the best job of explaining why white-collar criminals are treated differently from street criminals? Is your answer to this question different from your answer to Question 1? Explain.

3. Do you think that violent criminals should be treated differently from nonviolent criminals in terms of punishment? Why or why not? Consider the case of the criminally negligent manufacturer whose product kills people but who has no actual contact with victims versus the street criminal who kills someone during a robbery.

4. Which of the four basic approaches to treating criminals (retribution, deterrence, rehabilitation, and incapacitation) do you think is the most appropriate? Why?

CHAPTER 7

Economic Problems:
Wealth and Poverty

At age 17, Julie Treadman faced more than her share of problems. Her boyfriend—her "first love"—had deserted her when she told him that she was pregnant. Exhausted and depressed, Julie dropped out of high school. Now five months' pregnant, she wondered about her child's future.

When Julie had severe stomach pains, a neighbor called an ambulance, and she was rushed to Lutheran Hospital. When hospital administrators discovered that neither Julie nor her mother had insurance,

> # Julie gave birth to a stillborn baby.

money or credit, they refused her admission. Before they could transfer her to a public hospital for the poor, however, Julie gave birth to a stillborn baby.

This perplexed hospital administrators. They didn't want patients who could not pay their bills, but what could they do at this point? They quickly hit upon a Machiavellian solution: They ordered the ambulance driver to take Julie—dead baby, umbilical cord, and all—to the public hospital.

—Based on an event in St. Louis, Missouri

The Problem in Sociological Perspective

In this chapter, we examine economic problems facing our nation. Our primary focus will be on the unequal distribution of society's resources, especially as this produces the twin problems of wealth and poverty.

Economic Systems and Changes

COMPARING CAPITALISM AND SOCIALISM. The United States, where "all 'men' are created equal," has always had **social classes**—groups of people who occupy the same rung on the economic ladder. Where you are located on that ladder makes a vital difference in what your life is like. We have the *working poor,* full-time workers who depend on food stamps to survive, and we also have Bill Gates, the richest man in the world, who spent $75 million for a house and $30 million for a Winslow Homer painting to decorate his living room. Most of us fall somewhere in between, of course—and not toward Gates' end of the spectrum. In this chapter, we shall look at sociological research and theory on the rich and the poor, the powerful and the powerless. Let's start by considering how the economy affects all our lives.

The **economy** is not only money and jobs; it is the entire social institution that produces and distributes goods and services. How the economy functions affects the welfare of every individual, group, and community in the entire nation. At any given time, the U.S. economy is in a "boom," when everything seems to be percolating, or a "bust," when nothing seems to be going right. These "boom–bust" cycles plague **capitalist economies,** which are based on the private ownership of property and the investment of capital for the purpose of making a profit. Some students who are taking this course will graduate during a "boom" and will have their choice of jobs. Others will graduate during a "bust," and even though they have worked just as hard as the others and earned the same degrees, they will end up driving cabs, working in fast-food restaurants, or standing in unemployment lines.

Many nations, primarily eastern European countries under the domination of the former Soviet Union, used to have **socialist economies;** the government owned the property, profit was illegal, and government committees decided what items—from cars to toilet paper—would be produced and where they would be distributed. The government also set the price for the items—taking into consideration neither the quality of the goods nor the demand for them. Everyone was guaranteed a job, and everyone worked for the government, which owned everything. It was also a crime to miss work when you weren't sick.

The socialist and capitalist economies were almost mirror images of one another. Capitalists believed that socialism was immoral, that socialism denied people the freedom of choice—including the right to choose where you were going to live and work. Socialists believed that capitalism was immoral, that capitalism put profit ahead of the welfare of people, and that the poor were left to suffer. In what was known as the cold war, proponents of each ideology viewed the other as a mortal enemy and threatened one another with nuclear destruction.

THE TRIUMPH OF CAPITALISM. Production in the socialist countries was inefficient. Central committees decided what goods would be produced and how they would be distributed. Workers could not be fired; they could be jailed for not showing up for work, but not fired for producing less than others. Capitalism proved much more efficient, and the workers' standard of living in the capitalist countries grew. Workers in the socialist countries, in contrast, saw their living conditions—already at a low level—decline. As the Soviet economy deteriorated in the late 1980s, its leaders, under Mikhail Gorbachev, abandoned socialism and reluctantly turned to capitalism. The Soviet Union broke up into fifteen independent states, which followed Russia into the pursuit of capitalism. China has maintained the façade of socialism, but it is well on its journey to capitalism. The Chinese are now encouraged to own property and to pursue profit.

At this stage in world history, then, capitalism has triumphed. The newly independent states that are traveling the road to capitalism, however, have encountered torturous economic problems. Russia was thrown into such economic and political disarray that its central authority was threatened. Organized crime figures, mentioned in the last chapter, in cooperation with corrupt politicians and military, took control of a large part of the Russian economy. They assassinated politicians and business leaders who stood in their way, as well as journalists who tried to expose them. This put the security of Russia's nuclear weapons in jeopardy, a matter to which we shall return in Chapter 15.

As capitalism has come to dominate the globe (with the primary holdouts being China, North Korea, and Cuba), the leaders of the major capitalist countries have divided the world's nations into three primary trading blocs: North and South America, dominated by the United States; Europe, dominated by Germany; and Asia, dominated by Japan, with

Foreign investment in Asia made its economies boom. The wealthy search for ways to display their status, such as by driving this car in Brunei.

Poverty is a global issue, and every country has huge disparities between its wealthy and its poor. These young people in Siliguri, India, have no home. For them, every day is a fight for survival, as they scrounge for scraps to eat, followed by fitful nights spent on the sidewalks.

China the newest contender. To try to control capitalism's troublesome cycle of "booms" and "busts," the most powerful eight nations, known as G-8 (the Group of 8) hold an annual summit, where they try to regulate the global markets. This organization used to be called G-7, until Russia was invited to join. Soon it will be called G-9: China has been invited to be an observer, the first step toward becoming a partner in world domination.

Capitalism's certainty of a "boom–bust" cycle is matched by the uncertainty of knowing when the economy will switch from "boom" to "bust" and back again. To try to control this cycle, G-8 uses the *International Monetary Fund*, a world bank that lends to nations that are in economic trouble. The "boom–bust" cycle continues, however, and entire regions experience prosperity or poverty. In the 1990s, the region dominated by Japan went into the "bust" part of this cycle, and formerly booming factories in Thailand, Indonesia, and South Korea closed their doors. As the value of these countries' currencies shrank, capitalist leaders feared a global "bust." Although G-8 (then G-7) was able to pull this region out of the "bust," a danger with global capitalism is that most of the world will be engulfed in these cycles.

The socialist economies had a primary advantage: greater equality. They guaranteed jobs for everyone (although the jobs paid little) and provided medical care for almost everyone; if there was no wealth, neither was there hunger. With these benefits, why did capitalism win the war? The simple answer is that capitalism is more efficient at producing wealth. There certainly was greater equality in the socialist nations—almost everyone was poor. The capitalist countries are marked by tremendous **social inequality**—the unequal distribution of wealth, income, power, and other opportunities—but most people under capitalism have a high standard of living.

FOCUSING ON PROBLEMS. Capitalism offers both individual freedoms and the opportunity for economic success. These features are so appealing that millions of people beat down the door to enter the United States, whether legally or illegally. For some people, however, such as Julie Treadman in our opening vignette, the social inequality of a capitalist system has dire consequences. Because Julie couldn't pay, she was denied medical treatment and human dignity. Because this book is about social problems, not social opportunities, our focus is on the negative consequences of social inequality.

Economic Problems Facing the United States

Because the U.S. economy is essential to our well-being, it is important to try to understand the issues that affect its future. Let's look at four problems that spell trouble.

STAGNANT INCOMES. The first is that people's **real income** (income adjusted for inflation) is stagnant. For 25 years, from the end of World War II until 1970, the real income of U.S. workers rose steadily. Even after you subtracted inflation from their paychecks, workers still had more money to spend. Since then, the paychecks of workers have continued to grow, but those paychecks contain dollars without calories. Although the paychecks show more and more dollars, making workers feel as though they are earning more than they used to, as Figure 7-1 on the next page shows, the real income of today's workers is little more than it was in 1970. In short, the raises that U.S. workers have been receiving have been eaten up by inflation. Look closely at Figure 7-1. You will see that it took 35 years for workers to get a real raise of 14 cents an hour.

What has softened the blow for the average family is that more family members are working. In 1940, only 16 percent of wives worked for wages. Today, about 60 percent of wives work for wages either full- or part-time (Davis and Robinson 1988; *Statistical Abstract* 2006:Tables 584, 585, 586, 587). How much do you think that having this extra worker has added to the average family's income? Do you think it doubled it? Maybe increased it by half? Despite two incomes, after adjusting for inflation, the average household today brings in just 16 percent ($6,000) more a year than it did in 1980 ($43,000 versus $37,000) (*Statistical Abstract* 2006:Tables 585, 674). Despite 11 million more wives working for wages now than in 1980, the net gain to the average family's income is only 16 percent. This additional income is *before* the costs that jobs require: child care, second car, additional clothing, lunches, and so forth. After these costs are subtracted, one wonders whether there has been any gain at all.

FIGURE 7-1 Average Hourly Earnings, in Current and Constant Dollars

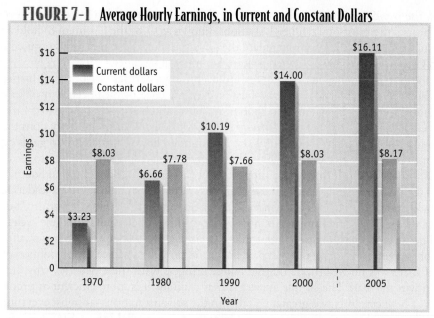

Note: *Current dollars* are the number of dollars a worker earns. *Constant dollars* means those dollars have been adjusted for inflation.

Source: By the author. Based on *Statistical Abstract* 1999:Table 698; 2007:Table 626.

TAXES. The second major problem is taxes. Someone coined the term *Tax Freedom Day* to refer to the day when the average worker has earned enough to pay his or her annual taxes. Politicians keep promising tax cuts, but they seldom deliver on that promise. Tax Freedom Day falls on April 26 (Tax Foundation 2006). On average, each of us must work for the government for almost four months before we have a cent for our own needs!

THE SAVINGS RATE. Figure 7-2 illustrates the third major problem. Americans are saving very little, even less than what they saved in the midst of the Great Depression of the 1930s. Americans save less than the citizens of all other industrialized nations. The drop in savings shown in Figure 7-2 has significant consequences. It isn't just that the average family has less

FIGURE 7-2 How Much Do Americans Save?

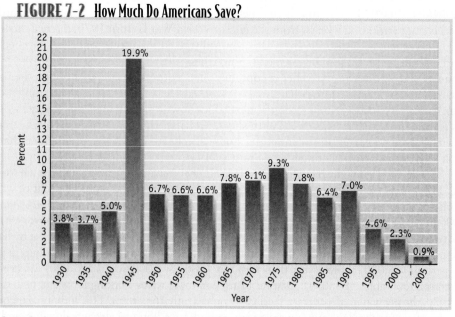

Source: By the author. Based on American Savings Education Council, 1999; *Statistical Abstract* 1990:Table 700; 1995:Table 710; 2007:Table 658.

to draw on when that inevitable "rainy day" arrives. That is true, and serious enough. It is also that workers' savings are put to work in the society. Reduced savings mean that we have less money to invest in new plants and equipment, and this can undermine our ability to compete in today's global markets. This, in turn, undermines our standard of living.

A DEBTOR NATION. Fourth, we buy goods from other nations at such a frenzied pace that the United States has become the largest debtor nation in the world. When you add up what we pay for the products we buy from other nations and what we receive for the products we sell to those nations, at the end of year we end up about $600 billion short (*Statistical Abstract* 2006:Table 1273). Year after year, we sell less than we buy. These mountains of debt have been piling up, and this cannot go on indefinitely. Just as individuals must repay what they borrow or else get into financial trouble—and perhaps financial ruin—so it is with nations. To finance the **national debt** (the total amount the U.S. government owes), we pay about $180 billion a year in interest (*Statistical Abstract* 2006:Table 460). These billions are money that we cannot use to build schools and colleges, hire teachers, pay for medical services or job programs for the poor, operate Head Start, or pay for any other services to help improve our quality of life.

The Nature of Poverty

TYPES OF POVERTY. With this broad background, let's analyze poverty. You might think that poverty would be easy to define, but its definition is neither simple nor obvious. There are three types of poverty. The first is **biological poverty,** which refers to starvation and malnutrition. It also refers to housing and clothing so inadequate that people suffer from exposure. Our homeless endure biological poverty.

More common is **relative poverty.** This term refers to people living below the standards of their society or group. Some relative poverty is serious, such as the poverty experienced by the Americans who try to get by on only half or even one-quarter of the average national income. On another level is the relative poverty of the members of country clubs, those who feel "poor" because they are among the few whose Jaguar or Porsche is two years old. Relative poverty also exists on a world scale: What is poverty in the United States would mean comfortable living in India, where most families have little clothing and little food, and many people live in just a room or two.

The United States and some other countries also have a third type of poverty. **Official poverty** refers to the income level at which people are eligible for welfare benefits. People below this **poverty line** are defined as poor; those above it are not. The United States developed its definition of official poverty in 1962. The poor at that time spent about one-third of their incomes on food, so the Social Security administration determined the poverty line by multiplying a low-level food budget by 3 (Fisher 1988). The U.S. government has kept this rough figure, adjusting it annually to match the Consumer Price Index, the official gauge of inflation.

PROBLEMS WITH THE POVERTY LINE. Critics point out that the poverty line is stuck in a time warp. Sociologist William Julius Wilson (1992) and policy analyst Patricia Ruggles (1990, 1992) point out that food preferences and cooking patterns have changed since the 1960s, but not the government's definition of poverty. They say that because poor people actually spend only about 20 percent of their incomes on food, to determine a poverty line we ought to multiply their food budget by 5 instead of 3 (Uchitelle 2001). Sociologist Michael Katz (1989) notes that the official poverty line assumes that everyone is a careful shopper who cooks all the family meals at home and never has guests. Who lives like this, he asks? Others point out that except for Alaska and Hawaii, the poverty line is not adjusted for different costs of living. It costs a bit more to live in Albany, New York, than it does in Albany, Georgia, or in Philadelphia, Pennsylvania, than in Philadelphia, Mississippi. Finally, the poverty line does not even distinguish between urban and rural families. Despite decades of criticism, this magical line continues to be drawn across the income spectrum, supposedly separating the "poor" from the "nonpoor." Using this rock-bottom definition, let's look at official poverty in the United States.

The Scope of the Problem

Subjective Concerns and Objective Conditions

We first need to stress again that objective conditions alone—whether defined officially or not—are not enough to make poverty a social problem. Subjective concerns are also essential and, actually, are more important. How can subjective concerns be more important than objective conditions? Consider the extremes: On the one hand, according to our definition of social problems, if poverty is extensive but few people are concerned about it, poverty is *not* a social problem. On the other hand, if poverty is rare but its existence bothers many people and they want to address it, poverty *is* a social problem. Let's look at examples.

CHANGES IN CONCERNS AND CONDITIONS. During the early years of the United States, *most* people were poor. Yet at this time poverty was not considered to be a social problem. Life had always been a struggle for most of the population, so *people assumed that poverty was a natural part of life.* As industrialization progressed in the nineteenth century, it produced an abundance of jobs and wealth. As poverty declined, though, masses of poor people migrated to U.S. cities. Even though the standard of living had increased, this migration made poverty more visible, leading public leaders to declare that poverty was a social problem. As the immigrants were absorbed into the expanding workforce, once again poverty receded from sight. Then the Great Depression of the 1930s hit with the force of Hurricane Katrina, throwing millions of people out of work.

As the ranks of the poor swelled and citizens protested not having work, poverty was "rediscovered." Declaring poverty to be the greatest problem facing the nation, government officials rushed through legislation, establishing emergency programs and creating millions of jobs. Then came World War II, when factories began to operate at full capacity and millions of men were sent overseas. Postwar prosperity followed, and poverty continued to recede from sight. Even though the objective condition remained—poverty didn't go away, and millions of people remained poor—subjective concerns receded. Tucked in out-of-the-way rural areas and isolated in urban slums, the poor once again dropped from sight.

LAUNCHING THE WAR ON POVERTY. In 1960, President Kennedy tried to make poverty a campaign issue, but subjective concerns were not really aroused until Michael Harrington wrote *The Other America* in 1962. Rarely has a single volume of social science transformed people's consciousness as this one did. Harrington passionately argued that in the midst of "the affluent society," one-quarter of the nation lived in squalor. Policy makers read this book, the media publicized it, and sociologists assigned it to their students.

Within two years of the book's publication, President Johnson declared a "war on poverty." The federal government began a raft of programs for the poor: child care, Head Start, legal services, medical services, job training, subsidized housing, and community health centers. The result was dramatic. As you can see from Figure 7-3, in just 10 years the number of Americans below the official poverty line dropped from 22 percent to 13 percent. This reduction made it clear that poverty could be solved. We simply need the right social policies.

The Situation Today

Currently, poverty is a sputtering sort of affair. With the war on terrorism being conducted amidst global economic threats, subjective concerns are low, and once again poverty has largely receded from sight. Although the media occasionally highlight the plight of workers in the steel, textile, or automobile industries, for the most part poverty has been relegated to tales of woe featured during Thanksgiving and Christmas.

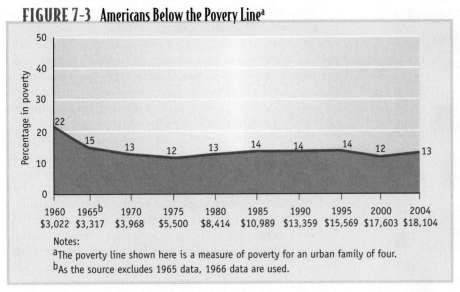

FIGURE 7-3 Americans Below the Poverty Line[a]

Notes:
[a]The poverty line shown here is a measure of poverty for an urban family of four.
[b]As the source excludes 1965 data, 1966 data are used.

Source: By the author. Based on *Statistical Abstract of the United States* 1992:Table 724; 2007:Table 694.

REACHING A PLATEAU. Since the initial and dramatic reduction in poverty, little or no progress has been made. From Figure 7-3, you can see that during the past 30 plus years, the percentage of people below the poverty line has hovered between 12 and 14 percent. Currently, it is again at 13 percent. With our larger population, today's 13 percent represents 37 million people, about the same number who were poor before the "war on poverty" began in the 1960s.

CONTROVERSY OVER NUMBERS. The poverty line, of course, is arbitrary in the first place, and the number of "poor" people can be reduced or increased at will by changing this official definition. Although some argue that the number of poor is higher than the official measure, others claim it is less. They point out that the government does not count as income many benefits that people receive from antipoverty programs. Medicare, Medicaid, food stamps, and HUD vouchers (the amount the government pays in rent for poor families) are not counted as income. If such items were counted, many people would no longer be officially poor.

THE SIGNIFICANCE OF POVERTY. You can see the problem. Where should the cutoff for poverty be, and what should we count as income? As a consequence, experts disagree about how many poor people there are. Despite this fuzziness of definition, three facts stand out: First, no matter how we compute poverty, millions of Americans are poor. Second, how we define poverty has serious consequences for people's lives. The definition we use determines who will receive help and who will not. Third, poverty lies at the root of many of our other social problems. In earlier chapters, we saw the connection between poverty and prostitution, rape, murder, and alcoholism and other forms of drug addiction. In coming chapters, we shall see how poverty is related to other social problems such as racism, physical and mental illness, and abuse in the family.

Social Inequality

The existence of poverty and other forms of social inequality contradicts our ideals. Americans often cope with this contradiction by denying it. For example, when researchers ask people what social class they belong to, most Americans—whether rich or poor—say that they are middle class. This tendency is fascinating, especially in its extremes. When Ann Getty, a former saleswoman who married an heir to the Getty oil fortune, was being interviewed, she said to the reporter, "I lead a very ordinary life" (*New York Times,* Sept. 7, 1980). Ordinary? Her "ordinary life" included not only living in a San Francisco mansion but also flying to Paris to shop for clothing by top designers—and taking her personal chef with her.

Poverty is much more than having little money. Poverty means the reduction of life's chances—including the greater likelihood of disease, death, and divorce. This photo was taken in Texas, a region where poverty persists generation after generation.

We know that all Americans are not equal, of course, and that the life chances of a waitress' daughter differ immensely from those of a son born to wealthy parents. We all know that the rich and politically connected pass advantages to their children and that the poor and powerless pass disadvantages to theirs. Because of this, we have social programs to help level the playing field. Affirmative action, as well as college scholarships and community colleges, are attempts to make opportunity more equal.

Such programs run up against **structural inequality,** the inequality that is built into our economic and social institutions. Differences in wages are an example. If a society has 100 million jobs and 20 million pay excellent wages, 50 million pay good wages, and 30 million pay low wages, the job market has inequality built into it. Unemployment is another example. If a society has 107 million workers but only 100 million jobs, then 7 million workers will be unemployed, regardless of how hard they look for work. Job training programs will not solve this structural problem. The solution requires changes in the structure—that is, more jobs. No workable social system has been devised, however, that eliminates the structural inequality of different pay for different positions.

Distribution of Income and Wealth

INEQUALITY OF INCOME. A major consequence of structural inequality is the vast inequality in the income of Americans. Look at Figure 7-4. The poorest fifth of Americans receive only 4.1 percent of the nation's income, whereas 47.6 percent of the country's entire income goes to the richest fifth. Despite numerous antipoverty programs, *income inequality today is greater than it was in the 1940s.* The poorest fifth of Americans now receive less of the nation's income than they did in the 1940s (a drop from 5.4 percent to 4.1 percent). The richest fifth receive more than ever (an increase from about 41 percent to 47.6 percent).

INEQUALITY OF WEALTH. Another way to view financial inequality is to look at the distribution of **wealth,** what people own—their property, savings, investments, and other economic assets. Americans are worth about $50 trillion, mostly in the form of real estate, corporate stock, mutual funds, and checking and savings accounts (*Statistical Abstract* 2006:Table 703). As you know from your own bank account, this

FIGURE 7-4 Who Gets What? How the Income of the United States Is Distributed

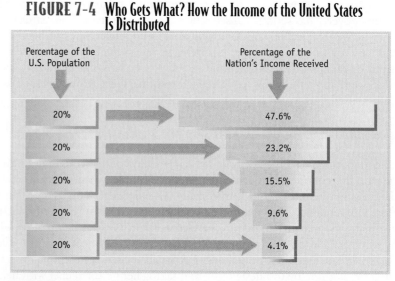

Percentage of the U.S. Population	Percentage of the Nation's Income Received
20%	47.6%
20%	23.2%
20%	15.5%
20%	9.6%
20%	4.1%

Source: By the author. Based on *Statistical Abstract of the United States* 2006:Table 680.

wealth is not evenly divided among Americans. To give you an idea of how concentrated these assets are at the upper levels of wealth, look at Figure 7-5. You can see that one-third of the nation's wealth is in the hands of just 1 percent of U.S. families. This 1 percent virtually controls corporate America.

With $50 billion, the richest person in the United States—and the world—is Bill Gates, who dropped out of Harvard to cofound Microsoft Corp., the world's largest software company. (Gates' wealth fluctuates a few billion dollars up and a few billion dollars down as the price of Microsoft stock changes.) Gates and his employees developed MS-DOS and Windows, two computer operating systems. Microsoft gets a licensing fee each time a computer that uses these systems is sold. Having already given $30 billion to the Gates Foundation and in the process of giving away most of his wealth, Gates is also the most generous man in human history (Strom 2006).

How much is a billion dollars? Because neither you nor I is likely to have a bank account this size, an illustration can help us grasp the enormity of a billion dollars—*one thousand million dollars:*

> Suppose you were born on the day Christ was born, that you are still alive today, and that you have been able to save money at the fantastic rate of one cent for every second that you lived—that is, 60 cents for every minute, $36 for every hour, or $864 for every day of your life during these past two thousand years. At that rate, it would take you another thousand years to save one billion dollars. (Shaffer 1986)

WEALTH AND POWER. As research scientist James Smith said, "Wealth is a good thing, and everyone ought to have some" (Stafford et al. 1986–87:3). Then what is the problem? Part of the problem is that vast wealth brings vast power. Because owning 10 or 20 percent of a company's stock is enough to control it, the 1 percent of Americans who own over half of all corporate stock wields immense power over the economy (Beeghley 2005). In their pursuit of even more wealth, this elite can move production to Mexico, India, or China, where labor is cheaper, closing down factories here and throwing thousands of people out of work. Most designer jeans, for example, which used to be made in the United States, are now made in Asian nations. The U.S. workers who lose their jobs in this global game of monopoly don't make these decisions, but they must live with the consequences.

Finally, because the rich can hire top financial advisers, attorneys, and lobbyists, they perpetuate their advantages. In their world of privilege, they are protected from unemployment, not being able to pay the rent, having their utilities cut off or their family car breaking down, injustice in the courts, and an unresponsive political system. This, in contrast, is the life some others live. Let's turn our attention to those who must cope with such conditions as part of everyday life.

The Impact of Poverty

Let's consider the impact of poverty. Being poor does not simply mean having less money and therefore going to fewer movies, buying fewer video games, and eating steak less often. Rather, people's economic circumstances envelop

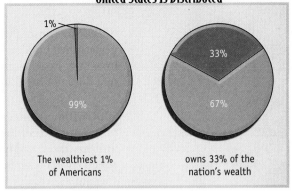

FIGURE 7-5 Who Owns What? How the Wealth of the United States Is Distributed

The wealthiest 1% of Americans

owns 33% of the nation's wealth

Source: Beeghley 2005.

"*The poor are getting poorer, but with the rich getting richer it all averages out in the long run.*"

How we define reality depends to a large extent on where we are located in the social class structure. Poor Americans are not likely to have the view illustrated in this cartoon.

© The New Yorker Collection 1988. Joseph Mirachi from cartoonbank.com. All Rights Reserved.)

them, affecting profoundly every aspect of their lives. Let's look at some of these consequences.

HOUSING. Most of the poor live in substandard housing. Many rent from landlords who neglect their buildings. The plumbing may not work. The heating system may break down in winter. Roaches and rats may run riot. And, unlike mortgage payments, the monthly rent does not build up equity in a home.

EDUCATION. Although public schools are supposed to give all children an equal opportunity to succeed, the poor are at a disadvantage. Because our schools are supported by property taxes, and property in poorer areas produces less taxes, the schools that the poor attend have smaller budgets and often outdated textbooks and inexperienced teachers who are paid less (Kozol 1999). This, of course, is common knowledge, and everyone knows how superior the schools are in the areas where the rich live.

Everyone also knows that poverty affects people's chances of going to college. Few, however, know that college and income are matched this closely: If you rank families from the poorest to the richest, at each level of family income the likelihood that their children will go to college increases (Manski 1992–93; Reay et al. 2001). Similarly, the wealthier a family is, the more years of schooling that their children complete (Conley 2001).

And then there is the *type* of college that children attend. Most poor children who go to college attend community colleges where they are funneled into vocational programs. In contrast, most children of the middle classes attend state universities, while the children of the wealthy go to elite private colleges. Before they go to college, some of the children of the very wealthy first attend private boarding high schools, where the classes are small and the teachers well-paid (Persell et al. 1992). The college advisers at these schools have ties with the admissions officers of the nation's most elite colleges. Some have networks so efficient that *half* of a private high school's graduating class will be admitted to just Harvard, Yale, and Princeton (Cookson and Persell 1985/2005).

JOBS. Unlike the career paths that are open to the children of the middle class and the rich, the low-paying jobs of the working poor lead nowhere. Because workers are often laid off from these dead-end jobs, their incomes, already low, are erratic. During unemployment, they have to cope with the complex bureaucracies of unemployment insurance, welfare, and other social programs that are designed to carry them along. Such experiences add to the stress of lives that are already filled with anxiety.

CRIMINAL JUSTICE. The poor are also given a different walk through the halls of justice. As discussed in Chapter 6, their life experiences make them more likely to commit robberies and assaults, crimes that are especially visible and for which offenders are punished severely. White-collar crime may be more pervasive and costly to society, but it is less visible and carries milder punishments. As mentioned in the previous chapter, when the poor are arrested, they lack the resources to hire good lawyers to defend themselves. Often, they cannot even post bail.

IN SHORT: QUALITY OF LIFE. Wealth and income represent privileges—received or denied. The net result is a quality of life that goes right to the core of one's being. Job insecurity brings nightmares to the poor. Their jobs offer no pension plans and often no medical benefits. They live one paycheck away from eviction. If they get sick, they are laid off, and their job may not be there when they return to work. Among the stark repercussions: Those at the lower end of the income scale don't eat as well, their children are more likely to die in infancy, they are more likely to have accidents at work and at home, and they die younger. And, like Julie Treadman in the opening vignette, they have less access to good medical care, which further jeopardizes their well-being.

Looking at the Problem Theoretically

As we saw in earlier chapters, each of the theoretical perspectives gives a different view of a social problem. Let's look at poverty through these three lenses.

Symbolic Interactionism

THE RELATIVITY OF POVERTY

Andy, Sharon, and their two children live in a small house in a rural area. Andy farms 65 acres and works part-time at the local grocery store. Sharon works part-time as a cook at the Dew Drop Inn. She sews some of the children's clothing. Between their jobs and the farm, they make about $16,000 a year. They grow their own vegetables, buy milk from a neighbor, and fish in a nearby pond. Integrated into the community and with their basic needs satisfied, they don't think of themselves as poor. Neither do their friends and neighbors.

Leslie attends a private college. Her parents pay her tuition, fees, books, rent, utilities, insurance, medical bills, and transportation. They also pay about $800 a month for "extras." Unlike many of her friends, Leslie has no car, and she complains about how hard it is to get by. Her affluent friends feel sorry for her.

Between auditions, Keith, a struggling young actor works as a waiter. He earns about $900 a month, which has to cover his rent, food, and all other expenses. To make ends meet, he rooms with three other aspiring actors. "It's difficult to make it," he says, "but one day you'll see my name in lights." Keith sees himself as "struggling"—not poor. Nor do his actor friends think of him as poor.

Maria and her two children live in a housing project. Her rent is subsidized and cheap—$97 a month. Her welfare, Medicaid, and food stamps total $14,287 a year, all tax-free. Her two children attend school during the day, and she takes classes in English at a neighborhood church. Maria considers herself poor, and so do the government and her neighbors.

By the government's standards, all but Leslie are poor, and yet it is Leslie (and Maria) who *feel* poor. Why?

Symbolic interactionists stress that to understand poverty we must focus on what poverty *means* to people. All of us try to evaluate where we are in life. To do so, we *compare* ourselves with others. In some rural areas, simple marginal living is the norm, but in Leslie's cosmopolitan circle people *feel* deprived if they cannot afford the latest upscale designer clothing from their favorite boutique. The meaning of poverty, then, is *relative:* What poverty is differs from group to group within the same society, as well as from culture to culture and from one era to the next.

To understand poverty, we must focus also on how the middle class views the poor. The dominant view might be that the poor are good people who are down on their luck and need a helping hand. Or they might view the poor as "no-goods" who refuse to work and are a drain on society's resources. Such differences in perception and meaning are significant, for they have an impact on social policy. Let's look at how views about poor people have changed.

CHANGING MEANINGS OF POVERTY. The view of poverty in the early 1700s stands in marked contrast to today's perspective. At that time, Americans viewed poverty as God's will, and clergy preached that God put the poor on earth to provide an opportunity for the rest of us show Christian charity (Rothman and Rothman 1972). Poverty was viewed not as a social problem, but as a personal problem. Poverty was considered to be an ordinary part of life that required compassion on the part of others.

After the European settling of North America, the poor were scattered among hundreds of villages along country roads. By the time of the American Revolution, however, the poor started to be concentrated in colonial cities such as Boston, Philadelphia, and New York City. Authorities set up welfare committees, and following the view of the time, the members of these committees distinguished between the deserving and undeserving poor. The deserving poor were the blind, the handicapped, and the deserted mothers. The undeserving poor were the beggars, peddlers, idlers, drifters, and prostitutes. At this point, the meaning of poverty began to change. Increasingly, poverty was viewed not just as God's will, but also as the result of flawed character.

As the United States industrialized and more people moved to the cities, the squalor bothered people of good intentions. Reformers launched campaigns to help the poor—and again the meaning of poverty changed. The reformers saw poverty as the product of corrupt cities. Urban temptations—alcohol, crime, and debauchery—held people in the bondage of poverty (Rothman and Rothman 1972).

Although we no longer believe that poverty is God's will, the idea that poverty ought not to exist—and the suspicion that it is due to the character of the poor—remain part of our symbolic heritage. We have vacillated between viewing the poor as worthy people who deserve our help and as worthless people who deserve nothing but a kick in the pants. Symbolic interactionists make us aware that the meanings of poverty change as social conditions change.

Functionalism

HOW INCOME INEQUALITY HELPS SOCIETY. In a classic essay in 1945, sociologists Kingsley Davis and Wilbert Moore developed the functionalist perspective on social inequality. Their argument was simple. Some tasks in society are more important than others. These positions require talented people who are willing to make a sacrifice to prepare for them. To attract such talented people, the positions must offer high income and prestige. Oil, for example, is vital to keeping the economy going, but to learn the advanced techniques to find oil or to manage oil fields takes years of training in geology. Consequently, petroleum geologists, especially geophysicists, must be offered both a substantial salary and the respect of others. Anyone can wash dishes, so unskilled workers earn poverty wages at these jobs. Thus, disparities in income help society function.

HOW POVERTY IS FUNCTIONAL FOR SOCIETY. Functionalists go beyond this by saying that poverty itself is functional for society. Sociologist Herbert Gans (1971/2007) points out that we need poor people because their poverty leads to unique contributions to society's well-being. For a summary of this view, see the Thinking Critically box on the next page. Functionalists also analyze the dysfunctions of poverty, including alienation and despair, drug abuse, street crime, suicide, and mental illness. In the Spotlight on Social Research box on page 222, Gans explains how he has struggled against arguments that victimize the poor.

Conflict Theory

THE CAUSE OF SOCIAL INEQUALITY. Conflict theorists view the functionalist argument as wrong-headed. To say that inequality comes from a basic social need to offer higher rewards to fill some positions is to justify the power of the wealthy and the deprivation of the poor. Social inequality, argue conflict theorists, comes from a basic struggle over limited resources. At any point in history, some group has gained control of society's resources, and that group uses its power to secure its gains and to exploit those who are weaker. The result is a social class system in which the wealthy pass advantages to their children, whereas the poor pass disadvantages to theirs.

A GENERAL THEORY OF SOCIAL CLASS. Karl Marx (1818–1883) was the first sociologist to develop a general theory of social class and class relations. He argued that social class depends on a single factor, the *means of production*—the tools, factories, land, and capital used to produce wealth (Marx 1867/1967; Marx and Engels 1848/1964). People are either capitalists (or bourgeoisie), who own the means of production, or they are workers (*proletariat*), employed by the capitalists. The history of a society is best understood as a conflict between owners and workers, the wealthy and the poor. Because the capitalists

Functionalists argue that the highest salaries go to the positions that perform the most important functions for society. Critics respond that if this were true then garbage collectors would be among the most highly paid members of society. The garbage collectors shown here, needless to say, do not receive the salaries and stock options awarded to CEOs.

IN SUM Conflict theory comes in several versions. But no matter the form that it takes, conflict theorists always stress the relationship between those who have power and those who do not. The problems of the poor are due to their deprived position in a system of stratification, to their relative powerlessness and oppression.

IN SUMMARY
Each of the three theoretical lenses provides a unique understanding of wealth, poverty, and social inequality. Symbolic interactionists, who focus on the individual level, make us more sensitive to how social class works in our everyday lives. They explain, for example, why the amount of income that people have (the objective condition) is not the same as the ways that people see themselves (subjective views that lead to relative poverty). Functionalists and conflict theorists look at the bigger picture. They examine social structure, the ways that society's parts fit together—in this case, the poor and the wealthy, the powerful and the powerless. Where functionalists see inequality as originating from a broad social need to reward society's important positions, however, conflict theorists stress that poverty originates and is maintained in the means of production.

Research Findings

Who Are the Poor?

PERMANENCE AND POVERTY. It comes as a surprise to many that most people who fall below the poverty line are not poor permanently. Most are poor only for short periods—for example, when they are injured or sick, or during layoffs or slow seasons, such as in winter in the northern states, when there are few construction jobs. Although the total of poor people in the United States remains fairly constant from year to year, there is much change within this total. Each year millions of people rise above the poverty line, while millions of others fall below it.

GEOGRAPHY. A striking characteristic of poverty is how it is distributed. The poor are concentrated in the inner city and in rural areas such as Appalachia. The Social Map on the next page shows how the rates of poverty differ among the states. As you can see, the regional differences are striking.

FIGURE 7-6   The Geography of U.S. Poverty

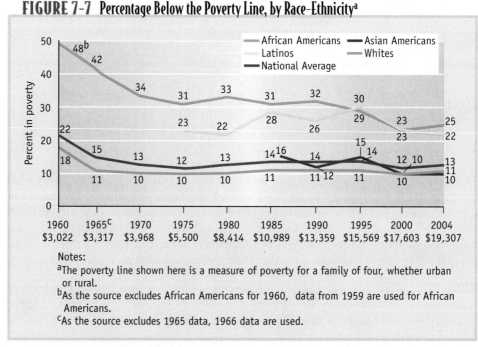

The Geography of U.S. Poverty

- States with the least poverty, 5.1% to 7.5%
- States with average poverty, 7.6% to 9.9%
- States with the most poverty, 10.5% to 16.6%

WA 7.9
OR 9.7
ID 9.8
MT 9.9
ND 8.4
MN 5.6
WI 7.2
MI 8.6
VT 6.4
NH 5.1
ME 7.6
NY 10.7
MA 7.5
RI 8.2
CT 6.4
NJ 6.6
DE 5.8
MD 6.1
PA 8.2
OH 9.4
WV 5.5
VA 6.6
SD 7.2
WY 7.3
NE 8.2
IA 6.9
IL 8.5
IN 7.5
KY 14.2
NV 8.7
UT 7.6
CO 7.3
KS 7.1
MO 8.6
NC 10.7
CA 10.5
AZ 11.9
NM 14.8
OK 12.4
AR 12.1
TN 10.6
SC 11.3
DC 18.5
MS 16.4
AL 13.7
GA 10.8
TX 13.1
LA 16.6
FL 9.7
AK 8.0
HI 7.4

Source: Statistical Abstract of the United States 2006:Table 692.

RACE-ETHNICITY. As you can see from Figure 7-7, poverty also follows lines of race-ethnicity: African Americans and Latinos, who have about the same rate of poverty, are about twice as likely as whites to be poor. The poverty rate of both Latinos and African Americans has dropped considerably in recent years, and their rates are now close to where the national average was in 1960. The drop in poverty among African Americans is especially striking. It is now about half of what it used to be.

I would like you to compare Figure 7-7 with Figure 7-3 on page 215. In both of these figures, we trace poverty over the same period of time. But look at how the national average covers up significant information. Figure 7-7 shows how remarkably different some

FIGURE 7-7   Percentage Below the Poverty Line, by Race-Ethnicity[a]

Legend:
- African Americans
- Asian Americans
- Latinos
- Whites
- National Average

Percent in poverty (y-axis): 0, 10, 20, 30, 40, 50

Year	1960	1965[c]	1970	1975	1980	1985	1990	1995	2000	2004
	$3,022	$3,317	$3,968	$5,500	$8,414	$10,989	$13,359	$15,569	$17,603	$19,307

Data points shown: 48[b], 42, 34, 31, 33, 31, 32, 30, 23, 25; 22, 23, 22, 28, 26, 29, 23, 22; 22, 15, 13, 12, 13, 14, 16, 14, 15, 14, 12, 10, 13; 18, 11, 10, 10, 10, 11, 11, 12, 11, 10, 11, 10

Notes:
[a]The poverty line shown here is a measure of poverty for a family of four, whether urban or rural.
[b]As the source excludes African Americans for 1960, data from 1959 are used for African Americans.
[c]As the source excludes 1965 data, 1966 data are used.

Source: Statistical Abstract of the United States 1992:Table 724; 2007:Tables 691, 694.

groups are from the national averages. It is the same with all social problems.

CHILDREN IN POVERTY. Poverty is also related to age. The poverty rate of children is one-third *higher* than that of adults. Overall, 13 percent of U.S. adults are poor, but 17 percent of children live in poverty (*Statistical Abstract* 2006:Tables 693, 694). Figure 7-8 shows how poverty among children mirrors the nation's racial-ethnic pattern: About one of seven or eight white and Asian American children lives in poverty, but for African American and Latino children the total is closer to one of three. For any child to have to live in poverty is unfortunate, but such extensive poverty among children has severe implications for an entire generation of Latinos and African Americans. It is the same for Native American children, but the source does not list this group separately.

THE FEMINIZATION OF POVERTY. Children who live with both parents are seldom poor, while children who live in single-parent families are often poor. The reason for this is fairly simple: On average, two parents earn more. In addition, as you know, it is almost always the mother who heads single-parent families, and these women average *less than half* (43 percent) of what two-parent families earn (*Statistical Abstract* 2006:Table 681). Figure 7-9 illustrates how single-parent families headed by women increased sharply from about 1950 to 1980, when the divorce rate and births to single women were increasing. You can also see that there has been a plateau since that time.

Life for a single mother can be brutal: She has a baby and herself to care for, and many receive little or no help from the father. If she is unskilled and undereducated, how can she compete in the labor market? If previously married, her income usually takes a nose-dive after divorce. And if a woman has been out of the workforce, her skills might be rusty. How about child support? As Figure 7-10 shows, only about half of single mothers receive what the court orders the fathers to pay. A fourth of these fathers skip out and pay nothing. Add all these factors together, and you can see why women and children are much more likely to be poor. Sociologists call this the **feminization of poverty.** (If you want to avoid poverty, see the Thinking Critically box on page 227.)

Poverty in the United States has become concentrated among women and children. Sociologists call this pattern *the feminization of poverty*. Poverty is especially high among teenage mothers.

FIGURE 7-8 U.S. Children in Poverty

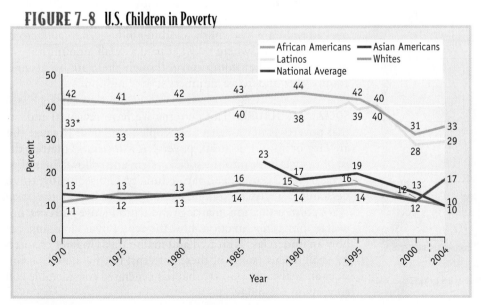

Source: *Statistical Abstract of the United* States 1994:Table 727; 2007:Table 693.

FIGURE 7-9 Families Headed by Women

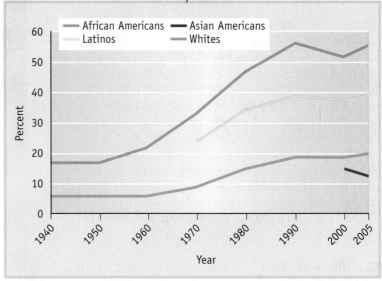

Note: Asian Americans include Pacific Islanders. Beginning with year 2000, the category for white is white, non-Hispanic.

Source: By the author. For 1940, 1950, and 1960, based on U.S. Bureau of the Census, Current Population Reports, Series P-20, various numbers; for 1970, 1980, 1990, 2000, and 2005 *Statistical Abstract* 2007:Table 62.

THE ELDERLY. Poverty also used to plague the elderly, but, as mentioned in Chapter 2, their economic situation has improved. At 10 percent, the poverty rate of Americans over age 65 is now *lower* than that of the nation as a whole (*Statistical Abstract* 2006:Table 696). Social Security and Medicare are the primary reasons for the reduction in poverty among the elderly. This change shows that social legislation can work and that we can either allow a group to stay in poverty or not. We shall consider social policy later.

AN UNDERCLASS. Finally, there is the obvious pattern of low wages and dirty work. People who earn the minimum wage are likely to be poor. I am not referring to college students who take minimum-wage jobs while they are preparing for careers that pay well. Rather, the United States has an *underclass,* people who are locked into low-paying, dirty work. They do the "stoop labor" on farms and fill the sweatshops of our cities. Many work in the clothing industry's small factories or even at home, where they get paid a small amount for each piece of work they complete. Although there are no accurate counts, this underclass numbers several million.

SOCIAL STRUCTURE. The patterns we have reviewed indicate that poverty is not a matter of people being poor because they are lazy or stupid. Instead, poverty is a *structural* matter; that is, poverty is built into the social system and follows lines of geography, age, gender, and race-ethnicity. Consequently, to understand poverty, sociologists examine features of the *social system*: discrimination, marriage and reproductive patterns, how welfare programs function, how the economy is changing, and how an underclass is created and maintained. In later chapters, we shall discuss some of these patterns, but for now let's consider an analysis of poverty that has generated considerable controversy in sociology.

FIGURE 7-10 Child Support Payments

From what the court ordered, the mother received	Percentage of mothers who received this	In one year, the mothers received
No payment	25%	$0
Partial payment	29%	$2,100
Full payment	46%	$5,700

Source: By the author. Based on *Statistical Abstract of the United States* 2006: Table 558.

THINKING CRITICALLY About Social Problems

If you want to avoid poverty, follow these three rules:

1. Finish high school.
2. Get married before you have your first child.
3. Don't have a child until after you reach the age of 20.

This message is being delivered to the black community by African American leaders (Herbert 1998). Hugh Price, president of the National Urban League, and retired General Colin Powell say that 80 percent of African Americans who ignore these principles end up poor, but only 8 percent of those who follow them are poor. Although their statistics may not be exact, the rules are sound—and they apply to all racial-ethnic groups.

To not only avoid poverty but to also develop a financially secure life, I would add four more "rules":

4. Go to college.
5. Stay married.
6. Avoid the misuse of drugs, including alcohol.
7. Avoid credit card debt.

Poverty among people who follow these seven rules is practically nonexistent.

Is There a Culture of Poverty?

> We boast of vast achievement and of power,
> Of human progress knowing no defeat,
> Of strange new marvels every day and hour—
> And here's the bread line in the wintry street!
>
> Berton Braley, "The Bread Line"

BLATANT POVERTY IN THE MIDST OF PLENTY. How things have changed! A generation ago, Americans associated bread lines and soup kitchens with the Great Depression, or perhaps with Charles Dickens' description of nineteenth-century London. Now the homeless are part of every large city across this rich land. Some are tucked out of sight, but the blatant presence of others on our cities' sidewalks, ravaged by hunger and dressed in mismatched layers of out-of-date clothing, reveals the contrast between the American dream and its stark reality—between "us" and "them." Who are these homeless people, and how did they get that way? I wanted to find out, so I stayed in homeless shelters across the nation. The Thinking Critically box on the next page summarizes some of what I discovered on this sociological adventure.

THE CULTURE OF POVERTY. Why do some people remain poor in the midst of plenty? After years of doing participant observation with poor people and gathering extensive life histories, anthropologist Oscar Lewis (1959, 1966) concluded that people who remain poor year after year develop a way of life that traps them in poverty. He called this way of life the **culture of poverty.** Perceiving a gulf between themselves and the mainstream, these people feel inferior and insecure. Concluding that they are never going to get out of poverty, they become fatalistic and passive. They develop low aspirations and think about the present, not the future. They also become self-destructive, as illustrated by their high rates of alcoholism, physical violence, and family abuse. Their lives become marked by broken marriages, desertion, wife beating, single-parent households—and self-defeating despair. Their way of life, this culture of poverty as Lewis called it, makes it almost impossible for these people to break out of poverty.

TESTING THE CONCEPT. This is an interesting concept, but is it true? To find out, economist Patricia Ruggles examined national statistics. Her findings both challenge and support the idea of a culture of poverty. Contrary to popular belief, few people pass poverty on to the next generation: *Most children of the poor do not grow up to be poor.* Only about one of five people who are poor as children are still poor when they are adults (Corcoran

BEING HOMELESS IN THE LAND OF THE AMERICAN DREAM

When I met Larry Rice, who runs a shelter for the homeless in St. Louis, Missouri, he said that as a sociologist I needed to know firsthand what was happening on our city streets. I resisted his "invitation," reluctant to leave my comfortable home and office to see who knew what. Then Larry hooked me: He offered to take me to Washington, D.C., where he promised that I would see people sleeping on sidewalk grates within view of the White House. Intrigued at the sight of such a contrast, I agreed to go with him, not knowing that it would change my own life.

When we arrived in Washington, it was bitter cold. It was December, and I saw what Rice had promised: sorrowful people huddled over the exhaust grates of federal buildings. Not all of the homeless survived that first night I was there. Freddy, who walked on crutches and had become a fixture in Georgetown, froze to death as he sought refuge from the cold in a telephone booth. I vividly recall looking at the telephone booth where Freddy's stiff body was found, still upright, futilely wrapped in a tattered piece of canvas. I went to Freddy's funeral and talked with his friends. To me, Freddy became a person, an individual, not just a faceless, nameless figure shrouded by city shadows.

This experience ignited my sociological curiosity. I was driven to find out more. I ended up visiting a dozen skid rows in the United States and Canada, sleeping in filthy shelters across North America. I interviewed the homeless in these shelters—and in back alleys and on street corners, in parks, and even in dumpsters. I became so troubled by what I experienced that for three months after I returned home, startled by disturbed dreams, I couldn't get through an entire night without waking up.

Among the many things that impressed me was that there are many routes to homelessness. Here are the types of homeless people whom I met:

1. *"Push-outs":* These people have been pushed out of their homes. Two common types of "push-outs" are teenagers who have been kicked out by their parents and adults who have been evicted by landlords.
2. *Victims of environmental catastrophe:* This type really surprised me, but they, too, live on our streets. The catastrophes I came across ranged from fires to dioxin contamination.

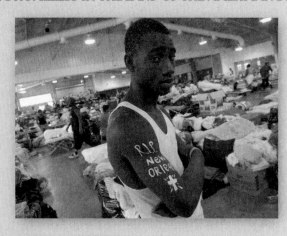

Like other people, the homeless consist of diverse people from many backgrounds. Some of the homeless have jobs and work regularly. Some are people with disabilities or elderly people trying to live on inadequate incomes. Similarly, there is no single route to homelessness. One route is environmental disaster.

3. *The mentally ill:* These people have been discharged from mental hospitals. They are given little or no treatment for their problems, and they are unable to care for themselves.
4. *The new poor:* This group consists of unemployed workers whose work skills have become outmoded because of technological change.
5. *The technologically unqualified:* Unlike the new poor, these unemployed workers never possessed technological qualifications.
6. *The elderly:* These people have neither savings nor family support; they are old, unemployable, and discarded.
7. *Runaways:* After fleeing intolerable situations, these boys and girls wander our streets.
8. *The demoralized:* After suffering some personal tragedy, these people have given up and retreated into despair. The most common catalyst to their demoralization was divorce.
9. *Alcoholics:* The old-fashioned skid-row wino is still out there.
10. *Ease addicts:* These people actually choose to be homeless. For them, homelessness is a form of "early retirement." They have no responsibilities to others, and they can do mostly as they please. Some, in their twenties, spend their days playing chess in the parks of San Francisco.
11. *Travel addicts:* These people also choose to be homeless. Addicted to wanderlust, they travel continuously. They even have their own name for themselves: "road dogs."
12. *Excitement addicts:* These people, among the younger of the homeless, enjoy the thrill of danger. They like the excitement that comes from "living on the edge." Being on the streets offers many "edge" opportunities.

As you can see, the homeless are far from being one-dimensional. The homeless are not a single group, but rather are people who have arrived on our city streets by many "routes." Note how different the "routes" are for the last three types (those who choose homelessness, a minority of these people) than for the first nine types, those who do not want to be homeless. Because there are many "causes" of homelessness, it should be obvious that there can be no single solution to this social problem. We need multifaceted programs that are based on the various "routes" by which people travel to this dead-end destination.

Is there a *culture of poverty,* a way of life that encourages poverty and is transmitted across generations? Most sociologists dislike this controversial theory because it seems to blame the victims of social arrangements. But see the caption for the cartoon on page 232.

et al. 1985; Sawhill 1988; Ruggles 1989, 1990). But in support of a culture of poverty, Ruggles also found that about 1 percent of the U.S. population remains poor year in and year out. They were poor 20 years ago, they are poor today, and they will be poor tomorrow. This group has three primary characteristics: Most are African American, are unemployed, and live in female-headed households. About half are unmarried mothers with children.

How do we reconcile Ruggles' findings? The fairest conclusion seems to be this: Some people apparently do have a culture of poverty that perpetuates itself. These people learn behaviors that keep them poor, and they pass this way of life to their children. Because most people who are poor today—regardless of their gender, race-ethnicity, or age—will not be poor in just a few years, however, we can conclude that *most* poor people do not have such a culture.

Who Rules America?

WHO HAS THE POWER? Conflict theorists stress that to understand social life, we must understand who controls its scarce resources, especially power. Like wealth, power is a scarce resource, and some people have much of it, whereas others have little or none. The possession of power is especially significant, because it determines who gets the lion's share of the other resources of society. Let's ask, then, who makes the big decisions in the United States?

This question is not easy to answer. In the past, societies had a simpler organization. In feudal societies, the serfs formed a working class and the feudal lords an ownership class. The feudal lords controlled both the means of production and the political system. Today, in contrast, the owners of the means of production do not run the political system directly. Connections between business and politics are complex, with numerous, indirect lines running from one to the other. Let's see what answers sociologists have come up with.

THE POWER ELITE. Sociologist C. Wright Mills (1959a) argued that a **power elite** rules the United States. He said that a small group, with access to the center of political power, makes the decisions that direct the country—and shake the world. Figure 7-11 on the next page illustrates Mills' view of the power elite. As you can see, it consists of the top leaders of the largest corporations, the top commanders of the armed forces, and a few elite politicians—the president, his cabinet, and members of Congress who chair the major committees.

Mills stressed that the power elite is not a formal group. It meets neither in secret nor in public. In fact, some members may not think that they belong to it. But, structurally, it exists. The power elite consists of people whose interests have coalesced. As people move from

FIGURE 7-11 How Is Power Distributed in the United States? The Model Proposed by C. Wright Mills

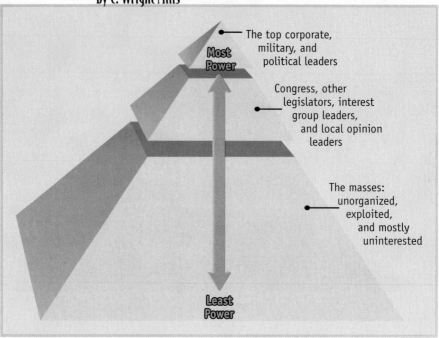

The top corporate, military, and political leaders

Congress, other legislators, interest group leaders, and local opinion leaders

The masses: unorganized, exploited, and mostly uninterested

Most Power

Least Power

Source: Based on Mills 1959a.

top posts in business to government and back again, or from the military to management positions in the defense industry, the power elite gains cohesion. White House aides join powerful law firms. A law partner joins the president's cabinet or is appointed secretary of the treasury. The head of the treasury becomes the CEO of a leading bank or corporation. An air force colonel retires and then takes over the sales division of Boeing or General Dynamics.

Because these people share interests and experiences in business and politics, they think alike on major issues. In addition, they come from similar backgrounds in which they learned similar values and ways of looking at life. Most are white Anglo-Saxon Protestants who attended exclusive prep schools and Ivy League colleges. Many belong to the same private clubs and vacation at the same exclusive resorts. Some even hire the same bands for their daughters' debutante balls. These people, then, are united by shared backgrounds, contacts, ideologies, values, and interests (Domhoff 1974, 1990, 2001).

Mills said that the three groups that make up the power elite—the top political, military, and corporate leaders—are not equal in power. Identifying who was dominant, Mills did not point to the president, however, or even to the generals and admirals, but, rather, to the heads of the top corporations. Because all three segments of the power elite view capitalism as essential to the welfare of the country, national policy centers on businesses' interests. Making decisions that promote capitalism works to the mutual benefit of all three groups.

Sociologist William Domhoff (1990, 1998, 2001), who prefers to use the term "ruling class" instead of power elite, has studied the 1 percent of Americans who belong to the superrich. These are people so wealthy that *they are worth more than the entire bottom 90 percent of the nation* (Beeghley 2005). This 1 percent controls the nation's top corporations and foundations, even the boards that oversee our major universities. They also own the nation's major newspapers and magazines and radio and television stations. Members of this powerful group attempt, quite successfully, to shape the consciousness of the nation. It is no accident, says Domhoff, that from this group come most of the president's cabinet and top ambassadors.

Conflict theorists stress that we should not think of the power elite or ruling class as a group that meets and makes specific decisions. Rather, with their interlocking economic and political interests and similar worldview, their behavior stems not from a grand conspiracy to control the country but from a mutual interest in solving the problems that face large businesses (Useem 1984). Able to ensure that the country adopts the social policies that it deems desirable—from fixing interest rates to sending troops abroad—this powerful group sets the economic and political agenda under which the rest of the country lives (Domhoff 1990).

THE PLURALIST VIEW. Not all sociologists agree with this view. *Pluralists* argue that there is no power elite that pulls the strings behind the scenes. Instead, many **interest groups** compete for social, economic, and political power. There are unions, industries, professional associations, ecologists, hawks, doves, and the like. *No one group is in control,* they stress. Sociologist David Riesman (1951) and his colleagues, who developed this *pluralist view of power,* said that power is dispersed because the country's many groups are divided by essential differences. This makes a united policy or action impossible (Kornhauser 1961; Marger 1987; Beeghley 2005). Mills replied that members of the power elite settle important questions and differences among themselves.

CONTINUING RESEARCH ON THE CONTROVERSY. The controversy between the pluralists and the sociologists who support the view of the power elite is long-standing and unresolved. In 1961, sociologist Robert Dahl published a study on power in New Haven, Connecticut, the home of Yale University, which he felt proved that the power elite did not exist. Dahl found little overlap between the social elites of the university and the town and little influence by either of them on the city's policies. Dahl's research became a classic in support of the pluralistic view of U.S. power.

Conflict theorists remained unconvinced. William Domhoff (1978b), who, as you have seen, supports the power elite view, decided to reanalyze Dahl's data and to collect more data for the same period. Unlike Dahl, Domhoff found that Yale University, New Haven's businesses, and its other social institutions are interlocked extensively. Domhoff concluded that a power elite of corporate heads, bankers, social leaders, and politicians shape New Haven's economy. He documented not only how the New Haven elite shapes local decisions but also how they are connected to national elites. Domhoff believes that each major city in the United States has such a power center and that lines run from these cities to the national power structure.

How about each industry? Does it, too, have such links? Economists produced a study that has intriguing implications. When they examined the relationships among the 72 U.S. companies that deal with low-level radioactive waste, they found extensive connections among the corporate directors. These companies are so bound together, the researchers concluded, that they form a power bloc (Hayden et al. 2002). It is possible, and perhaps likely, that each type of industry in the United States has its own interlocking power structure. If so, and this has yet to be determined, the next question will be how the various blocs of power are related to each other and to the national power structure.

To see how extensively the corporate elite is tied together on a national level, sociologist Michael Useem (1979) examined the nation's 797 largest corporations. These corporations had 8,623 directors. Of these, 1,570 were directors in two or more of the corporations. Most of those who did not hold multiple positions in these largest corporations held directorships in smaller firms. In another study, sociologist Gwen Moore (1979) examined the 545 top positions in key U.S. institutions. They were clustered into 32 issue-oriented cliques (see Table 7-1). One core circle of 272 people was linked to almost all the smaller cliques. Moore (1979:689) concluded,

> the evidence examined here indicates that considerable integration exists among elites in all major sections of American society. . . . The existence of a central elite circle facilitates communication and interaction both within that large, diverse group and between its members and those in more specialized elite circles and cliques.

Useem and Moore concluded that there is a national interlocking power elite. Yet, because they were unable to study how decisions are made (for example, policy on the Middle East), their studies do not demonstrate that U.S. elites form a cohesive ruling group.

TABLE 7-1 Members of the National Elite[1]

SECTOR	POSITION
Congress	Senators and members of the House of Representatives who are the chairpersons of major committees; all members of the Rules, Appropriations, and Ways and Means Committees.
Federal administration— Political appointees	Secretaries and general counsel of cabinet departments; heads and deputy heads of independent agencies.
Civil service	The two highest civil service grades from all cabinet departments and independent agencies.
Industrial corporations	Fortune 500 largest industrial corporations.
Nonindustrial corporations	Fortune 300 largest nonindustrial corporations.
Wealthy individuals	Holders of fortunes worth at least $100 million.
Labor unions	Presidents of unions with at least 50,000 members; top officials of the AFL-CIO.
Political parties	The members of the Democratic and Republican National Committees; state and major city chairpersons of these parties.
Voluntary organizations	The directors of certain public-affairs organizations including professional societies, farmers' organizations, women's groups, religious organizations, civil rights organizations, and business groups.
Media	Editors of the largest-circulation newspapers and public affairs periodicals, including their major syndicated columnists and news executives; broadcasters and commentators of national networks.

[1]This table lists the categories of people who, according to one study, make up the national elite of the United States.

Source: Based on Moore 1979.

THE CULTURE OF WEALTH. Although the question of a cohesive ruling group must remain open until we have more evidence, this brings us to another significant question: Does the culture of the elite—its set of institutions, customs, values, worldviews, family ties, and connections—allow the rich and powerful to perpetuate their privileges? In other words, is there a **culture of wealth** that keeps people from falling down the social class structure, just as some claim that a culture of poverty makes it difficult for poor people to pull themselves up? Of course there is. The elite of any city, region, or nation—indeed of any group—tend

"Actually, it's one giant organism connected by blood, genes, and a common source of old wealth."

Is there a *culture of wealth,* one that locks its members into wealth and privilege and is transmitted across generations? Sociologists have no difficulty in agreeing that such a culture (or, more accurately phrased, subculture) exists. We sociologists, like the rest of society, perceive through colored lenses, and a culture of wealth matches our bias in favor of the oppressed of society. As symbolic interactionists point out, it is impossible to perceive events except from some perspective. We use the research methods described in Chapter 1 to overcome our biases.

(© The New Yorker Collection 2001. Warren Miller from cartoonbank. com. All Rights Reserved.)

to develop common sentiments and share similar values and goals. The sociological problem is not to determine whether this occurs but to discover how it operates.

That a culture of wealth exists, however, does not mean that the elite work together to rule the country. This is another matter entirely. You can take for granted that power and wealth go together. Who doesn't know that few poor people are powerful, and few powerful people are poor? Whether this concentration of power and wealth exists is not the question. The question is whether this concentration is a problem.

It is precisely here that many sociologists see a danger—that the concentration of wealth and power violates the democratic processes on which our country is premised. Interlocking interests by wealthy people in powerful positions can result in a few nonelected individuals being able to wield immense control over the country. There are just too many unanswered questions in this area, though, and one of the major needs in the study of social problems is more research on the relationship of wealth and power.

Inequality and Global Poverty

GLOBAL STRATIFICATION. Just as the United States is stratified into social classes, so the world's nations are stratified into rich and poor nations. The Most Industrialized Nations, which are wealthy, have **residual poverty,** or pockets of poverty. Most of the Least Industrialized Nations, in contrast, have **mass poverty:** Most of their citizens live on less than $1,000 a year. Most are malnourished, are chronically ill, and die young. The Global Glimpse box on the next page reports on the abysmal conditions of some children in nations that experience mass poverty.

An intriguing question is why some nations remain poor year after year. Let's look at three answers that sociologists have suggested.

ECONOMIC COLONIALISM. The *first* proposed answer is that the rich nations exploit the poor nations. To obtain raw materials, the more powerful nations used to invade and conquer weaker nations *(political colonialism)*. Today, instead, they use **economic colonialism.** The Most Industrialized Nations import raw materials from the poor nations and export industrial products to them. With the Most Industrialized Nations dominating the global markets, the poor nations sell their food and natural resources—from bananas and coffee to tin and manganese—at prices so low that they are lucky if they can keep up with their expanding populations. Few actually do, and each year they find themselves deeper in debt to the Most Industrialized Nations. As a result, they do not have the capital to develop their own industries, and they remain poor.

The oil-rich nations are a special case. Their income is high, but they remain economic colonies. What do you think would happen if one of these nations were to break out of this system? What if it were to gain control over the region's resources? If that nation could control the flow of oil and set oil prices, it could lead the Most Industrialized Nations by the nose. Do you think that the Most Industrialized Nations would allow this? The answer should be obvious. When Iraq made an attempt to dominate its region, the result was the First Gulf War. At the time of that brief war, few Americans took the U.S. government's statements about "protecting Kuwait" at face value. Even the person on the street talked cynically about the bottom line being lower oil prices. During the Second Gulf War, on the heels of September 11, such statements were not made as openly.

AN EXPLOITING NATIONAL POWER ELITE. A *second* answer as to why some nations remain poor is that their own power elite exploits them. Although these nations are dirt poor, each has a wealthy elite that lives a sophisticated, upper-class lifestyle in the major cities of its home country. This elite identifies with elites abroad and even sends its children to Oxford, the Sorbonne, or Harvard. The multinational corporations channel their investments through these national elites, which profit from exploiting their own country's resources. These power elites build laboratories and computer centers in their capital cities, projects that do not help the majority of their people, who continue to live in poverty in remote villages.

What is childhood like in the Least Industrialized Nations? As in the United States, the answer depends primarily on who your parents are. If your parents are rich, childhood can be pleasant. If you are born into poverty but live where there is plenty to eat, life can still be good—although you will lack books, television, and education. But you probably won't miss them. If you live in a slum, however, life can be horrible, worse than in the slums of the Most Industrialized Nations. Let's look at the slums of Brazil.

You can take for granted alcoholism, drug abuse, child abuse, wife beating, a high crime rate, and not having enough food. Even in the inner cities of the Most Industrialized Nations, you would expect these things.

You might not expect the brutal conditions in which Brazilian slum (*favela*) children live. Poverty is so deep that children and adults swarm over garbage dumps to find enough decaying food to keep them alive. Sociologist Martha Huggins (1993) reports that the owners of these dumps hire armed guards to keep the poor out—so they can sell the garbage for pig food. The Brazilian police and death squads murder some of these children. Some associations of shop owners even put assassination teams on retainer and auction victims off to the lowest bidder! The going rate is half a month's salary—figured at the low Brazilian minimum wage.

Life is cheap in the Least Industrialized Nations—but death squads for children? To understand how this could possibly be,

I took this in a garbage dump in Cambodia. This is a typical sight—family and friends working together. The trash, which is constantly burning, contains harmful chemicals. Why do people work under such conditions? Because they have few options. As in Brazil, it is either this or starve.

we need to note that Brazil has a fragile political structure and a long history of violence. With high poverty and a small middle class, mob violence and revolution always lurk just around the corner. The "dangerous classes," as they are known, threaten the status quo. Groups of homeless children, who have no jobs or prospects of getting work, roam the streets. To survive, these children clamber in and out of traffic to wash the windshields of cars that are stopped at red lights. They shine shoes, beg, steal, and sell their bodies.

These children annoy the "respectable" classes, who see them as trouble. Sometimes the children break into stores. They hurt business, for customers feel intimidated when they see poorly dressed adolescents clustered in front of a store. Some children even sell items in competition with the stores. Without social institutions to care for these children, one solution is to kill them. As Huggins notes, murder sends a clear message to the children, especially if it is accompanied by torture—gouging out the eyes, ripping open the chest, cutting off the genitals, raping the girls, and burning the victim's body.

FOR YOUR CONSIDERATION

Can the Most Industrialized Nations do anything about this situation? Or is it none of our business? Is it, though unfortunate, an internal affair for the Brazilians to handle?

A CULTURE OF POVERTY. As a *third* answer to why poverty continues in the Least Industrialized Nations, some analysts have proposed that they suffer from a culture of poverty (Landes 1998). As ambassador to India, John Kenneth Galbraith (1979), a social economist, observed what he described as a culture of fatalistic resignation, reinforced by religion. He pointed out that most of the world's poor eke out a living from the land. With barely enough to live on, they are reluctant to experiment with different ways to farm: If an attempt fails, it will lead to hunger or death. Their religion also teaches them to accept their lot in life as God's will and to look for rewards in the afterlife. Galbraith emphasized that the poor countries do not lack resources. Most have many natural resources—most much greater than resource-starved

Japan. Their weakness in world markets, however, combined with their fatalistic culture, makes it unlikely that they will rise from poverty.

These three reasons—economic colonialism, an exploiting local power elite, and a culture of poverty—remain a matter of debate among social scientists. Rather than being exclusive, however, they are probably complementary. Each probably holds part of the truth.

Social Policy

Historical Changes in Social Policy

SHIFTING VIEWS OF CAUSE AND POLICY. Our views of what causes a social problem influence the social policies that we favor. We reviewed how people's ideas about poverty have changed—how poverty was once considered God's will, then was thought to result from character flaws, and how it was even attributed to the evils of the city. As people's views of cause changed, so did their ideas of what social policies were appropriate. In colonial times, when poverty was thought to be God's will, the proper response was thought to be the individual's religious duty to shelter, feed, and clothe the poor. The poor were cared for on a personal, individual basis.

During the American Revolution, when the poor were considered to be lazy and wayward people who needed discipline, Boston opened a workhouse. There the poor had to work until they showed that they had acquired self-discipline and appreciated hard work. Philadelphia Quakers took a gentler view and built almshouses that took in poor women and children. These social policies marked a departure from providing relief on an individual basis; instead, the government established institutionalized care of the poor (Nash 1979).

In the 1830s, when people believed that the squalor of cities caused poverty, they developed a policy that matched this belief. The logical solution was to take the poor away from the corrupting influence of the city. In the country, their basic sense of decency and order would be restored (Rothman 1971). This attempt failed because the institutions that were built for this purpose filled up and budgets were cut. The institutions became human warehouses of the worst sort.

To appreciate the attitudes of the time, consider this statement from Henry Ward Beecher, the most prominent clergyman of his day:

> It is said that a dollar a day is not enough for a wife and five or six children. No, not if the man smokes and drinks beer. . . . But is not a dollar a day enough to buy bread with? Water costs nothing, and a man who cannot live on bread and water is not fit to live. A family may live on good bread and water in the morning, water and bread at midday, and good water and bread at night. (quoted in Thayer 1997)

A dollar went a lot farther in those days, to be sure, and people did pump water freely from backyard wells. But to live on only bread and water?

Then came the 1930s, when the United States was thrown into the Great Depression. As businesses closed up all over the country and unemployment skyrocketed, so did poverty. Not having enough food to eat became common. So did bread lines. Finding their economic security pulled out from beneath them, people who had been middle class lined up with the other poor for a handout. At his 1937 Inaugural Address, President Franklin D. Roosevelt said,

> Millions of families are trying to live on incomes so meager that the pall of family disaster hangs over them day by day. . . . I see one-third of a nation ill-housed, ill-clad, ill-nourished. (quoted in Fisher 1988)

As masses of people became poor, the nation was shocked into a different view. No longer was poverty viewed as the result of God's will, flawed character, or the corruption of the city.

Rather, poverty came to be seen as the result of institutional (economic) failure—the lack of jobs. To match this shift in view, the Roosevelt administration created basic welfare to help families survive until the husband-father could get a job, established massive work projects across the nation, and tried to revive the economy to create jobs. During World War II, the economy picked up and poverty declined sharply.

As work became available and men went back to work—and, during World War II, women also—less-visible and more permanent kinds of poverty remained. As described earlier in this chapter, the rediscovery of poverty in the 1960s led to new social policies based on the idea that the poor had been left behind during the country's rise to prosperity. Some programs provided education and training so the poor could get jobs. Other programs were based on the assumption that some of the poor, such as single mothers, children, and the elderly, needed to be subsidized.

THE BASIC DIFFERENCE—CAUSE AS WITHIN OR OUTSIDE OF PEOPLE. Views have shifted between attributing poverty to forces within the individual (laziness, stupidity, evil) and attributing poverty to forces outside the individual (God, evil cities, the economy). These differing assumptions bring with them contrasting ideas of appropriate social policy. Explanations of poverty that assume that the cause lies *within* people lead to such policies as doing nothing (because no social policy will help) to developing ways to teach people to be more self-disciplined. Sterilization was even practiced—so that these types of people could not reproduce and flood the society with *that* kind of children. Explanations that are based on causes *outside* the individual lead to programs of education, aid, social reform, job retraining, and stimulating the economy. Our cycles of social reform still reflect this duality of internal and external forces.

Although different generations define poverty differently, in each era these two core issues remain: What is the cause? and What shall we do about it?

Let's review today's social policies.

Progressive Taxation

A broad policy to help reduce inequality is **progressive taxation,** tax rates that progress (increase) with income. The federal and state governments tax wealthier people at higher rates and redistribute some of this money to the poor through welfare, Medicaid, housing subsidies, child care, and food stamps. Table 7-2 shows that as Americans earn more, they not only pay more dollars in taxes but also pay a larger percentage of their incomes in taxes.

TABLE 7-2 Income Taxes Paid by Americans

ADJUSTED GROSS INCOME	NUMBER OF RETURNS	TAX PAID AS A PERCENTAGE OF ADJUSTED GROSS INCOME	APPROXIMATE TAX PAID BY EACH INDIVIDUAL	TOTAL TAX PAID
Less than $5,000	13,562,000	2.6%	$89	$162,744,000
$5,000–$10,999	15,058,000	2.7%	$209	$3,147,000,000
$11,000–$18,999	18,697,000	4.5%	$686	$13,000,000,000
$19,000–$29,000	20,748,000	6.7%	$1,550	$32,000,000,000
$30,000–$39,999	13,980,000	8%	$2,600	$36,000,000,000
$40,000–$49,999	10,550,000	9%	$3,800	$38,000,000,000
$50,000–$74,999	17,397,000	10%	$6,000	$104,000,000,000
$75,000–$99,999	9,248,000	12%	$10,000	$92,000,000,000
$100,000–$199,999	8,423,000	16%	$21,000	$177,000,000,000
$200,000–$499,999	1,908,000	23%	$65,000	$124,000,000,000
$500,000–$999,999	337,000	28%	$188,000	$63,000,000,000
$1,000,000 or more	169,000	29%	$805,000	$136,000,000,000

Source: Statistical Abstract of the United States 2006:Table 474.

Few wealthy people approve of the government taking their money in order to distribute it to the poor, and to retain more of their incomes they hire legal experts to find loopholes in the tax laws. A few wealthy individuals and corporations are so successful at finding loopholes that in some years they manage to pay no taxes. These are exceptional cases, however.

Public Assistance Programs

SOCIAL INSURANCE. We can divide public assistance programs into four types. The first is designed to help people help themselves. This type includes social insurance programs such as unemployment compensation and Social Security, Money is deducted from paychecks, and workers draw on this pool when they need it. Few argue that workers who are laid off when an entire industry, such as steel or automobiles, is hit by recession don't deserve help.

TEACHING JOB SKILLS. The second type of program is intended to help the poor become self-supporting so that they no longer need social welfare. Most of these programs, such as Job Corps, center on teaching job skills. Some teach personal grooming, punctuality, and politeness so that prospective workers can meet employer expectations.

WELFARE. A third type of program is *welfare*—money, food, housing, and medical care given to people who have a low-enough income to qualify for them. Here the distinction between the deserving and the undeserving is replaced by a humanitarian notion that people in severe need should be helped regardless of who is responsible. These programs, such as Temporary Assistance to Needy Families (TANF), food stamps, and public housing, generate controversy because people think that they encourage laziness and unwed motherhood. They also think that the people who receive this money really could work and take care of themselves. One consequence is a disparaging of people on welfare, the topic of the Issues in Social Problems box on the next page.

To keep people from starving and to stimulate the dormant economy during the Great Depression of the 1930s, the federal government began the Works Progress Administration (WPA). Men were put to work constructing public buildings, parks, and roads; women were put to work picking garden crops and canning food. Even artists were put to work. Shown here is a mural painted by WPA artists in the public school in Wilton, Connecticut.

Issues in Social Problems

WELFARE: HOW TO RAVAGE THE SELF-CONCEPT

My husband left me shortly after I was diagnosed with multiple sclerosis. At the time, I had five children. My oldest child was 14, and my youngest was 7. My physician, believing I would be seriously disabled, helped get me on Social Security disability. The process took several months, and so it became necessary for me to go on public aid and food stamps.

By the time I needed to depend on my family in the face of a crisis, there weren't any resources left to draw on. My father had passed away, and my mother was retired, living on a modest income based on Social Security and my father's pension. Isn't it funny how there is no social stigma attached to Social Security benefits for the elderly? People look at this money as an entitlement—"We worked for it." But people who have to depend on public aid for existence are looked at like vermin and accused of being lazy.

I can tell you from my own experience that a great deal of the lethargy that comes from long periods on welfare is due primarily to the attitudes of the people you have to come into contact with in these programs. I've been through the gamut: from rude, surly caseworkers at Public Aid, to patronizing nurses at the WIC [Women, Infants, and Children] clinic ("You have *how* many children?"), to the accusing tone of the food pantry workers when you have to go begging for a handout before the thirty-day time span has expired. After a while your dignity is gone, and you start to believe that you really are the disgusting human trash they all make you out to be.

Christine Hoffman, a student in the author's introductory sociology class.

WORKFARE. A fourth type of program is *workfare*. Critics claim that welfare reduces people's incentive to work. They say, "Why will people work if they can get money free?" As U.S. welfare rolls swelled to 14 million people in the early 1990s, criticism grew louder. The media ran stories about "welfare queens," "welfare Cadillacs," teenaged girls getting pregnant so they could get away from their parents, and women having more babies to get bigger welfare checks. As criticism mounted, the federal government passed the 1996 *Personal Responsibility and Work Opportunity Reconciliation Act.* This law requires states to place a lifetime cap on welfare assistance and compels welfare recipients to look for work and to take available jobs. The maximum length of time that someone can collect welfare is five years. In some states, it is less. Unmarried teen parents must attend school and live at home or in some other adult-supervised setting.

Workfare was met with severe criticism ("It's just a way of throwing the poor into the streets"), but national welfare rolls plummeted. Overall, the number of Americans on welfare was cut by about 60 percent (Haskins 2006). This huge reduction carries a lot of hidden elements. About a third of people who have been forced off welfare have no jobs (Hage 2004). I'm sure there are a few who don't want to work, but most of these people can't work because of bad health, lack of transportation, being trapped in communities where there are no jobs, or because they are addicted to alcohol or other drugs. Many of those who do have jobs earn so little that they remain in poverty. On the bright side, however, about two of five who have left welfare have also left poverty.

This reduction of the welfare rolls, with both its problems and successes, occurred during the longest "boom" period in U.S. history. We know that recessions are inevitable and, with them, unemployment. When this next "bust" period comes, these former welfare recipients, most with marginal jobs, are going to be hit hard.

The Feminization of Poverty

The poverty that clusters around women and children is a special problem. To alleviate it, women whose job skills are rusty or nonexistent need job training. Many of these women also need child care facilities, and policies that promote child care will help. It also seems reasonable that absent fathers, whether or not they were married to their children's mother, should support the children they fathered, rather than letting these children become the government's responsibility. The courts can award child care that better reflects the father's earnings, and as we saw in Figure 7-10 (page 226), they can also do a much better job of making sure that fathers pay child support. Unfortunately, some unemployed fathers can pay little or nothing. Their own poverty is a related problem that must be solved.

Private Agencies and Volunteer Organizations

When we think of aid for the poor, we generally think of the government. The United States also has thousands of private agencies and volunteer organizations that work to help the poor. Because these groups work mainly with the desperate poor, who are tucked in out-of-the-way corners of our urban centers and rural areas, few Americans see them in action. The Salvation Army, for example, runs soup kitchens and homeless shelters, as do other religious groups. The Salvation Army's efforts on behalf of the poor include alcohol counseling and job training.

Over the years, attempts to get the government to fund religious charities have run into opposition on the basis that they violate the separation of church and state. Under the George W. Bush administration, religious charities were allowed to compete for federal funds. "Faith-based" organizations were awarded about $2 billion a year to help the poor (Loven 2006).

Without weighing in on the issue of the government funding religious charities, we can note that the efforts of religious groups are well intentioned, and without them the social problem of poverty would be much worse. The quality of what these groups do, however, varies widely.

The Purpose of Helping the Poor

What is the purpose of helping the poor? For faith-based organizations, the purpose is often connected with ideas of what God wants. For private groups, the purpose is often simply humanitarian. While not denying that some people and groups have these motives, conflict sociologists suggest that when the government offers welfare the underlying motive is quite different.

REGULATING THE POOR. Conflict sociologists Frances Piven and Richard Cloward (1971, 1982, 1989, 1997) argue that because capitalism expands and contracts, it needs a dependable supply of unemployed, low-skilled, temporary workers. These people can be put to work when the economy is booming and laid off when the economy slows. At a minimal cost, welfare maintains this pool of workers for the capitalists. Welfare keeps the poor alive during business downturns so they can be used during the next business expansion. To support this assertion, Piven and Cloward point to the changing rules of welfare: In times of high unemployment, when political disorder looms, welfare rules soften. This makes the impoverished, who might band together in protest, quiet and submissive so they can receive their weekly check. In "boom" times, these workers are needed, so welfare rules are tightened. In short, conclude these theorists, the purpose of welfare is to control the unemployed, to maintain social order, and to provide capitalists a pool of cheap labor.

Following Piven and Cloward's analysis, we would conclude that it is no coincidence that the *Personal Responsibility and Work Opportunity Reconciliation Act* was passed during the longest "boom" in U.S. history. Because more workers were needed, the federal government required states to force the unemployed into the labor market by tightening their rules for welfare eligibility. Some states even began to fingerprint applicants for welfare and to send investigators to their homes. During this time, as the states began to emphasize job training instead of welfare, New York City even changed the name of its locations from "welfare centers" to "job centers." Following this conflict analysis, then, it is reasonable to assume that the states will loosen their rules for welfare eligibility during the next recession so that the expanding pool of unemployed, marginal workers, superfluous at the moment, can survive until capitalists need them again.

Providing Jobs

Perhaps the most direct way to deal with poverty and to meet the common criticism of welfare that "people are getting something for nothing and they ought to contribute to society" is to provide jobs. President Roosevelt lifted millions out of poverty during the Great Depression by providing jobs building bridges, roads, parks, and public buildings. Programs to create jobs have the added benefit of stimulating the economy, for these workers spend the money that they earn. This, in turn, produces even more jobs. People who approve of job creation disagree violently, however, about how those jobs should be created. One group says that it is the government's responsibility to create jobs, while the other insists that this is the role of private business.

This debate never will be resolved. Rather than becoming embroiled in it, let's note two principles. First, regardless of the path we choose to get there, what is important is that the jobs be available. Second, to be really effective in fighting poverty, the jobs should either provide a wage that lifts people out of poverty or else serve as a stepping-stone to jobs that will. Dead-end jobs that keep people in poverty do not meet the goal. Additional factors affect whether job creation will help the poor. For example, good jobs are often in the suburbs, where they are inaccessible to the inner-city poor. To overcome this limitation, we would need to provide transportation that helps move the poor to the jobs. Finally, because much poverty clusters around women with children, quality child care facilities also need to be made available.

What is the solution to poverty? Although no one has come up with *the* answer, giving the poor a few groceries and some castoff clothing does not solve the problem. Perhaps the solution is given in the box on page 242. What do you think?

Education Accounts

A promising proposal is *education accounts.* The government would establish a credit of, say, $40,000 for *everyone* at age 18 who graduates from high school (Haveman and Scholz 1994–95; Oliver and Shapiro 1995). Based on their background, abilities, and preferences, students would choose from approved colleges and technical and vocational schools. This money (which would be adjusted annually for inflation) could be spent only for direct educational costs, such as tuition, books, and living expenses. Besides allowing individual choice, an attractive aspect of this proposal is that ultimately it would cost little or nothing: Not only would this program reduce welfare, but it would also increase people's earning power *for their entire lives.* The additional taxes from those larger earnings could be adequate to pay for the program. If any proposal is a "no-brainer," this one is. (Of course, I must admit that I have a bias toward encouraging people to go to college.)

Giving the Poor More Money

For our final social policy, let's consider a radical proposal. Why don't we eliminate poverty by giving poor people enough money so they are no longer poor?

This is such an obvious solution. But what would happen if we did give people enough money to remove them from poverty?

THE INCOME MAINTENANCE EXPERIMENTS. As some social scientists were considering this obvious solution, they wondered what poor people would do in such a situation. To find out, they developed what are known as the *income maintenance experiments,* and they convinced the government to go along with their plans. In the 1970s, thousands of poor people were given weekly checks to find out what they would do with their money. Would they spend it on liquor or food for the kids? Would they work less? How would the free money affect relations between husbands and wives?

The studies were well done. Random samples of poor people in Denver, Seattle, and New Jersey were given different amounts of money (West and Steiger 1980; Moffitt 2004). Both urban and rural people were selected. If people got jobs or earned more money, only part of the amount they received was cut. This was to help avoid the **welfare wall**—the disincentive to work that comes when the amount that people earn from working is not much more than what they get on welfare. The families were guaranteed this money for either three or five years—no matter how they spent the money—so they could change their living habits without worrying that the program might suddenly end.

What were the results? Some people did work less or drop out of the labor market. The reduction in work averaged 9 percent for husbands, 23 percent for wives, and 15 percent for female heads of households (West and Steiger 1980). The people who quit their jobs enjoyed the extra money and were glad to get away from unpleasant jobs that paid poorly. Most people, however, continued to work as much as before.

Compared with control groups, the people in this program spent more on durable goods (cars, refrigerators, TVs) than they did on nondurable goods (food, entertainment) (Pozdena and Johnson 1979). They also bought more housewares and clothing (Johnson et al. 1979). In households headed by women, most of the new spending went for better housing. With the security that came from a regular income over several years, they also saved less and went into debt more—just like many families who are not poor.

ENDING POVERTY. Liberals and conservatives have engaged in endless verbal battles over welfare and every other program designed to help the poor. Liberals consistently favor giving more money or aid to the poor, while conservatives consistently favor programs that emphasize work and what they call personal responsibility. Now conservatives have come up with a plan so radical that it outliberalizes most liberals. In the Thinking Critically box on the next page, we examine this plan.

The Future of the Problem

Poverty begs for a solution. The homeless, the rural poor, and those trapped in the inner cities can't be wished away. But no solution comes without a high price tag.

Some say, "Let's spend whatever it costs, because it's right. We can worry about the bill some other time. Besides," they add, "if we can afford all those weapons for the military, we can afford any program that will help the poor." Others, in contrast, argue that we should establish effective programs to help the poor, but that it is not right to saddle future generations with our spending. Their position is, "If we can't pay for programs now, we can't afford them."

Most Americans seem to find themselves somewhere between these positions—feeling that it is not right to have homeless people huddled over heating grates or children's futures blocked or their lives cut short because of their parents' poverty—but not knowing what to do about the situation. With the politicians and the public not seeing any clear solutions, and with the poor remaining disorganized and having little political clout, I anticipate that we will continue to muddle along with our present programs. From time to time, there will be a little tinkering, of course, and perhaps even the illusion of progress. Current tinkering includes limits on how long people can receive welfare and some modest job training programs.

It would be much more satisfying for you—and for me—if I were to see Utopia Ahead: Politicians of all political stripes join to eliminate poverty. Whether their program is something like the one outlined in the Thinking Critically box below or something else, their solutions work, and everyone enjoys a decent standard of living. There are no more poor people. Everyone is prosperous and happy. Such a future, though, does not match any reality that I envision.

When hundreds of thousands across the land reach the new time limits of welfare and are cut off from benefits, what will happen? If the times are prosperous, jobs will be available and a crisis will be averted. Imagine, though, that our inner cities start to explode like a series of powder kegs across the United States—or even that we face such a threat—and the choice is to call out the National Guard to stop the burning and looting or to change the eligibility rules of welfare. Do you think that there will be any question regarding the choice that will be made?

THINKING CRITICALLY About Social Problems

THE UNIVERSAL GUARANTEED INCOME PLAN TO ELIMINATE POVERTY

Charles Murray (2006), a conservative who has been soundly criticized by liberals for various positions he has taken, has proposed the Universal Guaranteed Income Plan. The plan, designed to put an end to poverty, would work like this: First, we would end *all* services, subsidies, and programs for the poor, including housing, food stamps, and Medicaid. They wouldn't be needed because the plan is designed to eliminate poverty. Second, *all* U.S. adults would receive a cash grant large enough so no one would be poor. The grant would be large enough so everyone could live comfortably and afford health care and retirement. The grant would not be reduced for anyone's earnings, which would be unlimited.

That's the skeleton. The particulars go something like this: A health insurance policy would be purchased for everyone from private companies. With guaranteed payments for the entire life of each individual, companies would compete for this business, reducing the cost. At current rates, each policy would cost about $3,000 a year. For retirement, here's how everyone would have a comfortable income: Beginning at age 21, each person would get a retirement account, with $2,000 placed into it each year. This money would be invested in an index-based stock fund. This money would accumulate, with earnings, for 45 years until the individual retired at age 66. The worst that the stock market has ever done for *any* 45-year period, including the Great Depression, is 4.3 percent a year (1887–1932). If an individual were unlucky enough to get this worst historical return, he or she would have about $250,000. This would purchase an annuity, giving the individual $20,000 a year. On average, the return would be considerably better, giving each person closer to

$30,000 or $40,000 a year at retirement. But at its worst, an elderly couple would have an annual income of $40,000.

The Universal Guaranteed Income Plan certainly sounds like pie-in-the-sky. How could we ever afford it? According to Murray, we are a rich country going broke, and we have to do something about the situation. At current rates, by the year 2050 Social Security, Medicare, and Medicaid will consume 28 percent of the entire economic production of the nation (our gross domestic product), and this is what we can't afford. At first, says Murray, the Universal Basic Guaranteed Income Plan would be costly, but we could afford the additional taxes. Then in just five years, the cost of the plan would run about the same as what our current system is projected to cost at that time. In ten years, this plan would run $500 billion a year *less* than the projected cost of our current system. In another eight years, the savings would be twice this amount.

I don't know how accurate these projections are or how the assumptions on which they are based would hold over the years. No one does, as assumptions projected into the future are unknowns that often fail to follow projected paths. I do know, however, that if any plan holds the possibility of eliminating poverty—or even of reducing it to practically nothing—we should consider it. I also know that conservatives and liberals, who seem to have dog-cat natures when they try to communicate, will continue to quarrel. The one will continue to insist that individuals be responsible for their lives, while the other will stress the government's responsibility. If there is any possibility of actually eliminating poverty, perhaps both sides can put aside their biases and work together develop a workable plan.

SUMMARY AND REVIEW

1. There are several types of *poverty*. *Biological poverty* refers to starvation and malnutrition. *Relative poverty* is the feeling of being poor in comparison with others, although one may be objectively well off. *Official poverty* refers to falling below arbitrary standards set by the government. Poverty follows lines of age, gender, geography, and race-ethnicity.

2. Symbolic interactionists examine how the *meaning* of income (for example, whether people see themselves as being rich or poor) differs from its objective measures. Functionalists emphasize that social inequality is a way of allocating talented people to society's more-demanding tasks and less-talented people to its less-demanding tasks. They point out that although poverty may be dysfunctional for individuals, it is functional for society. Conflict theorists stress that those who win the struggle for society's limited resources oppress those who lose. They also stress that a *power elite* of top politicians and corporate and military leaders make society's big decisions. Pluralists disagree. They view society as made up of many groups that compete with one another in a marketplace of power and ideas.

3. Why do some people remain in poverty year after year? Some suggest that the reason is a *culture of poverty,* self-defeating behaviors that parents pass on to their children. Most sociologists, however, view what is called the culture of poverty not as the *cause* of poverty but, rather, as the *result* of poverty. Why do some countries remain in poverty year after year? Some suggest that this is due to a national culture of poverty. Others look to *economic colonialism* and exploitation by national elites.

4. Policies for dealing with poverty have been as diverse as the beliefs about its causes. In the seventeenth century, poverty was considered God's will, and it was a person's religious duty to help the poor. Personal moral failure has also been considered to be a cause of poverty. During the Great Depression, the poor were considered victims of economic conditions and were helped on a mass basis. Today, our welfare programs cause bitter debate. Rules have been tightened to make fewer people eligible for welfare and to "encourage" the poor to take jobs. Where conservatives think that individuals should take more personal responsibility, liberals view government action as more appropriate.

5. The future is not likely to bring an end to poverty but, rather, a continuation of our piecemeal welfare programs. It is likely that Americans will continue to be divided on the matter of the "deserving" and "undeserving" poor and to what extent they should be helped.

KEY TERMS

Biological poverty, 213
Capitalist economy, 209
Culture of poverty, 227
Culture of wealth, 232
Economic colonialism, 233
Economy, 209
False class consciousness, 222
Feminization of poverty, 225

Interest groups, 231
Mass poverty, 233
National debt, 213
Official poverty, 213
Poverty line, 213
Power elite, 229
Progressive tax, 236
Real income, 211

Relative poverty, 213
Residual poverty, 233
Social class, 209
Social inequality, 211
Socialist economy, 209
Structural inequality, 216
Wealth, 216
Welfare wall, 241

THINKING CRITICALLY ABOUT CHAPTER 7

1. What is your reaction to Herbert Gans' observations on how poverty helps society? Do you think Gans is serious? (See the Thinking Critically box on page 221.)

2. Review the different rates of poverty by age, sex, geography, and race-ethnicity (Figures 7-6 to 7-9). Now explain them. To answer this question sociologically, you might want to begin by asking, "Why don't all groups have the same rate of poverty?"

3. A central debate in sociology has been whether the power elite or pluralist view is correct. Which do you think is right? Why?

4. What do you think can be done to solve the social problem of poverty?

CHAPTER 8

Racial-Ethnic Relations

Damn right I'm teaching violence! It's about time somebody is telling you to get violent, whitey. You better start making dossiers, names, addresses, phone numbers, car license numbers on every damn Jew rabbi in this land.

—William Potter Gale, a former colonel who served under General Douglas MacArthur in the Philippines in World War II

> # Damn right I'm teaching violence!

The Klan called the mother of a white teenage girl who had been seen with black companions and warned her: "If you can't do anything about it, the Klan can, and will."

—According to Bill McGlocklin, the Grand Kaliff of the Invisible Empire, Knights of the Ku Klux Klan in Denham Springs, Louisiana

Today we see the evil is coming out of government. To go out and shoot a Negro is foolish. It's not the Negro in the alley who's responsible for what's wrong with this country. It's the traitors in Washington.

—Thomas Robb, publisher of *The Torch,* a Klan newsletter

Hitler is the reincarnation of the prophet Elijah. *Mein Kampf* is part of the Bible. The "terrible day of destruction" is coming.

—Keith Gilbert, who started his own church, Restored Church of Jesus Christ, in Post Falls, Idaho

Outside Hayden Lake, Idaho, a neatly lettered sign—"Whites Only"—used to mark the entrance to the Church of Jesus Christ Christian. Members of the congregation carried rifles and wore Nazi swastikas. The group lost its property in a lawsuit. Richard Butler, the church's leader, argues that Jesus Christ was an Aryan, not a Jew, and Jews should be destroyed as the children of Satan. He keeps a photo of Adolf Hitler in his living room.

Based on King 1979; Starr 1985; Murphy 1999

The Problem in Sociological Perspective

Prejudice, discrimination, and racial violence are facts of life in the United States. Hostilities and tensions among groups surface in street confrontations, disturbances in our schools, and the media-captivating activities of extremist groups like those profiled in the opening vignette.

A WORLDWIDE PROBLEM. Prejudice and discrimination abound throughout the world. In Northern Ireland, Protestants and Roman Catholics discriminate against one another; in Israel, wealthier Jews, primarily of European descent, discriminate against poorer Jews of Asian and African backgrounds; in Japan, the Japanese discriminate against just about anyone who isn't Japanese, especially the Koreans and Ainu who live there (Spivak 1980; Fields 1986; "Law Enacted . . ." 1997). And to move beyond any specific group, we note that in every society around the world, men discriminate against women.

Prejudice and discrimination are terms in common usage, and they often are confused with one another. The distinction is simple. **Prejudice** is an attitude—a prejudging of some sort. The prejudging is usually negative, but it can be positive. **Discrimination,** in contrast, is an action. It refers to treating someone or some group unfairly. The unfair treatment can be based on almost anything. Discrimination is often based on appearance—age, race-ethnicity, sex, height, weight, disability, even clothing and facial hair. People also discriminate against others on the basis of their income, education, lifestyle, habits, and religious or political beliefs.

People who are discriminated against because they belong to a group are called a minority. **Minority groups,** as sociologist Louis Wirth (1945) defined them, are groups of people who are singled out for unequal treatment on the basis of their physical or cultural characteristics and who regard themselves as objects of collective discrimination. Discrimination denies minorities full participation in their society.

Minority in this sense does not necessarily mean a *numerical* minority in a society. In South Africa, the descendants of the Dutch settlers used to be in political control of the country. They discriminated against the much larger population of blacks in housing, jobs, education, and social relations. Perhaps the most startling example of numbers is colonial India, where a handful of British discriminated against several hundred million Indians. The most universal example is men and women. Although there are more women than men, in every society men discriminate against women. Accordingly, we will refer to those who do the discriminating as the **dominant group.** This group, which has more power and privileges and higher social status, can be either larger or smaller than the minority group.

THE ORIGIN OF MINORITY GROUPS. There are two ways minority groups come into being: either political expansion or migration. Some groups become minorities when a government expands its political boundaries. As anthropologists Charles Wagley and Marvin Harris (1958) pointed out, there are no minority groups in small tribal societies (except for females, whom we discuss in the next chapter). This is because everyone in a tribal society is "related"; they all speak the same language, practice the same customs, share similar values, and belong to the same physical stock. A second way that minority groups originate is through migration—when people who have different characteristics move into a political unit. The migration can be involuntary, as with Africans who were forcibly brought to the United States, or voluntary, as with Turks who chose to move to Germany for work.

Minorities come into existence, then, when people who have different customs, languages, values, or physical characteristics come under control of the same political system. There, some groups who share physical and cultural traits discriminate against those who have different traits. The losers in this power struggle are forced into minority-group status; the winners enjoy the higher status and greater privileges that dominance brings.

CHARACTERISTICS OF MINORITY GROUPS. Wagley and Harris noted that minority groups share these five characteristics:

1. Membership in a minority group is not voluntary but comes through birth.
2. The physical or cultural traits of the minority are held in low esteem by the dominant group.
3. Members of the group are treated unequally by the dominant group.
4. Minority members tend to marry within their group.
5. They tend to feel group solidarity because of their physical or cultural traits—and the disadvantages that these traits bring.

Let's consider this last characteristic. Because members of minority groups possess similar cultural or physical traits, tend to marry within their own group, and experience discrimination at the hands of a dominant group, a feeling of common identity often unites them. This identity (a sense of "we" versus "them") may be so strong that members of a minority group feel that they share a common destiny.

OBJECTIVES OF MINORITY GROUPS. Although minority groups share these characteristics, they can end up having quite different goals. Wirth (1945) identified four objectives of minority groups:

1. **Pluralism:** The group wants to live peacefully with the dominant group, yet maintain its distinctive culture—the differences that set it apart and that are so important to its identity.
2. **Assimilation:** Focusing on the culture that they share with the dominant group, members of the minority group want to be absorbed into the larger society. They want to be treated as individuals, not as members of a separate group.
3. **Secession:** Wanting cultural and political independence, the minority seeks to separate itself and form a separate nation.
4. **Militancy:** Convinced of its own superiority, the minority wants a reversal in status and seeks to dominate the society.

POLICIES OF DOMINANT GROUPS. Dominant groups can differ not only in how they view minority groups, but also in the policies they adopt toward them. Figure 8-1 outlines six policies that sociologists George Simpson and J. Milton Yinger identified. As you can see from this figure, these policies can parallel or oppose the goals of minorities. Let's examine the policies, beginning with the most humane.

1. **Pluralism. Pluralism** means that a dominant group permits or even encourages cultural differences. The United States' "hands-off" policy toward immigrant associations and foreign-language newspapers is an example of pluralism. (During times of war or terrorism, however, the government infiltrates and spies on immigrant groups.) Switzerland provides an outstanding example of successful pluralism: Although the French, Italian, German, and Romish Swiss have retained their separate languages and other customs, they live peacefully together in a political and economic unit. None of these groups is a minority.
2. **Assimilation. Assimilation** is an attempt to "eliminate" the minority by absorbing it into the mainstream culture. In its more severe form, *forced* assimilation, the dominant group bans the minority's religion, language, and other distinctive customs. In the former Soviet Union, the Russians treated Armenians this way. *Permissible* assimilation, in contrast, permits the minority to adopt the dominant group's patterns at its own speed. In the United States, cultural minorities are expected to gradually give up their distinctive customs such as unique clothing and language and adopt the customs of the dominant group.
3. **Segregation.** Also known as *continued subjugation,* segregation is an attempt by the dominant group to keep a minority "in its place," that is, subservient, exploitable, and "off by itself." The whites who used to control South Africa despised the blacks

FIGURE 8-1 Policies of Dominant Groups Toward Minority Groups

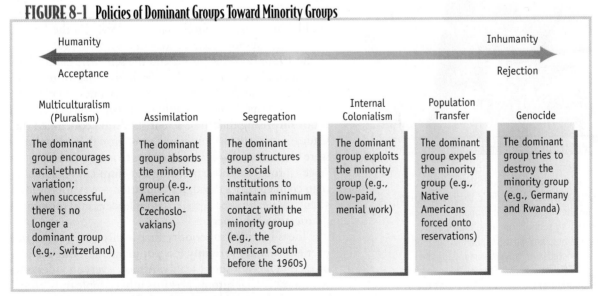

Source: By the author. Based on Simpson and Yinger 1972; Henslin 2007.

and their culture, but they found their presence necessary. As Simpson and Yinger (1972) put it, who else would do the hard work? This small group established **apartheid** (ah-par'-tate), a system of elaborate rules to maintain social distance from the blacks and to force the segregation of blacks and whites in almost all spheres of life. In the face of international sanctions that threatened the nation's economy, the whites dismantled apartheid.

4. **Internal colonialism.** This policy refers to exploiting the minority group's labor. Internal colonialism accompanies segregation and precedes the next two policies, population transfer and genocide.

5. **Population transfer.** In *direct* **population transfer,** the dominant group forces the minority to leave. In the 1400s, for example, King Ferdinand and Queen Isabella (who financed Columbus' voyage to North America) drove the Jews and Moors out of Spain. Another notorious example occurred during World War II when the U.S. government placed Japanese Americans in internment camps. *Indirect population transfer* refers to the dominant group making life so miserable for a minority that its members "choose" to leave. Facing the bitter conditions of czarist Russia, for example, millions of Jews made this "choice."

6. **Genocide.** Hatred, fear, or greed can motivate the dominant group to turn to a policy of extermination, or **genocide.** The most infamous example is the Holocaust, when the Nazis ran death camps to systematically exterminate minorities. Between 1933 and 1945, the Nazis slaughtered about 6 million Jews, a quarter of a million Gypsies, hundreds of thousands of Slavs, and unknown numbers of homosexuals, communists, people with disabilities, and the mentally ill—all people whom Hitler did not consider "pure" enough to be part of his mythical Aryan race.

Before and during World War II, Adolf Hitler, the chancellor of Germany, was determined to create hatred of Jews. To do so, he harnessed the propaganda machine of the state, including schools, movies, radio, books, newspapers, magazines, and posters, such as the one shown here. This poster is an advertisement for the notorious anti-Semitic movie, *The Eternal Jew*, which in 1937 was shown daily from 10 a.m. to 9 p.m. at the Munich Museum.

IDEAS OF RACIAL SUPERIORITY. Hitler was convinced that **race**—the inherited physical characteristics that identify a group of people—was reality. He believed that a race called the Aryans was responsible for the cultural achievements of Europe. These tall, fair-skinned, mostly blond-haired people—a biologically superior "super race"—had a destiny: to establish a still higher culture, a new world order. To fulfill their destiny, the Aryans had to avoid the "racial contamination" that breeding with "inferior races" would engender and isolate or destroy the "inferior races" so they would not endanger Aryan biology or culture. Some "lower races" could remain to perform the tasks too lowly for the Aryans.

Although most people today find Hitler's ideas bizarre, in the 1930s both the public and the scientific community took such ideas seriously. Many biologists and anthropologists, for example, believed that sharp lines divided the "races" and that some were inherently superior to others. It is not surprising that these scientists always concluded that Caucasians were the superior "race," for they themselves were Caucasian. *Eugenics*—attempts to improve the human "race" through selective breeding and eliminating faulty human characteristics through sterilization—was approved by scientists, health specialists, religious leaders, and prominent politicians of this period.

Ideas of racial superiority that justify one group's rule over another are certainly less popular today, but the idea of race remains a social reality. Almost everyone identifies with some "racial" group, classifies other people into "racial" groups, and treats them accordingly. Everyone has ideas, opin-

To educate the (white) public on eugenics, "proper breeding," activists in this social movement, backed by scientists, took to the road. This meeting, sponsored by the American Eugenics Society, was held in Topeka, Kansas, in 1929.

ions, and attitudes on this topic, feelings and beliefs that motivate behavior. In this sense race remains very real.

RACE AS AN ARBITRARY SOCIAL CATEGORY. In modern biology, however, pure race is a myth. People show such a mixture of physical characteristics—skin color, hair texture, nose and head shapes, height, eye color, and so on—that no pure races can be substantiated. Instead, biologists have found that human characteristics flow endlessly into one another, and this melding makes any attempt to draw sharp lines arbitrary. Large groupings of humans, however, can be classified by blood type and gene frequencies. Depending on the criteria, biologists and anthropologists can develop arbitrary listings that contain any number of "races." Some scientists have classified humans into as few as two "races," others into as many as 2,000 (Montagu 1964). The Thinking Critically box on the next page illustrates just how arbitrary our racial classifications are.

CLARIFYING TERMS. Because the idea of race is so embedded in our culture, race is a social reality that sociologists must confront. Preferring to avoid a term so imprecise and sometimes provocative as *race,* many sociologists, as I will do in this chapter, use the term *ethnic group* or *racial-ethnic group.* The term *ethnic* is derived from the Greek word *ethnos,* meaning "people" or "nation." A **racial-ethnic group** refers to people who identify with one another on the basis of their ancestry and cultural heritage. Their sense of belonging may center on unique physical characteristics, foods, dress, names, language, music, and religion. As we just reviewed, collective discrimination and intermarriage may also be significant factors in shaping that common identity.

The Scope of the Problem

Many racial-ethnic groups with different histories, customs, and identities populate the United States. The largest groups are listed in Figure 8-2 on page 251.

THE MELTING POT. For most of the nation's history, U.S. immigrants, whatever their background, confronted **Anglo-conformity;** that is, they were expected to maintain English institutions (as modified by the American Revolution), speak the English language, and

THINKING CRITICALLY About Social Problems

CAN A PLANE RIDE CHANGE YOUR RACE?

According to common sense, the title of this box is nonsense—our racial classifications represent biological differences. Sociologists, in contrast, stress that what we call races are *social* classifications, not biological categories.

Sociologists point out that *our "race" depends more on the society in which we live than on our biological characteristics.* For example, the racial categories that are common in the United States are merely one of *numerous* ways by which people around the world classify physical appearances. Although groups around the world use different categories, each group assumes that its categories are natural, merely a logical response to visible physical differences.

To better understand this essential sociological point—that race is more social than it is biological—consider this: In the United States, children who are born to the same parents are all of the same race. I am sure that you are thinking, "What could be more natural?" This is the common view of Americans. But in Brazil, children who are born to the same parents can be of different races—if their appearances differ. "What could be more natural?" assume Brazilians.

Consider how Americans usually classify a child who has a "black" mother and a "white" father. Why do they usually say that the child is "black"? Wouldn't it be equally logical to classify the child as "white"? Similarly, if a child's grandmother is "black" but all her other ancestors are "white," the child is often considered "black." Yet she has much more "white blood" than "black blood." Why, then, is she considered "black"? Certainly not because of biology. Rather, such thinking is a legacy of slavery. Before the Civil War, numerous children were born whose fathers were white slave masters and whose mothers were black slaves. In an attempt to preserve the "purity" of

What "race" are this mother and her daughter?

their "race," whites classified anyone with even a "drop of black blood" as "not white."

Race is so social—and fluid—that even a plane ride can change a person's race. In the city of Salvador in Brazil, people classify one another by the color of their skin and eyes, the breadth of their nose and lips, and the color and curliness of their hair. They use at least seven terms for what we call white and black. Consider again a U.S. child who has one "white" and one "black" parent. Although she is "black" in the United States, if she flies to Brazil, she will belong to one of their several "whiter" categories (Fish 1995).

On the flight just mentioned, did the girl's "race" actually change? Our common sense revolts at this, I know, but it actually did. We want to argue that because her biological characteristics remain unchanged, her race remains unchanged. This is because we think of race as biological, when *race is actually a label we use to describe perceived biological characteristics.* Simply put, the race we "are" depends on *where* we are—on who is doing the classifying.

"Racial" classifications are so fluid, not fixed, that you can see change occurring even now. In the United States, we recently began to use the term "multiracial." This new category indicates changing thought about race, a change picked up by the new classification on U.S. census forms, "two or more races."

FOR YOUR CONSIDERATION

How would you explain to "Joe Six-Pack" the sociological point that race is more a social classification than a biological one? Can you come up with any arguments to refute this view? How do you think our racial-ethnic categories will change in the future?

---

adopt other Anglo-Saxon ways of life. The United States was supposedly destined to become a modified version of England. Many thought that the evolving society would become a **melting pot,** that it would "melt" the European immigrants together into a new cultural and biological blend. As sociologist Milton Gordon (1964) put it,

> the stocks and folkways of Europe [would be], figuratively speaking, indiscriminately mixed in the political pot of the emerging nation and melted together by the fires of American influence and interaction into a distinctly new type.

For most European immigrants, the melting pot became a reality. Most lost their specific ethnic identities and merged into a mainstream culture. Although individuals might

FIGURE 8-2 U.S. Racial-Ethnic Groups[a]

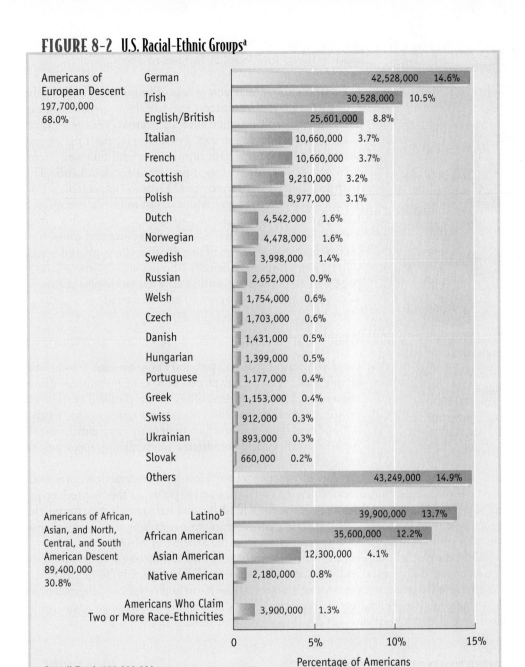

Americans of European Descent
197,700,000
68.0%

German	42,528,000	14.6%
Irish	30,528,000	10.5%
English/British	25,601,000	8.8%
Italian	10,660,000	3.7%
French	10,660,000	3.7%
Scottish	9,210,000	3.2%
Polish	8,977,000	3.1%
Dutch	4,542,000	1.6%
Norwegian	4,478,000	1.6%
Swedish	3,998,000	1.4%
Russian	2,652,000	0.9%
Welsh	1,754,000	0.6%
Czech	1,703,000	0.6%
Danish	1,431,000	0.5%
Hungarian	1,399,000	0.5%
Portuguese	1,177,000	0.4%
Greek	1,153,000	0.4%
Swiss	912,000	0.3%
Ukrainian	893,000	0.3%
Slovak	660,000	0.2%
Others	43,249,000	14.9%

Americans of African, Asian, and North, Central, and South American Descent
89,400,000
30.8%

Latino[b]	39,900,000	13.7%
African American	35,600,000	12.2%
Asian American	12,300,000	4.1%
Native American	2,180,000	0.8%

Americans Who Claim Two or More Race-Ethnicities

	3,900,000	1.3%

Percentage of Americans

Overall Total: 290,800,000

[a]Because of inconsistencies by the U.S. Census Bureau, the totals shown here should be taken as approximate.
[b]Most Latinos trace at least part of their ancestry to Europe.

Source: By the author. Based on *Statistical Abstract of the United States* 2005:Tables 13, 47.

identify themselves as "three-quarters German and one-quarter mixed Italian and Greek—with some English thrown in," they tend to think of themselves as "American." Some groups, however, have retained their unique cultures and ethnic identities. In recent years, large numbers of immigrants, especially those from Mexico, Cuba, Haiti, Vietnam, Laos, and India, have retained a strong ethnic identity.

Despite their desire to melt into U.S. culture, some non-European Americans find the melting to be elusive. Differences in appearance evoke stereotypes, as Nazli Kibria, who did research on Asian Americans, explains in the Spotlight on Research box on page 255.

The concept of a melting pot also conceals as much as it reveals, for it referred only to some groups of Americans. Americans of Western European background never intended for those of other ethnicities to become part of a "biological mix." On the contrary, they

Underlying some aspects of U.S. race relations was the ideal that the United States would become a melting pot of the nations of the world. Sifted together, immigrants would become a new people. As discussed in the text, this ideal was more *ideology* than reality and did not apply to everyone.

wanted to enforce "racial" purity; they even passed laws that made it illegal for blacks and whites to marry.

STEREOTYPES. As each new group of immigrants entered the United States, it confronted prejudice. New arrivals still do. Helping to keep prejudice alive are **stereotypes,** generalizations of what people are like. For example, the English immigrants despised the Irish immigrants who followed them, viewing them as dirty, lazy, untrustworthy drunkards. The Irish overcame their stereotypes, became "respectable," and joined mainstream society. Members of minority groups also hold stereotypes of the dominant group; and, as you probably know from personal experience, whites and minorities hold debasing stereotypes of one another (Leonard and Locke 1993). The Thinking Critically About Social Problems box on page 256 explores the question of what to do about people who manipulate stereotypes to stir up hatred.

What Is the Problem?

Prejudice, negative stereotypes, and discrimination are not necessarily social problems. Even people who are prejudiced against one another can coexist peacefully. A social problem exists when people get upset because prejudice and discrimination deprive minorities of the rights to which their citizenship entitles them. And if prejudice turns into hatred or conflict, group relations are severely troubled.

As with other social problems, however, exactly what is problematic about racial-ethnic relations depends on one's vantage point. As the chapter's opening vignette indicates, for members of the Ku Klux Klan and its sympathizers, minorities are the source of the social problem. These people think that members of minority groups who mix with the mainstream and prosper do so at the expense of whites.

Others are upset that prejudice and discrimination have thwarted the American ideal of equality of "life, liberty, and the pursuit of happiness." They see this failure of principles that the Constitution guarantees, along with the harm and tensions it engenders, as the social problem of racial-ethnic relations. This is how we shall look at the social problem of racial-ethnic relations—as discrimination that hurts people.

TRYING TO MEASURE DISCRIMINATION. The significance of discrimination goes far beyond any statistics about how many people are denied some particular benefit of society. Too often, we end up focusing on such cold numbers. Although numbers are important, what we often miss is how discrimination affects the lives of its victims. Because of discrimination, people often see themselves through the very lens that the dominant group uses to view them. They can come to deprecate ("put down") their own abilities, to think of themselves as less capable, less worthy, and, ultimately, as less human. Discrimination, in short, can detract from people's sense of being, the sense of their own self-worth and humanity.

We don't have adequate measures of this vital aspect of discrimination, however, so we will have to concentrate on its surface manifestations. As we do so, keep in mind that millions of Americans live with prejudice and discrimination. These twin aspects of group relations pierce deeply, touching almost every facet of people's lives, including their self-concept and their personal aspirations in life.

Let's first consider the highly visible area of economic well-being. As Table 8-1 shows, family incomes of African Americans, Latinos, and Native Americans are only 60 percent of the average income of white families, and their poverty is more than triple that of whites. Such measures of economic well-being produce cold statistics. Behind these abstract

TABLE 8-1 Indicators of Relative Economic Well-Being

	FAMILY INCOME		FAMILIES IN POVERTY	
	Median Family Income	Percentage of White Income	Percentage Below Poverty	Percentage of White Poverty
White	$58,131		6.1%	
Asian American	$63,251	109%	9.2%	151%
Native American	$34,641[1]	60%	20.1%	330%
African American	$34,369	60%	21.9%	359%
Latino	$35,600	61%	20.4%	334%

[1]I doubt the accuracy of this total. It conflicts too greatly with the lower incomes for Native Americans that were reported in preceding years; it is suspiciously close to the incomes reported for African Americans and Latinos; and it does not account for the greater poverty of Native Americans. The explanation could be Indian casinos. If so, this total would mask huge disparities of income among tribes.

Source: By the author. Based on *Statistical Abstract of the United States* 2006:Tables 37, 678.

measures are people whose lives are affected adversely. At issue is whether they can afford health care, nourishing food, and education—not whether they can afford a boat or a new car or whether they can afford to vacation out of state—economic decisions that middle-class people might make.

Economic matters are so significant that they can translate into life and death. Look at Table 8-2. As you can see, an African American baby has *more than twice* the chance of dying as does a white baby, and the chances of a mother dying during childbirth are *four* times higher for African American women. You can also see that, on average, African American women die about four or five years younger than white women, African American men six years younger than white men. Unfortunately, the source does not contain data for other racial-ethnic groups. In short, higher incomes buy better nutrition, housing, and medical care—and a longer life.

INSTITUTIONAL DISCRIMINATION IN THE PAST. To understand the effects of discrimination, we need to move beyond thinking in terms of **individual discrimination,** one person treating another badly on the basis of race-ethnicity. Although this certainly creates problems, it primarily is a matter for the individuals to resolve. The law, however, may become involved if one person withholds something illegally—say, employment or housing—from someone on the basis of race-ethnicity.

Sociologists encourage us to move beyond individual situations and to think in broader terms. They point to **institutional discrimination** as the essence of the social problem. This is discrimination that is built into the social system that oppresses whole groups. For example, for generations whites denied African Americans the right to vote, join labor

TABLE 8-2 Health and Race-Ethnicity

	INFANT DEATHS[1]	MATERNAL DEATHS[1]	LIFE EXPECTANCY MALE	FEMALE
White	5.8	6.0	75.4	80.5
Black	14.4	24.9	69.2	76.1

[1]The death rates given here are the number per 1,000. Infant deaths refer to the number of infants under 1 year old who die in a year per 1,000 live births. The source does not provide data for other racial-ethnic groups.

Source: *Statistical Abstract of the United States* 2006:Tables 96, 104.

Realty companies pose happy minority home buyers as part of their advertising campaigns. As indicated in the text, minority families are less likely to be approved for a loan even when their qualifications are identical to white applicants.

unions, work at higher-paying and more prestigious jobs, attend good schools, or receive care at decent hospitals.

To better understand how pervasive and socially acceptable institutional discrimination used to be, it is enlightening to consider the group that controls most real estate sales in the United States, the National Association of Real Estate Boards (NAR). This organization used to support racial discrimination as a *moral* act. Here is a statement from its 1924 code of ethics:

> A Realtor should never be instrumental in introducing into a neighborhood . . . members of any race or nationality, or individuals whose presence will clearly be detrimental to property values in that neighborhood. (Newman et al. 1978:149)

It wasn't just business organizations that practiced institutional discrimination. The federal government followed the same policy. If developers of subdivisions wanted to obtain a loan from the Federal Housing Authority (FHA), they had to exclude nonwhites (Valocchi 1994; Oliver and Shapiro 1995). Even after World War II, the FHA denied loans to anyone who would "unsettle a neighborhood." Again, the discrimination was considered a *moral* act, done to protect people. The FHA manual was explicit about this:

> If a neighborhood is to retain stability, it is necessary that properties shall continue to be occupied by the same social and racial classes. (Duster 1988:288)

How times have changed. And with them, so have federal agencies and the NAR. In 1950, under pressure, the NAR deleted the reference to race or nationality. The NAR continued its pattern of discrimination, however, and it took until 1972 for the NAR to adopt a position that supported fair housing.

INSTITUTIONAL DISCRIMINATION TODAY. Do we still have institutional discrimination, or is it long gone, a memory from our past? With laws and practices so changed, it would seem so. Many aspects of institutional discrimination, as we have just seen with the NAR, certainly are a thing of the past, but institutional discrimination remains. Figure 8-3, which summarizes a study of 9,000 U.S. financial institutions, shows that institutional discrimination is alive and well. This figure illustrates how discrimination is built into our social system.

Spotlight on Social Research
BEING A "FOREIGN" AMERICAN

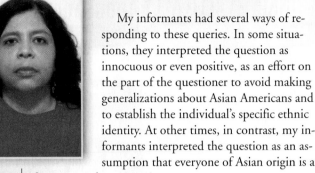

Nazli Kibria, *Professor of Sociology at Boston University, did research on second-generation Chinese and Korean Americans. She explored their experience of being identified by others as "Asian." In this essay, she reports on how "racial identities" serve as markers (or signals) in everyday social encounters. These "markers" are based on how people perceive the physical characteristics of others.*

I use the term "second-generation Chinese and Korean Americans" to refer to people of Chinese and Korean ancestry who were born and/or from a young age reared in the United States. Based on their encounters with people of non-Asian origin, I explored the ways in which they experience the identity marker of "Asian race" in their daily lives.

In their everyday social encounters, non-Asian Americans often assume that Chinese and Korean Americans are "foreigners." With the perception of "Asian" often comes an image of an unassimilable alien— a presence that is fundamentally and unalterably outside of, if not diametrically opposite to, what is "American." Many of my informants said that they frequently were asked, "Where are you from?" While this question may be intended as an inquiry about one's regional origin in the United States (e.g., "Are you from Southern California?"), when asked of Asian Americans it is often meant as a question about nationality and ethnic origins. In fact, informants told me that if they answered the question in local terms (such as, "I'm from Boston"), the person often followed up with something like, "Yes, but where are you really from?"

My informants had several ways of responding to these queries. In some situations, they interpreted the question as innocuous or even positive, as an effort on the part of the questioner to avoid making generalizations about Asian Americans and to establish the individual's specific ethnic identity. At other times, in contrast, my informants interpreted the question as an assumption that everyone of Asian origin is a foreigner and not American.

Among the strategies that my informants used to neutralize or at least to deflect the assumption of their foreignness were disidentifiers. To remove an identity of "foreignness" and provide an identity of "American," they used symbols, such as language, dress, demeanor, and even the people with whom they were seen or associated. Language was one of their main disidentifiers. During an encounter with strangers, they would deflect their presumed foreignness by speaking fluent and unaccented English. The need to use disidentifiers produced an awareness among my informants that for Asian Americans, the achievement and acceptance of an American identity requires vigilance and work.

Ascribing "foreignness" to second-generation Chinese and Korean Americans not only casts doubt upon their identity as Americans, but also it signals authentic ethnicity. That is, the dominant society assumes that second-generation Chinese and Korean Americans have ties to a community and culture that is either located or rooted outside the U.S. mainstream. These ties are assumed to be strong and genuine—authentic, rather than contrived or fake. My informants were especially aware of this assumption of ethnic authenticity when a non-Asian American would ask them to interpret Asian, Korean, or Chinese cultural practices, or in some other way to display their ethnic cultural knowledge.

When bankers were shown the findings reported in this figure, they cried foul, denying that they had a discriminating bone in their collective bodies. They claimed that they were fair to everyone, that they gave more loans to whites because they had better credit histories. If this were true, it could account for the findings without pointing to racial-ethnic discrimination. To find out, the researchers went back to their data. To be even more thorough, they compared the history of late payments of the applicants, and even the loan size, to their incomes. The results? When two applicants for a mortgage were identical in terms of debts, loan size relative to income, and even characteristics of the property they wanted to buy, African Americans and Latinos were 60 percent more likely to be rejected than whites (Thomas 1992; Passell 1996).

UNINTENDED INSTITUTIONAL DISCRIMINATION. I don't know how many bankers intended to discriminate and how many did so without such intentions. I do know, however, that a fascinating aspect of institutional discrimination is that *it can occur even when those who are doing the discriminating and those who are its objects are unaware of it.* Let's look at an example.

THINKING CRITICALLY About Social Problems

WHAT SHOULD WE DO ABOUT HATE SPEECH?

The Internet has proven a marvelous source of information. As a sociologist, I am pleased that we have this tool. It enables me to live and travel in other countries and still have libraries, government agencies, and other sources at my fingertips—vast research that can be downloaded onto my computer.

The Internet is also a remarkable source of misinformation. Anyone can put up a Web site and fill it with distortions of truth or with outright lies. People can nurse grudges, seek revenge for perceived wrongs, and fan hatred.

These negative communications are upsetting, especially the hatred. Consider these statements:

> Civil Rights come out of the barrel of a gun, and we mean to give the niggers and Jews all the civil rights they can handle. . . . Our security team will see that no live targets escape from the range. Any who refuse to run or can't for any reason will be fed to the dogs. The dogs appreciate a good feed as much as we do.
>
> —An invitation to a summer conference held by the Aryan Nations at Hayden Lake, Idaho. The group's founder, Richard Butler, is a former Lockheed executive (quoted in Murphy 1999)

> Who's pimping the world? The hairy hands of the Zionist. . . . The so-called Jew claims that there were six million in Nazi Germany. I am here today to tell you that there is absolutely no . . . evidence to substantiate, to prove that six million so-called Jews lost their lives in Nazi Germany. . . . Don't let no hooked-nose, bagel-eating, lox-eating, perpetrating-a-fraud so-called Jew who just crawled out of the ghettoes of Europe just a few days ago. . . .
>
> —Statements of Khalid Abdul Muhammad (quoted in Herbert 1988)

Should hate speech be a protected right?

Hatred knows no racial-ethnic boundaries; the first statement was made by a white, the second by an African American.

Should we ban such statements from the Internet and other forms of the mass media? Should we punish their authors as lawbreakers? Should we allow such statements to be circulated as part of free speech, regardless of their inflammatory rhetoric, the twisting of fact, or the hatred they spew?

Canada has taken steps to ban hate speech. Ingrid Rimland of San Diego runs a Web site on which she sells anti-Semitic literature and publicizes the views of Ernst Zundel. An immigrant from Germany who lived in Canada for 40 years, Zundel denies the Holocaust took place and preaches anti-Semitism. Canadian authorities accused Zundel of controlling Rimland's Web site and charged him under laws that prohibit the use of telephone lines to spread hate messages based on race, religion, or ethnic origin ("Canada Tries to . . ." 1998). Zundel was arrested in the United States on a charge of overstaying his visa and deported to Canada. Canadian authorities then deported Zundel to Germany, where it is illegal to deny the Holocaust or to display Nazi symbols. Zundel was put in prison at Mannheim (Zundel 2004).

FOR YOUR CONSIDERATION

Some say that in order to expose the ridiculousness of bad ideas, we should let them be viewed in the cold, hard light of logic. Others take the position that censorship even of hatred is wrong; as an attack on free speech, it threatens us all. That people can be put in prison for expressing ideas, as with Zundel in Germany, sends a chill up the spine of the advocates of free speech. They point out that it might be *your* ideas that are banned in the future. Still others say that hatred needs to be fought in any way possible, even by passing laws against certain kinds of speech and punishing those who express those ideas.

What do you think?

Imagine that you are in the fifth grade and your school is giving your class an IQ test. For "politically correct" reasons, the test is no longer called an IQ test. It has been renamed The Achievement Predictor (TAP). Your teacher tells everyone to do their best because your results on TAP are going to affect your future. This is rather vague, but it makes you feel a

FIGURE 8-3 Race-Ethnicity and Mortgages: An Example of Institutional Discrimination

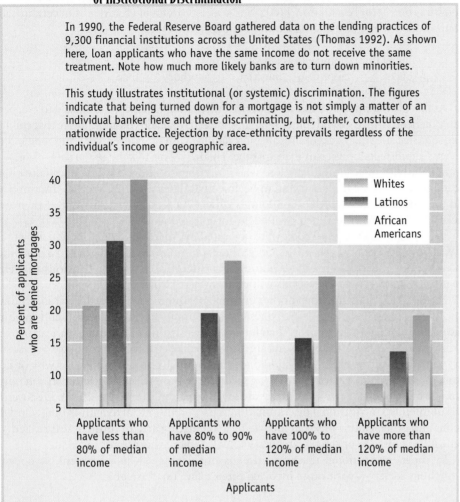

In 1990, the Federal Reserve Board gathered data on the lending practices of 9,300 financial institutions across the United States (Thomas 1992). As shown here, loan applicants who have the same income do not receive the same treatment. Note how much more likely banks are to turn down minorities.

This study illustrates institutional (or systemic) discrimination. The figures indicate that being turned down for a mortgage is not simply a matter of an individual banker here and there discriminating, but, rather, constitutes a nationwide practice. Rejection by race-ethnicity prevails regardless of the individual's income or geographic area.

little nervous. You intend to do your best anyway. You don't want anyone to think you're a dummy.

The booklets are passed out face down. You fill out the blanks on the back, carefully printing the date, your name, class, school, and teacher. At your teacher's command, for this is a timed test, you turn the booklet over, open it, and eagerly read the first question. You can hardly believe your eyes when you read:

1. If you throw the dice and "7" is showing on the top, what is facing down?
    ___ seven ___snake eyes ___box cars ___little Joes ___eleven

This question confuses you. You haven't the slightest idea of what the correct answer might be. When you play Monopoly, you never look *under* the dice.

Since your teacher said that it is better to guess than to leave an answer blank, you put a check mark on something. Then you go to the second question, which only increases your confusion and frustration. Here is what you read:

2. Which word is out of place here?
    ___ splib ___blood ___gray ___spook ___black

Again, you have no idea of what choice is correct, so you put a check on anything. The questions that follow are just like these first two. You continue to make marks, for the most part, meaninglessly. As this seemingly endless nonsense continues, somewhere in the process you realize that you've given up. No longer are you reading the questions thoroughly, for it doesn't seem to affect which blank you check.

It is obvious that you performed poorly on this test. It should also be obvious why—you were being tested on things that were not from your background of experiences. This is how it is on IQ (or "evaluation") tests. Some questions favor children from certain backgrounds. Consider this question from a standardized IQ test:

A symphony is to a composer as a book is to a(n) _____:
___paper ___sculptor ___musician ___author ___man

At first glance, this seems like an objective question, one that applies equally to everyone. Your experience with dice and splibs, though, should have made you more aware that children from some racial-ethnic backgrounds are more familiar with the concepts of symphonies, composers, sculptors, and musicians than are other children. This tilts the test in their favor.

It is important to note that those who write the questions for these evaluative tests are doing their best. They are trying to be objective. They do not intend to discriminate, and they are unaware that they are doing so. They are simply working out of their own backgrounds, from within their own taken-for-granted worlds.

The questions that "you" took were suggested by Adrian Dove (n.d.), a social worker in Watts (East Los Angeles). As is obvious, these questions are slanted toward a nonwhite, lower-class experience. With these *particular* cultural biases, is it not obvious that children from some social backgrounds will perform better than others?

Medical decisions provide another example of unintended institutional discrimination. Researchers have found that physicians are more likely to recommend knee replacements for their white patients than for either their Latino or African American patients (Skinner et al. 2003). White patients are also more likely to receive coronary bypass surgery (Smedley et al. 2003). Why should this be? Actually, no one yet knows why or how race-ethnicity becomes a factor in making medical decisions. Even African American physicians are more likely to give preventive care to white patients (Stolberg 2001). Discovering how unintended institutional discrimination is part of interracial dynamics in medical decisions and other aspects of social life will be a fascinating area of future research. Perhaps you will become one of the researchers who will explore this area of social life.

In short, institutional discrimination is built into our social system. It operates throughout society—with those involved often being unaware of it.

Looking at the Problem Theoretically

Prejudice, discrimination, hostility, and tensions characterize many relations between racial-ethnic groups in the United States. To account for them, social scientists have developed contrasting theoretical views. Although separately each of our three theoretical perspectives presents a limited perspective, taken together they bring more of the picture into focus.

Symbolic Interactionism

"What's in a name?" asked Juliet. "That which we call a rose, by any other name would smell as sweet."

What Juliet said might be true of roses, but in human relations words are not meaningless labels. The labels we learn color the way we see the world and influence what we experience.

SOCIALIZATION INTO PREJUDICE. Symbolic interactionists examine how we are socialized into prejudice and discrimination. No one is born with prejudice or with a desire to discriminate. Indeed, we are born without standards, values, or beliefs. But all children are born into particular families and racial-ethnic groups. There they learn values, beliefs, and ways to perceive the world. If their group is prejudiced against another group, children learn to dislike that group and to perceive its members negatively. Similarly, if discrimination is common, children learn to practice it routinely. As part of their socialization, children learn the labels that accompany their journey into social life.

LABELS AND SELECTIVE PERCEPTION. Symbolic interactionists stress that labels (such as stereotypes) affect prejudice by causing **selective perception.** Stereotypes lead us to see certain things while they make us blind to others. As we view people through the lens of a stereotype, it shapes our perception, and we tend to look at the members of a group as though they all were alike. As Simpson and Yinger (1972) put it: We fit new experiences into old categories by selecting only those cues that harmonize with our prejudgment or stereotype.

THE SELF-FULFILLING PROPHECY. Stereotypes can be so powerful that they justify prejudice and discrimination. The negative stereotypes that characterize a group can legitimate the withholding of opportunities from its members and justify placing them into positions considered appropriate for people "like them." Stereotypes create a **self-fulfilling prophecy.** For example, if a stereotype defines members of group X as lazy, then it legitimizes keeping them out of jobs that require dedication, industry, and energy. If "appropriate" jobs are not available, members of group X are liable to be seen standing around street corners while members of groups Y and Z are working. Seeing members of group X idle reinforces the original stereotype of laziness, whereas the basic discrimination that created the "laziness" passes unnoticed.

LABELS AND MORALITY. Racial-ethnic labels have special power over people. They are shorthand for emotionally laden stereotypes. "Nigger," for example, has numerous connotations. By no means is it neutral. This term is so loaded with negative emotions that television commentators won't say the word, using the phrase, "the N word," instead. Nor are "honky," "spic," "mick," "limey," "kraut," "dago," "wetback," or the many other words that people use to refer to members of racial-ethnic groups neutral. The emotional impact of such words overpowers us, blocking out other kinds of realities about people (Allport 1954).

Racial-ethnic labels can be so powerful that they even block out the morality that people learn early in life. In the 1960s and 1970s, for example, young U.S. men were sent to a small Asian nation where they were required to kill. Labels helped these young soldiers overcome their deeply rooted taboo against killing. Calling the Vietnamese "the enemy," "slopes," and "gooks" helped U.S. soldiers to perceive these people not as individuals but as members of an inferior group. The army bureaucracy adopted a similar strategy: Weekly it would release reports, not of *people* killed, but of "body counts" and "kill ratios." Such labels help people **compartmentalize:** They allow people to separate negative acts from other aspects of their lives. This helps them to maintain feelings of goodness and self-respect, even when they do horrible things.

Dominant groups can be quite effective in using labels for this purpose. For instance, if a group is targeted for slaughter, dehumanizing labels can help relegate that group to subhuman status. In this way, the people who are given the "dirty work" of killing are not killing "real" people. The act of labeling helps them commit acts that are incompatible with their moral training and self-concept. Just as terms that dehumanized the Vietnamese helped U.S. soldiers commit acts that otherwise would have challenged their identities as moral people, so in the 1700s and 1800s white authorities and settlers labeled Native Americans "savages." Viewing Native Americans as something less than human, troops and settlers destroyed tribe after tribe (Garbarino 1976). The Boers, Dutch settlers in South Africa, characterized the native Hottentots as jungle animals and wiped them out. Holding similar views, British settlers in Tasmania hunted the local population for sport and even for dog food. Today, much as in earlier U.S. history, miners, ranchers, and loggers in Brazil are wiping out Indian tribes as they seize their lands (Linden 1991; "Guardian of Brazil Indians . . ." 1997).

Negative terms to describe a group of people, then, are dangerous. Not only do they create selective perception, but they can also lead to discrimination and mass murder. Groups that build an identity around the hatred that can accompany such terms pose a special threat to society. In the Spotlight on Research box on the next page, Raphael Ezekiel discusses his research of such groups.

IN SUM Symbolic interactionists examine how labels (or symbols) affect our relationships: how we learn labels, how we use labels to classify one another, how our classifications affect our perceptions and sort people out for different kinds of life experiences, how symbols of race-ethnicity change, and how symbols are used to justify discrimination and violence.

Functionalism

Why does racial-ethnic discrimination persist in the United States—and in other parts of the world? As you will recall, functionalists argue that the benefits of a social pattern (some characteristic of society) must be greater than its costs, or else that pattern would disappear. The benefits (or functions) of discrimination, then, must outweigh its costs (or dysfunctions). Let's see how this could be.

FUNCTIONS AND DYSFUNCTIONS OF PAST DISCRIMINATION. It is easy to see the functions of past discrimination, how it benefitted the dominant group. Whites gained free land by killing Native Americans or by driving them west. Whites benefitted from owning slaves. They had cheap labor (not free, as by law they had to provide specified amounts of housing, food, and clothing), sold the cotton and other products the slaves produced, and sold the slaves' labor as masons, carpenters, or factory workers. Slave labor allowed many owners to live a "genteel" life of leisure or to pursue art, education, and other "refinements."

And today? The legacy of hatred that slavery bequeathed is a dysfunctional one—tension, hostility, hatred, and fear among racial-ethnic groups. There also are urban **riots,** which exact a high cost in property and lives. It would appear that the high costs of discrimination would lead to its elimination. Because racial-ethnic discrimination remains a fact of life in the United States, however, functionalists search for its benefits, or functions. Just as discrimination was functional for the dominant group in the past, functionalists look for how today's dominant group benefits from it.

DISCRIMINATION AND DIRTY WORK. **Racial-ethnic stratification,** the unequal distribution of a society's resources based on race-ethnicity, has three major functions. The first is to ensure that society's **dirty work** gets done. Sociologist Herbert Gans (2007) defines dirty work as society's "physically dirty or dangerous, temporary, dead-end and underpaid, undignified and menial jobs." Sociologist Emile Durkheim (1893/1964, 1897/1965) stressed that society needs a **division of labor,** people performing specialized tasks. Dirty work, such as garbage collection, is a necessary but disagreeable task within this division of labor.

Society can fill its dirty-work jobs either by paying high wages to compensate for the work's unpleasantness and degradation or by forcing people to do them for low wages. To get society's dirty work done, then, it is functional for it to be difficult for some group to attain higher positions. This ensures that these jobs will get done and get done cheaply.

RACIAL-ETHNIC SUCCESSION IN DIRTY WORK. When a racial-ethnic group climbs the social class ladder, it leaves the dirty work behind. Because the dirty work still has to be done, other groups are recruited to perform those tasks. For example, many African Americans have moved into the middle class, and unauthorized immigrants are doing much of the work they used to do. Mexicans and others who have entered the United States illegally have little control over their working conditions. They take jobs that practically no one else will accept, often working long hours in crowded, dirty, sometimes dangerous conditions. And they work cheaply, for many employers don't have to provide unemployment

Spotlight on Social Research

STUDYING NEO-NAZIS AND KLANS

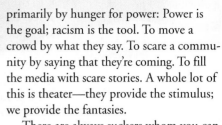

RAFAEL EZEKIEL, *a Senior Researcher with the Harvard School of Public Health, says that his interest in racism was stimulated by the contradictions he experienced as a child growing up with liberal, Northern, Jewish parents in a deeply racist East Texas town.*

Dear students,

Jim Henslin asked me to write about my fieldwork. I got stuck, so I decided to interview myself.

Interviewer: What did you do, Professor?

Rafe: I spent three years hanging out with a neo-Nazi group in Detroit. After that, I interviewed national leaders from neo-Nazi groups and from Klans. I also went to their national and regional meetings. My book, *The Racist Mind,* comes from that work.

Interviewer: Did they know you were a Jew?

Rafe: I made sure they knew I was a Jew and opposed to racism. Good interviewing is interplay between you and your respondent—kind of a dance. That requires trust; trust requires openness and honesty.

Interviewer: But, then, why did they talk with you?

Rafe: Because I told them the truth—that I believe every person creates a life that makes sense to him or her, and my professional work is to go onto the turf of people whose lives seem unusual to most folk and let these people tell me, in their own words, the sense their lives make to them. That made sense to them.

Interviewer: Did you find anything out?

Rafe: Yeah. The leaders and members are real different. The leaders are men—this is essentially a male movement—force, macho, blood, all that. The leaders are not motivated primarily by hate or by racism. They are motivated primarily by hunger for power: Power is the goal; racism is the tool. To move a crowd by what they say. To scare a community by saying that they're coming. To fill the media with scare stories. A whole lot of this is theater—they provide the stimulus; we provide the fantasies.

There are always suckers whom you can recruit by talking racism. If you line up 100 white Americans, ranked by how much they fear and dislike African Americans, the big leaders wouldn't be at the head of the line—they'd be about 30 places back.

Interviewer: And the ordinary members?

Rafe: That's a whole different story. This is not a movement built on hate. It's a movement built on fear. When you talk with a member, talk honestly about his life—his, again—the emotion you sense under the surface is fear. The kids in the Detroit group felt, deep down, that their own lives might be snuffed out at any moment, like a candle in the wind.

Interviewer: Do you have any hints on how to do good fieldwork?

Rafe: Yeah. First, check yourself out—why are you doing this? What does it mean to you? Second, be real—with them, with yourself. Third, field notes. When you finish your interview and start home, roll the interview around in your mind. Don't analyze, just let it play in your mind. Like remembering a dream. Don't talk to anyone—no phoning—don't listen to the radio—just keep the interview rolling around. Go straight home and start writing. Write first pure emotion—primary process stuff—associations, feelings. What's going on inside you after this interview? What does it remind you of? Then write your secondary process stuff—what went on and what you think it means. Then, in terms of your project, where does this take you? Do you need more questions? Respondents? Finally, ask yourself: "So what?" What difference does it make to the world what you think you are understanding? As you write that, you will be writing much of your book.

---

compensation, Social Security, hospitalization, overtime pay, disability compensation, or vacations.

Apart from what one could say about the injustice of this situation, it is functional. The dirty work gets done, and *most* Americans benefit: They eat the produce that the unauthorized immigrants pick and wear the clothing they make. The immigrants also benefit: They earn far more than they would in their home country. Their families, left behind in desperate conditions, also benefit, as their relatives in the United States send them part of their earnings. Even the government of Mexico benefits, for this vast migration siphons off millions of its more ambitious and dissatisfied citizens—those who otherwise might direct their energies toward overthrowing an oppressive Mexican elite.

Another example of ethnic succession in dirty work is boxing. Although boxing produces large advertising revenues and can bring high pay for those who are successful at this sport, because of the harsh discipline it requires and the danger it entails, few are willing to box. Accordingly, most fighters come from groups that find it difficult to reach the more socially approved avenues of success. As a group climbs the social class ladder, fewer of its members are willing to seek fame and fortune by boxing. As a result, boxing has an "ethnic succession" (Weinberg and Arond 1953). As one group moves up the ladder, new fighters come from an ethnic group that is still struggling at the lower rung of the ladder. In general, Irish boxers gave way to Germans, then to Italians, then to African Americans, who now are being rivaled by Latinos.

ETHNOCENTRISM. Another function of racial-ethnic inequality is **ethnocentrism,** a sense of group identity so strong that members of other groups are viewed as inferior. Ethnocentrism helps the dominant group justify its higher social positions and greater share of society's resources. Members of the group don't have to question why they get more than others or feel guilty about it, for aren't they superior? And aren't they performing the more responsible tasks that society requires?

Racial-ethnic stratification also produces ethnocentrism among minority group members. Their visible differences and the discrimination they face because of their distinctiveness create cohesion, a sense of identity with one another. Seeing that other groups have "made it" nourishes the hope that they, too, will succeed. This hope for the future strengthens the social system: It encourages minority groups to work hard, minimizes rebellion, and makes them willing to put up with demeaning circumstances—for the time being.

DYSFUNCTIONS. Discrimination is also dysfunctional; that is, it interferes with people's welfare and even the functioning of society. If a group becomes too alienated, it might disrupt society through strikes and riots. Another dysfunction is the destruction of human potential. Prejudice and discrimination can lower children's self-esteem, discourage high goals, and decrease the capacity to compete in school and work. Because they confront discrimination, many minority children drop out of school and waste their potential in low-level jobs or street crime. Society is the loser, for it is denied the contributions that these youngsters could have made.

IN SUM Functionalists are sometimes misunderstood: To identify social benefits that come from some negative behavior, such as discrimination, can be seen as justifying or even promoting that behavior. The functionalists' main point, however, is that social characteristics persist only because they are functional. By analyzing the functions and dysfunctions of racial-ethnic stratification, functionalists uncover some of the hidden consequences of institutional arrangements.

Conflict Theory

> What had seemed a personal hatred of me, an inexplicable refusal of southern whites to confront their own emotions, and a stubborn willingness of blacks to acquiesce, became the inevitable consequence of a ruthless system which kept itself alive and well by encouraging spite, competition, and the oppression of one group by another. Profit was the word: the cold and constant motive for the behavior, the contempt and despair I had seen. (Davis 1974)

With these words, Angela Davis, an African American Marxist, recounted her new understanding of U.S. racial-ethnic relations. What does she mean?

PITTING WORKERS AGAINST ONE ANOTHER. According to Marxist conflict theory, the dominant group pits racial-ethnic groups against one another in order to exploit workers and increase profit. Here is how the process works:

The United States is a **capitalist** society; that is, our economic system is based on investing capital with the goal of making a profit. Profit depends on selling items for more than they cost to produce. In conflict theory, this is called extracting the **surplus value of labor.** For example, if each item that a factory produces costs the owner of the factory $1 for materials; $1 for rent, utilities, and transportation; $1 for advertising, transportation, insurance, and the cost of borrowing money; and $1 for a worker to run a machine, the total cost of the item is $4. If the owner sells the item for $5, he or she makes $1 profit. Conflict theorists say that the profit represents a surplus value that came from the labor used to produce the item. That is, the item increased in value because the worker added his or her labor to the item.

THE SPLIT-LABOR MARKET. Lower wages help investors and owners increase their profit. To keep wages low, capitalists use a **split-labor market;** that is, they weaken the bargaining power of workers by splitting them along racial-ethnic or gender lines (Reich 1972, 1981; Shafir and Peled 1998). If employers can keep workers fearful and distrustful of one another, they can prevent them from uniting to demand higher wages and more benefits.

The unemployed are especially valuable in maintaining a split-labor market. If everyone who wanted to work had a job, workers could threaten to quit unless they received higher pay and better working conditions. But if there are workers who don't have jobs, the owners have a pool of needy workers that they can dip into when they need them—to expand production or to break a strike. When the economy contracts or when the strike is settled, these workers—called a **reserve labor force**—can be laid off to rejoin the unemployed, with no unsettling effects on society. Ideal for the reserve labor force are minority workers, as white workers seldom object to what happens to members of minority groups, especially to the unemployed (Willhelm 1980).

FALSE CLASS CONSCIOUSNESS. Besides the threat of unemployment, workers are also held in check by **false class consciousness,** identifying themselves with employers. Many workers think that one day they will own a business and be rich. Such false class consciousness prevents workers from seeing that their welfare is bound up with that of all workers, regardless of their race-ethnicity. If workers identify with the property interests of capitalists instead of with their true working-class interests, they cannot unite to bring about social change for the improvement of all workers. If white workers believe that their living standards will fall if minorities get good jobs, they can even feel that they have a stake in discrimination.

CONSEQUENCES OF A SPLIT-LABOR MARKET. The consequences of splitting labor along racial-ethnic lines are devastating, say conflict theorists. The system so distorts reality that it leads minorities and whites to view one another as enemies, each able to gain some advantage for itself only at the expense of the other. Whites can come to think of themselves as moral, hardworking taxpayers and view a competing minority as lazy and sexually promiscuous, as people who swell the welfare rolls and have to be supported by the taxes that the whites pay. The minority, in turn, can come to view whites as ruthless, untrustworthy, hate-mongering hypocrites.

Dividing workers in these ways fosters disunity, keeping people from identifying with "the other." When this method is successful, whites and minority group members fail to see that "the other" is an essential part of their own class interests. The reality, say conflict theorists, is that they both have a common enemy, the wealthy, who, to line their own pockets, use racial-ethnic divisions and hatred to oppress both.

Riots and other violence that result from this situation sometimes put pressure not just on individuals or on some city or area, but also on the social system. When the elite feel threatened, they try to defuse the bomb that might disrupt their power. A favorite tactic is concessions, giving a little here and there, whatever seems necessary to quiet the workers. They might increase welfare benefits, assign token representation on committees, offer government aid to reconstruct the inner cities—or build swimming pools and gyms or even offer "night basketball." From the conflict perspective, these acts are not intended to change anything, only to protect the privileged position of the powerful.

IN SUM Racial-ethnic antagonisms, then, encouraged, say conflict theorists, by the powerful, divide the working class and strengthen the position of the powerful. A racist environment not only deflects working-class hostilities but also prevents working-class consensus, the solidarity that would allow workers to challenge control of the United States by the wealthy who own the means of production. Racial-ethnic discrimination will end only when white and minority workers see that they both are oppressed and that they have the same oppressor. If they lose their false class consciousness, workers of all groups will see the true source of their oppression. Then they can unite and create a new social order in which they will receive the full value of their labor. Workers can then create a new racial-ethnic harmony, a society that will no longer have minority and dominant groups.

IN SUMMARY

None of the three theoretical perspectives has an exclusive claim to truth. Rather, each presents a particular truth. Each focuses on selected aspects of racial-ethnic relations, emphasizing those aspects above any other. Symbolic interactionists alert us to the powerful role of labels in defining human relations, how they are lenses through which we view ourselves and others. If those labels are demeaning, they help people discriminate with a clear conscience. Functionalists turn our attention not only to the dysfunctions of discrimination, but also to its benefits—its role in the division of labor and the consequences of the ethnocentrism that it produces. Conflict theorists stress how the powerful of society use prejudice and discrimination to destroy worker solidarity so they can hold down wages and increase profits. Each theoretical lens, then, produces a unique understanding of racial-ethnic relations. Combined, these perspectives provide greater understanding of discrimination than does any one of them alone.

Research Findings

As you saw on Figure 8-2 on page 253, whites make up 68 percent of the overall U.S. population, minorities 31 percent (African Americans 12 percent, Latinos 14 percent, Asian Americans 4 percent, and Native Americans 1 percent). About 1 percent of Americans claim two or more races. These groups are far from distributed evenly across the nation. As the Social Map on the next page shows, their distribution among the states seldom comes close to the national average. This is because minority groups tend to be clustered in regions. The extreme distributions are represented by Maine, which has only a 4 percent minority population, and Hawaii, where minorities outnumber European Americans 77 percent to 23 percent.

What major problems do minority groups in the United States face? How do the groups differ from one another? In what ways are relationships changing? What strategies are minority groups using to bring about social change? To answer these questions, we shall present an overview of the four largest minority groups in the United States: Native Americans, Latinos, African Americans, and Asian Americans.

Native Americans

NUMBERS. When Columbus arrived on the shores of the "New World," Native Americans numbered about 10 million (Schaefer 2004). About 400 years later, in 1900, the number of Native Americans reached a low of just a quarter of a million. Today, as you saw on Figure 8-4 on the next page, there are a little over 2 million Native Americans. Native Americans belong to more than 500 tribes (O'Hare 1992).

CONFLICT. At first, relations between the European settlers and the Native Americans were peaceful. Some American (and Canadian) authorities even encouraged marriage between whites and Native Americans. In 1784, Patrick Henry introduced a bill in the Virginia House of Delegates to offer tax relief, free education, and cash bonuses to whites and Indians who intermarried (Kaplan 1990). As more Europeans arrived, they began a relentless push westward. Native Americans stood in the way of this expansion, and the Europeans began a policy of genocide. As part of this policy (which they called "pacification"), the U.S. Cavalry slaughtered tens of thousands of Native Americans. When the cavalry

FIGURE 8-4 The Distribution of Dominant and Minority Groups in the United States

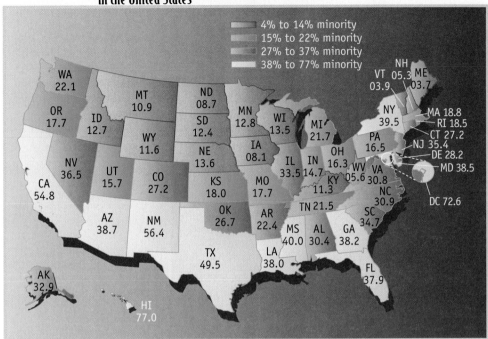

This social map illustrates how unevenly minority groups are distributed among the states. The extremes are Maine with 4 percent minority and Hawaii with 77 percent minority.

Source: By the author. Based on *Statistical Abstract of the United States* 2005:Tables 13, 47.

butchered the huge herds of buffalo on which the Great Plains Indians depended, many thousands more died from malnutrition and disease. Because the Native Americans had no immunity to the European diseases, apparently more of them died from smallpox, measles, and the flu than from bullets (Kitano 1974; Dobyns 1983; Schaefer 2004).

In reading the accounts of this period, I was struck by the barbarity of the European Americans. One of the most grisly acts was the distribution of blankets contaminated with smallpox. The blankets were given as a peace offering. Another was the forced march along the Trail of Tears, which took place after the government changed its policy from genocide to population transfer and began to relocate Native Americans to specified areas called "reservations." The march along the Trail of Tears took place in midwinter from the Carolinas and Georgia to Oklahoma, a journey of 1,000 miles. Fifteen thousand Cherokees were forced to make this march in light clothing. Falling exhausted, 4,000, mostly elderly and children, were left to die.

TREATIES. Because each tribe was a nation, the U.S. government signed treaties with the tribes. These treaties, ratified by the U.S. Senate, granted the Native Americans specified lands forever. The treaties often were broken when white settlers demanded more Indian land and natural resources. In 1874, for instance, when gold was discovered in South Dakota's Black Hills, whites flooded the reservation lands. The cavalry supported the settlers, resulting in the well-known defeat of "General" (actually, Lt. Colonel) Custer at Little Big Horn in 1876 (Churchill and Wall 1990). The symbolic end to Native American resistance may have been the 1890 massacre at Wounded Knee, South Dakota, where the cavalry killed 300 (out of 350) Native American men, women, and children (Kitano 1974; Olson et al. 1997).

STEREOTYPES. As noted earlier, people use stereotypes and labels to justify their inhumane acts and to keep their acts from conflicting with favorable definitions of the self. So it was with the U.S. Indian policy. The Europeans who populated the Americas viewed Native Americans as stupid, lying, thieving, murdering, pagan "savages" (Simpson and Yinger 1972). Killing dangerous savages was viewed as a way to make the world a safer place for

To "civilize" the Native Americans, the U.S. government forcibly took children away from their parents and placed them in schools to learn "white" skills. This 1882 photo of a blacksmithing class was taken at Forest Grove School in Oregon.

intelligent, civilized people. The victors—who write the history books—labeled whites as "pioneers," not "invaders"; their military successes, they called "victories," those of the Native Americans "massacres"; they didn't call their seizure of Native American lands "invasion," but, rather, "settling the land"; and they labeled the Native Americans' defense of their homelands against overwhelming numbers not "courageous" but "treacherous" (Josephy 1970; Henslin 2007b).

EDUCATION AND CULTURE CONFLICT. After the federal government moved the Native Americans to reservations, the Bureau of Indian Affairs (B.I.A.), an agency of the federal government assigned the responsibility of overseeing Native Americans, opened schools in an attempt to "civilize" the Indians—that is, to replace the Native American cultures with that of the European Americans. The B.I.A. opened some schools on reservations, but in an attempt to make this effort more effective, the B.I.A. took thousands of Native American children from their parents and forced them to attend school at off-reservation boarding schools. Effects of these efforts to replace the Native American cultures linger today, with the intentions of white authorities often distrusted.

A generation ago, when the boarding schools had been mostly abandoned, anthropologists Murray and Rosalie Wax (1964, 1965, 1967, 1971) found that a huge cultural gap still existed between the home and school life of Native American children. The parents teach their children to be independent, but at school they are rewarded for being dependent on their teachers. Native American parents teach their children not to embarrass their peers, but their teachers expect them to correct one another in public. Geared to urban middle-class values, the schools prepare Native American children for a life that few will lead. Because the school system, which is based on the values of the dominant group, denigrates Native American culture and teaches concepts that are largely irrelevant to reservation life, the parents are alienated from it and refuse to visit their children's schools. The teachers, alienated by the rejection of their well-intended efforts, avoid the homes of their students.

Dead center in this value conflict between the schools and the reservation are the children. Torn between home and school, they generally choose the family and tribe. Lacking motivation to do well in school, they tend to drop out. As the Waxes expressed it, the deck is so stacked against Native American children that they are, in effect, pushed out of school. Their continuing low rate of college graduation indicates that such contrasting orientations continue.

ECONOMIC WELL-BEING. Table 8-1 on page 253 shows how Native Americans rank on indicators of economic well-being. As you can see from this table, their income is only

60 percent that of whites, while their rate of poverty is *three* times higher than that of whites. In addition, and not shown on this table, the life expectancy of Native Americans is less than that of the nation as a whole: One in four Native Americans dies before the age of 25, compared with the national average of one in seven. Their suicide rate is higher than that of any other racial-ethnic group, and their rate of alcoholism runs perhaps five times that of the nation (Snipp and Sorkin 1986; O'Hare 1992; Wallace et al. 1996). It seems fair to conclude that Native American life in the dominant white society is far from satisfying.

CONTEMPORARY STRUGGLES. Native Americans are sometimes called the invisible minority. Because a third of Native Americans live on reservations, half in just four states—Oklahoma, California, Arizona, and New Mexico—most Americans are hardly aware of their presence (O'Hare 1992). In addition, for the past 100 years or so, seldom have Native Americans made headlines by disrupting the white-dominated society that they have refused to join. Today's conflicts are primarily legal. They center on the Native Americans trying to enforce the treaties they made with the United States. Minor legal skirmishes have centered on maintaining traditional fishing and hunting rights. Major legal battles are being fought over the Native Americans' demand for the waters of the Arkansas, Colorado, San Juan, and Rio Grande rivers—which were guaranteed by treaty. What most upsets whites, however, are the lawsuits that Native Americans have filed to reclaim millions of acres of land ranging from New England to the Southwest. By treaty, Congress guaranteed these lands to Native American tribes "in perpetuity."

The federal government's primary legal strategy has been to obstruct the justice system by postponement. In some instances, legal cases are never heard, for those who filed the motion die and others lose interest as proceedings drag on for years, sometimes for generations. Some tribes, however, have won their legal battles. Blue Lake, in New Mexico, a heavily forested area sacred to the Taos Pueblo tribe, has been returned to the tribe. Alaskan Native Americans, primarily the Inuits and Aleuts, were awarded a cash settlement of nearly $1 billion and legal title to 40 million acres. Other tribes have received smaller settlements.

Because real estate is so significant for the country's welfare, and clouded titles interfere with the transfer of property, whites in the affected areas are upset—and understandably so. In the state of New York, clouded titles have even made it difficult for owners to sell their land, even though it has been in their family for 200 years (Olson 2002). Some whites have hit upon a legal strategy that goes straight to the jugular—trying to strip Native

The ironies of history! The success of some casinos operated by Native Americans has aroused resentment among some whites who feel that the Native Americans are enjoying an advantage they don't have.

Americans of their legal status as separate nations and remove their immunity to lawsuits. So far, such attempts have failed (Anderson and Moller 1998).

CASINOS. In 1988, the federal government passed a law that allows Native Americans to operate casinos. Now over 400 tribes do so, with their casinos bringing in about $18 billion a year. This is *twice as much as all of Nevada's casinos take in* (Butterfield 2005).Some tribes have hit it rich. An outstanding example is the Oneida tribe of New York, whose 1,000 members used to live in trailers on 32 acres. Now their casino nets $232,000 a year for *each* man, woman, and child. This tribe employs 3,000 people in their casino, hotels, convention center, gasoline stations, and bars and restaurants. Not surprisingly, poorer white neighbors have grown resentful of the tribe's affluence (Dao 1999; Peterson 2003). Then there are the gambling profits of the Mashantucket Pequots of Connecticut. With only 310 members, this tribe brings in more than $2 million *a day* (Zielbauer 2000). Native Americans who are wealthy, much less have an income higher than the national average, are an exception, of course, as is evident from the data we reviewed in Table 8-1 (on page 253).

SELF-DETERMINATION. Native Americans had no overarching term for the many tribes that inhabited North and South America. The term *Indian* was given to them by Columbus, who mistakenly thought that he had landed in India. The name stuck, and many Native Americans still use it to refer to themselves (Shively 1999). The term *Native American* was also made up by whites. Thinking of the 500 culturally distinct tribes as "one people," then, is a European American way of viewing matters. The tribes see themselves as many nations, many peoples, and they insist on the right to self-determination—to remain unassimilated in the dominant culture if they wish and to run their own affairs as separate peoples.

These many separate identities have served the dominant whites well, for they have not had to face a united Native American population. Perhaps, then, the most significant change in this aspect of group relations is the development of **pan-Indianism.** Moving beyond identification with only a particular tribe, some Native Americans emphasize common elements that run through their cultures. They are trying to utilize these themes to build a united identity and to work toward the welfare of all Native Americans. If effective, national Native American organizations will develop. These groups could help force the courts to act on the many Native American lawsuits, file hundreds or thousands more lawsuits, and develop self-help measures that center on Native American values. Pan-Indianism, however, is a controversial issue among Native Americans. Some reject it in favor of ethnic diversity, preferring to stress the many Native American histories, languages, and even musical styles (Rolo n.d.).

Latinos (Hispanics)

ARTIFICIAL TERMS. The largest ethnic group in the United States is the Latinos (or Hispanics), people who trace their origins to the Spanish-speaking countries of Latin America and to Spain. Like Native Americans, few Latinos consider themselves to be a single people. They think of themselves as Americans of Mexican origin (*Mexicanos* or *Chicanos*), Americans of Cuban origin (*Cubanos*), Americans from Puerto Rico (*Puertoricanos*), and so on. Nor do most identify readily with *Latino* or *Hispanic*. Most consider these terms to be an artificial grouping of peoples. And so they are. In the dominant group's effort to pigeonhole everyone, using dozens of separate classifications is cumbersome. *Latino* and *Hispanic,* in contrast, are umbrella terms that lump many peoples into a single category. It is also important to stress that *Latino* and *Hispanic* do not refer to a race, but to *ethnic* groups. Latinos may identify themselves as African American, white, or Native American. Some even refer to themselves as *Afro Latino.*

COUNTRY OF ORIGIN. In addition to 25 million people whose country of origin is Mexico, Latinos include about 3 million people from Puerto Rico, 1 million from Cuba, and 5 million from Central and South America (*Statistical Abstract* 2005:Table 40). Although most Latinos of Mexican origin live in the Southwest, most Latinos from Puerto Rico live in New York City, and those from Cuba live primarily in the Miami area of Florida.

UNAUTHORIZED IMMIGRANTS. Officially tallied at 37 million, the number of Latinos in the United States is considerably higher than this. Although most Latinos are U.S. citizens, about 8 million have entered the country illegally, about 6 million from Mexico and 2 million from Central and South America (Passel 2005). Each year, over 1 million Mexicans are deported to Mexico (*Statistical Abstract* 2006:Table 521). Some come to the United States for temporary work and then return home. Most do not. In 1986, the federal government passed the Immigration Reform and Control Act, which permitted unauthorized immigrants to apply for U.S. citizenship. Over 3 million people applied, the vast majority from Mexico (Espenshade 1990). Similar proposals of amnesty and citizenship are being made today. To understand better what stimulates this vast subterranean migration, see the Issues in Social Problems box on the next page.

FIGURE 8-5 Geographic Distribution of the Latino Population

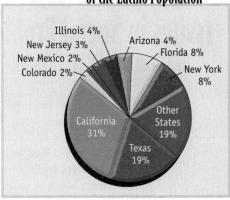

Source: By the author. Based on *Statistical Abstract of the United States* 2005:Table 21.

RESIDENCE. Although there are vast stretches of Middle America in which no Latinos can be found, the United States has more Latinos than Canada has Canadians. As Figure 8-5 shows, two-thirds of Latinos are concentrated in just four states—California, Texas, Florida, and New York. The migration of Latinos into the United States is so vast that Latinos have become the largest minority group in the United States. They have brought seismic changes to some areas, such as Florida's Dade County, which contains Miami. With its prominent Latino presence, especially with regard to the amount of Spanish that is spoken, Miami has been called "the capital of South America."

SPANISH. The factor that clearly distinguishes Latinos from other U.S. minorities is the Spanish language. Although not all Latinos speak Spanish, most do. About 30 million Latinos speak Spanish at home (*Statistical Abstract* 2006:Table 47). Many cannot speak English or can do so only with difficulty. Being fluent only in Spanish in a society where English is spoken almost exclusively is a severe obstacle to getting a good job.

In some areas, teachers used to punish children who spoke Spanish at school. Despite the 1848 Treaty of Hidalgo, which ended the Mexican War and guarantees Mexicans the right to maintain their culture, from 1855 until 1968 California banned teaching in any language other than English. In a 1974 decision (*Lau v. Nichols*), the U.S. Supreme Court ruled that to use only English to teach students who cannot understand English violated their civil rights. This decision, which paved the way for bilingual instruction for Spanish-speaking children, resulted from a lawsuit by Chinese students who wanted to receive instruction in Chinese (Vidal 1977; Lopez 1980).

The growing use of Spanish has become a social issue. Senator S. I. Hayakawa of Hawaii initiated an "English-only" movement in 1981. Supporters of this movement have succeeded in getting 26 states to pass a law declaring English their official language (Schaefer 2004).

ECONOMIC WELL-BEING. Latinos fare poorly on the indicators of economic well-being shown in Table 8-1 on page 253. Their family income averages only three-fifths that of whites, and they are three times as likely as whites to be poor. In addition, their unemployment rate is almost double that of whites, and only one of nine is a college graduate. At *every* level of education, whether it be a high school diploma or a doctorate, whites earn more (*Statistical Abstract* 2006:Table 217). In response to their position in U.S. society, some Latinos have begun a movement that rejects assimilation and emphasizes the maintenance of Latino culture. Others insist on greater assimilation. Hundreds of thousands of unauthorized immigrants have taken to the streets to protest their illegal status, demanding the right to citizenship.

POLITICS. Despite their numbers, Latinos hold only a tiny fraction of elected offices. Because of their huge numbers, we might expect about 14 of the 100 U.S. senators to be Latino. How many are there? *Three.* Of the 435 representatives, 27 are Latino. Overall, of the 500,000 elected public officials in the United States, only 4,700 are Latino. Most serve on the county level and on school boards. Only 231 are on the state level (*Statistical*

Issues in Social Problems
THE ILLEGAL TRAVEL GUIDE

Manuel was a drinking buddy of Jose's, a man I had met in Colima, Mexico. At 45, Manuel was friendly, outgoing, and enterprising.

Manuel, who had lived in the United States for seven years, spoke fluent English. Preferring to live in his home town in Colima, where he palled around with his childhood friends, Manuel always seemed to have money and free time.

When Manuel invited me to go on a business trip with him, I accepted. I never could figure out how he made his living and how he could afford a car, a luxury that none of his friends had. As we traveled from one remote village to another, Manuel would sell used clothing that he had heaped in the back of his older-model Ford station wagon.

At one stop, Manuel took me into a dirt-floored, thatched-roof hut. While chickens ran in and out, Manuel whispered to a slender man of about 23. The poverty was overwhelming. Juan, as his name turned out to be, had a

Illegal immigration is destined to continue—unless the root causes are addressed.

partial grade school education. He also had a wife, four hungry children under the age of 5, and two pigs—his main food supply. Although eager to work, Juan had no job, for there was simply no work available in this remote village.

As we were drinking a Coke, which seems to be the national beverage of Mexico's poor, Manuel explained to me that he was not only selling clothing—he was also lining up migrants to the United States. For $200 he would take a man to the border and introduce him to a "wolf," who, for another $200 would surreptitiously make a night crossing into the promised land.

When I saw the hope in Juan's face, I knew nothing would stop him. He was borrowing every cent he could from every friend and relative to scrape the $400 together. Although he risked losing everything if apprehended, and he would be facing unknown risks, Juan would make the trip, for wealth beckoned on the other side. He knew people who had been there and spoke glowingly of its opportunities. Manuel, of course, stoked the fires of hope.

Looking up from the children playing on the dirt floor with the chickens pecking about them, I saw a man who loved his family. In order to make the desperate bid for a better life, he would suffer an enforced absence, as well as the uncertainties of a foreign land whose customs he did not know.

Juan opened his billfold, took something out, and slowly handed it to me. I looked at it curiously. I felt tears as I saw the tenderness with which he handled this piece of paper. It was his passport to the land of opportunity: a Social Security card made out in his name, sent by a friend who had already made the trip and who was waiting for Juan on the other side of the border.

It was then that I realized that the thousands of Manuels scurrying about Mexico and the millions of Juans they were transporting could never be stopped, for only the United States could fulfill their dream of a better life.

Abstract 2006: Tables 395, 404; "Some Facts . . ." 2007). Yet, compared with the past, even these small totals represent substantial gains in the political system.

It is likely that Latinos soon will play a larger role in U.S. politics, perhaps one day even beyond their overall numbers. This is because they are concentrated in four states that hold one-fourth of the 538 electoral votes: California (55), New York (31), Texas (34), and Florida (27). Already, presidents have seen the political wisdom of appointing Latinos to major federal positions, such as Secretary of Transportation and Secretary of Housing and Urban Development. In addition to their ritual kissing of babies, presidential candidates now ritually utter a few Spanish phrases.

The potential political power of Latinos has not been realized because of severe divisions of national origin and social class. These distinctions nourish disunity and create disagreements about social and economic policy. As mentioned, Latinos do not think of themselves as a single people, and national origin is highly significant. People from Puerto Rico, for example, feel little sense of unity with people from Mexico. It is similarly the case with those from Venezuela, Colombia, or El Salvador. Latinos from rural and urban areas also have different cultural traditions and, often, political views. It used to be the same with those who had immigrated from Germany and Sweden or from England and France. With time, however, identifying with the country of origin was mostly lost to the descendants of these immigrants, and they came to think of themselves almost exclusively as Americans. I anticipate that, for the most part, this will happen to Latinos as well.

Social class divisions also obstruct united action. Like people of other ethnic backgrounds,

Immigrants from Central America don't arrive with a Latino identity. They identify themselves, rather, as Salvadorans, Hondurans, Guatemalans, and so on. As this photo illustrates, their identity may broaden to Central American. The umbrella terms, Latino and Hispanic, were invented by Anglos, who lump immigrants who speak Spanish together. As Spanish-speaking immigrants assimilate, they may come to adopt these encompassing terms and establish a broader identity.

Latinos are divided by education and income. In some cases, even when they come from the same country, the differences in their backgrounds are severe. Most of the half million Cubans who fled their homeland after Fidel Castro came to power in 1959 were well-educated, financially comfortable professionals or businesspeople. The 100,000 "boat people" who arrived twenty years later, in contrast, were mainly lower-class refugees to whom the earlier arrivals would hardly have spoken in Cuba. The earlier arrivals have prospered in Florida and control many businesses and financial institutions: There continues to be a vast division between them and the more recent immigrants.

African Americans

It was 1955, in Montgomery, Alabama. As specified by law, whites took the front seats of the bus, while blacks went to the back. As the bus filled up, blacks had to give up their seats to whites.

When Rosa Parks, a 42-year-old African American woman and secretary of the Montgomery NAACP, was told she would have to stand so white folks could sit, she refused. She sat there stubbornly while the bus driver fumed, whites felt insulted, and blacks, observing from the back of the bus, also wondered what she was doing.

Mrs. Parks was arrested. Instead of passing as an incident of little importance, her arrest touched off mass demonstrations, led 50,000 blacks to boycott the city's buses for a year, and thrust onto the stage of history Rev. Marin Luther King, Jr., an unknown preacher who had majored in sociology at Morehouse College in Atlanta, Georgia.

Dr. King, who was later murdered in Memphis, Tennessee, organized car pools and preached nonviolence. Incensed at this organizer and at the unfamiliar stirrings in the normally compliant black community, the segregationists also put their beliefs into practice—by bombing homes and dynamiting churches.

CIVIL DISOBEDIENCE AND AMERICAN APARTHEID. In the 1950s, the South was still practicing apartheid. African Americans, then called Negroes, were not allowed to stay at hotels or to eat in restaurants that whites patronized. They had to use separate toilets, water fountains, and swimming pools. It was only a few years earlier, in 1944, that the U.S.

The segregation of whites and blacks in the United States used to be a matter of law. As you can see in this photo, which was taken in Belle Glade, Florida, in 1945, it would have been illegal for a white to buy a soda from this store.

Supreme Court had decided that African Americans could vote in the southern primaries. Just one year earlier, in 1954, the Court had ruled that African Americans had the legal right to attend public schools with whites. Before this, they had to go to "colored" schools. Virginia and South Carolina still had laws that prohibited marriage between blacks and whites (O'Hare 1992). These wouldn't be struck down until 1967.

In order to break the institutional barriers that supported American apartheid, King led African Americans in a strategy called **civil disobedience,** deliberately but peacefully disobeying laws that are considered unjust. Inspired by the writings of Henry David Thoreau and the acts of Mahatma Gandhi, who had used this tactic to help win India's independence from Great Britain, King (1958) based his strategy on these principles:

1. Actively resisting evil, but nonviolently
2. Not seeking to defeat or humiliate opponents, but seeking instead to win their friendship and understanding
3. Attacking the forces of evil rather than the people who are doing the evil
4. Being willing to accept suffering without retaliating
5. Refusing to hate the opponent
6. Acting with the conviction that the universe is on the side of justice

King found no overnight success, but he and his followers persisted. Gradually the barriers did come down. In 1964 Congress passed the Civil Rights Act, making it illegal to discriminate in hotels, theaters, and other public places. Then, in 1965, the Voting Rights Act banned the literacy and other discriminatory tests that whites had used to keep African Americans from voting.

Encouraged by these gains, African Americans experienced **rising expectations;** that is, they expected better conditions to follow right away. The lives of poor African Americans, however, changed little, if at all. Frustrations built, finally exploding in Watts in 1965, when residents of this central Los Angeles ghetto took to the streets in the first of what have been called the "urban revolts." The violence, which occurred despite the protests of Dr. King, precipitated a white backlash that threatened the interracial coalition that King had spearheaded. Congress refused to enact civil rights legislation in both 1967 and 1968. When King was assassinated on April 4, 1968, ghettos across the nation erupted in fiery violence. Under threat of the destruction of the nation's cities, Congress reluctantly passed the sweeping Civil Rights Act of 1968.

MILITANCY. After King's death, black militants rushed in to fill the void in leadership. Like King, they emphasized black unity and black pride, but, unlike King, some of them proclaimed that violent confrontation was the way to gain equality. Flashed across the nation's television screens were images of the Black Panthers, brandishing rifles and parading in military-style uniforms. The statements and acts of black militants stirred up fear and hostility among whites. As a result, the authorities turned violently on the most outspoken leaders. Some leaders the police assassinated in nighttime raids, shooting them to death in their beds. Others the politicians co-opted, buying them off with job titles and government paychecks.

With violence turned against them—and with photos of the bloodied bodies of their associates circulating in the mass media—the leadership fragmented, disagreeing even about basic purposes. Some argued for secession from the United States, others for total integration. Leaders also disagreed about methods, some insisting that violent confrontation was the way to go, others arguing for peaceful protest. In the end, those who made the case for integration and political action won. As more moderate approaches replaced militancy, even the Black Panthers changed their tactics. Instead of challenging white authority and confronting the police, they switched to community organizing, providing breakfasts for schoolchildren and running for political office. Lacking a charismatic leader to replace King, the momentum that had propelled the struggle for equality faded.

POLITICS. Change has been gradual, but over time the change has been so incremental that today's race relations are vastly different from those that Rosa Parks experienced when she refused to move to the back of the bus. The change, however, has been uneven. Consider politics. On the positive side, the governor of Massachusetts and the mayors of many major U.S. cities are African American. Of the nation's 435 representatives, 42 are African American. And 9,000 African Americans hold lower-level political office, including over 600 at the state level (*Statistical Abstract* 2006:Tables 395, 403; "Some Facts . . ." 2007). Because African Americans make up about 12 percent of the U.S. population, though, we would expect about 12 African American senators. How many are there? *One.* Although far from equitable, compared with the past this change in political representation represents substantial gains in the U.S. political system.

EDUCATION. An elusive goal is an integrated public school system. In one of the ironies of race relations, the pathbreaking 1954 Supreme Court decision to integrate U.S. schools led to the schools becoming even more segregated. Following the 1954 decision, whites fled the cities and relocated in all-white suburbs. Others remained in the city but opened all-white private schools. In Atlanta, Georgia, for example, "white flight" changed the school system from 55 percent white to 90 percent black (Stevens 1980). As white flight continued, most schools of the major U.S. cities became primarily African American. Facing this unanticipated result of the 1954 decision, in 1986 courts across the nation began to ease up on desegregation rulings. The result of these court actions has been the same as the 1954 ruling: even greater segregation (Frankenberg and Lee 2002).

African Americans, however, have made strong gains in education. The percentage of African American high school graduates who attend college increased from 43 percent in 1980 to 62 percent in 1998. Since then, however, the numbers have moved backward, and today 58 percent of African Americans who graduate from high school go to college (*Statistical Abstract* 2006:Table 263). The reasons for this setback are uncertain, but it is ominous. To continue their hard-won economic gains, African Americans must reverse this decline: It is the college graduates who enter the better-paying positions and join the middle class. Because African Americans are more likely than whites to drop out of high school and now less likely to attend college than just a few years ago, a smaller proportion of African Americans will be prepared to compete for the better jobs.

RACE OR SOCIAL CLASS? A SOCIOLOGICAL DEBATE. The overall changes are stunning when one realizes that in the 1950s whites in some areas kept African Americans from voting, forced them to sit at the back of the bus, refused to serve them in restaurants, and would not allow them to attend "their" schools financed by public taxes—and the law stood on the side of discrimination. With the progress that African Americans have made in education, employment, politics, and legislation, the question has been raised whether race still underlies the relations between African Americans and whites. Some sociologists have suggested that, rather than race, the significant factor has become social class.

The social class view is supported by this event:

> In Westland, Michigan, the residents of Annapolis Park—a subdivision of expensive homes owned by African Americans—banded together to keep out whites as neighbors. The city council had voted to allow the construction of a trailer park near the Annapolis Park neighborhood. Residents of this neighborhood protested against the trailer park, in which whites would live, because of the social class of the whites, not their race-ethnicity. As one Annapolis Park homeowner said: "Let's face it. These are going to be lower-class whites. You wouldn't want a $15,000 [trailer] home next to your place, would you?" (Associated Press, February 5, 1981).

Sociologist William Wilson (1978), who proposed this view, put the matter this way: "Race relations in America have undergone fundamental changes in recent years, so much so that the life chances of individual blacks have more to do with their economic class position than with their day-to-day encounters with whites." Wilson uses the term **social class** to refer to "any group of people who have more or less similar goods, services, or skills to offer for income in a given economic order and who therefore receive similar financial remuneration in the market-place." He says that the changes have been so great that social class, not race, is what most determines African Americans' **life chances**—their quality of life and experiences. Neither Wilson nor any other sociologists denies that race is significant in social life today, just that social class is more significant.

Wilson (1978, 1987) points out that social class now separates African Americans into two main groups—those with money and those without. Official statistics support this. Most African Americans are not poor. The African American middle class has expanded so greatly that it now holds three times the proportion of African Americans than it did in 1940. One of every three African American families makes more than $50,000 a year. Yet there is another side to the income statistics: One of every seven African American families makes less than $10,000 a year (*Statistical Abstract* 2006:Table 36). These figures indicate a division of African Americans into the "haves" and the "have-nots" and, with it, two contrasting worlds.

One world consists of the middle class. These people work at jobs that offer advancement, earn good incomes and benefits, and live in middle-class suburbs or in exclusive areas of the city. They face little crime, and their children, who go to better schools, are motivated to go to college and prepare for good jobs. Not sociologically surprising, their orientations follow their middle-class experiences and middle-class lifestyles. They represent and believe in the "American dream." The second world consists of those who are stuck in poverty in the inner city. Violent crime is a part of life, the schools are terrible, their jobs are dead-end, and they feel despair, as well as either apathy or hostility. The aspirations and values of these two groups have little in common.

Many sociologists take hearty exception to the idea that social class has replaced racial oppression. They say that this analysis misses the vital element, the discrimination that continues to underlie the relative deprivation of African Americans. They emphasize that at *all* levels of work—whether among factory workers, managers, or supervisors—an income gap separates African Americans and whites. They point out that without exception whites are on top. They also point out that at every level of education, whether it be a high school diploma or a doctorate, whites earn more (*Statistical Abstract* 2006:Table 217). Both Wilson and his critics agree that an African American child's chance of growing up poor is much greater than that of a white child. In Wilson's view, however, social class, not racial-ethnic discrimination, is mainly responsible for perpetuating this situation.

It seems fair to conclude that each position is partly correct, that each pinpoints part of today's reality. It is likely that both discrimination and a disadvantaged social class position make their relative contributions: Those who are poor face far fewer opportunities and much greater discrimination; those who enjoy an advantaged class position face more opportunities and considerably less discrimination.

Asian Americans

It was a quiet Sunday morning, the seventh of December, 1941, a day destined to live in infamy, as President Roosevelt was later to say.

At dawn, waves of Japanese bombers began an attack on Pearl Harbor, the United States' major naval station in the Pacific Ocean. At Oahu, Hawaii, the Japanese pilots found the U.S. Pacific Fleet anchored in shallow waters, unprepared for battle. The Americans were sitting ducks.

In response, the United States declared war on Japan, entering World War II and leaving no American untouched. Some left home to battle overseas; others left their farms to work in factories that supported the war effort. All lived with the rationing of food, gasoline, sugar, coffee, and other essentials.

DETENTION CAMPS. This event touched Americans of Japanese descent in a special way. Just as waves of planes had rolled over Pearl Harbor, so waves of suspicion and hostility rolled over the 110,000 Japanese Americans who called the United States "home." Overnight, Japanese Americans became the most detested racial-ethnic group in the country (Daniels 1975). Many Americans feared that Japan would invade the United States and that Japanese Americans would sabotage military installations on the West Coast. Although not a single Japanese American had committed even one act of sabotage, on February 1, 1942, President Franklin Roosevelt signed Executive Order 9066, authorizing the removal of people considered threats to military areas. All people on the West Coast who were *one-eighth* Japanese or more were jailed in detention centers called "relocation camps." These people were charged with no crime; they were neither indicted nor given a trial. Having a Japanese great-grandmother on either your mother's or father's side of the family was sufficient reason to be put in prison.

In 1942, Japanese Americans were considered a threat to the security of the United States. They were taken from their homes and moved to internment camps.

EARLIER DISCRIMINATION. This was not the first time that Asian Americans had met discrimination. For years, differences in appearance and lifestyle had prompted Americans of European background to discriminate against Americans of Asian ancestry. Lured by gold strikes in the West and a huge need for unskilled labor, about 200,000 Chinese immigrated between 1850 and 1880. There was a rush to unite the West with the East, and the Chinese were put to work building the East-West railroad. Although 90 percent of the workers for the Central Pacific Railroad were Chinese, when the famous golden spike was driven at Promontory, Utah, in 1869 to mark the joining of the Union Pacific and the Central Pacific railroads, white workers prevented the Chinese from being present (Hsu 1971). After the railroad was finished, many Chinese settled in the West. To intimidate their new competition, white workers formed mobs and vigilante groups.

As fears of "alien genes and germs" grew, legislators passed anti-Chinese laws (Schrieke 1936). In 1850, the California legislature passed the Foreign Miner's Act, levying a special tax on Chinese (and Latinos) of $20 a month. At this time, wages were a dollar a day. The Chief Justice of the California Supreme Court ruled that Chinese could not testify against whites in court (Carlson and Colburn 1972). In 1882 Congress passed the Chinese Exclusion Act, suspending all Chinese immigration for 10 years. Four years later, the Statue of Liberty was dedicated. The tired, the poor, and the huddled masses it was to welcome obviously did not include the Chinese.

Facing such severe discrimination, Chinese immigrants turned inward, forming segregated communities called "Chinatowns." Four stages were involved in their development (Yuan 1963). The first was *involuntary segregation:* Discrimination forced the immigrants into separate living areas. The second was *defensive insulation:* The immigrants banded together for mutual help. The third was *voluntary segregation:* They chose to remain in the segregated community because that was where their friends and relatives lived, it avoided language difficulties, and it allowed them to follow their customs and religion (Buddhism), which were strange to the dominant group. The final stage, now in process, is *gradual assimilation:* As they become acculturated, individuals move out of Chinatown and adopt even more mainstream customs.

When the Japanese began to immigrate, they met spillover bigotry that had been directed against the Chinese. They also confronted discriminatory laws. Even the U.S. Constitution became a tool that was used against them. Initially a document that allowed only whites to be citizens, the Constitution was amended in the 1860s to include African Americans (Amott and Matthaei 1991). Because Asians had not been named in the amendments, the Supreme Court ruled that this prohibited them from becoming citizens (Schaefer 2004). This ruling provided an opportunity for California politicians. In 1913, they passed the Alien Land Act, prohibiting anyone who was ineligible for citizenship from owning land. (Most Native Americans were not granted citizenship in their own land until 1924; the Chinese gained citizenship in 1943; for those born in Japan, the exclusion remained until 1952.)

FIGURE 8-6 The Country of Origin of Asian Americans

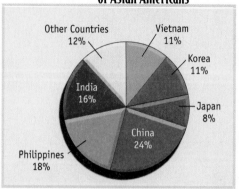

Other Countries 12%
Vietnam 11%
Korea 11%
Japan 8%
China 24%
Philippines 18%
India 16%

Source: By the author. Based on *Statistical Abstract of the United States* 2005:Table 22.

DIVERSITY. Contrary to stereotypes that prevail in our society, the 12 million Asian Americans are diverse peoples. As you can see from Figure 8-6, they come from many different lands. As a result, Asian Americans are divided by many cultural heritages, including different languages and religions. Half of Asian Americans live in the western states, one of three in California (*Statistical Abstract* 2006:Tables 23, 24). The two largest groups of Asian Americans, those of Chinese and Filipino descent, are concentrated in New York City, Los Angeles, San Diego, San Francisco, and Honolulu. The third largest group, those of Asian Indian descent, is the most geographically dispersed.

REASONS FOR SUCCESS. As you can see, like the terms *Latino (Hispanic)* and *Native American,* the category of Asian American also lumps a lot of different groups together. As a result, any "average" that is computed for Asian Americans conceals a lot of differences. As you saw on Table 8-1 on page 253, the average family income of Asian Americans is higher than that of whites, and their poverty is 9 percent. Sociologists, however, stress that the income and poverty of Asian Americans differ according to country of origin: Poverty is the greatest among the Cambodians and the Hmong and least among those whose origin is China and Japan (Lee 1998; Zhou and Xiong 2005). Many of the Chinese who live in the urban settlements known as "Chinatowns" face the usual problems of ghetto poverty: poor health, high suicide, poor working conditions, and bad housing.

One general conclusion that we can make, with the caution I just indicated, is that most Asian Americans are remarkably successful. The general economic success of Asian Americans seems to be rooted in three factors: family life, education, and assimilation.

The divorce rate of Asian Americans is low, less than half the rate of whites (Reeves and Bennett 2003). One result is that of all racial-ethnic groups, including whites, Asian American children are the most likely to grow up with two parents. They also are the least likely to be born to single mothers (Lee 1998; Zhou and Xiong 2005). Most Asian American children grow up in closely knit families where they are socialized into values that stimulate cohesiveness and high motivation to succeed (Bell 1991). Within a framework of strict limits and constraints, they are taught self-discipline, thrift, and industry (Suzuki 1985). This early socialization provides strong impetus for the next two factors.

The second factor is educational achievement. Asian Americans are the most likely of any racial-ethnic group in the United States to complete college. Assimilation, the third factor, is indicated by several measures. Asian Americans have the highest intermarriage rate of any minority group: About two of five marry someone who is not an Asian American. Asian Americans are also the most likely to live in integrated neighborhoods (Lee 1998). Japanese Americans, the financially most successful of Asian Americans, are the most assimilated (Bell 1991). About 75 percent say that their best friend is not a Japanese American.

POLITICS. Asian Americans are underrepresented in U.S. politics. With their percentage in the population, we could expect 17 of the nation's 435 representatives and 4 senators to be Asian Americans. The actual numbers: 7 and 2 ("Some Facts . . ." 2007). They are becoming more prominent in politics, however. With 60 percent of its citizens being Asian American, Hawaii has elected Asian American governors and sent several Asian American senators to Washington (Lee 1998; *Statistical Abstract* 2006:Table 395). The first Asian American governor outside of Hawaii was Gary Locke, who in 1996 was elected governor of Washington, a state in which Asian Americans make up less than 6 percent of the population. Locke was reelected in 2000, and after that decided not to seek another term.

Social Policy

Although the goal of a unified society is laudable, we have more than adequate experience to know that it is futile to attempt to use our social institutions to force everyone into a white mold. Accordingly, it seems reasonable for social policy to center on the twin goals of encouraging cultural pluralism and preventing discrimination.

Encouraging Cultural Pluralism

APPRECIATING DIFFERENT BACKGROUNDS. The first goal of a social policy that encourages cultural pluralism would be "cultural integrity"; that is, it would encourage pride and appreciation of different backgrounds. Here are possible specifics:

1. Establishing national, state, and local "cultural centers" that feature a group's heritage
2. Holding "ethnic appreciation days" in the public schools, where ethnic customs, dress, dances, history, and food are featured

3. Teaching history (and all courses with an historical emphasis) in ways that recognize the contributions of the many groups that make up the United States
4. Teaching foreign languages in our public schools, from grade school through high school—starting so early that all students could learn two foreign languages

The first two suggestions are easy to implement, and they can go a long way toward encouraging appreciation of cultural differences and pride in one's own heritage. Because of the segregation of our urban schools, for the second proposal to be more effective, it should include cultural exchanges among our public and private schools. The third requires a changed emphasis in how we train teachers. For this third proposal to be effective, the approach must be honest. Students will see through it if any group's historical contributions are "stretched" so they can be included. The fourth proposal, which is the most extensive, would ordinarily require vast retraining of our teachers. With the technical capacity for teaching foreign languages that we now have, however, not only students but also teachers can be taught more easily and efficiently. With the lowering of cultural boundaries and our developing global society, this fourth proposal carries significance beyond racial-ethnic relations in the United States.

PRIDE AND PARTICIPATION. Although one of the emphases of cultural pluralism is pride in one's own racial-ethnic heritage, this does not mean a retreat into one's racial-ethnic culture. Like members of the dominant group, members of minority groups need to be prepared to compete within the dominant white institutions. Although children of minority groups should be encouraged to retain and to take pride in their rich heritage, like the children of the dominant group, they, too, need to become proficient at English and other basic skills that make them competitive in the marketplace. The school system is uniquely situated to equip them with these tools. Without them, members of minority groups find themselves at a severe disadvantage in meeting their number-one need—competing with whites for jobs, especially positions that pay well and offer advancement.

Preventing Discrimination

USING THE LEGAL SYSTEM. The second social policy, preventing discrimination, involves using the legal system to ensure that minorities are not discriminated against in jobs, housing, education, or any other areas of life that pertain to all citizens. This requires that our local, state, and federal governments be watchdogs. The Civil Rights Act of 1964, which forbids discrimination by race, color, creed, national origin, and sex, must be enforced. This law covers unions, employment agencies, and, as amended in 1972, all businesses with 15 or more employees. This law also prohibits discrimination in voting, public accommodations, all federally supported programs such as road construction, and federally supported institutions such as colleges and hospitals. Preventing discrimination also means funding the Equal Employment Opportunity Commission (EEOC), the organization that is empowered to investigate complaints of discrimination and to recommend action to the Department of Justice.

EDUCATION VOUCHERS. As noted, "white flight" was a common reaction to the forced integration of the public school system. U.S. parents have the right to send their children to any schools they can afford, and this right needs to be protected. Although controversial, there is an effective solution to white flight. If education vouchers in the amount of the average cost per student in a district's schools were given to each student, their parents could choose any school they wanted their children to attend, private or public. Some voucher programs already exist, but none as generous as what I am suggesting. All schools, without exception, must be open to students of any racial-ethnic background.

The Dilemma of Affirmative Action

THE *BAKKE* CASE. The Civil Rights Act of 1964 created a dilemma: how to make up for past discrimination without creating new discrimination. The first dispute to catch the public's attention was the precedent-setting *Bakke* case (Sindler 1978). In 1972 and again in 1973, Allen Bakke was denied admission to the medical school of the University of California at Davis. Bakke sued when he learned that the school had admitted African Americans, Asian Americans, and Latinos who had scored lower than he had on the entrance exam and who had lower grade point averages than his. Bakke argued that had he been a member of a minority group he would have been admitted. In other words, the university was racist—it had discriminated against him because he was white. The U.S. Supreme Court ruled that the Davis medical school had to admit Bakke because it was illegal to use quotas for minorities.

CLOUDY GUIDANCE. Following the *Bakke* case, the U.S. Supreme Court handed down a series of inconsistent rulings. It ruled that colleges cannot use quotas to determine whom they admit, but they can use race as a factor to create a diverse student body (Walsh 1996). In a 1989 precedent-setting *City of Richmond* decision, the Court ruled that state and local governments "must almost always avoid racial quotas" in awarding construction contracts. "Almost always" means that it might be okay, but then again it might not, which left everyone confused about where and when and in what ways preferential treatment is or is not constitutional.

PROPOSITION 209. With the U.S. Supreme Court giving such cloudy guidance, the national debate continued. Few were fond of affirmative action, but no one saw alternatives to erase the consequences of past discrimination. Then during the 1990s, the tide turned against affirmative action, with a series of rulings by circuit courts and the U.S. Supreme Court. Perhaps the most significant development was *Proposition 209*, a 1996 amendment to the California state constitution that banned race and gender preferences in hiring and in college admissions. Despite appeals by a coalition of civil rights groups, the U.S. Supreme court upheld the California law.

THE UNIVERSITY OF MICHIGAN CASE. Another significant ruling was made in 2003. White applicants who had been denied admission to the University of Michigan claimed that they had been discriminated against because applicants from underrepresented minority groups had been given extra points just for being members of the group. Again, the Court's ruling was ambiguous. The Court ruled that the goal of racial diversity is laudable and that universities can give minorities an edge in admissions, but they cannot use an automatic system to do so. Race can be a "plus factor," but in the Court's words, there must be "a meaningful individualized review of applicants."

Such a murky message left university officials—and, by extension, those in business and other public and private agencies—scratching their heads. Trying to bring about racial-ethnic diversity is constitutional, but using quotas and mechanical systems is not. Michigan voters didn't like this ambiguity, and in 2006 they amended their constitution to make it illegal to use race-ethnicity (or gender) in college admissions (Golden 2006).

Absent constitutional amendments like those in Michigan and California, states that want to use race-ethnicity in college admissions must follow the Supreme Court's decision. Because the Court's ruling provides no specific guidelines and its University of Michigan ruling remains open to interpretation, we obviously have not yet heard the final word from the U.S. Supreme Court on this topic. And what we hear will likely depend not on the Constitution, which in this matter is open to contradictory interpretations, but, rather, on the political makeup of the Court—on who retires and what justices of what political persuasion are the replacements.

Principles for Improving Relations

Social policies should follow sound sociological principles. The principles developed by social psychologist Gordon Allport (Pettigrew 1976), which are based on experimental evidence, can provide a basic map for developing social policy:

1. People of different racial-ethnic backgrounds should possess equal status in the situation (similar income and education for example). The occupants of interracial (or interethnic) housing, for example, should have similar incomes.
2. People in interethnic contact should be seeking the same goals. Parents from different racial-ethnic backgrounds, for example, should work together to improve their children's school.
3. To attain their goals, the groups must pull together. (Allport calls this cooperative dependence.) For example, to improve an integrated school system, voters from different racial-ethnic groups must vote for a bond proposal.
4. Authority, law, and custom should support interaction among the groups. If authorities stand behind school integration, for example, positive interaction among the groups is more likely.

The Future of the Problem

PROGRESS. Most Americans today reject the patterns of discrimination that were taken for granted at earlier times or—strange to our ears—that were even assumed to be morally correct. Progress has been uneven, at times sideways or even backwards, but the result has been expanding opportunities for minority groups. Even with our halting, hesitant progress and even though huge gaps remain between our ideals of equality and the reality of racial-ethnic relations as we actually experience them, the United States has moved toward greater equality.

World War II was especially significant for racial-ethnic relations. Prior to the war, the U.S. government, dominated by racist policies, supported apartheid. The war's effects on minority groups profoundly changed relations with the dominant group, and U.S. society was never the same. To work in the expanding war industries where there was a severe labor shortage, hundreds of thousands of African Americans migrated from the South to the North. Although they fought in all-black units at this time, the several hundred thousand African American soldiers, dislodged from the apartheid of home, were thrust into unexpected cultural experiences. Exposed to new ways of life in Europe, they returned home with visions of the possibility of change. After the war, the federal government, moving gradually from apartheid to a policy of integration and social equality, broke many of the institutional barriers that had been directed against minorities. The future will not bring a return of these barriers.

AN ONGOING STRUGGLE. Stubborn barriers to equality do remain, however, and racial-ethnic relations are haunted by them, as well as by the consequences of past discrimination. Affirmative action was designed to overcome these barriers, but, as you know, it has come under heavy attack. By their very nature, court rulings are victories for one and defeat for the other. The disappointment is especially severe when the two sides hold incompatible philosophical positions. Inconsistent and vague court rulings, however, sow confusion. With effective mechanisms to remedy inequalities yet to be developed, the proper role of affirmative action in a multicultural society is likely to remain center stage for quite some time.

The major struggle in racial-ethnic relations will center on jobs. The outcome is of fundamental importance because access to good jobs determines so much of people's quality of life. Two issues will be central to the outcome, the dismantling of remaining structural barriers, which is likely to be slow, and the preparation of workers. Increasingly, workers must be prepared to compete in a world that demands more technical expertise. What occurs in education, then, is of vital importance for the future of racial-ethnic relations.

DISPARITIES IN EDUCATION. Education is so important that we should try to catch a glimpse of its potential and likely impact on racial-ethnic relations. For most Americans, education holds the key to the future. Those who receive the better education get the better jobs and enjoy the more satisfying lifestyles. Any group that receives less schooling than the national average faces disadvantages in our technological society.

Granted this principle, then, look at Table 8-3 on the next page. You can see that the rate of college graduation of Asian Americans outstrips those of other groups: It is about

TABLE 8-3 Race-Ethnicity and Education

Racial-Ethnic Group	EDUCATION		COMPLETED		DOCTORATES		
	Less than High School	High School	Some College	College (BA or Higher)	Number Awarded	Percentage of all U.S. Doctorates[1]	Percentage of U.S. Population
Whites	14.6%	30.0%	28.5%	27.0%	26,905	81.0%	68.0%
Latinos	47.6%	22.1%	19.9%	10.5%	1,432	4.3%	13.7%
Country or Area of Origin							
South America	23.8%	24.0%	27.0%	25.2%	NA	NA	
Cuba	37.0%	20.0%	21.7%	21.2%	NA	NA	
Puerto Rico	36.7%	26.2%	24.6%	12.5%	NA	NA	
Central America	54.0%	19.1%	17.4%	9.5%	NA	NA	
Mexico	54.2%	20.9%	17.5%	7.5%	NA	NA	
African Americans	20.0%	35.2%	27.4%	17.3%	2,397	7.2%	12.2%
Asian Americans	16.8%	18.9%	21.3%	43.1%	2,317	7.0%	4.1%
Native Americans	29.1%	29.2%	30.2%	11.5%	180	0.5%	0.8%

Source: By the author. Based on *Statistical Abstract of the United States* 2005:Tables 34, 37, 38, 41, 283, and Figure 8-2 of this text.

four times higher than that of Latinos and Native Americans, and between *two and three* times that of Native Americans, almost *three* times that of African Americans, and more than half again as much as that of whites. Note also that although the number of Asian Americans is less than a third that of Latinos, they earn almost twice the number of doctorates. This high achievement in education brightens the future for Asian Americans, opening doors to the professions and managerial positions.

From the same table and for the same reasons, we can conclude that the future looks good for whites, less bright for African Americans, and the worst for Latinos and Native Americans. Mentioned earlier was the decline in the percentage of African American high school graduates who go to college. This is ominous and must be addressed.

The indicators of relative economic well-being of the various groups shown in Table 8-1 on page 253 are related to education. Note from this table how closely each group's relative well-being in income and poverty matches its attainment in education as shown on Table 8-3. It isn't difficult to figure out why, since we all know that education opens doors of opportunity, and the lack of education closes them. Obviously, we need policies that produce greater educational achievement. To develop these policies, I suggest that we fund a "think tank" composed of top educators from our various racial-ethnic groups, whose purpose will be to propose such policies. There likely are already sufficient studies of how education works and how cultures function so that the members of the think tank need not do any more research, just evaluate what already exists and suggest creative, testable policies.

AN UNDERCLASS. I have severe reservations that, as a nation, we have sufficient desire to solve this problem of mismatched educational attainment. A disturbing possibility is that we already have a permanent **underclass** (Wilson 1978, 1987). That is, society may already have thrown up its collective hands and consigned to the ghetto an underclass that will endure. This alienated group, especially visible in our inner cities, has little education, lives primarily in single-parent families, and has high rates of violent crime, drug abuse, disease, births to single mothers, and death by murder. These behaviors are self-defeating, if the goal is to succeed in mainstream society. Educational attainment, to put it mildly, is not one of this group's values.

Unless ways are found to reach this group, which was left behind as residents of the inner city moved into middle-class jobs and middle-class neighborhoods, the tragic cycle will perpetuate itself. Many of the children who are born in those conditions will be fated to repeat their parents' lives. A primary structural factor that makes this sorry possibility likely is that most jobs are located in the suburbs. Those who live in the urban ghettos lack the means of transportation to reach those jobs and the financial ability to move closer to them.

These conditions carry severe implications for society as a whole. If large groups of people remain isolated from mainstream society, receive a meager education, can't get jobs, and are denied even proper police protection, a spark could ignite collective violence. With little being done about the problems of our inner cities, it is likely that there will be sparks. More riots, then, are likely, and at some point we will see a repeat of the 1992 riots in Los Angeles.

MILITANCY. Militants, whether from a minority group or the dominant group, are an unpredictable factor in future racial-ethnic relations. Although racial-ethnic pride is laudable—as I indicated in the social policy section, such pride should be encouraged—some people mistake such pride as hatred of others. Any group—no matter its racial-ethnic background—that preaches hatred intends to create significant divisions by building on hostilities and negative stereotypes. The resurgence of the Ku Klux Klan, though involving only a handful of people, indicates an alarming potential for violence. I anticipate, however, that the occasional outbursts of such groups, though dramatic, will be limited primarily to headline grabbing and will pose no serious threat to the future.

THE AMERICAN DILEMMA. In 1944, Gunnar Myrdal (1898–1987), a sociologist from Sweden, wrote that the United States was caught between two major forces. In his classic, *An American Dilemma,* Myrdal contrasted the "American creed," as expressed in Christian ethics and the Declaration of Independence, with the un-Christian and undemocratic behavior he observed. Myrdal was confident that Americans would resolve the dilemma in favor of the higher values of the American creed, rather than the lower ones of discrimination and prejudice. Myrdal's prediction was right, and conditions are remarkably better today than they were in the 1940s. The dilemma that Myrdal identified back then, however, remains with us.

Valleys of hatred and despair follow peaks of goodwill and high hopes. We have seen this in the past, and the future will bring more of the same. Although as individuals we have little power or influence, our actions, collectively, are significant. Ultimately, it is these actions that give shape to racial-ethnic relations. None of us can overcome structural barriers, yet, together, we can dismantle them. I do not mean to sound Pollyannaish, but as C. Wright Mills realized, we can at least ask how we can help to create a more positive future.

SUMMARY AND REVIEW

1. *Discrimination* occurs worldwide, as *racial-ethnic groups* living in the same society struggle for dominance. *Dominant groups* develop *ideologies* and *stereotypes* to support their dominance.

2. *Minority groups* share five characteristics: unequal treatment, distinctive traits, solidarity, membership by birth, and marriage within their own group. Minority groups have four objectives: *pluralism, assimilation, secession,* and *militancy.* Five objectives of dominant groups are *assimilation, multiculturalism (pluralism), population transfer,* continued subjugation, and *genocide.*

3. Although the idea of *race* is significant in human behavior, biologically speaking, no human group represents a "pure race."

4. Discrimination is a life-and-death matter, affecting both the quality of life and mortality rates.

5. *Individual discrimination* consists of overt acts by individuals. *Institutional discrimination* is discrimination that is built into the social system.

6. Symbolic interactionists focus on how symbols of race and ethnicity divide people and influence their behavior, particularly how they affect perception, sort people into different life experiences, and justify discrimination and violence. Functionalists analyze functions of discrimination, such as fostering *ethnocentrism* and ensuring that society's *dirty work* gets done. They also analyze its dysfunctions, such as destroying human potential. Marxist conflict theorists stress that racial-ethnic divisions among workers help capitalists control workers and increase their profits.

7. Discrimination in the United States is especially severe for Native Americans, Latinos, and African Americans.

Members of these groups have less education, higher unemployment, lower incomes, and higher rates of poverty than whites and Asian Americans. The pressures that these groups have placed on white-controlled social institutions have forced social change. Asian Americans have made the most social and economic gains—primarily through assimilation and family values that stress hard work, thrift, and education.

8. Major cleavages along social class lines divide U.S. racial-ethnic groups. Some sociologists argue that *social class* has become more significant than race-ethnicity in determining an individual's *life chances*.

9. Social policies to encourage cultural pluralism and prevent discrimination were suggested. Groups that attain the most education have the brightest future. The major struggle is over jobs. Dilemmas over affirmative action continue.

10. With the creation of an *underclass,* we can expect urban riots. In no foreseeable future will *prejudice* and discrimination be eliminated. A storm cloud on the horizon is the resurgence of groups that preach division and hatred.

KEY TERMS

Anglo-conformity, 250
Apartheid (ah-par'-tate), 248
Assimilation, 247
Civil disobedience, 272
Compartmentalize, 259
Dirty work, 260
Discrimination, 246
Division of labor, 260
Dominant group, 246
Ethnocentrism, 262
False class consciousness, 263
Genocide, 248

Individual discrimination, 253
Institutional discrimination, 254
Life chances, 274
Melting pot, 250
Militancy, 247
Minority group, 246
Pan-Indianism, 268
Pluralism, 247
Population transfer, 248
Prejudice, 245
Race, 248
Racial-ethnic group, 249

Racial-ethnic stratification, 260
Reserve labor force, 263
Riot, 260
Rising expectations, 272
Secession, 247
Selective perception, 259
Self-fulfilling prophecy, 259
Social class, 274
Split-labor market, 263
Stereotype, 252
Surplus value of labor, 263
Underclass, 281

THINKING CRITICALLY ABOUT CHAPTER 8

1. On page 246 is a list of five characteristics that minority groups share. Pick any minority group in the United States and give examples of how these five characteristics apply to that group.

2. On page 247 is a list of four objectives of minority groups. Explain how each objective applies to African Americans, to Asian Americans, to Latinos, and to Native Americans. Do these groups emphasize these objectives in the same way? If not, why do you think there are differences?

3. Which of the six policies of dominant groups that Simpson and Yinger identify (pp. 247–248) do you think that whites are directing toward African Americans? Toward Native Americans? Toward Latinos? Toward Asian Americans?

4. What is your opinion about the laws against hate speech? Do you think that these laws should be eliminated or that they should be strengthened and enforced? Explain.

5. Which of the three sociological perspectives (symbolic interactionism, functionalism, or conflict theory) do you think best explains why prejudice and discrimination exist in the United States? Explain.

CHAPTER 9

Sex
Discrimination

Let's eavesdrop on a birth in India, what should be a happy event, the birth of a healthy child after what seemed to be a never-ending pregnancy.

Just outside the delivery room of a Delhi hospital, the expectant mother's family keeps vigil. The woman's husband is smoking and playing cards with the men. They tell a few jokes and laugh. None of the men mentions what everyone knows might happen. The women are knitting and recalling their own deliveries. They, too, don't bring up the taboo topic, although all are thinking about it.

When the nurse brings the news, everyone falls silent. Faces drop—the newborn is a girl. Some relatives console the father; others curse the mother.

This scene is familiar in India. The birth of a son is seen as a gift from God; the birth of a daughter, at best, a disappointment.

This attitude persists, especially in India's tens of thousands of tradition-locked villages. As a result, many

> **Strangling baby girls . . . might be a thing of the past.**

girls face hardships and even early death.

Female infanticide is not uncommon, although the authorities seldom document specific instances. They leave such sensitive family matters alone.

"Strangling baby girls at birth might be a thing of the past," says Promilla Kapur, a sociologist who specializes in research on Indian women. "However, what used to be done in a fairly crude manner is still often achieved indirectly."

A female infant can be deprived of milk or ignored if she falls sick. The male child gets the most nourishing food and preferential treatment from his mother.

The Indian girl stands little chance of earning money for her family. In Hindu society almost all women are expected to remain at home with their family. Jobs for women, especially uneducated women, are few—and most Indian women are uneducated.

—Based on Chacko 1977.

The Problem in Sociological Perspective

You can see how important the sex of a child is in India. Parents who live on the edge of survival despair at the birth of a girl: They must feed and clothe her, but she can contribute little to the family's income. They rejoice at the birth of a boy, for his birth signals the arrival of a child who can help sustain them in their old age.

WOMEN AS A MINORITY GROUP. Although the Indian situation is extreme, *sex is the major sorting device in every society in the world.* In our own society, as we'll examine in this chapter, men are paid more for the same work; and, despite changes, they continue to dominate politics and public life. Even though females make up 50.9 percent of the U.S. population (*Statistical Abstract* 2006:Table 12), sociologists consider women to be a minority group because of their position relative to men, the dominant group.

THE DEVELOPMENT OF SEXISM AS A SOCIAL PROBLEM. Sociologists have not always referred to women as a minority group. This came about only gradually, as they began to note parallels between the social positions of women and men and those of African Americans and whites. In 1944 Gunnar Myrdal, a Swedish sociologist who studied U.S. race relations, mentioned the parallels in *An American Dilemma*. He also noted the historical connection: The legal status of African American slaves was derived from the legal status of women and children in the seventeenth century, whose lives were controlled by the male heads of family. In 1951 an American sociologist, Helen Hacker, was the first to apply the term *minority* to women. Noting that discrimination against women "takes the form of being barred from certain activities or, if admitted, being treated unequally," Hacker said that women were marginal to a society that was dominated by men.

Just as the perception of sociologists was changing, so was that of women, who began to challenge the traditional relations between the sexes. Many came to see themselves not as *individuals* who had less status than men, but as a *group* of people who were discriminated against. During the 1960s and 1970s, women discussed and publicized their grievances with being second-class citizens in a society dominated by men. Subjective concerns grew as large numbers of women in the United States and around the world concluded that something needed to be done. Recalling our definition of social problems, you can see that this new evaluation of the relative positions of women and men transformed what had been an objective condition of society into a social problem. Taking this issue seriously, sociologists started to investigate **sexism,** the belief that one sex is innately superior to the other, and the discrimination that results from this belief.

Many social conditions have changed since the period of unrest and agitation of the 1960s and 1970s, when the activities of protest groups often dominated the evening news, so let's see how extensive this problem is today.

The Scope of the Problem

IS MALE DOMINANCE UNIVERSAL? When did sexism begin? Some social scientists, such as anthropologist Marvin Harris (1977:46), claim that men's domination of society "has been in continuous existence throughout virtually the entire globe from the earliest times to the present." After reviewing the evidence, historian and feminist Gerda Lerner (1986:31) agreed, saying that "there is not a single society known where women-as-a-group have decision-making power over men (as a group)." She also concluded that horticultural and hunting-and-gathering societies had the least gender discrimination, that in those societies women contributed about 60 percent of the group's total food.

Conclusions of universal domination by men make some social analysts apprehensive: If people think that men have always dominated every society around the world, perhaps they will conclude that this behavior is innate. They might then use this conclusion to justify men dominating women today. Not all sociologists accept the conclusion of the universality of male dominance (Epstein 1989), a point to which we shall return shortly.

Don't women presidents, prime ministers, and monarchs disprove the universal domination of society by men? Sociologists point out that these are *individual* women in positions of power, not examples of women-as-a-group in control of a society. Even those societies led by a woman are dominated by men, for men hold almost all the key positions. Sweden comes closest to exhibiting political equality between the sexes: Forty-five percent of its cabinet ministers and 45 percent of its parliament are women ("Women in the Riksdag" 2003). Women hold so many positions of power because Swedish laws limit the percentage of offices that men can control.

THE SEXUAL STRATIFICATION OF WORK. *Every* society stratifies its members by sex; that is, they single out males and females for different activities. Around the world, for example, most work is **sex-typed,** associated with one sex or the other. Because of this, it was easy to believe that anatomy required men and women to be assigned particular work. In 1937, anthropologist George Murdock reviewed information on 324 societies. He found that what is considered "male" or "female" work differs from one society to another. For example, in some societies the care of cattle is women's work; in others, it is men's work. The only exception was metalworking, which was universally men's work.

When men do an activity that is usually assigned to women, the prestige of the activity increases. With but a few exceptions, the acclaimed chefs of the world are men. Shown here is Gordon Ramsey, an eminent television chef. Does his food taste better because it was cooked by a man?

Three pursuits—making weapons, pursuing sea mammals, and hunting—were almost always men's work. No specific work was universally assigned to women. Making clothing, cooking, carrying water, and grinding grain were commonly women's work, but not always. Biology, then, does not determine occupational destiny.

That one society assigns a certain kind of work to men while another assigns it to women—isn't this a type of equality? How is this relevant to a discussion of sexism? Social scientists, however, have discovered a startling principle: *Universally, men's activities are always given greater prestige.* Whatever work is assigned to men is considered superior (Linton 1936; Rosaldo 1974). If taking care of cattle is men's work, then cattle care is thought to be important and carries high prestige. If taking care of cattle is women's work, however, it is considered less important and carries less prestige. To cite an example closer to home, when delivering babies was "women's work," the responsibility of midwives, this job was given low prestige. But when men took over delivering babies (despite opposition from women), its prestige shot up (Ehrenreich and English 1973). *It is the sex that is associated with the work that provides its prestige, not the work itself.*

MAJOR AREAS OF DISCRIMINATION. Sexism pervades every society in the world, and it touches almost every aspect of our social life. In her classic 1951 article, Helen Hacker, analyzing the situation at that time, listed these areas of discrimination against U.S. women:

1. *Political and legal.* Women are often barred from jury duty and public office.
2. *Education.* Professional schools, such as architecture and medicine, apply quotas for women.
3. *Economic.* Women are usually relegated to work that falls under the supervision of men, for which they get unequal pay, promotion, and responsibility.
4. *Social.* Women are permitted less freedom of movement, fewer deviations in dress, speech, and manners, and a narrower range of personality expression.

Hacker also described how women's three major roles—sister/daughter, wife, and mother—fit this pattern of discrimination. She said that a sister does more housework than her brother, a wife is expected to subordinate her interests to those of her husband, and a mother bears the stigma for an illegitimate child.

Sex discrimination in U.S. society has changed so drastically since Hacker did her analysis that some of her description sounds as though she were speaking about another society—and in a sociological sense she was. Women are no longer barred from jury duty and public office, nor do they face quotas in professional schools. You probably noticed that on a couple of significant levels, though, Hacker's analysis remains remarkably current. Women still struggle against unequal treatment in jobs, politics, and informal social life.

Looking at the Problem Theoretically

Why are societies sexist? Let's apply our three theoretical lenses to see what contrasting perspectives emerge.

Symbolic Interactionism

BASIC TERMS. We must distinguish between two terms. When we consider how males and females differ, we usually think first of **sex,** the different *biological* equipment of males and females. Then we might think about **gender,** how we express our "maleness" or "female-ness." Symbolic interactionists stress that sex is biological, and gender is learned, or social.

SOCIALIZATION INTO GENDER ROLES. Symbolic interactionists study how we are socialized into **gender roles,** the attitudes and behaviors that are expected of boys and men because they are males and of girls and women because they are females. Each society has ideas that some activities are "male" and others "female." To enforce these ideas requires that a society's institutions work together. The result is so effective that people feel shame if mismatching occurs in their own behavior and sometimes insulted and angry if they see it in others. In the short space we have, I can indicate only a few of the elements involved in this orchestration of a society's institutions.

The process begins *before* birth (Henslin 2007a). The expectant parents mentally project their child's participation into activities that are sex-typed. The father may see himself teaching his son how to play baseball; the mother may imagine dressing her daughter in frilly dresses and hearing people say how cute she looks.

When their child is born, the parents announce its sex to the world. Through cards, telephone calls, and e-mail, they proclaim: "It's a girl!" or "It's a boy!" Even the newspapers report this momentous event. And momentous it is, for *in every society of the world this announcement launches people into their single most significant life-shaping circumstance.* Sex is a **master trait,** cutting across all other identities in life. Whatever else we may be, we always are a male or a female.

Cast onto the stage of life with an assigned role to play, we spend much of our childhood and young adulthood learning what this role requires. Throughout the world, parents are the first "significant others" to teach children their gender role. The specifics vary from one society to another, but in our society parents begin by using pink and blue, colors that have been imbued with gender-role significance. Parents continue to coach us in our expected roles for longer than most of us want their help.

Difficulties of Interpretation ■ In a classic study, psychologists Susan Goldberg and Michael Lewis (1960) observed how parents teach gender roles subconsciously—that is, without being aware that they are doing so. Goldberg and Lewis recruited mothers of 6-month-olds to come into their laboratory so they could observe the development of their children. They also observed how the mothers interacted with their babies, although the mothers didn't know this. They found that the mothers kept their girls closer to them and that they touched and spoke more to them than to their sons. By the time the children were 13 months old, the girls were more reluctant than the boys to leave their mothers. During play, they remained closer to their mothers and returned to them sooner and more often than the boys did.

Goldberg and Lewis then did an interesting experiment. They surrounded each mother with colorful toys and placed her child on the other side of a small barrier. The girls were more likely to cry and motion for help, while the boys were more likely to try to climb over or go around the barrier. The researchers concluded that without knowing it, the mothers had rewarded their daughters for being passive and dependent and their sons for being active and independent.

But is this the right conclusion to draw from these observations? Were these differences brought about by the mother's behavior, as the researchers suggest? Or did the researchers observe biological differences that were showing up at the age of 13 months? In short, were the mothers responding to differences inherent in their children (the boys wanting to get down and play more, and the girls wanting to be hugged more), or were the mothers creating those differences? In view of the sociological debate recounted on pages 296–297, this study could be interpreted either from the cultural or biological perspective. We don't yet have enough evidence to draw a firm conclusion.

In childhood, boys are generally allowed to be more active and to express more independence. Preschool boys, for example, are given more freedom to roam farther from home than their preschool sisters. They are also allowed to participate in more rough-and-tumble play—even to get dirtier and to be more defiant (Henslin 2007a). Again, we face the same problem. Are the parents and teachers creating these differences in behavior? Or are the children responding to biological predispositions?

The Dominant Symbolic Interactionist Position ▪

Most symbolic interactionists assume that the differences are learned. They emphasize that stereotypes tend to become reality. If males are considered to be aggressive and dominant and a person knows that he is male, he tends to fulfill those expectations by being aggressive and dominant. If females are considered to be passive and submissive and a person knows that she is female, she tends to fulfill those expectations. Not everyone follows the script, but so many do that to most members of a society it is evident why *their particular stereotypes* represent what biology "really" is.

IN SUM Symbolic interactionists emphasize that every society uses symbols of male and female to sort its members into separate groups. This process starts within the family and is reinforced by other social institutions. As a result, males and females acquire different ideas of themselves and of one another. As children, all of us learn the meanings that our society associates with the sexes. These symbols then become an essential part of how we picture life—an image that forces an interpretation of the world into "proper" activities for males and females.

Functionalism

TWO THEORIES OF MALE DOMINANCE. If male dominance is universal, or even nearly universal, how did it come about? Although the origins of sexism are lost in history, functionalists have two theories to account for it.

Rewards for Warriors ▪ The first theory was proposed by anthropologist Marvin Harris (1977). He said that male dominance is universal because it is based on two universal conditions. The first is social—the necessity to survive warfare. The second is biological—innate differences in the physical strength of men and women.

Harris' controversial explanation goes like this: In preliterate times, humans lived in small groups. Because each group was threatened by others, to attempt to survive, it had to recruit people who would fight in hand-to-hand combat. People feared injury and death, of course, so the recruiting wasn't easy. To coax people into bravery, groups developed rewards and punishments. Because an average woman is only 85 percent the size of an average man and has only two-thirds his strength, men were better at hand-to-hand combat. Men became the warriors—and females became their reward—for both their sex and their labor. Some groups allowed only men who had faced an enemy in combat to marry. Even today, in some tribal groups such as the Barabaig of Tanzania, women are a reward for men who show bravery (Aposporos 2004).

"Sex brought us together, but gender drove us apart."

The distinctions between sex and gender that sociologists have drawn are becoming part of public consciousness.

(© The New Yorker Collection 2001. Barbara Smaller from cartoonbank.com. All Rights Reserved.)

Because some women are stronger than some men, to exclude all women from combat might seem irrational. But if women were to be the chief inducement to get men to fight, this was necessary. To make the system work, men had to be trained from birth for combat, and women had to be trained from birth to give in to men.

According to this explanation, the reward for male bravery came at the expense of females. In almost all band and village societies, men assigned the "drudge work" to women—weeding, seed grinding, fetching water and firewood, doing the routine cooking, and even carrying household possessions during moves. Because men preferred to avoid these onerous tasks—and could if they had one or more wives—women were an excellent bait to induce men to bravery.

Reproduction ▪ The second theory is based on human reproduction (Lerner 1986; Hope and Stover 1987; Friedl 1990). It also goes back to early human history. Life used to be short, and women gave birth to many children. Because only women get pregnant, carry a child for nine months, give birth, and nurse, for a considerable part of their lives women were limited in what they could do. To survive, an infant needed a nursing mother. With a child at her breast or in her womb and one on her hip or on her back, a woman was encumbered physically. Thus women everywhere took on the tasks associated with the home and child care, while men took over hunting large animals and other tasks that required more speed and longer absence from the base camp (Huber 1990).

Men gained both power and prestige. They made and controlled the weapons used for hunting and warfare. They left the camp to hunt animals, returning triumphantly with prey. Leaving the camp, they also made contact with other tribes and accumulated possessions in trade. Men also gained prestige by returning with prisoners from warfare. In contrast, little prestige was given to the routine activities of women, who didn't do such showy and triumphant things and were not seen as risking their lives for the group. The men's weapons, their items of trade, and the knowledge they gained from their contacts with other groups became sources of power.

The result was that men took over society, creating a fundamental change in the relations of the sexes. As women became subject to the decisions of men, men justified their dominance. They developed ideas that because biology gives men superior strength, it also imbues manhood with superiority. To avoid "contamination" by females, who had become a lower class of people, men shrouded some of their activities in secrecy and established rules and rituals that excluded women.

IN SUM If either of these theories is true, the *origin* of male dominance is rooted in both biological and social factors. The *maintenance* of male dominance, however, is purely social—a perpetuation of millennia-old patterns. Although tribal societies developed into larger groups and hand-to-hand combat and hunting dangerous animals ceased to be routine, men, enjoying what they had, held on to their privileges and power. Reluctant to abandon their privileged position—a dominance rooted in ancient custom—men use cultural devices to control women. For an example, see the Global Glimpse box on the next page.

Conflict Theory

PRINCIPLES OF POWER. Conflict theorists provide a contrasting view of sexism. For background, consider these four principles.

1. Power yields privilege. In every society, the powerful enjoy the best resources available.
2. The privileged lifestyles of those in power encourage them to feel that they are superior beings.
3. To bolster their feelings of superiority, the powerful clothe themselves with ideologies that justify their position.
4. As the powerful cling to their privileges, they utilize the social institutions to maintain their power.

A Global Glimpse
FEMALE CIRCUMCISION

This is how one woman, who was circumcised at 12, described her experience:

"Lie down there," the excisor suddenly said to me, pointing to a mat stretched out on the ground. No sooner had I laid down than I felt my frail thin legs tightly grasped by heavy hands and pulled wide apart. I lifted my head. Two women on each side of me pinned me to the ground. My arms were also immobilized.

Suddenly I felt some strange substance being spread over my genital area. . . . I would have given anything at that moment to be a thousand miles away; then a shooting pain brought me back to reality. . . . I underwent the ablation of the labia minor and then of the clitoris. The operation seemed to go on forever. . . . I was in the throes of agony, torn apart both physically and psychologically.

It was the rule that girls of my age did not weep in this situation. I broke the rule. I reacted immediately with tears and screams of pain. . . . Never have I felt such excruciating pain!

[After the operation] they forced me, not only to walk back to join the other girls who had already been excised, but to dance with them. . . . I was doing my best . . . then I fainted. . . . It was a month before I was completely healed. . . . When I was better, everyone mocked me, as I hadn't been brave, they said. (Walker and Parmar 1993: 107–108)

Female circumcision, often called female genital mutilation by Westerners, is common in parts of Africa, Malaysia, and Indonesia. Worldwide, about 130 million women have been circumcised. As you can see from Figure 9-1, in Guinea 99 percent of the women have been circumcised.

In some cultures only the girl's clitoris is cut off; other groups remove the clitoris, the labia majora, and the labia minora. The Nubia in the Sudan cut away most of the girl's genitalia, then use silk or catgut to sew together the remaining outer edges, so that as the wound heals the vagina fuses together. They leave a small opening—the size of a matchstick—for urine and menstrual fluids. In East Africa the vaginal opening is not sutured shut, but the clitoris and both sets of labia are cut off.

Among most groups, the surgery takes place when the girls are between the ages of 4 and 8. In some cultures, it occurs 7 to 10

A woman who circumcises girls poses by a poster supporting the abolition of female genital mutilation. Forty percent of women in Ivory Coast undergo genital mutilation.

days after birth; in others, not until girls reach adolescence. Most circumcisions are done by traditional practitioners, such as midwives and barbers, who use a variety of cutting instruments, including scissors, knives, razor blades, and broken glass (UNICEF 2005).Where the surgery is done without anesthesia, the pain is so excruciating that adults must hold the girl down. In Egypt, most circumcision is done in hospitals.

Immediate complications include shock, pain, bleeding, infection, infertility, and death. Ongoing complications include vaginal spasms, painful intercourse, and lack of orgasms. The tiny opening makes urination and menstruation difficult. Frequent urinary tract infections result because urine and menstrual flow build up behind the opening.

When the woman marries, the opening is surgically enlarged to permit sexual intercourse. In some groups, this is the husband's responsibility. Before a woman gives birth, the opening is enlarged further. After birth, the vagina is again sutured shut, a cycle of surgically closing and opening that begins anew with each birth.

What are the reasons for this custom? Some groups believe that circumcision enhances female fertility. Others think that it reduces female sexual desire, making it more likely that a woman will be a virgin when she marries and, afterward, remain faithful to her husband. Feminists, who call female circumcision "ritual torture to control female sexuality," point out that men dominate the societies that practice it.

Change is coming. The first ladies of four countries—Burkina Faso, Guinea, Mali, and Nigeria—have condemned the practice (Lacey 2003). In Kenya, two girls obtained a court order to stop their father from having them circumcised. Their community was shocked, but an attorney reminded the court that Kenya had signed human rights agreements.

What do you think?

Based on Mahran 1978, 1981; Ebomoyi 1987; Lightfoot-Klein 1989; Merwine 1993; Walker and Parmar 1993; Chalkey 1997; Lacey 2003; UNICEF 2005.

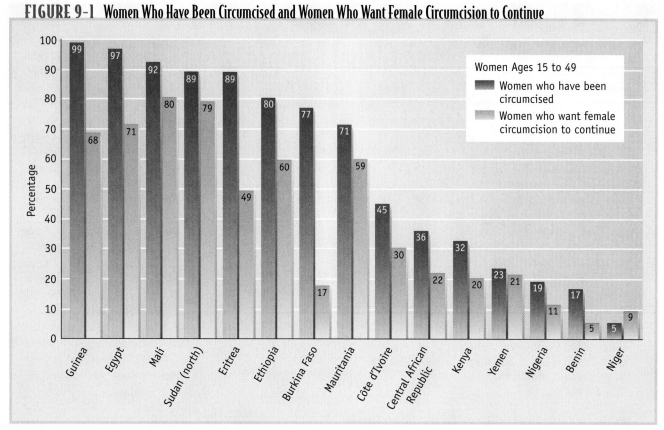

Source: UNESCO 2005:18.

As a group, men are no exception to these principles. They, too, cling to their positions, cultivate images of female inferiority to justify their greater privilege, and use economic and legal weapons against women. As Helen Hacker (1951) put it:

> In the wake of the Industrial Revolution, as women acquired industrial, business, and professional skills, they increasingly sought employment in competition with men. Men were quick to perceive them as a rival group and made use of economic, legal, and ideological weapons to eliminate or reduce their competition. They excluded women from the trade unions, made contracts with employers to prevent their hiring women, passed laws restricting the employment of married women, caricatured the working woman, and carried on ceaseless propaganda to return women to the home or keep them there.

THE STRUGGLE FOR EQUALITY. Now that greater sexual equality is a part of U.S. life, it is easy to lose sight of the prolonged and bitter struggle by which women gained their rights. In the 1800s, females were under the legal control of a man, either a father or a husband, and possessed no legal or social right to self-determination. Women could not vote, make legal contracts, testify in court, hold property in their own name, or even spend their own wages (which by law belonged to the husband). To secure these rights, women had to confront men and the social institutions that men dominated. Men first denied women the right to speak in public, spat upon those who did, slapped their faces, tripped them, pelted them with burning cigar stubs, and hurled obscenities at them. Despite the opposition, leaders of the women's movement persisted. They chained themselves to the iron grillwork of public buildings and went on talking while the police sawed them loose. If arrested, these women would go on hunger strikes in jail.

In 1916, feminists (then called *suffragists*) formed the National Women's Party. In January 1917, they began to picket outside the White House. After the women had protested for six months, authorities were tired of "the nonsense" and arrested them.

Universally, children imitate the adults around them. This process of modeling or role playing helps children prepare for roles that they will play as adults.

The women refused to pay their fines, and judges sent hundreds to prison, including two leaders, Lucy Burns and Alice Paul. Their treatment in jail illustrates how seriously these women had threatened male privilege:

> The guards from the male prison fell upon us. I saw Miss Lincoln, a slight young girl, thrown to the floor. Mrs. Nolan, a delicate old lady of seventy-three, was mastered by two men. . . . Whittaker (the Superintendent) in the center of the room directed the whole attack, inciting the guards to every brutality. Two men brought in Dorothy Day, twisting her arms above her head. Suddenly they lifted her and brought her body down twice over the back of an iron bench. . . . The bed broke Mrs. Nolan's fall, but Mrs. Cosu hit the wall. They had been there a few minutes when Mrs. Lewis, all doubled over like a sack of flour, was thrown in. Her head struck the iron bed and she fell to the floor senseless. As for Lucy Burns, they handcuffed her wrists and fastened the handcuffs over her head to the cell door. (Cowley 1969:13)

Today it is difficult to imagine U.S. women being treated this way for trying to gain rights that men already possess. The early suffragists were persistent and outspoken, however, and they used bold tactics to force a historical shift in the balance of power.

Since those days, there has been no overt conflict between men and women as a group (Hacker 1951). Today's discrimination is more subtle: hidden quotas, jokes, glass ceilings, and the "purely personal preference" that men occupy the more responsible positions. Women continue to press for a greater share of society's power and privileges, but the struggle has changed. Women today pressure lawmakers, compete for positions in good colleges and graduate schools, and fight obstacles that inhibit advancement at work, including sexual harassment.

IN SUM From the conflict perspective, society is divided into those who control society's resources and those who are controlled by this elite group. Social equality comes about by forcing those in power to yield—for those in power do not willingly cede their control of society's institutions. So it has been with women's struggle for equality with men-as-a-group.

Let's examine this struggle, pausing first to consider again the question of natural differences between the sexes.

Research Findings

Are There Natural Differences Between the Sexes?

Apart from obvious physical differences between males and females, what are the natural differences between the sexes? Is one sex innately more intelligent? More aggressive? Dominant? Protective? Nurturing? Tender? Loving? Passive?

STUDIES OF CHILDREN. The difficulty of separating culture from biology has plagued researchers in their attempt to answer such intriguing questions. Because each society places males and females on different roads in life, the society in which they are reared shapes any innate differences that may exist. To untangle this knotty problem, researchers have taken four approaches. The *first* focuses on children. If girls and boys show consistent differences at early ages, biology may be at work. Researchers have found that girls generally score higher than boys on verbal skills (Goleman 1987). Most girls begin to speak earlier than boys. They are also quicker to talk in short sentences and then to use longer sentences. They also read earlier and do better in grammar, spelling, and word fluency. And young boys? They tend to do better on spatial tasks (Bardwick 1971).

Test results in mathematics have provided a puzzle for researchers. When boys and girls are compared nationally, boys always outperform girls. This holds true if we compare their overall scores or if we compare the scores of those who have taken specific courses: general math, algebra, advanced algebra, geometry, or calculus (*Digest of Education Statistics* 2005:Table 120). It is the same on the SATs. Year after year, boys score higher in math on these college entrance tests. In 1967, boys scored 40 points higher; in 2004, it was 36 points higher *(Statistical Abstract* 2006:Table 252).

Do such differences reflect innate abilities? Some researchers think so. For fifteen years, psychologist and feminist Camilla Benbow searched for an environmental explanation. Gradually, she ruled out all possibilities and concluded—reluctantly, she said—that these results are due to "a basic biological difference between the sexes in brain functions" (Goleman 1987). Other social scientists insist that cultural factors explain such differences. To explain girls' higher verbal performance, they point to three social causes: (1) girls identify more with their mothers (who are themselves more verbal), (2) both mothers and fathers hold and speak to their daughters more than to their sons, and (3) little girls' games are more linguistic than boys' games (Bardwick 1971). As Carole Whitehurst (1977:36) put it: "All *apparent sex* differences in intelligence *may* be explained by early learning and continual reinforcement."

This likely is true of verbal differences. In 1967 and 1970 girls outscored boys on the verbal portion of the SATs, but in 1975 boys outscored girls, and boys have held the lead ever since (*Statistical Abstract* 2006:Table 252). The explanation must be environmental, for certainly there was no switch in male–female brain functions during this time. The environmental explanation is also supported by this observation: Although the boys are consistently outscoring the girls, the scores of both vary from year to year. In the years that the boys' scores decline, so do the girls' scores, and in the years in which the boys' scores increase, so do the girls' scores. What is the environmental explanation? No one has yet come up with a satisfactory answer.

During this same period, from 1967 to the present, in no year have girls outperformed boys in mathematics. For this consistent difference, a biological explanation seems to be an excellent candidate. If girls catch up or take the lead in mathematics, as boys did in verbal scores, however, this would be strong evidence of environmental causes. Again, we really don't know the answer.

Boys and girls also show differences in aggression. As Judith Bardwick (1971) pointed out, from early childhood to adulthood males tend to be more active and extraverted, females more passive and introverted. Again, the question is, Does this mean that males are *innately* more "aggressive" than females? Some researchers point to cultural factors. Parents may subtly (or not so subtly) encourage their sons to be aggressive, believing that "sticking up for your rights," "showing you're not a sissy," "not letting yourself get pushed around," and so on, are signs of masculinity. Parents may also express pleasure when their daughters are less demanding and more compliant—traits that are not only considered feminine but that also make parenting easier. From infancy on, then, parents mold their children into cultural stereotypes of masculinity and femininity. But, to be fair—and we sociologists don't like this conclusion, but we do want to be objective—these cultural factors do not rule out biology. Parents may be responding to biological differences and even reinforcing them. We simply don't yet know.

CROSS-CULTURAL STUDIES. A second approach that researchers have taken is to compare men and women cross-culturally. In this part of the nature–nurture controversy, researchers also fail to agree. In our review of this approach in the Issues in Social Problems box on pages 296–297, you will see how sharply sociologists disagree on the meaning of anthropological findings.

STUDIES OF ANIMALS. The third approach researchers have taken to separate innate biological factors from cultural molding has been to observe animals, with monkeys a favorite object of study. The findings about aggression among monkeys are noteworthy, for differences show up early and consistently: "Within a month after birth, male rhesus monkeys are wrestling, pushing, biting, and tugging, while the female monkeys are beginning to act shy, turning their heads away when challenged to a fight by young males" (Bardwick 1971:91). Bardwick adds,

> The males quickly surpass the females in the rate of achieving independence from their mothers (helped by the way the mothers punish them more, pay less attention to them, and hold and carry them less). The males had higher general activity levels, did more biting, pushing, shoving, yanking, grabbing, and jerking. They also did more thumbsucking and more manipulation of their genitals.

We must always be cautious when drawing conclusions about humans from animal research, of course. To understate the matter, humans are not monkeys. Aggression, however, is related to the level of male hormones (Bardwick 1971; LeVay 1993), a factor that we shall now consider.

THE STUDY OF VIETNAM VETERANS. The fourth and most recent approach is intriguing. In 1985, the U.S. government began a health study of Vietnam veterans. To be certain the study was representative, the researchers chose a random sample of 4,462 men. Among the data they collected was a measurement of testosterone for each veteran. Until this time, research on testosterone and human behavior was based on very small samples. Now, unexpectedly, sociologists had a large random sample, one that is turning out to hold surprising clues about human behavior.

When the veterans with higher levels of testosterone were boys, they were more likely to get in trouble with parents and teachers and to become delinquents. As adults, they are more likely to use hard drugs, to get into fights, to end up in lower-status jobs, and to have more sexual partners. Not surprisingly, this history makes them less appealing candidates for marriage, and they are less likely to marry. Those who do marry are less likely to share problems with their wives. They also are more likely to have affairs, to hit their wives, and, it follows, to get divorced (Dabbs and Morris 1990; Booth and Dabbs 1993).

This study of Vietnam veterans does *not* leave us with biology as the sole basis for behavior, however. Not all men who have high testosterone levels get in trouble with the law, do poorly in school, or mistreat their wives. A chief difference, in fact, is social class. High-testosterone men from higher social classes are less likely to be involved in antisocial behaviors than are high-testosterone men from lower social classes (Dabbs and Morris 1990). Social factors (socialization, life goals, self-definitions), then, also must play a part. Uncovering the social factors and discovering how they work in combination with biological factors such as testosterone will be of high sociological interest.

RECONCILING THE FINDINGS. From our current evidence, we can conclude that *if* biology provides males and females differences in temperament, personality, or some type of predisposition in behavior, culture overrides those differences. Culture shapes people into the types of men and women that predominate in a particular society. Because people wear

Issues in Social Problems

THE NATURE–NURTURE CONTROVERSY: BIOLOGY VERSUS CULTURE

What causes differences between men and women? Answers that are commonly given in discussions from cocktail parties to locker rooms fall roughly into either biological or cultural explanations. So do the answers given by the experts. Most but not all sociologists favor the cultural side. Here are the basic arguments among sociologists.

BIOLOGY IS THE ANSWER

Sociologist Steven Goldberg (1974, 1986, 1989) finds it astonishing that anyone should doubt "the presence of core-deep differences between men and women, differences of temperament and emotion we call masculinity and femininity." He argues that inborn differences, not the environment, "give masculine and feminine direction to the emotions and behavior of men and women." Here is his argument:

1. The anthropological record shows that all societies for which evidence exists are (or were) **patriarchies** (societies in which men dominate women). Stories about **matriarchies** (societies in which women dominate men) are myths.

2. In all societies, past and present, the highest statuses are associated with males. All of them are ruled "by hierarchies overwhelmingly dominated by men."

3. The reason for this one-way dominance of societies is that males "have a lower threshold for the elicitation of dominance behavior . . . a greater tendency to exhibit whatever behavior is necessary in any environment to attain dominance in hierarchies and male–female encounters and relationships." Males are more willing "to sacrifice the rewards of other motivations—the desire for affection, health, family life, safety, relaxation, vacation and the like—in order to attain dominance and status."

Steven Goldberg, whose position in the ongoing "nature versus nurture" debate is summarized here.

4. Just as a six-foot woman does not prove that women's height is due to social factors, so an exceptional individual, such as a highly achieving and dominant woman, does not refute "the physiological roots of behavior."

In short, only one interpretation of why every society, from the Pygmies to the Swedes, associates dominance and attainment with males is valid. Male dominance of society is "an inevitable resolution of the psychophysiological reality." Socialization and social institutions merely *reflect*—and sometimes exaggerate—inborn tendencies. Any interpretation other than inborn differences is "wrongheaded, ignorant, tendentious, internally illogical, discordant with the evidence, and implausible in the extreme." The argument that males are more aggressive because they have been socialized that way is equivalent to claiming that men can grow mustaches because boys have been socialized that way.

To acknowledge this reality is *not* to condone or to defend discrimination against women. Whether one approves what societies have done with these biological differences is not the point. The point is that biology leads males and females to different behaviors and attitudes—regardless of how we feel about this or wish it were different.

cultural blinders that mask the workings of their culture, in each culture people consider the characteristics that are implanted into their males and females to be overwhelming evidence of the "natural" differences between the sexes.

In the years to come, unraveling the influences of socialization and biology should prove to be an exciting—and controversial—area of sociological research. One level of research will be to determine whether there are behaviors that are due only to biology. The

CULTURE IS THE ANSWER

For sociologist Cynthia Fuchs Epstein (1986, 1988, 1989), the answer lies solely in social factors, especially socialization and social control. Here is her argument:

1. The anthropological record shows more equality between the sexes in the past than we had thought. In earlier societies, women, as well as men, hunted small game, devised tools for hunting, and gathered food. Studies of today's hunting and gathering societies show that "both women's and men's roles have been broader and less rigid than those created by stereotypes. For example, the Agta and Mbuti are clearly egalitarian. . . ." This proves that "societies exist in which women are not subordinate to men. Anthropologists who study them claim that there is a separate but equal status of women at this level of development."

2. Not biology but rigidly enforced social arrangements determine the types of work that women and men do in each society. Few people can escape these arrangements to perform work outside their allotted range. Informal customs and formal systems of laws enforce this gender inequality of work, which serves the interests of males. Once these socially constructed barriers are removed, women can and do exhibit the same work habits as males.

3. The human behaviors that biology "causes" are only those that involve reproduction or differences in body structure. These differences are relevant for only a few activities, "such as playing basketball or crawling through a small space."

4. Female crime rates, which are rising, indicate that the aggressiveness that often is considered a biologically dictated male behavior is related to social, not biological, factors. When social conditions permit, such as with women attorneys, females also exhibit "adversarial, assertive, and dominant behavior." Not incidentally, their "dominant behavior" also shows up in their challenging the biased views about human nature that male scholars have proposed.

In short, not "women's incompetence or inability to read a legal brief, to perform brain surgery, [or] to predict a bull market," but social factors—socialization, gender discrimination, and other forms of social control—are responsible for differences in the behavior of women and men. Arguments that assign "an evolutionary and genetic basis" to explain gender differences in social status "rest on a dubious structure of inappropriate, highly selective, and poor data, oversimplification in logic and inappropriate inferences by use of analogy."

Cynthia Fuchs Epstein, whose position in the ongoing "nature versus nurture" debate is summarized here.

second will be to discover how social factors modify biology. The third will be, in sociologist Janet Chafetz's (1990:30) phrase, to determine how "different" becomes translated into "unequal."

AVOIDING IDEOLOGY. At this point, we have no final answer to the question of natural differences between the sexes in aggression, nurturing, forms of intelligence, and so on. Some researchers are convinced they are innate, others that they are learned. Like other areas of science, we must examine the data with an open mind, not try to make the evidence fit ideologies that favor either biology or culture. Unfortunately, the research on differences between males and females has become emotionally charged, and to draw conclusions on one side or the other indicates to some that one is "faithful" or "unfaithful" to an ideology. This, of course, is not science. One would hope that data, not ideology, will one day answer this question once and for all.

Let's examine inequality between the sexes, with a focus on U.S. society.

Everyday Life

> Leaning against the water cooler, two men—both minor executives—are nursing cups of coffee, discussing last Sunday's Giants game, postponing the moment when they have to go back to work.
>
> A vice president hears them talking about sports. Does he send them back to their desks? Probably not. Being a man, he is likely to join in the conversation and prove that he is "one of the boys," feigning an interest in football that he may not share at all. These men—all men in the office—are his troops, his comrades-in-arms.
>
> Now, assume that two women are standing by the water cooler discussing whatever you please: clothes, work, the glass ceiling, any subject except football or some other sport. The same vice president sees them and wonders whether it is worth the trouble to complain that they are standing around gabbing when they should be working. "Don't they know," he will ask, in the words of a million men, "that this is an office?" (Korda 1973:20–21, paraphrased)

In everyday life, women often encounter antagonistic attitudes from men. They find their interests, attitudes, and contributions held in low regard. Masculinity is highly valued; it represents success and strength. Femininity is devalued; it is perceived as failure and weakness.

Let's look at two areas of life, the military and sports, to observe the devaluation of females. During World War II, a team of researchers headed by sociologist Samuel Stouffer studied the motivation of combat soldiers. Out of this research came a sociological classic, *The American Soldier*. Stouffer and his colleagues reported (1949:132) that officers used feminine terms as insults to motivate soldiers:

> To fail to measure up as a soldier in courage and endurance was to risk the charge of not being a man. ("Whatsa matter, bud—got lace on your drawers?")

A generation later, during the Vietnam war, military officers still used accusations of femininity to motivate soldiers. Drill sergeants would mock their troops by saying, "Can't hack it, little girls?" (Eisenhart 1975). This practice continues. In the Marines, the worst insult to male recruits is to compare their performance to a woman's (Gilham 1989). If a male soldier shows hesitation during maneuvers, others mock him, calling him a girl (Miller 2007).

Social scientists have observed this same behavior in sports. Watching basketball, sociologists Jean Stockard and Miriam Johnson (1980) heard boys shout to boys who missed a basket, "You play like a woman!" Anthropologist Douglas Foley, who studied Texas high school football, heard ex-football players tell boys who had a bad game that they were "wearing skirts" (Foley 1990/2006). And sociologist Donna Eder (1995) reports that junior high boys call one another "girl" if they don't hit hard in football. You've probably heard things like this yourself.

Most people dismiss such remarks as insignificant: "That's just people talking." Stockard and Johnson point out, however, that such comments reveal a basic derogatory attitude toward women and things feminine, an attitude that women face as part of their everyday lives. To make this idea clearer, they make this telling point: "There is no comparable phenomenon among women, for young girls do not insult each other by calling each other 'man.'"

Although we are seeing changes in male–female relationships, the devaluation of women continues to be a background feature of social life. As sociologist Carol Whitehurst (1977) stressed, this devaluation is important because it underlies all other forms of oppression.

Education

LOOKING AT THE PAST. To get a better picture of today's situation in education, we can take a glimpse of the past. About a century ago, leading educators claimed that women's wombs dominated their mental life. This sounds ludicrous today, but these people were serious. And they weren't nut cases. They were highly respected in their profession and were considered to be experts. Dr. Edward Clarke, for example, a member of Harvard University's medical faculty, warned women that studying was dangerous for them. He wrote:

A girl upon whom Nature, for a limited period and for a definite purpose, imposes so great a physiological task, will not have as much power left for the tasks of school, as the boy of whom Nature requires less at the corresponding epoch. (Andersen 1988:35)

To preserve their fragile health, Clarke added that young women should study only one-third as much as men. And during menstruation, they shouldn't study at all.

Views like Clarke's certainly put women at an educational disadvantage. Women who followed his warning and studied less than men would obviously do worse on papers and exams. This, of course, would confirm the stereotype of the time that women's brains weren't as capable as men's and that women didn't need a college education in the first place because their proper place was the home.

LOOKING AT OTHER COUNTRIES. We don't face anything even remotely close to the stereotypes and discrimination that we had in the past, but in some countries, women are still discriminated against in education. Table 9-1 provides a glimpse of how education is disproportionately reserved for boys in some countries. This table lists the twenty-one countries of the world in which girls make up less than 45 percent of secondary school students. You can see that sixteen of those countries are located in Africa, three are in Asia, and one (Turkey) straddles Asia and Europe.

ACTIVE BOYS AND CHEERING GIRLS. What a vital contrast we find when we turn to the United States. There are *2.5 million* more women than men in U.S. colleges (*Statistical Abstract* 2007:Tables 268). With such vast numbers of women in college, how can anyone say that there is sexism in education?

We certainly have to look more deeply for it than we used to, but it is still there. Some of it shows up in school sports: Boys become the football players, and girls join the drill team, drum majorettes, and pep squads (Foley 2006). As Carol Whitehurst (1977) put it, "The boys perform, the girls cheer." It is difficult to imagine girls playing a sport, while boys sit on the sidelines with bated breath, jumping eagerly to their feet and even throwing themselves into the air when some girl makes a great play.

GENDER TRACKING. Apart from this rather visible and interesting demonstration of men being the active masters fighting one another while women cheer them on, in college we see what sociologists call *gender tracking;* that is, women and men tend to cluster in different educational specialties. Women earn 92 percent of associate's degrees in home economics, for example, whereas men earn 95 percent of associate's degrees in the building trades. Similarly, men dominate engineering, while women dominate library "science" (*Statistical Abstract* 2006:Table 288). It is socialization—rather than any presumed innate characteristics—that channels males and females into sex-linked educational paths.

A MAN'S WORLD. Another factor is significant. When they enter college, most students face a man's world. Not only are most of their professors men, but they also study mostly male authors in their literature courses, discuss the thinking of men in their philosophy courses, and read almost exclusively about famous men in their history courses. The social sciences, including sociology, also concentrate on the contributions of men. Little is known about how this affects the orientations of female and male students, but it certainly has to be significant. Men who have taken courses in gender studies taught by women have told me how upsetting it was to be immersed in a "women's world of thought." Women's immersion in what we can call the "men's world of thought" is gradual and taken for granted, but the impact is just as severe, although not as apparent.

COMPLETING THE DOCTORATE. Although women now outnumber men in college and earn 58 percent of all bachelor's degrees (*Statistical Abstract* 2006:Table 286), something happens

TABLE 9-1 Of Students Enrolled in Secondary School, What Percentage Are Girls?

PERCENTAGE	COUNTRY
32%	Benin
36%	Equatorial Guinea
37%	Cambodia
38%	Djibouti
38%	Ethiopia
38%	Niger
39%	Burkina Faso
39%	Eritrea
39%	Mozambique
40%	Senegal
41%	Gambia
41%	Laos
41%	Nepal
41%	Papua New Guinea
42%	Burundi
42%	Congo
42%	Turkey
43%	Mauritania
44%	Angola
44%	Malawi
44%	Zambia

Note: These are the world's countries in which less than 45 percent of the students are females.

Source: By the author. Based on U.S. Agency for International Development 2004.

TABLE 9-2 Doctorates in Science, by Sex

Field	STUDENTS ENROLLED IN DOCTORAL PROGRAMS		DOCTORATES CONFERRED		COMPLETION RATIO* (HIGHER OR LOWER THAN EXPECTED)	
	Women	Men	Women	Men	Women	Men
Computer sciences	27%	73%	20%	80%	−26	+10
Mathematics	36%	64%	27%	73%	−25	+14
Agriculture	45%	55%	34%	66%	−24	+20
Engineering	21%	79%	17%	83%	−19	+5
Biological sciences	55%	45%	46%	54%	−16	+20
Social sciences	53%	47%	45%	55%	−15	+17
Physical sciences	31%	69%	27%	73%	−13	+6
Psychology	74%	26%	67%	33%	−9	+27

Note: The formula for the completion ratio is *X* minus *Y* divided by *X*, where *X* represents the doctorates conferred and *Y* represents the proportion enrolled in a program.

Source: By the author. Based on *Statistical Abstract of the United States* 2006:Tables 781, 783.

between the bachelor's and the doctorate. Look at Table 9-2, which gives us a snapshot of doctoral programs in the sciences. This table shows us how aspirations (enrollment) and accomplishments (doctorates conferred) are sex linked. In five of the eight doctoral programs, men outnumber women; in three, women outnumber men. Note that in *all* of them women are less likely to complete the doctorate.

We don't have conclusive answers as to why women are less likely to complete the doctorate degree, but we do have indications of the reasons. No one is suggesting that graduate faculties purposely discriminate against female students. Perhaps what I mentioned earlier about most faculty being men and most of the researchers, theorists, and writers being studied in the academic disciplines also being men has something to do with it. Perhaps. Apparently, though, the main answer is simpler, that women are more likely to get sidetracked with marriage and family responsibilities.

A DEVELOPING SOCIAL PROBLEM? I would like to conclude this section by going back to an earlier point, the decrease in men's college enrollments. That we now have over 2 million more women than men enrolled in college and that they are earning 58 percent of all bachelor's degrees might indicate that we are glimpsing the beginning of a fundamental change in how we view the sexes in education. Following the basic model of social problems that I have stressed throughout this text, at this point we have only an objective condition. If enough people become upset about this condition, however, we will have a full-blown social problem, this time with the focus on men as the objects of discrimination. If this occurs, and we might be close, do you think that men might need affirmative action, scholarships, remedial help, and retention programs?

The Mass Media

The mass media help to shape gender roles. The media give messages to children—and to the rest of us—that certain behaviors are considered "right" for boys and other behaviors "right" for girls. They also send messages about the "proper" relationships between men and women. To get some insight into how this occurs, we will look first at children's books, then at television, music, video games, and advertising.

CHILDREN'S BOOKS. Children's picture books have been a major focus of sociologists. It is easy to see that illustrated books for children are more than just entertainment. Little children learn about the world from the pictures they see and the stories read to them.

Role models are important for what we aspire to, what we become, and how we evaluate ourselves. Shown here is Jennifer Lopez with some young women who are modeling her line of clothing.

What the illustrations show girls and boys doing becomes part of their picture of what is "right" for the sexes.

When sociologists first examined children's picture books in the 1970s, they found that it was unusual for a girl to be the main character. Almost all the books featured boys, men, and even male animals. When pictured at all, the girls were passive and doll-like, whereas the boys were active and adventurous. While the boys did things that required independence and self-confidence, most girls were shown trying to help their brothers and fathers (Weitzman et al. 1972). Feminists protested these stereotypes and even formed their own companies to publish books that showed girls as leaders, as active and independent.

As a result of these efforts—as well as the changing role of women in society— today's children's books have about an equal number of boy and girl characters. Girls are also now depicted in a variety of nontraditional activities. A gender stereotype continues to linger in children's books, however: As researchers have pointed out, females are now portrayed as doing things that males do, but males are not portrayed as doing things that females do (Dickman and Murnen 2004). Males, for example, are seldom depicted as caring for the children or doing grocery shopping, and they never are seen doing housework (Gooden and Gooden 2001). As gender roles continue to change, I am sure that this, too, will change.

TELEVISION. More powerful than picture books is television, both because of its moving images and the number of hours that children watch television. In the cartoons that so fascinate young children, males outnumber females, giving the message that boys are more important than girls. A children's TV show that ran from 1987 to 1996, *Teenage Mutant Ninja Turtles,* captures the situation. The original turtles were Michelangelo, Leonardo, Raphael, and Donatello—named after male artists whose accomplishments have been admired for centuries. A female turtle was added. Her name? Venus de Milo. The female turtle was named not for a person, but for a statue that is world famous for its curvaceous and ample breasts. She never did anything. And how could she—she has no head or arms ("Getting the Message" 1997).

Adult television reinforces stereotypes of gender, age, and sexuality (Butler et al. 2006). On prime time, two-thirds of all characters are male, and men are more likely to be portrayed in higher-status positions (Glascock 2001; "Fall Colors" 2004). Women are depicted as losing their sexual attractiveness earlier than men; and starting at age 30, fewer and fewer women are shown. About nine out of ten women on prime time are below the age of 46, and older women practically disappear from television (Gerbner 1998). Men are portrayed as aging more gracefully, with their sexual attractiveness lasting longer.

Body image is part of gender roles, and television is effective in teaching us what we "should" look like. Sociologists who studied situation comedies found that most female characters are below average in weight. They are also portrayed as dieting and as driven to be slender. Viewers not only learn that thinness is desirable, but, compared with what most women actually look like, they also learn a "distorted and unrealistic picture of women's bodies" (Fouts and Burggraf 1999).

Sociologists who studied televised sports news in Los Angeles found that it maintains traditional stereotypes (Messner et al. 2003). Women athletes rarely receive coverage. When they do, the stories sometimes trivialize them by focusing on humorous events in women's sports or by turning the women into sexual objects. Newscasters even manage to emphasize breasts and bras and to engage in locker-room humor.

At the same time, though, stereotypes are being broken. On comedies, women are more aggressive verbally than men (Glascock 2001). Buffy the Vampire Slayer saved her classmates from Evil, while, with tongue in cheek, the Powerpuff Girls are touted as "the most elite kindergarten crime-fighting force ever assembled." Perhaps the most stereotype-breaking of all was *Xena, Warrior Princess*, a television series imported from New Zealand. Portrayed as super dominant, Xena overcame all obstacles and defeated all foes—whether men or women.

MUSIC. There are so many kinds (genres) of music that it is difficult to summarize sex roles in music accurately. In many songs for teens and preteens, the boys learn that they should dominate male–female relationships. Girls often hear the message that they should be sexy, passive, and dependent—and that they can control boys by manipulating the boys' sexual impulses. In music videos, the females typically are background ornaments for the dominant males, and those who watch these videos the most also hold more traditional sex role stereotypes (Ward et al. 2005). Some rap groups glorify male sexual aggression and revel in humiliating women. A common theme in country-western music is that men are aggressive and dominant, whereas women are passive and dependent. These dominant men do have a tender side, however: They cry into their beers after their cheating women have left them. But, never mind, some honky-tonk woman is waiting to revel in her newly found dominant man.

VIDEO GAMES. More than any other medium, video games give the message that women are not important. In these games, male characters outnumber female characters seven to one (Beasley and Standley 2002). Just as in other media, women in video games show more skin than men do.

ADVERTISING

> Advertising is an insidious propaganda machine for a male supremacist society. It spews out images of women as sex mates, housekeepers, mothers, and menial workers—images that perhaps reflect the true status of most women in society, but which also make it increasingly difficult for women to break out of the sexist stereotypes that imprison them (Komisar 1971:304).

How has the portrayal of the sexes in advertising changed since this observation was made in the 1970s? Although fewer women are now depicted as "housekeepers, mothers, and menial workers," television advertising continues to reinforce stereotypical gender roles. Commercials aimed at children are more likely to show girls as cooperative and boys as aggressive. They are also more likely to show girls at home and boys at other locations (Larson 2001). Men are more likely to occupy higher status positions (Coltrane and Messineo 2000). Women make most purchases, they are underrepresented as primary characters, and they are still shown primarily as supportive counterparts to men (Ganahl et al. 2003). Even when they are depicted as professionals, women are apt to be shown as less engaged in the situation or as weaker or as needing men in some way (Lindner 2004).

The use of the female body—especially exposed breasts—to sell products also continues. Feminists have fought back. In one campaign, they spray-painted their own lines

Feminists have protested the degradation of women, including the exposure of the female body to sell products. The resulting change, however, has not been a decrease in the number of such ads. Instead, we now have ads that explicitly display the male body to sell products. This is a form of equality, although not the one that was intended.

on billboards (Rakow 1992). One billboard featured a new car with a woman reclining on its roof saying, "It's so practical, Darling." Feminists added the spray-painted line, "When I'm not lying on cars, I'm a brain surgeon."

Such resistance, as you know from the average 1,600 ads that pummel you each day (Draper 1986), has had little impact. The major change in how bodies are depicted in advertising is that the male body has become more prominent. More than ever, parts of the male body are also selected for exposure and for irrelevant association with products.

IN SUM The essential point is that the mass media—children's books, television, music, video games, and advertising—influence us. They shape the images that we hold of the way people "ought" to be—how they should act and even feel—and we tend to see both one another and ourselves as men and women through those images. Perhaps the most significant and influential change that researchers of gender are documenting is the portrayal of girls with more masculine characteristics. This appears to parallel the changes occurring in the ways that parents are socializing their children—continuing to encourage traditional masculine characteristics in their sons while encouraging their daughters to display some of these same characteristics (Kane 2006).

The images of the sexes that we learn as children and continue to assimilate as adults channel our behavior, becoming part of the process by which traditional sex roles are both maintained and changed. This includes politics, to which we now turn.

The World of Politics

THE CURRENT SITUATION. Despite the many changes that mark greater equality between the sexes, men remain dominant. Politics gives us an excellent illustration of the relative position of men and women in the United States. Figure 9-2 on the next page illustrates how vastly underrepresented women are in political decision making. As you can see, the higher the office, the fewer the women. Only a handful of women have been governors or mayors of large cities. Despite the gains women have made in recent elections, since 1789, 1,858 men have served in the U.S. Senate, but only 35 women have served, including the 16 current senators (Baumann 2006; election results 2006). Not until 1992 was the first African American woman (Carol Moseley-Braun) elected to the Senate. No Latina or Asian American woman has yet been elected to the Senate (National Women's Political Caucus 1998; *Statistical Abstract* 2006:Table 395).

FIGURE 9-2 Who Controls U.S. Politics?

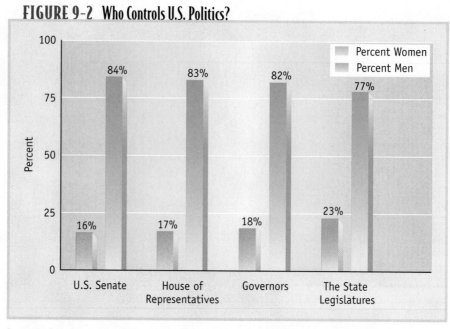

Source: By the author. Based on National Governors' Association (nga.org); *Statistical Abstract of the United States* 2006:Table 395; 2006 election results.

The social map below shows the percentage of women who make up the state legislatures of the United States. This is a rough indicator of how political power is distributed between men and women on the state level. It is difficult to perceive patterns in this distribution of power among the states, but one does stand out. As you can see, the states in which women hold the highest percentage of the state offices tend to be in the West. You can also see the wide variance in the political power of women, as represented by this measure, from 0 percent in South Carolina to 33 percent in several states.

FIGURE 9-3 Women in State Legislatures

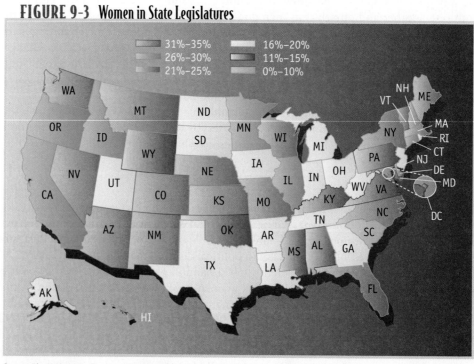

Source: The National Conference of State Legislatures

WHY DON'T WOMEN DOMINATE POLITICS?   Consider these two facts. The first: About *8 million* more women than men are of voting age. The second: Because a larger percentage of women vote in national elections, women voters outnumber men voters by *9 million* (*Statistical Abstract* 2006:Table 405). With their overwhelming numbers, why don't women take political control of the nation?

The Syllogism of Masculinity ■ A good part of the reason that women are underrepresented in political power appears to be socialization. As we have seen, our social institutions help to socialize males into dominance. This leads to the following syllogism:

> Dominance is masculine;
> politics is a form of dominance;
> therefore, politics is unfeminine.

This perception imposes severe restraints on women's recruitment, participation, and performance in politics.

The Power of Sex Roles ■ Other significant reasons center on sex roles and the relative positions of men and women. First, women are underrepresented in law and business, the careers from which most politicians come. Further, most women do not perceive themselves as a class of people who need political action to overcome domination. Most women also find the irregular hours that it takes to run for elective office incompatible with being a wife and mother. For fathers-husbands, in contrast, whose ordinary roles are more likely to take them away from the home, this conflict is not as severe. Women are also less likely to have a supportive spouse who will play an unassuming background role while providing child care, encouragement, and voter appeal. Finally, men prefer to keep their power and have been reluctant to bring women into decision-making roles or to regard them as viable candidates.

Changes ■ These factors are changing, which indicates that we can expect more women to seek and win political office. More women are going into law and business, where they are doing more traveling and making statewide and national contacts. Child care is increasingly becoming the responsibility of both parents. A main concern of many party leaders today is not the sex but the "winnability" of a candidate. This generation, then, is likely to see a fundamental change in women's political participation—and a woman occupying the Oval Office.

The World of Work

THE HISTORICAL PATTERN. To glimpse the overall historical pattern of women in paid work in the United States, look at Table 9-3 on the next page. As you can see, with one exception, for more than 100 years the number of U.S. women employed outside the home has increased consistently. The exception is the period immediately following World War II. By 1945, 38 percent of women were in the labor force, working in factory and office jobs while the men fought in World War II. After the men came home from the war, they reclaimed many of these jobs, and the percentage of women in the paid workforce dropped. As you can see, it took about 20 years for the percentage of women who work for wages to get this high again.

The percentage of the population age 16 and over that is in the labor force at least part-time is known as the **labor force participation rate.** For women, the watershed year was 1985. In that year, for the first time in U.S. history, half of all U.S. women were employed outside the home at least part time. Today, close to half of

One of the major changes occurring in the United States is the ascent of women into positions of power. Although we are not even close to a balance of men and women of power, the candidacy of Hillary Clinton for the presidency of the United States illustrates a fundamental change.

TABLE 9-3 Women in the Civilian Labor Force

YEAR	NUMBER	AS A PERCENTAGE OF ALL WORKERS	PERCENTAGE OF WOMEN IN THE LABOR FORCE	PERCENTAGE OF WOMEN NOT IN THE LABOR FORCE
1890	4,000,000	17%	18%	82%
1900	5,000,000	18%	20%	80%
1920	8,000,000	20%	23%	77%
1930	10,000,000	22%	24%	76%
1940	14,000,000	25%	29%	71%
1945	19,000,000	36%	38%	62%
1950	18,000,000	30%	34%	66%
1960	23,000,000	33%	36%	64%
1970	32,000,000	37%	41%	59%
1980	45,000,000	42%	48%	52%
1990	57,000,000	45%	54%	46%
2000	63,000,000	46%	60%	40%
2010*	76,000,000	48%	60%	40%

Note: Pre-1940 totals include women 14 and over; totals for 1940 and after are for women 16 and over.
*Estimate by the U.S. Dept. of Labor.

Sources: By the author. Based on *1969 Handbook on Women Workers* 1969:10; *Manpower Report to the President 1971:203,* 205; Mills and Palumbo 1980:6, 45; *U.S. Bureau of the Census,* various years; *Statistical Abstract* 2003:Table 588; 2006:Table 577.

all U.S. workers are women. As the Social Map on the next page shows, the percentage of women working for wages differs by state. The rate ranges from 49 percent in West Virginia to almost 70 percent in South Dakota.

The world of work is no exception to the general pattern of discrimination against women. Women come up against an "old boys' network," social contacts that keep jobs, promotions, and opportunities circulating among men. To overcome this exclusion, some women professionals have developed a "new girls' network." They pass opportunities among one another, purposefully excluding men in order to help the careers of women.

THE GENDER PAY GAP. But we need more than anecdotes to pinpoint discrimination at work. Someone can always provide an anecdote about a woman who is paid more than a man for the same work. What we need are hard numbers, and the one that really stimulates the sociological imagination is the *gender gap* in wages. Let your mind grapple with this startling statistic: *At all ages and at all levels of education and no matter the type of work, the average man is paid more than the average woman.* If we consider all jobs in the nation, and if we look only at full-time, year-round workers, we find that women average only *70 percent* of what men earn (*Statistical Abstract* 2006:Table 686). Think about this—the average woman earns only a little over two-thirds of what the average man earns. Until the 1980s, women's earnings hovered between 58 and 60 percent of men's, which means that to be paid 70 percent of what men make is an improvement! The European nations also have a gender gap in pay, but only Portugal has a gap as great as that of the United States (Clarke 2001).

We don't want to confuse things by comparing better educated men with poorer educated women, or some such thing, so look at Figure 9-5. Here we compare men and women who have the same level of education. Despite matching educations, the average man earns more than the average woman. This is true not only of all levels of education but also of all occupations. There isn't a single occupation in which the average woman outearns the average man. How powerfully gender affects earnings!

From Figure 9-5, which shows annual earnings, you can see that we are talking about a lot of money. The gender gap in pay translates into an astounding lifetime total in favor of men: *Between the ages of 25 and 65, the average man who graduates from college earns about a million dollars ($1,100,000) more than the average woman who graduates from college.*

FIGURE 9-4 How Likely Are Women to Work for Wages?

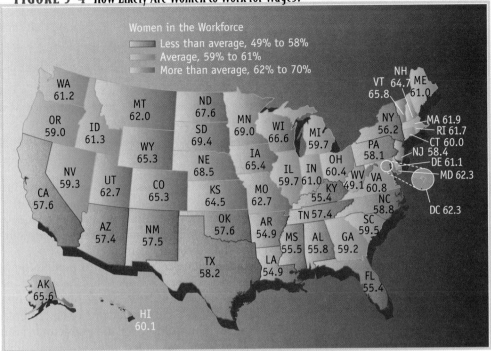

Note: Refers to women who are 16 years old and over who work for wages at least part-time in the civilian labor force; commonly called the *labor force participation rate.*

Source: By the author. Based on *Statistical Abstract of the United States* 2007:Table 684.

REASONS FOR THE GENDER PAY GAP. Why do we have a pay gap between women and men? Recall the gender tracking in education that I mentioned earlier. Perhaps this leads to occupational tracking, and women are more likely to work at the types of jobs that pay less. You know that most secretaries and food servers are women, for example, and that few people who do these jobs earn much. Another possibility is that the gender gap in

FIGURE 9-5 The Cash Penalty for Being Female (Or the Cash Reward for Being Male)

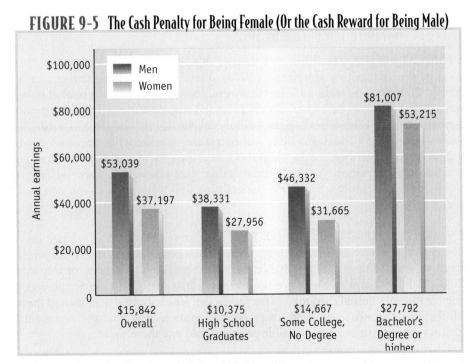

Note: These are the average (median) annual earnings of full-time workers.

Source: By the author. Based on *Statistical Abstract of the United States* 2007:Table 684.

pay exists because women professionals, such as physicians, work fewer hours than the men in the same profession (Steinhauer 1999b). Researchers considered these possibilities and did research to "control for these variables," as they put it. They found that such factors are important. They account for about half the pay gap (Kemp 1990). The balance is apparently due to gender discrimination.

THE FULLER-SCHOENBERGER STUDY. How does discrimination work to create this gap in income between men and women? The most insightful research I have come across was done in 1991 by economists Rex Fuller and Richard Schoenberger. Unfortunately, they retired from the university and have not updated their research, and I can't find anyone else who has done so. Let's look at what they found to help us understand how the gender gap in pay comes about.

Fuller and Schoenberger who were teaching in the business school at the University of Wisconsin, noticed that the women graduates seemed to be starting off at lower salaries. To find out if their informal observation was true, they examined the starting salaries of 230 business majors, of whom 47 percent were women. They found that the women's starting salaries averaged 11 percent ($1,737) less than those of the men.

One possibility that these researchers considered was that the women were less qualified than the men. Perhaps they had lower grades. There was also the possibility that the women had done fewer internships. If so, they deserved their lower salaries. As faculty members, Fuller and Schoenberger were able to gain access to the students' college records. They compared the men's and women's grades and internships. What they uncovered can be described as *deep* gender discrimination: The *women* had earned *higher* grades and done *more* internships. In other words, the women had to have higher qualifications than men in order to be offered lower salaries!

What happened after these graduates were on the job? Did their bosses realize that the recruiters had made a mistake, so that after a while these initial salary differences were wiped out? On the contrary. The gender gap grew. In four years, the women were earning 14 percent ($3,615) less than the men.

IN SUM Sociologically, it seems fair to conclude that "maleness" is so valued by employers that they pay hard cash for it—a conclusion that applies to other industrialized nations as well (Rosenfeld and Kalleberg 1990; Sorensen 1990; Shellenbarger 1995).

Why Is Our Workforce Segregated by Sex?

THE CONFLICT PERSPECTIVE. Two explanations compete for why our labor force is segregated by sex (Blau 1975; MacKinnon 1979). The first is based on conflict theory. As we saw in Chapter 7, Marxist conflict theory emphasizes how having a pool of low-paid labor helps the owners of businesses. They draw on those workers during periods of economic expansion, then lay them off when the economy slows down. The result is a **dual labor market**—better-paid workers who are employed regularly coupled with temporary, marginal, low-paid workers. Women are not singled out because they are women, nor are African Americans and Latinos singled out because of their race-ethnicity. All are singled out for the underpaid and underutilized pool of marginal labor because, as minorities, they are relatively powerless.

THE SYMBOLIC INTERACTIONIST PERSPECTIVE. The second explanation is based on symbolic interactionism (MacKinnon 1979). Because men *perceive* women as less capable, less productive, and ultimately, less profitable, they pay them less. This stereotype is based partially on childbirth and women's greater responsibilities for child care: Employers view women as more dedicated than men to the family and less dedicated than men to the firm. With these perceptions, employers assign women more menial jobs and pay them less, while they assign men more responsible positions and pay them more.

IN SUM Each explanation probably holds part of the answer. Businesses do profit from marginal pools of labor, and women do confront structural barriers in the marketplace.

Stereotypes of men and women do affect employers' expectations, influencing their reactions, including what they pay their workers. Whatever the factors that created the situation, sex discrimination tends to be self-perpetuating. And, we might add, regardless of their personal opinions, employers generally pay the least they can.

Sexual Harassment

Another form of sex discrimination that women face is **sexual harassment,** using one's position to make unwanted sexual demands. If power is unequal, the less powerful person is at a disadvantage in warding off such demands. The most vulnerable women are those who lack job alternatives.

A PERSONAL PROBLEM. The traditional view of sexual harassment makes it a *personal* problem, a matter of individual sexual attraction. A man gets interested in a woman and makes an advance; the woman accepts, rejects, or says "maybe." Perhaps her body language even "signals" that she *wants* to be approached sexually. There are always sexual attractions between men and women; some just happen to take place at work. These are events between individuals and are not a *social* problem.

A SOCIAL PROBLEM. In 1979, Catharine MacKinnon, an attorney and professor, wrote a book on sexual harassment that changed our thinking. Rejecting the traditional view, MacKinnon argued that sexual harassment is a *structural* matter; that is, it is built into the marketplace. She noted that two conditions encourage sexual harassment. The first is that most women occupy an inferior status in boss–worker relations. The second is an emphasis on women as sex objects at work. Women are often hired because of their sexual attributes, a precondition that usually is hidden under the requirement that the newly hired be young, "attractive" women who can make a "good appearance" to the public. In short, sexual harassment begins with hiring procedures that judge women on factors other than their job qualifications and that then places them in a position where they are responsible to men (Silverman 1981).

Although MacKinnon's analysis is accepted widely now, at the time it was new and controversial. Until 1976, sexual harassment was literally unspeakable—because it had no name. The traditional view dominated, and women considered unwanted sexual advances as something that happened to them as individuals. They did not draw a connection between those advances and their lower position in the marketplace. As women's liberation

Most charges of sexual harassment are settled quietly, but some make headlines. Shown on the left is Tim Nardiello, coach for the U.S. Olympic bobsled team, who was accused of sexual harassment by some of his female bobsledders. Denying the charges, he was suspended, reinstated, and then fired.

groups raised awareness of the *group* basis of these objective conditions, women gradually concluded that the sexual advances by men in more powerful positions at work were part of a general problem. As more women came to the same conclusion—and became upset about it and demanded that something be done—sexual harassment as a *social* problem was born. To catch a glimpse of how this definitional process is occurring in Japan, see the Global Glimpse box on the next page.

DEFINING SEXUAL HARASSMENT. As MacKinnon pointed out, sometimes sexual harassment is just a single encounter at work, but sometimes harassment consists of a series of incidents. At times, sexual relations are made a condition for being hired, retained, or advanced. Sexual harassment can include

> verbal sexual suggestions or jokes, constant leering or ogling, brushing against your body "accidentally," a friendly pat, squeeze, or pinch or arm against you, catching you alone for a quick kiss, the indecent proposition backed by the threat of losing your job, and forced sexual relations. (MacKinnon 1979:2)

MacKinnon (1979:29) added,

> Sexual harassment takes both verbal and physical forms. . . . Verbal sexual harassment can include anything from passing but persistent comments on a woman's body or body parts to the experience of an eighteen-year-old file clerk whose boss regularly called her in to his office "to tell me the intimate details of his marriage and to ask what I thought about different sexual positions." Pornography is sometimes used. Physical forms range from repeated collisions that leave the impression of "accident" to outright rape. One woman reported unmistakable sexual molestation which fell between these extremes: "My boss . . . runs his hand up my leg or blouse. He hugs me to him and then tells me he is 'just naturally affectionate.' "

The Equal Employment Opportunity Commission has broadened the definition of sexual harassment to include all unwelcome verbal or physical conduct of a sexual nature that explicitly or implicitly affects an individual's employment, unreasonably interferes with an individual's work performance or creates an intimidating, hostile or offensive work environment. The offender does not have to be a boss, nor does the victim have to be a female. The intimidating, hostile, or offensive behavior can be from fellow workers or agents of the employer ("Facts About . . ." 2006). The definition has also been broadened to include unwanted sexual behavior from fellow students.

You can see that some of the key terms in this definition are broad and subject to interpretation. One person can find some behavior intimidating, hostile, or offensive, while another person can view that same act quite differently. The legal concept has become so fuzzy that a woman whose boss did *not* ask her for sexual favors—while he asked all the other women—was ruled a victim of sexual harassment (Hayes 1991). In addition, as sociologist Kirsten Dellinger discusses in the Spotlight on Social Research box on page 312, what passes for acceptable behavior in one work setting can be taken as sexual harassment in another.

THE MITSUBISHI CASE. If a worker is sexually harassed by a boss, she or he has limited options. Objecting, submitting, or ignoring the act are all risky (MacKinnon 1979:52). Let's say that the victim is a woman. If she objects, she may be hounded into quitting or get fired outright. If she submits, the man may tire of her. If she ignores it, she can get drawn into a cat-and-mouse game with few exits: He may tire of the game and turn to someone else, or he may fire her so he can hire a more willing victim.

Or she can file a claim of sexual harassment. These claims are often settled privately, as they are usually difficult to prove. In addition, women who make legal claims run the risk of frustration, embarrassment, and retaliation at work. Victims who have taken these risks, however, have gradually transformed the workplace. The landmark decision came in 1998. Three hundred women who worked at the Illinois plant of Mitsubishi Motors claimed that the company tolerated a hostile work environment. Some claimed fellow

A Global Glimpse
SEXUAL HARASSMENT IN JAPAN

The public relations department had come up with an eye-catcher: Each month the cover of the company magazine would show a woman taking off one more piece of clothing. The men were pleased. Never had they so looked forward to the company magazine.

Six months later, with the cover girl poised to take off her tank top, the objections of the female employees had grown too loud to ignore. "We told them it was a lousy idea," said Junko Takashima, assistant director of the company's woman's affairs division. The firm dropped the striptease act.

The Japanese men didn't get the point. "What's all the fuss about?" they asked. "Beauty is beauty. We're just admiring the ladies. It just adds a little spice to boring days at the office."

"It's degrading to us, and it must stop," responded women workers, who, encouraged by the U.S. feminist movement, broke their tradition of silence.

The Japanese (like Americans until the 1970s) have no word of their own to describe such situations. They have borrowed the English phrase "sexual harassment" and are struggling to apply it to their own culture. This is difficult, because a pat on the bottom has long been taken for granted as a boss's way of getting his secretary's attention.

The cultural expectation that all Japanese workers are part of a team that works together harmoniously also makes it difficult to complain. But some women have begun to speak out, using their new vocabulary—and the changed perception that comes with it. As a result, the Japanese government has designated a week in December as "Week for Prevention of Sexual Harassment of National Civil Servants."

Based on Graven 1990; "Implementation of Measures . . ." 2000.

What is considered sexual harassment can differ from one culture to another. Do you think that the striptease in the company magazine, discussed in this box, is sexual harassment? How about the photos at this magazine stand in Tokyo? What is the difference?

workers had groped them, others that bosses had threatened to fire them if they didn't agree to have sex. The women were awarded $34 million, an average of $113,000 each. The size of the award caught employers' attention nationwide. They became aware that tolerating a hostile work environment can affect the corporate bottom line.

RACIAL-ETHNIC LINES. When sexual harassment crosses racial lines, victims are put at a special disadvantage. If they protest, they can be accused of being insensitive to cultural differences—they have misunderstood what is a "normal" sexual invitation in another racial-ethnic group. Or they can be perceived as prejudiced—offended by the sexual offer because

Spotlight on Social Research

SEXUAL HARASSMENT AT TWO MAGAZINES

KIRSTEN DELLINGER, *Associate Professor of Sociology at the University of Mississippi, says that her interest in gender and sexuality in organizations emerged from her own early work experiences. As she worked with autistic adults in one setting and children in another, she wondered why most workers were women and why they earned little and received little respect. From these initial observations, she turned her attention to how work is organized and the role of gender and sexuality in the work setting.*

I have been intrigued by the research that explores how organizations are "gendered" and "sexualized." One of the themes in this literature is how workplace policies create and maintain ideologies about masculinity and femininity. Another is how workers construct their gender identities through their everyday interactions. What is acceptable or not differs from one work setting to another. Take the example of sexual harassment.

Have you ever heard people say that sexual harassment is impossible to solve in the workplace because "it all depends on what an individual finds offensive"? Sally finds the joke about women's bodies funny, but Julie doesn't. Harry likes to tell stories about homosexuals, but Frank cringes when he hears them. Julie and Frank keep their mouths shut, because they hold lower positions at work. Much survey research on sexual harassment emphasizes this individualistic level. Researchers ask people if, in their opinion, certain behaviors (such as patting someone's butt) are sexual harassment or not.

Instead of taking this individualistic perspective, in my research I examine how the *social context* influences how people define sexual harassment. The research that I did with Christine Williams underlines the symbolic interactionist perspective that whether a behavior is sexual harassment or not depends on the definitions that people apply to it. And those definitions, as we found out, depend more on the social context than on individualistic perspectives.

We studied workers at two magazines who were doing the same jobs: editors, accountants, and administrative assistants. The magazines were quite different: a heterosexual men's pornographic magazine and a feminist magazine. Workers at the men's magazine, *Gentleman's Sophisticate,* worked in a "locker room" culture. Sexual joking was common, even about the magazine itself. At the same time, these workers had strict norms against discussing highly personal aspects of their own lives. Sexual harassment was defined as a violation of personal boundaries, not by how sexual a conversation was. In contrast, workers at the feminist magazine, *Womyn,* worked in something that was closer to what you find in an all-women's dorm: They expected one another to share personal aspects about their sexual lives. They wanted to analyze them through a feminist framework. These women defined sexual harassment as an abuse of power. Editors talked about being careful with the power that they had over interns, most of whom were college students. Workers at *Gentleman's Sophisticate* and at *Womyn* were using different workplace norms to define and to deal with sexual harassment.

it was made by someone of a different race-ethnicity—with the implication that they would have welcomed the suggestion had it been made by someone of their own race-ethnicity.

NOT JUST A WOMAN'S PROBLEM. Sexual harassment used to be perceived as an exclusively female problem. With more women in positions of power, men have also found themselves victims (DeSouza and Fansler 2003; Hill and Silva 2005). One man claimed that his chief financial officer, a woman, made sexual overtures to him "almost daily." Another objected that his supervisor told him that she had dreamed about him naked. Some men who are victims receive little sympathy. Many men don't understand why a man would take offense at a woman's sexual advances, even from his boss (Carton 1994). "Why not have some fun?" is a typical response. I anticipate that norms will change to account for women's growing power.

In 1998, the Supreme Court broadened sexual harassment laws to include people of the same sex. The Court ruled that sexual harassment is not limited to behavior between men and women, and it does not have to include sexual desire. The law now covers the harassment at work of homosexuals by heterosexuals (Felsenthal 1998). By extension, the law includes the sexual harassment of heterosexuals by homosexuals.

Violence Against Women

RAPE AND MURDER. Fears of rape and murder stalk women in this society. Women know that they can disappear while they are on their way to school or just out getting groceries. Some victims resurface raped and brutalized, but alive. Others are found dead, stuffed in the trunk of their own car or thrown alongside the road. We reviewed rape and murder in Chapter 5, and there is no need to go beyond that chapter's materials. We need to stress one of the main points of that chapter, though: Women tend to be the victims, men the rapists and killers.

FAMILY VIOLENCE. Looking ahead, in Chapter 11 we will review family violence. There, too, females are disproportionately the victims. A form of violence against women that is family centered, but a stranger to the Western world, is genital mutilation, the focus of the box on page 291. Another form of violence that is also family centered and alien to Western culture is known as "honor killings." These are the killings of girls and women who have violated the family's honor by stepping outside the culture's sexual boundaries. In the typical case, the daughter or mother has had sex outside of marriage or has been accused of doing so. It is the duty of a male family member, ordinarily the father, brother, or uncle, to restore the family's honor by killing the accused girl or woman. Honor killings are common in the Islamic world, especially in Pakistan.

APPLYING THE CONFLICT PERSPECTIVE. To explain why girls and women are the typical victims of violence, some sociologists use conflict theory. They argue that we can understand a lot of violence against women if we view it as an expression of power. Family violence, for example, usually involves a misuse of power. That is, men usually have greater power than women in the family, and it is they who are the usual perpetrators of violence, with wives and children their victims.

APPLYING SYMBOLIC INTERACTIONISM. Sociologists also use symbolic interactionism. They stress that in U.S. culture men learn to "associate power, dominance, strength, virility, and superiority with masculinity" (Scully 1990). Strength and virility are held out as goals for boys to achieve. Surrounding us are men in positions of power, men who dominate society. The evidence of male superiority oozes from all sectors of society.

But how does this association of masculinity with strength, virility, and dominance turn into violence? The process is unknown at present, but we do know that males are also surrounded with models of violence. Of the many examples that we could select, let's point to just one, video games. In many of these games, the goal is to hunt down and kill enemies—from mythical creatures to men and women. In some games, those who are to be hunted down and killed are barely clad young women. The form varies, and in one game, zombies suck the blood of scantily dressed sorority sisters (Pereira 1993).

In a typical game, players can choose the characters they wish to play. The choice may include both men and women. As a sign of changing times, I see men players choosing to be women characters. Bob may choose to "be" "Melissa, the hot-tempered, evil, axe-wielding killer," so he can see how she compares with "Annie, the mean strumpet who packs a .45," or whether she can bring down "Fred, the escaped loony with a chain saw." Apart from what such characters might indicate concerning changing views of women, we need to stress that most players of video games are boys and young men. Although the form may change, symbols of violence continue to be a feature of the male world.

For killing his 16-year-old sister, shown in the photo he is holding, this Pakistani man served 6 months in jail. The girl's offense? Being raped by her brother-in-law.

Social Policy

Irreconcilable Ideologies

As we saw in Chapter 7, with the improvement in the poverty rate of the aged, social policy can be effective in reducing inequality and in achieving a more equitable society. Let's turn now to an overview of social policy as it applies to sex discrimination.

As stressed in Chapter 7, proposals for social policy depend on assumptions of cause. They also depend on people's assumptions of justice, of what is right or how things in life should be. To see the range of suggestions for reducing sex discrimination, let's look at the extremes. I will call these the *radical extremists* and the *conservative extremists*. Each term lumps together the thinking of several groups and organizations.

THE RADICAL EXTREMISTS. The radical extremists insist that our society is so rotten at the core that it must be restructured. As sociologist Jessie Bernard (1971) stressed, it is not enough to simply tinker with some parts of society, such as demanding equal pay or knocking a hole in the glass ceiling. As good as they are in their intent, policies to bring such things about are superficial. Our current social arrangements threaten to destroy the basic humanity of women and men, she said, and we need social policies that eradicate the social roots of sexism.

Because the roots of sexism go back to childhood, we would need social policies designed to remove distinctions between boys and girls and men and women. Girls and boys would have to be socialized in the same way. They would have to be treated equally throughout education, from preschool to graduate school. This would include athletics and sports. Husbands and wives would also have to share housework equally, and both parents would have to compete equally in the world of work. Ultimately, men and women would hold all positions in our social institutions equally.

If we fail to restructure society, but only tinker with parts of it, as Bernard said, women will continue to "end up in service positions or servant roles, no matter what class of job they hold—factory work, technician, secretary, research assistant." Women will still perform the supportive or stroking functions, continue to be "the restorers, the healers, the builder-up-ers" and be disqualified from the top positions (Bernard 1971).

It should be obvious that such extreme social policies are not possible in our society—unless we had a dictator to enforce them. Consequently, these goals will not be achieved.

THE CONSERVATIVE EXTREMISTS. Standing on the other side of the gulf are the conservative extremists. They believe that gender distinctions are natural and desirable and ought to be encouraged. They hold that a woman's proper role is to be a homemaking wife and mother; a man's to be a breadwinning husband and father. This ideology would require an antithetical set of social policies. Their policies would require parents to take full responsibility and care for their own preschool children. There would be no publicly supported child care. Girls would be encouraged to become full-time wives and mothers and boys to become the protectors and primary source of financial support of their wives and children. Children's picture books and school texts would present women and men in these traditional roles. Full-time homemakers would receive tax breaks, and job preference would be given to men who are supporting dependents.

Again, absent their enforcement by a dictator, these social policies, too, will never become the law of the land.

MIDDLE-OF-THE-ROAD POLICIES. Innumerable positions fall between these two extremes. It is likely that some of the more middle-of-the-road policies reflect your own views and the causes you support: well-run child-care facilities for working parents, policies that foster closer relations of fathers with their children, the right for both mother and father to take extended leaves from work when a child is born or sick, summer camps for all children, enforcement of child support that has been awarded by the courts, the end of the gender pay gap, and, at home, a more equitable distribution of housework.

The Battle Lines

Probably most of us would agree with most of these middle-of-the-road proposals. And most of us probably would also agree with the principle that we should have equality between the sexes. Few of us, however, realize how radical the view of sexual equality is.

THE ERA. To see why I say this, let's look at how the United States reacted to the proposal of an equal rights amendment (ERA). Between 1924 and 1971, Congress held twelve hearings on this amendment, and in 1972, the House and Senate passed this version:

Section 1 Equality of rights under the law shall not be denied or abridged by the United States or by any State on account of sex.

Section 2 The Congress shall have the power to enforce, by appropriate legislation, the provisions of this article.

Section 3 This amendment shall take effect two years after the date of ratification.

Within hours after the Senate passed this resolution, Hawaii ratified the amendment. Twenty-one additional states ratified in 1972, eight in 1973, three in 1974, one in 1975, none in 1976, and one, the thirty-fifth, in 1977. With only three states short of the required three-fourths majority, the amendment hit a roadblock, and no further states ratified. When the seven-year limit for ratification expired in March 1979, Congress extended the time for ratification by three years and three months. Momentum and sentiment had swung the other way, however, and five states rescinded their ratification.

Why did this simple statement proposing equality of rights under the law for the sexes fail? Does it not simply match what any decent, fair-minded person would want? The problem is that no one knew what the consequences would be if the ERA became law. Its terms were so broad that its meaning could be determined only through court decisions in lawsuits. The interpretation process might have extended over centuries (Lee 1980). Consequently, no one knew the details of what they were fighting for or against.

This, however, did not deter groups from lining up on either side of the ERA, each convinced that it understood the consequences of the amendment. Women were not on one side, opposed by men on the other. Rather, women were on both sides, as were men. In the forefront of the battle were two groups: feminists, largely represented by the National Organization for Women (NOW), and traditionalists, largely represented by the Eagle Forum. Most women, however, watched from the sidelines, passively silent and strangely acquiescent about the outcome that affected them so vitally.

The convictions of these two main groups of activists appear to have been based on hopes and fears. The feminists *hoped* that the amendment would bring equality of the sexes, help eliminate sexual stereotypes, and give women access to all areas of participation and leadership in society. The traditionalists, in contrast, *feared* that the amendment would lead to the elimination of protective work legislation (such as that preventing women from lifting weights in excess of designated amounts); to the drafting of women for combat; to unisex sleeping arrangements in military barracks, college dormitories, and prisons; and to unisex public restrooms.

As these groups argued and fought on opposing sides of the ERA, they were blinded to what they had in common. For example, both groups agreed that pornography degrades women and encourages violence against women, and that it should be highly restricted, if not banned. Each group also wanted the best for women. But because each viewed what is best from the lens of its own ideology, neither was able to see the point of view of the other. Women were divided by this controversy.

The defeat of the ERA in 1982 did not end the matter. ERA is very much alive. In every Congressional term since then, some form of the ERA has been proposed by feminists—and opposed just as strongly by conservatives. In the current political climate, these proposals are given little consideration, and they die a quiet death.

Ideology and Social Policy

Ideology colors all aspect of relations between the sexes and the roles of women and men in society. Within this ideological morass, no social policy is viewed as neutral. With irreconcilable points of view abounding, every proposal seems subversive to someone. To be sound, social policy must consider these cleavages. It must also be based on the principle that both men and women deserve the right to make informed choices about their roles in life. For example, forcing a woman to be a homemaker is no more an example of freedom than is forcing her to be a paid worker. To move beyond ideological rhetoric, then, social policy ought to support an environment in which neither men nor women are forced into predetermined roles.

The Future of the Problem

Although sexism will remain a fact of life, the historical trend is toward greater equality between women and men, and I anticipate that this will continue. Previous generations of women fought hard to win rights that we now take for granted, such as the right to vote and to own property. Today's and tomorrow's struggle centers on removing stereotypes, eliminating the gender gap in pay, and gaining greater access to leadership, especially in business and politics.

THE WORLD OF WORK. The most significant social trend that will affect this social problem is the employment of women. As even larger numbers of women join the paid workforce, women will continue to reshape social relationships. Power relationships between husbands and wives will be altered, because wives who work outside the home have more control over family decisions than wives who do not. As more wives work outside the home, husbands will gradually take on greater responsibilities for the housework and children. This will not mean equality in household responsibilities any time soon, however, for men resist doing housework and even in dual-earner families, husbands do considerably less housework than their wives (Bianchi et al. 2000; Batalova and Cohen 2002).

Women are likely to make greater use of the Equal Pay Act of 1963 (forbidding discrimination in salaries), Title VII of the Civil Rights Act of 1964 (forbidding discrimination on the basis of sex), and the Fourteenth Amendment (forbidding a state to "deny any person within its jurisdiction the equal protection of the laws"). Such legal pressures will not eliminate the problem, but they will continue to undermine the structure of sexism.

BREAKING GENDER STEREOTYPES. The increasing numbers of women in the workforce are already changing gender stereotypes, a change that will continue. More children are growing up with the model of a mother who more fully participates in family decisions. Children who see both mother and father bringing home paychecks take it for granted that a man is not the exclusive breadwinner and that a woman is more than a mother and a wife. As stereotypes continue to fall, both men and women will be free to do activities compatible with their desires or proclivities as *individuals*—not because the activity matches a stereotype. This will free more men to play more supportive roles and "get more in touch with their feelings" and more women to take leadership roles and become more assertive.

NEW ORIENTATIONS. As sociologist Janet Giele said in the 1970s, the ultimate possibility for the future is a new concept of the human personality (Giele 1978). Stereotypes and gendered roles push us into activities dictated by our culture. As stereotypes are abandoned and as activities become gender-neutral, men and women will develop a new consciousness of who they are and of their potential. New paths will open, ones that allow feelings and expressions of needs that our current stereotypes deny. Women are likely to think of themselves as more active masters of their environment, men to feel and express more emotional sensitivity. Each will be free to explore these other dimensions of the self. As the future unfolds, it will reveal exactly what such "greater wholeness" of men and women looks like.

SUMMARY AND REVIEW

1. Although females make up 50.9 percent of the U.S. population, men discriminate against them. Consequently, sociologists refer to men as a dominant group and women as a minority group.

2. Every society *sex-types* occupations. That is, around the world, some work is thought suitable for men and other work appropriate for women. There is no inherent biological connection between work and its assignment to women or men, for "women's work" of one society may be "men's work" in another. In all societies, "men's work" is given greater prestige than "women's work."

3. Symbolic interactionists examine *gender* (masculinity and femininity), looking at how each society socializes the sexes into its ideas of what men and women ought to be like. Socialization includes learning *sexism,* the belief that one sex is innately superior to the other and the discriminatory practices that result from that belief.

4. Functionalists theorize that sexual discrimination is based on the need of early human groups to engage in hand-to-hand combat. Men had the physical advantage but needed to be motivated to become warriors. Women, offered as inducements for men to fight, were assigned the drudge work of society. A second functionalist explanation is that because women were encumbered physically through childbearing and nursing, men became dominant as they took control of warfare and trade.

5. Conflict theorists emphasize that the rights that U.S. women enjoy came out of a power struggle with men. The confrontations and violence between the sexes in the late 1800s and early 1900s have been replaced by legal pressure and economic and educational competition.

6. Given the inextricability of nature and nurture, we do not know the extent to which natural differences exist between the sexes. Both genetics and socialization can explain females' earlier proficiency in verbal skills and males' greater aggressiveness and abilities at mathematics. The door to biological explanations in sociology has been pried open a bit by the studies of Vietnam veterans.

7. Women confront discrimination in most areas of life, including a belittling attitude from men. The educational system and the mass media generally support existing gender roles. Although women outnumber men voters, men dominate politics; women tend to see politics as incompatible with femininity and motherhood.

8. Women often work at jobs that pay less and that offer less advancement. They also confront *sexual harassment* at work. As more women have moved into power positions at work, men, too, experience sexual harassment.

9. All social policies to deal with sex discrimination have ideological implications. Different groups of women propose antithetical social policies.

10. In the future, even larger numbers of women will be employed outside the home. This will continue to change power relationships at home and break down traditional stereotypes. The direction of the future is toward greater equality between the sexes.

KEY TERMS

Dual labor market, 308
Gender, 288
Gender roles, 288
Labor force participation rate, 305

Master trait, 288
Matriarchy, 296
Patriarchy, 296
Sex, 288

Sex-typing, 286
Sexism, 286
Sexual harassment, 309

THINKING CRITICALLY ABOUT CHAPTER 9

1. List ten examples of sexism in the United States. In what ways do you think that your list would be different if you had written it ten years ago? In what ways do you think it will be different if you were to write it ten years from now?

2. Which of the three theoretical perspectives (symbolic interactionism, functionalism, or conflict theory) do you think best explains sexism in the United States? Why?

3. What are the main changes that you see occurring in gender roles? Why do you think we are experiencing these changes?

4. A developing social problem is mentioned on page 300: two million more women in college than men and women earning 58 percent of all bachelors degrees. Do you think we should start affirmative action and special remedial and motivational courses for men? Why or why not?

10

Medical Care: Physical and Mental Illness

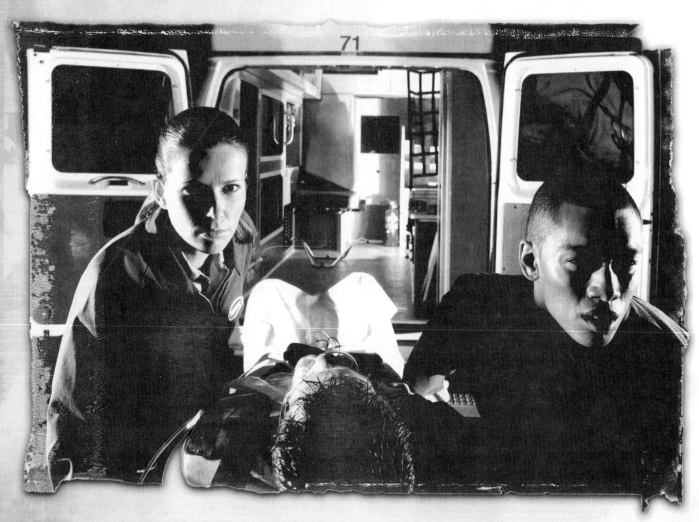

To prepare for the birth of their first child, Kathie Persall and her husband, Hank, read books and articles about childbirth and took childbirth classes together. At 5 o'clock one morning, waking Kathie from a fitful sleep, the protective "bag of waters" that surrounds the fetus broke.

By 10 A.M., Kathie was on the maternity ward, hooked up to an electronic fetal monitor (EFM) and an intravenous feeding tube. She was informed of the hospital's rule that to prevent infection, delivery must take place within twenty-four hours after the waters break. At 11 A.M. the resident physician (not her own doctor) said that they would speed up Kathie's labor by using Pitocin, a powerful drug.

Kathie's sister, Carol, knew that inducing labor could lead to cesarean section. She urged Hank to get Kathie off Pitocin, but Kathie and Hank felt that they couldn't tell the doctor what to do. By evening, doctors decided that Kathie's cervix was not dilating rapidly enough. They increased the Pitocin. One nurse thought that the flow of Pitocin looked blocked. She wiggled the bottle, and a large dose sped through Kathie's veins. Kathie writhed in pain as a massive contraction took over her body. Five or ten minutes later, the fetal monitor indicated that the baby's heartbeat had

> **Kathie was in pain and exhausted.**

dropped from 160 to 40 beats per minute. The doctor rushed in, cut off the Pitocin, and gave Kathie another drug to stop the contraction. He told them that a cesarean might be necessary. Hank, who had been trying to comfort Kathie, protested. The doctor told them that they could face an emergency, and they had to sign a consent form. On the form, Hank and Kathie read a long list of things that could go wrong. They did not want to sign the form, but how could they resist? Kathie was in pain and exhausted.

At midnight, the doctor told Kathie that a cesarean was necessary because she had dilated only 5 centimeters in 13 hours of labor and would need another 13 hours to dilate enough to have a vaginal birth. Kathie knew it was wrong to assume that just because the first 5 centimeters had taken 13 hours that the next would take as long. Nevertheless, she felt overpowered, and at 1:10 A.M. Kathie went into surgery.

When the baby was born, Kathie was vomiting too severely from the anesthetic to even look at her new son. It took Kathie seven weeks to recover physically from the cesarean surgery. She was left with a disfiguring scar, but this was nothing compared with her anger at the doctors, the hospital, and the medical procedures that had created the need for surgery.

The Problem in Sociological Perspective

In Chapter 6, we focused on the twin problems of crime and the criminal justice system that is set up to deal with crime. As we consider medical care, we again need to focus on twin problems: illness and the medical care system that is set up to deal with illness. Our focus is on how *social* factors affect health.

Subjective concerns about this medical problem run high. As Table 10-1 shows, the U.S. public sees health care as the third most pressing social problem that it wants the

TABLE 10-1	**The Ten Most Important Problems Facing the Nation**	
RANK	**PROBLEM**	**PERCENT WHO RANK IT NUMBER ONE OR TWO**
1	The Economy[1]	47%
2	War[2]	24%
3	Health Care[3]	18%
4	Terrorism[4]	12%
5	Education	11%
6	Taxes	5%
7	Budget Deficit	5%
8	Environment	4%
9	Crime	3%
10	Drugs	3%

A random sample of Americans was asked: "What do you think are the two most important issues for the government to address?" To compute these rankings, I have combined similar categories, namely:
[1] The Economy (general) and unemployment
[2] War, Iraq, and defense (military)
[3] Health care and Medicare
[4] Terrorism and domestic security

Source: By the author. Based on *Sourcebook of Criminal Justice Statistics* 2005:Table 2.2.

government to solve. Health care even outranks taxes, terrorism, and crime as a problem for the government to address.

The Social Nature of Health and Illness

NOT JUST BIOLOGY. Most of us think of illness in biological terms, but much more is involved. What is considered health or illness depends on cultural ideas. This may seem strange. Isn't fever, for example, always a sign of illness? Not always. Many people dismiss a low-grade fever as "just a little temperature." Whether a fever is considered a sign of illness depends on how high it is and how long it lasts. Even when it is considered to be illness, interpretations of what fever means and how to treat it differ—among medical authorities as well as patients.

INDUSTRIALIZATION AND LIFESTYLE. The social nature of health and illness is also apparent when we consider industrialization and lifestyle. When the United States industrialized, heart disease became our number one killer. What happened was that industrialization brought greater affluence, and people began to eat richer foods and to get less exercise. One consequence was more heart attacks. Similarly, the pursuit of pleasure is a major cause of disease. Consider gonorrhea, syphilis, and AIDS. Then, too, there is the whole array of diseases that we reviewed in Chapter 4 that come from smoking and the misuse of alcohol.

IATROGENESIS. Another example of the social nature of illness is injuries caused by medical care, called **iatrogenesis**. This occurred when the nurse jiggled Kathie's bottle of Pitocin and the baby's heartbeat plummeted. Iatrogenesis is not trivial. Each year, about 90,000 Americans die at the hands of doctors. *If the number of Americans who are killed by medical errors were an official classification of death, it would rank as number six in the top ten leading causes of death* (Health Grades 2005). The discussion on medical incompetence in the Thinking Critically box on the next page focuses on another aspect of iatrogenesis.

CHANGING IDEAS ABOUT HEALTH AND ILLNESS. The way pregnancy is handled by physicians also highlights the *social* nature of health and illness. Physicians have defined a natural process (pregnancy and birth) as something that requires fetal monitors and powerful drugs. Many doctors also define a woman as "ill" if she does not deliver within twenty-four hours after her water breaks. This arbitrary definition of "illness" is imposed on a natural process in which some women deliver a baby in one hour, but others not for forty-eight hours or longer.

Even ideas of what a disease is are not fixed. A good example comes from coal miners, who used to think of lung cancer as an almost inevitable consequence of their job. Becoming short of breath and coughing up blood was something that "just happened" to longtime coal workers. They even wrote folk songs about "black lung." Eventually, however, coal workers concluded that their symptoms constituted a disease and that the illness need not be inevitable. To get their symptoms recognized as a disease so they could get adequate medical care and compensation, unions had to fight not only management, as you would expect, but also the medical profession. Doctors refused to acknowledge that coal mining caused these health problems. The coal miners' subjective concerns and their struggle to get their disease recognized brought about a new understanding, not just of black lung disease but also of how the environment can create disease (Smith 1987).

THINKING CRITICALLY About Social Problems

HOW INCOMPETENT ARE DOCTORS?

What do you think about these three statements?

1. Most physicians are competent, but all physicians make mistakes.
2. Some physicians are so incompetent that they should not practice medicine.
3. Some of the most incompetent physicians are so admired by their medical colleagues that they are promoted to the leadership of their state medical associations.

You probably agree with the first statement, you likely find the second statement to be somewhat controversial, and the third statement you probably find outrageous. I once had such confidence in the competence of the medical profession (the tough entrance requirements of medical schools, the rigorous training, the years of study) that I thought that the last two statements could not possibly be true. Then on a postdoctoral fellowship I studied suicide in Missouri. As I pored over the coroner's records, I was awestruck by the decision that a person who had been shot several times might have committed suicide. Later, I read about a father in Warren, Ohio, who was convinced that his 20-year-old daughter, who was found dead in a field, had not committed suicide. For seventeen years, this man kept the case alive. As he doggedly pursued the issue, it eventually became apparent that the coroner had missed "obvious" clues to the cause of the woman's death—like "suspicious marks" on her neck. The woman's former boyfriend was charged with strangling her.

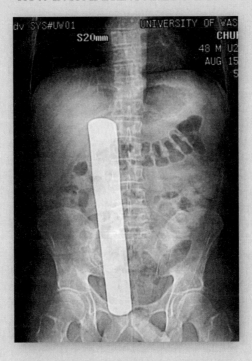

Supposedly, the surgeon at the University of Washington Medical Center who left this 13-inch steel retractor in a patient became "distracted" during the surgery. Some distraction!

When this incompetence became public, the sheriff's department investigated the coroner. Among their findings were these unusual rulings:

- Suicide—the man had been run over with a bulldozer and shot
- Suicide—an inmate was found hanged on his knees with toilet paper stuffed in his mouth
- Death by carbon monoxide from a lawn mower—the lawn mower didn't work
- Death by carbon monoxide—no carbon monoxide was found in the person's blood

This coroner had served as president of the Ohio State Medical Association three years before his exposure.

Makes you wonder, doesn't it?

There are other types of medical blunders. A woman entered a New York City hospital because of a problem with her lungs: Her surgeon did a hysterectomy. In another hospital, a doctor removed the wrong kidney—leaving the cancerous one intact. In yet another hospital, a woman awoke from surgery to find that the surgeon had removed the wrong breast. In a Tampa hospital, a respiratory technician was supposed to disconnect a man from a ventilator. The technician disconnected the wrong patient. He died an hour later.

I trust that these surgeons and the respiratory technician will not be promoted. But that coroner did become president of the state medical association. . . .

What do you think?

Based on "Father's Persistence Pays Off" 1995; Steinhauer 2001; Steinhauer and Fessenden 2001.

ENVIRONMENT AND DISEASE ON A GLOBAL LEVEL. Medical researchers are investigating how the environment affects human disease. Specifically, they are looking at how human activities reshape the environment, which, in turn, has profound effects on the diseases that humans experience. This is the topic of the Global Glimpse box on the next page.

IN SUM We usually think of illness and disease as biological matters. Biology is certainly involved, but what is considered health and illness is a *social* matter. At one point

A Global Glimpse
A MEDICAL MYSTERY: ON BATS, FRUIT FLIES, AND ASTHMA

Why has the rate of asthma jumped in the United States? Our preschool children are more than twice as likely to have asthma today than just ten or fifteen years ago. Why were people in Malaysia suddenly struck by the Nipah virus? Why has Lyme disease become a danger to Boy and Girl Scouts and other wilderness campers?

Such changes in diseases have alarmed the public and perplexed medical researchers. There has to be a cause. Such things don't spring from nothing. They happen because of something; and, as medical researchers are discovering, that something is social change. Let's explore some of the conclusions that medical researchers are arriving at as they study the intricate relationship between the environment and disease.

One of their most remarkable findings is how human activities have unexpected consequences for human disease. Deforestation, for example, the extensive cutting down of trees, can bring disease to humans. The early 1990s saw extensive deforestation in Malaysia and huge forest fires in Sumatra. These events destroyed much of the natural habitat of the fruit bats, which carry the Nipah virus. In their search for food, the bats moved closer to where humans live, settling in backyard fruit trees. From this contact, the Nipah virus jumped to pigs and then to people.

Human activity can be linked to the increase in malaria in several parts of the world. Here, too, deforestation has been traced as a cause of the increase. The reason is simple: Clearing forests leaves holes that fill with water when it rains, and these pools of standing water become breeding grounds for mosquitoes that carry malaria. Even plastic bags have been pinpointed as a culprit. Plastic bags are so handy and cheap that they are now found around the world. Widespread use of such an inexpensive item means that millions upon millions of bags are being discarded. These bags collect water, again increasing breeding sites for mosquitoes.

Globalization, too, is leaving its impact on disease. The world's increasing trade introduces plants and animals to new parts of the world, disrupting the balance of the ecosystem. Ships, for example, suck up water for ballast at some port and then disgorge the water at their destination in another region of the globe. The ballast contains plant and animal species, and the ships transfer them from one part of the world to another. In their new homes, some of these species don't have natural enemies to keep them in check, as they would in their home ecosystem. Algae from Asia, for example, have been transferred

Researchers are studying the relationship of disease and the environment. How does clearing the forests lead to humans getting diseases from bats?

to Europe's North Sea. There they contaminate shellfish, which, when eaten, make humans sick.

Let's go back to one of the puzzles with which we opened this box, one that might have affected you or your friends. Why has asthma more than doubled among U.S. preschool children? The answer to this huge increase has proved elusive to medical researchers, but they now think they are unraveling its cause. The major suspect turns out to be diesel emissions. These emissions allow pollen to be delivered deep into the lungs, increasing asthma among children.

Diesel emissions, of course, are related to global warming, which in itself is having an impact on disease. Consider ticks. As the earth warms, ticks find more hospitable environments, and they multiply. The more ticks, the more humans get bitten. The more that humans get bitten, the more Lyme disease there is. Global warming is expected to continue, and researchers expect this to have another impact on Lyme disease. With continued warming, the ticks that carry Lyme disease will move northward, from the United States into Canada. Soon not just U.S. Boy and Girl Scouts and campers will be at risk, but so will their Canadian counterparts.

Medical sleuthing is not new. Back in the 1800s, London physicians were perplexed at the city's outbreak of deadly cholera. There was no cure, and healthy Londoners were struck dead almost overnight. The disease wasn't hitting the countryside, and it was spotty in London. Some areas were hit hard, while others had only a few cases. John Snow, a physician, painstakingly plotted the outbreak, noting on a map of London where each victim had lived. As he studied the map, it became apparent that the victims were clustered around certain wells. Snow speculated that some wells were contaminated and that if they were shut down, the epidemic could be halted. He removed the pump handle from one well in an area where 500 people had died in ten days. The cholera was stopped in its tracks, defeated not by medicine but by medical sleuthing.

Today medical researchers are trying to tease out more of these intricate connections between human activities and disease. One conclusion that we will be stressing in the coming chapter on the environment (Chapter 14) is that "everything is connected to everything else." Human activities, the environment, and disease are an example of this principle.

Based on Cooper 2002; Lloyd 2006.

in time, a physical condition such as pregnancy can be considered a natural condition, and at another time it can be considered a medical matter. Similarly, what is considered to be the cause of health problems goes beyond biology. The health problems of coal miners were once viewed as the result of some men's "weakness," but were later redefined as a disease caused by environmental conditions.

The Social Organization of Medicine as a Source of Problems

The second part of this social problem is the social organization of medicine. We'll review various aspects of this part of the problem later in this chapter, but for now let's consider medical costs, cesarean births, and the quality of medical care.

AN EXPLOSION IN MEDICAL COSTS. As we all know, it's expensive to visit a doctor, but it wasn't always this way. If you want to see how little it used to cost to have a baby, look at Figure 10-1. The total bill of $113.85 in 1962 included three days in the hospital for the mother, her anesthetic, the lab fees, medicines, dressings, delivery room, nursery, even the circumcision of her son. Because of inflation, the dollar today buys what 19 cents would have bought in 1962. If you had a baby today at 1962's medical costs, even after adjusting for inflation, your hospital bill would run $730.

Figure 10-2 provides another illustration of how medical costs have soared. In 1960, the nation's medical bill was $27 billion, but by 2006 it had exploded to $2.1 trillion,

FIGURE 10-1 Hospital Bill for Childbirth, 1962

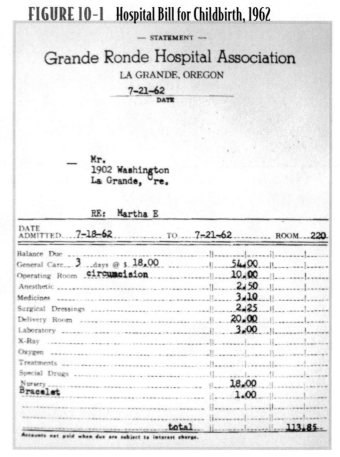

FIGURE 10-2 The Nation's Medical Bill: Soaring Costs

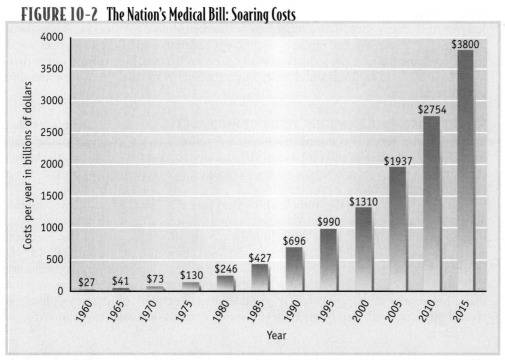

Note: Year 2010 is an estimate by the U.S. Centers for Medicare and Medicaid Services. The source also contains an estimate for 2015, to which I added a moderate increase.

Source: By the author. Based on *Statistical Abstract of the United States* 2006:Table 118.

Part of our new health consciousness includes changed attitudes toward people with disabilities—and the attitudes of people with disabilities toward themselves. Shown here are members of the U.S. team that competes in the paralympics wheelchair rugby.

78 times higher. During this time, the cost of the average goods we buy increased a little over six times. If medical costs had increased at the same rate as the average inflation, and we take into account that our country's population increased by 60 percent, the nation's annual medical bill would be about $260 billion, one-eighth of what it is now.

Reasons for the Explosion in Costs ■ Why did the nation's medical bill explode? First, as the standard of living improved, people lived longer. As a result of longer lives, there are many more older people in our population—and older people require more medical treatment than others. Three other factors also contributed to this explosion in medical costs: the development of expensive technology accompanied by the patients' demand for the latest treatment; a preoccupation with last-minute heroic intervention rather than with the prevention of illness and disease; and the view that medical care is a commodity to be sold for a profit.

MEDICINE FOR PROFIT: A TWO-TIER SYSTEM OF MEDICAL CARE. Medicine for profit is called a *fee-for-service system.* This means that physicians collect a fee for each service they perform. Just like mechanics and plumbers, the more services that physicians sell, the higher their profit. The fee-for-service system makes health care a commodity to be sold, not a right that people have.

This has led to a **two-tier system of medical care:** One kind goes to those who can afford it, and another kind goes to those who cannot. You might want to review the opening vignette of Chapter 7 (page 209). Julie Treadman, who is featured in that vignette, was at the lower end of this two-tier system. Refused admission to one hospital, she was transferred with her dead baby to another. Because we treat health care as a commodity to be sold to the highest bidder, our medical care ranges from the finest in the world at major universities to that provided by an underground network of unlicensed, foreign-trained physicians who can barely understand their patients and who have flunked their U.S. exams.

MEDICINE FOR PROFIT: CESAREAN DELIVERY. Consider our opening vignette: Do you think that Kathie's physician created a crisis so that cesarean surgery would be "required" and she could earn a larger fee? This is unlikely. But some physicians really are that crass, and

FIGURE 10-3 The Growth in Cesarean Births

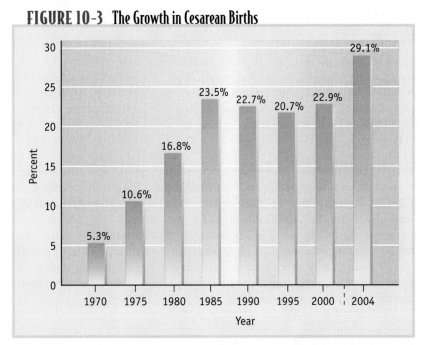

Source: By the author. Based on *Statistical Abstract of the United States* 1990:Tables 88, 89; 2000:Table 90; 2007:Table 86.

they perform unnecessary surgery to increase their profits. As shown in Figure 10-3, in 1970 about 1 of 19 babies was delivered by cesarean section. Now the total is 1 of every 3 or 4 (29 percent).

Why have Cesarean Births Increased? ■ Have women in the United States become less healthy than they used to be, and therefore less able to deliver babies naturally? After all, today's rate of cesarean births is more than *five* times higher than it used to be, and there has to be some explanation. There is no reason to make the assumption that today's women are less healthy, however, for they are living longer now than they did in the 1960s. The answer, then, must have something to do with the medical profession, with its approach to childbirth. In some hospitals, for example, the percentage of cesarean births is *five* times that in other hospitals (Kilborn 1998). Then, too, there is this interesting finding: In Puerto Rico, the rate of cesarean delivery is 45 percent of all births—yet the rate among Puerto Rican women who give birth on the U.S. mainland is the same as that of other women ("Rates of . . ." 2006). The difference is not the mothers, but how medicine is practiced in different areas.

To better understand the increase in cesarean births, we should note that the number has risen despite their carrying greater risks for the mother. Compared with women who give birth vaginally, women who have cesarean births have a higher death rate, have to stay in the hospital longer, and are more likely to be rehospitalized after childbirth ("Rates of . . ." 2006). Finally, and most significantly, *most cesarean deliveries are medically unnecessary.*

Then why are so many U.S. births by C-section? You might think that being able to charge a lot more for such births motivates doctors to encourage them. Certainly, this is a major factor, and the income of obstetricians (doctors who specialize in childbirth) jumped as they performed more cesarean deliveries. Their income has increased so much that, with the exception of anesthesiologists and surgeons, it is higher than that of all the other medical specialties ("Physicians and Surgeons" 2006).

This is just part of the picture. Perhaps equally significant is that cesarean births *allow doctors to take control* of the delivery process. Instead of being called at midnight or 3 A.M.—and no one likes this—the doctor can decide when the baby will be born. *Both* convenience and higher profits? You can see how this can motivate doctors to do C-sections.

Because these births are designed to fit the physician's schedule, more births now occur on Tuesday than any other day of the week.

Medical Technology ■ In addition to the motivations to perform cesarean surgery that come from the medical profession, medical technology is also a cause. Almost all U.S. women who give birth do so in a hospital, and almost all of these women are attached to a fetal monitor prior to delivery. This monitor sets off an alarm when the fetus is in distress, which can call for a cesarean delivery. Almost all such distress signals are false (Beckett 2005).

A Feminist Controversy ■ Cesarean birth has become not only a social issue, but also cause for controversy among feminists. The central issue is the relative power of women (Beckett 2005). Some say that cesarean delivery takes power over childbirth away from women and places it in the hands of doctors. This was the case with Kathie Persall in our opening vignette. Some feminists, in contrast, take the opposite view. They say that cesarean delivery can empower women. They point out that it isn't always the physician who decides that a woman will have a cesarean delivery: Women also tell their doctors how they want to deliver their children. Because this argument is rooted in deep-seated ideology, it is likely to continue for some time.

The Scope of the Problem

To better understand the scope of the problem, we will look first at aspects of physical illness, then consider issues that pertain to mental illness.

Physical Illness as a Social Problem

LIFE EXPECTANCY AND INFANT MORTALITY. A key measure of a nation's health is life expectancy at birth. In the United States, this measure has been rising for over a century, and for those born today it now stands at about 75 years for males and 81 years for females (*Statistical Abstract* 2006:Table 96). These are national averages, however, and they conceal as much as they reveal. As with so many other conditions in our

In the United States, health care is a commodity to be sold. The result is a two-tier system of medical care—one for those who can pay, another for those who cannot. Shown here are two waiting rooms for medical patients, one way to illustrate the social class difference in medical care.

society, life expectancy is related to income: Those who have more money live longer. In addition, life expectancy is related to race-ethnicity, with Asian Americans living the longest, whites next, and African Americans and Native Americans dying at the youngest ages. Then there is also the matter of geography, for where you live also makes a difference. The extremes are Asian American women in Bergen County, New Jersey, who, on average, live to see their 91st birthday, and Native Americans in South Dakota who, on average, die before they reach their 59th birthday (Murray et al. 2006).

While our life expectancy has been rising, our infant mortality rate has been falling. The *infant mortality rate* (of each thousand babies, the number who die before their first birthday) is one of the most accurate measures of a group's health conditions: It reflects the quality of nutrition, the health of mothers and babies, and the quality of health care. In 1960, the U.S. rate was 26 deaths per 1,000 births. Now it has dropped to just 6.6 per 1,000 births (*Statistical Abstract* 1990:Table 110; 2006:Table 1318). As the Social Map below shows, infant deaths are not distributed evenly across the United States. The range is so broad that it is just 4.4 in Maine and Vermont but 10.3 in Louisiana and Mississippi. As you can see from this map, the states with the highest death rates cluster in the Southeast, and those with the lowest rates cluster in the North and West. This, again, shows the *social* basis of health, illness, and even death.

Considering that our life expectancy is increasing and our infant mortality is dropping, we can conclude that the United States has no *health* crisis. (It does have a *health care* crisis, however, which we shall discuss.) There are health problems, to be sure, and some are severe—cancer, AIDS, suicide, and medical problems from drug abuse. Tremendous battles have been won against most infectious diseases, however, and many people survive even cancer and AIDS. Overall, the nation's physical health has been improving.

All of the Least Industrialized Nations have higher infant mortality rates and a shorter life expectancy than we do (*Statistical Abstract* 2006:Table 131). Life expectancy in some of these nations is less than 50 years, and some infant mortality rates run 15 to 20 times higher than ours. That life expectancy and infant mortality improve with industrialization is another example of how *social* conditions affect the *biology* of health.

FIGURE 10-4 The Geography of Death: Infant Mortality Rates

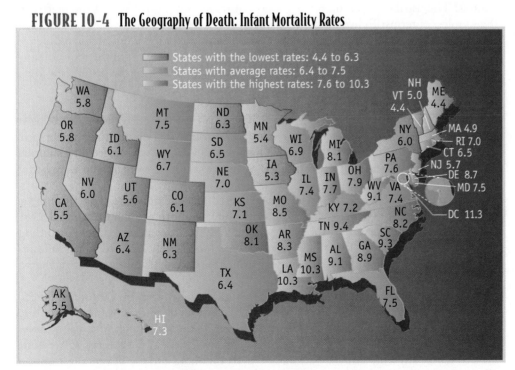

Source: By the author. Based on *Statistical Abstract of the United States* 2006:Table 105.

FIGURE 10-5 Infant Mortality Rates

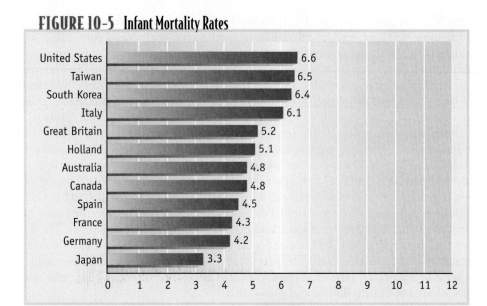

Note: These totals are infant deaths (babies who die before their first birthday) per 1,000 live births. For some reason, seven countries that had a lower rate of infant mortality than the United States have been dropped from the source. These countries are Belgium, Cuba, Czech Republic, Greece, Portugal, Sweden, and Switzerland.

Source: By the author. Based on *Statistical Abstract of the United States* 2006:Table 1318.

Although our infant mortality rate has improved so greatly, many medical experts still find it a cause for concern. To see why, look at Figure 10-5, which compares our rate with nations that have a better record of saving babies than we do. The cold numbers in this figure translate into needless deaths. If our rate were the same as Japan's, half of the 28,000 U.S. infants who die each year would live (*Statistical Abstract* 2006:Table 72). Our overall life expectancy (males and females combined) of 77.3 years is also less than the life expectancy in most of the nations shown on Figure 10-5. Japan, with a life expectancy of 81.0 years, holds the world record.

Why are infant mortality and life expectancy rates better in some other industrialized nations? The usual explanation is the poverty of many Americans. To put the matter in the simplest of terms: To live on the edge of survival is not good for people's health. Poor people are sick more often. They experience more stress, have more emotional problems, suffer more accidents and violence, and don't eat as well. Poverty lies at the root of many health problems, and our advances in medical care are not reaching the poor to the same extent that they are reaching those who are better off.

LIFESTYLE. Although poverty is important, lifestyle is even more significant. Sociologist Ruben Rumbaut and geographer John Weeks (1994) found that despite their higher rates of poverty, unemployment, and welfare, Vietnamese and Cambodian refugees in California had lower infant mortality rates than did U.S.-born California women who were better off financially.

This puzzled the researchers, for they expected just the opposite. They found the answer not in biology but in *social* conditions. The U.S.-born women had gained more weight during pregnancy, and they were more likely to have abused drugs, including alcohol. In addition, the U.S.-born women were more likely to have what these researchers called a "surgically scarred uterus" from abortion. The immigrant women had fewer abortions.

It is difficult to overstate the importance of lifestyle in determining health and illness, for *lifestyle is the major cause of illness and death.* To mention the most obvious: Overeating and lack of exercise lead to heart attacks and strokes. So does smoking, which also causes cancer. We reviewed the effects of smoking and alcohol abuse in Chapter 4, so we don't need to repeat anything but the bottom line here: Smoking and the heavy consumption of alcohol harm essential body organs and are part of the *social* nature of physical illness.

Sexually transmitted diseases (STDs) also illustrate how lifestyle is related to health. To again state the obvious: Singles who practice abstinence run zero risk of STDs, as do couples who have sex exclusively with one another. All others are at risk, a risk that increases with the amount of promiscuity and unprotected sex. As with catching a cold, chance also plays a role—being in the wrong place at the wrong time or, in this case, being with the wrong person at the wrong time. Although the greater someone's promiscuity and unprotected sex, the greater that person's chances of acquiring an STD, some have contracted gonorrhea, syphilis, and even AIDS after their first act of sexual intercourse. We shall examine the relationship of AIDS and lifestyle later.

HEROIC MEDICINE. At the center of our social problem of physical illness and medical care is this contradiction: We live in an age of *chronic* illnesses (that is, lingering and ongoing medical problems), but our medical services are geared for *acute* illnesses (those that have a sudden onset, a sharp rise, and a short duration). Our approach to cancer, heart disease, and other chronic disorders is heroic, hospital based, and expensive. Intervening at advanced stages of a disease requires costly medical teams, highly trained specialists, technical equipment, and costly drugs. Patients who have serious illnesses want the best care, and the medical world has taught us that "the best" means complex, technical, and expensive. By promoting exotic "cures," companies that manufacture medical equipment and drugs feed this surge in cost.

Prevention lacks the drama and heroics of such interventions as open-heart surgery, but it is much more effective. We could save untold suffering and lives through public health measures that reduce pollution, smoking, and alcohol abuse and that increase healthier eating and exercise. Such efforts at prevention, however, account for only a small fraction of what we spend on heroic measures to deal with health problems *after* people are stricken with them.

EMERGENCY ROOMS AS DOCTORS' OFFICES. Our emphasis on specialists and hospital care has also led to a shortage of primary care doctors who treat routine problems. Consequently, for their basic medical needs some patients go to hospital emergency rooms, which stay open day and night and do not require appointments. These services, however, are more expensive than office care; treating a fever or a splinter runs three to five times more. Insurance companies have rebelled at using hospital emergency rooms as doctors' offices and refuse to pay for routine treatment given there. This has created an ironic situation: Many insured patients now have to prove that their visit to an emergency room was an emergency, but with laws that prohibit hospitals from turning away patients who cannot pay, the poor who show up in emergency rooms but have no insurance are treated. States like California, Texas, and Arizona, which are spending billions of dollars each year on the medical treatment of undocumented migrants, have become vocal critics of these laws.

UNEVEN DISTRIBUTION OF MEDICAL SERVICES. A problem with the medical delivery system is its uneven distribution of medical services. Some areas revel in an abundance of physicians, while in others it is difficult to even find a doctor. Consider this extreme: Beverly Hills, California, has one doctor for every 275 residents, while just down the road is Bell Gardens, where poor people live. They have one doctor for every 27,000 residents, worse even than Haiti (Olivo 1999). The Social Map on the next page shows the national distribution of physicians.

Mental Illness as a Social Problem

MEASURING MENTAL ILLNESS. Some experts conclude that mental illness has become more common because people today experience higher stress, and their social support system (family, friends, place in the community) has grown weaker. Such an answer might be right, but, frankly, we don't even know if mental illness is more common today. We have no firm measurements of how much mental illness there used to be, so we can't compare that number with the prevalence of mental illness today. The measurement problem is actually worse than this: We don't even know how much mental illness there is today,

FIGURE 10-6   Where the Doctors Are

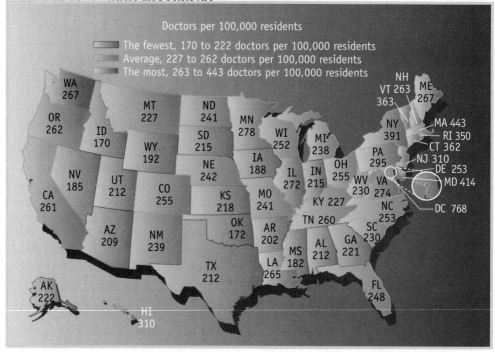

Source: By the author. Based on *Statistical Abstract of the United States* 2006:Table 153.

much less in the past. Any total you have ever read is a speculation. Experts even disagree on how to determine that someone is mentally ill, much less how to classify that person's mental illness. We can dispense, then, with the argument that mental illness is more common today, as there is no way of knowing one way or the other.

THE SOCIAL NATURE OF MENTAL ILLNESS. Whatever mental illness is—and this is a matter of dispute, with some critics of the mental health establishment even denying that mental illness exists (Szasz 1961; Caplan 2006)—we do know that it has a strong social basis. That is, people who experience more stress are more likely to also experience what are known as mental problems. Mental problems, of course, would be part of the objective conditions of a social problem. Where are the subjective concerns that make mental illness a *social* problem? This is the focus of the Issues in Social Problems box on page 332–333. From this box, you can see why even the intensely personal act of suicide can be part of a *social* problem.

A TWO-TIER SYSTEM OF MENTAL HEALTH DELIVERY. Just as problems of physical illness have two parts—the illnesses and the medical delivery system to treat them—so do problems of mental illness. Let's see how the medical delivery system is part of this problem. Here is something I observed when I did research on the homeless:

> Standing to the side, I watched as the elderly nude man, looking confused, struggled to put on his clothing. The man had ripped the wires out of the homeless shelter's main electrical box and then, with the police in pursuit, had run from one darkened room to another.
>
> I asked the officers where they were going to take the man, and they replied, "To Malcolm Bliss" (the state hospital). When I commented, "I guess he'll be there for quite a while," an officer replied, "Probably for just a day or two. We picked him up last week—he was crawling under cars at a traffic light—and they let him out in two days."

The police explained that to be admitted as a long-term patient one must be a danger to others or to oneself. Visualizing this old man crawling under cars in traffic and risking electrocution by ripping out electrical wires with his bare hands, I marveled at the definition of "danger" that the psychiatrists must be using.

Here in front of me, the two-tier medical system was stripped of its coverings. A middle-class or wealthy person would have received different treatment. Of course, such a person would not be in a shelter for the homeless in the first place.

Back in the 1970s, state mental hospitals discharged tens of thousands of seriously disturbed patients. The idea behind **deinstitutionalization,** as these discharges were called, was that these people could lead more normal lives in the community than they could in mental hospitals. The plan was to support them with medications and community mental health services. To save money, however, few of the planned community centers were ever built. Most patients were simply abandoned on the streets to fend for themselves. They did the best they could—living in fleabag hotels when they could afford it or in bus stations or cardboard boxes in back alleys. A few were sent back to mental hospitals when no one around could tolerate them; but most were left to wander the streets, no matter how bizarre their behavior.

I know that it is difficult to grasp that medical and governmental authorities would simply abandon disoriented mental patients on the streets, but they did precisely this. The unfeeling, cruel way that deinstitutionalization was carried out is illustrated by what occurred in Austin, Texas. Patients from the state mental hospital were loaded in a van and driven to Houston (so they wouldn't bother Austin residents). There they were dumped at the Greyhound bus station on skid row (Karlen and Burgower 1985).

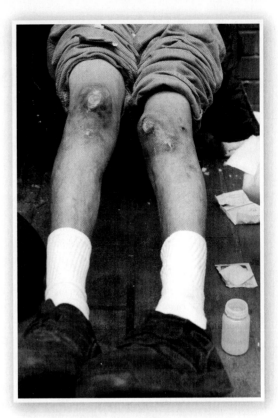

The homeless are the castoffs of postindustrial society. Unwanted and unneeded, they are left to wander the city streets and countryside. Only grudgingly are their needs attended to.

Looking at the Problem Theoretically

Let's look at how the three theoretical perspectives that we have been considering in this text apply to health, illness, and the practice of medicine.

Symbolic Interactionism

DETERMINING THE MEANING OF SYMPTOMS AND BEHAVIOR. As you will recall, symbolic interactionists study how people use language and other symbols to define social reality. When we self-diagnose, for example, we are trying to figure out what our symptoms mean. Should we go to bed, call a doctor, or just carry on with everyday life? To determine the meaning of some symptom, then, we use the symbols (or system of meaning) that our culture provides.

Because the different social classes and subcultures equip their members with distinct ways of thinking, people from different backgrounds make these decisions differently. People from the lower class, for example, are more likely to regard back pain as part of life. "This is what happens to people when they get a little older." People from the middle class, in contrast, are more likely to view back pain as a health problem that needs to be treated by medical professionals. Similarly, to many people, cold or flu symptoms indicate that they should go to the doctor to "get a shot," but to adherents of alternative medicine those same symptoms indicate a need for drinking more water and taking more vitamin C and other antioxidants. In short, symptoms don't force their meaning on us, but we use cultural and subcultural symbols to determine what the symptoms mean.

THE SIGNIFICANCE OF DEFINITIONS. Just as social classes and subcultural groups perceive health and illness differently, so groups compete to get their view of health accepted. This, in turn, changes the way we view health, illness, and medicine. For

Issues in Social Problems
SUICIDE: THE MAKING AND UNMAKING OF A SOCIAL PROBLEM

Suicide—deliberately drawing a razor blade across one's arteries, putting a gun in one's mouth and pulling the trigger, or swallowing a lethal dose of pills—chills the imagination. As sociologist Emile Durkheim (1897/1951) documented more than 100 years ago, suicide is more than an individual inclination or a sign of personal problems. Suicide, concluded Durkheim, is based on social conditions. Durkheim drew this conclusion when he noticed that countries have different suicide rates and that year after year a country's rate remains about the same. Look at Figure 10-7. From one year to the next, these rates show little change. You can expect 30,000 to 32,000 Americans to kill themselves this year, and the next year, and the year after that (*Statistical Abstract* 1994:Table 125; 2006:Table 109).

The funeral of a young man who committed suicide.

From Figure 10-7, you can also see that in each country men have a much higher suicide rate. In the United States at least, many more women than men attempt suicide, but more men succeed at it. This is often interpreted as meaning that the women's attempts are more a "cry for help," whereas the men are more serious about accomplishing the act. This assumption is likely true, but there is also another factor: Men are more likely to use guns to kill themselves, whereas women are more likely to take pills. Guns obviously allow people less time to change their mind or to let someone intervene.

FIGURE 10-7 International Suicide Rates

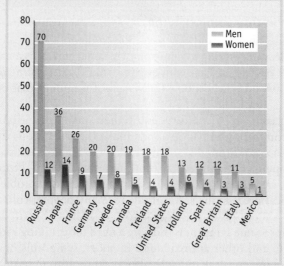

Note: The rate is per 100,000 people, as of 2003.

Source: By the author. Based on "Suicide Rates" 2004.

Suicide illustrates the making and unmaking of a social problem. In the 1960s, mental health professionals began to publicize the idea that suicide was a national problem. There were no major changes in objective conditions at this time, but subjective concerns had grown. The National Institute of Mental Health (NIMH) took these new subjective concerns to heart and began to finance an innovative idea—suicide prevention centers. The idea of swift intervention when people contemplate or attempt suicide was appealing, and across the nation suicide prevention centers were established to conquer what had become a social problem.

The suicide prevention centers failed. The suicide rate didn't budge. For example, today suicide is the third most common cause of death among 15-to-24-year-olds in the United States, about the same as it was back then (*Statistical Abstract* 2006:Table 108).

To prevent suicide, a major problem is managing patients who are known to be suicidal. This is difficult because psychiatrists receive inadequate training in how to treat suicidal patients. Some psychiatrists even contribute to their patient's suicide through a pattern of engagement and abandonment. The therapist initially responds to a suicidal patient with sympathy and concern, and the troubled individual begins to depend on the therapist as a helper. As treatment continues, the patient grows not only more dependent but also more demanding. Disliking this pressure, the therapist pulls back, calling the intense dependency "infantile regression." The therapist becomes less accessible just when the patient is most vulnerable. Feeling abandoned, the patient commits suicide (Light 1973).

These treatment failures and the lack of new techniques kept the suicide prevention centers from fulfilling their optimistic promise. Gradually, suicide as a social problem faded from the limelight. The government reduced its funding, and most of the suicide prevention centers closed. Some kept their doors open by broadening their focus to general crisis intervention.

IN SUM

Suicide illustrates how social problems are socially constructed. As Figure 10-7 shows, our suicide rate is not exceptional. Compared with other industrialized nations, our rate falls in the lower middle. Today's suicide rate is also about the same as it used to be. (The overall rate, males and females combined, was 12.5 in 1960 and also 12.5 in 1990. Since then, for reasons unknown we have had a significant decline, and today's overall rate is 11.0 [*Statistical Abstract* 2006:Table 110.]) Suicide became a social problem in the 1960s and 1970s not because of an increase in suicide but because of political activity that increased subjective concerns: Mental health professionals and government officials used the mass media to arouse the public. With the resulting public outcry about the "epidemic" of suicide, suicide prevention centers were invented. Today we take our rate for granted, and no longer consider suicide a pressing social problem.

example, the American Psychiatric Association (APA) used to list homosexuality as a mental illness and had specialists who treated it. Homosexuals objected to being defined as ill. As homosexuals became more of an organized group, they lobbied and put intense pressure on the APA to drop homosexuality as a mental illness. Their efforts succeeded, and since 1973 the APA has not classified homosexuality as a mental illness. Establishing official definitions is a two-way street: Just as medicine and psychiatry can declassify a behavior that had been considered an illness, so they can declare other behaviors to be illnesses. Asserting that alcohol abuse is a disease (not "drunkenness") is an example, as is defining children's unruly behavior as a symptom of "attention deficit disorder" (see Chapter 4).

How we define health and illness has an impact on how we see the world and on our behavior. If we define alcohol abuse as a disease, we perceive an alcohol abuser as sick, but if we define this person's behavior as drunkenness, we perceive him or her as a drunkard. With such contrasting ways of viewing reality, the behavior that is thought appropriate in response to these definitions also differs: If alcohol abuse is defined as a disease, sympathy and help might be viewed as appropriate responses, but if it is defined as drunkenness, condemnation or humor might be viewed as appropriate. As with the classification of homosexuality by the American Psychiatric Association, a political process (the relative power of groups) sometimes determines what symbols we will use. In short, definitions are not inherent in human behavior; determining what symbols are appropriate to apply to some situation develops out of social interaction. We use the symbols available to us, and their use helps to determine whether we view something as a problem and what we think are appropriate ways to deal with it.

DIFFERENT REFERRAL NETWORKS. As they study how meaning is determined in the practice of medicine, symbolic interactionists analyze interactions between doctors and patients. In classic research, Eliot Freidson (1961) examined how patients and doctors use different frames of reference. Patients come from a **lay referral network,** a set of friends, relatives, neighbors, and co-workers with whom they talk over their medical problems. This network helps them decide which doctor to see—or even whether to see a doctor at all. In this lay referral network, a physician's knowledge is considered important, but so is the physician's personality. People want someone who shows an interest in them; they don't want to become some faceless patient on a cold medical assembly line. Also important is the amount of confidence that the doctor exhibits. Doctors who show uncertainty create fears, while those who appear confident instill confidence in their patients. People also want to be sure they won't come away empty-handed: They want to get a shot or a prescription, not just advice to get more rest or to go on a diet.

The physician, in contrast, uses a **professional referral network,** one made up of other physicians and medical professionals. Here the meaning of "doing doctoring" is different, for medical schools put the emphasis on organs, symptoms, and diseases apart from the person. Sympathy for the patient and understanding an illness from the patient's point of view are less important to doctors than determining what and why some organ is malfunctioning and prescribing appropriate treatment (Haas and Shaffir 1993; Conrad 1995).

You can see, then, how the patients' and physicians' referral networks produce definitions so contradictory that the expectations of patients and doctors can come crashing into one another.

DEPERSONALIZATION. One consequence of the professional referral network is that some doctors treat patients not as persons, but as objects with sick organs, a process referred to as **depersonalization.** Patients detest being depersonalized, for it strips away their humanity. To doctors who see patients as objects, the psychological and aesthetic costs of procedures are of little importance. This is what happened with Kathie Persall's cesarean surgery, and it is one reason that midwifery has reemerged as an appealing alternative for delivering children. Because depersonalization breaks a social bond between patient and physician, patients have a greater tendency to sue their doctors. The threat of malpractice suits, in turn, has produced **defensive medicine;** that is, physicians order lab tests and consultations that may not be needed, in order to leave a "paper trail" that shows they did everything reasonable in case they are sued.

PROBLEMS IN COMMUNICATION. These different backgrounds and expectations often make it difficult for patients and physicians to communicate with one another. In an age of specialized medicine characterized by brief encounters between people from different walks of life, doctors often neglect the personal or emotional needs of their patients. Their long, strange-sounding words don't help the matter:

> When Mrs. J., a 47-year-old Queens schoolteacher, was told in a routine examination that she had a "uterine fibroid" and needed a hysterectomy (removal of her uterus), the only thing she could think of was "tumor." She asked the doctor if it was cancerous, and he frightened her more by saying, "Sometimes when we go in, we find them to be cancerous." Fearing

cancer of the uterus, she consulted two other physicians and learned that the fibroid was small, common in middle-aged women, and soon likely to shrink on its own as she went into menopause. (Larned 1977:195–196)

On the lighter side, one patient was unhappy after being put on a low-salt diet. As if that weren't bad enough, when she was hospitalized she was further dismayed to find that she was also put on a low-sodium diet (Silver 1979:4).

Functionalism

WHO BENEFITS? Because functionalists assume that customs or social institutions persist only if they fulfill social needs, this perspective raises some interesting questions. Whose needs are met by a health care system that is hospital based and oriented toward acute illnesses? Who benefits from allowing environmental diseases to flourish? What are the benefits of depersonalizing patients such as Kathie Persall, of making childbirth a rigorous medical procedure?

FEE-FOR-SERVICE MEANS PROFITS. Let's start with the obvious: It is difficult for doctors to make money from healthy people. Patients who get well quickly also mean less profit. But an expensive, hospital-based system oriented toward acute illness—now that's a dream come true. Everyone—physicians, medical suppliers, hospitals, and drug companies—makes money from giving patients intensive care. Each year, about one of every eight Americans is admitted to a hospital and stays an average of six days (*Statistical Abstract* 2006:Table 163). The average daily cost is shown in Figure 10-8. The shorter bars on this figure represent what a day's stay in the hospital would cost if medical costs had not outpaced inflation. This figure illustrates the skyrocketing costs of medical care better than words can say.

Despite feeble pretensions to the contrary, profits, not health care, are the engine that drives the U.S. health care system. Our fee-for-service system means that the more services doctors sell and the higher price they charge, the more they earn. One result is unnecessary surgery, such as *most* of the cesarean surgeries mentioned earlier (see Figure 10-3 on page 325). Another example is hysterectomies, which we will review in the next section on conflict theory.

Physicians, nurses, and investors in the U.S. health care industry, then, benefit from our fee-for-service system. Patients benefit, too, however, for this system lets them shop around. They can choose which doctor to see and what services to purchase. That this system is functional for patients is indicated by our rising life expectancy and our decreasing infant mortality.

A SELF-CORRECTING SYSTEM. There are problems with a fee-for-service system, of course, and I've mentioned some of them, but functionalists point out that the system is self-correcting. For example, although the medical system is oriented to acute illnesses, after environmental health problems were recognized as serious, the government passed antipollution laws and formed the Environmental Protection Agency (EPA). Medical schools also responded, developing training programs in environmental medicine. Likewise, runaway costs have led to cost controls: HMOs (discussed later), new forms of medical care such as outpatient surgery, and limitations on the number of days Medicare and Medicaid pay for hospitalization. In short, functionalists view our fee-for-service health care as a system that responds to the shifting needs of the nation.

THE GLOBAL LEVEL. Functionalists also analyze functions and dysfunctions of medicine on a global level. Exporting modern Western medicine to the Least Industrialized Nations provides an excellent example. The vaccines, immunizations, and medicines sent to these nations were functional: They reduced those nations' death rates. But they were also dysfunctional: They helped to produce conditions that allowed the populations of these

FIGURE 10-8 How Much Does It Cost to Stay in the Hospital? One Day's Cost Compared to Inflation

How the cost of an average day in a hospital compares with the cost of buying the same products over time.

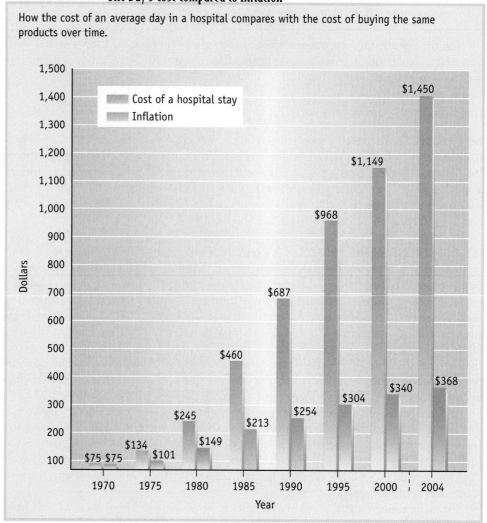

Source: By the author. Based on *Statistical Abstract of the United States* 1998:Table 137; 2007:Table 163.

nations to surge. The populations grew so fast that they outpaced the nations' food production, leading to mass starvation and political upheaval.

Conflict Theory

Conflict theorists shake their heads in disbelief when they hear anyone refer to the U.S. medical system as self-correcting. They view our patterns of illness and health care as the outcome of clashes between interest groups—which the most powerful have won. They argue that the poor are sicker than others because they have lost the struggle for the better income, education, food, housing, jobs, and medical services.

MEDICAID. What about Medicaid, which benefits the poor? Conflict theorists see this program, too, as the result of conflict. In the 1960s, resentment about the treatment of the poor had grown so vocal that politicians were forced to do something. With these pressures accompanied by a growing sentiment favoring socialized medicine, the U.S. medical establishment felt that its profitable fee-for-service system was threatened. Physicians used their union, the American Medical Association (AMA), to campaign to preserve the fee-for-service system. Viewing Medicaid as a first step to socialized medicine, the AMA fought its passage tooth and nail. Caught between the public's demand for change and the intense lobbying of the AMA, Congress designed Medicaid to satisfy the public's criticism yet to provide profit for doctors. To consider, as functionalists would, that Medicaid was passed because health care providers wanted the poor to get free medical services is naive. It ignores the millions of dollars that the AMA spent lobbying to *prevent* the federal government from funding health insurance for the poor.

COLLIDING INTERESTS OF DOCTORS AND PATIENTS. Conflict theorists also have a different view of the doctor-patient relationship. Those with a Marxist perspective emphasize that patients and doctors form two classes in regard to medicine—those who control it and those who receive it. To maximize their incomes, physicians try to control the doctor-patient relationship. It is no accident that physicians commonly fail to explain their procedures and diagnoses but instead simply say a few words and send patients on their way. This is one way that physicians try to keep the oppressed class of patients ignorant and dependent (Waitzkin and Waterman 1974). In a capitalist system of production for profit, the alienation of patient and physician is like that of owner and worker, an inevitable result when the interests of the one (making a profit) oppose those of the other (getting well at the least expense).

When Western medicine was exported to the Least Industrialized Nations, life expectancy there increased dramatically. One reason was the sharp drop in the death rate of children. Shown here are medical workers in Nigeria as they deliver medical services to a low-rent district.

WOMEN'S REPRODUCTIVE ORGANS. Sociologists who have done participant observation of doctors report a bias *against* women's reproductive organs. Sociologist Sue Fisher (1986), for example, was surprised to hear surgeons recommend total hysterectomy (the removal of both the uterus and the ovaries) even when no cancer was present. She found that male doctors regard the uterus and ovaries as a "potentially disease-producing" organ—useless and unnecessary after the childbearing years. Some surgeons routinely recommend this profitable operation for every woman who has finished bearing children. *Most* of the 600,000 hysterectomies performed each year in the United States are unnecessary (Broder et al. 2000). It is no wonder that feminists refer to hysterectomies as a "war on the womb" (Fisher 1986).

Many surgeons view hysterectomies as a money machine. To increase their profits, they drum up business by "selling" the operation. Here is how one resident explained it to sociologist Diana Scully (1994):

> You have to look for your surgical procedures; you have to go after patients. Because no one is crazy enough to come and say, "Hey, here I am. I want you to operate on me." You have to sometimes convince the patient that she is really sick—if she is, of course [laughs], and that she is better off with a surgical procedure.

Some surgeons try to convince women to "buy" the operation they are offering for sale by scaring them. They tell a woman that her fibroids *might* turn into cancer. This statement is often sufficient, for the woman can picture herself lying in a casket, her tearful family inconsolable after the loss of their wife and mother. What the surgeon does *not* say is the rest of the truth—that the fibroids are not likely to turn into cancer and that several nonsurgical treatments are available.

IN SUM From a Marxist conflict perspective, the entire medical system is an industry whose goals are profit and power. To reach these goals, its practitioners exploit sick people (Reynolds 1973). Marxists argue that their perspective best explains why medical care for the rich is so much better than that for the poor: Health care is *not* the goal of the U.S. medical system—the goal is profit for those who practice it. Physicians are businesspeople, patients are customers, and health care is the commodity they sell. Health care is like cars: Some people can afford new convertibles, but others can afford only old junkers.

The government pays an increasing proportion of the nation's health care bill because government in a capitalist society perpetuates and underwrites the interests of capitalist industries—including medicine. Conflict theorists argue that health care should be a right of *all* citizens and that people's illnesses and diseases should never be exploited for profit.

Research Findings

Afteer a brief overview of physical health problems in the United States, we will concentrate on social inequalities of health and health care. We will discuss inequalities by age, race, and social class; examine our two-class system of medicine; and consider how health insurance creates its own inequalities. We will also discuss social inequalities in mental illness.

An Overview of Physical Health Problems

HISTORICAL CHANGES IN HEALTH PROBLEMS. Figure 10-9 on the next page compares today's ten leading causes of death with those of 1900. This figure makes the *social* nature of death evident. As you can see, only six of the ten leading causes of death are the same. As a symbolic interactionist would point out, these categories of death are arbitrary, and by using different classifications we would produce a different list. In fact, the CDC (Centers for Disease Control and Prevention) has revised these categories almost a dozen times since 1900. To see how arbitrary the categories are, note the ninth leading cause of death in 1900. Today's definition of senility is obviously different from the one used in 1900. Today, senility doesn't kill anyone, but it must have been a raging menace back then. Actually, senility seems to have been the 1900 catch-all category for old age. When old people didn't die from diarrhea or pneumonia or something else recognizable, doctors lumped their deaths together and said they were due to senility.

As arbitrary as these lists are, you can note that several of the top killers—heart diseases, cancer, and accidents, which made the top ten lists in both 1900 and 2003—are caused primarily by people's behavior or by environmental pollution. You can also note that in 1900 smoking wasn't very common, and lung diseases didn't make the top ten list. At this point in time, in contrast, we are seeing the fatal results of all those cigarettes people smoked in earlier decades. Another behavioral cause of death, suicide, edged into the top ten during the 1990s. In some years when I produce Figure 10-9, suicide shows up as the tenth leading cause of death in the United States, while in other years it drops to number 11. These changes in leading causes of death reinforce the point made earlier about how health and illness are related to lifestyle and the environment.

THE INFECTIOUS DISEASES. Figure 10-9 also reveals how significant infectious diseases used to be. As you can see, a hundred years or so ago pneumonia was the number one killer, with tuberculosis (TB) close behind. Diarrhea was also a huge killer. Every family also feared polio, whooping cough, German measles, smallpox, and diphtheria. Then, during the first half of the twentieth century, these diseases receded, death rates plummeted, and life expectancy rose from 47 years to over 70. What happened?

Reasons for the Decline in Infectious Diseases ▪ The usual answer is that modern medicine wiped out these diseases. I do not want to detract from the many accomplishments of modern medicine, for most of us know someone who would not be alive today if it weren't for bypass surgery or some organ transplant. And drugs have played a significant role in treating some diseases, such as syphilis, bacterial pneumonia, and hypertension. Some vaccinations, too, such as the one for polio, have reduced deaths dramatically.

Most of the infectious killers of the nineteenth century, however, had been declining for decades *before* antibiotics, immunizations, or specific drugs had been developed (McKeown 1980). Although medical myth has it that new drugs and vaccinations

FIGURE 10-9 The Ten Leading Causes of Death in the United States

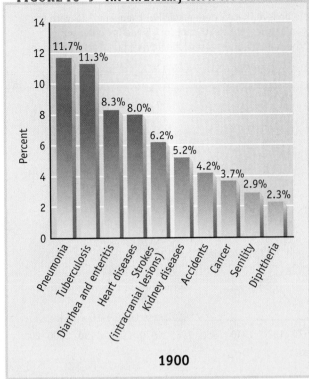

1900

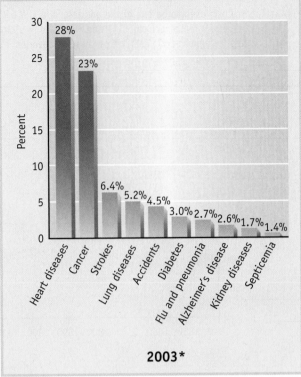

2003*

Note: Latest year available

Sources: By the author. Year 2003 is based on Centers for Disease Control 2006a; year 1900 is based on Centers for Disease Control 2006b.

conquered TB in the 1950s, as Figure 10-10 on the next page shows, TB had been declining since the 1800s. If modern medicine did not conquer the infectious diseases so feared by earlier generations of Americans, what did? The answer is not dramatic: cleaner public water supplies and improved social and economic conditions. Infectious killers declined as people became healthier and stronger from cleaner water, better and more food, and better housing.

The Resurgence of Infectious Diseases ■ Infectious diseases, however, have a way of fighting back. They can go underground and develop new strains that are resistant to known drugs and vaccines. The Technology and Social Problems box on page 341 discusses worldwide implications of this problem. Even TB has resurfaced with deadly strains. More people around the world (about 1.7 million) die of TB now than when the vaccine was discovered (Garrett 1999). Some strains have become resistant to *all* known treatment (Rosenthal 2006). Health officials in New York City so fear the possibility of an outbreak of tuberculosis that they order the arrest of TB patients who refuse treatment or who terminate care before their course of treatment is completed. They lock these patients in hospital rooms where guards sit at their door every hour of every day (Specter 1992). TB patients in other states who refuse treatment are also being arrested (Hench 2006).

The most feared infectious disease today, however, is HIV/AIDS. Let's look at how this disease is related to behavior.

How Disease Is Related to Behavior and Environment: The Case of HIV/AIDS

BACKGROUND. HIV/AIDS is an excellent example of the relationship between behavior, environment, and disease. This disease was first noted in male homosexuals. One person, Gaetan Dugas, an airline steward from Canada, played a key role in its rapid transmission, for he or one of his sex partners had sex with 40 of the first 248 AIDS cases reported in the United States (Shilts 1987). The disease then hit another group whose lifestyle also encouraged its transmission—intravenous drug users who shared needles. The third of the

FIGURE 10-10 The "Conquest" of Tuberculosis

Tuberculosis used to be one of the greatest killers. Many people believe that modern medicine "conquered" TB with the discovery of streptomycin in 1947 and a vaccine in 1954. As you can see, the death rate for TB had been declining steadily for almost 100 years before these discoveries. Many other infectious diseases "conquered" by modern medicine follow a similar pattern.

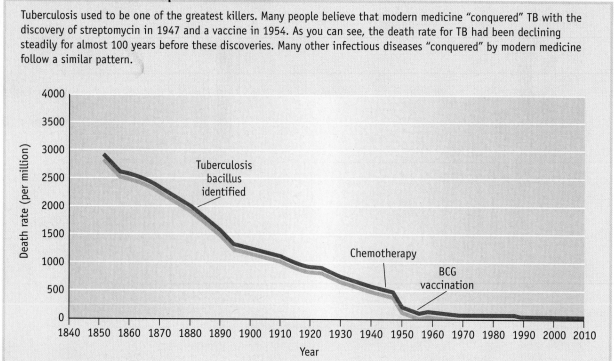

Source: McKeown 1980; *Statistical Abstract of the United States* 2006:Table 107.

groups that were the hardest hit represents an environmental risk: Hemophiliacs, who need regular blood transfusions, were exposed to the disease through contaminated blood. Lifestyle was also central to how the disease entered the general population; the bridge was prostitutes who had sex with intravenous drug users and with bisexual and heterosexual men. Lifestyle and environment continue to be significant: HIV/AIDS is more common among drug users who share needles and among people who have multiple sexual partners.

A GLOBAL EPIDEMIC. HIV/AIDS is a global epidemic, perhaps the worst in the history of the world. About 25 million people have died from this disease, about 40 million people around the world are infected now, and about 5 million more people will be infected this year (Lamptey et al. 2006). Of all regions in the world, sub-Saharan Africa has been hit the worst. There, HIV/AIDS is the leading cause of death. The primary reason that HIV/AIDS is so common in this region is the common practice of men having sex with prostitutes. In some African countries, HIV/AIDS is expected to wipe out half the teenagers. Hardest hit is Swaziland, where two of every five adults are infected with HIV/AIDS.

HIV/AIDS IN THE UNITED STATES. A combination of retroviral drugs, including protease inhibitors and reverse transcriptase inhibitors, has dropped yearly AIDS deaths in the United States from a high of 50,000 in 1995 to 14,000 now (*Statistical Abstract* 1998:Table 144; 2006:Table 108). The new drugs—at a cost of $20,000 per year per patient—prevent people who are infected with the HIV virus from developing full-blown AIDS and keep those who have the disease from dying from infections (such as the flu or pneumonia) that used to kill people who had HIV/AIDS. They do *not* prevent people from infecting others with HIV. With changed lifestyles, new infections have dropped to a third of what they were.

Figure 10-11 on page 342 shows how HIV/AIDS is related to race-ethnicity. The reason that these groups have different rates of HIV/AIDS is not genetic. No racial-ethnic group is more susceptible to HIV/AIDS because of biological factors. Rather, the reason is *social*. The members of some groups have higher rates of the three main ways by which HIV is transmitted: sharing needles when injecting drugs, having sex with multiple partners, and having unprotected (condomless) sex.

Technology and Social Problems
SUPERBUGS IN THE GLOBAL VILLAGE

Simon Sparrow, a 17-month old robust toddler, was just learning to feed himself. His family was startled out of their sleep one early morning when Simon let out a primal scream. They rushed Simon to the hospital, where he was diagnosed with a virus and asthma and sent home. Fifteen hours later, he was dead. (Chase 2006)

What killed Simon? It was a new strain of staph infection. This germ can penetrate bones and lungs, leaving abscesses that require surgery. Simon died so quickly that he was spared this suffering.

This new form (community-associated methicillin-resistant staphylococcus aureus, which, fortunately has a shortened name—CA-MRSA) has also cropped up in Japan, France, England, and other countries. Health authorities are uncertain how to treat CA-MRSA and the other drug-resistant bacteria that are appearing at various spots around the world.

Their fear is that someone, somewhere, will come down with a germ that is resistant to every antibiotic—that with global travel, in just a matter of days that strain will spread throughout the global village.

Following the discovery of penicillin in the 1940s came a series of effective microbe killers. By the 1970s, more than 100 antibiotics sat on pharmacy shelves. The war against microbes had been won, or so the medical industry thought. Researchers relaxed and stopped developing new antibiotics. Promising new drugs, already in development, were even canceled as superfluous.

In the presence of antibiotics, the weaker germs die off, but the stronger ones can mutate, survive, and proliferate. This is especially likely to happen if people do not complete the full course of their medical treatment and stop taking a drug when they feel better. The more that antibiotics are used and misused, the more that drug-resistant bugs proliferate (Chase 2006).

Are antibiotics misused? The Institute of Medicine reports that 20 to 50 percent of the 145 million prescriptions given to U.S. outpatients each year are unnecessary. The same goes for the 190 million doses of antibiotics given to hospital patients.

We all carry staphylococcus germs on our skin and in our nose. There they are harmless. When we get a scrape or cut or

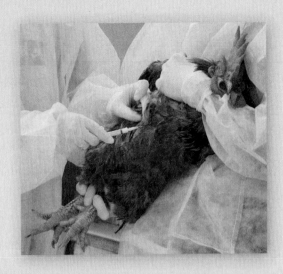

Bird flu is one of the diseases medical authorities fear can circle the globe and cause millions of deaths.

have a surgical incision, however, they can penetrate our body and attack our internal organs. This seldom leads to serious problems, as most of these staph germs are relatively mild. But when some of these are replaced by a mutant, virulent strain, simple cuts and scrapes can become mortal wounds. A patient who goes to the hospital for some strange pain, a sore throat, or routine surgery can be carried out in a coffin.

This threat has broken through the apathy of the medical industry. Pharmaceutical firms are searching for the next generation of antibiotics to fight the next generation of microbes. The race is close. Let's suppose that we win and are able to develop new antibiotics in time to prevent a global epidemic. Will we then repeat this process—overprescribing, not completing the course of treatments—with the microbes again mutating and developing resistance to the new drugs?

Granted the folly of much human behavior, I am certain that this will happen. In addition certain social factors promote this self-defeating behavior—especially a medical establishment eager for profits and the tendency of patients to quit taking medicine when they feel better, but before invasive microbes are destroyed totally. A sage once said that those who do not learn from history are doomed to repeat it. I would add that although we study history, and even know its lessons, in some instances we set ourselves on a course destined to repeat it. This is one such case.

A startling statistic illustrated on Figure 10-11 is that although African Americans make up just 12 percent of the U.S. population, they account for almost *half* of HIV/AIDS infections. Why? The first reason is a combination of cultural-behavioral factors: disbelief that it can happen, distrust of doctors, reluctance to talk about AIDS, lack of knowledge about its transmission, higher-than-average use of injected drugs, and a reluctance

FIGURE 10-11 Adults Living with HIV/AIDS

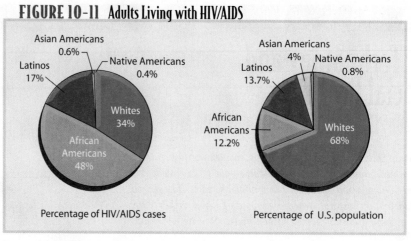

Percentage of HIV/AIDS cases

Percentage of U.S. population

Source: By the author. Based on Centers for Disease Control and Prevention 2005:Table 19.

to use condoms. The second reason is organizational: Most money for HIV prevention bypassed African Americans, going instead to AIDS organizations with roots in the gay community (Stolberg 1998).

OMINOUS CHANGES. The HIV virus mutates rapidly, and medical researchers fear that the drugs being used to fight HIV/AIDS might prove to be only a stopgap measure. Some individuals have contracted strains of HIV that are resistant to protease inhibitors (Bhattacharya 2005). If drug-resistant strains become widespread, as is likely, the epidemic could surge again. Several new drugs, however, hold the promise of taking over where the protease inhibitors leave off.

Social Inequalities in Physical Illness

POVERTY AND HEALTH. Let's look more closely at the social inequalities that underlie the U.S. health picture. From your reading of earlier chapters, you should not be surprised to learn that economic factors largely determine who will be healthy and who will be sick. Poor children, for example, are more likely to be undernourished or to lack a balanced diet. As a result, they are more vulnerable to disease. In general, the poorer people are, the sicker they are. Even their death rates are higher.

This takes us to the heart of the matter. *Social* inequality—the essential factor that underlies our patterns of disease and death—is seldom considered a problem for our health care system to deal with. Instead, our system focuses on acute health problems, patches people up, and sends them back to the same environment from which they came.

OCCUPATIONAL HEALTH HAZARDS. Health problems that come from work are also distributed unequally. For example, the workers in manufacturing plants, not the managers, are more likely to be exposed to dangerous working conditions and toxic chemicals. Some chemicals merely irritate the skin; others cause skin cancer or attack vital body organs. Carbon monoxide, mercury, and uranium destroy the kidneys; the ethers, chlorines, and the heavy metals invade the nervous system.

Machinery and equipment also can be harmful to health. The noise level of some factories causes hearing loss—for workers (bosses are usually sheltered behind protective partitions or located in quieter buildings). Arc welding, lasers, and radar all produce radiation and damage the eyes. Increasingly considered a social problem, occupational illnesses will receive more attention in the future.

PAYING THE BILL. Looking at who pays the medical bill helps to expose social inequalities of health care. Before today's patchwork insurance coverage, there were private hospitals and clinics for those who could pay (considered "the worthy") and public facilities for those who could not (considered "the unworthy") (Rosenberg

1987). Because medical students need patients to practice on and public hospitals provided them, some public facilities were affiliated with medical schools. The medical care at these facilities was often superior. On the whole, however, with lower salaries, worse working conditions, and outdated equipment, public hospitals attracted the less-qualified doctors and nurses. Iatrogenesis, injury caused by medical care, was common; it included death due to a low level of medical knowledge and incompetent physicians.

Before World War II, professional health care was still fairly primitive. Most health care took place at home, and doctors made house calls to supplement and direct home health care. Hospitals, which were considered a last resort, were feared. They were known as "the place where people go to die."

After World War II, medical technology improved, and the costs of treating illness increased. Many middle-class people who had serious health problems found that they could no longer afford hospital care. Coupled with the desire of physicians and hospital owners to increase their income, this problem led to the creation of medical and hospitalization insurance. The idea spread, and such insurance eventually became a standard benefit for business and government employees. As a result, most working-class and middle-class people who had steady jobs received medical care. The poor were still left out in the cold, with only charity to take care of the worst cases.

Those who suffered the most health problems, the poor and the elderly, were passed over. In 1966, Congress tried to remedy this sorry situation by passing Medicaid for the poor and Medicare for the elderly. Neither is comprehensive or generous, but overnight these plans provided medical coverage for millions who needed it the worst. Because these programs did not control what health providers could charge, however, the cost of medical care rose rapidly. Soon people's out-of-pocket expenses were as much as they had been before the government began these programs.

Unanticipated Consequences of Medicaid and Medicare ■ As functionalists stress, human actions have unanticipated consequences. One of Medicaid's was that it undermined public hospitals. City and county officials figured that because the poor now had medical insurance, they no longer needed free facilities. Eager to save money, many cities and counties closed their public hospitals and clinics. This left many of the poor in the lurch; because Medicaid's rates were low, many doctors and private hospitals refused to accept Medicaid patients. The working poor have been especially hard hit—their income is so low that they cannot afford to buy insurance, but not so low that they qualify for Medicaid. Sixteen percent of the nation, or about 45 million people, have no health insurance (*Statistical Abstract* 2006:Table 142).

MEDICAL INSURANCE. Lack of medical insurance highlights the racial-ethnic inequalities that run through U.S. society. Because African Americans and Latinos have a larger proportion of working poor, they are more likely to lack medical insurance. Whereas 15 percent of whites are not covered by insurance, the rate for Asian Americans is 19 percent, for African Americans it is 20 percent, and for Latinos it is 33 percent (*Statistical Abstract* 2006:Table 142).

Social Inequalities in Mental Illness

SOCIAL CLASS AND MENTAL ILLNESS. Do some social classes have more emotional problems than others? This intriguing question has a consistent answer. Since 1939, sociologists have found that people's emotional well-being gets worse as you go down the social class ladder. Those in the lower social classes are more likely to be depressed, anxious, or nervous and to have phobias. (In sociological parlance, this is known as an "inverse correlation between mental problems and social class.") This finding has been confirmed in numerous studies (Faris and Dunham 1939; Srole et al. 1978; Lundberg 1991; Starfield et al. 2002).

As mentioned, the term *mental illness* is so imprecise that we have to be suspicious of what is being measured. To overcome this problem, in 1978 sociologist Leo Srole and his colleagues at Columbia University did a study that became a classic in sociology: the

FIGURE 10-12 Social Class and Mental Problems

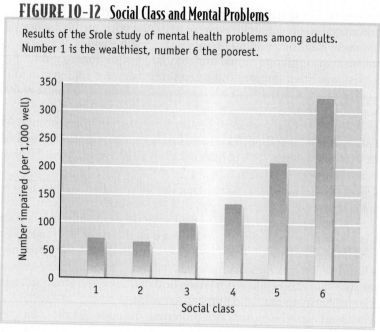

Results of the Srole study of mental health problems among adults. Number 1 is the wealthiest, number 6 the poorest.

Source: Srole 1978.

Midtown Manhattan Project. The Srole team developed its own scale of symptoms, trained its own interviewers, and then interviewed a representative sample of New Yorkers. As shown in Figure 10-12, like both earlier and later studies, these researchers found that the poor have considerably more emotional problems.

FOUR EXPLANATIONS FOR THE GREATER EMOTIONAL PROBLEMS OF THE POOR. Why do the poor suffer more mental disorders than people in other classes? Four explanations have been suggested.

The Drift and Genetic Hypotheses ▪ According to the *drift hypothesis,* people with emotional difficulties tend to be less successful in life, so they drift from higher-income families down into the lower classes (Fox 1990). According to the *genetic hypothesis,* faulty genes cause schizophrenia, manic depression, and other severe disorders. Therefore, the poor have more of these genes. Why should this be? The answer is provided by the drift hypothesis: Even if these genes once were distributed evenly among the social classes, many of the people who have these genes would drift downward, leaving a disproportionate number of poor families with these traits.

The Socialization Hypothesis ▪ According to a third explanation, the *socialization hypothesis,* children who are reared by disturbed parents are more likely to learn pathological ways of coping with the world. They are less equipped to deal with the challenges of education and career. People in the higher classes who are reared in such homes drift to the lower classes, whereas lower-class children from such homes remain in the lower class.

The genetic explanation for the most severe disorders, such as schizophrenia and manic depression, is influential in the medical community. But since the family that rears the child is usually the biological family, it is difficult to separate genetic influences from the effects of socialization. To try to do so, researchers have studied twins. They have found that identical twins who have been reared in different families have more mental problems than fraternal twins who were reared in the same family. They conclude that their research validates the genetic hypothesis. Critics of this explanation say that there are too many problems with the research to accept this conclusion. With the decoding of the human genome system, researchers are hopeful that they will be able to match specific genes with mental illnesses (Pestka 2006).

The Environmental Hypothesis ▪ Sociologists prefer an explanation called the *environmental hypothesis.* Here the focus is on how the environments of the social classes differ. Let's rephrase the basic finding that the lower classes have more "mental illnesses": Another way to say this is that the social classes that are better off financially are happier, less depressed, less filled with anxiety, and less phobic (that is, they have fewer fears). In short, they are "mentally healthier." And why shouldn't they be? For them, life is better—less "nasty, brutal, and short." People who are in the middle classes and above enjoy better job security, finances, physical health, medical care, and marriages. Not only do they have greater security at the present time (not absolute security, of course, but much greater security than the poor have), but they also have greater hopes for the future. They realistically plan and look forward to a larger house, better cars, exotic vacations, their children completing college, and a relaxing, enjoyable retirement. Of course, sociologists say, their mental health is better. Why would anyone expect anything less?

Compare this situation with the stress-filled package that comes with poverty: jobs that can quit on you anytime, low wages, unpaid bills, trouble paying the rent, and insistent bill collectors; more divorce, alcoholism, and violence; and greater vulnerability to crime combined with worse physical health and less access to good medical care. Such conditions certainly deal severe blows to people's emotional well-being.

To be fair (and my bias as a cultural sociologist certainly shows up here), as with some of the issues raised regarding gender differences in Chapter 9, environment versus heredity must remain an open question.

THE DELIVERY OF MENTAL HEALTH SERVICES. In order to understand how mental health services are related to social inequality, let's consider types of therapy and health care institutions. In **individual psychotherapy,** a therapist listens and tries to guide the patient toward a resolution of emotional problems. One type of psychotherapy is **psychoanalysis,** which Sigmund Freud pioneered as a way to uncover the subconscious motives, fantasies, and fears that shape people's behavior. The patient meets an analyst several times a week and talks about whatever comes to mind, while the analyst listens for hidden patterns, particularly those that reveal unresolved conflicts from early childhood. More common is **short-term directive therapy,** in which a counselor focuses on current situations to help clients understand their problems. In **group therapy,** several patients, with the guidance of a therapist, help each other to cope with their problems.

Another option is **drug therapy,** the use of tranquilizers, antidepressants, and antipsychotic drugs to relieve people's problems and help them cope with life. As discussed in Chapter 4, some of these drugs have serious side effects. Drug therapy is often criticized for being a way to treat the symptoms of troubled people without getting at their underlying problems.

In some cases, especially depression, **electroconvulsive therapy (ECT)** (also known as electroshock therapy) is used. Wires are attached to either side of a patient's skull, and low-voltage electric shocks are sent repeatedly through the brain. A side effect is memory loss. I used to be an orderly at Renard Hospital in St. Louis, a private mental hospital affiliated with Washington University Medical School. Occasionally, I held patients down during ECT treatment. I vividly recall how they convulsed wildly as the electricity surged through their brains and how disoriented they were afterward.

Consequences of Ability to Pay ■ The type of therapy that a troubled person is likely to receive does not depend on the person's problems, but on the person's ability to pay. People who have money and good insurance are more likely to be guided through their problems with **talk therapy**—psychotherapy, group therapy, and so on. "Talk" therapy is expensive, and it would be rare for a poor and uninsured person to receive it. The poor and uninsured are likely to receive no help at all, but when they do receive help, they are likely to be given drug therapy, which has been called a "pharmaceutical straitjacket." (The drugs given in mental hospitals make patients drowsy, lethargic, and easier to handle. They also often make them confused.)

It is difficult, however, to say that these patterns of therapy and social class represent inequality: *We do not know which therapies work.* Costly psychoanalysis may be no more effective than drug therapy or even no therapy at all. Psychoanalysis may even be less effective. Consequently, we cannot say whether the poor are receiving worse—or better—treatment for their emotional problems. The rigorous studies that demonstrate the

Neither long-term counseling with psychiatrists nor quick-takes with pop counselors has been proven to be effective.

effectiveness of therapy are yet to be done. An emerging type of therapy, described in the Technology and Social Problems box on the next page, is also likely to be claimed a success by its practitioners but remain unexamined and unproven.

Health care facilities for treating mental illness used to parallel the facilities for treating physical problems: public hospitals for the poor and private hospitals or office visits for the affluent. The state and county hospitals had so many patients and so little money that thousands of patients languished in back wards, where they were driven as crazy by the disturbed people around them and the stark rooms they called home as they were by their own inner turmoil. Few received anything that could be called treatment.

With deinstitutionalization, described earlier in this chapter, the population of state and county mental hospitals shriveled. Although such places now offer short-term treatment and outpatient services, they still warehouse chronic patients who cannot cope in other environments.

As with physical illness, the type of payment that is available shapes what happens in the care of mental patients. Medicare allowed the states to transfer the cost of treating the poor to the federal government. Because many of these patients were elderly and qualified for nursing homes, some nursing homes became what psychiatrists Fritz Redlich and Stephen Kellert (1978) called decentralized back wards. People who would have been placed in mental hospitals under previous practices now are placed in nursing homes. The primary force behind this change was not an improvement in therapy, but Medicare legislation.

IN SUM Social inequalities in the treatment of mental problems continue, but today far more services are available over a wide range of facilities. Because we don't know which therapies are effective, we cannot say that the poor are getting less effective ones. As with the treatment of physical illness, however, the poor are less likely to receive mental health services.

Social Policy

We have reviewed conditions that have pushed up the cost of health care. The fee-for-service system encourages physicians to sell specialized services and to get patients to come back for visits. Doctors who are paid for every office visit, whether a visit

Technology and Social Problems
CYBERBABBLE, CYBERSHRINKS, AND CYBERSHAMS

The effectiveness of therapy is questionable. Talking to a friend or member of the clergy (or your mother-in-law, for that matter) may be as effective (or ineffective) as psychotherapy. Talking, in other words, may be helpful regardless of who the listener is—or it may not be helpful. We just don't know. It certainly is more pleasant to talk to a supportive, sympathetic, and understanding listener than to someone who challenges what you say—but even which type of listener is more effective in helping with problems has not been demonstrated.

E-mail therapy has now made its appearance; patient and therapist send e-mail back and forth. Some therapists and patients use chat rooms. Others add video links so they can see each other. Some therapists offer a one-shot deal for a flat rate. Some sell their virtual couches by the minute, others by the month (Cohen 1997).

Cybertherapy offers an advantage that the telephone does not: Time zones make no difference. Patients who are traveling around the world can zap off an e-mail whenever they like without waking the therapist in the middle of the night.

Because cyberbabble offers another profit center for therapists, it is being taken seriously by the American Psychological Association (APA). The APA has set up guidelines, and California requires that insurance companies pay for online therapy (Cohen 1997). Therapists are also establishing ethical guidelines, which a skeptic might call rules for avoiding problems so the profits can flow without interruption (King and Poulos 1999).

Cybertherapists are developing their own professional associations, such as the Interactive Media Institute. They hold national and international "telehealth" conferences, where they discuss such issues as how video games and robotics can "heal" patients.

There are also academic signs of acceptance: Some universities have set up programs in virtual counseling. The one at Duke University, called the Virtual Reality Program, recruits patients by saying that this type of therapy is more efficient, easier to schedule, and more confidential. (Efficient it may be—perhaps in bringing in profits—but in terms of results, totally unknown). In the Duke program, the patients actually come to a university office, where they use computer simulations. The therapist, says an online ad for the program, can treat people who have a fear of flying by having the patient "repeatedly land the virtual airplane."

We have just entered the age of virtual therapy, barely able to envision its future. One form that is being developed is fascinating. In computer-enhanced therapy, the therapist and patient engage in discussions through computer-animated characters that represent themselves. From a supply of images, the patient chooses his or her character, as well as the character of the therapist and the online setting where their session takes place. The animated characters then talk to one another. Supposedly, this format reduces embarrassment for patients, encouraging them to talk about unflattering problems and feelings (Onion 2004). I might add that it will also allow the therapist to express emotions. Sequestered from the patient, the therapist can show shock, take offense, or even laugh at the patient—who is none the wiser.

Does cyberbabble work? No one knows. But, then, no one knows if other forms of therapy work either. So therapists might as well collect fees this way as any other. And in most forms, the cybershrink doesn't even have to leave home or have patients drop by. Quite a deal.

---

is necessary or not, tend to encourage visits rather than dissuade them or promote preventive medicine. Focusing on acute problems is also profitable for hospitals. In our litigious society, when depersonalization breaks the bonds between physician and patient, many patients look for reasons to sue. Malpractice insurance is expensive, and it further drives up the cost of medical care. Concentrating on disease intervention is more expensive and less effective than prevention. Let's look at policies that address these basic forces.

Being Paid to Stay Healthy

Some employers give their workers a rebate for staying healthy—or at least for staying away from doctors. In return for accepting a high annual insurance deductible, employees who spend less than the deductible are paid the difference between it and their insurance claims. If the deductible is, say $1,500, workers who claim only $100 for medical treatment collect $1,400, a very nice bonus. Where this program has been tried, employee health costs go down. As one teacher said, "Before, I kind of overdid it. Now I feel I have an investment in my own health."

Prepaid Medical Care: The Example of HMOs

In the best-known type of prepaid medical care, the **health maintenance organization (HMO),** a medical corporation (sometimes owned by physicians) bids to take care of the health needs of a company's employees. The business pays a monthly fee for each employee. If the health care of an employee runs more than this fee, the medical corporation loses money; if it costs less, it makes money. Because the medical corporation receives no more than this fee, its directors are motivated to reduce medical costs. Doctors are paid salaries, but they can receive bonuses if they reduce patient costs. The doctors try to strike a balance between ignoring trivial and self-limiting symptoms and giving good health care. They are also motivated to treat medical problems before they become serious and their remedy grows expensive. Where fee-for-service doctors are happy to charge $45 each time a patient runs to them with the sniffles and will hold their hands for a few minutes and prescribe the same medication that is available over the counter, HMO doctors don't feel the same way about the matter.

THE POSITIVE SIDE. Because the doctors make more money if patients stay well, they encourage preventive care, such as immunizations, well-baby checkups, mammograms, and physicals (Ilminen 2006). They urge patients to adopt a lifestyle that improves health, one based on better diet, exercise, rest, and avoiding the abuse of drugs, including alcohol. Unnecessary tests, surgery, and hospital admissions represent costs to the physicians and medical corporations, so they avoid them. For the same reason, they also keep the length of hospital stays to the bare minimum. The reduction in costs can be dramatic, as HMO patients have less surgery and fewer hospitalizations than fee-for-service patients (Ward 1991; Cuffel et al. 1999).

PROFITS AND A CONFLICT OF INTEREST. As you read this description of HMOs, you may have perceived the built-in conflict of interest. The physicians face a dilemma: profits or patient care? An unintended consequence of avoiding hospitalizing patients and conducting expensive tests or treatments is that HMO doctors withhold some *necessary* treatments, tests, and hospitalizations. For example, a woman I know was sent home from the hospital even though she was still bleeding from her surgery. If she had remained longer,

Patients demand—and doctors like to deliver—high-tech care. There is something glamorous about the latest technology. Such technology, however, has driven up the cost of medical care, and, as I found out from personal experience, a week's stay in a hospital can now run over $50,000. HMOs represent an attempt to hold medical costs in check.

she would have used up more than her "share" of allotted costs and eaten into the corporation's profits. This would not have happened to a fee-for-service patient who could afford to pay for the health care.

Physicians are chafing at HMOs. Their two major concerns are loss of autonomy and reduced quality of health care. Doctors have to call their HMO for permission to give certain treatments. This puts administrators of HMOs, even low-level ones, in the position of dictating to doctors what treatment they can give their patients (McGinley 1999). ("You can do that if you want, but we won't pay for it.") Some HMOs even determine how many patients the doctors must see each day. One HMO, for example, insisted that its physicians see eight patients an hour, limiting them to 7½ minutes per visit. This did not leave the doctors enough time for completing paperwork, analyzing lab results, and of course, for calling HMO officials to get approval for treatments (Greenhouse 1999).

Limiting medical treatment in order to increase profits has led to severe problems. A mother tried to get her HMO doctor to refer her toddler to a specialist because of a persistent ear infection. She succeeded—after a year (Kilborn 1998). A physician recalls how he fought with his HMO for three hours to get permission to do a procedure. The HMO officials kept refusing, even though the woman was coughing up life-threatening amounts of blood (Steinhauer 1999a). Then there is the doctor who noticed a lump in one of her breasts. When she called the radiology department of the hospital where she worked to schedule a mammogram, she was told that she would have to wait six months. The hospital's HMO allowed one mammogram every two years, and she had had a mammogram eighteen months earlier. She had to appeal to the HMO's board of directors, who agreed to let her be an exception to the rule. She had breast cancer (Gibbs and Bower 2006).

Physician Assistants

Another strategy for controlling costs is to use *physician assistants.* Half to three-quarters of all the problems that are dealt with in a typical doctor's office are medically trivial. Physician assistants and nurses can provide much of this medical care and educate patients who have chronic disorders. To delegate routine and time-consuming responsibilities to assistants makes more sense than making sure that everyone who has the sniffles is seen by a physician whose job requires twenty-three years of education and commands one of the highest salaries of any occupation.

The use of physician assistants has led to an in-house rivalry, however, and the first volleys in a battle over turf have been fired. Physician assistants must work under the supervision of physicians, but they don't like doctors breathing down their necks. They want to be able to give more independent care, but their efforts at establishing greater autonomy have been met with hostility from doctors (Aston and Foubister 1998). At this point, the attitude of the medical profession is, "If they want to do more, they can go to medical school."

Training Physicians

Medical schools graduate about 15,000 physicians a year, the same today as in 1980 (Statistical Abstract 2006:Table 291). As Figure 10-13 shows, a startling change has occurred in the gender makeup of those graduates: In 1960, only 6 percent of medical school graduates were women. Today, women make up almost half of the nation's medical school graduates, and I anticipate that women will soon outnumber men in the nation's medical schools.

It is doubtful that this change in gender will have any significant effect on how medicine is practiced. The medical delivery system is in place, the characteristics we reviewed are firm, and gender is mostly irrelevant to the medical system. Female doctors are as likely as male doctors to be generous or greedy, patient or profit oriented, in favor of heroic medicine or preventive medicine. They, too, will prefer fee-for-service medicine

FIGURE 10-13 M.D. Degrees, by Sex

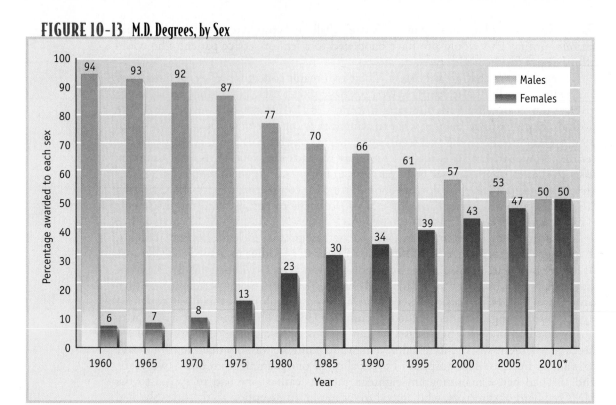

Note: Asterisk indicates the author's estimate..

Source: Statistical Abstract of the United States 1994:Table 295; 2007:Table 293.

and will be just as likely to avoid the poor and to set up practices where they make more money. Such orientations are consequences of core values in the general society and of those passed on in medical schools. Gender does not make someone lean in one direction or the other.

A social policy that might reduce costs and help get more doctors to the poor, where they are needed the most, would be to overproduce physicians. The government could encourage the opening of new medical schools. It could either finance them or offer tax breaks to investors. I suggest that students be allowed to go to college and medical school free of charge in return for spending a specified amount of time in areas where there is a doctor shortage. They would also be paid a monthly salary while they are in school. New physicians trained under this program can be required to give four years back for the eight that they spend in college and medical training. These graduates would not be given their final certification until they completed those four years. During their years of service, the government would pay for their medical malpractice insurance and pay them a salary equal to the average U.S. wage. The United States has the National Health Service Corps, which offers support for students in medical school or repayment of loans, but we need a more extensive program.

Not only would such a program help to get doctors to the areas where the need is the greatest, but it would also increase competition among doctors. Currently, the American Medical Association stifles competition by limiting the number of medical graduates. If more doctors graduated, patients would have a greater choice of physicians. As competition among doctors grew, doctors would likely reduce their prices, and the rise in medical costs would slow. The waiting period in doctors' offices would also lessen as overcrowding and overscheduling decreased. If patients have more choice, some of the more incompetent physicians should be driven out of medicine. Communities that have not been able to lure physicians to their town should be able to recruit them.

The outcry of physicians to such a proposal would be loud, for their income would drop as prices for their services fell. The physicians' labor union (or more accurately, their business organization), the American Medical Association, would mobilize to fight such a proposal. By controlling the nation's medical schools, the AMA limits the supply of physicians, guaranteeing high medical costs. An oversupply is not in the interest of this powerful monopoly.

Outreach Services

Because hospitalization is expensive and many hospital stays are unnecessary, whenever possible outreach services are replacing hospitalization. **Home health care,** for example, is less expensive and often more humane than the care that is available in nursing homes and hospitals. Many elderly people are put in nursing homes not because they are ill but because they can no longer live independently at home. Home health care lets them remain at home, in the environment they are used to and that they prefer. On the negative side, home health care encourages profiteering. For instance, a home health care company may pay its workers $14 an hour to care for the homebound, yet charge Medicare $30 an hour and pocket the difference.

Outreach programs for the mentally ill can be improved. We can provide ex-mental patients the community care that was supposed to accompany deinstitutionalization. The need is great, as anyone who takes time to talk to the homeless can attest. Group homes and supervised apartments can be established for the mentally disturbed, the mentally handicapped, and the chronically ill who have difficulty living in the community on their own.

Such programs are costly, of course, but cost is not the primary obstacle. If we refer to a "worthy" group, such as wounded veterans, hardly anyone objects. But if we suggest establishing such services for the homeless, who are viewed as "unworthy," the objections are never-ending. I suggest that it is not the cost, but the beneficiaries, that are people's concern.

Preventive Medicine

PREVENTABLE DEATHS. *Half* of all deaths of Americans are preventable. (Preventable is a strange term to use in this context, I know, but it is the standard term. It would be more accurate to say that these deaths are postponable, as each of these people would die eventually.) The two main causes of preventable deaths are deaths from smoking (435,000 a year) and deaths from improper diet and lack of exercise (400,000 deaths a year) (Mokdad et al. 2004). As subjective concerns and greater knowledge about health have increased—and because it senses profit—the AMA has begun to stress preventive medicine.

THREE TYPES OF PREVENTIVE MEDICINE. Preventive medicine sounds ideal as a way to ensure good health and reduce medical costs, but how do you put it into practice? Health planners distinguish among three types of prevention. **Primary prevention,** such as improved nutrition and childhood vaccinations, keeps a disease from occurring in the first place. **Secondary prevention,** such as self-examination for breast cancer, involves detecting a disease before it comes to the attention of a physician. **Tertiary prevention** is not very different from medical care. It means to prevent further damage from an already existing disease. Examples are controlling pneumonia so that it does not lead to death and maintaining a diabetic on insulin.

FOOD AND HEALTH. Primary prevention is promising because with proper nutrition and exercise, and avoidance of tobacco, people can greatly reduce their susceptibility to many diseases. For example, only about 15 percent of people who get lung cancer are non-smokers. A diet rich in beta-carotene, raw fruits and vegetables, and vitamin E supplements reduces the risk of cancer. Wheat bran, canola oil, soy milk, cantaloupe, avocados, olive oil, and green vegetables such as cabbage also appear to reduce the risk. And those leafy green vegetables that are hardly anyone's favorite—broccoli, brussels sprouts, and spinach—also seem to fight cancer (Biello 2006).

Studies on the effects of milk on health show mixed results. Some studies indicate that milk can reduce cancer (Cho et al. 2004; Larsson 2004), whereas other research indicates that milk might increase the risk of cancer (Mayne et al. 1995). If milk does increase the risk of cancer, this could be due to the pesticides and herbicides in the cows' fodder or even to the hormones that cows are given to promote their growth. Some researchers claim that bovine growth hormones pave the way for cancer by inhibiting the body's natural cancer fighters (Epstein 2001). Some researchers also accuse Monsanto, a global corporate giant that produces bovine growth hormones, of caring more about profits than people's health. To this some reply with a yawn, "Big surprise."

IMMUNIZATIONS. Immunizing children is also an effective technique of primary prevention. Not only do immunizations save lives but also they save vast sums that would have been spent on medical care. Yet about one of ten U.S. children has not been immunized against measles, mumps, diphtheria, hepatitis, and polio (*Statistical Abstract* 2006:Table 178). For many rural and poor areas, the figure is worse.

More Americans are overweight today than ever before in the history of the United States. The likely causes are a surplus of income, an abundance of food, less physically active occupations (a reduction in farming), more leisure, and more sedentary lifestyles (television watching), accompanied by more sugary foods and a custom called "snacking." Being overweight produces a variety of health problems, from weakened knee joints to heart attacks.

PREVENTING DRUG ABUSE AND HOMICIDE. Although not usually thought of as preventive medicine, no program would be complete unless it also focused on preventing drug abuse and homicide. From what we learned in Chapters 4 and 5, to reduce drug abuse is to prevent many serious health problems. Such programs could prevent the untimely deaths of many inner-city youths. In addition, drug abuse prevention programs that are directed against smoking and alcohol abuse could save hundreds of thousands of middle-class lives. Drug abuse programs, then, are one way to improve the nation's health.

EATING OURSELVES TO DEATH. Something disturbing is happening in the United States, and it does not bode well for our health:

In Cape Canaveral, Florida, while waiting for a space shot, I struck up a conversation with a British couple in their twenties. As we chatted while awaiting the delayed launch, I asked them what they thought about the United States. They looked at each other in that knowing way that couples do, and asked if I really wanted to know. I said I did. They replied, hesitatingly, that they had never seen so many overweight people in their lives.

When a friend from Spain visited me, he commented on the things that struck him as different. He was surprised to see people living in metal houses (he had never seen a mobile home). He also asked why there were so many overweight Americans.

Are these valid perceptions, or just twisted ethnocentric observations by foreigners? I wish I could say that the perceptions aren't true, but the statistics bear them out. In 1980, one of four Americans was overweight. By 1990, the percentage of overweight

Americans had jumped to one of three. Now, incredibly, it is *two of every three* (65 percent) (*Statistical Abstract* 1998:Table 242; 2007:Table 198).

Perhaps we should just shrug our shoulders and say, "So what?" Are the concerns being raised anything more than someone's arbitrary idea of how much we should weigh? It is a great deal more. Being overweight is more life threatening to Americans than AIDS or even alcohol abuse. Health experts estimate that the extra weight kills 365,000 U.S. adults die each year. Some say that this total is exaggerated, that deaths from being overweight are actually 112,000 a year (Saguy 2006). Regardless of the exact number, it is large. People who are overweight are more likely to have strokes, to suffer heart attacks, and to come down with diabetes (Kumanyika 2005). And compared with thinner people, when people who are overweight come down with these health problems, they are more likely to die (Calle et al. 2003). The problem has become so extensive that some experts are predicting that the life expectancy of Americans will start to decline (Olshansky et al. 2005).

This increase in the weight of Americans, so apparent to people from other cultures, flies in the face of what we know about preventing health problems. Our knowledge has gone one way, but our lifestyles another. For example, the average American drinks 46 gallons of soft drinks a year—more sugared, caffeinated, and carbonated water with harmful chemicals than milk and fruit juices combined (*Statistical Abstract* 2006:Table 201). Because this lifestyle is firmly ingrained—and continuously reinforced by appealing advertising—it is more difficult to implement preventive medicine than it is to continue the less effective but more dramatic medical procedures called heroic medicine. To put this in plain English, most people apparently prefer to go to a doctor to be treated for health problems than to exercise and eat healthier.

While obesity is a growing problem in the Western world, especially the United States, its opposite is also a medical problem. *Anorexia nervosa*, a pathological fear of becoming fat that leads to a distorted body image, excessive dieting, and emaciation, primarily affects adolescent girls and young women.

THE PROBLEM WITH PREVENTIVE MEDICINE. Preventive medicine is quiet and unassuming. It often is obscured by the drama of heroic medicine—open-heart surgery, screaming ambulances, and doctors and nurses rushing about in emergency rooms. If you take care of your body and manage to stay well, no one thinks much about it. Become seriously ill, however, and people jump to attention. Preventing something from happening means that you never see it happen. In fact, this is what most people want—not to get sick. Yet most people only talk about this goal, and few are willing to work to reach it. Although entire communities could reduce their risk of heart disease, unhealthy habits such as fatty foods, booze, and the boob tube are much more appealing to most of us than are vegetables, fruit juices, and aerobic exercise.

To see how severely lifestyle can affect people's health on a national basis, read the Spotlight on Social Research box on the page 355.

Humanizing Health Care

Mary Duffy was lying in bed half-asleep on the morning after her breast surgery, when a group of white-coated strangers filed into her hospital room. Without a word, one of them, a man, leaned over her, pulled back her blanket, and stripped her nightgown from her shoulders. He began to talk about carcinomas to the half-dozen medical students who had encircled her bed, staring at her naked body with detached curiosity. Abruptly, the doctor said to her, "Have you passed gas yet?" (Carey 2005).

It's almost incredible that such an event could happen, but it did. No one likes being *depersonalized*, treated as a thing or as an object, yet this happens routinely in medical settings. It is as though medical personnel think that when people check into a hospital, they have also checked their feelings and personal needs into their medical folder.

Sociologists who have studied depersonalization in public clinics note how the poor not only have to wait for hours to be seen, but aren't even given normal eye contact. Nurses address them by number and don't look in their direction when they respond. If they aren't able to see a doctor that day, it's just one of those things. After all, what do poor people have to do that's important, anyway?

If depersonalizing medical care is a problem, then the solution is to repersonalize it. This process has to begin in medical school or even in pre-med training. The medical establishment recognizes depersonalization as a problem, and some medical schools have incorporated "bedside manner" training into their curriculum. So far, such efforts have been feeble and ineffective. Even when medical students have a strong desire to treat patients as people, the pressures of their rigorous training accompanied by their faculty's stress on organs, disease, and dysfunctions changes the students' attitude and approach to patients. Listen to a medical student describe this change in her orientation:

> Somebody will say, "Listen to Mrs. Jones's heart. It's just a little thing flubbing on the table." And you forget about the rest of her . . . and it helps in learning in the sense that you can go in to a patient, put your stethoscope on the heart, listen to it, and walk out. . . . The advantage is that you can go in a short time and see a patient, get the important things out of the patient, and leave (Haas and Shaffir 1993:437, emphasis added).

Ultimately, medical training needs to stress the *inherent worth* of patients—that each individual is valuable and deserves personal attention. Physicians and nurses also need to learn *holism,* the view that a person's body, feelings, attitudes, and actions are intertwined and should not be segregated into separate organ systems for the convenience of clinicians. Waiting rooms can be made more humane by having adequate lighting, comfortable seats, appropriate reading materials, warm decor, convenient bathrooms, and noninstitutional furniture. Hospital rooms can be made more homelike (Howard 1975; Carey 2005).

Repersonalizing patients is certainly an uphill battle. Depersonalizing them has become an institutionalized attitude, built into the medical approach so strongly that it seems instinctive to medical personnel. Consider this event:

> Jeanne Kennedy, the chief patient representative at Stanford Hospital in Palo Alto, California, broke her knee cap rushing to a meeting. A member of her staff wheeled her to the employee health department, where a nurse practitioner she had worked with for years began to arrange for her care. But the nurse spoke to the woman pushing the wheelchair and ignored Mrs. Kennedy.
>
> "It was crazy," she said, "Here I was in my own hospital, hurt but perfectly capable, and she's being very professional, but she's talking over my head as if I were a child. And we worked together. She knew me!" (Carey 2005)

The key to changing such deeply ingrained attitudes is probably profits. Until physicians make more money by giving holistic treatment, this change is unlikely to come about. This could happen, as there are indications that patients who feel their physicians have a personal interest in them and in the outcome of their treatment are less likely to sue for malpractice, even when doctors make mistakes. In addition, many people with medical problems are turning away from traditional medicine, which is eating at the profits of traditional medical practitioners. Let's look at one of these alternatives.

Self-Care Groups

One reaction to depersonalization and the high costs of health care is the emergence of self-care groups. The goals of self-care groups are to maintain health, prevent disease, and do self-diagnosis, medication, and treatment. Among the many who have formed groups to help each other are people with diabetes, heart attack victims,

Spotlight on Social Research
SOLVING A HEALTH MYSTERY

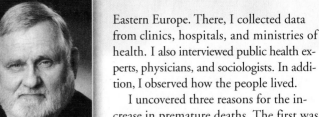

WILLIAM COCKERHAM, *Professor of Sociology at the University of Alabama at Birmingham, studies international aspects of health. He has done research on health and lifestyles in Russia and Eastern Europe, and he is doing similar research in Japan.*

In the mid-1990s, I attended a medical sociology conference in Vienna. Sociologists from the former socialist countries in Eastern Europe reported that their countries were in the midst of a health crisis, They said that men were dying prematurely and that the life expectancy for women had either declined or stagnated. What was striking about their presentations and in the discussions that followed was that no one could explain why this was occurring. That in peacetime an entire group of industrialized societies was experiencing a prolonged deterioration in the health of the population was unexpected.

The lack of an explanation for this crisis presented an intriguing research question. The killer turned out to be an increase in heart disease that had begun in the mid-1960s. A review of the evidence showed that infectious diseases, environmental pollution, and poor medical care were not enough to cause this surge in mortality. A clue that social factors were important was the fact that the rise in death rates was not universal. Heart disease differed by gender, age, urban-rural locale, education, and region. The group most affected was middle-aged, urban men who did manual work.

We now knew the "what" and the "who," but not the "why." To discover the "why," I traveled to Russia and

Eastern Europe. There, I collected data from clinics, hospitals, and ministries of health. I also interviewed public health experts, physicians, and sociologists. In addition, I observed how the people lived.

I uncovered three reasons for the increase in premature deaths. The first was policy failures: the failure to address the increase in heart disease and to adopt measures to lower smoking and drinking. The second seemed to be stress, which had increased with the collapse of communism: Workers had lost jobs and state benefits, such as housing and food subsidies. In addition, inflation had made their money worth less, driving down the value of their pensions and salaries. The third—and the primary reason—turned out to be unhealthy lifestyles. Heavy drinking and smoking and lack of exercise characterized the people who died prematurely from heart disease. To say "heavy" drinking is an understatement: Russian adult males, who comprise 25 percent of the population, drink 90 percent of the alcohol consumed in a country that averages 14 gallons per person annually.

I did not have enough data, however, to determine conclusively that stress—which has a well-established connection to heart disease—was especially important. A grant from the European Union provided funds to survey 18,000 people in eight countries of the former Soviet Union. This survey showed that women actually are more stressed than men. While stress undoubtedly makes the women's lives less pleasant and has consequences for their health, it is not killing enough of them prematurely to come close to the mortality rates of the men. As bad as the situation may be for the women, the key to explaining the health crisis ultimately lies in the men's behavior.

---

cancer patients, people who have had breast surgery, smokers, alcoholics, and people who suffer from rheumatism, arthritis, AIDS, disabilities, mental illnesses, and genetic problems. In these groups, members discuss new developments in their diseases or problems, encourage one another to take preventive measures, and support one another emotionally.

IN SUM The social policy ideas we have discussed focus on three major problems of health and medical care: high costs, the general lack of preventive medicine, and depersonalization. The aim of these policies is to move health care away from the hospital with its emphasis on acute care and dysfunctional organs and back to changes in lifestyle, with an emphasis on preventing problems and treating the whole person. These policies offer low technology and inexpensive alternatives to highly technological and costly medical care. For a comparative context to evaluate the U.S. medical system and the policies discussed here, see the following Global Glimpse box.

A Global Glimpse
HEALTH CARE IN SWEDEN, RUSSIA, AND CHINA

To better understand our own medical system, it helps to examine health care in other nations. Sweden, Russia, and China illustrate contrasting themes in health care around the world, helping us to place the U.S. medical system in cultural perspective.

HEALTH CARE IN THE MOST INDUSTRIALIZED NATIONS: SWEDEN

Sweden has the most comprehensive health care system in the world. National health insurance, which is financed by contributions from the state and employers, covers all Swedish citizens and alien residents. The government pays most physicians a salary to treat patients, but 5 percent work full time in private practice (Swedish Institute 1992). Except for a small consultation fee, medical and dental treatment by these government-paid doctors is free. The state also pays most of the charges of private physicians. The government reimburses travel expenses for patients and for the parents of a hospitalized child. Only minimal fees are charged for prescriptions and hospitalization.

Medical treatment is just one component of Sweden's broad system of social welfare. For example, people who are sick or who must stay home with sick children receive 90 percent of their salaries. Swedes are given parental leave at the birth of a child and when a child is sick. They also are guaranteed a pension.

Sweden's socialized medicine, however, is inefficient. Swedes have not solved the twin problems of getting rid of waiting lines and motivating physicians to work hard. Because medical personnel know how much their pay will be, regardless of how many patients they see, they are not productive. When reporters visited Sweden's largest hospital on a weekday morning, when 80 of 120 surgeons were on duty, they found 19 of the hospital's 24 operating rooms idle. Their photos of empty operating rooms—at a time when there was a one- to two-year waiting period for hip replacements and cataract operations—provoked a public outcry (Bergström 1992). The waiting list for cataract surgery has grown to 30,000 Swedes—in a population of 9 million ("Swedish Health Care . . ." 2002). If the same percentage of Americans were waiting for surgery, the U.S. line would be 600,000 people long.

Swedish lawmakers decided that to improve efficiency they need to abandon the socialized model, and they are gradually

A doctor in China applying herbs on acupuncture points.

turning the health care system over to the private sector. The government has begun selling hospitals to private companies ("Social Darwinism . . ." 2001). We don't yet know what the Swedish medical system will look like by the time this transition is complete.

HEALTH CARE IN THE INDUSTRIALIZING NATIONS: RUSSIA

Russia's medical system is in tatters. Under the Communist party, Russia had established a system that made free health care available to most people. Doctors would even visit patients at their homes (Gaufberg 2004). Like the rest of the nation's production, the health care system was centralized. The state owned the medical schools and determined how many doctors would be trained in what specialties. The state paid medical salaries, which it set, and determined where doctors would practice. Physicians were poorly trained, had low prestige, and earned less than bus drivers.

Under Russia's fitful transition to capitalism, its health care system has deteriorated, and the health of the population has declined. An example is Moscow's ambulance system. It used to be efficient—dial 03, and an ambulance would arrive within minutes. When Russia turned to capitalism in 1991, ambulances sometimes took eight hours to arrive because the drivers were using the ambulances as freelance cabs, and they kept emergency cases waiting (Field 1998). Since then, ambulance service has improved, especially in Moscow (Gaufberg 2004).

The only hospitals comparable to those of the United States are reserved for the elite (Light 1992; Gaufberg 2004). In the rest, conditions are deplorable. To be assured of care, some patients bring their own linens, medicines, and syringes with them to the hospital (Paddock 1999). In some hospitals, surgeons resharpen scalpels until they break. Some even use razor blades for surgery (Donaldson 1992). Outdated and broken equipment is not replaced. Some doctors face the choice of operating without anesthetic or not operating at all (Paddock 1999). Physicians are paid so little that in order to have food, they have to grow potatoes. They walk to work because they cannot afford the equivalent of a dime to take a bus (Goldberg and Kishkovsky 2000).

The bright spot is that physicians continue to work despite their low status and miserable pay. Many are motivated by idealism and the desire to help, coupled with the hope that things will get better. A second bright spot is that some doctors are making the transition to private practice, which could be the beginning of a new medical system built on the rubble of the old (Goldberg and Kishkovsky 2000).

In the meantime, Russia's medical system remains broken. Perhaps no event more pinpoints the disarray than this:

> Three patients lay unconscious in the intensive care unit, kept alive only by the Siberian hospital's life support system. Two were elderly; one was 39.
>
> On Wednesday, the hospital received a telegram from the local power company: "You haven't paid your bill for five years. You owe us $94,931. Pay up, or we'll shut off your electricity." The next morning, at 6 A.M., the company shut off the power. Forty minutes later, all three patients were dead. (Paddock 1999)

The years of environmental degradation under the Communists have also taken their toll. Serious birth defects have jumped to four times the U.S. rate. A likely culprit is radiation pollution from decades of nuclear irresponsibility (Specter 1995). Perhaps the single best indicator of the deterioration of health is the drop in life expectancy that began in the 1960s (Cockerham 1997). As shown in Table 10-2, the health of Russians is more like that of the Chinese than that of citizens in the Most Industrialized Nations. Life expectancy is not only a medical issue, but also a barometer of a society's health.

HEALTH CARE IN THE LEAST INDUSTRIALIZED NATIONS: CHINA

Because this nation of 1.3 billion people has a vast shortage of trained physicians, hospitals, and medicine, most Chinese see "barefoot doctors," people who have only a rudimentary knowledge of medicine, are paid low wages, and travel from village to village. Until a few years ago, physicians were employees of the government, and the government owned all the country's medical facilities. With its emphases on medicinal herbs and acupuncture, Chinese medicine differs from that of the West. Although Westerners have scoffed at the Chinese approach, some have changed their minds, and on a limited basis, medicinal herbs and acupuncture are used in the United States.

Like Russia, China has begun the journey to capitalism. Physicians earn so little that, like U. S. college students, some take "after work" part-time jobs. Deciding that profits should be part of the medical system, Chinese authorities withdrew government financing from the local health centers, which are now expected to sell their services (Beech 2004). Most patients who cannot pay for their medical care go untreated. In one hospital, doctors insisted on being paid before they would give emergency care to a 3-year old who had swallowed pesticides. The boy died, and the villagers rioted, ripping the hospital apart (Kahn 2006a).

At this point in its transition, China's medical system has deteriorated so greatly that the World Health Organization ranked it 144 of 191 nations. WHO ranked the medical care system of Bangladesh higher (Beech 2004).

FOR YOUR CONSIDERATION

In what ways would you say that the U.S. medical system is superior—and inferior—to each of these systems? Would you prefer to be treated within one of these three systems rather than in the U.S. system? Why or why not? Short of socializing medicine, which goes against the values of Americans, how do you think the U.S. medical system can overcome the deficiencies reviewed in this chapter—and maintain its strengths?

TABLE 10-2 Indicators of Health

	SWEDEN	UNITED STATES	RUSSIA	CHINA
Life expectancy, years	79.2	77.3	66.8	71.6
Infant mortality[1]	3.9	6.6	16.0	26.4
Birthrate[2]	11.7	14.1	9.6	13.0
Death rate	10.8	8.3	14.7	6.9
Health costs as a percentage of Gross Domestic Product	9.2	15.0	2.3	4.8

[1]Per 1,000 live births.
[2]Per 1,000 population.

Sources: By the author. Based on Field 1998; Liu 2004; *Statistical Abstract of the United States* 1998:Tables 1345, 1348; 2000:Tables 1355, 1358; 2006:Tables 98, 1318, 1323.

The Future of the Problem

To try to catch a glimpse of the future, let's look at trends in medical technology and in redirecting medicine.

Technology

MORE TECHNOLOGY. Just as the practice of medicine has been driven by the development of new technology, so it will be in the coming years. Patients will not stop demanding cutting-edge technology when their lives are threatened—regardless of the cost. Cost is a factor only when the emergency is over and the bills arrive. With this demand from patients—and from doctors and hospitals in competition with one another and wanting the latest technology to give them a competitive edge—the manufacturers of medical equipment will continue to find the development and sale of new products a profitable venture.

ETHICAL DILEMMAS. Out of these technological advances have arisen ethical problems that plague medical professionals and laypeople alike. If people can be kept alive artificially, must doctors keep them alive? Does "brain dead" really mean "dead"? If so, should physicians be allowed to "harvest body parts" from people who (only because of machines) are still breathing? (In some hospitals, they already do this.) Should medical researchers be allowed to test dangerous drugs on these people, because, after all, they are "really" dead? (They already do this in some hospitals.) Another ethical controversy, **euthanasia,** is discussed in the Thinking Critically box on the next page.

THE INTERNET. The Internet has helped some patients regain control over their medical care. People who have rare diseases, for example, can participate in online discussion groups. Although people don't meet personally in this new type of self-care group, they share their experiences and knowledge with one another. Some doctors are surprised—and dismayed—when their patients know more than they do about a new treatment or some new research. Not only do physicians feel threatened because they no longer are the sole possessors of esoteric knowledge on rare diseases or even the treatment of common disorders, but they also fear that patients can be picking up misinformation on the Internet. Medical experiments can also be contaminated: By sharing information online, some patients are able to determine whether they are receiving an experimental drug or a *placebo,* a substance that is designed to look like a medicine but that has no medical value (Bulkeley 1995).

Redirecting Medicine

THE CARLSON PREDICTIONS. In the 1970s, Rick Carlson (1975) said that in the year 2000 we would be living in a more complex and stressful society, we would have a large aging population with incurable degenerative diseases, and we would have more illnesses resulting from lifestyle and environmental deterioration. Carlson also held out little hope that our medical system would turn to preventive medicine and work on overcoming the environmental and lifestyle causes of illness. He concluded that poverty would not be cured and that the poor would continue to have more illnesses than the affluent. He was right on all counts.

THE POTENTIAL. Carlson argued, however, that we can change our health care system, transforming it into a much better system for meeting our medical problems. His ideas are worth repeating. An effective system, he said, would *encourage people to demand better health rather than more medicine.* This requires an awareness of factors that influence health, from those under the individual's control to environmental factors under the community's control.

To take this essential element of an effective health care system seriously, we would need more research on self–health care and disease prevention. Some physicians would continue to provide acute and emergency care, but others would be retrained in preventive

THINKING CRITICALLY About Social Problems

SHOULD DOCTORS BE ALLOWED TO KILL PATIENTS?

Except for the name, this is a true story:

Bill Simpson, in his 70s, had battled leukemia for years. After his spleen was removed, he developed an abdominal abscess. It took another operation to drain it. A week later, the abscess filled, and required more surgery. Again the abscess returned. Simpson began to go in and out of consciousness. His brother-in-law suggested euthanasia. The surgeon injected a lethal dose of morphine into Simpson's intravenous feeding tubes.

Dr. Jack Kevorkian illustrating his suicide machine.

At a medical conference in which euthanasia was discussed, a cancer specialist who had treated thousands of patients, announced that he had kept count of the patients who had asked him to help them die. "There were 127 men and women," he said. Then he added, "And I saw to it that 25 of them got their wish." Thousands of other physicians have done the same (Nuland 1995).

When a doctor ends a patient's life, such as by injecting a lethal drug, it is called *active euthanasia*. To withhold life support (nutrients or liquids) is called *passive euthanasia*. To remove life support, such as disconnecting a patient from oxygen falls somewhere in between. The result, of course, is the same.

Two images seem to dominate the public's ideas of euthanasia: One is of an individual devastated by chronic pain. The doctor mercifully helps to end that pain by performing euthanasia. The second is of a brain-dead individual—a human vegetable—who lies in a hospital bed, kept alive only by machines. How accurate are these images?

We have the example of Holland. There, along with Belgium, euthanasia is legal. Incredibly, in about 1,000 cases a year, physicians kill their patients without the patients' express consent. In one instance a doctor ended the life of a nun because he thought she would have wanted him to but was afraid to ask because it was against her religion. In another case, a physician killed a patient with breast cancer who said that she did *not* want euthanasia. In the doctor's words, "It could have taken another week before she died. I needed this bed" (Hendin 1997, 2000).

Some Dutch, concerned that they could be euthanized if they have a medical emergency, carry "passports" that instruct medical personnel that they wish to live. Most Dutch, however, support euthanasia. Many carry a different "passport," one that instructs medical personnel to carry out euthanasia (Shapiro 1997).

In Michigan, Dr. Jack Kevorkian, a pathologist (he didn't treat patients—he studied diseased tissues) decided that regardless of laws, he had the right to help people commit suicide. He did, 120 times. Here is how he described one of those times:

I started the intravenous dripper, which released a salt solution through a needle into her vein, and I kept her arm tied down so she wouldn't jerk it. This was difficult as her veins were fragile. And then once she decided she was ready to go, she just hit the switch and the device cut off the saline drip and through the needle released a solution of thiopental that put her to sleep in ten to fifteen seconds. A minute later, through the needle flowed a lethal solution of potassium chloride. (Denzin 1992)

Kevorkian taunted authorities. He sometimes left bodies in vans and dropped them off at hospitals. Although he provided the poison, as well as a "death machine" that he developed to administer the poison, and he watched patients pull the lever that released the drugs, Kevorkian never touched that lever. Frustrated Michigan prosecutors tried Kevorkian for murder four times, but four times juries refused to convict him. Then Kevorkian made a fatal mistake. On national television, he played a videotape showing him giving a lethal injection to a man who was dying from Lou Gehrig's disease. Prosecutors put Kevorkian on trial again. This time, he was convicted of second-degree murder and was sentenced to 10 to 25 years in prison.

In 1997, Oregon became the only U.S. state where medically assisted suicide is legal. If Kevorkian had lived in Oregon, and he hadn't begun killing patients until 1997, he would be a free man today.

FOR YOUR CONSIDERATION

Do you think Michigan or Oregon is right? Why? In the future, do you think we will go the way of Oregon or Michigan?

As is evident in Holland, physician-assisted deaths have a way of expanding. In addition to what is reported here, Dutch doctors also kill newborn babies who have serious birth defects (Smith 1999). Their justification is that these children would not have "quality of life." Would you support this?

and environmental medicine. The infirm aged would be cared for in residential complexes that are humane and pleasant, such as those in Denmark and Sweden. Funds saved from spending less on acute and emergency medical care could go to programs that feature accident prevention, food safety, occupational safety, nutrition, and exercise. Efforts would be made to reduce the stresses of modern life by designing more relaxing work environments in offices and schools; building hiking and bike paths, tennis courts, and parks in our communities; and reducing noise pollution. Schools would be an essential element, teaching nutrition and the benefits of a healthy lifestyle, while requiring students to get exercise through rigorous physical education.

The potential for improving the general health of our people is immense. With the public's growing awareness of the social factors that underlie health and illness, the demand for better health through preventive action will grow. The focus on preventive medicine, however, runs counter to our current emphasis on heroic intervention in acute cases. We will experience a cultural clash, with both emphases existing alongside one another.

SUMMARY AND REVIEW

1. What people consider to be health and illness varies with culture and social class. Health problems are based on both biological and social factors.

2. Industrialization has brought better health, but with it has come an increase in some health problems—cancer, heart disease, drug addiction, and other chronic illnesses caused by lifestyle, aging, and environmental pollution. HIV/AIDS illustrates the relationship among behavior, environment, and disease. Physical and emotional problems are more common among the poor. To explain the relationship between social class and mental illness, sociologists prefer environmental explanations rather than genetic ones.

3. The U.S. medical system is centered on specialized, hospital-based, and heroic intervention. A fee-for-service system increases cost. In preventive medicine, the emphasis is on changing people's lifestyles and environment.

4. Social inequalities in medical and mental health services stem largely from the way we pay medical bills. In our fee-for-service system, health care is not a right but a commodity sold to the highest bidder. The United States has a *two-tier system of medical care*—public clinics and poorer treatment for the poor and private clinics and better treatment for the more affluent.

5. Two policies designed to control medical costs are to pay patients to stay healthy and to pay doctors to reduce unnecessary medical care. HMOs are a form of prepaid health care that provides a fixed amount of money to a medical corporation to attend to the health needs of a group of people. Medical services and tests come directly off the corporate bottom line, leading to a conflict of interest in treating patients. On the other hand, if HMO practitioners let their patients become too sick, it costs the medical corporation more than if they catch problems early.

6. The medical profession is experiencing a tension among its traditional focus on heroic intervention in acute problems, the need to treat chronic problems, and the emerging focus on medical problems caused by lifestyle and environmental pollution. Within this tension, there is likely to be increased emphasis on preventive medicine—better health habits, a cleaner environment, and education designed to teach people how to take care of themselves and to manage their illnesses.

KEY TERMS

THINKING CRITICALLY ABOUT CHAPTER 10

1. What do you think the government's role should be in medical care? Why?
2. Why do you think the United States is the only industrialized country that doesn't have a national health care system?
3. Why do you think women live longer than men?
4. Which of the theoretical perspectives (symbolic interactionism, functionalism, or conflict theory) do you think best explains health care problems in the United States? Explain.

CHAPTER 11

The Changing Family

Nancy and Antoine were pleased. Their 4-year-old daughter, Janelle, had been accepted at Rainbow Gardens Preschool in Manhattan Beach, California, a prosperous suburb of Los Angeles. The preschool came highly recommended by their close friends, whose son was attending the school. With Nancy's promotion and Antoine's new job, schedules had become more difficult, and Rainbow Gardens was able to handle their need for more flexible hours.

At first Janelle loved preschool. She would happily leave whichever parent drove her to school for the pleasures of her little friends and the gentle care of loving teachers. Then, gradually, almost imperceptibly, a change came over her. At first, Janelle became reluctant to leave her parents. Then she began to whimper in the mornings when they were getting her ready. And lately she had begun to have nightmares, waking up crying and screaming several times a week, something she had never done. The counselor they took Janelle to said it

> ## She had begun to have nightmares.

was nothing to worry about; all kids go through things like this from time to time. Janelle was going through a "developmental adjustment," and she would be just fine in a little while.

When allegations of sexual abuse of 3-, 4-, and 5-year-olds at Rainbow Gardens made headlines, it was devastating to parents around the nation. The unthinkable had become real. Had it happened at their preschool, too—with their child? But for Nancy and Antoine, it was more than a nagging question. Overnight, Janelle's nightmares, her crying, and her bed-wetting took on new meaning. Those gentle teachers, so affectionate with the children, child molesters? Janelle undressed, photographed, forced to commit sexual acts with adults, and threatened with the death of her puppy if she told?

Nancy and Antoine don't know. It is either this or simply a "developmental adjustment." Now it is Nancy's and Antoine's turn for nightmares.

The Problem in Sociological Perspective

"Nightmare at Rainbow Gardens" could be the title of a horror movie, a real-life one for some parents. Each year, some unknown number of children are abused sexually at day care centers. Back in the 1980s, a kind of hysteria swept the country. Rumors spread that day care centers were packed with child molesters. Teachers were tried and convicted, sometimes on flimsy evidence (Rabinowitz 2004). A Massachusetts man served eighteen years in prison before his pleas of innocence were finally acknowledged. Despite the hysteria, some children are abused at day school, a frightening prospect for parents. Why aren't the children with their families? Why are 5 million U.S. children entrusted to the care of strangers in a new social institution called day care (*Statistical Abstract* 2006:Table 568)?

Day care—and its risks—is part of a sea of change that has swept our society, engulfing families and forcing them to adjust. For the family, change is nothing new. As the basic social institution (also called the basic building block of society), the family always feels changes that occur in other parts of society.

Effects of the Industrial Revolution on the Family

The most significant event to affect the family was the Industrial Revolution. Because its consequences were so extensive and because they continue to affect family life today, let's explore its significance. Before industrialization, economic survival was perilous. Almost everyone worked at home. The entire family was involved, both the parents and their children. When industrialization moved production to factories, it had a dynamic effect on family life. Here are some of those effects:

MEN LEAVING HOME. Men left home to work in factories. This opened a major gap between the husband-father and other family members. For most of the day they now lived different lives, one at work and the others at home. Husband and wife no longer shared activities during their working hours. Separated from the household, the husband-father's orientation to life changed.

CHILDREN—FROM ECONOMIC ASSETS TO ECONOMIC LIABILITIES. Industrialization turned children from an economic asset into an economic liability. When production was farm based, children contributed to their family's survival—from feeding chickens and milking cows to working in the fields. In some of the first factories, children still worked alongside adults. Throughout the late 1800s, a social movement to "save" children gained momentum, resulting in child labor laws that ended the employment of most children. There were a few exceptions, such as selling newspapers and helping at the family's business. Although children could no longer bring home a paycheck, they still consumed much of the family's limited resources. This made children nonproductive and expensive.

FORMAL EDUCATION. Industrialization brought a need for more formal education and opened opportunities to acquire it. As children spent more years in school than ever before, they became dependent on their parents for a longer period. Their prolonged education and longer dependency made children even more expensive.

A LOWER BIRTHRATE. The discovery of vulcanized rubber during the 1840s made large-scale production of the condom possible. With further refinements in design and manufacture in the 1920s, the condom allowed couples to limit the number of their children (Douvan 1980; Laslett 1980). Because children had become nonproductive and expensive, the birthrate plunged. As Figure 11-1 on the next page shows, our birthrate is now the lowest in our history, and it is expected to fall still further.

FROM RURAL TO URBAN. Industrialization changed people's settlement patterns. Until about 100 years ago, almost everyone in the world lived in the country. As production moved to factories, workers moved where the work was. With housing in the city expensive, people reduced the size of their families even more.

LOSS OF FUNCTIONS. As industrialization continued, other institutions grew stronger and stripped the family of many of its traditional functions, such as producing food, educating the young, providing recreation, and nursing the old and sick. As family functions were taken over by other social institutions, the family weakened.

CHANGES IN WOMEN'S ROLES. Industrialization changed women's roles. The wife-mother had been responsible for basic food production (milk, butter, eggs, vegetables), preparation (baking and cooking), and storage (canning). She also made, washed, ironed, and mended the family's clothing, cleaned the house, and took care of the children, the sick,

What is a "normal" family? The answer depends on culture. Shown here in Baranama, Upper Guinea, are two wives with their husband and children.

FIGURE 11-1 U.S. Birthrate, 1890–2050

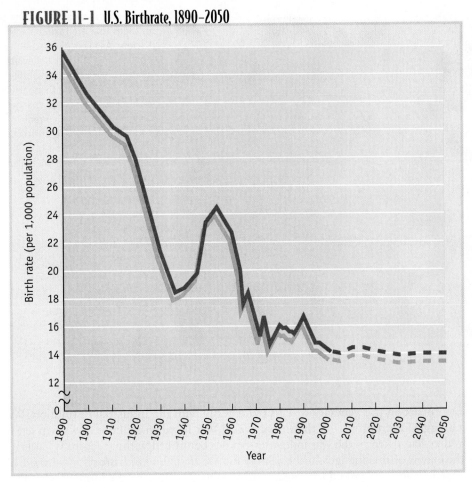

Note: Broken line indicates U.S. government projections.

Source: By the author. Based on *Statistical Abstract of the United States,* various editions; 2001:Table 4; 2006:Table 76.

and the elderly. As her functions were reduced, she increasingly became an "emotional provider"; that is, the wife-mother was expected to be the stable counterpoint to the husband's pressures at work and to lavish attention on a diminishing number of children.

GREATER EQUALITY. Industrialization brought greater equality to the family. As traditional roles changed, so did feelings about how things "ought to be" between husband and wife and between parents and children. This gradual change did not happen without struggle, for men were reluctant to give up their more privileged positions. Indeed, the struggle over equality (or authority, decision-making) is still a primary source of marital tension.

MORE DIVORCE. Industrialization increased divorce. Before industrialization, divorce was rare. But with the changes just outlined, especially the reduced functions of the family and the lower birthrate, marriages became fragile.

LONGER LIVES AND MORE INTERGENERATIONAL TIES. Industrialization improved health and brought longer lives. One consequence is that today's grandparents are more likely to be alive and to participate in the lives of their grandchildren than at any other time in history (Bengtson et al. 1990). It is even becoming more common for grandparents to rear their grandchildren.

THE "QUIET REVOLUTION." The changes continue. One of the most fundamental changes ever to affect the family—women leaving home to take paid employment—is having a

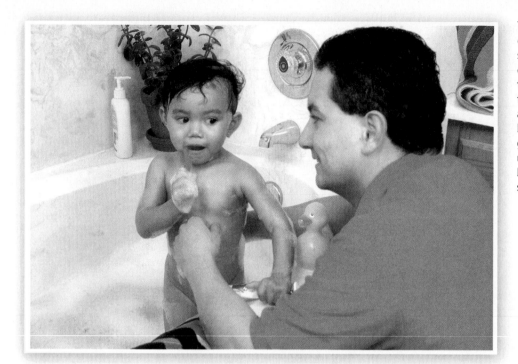

The family is always adjusting to changes that are taking place in society. As ideas of masculinity change, for example, behaviors that once were not acceptable for men come to be thought of as normal. After those changes become standard, a current generation may have difficulty understanding why such behaviors ever threatened men's sense of "masculinity."

major impact on this generation. This trend began with the Industrial Revolution. With but a single interruption—at the end of World War II, when millions of women left the jobs they had taken in the war industries—it has continued without letup. What is new is the extent of the change: In the 1980s, for the first time in history, more than half of married women worked for wages at least part-time outside the home. Today about 61 percent do (*Statistical Abstract* 2006:Table 584).

That so many married women work for wages reinforces most of the trends we have discussed, especially changes in husband–wife roles and relationships, divorce, and the birthrate. It also complicates rearing children, which some consider *the* social problem of today's family. Because the movement of wives and mothers from the home is part of a gradual historical trend, and yet is so fundamental—forcing change in all family relationships— it sometimes is called the *quiet revolution.*

IN SUM The family is always in transition. Just as the family adapted to large-scale social events that began centuries ago, so it adapts to today's current events. The family is not an independent unit, and to survive it must adapt to what is happening in society. Because the family provides for the economic well-being of its members, as with industrialization of years past, the family is especially sensitive to economic changes.

The Scope of the Problem

A lot of people are bothered by what is happening to the contemporary family. Some think that the changes in society are so extensive that the family isn't going to be able to adjust to them. Some even feel that the social changes are causing the family to disintegrate. The family used to be a viable social institution, goes this thinking, but social change has been so far-reaching that the family no longer fits today's society. Unfortunately, the family is doomed to be a relic of a past way of life. It has failed to meet its evolutionary challenges, and, like all dinosaurs, it will be replaced, in this instance, by more suitable forms of association.

As you will see, we will not take these positions, but, as with all the topics we've discussed in this text, we want to move beyond subjective concerns and examine objective conditions. What indications are there that the family is in trouble?

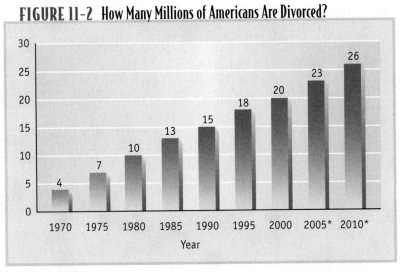

FIGURE 11-2 How Many Millions of Americans Are Divorced?

Note: Asterisk indicates the author's estimate.

Source: By the author. Based on *Statistical Abstract of the United States* 1989:Table 50; 2003:Table 61; 2006:Table 51.

Divorce

If you ask people why they think today's family is in trouble, usually the first thing to pop into their minds is divorce. As Figure 11-2 shows, perceptions that divorce has become more common are true. In 2004, there were five times more divorced Americans than in 1970. During this time, the population increased only 45 percent. Another way to look at the trend in divorce is to compare the number of Americans who are getting married with the number who are getting divorced. As Figure 11-3 shows, for every two couples getting married, another couple is ending its marriage.

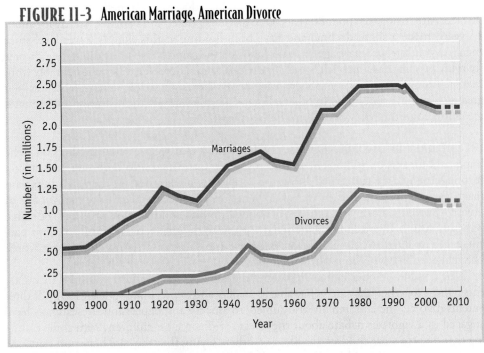

FIGURE 11-3 American Marriage, American Divorce

Note: Broken lines indicate the author's estimates.

Source: By the author. Based on *Statistical Abstract of the United States,* various years, and 2006:Table 72.

FIGURE 11-4 Variations in Divorce

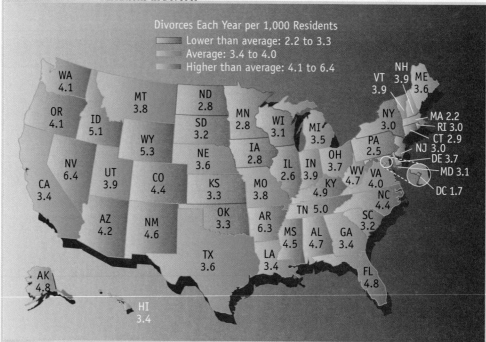

Note: The most recent rates available for California, Georgia, Hawaii, Indiana, Louisiana, and Oklahoma have been reduced by the average decrease in U.S. divorce since that date.

Source: By the author. Based on *Statistical Abstract of the United States* 2006:Table 117.

IS DIVORCE A SIGN OF WEAKNESS OR STRENGTH? We can interpret divorce statistics in different ways. Some see our increase in divorce in a positive light: More divorce means that families are becoming *stronger*. How could anyone interpret divorce this way? Here's the thinking: No longer willing to put up with miserable marriages, men and women terminate them. They then look for new partners, and most end up with more satisfying marriages. Even if this interpretation is not correct, Figure 11-3 does show something positive about divorce. After rising for about 80 years, U.S. divorces peaked in 1980, held steady for about 15 years, made a slight decline, and have been holding at this slightly lower level since then. As you can see, marriage has also followed the same path. The ratio of one divorce for every two marriages has held steady. Individual states, however, differ considerably from these national statistics. As the Social Map above shows, divorce is considerably less—or greater—in some states than in others. In general, the states with the lowest divorce rates are clustered in the Midwest and in the Northeast.

THE CHILDREN OF DIVORCE. Divorce involves things that we can't put numbers on—the hopes and dreams of millions of adults crushed, transformed into bitterness and rancor. Although people are concerned about the couples involved, they see them as adults who make their choices—and their mistakes. What really concerns people are the *children* of divorcing parents. Each year, the lives of about 1 million children are disrupted by divorce (Cherlin 2002). These children are filled with unsettling fears of the future as their parents break up. Divorce is so extensive that, as Figure 11-5A shows, only about two of three U.S. children live with both of their parents.

The children of quarreling parents find themselves in a no-win situation. If their parents remain together, they are vulnerable to anxiety and depression (Jekielek 1998). If their parents divorce, the children are also subject to anxiety and depression. Researchers have engaged in a vigorous debate about the effects of divorce on children, with some claiming that divorce scars children for life, and others saying that they are better off removed from unhealthy relationships. To unravel this thorny issue, researchers must know why the children of divorce have additional emotional problems: Are they from the divorce or

FIGURE 11-5 Where Do U.S. Children Live?

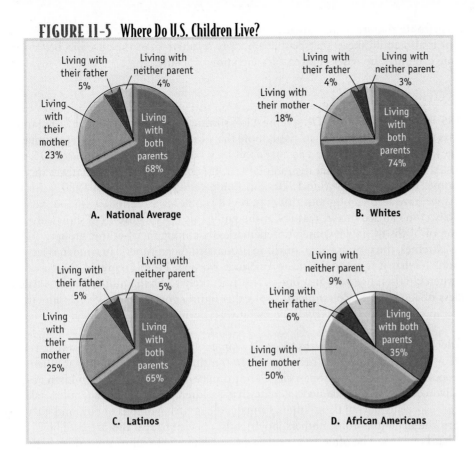

A. National Average

Living with their father 5%
Living with neither parent 4%
Living with their mother 23%
Living with both parents 68%

B. Whites

Living with their father 4%
Living with neither parent 3%
Living with their mother 18%
Living with both parents 74%

C. Latinos

Living with their father 5%
Living with neither parent 5%
Living with their mother 25%
Living with both parents 65%

D. African Americans

Living with neither parent 9%
Living with their father 6%
Living with their mother 50%
Living with both parents 35%

Note: Only these groups are listed in the source.

Source: By the author. Based on *Statistical Abstract of the United States* 2006:Table 60.

from the trauma of living with quarreling parents before the divorce? (Strohschein 2005). For most children, divorce also means a reduced standard of living. For some, it means poverty.

THE NAGGING DILEMMA OF DIVORCE. Few adults enter into divorce lightly. The decision to divorce is usually painful, preceded by years of dissatisfaction and unhappiness. Couples who divorce find themselves on an emotional roller-coaster, filled with fears and anxiety about an uncertain future, perhaps with thoughts that they might be able to patch things up. They can feel as though they are being torn apart, that their identities are being shredded. No longer can they depend on many of the identity markers that had become part of their stability in life. They can be ripped apart by feelings of guilt, of "what might have been," of what they did wrong, of years wasted with the wrong person, or of how their children are going to adjust.

THE SLOWING RATE OF REMARRIAGE. The pattern of remarriage has changed rapidly. In the 1960s, a third of divorced women remarried during the *first* year after their divorce. Within two years, half had remarried (*Statistical Abstract* 1998:Table 161). Today, women take a longer time to remarry, and half of women who divorce never do marry again (Bramlett and Mosher 2002). Figure 11-6 illustrates how significant race-ethnicity is in determining whether women remarry. (Comparable data are not available for men.) Some take this change as a negative sign, an indication that people distrust

FIGURE 11-6 The Probability That Divorced Women Will Remarry in Five Years

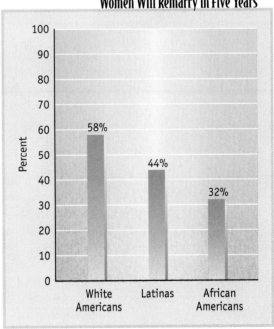

White Americans 58%
Latinas 44%
African Americans 32%

Note: The source does not include other groups and men.

Source: By the author. Based on Bramlett and Mosher 2002.

marriage more than they used to and are, therefore, more hesitant to marry. This could be, but it also could mean that people are more selective than they used to be. Perhaps they are even making wiser choices. No one knows for sure.

One-Parent Families

BIRTHS TO UNMARRIED WOMEN. Figure 11-7 summarizes a statistic about U.S. families that has greatly upset people. Each year, more than 1 million babies are born to unmarried mothers. This is one-third (35 percent) of all U.S. babies (*Statistical Abstract* 2006:Table 82). This rate is sharply higher than in our past: It is *six* times higher than it was in 1940, *three* times higher than it was in 1970, and about *double* what it was in 1980.

As we have seen throughout this text, social problems often follow lines of race and ethnicity. You can see this in matters of the family also. As Figure 11-7 shows, the proportion of births to single women differs markedly among racial-ethnic groups. To look at the extremes, the proportion of births to unmarried Asian American women is less than one-fourth what it is among African American women. From Figure 11-5, you can see that when children live with just one parent it is likely to be the mother. This is true regardless of the child's race-ethnicity. From this figure, you can also see that an African American child is the least likely to be living with both parents.

HAVING JUST ONE PARENT. Births to single women and divorce can be looked at as individual matters, of course, and they are. When multiplied by millions, though, their consequences reverberate throughout society. The primary problem is that the children of single and divorced parents are denied benefits that children in two-parent families take for granted, especially having their father as a male role model. Millions of boys and girls have to learn the male role from mothers, boyfriends, television, and the streets. This is especially hard on boys, who often end up with grossly inadequate substitutes. With high rates of divorce and births to single women, *17 million* children live without fathers at home. Another *3 million* live without their mothers (*Statistical Abstract* 2006:Table 60). As always, overall statistics conceal significant variations. The Social Map on the next page shows how the states compare in the percentage of families that are headed by single parents.

FIGURE 11-7   Of All Births, What Percentage Are to Single Women?

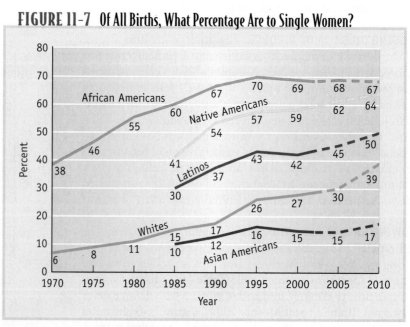

Note: Broken lines indicate the author's estimates.

Source: By the author. Based on *Statistical Abstract of the United States* 1992:Table 87; 1998:Table 100; 2006:Table 73.

FIGURE 11-8 Families Headed by Single Parents

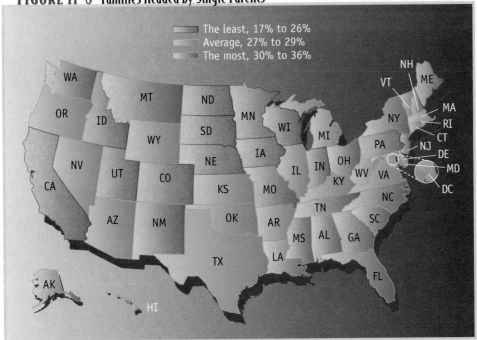

The least, 17% to 26%
Average, 27% to 29%
The most, 30% to 36%

Source: By the author. Based on "Kids Count Data Sheet" 2004.

Impact on Children ■ Being reared by only one parent has a significant impact on children. Sociologists may argue (as they do) about cause and effect, that this or that is not proven and could be due to something else, but every year of every decade children who come from mother-headed families are more likely to drop out of school and get in trouble with the law. This statistic applies to every region of the country and to every racial-ethnic group. There just are no exceptions. I know of no group in which children reared by both parents are more likely to drop out of school or to get into trouble with the law.

Life for single mothers is usually filled with difficulties. In the typical case, these mothers are younger, have little education, and have an inadequate income. Although their resources are highly limited, their responsibilities are great.

Absence of the Father ■ The absence of the father is proposed by some as the major explanation for some of the problems we analyzed in other chapters. The higher a group's rate of mother-headed families, for example, the higher is that group's rate of violent crimes. Such a statistic says nothing about the individual child, of course. Although children from mother-headed homes are more likely to drop out of school and get in trouble with the law, any particular child may grow up to become an artist, an astronaut, or (and what can you expect of this author!) a sociologist. But, *on average,* which is what sociologists deal with, the absence of a father is more likely to lead to such problems.

We don't understand the mechanisms by which this occurs, and as much as we would like it to be otherwise, on average, a mother by herself does not do the same job of rearing children that a mother and father do together. On a personal note, let me add that it was difficult for my wife and me to guide a son through the turbulence of adolescence. To counteract the effects of peer groups required countless discussions, and even our combined efforts were at times barely sufficient to keep him in school and out of trouble with the law. But for so many, the burden falls on just one parent, who finds it too much to cope with.

Sociologist Travis Hirschi (Pope 1988:117–118) says that, all else being equal, one parent is probably sufficient. The problem, he says, is that rarely is all else equal:

> The single parent (usually a woman) must devote a good deal to support and maintenance activities that are at least to some extent shared in the two-parent family. Further, she must do so in the absence of psychological or social support. As a result, she is less able to devote time to monitoring and punishment, and is more likely to be involved in negative, abusive contacts with her children.

Equality is a goal with which most of us agree in principle. Because we all perceive reality from particular corners in life, however, putting "equality" into practice is problematic: What some see as gaining equality, others view as a demand for privileges. For one group to gain equality, then, some other group might undergo a reduction in privileges. Shown here is one example of this problem.

Trying to be Two Parents ■ One-parent families are not limited to fatherless families, of course. Our 3 million motherless households also present tremendous obstacles to fathers who rear children alone. How should a single father teach female roles to his daughter? Whether man or woman, the single parent must try to be both mother and father, which, if not impossible, is certainly a formidable task. (We don't have enough studies on the consequences of father-headed families.)

Discipline ■ The essential problem appears to be defective discipline—in either direction, excessive leniency or excessive control (Pope 1988). To find the proper balance is difficult for any family, but more difficult for one parent to achieve than for two.

The Cross-Cultural Context ■ As always, it is difficult to determine cause and effect, and sociologists are especially good at complicating explanations by adding more data. In this case, when we add cross-cultural data, we see that explanations based around father absence are not adequate. Look at Figure 11-9 on the next page, which compares births to single women in ten Most Industrialized Nations. Four of these nations have a rate higher than ours. Yet in none of them is the rate of juvenile delinquency or violent crimes as high as ours. Therefore, something else also has to be at work. That "something else" is the culture within which one-parent families live—family support systems, subcultures of violence, access to guns, and views of life. Sociologists have not unraveled this thorny problem.

FIGURE 11-9 Births to Single Women in Ten Most Industrialized Nations*

Note: *As a percentage of all births. For some countries, the latest year available is 2003.

Source: By the author. Based on *Statistical Abstract of the United States* 2007:Table 1311.

Other Problems

RUNAWAY CHILDREN. Although some might disagree that divorce, a slowing rate of re-marriage, births to single women, and families headed by one parent indicate a social problem, no one disputes that runaway children offer evidence that something is wrong with many U.S. families. No central agency keeps track of runaways, so we lack firm figures. The media sometimes say that one million children run away from home each year, but this is simply a round number used to gain the public's attention. No one knows the total, but whatever it is, each year the police arrest about 70,000 children on charges of running away from home (*Sourcebook of Criminal Justice Statistics* 2005:Table 4.6). At a minimum, we can say that runaways are not fleeing happy homes. They are trying to escape from intolerable situations—incest, beatings, and other debilitating family conditions.

The streets are tough, and survival is precarious. Some runaways (and "pushouts," children who have been shoved out by parents who no longer want them) fall into the hands of predators, making their already bruised lives even more desperate. Pedophiles (adults who want sexual relations with children) and pimps search bus stations for victims, looking for children who appear lonely, confused, and vulnerable. As adults who work with runaways have observed, when children tire of sleeping in doorways, their alternative to starvation is to steal or to turn to the only thing they have—their bodies. Many runaways get involved in prostitution and pornography when they have no money and no place to go.

FAMILY VIOLENCE. Another indication of family problems is violence. Police and welfare workers know the scene all too well: the battered child, wife, husband, parent, or even grandparent. About 75,000 people are arrested each year for "offenses against family and children" (*Sourcebook of Criminal Justice Statistics,* 2005:Table 4.6). Sociologists Suzanne Steinmetz and Murray Straus (1974; Straus 1992) stress that it would be hard to find a group or institution in the United States in which violence is more of an everyday occurrence than in the family. They add that our data expose is only the tip of the iceberg.

IN SUMMARY

Problems of violence, divorce, runaways, and so on indicate severe problems in the U.S. family. They do *not* indicate, however, that the family is disintegrating. Although the contemporary family is in trouble, as a social institution it will endure its present crisis. Despite family problems, humans have found no satisfactory substitute for the family, and millions of people report that marriage and family meet their needs for intimacy and sense of identity and belonging. In this book, however, we examine *problems,* not the joys of marriage and family. At this point, let's turn our theoretical lenses on these problems.

Looking at the Problem Theoretically: Why Is Divorce Common?

For most of us, the family is our major support system. Our family nourishes and protects us when we are young. It gives us security and love and shapes our personality. Sociologists call the family that rears us our **family of orientation** because it introduces us to the world and teaches us ways to cope with life. As a result, most people around the world try to establish stability, identity, and intimacy through marriage. When we marry, we form what is called a **family of procreation.**

With the high value we place on marriage and family and the many benefits they give us, why is divorce common? Sociologists have used their three theoretical lenses to examine how divorce is related to changes in society. As always, each lens yields a unique interpretation, but, as you will see, in this case the theoretical contribution of each dovetails neatly with the others.

Symbolic Interactionism

AN OVERLOADED INSTITUTION. To explain why our divorce rate is so high, symbolic interactionists examine what people expect out of marriage. In 1933, sociologist William Ogburn noted that personality was becoming more important in people's choice of a husband or wife. A few years later, in 1945, sociologists Ernest Burgess and Harvey Locke observed that affection, understanding, and compatibility were becoming more central to marriage. These sociologists had documented a major change: Society had become more complex and impersonal, and increasingly people were looking for marriage to satisfy their needs for intimacy.

These trends have escalated. Society has grown more impersonal, and today husbands and wives expect even greater emotional satisfaction from one another. Having come to view marriage as a solution to the tensions produced by our problem-ridden society (Lasch 1977), we are likely to expect our spouse to meet most of our personality and emotional needs. Because these expectations place a heavy burden on marriage, often more than it can carry, sociologists say that marriage and family have become an *overloaded institution.* Let's see how marriage and family have become "overloaded."

The Love Symbol: Engulfment into Unrealistic Expectations ■ The "affection, understanding, and compatibility" that Burgess and Locke observed in 1945, saying that they were becoming more central to marriage, escalated into *the* central component of today's marriage. They coalesced into a concept called love, as in "Love conquers all." Our ideas of love encourage us to expect marriage to deliver more than it possibly can, setting us up for inevitable disappointment. The American idea of love carries an expectation of total happiness: If we are "truly in love," we will be satisfied emotionally and, somehow, enjoy a continuous emotional high. For Americans, love has become *the* reason for marriage. The unrealistic expectations associated with such ideas of love, however,

Ideas of love permeate our culture, often creating sentimental feelings when we see symbols of love. These feelings, in turn, motivate couples to marry and to take on the responsibilities of rearing children.

must at some point come down to earth, and, when they do, the consequences can be tragic. When dissatisfactions arise in marriage, as they inevitably do, spouses tend to blame one another, believing that the other has somehow failed them. Their engulfment in the symbol of love blinds them to the unreality of their expectations. In effect, our culture's lesson is that we should base a lifelong relationship on a temporary emotional state. (Of course, when we are "madly in love," we hope it isn't temporary.)

Changing Ideas About Children ◼ Ideas about children have undergone a historical shift so profound that the customs of earlier generations seem strange to us. This change, too, has deeply affected the family. In medieval society, children were seen as miniature adults (Aries 1962). With no sharp separation between their worlds, adults and children mixed freely with one another. At about age 7, boys became apprentices in some occupation, whereas girls of this age learned the homemaking duties that were associated with their cultural role. These practices don't make sense to us. We consider age 7 to be a tender phase of early childhood. In short, from being viewed as miniature adults, children have been culturally transformed into impressionable, vulnerable, and innocent beings.

Changing Expectations of Parenting ◼ Ideas about children—what they are like and what we can expect of them—lie at the root of what we expect of parents. Three generations ago, until about 1940, U.S. children "became adults" when they graduated from eighth grade and took a job. Because we now view children as more vulnerable and expect them to be dependent much longer, we expect parents to give their children greater protection and to nurture them for many more years. We even expect parents to help their children "reach their potential." As the tasks associated with child rearing have expanded, and as the expected emotional ties between parents and children have become more intense, the family has been thrust into even greater "emotional overload" (Lasch 1977).

Changing Marital Roles ◼ The past is being wiped away as change also sweeps over traditional ideas of the "right" way to be a wife or a husband. It used to be that everyone (including the neighbors and in-laws) expected the husband to assume the role of breadwinner. It was his responsibility to provide for the family. If he did that well, he was considered a good husband and father. Those same neighbors and in-laws expected the wife to stay home, to take care of the house and children, and to attend to the personal needs of her husband. If she did those things well, she was considered a good wife and mother. Traditional roles—whatever their faults, and there were many—provided clear-cut guidelines for behavior. Newlyweds knew what to expect of one another—because they, too, held these same ideas—and neither they nor their friends and relatives questioned those basic expectations. No longer.

Today's newlyweds are expected to work out their own roles. Although this gives them a great deal of freedom and flexibility, it also produces a major source of tension and conflict. A couple's ideas might not mesh. They may disagree over who should do what housework, whether the wife should be career oriented, or to what extent, how to make spending decisions, or how to divide responsibilities for the children. Because guidelines are still unclear, couples face a role vacuum that can create discontent. How can you adequately fulfill your marital role if you can't agree on what that role is?

IN SUM Collectively, then, these fundamental changes in the meaning of marriage—our ideas about love, children, parenthood, and the roles of husband and wife—put tremendous pressure on spouses and provide a strong push toward divorce. These changes have created an "emotional overload" that becomes a burden to today's couples. We expect marriage to provide unlimited emotional satisfaction, something that it just cannot deliver.

PERCEPTION OF ALTERNATIVES. While these fundamental changes were taking place, another change also occurred that affected marriage deeply. More women were taking jobs outside the home, and this, too, had a fundamental effect on people's ideas about marriage.

As wives earned paychecks of their own, they began to perceive alternatives to putting up with unhappy marriages. Symbolic interactionists consider the *perception of alternatives* as an essential first step to making divorce possible.

CHANGING IDEAS ABOUT DIVORCE. It is difficult for us to grasp how seriously divorce was once taken. Divorce used to represent failure, irresponsibility, and immorality. Divorced people were social outcasts. They were suspected of immoral behavior and were no longer welcome as dinner guests. As divorce became more common, its meaning changed: Divorce was transformed from being a symbol of failure to one of self-fulfillment, of opportunity rather than shame. This symbolic leap added one more push toward divorce. When being a divorced person carried a stigma, divorce was held in check. As divorce became a sign of personal change and development, the stage was set for widespread divorce.

Legal Changes ■ The law also used to hold divorce in check, for divorce was granted only on rigorous grounds. In some states, such as New York, obtaining a divorce required that one spouse prove that the other had committed adultery. This proof required witnesses and a trial. As people's ideas about divorce changed, the laws against it were relaxed. Today, in most states, "incompatibility," as vague as that term is, is adequate grounds for divorce. In many states, couples can work out their own "no-fault" divorce, and judges "compatibly" divorce them. In Florida, the couple can sign papers in a lawyer's office, and they don't even have to appear in court. Such legal changes have further reduced the stigma attached to divorce, which, in turn, has contributed to the divorce rate.

Are These Changes Good or Bad? ■ Symbolic interactionists take the position that nothing is good or bad in and of itself. They view "goodness" and "badness" as value judgments that are imposed on people's behavior. Thus, different groups evaluate divorce differently. Depending on its assumptions, one group is alarmed at increases in divorce and changes in sex roles, ideas of what children are, parenting, and so on, whereas another group looks at these same changes and feels pleased that the family is evolving. Symbolic interactionists can't say which view, if either, is correct, for symbolic interactionism provides no framework to make value judgments about anything.

IN SUM To explain why divorce increased, symbolic interactionists analyze how the symbols (that is, ideas or expectations) associated with the family have changed. They stress that symbols both reflect and create reality. That is, symbols not only represent people's ideas, but those same symbols also influence people's behaviors and ideas. Although symbolic interactionists can analyze social change, they cannot pass judgment on it.

Functionalism

When functionalists analyze social change, they look at how change in one part of a social system affects its other parts. Earlier, in "The Problem in Sociological Perspective," pages 363–366, we examined the impact of industrialization and urbanization on the family. We saw, for example, how the birthrate fell as children became more dependent, unproductive, and costly.

HOW CHANGES IN THE TRADITIONAL FUNCTIONS OF THE FAMILY ARE RELATED TO DIVORCE.
Functionalists have identified seven traditional functions of the family. They point out that around the world the family provides

1. Economic production
2. Socialization of children
3. Care of the sick and injured
4. Care of the aged
5. Recreation
6. Sexual control of family members
7. Reproduction

Let's see what effects the Industrial Revolution and urbanization have had on these seven traditional functions of the family—and how these changes are related to divorce. We will examine each of the seven functions in the order they were just listed.

Economic Production ▪ Before industrialization, the family was an economic team. Unlike today, survival was precarious. Even getting enough food and adequate clothing were problems. For survival, the members of a family—like it or not—were forced to cooperate. *Industrialization moved production from home to factory, disrupting this team.* This isolated the husband-father from the daily activities of the family, separated the wife-mother from the production of income, and made older children, who went to work for wages, less dependent on their family.

Socialization of Children ▪ While economic production was changing, the state and federal governments were growing larger, more centralized, and more powerful. One consequence was that the government began to take over some of the family's functions, weakening family relationships. For example, lawmakers passed mandatory education laws, making it illegal for parents not to send their children to school. Parents faced fines and jail if they did not put their children in the government's care. In this way, the government took over much of the responsibility for socializing children.

Care of the Sick and Aged ▪ Care of the sick and aged followed a similar course. Before industrialization, there were few trained physicians, and medicine had been a family matter. When someone was sick, the individual was cared for at home. As medical schools developed, along with hospitals and drugs, medicine came under government control. Gradually medical care shifted from the family to medical specialists. It was similarly the case with care of the aged. As the central government expanded and its agencies multiplied, care of the aged, too, became a government obligation.

Recreation ▪ As industrialization progressed, the country became more affluent. The family's disposable income increased, and businesses sprang up to compete for that income. Before the industrial age, entertainment and "fun" had consisted primarily of home-based activities—card games, parlor and barn dances, sleigh rides, and so on. As family-centered activities gave way to public-centered paid events, the family lost much of its recreational function.

Control of Sexuality ▪ The family had also controlled the sexuality of its members, but even this changed. Sexual relations in marriage were the only ones that were viewed as legitimate. Sexual relations outside marriage—even between an engaged couple who planned to marry shortly—were considered immoral. Although this was only an ideal, and marriage never enjoyed a monopoly on sexual relations, the "sexual revolution" opened many alternatives to marital sex. Consequently, to understate the matter, marital control over sexuality is considerably weaker than it used to be.

Reproduction ▪ At first glance, the seventh function, reproduction, appears to remain solidly in the family's domain. Yet even this vital and seemingly inviolable function of the family is not going unchallenged. Review Figures 11-7 and 11-9 (on pages 370 and 373), which show that giving birth outside marriage has become much more common. In the United States, one-third of reproduction has moved away from the traditional family unit of husband and wife. In addition, married women can get abortions without informing their husband, and teenagers can obtain birth control and, in most states, abortions without parental consent. Buttressed by laws and government funding, then, some control over reproduction has been removed from the family.

Can reproduction move even farther away from the sphere of the family? Some envision a future in which women, single or married, homosexual or heterosexual, order semen to match their specifications: sex, race-ethnicity, height, hair color, eye color, body type, even intelligence, personality traits, and ability in music, art, poetry, and sports (Bagne 1992). Sociologist Judith Lorber (1980:527) proposed a system of "professional breeders":

A system of completely professional breeders and child rearers could be conducted with the best of modern technology—fertility drugs for multiple births, sperm banks, embryo transfers, and uterine implants to expand the gene pool and so on. Professional breeders could be paid top salaries, like today's athletes, for the 15–20 years of their prime childbearing time. Those who were impregnated could live in well-run dormitories, with excellent physical care, food, and entertainment.

We are caught in the middle—somewhere between our fast-paced, changing present, and a fast-approaching mind-boggling, largely technology-driven future. Although we can speculate about what the future will look like, none of us knows its specifics. Perhaps Lorber's vision may come about—although such a future could be the fulfillment of a dream for those who want to usher in a *1984*-like Big Brother or a Hitleresque *Lebensraum*.

IN SUM The family has lost many of its traditional functions, and other functions are under assault. From a functionalist perspective, such changes have weakened the family unit. The fewer functions that family members have in common, the fewer are their "ties that bind." As these bonds have weakened, the family has become more fragile. Divorce, then, has become more common—the inevitable consequence of eroded functions in a context of greater social strain.

Conflict Theory

Conflict theorists point us in a different direction. They stress that marriage and family reflect a basic social inequality of men and women. In general, men control, dominate, and exploit women, and marriage is one of the means by which they do this.

MALE DOMINATION OF MARRIAGE AND FAMILY. Historically, men have dominated women. The home was a place where women served their fathers, husbands, and brothers. Fathers decided whom their daughters would marry—often on the basis of the benefits that they themselves would derive, such as gaining favor with more powerful men. A common example is how kings forged alliances with other kings by giving their daughters in marriage. Both custom and the law allowed men to discipline not only their children, but also their wives. A husband could spank his wife—if she "needed" it. Even beating a wife was considered permissible if she became rebellious or had an affair. In some areas, killing an unfaithful wife was within the community's norms. In some places, such as Pakistan, it still is.

Our own forms of marriage and family reflect these millennia-old patterns of power. One of the most striking examples is the traditional U.S. wedding ceremony. While the mother sits passively on the side, the father walks down the aisle with his daughter and "gives" her to her husband. This is but a pale reflection of the power men once wielded—when fathers were able to choose their daughters' husbands—but it is a reflection nonetheless.

Marriage as an Arena for a Continuing Historical Struggle ■ Although men's power has eroded severely, inequality between men and women remains, making marriage an arena for this ongoing struggle between the sexes. This, say conflict theorists, is the key to understanding today's family problems. In individual marriages, historical causes drop from sight. As husbands and wives argue and fight, they don't view their personal problems as rooted in broad historical change. They experience personal disagreements with their spouse, not something historical or in the abstract. At the root of personal marital disagreements, however, stress conflict theorists, lies this historical struggle between men and women over rights, obligations, and privileges.

As industrialization progressed, women's roles changed. As their experiences expanded beyond home, church, and neighbors, women came to resent arrangements that they had taken for granted. Housework became one of these sources of resentment. Sociologist Arlie Hochschild (2001) points out that even today, most wives, after returning home from an eight-hour shift of work-for-wages, put in a "second shift" doing cooking, cleaning, and child care. In two-paycheck families, wives average 15 hours more work each week than their husbands. The cumulative total is incredible: Over a year, wives work an *extra month of twenty-four hour days*. Husbands resist attempts to reduce their power, and wives resent their husband's reluctance to share responsibilities. Within the intimacy of the family, then, this historical struggle is being played out. At times, this competition between the sexes breaks into open conflict, taking the forms of spouse battering and child abuse.

Consciousness of Oppression ▪ This analysis may fly in the face of your own experience. Many wives do not *feel* oppressed, and some husbands feel that *they* are oppressed. A woman who does not feel oppressed, say conflict theorists, is blind to her real situation and is suffering from false consciousness. A man who feels oppressed, however, may be expressing social reality, for the social system oppresses both males and females. The difference, however, is that although society may torment both sexes, society is the creation of men and reflects their reality (de Beauvoir 1953).

Power and the Marital Experience ▪ This unequal balance of power has caused men and women to experience dating and marriage differently. In traditional arrangements, women expected their lives to revolve around being a wife and mother. Consequently, with their goal of finding a husband who would provide security, they felt more anxious than men about dating, finding a mate, and the resulting quality of family life (Greer 1972). One consequence was that wives tended to invest more time and effort in making the marriage work (Firestone 1970). For the sake of maintaining security, including their status in the community, they would put up with unsatisfying relationships. Today's women, who are more career oriented and less dependent on marriage for their status and welfare, are not as willing to put up with relationships that don't provide fulfillment.

The 1950s marked a watershed era in U.S. middle-class families. With the husband's income adequate to support a family comfortably, the wife was expected to focus on the home. This historical period is bathed in images that characterized only a minority of families, images that form a mythical lens through which we view that "ideal" period of family life.

IN SUM Conflict theorists stress that marriage and family reflect fundamental, historical relationships between men and women. Historically, men have dominated marriage. Women's greater willingness—or capacity—to divorce is part of this historical struggle. High divorce rates are not a sign that the family is weakening but, rather, that women are making headway in their millennia-old struggle with men; they are an indication of increasing equality in marriage (Zinn and Eitzen 1990).

Research Findings

Let's look at major characteristics of marriage and family today: age at first marriage, cohabitation, remaining single, childlessness, family violence, sexual abuse, and abandonment of the elderly. Then let's consider whether these characteristics indicate the death of the family.

Cohabitation and the Changing Age at First Marriage

CHANGES IN AGE AT FIRST MARRIAGE. From 1890 to 1950, Americans married at younger and younger ages. By 1950, brides were younger than at any other time in U.S. history: The typical bride had just left her teens. By 1970, the grooms were also the youngest since the U.S. government kept records. After plateauing for about twenty years, there was an abrupt reversal, and *today's average first-time bride and groom are older than at any other time in U.S. history.*

FIGURE 11-10 Cohabitation in the United States

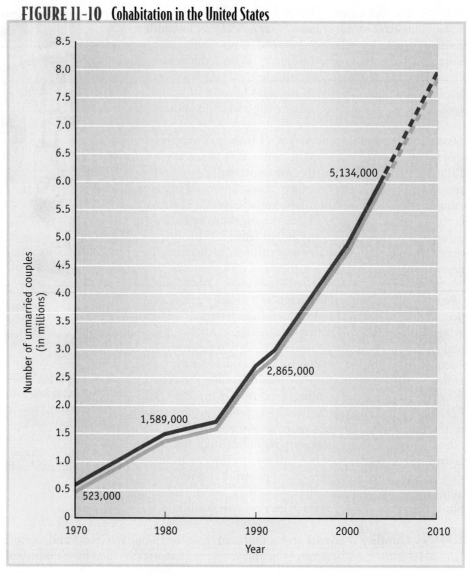

Note: These are totals for heterosexual cohabitation. The source indicates that 700,000 homosexual couples are also cohabiting. The broken line is the author's estimate.

Source: By the author. Based on *Statistical Abstract of the United States* 1985:Table 54; 2007:Table 61.

COHABITATION. Why this reversal? Sociologists point to Figure 11-10 as the answer. Look at the sharp increase in the number of unmarried couples who are **cohabiting,** living together in a sexual relationship. Some sociologists estimate that if cohabitation had not increased so much, the average age at first marriage might show little change.

It is not that most cohabitants are opposed to marriage. They are opposed, rather, to marriage for themselves at this particular time. For a variety of reasons, they do not feel that they are ready to handle the commitments and responsibilities of marriage. Although attracted to one another and wanting more than to be just "going together," many couples fear that their relationship isn't solid enough for marriage. They feel that they might develop this commitment, however, while they cohabit. Finances are also a major concern. Some couples fear that marriage will tie them down financially, but cohabitation doesn't require this same commitment. Marriage is also considered a declaration of financial independence from parents, and for many young people, especially college students, cohabitation keeps them eligible for support from their parents. For some, of course, cohabitation is simply a way to enjoy regular sex with a dependable partner minus the hassles of dating.

THE INCREASING NUMBER OF SINGLES. So many Americans have postponed their wedding day that the percentage of single young people has surged. The percentage of women age 25 to 29 who are single today is almost *four* times higher than it was in 1970 (only 11 percent unmarried in 1970 compared with 41 percent today). The percentage of single men of this age group has jumped *three* times (19 percent unmarried in 1970 and 57 percent today) (*Statistical Abstract* 1993:Table 52; 1998:Table 62; 2006:Table 51).

REMAINING SINGLE. Few people look at being single as a permanent alternative to marriage. Some do, however, and as sociologist Peter Stein (1992) found, those who plan on remaining single all their lives still feel a strong need for intimacy, sharing, and continuity. To attain these satisfactions, which marriage and family ordinarily provide, the permanent singles cultivate a network of people who feel as they do about marriage. Through these friendships, they satisfy their needs for intimacy.

Childlessness

PRESSURES TO HAVE CHILDREN. Although most married women give birth, about one of five (19 percent) does not (DeOilos and Kapinus 2002). Childlessness has grown so fast that this statistic is *twice* what it was twenty years ago. Most of these couples choose not to have children, but many couples are infertile. Sociologist Charlene Miall (1986), who studied infertile couples, found that they feel stigmatized because childlessness goes against strong cultural expectations that married couples will have children. In their everyday interactions, these couples maneuver defensively. They find topics of pregnancy and parenthood especially threatening or potentially embarrassing, and they tiptoe around them in their conversations with friends, relatives, and fellow workers. They even select friends who are comfortable with childlessness.

THE PROCESS OF REMAINING CHILDLESS. Sociologists have also studied couples who choose to remain childless. Sociologist Jean Veevers (1973, 1980) found that of fifty-two wives who had been married at least five years and had not given birth deliberately, about a third had made an agreement with their husbands before they married not to have children. In fact, they had sought husbands who would agree to remain, in their terms, child free. (They prefer the term "child free," as it carries a sense of freedom, not the stigma that they feel accompanies the term "childless.")

About two-thirds of the wives that Veevers studied, however, had planned to have children, but never did. Their permanent childlessness was the result of a four-stage process. First, these women had postponed the decision to get pregnant while they worked toward a specific goal, such as graduating from college or buying a house. Then they shifted their postponement to a vague future, a "sometime" (such as when they would feel financially independent) that never seemed to arrive. During the third stage, they decided that not having kids wasn't so bad, that they *might* want to remain childless. When they reached the fourth stage, they viewed their childlessness as a permanent rather than a temporary state.

The Mythical Child ■ All the wives who decided to remain childless felt stigmatized. Friends and relatives put pressure on them to bear children and made negative comments because they weren't pregnant. These pressures peaked during their third and fourth years of marriage, then decreased after they were married for five or six years. To help cope, the couples talked about what Veevers calls their "mythical child," the one that they would adopt "one day." Few couples, however, made an effort to contact an adoption agency, and none of those who did followed up their initial contact. The "mythical child" helped the couples to adjust, for it made their childlessness seem temporary. Talking about adoption affirmed to themselves and others that they were "normal" people who liked children. Even after the wives became too old to bear children, adoption remained a symbol that held open the possibility of socially altering biological facts.

Family Violence

When she refused to give him money, the middle-aged man pushed the frail 70-year-old woman to the floor. She sprawled there, stunned and helpless, while he screamed insults. The woman became even more upset when the police arrived. She told them that she didn't want her attacker to be arrested.

This was not the first time—nor would it be the last—that this man would attack her. He was her son.

A NATIONAL STUDY. Murray Straus heads the Family Violence Research Program at the University of New Hampshire. He and fellow sociologists Susan Steinmetz and Richard Gelles have studied this cruel irony—that the social group we most often look to for intimacy and love is sometimes characterized by cruelty and violence. To determine the amount and types of violence in U.S. homes, they interviewed nationally representative samples of couples. Their questions about acts of intentional physical injury ranged from slapping, pushing, kicking, biting, and beating to attacking with a knife or gun (Straus et al. 1980; Straus and Gelles 1988; Straus 1992).

EXTENT OF VIOLENCE. Here is one of the most startling aspects of their research: The FBI reports violence in numbers per 100,000 people, but violence among family members is so common that these researchers reported incidents per 100 people. They found that each year, 16 of every 100 spouses physically attack their husband or wife. This is 1 spouse out of every 6. No other violent crime even approaches this rate.

Because most couples (84 percent) were not violent during the past year and most violence is mild (such as slapping), some dismiss these figures with a "so what" attitude. To this, Straus and Gelles (1988) reply (paraphrased):

> Let's suppose we are talking about a university. Would anyone say that there wasn't much of a problem because, after all, 84 percent of the faculty didn't hit a student last year? Or would anyone argue that this isn't significant because, after all, most of the 16 percent of faculty members who were violent only slapped students, rather than punching or beating them?

Violence among spouses, whatever its forms, is a topic of research by sociologists. Sometimes sociologists become interested in a social problem because of personal experience with it. This is how it was for sociologist Kathleen Ferraro, who shares her experiences in the Spotlight on Social Research box on the next page.

THE MOST VIOLENT. The most violent family members are the children. During the year preceding the interview, two-thirds of the children had attacked a brother or sister. Most had shoved or thrown things, but one-third had kicked or bitten a sibling. In rare instances, the attack involved a knife or gun. Straus suggests that these totals are severe underestimates.

EQUALITY BETWEEN THE SEXES? This surprises some people, but husbands and wives are about equally as likely to attack one another (Gelles 1980; Straus 1980, 1992). It is a different matter, when we look at the *effects* of violence. Then sexual equality vanishes. As Straus points out, even though she may cast the first coffeepot, he usually casts the last and most damaging blow. Because most men are bigger and stronger than their wives, women are at a disadvantage in this literal battle of the sexes, and after episodes of spousal violence more women than men need medical attention. Like other crimes, marital violence has dropped in recent years, so much so that it is now *less than half* of what it was just ten years ago (*Statistical Abstract* 2006:Table 304). When the worst happens, and one spouse kills another, four times out of five the wife is the victim (*FBI Uniform Crime Report* 2006:Table 9).

SOCIAL CLASS AND VIOLENCE. When it comes to social class and violence, you might hear someone say, "Violence occurs in all social classes." This statement is true, because, like everything except poverty, all social classes have some of it. But such a statement hides much more than it reveals. Like everything else, including money, violence is not distributed equally among the classes. Violence follows well-worn "social channels," which makes spouses in some social classes much more likely to be abusers—or victims—than others. The highest rates of violence (Gelles 1980) are found among

Families with low incomes

Blue-collar workers

Families in which the husband is unemployed

Families with above-average numbers of children

People with less education

Individuals who have no religious affiliation

People under 30

Poverty and Violence ■ Poverty is the theme running through the first five of these findings. Poverty opens only some of the doors, however, for, as you can see, age and religion are also factors. Although family violence occurs in all social classes, blue-collar spouses,

Spotlight on Social Research
INTIMATE PARTNER VIOLENCE

KATHLEEN FERRARO, *Professor of Sociology at Northern Arizona University, wanted to be a sociologist from the time she was 12. She never imagined, though, that her research would focus on "intimate partner violence," because she never knew that this existed.*

I found out about "intimate partner violence" at age 23 when I married my first husband. He went to high school with me and came from a well-respected family. He was a naturalist and a bird-watcher, did not drink or use drugs, and showed no violent tendencies. After we exchanged vows, however, he changed almost immediately, displaying the "power and control" tactics that have become so well known today. He monitored my movements, eating, clothing, friends, money, make-up, and language. If I challenged his commands, he slapped or kicked me or pushed me down.

I left him on these occasions, staying with other graduate students at Arizona State University, but I had no way to understand what was happening. My husband always convinced me to return. He stalked and threatened to kill me, even in front of police officers, but my faculty mentor, Albert J. Mayer, and my friends hid me until my father-in-law came to take my husband back to our hometown on the other side of the country. I obtained a single-party, no-fault divorce and never saw him again.

These events took place in 1974 and 1975, before the battered women's movement transformed public understanding of "domestic violence." In a graduate class on

social deviance, Erdwin Pfuhl required us to write a paper on a form of deviance with which we had personal experience. I could not think of anything. While I waited outside his office to ask for help, another woman struck up a conversation with me, and I learned that her boyfriend abused her. That was the moment that I began to think sociologically about my own experience. I discovered that there was a battered women's shelter in my city, and I began to volunteer there and to interview staff members. This was the beginning of the battered women's movement and the beginning of a lifetime of research, teaching, and activism for me. I joined with a group of people to establish another shelter, and that is where I conducted the interviews and ethnographic work for my dissertation, *Battered Women and the Shelter Movement*, and for the *Social Problems* article, "How Women Experience Battering: The Process of Victimization."

The women taught me how difficult it is to make sense of the violence and emotional abuse that come from a person they love and believe loves them. The rationalizations the women used to understand what was happening to them were similar to those used by people who commit crimes, the "techniques of neutralization" described by Gresham Sykes and David Matza [reviewed in Chapter 6 in this text]. For women at the shelter, these techniques included denial of victimization, denial of the victimizer, denial of injury, denial of options, appeal to higher loyalties, and the salvation ethic. Because of fear, lack of resources, and institutional failure to respond to battering, the women found escape from violent relationships to be difficult and precarious. Leaving an abuser does not necessarily end the violence—women are often at most risk during the time they are leaving the abuser.

FIGURE 11-11 How Is Marital Violence Related to the Family Violence That Teenagers Experience?

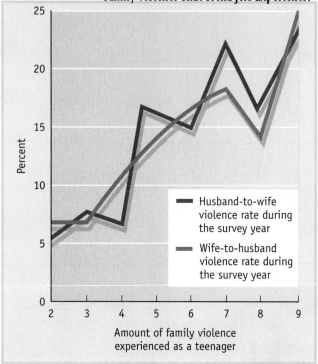

Legend:
- Husband-to-wife violence rate during the survey year
- Wife-to-husband violence rate during the survey year

Y-axis: Percent
X-axis: Amount of family violence experienced as a teenager

Source: Straus, Gelles, and Steinmetz 1980:112.

especially husbands, are considerably more violent than white-collar spouses. The researchers suggest that this is because blue-collar husbands experience more stress than their white-collar counterparts. Although it is likely that blue-collar husbands do experience much more stress, this does not explain why that stress is translated into violence toward their wives. For this, we need more research that uses symbolic interactionism, research that tries to understand life from the perspective of blue- and white-collar husbands. Perhaps you will be the researcher who does such an enlightening study.

ALCOHOL AND VIOLENCE. Sociologists Glenda Kantor and Murray Straus (1987) also found another key to spousal violence: alcohol. Based on a national probability sample, they found a direct relationship between alcohol consumption and wife battering; that is, the more a husband drinks, the more likely he is to beat his wife. The lowest rates of violence against wives are by husbands who do not drink, the highest among those who go on binges.

THE SOCIAL HEREDITY OF VIOLENCE. Straus, Gelles, and Steinmetz also discovered what they call the *social heredity of violence.* By this term, they mean that children learn from their parents that violence is a way to solve problems. After the children grow up and marry, they apply this lesson to their own family life. As Figure 11-11 shows, the more violence that children experience during their teen years, the more likely they are to be violent after they marry. Let's hear how the researchers (1980:113) explain Figure 11-11:

> Those with scores of zero are the people whose parents did not hit them and did not hit each other. At the other extreme are people with scores of 9. They are the people whose parents frequently hit them when they were teenagers and whose parents were frequently violent with each other.

The researchers stress how powerful the social heredity of violence is by saying:

> When one member of a couple had experienced the double whammy of being hit as a child and observing his or her parents hitting each other, there was a one in three chance that at least one act of violence had occurred during the year of the study!

WHY DOESN'T SHE JUST LEAVE? Why does a woman remain with a husband who abuses her? This question has intrigued members of the public and sociologists alike. Researchers have studied many samples of women, and they have found remarkably consistent answers. Findings from one of these studies are featured in the Issues in Social Problems box on the next page.

SPOUSE ABUSE AS A DEFENSE FOR HOMICIDE. Some wives, of course, leave their husbands after the first blow and never return. Others remain, but after being brutalized for years, they kill their husbands. Wife beating has become a controversial defense for wives who have killed their husbands. Listen to Cindy Hudo, a 21-year-old mother of two in Charleston, South Carolina, who was charged with the murder of her husband, Buba. Here is what she said:

> I start in the car and I get down the road and I see Buba walking, and he's real mad. I just look at him. So, I pull over, you know, and I'm trying, you know—"I didn't know to pick you up. You know, I'm sorry." And he didn't even say nothing to me. He just started hitting on me. And that's all I wanted to do, was just get home, because I was just self-conscious. I don't want nobody to see him hitting me, because I didn't want him to look bad. I had to go to work in a half-hour, because I was working a double-shift. And he told me I had forty

Issues in Social Problems
"WHY DOESN'T SHE JUST LEAVE?"
THE DILEMMA OF ABUSED WOMEN

"Why would she ever put up with violence?" is a question on everyone's mind. From the outside, it looks so easy. Just pack up and leave. "I know I wouldn't put up with anything like that."

Yet this is not what typically happens. Women tend to stay with their men after they are abused. Some stay only a short while, to be sure, but others remain in abusive situations for years. Why?

Sociologist Ann Goetting (2001) asked this question, too. To get the answer, she interviewed women who had made the break. Goetting wanted to find out what it was that set these women apart. How were they able to leave, when so many can't seem to? She found that:

Husbands or wives who are violent are likely to have been reared in homes in which their own parents were violent, a process sociologists call the "cultural transmission of violence."

1. These women had a positive self-concept.
   Simply put, they believed that they deserved better.
2. They broke with traditional values.
   They did not believe that a wife had to stay with her husband no matter what.
3. They found adequate finances.
   For some this was easy, but for others it was not. To accumulate enough money to move out, some of the women saved for years, putting away just a little each week.
4. They had supportive family and friends.
   A support network served as a source of encouragement to help them rescue themselves.

If you take the opposite of these four characteristics, you have the answer to why some women put up with abuse: They don't think they deserve anything better; they believe it is their duty to stay no matter what; they don't think they can make it financially; and they lack a supportive network. These four factors are not of equal importance. For some women, the lack of finances is the most significant, whereas for others it can be a low self-concept. For all women, the supportive network—or the lack of one—plays a significant role.

FOR YOUR CONSIDERATION

On the basis of these findings, what would you say to a woman whose husband or partner is abusing her? How do you think women's shelters fit into this explanation? What other parts of this puzzle can you think of—such as the role of love?

minutes to get all my furniture out of the house and get my clothes and be out or he was going to throw them out.

And I was sitting there, because I could talk him down. You know, because I didn't want to leave him. I just talked to him. I said, "Buba, I don't want to leave." I said, "This is my house." And then he told me . . . (unclear) my kids. And I said, "No, you're not taking my kids from me. That's too much." And so I said, "Just let me leave. Just let me take the kids. And, you know I'll go, and you know, I won't keep the kids from you or nothing like that." And he said, "I'm going to take them and you're getting out."

[Buba then loaded a shotgun, pointed it at Cindy, and said:] "The only way you're going to get out of this is if you kill me and I'll—I'll kill you." [Buba then gave the shotgun to Cindy and] just turned around and walked right down the hall, because he knew I wouldn't do nothing. And I just sat there a minute. And I don't know what happened. I just, you know, I went to the bedroom and I seen him laying there and I just shot him. He moved. I shot him again because I thought he was going to get up again. . . .

I loved him too much. And I just wanted to help him. (20/20, October 18, 1979)

Although Cindy had shot and killed her husband, who at the time was unarmed and unresisting, a jury acquitted her on the basis that she was a battered wife.

As with Cindy Hudo, in a few celebrated cases wife battering as a defense for homicide has worked, and wives have been acquitted for killing their husband. No matter how understandable the desire to kill may be under conditions of extreme duress, brutality, and fear, this defense raises nagging questions about justifying the killing of spouses.

Sexual Abuse in the Family

MARITAL RAPE. How common is marital rape? This area of human behavior is shrouded in secrecy, making it difficult to gather information (Bennice and Resick 2003). Sociologists David Finkelhor and Kersti Yllo (1983, 1989) broke through that shroud. They interviewed a representative sample of 330 women in the Boston metropolitan area. Ten percent of the women reported that their husbands had used physical force to compel them to have sex. Based on another sampling technique from which we can generalize, sociologist Diana Russell (1980) estimates that 12 percent of married women have been raped by their husbands. If 10 to 12 percent is even close to being accurate, we are talking about 8 or 10 million married women who have suffered this form of sexual abuse (*Statistical Abstract* 2006:Table 50).

Types of Marital Rape ■ From interviews with fifty women whose husbands had raped them, Finkelhor and Yllo found three types of marital rape:

1. *Nonbattering rape.* In about 40 percent of the cases, the husband raped his wife without intending to do physical harm. The attack was usually preceded by a conflict over sex, such as the husband feeling insulted when his wife refused to have sex.
2. *Battering rape.* In about 48 percent of the cases, the husband intentionally inflicted physical pain during the rape. He was retaliating for some supposed wrongdoing on his wife's part.
3. *Perverted rape.* In these instances, about 6 percent, the husband seemed to be sexually aroused by the violence. These husbands forced their wives to submit to unusual sexual acts. (The remaining 6 percent contain elements of more than one type.)

Effects of Marital Rape ■ How did the rapes affect the wives? The short-term effects were anger, accompanied by grief, despair, shame, and a feeling of "dirtiness." The most common long-term effect was the woman's inability to trust intimate relationships or to function sexually.

The Timing of Marital Rape ■ Marital rape most often occurs during separation or when a marriage is breaking up. In rare instances, however, husbands rape their wives throughout marriage. One woman, for example, had endured marital rape for twenty-four years—her marriage ended only when her husband divorced her!

Why do Some Women Put Up with Marital Rape? ■ Although most women quickly leave a marriage after being raped by their husbands, some remain. Why? The answer reflects the reasons why women who are physically but *not* sexually abused remain with their husbands, which we reviewed on the previous page. They are afraid to leave. They fear they do not have the skills to make it on their own. They don't have a supportive network. Or they have children, and with their low self-esteem, they feel they cannot survive without their husbands.

INCEST. Another area that sociologists have investigated is **incest**—forbidden sexual relations between relatives, such as brothers and sisters or parents and children. Sexual relations between siblings or with one's own children are condemned almost universally. If a social group allows incest, it is for specific categories of people and often under limited circumstances. Examples include brother-sister marriages among the Egyptian pharaohs and the Incas of Peru. In East Africa, Thonga lion hunters may have sex with their daughters on the night before a big hunt (La Barre 1954; Beals and Hoijer 1965). Apart from such rare exceptions, incest is viewed as abhorrent, sinful, or unnatural. Revelations of incest are met with repugnance, and incest is one of the few issues on which most Americans strongly agree.

Extent of Incest ▪ With such strong condemnation, incest should be rare, but is it? Sociologist Diana Russell (1986) interviewed a probability sample (from which we can generalize) of 930 women in San Francisco. She found that before these women turned age 18, 16 percent had been victims of incest. Before you conclude that 16 percent of all the women you know or meet have been victims of incest, you need to know that Russell's definition of incest was curiously broad. Not only did her definition include sexual relations with a relative, but also it included unwanted kisses. Russell found that in only 5 of 100 cases were the police informed. Although this study does not reflect common assumptions about what incest is, we can conclude that incest is much more common than the numbers that are officially reported.

This Utah man, Jeremy Kingston, was convicted of marrying his cousin, which is incest in some states but not in others. He was convicted because she was underage when they married. (She was 15 years old and he was 24.) His wife and cousin is also his aunt.

Who Are the Offenders? ▪ Russell found that the most common offenders are uncles, followed by first cousins, then fathers (biological, adoptive, step, and foster), brothers, and finally other relatives from brothers-in-law to stepgrandfathers. In Russell's sample, incest between mother and son was rare, a finding confirmed by other researchers (Lester 1972).

Effects on Victims ▪ Incest creates enormous burdens for its victims (Bartoi and Kinder 1998; Lewin 1998). Susan Forward, a psychotherapist who was herself a victim of incest, reports:

> I understand incest not only as a psychotherapist but as a victim. When I was fifteen my father's playful seductiveness turned into highly sexualized fondling. This is a difficult admission for me to make, but even more painful is the fact that I enjoyed my father's attentions.
>
> I felt enormously guilty about my participation in the incest, as if I had been responsible. I know now I was not. It was my father's responsibility as an adult and as a parent to prevent sexual contact between us, but I didn't understand that at the time.
>
> I also felt guilty about competing with my mother—who was only thirty-three and very attractive.
>
> I was flattered by my father's attraction to me, and his caresses felt good, but after several months my guilt became too great. I somehow found the courage to tell him to stop, and he did. The psychological damage, however, had already been done.
>
> As my guilt feelings accumulated, my self-image deteriorated. I felt like a "bad girl." I began to punish myself unconsciously, most prominently by marrying an unloving man instead of pursuing the acting career I had dreamed of since I was five. Later, when my children were in school, I finally got a job on a television series. Good jobs followed and success was within my grasp. But my guilt still fought me on a [sub]conscious level, telling me that I didn't deserve success. So I allowed myself—[sub]consciously, of course, to become overweight and matronly at twenty-eight. My acting career stagnated. My marriage was a mess. I was desperately unhappy. Yet I had absolutely no idea that there was any connection between what my father had done to me and the problems in my life. (Forward and Buck 1978:1)

The Pro-Incest Lobby ▪ A tiny minority takes the position that incest is not a problem. The problem, they say, is the *attitude* toward incest. If people's attitude were different and incest were allowed, no one would have a problem. This small "pro-incest lobby," sometimes called the "new permissivists," claims that there should be no laws against incest because such laws are based on outdated biblical ideas. People who have this view also argue that prohibiting incest chills affectionate relationships of sexual love that can bind people to one another (De Mott 1980).

If the pro-incest lobby ever were to succeed in removing what has been called the "last taboo," the change certainly would affect family life—and, as most would say, devastatingly. The chances of this happening range from impossible to remote.

Old Age and Widowhood

PROBLEMS OF ADJUSTMENT. In contrast with our past, most Americans today survive to old age. Old age brings many problems of adjustment, especially the need to adjust to deteriorating health, the death of loved ones, and the knowledge of one's own impending death. When the elderly retire (or disengage from their usual productive roles, as sociologists put it), their sense of social worth can be challenged. They may even face subtle and less-subtle accusations of being parasites—of robbing younger workers by bankrupting the Social Security system.

THE FAMILY AS BUFFER. The family stands as a buffer between the individual and outside forces. Families that function well give their members a sense of belonging and personal worth. Most adults thrive on the love and acceptance that they find within their family. As it is for young children, for the elderly, this is especially important: The family is their chief source of identity. The warmth and acceptance they find in family life—if they do—counteracts the negative stereotypes by which the elderly are portrayed in the general society.

FROM EXTENDED TO NUCLEAR. Several generations ago, Americans lived in **extended families;** that is, other relatives, perhaps a grandmother or an uncle, lived with the parents and their children. During this agrarian period, the aged, who owned the land, could maintain positions of authority, gradually relinquishing control while easing younger family members into responsible roles. Although we cannot be sure, the transition to old age may have been smoother and perhaps less painful than it is today. We have to be careful about picturing a rosy past that never was, however. Even if individuals were located within a larger family unit, their adjustment to deteriorating health, the death of loved ones, and the knowledge that they, too, would soon die could not have been easy.

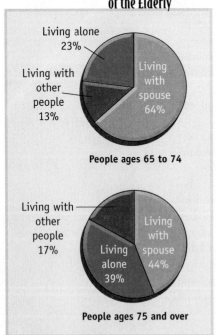

FIGURE 11-12 Living Arrangements of the Elderly

Living alone 23%

Living with other people 13%

Living with spouse 64%

People ages 65 to 74

Living with other people 17%

Living alone 39%

Living with spouse 44%

People ages 75 and over

Source: By the author. Based on *Statistical Abstract of the United States* 2006:Tables 52, 67.

THE MYTH OF FAMILY ABANDONMENT. Today, the "older generation" no longer lives with their adult children, and the **nuclear family,** consisting of parents and children, has become our dominant family form. This living arrangement has led to stereotypes of relationships between adult children and their parents. Many have images of people living in dispersed family units, with the elderly alienated and isolated from the ungrateful children they reared. The media often paint a picture of the elderly, abandoned and embittered, living out their last remorseful years stowed away in some isolated apartment, crammed full of newspapers and memorabilia from the past. Another popular image is of the elderly who are cast away in some dreary nursing home, surrounded by beastly attendants.

We noted in Chapter 2 that such images are far from the truth. A team of sociologists who studied the residents of Muncie, Indiana, found that the elderly maintain contact with their adult children (Caplow et al. 1982). As you can see from Figure 11-12, 64 percent of Americans age 65–74 are still living with their spouse. Only one of four lives alone. Even among people age 75 and over, 44 percent are still living with their spouse. With increasing age and the death of spouses, the percentage of the very old who live alone increases, but even among this group it is only two of five.

"Intimacy at a Distance" ■ Sociologist Elaine Brody (1978) reported that abandonment of the elderly is about as true as the illusion of a golden past in which the whole family lived idyllically on a farm, joyfully meeting each other's every need. She says that in the United States both the elderly and the young *prefer* to live apart. The elderly prefer to live near, but not with, their children—described as "intimacy at a distance." As an elderly person I interviewed put it, "We live just far enough away to have our privacy. We don't want to be on top of each other."

Sociologist Suzanne Steinmetz (1988) reports that parents and their adult children who live together tend to get on one another's nerves. The elderly appear to be acting on a good "sixth sense," then, when they want to live near, but not with, their children. Far from abandoning their aged parents, children remain key figures in their support system (Bengtson et al. 1990).

THE INSTITUTIONALIZED ELDERLY. As was discussed in Chapter 2, the 3 percent of the aged who live in nursing homes are *not* typical of older people (*Statistical Abstract* 2003:Tables 11, 68). Most need help with bathing (95 percent), dressing (88 percent), and even going to the toilet (58 percent). Most (63 percent) are in wheelchairs, and another 26 percent have to use walkers to get around. Seven out of ten can no longer manage money or take care of their personal possessions. Most of them even need help to use the telephone (*Statistical Abstract* 2003:Table 185).

Nursing home residents, then, confirm common stereotypes about the elderly. They certainly are not a healthy group, but remember that nursing home residents do *not* represent elderly people in general. On the contrary, *most* elderly Americans enjoy good health and the company of their family and friends.

Although most of the elderly who end up in nursing homes do not have families to take care of them, some do. Contrary to stereotypes, the elderly people who have families have not been "dumped" by ungrateful children. As Elaine Brody reported (1978:20–21):

> Prior to institutionalization, most families have endured severe personal, social, and economic stress in attempting to avoid admission [to a nursing home]; it is typically the last, not the first, resort; and the decision is made reluctantly. The "well" spouse usually is in advanced old age. The adult children are often approaching or engaged in the aging phase of life with attendant age-related stresses and often are subjected to competing demands from ill spouses or their own children.

ADJUSTING TO WIDOWHOOD. Even for people who enjoy good health and family relationships in their older years, death comes eventually. When death ends a marriage, the survivor is forced to face life without the partner who had become such an essential part of life. In the midst of disrupted family relationships and the loss of social roles, the widowed face three main problems: loneliness, anxiety, and money (Hiltz 1989).

Sociologist Robert Atchley (1975) studied retired schoolteachers and retired employees of a telephone company who were in their 70s. He found that the widowers generally did better than the widows. The men were more likely to be active in organizations, to have more contact with friends, and to be less anxious. The key, Atchley found, was money. The men were more secure financially, which made them less anxious about life. Atchley also found a surprising variable—the ability to afford a car. Those who had cars, whether widows or widowers, got out of the house more, participated in more group activities, and visited their friends more often. The mobility that a car offered was *the* key factor in reducing social isolation, loneliness, and anxiety.

Atchley's findings can be summarized as a principle that runs through social life: In general, the more adequate people's income, the better they adjust to whatever challenges they face.

The Death of the Family?

MARRIAGE IN DECLINE. Marriage is doomed. Our high divorce rate shows that marriage is no longer a viable social institution. The many problems that we have reviewed in this chapter signal the end of the contemporary family. As Figure 11-10 (on page 380) shows, *ten times* more couples are cohabiting today than in the 1970s. If this trend continues, eventually most people will live together, not marry. Another indication: Throughout U.S. history, most households have consisted of married couples with or without children. Then in the year 2006,

TABLE 11-1 Average Size of U.S. Households

1960	1970	1980	1990	2000	2005
3.67	3.62	2.75	2.63	2.62	2.57

Source: By the author. Based on *Statistical Abstract of the United States* 1971:Table 44; 1989:Table 58; 1991:Table 61; 2007:Table 59.

these households slipped below 50 percent, and now *most* households consist of people in other living arrangements (alone, with other friends or relatives, cohabiting) (Roberts 2006). Table 11-1 also illustrates that the family is dying: The average household has been *shrinking*, indicating that there is little left of the family. Then, too, there is that interesting statistic that we reviewed, that one-third of U.S. children are born to unmarried mothers. As more unmarried women bear children, marriage will become a quaint custom reserved for a few traditionalists.

Are such proclamations of the death of the family true? Let's look at sociological research.

MARRIAGE FLOURISHING. Although households consisting of married people have dropped below 50 percent (to 49.7 percent), because the population has grown, more Americans are married than ever before. Young Americans are certainly taking longer to say "I do," but they are still taking those vows. Look at Figure 11-13, which certainly gives you a different picture of marriage today. By the time they reach age 26 or 27, one half of all women are married. For men, that halfway mark hits at about age 29. Then comes a rush to the altar: By the end of their 30s, just one of seven women and one of five men remain unmarried. Overall, about 96 percent of Americans marry—perhaps the *highest* percentage in our history.

The Middletown Studies ▪ Other sociological research also indicates that the U.S. family is not disintegrating. Muncie, Indiana, is one of the most thoroughly researched of U.S. cities. In the 1920s and 1930s, sociologists Robert and Helen Lynd (1929, 1937) analyzed family life in this middle-American city, which they called "Middletown." In the 1980s, other sociologists went back to Muncie to find out whether the family had declined during those 50 years. To see whether it had, they checked the rates of suicide, mental breakdown, and domestic violence.

To their surprise, Theodore Caplow and his fellow researchers (1982) found that these problems were *less* frequent in Middletown than they had been two generations earlier. They also found that people are not living in isolated nuclear families, as some stereotypes indicate.

FIGURE 11-13 The Percentage of Americans Who Have Never Married

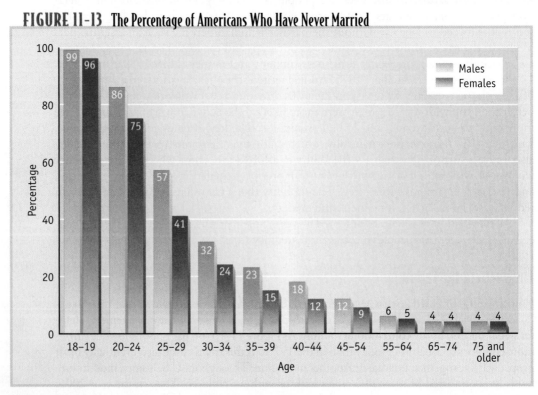

Source: By the author. Based on *Statistical Abstract of the United States* 2006:Table 51.

Rather, the nuclear families are embedded in larger kin networks, where people find economic support and satisfying personal relationships. Most parents and their grown children keep in close touch. Perhaps these researchers' most surprising finding was that marriage had become more vibrant. Marriage in the 1920s was shallower; husbands and wives didn't talk as much with one another. Now that male and female roles are less segregated, husbands and wives talk things over more— and they are *more satisfied* with marriage. Caplow concludes that "for most of their members most of the time, Middletown's composite families provide a safe and comfortable niche in a hazardous world." *The idea that the family has declined is a "sociological myth."*

VAST CHANGES, CHALLENGES, AND PROBLEMS. Despite such a rosy assessment, in this chapter you've seen some of the problems that U.S. families are struggling against. These challenges are severe. As I stressed earlier, the family always has been in transition, but recent transitions are startling. Figure 11-14 on the next page shows that less than a quarter of U. S. households consist of a married couple with their children. Don't interpret the category—"Married couple, no children"—as meaning childless couples. Married couples who have never had children are included in this category, to be sure, but most of these couples are "empty nesters": Their children have grown and left home.

Table 11-2 is another way of summarizing some of the vast changes that are engulfing the family. As you can see, the three largest increases are in cohabitation, people who are living alone, and children who are living with only one parent.

"Money can't buy happiness" is an old saying. But it is not true. Money does buy happiness. Compared with poor people, wealthier people are more satisfied with life—and more optimistic about the future. Their health is better, they live longer, and even their marriages last longer.

IN SUM As symbolic interactionists stress, objective conditions never come with built-in meanings. Meanings are always given by people, and it is no different in the case of the changes occurring in the family. We could become alarmed at these figures, wring our hands, and say that the family is in serious trouble or even that it is about to collapse. I see nothing to indicate this. The family is experiencing severe problems, but it seems to me that the fairest conclusion is that the family is doing what it always does—adjusting

TABLE 11-2 How U.S. Families Are Changing

	1970	1980	1990	2000	2004	Change Since 1970
Marriages	2,159,000	2,390,000	2,443,000	2,329,000	2,187,000	+1.3%
Divorces	708,000	1,189,000	1,182,000	1,179,000	1,108,000	+56%
Married couples	47,500,000	52,300,000	56,300,000	56,497,000	57,719,000	+22%
Unmarried couples	523,000	1,589,000	2,856,000	4,900,000	5,571,000	+1,065%
People living alone	10,851,000	18,296,000	23,000,000	28,724,000	29,586,000	+273%
Married couples with children at home	25,541,000	24,961,000	24,537,000	25,248,000	25,793,000	+1%
Children living with both parents	58,787,000	48,648,000	46,499,000	49,760,000	49,632,000	−16%
Children living with one parent	8,300,000	12,495,000	15,841,000	19,155,000	20,424,000	+246%
Average size of household	3.14	2.76	2.63	2.62	2.57	−18%
Married women who are employed	18,475,000	24,980,000	30,970,000	35,146,000	35,845,000	+194%

Source: By the author. Based on *Statistical Abstract of the United States* 1989:Table 58; 1992:Tables 49, 52, 56, 69, 73, 127, 619; 2001:Table 59; 2006:Tables 53, 57, 60, 72, 585.

to social change. As the family faces challenging changes and is buffeted from one side and another, I see both signs of distress and signs of health.

Despite divorce, cohabitation, births to unmarried women, family violence, and forces that pull people apart and even make them flee, Americans still have high hope for marriage and family life. As you saw on Figure 11-13 on page 390, Americans are marrying at a high rate. However, they aren't running into marriage at the pace they used to—they are postponing the age at which they first marry, and fewer divorced people marry. At the same time, as we saw, some sociological research documents areas of family life that have improved over the years, especially more satisfying interaction between husbands and wives.

FIGURE 11-14 What Are Americans' Living Arrangements?

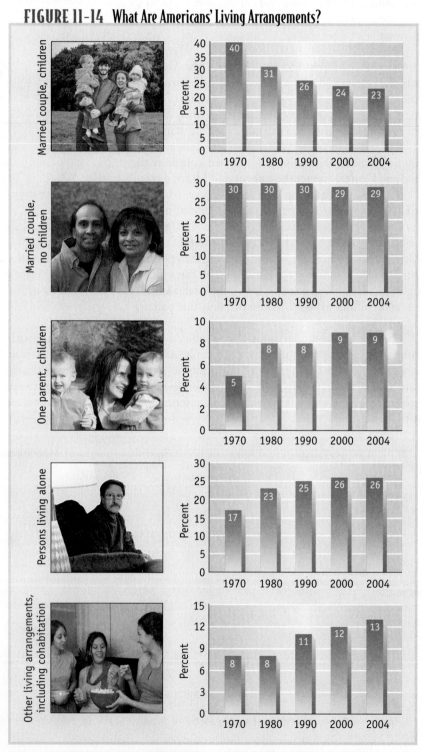

Source: By the author. Based on *Statistical Abstract of the United States* 2000:Table 60; 2006:Table 53.

Social Policy

THE LASCH ACCUSATIONS: INTRUSIONS BY PROFESSIONALS. Social policy for the family is mired in controversy, for every policy steps on someone's toes. In *Haven in a Heartless World* (1977), social historian Christopher Lasch said that people are trying to find in the family a refuge of love and decency in a cruel and heartless world. The family, however, often cannot provide these comforts because it has been besieged by professionals—doctors, social workers, and "counselors" of various sorts. What Lasch meant was that these professionals have been trying to enlarge their own domains at the expense of the family. Under the guise of helping, they have stripped the family of some of its functions, eroding its capacity to provide protective intimacy.

How could Lasch draw this conclusion? One example is professionals who claim to be experts in sex. These sexperts write books and magazine articles about what sexual relations between husband and wife "ought" to be like. Hundreds of "Dr. Phils" and "Phil wannabes" appear as self-styled experts on radio and television, where they proclaim their expertise. As a result, husbands and wives feel less capable of working out their own sexual problems, for only "sexual experts" have the "real" answers. Another example is the professionals who stake claim to child rearing. They profess to know the best ways to rear children, sometimes even "the" correct way to do so. This makes parents worry that, as mere laypeople, they might be damaging their children through clumsy, improper parenting. They then turn to "professionals" who intrude into this traditionally private area of family life.

In short, Lasch says, we are on a road that leads to a "therapeutic society," one in which "experts" claim that all problems—including those in the family—are their domain. This "concern" by "experts" about the plight of the family, publicized on television and radio, in magazines and books, masks what is really happening—outside agents trying to take away the family's authority and place the family under their control. The situation is even worse than this, Lasch says, for there is no evidence that these so-called "experts" have benefited the family. What they have done is to market their services and products and establish self-serving mini-empires.

As you would expect, professionals have reacted bitterly to this attack on their expertise, skills, accomplishments, and motives. They deny that they have self-serving motives or that they intrude into family life, undermine its authority, and cause families to have less "self-sufficiency" (Joffe 1978). On the contrary, their goal is to empower the family so it can handle the problems of life successfully, making its members more competent and happy. The troubled family needs them, they reply.

THE DILEMMA OF FAMILY POLICY: TAKING SIDES. Lasch's denunciations expose a core dilemma. Any social policy for the family finds itself on one side or the other of issues that divide fair-minded people who have the best interests of the family at heart. For example, consider what seems to be a neutral matter, making financial aid available to troubled families. One side suggests that such a policy would aid the family; another side, however, sees it as an attack on family self-sufficiency, saying that it discourages families from looking out for themselves and makes them further dependent on "Big Brother."

THE BATTLEGROUND OF DEFINITIONS: INTERVENTION OR INTERFERENCE? Consider a book that became a best seller and stimulated national policy discussions—*It Takes a Village: And Other Lessons Children Teach Us* by Hillary Rodham Clinton. Clinton's declared purpose was to make the public aware of the need for community involvement in child care. Yet the book set off a storm of controversy: Some people were alarmed that the book was a rallying cry for the state to intrude on the family, to eventually take child rearing away from parents.

Almost all policy falls on one side or the other of this explosive issue. Consider this case:

Parents tell their 14-year-old girl that she cannot have sex because premarital sex is a sin. The daughter faces a dilemma. She is afraid that if she does not have sex with her boyfriend, he will date more cooperative girls. She also is "in love" and wants to please him. The girl goes to a family planning clinic and explains her plight. Counselors encourage her to assert herself against domineering and old-fashioned parents. They assure her that she can come to them for a free and confidential abortion if she becomes pregnant. They also offer her a Norplant.

Who is "right" in this example? As symbolic interactionists stress, our understanding of what "ought" to be depends on our values. Sociologist Carole Joffe (1978), who originated this example of the 14-year-old, put it this way: From one perspective, the decision of a teenager to seek out contraception is a step forward in gaining her independence. From another standpoint, to talk about giving contraceptives to a young teenager is to prejudge the issue. From this perspective, contraception does not represent a step toward independence but, rather, an intrusion on family privacy.

With the nation divided along conservative and liberal lines, we face divisive issues when it comes to social policy for the family. The matter is even more complicated than such ideological divisions. As symbolic interactionists stress, different family members experience family life differently. Arrangements that some family members find comfortable and satisfying, others can find oppressive (Joffe 1978). As the Thinking Critically box on children's rights on the next page highlights, what is government intervention to some is government interference to others. In the midst of this intense controversy and clash of values and opinions, there is an area on which most people agree—that the young and defenseless need to be protected from physical and psychological harm and exploitation, as well as from anything that deprives them of their health and well-being. But even here, a basic dilemma plagues social policy: encouraging families to be responsible and independent versus protecting individuals within the family (Chilman 1988). How do we protect individuals without a "Big Brother" to watch over every family's shoulder?

THE ISSUE OF POVERTY. Apart from certain family problems, such as marital rape and child abuse, many sociologists see poverty as the root of family troubles. Social policies to help families escape poverty are a central concern to many. Some sociologists suggest that a guaranteed family income is the best solution to family poverty. Others see the solution as a robust economy with full employment. To this, we might add educational opportunities open to all. Income, jobs, and education would not solve all the family's problems, especially, say conflict theorists, those that are rooted in sexist-power orientations. They would, however, go a long way toward solving many of them.

The Future of the Problem

RAPID SOCIAL CHANGE AS NORMATIVE. Social change is the hallmark of our society. Seemingly overnight, familiar landmarks are torn down and replaced by a strip mall or by another of an endless series of fast-food outlets. Computers recognize your speech, type your message, and check your grammar; devices connected to the Global Positioning System announce your location, even guide you through traffic in a strange city. On the Internet, type something in English, and it can be translated instantly into German or Spanish or any major language before being transmitted to someone in a distant part of the world. (It often comes out garbled, but that will change.) Soon you'll be able to have one telephone number that will stay with you for life and will be valid throughout the world. Change is so rapid and extensive that parents and children live in different worlds—so much so that grown children who are visiting their parents after an absence of months or even years often find that after the first hour or two they have little left to talk about.

FUTURE SHOCK. The speed, extent, and intensity of today's social change are mind-boggling. We barely get used to one idea, object, or relationship when another overpowers it—and us. Alvin Toffler (1971) coined the term *future shock* to refer to this dizzying barrage of change to which we have no leisure or opportunity to adjust. **Future shock** is the vertigo, the confusion, the disorientation that we experience when our familiar world is transformed.

THINKING CRITICALLY About Social Problems

CHILD RIGHTS

In 1943, the U.S. Supreme Court determined that a cardinal principle of U.S. law is that "the custody, care, and nurture of the child reside in the parents." This decision is usually interpreted to mean that parents have a total right to decide matters concerning the welfare of their children, with the state able to intervene only to stop abuse or neglect.

Americans, however, are divided over the rights that parents should have over their children. The central question is, At what point does the authority of the state supersede the authority of parents? When does the privacy of the family take precedence over the concern of well-intentioned outsiders? Let's look at the major arguments.

TO PROTECT CHILDREN FROM DOMINEERING PARENTS, WE MUST STRENGTHEN CHILDREN'S RIGHTS

In the journal *Human Rights,* Patricia Wald (1974) wrote that a "very young child" has the right "to be consulted and informed about critical decisions in his life, and (the) right to be represented in those decisions." To protect the child from the "consequences of unilateral parental actions . . . the child's interests deserve representation by an independent advocate before a neutral decision maker."

Wald also suggested that communities provide homes for runaways under age 16 who do not want to return home. "Parents would have no right to forcibly take their children away from such homes," she proposed. A child ought to be able to seek legal advice to redress grievances against his or her family. Some also propose that children should be able to sue their parents for poor child rearing.

These proposals are designed to balance a system that currently favors the parents at the expense of children. For example, as things now stand, if parents want to take a job out of town, they do. The child has no choice in the matter and simply has to move with them. This, say critics, is a "crucial decision that affects the child's life." If the parents move, the child has to leave friends and attend a new school. The child should have the right to "an independent advocate to argue his or her case before a neutral decision maker." If the child does not want to go and the parents insist on moving, the independent advocate should be able to remove the child from the family.

TO PROTECT FAMILIES FROM DOMINEERING PROFESSIONALS WE MUST STRENGTHEN PARENTS' RIGHTS

To accomplish this, Phyllis Schlafly (1979) proposed The Family Protection Act. This Act would guarantee that

1. Parents have the right to visit public school classrooms and school functions.
2. Parents can review textbooks before public schools adopt them.
3. No federal funding will be given for courses that encourage children to rethink the values that their parents have taught them, courses often called "values clarification" or "behavior modification."
4. Parents must give their consent for their children to enroll in courses about religion or "ethics," and they can keep their children out of such courses that they find offensive.
5. Parents must give consent for unmarried minors to get contraceptives or an abortion and must be informed if their child is treated for a venereal disease.
6. If a child's "right to self-expression" conflicts with the parents' "right to educate or discipline," in the absence of compelling evidence of parental unfitness, the courts must rule in favor of the parents.

The U.S. family is experiencing future shock. With industrialization and urbanization, the family has already had to adapt to social change so extensive that it left little of human relationships untouched. Now computers are changing the worlds of work, education, recreation, and entertainment. Parents and children e-mail one another from office, school, and home, giving brief updates on changing plans. Because the family is continuing to adapt to changing social conditions, its future is unclear. But let's venture into these uncharted waters.

CHANGES WE CAN EXPECT. The lofty goals of love and marriage are established firmly in our culture, and love will continue to be the "proper" basis for marriage. People will also continue to marry at a rate close to what we see today. The age at first marriage will continue upward a while longer, then stabilize. Cohabitation will continue to increase for about another decade, and then level off. The proportion of married women who are employed outside the home will continue to increase, eventually plateauing at about 75 to 80 percent. Marriage will become even more oriented around companionship. This orientation, coupled with more wives working outside the home and their incomes increasing relative to those of men, will be a stimulus for husbands and wives to develop more equal relationships. Marriage will remain brittle, and the United States will continue to have one of the highest divorce rates in the world. With our older age at first marriage, accompanied by more years of education, the divorce rate will decline. Day care will become more common for children of working parents (see the Issues in Social Problems box below). Whether you interpret such changes as good, bad, or indifferent depends, of course, on your values.

THE IDEOLOGICAL STRUGGLE. The struggle by ideologically committed groups to influence family orientations and to control family policy will intensify. With their incompatible views of right, justice, and the good life, oppositional groups will continue to try to make family policy match their own vision of reality. Regardless of who wins in the short term, this competition of ideas and values will continue. The future looks exciting, the outcome uncertain. This struggle is not theoretical or abstract: Much of your own family life hangs in the balance.

Issues in Social Problems
WHAT DOES DAY CARE COST A COMPANY?

Suppose that you are the president of Union Bank in Monterey, California. Some of your employees have asked you to provide a day care center. You would like to do so, but you can't spend stockholders' money on day care simply because you think it is a nice idea. You are accountable for the performance of your stock, and you have to know the bottom line.

"Find out what it would cost us to have a day care center," the manager told Sandra Burud, a social science researcher. At first, determining costs may sound fairly easy. You simply add the cost of the facilities and personnel, and you have the answer. But what you want to know is the *net* cost. After all, day care is supposed to benefit the company. Will the benefits be greater or less than the cost? How much in either direction?

Now the problem becomes difficult. How can you accurately estimate changes that the day care center will make in employee turnover? This, in turn, will change interview costs, hiring bonuses, and job advertisements. Then, too, you have to try to measure the productive time that will be lost while an employee is on maternity leave or is job hunting, while a job goes unfilled, or while a new employee is learning the ropes. Employee turnover is costly: Merck Pharmaceuticals has determined that during their first fourteen months on the job new employees cost the company five months of work. Some costs are impossible to measure, such as poor morale and loss of reputation with the community if a lot of employees quit. In fact, Burud decided that she couldn't put numbers on these variables and had to skip them.

In the midst of such uncertainties, Union Bank decided to go ahead and open a day care center. This cost the bank $105,000. Then Burud compared 87 employees who used the center with a control group of 105 employees who didn't use the center. She found that employee turnover among the center's users was 2 percent; among the control group, it was 10 percent. Employees who used the center were also absent an average of two days a year less than the control group. Their maternity leaves were also one week shorter.

The bottom line? After subtracting its costs of running the day care center, the bank saved $232,000. Should you, the president, have your bank open a day care center? *Now,* that is an easy decision.

Such companies as Marriott Hotels have paid attention to the bottom-line results of corporate day care and have opened their own centers. Other companies, such as Levi Strauss and AT&T, subsidize their employees' child care.

Based on Solomon 1988; Shellenbarger 1994.

SUMMARY AND REVIEW

1. The family is always adjusting to social change. One of the most significant effects of the Industrial Revolution was the removal of economic production from the household.

2. Whether change within the family is perceived as a social problem or as merely a form of adaptation depends on people's values. Indicators that many see as evidence of a social problem are divorce, runaway children, births to single women, one-parent families, and violence and sexual abuse in the family.

3. In analyzing why the U.S. divorce rate is high, symbolic interactionists stress the changing ideas of sex roles and expectations of marriage; functionalists, the declining functions of the family; and conflict theorists, the unequal distribution of power in the family.

4. The average age at first marriage declined from 1890 to about 1950, then began to increase in about 1970. Today, the average age at first marriage is the highest in our history. The primary reason is *cohabitation.* As many people postpone marriage, a growing proportion of the young remain single.

5. Married couples remain childless because of infertility, the decision not to have children, or the continuous postponement of children until childlessness becomes inevitable. Childless couples face a stigma.

6. Physical violence between family members is common. Although wives initiate about as much violence as husbands, they are injured more often. People reared in violent homes are more likely to be violent to their own spouses and children. Incest and marital rape are more frequent than commonly supposed.

7. That the elderly are abandoned by their families is a myth: Most adult children and their parents keep in close touch. The elderly prefer to live near their children, but not with them, a preference called "intimacy at a distance." Widowhood appears to be easier for men than women; this is not due to gender—rather, those who are better off financially adjust better to the death of a spouse.

8. Despite its problems, the family is far from doomed and is much healthier than most imagine. More Americans are marrying today than ever before. The "Middletown" studies indicate that husbands and wives are more satisfied with married life than they were 50 years ago.

9. Social policy on the family is controversial because it pits individual rights against government intervention. Some even accuse "family professionals" of expanding their domain at the expense of the family.

10. These trends are likely to continue: increases in cohabitation, later age at first marriage, more wives working outside the home, more day care, and greater marital equality. Groups that are concerned about the family differ in their ideas about the way the family "should" be, and it remains to be seen which groups will be most influential in determining social policy.

KEY TERMS

Cohabitation, 380
Extended family, 388
Family of orientation, 374

Family of procreation, 374
Future shock, 394
Incest, 386

Nuclear family, 388

THINKING CRITICALLY ABOUT CHAPTER 11

1. What do you consider to be the five greatest benefits and the five greatest downsides of the changes in the composition of U.S. families? Do you think that these changes are bringing more negatives or positives? Explain.

2. Which perspective (symbolic interactionism, functionalism, or conflict theory) do you think does the best job of explaining the changes that are taking place in U.S. families? Explain.

3. Rank the seven traditional functions of the family according to how important you think they are in today's family. Explain your rankings.

4. With the huge increase in cohabitation, the high divorce rate, the number of runaways, and the extent of abuse in families, how can the author not conclude that marriage is doomed? Explain.

CHAPTER 12

Urban
Problems

Kellie Moiser was a 17-year-old high school student who worked part time at the corner ice-cream store. From childhood, she had dreamed of becoming a model. Kellie's mother encouraged her dream, hoping that it would be a way out of the ghetto.

But Kellie never got the chance.

Michael Hagan, 23, also lived in the slums of south-central Los Angeles. He liked Olde English "800" Malt Liquor, especially when he smoked PCP.

He also liked guns.

And a little blood didn't bother him, either.

One Monday evening, Hagan was on a binge with other members of his gang, when they decided to go after a rival gang. They piled into an old Buick and sped toward enemy turf. There they spotted four teenagers, two boys and two girls.

The teenagers were not gang members. They were just kids who had gone out for ice cream. When they saw the gun, they ran. Kellie didn't run fast enough. Hagan methodically pumped fifteen slugs into her, six into her back.

The cops took the killing in stride. For them, it was just one more in an endless stream of murders that occur in this part of the city. They didn't have much to go on, witnesses clammed up, and the detectives had other priorities.

> ## And a little blood didn't bother him.

Kellie's mother didn't have much to go on either, but she set out to solve her daughter's murder. Out of a fury born of grief, she stormed the streets in search of the killers. She even barged into local drug houses. The word got around, and a sympathetic inmate in the county jail sent her a letter telling her the name of the shooter.

Kellie's mother shook her head in disbelief when she found out who had killed her daughter. She said, "I knew these gang members when they were just babies. Now look at them. They've turned into killers."

Hagan, the shooter, says, "Jail ain't bad. To me, life ain't much better on the streets than in jail. I can live here; no problem."

"The gang is your family," Hagan explains. "If you're a Crip, I fight for you, no matter what the odds. If you're the enemy, it's do or die."

Hagan adds, "If I had a son, I'd give him a choice: Either he can go to school and be a goody-goody, or he can hit the streets."

Hagan smiles broadly as he adds, "I done did something, and I'm known. I consider myself Public Enemy Number 1."

—Based on Hull 1987.

The Problem in Sociological Perspective

Hagan is part of the American nightmare—the unsafe streets, the drive-by shootings, the senseless killings, without conscience, that destroy those who are trying to build a future. Before we get to Hagan, however, let's look at the history of cities.

THE EVOLUTION OF CITIES. Although almost everyone lives in an urban world today, cities developed only slowly in human history. Somewhere between 6000 and 8000 B.C., people may have built cities with massive walls, such as biblically famous Jericho (Homblin 1973). Some historians, however, think that cities originated later, in conjunction with the invention of writing. For certain, by 3500 B.C. cities had been established in several parts of the world. They appeared first in Mesopotamia, then in the Nile, Indus, and Yellow River valleys, around the Mediterranean, in West Africa, Central America, and the Andes (Fischer 1976).

Agriculture was the key to the development of cities. Only when a society produces a surplus of food are some people able to stop farming and gather in cities to pursue other occupations. A **city,** in fact, can be defined as a large number of people who live in one place and do not produce their own food. As agricultural techniques become more efficient, they spur urban development. During the fourth millennium B.C., the plow was invented: As this invention spread, the resulting agricultural surplus stimulated the development of towns and cities across wide areas of the world.

Early plows, although a great improvement on the digging sticks that had been used, were primitive, and for the next 5,000 years, the food surplus was only enough to allow a small minority of the world's population to live in urban areas. Then came the Industrial Revolution of the 1700s and 1800s, which sparked the urban revolution that we are still experiencing. The Industrial Revolution stimulated not only the invention of mechanical means of farming, which brought food in abundance, but also mechanical means of transportation and communication. These allow people, resources, and products to be moved efficiently—essential factors on which the modern city depends.

FROM RURAL TO URBAN. Two hundred years ago, almost everyone in the world lived in rural areas. Only 3 percent lived in towns of 5,000 or more (Hauser and Schnore 1965). By 1900, the total of city dwellers was up to 13 or 14 percent. Today, about half of the entire world lives in cities (Massey 2001).

In its early years, the United States, too, was almost exclusively rural. In 1800, only about 6 of 100 Americans lived in towns of 2,500 or more. As Figure 12-1 shows, cities became increasingly popular as places to live, and by around 1920 half of Americans lived in cities. Today, four of every five Americans do. As you can see from the Social Map on page 402, rates of urbanization differ considerably from state to state.

Cites are designed to solve problems, to make life better by transcending the limitations of farm and village. Cities offer the hope of a better life, of gaining work, education, and other advantages. With these benefits, cities are growing around the world. Table 12-1 on page 403 lists the world's ten largest cities in 1950 and the projected ten largest cities in 2015. You can see how vast the geographical switch is. In 1950, four of the world's largest cities were in Europe, and two in North America. In 2015, none will be in Europe, and the one in North America is not in the United States. Seven of the world's largest cities will be located in Asia (four) or the subcontinent (three). The major shift has been from the Most Industrialized Nations to the Industrializing and Least Industrialized Nations.

There are two primary reasons for this global switch in the location of the world's largest cities. The first is the lack of population growth in the Most Industrialized Nations, which is basically at a standstill, accompanied by the tremendous growth in the populations of the Industrializing and Least Industrialized Nations. We will discuss this in the next chapter. The second is the "push" from the rural areas (their poverty and lack of opportunities) accompanied by the "pull" of the urban areas (their economic opportunities). In the Global Glimpse box on page 404, we explore why people in the Least Industrialized Nations are deserting their rural way of life and flocking to urban areas.

URBAN PROBLEMS. In the next section, we will survey the scope of urban problems, but first I want to stress that this principle underlies many of these problems: Cities have a

FIGURE 12-1 U.S. Population, Rural and Urban

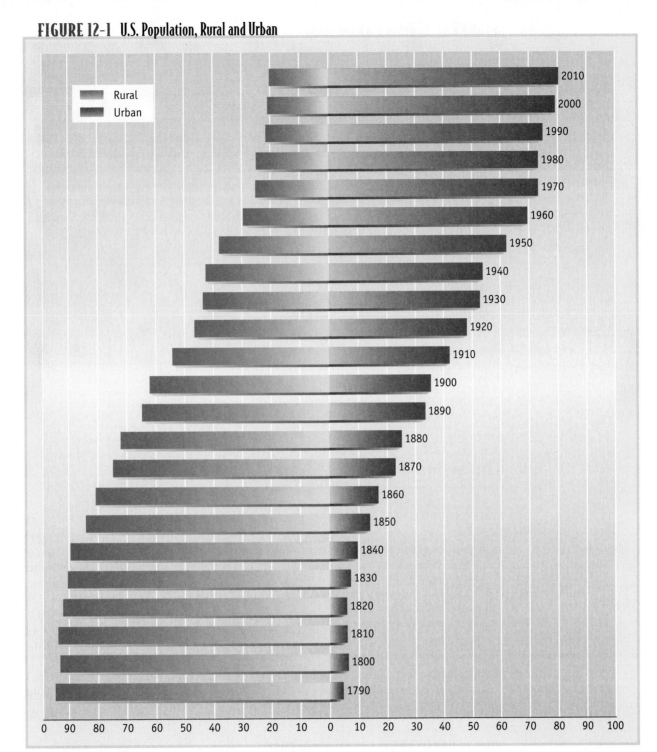

Rural
Urban

| | | | | | | | | | | | | | | | | | | | | |
2010
2000
1990
1980
1970
1960
1950
1940
1930
1920
1910
1900
1890
1880
1870
1860
1850
1840
1830
1820
1810
1800
1790

0 90 80 70 60 50 40 30 20 10 0 10 20 30 40 50 60 70 80 90 100

Note: The indicated change from 1990 to 2000 is misleading. In the year 2000 census, the U.S. Census Bureau began to use a more inclusive definition of "urban." Smaller areas that are dense ("urban clusters") are now counted as urban. If the old definition were used, the figure would show a 1 percent increase in urban population, not the 4 percent shown here.

Source: By the author. Based on U.S. Bureau of the Census; *Statistical Abstract of the United States* 2006:Table 27. The projections from 2000 to 2010 are by the author.

difficult time meeting people's needs for **community,** a feeling of belonging, the sense that others care what happens to you and that you can depend on the people around you. Some people do find community in the city, but others find alienation, and they live in isolation and fear. Some people, like Hagan, even band together to create fear, making the city, for many, a miserable place to live.

FIGURE 12-2 Urban and Rural States

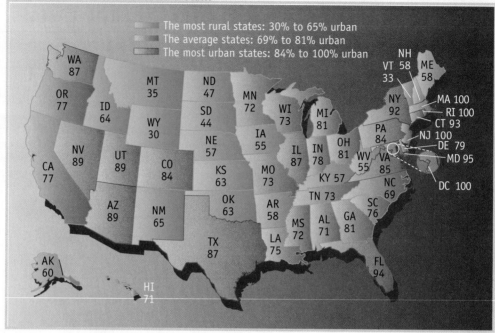

Note: The most rural state is Wyoming, where 70 percent live in rural areas. The most urban states are Massachusetts, New Jersey, and Rhode Island, which are 100 percent urban. The percentage refers to residents living in urban areas, not the amount of geographical area used for cities. For instance, Connecticut is 80 percent urban by this map, and yet it is also about two-thirds woodlands.

Source: By the author. Based on U.S. Bureau of the Census 2006.

The Scope of the Problem

A DEEP AMBIVALENCE. Thinking of the city as a source of problems is nothing new. In 1780, Thomas Jefferson said that cities contribute to the good government of a nation about as much as sores contribute to the strength of the body. He said that cities were "pestilential to the morals, the health, and the liberties of man" (1784/1977). The other extreme is an image that many Americans carry of rural life as the serene source of virtue, an agrarian paradise where life is innocent, simple, and happy (Hadden and Barton 1973). The cold brutality of urban life—the Hagans wandering the streets in search of victims—makes people long for something better. The bottom line is a deep ambivalence toward the city: People dream of fleeing the city to find safety and security in a simpler life, yet they remain fascinated with the city, seeking it for work, cultural attractions, and diversions.

This ambivalence toward the city—its threat and its allure—will be woven throughout this chapter as we examine major problems that face our cities.

WHAT IS URBAN ABOUT URBAN PROBLEMS? In one sense, almost all social problems are urban. Because most Americans live in cities, poverty, crime, unemployment, divorce, drug addiction, violence, and so forth are concentrated in cities. None of these problems is urban by nature, because these problems can—and do—occur everywhere.

What, then, is *urban* about social problems? First, city life *increases* social problems. For example, the *rates* of burglary, robbery, suicide, alcoholism, and rape are *higher* in cities than in rural areas. Why do cities increase such behaviors and even produce people like Hagan? Or, conversely, why do rural areas inhibit them? We will return to this question, for it is central to understanding urban problems.

Second, the United States is facing an *urban crisis*. U.S. cities have areas that almost everyone fears and avoids. There, amidst burned-out and boarded-up buildings, addicts and the unemployed slouch on apartment steps. Drug dealers openly work "their" street

TABLE 12-1 The World's Ten Largest Cities, 1950 and 2015

1950				2015			
Rank	City	Population	Country	Rank	City	Population	Country
1	New York	12.3 mill.	United States	1	Tokyo	28.7 mill.	Japan
2	London	8.7 mill.	England	2	Mumbai (Bombay)	27.4 mill.	India
3	Tokyo	6.9 mill.	Japan	3	Lagos	24.4 mill.	Nigeria
4	Moscow	5.4 mill.	Russia	4	Shanghai	23.4 mill.	China
5	Paris	5.4 mill.	France	5	Jakarta	21.2 mill.	Indonesia
6	Essen	5.3 mill.	Germany	6	São Paulo	20.8 mill.	Brazil
7	Shanghai	5.3 mill.	China	7	Karachi	20.6 mill.	Pakistan
8	Buenos Aires	5.0 mill.	Argentina	8	Beijing	19.4 mill.	China
9	Chicago	4.9 mill.	United States	9	Dhaka	19.0 mill.	India
10	Calcutta	4.4 mill.	India	10	Mexico City	18.8 mill.	Mexico

Source: United Nations 2006.

corners, a lucrative turf that they defend by violence. The Hagans prowl filthy streets, mugging and raping and killing. Anyone who enters these areas is at peril—in some, even the police. There are other indications of an urban crisis. During economic downturns, some cities shorten the school year because they cannot meet the payroll. Some slash budgets for the public library and garbage collection. Some even reduce police and fire protection. Across the nation the middle class has rushed to the suburbs, abandoning the inner city to the poor, a flight that has impoverished the city. Another problem is **urban sprawl;** as cities expand, they invade the countryside, devouring farmland, leaving in its place asphalt and buildings. The term **urban crisis** refers to this cluster of interrelated urban problems.

Looking at the Problem Theoretically

As usual, our three theoretical perspectives yield contrasting insights. As we apply symbolic interactionism to the inner city, we will glimpse the "slum's" social organization, which ordinarily remains invisible to outsiders. Using functionalism will make visible the zones of activity that develop as a city expands. Finally, from the conflict perspective, we will see how class conflict creates urban problems.

Symbolic Interactionism

If Americans are ambivalent about the city, they are not so when it comes to the inner city. Most fear it, and everyone avoids it. Most middle-class Americans shake their heads and say that they can't understand why anyone would live "like that."

A Global Glimpse

WHY CITY SLUMS ARE BETTER THAN THE COUNTRY: THE RUSH TO THE CITIES OF THE LEAST INDUSTRIALIZED NATIONS

Thoughts of the Least Industrialized Nations often bring images of people tending animals or harvesting crops, enjoying a peaceful life in the lush countryside or along babbling brooks. Such images no longer represent the reality that most people in the Least Industrialized Nations face—if ever they did. The rural poor of these countries are flocking to the cities at such a rate that, as we saw in Table 12-1, the Least Industrialized Nations now contain most of the world's largest cities. In the Most Industrialized Nations, industrialization generally preceded urbanization, but in the Least Industrialized Nations *urbanization is preceding industrialization*. These cities cannot support their swelling populations.

The settlement patterns are also different in these cities. When rural migrants and immigrants move to U.S. cities, they usually settle in deteriorating housing near the city's center. The wealthy reside in suburbs and luxurious city enclaves. Migrants to cities of the Least Industrialized Nations, in contrast, establish illegal squatter settlements outside the city. There they build shacks from scrap boards, cardboard, and bits of corrugated metal. Even flattened tin cans are scavenged for building material. The squatters enjoy no city facilities—roads, public transportation, water, sewers, or garbage pickup. After thousands of squatters have settled an area, the city reluctantly acknowledges their right to live there and adds bus service and minimal water lines. Hundreds of people use a single spigot. About *5 million* of Mexico City's residents live in such squalid conditions, with hundreds of thousands more pouring in each year.

Why this rush to live in the city under such miserable conditions? At its core are the "push" factors that arise from a breakdown of traditional rural life. With a safer water supply and the importation of modern medicine, the death rate in rural areas dropped. As a result, their populations multiplied, and no longer

is there enough land to divide up among children. Without land, there is hunger. People are deeply dissatisfied with the resulting hardscrabble character of rural life. Then, too, there are the "pull" factors that draw people to the cities—jobs, schools, housing, and even a more stimulating life.

At the bottom of a ravine near Mexico City is a dismal bunch of shacks. Some of the parents have 14 children.

"We used to live up there," Señora Gonzalez gestured toward the mountain, "in those caves. Our only hope was one day to have a place to live. And now we do." She smiled with pride at the jerry-built shacks . . . each one had a collection of flowers planted in tin cans. "One day, we hope to extend the water pipes and drainage—perhaps even pave. . . . "

And what was the name of her community? Señora Gonzalez beamed. "Esperanza!"(McDowell 1984:172)

Esperanza is the Spanish word for hope. This is what lies behind the rush to these cities—the hope of a better life. And this is why the rush won't slow down. In 1930, only one Latin American city had over a million people—now fifty do! This change is so vast and so rapid that the world's cities are growing by one million people each week (Brockerhoff 2000).

How will the Least Industrialized Nations ever be able to adjust to such extensive migration? They have no choice. Authorities in Brazil, Guatemala, Venezuela, and other countries have sent in the police and even the army to evict the settlers. It doesn't work. It does lead to violence, and sometimes the temporary removal of people, but the settlers keep streaming in. The adjustments that these nations must make will be painful. The infrastructure (roads, water, sewers, electricity, and so on) must be built, but these poor countries don't have the resources to build them. As the desperate rural poor flock to the cities, the problems will worsen.

Do you see any solutions?

GAINING AN INSIDER'S VIEW. These are outsiders' views. Symbolic interactionists try to see how life looks to the people who live it. They try to discover the meanings that people give to their experiences, how they feel about their situation, and how they cope with their problems. As symbolic interactionists study the worlds of the urban poor, they try not to impose their own values or views on others. This approach to understanding urban life is called the **Chicago school of sociology,** because it represents the approach used by the sociology department of the University of Chicago in the 1920s and 1930s. This department produced classic studies of urban life. In 1923 Nels Anderson wrote *The Hobo,* followed in 1927 by Frederic Thrasher's *The Gang.* In 1929 Harvey Zorbaugh's *The Gold Coast and the Slum* contrasted the poor and the rich in Chicago. Then in 1932, Paul Cressey published *Taxi-Dance Hall,* about women who made their living by dancing with men. Making the city their sociological laboratory, these sociologists, as others have done since, focused mostly on the lives of the poor.

DISTINCTIVE SOCIAL WORLDS. The contrasts of the city—its many groups with their distinctive ways of life—fascinated sociologists at Chicago. They were impressed with how people of different backgrounds develop unique subcultures and live in separate areas of the city. As Louis Wirth (1938) put it, the city is made up of "a mosaic of social worlds." Sociologists today are also fascinated by these contrasting social worlds, and they remain topics of sociological research. In these smaller social worlds, urban people live with unique codes and understandings of social life. Their differing interpretations of life and expectations of how to interact make it easy for people from different areas of the same city to misunderstand one another.

WHYTE'S CLASSIC STUDY. In this tradition, sociologist William Foote Whyte lived as a participant observer in an inner city for two or three years. In the classic book that he wrote to recount his experiences, *Street Corner Society* (1943, 1995), Whyte explains that what may look to outsiders to be disorganized is, in fact, a tightly knit way of life. By participating in the residents' lives—hanging around the street corner with "the boys," going to dances, bowling, playing baseball—Whyte was able to identify the various types of people who lived there. The young men separated themselves into two main groups: the college boys, who were upward bound, and the corner boys, who remained in their old neighborhood. Each group was further subdivided into smaller worlds, such as the group of young men whom Whyte met each evening. Other major groups were the racketeers and the politicians. Each group had its own statuses, its own norms, and its own ways of controlling its members.

SUTTLES' STUDY. Thirty years later, sociologist Gerald Suttles did participant observation in an inner city of Chicago. He found social statuses and forms of communication equally as complex as those Whyte had uncovered among the Italians he studied. Suttles documented how African Americans, Puerto Ricans, Chicanos, and Italians, although sharing the same physical space, have their own forms of communication. One group's customary ways of expressing itself—its distinctive language, gestures, and clothing—can be offensive to members of another group. Even how people make eye contact can be a problem. Here's what Suttles (1968:66–67) says:

> Whites say that Negroes will not look them in the eye. The Negroes counter by saying the whites are impolite and try to "cow" people by staring at them. . . . The most subtle accounts are those which describe almost entirely nonverbal encounters: "When I went over to the Negro nurse, she didn't even look up," "I'd go again (to an Italian restaurant) but they really stare you down," "I can understand why those guys (older Italians) can't half speak English, but why they gotta eyeball everybody walk past?"

Within each area of the city, different groups stake out a unique existence. They develop their own ways to express themselves, live by their own codes, and evaluate their members accordingly. Although these background assumptions unite a group's members, they separate them from others and hinder communication with other groups. This can create misunderstandings and hostility among the diverse groups that compose the urban mosaic. As the quotation from Suttles shows, these differences lead to suspicion and misunderstanding. They can even lead to death.

ANDERSON'S STUDIES. In the Spotlight on Social Research box on the next page, Elijah Anderson discusses the participant observation that he did in yet another Chicago slum. He, too, emphasizes how you cannot understand a group of people unless you see the world

Spotlight on Social Research
THE CODE OF THE STREET

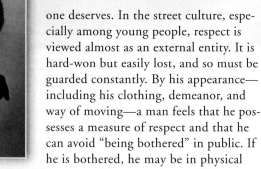

*While a graduate student at the University of Chicago, **ELIJAH ANDERSON** began to study the men who hung around a Southside bar named Jelly's. As an outsider, he drew attention the first time he entered the bar, but after he ordered a drink, the curiosity of others seemed temporarily satisfied. It was here where Anderson, now a professor at the University of Pennsylvania, learned about the social world of the urban ghetto and the "code of the street."*

Of all the problems that beset the inner-city poor black community, none is more pressing than that of interpersonal violence and aggression. Violence wreaks havoc with the lives of community residents and increasingly spills over into downtown and residential middle-class areas. The inclination to violence springs from the circumstances of life among the ghetto poor: the lack of jobs that pay a living wage, the stigma of race, the fallout from rampant drug use and drug trafficking, and the resulting alienation and lack of hope for the future.

Out of this pervasive despair has evolved a street culture. This code of the street consists of informal rules that govern behavior in public, including violence. By regulating the use of violence, the code allows those who are inclined to aggression to precipitate violent encounters in an approved way.

At the heart of the code is the issue of respect—of being treated "right," or granted the deference that one deserves. In the street culture, especially among young people, respect is viewed almost as an external entity. It is hard-won but easily lost, and so must be guarded constantly. By his appearance—including his clothing, demeanor, and way of moving—a man feels that he possesses a measure of respect and that he can avoid "being bothered" in public. If he is bothered, he may be in physical danger, but he also has been disgraced or "dissed" (disrespected).

The code of the street is a cultural adaptation to the profound sense of alienation from mainstream society and its institutions that many poor inner-city black people feel. This includes their lack of confidence in the police and the judicial system. When called, the police may not respond, which is one reason that many residents feel that they must be prepared to defend themselves and their loved ones against those who are inclined to aggression. Thus the person who is believed capable of "taking care of himself" is accorded respect.

The code of the street has emerged as a result of the breakdown or weaknesses of civil law in the most distressed inner-city communities. It is a survival strategy that centers on reputation, respect, retribution, and retaliation. When people rely on themselves and their reputation for protection, we have a situation that leads to high rates of violence. A legacy of institutionalized racism, joblessness, and alienation suffuses distressed inner-city neighborhoods and exacerbates these conditions.

as they see it. For example, at Jelly's, a bar and liquor store in an African American area, Anderson (1978) uncovered intricate boundaries that separated people from one another. He found three main groups at Jelly's:

The regulars. These men see and present themselves as hard-working. They subscribe to mainstream values, are proud of their involvement in families, and have aspirations of getting ahead. Their values can be summed up with the single word *decency*—working regularly and treating other people right.

The wineheads. These men neither value work, nor do they work regularly. Their main concern is getting enough money to buy wine. They beg from others and have low status.

The hoodlums. These men pride themselves on "being tough" and having access to easy money. Few work regularly. They are involved in petty theft, stickups, burglaries, and fencing stolen property. The other men at Jelly's do not trust them, nor do they trust one another.

When Anderson (1990, 2006) was hired as a sociologist at the University of Pennsylvania, he moved into what he calls the Village-Norton, a neighborhood in Philadelphia that was being "gentrified"; that is, more affluent people were moving into the area and rehabilitating its buildings. **Gentrification** creates tensions because it raises property values, taxes, and rents, forcing the poorer residents to move to lower-rent areas. Although the area begins to look prettier, the poor resent the invasion of their neighborhood and do not benefit from it.

The Village-Norton bordered an African American ghetto, and tension between residents of the two areas was high. Both African American and white residents were suspicious about the African Americans they saw on the streets of the Village-Norton. Just as Suttles had documented a couple of decades earlier, eye contact was a significant source of tension. Whites were afraid to look too long at African Americans that they didn't know, fearing that their look might be interpreted as an invitation to interact. To avoid this problem, whites either pretended not to see African Americans or else they looked right through them without speaking. African Americans, in contrast, were used to more outgoing interaction, and they found this eye contact offensive. Only after people lived in the area for a while did they become adequately familiar with what Anderson calls the *code of the street*—that is, its norms and etiquette, which reduce tension and allow the two groups to coexist. The coexistence, though, was never easy, and tensions remained.

IN SUM Groups living within each area of the city stake out territory, establish social boundaries between themselves and others, and work out a sense of identity and belonging. This is no less true of the residents of the inner city. If you look beyond the run-down buildings, you will find intricate patterns of interaction. People there, like people everywhere, interact on the basis of background assumptions and within social networks of associations and friendships. The assumptions, codes, and norms of inner-city residents, however, often differ sharply from those of the middle class.

Symbolic interactionists also remind us that the poor do not experience urban problems in the abstract. They encounter specific problems. For example, the poor do not experience the *concept* of urban decay. Rather, they deal with cutbacks in city services; buses that run late or not at all; factories that move to Mexico or China and wipe out their jobs overnight—and killers like Hagan who stalk their neighborhood, hallways, and elevators. In short, symbolic interactionists focus on how people make sense of their experiences as they attempt to cope with urban life.

Functionalism

BURGESS' MODEL OF CONCENTRIC ZONES. The University of Chicago also produced urban studies that reflect the functionalist perspective. Ernest Burgess, whose study became a classic, analyzed how cities grow. Figure 12-3 on the next page is taken from one of his books. As you can see, Burgess identified five urban zones, each with distinct functions. Burgess visualized the city as expanding outward from its center, the central business district (Zone I). Zone II, which encircles the downtown area, contains the city's slums. To escape the slum, skilled and thrifty workers move to Zone III. Zone IV contains the better apartment buildings, residential hotels, single-family dwellings, and gated communities where the wealthy live. Still farther out, beyond the city limits, is Zone V, a commuter zone of suburbs or satellite cities.

Burgess intended his **concentric zone theory** to represent the "tendencies of any town or city to expand radially from its central business district." He noted, however, that no "city fits perfectly this ideal scheme." Some cities face physical obstructions such as lakes or rivers that make their expansion depart from this model. As Burgess also noted, businesses deviate from this model when they locate in outlying zones. This was in 1925. Burgess didn't know it, but he was seeing the beginning of a major shift that led to today's suburban shopping malls, strung like beads around the city. This shift has been so strong that malls today account for most of the country's retail sales.

MOBILITY AND THE CITY. This classic model of urban growth helps us understand urban problems. Burgess stressed that city dwellers are always on the move. In addition to commuting for work, school, shopping, and recreation, they move into better zones when they can afford to. This creates an **invasion-succession cycle,** one group moving into an area that is already occupied by people who have different characteristics. The invasion creates antagonisms between the groups: The one resents displacement; the other feels

FIGURE 12-3 Burgess' Concentric Zones: Illustrating the Growth of the City

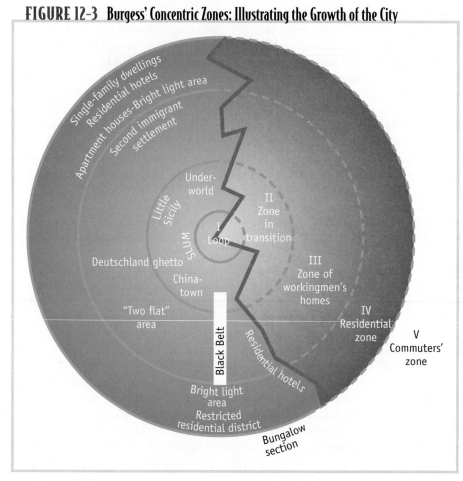

Note: This is Burgess' depiction of how concentric zones flow from the central business district as a city expands. The left side shows the city of Chicago in 1925. The jagged vertical line represents the shore of Lake Michigan.

Source: From Ernest W. Burgess, "The Growth of the City: An Introduction to a Research Project" in *The City,* Robert E. Park, Ernest W. Burgess, and Roderick D. McKenzie, eds. Chicago: University of Chicago Press, 1925. (Pages 47–62 in the 1967 edition). Reprinted with the permission of the University of Chicago Press.

unwelcome. Burgess did his analysis a long time ago, but this same process continues today. Today, however, people move not only outward, away from a city's center, but also toward it, in this process we call gentrification.

THE ZONE IN TRANSITION. Burgess also noted that the most mobile areas have the most severe social problems: These areas lack a sense of community, they have fewer controls over people's behavior, and they suffer from *anomie,* or alienation. As Burgess put it, high mobility leads to demoralization, which is accompanied by promiscuity, vice, juvenile delinquency, gangs, crime, poverty, and the breakup of families. Mobility and its accompanying problems are concentrated in Zone II, which Burgess called a *zone in transition.* He said that here we find the city's "poverty, degradation, and disease," the "underworlds of crime and vice." In Burgess' colorful phrase, this zone is "the purgatory of lost souls."

The zone in transition also contains the seeds of its own regeneration. There you can also find social workers, preachers, artists, and political radicals—all, says Burgess, "obsessed with the vision of a new and better world." To this, we can add that in recent years financiers have seen value in this area; and, in a process called *urban renewal,* they have constructed office buildings, financial centers, stadiums, and luxury hotels. This is another movement *toward* the city center.

Because many cities diverge from Burgess' concentric zone model, his theory has many critics (Alihan 1938; Harris and Ullman 1945; La Gory et al. 1980). All cities, however, have zones of functional specialties—areas dominated by a type of business or activity—

clusters of warehouses, auto dealerships, repair shops, boutiques, or fast-food restaurants. Cities also have zones that "specialize" in urban problems—skid rows, red-light districts, and regions of high crime and delinquency. If you know how to read urban graffiti, you know that some of these areas are even set off by their own signs.

It is significant that the functionalist approach implies that a city's problems are temporary. Over time, a city will absorb its dispossessed and poor and equip them for a better life.

Conflict Theory

CLASS CONFLICT AND URBAN PROBLEMS. Conflict theorists say that the functionalists overlook the basic class conflict that underlies urban problems. Manuel Castells (1977, 1983, 1989), for example, says that the problems that our cities face are the consequence of our capitalistic system. Businesses began with mom-and-pop operations, but they outstripped those humble origins—expanding, merging, and growing powerful. Today, business leaders dictate government policy and tap the public treasury. Here are two examples of how they do this: By insuring home mortgages, the government increases the profits of developers who build and market homes. By building interstate highways, the government finances a transportation system to move the goods that the wealthy manufacture.

As Castells points out, building interstate highways solved a major problem that confronted the wealthy. In the early 1900s, capitalists built multistory buildings to house their factories. When assembly-line techniques were developed, these buildings became obsolete: It was inefficient to move raw materials and manufactured goods from one floor to another. Interstate highways (or expressways), built at taxpayer expense, enabled factory owners to relocate their production to the suburbs, where lower land prices and taxes allowed them to build single-story factories. These highways also allowed the corporate elite to maintain access to the city. There they could do business with the marketing and financial institutions, as well as continue to enjoy its cultural benefits, such as professional sports, theaters, and concerts.

Moving factories and offices out of the city led to its decline. This flight by corporate management and skilled workers ravished the city's tax base, crippling the city's ability to maintain services and help the many poor who were left behind. To add insult to injury, after the corporate leaders moved their power base from city to suburb, they supported a coalition of rural and suburban districts that voted against proposals designed to aid cities. In effect, corporate leaders abandoned areas they no longer needed to the poor, about whom they did not care.

URBAN RENEWAL. A downtown cloaked in smoldering ruins, however, did not fit into the plans of the corporate elite, and they spearheaded plans to redevelop the downtown area. But such redevelopment has a bottom line: profits made through selling properties and operating businesses. To tourists—and indeed to a city's nearby comfortable suburbanites—the renaissance of the downtown area makes the city seem a phoenix, reborn from the ashes of destruction.

The city, however, remains the repository of the poor and powerless. Adjacent to the resurrected downtown live the huddled masses—the destitute in an affluent society. The poor are bypassed, some say oppressed, by leaders who pursue their own political and economic interests. This underclass, however, is not irrelevant, for if this group riots, it threatens the stability of society. This, in turn, threatens the position of the powerful and privileged. As a consequence, the police keep a sharp eye on the urban poor. A legion of social workers is also dispatched into their midst, not from altruism, say conflict theorists, but to keep the poor quiet and preserve the status quo.

Research Findings

As we look at research findings, let's first consider alienation and community in the city and then look in depth at the decline of the inner city, urban violence, and the changes that are affecting U.S. cities.

Alienation in the City

GEMEINSCHAFT AND GESELLSCHAFT. From early on, sociologists were fascinated by the sharp contrast between the intimacy and neighborliness of village life and the anonymity and self-centeredness of urban life. In the 1880s, Ferdinand Tönnies noted that agricultural people share a sense of community because they share the same activities and values. Tönnies (1957) used the term *Gemeinschaft* to refer to the bonds of intimacy and shared traditions that unite people. He used the term *Gesellschaft* to refer to the impersonality and self-interests that he said were associated with urban areas. (In German, *Gemeinschaft* means "community"; *Gesellschaft* means "society.")

IMPERSONALITY AND SELF-INTEREST. If you know urban life, you know that impersonality and self-interest are ordinary characteristics of the city. As you traverse city streets, you can expect people to avoid needless interaction with others and to be absorbed in their own affairs. These are adjustments that people have made to the crowds of strangers with whom they temporarily share the same urban space. Sometimes, however, these characteristics of urban life are carried to extremes. Here is an event that made national headlines when it occurred, upsetting the entire country:

> Twenty-eight-year-old Catherine Genovese, who was known as Kitty in her Queens neighborhood, was returning home from work. After parking her car, a man grabbed her. Kitty screamed, "Oh my God! He stabbed me! Please help me!"
> For more than half an hour, thirty-eight respectable, law-abiding citizens watched the killer stalk and stab Kitty in three separate attacks. Twice the sudden glow from their bedroom lights frightened him off. Each time he returned, sought her out, and stabbed her again. Not one person telephoned the police during the assault.
> When interviewed by the police, the witnesses said: "I didn't want to get involved," "We thought it was a lovers' quarrel," "I don't know," and "I was tired. I went back to bed." (*New York Times*, March 26, 1964)

It is possible that this incident was exaggerated, that due to darkness, distance, and obstructions people didn't understand that Kitty was being attacked ("Kitty Genovese" 2005). Regardless, anyone who lives in a large city knows that it is prudent to be alert to danger. You never know who that stranger near you really is. Even traffic accidents hold the danger of angry people whose wrath explodes:

> In crowded traffic on a bridge going into Detroit, Deletha Word bumped the car ahead of her. The damage was minor, but the driver, Martell Welch, jumped out. Cursing, he pulled Deletha from her car, pushed her onto the hood, and began beating her. Martell's friends got out to watch. One of them held Deletha down while Martell took a car jack and smashed Deletha's car. Scared for her life, Deletha broke away, fleeing to the bridge's railing. Martell and his friends taunted her, shouting, "Jump, bitch, jump!" Deletha plunged to her death. Whether she jumped or fell is unknown. (*Newsweek*, September 4, 1995)

HOW CITIES UNDERMINE COMMUNITY. Why should the city be alienating? In a classic essay, sociologist Louis Wirth (1938) said that urban dwellers live anonymous lives marked by segmented and superficial encounters. This undermines kinship and neighborhood, the traditional bases of social control and feelings of solidarity and identification with others. Urbanites then grow aloof and indifferent to other people's problems—as happened with the neighbors of Kitty Genovese. In short, the personal freedom that the city offers comes at the cost of alienation.

Community in the City

The city is not inevitably alienating. Most drivers who witnessed the tragedy that befell Deletha Word did nothing. But after Deletha went over the railing, two motorists jumped in after her, risking injury and their own lives in a futile attempt to save her. Some urbanites, then, are far from alienated.

THE GANS RESEARCH. The city also has enclaves of community. Sociologist Herbert Gans, a symbolic interactionist, did participant observation in the West End of Boston. He was so impressed with the sense of community that he titled his book *The Urban Villagers* (1962). Gans said:

> After a few weeks of living in the West End, my observations—and my perceptions of the area—changed drastically. The search for an apartment quickly indicated that the individual units were usually in much better condition than the outside or the hallways of the buildings. Subsequently, in wandering through the West End, and in using it as a resident, I developed a kind of selective perception, in which my eye focused only on those parts of the area that were actually being used by people. Vacant buildings and boarded-up stores were no longer so visible, and the totally deserted alleys or streets were outside the set of paths normally traversed, either by myself or by the West Enders. The dirt and spilled-over garbage remained, but, since they were concentrated in street gutters and empty lots, they were not really harmful to anyone and thus were not as noticeable as during my initial observations.
>
> Since much of the area's life took place on the street, faces became familiar very quickly. I met my neighbors on the stairs and in front of my building. And, once a shopping pattern developed, I saw the same storekeepers frequently, as well as the area's "characters" who wandered through the streets everyday on a fairly regular route and schedule. In short, the exotic quality of the stores and the residents also wore off as I became used to seeing them.

In short, Gans found a community, people who identified with the area and with one another. Its residents enjoyed networks of friends and acquaintances. Despite the area's substandard buildings, most West Enders had chosen to live here. *To them, this was a low-rent district, not a slum.*

Most West Enders had low-paying, insecure jobs. Other residents were elderly, living on small pensions. Unlike the middle class, these people didn't care about their "address." The area's inconveniences were something they put up with in exchange for cheap housing. In general, they were content with their neighborhood.

TYPES OF URBAN DWELLERS. Sociologists who do participant observation stress that the city is divided into little worlds that are knowable down to their smallest details (Lenz-Romeiss 1973; Karp and Yoels 1990; Keans 1991). These little social worlds are part of the urban mosaic that Wirth mentioned. People who feel that they fit into one of these little worlds and identify with it experience emotional security. Others never feel a good fit. Still others feel threatened by some "little world" that isn't theirs but in which they have to interact. The city is not a monolith, and people have different urban experiences.

As Gans did his research, he began to analyze the different kinds of people he met. He noted that the answer to the question about alienation and community depends on whom one is discussing. (To see what Gans says about his own research, go back to the Spotlight on Research box on page 222). Let's look at the five types of urban dwellers that Gans (1962, 1968, 1991) identified. The first three live in the city by choice and are not alienated; the latter two are outcasts of industrial society who live in the city despairingly, without choice or hope.

1. *The cosmopolites.* These are the intellectuals, professionals, and artists who have been attracted to the city. They value its conveniences and cultural benefits.
2. *The singles.* Roughly between the ages of 20 and their early 30s, the singles have not decided to settle in the city permanently. For them, urban life is a stage in their life course. Businesses and services, such as singles bars and apartment complexes, cater to their needs and desires. After they marry, many singles move to the suburbs.

Urban life can be alienating. To feel anonymous in a crowd of strangers can make people grow aloof and indifferent to other people's problems.

3. *The ethnic villagers.* Feeling a sense of identity, working-class members of the same ethnic group band together. They form tightly knit neighborhoods that resemble villages and small towns. Family and peer oriented, they try to isolate themselves from the dangers and problems of urban life.

4. *The deprived.* Destitute, emotionally disturbed, and having little income, education, or work skills, the deprived live in neighborhoods that are more like urban jungles than urban villages. Like Hagan, some of them stalk those jungles in search of prey. Neither predator nor prey has much hope for anything better in life—for themselves or for their children. The Issues in Social Problems box on the next page recounts the public housing experiment that isolated the deprived from the other residents of the city.

5. *The trapped.* These people don't live in the area by choice, either. Some were trapped when an ethnic group "invaded" their neighborhood and they could not afford to move. Others are "downwardly mobile"; they started in a higher social class but because of mental or physical illness, alcohol or other drug addiction, or other problems, they drifted downward. Many are elderly and are not wanted elsewhere. Like the deprived, the trapped suffer from high rates of assault, mugging, and rape.

IN SUM Gans' typology illustrates the complexity of urban life. The city is a mosaic of social diversity, and not all urban dwellers experience the city in the same way. Each group has its own lifestyle, and each has distinct experiences. Some welcome the city's cultural diversity and mix with a lot of groups. Others find community by retreating into the security of ethnic enclaves. Some, in contrast, feel trapped and deprived. To them, the city is an urban jungle. It poses threats to their health and safety, and they live lives of despair.

The Decline of the Central City

As people fled the central city for the suburbs, the city declined. It lost population, jobs, and political power. People moved out of U.S. cities to such an extent that more than half of Americans now live in the suburbs and twice as many manufacturing jobs are located in the suburbs as in the city (Palen 2005). Far from being utopias, the suburbs have their

Issues in Social Problems
A FAILED EXPERIMENT: CREATING ALIENATION

THE OLD EXPERIMENT: HIGH-RISE SEGREGATED HOUSING

Let's look at the problem of high-rise public housing as people lived it in the 1980s and 1990s.

It is a summer afternoon in the Robert Taylor Homes in Chicago, no different from most other days in the nation's largest public housing complex except for the intense heat.

Shots crackle from pistols near a play area. Laughter turns to screams as children dart for cover behind buildings and in stairwells crowded with craps shooters and winos.

The gunfire is soon over. The angry men bent on shooting each other have run off. The dice games and wine drinking resume. The basketball hoops again rattle above the scorching asphalt, and the children return to the dilapidated play equipment.

Fifteen blocks long and one block wide, Robert Taylor Homes is the world's largest public housing project. Taylor Homes consists of twenty-eight identical red and cream sixteen-story towers surrounded on all sides by other impoverished neighborhoods. Many residents view Taylor Homes as a separate city within Chicago, an island of poverty adrift in a city of plenty.

Mrs. Wallace has lived in Taylor Homes since it was built. "There are a lot of good people here," she says. "They go to work, come home, and close their doors. They take the attitude that if nobody bothers them, they won't bother anybody. They try to get their kids to do the right thing, which is hard when so many parents don't."

John Smith remembers better times at Robert Taylor Homes. He has reared his children here. "And I sent all twelve to college," he says proudly with a deep, resonant voice. "I worked two jobs to do it, but I did it. I was firm with them and demanded that they do the right thing. They never gave me any trouble."

"But things are different now," 68-year-old Mr. Smith says from the chair in which he sits each day. "Things are tense now. The young people have nothing to do. No jobs. No recreation programs. So they are rowdy. They don't go to school. They make trouble."

As he talks, a young man walks by several times wielding a metal pipe. Mr. Smith pauses and gives the youth a stern look. The youth leaves.

One of the few remaining buildings of Chicago's Cabrini-Green public housing project.

"You have to watch them or they will hurt you," he said. "If they think you have something, they will slash you or knock you over the head and take it."

Asked why he doesn't move, Mr. Smith says, "Son, things are bad all over. It's not just here."

One hundred fifty thousand people live in Chicago's public housing. Single mothers occupy most of the units. Most of the residents are unemployed. Gangs control many of the buildings. The police even gave up enforcing laws against drugs and burglaries. The head of Chicago's public housing put it this way:

As long as they don't go after and injure innocent people, it's fine. I can't stop them from using drugs. Everybody belongs to a gang. They are going to burglarize apartments to support their habits. You send a message. You don't say you can do these things, but over time they know that the only thing that's going to set me off is when they start hurting innocent people.

The Robert Taylor Homes, along with Cabrini-Green and other public housing projects in Chicago were badly mismanaged. Repairs weren't made, rats infested the apartments, and elevators broke down, leaving elderly people unable to get to their upper-level apartments.

THE NEW EXPERIMENT: MIXED INCOME INTEGRATED HOUSING

After many attempts at reform but continued mismanagement and high crime, authorities finally gave up on the Robert Taylor homes and similar public housing projects. They turned them over to the wrecking ball. The last of the Robert Taylor buildings was demolished in 2006. Its residents were dispersed to a new social experiment, a series of low-rise buildings, none over four stories. The essential change in the city's public housing is not the height but the mixed-income format of the new dwellings. Rather than piling poor family upon poor family in high rises where they are isolated from others, the residents are living among families that have a variety of incomes.

The end of this story is yet to be told. We'll have to wait to see the outcome of this new experiment in public housing.

Based on Sheppard 1980; J. Anderson 1995; "Granddaddy of All . . . " 2006.

own problems, especially the older ones. From traffic congestion to street crime and eroding tax bases, they have problems commonly associated with the city. Suburbs even have **suburban sprawl,** the disappearance of open areas as a suburb expands into the countryside.

DISINVESTMENT. As we saw, conflict theorists trace the decline of the city to capitalists, whose policies damaged cities and encouraged suburbanization. Banks and savings and loan associations tightened this noose by **redlining,** refusing to lend money for mortgages in areas they considered undesirable (Squires 2003). (Loan officers used to draw a "red line" around neighborhoods they considered bad risks.) Redlined areas are usually either in the inner city or in neighborhoods undergoing integration.

As sociologist John Palen (2005) noted, redlining creates a *self-fulfilling prophecy.* Because banks refuse to finance the sale of homes in the area, only people with cash or those who are eligible for government loans are able to buy homes. With few buyers, the inventory of homes for sale builds up, and prices drop. With home prices dropping and banks refusing to make loans for improvements, homeowners stop remodeling and making repairs to their homes. As the neighborhood declines, it justifies the decisions of the lending officials to avoid the area because it is a "bad risk." Bankers, of course, insist that **disinvestment,** their withdrawal of investments from an area, is the *result* of deteriorating housing, not its cause.

Redlining is now illegal, but it is still practiced covertly. A banker in southern Illinois told me that he would loan no money in a certain area. He then added, "If you tell anyone that I said this, I will deny that the conversation ever took place."

> "It just doesn't pay," said Linda Kutz as she looked mournfully around her. "This used to be a good business. I could get good rents and keep my building up. I knew my tenants, and they respected me. But now—nothing but animals!" Linda muttered as she looked despairingly at the shambles of what had been a nice apartment just a few days before.

Like many other urban landlords, Linda Kutz is abandoning her apartment building. She is caught between the cross-pressures of high taxes, the city insisting that she bring her buildings into conformity with the housing code, tenants who damage her property and refuse to pay their rents, and a costly and long eviction process.

When she went to the police, they asked, "Did you see them (the renters) do it?" She said, "No, I wasn't there." Pointing to holes in the wall and feces in the floor ducts, she said, "But you can see for yourself what they did." Their response: "If you didn't see them do it, we can't do anything about it." With three of her apartments vandalized during the past year, Kutz says she has no choice but to walk away and let the banks foreclose on her building.

ABANDONMENT. Each year, landlords abandon thousands of **housing units**—places of residence such as houses or apartments. Some of these buildings need only minor repairs. Why, then, are abandoned buildings part of the urban scene? As Kutz indicates, vandalism, high taxes, a slow eviction process, and housing codes that sometimes border on the quixotic all play a role. As another landlord told me:

> "Look at this building," he said, indicating the workers on the roof. "I don't know how long I can keep this up. I want to provide a nice place for my renters. Then comes the city inspector who says I have to add rain gutters. Every time someone moves in, an inspector examines my building. No one's ever said anything about gutters before. The building is over a hundred years old and has never had rain gutters. Why does it suddenly need them now?"

All these factors add up to higher risk and, sometimes, financial loss. Unable to find a buyer, some landlords stop paying their property taxes or making repairs. They collect as much rent as long as possible and then walk away from their deteriorating buildings. The abandoned buildings become a dangerous playground for children, a shelter for junkies, a target for looters, fun for vandals, and profit for arsonists.

Arson as a way of refinancing is discussed in the text. This fire at a landmark tavern in Beardstown, Illinois, was investigated as arson.

ARSON. Some owners of buildings and businesses who face huge losses see fire as the solution. Those afraid to set the fire themselves hire "torches" (professional arsonists), who are seldom apprehended because arson often destroys the evidence of the crime. Many insurance companies prefer to pay off a blaze of "suspicious origin" and recover the cost in their general rates than to fight a case in court and risk getting a reputation of not paying claims. Some cynically call arson the "modern way of refinancing."

Even when a company does fight a claim that is obviously arson, it can easily lose. As an insurance claims agent told me during an investigation:

> We won't have to pay on this one. The fire began in the basement on a pile of clothes. There was no source of fire [heating element or electricity] there. The insured was paid off on another fire just three years ago. The police have the case.
>
> I talked to the detective in charge of the case. The insured had lost his job, and the mortgage holder had begun foreclosure (the legal process of getting possession of the property), but the man stuck to his story. ("I don't know anything. I wasn't there.") The company paid.

Except when people are killed, urban arson receives little publicity or concern. The public shows little interest, and often neither do the police. Functionalists can well see the core truth in the statement that "arson is the modern way of refinancing." Perhaps it is functional for society to let entrepreneurs refinance their losses by spreading the cost over tens of thousands of policyholders.

Urban Violence: Youth Gangs

In addition to a physical decline, our urban centers also face violence. We have already discussed this topic in Chapters 5 and 6. Here we will examine violence by youth gangs and then move on to violence in the schools and riots.

The topic of gangs intrigues both the public and sociologists. We need to note that there is no such thing as *the* urban gang. There are many types of gangs, and not all of them are violent. In fact, not all of them are criminal. The purpose of some gangs is to protect their neighborhood, even to bring about social change that gives the poor a shot at the American dream—or at least makes life better for people who are clinging precariously to the edge of society (DiChiara and Chabot 2003; Martinez 2003). Our focus, though, is on gang violence.

THE THRASHER STUDY: HOW GANGS FORM. Gangs have been a sociological topic for almost a century. In the 1920s, sociologist Frederic Thrasher studied 1,313 gangs in Chicago. He (1927) found that gangs start as ordinary play groups that compete for space in crowded and deteriorating areas of the city. Boys band together because their participation in a group gives them a valued identity. The group then becomes the impetus for criminal activities.

Over and over since this classic research by Thrasher, sociologists have documented what the public has perceived, that it is primarily lower-class boys who are involved in gangs. They have also continuously documented the *alternative identity* that gangs offer. Let's try to understand why gangs hold such an attraction for lower-class boys.

THE COHEN STUDY: THE REJECTION OF MIDDLE-CLASS NORMS. In another classic study, sociologist Albert Cohen (1955) found a key that helps us to understand this attraction: Lower-class boys are measured by middle-class standards, but they lack the socially approved means to meet those standards. The schools these boys attend are immersed in middle-class values. They are run by middle-class teachers and administrators who use middle-class standards to judge the boys' speech, behavior, and performance on tests. The boys feel that they don't fit in, that their teachers look down on them. In self-defense, they form a subculture of like-minded boys in which they use different standards to judge one another, standards by which they can succeed. Their rejection of middle-class standards is so thorough that doing well in school becomes equated with girls and sissies, the opposite of the vibrant manliness and bravado that they expect of one another. As the boys twist the norms of the school into a shape by which they can succeed, they also reject the standards of other authority figures and give approval to violating the law.

THE MILLER STUDY: SUBSTITUTE VALUES. In what became another classic study, sociologist Walter Miller (1958) examined the norms that make gangs so attractive to lower-class boys. He found that the boys use gang membership to build identities on the basis of six values: trouble, excitement, toughness, smartness, autonomy, and fate. Making trouble not only provides excitement, relieving the monotony of everyday life, but also allows the boys to show that they are tough, smart, and autonomous (independent, defying authority). The boys also think of their lives as controlled by fate: If you get hurt or killed, this is simply because your number came up. The boys confer status on one another according to how they perform on these values. In short, through gangs lower-class boys reject the world of middle-class values that seems to crush their spirits with constant rejection and failure, replacing them with a world of alternative values. Activity in this world offers the boys the opportunity to achieve a sense of self-worth through the positive recognition of peers.

SUPERGANGS. For the most part, the gangs in these classic studies were groups of adolescents who did nothing worse than get high, skip school, write graffiti, steal from parked cars, get into a fight now and then, and vandalize property. I say "nothing worse" because today we have "supergangs" such as the Crips and Bloods. These gangs, and the many others like them, are no play groups occasionally wandering outside the law: Their members not only steal but also kill. The Crips and Bloods have gone national, and they now have affiliated gangs in most major cities and even in some smaller ones.

THE PRINCIPLES BENEATH THE FORMS. The findings of Cohen and Miller, however, remain firm. The El Rukins/Black P. Stone Nation, the Gangster Disciples, and the Vice Lords, as well as the more infamous Crips and Bloods, follow the same pattern. They are based on the boys' rejection of middle-class norms—which throw failure into their face and seem so irrelevant to their lives—and their replacement with a value system by which the boys can achieve positive recognition and a sense of self-worth. The form of gangs might change over time, but the basic principles on which they operate and by which they offer such attraction to lower-class boys remain the same.

GLOBAL ASPECTS OF GANGS. Gangs have been around for centuries and have operated throughout the world. There are local gangs in every large urban area around the globe. What is different is the growing global context of urban gangs. Today there are Muslim gangs in Norway, Latino gangs (their members exiled from the United States) in Honduras, and Hells Angels in Germany. The MS-13 gang in Los Angeles has expanded to El Salvador, and gangs tied to Chinese Triads are found in LA; Russian gangs operate in Chicago; the Crips are in Holland; and Mexican gangs have moved into San Diego (Hagedorn 2005).

Just as sociological studies have documented how gangs attract lower-class youth, so on the global level, gangs attract the disenfranchised, the neglected, those who are left out of the legitimate political process. Beyond establishing means of self-identity, which they do, on the global level gangs provide an alternative political structure. They give power to those who are bypassed by political systems. In some instances, the power of the gang is so great that the established political powers must take them into account when they develop social policy (Hagedorn 2005).

GIRL GANGS. Lower-class girls, coming from backgrounds similar to the boys', also find the middle-class values of the school oppressive. For them, too, the contrarian values of gangs beckon. The girls reject the "soft feminism" of the middle class, replacing it with expectations of acting tough and being aggressive. Within this framework, however, they are expected to be submissive to the boys (Vigil 2002). Here is one indication of how dominant the males in these groups are: When girls are initiated into the gang, the boys can require them to have sex with one or several of the male gang members. For the most part, girls play supportive roles in the boys' gangs, such as by hiding weapons and drugs and providing alibis and sex. Almost all girl gangs, then, are auxiliaries to boy gangs (Vigil 2002).

An occasional independent all-girl gang does appear on the urban scene, but this is unusual (Nurge 2003). An example is *Las Locas* (the Crazies), an all-girl gang in Los Angeles. The members of this gang were unpredictably dangerous, and the boys had to watch their step when they were around them. Although such cases are rare, the girls can be every bit as violent as the boys. Some girls will kill another girl just to get a pair of earrings (Faison 1991).

RACIAL-ETHNIC DIVERSITY. Youth gangs are not limited to any racial-ethnic group. Los Angeles has white gangs, African American gangs, Chicano gangs, even Colombian, San Salvadoran, and Vietnamese gangs. Over and over, it is the same: Banding together, the boys (or girls) form a group in which they can attain identity and protection, friendship, a "family," anonymity, and group support in criminal activities. The gangs also provide a way for members to protect themselves from rival gangs. In some areas, it is dangerous *not* to be a gang member.

Girl gangs have become more common, and not only in the United States. These girls in El Salvador, members of Gang 18, are making the symbol 18 with their hands.

NEIGHBORHOODS. It is difficult for members of the middle-class to understand what life can be like in a lower-class neighborhood. Life is so different that it is not too much of a leap from reality to say that lower- and middle-class youths live in different worlds. Certainly their worlds of experience are vastly different. To understand the violence of youth gangs, we need to start with the neighborhoods from which most gang members come.

Because gang members live in neighborhoods where violence is a normal part of life, they have learned an entirely different way of perceiving the world (Yonas et al 2006). They believe that people will be violent toward them and that they ought to be violent toward others. Life is uncertain and cheap, violence routine, and killing normal. Life can be destroyed for little or no provocation. For some, like Hagan in our opening vignette, a victim doesn't even have to be a gang member. Violence can be normative, the expected means by which members prove themselves and by which they receive valued recognition as worthy people (Scott 1994). Initiation into a gang can even require that the initiate do an anonymous drive-by shooting (Vigil 2002). No revenge is involved in such acts of violence; the gang drives up, and the initiate blindly shoots into a crowd. Violence for gangs, then, becomes a tool, a means both for getting their way and for expressing themselves.

NORMAL AND OUTRAGEOUS KILLINGS. As long as gangs limit their violence to their own area of the city, the public is seldom concerned. The common attitude is "let them kill each other." If violence spills into the downtown or some other area of the city that is used by the middle class, then the public demands that "something be done." Similar demands are made when there is an outrageous killing (a killing that the public does not define as "usual" or "normal"). Such killings generate publicity, and with the heightened subjective concerns youth gangs suddenly "become" a "problem." This murder provoked such concerns:

> Ben Wilson, the 17-year-old star forward of the Illinois state champion basketball team, was walking with his girlfriend during a school lunch break. Three teenage gang members confronted them. As the 6-foot 8-inch Wilson tried to move past them, one youth turned to his companion and said, "This guy pushed me. Pop him." The teenager pulled out a .22-caliber pistol and fired two shots into Wilson's stomach. Wilson died a day later—on Thanksgiving eve. (Starr and Maier 1985)

Urban Violence: Schools

That U.S. schools would need guards and metal detectors to protect their students used to be unthinkable. The worst kids in school used to carry a switchblade, but today those kids take guns to class. Some bring guns to defend themselves from classmates who carry guns! As a 15-year-old in a Baltimore junior high school said, "You gotta be prepared—people shoot you for your coat, your rings, chains, anything." He then proudly displayed his "defensive" .25-caliber Beretta (Hackett 1988).

And then, of course, there is Columbine—and the other schools where students have gone on killing sprees. In their wake, they have left dead students and teachers—and fear on the part of students, parents, and entire communities.

In some grade schools, teachers practice "duck-and-cover" drills to protect children from neighborhood shootings (Mydens 1991). In some high schools and even middle schools, rapes and assaults go unreported. Guilt stops some teachers from reporting that they were attacked; they feel that the assault would not have occurred if they had somehow done a better job in the classroom. Other teachers find it easier to ignore an attack, because assault cases usually require at least three appearances in court. Still others don't report attacks because they fear for their lives. Often there are no witnesses, and it is the teacher's word against the student's.

Except for incidents that cannot be hidden, such as shootings, school violence seldom comes to the attention of the police or public primarily because, like prison wardens—and I use this analogy purposefully—school administrators want to run "a nice, quiet school." The last thing they want is to arouse the community with stories about teachers versus students or to publicize unsafe conditions at school. Administrators hush up and downplay incidents. This relieves pressure on them and protects their jobs, for one sign of their success—or failure—is the amount of violence in their schools.

Urban Violence: Riots

The year was 1747. The place was the bustling port of Boston. The Royal Navy had been impressing (kidnapping legally) local men for forced service. Fed up, seamen and others armed themselves and rioted. For three days, they dominated the city, forcing the governor to flee. The mobs freed the impressed men, gaining another victory for the urban rioters of the time.

RIOTS IN HISTORY. Urban riots, seemingly so modern, go far back in history. The book of Genesis in the Old Testament recounts a riot in the city of Gomorrah. Two thousand years ago, riots occurred in the city of Rome. In the United States, riots have been with us since the 1700s. According to historian Richard Brown (1969), rioting by the lower-class urban population even helped start the American Revolution.

In their early history, Baltimore, Philadelphia, New York, and Boston were the sites of numerous riots. During the 1830s through the 1850s, at least thirty-five major riots and numerous minor ones took place in these cities. There were labor riots, anti-Catholic riots, and riots by volunteer firemen. Some riots were directed against the Irish, who were a despised immigrant group during much of the nineteenth century. In protest against Irish immigrants, in 1835 mobs in Boston burned the Ursuline convent and school in the Charlestown neighborhood (Wyatt-Brown 2003).

COMMUNAL RIOTS. Then, too, there is a type of riot commonly called a race riot. In this type, obviously, racial-ethnic groups are directing violence against one another. Competition for jobs underlie some of these, especially the riots of whites against blacks (Brown 1969). Until the 1960s, the most common type of race riot was the **communal riot.** In this type, also called a *contested area riot*, one group would contest another's control of an area of the city. According to sociologist Morris Janowitz (1970b), the cities in which communal riots occurred contained large numbers of migrants—both African American and white—who were living in segregated areas. The police had little capacity to deal with outbreaks of mass violence and often conspired with white rioters against African Americans.

BACKGROUND FACTORS AND PRECIPITATING INCIDENTS. Sociologists have found that riots are preceded by a background of tensions between groups, an increase in those tensions and minor outbursts of violence. Then comes a **precipitating incident,** something that triggers the riot. For example, between 1917 and 1919 whites bombed more than twenty-seven homes of Chicago blacks. None of these incidents led to riots. What did, however, was the death of a 17-year-old black youth who swam into an area of Lake Michigan used exclusively by whites. When other blacks challenged the whites' use of this part of the beach, crowds of blacks and whites began throwing stones at one another. The black youth, still

Although riots are often thought of as a recent development in the United States, they are rooted in our history. Shown on the left is a riot in New York City in 1863. Rioters also looted stores—another behavior that is not new. The photo on the right is from a riot in Los Angeles 1992, discussed in the text.

in the water, drowned. Rumors abounded that he had been stoned to death, and blacks rioted. Thirty-eight people were killed, 537 injured, and about 1,000 left homeless.

The 1960s saw a major change in riots. Until this time, riots had been sporadic, but during the 1960s riots erupted across the nation. Harlem, Brooklyn, Watts, Newark, and Detroit were hit. These riots were different. Instead of challenging the control of some area of the city, as in communal riots, the rioters looted stores. Because of this, they are referred to as **commodity riots** (Janowitz 1970a). Commodity riots peaked in 1967, with 41 major riots and 123 lesser ones.

The 1960s riots so upset the nation that President Johnson appointed a National Advisory Commission on Civil Disorders to study them. The commission identified five main background factors (Kerner 1968):

1. *Discrimination and segregation* in employment, education, and housing that excluded many blacks from economic benefits.
2. *Isolation* due to black in-migration and white flight; poor blacks were concentrated in the city, with deteriorating facilities and services and unmet human needs.
3. *Destroyed opportunity* from segregation and poverty, which enforced failure on the young. Life in the ghetto often culminated in crime, drug addiction, welfare, and bitterness and resentment against society in general and white society in particular.
4. *Frustrated hopes* following the judicial and legislative victories of the civil rights movement. These had stimulated hopes of extensive social change, which, unfulfilled, increased frustration.
5. *Powerlessness,* combined with alienation and hostility to authority. These attitudes created further seething resentments that led to the conviction that only violence could change the "system."

These are *background* factors. By themselves, they do not cause riots. The poor and minorities are not strangers to these six factors: discrimination, segregation, isolation, destroyed opportunity, frustrated hopes, and powerlessness. They encounter these conditions as part of their everyday lives. Rioting, in contrast, is rare. Despite their disadvantages and oppression, poor people usually live lives of quiet desperation. For people to riot, their anger must rise to fever pitch (Piven and Cloward 1977). It takes some *precipitating incident* to ignite their underlying anger and frustration.

But there always are incidents. Why does one incident set off a riot, whereas others do not? Social psychologists Kurt and Gladys Lang (1968) identified two necessary conditions for an incident to precipitate a riot: It must be perceived as a threat to the group's well-being and evoke moral outrage. The precipitating incident is often a confrontation between African Americans and white police officers. Rumors sweep the area, and the incident escalates in people's minds as they talk excitedly about it. As they conclude that "this time it has gone too far, and we won't take it any more," violence erupts.

THE LOS ANGELES RIOT OF 1992. The riot in Los Angeles in 1992 followed this scenario perfectly. The background conditions were the long-term poverty of African Americans and Latinos and their oppression by the police. The precipitating incident that inflamed passions was the acquittal of the policemen who had been accused of assaulting Rodney King, an African American who was being arrested on traffic violations. A passerby had videotaped the police as they beat King. The videotape showed the officers as they pounded King with their nightsticks. Television stations repeatedly broadcast the videotape to stunned audiences across the nation. *Everyone* knew that the police officers were guilty.

Within minutes of the verdict of acquittal, angry crowds gathered. That night, mobs set fire to businesses in south-central Los Angeles, and looting and arson began in earnest. The rioting spread to other cities—Atlanta, Tampa, and even Madison, Wisconsin, and Las Vegas, Nevada. Whites and Koreans were favorite targets. The LA riot was spectacular— 4,000 fires; dramatic footage of looting and beatings; the president appearing on television federalizing the California National Guard and ordering the Seventh Infantry, SWAT teams, and the FBI into Los Angeles; and sixty dead, the most victims of a U.S. riot since the Civil War. The LA riot seemed different, but sociologically it was a "routine" riot. That is, it followed the patterns that sociologists have identified.

THE RESULTS OF RIOTS. Beyond the obvious—the burning, looting, and killing—what are the results of riots? First, rioting can have positive consequences: Federal funds sometimes flow to the inner city. Most positive consequences, however, are short-lived. Second, as sociologists George Simpson and Milton Yinger noted (1972), riots increase segregation, for whites flee the area. Although rioters may gain a sense of having struck a blow for freedom, they have only indicated their need for freedom: They have not shaken the basic institutions that support their oppression and enforce their poverty (Piven and Cloward 1977). Not one riot in the history of the United States has eliminated the underlying discrimination and poverty that are the background factors of riots.

THE CONTINUING PROBLEM. I don't want to seem cynical, but because these background conditions remain—the poverty of the inner city, its segregation, and the lack of opportunities for legitimate work—and precipitating events are bound to occur, riots have not come to an end in the United States. Periods of calm will inevitably be followed by more riots. When this occurs, there will be more commissions, more studies, more recommendations—all about the same as those we've already had. The same background conditions will be newly "discovered," the same hand-wringing will occur, the same public denunciations of deplorable conditions will be uttered by politicians and other public officials; money will be funneled into emergency federal programs for the inner city, which will give the appearance of solving the problem. These will be but temporary measures. When the inner city is quiet, and some of it rebuilt, there will be no headlines about the debilitating poverty, the hopelessness and despair. The rest of the nation will go about its business as usual, with the inner city off the national radar, out of sight and out of mind. However, the same underlying background conditions will remain, festering in frustration and anger, destined to be ignited yet again by some other unexpected precipitating incident.

The City in Change

In addition to violence and general decline, U.S. cities face extensive change. In this section we will examine the transition in power, changes in urban government, the emerging megalopolis, and the brightening of the sunbelt.

THE END OF THE CITY? "Are U.S. cities becoming obsolete?" John Teaford (1986), an urban historian, posed this question. He was referring to the problems we have reviewed here and in earlier chapters—gangs, rape, murder, drug addiction—that often make U.S. cities threatening, alienating places to live. Our inner cities have become places that inspire such fear that they are avoided by all except those who live there and those who must transact business there. Locked in these pockets of poverty, many inner-city residents live short, brutal lives.

Although the cities face severe challenges, no one need erect a grave marker over them. They are located on valuable land, which draws resources for renewal when the price is right. Just as the World Trade Center will be replaced after its destruction, so U.S. cities will be renewed after they reach a certain point of decay. Consider the reversal of fortunes in Harlem, the topic of the Thinking Critically box on the next page.

GOVERNING THE CITY. Regardless of its problems, the city must be governed. To help accomplish this task, the **political machine** emerged during the 1800s. This term refers to an organization headed by a "boss" that operates behind the scenes to circumvent the city's official procedures. In return for loyalty, the political machine distributes government jobs and favors. In a practice called *patronage*, the machine puts its members on the city payroll. Their official job is a subterfuge; their real job is to promote the political machine.

Merton's Study: "Machine Politics" ■ In a classic functional analysis, sociologist Robert Merton (1968) examined big-city "machine politics." He wanted to know why, despite repeated attempts at reform, the political machine was able to continue year after year. Merton applied two basic assumptions of functionalism: (1) something does not exist in a society unless it contributes to that society, and (2) no part of society exists in isolation; each part is related to the other parts of the social system.

RECLAIMING THE CITY: THE NEW HARLEM

The story is well known. The inner city is filled with crack, crime, and corruption. It stinks from foul, festering garbage strewn on the streets and piled up around burned-out buildings. Only those who have no choice live in this desolate, despairing environment where danger lurks around every corner.

What is not so well known is that affluent African Americans are reclaiming some of these areas.

"Brownstones" in a gentrified Harlem neighborhood. This photo was taken on West 132nd Street.

Howard Sanders was living the American Dream. After earning a degree from Harvard Business School, he took a position with a Manhattan investment firm. He lived in an exclusive apartment on Central Park West, but he missed Harlem, where he had grown up. He moved back to Harlem, along with his wife and daughter.

African American lawyers, doctors, professors, and bankers are doing the same.

What's the attraction? The first is nostalgia, a cultural identification with the Harlem of legend and folklore. It was here that black writers and artists lived in the 1920s, here that the blues and jazz attracted young and accomplished musicians.

The second reason is a more practical one. Harlem offers housing value. Five-bedroom homes with 6,000 square feet are available. Some feature Honduran mahogany. Some brownstones are only shells and have to be renovated; others are in good condition. Prices, though, have soared.

What is happening is the rebuilding of a community. Some people who "made it" want to be role models. They want children in the community to see them going to and returning from work.

When the middle class moved out of Harlem, so did its amenities. Now that young professionals are moving back in, the amenities are returning, too. There were no coffee shops, restaurants, jazz clubs, florists, copy centers, dentist and optometrist offices, or art galleries—the types of things urbanites take for granted. Now there are.

The police have also returned, changing the character of Harlem. Their more visible presence and enforcement of laws have shut down the open-air drug markets. With residents running a high risk of arrest if they carry guns, the shootouts that used to plague this area have become a thing of the past. With the enforcement even of laws against public urination, the area has become much safer, further attracting the middle class.

The same thing is happening on Chicago's West Side and in other U.S. cities.

The drive to find community—to connect with others and with one's roots—is strong. As an investment banker who migrated to Harlem said, "It feeds my soul."

"But at what cost?" ask others. This change might be fine for investment bankers and professionals who want to move back and try to rediscover their roots, but what about the people who are displaced? Gentrification always has a cost: residents of an area being pushed out as the area becomes middle class and more expensive. Tenant associations have sprung up to protest the increase in rents and the displacement of residents.

The "invasion-succession cycle," as sociologists call it, is continuing, this time with a twist—a flight back in.

Sources: Based on Cose 1999; McCormick 1999; Scott 2001; Taylor 2002; Leland 2003; Hampson 2005.

Merton found that the political machine helped three groups: the disadvantaged, businesspeople, and individuals who wanted to get ahead. The machine helped the disadvantaged obtain food, welfare, jobs, scholarships, and legal assistance when children ran afoul of the law or when bill collectors became too threatening. Those who received such favors knew without question whom to vote for in the next election.

Businesspeople also needed favors. They wanted to bypass building codes and the many bureaucratic regulations that impeded their efforts to expand their businesses. In return for under-the-table payoffs, the political boss would pull strings at the appropriate government agency. The boss served as a mediator between the demands of urban bureaucrats and the needs of businesspeople.

The machine also helped the third group, people who wanted to move up the social-class ladder. Ambitious people always confront obstacles in their pursuit of success, and the ambitious poor are no exception. They don't have the money to start their own businesses, and many don't have the grades to attend professional schools. In return for their loyalty, the machine helped some get jobs at local businesses. Others went to work for the machine.

In short, Merton found that the political machine existed because the official channels of society failed to provide needed services; the machine stepped in to fill the void left by the more culturally approved structures of society.

As functionalists also stress, something that is functional for some may be a source of problems for others. The political machine, headed by whites, passed over minorities when it handed out political favors. It also made certain that minorities were "contained" to specified areas of the city, ordering real estate agents to keep designated areas "pure" (Royko 1971). Fire marshals and city inspectors enforced city and state codes strictly when property was scheduled to pass into the "wrong hands," but overlooked violations for buyers whose race-ethnicity was approved. The machine may also be dysfunctional to the general public if it sacks the city treasury or diverts tax monies while streets, sewers, bridges, lighting, libraries, and other public services deteriorate.

The Decline of the Political Machine ■ The machine, which had dominated politics during the first half of the twentieth century, gradually declined. With the death of Chicago's Mayor Richard J. Daley in 1976, the last of the old-fashioned political machines began to pass into history. The transition is not yet complete, however, as Daley's son eventually took over Chicago politics. Richard M. Daley, however, inherited a machine greatly weakened by social change. Here is why the political machine has declined:

1. Immigration slowed in the middle part of the twentieth century. This removed a major function of the machine (serving unmet needs in return for loyalty) and undermined one of its major bases of power.
2. Education increased. As many people moved into the mainstream of society, they became less dependent on favors from the machine.
3. Suburbanization occurred. As whites and jobs left the city, the machine lost the broad revenue base on which its power depended.
4. Civil service laws were passed. As city workers came under the protection of these laws, it became difficult for the machine to demand their loyalty.
5. New standards of city management came into vogue. The public wanted the heads of city agencies to be professionals rather than political operatives being rewarded for their service.

The political machine may be down, but as I mentioned, it isn't dead. City bosses, sometimes called "power brokers," continue to operate behind the scenes of city politics. New Jersey is famous for continuing this tradition (Kocieniewski and Sullivan 2006). In Chicago, the son of Richard J. Daley, who was barely able to pass the Illinois bar exam, has been re-elected mayor several times. In Boston, rumors abound about political connections so corrupt that during the construction of a highway tunnel (the "big dig") millions of dollars were siphoned off for payoffs. The machine might even be due for a resurgence. Our cities are again being flooded with immigrants, legal ones as well as millions of undocumented workers from Mexico and central and South America. Their unmet needs and difficulty with English and U.S. customs may be planting the seeds for the renewal of the political machine.

The New City Management ■ In most cases, the political machine has been replaced by professional city management. This development has not only weakened the political machine, but has also produced its own problems. Mayors or city managers head a complex bureaucracy of urban departments. Each department is assigned a particular task and works fairly independently of the others. Communication breaks down, and with department chiefs and their workers being more loyal to their own department than they are to the city or the mayor, they perform their work without concern for how it fits into the larger picture (Lowi 1977). Here's an example from Granada, Spain. The rundown buildings on one of its main streets were an eyesore. To present a better image to tourists, the city spent huge amounts painting and repairing the concrete, iron, and stonework on these buildings. The results were impressive. The only problem was that another unit of the government had slated these same buildings for demolition (Arías 1993).

The Transition to Minority Leadership ■ Another major change in city governance is the transition of power from whites to African Americans and Latinos. Statistics tell the story: In 1964, there were only 70 elected African American officials at all levels of government in the United States. Today there are 9,000. From 70 to 9,000 in forty years! Latinos have also increased their total, to more than 4,000 (Eisinger 1980; *Statistical Abstract* 2006:Tables 404, 404). It should be obvious from these totals that Latinos have a lot farther to go in gaining similar power in U.S. cities.

Sociologist Peter Eisinger (1980) studied this transition of power. If a city is to be governed, its major groups must cooperate. If whites were to withdraw their cooperation from an elected minority mayor, winning control of the formal apparatus of government would be a hollow victory. To see what happened after African Americans were elected as mayors of Detroit and Atlanta, Eisinger interviewed the business, political, and social leaders of these cities. Instead of engaging in confrontational politics, the white elite had chosen to cooperate and build coalitions.

This transition of power, Eisinger says, can be compared with what happened in Boston a century ago. At that time the Yankees, the white settlers from England, controlled the city. When thousands of poor Irish immigrants flooded Boston in the 1800s, the Yankees felt threatened, and they held onto their power. By 1900, however, the Irish held the political reins of Boston. Eisinger concludes that we are in the midst of a similar process. Although the players have changed, the game is the same—and the results are proving to be similar. With the continued transition to African American leadership in U.S. cities, and now increasingly to Latino leadership as well, Eisinger's conclusions are being borne out.

The Megalopolis

MERGING CITIES. Another major change is the development of the **megalopolis.** This term refers to urban areas spilling into one another. What once were small towns and cities become an interconnected mass. The first U.S. megalopolis runs from Boston to Washington, D.C., and includes New York City, Philadelphia, and Baltimore. It covers ten states, the District of Columbia, and hundreds of local governments. The areas between Chicago and Cleveland and between San Francisco and San Diego are becoming megalopolises.

These metropolitan areas are so intertwined that some people use air shuttles to taxi back and forth between the part of the megalopolis they work in and the part they live in. Air shuttles tie Washington, D.C., New York City, and Boston together. From dawn to dusk, commuters can catch a flight every few minutes between these cities. As sociologist John Palen (2005) has observed, in some instances these air shuttles make it faster to travel from city to city than to travel between parts of a single large city.

Regional Planning ■ As cities become more interconnected, regional governing structures are developing. These supersede the boundaries of the individual cities and suburbs, incorporating them into a single governed unit. In an endeavor called *regional planning*, several urban and suburban units work together through county boards. The boards pass laws to regulate the larger region's transportation, environment, housing, policing, and growth.

This new governing structure does not come without a struggle, as the many urban units that make up a megalopolis find it difficult to give up their autonomy. Often, each smaller urban unit clings to its historical rights, granted by state charter, and thinks of itself as independent. With profits at stake, though, there is little doubt about the outcome of these struggles: The larger governing unit will win out.

EDGE CITIES. Another way that cities are expanding beyond their traditional political boundaries is through *edge cities*. This term refers to a clustering of buildings and services near the intersection of major highways (Garreau 1991; Lang 2003). The shopping malls, hotels, office parks, and residential areas overlap political boundaries and can include parts of several cities or towns. Edge cities are not cities in the traditional sense; that is, they are not political units with their own mayor or city manager. Yet, edge cities provide a sense

TABLE 12-2 The 10 Fastest-Growing and Shrinking U.S. Cities

THE 10 FASTEST-GROWING CITIES	THE 10 SHRINKING OR SLOWEST-GROWING CITIES
1. +123% Las Vegas, NV	1. −50% New Orleans, LA
2. +95% Naples, FL	2. −5.7% Utica, NY
3. +71% McAllen, TX	3. −4.0% Scranton, PA
4. +68% Raleigh, NC	4. −3.9% Youngstown, OH
5. +67% Austin, TX	5. −2.9% Buffalo, NY
6. +66% Phoenix, AZ	6. −2.7% Pittsburgh, PA
7. +64% Boise City, ID	7. −0.9% Syracuse, NY
8. +64% Fayetteville, AR	8. −0.3% Huntington, WV
9. +53% Atlanta, GA	9. 0% Charleston, WV
10. +53% Provo, UT	10. +0.2% Dayton, OH

Note: The population change from 1990 to 2004 (except New Orleans, which is for 2006). A plus sign indicates a growth in population, a minus sign a loss of population.

Source: By the author. Based on *Statistical Abstract of the United States* 2006:Table 26, with New Orleans added for 2006, based on the rough estimates of various news reports.

of place to those who live or work there, and many of the nation's new jobs are developing in them. Two of the most well-known edge cities are those in Tysons Corner in Washington and those clustering along the LBJ Freeway in Dallas, Texas.

Regional Restratification ■ Another major change that is having a deep impact on U.S. cities is **regional restratification,** a shift in a region's population, wealth, and power. Tables 12-2 and 12-3 depict how the population has shifted. As you can see from Table 12-2, all ten of our fastest-growing cities are in the West and South. Of the cities that have lost population or are the slowest growing, except for New Orleans which is an exceptional case because of Hurricane Katrina in 2005, all are in the Northeast (and Ohio and West Virginia, which border this region). Table 12-3 illustrates this restratification on a *regional* basis. You can see how greatly the South and the West have grown and how little increase there has been in the Northeast and the Midwest. About half of the country's total population growth occurred in just the western states.

The political implications of this regional shift are enormous. Only during one other period of U.S. history—the Civil War—has the balance of power among the states undergone such rapid and deep transformation. With more population comes more wealth and power. Regarding wealth: The tax base is growing dramatically faster in the West and the South than in other regions. Regarding power: The West and South are gaining representatives in Congress whereas the Northeast and Midwest are losing representatives.

This change brings not only population, wealth, and power to the cities of the West and South, "the sunbelt," but also it brings problems, the same ones that the older urban centers face: traffic congestion, air pollution, urban sprawl, and pressures on educational

TABLE 12-3 Population Change of U.S. Regions

	MILLIONS OF PEOPLE				Increase in Millions	Increase in %
	1970	1980	1990	2000	1970–2000	1970–2000
West	35	43	53	63	28	80%
South	63	75	85	100	37	59%
Midwest	57	59	60	64	7	12%
Northeast	49	49	51	54	5	10%

Source: By the author. Based on *Statistical Abstract of the United States,* various years and 2006:Table 24.

systems. The capital and human resources flowing from the old industrial centers to the sunbelt states, however, have given them greater resources to solve their urban problems. As in the older cities, many problems in these newly expanding urban areas of the West and South mostly affect the poor. Leaders in these expanding areas are not unlike their counterparts in the older industrial centers: Few are willing to devote many resources to help the poor.

Let's look at the potential for improving the quality of life in U.S. cities.

Social Policy

Many despair that the crises facing our cities can be solved. Some say that the government has simply shuffled money from one fashionable urban program to another, with little, if anything, to show for it. Some even insist that government programs have made the problems worse. Shortly before she died, Jane Jacobs, an influential urban expert, warned that things were becoming so bad in our civilization that a dark age is threatening to engulf us and our cities. She indicated, however, that there was still hope (Jacobs 2004). A few have given up on cities altogether, saying that their problems are too complex and deep-rooted to be solved: We should abandon our cities and disperse the urban population throughout the countryside, to new, planned-from-scratch small cities with designated maximum populations (Webber 1973).

THE ESSENTIAL CONDITION: ESTABLISHING COMMUNITY. Let's stop short of such an extreme approach and take the view that urban problems are human problems that can be solved. Although outcomes of social policy are always uncertain, what steps seem reasonable? In an attempt to get at a root problem, sociologists stress that urban policy must create a sense of community (Karp et al. 1991). If social policy does not do this, it is doomed to fail, for community is the essence of quality of life, of social control over destructive tendencies, of the social support that provides the social nurturance on which we depend. If this is too vacuous a statement, let's just say that we need to create community, that we must preserve and develop neighborhoods that people enjoy living in. We must avoid "urban renewal" programs that destroy neighborhoods and social relationships, no matter what appealing names they may be given.

Granted the need and goal of preserving and developing community, then, what programs seem reasonable?

Specific Programs

Programs that can halt decline and revitalize urban areas are condominium in-filling, urban homesteading, tax reduction for improving property, enterprise zones, job deconcentration, and regional planning. Let's look at each of them.

CONDOMINIUM IN-FILLING. The exodus of the young middle class is a major loss to the snowbelt cities. To reverse this migration, policy analyst Jan Newitt (personal communication) proposes **condominium in-filling,** building small energy-efficient condominiums for older urban homeowners. Because many older people stay in the homes in which they reared their children, they often have more room than they need and more maintenance than they can handle. Building condominiums in the neighborhoods in which people reared their children—where many older people want to remain—would give these older people a place to live. Helping them to remain in the area would also help stabilize the neighborhood. The larger, older housing the elderly vacate would be available to younger families with children, who have the energy, enthusiasm, and incomes needed to maintain and improve these homes. Such quality housing would encourage more younger adults to remain in the city, often in the same neighborhoods where they spent their childhood. Of all programs, this has the most exciting potential, because it meets the sociological requirement to foster a sense of community.

URBAN HOMESTEADING.

Paul Gasparotti bought two abandoned adjacent houses from the city for a dollar each. After tearing everything out but the exterior bricks, roof rafters, and floor joists, he connected the two houses and dug out the basement. (Kirkpatrick 1981)

Urban homesteading is sometimes called "sweat equity," because people invest hard work rather than money for their down payment. In this program, a city sells (usually for $1) derelict housing that it has acquired by tax foreclosure. The buyer agrees to stay for some specified time, ordinarily at least three years, and to bring the house up to code within two years. As the mayor of Wilmington, Delaware, said, "We are not trying to provide housing for people. We are trying to find people for [abandoned] housing."

This program aims to stabilize neighborhoods by inspiring confidence. The idea is that salvaging buildings will encourage neighbors to stay and to improve their own properties. Deterioration will stop, neighborhoods will be rebuilt, and people will be lured back from the suburbs. Despite its promise, however, urban homesteading has been but a drop in the bucket of urban housing needs. A total of 75,000 homes have been reclaimed through urban homesteading, which sounds like a high number. To see the immensity of the problem, though, we can note that owners abandon approximately 150,000 homes and apartments in the inner city *each year* (Palen 2005).

Urban homesteading is a mixed blessing, because it does not include the very poor. Only people with good incomes and credit can undertake the cost of rehabilitating buildings. How can the poor repay the loans, unless they have jobs? And how can they even get loans if they don't have jobs? Even if times are prosperous and the unskilled poor get jobs, what happens when they lose them when the economy slows? Urban homesteading also threatens to displace the poor, for as a neighborhood is upgraded, rent and property values increase.

REDUCING TAXES. Another promising program is to reduce taxes. No one wants to abandon buildings. Walking away from a property means losing huge amounts of money, but the way the current tax system works discourages homeowners from making improvements. Because taxes are based on a percentage of a property's assessed value, when someone improves a property, the assessed value goes up and so do the taxes. To encourage owners to improve their properties, legislation can allow city and county officials to *reduce* taxes when specified improvements are made to buildings—say a new roof or an upgrade to the heating or electrical systems. Some may object that this policy would help landlords, and it would, but it also would make them a vehicle for improving and maintaining neighborhoods. Everyone wins. Social policies that penalize homeowners and landlords sow seeds of neighborhood destruction.

ENTERPRISE ZONES. The third program, **enterprise zones** (also known as *empowerment zones*), has been tried by most states. Here are the general principles of enterprise zones:

1. Businesses that locate in a designated zone—an economically depressed area with high unemployment—receive tax breaks and wage credits for each full-time, qualified employee they hire.
2. Businesses in the enterprise zone that improve their facilities receive credits on their property tax.
3. Businesses that locate in the enterprise zone, or that remain there, are eligible for low-interest loans.

Enterprise zones are designed to stimulate economic growth and generate employment. A danger is that enticing businesses to move into the zone may create blight in the areas they leave behind. It is also difficult to attract businesses, because the costs of additional security in the zone can outweigh the benefits offered for locating there. Another problem is that the enterprise zone can backfire, with local residents who get good jobs moving out of the neighborhood, as did earlier residents. The jobs usually available in the enterprise zones, however, are marginal, not paying enough for employees who are hired from the zone to move out.

Evaluating the results of enterprise zones has been difficult. The basic problem facing researchers is this: If you measure employment, earnings, or poverty in an enterprise zone, how do you know what they would have been if the enterprise zone had not been there? If the goal is to improve the lives of the residents in the enterprise zone, the results have been disappointing: Researchers have concluded that enterprise zones have had little impact on those who live in the zone (Ferguson 2001).

JOB DECONCENTRATION. Another promising policy is **job deconcentration**, the rational location of jobs through a master plan. This policy, which helps control urban and suburban sprawl, presupposes a regional master plan and a regional authority to enforce it. Job deconcentration also lets planning bodies develop public transportation that serves workers outside the central city. Toronto has such a plan. Factories, offices, shopping centers, and housing subdivisions can be built only in specified areas adjacent to the city. If there is no regional authority, however, this policy is impossible, and the fierce rivalries for power and resources between our urban and suburban areas make such a policy difficult. As policy analyst Jan Newitt said to me, "Can't you just see New York City adopting a policy of putting jobs in the suburbs!"

REGIONAL PLANNING. As you can see with job deconcentration, an overarching need is *regional planning* (Savitch and Vogel 2004). Metropolitan areas are fragmented into numerous small, competing political divisions. Each jealously guards its own turf against other jurisdictions. Governments responsible for regional development can be created without abolishing the individual, smaller governments. States, from which cities receive their charter to operate, can force cities to give some of their authority to regional bodies (such as decision making about water and sewer systems, police and fire protection, and building codes). These agencies would then implement policies for the region as a whole.

Educating the Poor

To be successful, urban programs must confront one of our major failures, the education of the poor. As sociologist Herbert Gans said back in the 1960s:

> The public-school system has never learned how to teach poor children, mainly because it has not needed to do so. In the past, those who could not or would not learn what the schools taught dropped out quietly and went to work. Today, such children drop out less quietly, and they cannot find work. Consequently, the schools have to learn how to hold them, not only when they drop out physically, but long before, in the early elementary grades, when they begin to drop out in spirit. (Gans 1968:292)

The directors of school systems in the United States still have not learned this lesson. And who will be the teachers to teach it? It is almost despairing to read Gans' policy suggestion made in the last century and to then look at today's educational system and to note that there is little or no change. As noted earlier, the educational system is still middle class, and it still bypasses the poor. Only now, with unskilled work seldom available, the educational dropouts live in greater despair—and with a greater propensity for violence.

PRINCIPLES FOR SUCCESS. When it comes to improving education, it is not that we don't have concerned teachers. We have good-hearted teachers in abundance, people with sincere intentions to make a difference in the lives of the children entrusted to their care (Gerstl-Pepin 2006). It is that educators seldom examine the results of their teaching or probe the consequences of their educational programs with the goal of improving their teaching effectiveness with the poor. Rather, what they usually propose is more money—vast funds—to improve buildings or to fund some fancily named educational gimmick. They propose such visible monuments to the public, which hasn't the slightest idea that the educators haven't the slightest idea of what works.

The United States is experiencing one of its largest waves of immigration (approximately a million immigrants a year). Like earlier arrivals, today's immigrants form ethnic neighborhoods in which they maintain customs from their homeland while they adjust to the norms of their new land. Today's immigrants, like those before them, also have special educational needs.

Good schools for the poor require more than new buildings or some catchy educational phrase. Teachers must nourish their students' motivation to learn. Few poor children lack the desire to learn when they begin school. As they stay in school, however, they often come to view education as irrelevant to their lives and future. To do a better job of educating the poor, Gans (1968) pointed out that we need

1. Motivated teachers
2. New teaching methods
3. Smaller classes
4. Innovative curricula that build on the aspirations of inner-city youth
5. A more decentralized and less bureaucratized school system
6. Work-study programs
7. Scholarships to encourage adult dropouts to return to school

We can add to this list: cooperative learning, child care facilities, and positive reinforcement. More controversial, but quite defensible, are a renewed emphasis on memorization in grade school (such as the multiplication tables), a de-emphasis on "feelings of self-worth" as an educational goal and its replacement with the learning of academic subjects, and a strong trades program that leads to apprenticeships. (Why assume that every high school student should go to college?) Certainly, we can all agree that to produce an effective learning environment, violence and gang activity must be reduced—or, better, eliminated.

ABC. A successful program is ABC (A Better Chance). Financed by corporations, foundations, and individuals, ABC identifies and recruits gifted inner-city students, starting in junior high school, and matches them with top prep schools. Given scholarships, these high-performing youngsters attend schools such as Phillips Academy in Andover, Massachusetts, and Cate Preparatory School in Carpinteria, California. The program is so successful that most graduates go on to college.

THE POTENTIAL VERSUS SHORT-TERM SOLUTIONS. ABC enrolls one or two thousand students, but we need to touch the lives of most poor children. As the Thinking Critically box on the next page shows, we *can* design and implement successful programs. Although these programs

EDUCATING FOR SUCCESS: REESTABLISHING COMMUNITY IN THE LEARNING PROCESS

Education is in crisis. Children are being promoted from one grade to another whether they learn or not. Some students graduate from high school illiterate, unable to even read help wanted ads. Many don't know how to do simple math, are unable to prepare a resumé, and have no idea how to prepare for a job interview. Budgets are cut, programs trimmed, teachers burned out, and students unmotivated.

"Sow the wind and reap the whirlwind," said Hosea, an Old Testament prophet. And sowing a future of illiterate children having babies and of unemployment, welfare dependency, crime, and despair will bring a whirlwind of shattered community. We can sever the nation into two, those who have and those who don't. Make this extensive enough, and it can destroy a society.

Can education make a difference in this sorry picture? How about for the most impoverished of society, the children of the inner city? To find out, a team from Yale worked with the staff and parents in two grade schools in New Haven, Connecticut. The schools were in low-income neighborhoods that were 99 percent black and plagued by the usual inner-city problems. Student achievement, which had been the lowest in the city, soared to the third and fourth highest. As measured on standardized tests, the students' achievement levels jumped to nine months *above* their grade level in one school, and twelve months ahead in the other. Attendance and behavior also improved dramatically.

How was this accomplished? First, the team made a radical assumption—that the problem was not "poor students," but, rather, the educational system. This is radical because it goes against the unspoken educational philosophy that

Regardless of their backgrounds, when students are challenged educationally, they can do well. Students in this highly disciplined and demanding inner-city school in The Bronx, New York, have 9 1/2-hour school days and 2 hours of homework a night. Is it any wonder that their test scores are the highest in The Bronx?

permeates U.S. education. It puts the responsibility on the shoulders of the staff. It made the staff responsible for meeting the needs that the children's background created. Second, the staff fostered a feeling of common cause. Leadership was transferred from a central office to the grass roots—to those who worked on the daily educational problems and rubbed shoulders with the students—and this group discussed problems and made decisions together. Third, parents, staff, and students interacted frequently. This allowed students to identify with adults who valued and encouraged learning, reflecting a solid educational principle that learning is based on modeling and imitation. Fourth, a sense of community was engendered as trust, mutual respect, and a sense of common cause developed among teachers, administrators, parents, and students.

Using this same assumption—that inadequate teaching, not inadequate students, is the reason the poor children do not do well in school—Jaime Escalante motivated his students in an East Los Angeles inner-city school to perform so well on national calculus tests that officials thought that they had cheated. It is obvious that students in poverty can do well—if the schools teach well.

FOR YOUR CONSIDERATION

How would you apply these principles to change a troubled school in your area? What other principles from this text would you use?

Based on Comer 1986, Escalante and Dirmann 1990; Hilliard 1991; J. Levine 2004.

---

appear expensive, they would pay back their cost many times over: Getting young people in school and out of criminal pursuits reduces the cost of crime and punishment. As working adults, former students would also pay taxes. The initial cost, however, would be high, and the basic question is where this money would come from. Both our leaders and the public have a short-term view of educating the poor and show little interest in solving fundamental problems.

IN SUM If we have learned anything from the recent past, it is that *replacing buildings does not cure urban ills.* Dilapidated buildings offer only surface appearances and don't reveal the basic social problems of the city. The real problems are poverty, crime, unemployment, dysfunctional families, gang violence, riots, arson, drug addiction, and juvenile delinquency—conditions whose origins are not local and that are not solved by fixing or replacing old buildings. As sociologist William Julius Wilson (1987) said, the key to solving urban problems is a revitalized economic system that offers work. Perhaps the simplest summary is this: Greater access to jobs, housing, education, and justice will reduce urban problems, but those problems will persist to the same degree that these inequalities persist.

The Future of the Problem

FOURTEEN TRENDS LIKELY TO CONTINUE. Based on current trends, I foresee the following.

1. The continued segregation of poor and minorities in the inner city
2. Further rebuilding ("renaissance") of downtown areas
3. The slum areas adjacent to downtown areas remaining slums with the same problems they have now
4. Poor young males still being attracted to gangs
5. More poor young females joining gangs and committing more street crimes
6. Street crimes that continue to make parts of the city unsafe for visitors and residents
7. Continued fear and avoidance of the inner city by the middle class
8. More middle-class flight to the suburbs, by both whites and minorities
9. Maintenance of racial-ethnic neighborhoods
10. More migration from the snowbelt to the sunbelt
11. Financial crises for city governments and deteriorating services
12. More gentrification as the middle class is drawn to cheaper housing
13. The growth of citylike problems in the suburbs
14. The continued failure of the educational system to meet the needs of the poor

INCREASING COSTS AND REDUCED INCOME. Many cities are confronting rising costs and demands for services in the face of reduced income. Our cities depend on federal money to finance many programs, from urban transit to rehabilitating buildings and even supervising playgrounds. Some of that federal money has dried up. Caught in a financial squeeze, some cities have cut back on education, street cleaning, recreation programs, and activities for children and the elderly. Because reducing services, except in the poor areas of the city, upsets voters, urban governments have deferred the maintenance of their infrastructure—their sewers, bridges, water systems, and city buildings. Although this cutback is less visible, making it less subject to voter outcry, deferred maintenance borrows from the future and is one of the most severe crises that U.S. cities face.

THE URBAN VILLAGERS. The maintenance of racial-ethnic neighborhoods flies in the face of predictions that sociologists used to make. As sociologist John Palen (2005) points out, for decades sociologists predicted the imminent disappearance of ethnic neighborhoods—but apparently no one told the people who live there. Neighborhoods based on race-ethnicity and social class will continue to provide a sense of community for their residents.

THE HOMELESS. The homeless will continue their sorry presence on our city streets, but they will be persecuted by city officials. To foster tourism and profits, politicians will disperse the homeless. This will create an outcry—not at the existence of such miserable poverty but at the presence of pitiful people in areas that the better-off would like to

Although ours is an affluent society, the problems of poverty—and of the very poor and the homeless—remain to be solved.

enjoy without having their consciences pricked. There will be calls to remove the homeless from sight, to put them in "asylums" somewhere, as though hiding them might solve the problem.

HOUSING COSTS. Two major forces will increase the demand for and cost of housing. First, each year about 4 million Americans turn age 30, the typical first-time home-buying age (*Statistical Abstract* 2006:Table 12). Second, the American dream of owning a home is deep, and it is nourished by developers and financial institutions. Middle-class Americans, although they have few children, want larger homes with more amenities (large master baths with his and her sinks, whirlpools, hot tubs, and so on). Although there will be fluctuations in cost due to speculation and overbuilding, these two factors will feed urban sprawl and inflate the cost of housing.

POTENTIAL IN-MIGRATION. Higher housing and commuting costs could spearhead a turnaround for our cities. The higher the cost of commuting to the city for work, the more attractive the lower-priced houses in deteriorated areas of the city. Gentrification holds the potential of reversing the exodus from the city. It may also signal another major racial-ethnic change, for it may increase the proportion of whites in our central cities. Gentrification, of course, will fuel another controversy, for it will mean accommodating the middle class at the expense of the poor, who are displaced.

REGIONAL RESTRATIFICATION. The future of the city depends on what city we are talking about. Because the regions of the country, and our cities with them, are undergoing restratification, their future will be region oriented. Sunbelt cities hold the brightest future. With their influx of capital, jobs, and workers, along with an expanding tax base and growing political power, they appear best equipped to weather problems.

As this proposed building for St. Petersburg, Russia, shows, future cities are unlikely to look like present ones. The text explains the human needs that must be paramount in developing cities.

PRINCIPLES FOR SHAPING THE FUTURE. I need to stress that no particular future is inevitable. The future of our cities depends partially on trends yet to appear and on the social policies we adopt. The following three principles provide a solid foundation for shaping that future:

1. As a cultural center of work and play, the city offers vast potential for human happiness.
2. The city is a social creation, and so are its negative features. As such, they can be overcome.
3. To design a future that overcomes urban problems, our policies must incorporate basic human needs—social, psychological, physical, and spiritual. As stressed in this chapter, the shorthand word for this is *community*.

These three principles can help us forge a future that enhances the quality of life, maximizes human potential, and creates urban areas that satisfy the human need for community. Or we can ignore sound principles and long-term planning, deal with problems on a piecemeal, haphazard basis, and leave a failed legacy to future Americans. The choice is ours.

As a final note, I want to stress that if we do not solve the problem of the poor who are isolated in the inner city—desperate people with little hope, who descend into drugs and crime, turning savagely on one another and on anyone within their reach—the city is doomed. If this is the case, U.S. cities will go up in flames.

SUMMARY AND REVIEW

1. The world is seeing an urban explosion. In 1900, about 13 percent of the world's population lived in *cities*. Today about 50 percent do. The U.S. figure is almost 80 percent.
2. Symbolic interactionists emphasize that areas of the city that appear undesirable, disorganized, and threatening to outsiders may be viable communities to their inhabitants. Slums are worlds in miniature, with their own hierarchies of status, standards, and controls over behavior. It takes an insider's frame of reference to understand such worlds.
3. According to functionalists, specialized zones develop naturally as a city grows. Each zone meets certain needs of a city's residents, and people with distinctive characteristics live there. Antagonisms result from the *invasion-succession cycle*, as one group displaces another. Urban problems are generally concentrated in the area adjacent to the central business district.
4. According to the conflict perspective, business leaders caused the decline of the inner city. They influenced politicians to subsidize the relocation of their businesses to the suburbs and to build a transportation system to move their products. Suburban development came at the city's expense; it reduced its tax base and spurred the flight of the middle class.
5. Many people find cities alienating and experience intense problems in them. Some people, however, find in cities islands of intimacy that yield high p[...] satisfaction.
6. The quality of life in our cities deteriorated because of *redlining*, the abandonment of buildings, the poor being locked out of opportunities, and the flight of the middle class. Older suburbs have similar problems.
7. Violence is such a problem that youth gangs even control some areas of our cities. Violence is also common in our urban schools. Poverty and discrimination remain background factors, but riots require a *precipitating incident*.
8. Ethnic minorities have gained political clout in our urban areas, and the transition of power has gone quite smoothly. *Megalopolises*, interconnected metropolitan centers that once were a series of smaller towns and cities, have emerged. The move to the sunbelt is forcing *regional restratification* in terms of capital, human resources, and political power.
9. To meet human needs better, urban policy can preserve neighborhoods and encourage new ones. Social policies include condominium in-filling, urban homesteading, enterprise zones, job deconcentration, and regional authority. To succeed, an urban policy must develop a sense of community and meet the needs of the poor.
10. Our cities have a troubled future. We are now at the crossroads in making decisions that will affect future generations.

KEY TERMS

Chicago school of sociology, 404
City, 400
Commodity riot, 420
Communal riot, 419
Community, 401
Concentric zone theory, 407
Condominium in-filling, 426
Disinvestment, 414

Enterprise zones, 427
Gemeinschaft, 410
Gentrification, 407
Gesellschaft, 410
Housing unit, 414
Invasion-succession cycle, 407
Job deconcentration, 428
Megalopolis, 424

Political machine, 421
Precipitating incident, 419
Redlining, 414
Regional restratification, 425
Suburban sprawl, 414
Urban crisis, 403
Urban homesteading, 427
Urban sprawl, 403

THINKING CRITICALLY ABOUT CHAPTER 12

1. Do you think that symbolic interactionism, functionalism, or conflict theory does the best job of explaining urban problems? Why?
2. If a bank finds that a certain area within a city contains many "risky" investments and makes a business decision to "redline" the area (refusing to give loans to people who live or work in the area), do you think it is proper for government to interfere with the bank's business and to ban such a practice? Explain.

3. Which of these programs do you think are the most appropriate and helpful in combatting urban decay?
   • Condominium in-filling
   • Urban homesteading
   • Enterprise zones
   • Job deconcentration
   • Regional authority
   Why?

CHAPTER 13

Population and Food

With her varicose veins and her blackened and missing teeth, Celia, only 30 years old, looked like an old woman. She beamed as she pointed to her distended stomach, indicating that her thirteenth child was on its way. Her oldest was only 14 years old! Looking at her smiling face, it was hard to imagine how she could be more delighted—even if she were expecting her first.

"The rich get richer—and the poor get children," I thought, as I looked around the tiny palapa, the single-room hut that housed this large family. I saw straw mats on the dirt floor where the older children slept, a double bed for the parents and younger children, and, for the oldest, a hammock strung between the poles that supported the thatched roof. The only furnishings were a stove, a cabinet where Celia stored her dishes and cooking utensils, and a table in the cooking area.

There were no chairs. This really startled me: The family was so poor that they could not afford even a single chair.

I found it difficult to swallow, as I ate the posole, swollen corn tasting something like hominy, that Celia and her husband, Angel, generously offered. "Surely the children are not receiving enough food on Angel's daily

> ## The rich get richer—and the poor get children.

wage of $5," I thought. And the family obviously could not afford adequate medical care. They had lost one child to polio, while their oldest daughter had been left disfigured by an injury to her right eye. Vainly trying to conceal her disfigurement, this 13-year-old would constantly sweep stringy locks of hair over the ghastly eye.

I was living in Armería, Mexico, and I had gotten used to many things. But I found Celia's situation depressing. I looked at the haggard face of her oldest son. Only 14 years old, he worked in the fields with the men. Each day I watched these men, machetes in hand, dragging themselves home at twilight. This was his fate, to work exhaustingly in fields for pennies a day. But Celia could not have been more proud of him. He was doing his part to help pay for the family's needs. She was as thrilled about her son's working as a U.S. mother is when her child graduates from college.

And then there was the coming child. Celia and her husband were genuinely delighted about this latest pregnancy. I congratulated them on the coming blessed event and decided that I still had much to learn about this culture. "Why is their thinking so different from ours?" I wondered.

How could Celia have wanted so many children, especially when she lived in such poverty? That question bothered me. I couldn't let it go until I knew why.

This chapter helps to provide an answer.

The Problem in Sociological Perspective

The definition of **demography**—the study of the size, composition, growth, and distribution of human populations—makes it sound like a pretty dry subject. Yet this area of sociology is anything but dry, for demographers study some of the most far-reaching changes taking place in today's world. Some are even warning that these changes might engulf us and our children and destroy our way of life.

A STARTLING CHANGE. Changes in population are especially important. For example, for most of history, the world's population increased at a snail's pace. When Jesus Christ was born 2,000 years ago, the population of the entire world was the same as that of the United States today. By 1750, all of Europe had only about 140 million inhabitants. Then there was an abrupt change: During just the next fifty years, Europe's population jumped by 48 million. Fifty years later, by 1850, it had shot up by another 68 million, reaching a total of 256 million. What caused this unprecedented change?

PUBLIC HEALTH OR THE POTATO? In 1926, G. T. Griffith argued that this increase was due to improved public health. Better medical knowledge, hospitals, housing, water, and sanitation, he said, lowered the *death rate*, the number of deaths per 1,000 people. More people lived longer, and the population jumped.

Griffith's explanation is widely accepted, but some demographers suggest a different explanation. Thomas McKeown (1977), for example, claimed that the population of Europe remained low until 1750 because Europeans practiced **infanticide,** killing infants shortly after birth. This practice declined after 1750, he said.

If McKeown is right, why did infanticide decline? His answer is surprising—because of the potato! McKeown's explanation goes like this: Europeans practiced infanticide because their food supply could not support more people. Infanticide kept their population in balance with their food supply, preventing widespread starvation. When the Europeans' food supply suddenly changed, they stopped practicing infanticide, and their population shot upward.

Could a lowly plant like the potato have had such an impact on history? It seems that this might be the case. When the Spaniards conquered South America in the 1500s, they discovered the potato, which was cultivated in the Andean highlands. When they brought the potato back home with them, Europeans first viewed this strange food with suspicion. Some grew it as a curiosity, but as the years passed Europeans gradually began to think of the potato as a good food. They then started to grow it in quantity. So sweeping was their change in diet that by 1800 the potato had become the main food of the poor in northern and central Europe. This "miracle" tuber expanded Europe's food supply, allowing the population to almost double in a century.

Demography, then, emphasizes the relationship between population and environment. If a population increases dramatically, demographers look for changes in people's customs. These can range from the adoption of new medical and sanitation practices to simply a change in their diet.

THOMAS MALTHUS, THE GLOOMY PROPHET. Thomas Malthus, an English economist, took Europe's surge in population as a sign of doom. In 1798, he wrote an influential book, *An Essay on the Principle of Population*. Malthus argued that although population grows geometrically, that is, from 2 to 4 to 8 to 16 and so forth, the food supply increases only arithmetically, that is, from 1 to 2 to 3 to 4 and so on. This means, he said, that if births go unchecked, the population of a country, or even of the world, will outstrip its food supply.

THE PESSIMISTS: THE NEW MALTHUSIANS. Malthus' conclusions were controversial at the time he made them, and they are still debated today. One group, whom we can call the *New Malthusians*, says that Malthus was right. We are still in the early stages of the process that Malthus identified, they say, and today's situation is as grim, if not grimmer, than he ever imagined. The world's population is out of control. It is following an **exponential growth curve.** This means that if growth doubles during approximately equal intervals of time, it suddenly accelerates.

To illustrate the implications of exponential growth, sociologist William Faunce (1981:84) told a parable about a man who saved a rich man's life. The rich man, of course, was very grateful, and he offered a reward:

The man replied that he would like his reward to be spread out over a four-week period, with each day's amount being twice what he received on the preceding day. He also said he

FIGURE 13-1 World Population Growth Over 2,000 Years

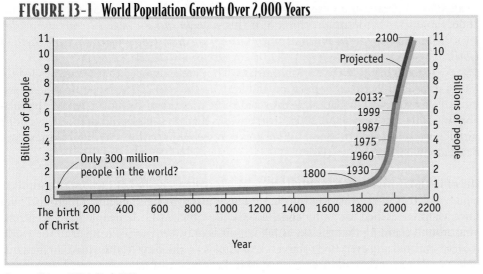

Sources: Piotrow 1973:4; Haub 2005.

would be happy to receive only one penny on the first day. The rich man immediately handed over the penny and congratulated himself on how cheaply he had gotten by.

At the end of the first week, the rich man checked to see how much he owed and was pleased to find that the total was only $1.27. By the end of the second week, he owed only $163.83. On the twenty-first day, however, the rich man was surprised to find that the total had grown to $20,971.51. When the twenty-eighth day arrived, the rich man was shocked to discover that he owed $1,342,177.28 for that day alone and that the total reward had jumped to $2,684,354.56!

This acceleration is precisely what alarms the New Malthusians. They claim that we have just entered the "fourth week" of an exponential growth curve. Figure 13-1 above shows why they think that the day of reckoning is just around the corner. It took from the beginning of time to 1800 for the world's population to reach its first billion. It then took only 130 years (1930) to add the second billion. Just 30 years later (1960), the world population hit 3 billion. The time it took to reach the fourth billion was cut in half, to only 15 years (1975). Then just 12 years later (in 1987), the total reached 5 billion, and in another 12 years it hit 6 billion (in 1999).

On average, every minute of every day, 151 babies are born. As Figure 13-2 shows, at sunset the world has 217,000 more people than it did the day before. In one year, this amounts to an increase of 79 million people. In just 4 years, the world increases

FIGURE 13-2 How Fast Is the World's Population Growing?

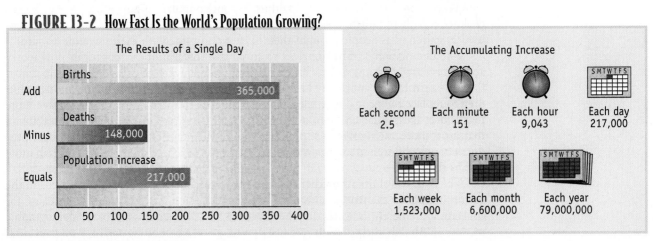

Source: By the author. Based on Haub 2005.

by an amount greater than the entire U.S. population (Haub 2005; *Statistical Abstract* 2006:Table 1314). You might think of it this way: *In just the next 12 years the world's population will increase as much as it did during the first 1,800 years after the birth of Christ.*

These totals terrify the New Malthusians. They are convinced that we are headed toward a showdown between population and food. In the year 2025, the population of just India, Pakistan, and Bangladesh is expected to be more than the entire world's population was 100 years ago (Haub 2005). It is obvious that we will run out of food if we don't curtail population growth. Soon we are going to see more pitiful, starving Pakistani and Bangladeshi children on television.

THE OPTIMISTS: THE ANTI-MALTHUSIANS. "You're wrong!" replies a much more optimistic group, which I call the Anti-Malthusians. "This is just scare talk," claims this group. "Ever since Malthus reached his faulty conclusions, like Chicken Little people have been running around claiming that the sky is falling—it is only a matter of time until the world is overpopulated and everybody starves. Year after year, the New Malthusians do the same song and dance, and, frankly, we're tired of it. Let's be realistic for a change."

And what is the counterargument of the Anti-Malthusians? They first point out that the way the New Malthusians perceive people is wrong, for the New Malthusians think of people as being comparable to germs that breed in a bucket:

> Assume there are two germs in the bottom of a bucket, and they double in number every hour. . . . If it takes one hundred hours for the bucket to be full of germs, at what point is the bucket one-half full of germs? A moment's thought will show that after ninety-nine hours the bucket is only half full. The title of this volume [The 99th Hour] is not intended to imply that the United States is half full of people but to emphasize that it is possible to have "plenty of space left" and still be precariously near the upper limit. (Price 1967:4)

Anti-Malthusians scoff at this image. They say that fitting the world's current population growth onto an exponential growth curve and then projecting it into the future indefinitely is totally incorrect. This approach ignores people's intelligence and their rational planning when it comes to having children. To understand what people really do, we need to study the historical record. Here we see an encouraging principle: People generally limit reproduction to match their available food. And this principle applies today, as shown in the Global Glimpse box on the next page. The current "explosion" in world population, then, is a hopeful sign. It means that the world is producing *more food* than ever before. As the Europeans did when they added the potato to their diet, people today are simply reacting to a growing food supply.

To understand the future, continue the Anti-Malthusians, consider Europe's **demographic transition.** As diagrammed in Figure 13-3, Stage I consists of a fairly stable population—high death rates offset by high birth rates. Throughout most of its history, Europe was in Stage I. Then about 1750 Europe entered Stage II, ushering in the "population explosion" that so frightened Malthus. Europe's population surged because death rates declined rapidly but birth rates remained high. When Europe moved to Stage III, its population stabilized as people brought their birth rates in line with their lower death rates.

The demographic transition was so successful that European countries now worry about *not having enough babies.* Having moved into Stage 4 of the demographic transition, Western European leaders fear **population shrinkage,** not producing enough children to replace the people who die. Italy was the first country in the world to have more people over age 65 than children under age 15. The transition has been like a small stream that turns into a raging river. Of the forty-two countries of Europe, forty no longer produce enough children to maintain their populations (McDonald 2001). They all fill more coffins than cradles.

The Anti-Malthusians predict that this demographic transition will also occur in the poorer nations of the world. The rapid growth of these nations today is not a cause for concern, for it merely indicates that they have reached the second stage of the demographic transition. Already their growth rate has slowed. Look again at Figure 13-1 on page 437.

A Global Glimpse
"I'D LIKE TO HAVE TWENTY CHILDREN"

In 1976, an anthropologist who was making a documentary of an African village in Kenya asked a 26-year-old mother of two how many children she wanted. The woman looked at her bulging stomach, giggled, and said, "I'd like to have twenty children."

The documentary then went into a freeze frame, with a subtitle stating that the woman had given birth to twins.

This image haunted John Tierney, a *New York Times* reporter. "What is wrong with her?" he wondered. "What would become of her family?" Ten years later, Tierney went to Kenya to follow up the story. He found the woman, Fanisi Kalusa, living in the same hut, the twins healthy. She was now 36, with seven children, aged 4 to 16.

When Tierney asked about her wanting twenty children, Fanisi laughed, and said, "I've rejected that idea because there is not enough food to meet the demand."

Most African men dislike birth control, but her husband had agreed to limit their family. He had his mother put a curse on his wife to make her barren—a standard practice in the area.

Fanisi went along with the curse—but without telling her husband, she visited a clinic for a free IUD.

This photo of eleven children of a Himba family in Namibia, posing in front of their home, says more about the population explosion in the Least Industrialized Nations than I could ever say.

Having twenty children made sense when children meant more hands to help farm the land and to support the parents in their old age. But now, children have become expensive in Kenya. For each child, parents must pay $10 a year in tuition, a burden in this poor land. In addition, many children are moving to the city, breaking the close family bonds and threatening the custom of adult children providing support for their aged parents.

Fanisi told her 16-year-old daughter to have only six children. Fanisi's daughter told Tierney that she thought four would be about right.

FOR YOUR CONSIDERATION

What do you think? Will Africa successfully make the demographic transition? The Anti-Malthusians point to Fanisi Kalusa as evidence that they will. But the New Malthusians retort that Kenya is growing at 2.3 percent each year—*four* times as fast as the United States.

Based on Tierney 1986; Haub 2005.

FIGURE 13-3 The Demographic Transition

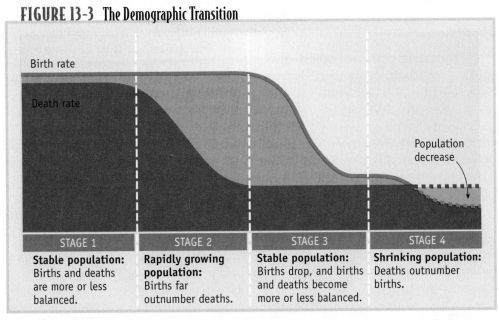

Birth rate

Death rate

Population decrease

STAGE 1	STAGE 2	STAGE 3	STAGE 4
Stable population: Births and deaths are more or less balanced.	**Rapidly growing population:** Births far outnumber deaths.	**Stable population:** Births drop, and births and deaths become more or less balanced.	**Shrinking population:** Deaths outnumber births.

Note: The standard demographic transition is depicted by Stages 1–3. Stage 4 has been suggested by some Anti-Malthusians.

It took the world's population twelve years to go from 4 to 5 billion, and then another twelve years to go from 5 to 6 billion. If population growth had kept accelerating as it had been doing, this last billion of people would have taken less than twelve years. Instead, population growth tapered off, the precise slowing that we would expect. These nations have just penetrated the third stage of the demographic transition. Soon we will be wondering what all the fuss was about.

One of the demographers whose work I have cited in this chapter is Carl Haub. Discussing his work in the following Spotlight on Social Research box. Haub touches on many of the issues that we have reviewed.

Spotlight on Social Research
EXPERIENCING THE DEMOGRAPHIC TRANSITION

CARL HAUB, *Senior Demographer at the Population Reference Bureau, became interested in population growth in the 1970s when he learned that the populations of some of the world's poorest nations would double in twenty-three years. He has conducted research in Belarus, Honduras, India, Jamaica, Trinidad and Tobago, and Vietnam.*

The populations of the world's poorest nations began to grow rapidly when their death rates declined because of factors like immunization campaigns, but their birth rates remained high. As a result, their growth rates shot up. In Europe, on the contrary, birth and death rates tended to decline together.

Most of the Least Industrialized Nations have adopted policies to slow their rates of growth. Without this, it would be impossible for them to improve health conditions and have any hope of feeding their people. A key point for demographers is the length of time it takes for a country's birth rate to decline to what we call the *replacement level.* This is achieved when couples average about two children each. When this happens, a country's population reaches zero growth, neither growing nor declining, since the average couple simply "replaces" itself.

Since most Least Industrialized Nations do not have thorough registration systems of their births and deaths, how do we know what a country's growth rate is? We glean trends in their population growth from their national census data. In addition, we take demographic surveys to fill the gaps in our knowledge.

Birth rates have declined remarkably in some countries, such as Brazil, South Korea, Thailand, and Tunisia. In others, especially the countries of sub-Saharan Africa, progress has been slow. In some sub-Saharan countries, progress has even stopped. In Asia and Latin America, the story is mixed. India, with one billion people, has seen some success, especially in its more educated areas. But in Uttar Pradesh, India's largest state with 170 million people, women still give birth to nearly five children each. In Costa Rica, the birth rate has declined to the replacement level, but in Guatemala it remains high.

The green revolution was truly a revolution; it improved food supplies in the Least Industrialized Nations. But the story does not end there. Poverty remains widespread in these nations, and malnutrition is still common. Without declines in population growth, alleviating poverty will be difficult. Consider these two countries: In Yemen, a country of high poverty, women still average about seven children. In Thailand, where much of the population is still rural, women average less than two.

Two recent developments are of major concern to demographers: HIV/AIDS and population shrinkage. HIV/AIDS has taken a toll, particularly in Africa, where, in some countries, over 30 percent (or more) of the population is infected. This has drastically changed the population outlook for these countries. The population of Africa, however, is still growing rapidly. In contrast, population shrinkage, not growth, is the situation in many of the Most Industrialized Nations. In all of Europe and in Japan, low birth rates are causing concern. In Germany and Italy, for example, women now average only 1.3 children. These low birth rates will lead to social problems.

Today's demographic trends will have significant impacts on society. The future will bring new developments, which will add to the developing demographic story.

The Scope of the Problem

SITTING ON THE SHOULDERS OF THE NEW MALTHUSIANS. Let's suppose that the world's population doubles during the next fifty years, as it will if present growth rates continue. Can the world support twice its present population? To answer this question, say the New Malthusians, let's look at how the world is doing with its current population. Famine and malnutrition stalk the earth. Six hundred million people are malnourished and go to bed hungry each night. Eleven million children die each year before they reach the age of 5. One half of these deaths are caused by hunger and malnourishment. One hundred twenty million children receive no schooling at all ("State of Food . . ." 2005). In some of the world's poorest nations, such as Bangladesh, *half* the population does not eat enough protein. Every year thousands of people in Africa, Asia, and Latin America are born deaf-mutes because of iodine deficiency (Pollack 2004). Several hundred million people survive on *less* than $1,000 a year. In Ethiopia, which is growing so fast that by the year 2050 it will be the tenth largest country in the world, the *average* income is less than $100 for the entire year (*Statistical Abstract* 2006:Table 1327).

As bad as it is now, add the New Malthusians, the future looks even bleaker. Urban sprawl is devouring productive farmlands. In the United States alone, each year developers turn about 3 million acres of farmland into subdivisions and businesses. This is enough land to form a corridor a mile and a half wide stretching from San Francisco to New York. The land chewed up by urban sprawl is lost to food production, further sealing the fate of the world's malnourished.

SITTING ON THE SHOULDERS OF THE ANTI-MALTHUSIANS. "It isn't like that at all," reply the Anti-Malthusians. The idea that the United States is being "paved over" is absurd, argued economist Julian Simon (1981). The United States has about 2 billion acres. All the land taken up by cities, highways, roads, railroads, and airports amounts to only 75 million acres—less than 4 percent of our total land. We are in no danger of running out of farmland.

Urban sprawl is not taking food out of the mouths of starving children, as the New Malthusians would have us believe. In fact, urban sprawl has not even slowed food production, add the Anti-Malthusians. The problem of starvation has nothing to do with the earth having too many people, nor with the earth failing to produce enough food. The amount of food available for every person on earth has actually been *increasing*, not decreasing. Every country records how much food it produces. As Figure 13-4 shows, *despite the billions of people who have been added to the earth's population, more food is available per person now than in the past.* The United States produces so much food that our problem is what to do with it all. The U.S. government even pays its farmers *not* to farm some land. Americans eat so much that obesity has become a major health problem. The bottom line is that efforts to reduce the world's population are misdirected.

What about those alarming images we see of starving children—those scrawny bony arms, protruding stomachs, and flies crawling over their faces? How can anyone deny that there is a food shortage? Of course, the starving people in those photos aren't getting enough food, reply the Anti-Malthusians. The reason for this, though, is not that the earth is failing to produce enough food for them. The problem is that the abundance of the earth is not distributed adequately. As we've known for a long time, if we were to redistribute a mere 3 to 5 percent of the grain grown in the Most Industrialized Nations, we could prevent *all* the malnutrition and starvation in the entire world (Conti 1980).

How about the common perception that Africa is overcrowded, that it has so many people that it is outstripping its resources? Again, reply the Anti-Malthusians, the starvation in Africa that upsets the world does *not* occur because there are too many people, but because of drought and civil war. Africa is rich in resources, and—contrary to common

FIGURE 13-4 How Much Food Does the World Produce Per Person?

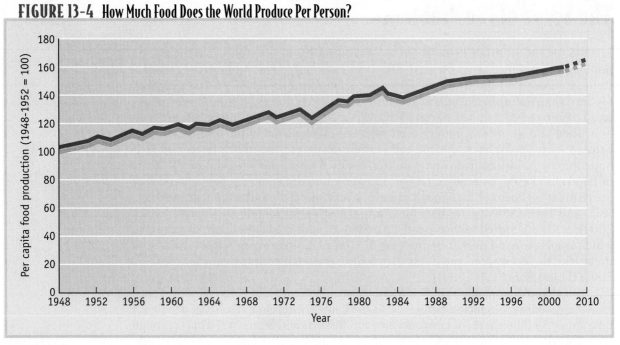

Note: Projections from 2004 are the author's.

Sources: Simon 1981:58; *Statistical Abstract of the United States* 1988:Table 1411; 1998:Tables 1380, 1381, 1382, 1383; 2006:Tables 817, 1346, 1350; recomputed to 1948–52 base.

belief promoted by those photos of starving children—*Africa has fewer people per square mile than either Europe or the United States* (Haub 2005). Civil wars in Africa disrupt food production and block humanitarian aid from reaching the dying. Look at the suffering depicted in this chapter's opening photo. This is totally unnecessary. There is plenty of food to feed this child—and all others like her.

To think that starvation comes about either because the earth has too many people or the earth does not produce enough food misses the mark entirely. The problem is a combination of agricultural inefficiency, inadequate incentives, political corruption, maldistribution of the earth's abundance, poor governments, and war—not too little food in the world.

As far as those statistics about deaf-mutes go, the Anti-Malthusians agree that the figures are horrible. They point out, however, that these people are born deaf-mutes because they lack iodized food, not because they are "excess" people. Their situation has nothing to do with the earth being overpopulated. The problem is how to get iodized food to people, not how to reduce population.

IN SUM The New Malthusians and the Anti-Malthusians draw different conclusions from the same evidence. Much like the pessimists who look at the water in a glass and conclude that the glass is half empty, the New Malthusians conclude that population growth is so great that we are about to run out of land and food. Like the optimists who consider the same glass of water half full, the Anti-Malthusians conclude that our era enjoys the greatest abundance that the world has ever known and that the abundance is growing. The scope of the population problem depends on one's perception—whether one sees the glass as half empty or half full.

No one can settle this argument for you. You will have to read the evidence and make up your own mind. As you do so, remember the symbolic interactionist principle that *facts never interpret themselves:* To interpret anything, we place it within a framework that gives it meaning. As we consider issues of population and food in the coming pages, we will return to this basic principle from time to time. For now, let's apply the frameworks of understanding called sociological theories.

Looking at the Problem Theoretically

As usual, our three theoretical lenses provide contrasting perspectives. We will use symbolic interactionism to better understand why the population of the Least Industrialized Nations is growing so fast. Functionalism illuminates the relationship between modern medicine and the twin problems of population and food. Finally, conflict theory yields a controversial analysis of food, profits, and international relations. Together, these perspectives help us understand the whole.

Symbolic Interactionism

WHY DO THE POOR HAVE SO MANY CHILDREN? Let's start with something that doesn't seem to make sense. Look at Figure 13-5, which shows population change over time. If you track the population increase of the Least Industrialized Nations, it looks as if you're going up a steep hill. In contrast, the population of the Most Industrialized Nations is standing still. Why is *almost all* the increase in the world's population coming from the Least Industrialized Nations?

Doesn't this seem obvious to you? If you are poor, you should have few children. Yet you can see that the world's population growth is driven by the poor nations of the world. Why don't hunger and disease, starvation and death, convince poor people to have fewer children? Do people in the Least Industrialized Nations *want* to have fewer children, but not know how to prevent them? This is not the case. Cheap and effective birth control techniques are available, but many of the poor won't use them. They continue to have many children because they *want* large families (Burns 1994).

TAKING THE ROLE OF THE OTHER. The focus of symbolic interactionism—trying to grasp people's perspective, to see the world as they see it—helps to explain this. What to us seems to be irrational behavior takes different shape when we examine what children *mean* for people in the Least Industrialized Nations.

FIGURE 13-5 Where Is the World's Population Growth Taking Place?

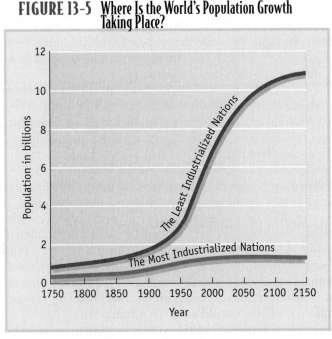

Sources: "The World of the Child 6 Billion," 2000; Haub 2005.

With political conflicts common, the world is awash in refugees, who need to be fed, clothed, and sheltered. Their care is usually a temporary matter, as in this scene from Afghanistan, but in some instances the turmoil continues or the refugees' government refuses to allow them back into the country. In such situations the "temporary" arrangement can continue for decades.

Recall Celia and Angel in the chapter's opening vignette. As you could tell, it was difficult for me to understand Celia's joy at being pregnant with her thirteenth child when her oldest child was only 14 years old and she was just 30. I was viewing her situation from my framework, not as she and her husband saw it. Only by **taking the role of the other**—that is, seeing things from another person's perspective—can we make sense of people's experiences.

To understand Celia and Angel's desire for more children, then—and the desires of billions of poor people like them—we must move beyond our own culture. We first need to see that in the Least Industrialized Nations people's identities center on their children. Motherhood is the most exalted status that a woman can achieve. It is what she was born for. Through childbearing, she fulfills this destiny and finds personal fulfillment. The more children she bears, the more she fulfills the purpose for which she was born. Similarly, the more children that a man fathers, the more he proves his manhood. It is especially sons that he desires, for through them, his name lives on.

There is more to the explanation, though: Most of these people live in small communities where they share values and identify with one another. It is in this *Gemeinschaft* community of like-minded people that they are given or denied the status that matters—their rank in the family and among friends and neighbors. Having many children is taken as a sign of God's blessing on their lives. As people produce more children, then, the community grants them higher status. The barren woman, not the woman with a dozen children, is to be pitied.

These are strong motivations for bearing many children. But there is yet another: For the poor in the Least Industrialized Nations, children are *economic assets*. This, too, is difficult for us to grasp. We live in an urbanized, postindustrialized world where children are economic liabilities. Long ago, we left the agrarian world where children helped on the family farm. In our society, children have become luxuries. They are expensive to bear and to rear—and with our requirement of college, and even graduate school, for economic success, they remain so for many years. In the Most Industrialized Nations, young adults consider whether to have children in much the same way that they consider buying a new car: "Can we afford one?" or "Should we put it off until later?"

How, then, can poor people afford to have many children, and why do they view children as economic assets? It is important to understand the world these people live in. They have no social security, no medical insurance, and no unemployment benefits. The lack of these benefits motivates people to have *more* children, not fewer, for when parents become too old to work, they rely on their adult children to take care of them. Their children are their social security, and the more children they have, the firmer their security is. In addition, children start to contribute financially to their family long before the parents are old. As you will recall, at age 14, the oldest son of Celia and Angel was contributing to his family. Figure 13-6 should help you take the role of the other, which is essential if we are to understand why the surge in the world's population is coming from the Least Industrialized Nations.

Our own situation in life, of course, is remarkably different, and for us it would be irrational to have many children. From the framework of the people involved, however—the essence of the symbolic interactionist position—having many children is rational. Consider this incident reported by a worker for the government of India:

> A water carrier . . . Thaman Singh . . . welcomed me inside his home, gave me a cup of tea (with milk and "market" sugar, as he proudly pointed out later), and said: "You were trying to convince me . . . that I shouldn't have any more sons. Now, you see, I have six sons and two daughters and I sit at home in leisure. They are grown up, and they bring me money. One even works outside the village as a laborer. You told me I was a poor man and couldn't support a large family. Now, you see, because of my large family I am a rich man." (Emphasis added) (Mamdani 1973:109)

IN SUM Our ideas of the right number of children make sense for us, for our perspectives match our life situation. To superimpose our ideas onto people in a different culture, however, is to overlook their situation and their perspectives. To understand the behavior of any group, we must see things as they see them, including—and perhaps especially—behavior that appears irrational to us.

Functionalism

CATASTROPHES ARE FUNCTIONAL. As we apply the functionalist perspective, keep in mind that functionalists want to determine *objectively* what the functions or consequences of events are, without the goal of judging those consequences as good or bad. As we saw in the instances

FIGURE 13-6 Why the Poor in the Least Industrialized Nations Want Many Children

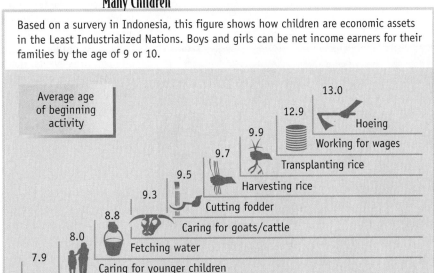

Based on a survery in Indonesia, this figure shows how children are economic assets in the Least Industrialized Nations. Boys and girls can be net income earners for their families by the age of 9 or 10.

Average age of beginning activity

13.0 Hoeing
12.9 Working for wages
9.9 Transplanting rice
9.7 Harvesting rice
9.5 Cutting fodder
9.3 Caring for goats/cattle
8.8 Fetching water
8.0 Caring for younger children
7.9 Caring for chickens/ducks

Source: U.N. Fund for Population Activities.

of poverty, rape, murder, drug addiction, and racial-ethnic discrimination, functionalists find that even deviant, illegal, or abhorrent events have functions. With regard to the social problem of population and food, functionalists stress that war, natural disasters, disease, and famine are functional. Historically, these mass killers held the world's population in check, keeping it to manageable levels and ensuring that humans did not outstrip their food supply.

MODERN MEDICINE AND PUBLIC HEALTH: LATENT DYSFUNCTIONS. Modern medicine, however, upset this precarious balance between population and food. The birth and death rates of the Least Industrialized Nations, both being high, had more or less cancelled one another out, leading to a stable population. Then came better nutrition and sanitation, coupled with Western drugs that brought under control those nations' major killers—smallpox, diphtheria, typhoid, measles, and other communicable diseases. As a result, the death rates in these nations plunged. These changes didn't touch their birth rates, though, which remained high. Not only did millions of people who otherwise would have died survive, but they also reproduced. This has forced the Least Industrialized Nations into the difficult second stage of the demographic transition (see Figure 13-3 on page 439).

POPULATION PYRAMIDS. If a country is in the second stage of the demographic transition, it has a lot of young people; if it is in the third or fourth stage, it has a lot of older people. Obviously, countries that have more young people will have higher birth rates, and those with more older people will have lower birth rates. Demographers use the term *age structure* to refer to countries having larger or smaller proportions of younger and older people. To illustrate age structures, demographers produce **population pyramids,** such as Figure 13-7, which contrasts Mexico, in Stage 2 of the demographic transition, with that of the United States, which is in advanced Stage 3. As you can see, different age structures produce different "shapes" of populations.

Let's consider one of the implications of Figure 13-7. If Mexico and the United States had the same number of people, Mexico would still grow faster than the United States. The reason? A larger proportion of Mexico's population is young, in the childbearing years. This is the case with all the Least Industrialized Nations, giving them what demographers call *population momentum.* What accounts for the growth that you saw in Figure 13-5 on page 444, then, isn't only that the families are larger in the Least Industrialized Nations. This is important, as we considered with Celia and Angel, but

As stressed in the text, events in life do not come with built-in meanings. All of us use frameworks of thought to interpret life's events. How do New Malthusians and Anti-Malthusians interpret this scene in India? Why do they see things so differently?

FIGURE 13-7 Population Pyramids of Mexico and the United States

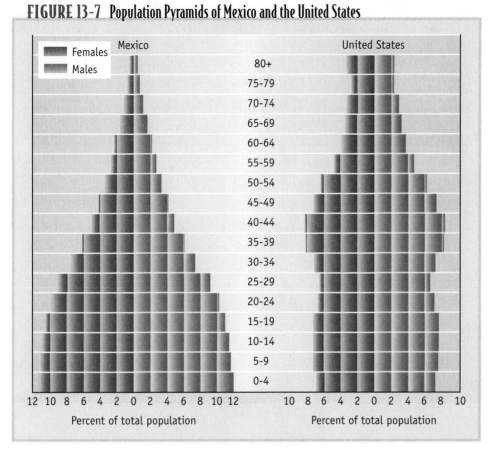

Source: By the author. Computed from the U.S. Bureau of the Census 2006b:Table 94.

underlying this surge in growth is also the population momentum of the Least Industrialized Nations.

DOUBLING TIMES. The combined force of larger families and population momentum has a tremendous impact on population growth. The Most Industrialized Nations average only 0.1 percent population growth per year. At this rate, it will take 583 years for their population to double. The Least Industrialized Nations, in contrast, are growing *fifteen times faster,* and they will double in just 40 years (Haub and Cornelius 1999). Table 13-1 on the next page shows some of the extremes: Chad will double its population in just 21 years, but it will take Austria 2,310 years to do so. The doubling time of the world's nations is shown on the Social Map on page 449.

The implications of a doubled population are mind-boggling. *Just to stay even* a country must double its food production and factories; its medical and educational capacities; its transportation, communication, water, gas, sewer, and electrical systems; its housing, churches, civic buildings, stadiums, theaters, stores, and parks; its automobiles, electronics, and household appliances; as well as jobs and all else that constitutes "decent living standards." This is just to stay even. If it fails to do this, a society's standard of living will fall.

The Least Industrialized Nations, then, appear destined to fall still farther behind the industrialized nations, for they start with less, and their swelling numbers drain their limited economic resources. In contrast, the Most Industrialized Nations, such as the United States, *can spend much more on fewer people.* With an annual growth rate of 1.0 percent, the United States is at the low end of the world's growth rate but at the high end of the rate for the Most Industrialized Nations. Much of the U.S. increase is due to immigration. The U.S. rate of natural increase (growth without immigration) is 0.6 percent (Haub 2005; *Statistical Abstract* 2006:Table 4).

TABLE 13-1 How Long Will It Take a Country to Double Its Population?

SOME MOST INDUSTRIALIZED NATIONS	POPULATION (IN MILLIONS)	BIRTHS (PER 1,000 WOMEN)	DEATHS (PER 1,000 POPULATION)	ANNUAL NATURAL INCREASE	YEARS IT TAKES TO DOUBLE
United States	290	15	9	0.6	116
Canada	31	11	7	0.4	162
Japan	127	10	7	0.2	318
Great Britain	59	12	10	0.2	423
Denmark	5	12	11	0.1	472
Belgium	10	11	10	0.1	693
Austria	8	10	10	Slightly over 0	2,310
SOME LEAST INDUSTRIALIZED NATIONS					
Chad	8	50	17	3.3	21
Nicaragua	5	38	6	3.2	22
Ethiopia	60	46	21	2.5	28
Algeria	31	30	6	2.4	29
Mexico	100	27	5	2.2	32
India	1,000	28	9	1.9	37
China	1,254	16	7	1.0	73

Source: By the author. Based on Haub 2005.

IN SUM Functionalists analyze how exporting Western medicine and public sanitation into the Least Industrialized Nations tipped a delicate balance. As these nations' traditional killers were curtailed while their birth rates remained high, the unanticipated consequence was a surge in their population. Their rapid population growth outstripped their food supply, resulting in malnutrition, mass starvation, and political unrest. Because these negative consequences were not anticipated or intended, sociologists call them **latent dysfunctions.**

The question arises, though, whether these consequences are functions or dysfunctions. The Anti-Malthusians believe that in the long run the increase in the world's population is functional. The Least Industrialized Nations are fighting through the difficult second stage in their demographic transition, but they will enter the third stage and limit their populations. Some nations have already begun to do so. Their growing populations will stimulate them to industrialize and to apply technology to food production. Consequently, they will increase their food supply to match their growing populations. Warnings to reduce world population are unwarranted, and the population surge that some now find so upsetting will turn out to be functional for humanity.

Conflict Theory

POWER AND PROFITS. Conflict theorists focus on the global distribution of power and resources. They stress that social and economic arrangements, not nature, produce poverty, hunger, and starvation. The Least Industrialized Nations have problems feeding their populations not because of Malthusian inevitabilities but because they have too little income. As sociologist Michael Harrington (1977) stressed, their income is restricted because global political and economic arrangements favor the rich nations. If they had more income, they could buy all the food they need but don't produce.

FIGURE 13-8 How Long Will It Take for Population to Double?

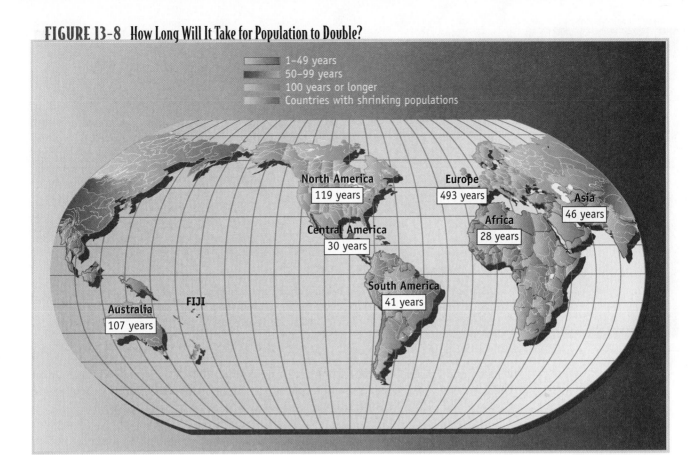

Source: By the author. Based on Haub and Cornelius 1999.

Conflict theorists point out that the Most Industrialized Nations exploit the Least Industrialized Nations today just as the European powers used to exploit their colonies. They extract the mineral and agricultural wealth of the Least Industrialized Nations at the lowest possible cost, turning those raw materials into products that they sell throughout the world. As the Most Industrialized Nations buy tin from Bolivia, copper from Peru, sugar from Cuba, coffee from Brazil, and so forth, the Least Industrialized Nations are mostly left out of this cycle of profits.

The poor nations even contribute to the diet of the rich nations. For example, each year the United States imports about $42 billion of food, much of it from the Least Industrialized Nations (*Statistical Abstract* 2003:Table 825). Although the ultimate consumers of these products pay dearly for them, the poor countries themselves receive little for the foods they sell. Long ago, social critic Michael Harrington (1977) pointed out a condition that has not changed, that global arrangements put the real profits in the pockets of the middlemen in the Most Industrialized Nations.

FOOD POLITICS. The United States also exports about $60 billion of food (*Statistical Abstract* 2006:Table 821). Like the other grain-exporting nations, it treats food as a money-making enterprise, not as a means of dealing with world hunger. The United States, which accounts for about 60 percent of the world's corn exports and 50 percent of its soybean exports, sells its grain surpluses first to those that can pay the highest prices, not to the most needy (Conti 1980; *Statistical Abstract* 2006:Table 817).

Why does the U.S. government pay farmers billions of dollars *not* to grow crops, even though people in some nations are starving? Conflict theorists say that the answer is *food politics*, controlling food production to control food prices. Paying farmers to leave their land fallow creates an artificial shortage and drives up grain prices. This also reduces the charges for storing grain—as there is less grain to store—and caters to the farm vote by

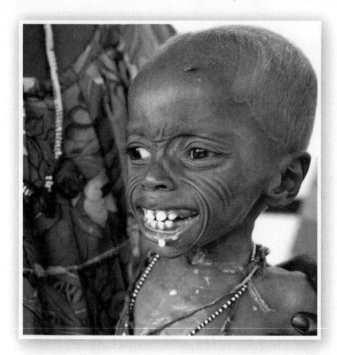

We have starvation not because the earth produces too little food, but because the earth's abundant food does not go to the starving. The photo on the left was taken in Tahoua, Niger, the one on the right in Bloomer, Wisconsin, where farmers dumped excess food to protest low prices.

keeping grain prices high. Food politics, stress conflict theorists, is pursued for political ends, with no concern for its moral implications. An indication that conflict theorists are correct is the U.S. government's own term for this practice: price supports.

IN SUM Conflict theorists conclude that food is a tool in the U.S. diplomatic kit. The food crisis that affects the undernourished masses of the world—and that so gnaws at our consciences as we see those shriveled bodies on television and in magazines—is the result of food politics, not Malthusian inevitabilities. Conflict theorists think in terms of a grain cartel headed by the United States, Canada, and Australia, which is as damaging to the Least Industrialized Nations as the OPEC oil cartel was to the industrialized world before the United States bombed it into submission. The United States, say conflict theorists, is engaged in a struggle of "agripower" against "petropower."

Research Findings

Let's first examine the position of the New Malthusians: the harm to fisheries, forests, and grasslands; the threat of plant disease and the intensification of natural disasters; and the built-in momentum in world population growth. Then, after considering the views of the Anti-Malthusians, we'll conclude by examining why it is difficult to predict population growth accurately. We'll also consider whether the United States has a population problem.

The New Malthusians

THREE NATURAL SYSTEMS. As you have seen, the New Malthusians are convinced that the world is outstripping its food supply. Their position is that the world's huge population has put unsustainable pressure on the earth's three natural systems—its fishing grounds, forests, and grasslands—on which we all depend for food. Each has a *carrying capacity*, limits fixed by nature, and we are straining those limits.

The Fishing Grounds ■ The first natural system seems to offer an endless supply of food. If you go to a fish market or order fish at a restaurant, you face a bountiful choice. There is no shortage. From flounder and catfish to lobster and shrimp, animals from the ocean are plentiful. What basis could there possibly be for concern? Certainly, there are those who point out that it is folly to view the ocean as a source of food that can supply our needs infinitely if we develop better harvesting techniques (Arnason et al. 2005). But there are always people who are issuing cautions about something. Even back in the 1970s, some "experts" were pointing out that 90 percent of the ocean is a biological desert (Ehrlich and Ehrlich 1972). The upper layer of open sea, which gets enough sunlight for photosynthesis, lacks nutrients for high productivity. They stressed that almost all our fish come from areas close to shore and that these are the most polluted waters. Then there are those who have been warning that we are devastating the world's fragile fishing populations with our far-ranging fishing fleets equipped with sonar and mile-long drift nets. Having gone on year after year while fish remain in abundance, these warnings have fallen mostly on deaf ears.

Then in 2006, the loudest alarm was sounded, one that just might wake the world up to see how close we are to the *collapse* of the world's fishing grounds. This report did not come from some wild-eyed radicals who continuously proclaim the end of something or other. It came from dispassionate scientists at Dalhousie University in Nova Scotia, who had plugged into a computer all the fishing data available from around the world from 1950 to 2003 (Worm et al. 2006). These data are so complete that they cover all sixty-four of the marine ecosystems worldwide, which produce 83 percent of the world's fish and invertebrate catches. The researchers were shocked at the results: If we continue to harvest fish at the rate we are doing now, more and more species will vanish, the marine ecosystems will unravel, and there will be a global collapse of all the species we currently fish. Unless we make changes, this collapse will occur in the year 2048.

The Forests ■ The second natural system, the forests, seems eternally renewable. On one level, this is true. For every tree cut down, a tree can be planted. Each year, however, the world's forests shrink by an area the size of Cuba. In many places, the cutting is not accompanied by replanting. In Peru and Chile, for example, which are following the earlier practice of the United States, vast areas have been cut for firewood and farming. With the soil unprotected against wind and rain, some hills have become as barren as the moon. Pressure on the world's forests continues to increase, as the demand for newsprint and packaging soars worldwide.

The Grasslands ■ The third global life-support system, the grasslands, is also under mounting pressure. Over the past four decades, individual family farms have been purchased by agricompanies, which operate farms of thousands of acres. To make these farms efficient, the corporate owners have joined field to field, bulldozing the windrows, the row of trees between the fields that farmers had planted to break the wind. By reducing the force of the wind, windrows keep topsoil from blowing away. Now that many are removed, some fear that the Midwest will see a repeat of the dust bowl of the 1930s. Back then, Oklahoma was the main victim; this time, much of the Midwest could be hit.

Much of the agricultural production of the Midwest and the West depends on the Ogallala aquifer, an extensive underground water system. Irrigation is depleting this reservoir. Wells are running dry, as we shall see in the next chapter. Soon we will have to curtail this extensive irrigation, which underlies much of the high productivity of the western United States.

Around the world, the pressing need for food is pushing into production land that is basically unsuitable for cultivation (Little and Horowitz 1987). The steep hillsides of Indonesia are being eroded; slash-and-burn agriculture is destroying tropical forests in many countries, including Brazil and the Philippines. Attempts to apply farming techniques that work in the temperate zone to the tropical soils of Brazil and Sudan have caused **laterization,** the transformation of soils into laterite, a rocklike material. This occurs when cultivation exposes certain soils to the air.

A DANGER: DISEASE OF SPECIALIZED STRAINS. In addition to pressure on the world's three natural systems, the expanding population of the world faces two other dangers. First, the world's agricultural system now depends on only a few specialized strains of crops. In the quest for higher yields, a few specifically bred, high-yield strains have replaced the world's wide range of traditional varieties of wheat and rice. Although these high-yield varieties allow farmers to produce more food, they also increase the potential of widespread crop failure from insects and disease.

Back in the 1970s, biologists John Holdren and Paul Ehrlich (1974) warned that what happened in Ireland during the last century could happen to our generation, but on a much larger scale:

> The Irish potato famine of the (1800s) is perhaps the best-known example of the collapse of a single agricultural ecosystem. The heavy reliance of the Irish population on a single, high productive crop led to 1.5 million deaths when the potato monoculture fell victim to a fungus.

In other words, if the right pest or plant disease comes along, we can have a worldwide calamity. Our extensive cultivation of single high-yield grains is "an accident waiting to happen." The benefits it now yields may come at the future cost of epidemic starvation, malnutrition, and disease. This could occur suddenly and in surprising ways. For example, the 2004 hurricane season was one of the worst that the United States ever experienced. These hurricanes spread to the United States from South America a fungus that attacks soybeans.

ANOTHER DANGER: INTENSIFICATION OF NATURAL DISASTERS. The second danger is the intensification of natural disasters. As human populations grow, they expand into areas less likely to protect them from the elements. The Ehrlichs (1972:243) provided this account of how overpopulation intensifies natural disasters:

> In November of 1970, a huge tidal wave driven by a cyclone swept over the Ganges Delta of East Pakistan. There a large, mostly destitute population lived exposed on flat lowland, in spite of the ever-present danger of climatic disaster for which the region is famous. They live in constant jeopardy because in grossly overpopulated East Pakistan the choice of places for them is greatly restricted. In November, 1970, 300,000 people died who need not have died if their nation had not been over-populated. This cataclysm has been described as the greatest documented national disaster in history.

Hurricane Katrina drove home to Americans how difficult it can be to deal with natural disasters. It is even more difficult to do so in the Least Industrialized Nations, where resources are so much more limited. This photo was taken in India.

In this poor, overcrowded nation, now called Bangladesh, evacuation was impossible. Because it was already nutritionally marginal, after the disaster people began to starve.

INCREDIBLY RAPID POPULATION GROWTH. Now consider this statistic on population explosion, which underscores the New Malthusians' point. Despite this huge death toll of 300,000 from the tidal wave, the population in Bangladesh grew so fast that in only five or six weeks new births made Bangladesh's population as large as it had been before the catastrophe (Waddington 1978). Then there was the tsunami of 2004, the one that captured the imagination of the world. By far, the country hardest hit was Indonesia, where 233,000 people died. With Indonesia's growth rate of over 3 million people a year, it took Indonesia just under four weeks (26 days) to replace all the people it lost to the tsunami (Henslin 2007b).

With such statistics, it is no wonder that the New Malthusians conclude that humanity must stop its population growth. Outstripping our food supply, they warn, will bring the worst catastrophe that the world has ever known. What we've seen so far is just the down payment on our foolhardy ways. Even our increased food supply is not doing anything other than buying us a little time. It allows us to postpone, but not avoid, the inevitable disaster. The only solution is to stabilize world population.

ZERO POPULATION GROWTH? Suppose that we achieve **zero population growth**—that is, adults having only enough children to replace themselves. It seems obvious that the world's population problem would disappear, right? The obvious, however, as the New Malthusians point out, is not true. *The population momentum that we discussed earlier would keep the world's population growing for 50 to 70 years before it leveled off.*

Certainly zero population growth combined with the population continuing to grow seems contradictory. Yet this strange combination is true. The reason is found in the population pyramids on page 447. In the Least Industrialized Nations, more people are in the younger age groups than in the older age groups. Consider Africa as an example. Forty-two percent of Africans are not yet age 15 (Haub 2005). This means that more Africans will enter the reproductive ages each year than will leave them. If Africa attained zero population growth, with each woman bearing an average of 2.1 children, the growth *rate* of Africa would fall for 50 or 70 years, but Africa's population would continue to increase during this time before it finally leveled off.

And, add the New Malthusians, Africa isn't even close to zero population growth. The average African woman gives birth to 5 children, not 2 (Haub 2005). Despite all those deaths from HIV/AIDS and the mass starvation, Africa has the fastest-growing population of any continent.

A BLEAK FUTURE FOR THE WORLD. The future looks desperate. Famine, malnutrition, and starvation are ready to strike the earth. We are also suffering from pollution and environmental destruction as too many people try to scratch a living from the earth's precarious surface. (We discuss this in the next chapter.) The world's swelling population even threatens world peace. When the governments of the Least Industrialized Nations cannot feed their people, riots will break out. Governments will topple, threatening the precarious balance of international power.

The Anti-Malthusians

LARGER POPULATIONS ARE GOOD. The Anti-Malthusians scoff at such conclusions. They just shake their heads and wonder how any sane person can make these interpretations. The Anti-Malthusians have a surprisingly different conclusion about the world's population: In the long run, more people are *good* for a country; larger populations lead to *higher* standards of living (Simon 1977, 1982, 1991).

This seems to fly in the face of reality. How can the Anti-Malthusians possibly take this position, wonder the New Malthusians, who, in their turn, scorn the Anti-Malthusians. All we have to do is look at India, Bangladesh, and China. To support their position, the anti-Malthusians make four points. First, a growing population means that more geniuses will be born, who will contribute to everyone's welfare. Second, population growth forces countries to use their land more efficiently, which increases productivity. Third, larger populations create larger markets. This promotes more efficient manufacturing, lowering the production cost per unit. This makes more goods available more cheaply. Fourth, a larger population makes many social investments profitable, especially railroads, highways, irrigation systems, and ports. Investments of this scale don't pay off for sparse populations. These investments, in turn, spur productivity and increase a country's capacity to deliver that productivity to its people.

FOOD PRODUCTION IS OUTPACING POPULATION GROWTH. The Anti-Malthusians stress that we should not lose sight of how the world's food production has *outpaced* the world's population growth. (Recall Figure 13-4 on page 442.) Today there is *more* food for each person in the entire world than there was 25, 50, or even 100 or 200 years ago. Moreover, this increase in per capita food occurred while the world's population "exploded." During this same time, the United States, the "breadbasket of the world," decreased the number of acres that it farmed. As Figure 13-9 below shows, the United States now has *less* land under the plow than in 1920, yet the food production of the United States continues to increase. If the world's population increase is dramatic—and it is—then the world's food increase is more dramatic still.

When it comes to fishing grounds, the Anti-Malthusians say that the numbers tell the story there, too. The world's fish harvest has not fallen, as one would expect from the alarms that the New Malthusians are trying to set off all over the world. According to U.S. government records, the world's fish harvest is now 36 percent *higher* than it was in 1990 (*Statistical Abstract* 2006:Table 1347). This increase does not make good headlines, of course, as it does not spread fear and sell newspapers. Therefore, the mass media ignore the good news and listen to the New Malthusians to try to find something to catch the public's attention by screaming the end of the world.

NOT EVEN A LAND SHORTAGE. And running out of land? Not in any realistic future, say the Anti-Malthusians. According to the U.N. Food and Agricultural Organization, more than 2 billion acres of rain-fed land go unfarmed (Livernash and Rodenburg 1998). Contrary to common belief, then, the world contains enough land to feed even more

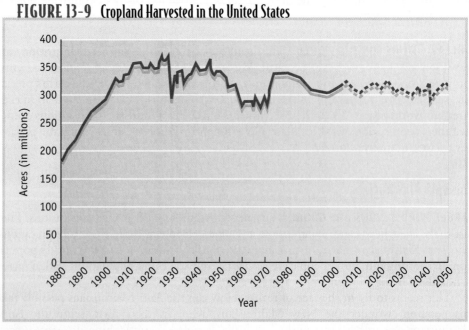

FIGURE 13-9 Cropland Harvested in the United States

Sources: By the author. Based on *Statistical Abstract of the United States* 1991:Table 1154; 1998:Table 1126; 2006:Table 797. Broken line is the author's estimate.

Food production has increased faster than population growth, and today the average person has more food than when the world had billions fewer people. New and Anti-Malthusians disagree sharply on what this means. Shown here is an automated milking line in Arizona. More than 3,000 cows are milked each day on these two rotating carousels.

people. If we should ever farm all this unused land, and need more, then we could reclaim wasteland and make it productive. The best example is Holland, whose success shows the potential of human endeavor. Originally Holland belonged more to the sea than the land; one would expect it to be filled with lagoons and dominated by sea fowl and migratory birds. Instead, it is a prosperous country with one of the highest population densities in Europe.

Has the Population Explosion Peaked?

THE ANTI-MALTHUSIANS. The Anti-Malthusians point out that the world's rate of population growth is slowing. The world's population grew 2 percent a year between 1965 and 1975. Then it dropped to 1.7 percent a year during the 1980s. Now it has dropped to 1.2 percent (*Statistical Abstract* 1991:Table 1434; Haub 2005). This means that the world's population growth has dropped by 40 percent. It is growing at only 60 percent the rate that it was just thirty or forty years ago.

Population growth has slowed not only in the industrialized nations of Europe and North America but also in the poorer nations on all continents. Population growth is still speeding along, but it is slowing—just as we would expect according to the demographic transition. Perhaps the most startling statistic is this: Today's birth rate in the Least Industrialized Nations is less than *half* what it was in the 1950s. Back then, the average woman in the Least Industrialized Nations gave birth to 6.2 children. The birth rate has dropped so drastically that today, the average women in these nations has just 3.0 children (Livernash and Rodenburg 1998; Haub 2005).

THE NEW MALTHUSIANS. The advocates of zero population growth agree that these figures are correct, but say they don't mean what the Anti-Malthusians think they do. These figures do indicate that the *rate* of population growth has slowed, but they don't mean that the world's population has leveled off or that it is getting smaller. On the contrary, the world's population is still exploding. The New Malthusians stress that we have to look at absolute numbers: The world's population is soaring beyond anything history has ever seen: We are still adding about 79 million people a year to our planet. The day of reckoning is on its way.

Problems in Forecasting Population Growth

WHY DEMOGRAPHERS HEDGE THEIR BETS. To forecast population growth is to invite yourself to be wrong (Conner 1990). Consider this:

> During the depression of the late 1920s and early 1930s, birth rates plunged as unemployment reached unprecedented heights. Demographers issued warnings about the dangers of depopulation almost as alarmist as some of today's forecasts of overpopulation (Waddington 1978). Because each year fewer and fewer females would enter the childbearing years, they felt that the population of countries such as Great Britain would shrink.

Instead, with the end of the Great Depression and the outbreak of World War II, the birth rate rose. After the war, both the United States and Britain had a "baby boom." The inaccuracy of the pessimistic prophets of the 1930s has made some skeptical of demographic forecasts. Population growth depends on people's attitudes and behavior, and how can anyone know what those will be?

To get around this, today's demographers hedge their bets. They make several predictions, each based on different assumptions. Look at Figure 13-10, which shows three projections of the U.S. population. Since the population of the United States hit 300 million in 2006, we already know that their low estimate is wrong.

CHANGES IN THE U.S. BIRTH RATE. Two remarkable changes shown in Figure 13-11 also illustrate how difficult it is to make accurate demographic projections. The first is this: As you can see from this figure, through the years the African American birth rate has been consistently higher than the white birth rate. Although the difference in the birth rates between these two groups fluctuated slightly, African American women always averaged more children than did white women. But look at how these birth rates have converged. Today, for the first time in U.S. history, white and African American women have the same birth rate. In projecting the U.S. population in past years, say in the 1970s, why would demographers have anticipated this?

Actually, the change is even more remarkable than this. For the first time since records have been kept, African American women have a *lower* birth rate than white women. The difference is slight, but it shows up in more precise data. The totals on Figure 13-11 are

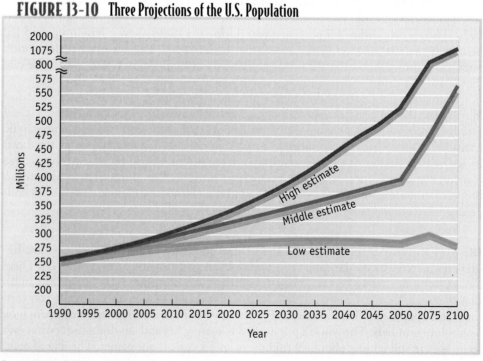

FIGURE 13-10   **Three Projections of the U.S. Population**

Source: Statistical Abstract of the United States 2006:Table 3.

FIGURE 13-11 The Birth Rates of African American and White Women

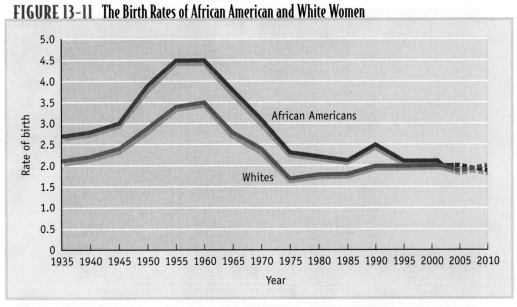

Note: These are the only groups listed in the source. For 1935 to 1960, the totals for African Americans are listed as Negro and Other. These are *fertility rates,* the number of births per woman. The source lists the number as per 1,000 women.

Source: By the author. Based on U.S. Bureau of the Census 1975:Series B 36-41; *Statistical Abstract of the United States* 1989:Table 87; 2007:Table 81.

rounded, and in 2004, the latest year available, the more precise totals were 2,033 children per 1,000 African American women and 2,055 children per 1,000 white women.

Figure 13-11 also shows another historical event: We have achieved the New Malthusian's dream of Zero Population Growth. Because some children die, for our population to stay even, the average woman must give birth to 2.1 children. (Or, as demographers say, every 1,000 women must give birth to an average of 2,100 children.) As you can see from Figure 13-11, although the U.S. birth rate has fluctuated slightly through the years, it has been on a solid downward track. About thirty years or so ago, the United States reached Zero Population Growth. Actually, the change is more extreme than this, and we are now below the replacement level of our population.

IMMIGRANTS OFFSET LOW BIRTH RATES. If U.S. women give birth to fewer children than it takes to replace the population, then the U.S. population should be shrinking. And it would be, except for immigration. Each year, about 1 million immigrants enter the United States legally (*Statistical Abstract* 2006:Table 6), and several hundred thousand more arrive illegally. This vast immigration is having dramatic effects on the United States. Figure 13-12 shows one of them, how immigration, combined with the natural increase from births minus deaths, is expected to change the U.S. racial-ethnic makeup.

FIGURE 13-12 U.S. Population by Race-Ethnicity

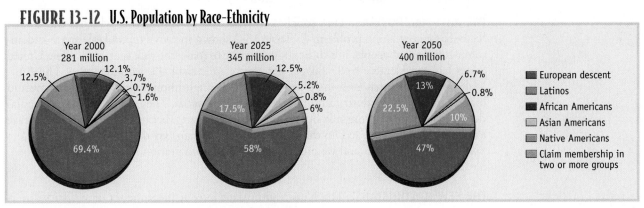

Source: Henslin 2007b.

Among the reasons that it is difficult to project population growth accurately is the uncertainty of immigration. Shown here are U.S. immigrants from Korea who are performing a traditional dance as they celebrate at a dance festival in Los Angeles, California.

DO IMMIGRANTS PAY THEIR WAY? People worry that immigrants depress wages and take jobs away from citizens. Because of concerns that immigrants are a drain on taxpayers, in 1997 a federal law made immigrants ineligible for welfare benefits (Martin and Midgley 1999). Some economists claim that after subtracting what immigrants collect in welfare and adding what they produce in jobs and taxes, they make a positive contribution to the economy (Simon 1986). Others find an "immigrant deficit," concluding that immigrants are a drain on taxpayers (Huddle 1993).

The situation is complicated, but the key seems to be education (Smith and Edmonston 1997). The fairest summary seems to be this: Immigrants with low education collect more in benefits than they pay in taxes, whereas those with high education pay more in taxes than they collect in benefits. On average, each adult immigrant who has less than a high school education costs taxpayers $89,000 over his or her lifetime. Immigrants who have more than twelve years of schooling provide a $105,000 lifetime gain (Martin and Midgley 1999).

Does the United States Have a Population Problem?

THE ANTI-MALTHUSIANS. Let's conclude this section by considering whether the United States has a population problem. As Table 13-2 shows, in terms of available space and absolute numbers of people, it is difficult for anyone to make the case that we do. The United States has considerably fewer people per square mile than the world average. The Anti-Malthusians stress that even if we continue to have high immigration, the country would have enough space, industry, and food to meet their needs. They say that a larger population would prove an economic boom to the United States, because industries would have to supply what they needed. In short, the Anti-Malthusians say that the United States does *not* have *enough* people, and we ought to encourage immigration, especially of skilled people (Simon 1991).

THE NEW MALTHUSIANS. The New Malthusians look at the same set of statistics differently, of course. They claim that we do have a population problem. It is not inadequate space, food, or industry, or even too many people, but, instead, the rate at which Americans deplete the world's resources and pollute the environment. The average American uses five times more energy than the average person in the world, twenty-six times more energy than a citizen of India (*Statistical Abstract* 2003:Table 1365). If each American costs the earth as much as 26 Indians, then in terms of energy our 300 million inhabitants use the same amount as 8 billion Indians. Put somewhat differently, if the population of India multiplied until it was larger than the earth's total population is now, only then would India put as much pressure on the earth's resources as we Americans already do.

THE ANTI-MALTHUSIANS. This analogy, reply the Anti-Malthusians, is irrelevant. We need to focus on what Americans contribute to the earth. Our science, technology, financing, and industry give the world the capacity to increase production and enhance the standard of living of even the poorest nations. If we had more people, we would have more geniuses, spurring even more creativity. We would then develop more of our potential, increase our capacity for production, including food, and help the poorer nations even more (Simon 1981).

OBJECTIVE CONDITIONS VERSUS VIEWPOINTS. How should we look at the matter? As with the optimist and the pessimist, the question again depends on definitions and viewpoints. These clashing views highlight the relevance of symbolic interactionism, for conclusions on both sides depend on how people interpret objective conditions. Although those conditions may be objective, how we choose to interpret them is not. Accordingly, the conclusions of both the New Malthusians and the Anti-Malthusians are biased.

TABLE 13-2 Density of Selected Countries

COUNTRY	NUMBER OF PEOPLE PER SQUARE MILE	COUNTRY	NUMBER OF PEOPLE PER SQUARE MILE
Macau	70,868	Turkey	232
Monaco	41,790	Greece	211
Hong Kong	19,126	Spain	209
Singapore	18,071	Egypt	198
Gibraltar	11,963	Morocco	187
Malta	3,202	Ethiopia	165
Bahrain	2,836	Iraq	151
Bangladesh	2,734	Ireland	149
South Korea	1,277	Mexico	141
Holland	1,245	Afghanistan	114
Puerto Rico	1,116	Iran	107
India	928	Colombia	106
Japan	835	South Africa	94
Israel	790	United States	83
Philippines	749	Zimbabwe	81
Haiti	746	Venezuela	73
Vietnam	658	Sweden	57
Great Britain	646	Brazil	56
Germany	609	Peru	56
Pakistan	529	New Zealand	39
Italy	511	Norway	38
North Korea	488	Argentina	37
China	361	Saudi Arabia	31
Nigeria	358	Russia	22
Indonesia	341	Guyana	10
Denmark	331	Canada	9
Poland	328	Australia	7
Portugal	297	Botswana	7
France	287	Mongolia	5
Cuba	264	**WORLD**	**126**

Source: By the author. Based on *Statistical Abstract of the United States* 2003:Table 1322; 2006:Table 1314.

Social Policy

Although the New and Anti-Malthusians disagree on almost everything, they do agree that we should increase food production. Let's consider the possibility of increasing food production by exporting Western agricultural techniques.

Exporting Western Agriculture

THE APPEAL OF EXPORTING WESTERN AGRICULTURE. Our farming techniques are so efficient that, as discussed, our problem is what to do with excess production. Because we have such advanced technology, why can't we help the world's nations to increase food production by exporting our agricultural techniques to the Least Industrialized Nations? Everyone knows the proverb, "Give people a fish and you feed them for a day. Teach them to fish, and you feed them for a lifetime." If these nations adopt our techniques, which are tried and proven, couldn't they produce food in abundance?

This solution has initial appeal, but it is unworkable. The **green revolution**—the rapid expansion in food production that occurred in the 1950s and 1960s—originated during a period of cheap energy and seemingly unlimited amounts of fresh water. The development of high-yield wheat and rice, coupled with effective fertilizers, raised hopes that impoverished nations could abolish famine. The U.S. Midwest could be reproduced in India, China, and Africa.

THE LACK OF WATER AND FERTILIZER. It didn't happen. Water and fertilizer, essential to these high-yield plants, are in short supply in the poor nations. To maximize yields, fields must be dosed with up to 150 pounds of nitrogen fertilizer per acre, and they also require massive amounts of water to keep the fertilizer from burning the crops.

Nitrogen fertilizer is expensive. Even some U.S. farmers find its cost prohibitive, and few farmers in the poor nations can afford it at all. What rural poverty is like in the Least Industrialized Nations is difficult for Americans to imagine. Many farmers cannot afford even gasoline or electricity to irrigate their fields:

> "Oh, yes, we know about the green revolution," said Patal Mukherjee, a primary-school teacher in India who farms a few acres of rice and wheat. "But it does not change anything here. We are too poor."

Mukherjee's primitive farming methods are typical of India's 700 million village dwellers. He knows that different fertilizers will increase crop yields. And he knows how to apply them. But he rarely has the money to buy them. He is locked into an endless cycle of defeat. When he most needs fertilizers—to make up for a bad harvest—he cannot afford to buy them. Thus, skimpy harvests often follow bad harvests (Wallace 1980).

THE LACK OF AN AGRICULTURAL INFRASTRUCTURE. Another factor also prevents the exportation of Western farming methods. As functionalists emphasize, food production is only one item in an interconnected system. Abundance is not enough; agricultural products must be distributed quickly to consumers or they rot. Our *agricultural infrastructure*—our network of railway and trucking, with many units refrigerated—allows us to move agricultural products from field to storage or directly to consumer. Our superhighways are subsidized by the federal government, which, in turn, depends on a vast system of tax collection. We also have regional and national systems of supermarkets to deliver products to consumers. It will not work to export to a poor nation one or two pieces of this interconnected, elaborate, and expensive support system of production, processing, and distribution (Harrington 1977).

Since exporting Western agricultural techniques is not the answer, let's look at the social policies that follow from the positions of the Anti- and New Malthusians.

Policy Implications of the Anti-Malthusians

ENCOURAGING POPULATION GROWTH AND TECHNOLOGICAL DEVELOPMENT. Few Anti-Malthusians will like the policy implications of their position, but if we take their position seriously, let's see what social policies follow. If larger populations are good for the world, then it follows that social policy ought to encourage larger families, that we need to avoid polices that would discourage women from having children. To implement their position, we could take the following steps:

1. Reduce the age of consent to have sex to match the age at which girls are biologically able to reproduce. This would get more young women pregnant.
2. Encourage teenagers to experiment sexually.
3. Offer incentives for women to become mothers. These might include reduced taxes, paid maternity leave, subsidized housing, free nannies and child care, and free education and medical care. Cash bonuses could be paid, with larger bonuses for each successive child.
4. Discourage the education of women, because the more education women attain, the fewer children they bear.
5. Make abortion and birth control illegal.

6. Export Western medicine and public health techniques to the Least Industrialized Nations, in order to reduce maternal deaths, infant deaths, and prolong the lives of the elderly.
7. Offer incentives to encourage science, technology, industry, and agriculture. Developments in these areas can help improve the standard of living of huge populations.

Policy Implications of the New Malthusians

Neither are New Malthusians likely to be pleased with the implications of their position, but let's also take their position seriously and extrapolate the policies that follow. Because their views are more widely held, let's examine their policy implications in more detail.

MALTHUS' MACHIAVELLIAN PROPOSAL. Malthus' main suggestion for limiting population was sexual abstinence, but in *An Essay on the Principle of Population* (1798/1926) he proposed a solution that most would find outrageous:

> We should . . . encourage . . . destruction. . . . Instead of recommending cleanliness to the poor, we should encourage contrary habits. In our towns we should make the streets narrower, crowd more people into the houses, and court the return of the plague. In the country, we should build villages near stagnant pools, and particularly encourage settlements in all marshy and unwholesome situations. . . . But above all, we should reprobate (abandon, reject) specific remedies for ravaging diseases.

EFFECTIVE BUT GENERALLY UNACCEPTABLE POLICIES. If we were to take Malthus' recommendations seriously, some rather severe social policies would be called for. Among them would be

1. Withdraw modern medicine from the Least Industrialized Nations, especially vaccines and antibiotics.
2. Refuse to train students from the Least Industrialized Nations.
3. Do not send food to areas of famine and starvation.
4. Encourage infanticide.
5. Raise the age of sexual consent and the age at which people are allowed to marry—or alternatively, lower the age of sexual consent and encourage promiscuous unprotected sex, while withholding medicines for HIV/AIDS.
6. Require a license to have children.
7. Require abortions for women who become pregnant without a license.
8. Encourage homosexual unions, since they don't produce children.
9. Sterilize enough baby girls to assure zero population growth.
10. Sterilize each woman who gives birth to a second child.
11. Establish a national system of free abortions on demand to any woman of any age for any reason.

Having read some of the social policies that follow from the New Malthusian position, you might be surprised to learn that some New Malthusians take even more extreme positions. Pentti Linkola, a Finnish botanist, suggests that we annihilate most of the human race (Milbank 1994). He compares humanity to a sinking ship with 100 passengers and a lifeboat that can hold only 10. He says, "We need to end aid to the Third World, stop giving asylum to refugees—and a war would be good, too." To prove that he is serious, he adds, "If there were a button I could press that meant millions of people would die, I would gladly sacrifice myself."

FOR DICTATORS, MACHIAVELLI STILL LIVES. I am certain that you find most of the social policies of both the New and Anti-Malthusians too far-fetched to ever be implemented, but we should note that as society changes, what is perceived as outrageous to one generation can become acceptable to another generation. Consider these social changes: Legal abortion in the United States, once unthinkable, is now common. Homosexual relations were once punished by law, but now they are supported by law.

It was once unthinkable for people of the same sex to marry, but such marriages are now legal in several countries.

It is conceivable, then, that other policy implications of the New Malthusians can similarly become accepted over time. Consider China, where the government launched a national campaign to reduce its population. The policy is simple: "One couple, one child." Steven Mosher (1983), an anthropologist who did fieldwork in China, observed how this policy was implemented:

> "Each population unit, such as a rural collective, is limited to a certain number of births per year, which it allots to couples who have yet to have children." Women who have had their allotted quota of 1 who get pregnant "are forced to attend round-the-clock 'study courses' until they submit to an abortion." In some cases abortions are physically forced on resisting women, some of whom are nine months pregnant. (Erik 1982)

Mosher also reports that

> families who actually have a second child must pay heavy fines, up to $2,000—several years' wages in mainland China—and run the risk of demotion or assignment to less desirable work as well.

One consequence is female infanticide:

> Among the peasants, especially, sons are more valued, as they still provide for their aged parents in a society that has no old-age security insurance. A daughter, in contrast, takes up residence with her husband's family upon marriage, severing all economic ties with her natal family. The birth of a son signals a relaxed and secure old age, while the arrival of a daughter portends poverty in one's declining years. Consequently, many peasants decide in favor of their own security, and trade the infant's life for their own.

The authorities not only overlook female infanticide but also practice it. Mosher provides this example:

> A young woman pregnant for the first time gave birth to twin boys. What should have been an occasion for rejoicing quickly turned tragic as the cadres (government representatives on the local level) present asked her which one she wanted. Both of them, she replied, but to no avail. One of the babies—she could not and would not choose which—was taken from her and put to death.

To solve social problems, leaders of an autocratic state can take steps that are out of bounds in a democracy. Remember that Hitler's murder of millions of Jews, Slavs, Gypsies, homosexuals, and people with disabilities was his "final solution" to what he saw as a social problem. Citizens of any nation that is ruled by a dictator, or any group that is not subject to the will of the people, can become captive to the *leaders' views of reality*. Although our system is far from perfect, it prevents leaders from enacting many policies that the people strongly oppose.

Chinese officials are serious about their "one couple—one child" policy. The Chinese landscape is dotted with billboards like this one—which translates to: "You will be happy and prosperous if you follow what the state says."

ZERO POPULATION GROWTH. The New Malthusians usually support zero population growth. To get people to go along with such a policy can be far from simple, however, for as we saw with Celia and Angel, peasant societies produce strong motives for wanting many children. There, children are interwoven so intricately with identity and security that few of us who don't live in such a society can comprehend their attitudes toward children. They consider our ideas selfish and shortsighted: From their perspective, for the sake of a higher standard of living, we are refusing the children that God wants to give us. Nor can they connect their desire to reproduce with some apocalyptic vision of a desperately overpopulated, starving world. Most people decide to have fewer children not because of a world population problem—but because of the attitudes, beliefs, and values produced by their location in an industrial or postindustrial society.

Perspectives Depend on Social Conditions ■ For zero population growth to occur in the Least Industrialized Nations, small families must be workable; that is, they must meet people's needs. Adults must be confident that they do not need their grown children to take care of them when they are sick or old. The reason we can have such a perspective is because we have a vast system of unemployment benefits, private and government retirement programs, and medical and disability insurance. With the exception of a few oil-rich nations such as Qatar, to have such a support system requires the extensive development of industry, which, as we shall examine in the next chapter, brings its own problems.

Proposals to Achieve Zero Population Growth ■ If we want to achieve zero population growth, here are some social policies that can help to achieve it. You are likely to find some of these policies quite acceptable and others quite unacceptable.

1. Encourage women to go to college and graduate school. Again, the more education that women attain, the fewer children they bear.
2. Encourage women to want careers. Careers reduce commitment to motherhood: Women find satisfactions in their careers, and their families become dependent on their income for a higher standard of living.
3. Distribute free or low-cost birth control devices to everyone, including teenagers.
4. Teach zero population growth to schoolchildren.
5. Pay women to be sterilized. The payment can be small, for $20 or $30 in the Least Industrialized Nations goes a long way when annual incomes are less than $1,000.
6. Make international aid, including the exporting of Western medicines, dependent on a country lowering its birth rates.
7. Tie food aid to agricultural reform.

In what might seem a very cold, brutal policy, this last principle was tried successfully in the 1960s. India faced mass starvation, and the United States used food to force agricultural reform: Each month's shipment depended on progress in meeting monthly agricultural goals. Today India can feed itself (Brown 1985).

The other Least Industrialized Nations also have the potential to produce enough food to feed themselves. Asia used to have famines that killed millions. Now Asia *exports* excess food. China broke up its communal farms and, using capitalist (profit-oriented) incentives, produces more food than it needs for its 1.3 billion people (Critchfield 1986).

NOT A PANACEA. Population control is not a panacea. First, as we reviewed earlier, if we were to achieve zero population growth, population momentum would keep the world population growing for another fifty years or so. Second, even if the world's population were to stabilize exactly where it is now, all the other social problems that we discuss in this text would remain. A population that was not growing would not solve poverty, sexism, racism, ageism, urban blight, drug addiction, violence, discrimination, and environmental decay. The New Malthusians, however, believe that to try to solve these problems is a lost cause without population control.

Restructuring Global Markets

Some New and Anti-Malthusians agree that the root of the problem is poverty, and that to eradicate poverty we need to restructure global markets. To do this, however, would mean that the rich nations would have to redistribute their wealth. Why would they do this? Their people do not want to lower their standard of living.

DEBTS, TRADE, AND STABLE PRICES. Other than redistributing the world's wealth, then, what can we do? Back in the 1970s, Michael Harrington pointed out the imbalance and suggested a moderate policy. He said that the imbalance in global trade loads crushing debt onto the shoulders of the Least Industrialized Nations. This debt prevents them from developing their own industrial infrastructure and increasing their standard of living. Harrington (1977) called for cancelling their debt and increasing trade with them. He also pointed out that nations with specialized economies (such as coffee, bananas, or oil) suffer from fluctuations in the price they receive for their commodities. To stabilize prices, he suggested that we create a world organization to buy commodities when the price dips below a specified level and to sell them when they rise to a certain point. He also suggested indexing, keying what the poor nations pay for industrial products to what they are paid for their own primary products. Indexing could lower the price that the poor nations pay for manufactured goods.

SELF-INTEREST, GLOBAL MARKETS, AND GEOPOLITICS. Such proposals require altruism on the part of the Most Industrialized Nations, which are more likely to act from self-interest. Long-term self-interest, however, is not always obvious. For example, it may well be in the interest of the wealthy nations to restructure global markets to give greater benefits to the Least Industrialized Nations. If they don't, they may face a more hostile world. The Iraqi invasion of Kuwait may have been an attempt by a Least Industrialized Nation to restructure global markets. The counterattack by the Western nations under the leadership of the United States (Desert Storm) may also have been an attempt by the Most Industrialized Nations to maintain the structure of global markets. Some conflict theorists say that the second invasion of Iraq had the same purpose. Regardless of those purposes, which have many different interpretations, as more Least Industrialized Nations gain access to nuclear, biological, and chemical weapons, it is going to be more difficult for the Most Industrialized Nations to maintain their control of global markets.

Illegal Immigration

To close this section, let's look at a population problem that has captured the public's attention, the vast illegal immigration into the United States. We should note that such immigration is also taking place around the globe: Russians enter Latvia illegally, Poles rush into Great Britain, and North Koreans settle in China. Let's look more closely at this problem in the United States—but with a twist—by focusing on the experience of the illegal immigrant. The Thinking Critically About Social Problems box on the next page should give you a different perspective.

The Future of the Problem

The future of food and population problems is murky. As we saw with the three projections of the U.S. population on Figure 13-10 (page 456), demographers cannot even agree what the future population of a given country will be, much less the future population of the world. With this caveat, let's plunge into the unknown.

The New Malthusian Viewpoint

THE PESSIMISTIC VIEW. If the New Malthusians are right, our future will bring wall-to-wall people. Do you think the life portrayed in the Global Glimpse box on page 466 is to be the fate of the world?

High Food Prices ■ If population outstrips food production, as the New Malthusians say it will, supply and demand will push the price of food upward. Some Americans

THINKING CRITICALLY About Social Problems

GOING NORTH: THE DREAM AND THE REALITY

Our news media are filled with accounts of the "invasion" of millions of Mexicans who thumb their nose at immigration laws, who fill jobs few others want, who work for so little they drive down the price of labor, who commit crimes here, and who demand citizenship despite their illegal status. But what is *their* experience? What is life like for them?

To Americans, it looks as though Mexicans, after crossing the border, disperse willy-nilly throughout the country. On the contrary, when Mexicans enter the United States most have a specific destination in mind, not just "someplace where I can find work." Some *migrant paths,* the routes between sending and receiving areas, are so established that they connect specific towns in Mexico with specific towns in the United States.

Nathan Thornburgh (2006), a reporter, studied the connection that has developed between Tuxpan, Mexico, and the Hamptons on New York's Long Island. It all started thirty years ago when a tourist from the Hamptons asked directions from a skinny Mexican kid, Mario Coria. The two struck up a conversation, and the tourist offered Mario a job as his gardener. He arranged for Mario to receive plane tickets and a visa.

Mario was a hard worker, and he prospered. He sent money back home and built a nice house. On his return visits, other men from Tuxpan asked for his help in getting to the United States. Their destination, of course, would be where Mario had experience, the Hamptons. A few friends found ways to cross the border and travel to Mario, who helped them find jobs. Over the years, the one grew into a dozen, and the dozen into the hundreds of Tuxpeños who now work in the Hamptons as gardeners, house cleaners, roofers, and day laborers.

You have to work hard to make it in the Hamptons. You have to line up on the street early in the morning and scramble to the cars that stop, ready to take any job anyone offers you—unless you're one of the lucky ones who had a relative come earlier and arrange a regular job for you.

It is crowded where you live. An entrepreneur has purchased a suburban house and placed a padlock on each of its four bedroom doors. You share one bedroom with two other men. The neighbors are angry that so many single men are living in one house, and they shout at you. Since they shout in English, you don't know what they are saying, but you do know that they are hostile.

You miss home. You knew everyone in Tuxpan, and life was so laid back. Some mornings you are so depressed that you can hardly force yourself out of bed.

But your dream keeps you going—to send enough money to your wife in Tuxpan so you can go back home and open your own little business. Maybe, even, if you work hard enough, you'll have enough money to build a pretty house, one with flowers and bright colors.

Right now, though, you've got to live with these other men and keep sending your wife enough money so she and the kids can keep eating.

You've heard the stories. Some of the wives back home have taken lovers while their husbands are up North. There's even a name for the guy, Sancho. And the running joke. "I've got to send more money to my wife. Sancho needs a new pair of shoes."

Your wife knows better. Your mother keeps you informed. But then there is that gnawing thought—would she really tell you, since she loves you and she knows how disturbed you would be? Then, too, she needs your remittances to survive, and if you came home the money would dry up.

And you know of the husbands here in the Hamptons who have found other women. After all, to achieve the dream, you have to be here for years, and with the increased surveillance at the border and that 700-mile-long wall being built, it has become more difficult to make the trip back home.

To make matters worse, you learn about some Tuxpeños who have achieved the dream. They've gone home and opened their businesses—and found there weren't enough customers to make a living.

To top it off, those who go home are seen as too American to be real Tuxpeños. Some neighbors even call them gringo.

You are caught in the middle. Too Mexican to be a gringo, and too gringo to be a Mexican. The dream of earning enough money to have a good life back home, though, keeps you going. It helps you get up in the morning, even though the dream recedes a bit each day.

FOR YOUR CONSIDERATION

The proposals to solve the problem of having millions of illegal immigrants in the United States range from hunting them all down and deporting them to granting amnesty to them all. What do you think we should do?

A Global Glimpse
WHERE WALL-TO-WALL MEANS PEOPLE

The Mong Kok section of Hong Kong may be the densest area on the face of the earth. Here, 200,000 people live in a bit more than half a square mile—a density rate of 300,000 people per square mile.

Officials have left a little strip of grass and a few wispy trees. People stand and stare at them. The trees are fenced off from the public.

How do the people feel about the crowding?

Winnie Choi, a hairdresser, says, "It's very crowded, but people like to live here because it's very convenient. It's a popular neighborhood." She adds that her family of five lived with two other families because her parents

A photo of Hong Kong, the focus of this box.

rented out two of the three rooms in their tiny apartment. Thirteen people shared one bathroom and a closet-sized kitchen. "But we didn't think we were crowded. The other families each stayed in their rooms, and we had ours."

Lee Chi-Kwong, a merchant, could move out of Mong Kok if he wanted to. But he stays. He says, "I don't mind crowds. Crowds mean prosperity."

When asked about crowding, some residents just gave a quizzical look. They had difficulty understanding what the interviewer was trying to get at.

Based on Basler 1988.

---

already find food expensive, but the burden on the Least Industrialized Nations will be greater. Already poor, and burdened by debt to the Most Industrialized Nations, they cannot afford to import much food.

More Famines ▪ If the New Malthusians are right, the famines of Africa are an omen of what is coming to other parts of the world. Millions of people will starve each year, and the world will face a flood of economic refugees. Neither the Least Industrialized Nations nor the Most Industrialized Nations will be willing to accept the stream of hundreds of thousands of poor, uneducated, culturally foreign people. To do so would deepen social tensions. Consequently, huge numbers of dislocated people will live in "temporary" refugee camps.

Riots, Revolutions, and Repression ▪ If efforts to stave off famine fail, or if there is insufficient food to feed the rural masses that are flocking to the cities in search of work and a better life, the Least Industrialized Nations will face riots and revolution. In response, these governments, controlled by their wealthy elites, will become more repressive. Because political and civil disorder can upset the global balance of power that the Most Industrialized Nations try desperately to control, these more powerful and wealthy nations may encourage such repression.

The Anti-Malthusian Viewpoint

THE OPTIMISTIC VIEW: THE FUTURE IS WHAT WE MAKE IT. The Anti-Malthusians, of course, foresee a different future. The idea that famines are inevitable if the world's population continues to grow is a bogeyman, they say. Such images are a scare tactic designed to get people to have fewer children. It is also a coldly calculated technique to raise money for political purposes (Simon 1981). The earth can support several times more people than it does now. Whether famines will be avoided, however, depends on political and economic arrangements. The future is what we make it.

TECHNOLOGY AND ABUNDANCE. Poorly managed, the earth's three natural systems (fishing grounds, forests, and grasslands) can collapse, losing much of their productivity and bringing terrible suffering to humanity. These are renewable resources, however, and, carefully managed, they can produce all that the world, even a growing one, will ever need. In the coming *biotech society*—the name some have given to the type of society that is presently emerging—bioengineering will produce pest-resistant plants that produce their own fertilizers. From gene splicing will come cereals that replace nitrogen in the soil, allowing farmers to bypass expensive petroleum-based fertilizers. We will produce low-fat cows and chickens that lay several eggs a day. Not only can the so-called inevitable cataclysm so widely touted by the New Malthusians be prevented, but the world will also be able to enjoy a future of abundance.

If any of this sounds unrealistic, we can note that the biotech future is already arriving. We have not just cloned animals, but we also have produced "designer animals," gene-spliced farm animals that produce more meat and milk. We even have a corn that makes its own insecticide (Kilman 2006). Consider what is on the drawing board (Elias 2001): tobacco that fights cancer and corn that fights herpes and is a contraceptive. Science fiction? The bioengineers don't think so. A few years ago, they were talking about developing goats that produce spider silk, as well as part-human animals that produce medicine. We now have them (Kristoff 2002; Osborne 2002).

The Long-Term Anti-Malthusian Viewpoint

THE FOURTH STAGE OF THE DEMOGRAPHIC TRANSITION: THE COMING POPULATION SHRINKAGE. If you want to peer into the future, look at the nations that have entered the fourth stage of the demographic transition. (This stage is illustrated on Figure 13-3 on page 439.) The populations of these nations have begun to shrink. The world's other nations will also enter this fourth stage; and, despite their current rapid population growth, they, too, will fill more coffins than cradles. As this process continues, the population of the world will reverse itself, and it will become smaller. When this occurs, we don't know at what point the world's population will stabilize.

UNBALANCED STAGES AND GLOBAL UPHEAVAL. Before this occurs, however, we will face a global realignment of nations which will bring the potential of global disorder. Consider the vexing dilemma facing the nations which will bring the fourth stage of the demographic transition. Because their birth rates are so low, they don't produce enough workers for their factories. Yet to maintain their standard of living, they need to keep those factories operating. Wanting those jobs—and waiting not so patiently—are masses of unemployed young people in the Least Industrialized Nations.

The Example of France ■ This situation is destined to bring conflict. Those who immigrate from the Least Industrialized Nations to the nations that have entered the fourth stage of the demographic transition bring with them customs that differ from their host nations. If the immigration is large, this can upset a society, as it has already begun to do in some European countries. Germany and France, for example, which have millions of workers from Turkey and other Muslim countries, are experiencing this kind of turmoil. Germany, mindful of the Holocaust and stepping tenderly on the world stage, remains quiet about the controversy. Without such historical baggage, the French are more vocal in their opposition to the "non-French" customs that the immigrants are bringing with them. French officials and politicians have spoken openly against Muslim women wearing veils in public, and they prohibit Muslim girls from wearing scarves in school. One political party, whose slogan is "France for the French," has even made anti-immigration its cornerstone. Within this context of hostility, Muslim youth throughout France have rioted.

PRONATALIST POLICIES. Fearful of a shrinking population and the arrival of more immigrants that don't share French culture, the French government has initiated **pronatalist**

The riots by Muslim immigrants in France, protesting their treatment as second-class citizens, also included an anti-American element. This is what was left of a McDonald's restaurant in a Paris suburb.

policies, policies that encourage women to bear children. It is trying to develop attitudes that favor higher fertility: If French women bear more children, there will be more French to operate the offices and factories. It is too late. Several million immigrants from Northern Africa have become French citizens. If the French government offers women benefits for giving birth, these benefits must also go to the "new" French. This will increase births among a group that already has a high birth rate, a group that is feared by the traditional French.

THE LONG-TERM FUTILITY OF PRONATALIST POLICIES. With the factors that lower the birth rate firmly in place around the globe, it is unlikely that social policies can have anything more than a short-term effect on a country's fertility. Facing a shrinking workforce amidst the increasing needs of a growing elderly population, accompanied by a possible wave of culturally distinct immigrants, countries in the fourth stage of the demographic transition are trying to increase their birth rates. To see the obstacles that these policies confront, consider Sweden, featured in the Global Glimpse box on the next page.

THE ROLE OF IMMIGRANTS. Earlier in this chapter, you saw why it is perilous to predict the future of populations. In addition to uncertain birth rates, a nation's policy toward immigrants can change. A nation may turn inward and exile immigrants, or it may welcome them. If the United States did not welcome immigrants, its population would be stagnant or shrinking. Only its million immigrants (or two million, counting those who enter the country illegally) a year keep it growing. The United States, however, is huge, one of the world's largest land masses, and as we have seen, it is relatively unpopulated. Perhaps only Russia and Canada face similar conditions.

Which Will It Be?

Will the earth be filled with so many people that there is not enough food for them all, with famine and suffering stalking the earth, as the New Malthusians anticipate? Or are the Anti-Malthusians right, and without curtailing population growth, the world's nations will be able to manage their resources, feed and clothe themselves, and provide a

A Global Glimpse
THE LOPSIDED SOCIETY: PRONATALISM IN SWEDEN

"What is happening now has simply never happened before in the history of the world," said Nicholas Eberstadt, a demographer (Specter 1998). Never before has a country's birth rate plunged so low that its population shrank. But this is now happening in several European countries.

Is a birth rate too low to replenish a population really new in history? We have had instances in the past when a country's leaders thought that their nation had too few children. Usually this was because many young men had been killed in war, and they wanted new soldiers to replace them. Officials would then initiate *pronatalism*, policies that favor or promote births. They were successful. Men and women responded to the rewards and had more children.

Today's situation is different. Populations are shrinking not because of war but because women are bearing so few children that they aren't replacing the people who die. What is happening in Sweden, one of these countries, helps us understand some of the implications of the fourth stage of the demographic transition—and why pronatalism is failing.

Reasons that Swedish couples, like this one, are choosing to have only one child or to remain childless are discussed in the text. Countries throughout Europe are experiencing similar low birth rates.

If any country is pronatalistic, it is Sweden. Health care for mothers and children is free. Maternity centers offer free health checks and free courses in preparation for childbirth. When a child is born, the parents are eligible for fifteen months' leave of absence with pay. They can divide the leave between them any way they want, as long as the father gets at least one of the months. When a child is sick, either parent can stay home to care for it and receive full pay for missed work—up to sixty days a year per child (The Swedish Institute 1992; Froman 1994; Bernhardt and Goldscheider 2001).

Births should be booming, families growing larger, the baby carriage industry prosperous. Instead, Sweden is becoming a lopsided society, one in which there are more old people than young, one in which there will not be enough workers to pay for the health care and pensions of the elderly.

The culprit? It is prosperity and freedom. Swedish women are staying in school longer, putting more emphasis on careers, marrying later—and having fewer children.

Like the Germans, Italians, Spanish, and other Europeans, the Swedes are developing different ideas about children and about what they want out of life. Here are some of their comments:

"People want their freedom. They see children as a burden, as an inconvenience."

"It's a sacrifice to have a child."

"Children cost more than they used to. Today you have to bring them to the pool, and you need to get a nanny, and they have to learn a foreign language. Children have more needs. Parents just didn't think of all these things before."

Ninni Lundblad, a biologist who works in Stockholm, said, "Did your parents sit down with a spreadsheet and figure out whether they could afford to have two or three children?"

No, they didn't. They just had them. But Ninni Lundblad, who said this so derisively, has no children (Specter 1998).

So why don't Sweden's generous pronatalist policies work? Perhaps this statement by Jan Delanor of Stockholm best sums it up:

"I am supposed to have an extra child to help the system? Nonsense. I'll have a child if and when it makes sense to me, not because the government thinks it's a good idea."

Swedes are finding so much more that makes sense to them—education, travel, career, money, spending time with friends. All these things come before having children.

I wonder who is going to live in Sweden after the Swedes are gone? The government is wondering, too—as they anxiously look over their shoulders at the vast Muslim migration into Europe.

high standard of living for everyone? Could the population problem of the future actually be not enough people, that the governments that now despair over too many children will be offering incentives for women to give birth?

I have no crystal ball. Like others, I must await the outcome. It certainly appears that the world has the potential to meet its nutritional needs, but this would require that the Most Industrialized Nations cooperate to meet the challenge. Perhaps they will rise to the occasion.

SUMMARY

1. *Demographers* study the size, composition, growth, and distribution of human populations. They disagree as to why Europe's population surged after 1750. Some cite improved public health, others a change in diet.

2. In 1798, Thomas Malthus predicted that the world's population would outstrip its food supply. His prediction is still controversial. The New Malthusians fear that the population of the world is entering the latter stages of an *exponential growth curve,* and most of this growth is in the nations least able to afford it. They favor an immediate cutback in population. The Anti-Malthusians claim that the world is producing more than enough food; the problem is the poor distribution of food due to political arrangements.

3. By applying symbolic interactionism, we can see why the birth rate is higher in the Least Industrialized Nations. There children are viewed as a blessing from God, they give the parents status in the present, and they provide security for the future.

4. By applying functionalism, we can see that exporting medicine and public health techniques from the Most Industrialized Nations was a *latent dysfunction* for the Least Industrialized Nations. It created problems by upsetting the balance between their birth and death rates.

5. Conflict theorists stress that the hunger that some nations experience is due to food politics, political and economic arrangements that favor the Most Industrialized Nations. Food politics creates and intensifies problems in the Least Industrialized Nations.

6. Demographers who take a New Malthusian position stress the pressures being placed on the earth's three natural systems: fishing grounds, forests, and grasslands.

Two dangers are the threat of famine as the result of our dependence on specialized strains of grains and the intensification of natural disasters. Even if we attain zero population growth, because of *population momentum* it would still take fifty to seventy years for the world's population to stabilize.

7. Demographers who take an Anti-Malthusian position argue that the earth can support many more people. Food production is outpacing population growth, fewer people are dying from famines, and much land remains uncultivated. A growing population can spur us to greater productivity.

8. Because of many cross trends and unexpected human action, demographers cannot forecast population growth accurately.

9. The United States is not overpopulated, but Americans place relatively great pressures on the earth's resources.

10. The New Malthusians recommend social policies to curb population growth. The Anti-Malthusians advocate policies that encourage (or do not discourage) population growth. Both sides agree that we should stimulate agricultural development. Exporting Western agricultural techniques to the Least Industrialized Nations is not viable, because it requires a vast support system that these nations cannot afford.

11. The New and Anti-Malthusians envision different futures. The New Malthusians anticipate widespread hunger in the Least Industrialized Nations, which may lead to more repression. The Anti-Malthusians stress that the world's nations hold the potential for meeting human needs, that one day the world will face the problem of population shrinkage.

KEY TERMS

1. Do you think the New Malthusians or the Anti-Malthusians are right? Explain.
2. Should the United States use its foreign policy to change the social and economic policies of other countries?
   - If yes, under what conditions and for what purposes? Under what conditions would you change your mind?
   - If no, why not? Under what conditions would you change your mind?
   - If yes, under what conditions and for what purposes? Under what conditions would you change your mind?
3. Should Russia, Germany, France, Iran, Iraq, or any other nation use its foreign policy to change the social and economic policies of the United States?

- If no, why not? Under what conditions would you change your mind?
- If your answer to this question is different from your answer to question 2, why the differences?

4. Which perspective (symbolic interactionism, functionalism, or conflict theory) do you think best explains the world's problems of population and food? Explain.
5. What is your reaction to Pentti Linkola's suggestion (on page 461) that we annihilate most of the human race to save the rest of the world? If such a policy were enacted, who would choose who lives and who dies?

CHAPTER 14

The Environmental Crisis

I hadn't been teaching very long at Southern Illinois University, Edwardsville, when I decided that I wanted to move to a farm. Living in a trailer in a low-rent, working-class mobile home park and driving a junker meant that for the first time in my adult life I had a money surplus.

I advertised for a farm in the county papers. The third one I visited was exactly what I was looking for. It was remote ("in the boonies," as the phrase goes), 165 acres of trees and pastures, with its own pond for swimming and fishing. (The pond was also my water source.) At $150 an acre, I knew I couldn't go wrong. My fellow professors were paying as much for a house as I would for the entire farm.

Being a town boy, I had a lot to learn about farm life. Eventually, I owned a dog, a horse, a sheep, and twenty-five head of cattle. My inexperience led to several humorous events (I can laugh at them now): the sharpie farmer sticking me with the runt of his herd, the horse I bought refusing to let me ride her, the cattle breaking through the fence and running away.

One of my most insightful lessons in farm life came one Saturday morning when I went to a cattle auction. Area farmers bring their excess cattle to these auctions, and fellow farmers—and meat companies, as it turned out—bid on them.

Standing amidst men wearing hats emblazoned with "Allis-Chalmers," "John Deere," and "Nutra-Feeds,"

> **Them's red-tagged, boys.**

I realized that I was entering a new culture. I was enjoying the moment, lost in reverie as I observed the auctioneer and the bidding. When one group of animals was brought into the ring, the auctioneer said, "Them's red-tagged, boys. Them's red-tagged."

I asked a man standing next to me what that meant. He said, "You can't buy 'em. They've got some disease. You can't take 'em back to your farm."

I nodded, then asked, "What happens to 'em, then?"

He replied, "Only guys from the meat packing plant can bid on 'em."

I let this sink in, relieved that I didn't eat much sandwich meat.

Then I recalled something my grandfather had told me when I was a child. He farmed on Minnesota's brutally cold Canadian border, and to earn money to buy his farm he had worked at a meat packing plant in St. Paul. I noticed that he always refused sandwich meat and had asked him about it. He said that it was because of what he had seen at the meat packing plant. He mentioned guys spitting into the meat.

I suppose I was too young for my grandfather to explain his revulsion, but I think I felt something similar on that Saturday morning. Animals too diseased to live on farms were judged by our government perfectly acceptable to be turned into lunch meat.

The Problem in Sociological Perspective

To better understand today's environmental problem, let's begin with a glimpse of the distant past.

Environmental Destruction in the Past: The Myth of the Noble Savage

THE MYTH. In early history, so the story goes, humans lived in harmony with their environment. They considered themselves one with the water, earth, sky, animals, and plants.

Many of our ideas of the past are shrouded in myth and painted in idyllic terms. An example is the view that early Native Americans lived in harmonic balance with nature. The text explains why this view is a myth. Today's situation is similar. When I visited an Indian settlement on an Arizona mesa, I peered behind the houses. There, at the bottom of the ravine, lay heaps of garbage—easier to dump down the hillside than to discard properly.

Unlike people today, who destroy their environment for short-sighted gains, people used to use earth's resources wisely. Their presence did not disrupt the earth's natural systems. An old woman of the Wintu tribe explained:

The White people never cared for land or deer or bear. When we Indians kill meat, we eat it all up. When we dig roots, we make little holes. . . . We shake down acorns and pine nuts. We don't chop down trees. We only use dead wood. But the White people plow up the ground, pull up the trees, kill everything. . . . How can the spirit of the earth like the White man?. . . Everywhere the White man has touched it, it is sore. (Lee 1959:163)

This view evokes a warm feeling about the good old days, some primitive past that is a part of us all. The problem is that it just isn't true. Sociologist William Burch (1971) called the image of "noble savages" a myth. He said that the social sciences should stop perpetuating romanticized views of the past and set the matter straight.

Okay. Let's try to do that.

EARLY HUMANS AND THE EXTINCTION OF ANIMALS. Humans have been destroying their environment for as long as they have existed. Carnivorous kangaroos, giant lizards, and horned turtles the size of automobiles disappeared from Australia about the time that humans arrived there. Environmental historians believe that humans destroyed these animals by setting fire to trees and shrubs to keep warm or to clear the land (Hotz 1999). It is likely that the same thing happened in North America, that its early inhabitants burned forests to help them in hunting and to control mosquitoes, even just to watch the flames. The result: Prehistoric hunters apparently wiped out three-fourths of the animals that weighed more than 100 pounds (Lutz 1959; Martin 1967; Hotz 1999). If so, this would mean that they extinguished more species of large animals than humans have in all the years since they invented writing and started to record their lives.

THE DESTRUCTION OF ENTIRE CIVILIZATIONS. Some of the past human destruction of the environment may have been so extensive that it brought down entire civilizations.

The Mesopotamians ▪ In the lush river basin of the Tigris and Euphrates, in what is now Iraq, the Mesopotamians developed a highly advanced civilization. Its fall has usually been attributed to invaders, but its destruction could have come from abuse of the environment (Ozturk et al. 2004). Their extensive irrigation system provided abundant food, allowing their civilization to flourish. Their irrigation system, however, did not have drainage. As water evaporated, it left the remaining water salty. Over the centuries, as the water seeped into the earth, the underground water table rose, making the land too salty for crops. Eventually, agriculture collapsed and, with it, so did the Mesopotamian civilization.

The Mayans ▪ In what is today Guatemala and Yucatán, another civilization may have met a similar fate. The Mayans developed their culture over seventeen centuries, reaching their peak in agriculture, architecture, and science around 900 A.D. Then, within decades, 90 percent of the Mayans disappeared, their population dropping from about five million to fewer than half a million. The cause may have been environmental destruction. Samples from lake beds indicate heavy soil erosion. As their population increased, the Mayans cleared the land of trees. The topsoil washed from the denuded land, and with it went the agricultural productivity on which their civilization depended (Fernandez et al. 2005).

The Anasazi ■ The story is the same for the Anasazi in what is now Arizona and New Mexico (Budiansky 1987). The Anasazi built roads, an irrigation system, and pueblos of stone and masonry. Some pueblos were four or five stories high and had up to 800 rooms. As they developed their way of life, the Anasazi cut down so many trees in the canyons that they had to travel fifty miles or more to gather wood for fuel. Having stripped the forest beyond its ability to replenish itself, their civilization collapsed.

The Tragedy of the Commons

Far from being thoughtful conservationists, then, good caretakers of their environment, earlier humans were like us. They, too, destroyed thoughtlessly. Because today's civilizations are larger, however, our capacity for destruction is greater. Many hope that there is another difference, too—that, having knowledge about the destruction of the environment on which our civilizations depend, we will act on this warning before it is too late.

Unfortunately, self-interest (or selfishness, if you prefer) works against the logic of environmental preservation. Biologist Garrett Hardin (1968) used to tell a parable known as *the tragedy of the commons*.

> Let us picture a pasture open to everyone. The number of cattle exactly matches the amount of available grass. Each herdsman, however, will seek to maximize his own gain. He thinks to himself: "If I add a cow to my herd, I will receive all the proceeds from the sale of this additional animal. The little overgrazing that this extra animal causes will be shared by all the other herdsmen."
>
> This herdsman adds another animal to his herd. This works, so he eventually adds another . . . and another. And, for the same reason, the other herdsmen who share the commons do the same. Each is part of a system that rewards individuals for increasing the size of their herds. And therein lies the tragedy of the commons. The pasture is limited, and additional stress eventually causes it—and the civilization that depends on it—to fail. As each pursues his or her own interest, all rush to their collective ruin.

IN SUM An irony of human existence is that our efforts to improve life can destroy the very environment on which life depends. Our civilization's contribution to environmental destruction is another event in a series that stretches back into prehistory, for as we have seen even the ancients confronted the dilemma of the commons. Today, however—with our new technology, incessant demands for an ever-rising standard of living, and more people on earth than ever before—we have magnified our destructive capacity.

The Scope of the Problem

To understand the scope of the problem, we must focus on interconnections. Because all of us are part of a worldwide, interdependent system, we need to perceive the environment in interconnected, global terms.

"Everything Is Connected to Everything Else."

PERCEIVING INTERCONNECTIONS. To perceive these interconnections is to see how even the "little things," such as local events, are part of a global problem. Consider this little example:

> Although my grandfather, whom I mentioned in the opening vignette, lived on a remote farm in northern Minnesota, his actions had global consequences. He sprayed his fields with DDT, the practice at the time. The excess DDT, a virulent pesticide, would run from his fields into a creek. The creek ran into a local river. That river led to a river that led to a river that ran into the Mississippi. From there, the chemicals flowed into New Orleans, helping to give its residents higher than average rates of cancer. From there, the chemicals flowed into the Atlantic, where they affected other nations.

None of us, then, is isolated. The connections between us and others are not always apparent, but we all are part of an interrelated system that encompasses humanity, technology, and the environment. To think in terms of individual small units ignores this encompassing reality.

THREATENING THE PLANET. Human actions are upsetting our planet's precarious balance. The population explosion we discussed in the last chapter, the industrialization emphasized throughout this text, and the drive for higher living standards are stark examples. If we deplete our natural resources, as some civilizations of the past did, our civilization, too, will collapse. This is the fear of some *ecologists*, scientists who study **ecology**—the relationship between living things and their environment.

For many, the primary threat to our environment and humanity's future is pollution. We all know what pollution is, but it is hard to define. A common definition of pollution is the accumulation in the air, water, and land of substances harmful to living things. This is a good definition, but for our purposes we want to look at pollution in *social* terms. Like all *social* problems, it is people who say that something is polluted, that they do not like what they see, and that they want to change it. Consequently, we can define **pollution** as the presence of substances that interfere with socially desired uses of the air, water, land, or food (Davies and Davies 1975).

Although pollution by humans is not new—it occurred when the first fires were lit for warmth, cooking, or visual delight—it has intensified beyond anything the world has ever seen. The world's industrial giants continue to be the primary polluters, but joining what some fear is a rush to destroy the world's environment are those nations that are industrializing rapidly. The two most significant examples are China and India, the world's two largest countries. Their headlong rush to industrialize is placing considerable additional strain on the earth's fragile environment.

LEAVING A LEGACY OF DEATH. As the tragedy of the commons reveals, the depletion of resources is due to shortsighted self-interest. So, too, is pollution. Ideology makes no difference. In the former Soviet Union, pollution was treated as a state secret (Feshbach 1992). Scientists and journalists could not even mention pollution in public. To demonstrate against pollution, even peacefully, could bring a prison term. With protest stifled, no environmental protection laws, and rigid production quotas, pollution was rampant.

Humans have been treating their environment as though it were garbage bag. The bill for the wanton destruction is coming due.

Citizens of Russia and those of the former Soviet states have been left a legacy of death—from abandoned factories that used to manufacture chemical and germ weapons to billions of pounds of nuclear waste that was simply dumped into rivers or holes in the ground (Garelik 1996; Miller 1999; Gessen 2001). Is the term "legacy of death" too strong? Consider this: Birth defects in Russia have jumped, and life expectancy has dropped. While lifestyle factors such as excessive alcohol consumption are involved, so is pollution. The effects are so devastating that the average Russian man dies at age 58, compared to age 75 in the rest of Europe. For Russian women it is 72, compared to 82 for the rest of Europe ("WHO/Europe" 2006).

How do we avoid a legacy of death? We humans are intelligent beings, and examples like this can motivate us to find the tools to avoid such lethal consequences of our actions. The materials in this chapter can contribute to this effort.

Looking at the Problem Theoretically

Each of our three theoretical perspectives helps us to understand the environmental crisis. Using symbolic interactionism, we will examine how the environment became a social problem. Through functionalism, we will focus on the interdependence of people and their environment. We will use conflict theory to examine the clashing interests of environmentalists and those who pollute.

Symbolic Interactionism

How did the environment become a social problem? To us, it seems obvious that the environment is endangered. On a simple, everyday level, for example, almost everyone seems to be aware of water pollution, making bottled water one of the most popular items in our supermarkets and convenience stores. On a broader level, people who have never seen a tropical rain forest are upset that they are being cut down to harvest lumber and to clear land for cattle and crops. Around the world, people are bothered by the harm that is done to whales, seals, dolphins, and owls and by the loss of plants and animals whose names they can't even pronounce. A worldwide protest movement has evolved.

But it was not always this way. Little more than a generation ago, people rarely thought of the environment as a problem. Let's find out what happened. How did the environment become a social problem?

OBJECTIVE CONDITIONS BUT LITTLE SUBJECTIVE CONCERN. As we saw in Chapter 1, even if objective conditions are widespread and harmful, they are not automatically considered social problems. Objective conditions must be translated into subjective concerns. For the environment, this translation did not come easily. In the 1800s, when hundreds of steel plants in the United States polluted the air, no one considered this a social problem. Ever since the automobile was invented, people have been discarding worn-out tires in gullies and creeks, but only recently have these actions been regarded as part of a social problem. The same is true of the disappearance of animal species, which began millennia ago: Many European Americans welcomed the near extinction of the bison, seeing it as a way to defeat the Indians. The passenger pigeon, during its mass annual migration, used to darken the skies for days. Its extinction in 1914 was seen as unfortunate—an interesting bit of history, perhaps—but not tragic.

THE GROWTH OF SUBJECTIVE CONCERNS. How did environmental decay and destruction become part of a pressing, worldwide social problem? That is, how did subjective concerns grow? Let's go back to the 1960s, when the environment became a hot topic. This period was characterized by high social activism of college students, who adopted the environment as one of their concerns. Students began to participate in environmental protests, and "earth days" began on college campuses. This is significant, but it doesn't

Humans have destroyed many animal species, extinguishing some without remorse. Few elephants are left in the wild. Poachers hunt them for their tusks, selling the ivory on the black market. Soon, the only elephants left will be those in zoos, circuses, and on state preserves (as in this one in the Kruger National Park, South Africa).

answer our question. How did this high subjective concern—marked by activism and demonstrations—come about? This is just what sociologists Clay Schoenfeld, Robert Meier, and Robert Griffin (1979) began to wonder. Let's see what they discovered.

The Conservation Movement ■ As these sociologists looked through the historical records, they found that the 1960s were not the first time that Americans had become concerned about the environment. The issue had emerged earlier—peaking around 1900. At that time, Theodore Roosevelt, who was the president of the United States from 1901 to 1909, spearheaded a conservation movement. Roosevelt was an avid hunter, and he had grown concerned that the wildlife he liked to kill was disappearing from our wilderness areas (Morrison et al. 1972; Gale 1972). In one of the ironies of history, Roosevelt, who liked killing animals so much that he also roamed Africa in search of elephants, tigers, and lions, supported bills that established our national park system, setting aside millions of acres for public use.

From Conservation to Environment ■ Obviously, there is a vast difference between conserving wilderness areas to make certain that hunters do not run out of moving targets and concern about the quality of our food, air, and water. How, then, did "conservation" change to "environmental concern"? Schoenfeld, Meier, and Griffin found that the change began with professionals and ended with an aroused public. Here are the five stages they uncovered:

1. *Professionals* were the first to become troubled by the environment. Knowing that we depend on natural resources, some professionals concluded that the situation was crucial. In 1959, geographers began to write journal articles about environmental problems and to present papers at their conventions.
2. *Interest groups* then began to form around specific issues.
3. *Government agencies,* aroused by the activities of the interest groups, began to issue environmental reports.
4. The *news media* discovered the issue. At first, reporters had difficulty understanding environmental issues. It was especially difficult for them to communicate the idea that people, resources, and technology are all part of a single, larger system. They tended to see things in terms of unrelated, flashy news items, such as an oil spill or a train wreck that spewed contaminants. As reporters began to understand the basic environmental principle that "everything is connected to everything else," they began to connect events.

5. *The public* was aroused by the stories in the mass media. As the media gave more coverage to what today are called environmental issues, three stories were especially significant. The first was the publication of Rachel Carson's *The Silent Spring,* in 1962. Focusing on the dangers of pesticides, this blockbuster alerted Americans to environmental hazards. The book, however, focused on a single-issue and didn't lead the public or the news media to explore the interconnections among environmental events. Then, in 1969 an oil well erupted off the coast of Santa Barbara, California. Each day for weeks 20,000 gallons of oil poured into the water. Americans were riveted by this environmental disaster as national headlines reported the oil's slow drift to the coast. When the oil finally hit Santa Barbara and blackened twenty miles of beautiful beaches, people were outraged (Davies and Davies 1975). Later that same year came the single most effective environmental message of the century—the view from the moon of earth. This helped make the public aware that we live on a fragile, finite "spaceship." With that first glimpse of us from the "outside," the public became much more aware that we all are partners on a small planet.

Shown in this 1910 photo is Teddy Roosevelt, president of the United States from 1901–1909. Roosevelt, who headed a conservation movement, loved to kill "big game." The text explains how "conserving" wilderness areas to prevent hunters from running out of moving targets changed to today's environmental concerns.

IN SUM Symbolic interactionists focus on the symbols that people use to communicate with one another, how those symbols develop and how they are used to create and maintain our ideas of reality. The social problem of the environment did not appear in a social vacuum. Rather, it is a "social creation." Over the course of the five stages summarized here, people's perceptions of the environment changed fundamentally. Professionals, reporters, and the general public began to see individual events as interconnected parts of the same problem. This changed perception has transformed our opinions of ourselves, our relationship with other living things, and even what we consider to be our place in the universe.

This change in how we symbolize ourselves and our world is still in process: We are still having a difficult time connecting what we do now with a distant future.

Functionalism

THE ESSENCE OF FUNCTIONALISM: INTERCONNECTIONS. The idea that everything is connected to everything else is becoming part of our intuitive understanding. We all know that though we are individuals, we are part of a larger group. We also know that the small groups to which we each belong are parts of a larger society and that our nation is part of a global network. Slowly, we are coming to grasp that we all are part of a global social system, that what each of us does—whether individual, group, or nation—affects the others.

This picture of humanity forming a global network is a functional analysis. Each unit is part of a larger structure, with the activities of one part having functional or dysfunctional consequences for the other parts. The more technical term for this interconnected system in the environment is **ecosystem**—all life on the planet is interconnected in the finely balanced cycles that occur on the dynamic layer of the earth's surface.

THE ECOSYSTEM. Both biologists and sociologists who work on environmental problems emphasize the interconnections between people and the earth's resources. No matter where we live on this globe, we need air, water, and soil to survive. Our survival depends on this ecosystem. Green plants produce oxygen for human and animal life. Plants, animals, and microorganisms purify the water in lakes and streams. Biological processes in the soil provide food and fuel. Anything that disrupts this interconnected system—the earth's ecosystem—threatens these finely balanced cycles. The major offender in disrupting the ecosystem has been industrialization.

FUNCTIONS AND DYSFUNCTIONS OF INDUSTRIALIZATION. Humans are intelligent and highly adaptable. We have multiplied and expanded into every habitable region of the globe. Our cultures have permitted us to adapt to mountains and plains, to deserts and oceans, even to steamy jungles and ice-bound regions. Our intelligence has allowed us to dominate the earth. We have domesticated plants and animals. To improve our lives, we have harnessed the energy of animals and rivers, the sun and the wind.

It was the steam engine, though, that allowed us to harness energy on a scale unknown in history. As we saw in Chapter 11, the Industrial Revolution that followed its invention created countless new jobs and great wealth. Because of this revolution, the average person today enjoys a standard of living that previously was attained only by the wealthy.

Industrialization, however, also brought severe dysfunctional consequences for the earth's ecosystem. Production of our material wealth damaged the air, water, and soil on which our existence depends. Our frenetic drive for a higher material standard of living has produced highly toxic industrial wastes, which we have strewn into almost every corner of the earth. In another irony of life, the expansion of our industrial systems to create a better life has damaged the environment that allows us life in the first place.

| IN SUM | Functionalists focus on how the parts of a social system are interconnected. As with earlier civilizations such as the Mesopotamians, the Mayans, and the Anasazi, our economic and political systems depend on a fragile ecosystem that is mostly below the level of our awareness. Although we still have problems conceptualizing it, we have begun to think in terms of our being part of a complex, living machine called the environment. If our ecosystem fails, our society will collapse.

Conflict Theory

Opposing sides are lining up on environmental issues. Some view us as being on the verge of catastrophe, and they act politically to protect the environment. Others resist what they consider arbitrary and irrational controls over their right to pollute. No one ever defends dirty water or filthy air, of course, for clean air and water have become like motherhood and apple pie. Nevertheless, some groups fight efforts to reduce pollution. Let's look at this conflict.

ON ONE SIDE: ENVIRONMENTAL GROUPS. On one side are the groups organized to fight what they view as environmental threats. These environmental action groups consist of such organizations as Greenpeace, the National Wildlife Federation, the Izaak Walton League, the Sierra Club, Americans for Safe Food, and Earth First! Here is a statement from the Izaak Walton League that expresses this position:

> There is no justification for water pollution. The people of the United States are entitled to wholesome surface and groundwater, usable for all human needs. At a minimum, surface water should be of suitable quality for both recreational contact and for the protection and propagation of fish and wildlife. . . . The public goal should be maximal removal of pollutants from all waters. (Izaak Walton . . . 2000:11)

The environmental action groups have become a powerful political force. With chapters across the nation, these groups maintain lobbyists in Washington and state capitals, they promote legislation aggressively, and they hire lawyers to fight environmental cases in the courts. Many politicians support their efforts.

ON THE OTHER SIDE: POLLUTERS. Other groups oppose pollution control. At their core are the industrial polluters. Their dilemma is obvious. Pollution control is expensive and adds nothing to the value of their products. Manufacturers in the Most Industrialized Nations must compete with businesses that are located in the Least Industrialized Nations. Manufacturers in these nations enjoy not only the advantage of low-cost labor, but also the additional edge of not having to pay for pollution controls in the manufacturing process.

Manufacturers in the Most Industrialized nations can't take a public stand in favor of pollution, of course. But they know how to work politicians behind the scenes. They, too, lobby in Washington and the state capitals—and they have deep pockets, always an allure for politicians. As the Technology and Social Problems box on the next page illustrates, in some instances the polluters even have enough political clout to get laws passed that allow them to profit from their own pollution.

The polluters also hire lawyers who specialize in finding loopholes in pollution controls. Consider the automobile industry:

> In 1951, when it was discovered that automobiles were the major cause of smog in Los Angeles, the suggestion was made to develop electric cars. The auto industry formed a committee to study this proposal. The White House stacked the committee with representatives from the auto and oil industries. Their "surprising" conclusion: a recommendation against research on electric vehicles. (Davies and Davies 1975)

The automobile industry's fight against pollution controls and alternative transportation—which continues today—illustrates a basic principle of conflict theory: that society is composed of competing groups whose interests often collide. It isn't just the interests of business and the public that collide, however. The interests of one business group can also conflict with those of another. Here is an obvious example:

> While the car manufacturers were opposing the control of automobile emissions, another group of manufacturers tried to pass laws that would require pollution control devices. This group was made up of the businesses that manufacture the pollution control equipment. For them, the more regulation the better—more stringent laws mean more profit.

A SPECIAL CONSEQUENCE: ENVIRONMENTAL INJUSTICE. Conflict and unequal power have led to a situation that sociologists call **environmental injustice**—the fact that pollution is more likely to hurt minorities and the poor (Ramo 2003; Stolz and Wald 2006). This is because polluting industries locate where land is cheaper, places where the wealthy do not live. As a result, low-income communities, often inhabited by minorities, are more likely to be exposed to pollution. Sociologists have studied, formed, and joined environmental justice groups that fight to stop polluting plants and to block construction of polluting industries.

IN SUM As conflict theorists examine environmental problems, they look at the groups whose interests are opposed to one another. The efforts of environmentalists to eliminate what they see as dangers to the public welfare conflict with what other groups see as their inherent right—to make profits regardless of pollution. Those who campaign to develop what they consider to be a more livable, healthy, even sane society run head on into the interests of powerful groups who see the cure as worse than the illness. This basic conflict runs throughout the environmental crisis.

Research Findings

How badly has our environment deteriorated? To answer this question, we will first examine the pollution of our air, land, water, and food. Then we will look at energy and resources. Finally, we will consider whether the whole matter is exaggerated.

Air Pollution

> A mixture of fog and smoke settled over Donora, Pennsylvania, during the last five days of October 1948. By Sunday, October 31, wind and rain finally cleared the smog.
> Of the 12,300 people who lived in this steel mill town, about half (5,910) became sick. Another 1,440 were "severely affected." Seventeen died.

Technology and Social Problems

HOW TO GET PAID TO POLLUTE: CORPORATE WELFARE AND BIG WELFARE BUCKS

Welfare is one of the most controversial topics in the United States. It arouses the ire of wealthy and middle-class Americans, who view the poor who collect welfare as parasites. But have you heard about *corporate welfare*?

Corporate welfare refers to handouts given to corporations. A state may reduce a company's taxes if it will locate within the state or remain if it has threatened to leave. A state may even provide land and factories at bargain prices. The reason: jobs.

Corporate welfare even goes to companies that foul the land, water, and air. Borden Chemicals in Louisiana has buried hazardous wastes without a permit and released clouds of hazardous chemicals so thick that to protect drivers, the police have sometimes had to shut down the highway that runs near the plant. Borden even contaminated the groundwater beneath its plant, threatening the aquifer that provides drinking water for residents of Louisiana and Texas.

Borden's pollution has cost the company dearly: $3.6 million in fines, $3 million to clean up the groundwater and $400,000 for local emergency response units. That's a hefty $7 million. But if we consider corporate welfare, the company didn't make out so badly. Its $15 million in reduced and canceled property taxes have brought Borden a net gain of $8 million (Bartlett and Steele 1998). And that's not counting the savings the company racked up by not having to properly dispose of its toxic wastes in the first place.

Louisiana has added a novel twist to corporate welfare. It offers an incentive to help start-up companies. This itself isn't novel; the owners of that little "mom-and-pop" grocery store on your corner may have gotten some benefits when they first opened. Louisiana's twist is in what it counts as a start-up operation. You might have even heard of one of these little start-up companies. It is called Exxon Corporation (now Exxon Mobil, the largest corporation in the United States, which in 2006 posted the largest quarterly profits of any U.S. company ever). Although Exxon opened for business about 125 years ago (under a different name and before multiple mergers), it had $213 million in property taxes canceled under this start-up program. Another little company that the state figured could use a nudge

Near Baton Rouge, Louisiana.

to help get started was Shell Oil Company, which had $140 million slashed from its taxes (Bartlett and Steele 1998). Then there were a few other mom-and-pop operations: International Paper, Dow Chemical, Union Carbide, Boise Cascade, Georgia Pacific, and another tiny one called Procter & Gamble.

Of course, you can always improve welfare programs. Can you imagine what a welfare program would be like if the recipients of welfare got the chance to design them? You can be certain that they would come up with some interesting ideas. Consider this one:

> Let's suppose that poor people were burning their old tires, fouling the air all around them, and the state said: "We know that we can't stop you from burning tires, so we'll give you a certificate for each tire that you don't burn. Other people want to burn tires, so you can make money by selling these certificates to them, giving them the right to burn a tire for each one that you don't burn."

This would be nonsense.

Yet this is just what U.S. businesses have arranged. When a treaty was negotiated in Kyoto, Japan, to reduce emissions of greenhouse gases, U.S. industries hit on a novel way to turn pollution on its head and reap billions of dollars. They proposed a new corporate welfare law. In this one, the government would issue credits to companies that reduce their emissions early—and even give them credits for reductions that took place years before the treaty. The companies could then sell the credits for billions of dollars to companies that didn't reduce their emissions, allowing them to continue to pollute (Cushman 1999). Now that's a great way to clean up—without cleaning up.

Front-page news stories compared Donora to the Meuse Valley in Belgium, where 60 people died in 1930. Both were heavily industrialized, and both had a **thermal inversion,** a layer of cold air sealing in a lower layer of warm air. Thermal inversions trap smoke, exhaust, and particles.

By Tuesday, November 2, most of Donora's dead were buried. The residents' reactions sound hauntingly familiar. The local doctor described the deaths as murder. An air pollution expert from a nearby university said the lungs of the people in the valley had suffered chronic damage. The superintendent of the steel factory, however, said, "I can't conceive how our plant has anything to do with the condition. There has been no change in the process we use since 1915." The workers, who saw the dense smoke and fog as part of their way of life, said, "That smoke coming out of those stacks is putting bread and butter on our tables." And most of the public shrugged their shoulders and went about their business. (Bowen 1972)

A few years later, in 1952, a "killer smog" settled on London. In just five days, 4,000 people were dead (Thorsheim 2004). People became fearful. Slowly, facts about air pollution emerged. Air pollution is essentially a poison that accumulates in the human body. Besides causing eye, nose, and throat irritations, it can cause bronchitis, emphysema, and lung cancer, which lead to a slow, agonizing death.

CAUSES OF AIR POLLUTION. With air pollution a problem for all of us, let's examine its main causes.

Fossil Fuels ▪ The main cause of air pollution is the burning of fossil fuels—substances such as wood, coal, petroleum, and natural gas that are derived from living things. To produce our electricity and to manufacture the goods we consume, power plants and factories pour pollutants into the air. The worst polluter, however, is the internal combustion engine. The exhausts of cars, trucks, and buses emit poisons—sulfur dioxide, nitrogen oxide, hydrocarbons, and carbon monoxide. The vehicles also leave behind **carcinogens** (cancer-causing substances) from the asbestos particles in their brake linings.

Pollution is almost always unintended. On occasion, however, pollution is the result of deliberate, spiteful acts. The most dramatic example occurred in 1991 after U.S.-led forces defeated the Iraqi army in Kuwait. During their retreat, the Iraqi military ignited 600 oil wells, storage tanks, and refineries. The soot from the fires circled the globe (Naj 1992).

Waste Incineration ▪ A second major source of air pollution is waste incineration. The burning of plastics is especially damaging to our health because it creates PCBs (polychlorinated biphenyls), a potent toxin. Plastics are not **biodegradable;** that is, they do not disintegrate after being exposed to normal bacteria. Even steel rusts, but plastics endure almost indefinitely. Consequently, we burn them.

Fluorocarbon Gases ▪ A third source of air pollution is fluorocarbon gases. These gases are suspected of damaging the **ozone shield,** the layer in the earth's upper stratosphere that screens out much of the sun's ultraviolet rays. High-intensity ultraviolet rays harm most life forms. In humans, they cause skin cancer and cataracts; in plants, they reduce growth and cause genetic mutations. When the danger of fluorocarbon gases was realized, their use in aerosol cans, refrigerators, and air conditioners was reduced or eliminated. The damage to the ozone is expected to be repaired (U.S. Department of State 1997).

The Taj Mahal in Uttar Pradesh, India, is considered by many to be the most beautiful building in the world. This mausoleum built by Shah Jehan in 1630–1648 for himself and his favorite wife, Mumtaz Mahal, is made of white marble inlaid with semiprecious stones. Along with other architectural masterpieces the world over, the Taj Mahal is threatened by acid rain.

GLOBAL WARMING. Besides damage to the ozone shield, another major consequence of air pollution is global warming. The pollutants in the air lead to what is known as the **greenhouse effect.** Carbon dioxide and water vapor form an invisible blanket around the globe that allows the sun's light to enter, but traps the heat. Without this blanket, temperatures would plummet, and the earth would be unable to support life. If the blanket is too thick, however, it traps too much heat and has devastating consequences for our environment.

And the blanket seems to be growing thicker. Because of the Industrial Revolution, we burn more fossil fuels than humans did in the past, releasing more carbon dioxide into the air. In effect, the carbon dioxide blocks the atmospheric window through which our earth's daily heat escapes to outer space. The increased temperature of the earth is known as **global warming.**

Peru's 7.5-mile-long mountain glacier, the Quelcayya, is the world's largest tropical glacier. Sitting at 18,600 feet above sea level, it often gets snow but never rain. The Quelcayya is shrinking by about 100 feet a year. As the ice receded, researchers discovered a moss-like plant that had been frozen in the glacier. Carbon dating showed the plant to be over 5,000 years old.

To get an idea of how extensive today's global warming is, consider this: The last time this plant wasn't covered with snow and ice, the Egyptians were busy inventing hieroglyphics. (Regaldo 2004)

Likely Consequences of Global Warming ▪ If global warming continues, some scientists say that it will disrupt the earth's climate and biological system (Brown 2001; Parmesan and Yohe 2003; Kluger 2006). If so, they say that we can expect these consequences:

1. Climate boundaries will move about 400 miles north, resulting in a longer growing season in the United States, Canada, and Russia.
2. The oceans will rise several feet as the polar ice caps melt.
3. The world's shorelines will erode. (Most of the beaches on the U.S. East Coast will be gone in a generation.)
4. Some small island nations will be destroyed, and the United States will lose an area of land the size of Massachusetts. Large portions of Florida will be under water.
5. Coastal fisheries will be damaged.
6. Summers will be hotter, increasing the demand for electricity.
7. There will be more forest fires, droughts, floods, and outbreaks of pests.
8. There will be more hurricanes.
9. There will be outbreaks of diseases—malaria, dengue fever, cholera.
10. Many species of plants and animals will become extinct.
11. Problems in the Least Industrialized Nations will be worse, as they have fewer resources to meet the crisis.

The Maldives is an island nation of just 270,000 people. The country's highest spot is about five feet above sea level. With the threat of the polar ice caps melting and the oceans rising, the ministry of tourism considered making this the national slogan, "Come see us while we're still here" (Dickey and Rogers 2002).

DIFFERENCES OF OPINION. Global warming is a fact, but what is causing it? Throughout its history, the earth has gone through periods of warming and cooling, and there is no one-to-one correlation between carbon dioxide and these periods. During the ice age at the time of the dinosaurs the atmosphere had even higher concentrations of carbon dioxide than we do today. With such inconsistent evidence, scientists disagree on whether global warming is due to natural or human causes. Some suggest that the cause might be changes in sun cycles or sea currents or even in the cosmic rays that bombard the earth (Broad 2006a).

In 1998, 15,000 scientists signed a petition asking the United States to revoke the Kyoto agreements to cut emissions of carbon dioxide. The petition was accompanied by a letter from a former president of the National Academy of Sciences. He said that higher carbon dioxide did not pose a threat to the climate and that it might actually benefit the world. More carbon dioxide would increase plant growth and be "a wonderful and unex-

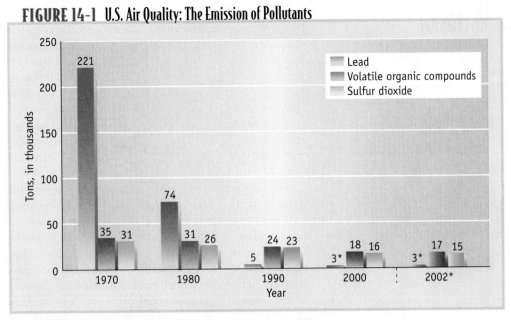

FIGURE 14-1 U.S. Air Quality: The Emission of Pollutants

*The last time the source lists a measurement for lead is 1996. Latest year available.

Source: By the author. Based on *Statistical Abstract of the United States* 2007:Table 360.

pected gift from the industrial revolution" (Stevens 1998). Confused, members of Congress called the National Academy of Sciences; its current president assured them that the greenhouse effect poses a threat to the world.

This argument is significant. If a natural cycle is the cause of global warming, we can't do anything about it. If the cause is human activity, however, we can take action to reduce or even reverse global warming.

CHANGES IN U.S. AIR POLLUTION. With today's pollution control devices and the agitation of environmentalists, is our air getting cleaner? Figure 14-1 shows some striking improvements. As you can see, emissions of sulfur dioxide and volatile organic compounds have been cut in half. The most stunning change is the amount of lead in our air; it is now only 1 percent of what it was in 1970. The primary reason for this change is lead-free gasoline. (Gasoline used to contain lead as an anti-knock additive.) With all of these improvements, we still have a long way to go. Carbon dioxide emissions continue to increase, and our air still contains 188 chemicals that have been linked to cancer, birth defects, and other health problems (Getter 1999; "U.S. Greenhouse Gas Inventory" 2006).

Land Pollution

It was such a beautiful day that Tamara and Bill decided to skip their social problems class and have a picnic on the beach. As they walked hand in hand, they found that they had to step around sewage that had washed ashore the night before. Their stomachs turned when they saw blood samples and contaminated needles that must have come from a hospital. All they could think of was AIDS.

They left hastily—without eating their lunch.

THE PROBLEM OF GARBAGE. Cities and towns across the nation have to dispose of their waste. From Figure 14-2 on the next page, which shows how much solid waste each American generates each *day*, you can see how our garbage has grown. At 4.4 pounds of solid waste per American per day, we produce *240 billion pounds* of garbage each year (*Statistical Abstract* 2006:Table 363). About a pound and a half of this waste is recovered (paper, glass, metals, plastics, rubber, wood), but each day each American still sends about 3 pounds of solid waste to landfills.

FIGURE 14-2 Ounces of Solid Waste Each American Generates Each Day

These totals are based on the solid wastes from residential and commercial trash collections. The totals do not include mining, agricultural, and industrial processing, demolition and construction wastes, sewage sludge, nor junked autos and obsolete equipment.

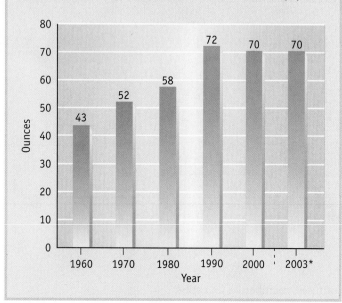

Year	Ounces
1960	43
1970	52
1980	58
1990	72
2000	70
2003*	70

*Latest year available.

Source: By the author. Based on Statistical Abstract of the United States 1994:Table 370; 2007:Table 362.

Humans have always dumped their wastes around them. We can identify many Stone Age villages by the mounds of oyster and mussel shells their inhabitants left behind. Today we produce so much trash that it is getting difficult to know what to do with it. Many towns bury their wastes in gullies and swampy areas, but areas convenient to urban centers are filling up—and groundwater contamination has become a problem. The land seems incapable of absorbing the huge amounts of garbage that we produce, and few want to turn the Grand Canyon into a giant landfill.

Cities used to throw their wastes into a pit and light it. But with today's awareness of how burning pollutes the air and adds to global warming, this is no longer allowed. Cities must now use garbage incinerators approved by the Environmental Protection Agency (EPA). (In an Orwellian twist, these incinerators are fancifully called resource recovery plants.) With federal regulations requiring utilities to buy power generated by these garbage-burning plants, they partially pay for themselves. When studies showed that these incinerators also spewed toxic gases into the air, the EPA required the installation of multimillion-dollar pollution controls. Many communities were unable to afford this bill, and they abandoned their incinerators (Schneider 1994).

Unable to burn their garbage, some states tried to ship their wastes to other states. When these states refused to accept the shipments, the case went to the Supreme Court. The Court ruled that the states to which the garbage was sent could not refuse the shipments. This decision opened landfills across the Midwest to the hard-pressed, more populated eastern states (Bailey 1992). As a consequence, some Midwestern states have become the "garbage cans" of other states.

Pollution is a global problem, taking many forms around the world. One of the most common is the dumping of human excrement around dwellings. This photo was taken in Manila, Philippines.

STRIP MINING. Another problem of land pollution is strip mining, which occurs where coal lies so close to the surface that it can be retrieved by stripping away the soil. Strip mining has scarred more than 5 million acres of U.S. land. Not only does strip mining make the land ugly, but stripped bare of its forest and plant life, the land is also poisoned as salt leeches from the coal. West Virginia was a special target of strip mining, which has left vast tracts of this state unfit for farming. Although current federal regulations require mining companies to return land to its original condition, many believe that doing so is impossible. Today the western areas of the United States and huge areas in Canada are vulnerable, for vast amounts of shale and coal lie just beneath the surface.

Water Pollution

A silent spring has fallen over parts of the western Adirondacks. Brook trout have vanished from Big Moose Lake—along with crayfish and frogs, loons, kingfishers, and most of the swallows.

Pollutants from Midwest factories, borne by rain, wind, and snow, have left more than 300 lakes devoid of fish. The acid rain is also killing the trees. (Blumenthal 1981; Ehrlich and Ehrlich 1981; Stevens 1996)

ACID RAIN. How do factory emissions in the Midwest destroy lakes in Canada and our northeastern states? Death at long distance begins when power plants in the Midwest burn coal and oil to generate electricity. Burning fossil fuels releases sulfur dioxide and nitrogen oxide into the atmosphere. Moisture in the air turns these emissions into sulfuric and nitric acid. After traveling hundreds of miles, these acids fall to the earth's surface as **acid rain.**

Acid rain is not new. Ice samples from glaciers show heavy concentrations of acids 350 years ago, probably from volcanic activity and organic decomposition (LaBastille 1979; Lynch 1980). Our intensified use of fossil fuels, however, has transformed acid rain into a global problem. To burn coal, utility companies in the Midwest built more than 175 smokestacks 500 feet tall or higher. These "megastacks" do a good job of reducing local pollution, but it is not as though the pollutants disappear as if by magic. Disgorged high into the air, these pollutants remain aloft for days, even weeks, before becoming part of a "chemical soup" that falls as rain on areas hundreds of miles away.

Canadians are upset by the "airborne sewer" that spills across their border from the United States. Acid rain has destroyed the fish and normal plant life of hundreds of lakes in the province of Ontario. Acid rain also damages crops and forests around the world, as well as such world-famous landmarks as the Colosseum in Rome, the Taj Mahal in India, the Parthenon in Athens, and the Lincoln Memorial in Washington. Acid rain also threatens human health. Apparently, acid rain produces chemical reactions that release toxic metals into the water table. From there, these metals go to the public water supply.

As you saw in Figure 14-1 on page 485, the emissions of sulfur dioxide have been cut in half. Although this has reduced acid rain, the problem continues. Some lakes are regaining the chemical balance that will support plant and animals, but for reasons that scientists are trying to figure out, some of the affected lakes are not recovering ("Acid Rain Called Peril . . ." 2006).

MERCURY RAIN. Then there is mercury rain. Half of the nation's electricity comes from burning coal. As coal burns, it releases traces of mercury, which becomes part of the smoke released by the coal-fired power plants. The mercury can stay airborne for up to two years, spreading around the globe. Some of the mercury reacts with chlorine and falls with rain. This rainwater washes into lakes, rivers, and oceans, where microorganisms ingest it. From there, it goes up the food chain into fish and from there into humans. As a result, some species of fish, especially swordfish and shark, are off limits to young children and to pregnant and nursing women (Levine 2004).

GROUNDWATER. As you know, pollution also contaminates groundwater, the source of drinking water for millions (Lewis 1990; Raloff 1990; Bartlett and Steele 1998). In addition to mercury, some of our drinking water also contains arsenic, asbestos, benzene, carbon tetrachloride, chloroform, PCBs, and other chemical wastes. Some wells on which large populations depend have had to be closed. For example, a well in the San Gabriel Valley of California that supplied drinking water to 400,000 people was closed after it became contaminated with the solvent TCE. Large portions of the water supplies of southern Michigan are so polluted that state officials have suggested that it might be "cheaper to simply write off the groundwater supplies" than to try to clean them.

LAKES AND STREAMS. If we have patience, the groundwater will rid itself of most pollutants. This self-cleansing process takes a bit of time, though, since groundwater recycles so slowly that it remains in aquifers for an average of 1,400 years (Bogo 2001). It is easier to solve the problem of the pollution of our lakes and streams, as these can be cleaned up.

The Missississippi River ■ The Mississippi River is a special case in point. Although thousands of industries discharge their wastes into this river, hundreds of cities pump their drinking water out of this putrid cesspool. To "purify" the water they send to their customers, the water companies add more chemicals. Water from the Mississippi and other rivers treated in this way passes the standards set by the EPA. One of ten Americans, however, does not have access to drinking water that meets even these minimal health standards (Duskin 2003).

The Great Lakes ■ The pollution of the Great Lakes is of special concern, for this giant network of waterways—Erie, Superior, Michigan, Huron, and Ontario—contains *one of every five gallons of the entire world's surface freshwater.* Yet hundreds of toxic chemicals are pouring into the Great Lakes (Ashworth 1987; Downing 2006). The pollution of these formerly pristine waters by industry is so bad that people are warned not to eat bottom-feeding fish (which are exposed to heavier concentrations of poisons in the lakes' sediment). Disturbed at this pollution, environmentalists put pressure on Congress, which mandated that the EPA clean up these lakes (Environmental Protection Agency 1994, 1998). Although the concentration of heavy metals has been reduced, the problem remains (McCool 2006).

While the problem of toxic chemicals was being addressed, an additional problem surfaced, that of foreign species introduced into the lakes through the ballast of boats. Some of these species, which have hitchhiked across the world, don't face the forces that keep them in check in their natural habitat. In the Great Lakes they multiply, threatening the native species ("To Restore . . ." 2005). Environmentalists are putting pressure on government bodies to work on this problem, too.

OIL SPILLS. Like a junkie, our industrial machine demands a continuous supply of oil. Transporting those vast quantities of oil is risky. Although industry and government assured environmentalists that they could handle oil spills, those promises proved hollow in 1989 when the *Exxon Valdez,* a 1,000-foot-long supertanker, ran aground and ruptured. Eleven million gallons of crude oil spewed into the pristine waters of Alaska's Prince William Sound, soiling 1,300 miles of coastline (Wells and McCoy 1989; Rosen 1999). Left dead were 250,000 sea birds, 2,800 sea otters, 300 harbor seals, 250 bald eagles, 22 killer whales, and vast numbers of fish (Rosen 1999). Exxon spent over $2 billion to clean up the mess (Wells 1990). Prince William Sound has largely recovered from the spill, but some species have not fully recovered (NOAA 2006).

Oil spills are a global problem. As huge and tragic as the Exxon oil spill in Prince William Sound was, oil spills in Russia have dwarfed it (Rosett 1994; Garelik 1996). When a cross-country oil pipeline burst in Siberia in 1994, it dumped 300 million gallons onto the tundra and into rivers. This is twenty-seven times more oil than was dumped in the Exxon spill. Russia's rusting oil pipes continue to spew oil.

Chemical Pollution

The incidents of pollution we have discussed so far all involve toxic chemicals. These chemicals are so poisonous to land, air, and water that it is difficult to overstate the extent to which they threaten our well-being. To grasp the potential destruction, let's look at a couple of examples.

LOVE CANAL. Perhaps the most infamous case of chemical pollution in the United States is Love Canal, New York, where

> Hundreds of families unwittingly purchased homes adjacent to a waste dump that had been covered over with clay. Over the years, deadly poisons seeped into their homes. Neurological damage was common. So were urinary tract infections, kidney damage, swollen joints, sleepiness, clumsiness, headaches, fragile bones, irritability, and loss of appetite. One-third of Love Canal residents suffered chromosome damage (Brown n.d.). One child was born with two rows of teeth, another with one kidney, and a third with three ears (Shribman 1989).
>
> Eventually, the federal government ordered all pregnant women and children under age 2 to move out of Love Canal (Brody 1976; Brown n.d.). In 1978, 239 families abandoned their homes, and in 1980 the federal government and the state of New York relocated another 710 families. The government bulldozed 128 homes (Shribman 1989).

How did a nice little community called Love Canal get so polluted?

> Beginning in the early 1940s, Hooker Chemical Company buried and covered with clay 44 million pounds of chemical wastes in a canal it owned (Mokhiber and Shen 1981). When Niagara Falls officials unwittingly chose the covered-over canal as the site for an elementary school, Hooker said that they had chosen a "desirable site" for the school and deeded the land to the city for a token $1. The company warned no one about the chemicals, but the deed stated that Hooker was not liable for any injuries or deaths that might occur at this site (Brown 1979).
>
> "That account," replied Hooker, "is only part fact, combined with a lot of lies." The truth, claimed Hooker, is that "we warned the board about the risk. We even told them on what part of the property to locate the school so they would not disturb the buried chemicals." Moreover, when the board considered selling part of the property, Hooker sent an attorney to the board meeting to warn them that the buried chemicals could have a "serious deleterious effect on foundations, water lines, and sewer lines" and that it was "quite possible that personal injuries could result from contact therewith." The attorney also stated that "only the surface of the land" should be used because "the subsoil conditions make it very undesirable and possibly hazardous if excavations are to be made therein" (Wilcox 1957).
>
> Despite these warnings, Niagara Falls' Board of Education approved the removal of dirt from the canal for top grading, the city constructed a storm sewer through the landfill, and the Department of Transportation built an expressway across part of the site. These construction projects disturbed industrial wastes that had been buried properly, causing the resulting damage, said Hooker.

Researchers are studying the long-term effects of chemical exposure on those who lived in Love Canal at the time of the contamination, but surprisingly, they have discovered little ("Serum Results . . ." 2006). Whoever is to blame—and there seems to be plenty of negligence and culpability to go around—we can draw several lessons from Love Canal. It seems reasonable to conclude that it is not good to bury chemical wastes and that we need to safeguard people from harm. How can we do this without having effective controls over the disposal of chemicals?

DISPOSING OF CHEMICAL WASTES. U.S. industries produce over a trillion pounds of hazardous chemical wastes each year (*Statistical Abstract* 2006: Table 380). Companies used to simply discharge wastes into the air or dump them into rivers and the oceans. This they have had to stop, but they do continue to bury them. In today's more environmentally aware climate, to say that companies *dump* their chemical wastes leaves a bad taste in our mouths. To help us feel better, the word *dump* has been changed to *landfill*. The containers buried in our dumps—that is, our landfills—disintegrate slowly, allowing lethal chemical wastes to rise to the surface or to leach into rivers and groundwater.

Not all chemicals can be buried, however, and some must go through expensive processes to render them into harmless substances. As officials have cracked down to make companies dispose of toxic wastes properly, it has opened opportunities for greedy money-grubbers—including members of organized crime (Brown n.d.). Legal disposal of a tankful of chemical wastes might cost $40,000, but underworld firms will do it for half that amount. Their disposal methods don't quite match those approved by the EPA, though: They drive an 8,000-gallon tank truck full of waste to a wooded area and dump it in eight minutes flat. The industrial company that produced the waste (a legitimate business) feigns ignorance. On twenty-one acres of marshland on Staten Island, men "well known to law enforcement agents" deposited 700,000 gallons of waste oil in barrels. There are even easier ways. In North Carolina, one "midnight dumper" simply opened the spigots on a tankload of PCBs and then drove until the tank was empty.

HAZARDOUS WASTE SITES: THE NATIONAL PRIORITY LIST. With inadequate disposal and thousands of toxic dump sites, chemical wastes are a ticking time bomb. You can check to see how your state ranks on the Social Map below, which shows the *worst* of the many hazardous waste sites in the United States. These are the sites that have been placed on the national priority list. Designated by authorities as posing such a risk to people's health that they need *immediate* attention, these sites will be cleaned up *when* and *if* Congress appropriates money to do so.

FIGURE 14-3 Hazardous Waste Sites on the National Priority List

Note: New Jersey is in a class by itself. This small state has 18 more hazardous waste sites than its nearest competitor, Pennsylvania, with 96.

Source: By the author. Based on *Statistical Abstract of the United States* 2006:Table 369.

Nuclear Pollution

THE WORLD'S FIRST NUCLEAR WASTE DISASTER: KYSHTYM. Russia's Ural River Valley is a remote place, and it was here that the Soviet government decided to develop its first atomic bomb. In Kyshtym, they built a nuclear reactor to obtain plutonium. Accounts vary as to how the Soviets disposed of the millions of gallons of nuclear waste produced by this reactor. Some say they bored holes into the ground and poured the liquid wastes into them (Solomon and Rather 1980). Others report that they piled the waste onto a dry lake bed (Clines 1998). Perhaps they did both. In the winter of 1957 a chemical reaction occurred, and the waste exploded, sending radioactive dust high into the sky.

The fallout from this explosion devastated the area. Maps before the explosion show thirty villages and towns around Kyshtym, but on maps printed after 1958, those communities are nowhere to be seen. Thousands of people had to be evacuated permanently from a 1,000-square-kilometer area.

THE PUNY NUCLEAR REACTOR ACCIDENT: THREE MILE ISLAND. By comparison, the worst nuclear accident in the United States was puny. It occurred in 1979 at Three Mile Island, Pennsylvania, when a reactor leaked. Panic ensued, and 100,000 residents fled (Rabinovitz 1998). The contamination was minimal, however, and people quickly moved back to their homes. Some say that this accident may cause up to fifty people to die from cancer (Milvy 1979), but others claim that the accident was simply a minor loss of coolant that exposed people to less radiation than they get at the dentist (Williams 1980).

THE WORLD'S WORST NUCLEAR REACTOR DISASTER: CHERNOBYL. Then there was Chernobyl, in the Ukraine:

> *Meltdown.* The word froze in the mouth of the operating engineer. No one wanted to even think it could happen. Yet the evidence was undeniable. An explosion had blown a 1,000-ton steel cover off a nuclear reactor. The containment structure was obliterated.
>
> It was too late to flee: No one could outrun the deadly radiation. For ten days, the world watched the drama, the fire raging and radioactive materials spewing into the air.
>
> Chernobyl's cloud of radioactive gases traveled slowly around the world. In two weeks, its airborne waste was detected in the United States and Tokyo (Flavin 1987). Canadians were advised not to drink rainwater, and farmers in Great Britain were ordered not to grow certain crops because of the radioactive fallout. (Dufay n.d.)

Over 300,000 people were evacuated. International medical teams rushed to the scene, and despite emergency transplants of bone marrow and fetal liver cells, thirty-one people died during the first months. About 12,000 square miles of farm- and forestlands were contaminated so badly that they may have been rendered useless for at least two generations. Unfortunately, some people have moved back into the contaminated areas around Chernobyl. They know the risk, but they still call it home (Dufay n.d.). Some farmers are again growing crops and raising livestock in areas contaminated by the Chernobyl disaster, which is presenting a concern for consumers. The residents of Eastern Europe are wary, and some avoid honey that comes from the Ukraine and Byelorussia. Since this honey is sold at a cheaper price, others buy it (author's notes, 2007).

Experts anticipated that the consequences on health would be devastating, that perhaps tens of thousands of people would die from radiation-caused cancers. United Nations researchers who did a twenty-year follow-up study of Chernobyl, however, found that the health effects were much milder than expected. The levels of leukemia—one of the main fears—turned out to be within the normal range. About 4,000 cases of thyroid cancer were found, primarily among adults who had been children at the time and had drunk milk from cows that had eaten radiation-contaminated grass. This disease, though, is treatable, and has resulted in only a few extra deaths ("Stakeholders and Radiological . . ." 2006).

Food Pollution

We may not be buying honey from the Ukraine, but you and I face **food pollution** daily. There are two types of food pollution: disease-causing germs in our food and chemicals added to food. A possible third source is genetically modified food. Let's look at all three.

DISEASE-CAUSING GERMS IN OUR FOOD.

I'll begin the first with a personal example.

> On Sunday, I had driven back to northern Florida from meetings in Miami. That evening, I didn't feel well. On Monday, I had a slight fever, and I didn't feel well enough to work. On Tuesday, I was experiencing pain, and I thought that I should see a doctor, but I decided to "tough it out." By Wednesday night, the pain had become so intense and my fever so high that I gave up and drove myself (I was living alone) to the emergency room of a local hospital. I was immediately given high doses of antibiotics intravenously.
>
> I had *E. coli,* a dangerous bacterium that comes from food or water contaminated from feces. Mine likely came from a restaurant worker who didn't wash his or her hands after defecating. Up to then, I had only read about this food contaminant, and I wish that were still the case.

The Example of Chickens ■ *E. coli* is only one of the many disease-causing substances in our food. If you have the stomach for it, consider how chickens are processed (Ingersoll 1990). Slaughter lines run so fast that inspectors have two seconds to scrutinize each carcass, inside and out, for signs of disease and feces. "After a while, it gets to be a blur," inspectors say.

Our food processing is supposed to reduce food contamination, but the way we process chickens can increase it. In one plant, 57 percent of chickens arrived contaminated with disease-causing bacteria such as salmonella. This is horrible to contemplate, but listen to this: *Seventy-six* percent left the plant infected. During their processing, contaminants are passed from carcass to carcass. The two primary culprits of this bird-to-bird contamination are automatic disemboweling knives, which spread chicken feces, and vats of chilled water in which the chickens are dipped before going into the freezer. Says a microbiologist, "Even if you chlorinate the chill water, it's still like soaking birds in a toilet." To this, industry officials reply reassuringly, "It may spread bacteria from bird to bird, but it also dilutes the overall dose level."

Why doesn't the U.S. poultry industry switch from chill water to blasting the chickens with cold air, as they do in Europe? The reason is profits. Federal regulations allow each chicken carcass to soak up to 8 percent of its weight in water. This allows the chicken industry to sell hundreds of thousands of gallons of disease-ridden water at poultry prices.

Is contaminated chicken a real problem? It is so bad that over one million Americans get sick each year from contaminated chicken. Scientists at *Consumer Reports* bought chickens at supermarkets in twenty-five cities nationwide ("Of Birds and Bacteria" 2003). These included major brands, supermarket brands, and chicken sold at health food stores. Tests showed that *half* of the chickens were contaminated with salmonella or *Campylobacter,* bacteria that can make people sick. To not get sick from the filthy chickens that are sold in our stores, the researchers suggest that we buy chickens that are located low in the supermarket freezer (where it is colder), separate raw chicken from other foods, not let any foods touch the area where we prepare the chicken, and cook the chicken thoroughly. They also warn us to wash our hands thoroughly to remove chicken juices—the blood and the filthy water (recall that "chill water") that the U.S. Department of Agriculture allows the chickens to absorb.

Our focus on chickens helps us to understand why some European nations refuse to import some food from the United States. This can come as a shock to some of us, as from our ethnocentric perspective, we are used to thinking of American food as the best. European resistance to U.S. food is the topic of the Technology and Social Problems box on the next page.

Technology and Social Problems

"DO YOU EAT PLASTIC FOOD?" WHY EUROPEANS DON'T LIKE U.S. FOOD

I didn't know what to say when a friend in Spain asked me if Americans eat plastic food. I was amused by the phrase and perplexed by what the question could mean.

The reason for the question became apparent as I became more familiar with Spanish food. I noticed that the egg yolks were brighter, almost orange. Fruits and vegetables are picked ripe. People buy them daily and eat them fresh. The meat is more tender and tasty. It doesn't come prepackaged or frozen. Each grocery store has its own butcher; in small stores, the butcher is also the owner. The butcher will cut the meat you order in the fashion you prefer. Bread is freshly baked and also purchased daily. The Spanish use a lot of fresh herbs—especially garlic and parsley. They also cook with olive oil—always.

But why should this contrast in food customs lead someone to ask, in sincerity, if Americans eat plastic food? A rumor had gone around Europe that U.S. food companies do strange things to our food, so much so that our food had become synthetic. The term *plastic* was my friend's innocent translation of *synthetic*. Perhaps this term is not too far off the mark.

It isn't only the common folk who wonder about our food. (My friend, who asked this question, runs one of the thousands of mom-and-pop bar–restaurants on Spain's many beaches.) Officials of the European Union (EU) are also suspicious about U.S. food. EU scientists claim that bovine growth hormones—BGF, the hormones fed to cattle to make them grow faster—can cause cancer. The EU banned beef with BGF. Since this ban was aimed primarily at U.S. beef, the United States retaliated by slapping millions of dollars in tariffs on EU food products ("Dispute Between EU . . ." 2004).

This dispute between proponents of "natural" versus "synthetic" foods, and the related positions that one is healthy and the other unhealthy, seems destined to continue for some time. The controversy has not yet played out on the political level, and the European Union and the United States continue to quarrel before the World Trade Organization. On the individual level, similar concerns are evidenced by the increasing numbers of "health food" stores and "organic" sections in our grocery stores.

FOR YOUR CONSIDERATION

How "synthetic" do you think U.S. food is? Do you have any concerns about the safety of the food you buy? Do you avoid foods with chemical preservatives?

To the left is a typical food store in Europe. This photo was taken in Madrid, Spain. It gives you a sense of the kinds of shopping and food that Europeans are accustomed to. Above is a protest outside the Federal Building in Oakland, California. Reasons that underlie such protests are discussed in the text.

THE DANGER IS REAL. It isn't just chickens, of course, that present such a threat to our health. Some of our food is so contaminated that it kills. Such a statement must sound like an exaggeration, but here are some cases: Twenty people died after they ate hot dogs produced by a subsidiary of Sara Lee—they were contaminated with *Listeria monocytogenes*. Forty people died after eating Jalisco brand soft cheese—this, too, was contaminated with listeria (Burros 1999). After eating Schwan's ice cream, 224,000 Americans became sick. The ice cream mix had picked up salmonella when it was transported in tanks that had been used to carry raw eggs (Neergaard 1998). Odwalla produced apple juice that was infected with *E. coli* bacteria—fourteen children developed a life-threatening disease that ravages kidneys, and a 16-month-old girl died (Belluck 1998). *Each year, about 75 million Americans get sick from contaminated food, 300,000 are hospitalized, and 5,000 die from it* (Widdowson et al. 2005).

CHEMICAL ADDITIVES. Let's turn to the second type of food pollution, the chemicals that are added to our food to process it, lengthen its shelf life, enhance its appearance, or alter its taste.

Food Flavorings and Colorings ▪ Food companies sprinkle our food with a lot of artificial additives. Just to flavor our foods, they use 2,000 different chemical compounds. The "cherry" flavor in soft drinks, pies, and shakes, for example, requires 13 different chemicals.

The information we have about the safety of food additives is not reassuring. The U.S. agency that is responsible for overseeing the safety of food, the Food and Drug Administration (FDA), has a sad history in regard to additives. For example, Red Dye No. 2 used to be the most common food coloring in the United States. Because it enhances colors, the food industry added more than a million pounds to our food each year. In 1970, researchers discovered that rats and mice fed Red Dye No. 2 developed cancer. It took five years for the FDA to ban this dye—and only after the agency was flooded with petitions from public interest groups.

Many find little comfort in knowing that Red Dye Nos. 3, 8, 9, 19, 37, and 40 replaced No. 2 to color food. Some of these dyes also damage DNA and cause cancer in animals—yet the FDA allows them to be used (Brooks 1985, 1987; Tsuda 2001). Red dye No. 40, for example, has been banned in Austria, Belgium, France, Germany, Norway, Sweden, and Switzerland—yet it continues to be added to our foods (Hanssen 1997).

Then there are the hundreds of dyes to make the colors blue, green, and yellow.

Food Preservatives ▪ The sulfites illustrate another example:

The food industry has found sulfites to be a handy chemical, for they are antioxidants. Because they keep foods from discoloring, the sulfites are spread over raw fruits and vegetables, especially at salad bars, to keep them "looking fresh." Sulfites are also added to beer, wine, and bakery goods, sprinkled over shrimp and fish, mixed with dairy and grain products, and added to fruit juices and frozen potatoes.

The problem is that the sulfites also make some people sick. A few even die from allergic reactions. Sulfites have been linked to deaths involving pizza, wine, and beer, and they pose a special danger to asthmatics. After years of complaints—and no regulation—the FDA decided to limit the amount of sulfites in our food and to require a warning label. (Dingell 1985; Ingersoll 1988; Food and Drug Administration 1994; Magee et al. 2005)

SYNERGISM AND CUMULATIVE EFFECTS. Because they are **synergistic**—that is, they interact with one another—chemical food additives are a complicated hazard. For example, the nitrites that give hot dogs, ham, and bacon their inviting red color appear to be safe in and of themselves. In the presence of amines, however, nitrites become nitrosamines— potent carcinogens. Every organ in every species of experimental animal ever exposed to the nitrosamines has shown cancer. Amines are commonly added to beer, wine, cereals,

FIGURE 14-4 Bon Appétit?

APPLES

captan*
parathion*
daminozide*
paraquat

POTATOES

chlorothalonil*
chlorpropham
aldicarb

CARROTS

trifluralin*
chlorothalonil*
parathion*
linuron*

MILK

aflatoxin*
clorsulon*
fenbendazole*
thiabendazole*
bacteria

GRAPES

captan*
parathion*
methyl bromide*

CHICKEN

antibiotics
gentian violet*
nitrofurans*
bacteria

These contaminants are often but not always in the items pictured above.
*Known or suspected carcinogen.

tea, fish, cigarettes, streptomycin, Librium, and Contac cold medicine. Thus, hot dogs and beer are an unhealthy combination, as are a ham sandwich and a cup of tea. See Figure 14-4 for another illustration of polluted food.

Many chemical additives are harmless until they build up in our bodies. When they reach a certain level, then they begin to destroy tissues and organs. That level varies from person to person.

PROFITS AHEAD OF HEALTH. The food industry adulterates our food with harmful chemicals not because it is necessary but because it is profitable. The chemicals retard spoilage and increase sales by making food that appeals to the public's conditioned taste and sight. Because the food industry can use alternative ways to preserve food, from a conflict perspective we can say that those who control the food industry put profits ahead of health. Certainly the *food chain* is long—that is, getting food from grower to consumer is a lengthy process—and we must have effective ways to preserve food. Ways to do so without harming people's health include older techniques such as pickling, smoking, salting, canning, freezing, and drying, as well as newer ways such as freeze-drying and vacuum packing.

Some of our food is polluted before it is processed and marketed. To keep cows, chickens, and other animals from getting sick and to get them to grow faster so they can be marketed sooner, they are fed antibiotics, hormones, and growth-promoting drugs. Some of these substances end up in our own bodies when we eat these animals or their products, such as milk and cheese. This use of antibiotics is also contributing to the rise of drug-resistant organisms (Iovine and Blaser 2004). Similarly, farmers spray pesticides on fruits and vegetables to prevent insect damage. Because the fruits and vegetables absorb some of these chemicals, they enter our bodies when we eat them.

The stakes are high. Food is the largest industry in the United States. Sales in our 120,000 grocery stores amount to about $475 billion a year (*Statistical Abstract* 2006:Table 1029). Adulterating our food is so profitable that our food industry adds more than 1 billion pounds of chemicals to our food each year—about five pounds of chemicals for every man, woman, and child in the United States. Researchers associate these chemicals with our high rates of cancer.

GENETICALLY MODIFIED FOODS. It does not take an expert to be aware that the first two sources of food pollution can be harmful to our health. At the very minimum, almost everyone agrees that we should avoid diseases in our foods and that at least some chemicals added to foods can be harmful to our health. When it comes to **genetically modified foods**—foods derived from plants or animals in which genetic materials have been transferred from one species to another or in which genes have been manipulated in a way that does not occur in nature—though, we land in the midst of controversy. Not only are governments and businesses, with their competitive power and economic interests, quarreling with one another, but so are scientists. They simply cannot agree whether genetically modified foods are harmful or not.

Even placing the topic of genetically modified foods in this section of the book is controversial. It might imply that modifying foods genetically is a form of food pollution. But locating this topic here is not intended to communicate such a message, only to stress that some scientists take this position.

The issue is simply this. Genetically modifying foods is a new technology. This technology seems to have the potential to greatly increase the world's food supply, but its consequences are unknown. U.S. companies have spearheaded the development of genetically modified foods, and they stand to reap huge profits if the new strains are accepted around the world. European agricultural interests, which fear the competition, spearhead the opposition. They are joined by environmentalists who fear both unknown health consequences of these foods and the harm they might bring to the environment if they replace natural varieties.

The quarrel has gone beyond scientific studies and has become an economic and political issue (Umberger 2005). Depending on the outcome of scientific studies, U.S. and EU agricultural interests stand to gain or lose hundreds of millions of dollars a year. The United States and the European Union don't order their scientists to produce studies that prove their position, but scientists on both sides of the Atlantic know the issue—that the EU wants to prove that genetically modified foods are harmful, whereas the United States (and Canada) want to show that they are not harmful. Although the research is being conducted within this highly charged political context, science—not economics or politics—will win. No matter who produces a study, the other side will examine it rigorously. Subjected to impartial, objective techniques of replication (repetition) and measurement, these studies will ultimately demonstrate that one or the other economic-political side is correct. My own prediction is that each side is partially correct—that is, that some genetically modified foods are harmful, while others are not. We will have to await the outcome to know.

Pollution in the Industrializing Nations

Although most pollution occurs in the industrialized nations, the nations that are industrializing also contribute to this problem. A third of the children in China have levels of lead in their blood that exceed the World Health Organization's limit (Oster and Spencer 2006). After the United Nations declared that Mexico City had the worst air in the world, Mexican authorities banned leaded gasoline, shut down some factories, and embarked on a tree-planting program (Mandel-Campbell 2001). Mexico City's air improved, and there now are fewer hacking patients admitted to hospitals.

For a snapshot of how harmful conditions can get in the industrializing nations, see the Global Glimpse box on the next page.

REASONS FOR THIS POLLUTION. Four main reasons underlie the extensive pollution of the industrializing nations. Let's look at them.

Use of Banned Chemicals ■ First, many of the chemicals that are outlawed in the industrialized nations remain legal to use in the industrializing countries. Although these chemicals cannot be used in the United States, U.S. chemical companies still manufacture them. They ship these chemicals to the industrializing nations, where they are used by workers who cannot read the warnings on the label. The chemicals poison the workers, the land,

A Global Glimpse
WHERE NEW LIFE BRINGS DEATH

"The factories, they give us life, but they kill us at the same time," sighs Maria Alves, who awakens at night to the sounds of her six children gagging in the polluted air. "It isn't fair, but what can we do? We need to work."

This is Cubatão, Brazil, a village nestled in the Serra do Mar mountains. It used to be pretty, but now people call it "the valley of death."

As nations rush to industrialize, they often skip health and safety standards. Their problems with hazardous chemicals don't grab the world's attention, but they still kill.

Cubatão is one of the most polluted cities on earth. With its factory pollutants and the worst acid rain ever recorded, half of its more than 100,000 people have respiratory ailments. Pollution is causing people to die from heart attacks and strokes.

This photo was taken in Cubatão, Brazil.

A benzene gas leak caused hundreds of workers to develop leukopenia, an abnormality of the blood cells. Three developed leukemia and died. The company was fined $4,000.

The phosphates spewing from the fertilizer factories make it look like winter—little white chemical flakes fluttering down, burning the skin.

Adimar dos Santos Lima, who works in a steel plant for $70 a month and is happy to have a job, says, "I make a living. But I live in a sewer."

A slum neighborhood blew up after gasoline leaked from an underground pipe owned by Petrobras, Brazil's national oil company. The recovery team found 90 bodies. Another 500 had been incinerated.

Based on Schuster 1985; Pereira et. al. 2004.

and the water. In a strange twist, they also often poison the food that you and I eat, for they return to us in our coffee, fruit, nuts, and so on.

The EPA banned domestic use of the pesticide ethylene dioromide (EDB) because it causes cancer. The State Department, whose concern is foreign relations, fearing bad relations with Mexico and Haiti, and, not incidentally, damages to U.S.-financed mango growers in Belize and Guatemala, pressured the EPA to allow foreign mango growers to continue using the pesticide. (Meier 1987)

Production of Banned Chemicals ■ Second, the industrializing nations manufacture chemicals that the United States bans or that can be made cheaper in those nations—often in factories that U.S. corporations own. Those factories mean jobs, and if an industrializing nation were to insist on stringent safeguards in manufacturing or in pollution controls, it would cut its own economic throat. Other nations would welcome the company—without the safeguards.

The cost of such practices, however, can be high. Consider Bhopal, the world's most infamous chemical accident:

It was an unseasonably cold night in Central India. In the shantytowns of Bhopal, thousands of poor families were asleep. At a nearby railway station, a scattering of people waited for early-morning trains. At the local Union Carbide plant, a maintenance worker noticed that a storage tank holding methyl isocyanate (MIC), a chemical used in making pesticides, was showing a high pressure reading. The worker heard rumbling in the tank, then the sound of cracking concrete. The plant superintendent was notified, and he sounded an alarm. But it was too late. A noxious white gas had started seeping from the tank and had begun to spread through the region on the northwesterly winds.

At the Vijoy Hotel near the railroad, sociologist Swapan Saha, 33, woke up with a terrible pain in his chest. "It was both a burning and a suffocating sensation," he said. "It was like breathing fire." Wrapping a damp towel around his nose and mouth, Saha went outside to investigate. Scores of victims lay dead on the platform at the train station. "I thought at first there must have been a gigantic railway accident," he recalled. Then he noticed a pall of white smoke on the ground, and an acrid smell in the air. People were running helter-skelter, retching, vomiting, and defecating uncontrollably. Many collapsed and died. Dogs, cows, and water buffaloes also lay on the ground, twitching in death agonies. Saha made his way to the railway office, only to find the stationmaster slumped over his desk. For a moment, he thought that an atom bomb had hit Bhopal. Staggering back to the hotel, half blind himself by now, he sat down to write a farewell letter to his wife.

Saha survived. More than 2,500 others did not. (Whitaker 1984; Spaeth 1989)

Not all the deaths took place at once. The leak contaminated the area's groundwater, claiming more lives over the following years. The Indian government estimates that this accident has caused about 22,000 deaths (Hertsgaard 2004).

Although this accident took place in India, it could happen anywhere that chemicals are manufactured. As an expert on workplace safety put it, "It's like a giant roulette wheel. This time the marble came to a stop in a little place in India. But the next time it could be the United States" (Whitaker 1984).

The Rush to Industrialize ▪ The third factor is the intensity with which these nations are trying to industrialize. Their pressing concern at the moment is to increase their standard of living and their position in the global power structure, not to manage pollution. China and India, the two most populous nations in the world, are industrializing at such a furious pace that they may well become the world's two largest polluters.

Dumping Grounds ▪ Fourth, the industrialized nations have found that some of these nations are a convenient dump for their toxic wastes. Corporate leaders make deals with dictators and weak governments and ship them chemical wastes that under our regulations make them expensive to dispose of (Polgreen and Simons 2006). We even send them the ships that we discard. In Alang, India, 35,000 men work for $1.50 a day breaking up ships whose parts are laden with asbestos, PCBs, lead, and toxic sludge (Englund and Cohn 1997). The men work unprotected, and each year two out of a thousand die from accidents, making ship-breaking the most dangerous occupation in India (Jain 2006). Without seeing such conditions firsthand, it is difficult to grasp the desperate misery that the poor of India face on a daily basis. One man who works in this setting, earning $1.50 for a full day's toil with the smell of death hovering over him, said: "It is better to work and die than starve and die."

Getting the Other Side

THE OPTIMISTIC ENVIRONMENTALISTS. Almost everything about the environment that I have reviewed to this point has reflected negative findings and opinions. There is another side, one that is seldom heard. Some experts, whom I shall call the optimistic environmentalists, say that groups of alarmist doomsayers have captured the attention of the media with their stress on negative findings, dire predictions, and exaggerations. Isolated incidents such as Bhopal, although tragic, have been blown out of proportion. If we take a more realistic, dispassionate view, they say, we will see that things are not so bad.

The Technological Fix ▪ This group believes that improved technology will solve whatever threat pollution may pose to the environment. We have had predictions of disaster in the past, they argue, and our technology has always seen us through. The present is no exception. To get their point across, some of them enjoy using a bit of humor. They point to the pollution problem of 1900. At that time, horses were common, and so was their manure. Huge amounts of this substance were piling up on city streets. When motorized vehicles replaced horses, that problem disappeared. The present is no different, and we will develop technology to counter threats to our environment.

FIGURE 14-5 Life Expectancy in the United States, by Year of Birth

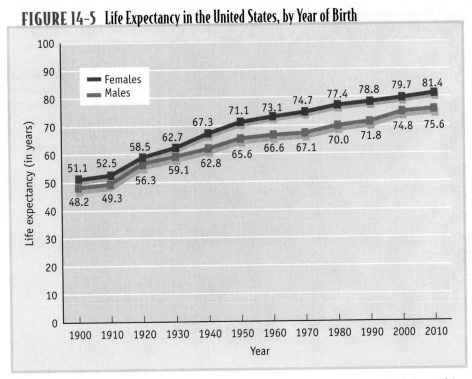

Sources: By the author. Based on *Historical Statistics of the United States* 1976:Table B 116, 117; *Statistical Abstract of the United States* 1989:Table 106; 2006:Table 96.

Environmentalism Can Cause Disease ▪ The optimistic environmentalists also point out that solutions can backfire, that they can do more harm than the problem they are supposed to be solving. Edward Teller (1980), the man most responsible for the hydrogen bomb, said that strict environmental regulations are not only expensive but also create poverty and disease in the poor nations. He made this point: When environmentalists objected to the use of DDT as environmentally harmful, it was banned. Look what happened in just Sri Lanka. The banning of DDT let mosquitoes multiply, and two million people came down with malaria. To combat this disease, DDT had to be brought back. Teller said, "I challenge anybody to show me a case where lack of environmental protection has made two million people as seriously sick as the disease caused by the environmentalists."

Things Are Getting Better ▪ The optimistic environmentalists also make this point: We can use a number of measures to evaluate the condition of the environment, but the best single one is life expectancy. When the environment deteriorates, life expectancy drops, as it did in Russia. If an environment improves, life expectancy increases. The quickest measure of the U.S. environment, then, is shown in Figure 14-5, where you can see a consistent upward march in U.S. life expectancy. Why are Americans living longer? Because our environment has improved, not deteriorated (J. Simon 1981). We need to stop worrying about what *might* go wrong, much less twist reality in order to match some woeful view of life. Life is getting better, so let's enjoy it.

Of Special Concern: The Tropical Rain Forests

We don't have to be alarmists to see that, at a minimum, we must deal with toxic wastes, provide wholesome food, and learn how to preserve, create, or—at least—not destroy a healthy environment. And we don't have to be alarmists to be concerned that plant and animal species are being extinguished. Especially ominous for humanity's future is the destruction of the tropical rain forests.

Ecotourism has developed to educate people about the environment and to generate profits to help sustain the environment. This ecotourist in Costa Rica's Rincon de la Vieja National Park is *zip-lining* over a rain forest canopy. Strapped in a harness, she uses the cable to propel herself to the next platform.

The tropical rain forests have been called the lungs of the earth. They help to regulate the earth's exchange of oxygen and carbon dioxide, and they absorb carbon gases that create global warming. The rain forests also help keep the earth's climate in balance by giving off water vapor that keeps the ground from drying out. Those lungs are gasping, and as the environmental pessimists would say, if action is not taken soon, they will collapse.

Although the rain forests cover just 7 percent of the earth's land area, they are home to *one-third to one-half* of all plant and animal species. Many species of plants, still unstudied, possess medicinal or nutritional value (Cheng 1995; Simons 2005). Some of the discoveries from the rain forests have been astounding: A flower from Madagascar is used in the treatment of leukemia, and a frog in Peru produces a painkiller more powerful, but less addictive, than morphine (Wolfensohn and Fuller 1998). A chemical from a rain forest plant in Panama is thought to be effective in treating malaria (Roach 2003).

Even knowing that the rain forests are essential for humanity's welfare, we keep clearing them. In the process, we extinguish thousands of plant and animal species (Durning 1990; Wolfensohn and Fuller 1998; "The Price of Success" 2004). As biologists remind us, a species lost is gone forever. Like Esau who exchanged his birthright for a bowl of porridge, we are exchanging our future for some lumber, farms, and pastures.

Let's turn to resource depletion. Here we find more disagreement among the experts.

Energy and Resources

THE WAY IT WAS. Americans used to think that gasoline was limitless. We even had "gas wars." To attract people to buy their gas, service stations kept undercutting one another's price. Gas stations even used to give away glasses and dishes with a gasoline purchase. This ended abruptly in 1973 when OPEC (Organization of Petroleum Exporting Countries) surprised the West with an oil embargo. Overnight, long lines appeared at U.S. gas stations, and for a moment, Americans became acutely aware of how fragile their energy supply was. But only for a moment. Although a few changes were permanent, such as more fuel-efficient cars and better-insulated homes, when the embargoes were removed, we mostly went back to our old habits.

How concerned should we be about energy and resources? It depends on whom you listen to. Let's examine the views.

THE PESSIMISTIC ENVIRONMENTALISTS. One group of experts feels that we are facing energy and resource shortages so vast that they will shatter the foundations of the industrialized world. They can't understand why most of us are so short-sighted that we become concerned only when the price of gasoline surges. Even then, our concern focuses not on the coming shortage of oil but on what it costs to fill our gas tank or heat our homes. We miss this bigger picture—that for its existence, our civilization depends on substances whose supply is limited.

The Water Shortage ▪ The coming shortage of oil is well known, but most of us are less aware that we are already running short of freshwater. We used to think that freshwater was endless, but gradually we are learning a bitter lesson. Of all the water on earth, 97 percent is salt water. A little over 2 percent is frozen in glacial ice. This leaves about 1 percent for all agricultural, industrial, and personal uses. Across the world, industrial societies are making huge and increasing demands on this limited supply of freshwater. In the United States, communities have even begun to quarrel about who has a right to the water in the Great Lakes (Barringer 2005).

To illustrate the coming crisis in freshwater, consider the Ogallala aquifer. As shown in Figure 14-6, this aquifer runs from South Dakota to Texas. It waters nearly 12 percent of the nation's corn, cotton, grain sorghum, and wheat (Frazier and Schlender 1980; Brown 1987). In this area, ranchers raise nearly half the nation's cattle. Yet we are depleting this underground formation (Stroud 2006). Some say that the natural condition of much of this area, now in pasture and farmlands, is Sahara-like desert, that eventually its outstanding characteristic will be its giant sand dunes (Stevens 1996). Frank Popper, the head of the Department of Urban Studies at Rutgers University, says that one day hardly anyone will live in this region. He suggests that the federal government buy huge chunks of the land, replant the native prairie grasses, reintroduce the buffalo, and turn off the lights (Farney 1989).

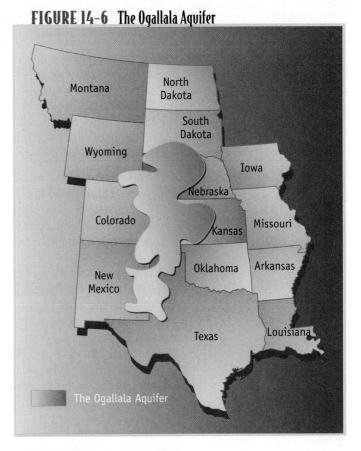

FIGURE 14-6 The Ogallala Aquifer

The Ogallala Aquifer

Minerals, Too ▪ The pessimistic environmentalists also foresee a bleak outlook for essential minerals. Economies around the world are expanding. India and China are joining the United States and the other industrialized nations in the competitive demand for the earth's limited, irreplaceable, essential resources. Unlike the economies of the world, however, the quantities of minerals in the earth are not growing. Soon we will run out of the metals—copper, zinc, aluminum, nickel, and so on—that we need to maintain our societies. Although substitute materials may buy us some time, we are reaching limits that will stop the expansion of the world's economies and bring our civilizations to a screeching halt.

IN SUM That our resources are finite and we are depleting them is so obvious that it stares us in the face: There is only so much oil, natural gas, and minerals. One day we are going to run out of them. When we do, our factories will grow silent, our cars will sit empty, and our homes will grow cold.

THE OPTIMISTIC ENVIRONMENTALISTS. Such a view misreads and distorts the evidence, reply the optimistic environmentalists. Why do they take this position?

Resources Are Not Getting Scarcer ▪ Seeming to fly in the face of logic and reality, economist Julian Simon insisted that raw materials are *not* getting scarcer. He said that when something that people want grows scarce, its price increases. To see whether raw materials are becoming scarcer, all we have to do is to look at their price. The long-term trend is lower prices, which means *less scarcity.* Here is how Simon put it (1980:11):

> The cost trends of almost every natural resource—whether measured in labor time required to produce the resource, or even in the price relative to other consumer goods—have been downward over the course of recorded history.
>
> An hour's work in the United States has brought increasingly more of copper, wheat, and oil (representative and important raw materials) from 1800 to the present. . . . These trends imply that the raw materials have been getting increasingly available and less scarce relative to the most important and most fundamental element of life, human work time.

This view so infuriated the pessimistic environmentalists that it led to one of history's famous bets. This fascinating bet is recounted in the Thinking Critically box on the next page.

To illustrate how the prices of raw materials have been falling relative to wages, Simon used the example of copper. As Figure 14-7 illustrates, it takes less and less time to earn enough to buy a pound of copper.

Energy ■ And energy? Here too, Simon stressed, the answer lies in long-term price trends. The historical prices of electricity and coal, for example, are downward, indicating a stable and even increasing supply of energy. Beware of short-term trends, which can yield a distorted picture. The escalation of oil prices in the 1970s, for example, did not indicate scarcity, but the futile attempt of OPEC to control prices. As Figure 14-8 on page 504 makes clear, OPEC's effort was but a blip on a long-term trend of declining oil prices. The higher oil prices of the early 2000s that also got people so excited will prove to be the same—increases because of war, political instability, higher demand, and the manipulation of output.

Technology ■ The optimistic environmentalists also count on technology. If we should ever exhaust a particular resource, our technology will produce a substitute. New technology will also exploit materials that were useless to older technology. In fact, technology is rushing so headlong into the future that it even produces new materials before the old ones are threatened. Fiber optic cable, for example, is replacing copper wire for the transmission of sound and images. Just a few years ago, the optimists point out, the pessimists were saying that we would run out of copper. Take another look at Figure 14-7.

FIGURE 14-7 The Price of Copper Relative to Wages

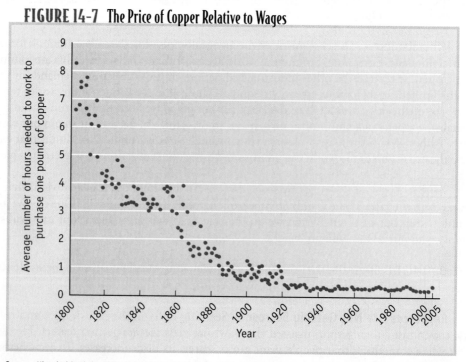

Sources: *Historical Statistics of the United States* 1976; Simon 1980; *Statistical Abstract of the United States* 2007:Tables 630, 865.

THINKING CRITICALLY About Social Problems

PUT YOUR MONEY WHERE YOUR MOUTH IS: THE SIMON–EHRLICH BET

To say that Professors Julian Simon and Paul Ehrlich didn't like each other would be an understatement. *Detest* would be a more appropriate term. Simon was an economist who taught at the University of Maryland. Ehrlich, a demographer and ornithologist, taught at Stanford.

Ordinarily, their paths would not have crossed. They lived a continent apart, and they worked in different fields.

But then life changed for both of them.

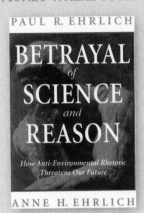

Ehrlich came out swinging. In 1968, he wrote a book that scared millions of people and fueled the environmental movement. He said that the world's population was growing so fast that food would soon be scarce. Prices were going to soar, and life expectancy would drop. His book, with the pop title, *The Population Bomb,* sold three million copies. The book scared the American public, aroused an environmentalist movement, and made Ehrlich rich. He was sought after as a guest on talk shows.

Fame and fortune. A prestigious job at Stanford. Unless he started to sexually harass his students or come to class drunk, how could that be spoiled?

Then along came Simon. Simon started grumbling in public, muttering that Ehrlich's book was a piece of, well, you know what—rotten catfish. Simon even claimed that the truth was the opposite of what Ehrlich had said. Larger populations, asserted Simon, would mean more abundance, not less. Prices would drop, not increase. Life expectancy would increase, not drop.

Simon and Ehrlich began to call each other names. They wrote nasty comments about one another in academic journals.

Ehrlich still had the public on his side. He kept repeating his predictions of doomsday. He was a founder of Earth Day, and he spoke to a crowd of 200,000 at the first gathering in 1970.

Simon was there, too, telling his side of the story. He had an audience of 16.

Simon didn't like this, but there wasn't much he could do about the public latching on to Ehrlich's ideas, not his.

Then Simon made an intriguing proposal. Without mentioning Ehrlich by name, he challenged any pessimistic environmentalist to a bet (Toth 1990). The opponent could select *any* commodity, and Simon would bet that its price would drop. "After all," he said, "contrary to common sense, resources are growing more plentiful, and they will drop in price."

"Put your money where your mouth is," Simon boasted, none too gently.

This was too much for Ehrlich—who knew that he was the target of the challenge. In October 1980, he accepted the bet. Then he did a little boasting of his own. He said, "I'll accept Simon's astonishing offer before other greedy people jump in" (Tierney 1990).

The bet was on. If the prices of chrome, copper, nickel, tin, and tungsten were higher in ten years, Ehrlich would win; if they were lower, Simon would win. To be sure there could be no misunderstandings, the two wrote their bet down, signed a contract, and publicized it widely.

During the ensuing years, the two kept goading one another—and the world's population kept growing. During the next ten years, it soared by more than 800 million people, the greatest increase in history.

Ten years later to the day, the two checked prices.

Ehrlich was chagrined. The price of all five metals had dropped. He quietly sent Simon a check. He enclosed no letter.

Simon gloated publicly. "Now you know who's right," he said. "And if you think this was just a fluke, let's do it again. And this time, let's put up some real money. How about $20,000?"

Ehrlich refused, saying that the matter was of minor importance.

Simon laughed and continued to poke fun at Ehrlich. Then students started to do the same, calling Ehrlich the nuttiest professor at Stanford.

Julian Simon died at age 65 in 1990. Paul Ehrlich stayed on at Stanford, where he still teaches. The two never reconciled.

IN SUM The price of commodities bounces around a little each year, and any given season will give you a distorted picture. It is necessary to focus on the larger picture—the historical price of resources relative to wages. The long-term picture indicates less scarcity and a growing standard of living.

FIGURE 14-8 The Price of Oil Relative to Wages

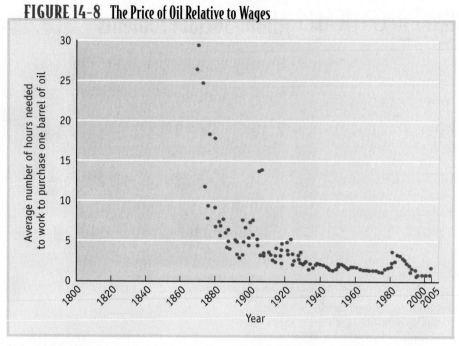

Sources: Historical Statistics of the United States 1976; Simon 1980; Statistical Abstract of the United States, various years, including 2007:Tables 632, 897.

Reconciling the Positions

In Chapter 13, where we discussed population and food, we saw that the experts fell into opposing camps. So it is with energy and resources. These topics, too, lead into controversy and debate. How do we reconcile the contrary positions of the "experts"?

FRAMEWORKS OF INTERPRETATION. As was stressed in Chapter 2, objective conditions—or the things that we call facts—do not come with built-in meanings. We have to interpret them. All of us, as the symbolic interactionists stress, fit "facts" into some framework. The framework that we choose colors our conclusions. This basic principle applies to "experts" and "nonexperts" alike.

Consider how this principle works when it comes to the environment—whether pollution, energy, or resources: If we assume that the environment is deteriorating and our vital resources are disappearing, we interpret data one way. If we assume, in contrast, that resources are infinitely abundant and will not shrink, other interpretations follow. The framework within which we interpret objective conditions makes all the difference in the world for how we view "facts."

Science at Work ■ Does this mean that we are left only with opinions, and opposing ones at that? Not at all. As I pointed out earlier about the controversy over genetically modified food, science is at work and objective studies will win out. Barring political interference, as opposing sides present their evidence, air their views, and try to disprove the other, the best data will become apparent. This isn't always the case, mind you, but it usually is. As scientists produce more data on the environmental crisis, the exaggerations of each side should become apparent, and which position has the better data on pollution, energy, and resources should become evident.

IMPLICATIONS OF THE FRAMEWORKS. Meanwhile, we must draw our own conclusions—which affect how we perceive the problem and the solutions we favor. On the individual level, our conclusions color our choices about energy use and lifestyles. On the political level, the conclusions have infinitely greater implications: The well-being of billions of people depend on them—including future generations. Everyone will benefit if this debate and its related research are allowed to continue, unencumbered by politics, so that social policies can be based on sound data and logic.

Social Policy

Before we examine specific social policies, let's first consider how—as with global population which we considered in the previous chapter—these contrasting frameworks of interpretation lead to vastly different social policies.

Oppositional Viewpoints and Overarching Solutions

Three primary approaches to social policy flow from these contrasting frameworks. Each also implies a different type of society.

THE STEADY-STATE SOCIETY. As we have seen, the pessimistic environmentalists say that it is folly to expect the world's economies and standards of living to increase endlessly. Based on their position that pollution is endangering the world and resources are diminishing, they have come up with an overarching solution called the **steady-state society.** When they use this term, the pessimistic environmentalists mean that we must stabilize industrial output approximately where it is now. If we do this, we will slow the rate at which we pollute the environment and use up resources. This will give us time to solve problems of pollution and to develop alternative resources before a crisis of shortages develops. To reach a steady-state society will require painful adjustments; it will require us to curb our growing appetite for the material goods that support our current lifestyles.

THE SCALED-BACK SOCIETY. An even more pessimistic group of environmentalists has developed a different overarching solution. It is not enough to develop a steady-state society. Our current rate of pollution and use of resources are so far beyond anything that the earth can sustain that we must develop a *scaled-back society*. That is, we must immediately reduce our industrial output and our standard of living. Only after we cut back to some optimal level—one that experts will determine—can we move to a steady-state society. This will require not "adjustments" but, rather, considerable sacrifice—yet it is necessary for the survival of earth. All of us, except the poorest, must learn to get by with less. To

To save the environment, some insist that we must drastically reduce the world's population and our standard of living. Few of us, however, want to go back to this way of life. There must be a balance that we can strike between population, standard of living, and the environment.

lower our material standards so we can reduce our dependence on depleting fossil fuels, we must scale back our expectations. Some who take this position add that once we have reduced our expectations and have learned to live simpler, less-materialistic lifestyles, we will find life more satisfying.

THE EXPANDING SOCIETY. The optimistic environmentalists scoff at the arguments of the pessimists. Their position is that not only can we solve the current environmental crisis but at the same time we can also enjoy high and even increasing standards of living. We can bring pollution under control through international agreements and develop alternative resources for any that are running short. As we do so, we can increase our industrial output and create a world of even greater material abundance. It is foolish to even consider a steady-state or scaled-back society. Such a society would deny billions of people a better life.

Regardless of whether we agree—partially, reluctantly, or wholeheartedly—with the pessimistic or optimistic environmentalists, it seems reasonable to take the position that we need social policies for pollution and energy. Let's consider them.

Pollution

PREVENTING THE MISUSE OF TOXIC CHEMICALS. A pressing problem is the misuse of toxic chemicals. Let's see what can be done.

International Controls ■ As the Global Glimpse box on the next page highlights, it is not enough to ban the use of some toxic chemical in the United States. That chemical will return to us by way of a food chain that stretches to us from the Least Industrialized Nations. To protect the people in these nations, hazardous chemicals need to be labeled in the language of the country to which they are shipped, their proper use and dangers clearly stated in plain words. To protect people everywhere, no company or its subsidiaries should be allowed to manufacture chemicals whose use is banned in the company's home country. The United States can call a summit to enact international controls.

Holding Industry Accountable ■ To prevent misuse, industry must be held accountable. Congress has already passed the Community Right to Know Act in 1986. It requires companies to annually submit to a state agency and to local fire departments a list of the hazardous chemicals they use or manufacture. Some states have passed their own right-to-know laws, requiring businesses to inform their employees of the hazardous chemicals they will be exposed to at work.

Some environmentalists say that this is not enough, They want a comprehensive policy for toxic chemicals. In this "cradle-to-grave" approach, all toxic chemicals would be approved for sale and use, registered as they enter the marketplace, and monitored throughout their lifetime. The public would have access to information on chemical releases, and the worst polluters would be publicized (Friends of the Earth, 2004).

PREVENTING FOOD POLLUTION. A second pressing problem is food pollution. Recall the chapter's opening vignette on the sorry state of our meat industry. No compelling reason exists to allow diseases to be transmitted in foods. With our alternative forms of food processing and preservation, there also is no compelling reason to add dangerous chemicals to make our food look or taste better, to make it easier to transport, or to lengthen its shelf life. At a minimum, no chemical should be added to our food until it is proven safe for human consumption.

State-of-the-art testing procedures can be used to detect banned chemicals in our food, whether imported or domestic. We can shut down U.S. companies that violate chemical restrictions and ban food imports from countries where this occurs. To be effective, the legal penalties need to be directed against the *managers and directors* of companies that violate such laws.

A Global Glimpse
THE CIRCLE OF POISON

In U.S. ports from Gulfport, Mississippi, to Oakland, Cal-ifornia, you can watch forklifts loading 55-gallon drums onto the decks of vessels bound for Central and South America.

What's in the drums? Heptachlor, chlordane, BHC, and other chemicals on their way to the plantations of Latin America. These pesticides, linked to cancer and sterility, are banned or severely restricted in the United States. U.S. companies, however, manufacture them here and in other nations and market them in the industrializing countries. There, most workers who handle these chemicals cannot read. They have no idea what the warnings on the labels say. Yet these chemicals will contaminate them, their family, and their food.

The pesticides that this girl in Pisco, Peru, is selling include DDT, which, although banned in the United States, is still manufactured for export.

Pesticides that are banned here don't disappear—they come back to haunt us. The fruit grown in these countries appears on our kitchen tables—along with the poisons used to protect them from insects. BHC comes back in your coffee. DDT, applied to cotton in El Salvador, shows up in beef carcasses imported through Miami. Nearly half of the green coffee beans we import are contaminated with pesticides, potential carcinogens. And the situation worsens, for the free trade zones that stimulate the globalization of capitalism increase the importation of these products.

Based on a newsletter from Frances Moore Lappe, founder of Food First; Ingersoll 1990; Allen 1991; "U.S. Pesticide Exports" 1994.

PREVENTING POLLUTION THROUGH INDUSTRIAL WASTES. A third pressing problem is how to safely dispose of the unwanted by-products of industrialization.

Detoxifying Wastes ■ We already know how to detoxify most industrial wastes. We probably could learn to detoxify the rest. Recycling waste products is especially promising because it turns noxious wastes into safe and usable products. To develop better technology to recycle and detoxify wastes, we could establish a superfund to finance cooperative research by scientists. Through a crash program—a "Manhattan Project" of industrial wastes—we might be able to decontaminate the world's chemical time bombs before they go off.

Hazardous Waste Sites ■ Scattered across the nation are thousands of sites where we have discarded oil, battery acid, PCBs, pesticides, paint, and radioactive wastes. As you saw on Figure 14-3 on page 490, the EPA has drawn up a National Priority List of the most dangerous of these hazardous waste sites. Table 14-1 ranks the states on the basis of the number of priority waste sites they contain. Congress established a superfund to clean up these sites and has spent $20 billion to begin the cleanup. Some estimate that the bill for cleaning up these sites will run $50 billion; others say that it will total $500 billion. No one knows, of course, but if the lower total is correct, that's $160 for every person in the United States. If the higher figure is right, the cleanup will cost each of us $1,600.

Nuclear Wastes ■ Because they stay lethal for thousands of years, leftover plutonium and other nuclear wastes have perplexed the experts. For decades, while scientists debated how to store something that was beyond human experience, *millions* of pounds of radioactive waste have been stored in temporary containers (Campbell 1987; Schneider

TABLE 14-1	How the States Rank in Number of Hazardous Waste Sites on the National Priority List

State	Number of Sites
1. New Jersey	114
2. Pennsylvania	96
3. California	95
4. New York	91
5. Michigan	69
6. Florida	52
7. Illinois	47
8. Washington	47
9. Texas	43
10. Wisconsin	39
11. Ohio	37
12. Massachusetts	32
13. Indiana	30
14. North Carolina	30
15. Virginia	30
16. Missouri	26
17. South Carolina	26
18. Minnesota	24
19. Maryland	20
20. New Hampshire	20
21. Colorado	18
22. Utah	17
23. Connecticut	16
24. Louisiana	16
25. Alabama	15
26. Georgia	15
27. Montana	15
28. Delaware	14
29. Kentucky	14
30. Tennessee	14
31. Iowa	13
32. New Mexico	13
33. Kansas	12
34. Maine	12
35. Nebraska	12
36. Rhode Island	12
37. Oklahoma	11
38. Oregon	11
39. Vermont	11
40. Arkansas	10
41. Arizona	9
42. Idaho	9
43. West Virginia	9
44. Alaska	6
45. Mississippi	5
46. Hawaii	3
47. South Dakota	2
48. Wyoming	2
49. Nevada	1
50. North Dakota	0
Total	**1,286**

Source: By the author. Based on *Statistical Abstract of the United States* 2006:Table 369.

1992). The waste's new home is supposed to be in Yucca Mountain near Las Vegas, Nevada. Storage chambers have been carved from an ancient salt bed, nearly half a mile below ground. Geologists assure us that this salt deposit has been stable for 250 million years (Brooke 1999). Critics point out that this may be so, but the waste will be stored in stainless steel containers lined with lead. No one knows if those containers will last a thousand years, much less ten thousand years. Others say that we have so much waste waiting to be buried that even this depository won't hold it all (Ashley 2002). Nevada officials don't want this waste, and they are suing to stop it from coming into their state (Tetreault 2006). To make the issue even more controversial, Las Vegas officials have said that they won't allow the waste to pass through their city on the way to the mountain. If necessary, they say, they will use armed force to stop the trucks and railroad cars carrying the waste.

THE GREENHOUSE EFFECT. What can we do to solve the greenhouse effect? An immediate step would be to plant vast numbers of trees around the world, for they thrive on carbon dioxide. To the extent that carbon dioxide is a danger to the world, nations must reduce the amounts that they produce. The 1997 environmental pact approved by 160 nations in Kyoto, Japan, was a giant step in this direction. As mentioned, this agreement proved controversial. Fearful that compliance could cost millions of jobs, the United States withdrew from it. Other nations seem ready to do so, too (Struck 2006). We will have to see what the future holds in this regard.

THE RAIN FORESTS. We must also develop social policies to help stop the destruction of the world's rain forests. I propose two policies. The first is to make it illegal to import timber that comes from these forests. This will require an international agreement; the ban won't work if only a nation here and there passes such laws. The second is for the industrialized nations to *purchase the rights to not develop the rain forests.* Because most of the rain forests are in nations that have not industrialized, those funds could pay off their huge debts, thus helping to solve another problem. This policy would preserve millions of acres and thousands of plant and animal species for future generations. The rights would extend indefinitely and be overseen by an international watchdog agency.

No social policy is simple, of course, and policies concerning the rain forests bring their own complications. Brazil, for example, which has extensive rain forests, knows that the United States prospered by cutting down most of its forests for farmland. Brazilian officials find it ironic that the United States wants them to preserve Brazil's forests for the benefit of Americans. Some Brazilian officials even fear that the concern the United States has expressed is a prelude to an invasion, and they have trained jungle forces to repel it (Goering 1998; Zibechi 2005). Paranoia? We have only to look at the long history of U.S. intervention in Latin America to understand such fears.

AN OVERARCHING SOLUTION. To hit this problem hard, we need to produce less of what harms the environment. We can change our production techniques and equipment, redesign our products, and do more in-process recycling (Doran 2006). We have the capacity to take these steps, but to take them we must be convinced that our fragile environment is being harmed and that it is worth the effort and cost to change our ways. Whether or not we have this perspective, of course, depends on the framework of interpretation we are using.

Energy

Aside from discovering new deposits of gas and petroleum, only two types of solutions for energy exist: alternative forms of energy and energy conservation.

ALTERNATIVE FORMS OF ENERGY. What forms of energy can be alternatives to our heavy dependence on gas and petroleum?

Coal ■ We have enough coal in the United States to satisfy our energy needs for centuries. We can transform coal into liquids and gases. South Africa already operates a coal liquefaction plant that produces a fuel that is competitive in cost with petroleum, and China is in the process of developing such plants (Wu 2006). We would have to assure that they did not contribute to pollution.

Synthetic Fuels ■ "Synfuels" can be developed from garbage, sawdust, and other waste. The decay of organic substances such as sewage and straw produces methane and methanol, gases that motors can burn efficiently. Synfuels offer the potential to solve two problems at once: the disposal of our organic garbage and the production of alternative fuels. We may see fields of common milkweed turn into flourishing "petroleum farms" as factories extract hydrocarbons—the backbone of motor fuels, lubricants, turpentine, and rubber—from those plants.

To encourage the development and production of synfuels, Congress offered huge tax breaks. This drew the scammers out of the woodwork. If you spray pine tar or latex on coal, you have met the IRS requirement that the new product be chemically different from the original. Although there is no new product, no real synfuel, the spraying meets the letter of the law and qualifies you for the tax break. Companies that conduct such scams have to sell their coated coal at a loss—otherwise, the utility companies they sell to could simply burn coal that doesn't have the coating. Although these supposed synfuel companies lose money on their fake product, they reap real profits from the tax credits that they sell to wealthy investors (Biddle 2001; Hogan 2001). The losers in this sweet setup are the taxpayers who have to ante up the taxes that the IRS doesn't collect from those who profit from this legal scam.

Other Alternative Fuels ■ Hydrogen, too, holds great potential. As a basic component of air and water, hydrogen is available in limitless amounts. Other alternative sources of energy include the wind, ocean tides, geothermal energy (heat from beneath the earth's crust), and nuclear fusion (combining atoms, as opposed to nuclear fission, which splits atoms). Especially promising is harnessing the sun. Solar power is infinite, and technologies such as the photovoltaic cell, which changes sunlight into electricity, can trap it.

Developing alternative sources of energy offers hope for our future, but the political climate blows hot and cold. When the price of gasoline goes up, the public clamors for something to be done. Politicians hint at developing alternative forms of energy, but they do little. If gasoline reaches $4 or $5 a gallon and remains there, it is likely that Americans will get serious about alternative forms of energy.

ENERGY CONSERVATION. The other solution is to conserve energy. Conservation involves everything from insulating homes, businesses, and factories to working four 10-hour shifts instead of five 8-hour shifts a week. Such a change in working patterns would cut commuting expenses by 20 percent and allow factories to fire up their boilers less often. The potential savings from conservation are dramatic, but it does involve changing patterns of behavior that are rooted firmly in culture, hardly an easy matter.

Our Homes ■ As the price of energy has gone up, we have made our homes more energy efficient (*Statistical Abstract* 2006:Table 896). But we still have a long way to go. The "Lo-Cal" house, developed at the University of Illinois, can cut fuel bills by about two-thirds. These savings are made simply through the design of the house, without help

Of the alternative sources of energy, wind power is one of the most promising. This photo was taken in India.

from solar equipment. About 85 percent of the total window area in the house faces south, the house is heavily insulated, and its roof overhangs by thirty inches, letting sunshine in during the winter but excluding it during the summer. Another home design is the "solar envelope." This house is built within a second set of walls that provide a "skin" to trap and distribute the sun's heat. Even in northern climates, a furnace is needed on only the cloudiest days of winter. Its ingenious design also cools the house in the summer by drawing in cool air from a chamber under the house.

Our Cars ▪ We have also increased the energy efficiency of our cars, and we get much better mileage than we used to. Although the automobile industry dragged its feet, after California increased its standards for cars sold in that state, car companies began researching alternatives in earnest. Their main innovation is the hybrid. Using both electricity and gasoline to propel them, hybrid cars burn about 25 percent less gasoline than regular cars. They even convert the car's motion to electricity when the brakes are applied ("Hybrid Car . . . " 2004). Other hybrids burn hydrogen. Toyota has even developed a car that can travel 300 miles on a single tank of compressed hydrogen (Murphy 2003). Propelling cars by burning hydrogen can also reduce global warming, because water flows out of the exhaust, instead of carbon dioxide.

Cogeneration ▪ Another form of conservation is **cogeneration,** producing electricity as part of normal operations, such as generating electricity from the heat and steam that industrial boilers produce. This is not a new idea. In 1900, cogenerators produced more than half of the nation's electricity. Now they produce only about 3 percent. To encourage cogeneration, federal law requires that utility companies purchase a firm's excess production at the utility's standard costs (Paul 1987). The advantage for utility companies is that they can add to their capacity to provide electricity without having to invest in building new power plants (Devine 2004).

IN SUM We seem to be at a watershed in social policy. If the pessimistic environmentalists are correct, we soon will see the end of some of the resources on which our civilization depends. If we haven't made the hard policy choices before this happens, these shortages will force us to make them. If the optimists are right, we won't have to make hard choices. Market forces will point us in the right direction. If we run short of something, the pursuit of profits will lead people to develop alternative sources. Those who are convinced of this view tell us, Just don't interfere with those market forces, and the balance will occur naturally.

Moral Issues in a Global Age

In addition to the fundamentally differing perspectives presented by the pessimists and optimists, determining social policy takes us into basic philosophical and moral issues.

THE DILEMMA OF GLOBAL SOLUTIONS. Because the environmental crisis is global, its solution requires global social policy of some sort. It seems inescapable that some organization—whether the United Nations or the World Trade Organization or some other international body—needs to take the lead in solving environmental problems by proposing international laws to benefit all nations. Because such laws will conflict with the individual sovereignty of nations, some nations are likely to reject this type of legislation as violating their national interest. This brings us face-to-face with philosophical, moral issues.

Consider these questions. Do nations have a fundamental right to use resources—whether from their own land or those they import—in any way they wish? Do they even have a fundamental right to pollute, if they choose to do so? If not, then do nations possess some fundamental right to impose their view of pollution and resources on others? If so, what is the basis of that right? Is it some "greater good" for the world's benefit? If so, who decides what that "greater good" is and how it should be enforced? Assumptions of a "greater good," as conflict theorists remind us, can be excuses for the Most Industrialized Nations to bully the world. If there is such a right, it certainly isn't likely that the weaker nations would be able to impose their ideas of pollution and resource depletion or use on the more powerful nations.

The Future of the Problem

As we try to glimpse the future, let's first examine energy conservation and pollution. After this, we'll again look through the eyes of the pessimists and optimists.

Energy

As our expectations of attaining higher standards of living continue to grow, we increase our demands for energy. Although since 1970, the average U.S. family has shrunk from 3.6 people to 3.1, the average size of a new home has risen by over 50 percent—from 1,500 square feet to over 2,350. We also furnish our homes with more energy-eating appliances. In 1970, 34 percent of new homes had central air conditioning; now 90 percent do (*Statistical Abstract* 1989:Tables 58, 1231; 2006:Table 932). Dishwashers have also changed from luxuries to "necessities." We might complain about the price of gasoline, but the higher cost doesn't show up in our driving. We drive our cars more than we used to, averaging 40 percent more miles per car today than in 1980 (*Statistical Abstract* 2006:Table 1084).

Our efforts at energy conservation have been quite effective. Although the size of an average new house has increased over 50 percent since 1970, it uses only 17 percent more energy (*Statistical Abstract* 2006:Table 896). Similarly, although we have increased our driving by 40 percent since 1980, our cars are so much more efficient that we burn only 6 percent more gasoline per car (*Statistical Abstract* 2006:Table 1985). You can see, however, that although we have made great strides in conservation, we have *not* reduced our energy usage. Instead, we have increased it.

It is likely that we and the rest of the industrialized world will continue our energy-wasteful ways. It is also likely that as shortages occur and prices go up that we will turn to alternative sources of energy, especially our vast reserves of coal. We likely will continue to develop technology to harness alternative forms of energy, making these sources of energy widely available at low prices. Doubtless, the international oil companies will turn the alternative forms into profitable enterprises.

Pollution

The picture for pollution is less positive. We continue to approach pollution on an emergency basis: When the leaching of a chemical dump or some other form of pollution becomes too public to ignore, we slap on an environmental Band-Aid. We have no overarching plan for chemical and nuclear pollution that ensures the long-range health of our population.

If bringing pollution under control required only law and technology, we could assume a future with cleaner air, water, and land. But more is required—particularly a national determination to make our environment as free of pollution as possible. Although this depends on public awareness, which ebbs and flows, it also depends on politics; any administration can strengthen or weaken standards.

THE GREENS. Environmentalists in Europe have formed their own political parties. The Green Party, as the one in Germany is called, holds seats in the parliament; and in several

Spotlight on Social Research
THE MARRIAGE OF COMMUNITY AND ENVIRONMENT

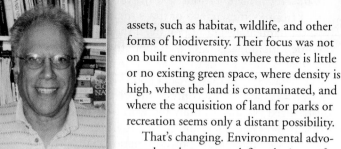

ROBERT GOTTLIEB, *Professor of Urban Environmental Policy at Occidental College, has found that something new is happening in the environmental movement. He calls it a marriage of community and environment. Living in Los Angeles and writing and teaching about the urban environment make this "marriage" particularly compelling for him.*

When I first arrived in Los Angeles in 1969, the city, with its sprawling landscapes of subdivisions and freeways, had a reputation as the "antienvironment." I never focused on the fact that Los Angeles had a river until the 1980s, when one of my students brought to my attention the growing advocacy around the revitalization of the asphalt-and-concrete-encased Los Angeles River. Since then, I've been able to document the creation in Los Angeles of a new kind of community-based environmentalism: where urban rivers and streams and other green spaces and community places in the City are re-envisioned.

This marriage of community and environment has made an impact on environmental groups. Open space has long referred to places outside urban areas or at the urban edge where there is little or no development. Earlier battles for open space sought to *preserve* environmental assets, such as habitat, wildlife, and other forms of biodiversity. Their focus was not on built environments where there is little or no existing green space, where density is high, where the land is contaminated, and where the acquisition of land for parks or recreation seems only a distant possibility.

That's changing. Environmental advocates have begun to redefine the issue of open space as the need to re-envision *community spaces* and to reclaim rather than simply preserve such places. Many environmentalists now embrace community gardens, farmers markets in low-income communities, relandscaping projects, and recreational opportunities in densely populated areas. I had the opportunity to direct an educational program on the Los Angeles River—the very symbol of both the antienvironment and efforts to re-envision the river as a community and environmental asset.

If you define the marriage of community and environment as an effort to re-envision—or reconstruct or reclaim—these kinds of community and environmental assets, then a different kind of environmental agenda begins to emerge. This agenda would focus on a neighborhood's transportation needs, on access to and quality of food, on health concerns like asthma, and on schools as relandscaped, livable places rather than fortresslike, asphalt jungles. In this marriage, the greening agenda becomes a justice agenda. It leads us to understand that nature belongs in the city as well as outside it.

---

of Germany's states it has become a key player in coalition governments. The United States, too, has a Green Party, but it has a difficult time mustering enough support to get on the ballot, much less to win a major election. Even the weak support for Ralph Nader, the closest we have had to a national Green candidate, dried up in the 2004 elections. That the U.S. Greens have not been able to muster strong political support does not mean that this will continue indefinitely. Some unexpected event could etch the environment into the national consciousness, making it a top political issue. In the meantime, as Robert Gottlieb discusses in the Spotlight on Social Research box above, environmentalists have begun to apply their perspective to urban life.

A LACK OF UNITY. As conflict theorists would stress, the future of pollution depends on a fragile balance of power among groups whose interests coalesce. At this point, there is little to indicate that people will drop their other political interests to join under a green banner. However, just as with the Santa Barbara oil spill in 1969 (see page 479), so some startling event yet to come could be the stimulus to unite fragmented groups around the world, forging them into a global political alliance. Certainly people are concerned about the world they will leave for their children, but environmentalists, often local in orientation or fragmented by multiple visions and political strategies, lack a unifying voice. Even so, groups split on issues can overcome differences to make the environment a top priority, as illustrated by the Christians and Jews who are joining forces under the banner "Creation Care." Their message: "We are called to be stewards, not exploiters, of the earth" (Watanabe 1998). Though the potential is present, the voice remains weak.

THE ENVIRONMENTAL PESSIMISTS AND OPTIMISTS. Finally, let's look at the future through the eyes of the two groups who see practically nothing alike.

The Picture Painted by the Pessimists ▪ The pessimists paint a gloomy future, of course. Pollution will continue with only superficial improvements here and there, and the depletion of resources will accelerate. The countdown has already begun, and "RDP Day" (Resource-Depletion and Pollution Day) is on its way. This is the day when we will have depleted our vital resources and pollution will have gone so far that we won't be able to fix it. With its industrial base undermined, modern society will disintegrate, bringing tragedy to all. Desperate, people will flee. But to where? Even the countryside will be too polluted to support anything but a minimum of life.

Can such a gloomy future be averted? Yes, reply the pessimists, but only if we develop a steady-state or scaled-back society. To either level off our energy consumption or to reduce it severely and eliminate much of our material gadgetry, however, will be like wrestling a bottle away from an alcoholic's gnarled hands. Because we have built a society on the assumption of inexhaustible resources, the withdrawal symptoms will bring enormous pain. But once we recover from the shock of being forced into a drastically different lifestyle, we may find that a simpler way of life is rewarding: We will be less rushed, enjoy social relationships more, and feel less compulsion to own things.

The Picture Painted by the Optimists. ▪ And what does the future look like to the optimists? Instead of using the gray and black colors of the pessimists, the optimists paint with bright, cheerful colors. Our present path is fine, they say. We already have more resources than we need for the foreseeable future, but as scientists continue to make breakthroughs, they will put even more energy at our disposal. Their

The future? This hybrid car runs on bioethanol. Delivering 260 horsepower, the car has zero emission of fossil carbon dioxide.

developments in hydrogen storage and fusion, for example, hold the potential of giving us energy in unlimited quantities. From this source alone, we can meet all the world's needs now and in the future (Bishop and Wells 1989; C. Stevens 1989).

For the optimists, neither is pollution a fearsome problem, not even nuclear waste. Scientists have discovered a bacterium that has adapted to fifteen times the dose of radiation it takes to kill humans. This bacterium, and others yet to come, *extremophiles,* will eat our nuclear wastes, breaking them down into relatively harmless components (Fialka 2004). The principle is this: Pollution will be solved to the extent that people demand a cleaner environment and are willing to pay for prevention and cleanup. Because people are demanding it, the environment is already getting cleaner—and it will continue to improve. Consequently, the future promises a healthier environment, an even higher standard of living, and a continued lengthening of our life expectancy.

WHO IS RIGHT? What *is* the future of the environmental crisis? Is humanity at a crossroads, as the pessimists insist, with our current course destining us to destruction? Or are the optimists right, and our current course is taking us to a delightful future? Could the future turn out to be even gloomier than imagined, with nuclear war, the worst pollution of all, destroying our ecosystem—and humanity? We consider that possibility in the next chapter.

We who are the audience—and either beneficiaries or victims of—this unfolding drama will have to await its outcome.

SUMMARY AND REVIEW

1. The destruction of the environment began millennia ago and may even have destroyed ancient civilizations. Industrialization has intensified this process.

2. The nations of the world share a common *ecosystem.* The environmental crisis is a global matter: Even individual acts of *pollution* can have international consequences. Pollution comes primarily from industrialization and is common in both capitalist and socialist nations.

3. Symbolic interactionists have studied how the environment became a social problem, how objective conditions were translated into subjective concerns. Concerns about the environment began with professionals, were picked up by interest groups and government agencies, and then by the press, which aroused the public.

4. Functionalists stress that all life on earth is interdependent. ("Everything is connected to everything else.") We all are part of a huge, complex living machine called the environment. Industrialization has dysfunctional consequences for the ecosystem.

5. Conflict theorists stress the conflict between environmentalists, who battle to reduce environmental threat, and industrial leaders, who fight for the right to pollute while earning a profit.

6. Some measures of air and water pollution show improvement, but the results are mixed, and pollution continues. The *greenhouse effect* could cause climatic change that would have far-ranging consequences for humanity.

7. Strip mining and the disposal of solid wastes despoil the land. Industrial wastes threaten our drinking water and many of our lakes and rivers. *Acid* and *mercury rain* imperil animal and plant life.

8. Chemical pollutants pervade our environment. Leaching from landfills is extensive. Nuclear pollution is ominous, as illustrated by the Kyshtym and Chernobyl disasters. Food additives are a form of pollution. Genetic modification might be another form.

9. Alarmed at the environmental crisis, pessimists advocate a *steady-state society*—one based on no economic growth—or a *scaled-back society,* based on deliberately shrinking the economy. Optimists, convinced that we can continue industrial growth and use technology to solve environmental problems, advocate an expanded economy. Regardless of who is right, pollution is a global problem that requires international social policies.

10. The environmental pessimists and optimists paint contrasting pictures of the future. We don't yet know who is right, but with our coal reserves and other alternative forms of energy, accompanied by developing technology, our energy future looks positive. The outlook for pollution, however, is less positive. The currently fragmented environmental movement has the potential to become a powerful global force.

KEY TERMS

Acid rain, 487
Biodegradable, 483
Carcinogen, 483
Cogeneration, 510
Corporate welfare, 482
Ecology, 476
Ecosystem, 479

Environmental injustice, 481
Food pollution (also called *food contamination*), 492
Genetically modified foods (GMF), 496
Global warming, 484
Greenhouse effect, 484

Ozone shield, 483
Pollution, 476
Steady-state society, 505
Synergistic (literally, "working together"), 494
Thermal inversion, 483

THINKING CRITICALLY ABOUT CHAPTER 14

1. Which of the perspectives (symbolic interactionism, functionalism, or conflict theory) do you think does the best job of explaining the environmental crisis? Why?

2. How far do you think the government should go to reduce pollution? Should the executives who run polluting corporations be jailed? Should the government shut down polluters? What else could or should the government do?

3. The scientists represented by, among others, the conservative think tank the Heritage Foundation, argue that problems of pollution and the scarcity of resources are best solved by free enterprise. They believe that the market is better equipped than governments to solve these problems. What do you think of their position? Explain.

4. Do you think that U.S. corporations should be allowed to manufacture and export to other countries chemicals that are banned in the United States? Explain.

5. Do you think that the U.S. government has the power or authority to demand a steady-state society? Do you think it is advisable? Why or why not?

CHAPTER 15

War, Terrorism, and the Balance of Power

Most of us can remember vividly where we were on September 11, 2001, a day that has become embedded in our own memories—and seared into the national consciousness. This day, which began like so many before it—a bright dawn, shining sun, and people going about their everyday lives—was destined to change the United States. No longer would our assumptions about life be the same.

When the commercial jets that had been transformed into lethal missiles struck the Twin Towers and the Pentagon, the United States was shaken to its roots. At dawn, these two global symbols, one of capitalism and the other of military power, had stood tall and proud. Just a few hours later, the one had been destroyed, the other crippled.

Americans shook their heads in dismay and confusion. Why had they been attacked? And who had done this? As confusion turned into anger, and the face of the enemy was beamed to the United States and the world, the nation's response was swift and violent. U.S. Special Forces, accompanied by missiles directed from remote locations, attacked al-Qaeda in Afghanistan.

The United States declared war on terrorism—as it steeled itself against further attacks by an enemy that, hidden in its midst, hit suddenly and without warning. Where would this unseen enemy strike next? The White House? A nuclear plant? Some NFL football game? Even the local mall?

Americans remembered 1941, the surprise attack at Pearl Harbor, which had led to the United States declaring war on Japan. This one did, too, but to a different kind of war. Instead of a country to counterattack, the enemy consists of small groups in many countries. Just as in 1941, Americans feared sleeper cells in the United States, with attacks launched at any time, from almost anywhere.

But how will we know when this new war has ended? After all, will there ever be an end to people who hold grudges against the United States? Will the United States try to track down groups around the world, without end?

It's a strange war—and strange times we live in.

> It's a strange war.

The Problem in Sociological Perspective

After the attack at Pearl Harbor, the United States entered World War II. The Soviet Union (a union of communist countries) and the United States (a capitalist country), although avowed enemies, became uneasy allies, fighting on the same side. From the end of that war in 1945 until the end of the 1980s, the Soviet Union and the West were caught up in an **arms race.** Each furiously developed and produced new weapons, threatening one another and trying to outmatch the other's war capabilities. During these decades, called the **Cold War,** the West and the Soviet Union built arsenals of nuclear weapons that had (and still have) the capacity to destroy the world many times over.

When the Soviet Union accepted capitalism in the 1980s, the Cold War came to an end, but the nuclear weapons that these nations developed did not. They remain, still so powerful that they threaten human existence. In an instant, these weapons could reduce major cities to rubble and transform world powers into barren deserts. If we could put all the catastrophes that the world has ever experienced throughout its history into a single pile, it would pale in comparison with nuclear war.

Why Is War Common?

Although the magnitude of the threat we face today is new, war itself is not. Human groups have always fought each other. Why do they do so?

AN INSTINCT TO FIGHT? Because war has been common in human history, some analysts suggest that humans have an instinct for aggression. Anthropologist Konrad Lorenz said (1960) that our instinct for aggression used to be functional. It helped ensure that the fittest survived. It also forced humans to colonize the whole world as they fled from one another's innate aggression. In modern society, however, as Lorenz put it, this instinct has become a "hereditary evil" left over from our primitive past.

THE SOCIOLOGICAL ANSWER: SOCIETIES CHANNEL AGGRESSION. To find the answer to why warfare exists, sociologists (and most anthropologists) do not look *within* people. Whether humans have an instinct for aggression is not the point. People will always disagree about something, so conflicts always arise among people who live together. *What is significant are the norms that groups establish to deal with those conflicts.*

To illustrate this principle, let's look at two extremes. The first is a society that nourishes aggression. As you read about the Yanomamö in the Global Glimpse box on the next page, you will see why they represent this extreme. The other extreme is represented by the Eskimos of East Greenland. Instead of fighting, their norms require that hostile individuals *sing* to one another! Actually, they sing about their grievances, and the contest goes like this:

> The singing style is highly conventionalized. The successful singer uses the traditional patterns of composition which he attempts to deliver with such finesse as to delight the audience to enthusiastic applause. He who is most heartily applauded is "winner." . . . One of the advantages of the song duel carried on at length is that it gives the public time to come to a consensus about who is correct or who should admit guilt in the dispute. . . . Gradually more people are laughing a little harder at one of the duelist's verses than at the other's, until it becomes apparent where the sympathy of the community lies, and then opinion quickly becomes unanimous and the loser retires. (Fromm 1973)

Other groups channel aggression into rituals in which violence becomes a form of drama. Here is an example of a spear-throwing duel among the Tiwi of northern Australia:

> When a dispute is between an accuser and a defendant, which is commonly the case, the accuser ritually hurls the spears from a prescribed distance, while the defendant dodges them. The public can applaud the speed, force, and accuracy of the accuser as he hurls his spears, or they can applaud the adroitness with which the defendant dodges them. After a time, unanimity is achieved as the approval for one or the other's skill gradually becomes overwhelming. When the defendant realizes that the community is finally considering him guilty, he is supposed to fail to dodge a spear and allow himself to be wounded in some fleshy part of his body. Conversely, the accuser simply stops throwing the spears when he becomes aware that public opinion is going against him. (Fromm 1973)

WAR IS NOT UNIVERSAL. Although hostilities, aggression, and even murder characterize all human groups, war does not. War is just one option that some groups have for settling disagreements, but not all societies offer this option. The Mission Indians of North America, the Arunta of Australia, the Andaman Islanders of the South Pacific, and the Eskimos of the Arctic, for example, have established ways to handle quarrels, but they do not have organized battles that pit one tribe against another. These groups don't even have a word for war (Lesser 1968).

NOURISHING AGGRESSION: THE YANOMAMÖ

The Yanomamö men of the Amazon rain forest often attack neighboring villages, killing the men and kidnapping the women. Villagers also fight with one another. Fights often begin over sex: infidelity, seductions, or failure to give a promised girl in marriage. Sometimes the men challenge one another to a duel. One man stands, muscles tensed, feet firmly planted, while the other hits him as hard as he can once in the chest. Then the other man gets his turn. This continues until one man can no longer return the blow. Sometimes men take turns pounding one another over the head with a long wooden club. At other times, they even use axes and machetes—and neglect to await their turn. When relatives are drawn in, fights turn into brawls. These games can trigger feuds between villages. When someone is killed, relatives seek revenge. A feud is self-feeding, for each killing requires retaliation.

Why do the men fight like this? Anthropologist Napoleon Chagnon, who lived with the Yanomamö and analyzed their relationships, concluded that the basic reason is *social status.* Because violence is considered to be the mark of a true man, a reputation for violence gives a Yanomamö man high status. Almost everyone everywhere wants more status, to be looked up to by others, and the Yanomamö have developed a system that integrates acts of violence and status.

There is also another factor, one that is less apparent: Success at violence brings men more access to women. Chagnon found

The origins of warfare go back to the origins of history. Because war is so common, some theorists suggest that aggression is a part of human nature. If so, it is socially channeled into cultural forms. Shown here are men of a Yanomamö tribe.

that the men in this northern Venezuelan jungle who have killed at least one other person have more wives and children than those who have never killed. An especially successful warrior may have six wives. The higher status that comes with killing makes a man an attractive candidate for marriages—which are arranged by the men.

"How primitive they are!" we might say, smugly acknowledging our higher technology and education. But the Yanomamö are not that different from us, as Chagnon points out. Although we don't reward our war heroes with additional wives, we do award them with medals, seats in the U.S. Senate, and even the presidency. As Chagnon points out and as presidential campaigns illustrate, the military record of candidates is important in U.S. politics.

Are we any different, then, from the Yanomamö—aside from being more indirect in the ways we reward "war behaviors"?

FOR YOUR CONSIDERATION

In what ways do we encourage (reward) and discourage human aggression? In what ways do we channel human aggression into socially acceptable forms? What prevents us from breaking down into little groups that are at war with one another?

Based on Allman 1988; Chagnon 1988.

Why Do Some Groups Choose War?

War—an organized form of aggression that involves armed conflict between politically distinct groups—is often part of national policy. Why do some groups choose war to handle disputes when less drastic solutions are available?

THREE ESSENTIAL CONDITIONS OF WAR. Sociologist Nicholas Timasheff became interested in this question. After studying armed conflicts, he (1965) identified three essential conditions of war. The *first* is a cultural tradition for war. Because war has become part of a people's thinking, they view war as a way to resolve conflict with another nation. The *second* is an antagonistic situation in which states confront incompatible objectives. Each, for example, might want the same land or resources. A cultural tradition for war and an antagonistic situation are essential, but they are not enough. They provide the fuel, but there also has to be a spark to ignite it. This *third* condition moves the nations from thinking about war to actually engaging in it.

SEVEN "SPARKS" THAT SET OFF WAR. To identify the "sparks" that ignite the fuel, Timasheff studied wars throughout history. He found seven "sparks" that ignite an antagonistic situation, causing it to flame into war. They are the opportunity to

1. Get revenge (to settle "old scores" from previous conflicts)
2. Dictate one's will to a weaker nation
3. Protect or enhance prestige (to preserve the nation's "honor")
4. Unite rival groups within one's country
5. Protect or exalt the nation's leaders
6. Satisfy the national aspirations of ethnic groups (to bring "our people" who are living in another country into our borders)
7. Convert others to religious and ideological beliefs

IN SUM To understand war, sociologists do not look for factors *within* humans, such as an instinct for war. Instead, they look for *social* causes—conditions in society that encourage or discourage aggression and that shape aggression into organized combat between nations.

The Scope of the Problem

Turn on the evening news or a twenty-four-hour news channel, and you almost always hear a report on a war being fought somewhere. And the United States always seems to be sending troops somewhere, sometimes to countries whose names we can't even pronounce or spell and, frankly, that most of us don't care about. Did countries fight this much in the past?

War in the History of the West

To find out how common war has been, sociologist Pitirim Sorokin (1937) listed the wars in Europe from 500 B.C. to A.D. 1925. He identified 967 wars, an average of one war every two to three years. Counting years or parts of a year in which a country was at war, Germany had the least warfare (28 percent) and Spain the highest (67 percent). Sorokin found that the land of his birth, Russia, had experienced only one peaceful quarter century during the previous 1,000 years. Since William the Conqueror took power in 1066, England had been at war for 56 of each 100 years.

And the United States? It turns out that we are one of the most warlike nations in the world. From 1850 to about 1980, we sent our military to other parts of the world more than 150 times (Kohn 1988). That's more than once a year. We continue to do this today, and at our current rate, it won't be long until the total reaches 200. Although we have been "at war" with no nation, in recent years we have "intervened" (as U.S. politicians like to call it) in this order: El Salvador, Honduras, Libya, Grenada, Panama, Afghanistan, Iraq, Somalia, Haiti, Bosnia, Sudan, Kosovo—and then back again to Afghanistan and Iraq, where, as I write this, we still have troops. And also as I write this, reports in the media keep mentioning the need for "military interventions" in Korea and Iran. The suggested target might have changed by the time you read this, but I anticipate that only the targets for our "military interventions" will be different, not our readiness to attack—excuse me, to intervene militarily.

Measuring War in Terms of Deaths

War may be hell, as William T. Sherman said, but some wars are more hellish than others. Consider the killing. Since 1829, there have been approximately

- 80 wars in which 3,000 to 30,000 people died
- 42 wars in which 30,000 to 300,000 people died

- 12 wars in which 300,000 to 3,000,000 people died
- 2 wars (World Wars I and II) in which 3,000,000 to 31,000,000 people died (Richardson 1960; updated to 2007)

If your father or mother dies in a war, of course, it matters little that there were 30,000 or 3 million other victims of that war. On a personal level, we measure things by how they affect us.

OUR GROWING CAPACITY TO KILL. Nevertheless, to understand war we need to recognize how industrialization has increased our capacity to kill. Consider bombs. During World War I, fewer than 3 of every 100,000 people in England and Germany died from bombs. During the next twenty years, scientists "advanced" this new technique of human destruction as well as the aircraft to deliver them, and during World War II bombs killed about 300 of every 100,000 English and Germans (Hart 1957). Scientists have continued to "advance" our technology in killing, and if nations were to unleash nuclear weapons against one another today, the deaths of past wars would seem as nothing. Some of our more "advanced" weapons supposedly have the capacity to destroy every living thing on earth.

THE SLAUGHTER CONTINUES. Many have hoped that war would become the relic of a primitive past. With the world's higher levels of education, many have thought that we humans would finally achieve a more advanced state, able to look back uncomprehendingly, and with a bit of smug superiority, at how people used to slaughter one another.

As we all know, this description doesn't even come close to matching life today. A generation or so ago, the United States fought in Vietnam for about seven years—at a cost of 58,000 American lives and several hundred thousand Vietnamese. The death toll of the Soviet Union's nine-year war in Afghanistan ran about 1 million Afghanistani and perhaps 20,000 Soviet soldiers (Armitage 1989). Iran and Iraq fought an eight-year war at a cost of 400,000 lives. We don't yet know the death tolls of our "interventions" in Afghanistan and Iraq, but they will be high. As I write this, about 3,000 U.S. and other coalition soldiers have died, while estimates of Iraqi deaths are running over a half million (Tavernise and McNeil 2006).

IN SUM War, then, as Sorokin sadly concluded in the 1930s, is normal. That is, war is a common element in the world's history. Sorokin added that his era was one of the bloodiest, most turbulent periods in the history of Western civilization—and perhaps in the history of humanity. Our era certainly provides no reason to correct Sorokin's sad judgment. In recent years, we have seen Serbs kill Bosnians, and Bosnians kill Serbs—each claiming rightful revenge for atrocities of years past. After generations and even hundreds of years, these groups claim the right to hate eternally—and to pass their bitter heritage to their children. Israelis and Palestinians do the same. As they kill one another, each is convinced that its views are just and that God is on its side. Among other nations, India and Pakistan also claim the right to perpetuate ancient hatreds—and to threaten to nuke one another to hell. The soldiers of the United States, NATO, Russia, and the European Union are armed and ready to battle their own "righteous" causes. On top of all this—as with 9/11, the train bombings in Madrid, and the bus bombings in London—small groups of individuals have gotten into the act. These suicide bombers who blow up civilians have begun to initiate the launching of armies across the globe.

Looking at the Problem Theoretically

Let's use our three theoretical perspectives to focus on the social problem of war. Using symbolic interactionism, we will examine the symbolic basis of the nuclear arms race. Applying functionalism, we will consider why nations go to war. Through conflict theory, we will explore how conflicting interests and the desire for more territory lead to war.

Symbolic Interactionism

Symbolic interactionists emphasize how significant *perceptions* are in human behavior. They stress that we choose courses of action based on how we perceive events. When we apply this principle to war, we see that, at times, the fate of the world can actually hinge on perceptions. Let's see how this worked during the Cold War.

PERCEPTIONS AND THE ARMS RACE. During the Cold War, the United States and the Soviet Union were constantly deciding which new weapons to build and how much to spend on them. To underestimate the enemy could prove fatal, so each magnified the evil intentions and destructive capacity of the other. Without hard information, each had to guess what the other intended, and they then used their guesses to choose what seemed to be the most practical response.

This guessing game led to an arms race. When one superpower thought that the other might build a certain weapon, it began to build that weapon itself. Sometimes, however, the other nation had no intention of building the weapon, and the so-called countermeasure turned out to be an aggressive step that stimulated the other nation to build the weapon. Robert McNamara, who was the U.S. Secretary of Defense, explained how such mistakes in perception led to a buildup of nuclear warheads (Kurth 1974).

> In 1961 when I became Secretary of Defense, the Soviet Union possessed a very small operational arsenal of intercontinental missiles. However, they did possess the technological and industrial capacity to enlarge that arsenal very substantially over the succeeding several years. We had no evidence that the Soviets did plan, in fact, fully to use that capability. But, as I have pointed out, a strategic planner must be conservative in his calculations; that is, he must prepare for the worst plausible case and not be content to hope and prepare merely for the most probable.
>
> Since we could not be certain of Soviet intentions, since we could not be sure that they would not undertake a massive buildup, we had to insure against such an eventuality by undertaking ourselves a major buildup of the Minuteman and Polaris forces. . . . But the blunt fact remains that if we had more accurate information about planned Soviet strategic forces, we simply would not have needed to build as large a nuclear arsenal as we have today.

This buildup of intercontinental ballistic missiles (ICBMs) illustrates a primary principle of symbolic interactionism—symbols are central to human behavior. Because U.S. officials perceived Soviet plans in a certain way, they decided to build missiles. That decision, in turn, signaled to the Soviets that they needed to build ICBMs. The nuclear arms race was based on symbolic interpretations of what the enemy might do.

This example illustrates how *symbols are so powerful that they can take on a life of their own.* Once put into play, symbols wield power over human affairs. Although McNamara's initial perception of Soviet intentions might have been wrong, our buildup of missiles became proof to the Soviets that they needed to build more missiles. This, in turn, became proof to us that our interpretation was right in the first place—and that we needed to build even more powerful weapons. *Perceptions, not facts, usually guide human behavior.*

PERCEPTIONS AND THE "FIRST STRIKE." This principle is significant in all of human life. You and I might like to think that we act on facts, but we really act on our perceptions of "facts," on how we "think" things "are." We are right often enough that we manage to get through everyday life, but we're not always right. This underlying uncertainty of perceptions takes on special significance when two rival nations are considering war. As long as these nations perceive war as a no-win situation, they are likely to avoid it. If there is hatred and fear between them, however, and one nation thinks that striking first can destroy the other's capacity to strike back, that nation is encouraged to strike first.

During the Cold War, generals of the U.S. Air Force advocated a "first-strike" if it meant that we could win the war (Kurth 1974). Apparently Soviet generals did the same. You can see how tense and dangerous the situation was at that time. Each nation felt that it had to signal to the other that it could not win, that a first strike would be foolish. As a result, both the Soviet Union and the United States would let information slip about their new weapons or defense systems like "Star Wars." It is scary to think that our lives—and those of the world—depended on mutual fear and the correct interpretation of one another's signals!

Functionalism

THE FUNCTIONS OF WAR. In 1939, the world was in turmoil. Hitler's tanks and *Luftwaffe* were rampaging through Europe. Japan had invaded China and was threatening the South Pacific. His sociological imagination piqued, Robert Park (1941) decided to analyze war's social functions. Here are the functions of war that he and others have identified.

Extension of Territory ■ Park surveyed the literature on war and found that the world's countries had been born in war. The nations that existed in 1939—like those of today—had come into being as one group extended its political boundaries by conquering other groups. What is today's United States, for example, would not exist if it hadn't been for the Indian wars and the wars with France, Great Britain, Spain, and Mexico. A major function of war, said Park, is the *extension of territory*, an enlargement of a group's political power.

Social Integration ■ Another function of war is *social integration*. If groups within a country are in conflict, war can give them a mutual enemy. The groups put aside their differences, close ranks, and cooperate to repel their common threat (Coser 1956; Timasheff 1965; Hoffman 2006). After the war, the factions turn back to unfinished business and try to settle old scores. Afghanistan, for example, was fragmented into groups separated by rigid lines and bitter divisions: religious, class, tribal, and clan loyalties that reached back for centuries. When the Soviets invaded Afghanistan in 1979, these groups put aside their differences to work together to repel their common enemy. As soon as they defeated the Soviets, which took ten years, they renewed their divisions and turned on one another. Today, the United States looks on in dismay as it tries to reproduce its own image in Afghanistan and Iraq, its presence uniting enemies throughout the Arab world.

Social Change ■ Sociologist Georg Simmel (1904) identified *social change* as a third function of war. One form of social change stimulated by warfare is the development of science and technology. Five centuries ago, for example, Leonardo da Vinci designed war machines for his patron. Since then, war has prompted aerodynamic designs, the harnessing of nuclear energy, and satellites. We even owe our interstate highways and the Internet to war. General Eisenhower was impressed by the *autobahns* he saw in Germany when he arrived after its defeat in World War II. When he became president of the United States, he decided that we needed highways like these so we could move soldiers, weapons, and supplies rapidly across the country in case the Soviets attacked. Military personnel developed the Internet as an alternative form of communications.

War also stimulates developments in surgical techniques: Officers want soldiers patched up as quickly as possible so they can return to battle faster. Currently under development is long-distance surgery: The surgeon can be in the United States and yet with the aid of computers actually operate on a wounded soldier in some remote region of the world.

Economic Gain ■ A fourth function of war is *economic gain:* access to treasure, trade routes, markets, raw materials such as oil, and outlets for investment (Pruitt and Snyder 1969). Industrialization has put a new twist on this function—increasing production, profits, and employment. The best example is how World War II put millions of unemployed people to work and helped lift the United States out of the Great Depression. Even the threat of war can bring economic gain. As sociologist C. Wright Mills (1958) noted back in the 1950s, "war readiness" requires high spending that benefits big corporations. Because this is still true today, we will look at this function in detail.

Other Functions ■ A fifth function of war is *ideological*—advancing a political or religious system or suppressing an opposing one. Between the eleventh and fourteenth centuries European Crusaders traveled to the Holy Land to fight to recover it from Islam. Today, al-Qaeda and its supporters have a similar agenda. A sixth function is *vengeance* or *punishment*—teaching another nation "a lesson" or avenging an injury or insult (Pruitt and Snyder 1969). Much of the warfare in Bosnia and Kosovo, including the rapes and other atrocities, served this function. A seventh function is to increase *military security*. That is, a nation does not desire an asset in and of itself, but attacks to prevent an enemy from using that asset against it. This is why Israel bombed Iraq's nuclear plants in 1981, and why trigger fingers have become itchy to do the same in Iran and North Korea. An eighth function of war is to *increase the credibility* of a nation's threats or guarantees. By going to war, other nations will see that a nation means what it says.

Multiple Functions ▪ No war serves a single function. The same war can involve territory, revenge, ideology, and military security. If a conflict is drawn out, functions can even change. The Crusades began in 1095 when Pope Urban II exhorted Christians to go to war and reclaim the Holy Land for Christians. Ideological purposes may have dominated at first, but the Crusades also functioned to provide treasure and territory. Nine Crusades and 200 years later, all the functions of war had become incorporated into this prolonged war. If the "war against terrorism" goes on for decades, as seems likely, it, too, will have served all the functions.

Functions for the Victors ▪ War is usually highly functional for the victors. Rome, for example, conquered most of the known world, subjugating one people after another to Roman power and exploiting their resources. To the acclaim of citizens and Caesar alike, generals would return in triumph to Rome, marching in formation down the main avenue and into the main square, laden with treasure and slaves. The treasure enriched the government and its elite, and the captives did their grunt work. Some of the slaves brought to Rome after the fall of Greece were educated Greeks, who served as tutors for the elite's children. In the latter part of the empire, slaves provided drama, their deaths in the Colosseum yielding pleasure for Rome's jaded and bloodthirsty citizens.

Functions for the Losers ▪ Although war is highly dysfunctional for the losers, especially in terms of deaths, property destroyed, territories lost, and humiliation, losers can benefit from war. One of the most remarkable examples is the social change in Japan. After their defeat in World War II, the Japanese embraced Western technology. This change not only increased their standard of living and life expectancy, but also gained them the world leadership that they had failed to win by going to war. No social change is without its dysfunctions, however, and Japan's, too, has come at a price: the disruption of its traditional ways of life.

The crusades were fought between the 11th and 13th centuries. The Christians' stated purpose was to recover the Holy Land from the Muslims, but motives of riches, revenge, and glory became intertwined. In 1212, the Children's Crusade took place. In this, the most pathetic of the Crusades, thousands of children set out from France for the Holy Land. The ships' captains sold them to the Muslims as slaves. German children met a different fate. Going overland, they died of hunger and disease.

Functions for Individuals ▪ War also has functions for soldiers and leaders. Soldiers often report that battle presents them with the challenge to "see what I'm made of." Some even report that when they enter a battle they feel an excitement that verges on sexual arousal. More significant, however, are the satisfactions that war brings its leaders. Although most leaders bemoan war, much of this is posturing, done for the sake of a public image. Officers who plan battles derive intense satisfaction from outmaneuvering the enemy, gaining advantage through surprise attacks, and being acclaimed as the victor. War can also be an avenue of social mobility. Generals George Washington, Andrew Jackson, Ulysses S. Grant, and Dwight D. Eisenhower, for example, moved from being generals in the army to being presidents of the United

States. Colin Powell went from general to national security advisor. From there, he became secretary of state, one of the most powerful positions in the world.

DYSFUNCTIONS OF WAR. Standing in stark contrast are the dysfunctions of war. Defeat is war's most well-known dysfunction, as are the destruction of cities and the deaths and the maiming. There also are the fatherless children, the interruption of education, and the bitterness that can span generations. Even military victory can bring dysfunctions. The victor can grow dependent on the exploitation of subjugated peoples; when that control ends, as inevitably it does, the economic pain is severe. Spain experienced this dysfunction when it lost its colonies in the 1820s. For decades, Great Britain suffered withdrawal pains after it lost many of its colonies as a result of the fervor for independence ushered in by World War II. With the breakup of the Soviet empire, forged by war, Russia is undergoing this same dysfunction today. No longer can Moscow's bureaucrats dispatch an order, and minions in satellite nations send the specified materials. The spigot has been turned off.

Conflict Theory

THREE REASONS THAT NATIONS GO TO WAR. Conflict theorists have developed three major explanations for why nations go to war.

Resources ■ The origin of the first explanation is lost in history. It was a common observation that one group would go to war to get another group's resources—its pastures, flocks, or other wealth. Back in the 1300s, Ibn Khaldun of Tunis, whom some count as an early sociologist, stressed that as human groups struggle to survive, they compete for scarce resources. Inevitably, they come into conflict with one another. War is simply one form that human conflict takes.

Conflict theorists have built on the explanation of conflict over resources. On it, they have developed what they see as the central force in human history, the struggle for control over society's resources. In each society, some group gains control. This group, which conflict theorists call the *bourgeoisie*, uses the resources of society to keep itself in power and to exploit the less powerful. As a bourgeoisie expands its power beyond its country, it comes into conflict with the bourgeoisie of another country. Their quarrel over resources sometimes leads to war. The bourgeoisie themselves don't fight, of course. They hold the power, so to do battle for them they send young men (today, in a few instances, also young women) from the groups that they control (the poor, the workers, the *proletariat*). The German generals used the term "cannon fodder" to refer to the young men of the poor who died in such outrageous numbers in their wars.

Expansion of Markets ■ The second explanation focuses on the expansion of markets. In 1902, John Hobson, an economist, noted that as capitalism grows, surplus capital develops. Business leaders want to invest this capital, so they look for ways to expand their markets. They then persuade the government to go to war and take over other lands. The result is **imperialism,** the pursuit of profits and markets by war and threat of war.

A Military Machine ■ Another economist, Joseph Schumpeter, proposed a third explanation in 1919. He said (1919/1955) that the military and political elite build a strong military machine because it brings them power and prestige. Because the military machine was built to be used–sitting around idle was not its purpose–its very existence encourages war. Its use also brings prestige to the elite.

The Military Machine Today

Conflict theorists have built on these explanations. They stress how today's military machine has increased the threat of war. They note that after World War I the United States dismantled its military, and U.S. war industries returned to their peacetime pursuits (Barber 1972). Then came World War II, which was a turning point in U.S. history. When this war was over, the United States did not dismantle its war machine, as it had previously (Eisenhower 1961/1972). Instead, the United States maintains *a couple of million* soldiers, each year pumping vast amounts of money into upgrading its weapons and equipment. After World War II, the Soviet Union, Great Britain, France, and others also kept their military machines.

A telling moment came after the fall of the Soviet Union in the late 1980s. With its archenemy turning away from communism and transforming itself into a capitalist ally, the West did not suggest that they and Russia disarm and join together in a new world of peace. Instead, the West continued to arm millions of its people and to develop new weapons, even those that are designed to turn space into a new venue of warfare. As the Russians reestablish their economy and regain some of their lost political might, primarily through the sale of oil, they are eager to rearm their military machine and reclaim a more prestigious place on the world scene.

THE MILITARY MACHINE, THE POWER ELITE, AND THE GLOBALIZATION OF CAPITALISM. To understand why such huge armies have become a fact of contemporary life, conflict theorists say that we need to look at the top levels of power. There we see the *power elite*—the top leaders of the military, business, and politics. As sociologist C. Wright Mills stressed, we should look closely at the power elite to see how the interests of these three groups have merged. The generals always want a more powerful military, of course: This is their reason for being, and greater power bolsters their position. Generals also perceive enemies on every side, so they give endless reasons for expanding the military.

This isn't new. But to this old picture has been added global capitalism. To protect their worldwide investments, today's business leaders also want a powerful military. At any moment, they might need armed intervention at home—or on the other side of the globe. Politicians are sensitive to what the business elite wants because, as conflict theorists stress, they owe their positions to the business elite. If business withdraws its support, politicians have little chance of being reelected. Consequently, politicians find it in their interest to support a strong military: In the name of national security, politicians levy taxes to finance the military machine so desired by the generals and business leaders. The term national security, being reborn as "homeland security," is often effective at deflecting opposition at budget time, for who can be against security of our homeland?

Today, stress conflict theorists, the U.S. military machine is used to advance capitalism around the globe. When you see U.S. armed forces in action, alone or, when not quarreling, accompanied by the United States' international capitalist partners—Great Britain, France, Canada, and Australia—you can be sure that the world is being made safe for capitalism. The result, says Mills (1958:2), is that "war is no longer an interruption of peace; in our time, peace itself has become an uneasy interlude between wars. . . ."

Research Findings

With war so common—and with today's weapons so powerful that they jeopardize even the existence of humanity—it is important to identify factors that can reduce the likelihood that nations will go to war. After trying to find out what these are, let's examine the costs of war, both economic and human. Finally, we'll consider the significance of the military-industrial complex, the possibility of accidental nuclear war, biological and chemical warfare, and terrorism. To get an idea of the variety of research by sociologists on this topic, see the Spotlight on Social Research box on the next page.

What Reduces War?

MAJOR FINDINGS ABOUT WAR AND PEACE. To see what reduces war, Quincy Wright (1942), a professor of international law, studied war throughout history. His findings, combined with those of physicist-mathematician Lewis Richardson (1960), are not encouraging. They can be summarized this way (Nettler 1976):

Spotlight on Social Research

ADVENTURES IN MILITARY SOCIOLOGY

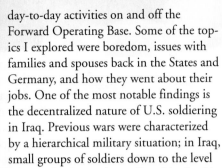

MORTEN ENDER, *Associate Professor at the United States Military Academy at West Point, does research on war, peace, and the military. In this essay, he discusses how he became interested in doing research on the military and his research experiences in Iraq.*

Although an American, I spent many years living in West Germany during the Cold War. I often reflected on the impact that World War II had on the German people as well as on the Americans living there. Both world wars had a profound impact on my own family. After WWI, my maternal great-grandparents were forced to move to the hinterland of Germany and a more meager lifestyle. U.S. bombers destroyed my paternal great-grandfather's printing plant during WWII, and a generation later, my mother married an American soldier stationed in Germany. I came to the United States for the first time on a U.S. troop ship. My family's many moves during my formative years and the stories I heard of war sparked my interest in social change, especially radical and intense change, at the individual level.

When I began studying the military I tried to develop knowledge in areas that had received little sociological attention, such as death and dying in a military context and military children. We learned that when a member of the military dies, the response is highly bureaucratic and task-focused, yet the notification and casualty officers keep the best interests of the survivors in mind. We also discovered that military children, who often live outside the country of their passport because of their parents' careers, have much in common with children of foreign service workers, missionaries, and those in international business.

I also had the opportunity to travel to Iraq and apply my sociological research skills to studying the Iraqi people. In a dangerous and compelling research environment, my research team helped assess the attitudes and opinions of Iraqis about their major social institutions—economics, politics, criminal justice, the family, education, the military, and medical care. We also studied Iraqi adolescents—their self-esteem and how they perceived their personal safety.

Because I was "embedded" with U.S. soldiers in Iraq, I was able to interview them, as well as observe their day-to-day activities on and off the Forward Operating Base. Some of the topics I explored were boredom, issues with families and spouses back in the States and Germany, and how they went about their jobs. One of the most notable findings is the decentralized nature of U.S. soldiering in Iraq. Previous wars were characterized by a hierarchical military situation; in Iraq, small groups of soldiers down to the level of 22-year-old platoon leaders make profound leadership decisions. For example, she might be responsible for training an entire police force for a neighborhood, or he might interact with the local leadership in a community, working with local mayors. This decentralized soldiering offers the opportunity to be creative and exercise autonomy. I asked soldiers an open-ended question on a survey about whether they use any creativity. A typical response was

> *Everyday! This place was not what we expected and therefore we have had to adapt on many occasions. One example is up armoring of vehicles. Soldiers are very adaptive and creative and come up with very good ideas that other units are now using. Scheduling is another example. We are short many soldiers and have had to develop shift work that fits the number of people we have.*

I also studied the soldiers' morale, cohesion, preparation, leadership, and attitudes toward the mission. In many of these areas I found evidence contrary to common expectations. For example, morale is high among soldiers in Iraq—in some cases higher than when they are at home. Further, many soldiers told me they enjoyed the mission in Iraq. They liked being a part of something larger than themselves. I found the soldiers to be very focused and committed to their jobs—the small-scale, daily missions. One day, at one of the larger post-exchanges (PX)—which is affectionately called Wal-Mart because it has everything—I struck up a conversation with a 23-year-old Army reserve specialist from Woodstock, New York. He owned a small business back home, and his brother and wife were managing it for him. He was headed home for his once-a-year two-week R&R (rest and relaxation), but with great misgivings. His job in Iraq involved responsibility for training two 44- and 47-year-old Iraqi police officers. He appeared genuinely worried that although his "guys" had received the proper socialization into the policing role, without his structure and discipline, although for only a short while, they would fall back into bad habits, possibly putting themselves and others at risk. I asked why he didn't stay and he said his sergeant was making him take some time off.

1. Type of religion does *not* reduce warfare. A nation in which Christianity is dominant does not go to war less than a nation in which Islam is dominant.
2. Type of government does *not* reduce warfare. Democracies and republics are neither more nor less peaceful than dictatorships and monarchies.
3. Prosperity does *not* reduce warfare. Prosperous nations are neither more nor less peaceful than poor nations. Nor do periods of prosperity reduce fighting.
4. A shared religion does *not* reduce warfare between nations.
5. A common language does *not* reduce warfare.
6. Education does *not* reduce warfare. Education does not create an "enlightened" preference for peace; countries with high education are as likely to go to war as those with low education.
7. Being "neighbors" does *not* reduce warfare. The opposite is true: Shared boundaries stimulate fights over territory, and the more boundaries that countries share, the more wars they fight with one another.

When we attempt to discover what reduces war, then, we face an uncomfortable and disheartening conclusion: No one knows. It seems only common sense that democracy, prosperity, increased education, and a shared religion would reduce war. They don't. So-called "experts" make up fancy-sounding terms such as "conflict resolution," but—despite all efforts to reduce war—the world's nations are *not* becoming more peaceful. And today's wars have become more lethal, killing more people than ever before in history. As sociologist Gwynn Nettler (1976) ruefully observed, the Nobel Peace Prize usually goes to a citizen of a nation with a long history of recent war. He said that perhaps we should consider this prize as awarded on the basis of need, rather than as a recognition of achievement.

The Costs of War

War takes a huge toll on humanity. Certainly, its costs cannot be measured only in dollars, but let's look at that cost first.

MATERIAL COSTS: MONEY. It is an understatement to say that war is costly. Table 15-1 summarizes what the United States has spent on its major wars. This huge amount does not include what it cost to "intervene" in places such as Bosnia, Kosovo, and Afghanistan. If you look at Figure 15-1 on the next page, you will see how much the United States spends each year to operate its military. The totals are in constant dollars, so you can easily compare one year to another. The higher spending during 1970 represents expenditures for the war in Vietnam; that of 1990, the ICBM defense called Star Wars. Today's higher spending represents the war on terrorism.

The expenditures shown in Figure 15-1 include the costs of veterans' benefits, but a more realistic total of what we spend on war and preparing for war would also include the costs of running the Central Intelligence Agency, the National Aeronautics and Space Administration, the Agency for International Development, and the Department of Homeland Security. A case could also be made to include what we spend on the Overseas Private Investment Corporation, the International Monetary Fund, and the World Bank (Greenberger 1994).

On average, since 1960 the United States has spent $334 billion a year on what is euphemistically called national defense. Such numbers roll easily off the tongue—with little realization of what they mean. This is because the concept of 1 billion of anything is beyond our experience. To gain an idea of how much we are spending, consider this:

Each dollar bill is about 6 inches long. If you laid a million of them end to end, you would just about cover the distance from Los Angeles to San Diego. A billion dollar bills would take you around the equator four times. If you laid the dollar bills of today's defense budget end to end, they would circle the earth more than 1,800 times! (Cf. Shaffer 1986)

TABLE 15-1 What Has the United States Spent on Its Wars?

War	Cost
War of 1812	$600,000,000
Mexican War	$1,100,000,000
American Revolution	$2,000,000,000
Spanish–American War	$6,000,000,000
Civil War	$46,000,000,000
Gulf War I	$145,000,000,000
Gulf War II	$250,000,000,000
Korean War	$260,000,000,000
World War I	$370,000,000,000
Vietnam War	$553,000,000,000
World War II	$3,000,000,000,000
Total	$4,590,000,000,000

Note: The costs listed in *Statistical Abstract* are in 1967 dollars. To account for inflation, I increased these amounts by 350 percent, and added the costs of service-connected benefits. Where a range was listed, the mean was used. The costs do *not* include interest payments on war loans, nor are they reduced by the financial benefits to the United States, such as the acquisition of territory such as California and Texas in the Mexican War.

Keep in mind that these are rough estimates, not actual costs. The costs of the many "military interventions" such as in Grenada, Panama, Somalia, and Haiti are not listed in the source.

Sources: By the author. Based on *Statistical Abstract of the United States* 1993:Table 553; this table was dropped after 1993. The cost for Gulf War I is from Conahan 1991, adjusted for inflation; for Gulf War II, the estimate is from Bilmes and Stiglitz 2006.

Lost Alternative Purchases ▪ Trying to grasp the concept of a billion is exceedingly difficult, so another way to measure our military expenditures is to compare them with what else we could buy with the same money. I could not find a comparison with today's dollars and have to rely on costs from the 1980s, but the same principle applies:

1. For the price of one aircraft carrier, we could build 12,000 high schools.
2. For the price of one naval weapons plant, we could build twenty-six 160-bed hospitals.
3. For the price of one jet bomber, we could provide school lunches for 1 million children for a year.
4. For the price of one new prototype bomber, we could pay the annual salaries of 250,000 teachers (de Silva 1980).

Money goes a lot further in the Least Industrialized Nations. There, the price of one tank would buy 1,000 classrooms. Many people dream of a world in which military dollars go to education, medicine, and the enlightenment of nations, but we certainly do not live in such a world—and from all indications, we never will.

Our armed forces employ about 1.4 million military personnel and about 650,000 civilians. Add the 1.1 million men and women in the reserves and National Guard, and the total comes to almost 3 million people (*Statistical Abstract* 2006:Tables 499, 500). For what it costs to pay these 3 million men and women to fight in or be ready for a war, we could pay 3 million people to work for the public good. We are already sending tens of thousands of soldiers abroad each year; for the same cost we could send tens of thousands of people to other countries to build schools and hospitals and to reduce the suffering of refugees. You might be able to think of other uses for these huge amounts of money and personnel.

But What Choice Is There? ▪ Like other nations, the United States finds itself boxed in. Although the military is costly in terms of money spent and benefits forgone, not spending this money would leave us vulnerable to attack. In light of the world's bellicose history, an assumption of danger appears well founded. Only if all nations were to become pacifists and all dangers of attack to cease would military preparedness become unnecessary. No such miracle seems in the offing.

MONEY SPENT BY OTHER NATIONS. The nations of the world spend about $1,100 billion a year to arm themselves (Stalenheim et al. 2006). This is about $165 a year for every man, woman, and child on the entire planet. Now let's mentally lay these dollars end to end to see what distance they would cover. The results are amazing: The dollars spent by the world's nations on war would stretch around the earth more than 4,000 times. Or if you laid them end to end, you could make over 200 round trips to the moon!

Any way you look at it, that's a lot of money.

Table 15-2 on the next page shows which countries spend the most and least on their military. The table holds some surprises. On a per capita basis, three of these countries outspend the United States; on the basis of gross national product, six do. Sweden, hardly a bellicose nation, is one of the world's top ten spenders. As you can see, the nations that spend the least have little industrialization. Although what they spend for their military on a per capita basis is tiny, these are poor nations. Most of their citizens live in poverty, and they need every dollar they can get for basic necessities. It is also true that some of these countries are so split by factions that only the power of their military holds them together.

HUMAN COSTS: DEATHS. War's greatest cost, of course, is not dollars, but lives lost. During the 1700s, wars were fought according to aristocratic ideals. Small professional armies

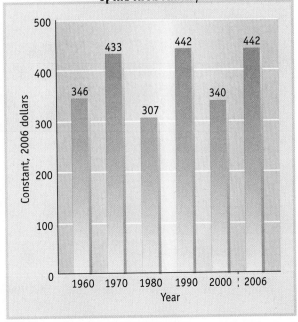

FIGURE 15-1 How Much Does the United States Spend on Its Military?

Note: These costs are in constant, 2006 dollars.

Source: By the author. Inflation-adjusted from the totals given in *Statistical Abstract of the United States* 2006:Table 490.

TABLE 15-2 What Do Countries Spend on Their Military?

COUNTRIES THAT SPEND THE MOST

RANK	COUNTRY	PER CAPITA	PERCENTAGE OF GROSS NATIONAL PRODUCT
1	Israel	$1,510	8.8%
2	Kuwait	$1,410	7.7%
3	Singapore	$1,100	4.8%
4	United States	$1,030	3.0%
5	Saudi Arabia	$996	14.9%
6	Taiwan	$690	5.2%
7	France	$658	2.7%
8	Great Britain	$615	2.5%
9	Sweden	$601	2.3%
10	Greece	$573	4.7%

COUNTRIES THAT SPEND THE LEAST

RANK	COUNTRY	PER CAPITA	PERCENTAGE OF GROSS NATIONAL PRODUCT
1	Tanzania	$4	1.4%
2	Bangladesh	$5	1.3%
3	Indonesia	$7	1.1%
4	Kenya	$7	1.9%
5	India	$11	2.5%
6	Nigeria	$13	1.6%
7	Philippines	$14	1.4%
8	Pakistan	$25	5.9%
9	Mexico	$27	0.6%
10	Egypt	$36	2.7%

Source: By the author. Based on *Statistical Abstract of the United States* 2003: Table 1383. This table was dropped in later editions of the source.

waged short, limited campaigns. In battle, the soldiers marched in formation, accompanied by flying flags and teenaged boys playing drums, flutes, and other musical instruments. War was like a chess game back then, with generals from an aristocratic background matching wits with opponents who also came from the upper class. Opposing generals had sometimes even been trained in the same military schools. Military officers, who considered warfare a test of bravery, referred to battle as the "field of honor." If townspeople knew when a battle would be fought, they rode in carriages to the site, eating picnic lunches and drinking wine while they watched the entertainment.

Napoleon changed this when he initiated **total war,** "no-holds-barred" warfare (Finsterbusch and Greisman 1975). This came home to Americans with the Civil War. During four brutal years, 620,000 Americans died, more than in all our other wars combined, from the Revolution to the present. No longer is there a field of honor, if ever there was one. With today's mass armies, and the capacity to deliver wholesale death, with industries spewing out weapons and with civilians not spared, an image of pageantry and games is far from reality.

Most fearful of all, today's weapons are so destructive that they threaten human existence itself. Although killing in the past was inefficient, since 1700 over 100 million people have died in war (Gartner 1988). This includes the total from our two world wars. If ever there were another world war, deaths could number in the hundreds of millions—if, indeed, anyone were left to count them.

HUMAN COSTS: DEHUMANIZATION. Although we can measure war in terms of money and deaths, war involves more than such gross measures. Among war's other costs is a loss in people's "quality of life." This factor is impossible to measure accurately, but at the very minimum war increases insecurity, paranoia, fear, and worry. As the ordinary expectations of what life is like begin to unravel, it becomes difficult to plan for the future. People ask themselves, for example, if it is worth getting married and starting a family. They don't know what lies ahead.

Morality is also part of our "quality of life," and war erodes this, too. It tends to break down the norms that regulate human behavior. Soldiers who are exposed to brutality and killing tend to **dehumanize** their opponents. That is, they come to see them as objects, not as people. This removes the obligation to treat them as human beings.

Characteristics of Dehumanization ▪ Social scientists have identified these four characteristics of dehumanization (Bernard, Ottenberg, and Redl 1971):

1. *Increased emotional distance from others.* The individual stops identifying with others, seeing them as lacking basic human qualities. They become not people, but an object called "the enemy."
2. *An emphasis on following procedures.* Regulations become all-important. Those who do the "dirty work" do not question their orders, even if they involve atrocities. A person will say, "I don't like it, but it's necessary," or "We all have to die some day."

Over the centuries, the form and weapons of war have changed. The result, however, is always the same: death and destruction.

3. *Inability to resist pressures.* Fears of losing one's job or the respect of one's group or of having one's integrity and loyalty questioned become more important than morality.

4. *Diminished personal responsibility.* People see themselves as a small cog in a large machine. They are not responsible, because they have no choice. They are simply obeying orders. The superiors know best, for they have the information to judge what is right and wrong. The individual reasons, "Who am I to question this?"

When dehumanization occurs, consciences become so numbed that people can dissociate killing—even torture—from their "normal self." Torture and killing, though remaining perhaps disagreeable, become "dirty work" that has to be done. Those who do this "dirty work" think of themselves being duty-bound to obey orders, not to question them. "The 'higher-ups' who make the decisions are responsible, not I, a simple soldier who does my duty."

Dehumanization in Prolonged Conflicts ■ Sociologist Tamotsu Shibutani (1970) pointed out that dehumanization is helped along by the tendency for prolonged conflicts to be transformed into a struggle between good and evil. People who don't want to torture or kill, for example, conclude that because the survival of good (democracy, freedom, the nation, our way of life) hangs in the balance, they must suspend moral standards. War, then, exalts treachery, brutality, and killing—and we give medals to glorify behavior that we would otherwise condemn.

Dehumanization by the Nazis and Japanese ■ To participate in such acts, soldiers distance themselves from the morality they learned as children. Their attempts at neutralization are often effective. During World War II, ordinary Germans—not Nazi ideologues—staffed the concentration camps. They began to view the inmates as vermin, lice, a blight on society. Surgeons who had been educated at top universities, whose profession called for them to be highly sensitive to people's needs, viewed the inmates they experimented on as lesser humans than themselves. Methodically and dispassionately, they would mutilate patients just to study the results. Some doctors immersed Jews in vats of

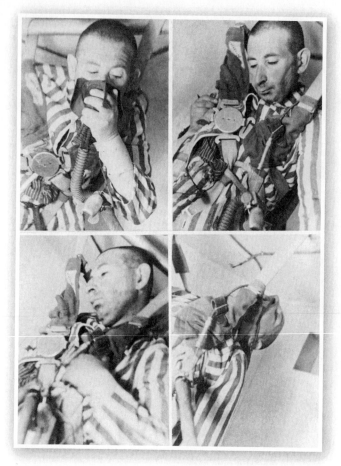

The extent that dehumanization can take is incredible. To measure the effects of compression and decompression, German doctors placed this inmate of a concentration camp in a pressure chamber. As the doctors manipulated the air pressure, they observed and photographed the man's death.

ice water in freezing weather, considering their deaths insignificant because the results of the studies would be used to save the lives of German pilots shot down over the North Atlantic (Gellhorn 1959). The photos on this page are part of the documentary that these educated and intelligent medical personnel produced.

One might think that the horrors of the Nazis were so great that no one could match them. Yet the Japanese did. They beheaded U.S. prisoners of war, and buried others alive (Chang 1997). They also tortured prisoners and performed medical experiments on them (Daws 1994). In one experiment, Japanese doctors pumped U.S. prisoners full of horse blood. In another, they injected them with typhus, typhoid, smallpox, and other diseases. In one test, they lined up ten prisoners "behind a protective screen with their naked buttocks exposed while a fragmentation bomb was detonated" (Leighty 1981). In China, the Japanese experimented with germ warfare, killing perhaps hundreds of thousands of Chinese with anthrax, typhoid, and plague (Harris 1994).

DEHUMANIZATION BY THE U.S. MILITARY. The Germans and Japanese carried dehumanization to horrifying limits, but they were not unique. U.S. soldiers in Vietnam also dehumanized their victims. To them, the Vietnamese became less than people; they became "gooks," "dinks," and "slants." Some soldiers became so effective at dehumanization that they were able to shoot mothers who were fleeing with their babies, the act dissociated from the self. For others, dehumanization was more difficult, but it was better not to question the morality of the act, better to think of the act as part of the larger scheme of things, such as saving a people from communism—or as rightful retaliation for buddies who had been killed: "I don't like doing this, but this is war."

Something similar is happening today. When U.S. (and coalition) forces bomb military targets, civilians are often killed unintentionally. The military does not refer to them as "dead children, mothers, and fathers" or even as "dead people" or "dead civilians." Instead, the military uses the term *collateral damage*. Talk about symbolizing people out of existence!

WHEN DEHUMANIZATION FAILS. Although such techniques of neutralization can protect the self, they are not foolproof, and their failure can lead to crippling guilt. Tim, for example, whose statement follows, was a Marine interrogator in Vietnam. Beating prisoners to elicit information was part of his job. When beating did not work, he would use electric shocks, attaching "two wires of a field telephone usually to the earlobe or the cheek or the temple, sometimes the balls or the crotch" (Smith 1980:27). Tim did not enjoy his work, and one day as he was beating a 16- or 17-year-old girl, he began to think:

Why are we killing all these people? These aren't soldiers. I'm beating on this girl—and it all hit me. I'm beating up this girl, what for? Who am I? . . . It was as if for the first time I was looking at myself. Here's this guy, slapping, beating on this girl—for what?

No longer seeing this prisoner as an object, Tim insightfully added: "For the first time I was looking at this person, a detainee, as a real human being, not as a source of information." This change of perspective directly affected Tim's job performance. As he said: "I wasn't a very good interrogator from that time on. I lost all motivation."

Being surrounded by army buddies who agree that the enemy is less than human helps maintain definitions that justify brutality. After returning home, however, the former soldiers find themselves being resocialized into more standard norms, and the definitions that worked for them during the war tend to break down. As this occurs, many former soldiers become disturbed by what they have done. Before putting a bullet in his head, here is what a soldier from California wrote:

> I can't sleep anymore. When I was in Vietnam, we came across a North Vietnamese soldier with a man, a woman, and a 3- or 4-year-old girl. We had to shoot them all. I can't get the little girl's face out of my mind. I hope that God will forgive me. I hope the people in this country who made millions of dollars off the men, women, and children that died in that war can sleep at night (I can't, and I didn't make a cent). (Smith 1980:15)

The norms of dehumanization also failed some of the Japanese soldiers who had participated in the atrocities of World War II. Although they had kept quiet for fifty years, some of them publicly confessed their mass rapes and killings. The confessions, which made international news, were accompanied by the denials of other soldiers that they had done anything wrong.

Let's turn from what has been a symbolic interaction analysis to a conflict perspective and examine how organizations and profit underlie modern warfare.

The Military-Industrial Complex

THE MILITARY AS AN ECONOMIC FORCE. The military requires a vast industrial backup. Those industries that specialize in armaments—the guidance systems, bombs, missiles, tanks, planes, guns, ships, submarines, and other weapons—have become a powerful force in the U.S. economy. Military weapons are like personal computers; they quickly become obsolete and need to be replaced with a new generation of even more powerful and sophisticated ones. This is so costly that *one of every four tax dollars* collected by the federal government goes to the Department of Defense and the Department of Veterans Affairs (*Statistical Abstract* 2006:Tables 464, 490).

The Military-Industrial Complex ▪ Like other businesses, the corporations that manufacture armaments want to increase their profits. Unlike other businesses, however, their main customer is the Department of Defense. This leads to a cozy relationship. The defense industry hires top-ranking military officers when they retire, people who know the military system inside and out. Some of them are even on a first-name basis with the officers who are in charge of military purchases, who may themselves be eyeing jobs with high salaries in the defense industry after their own retirement.

Their interests have so merged that the military and defense industries have become a power to be reckoned with by Congress. The **military-industrial complex,** as it is known, pressures Congress to increase military spending. Congress listens, because the Defense Department can channel contracts into their districts, which makes them popular at home and increases their chances of being reelected. Besides, "I'm soft on defense" doesn't make the best campaign slogan. Some use the term *Pentagon capitalism* to refer to this interlocking relationship between Pentagon armaments and U.S. business (Melman 1970).

Table 15-3 on the next page shows the ten states that receive the most income from military contracts. As you can see, they each receive several billions of dollars. The several hundred thousand employees of the military in these states spend huge sums for local purchases. Consider the impact of the military on Virginia. This state of just 8 million people has a payroll of $14 billion in military contracts. The state's 171,000 military and civilian workers connected with the military bring in several more billions of dollars a year. With such sums at stake, the threat to close a military base unites quarreling parties—unions and businesses and various chambers of commerce—who send lobbyists to Washington to fight to keep the base. NIMBY (Not In My Back Yard) has changed to KIMBY (Keep It In My Back Yard).

TABLE 15-3 Where Defense Dollars Go: The Top 10 States

RANK	STATE	PAYROLL FOR MILITARY CONTRACTS	MILITARY EMPLOYEES	CIVILIAN EMPLOYEES
1	Virginia	$14,000,000,000	93,000	78,000
2	California	$13,000,000,000	130,000	58,000
3	Texas	$10,000,000,000	114,000	38,000
4	Florida	$8,000,000,000	56,000	27,000
5	Georgia	$6,000,000,000	68,000	31,000
6	North Carolina	$6,000,000,000	97,000	17,000
7	Washington	$5,000,000,000	39,000	23,000
8	Maryland	$5,000,000,000	31,000	32,000
9	Hawaii	$3,000,000,000	34,000	17,000
10	South Carolina	$3,000,000,000	37,000	10,000

Note: Military employees refers to active-duty military personnel who are living in a particular state. *Civilian employees* refers to civilians employed by the military; the totals do not include workers in the defense industries who fulfill the military contracts listed in column 3.

Source: By the author. Based on *Statistical Abstract of the United States* 2006:Tables 497, 499.

THE GROWING CAPACITY TO INFLICT DEATH. With all the military contracts floating around the country and the employment they bring, it is easy to forget that the business of the military is death. Let's look at what those contracts represent in terms of death. During the arms race, the West and the Soviet Union put some of their top scientists to work to increase the destructive power of their weapons and the efficiency of their delivery systems. Our capacity for inflicting death grew so sharply that in 1970 a critic noted that *if a bomb the size of the one dropped on Hiroshima had exploded every single day from the birth of Christ until that year, the total force of those bombs would be less than the destructive capacity of the United States* (Melman 1970). Of course, our capacity to inflict death has increased since then.

That's just the United States. To this, we can add the nuclear weapons of Russia, France, Great Britain, and the other countries shown on the Social Map on pages 536–537. It is almost impossible to grasp the destructive capacity that these nations now possess, but imagery sometimes helps. Consider this. The explosive energy of nuclear weapons is measured in megatons. If you had 1 million tons of TNT, you would have one **megaton.** The United States has over 3,000 megatons of explosive power. Think of a freight train filled with gunpowder that stretches from the earth to the moon. Now *triple* that—make the train 925,000 miles long—and you have an image of the destructive power of the United States (see *Nucleus* 1981).

The length of the U.S. train is a matter of alarm for many. But then there is also this statistic: Russia's train is about just as long. France and Great Britain also have trains, although theirs are shorter. Israel, India, Pakistan, China, and a few other nations have these trains as well, although theirs are much shorter. North Korea and Iran are feverishly trying to build their own trains.

To better understand our inheritance from the Cold War, think of it like this. It is midnight on a cloudy night, and we are riding in trains that are running without lights, careening at full speed along the edge of a cliff. There has been a downpour, and a washout could be ahead. Yet the engineers keep the trains steaming full speed into the darkness. At any time, one of them might hit a washout, plunge off the cliff, and obliterate humanity.

A GLIMMER OF HOPE. In the midst of this dark futility lies a glimmer of hope. Like someone who has seen a washout ahead and is furiously waving a warning lantern, Russia and the United States have been heeding the danger. They have negotiated agreements to eliminate ICBMs with multiple warheads and to reduce their nuclear stockpiles. No longer do Russia and the United States target each other's major cities. (Since ICBMs have to be directed somewhere, one wonders just where those nuclear missiles are targeted.) Although Russia and the United States have destroyed some weapons, this is not disarmament. They

This is Hamburg, Germany, after the defeat of the Nazis in 1945. Note that there are no young men in this food line. They are either dead, wounded, or prisoners of war. The human and material costs of war are discussed in the text. Hamburg has been restored meticulously.

have destroyed outdated weapons and *reduced excess capacity:* Each nation can still destroy the other many times over—and take with them the rest of the world.

A GROWING DANGER. A special concern is nuclear weapons in the hands of a single individual or a small group. Part of that concern is terrorism, which we shall discuss shortly. Another concern is countries that are run by dictators. If such a country possesses nuclear weapons, what is to stop the dictator from launching those missiles? This, of course, is a primary concern of the West about the nuclear weapons being developed in North Korea. A cynic might add that this is not too different from the situation in other countries. If the president of one of the Western nations decided to launch nuclear-tipped missiles, could he or she really be stopped?

Another major concern is that nuclear proliferation increases the likelihood that nuclear weapons will be used. Not only do more countries possess these weapons, but in addition a few individuals (or governments) are willing to sell their knowledge of nuclear weapons and the materials for building them. Pakistan, for example, is thought to be the source of advanced technology behind North Korea's nuclear weapons program. Accompanying this dismaying situation is the proliferation of customers—from the quarreling ethnic groups that had been held in check by the military might of the former Soviet Union to al-Qaeda and similar organizations that have their own agendas of hatred.

Is it any wonder, then, that some see our civilization ending in one gigantic mushroom cloud? Look again at the Social Map on pages 536–537, which pinpoints the major sources of this danger.

The Possibility of Accidental War

COMPUTER FAILURE. As things now stand, we face not only the potential of some leader launching a nuclear attack or of terrorists detonating nuclear weapons, but also the possibility that missiles will be unleashed accidentally. We have come close to such unintended launchings in the past. Here is an actual event:

> Back in 1980, a military computer reported that Russia had fired missiles at the United States. The United States immediately went to red alert. U.S. bombers plotted courses toward preselected targets in the Soviet Union, and we prepared our missiles for launching. The countdown toward nuclear devastation had begun. (*U.S. News & World Report,* June 24, 1980)

Russia had *not* launched any missiles. A computer had malfunctioned, and the error was caught in time. It's a chilling thought—the end of the world due to a computer malfunction.

FIGURE 15-2 The Nuclear Club

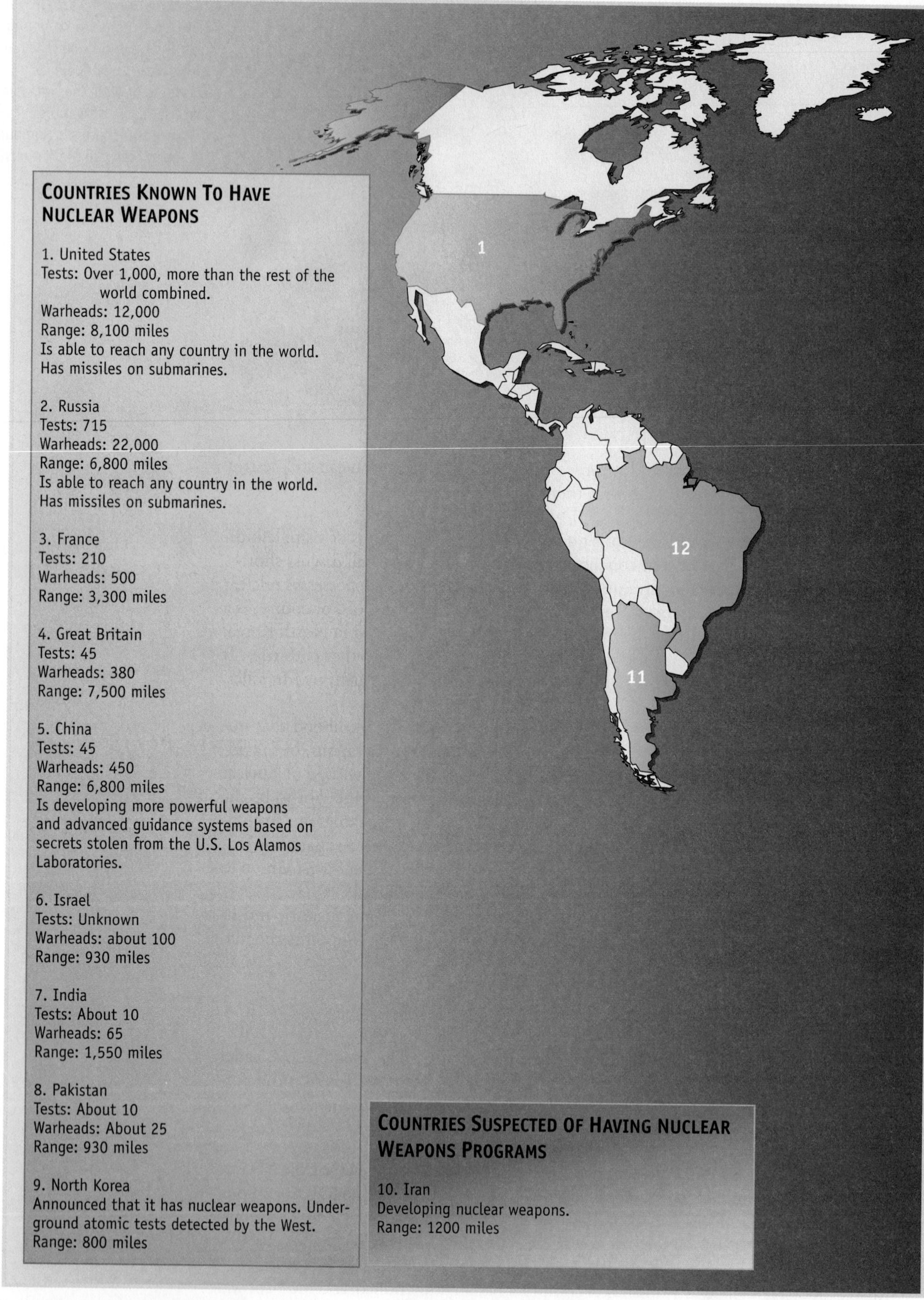

COUNTRIES KNOWN TO HAVE NUCLEAR WEAPONS

1. United States
Tests: Over 1,000, more than the rest of the world combined.
Warheads: 12,000
Range: 8,100 miles
Is able to reach any country in the world.
Has missiles on submarines.

2. Russia
Tests: 715
Warheads: 22,000
Range: 6,800 miles
Is able to reach any country in the world.
Has missiles on submarines.

3. France
Tests: 210
Warheads: 500
Range: 3,300 miles

4. Great Britain
Tests: 45
Warheads: 380
Range: 7,500 miles

5. China
Tests: 45
Warheads: 450
Range: 6,800 miles
Is developing more powerful weapons and advanced guidance systems based on secrets stolen from the U.S. Los Alamos Laboratories.

6. Israel
Tests: Unknown
Warheads: about 100
Range: 930 miles

7. India
Tests: About 10
Warheads: 65
Range: 1,550 miles

8. Pakistan
Tests: About 10
Warheads: About 25
Range: 930 miles

9. North Korea
Announced that it has nuclear weapons. Underground atomic tests detected by the West.
Range: 800 miles

COUNTRIES SUSPECTED OF HAVING NUCLEAR WEAPONS PROGRAMS

10. Iran
Developing nuclear weapons.
Range: 1200 miles

Sources: Various, including "Iran Test Fires . . ." 2006.

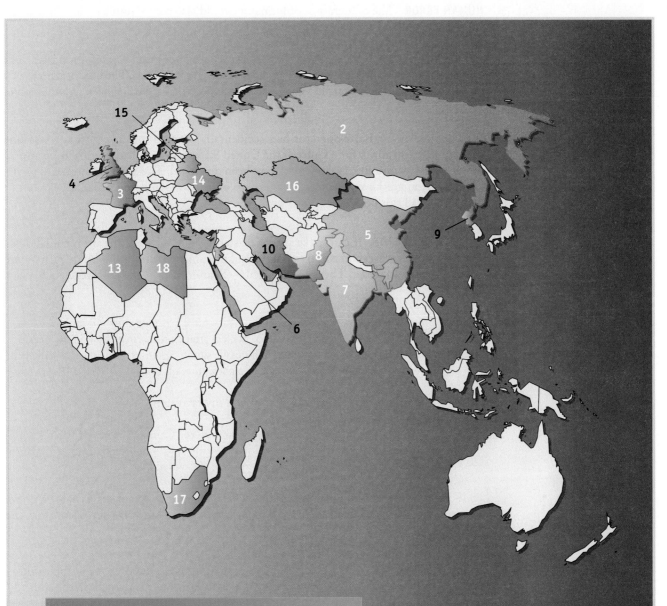

COUNTRIES THAT HAVE GIVEN UP NUCLEAR WEAPONS

11. Argentina
Stopped nuclear weapons development in 1990 and signed a nuclear weapons-free zone in Latin America.

12. Brazil
Stopped nuclear weapons development in 1990 and signed a nuclear weapons-free zone in Latin America.

13. Algeria
Stopped its program in 1991 and signed the Nuclear Proliferation Treaty.

14. Ukraine
Gave up the weapons the Soviet Union left when it broke up.

15. Belarus
Gave up the weapons the Soviet Union left when it broke up.

16. Kazakhstan
Gave up the weapons the Soviet Union left when it broke up.

17. South Africa
Dismantled its nuclear arsenal in 1991 and signed the Nuclear Proliferation Treaty.

18. Libya
Gave up its nuclear program in the face of economic sanctions.

HUMAN ERROR. The obliteration of humanity could also come from a simple human error. Here's another real-life event:

> On October 28, 1962, the North American Defense Command was informed that Cuba had launched a nuclear missile. It was about to hit Tampa, Florida. The U.S. began a countdown for its retaliatory strike. Then someone noticed that there had been no explosion in Tampa. (Sagan 1994)

It turned out that a radar operator had accidentally inserted into the system a test tape that simulated an attack from Cuba. If the United States had launched immediately, instead of waiting a few minutes, Cuba would have been destroyed. The Soviet Union, Cuba's ally at the time, might have responded with salvos of its own—and you probably would not be here to read this book.

NUCLEAR ACCIDENTS. It can make your hair stand on end—since the unintended detonation of a nuclear weapon could signal the end of human civilization—but here are some real-life nuclear accidents. These are reported by Rear Admiral Gene LaRocque, U.S. Navy (retired):

> The *George Washington,* a missile submarine, ran into a Japanese ship and sank it.
> The *Scorpion* and the *Thresher,* two other nuclear attack submarines, sank in the ocean.
> When a mechanic dropped a wrench in a missile silo in Arkansas, a missile was launched.
> Several nuclear weapons have fallen out of planes, through open bomb bays. (Keyes n.d.)

As a symbolic interactionist, though, this is my favorite:

> A nuclear weapon fell from a plane into a swamp in the Carolinas. The Air Force was unable to find it. The Defense Department bought the land, put a fence around it and, in Orwellian fashion, called it a "nuclear safety area." (Keyes n.d.)

Fortunately for us, in none of these incidents did a nuclear weapon detonate. We have no assurance that similar accidents will not happen again, and, if they occur, that the weapons will not explode.

NUCLEAR SABOTAGE. The U.S. government has repeatedly assured us—and the world—that a missile cannot be launched without proper authorization. Any talk to the contrary, they say, is alarmist. These assurances are either due to misinformation on the part of the speaker, or they are outright lies:

> The year was 1962. Kennedy had backed down in the Bay of Pigs invasion of Cuba, and the Soviet military thought that Kennedy would be a pushover. Khrushchev, the premier of the Soviet Union, decided to ship missiles to Cuba. The CIA reported that the missiles would be capable of destroying the Pentagon, New York City, and other U.S. cities. Kennedy warned Khrushchev to order the ships back and set up a blockade to intercept them. The world waited tensely, television reporting the location of the ships as they neared the blockade.

All the preceding is well known. What is not well known is this:

> At the height of the Cuban crisis, officers at Malmstrom Air Force Base in Montana, who also doubted the resolve of President Kennedy to give the order to bomb the Soviets, did what was supposedly impossible: They jerry-rigged their Minutemen missiles so they could launch them on their own.
>   After the crisis, the Air Force investigated the jerry-rigging. It then altered the evidence to prevent higher authorities from learning that officers at Malmstrom had given themselves the ability to launch missiles. (Sagan 1994)

THE SIGNIFICANCE OF SYMBOLIC INTERACTION. This hair-raising event demonstrates the significance of symbolic interaction. To have meaning, all events in life must be interpreted. If a missile were launched, or a city destroyed, as could happen with a computer malfunction or an unauthorized launch, military and political leaders would have to answer this question: Is this an accident, an unauthorized attack by a madman, or the opening salvo of an orchestrated attack? On that interpretation would hang the fate of the world.

Fortunately, the United States and Russia have agreed to notify the other if either spots a missile—and to help each other track and destroy it (Greenberger 1992). Although their intention is to protect one another against missile attacks by third nations, their cooperation also helps to prevent accidental nuclear war.

Biological and Chemical Warfare

It sometimes is difficult to fathom the human mind. One of the strangest quirks in human thinking is this: To kill by bullets and bombs is considered normal, but to kill by gas is deemed abnormal. During World War I, the French and Germans shocked the world by using poison gas. After that war, in 1925, the major powers met in Geneva, where they signed an agreement banning the use of poison gases in warfare. In 1972, they agreed not to use biological weapons (Seib 1981). In 1989, 145 nations met to try to ban chemical weapons (Revzin 1989). They failed.

USE OF BIOLOGICAL AND CHEMICAL AGENTS. Only a few nations have used biological and chemical agents during war. In World War I, it was mustard gas that France and Germany used on each other. In World War II, as I already mentioned, Japan used chemical and biological weapons against the Chinese. In the 1980s, Iran and Iraq used mustard gas against one another.

In the 1960s and 1970s, the United States rained chemical defoliants on the jungles of Vietnam. These chemicals, however, were not intended as a weapon, but as a tool to destroy crops and clear terrain. Spraying stopped when Vietnamese women began giving birth to deformed babies, such as the children shown in the photo below. After the war, thousands of Vietnam veterans claimed that Agent Orange had damaged their health. The Veterans Administration (VA) insisted that Agent Orange caused only a "severe skin rash" and could not be the cause of "cancer, birth defects in their children, miscarriages

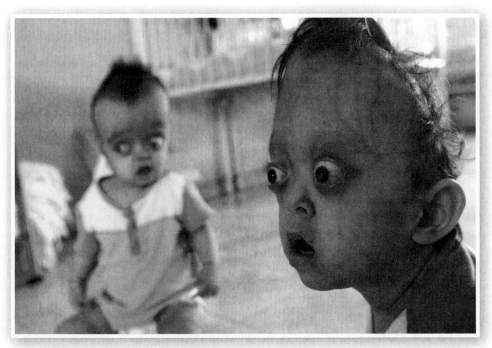

The human costs of war far outnumber the soldiers who are killed and maimed. Shown here are two victims of Agent Orange, a defoliant used by U.S. troops in Vietnam to clear the forests and disrupt the movement of troops and supplies from the north. Birth defects, especially the absence of vital organs (brains, eyes, kidneys, and so on) were a major factor in terminating the massive use of chemical defoliants during this war.

by their wives, impotency, respiratory problems, and liver, skin, nerve, and emotional disorders" (Feinsilber 1981). When the Department of Health and Human Services investigated the matter, it found that the United States had dropped 12 million gallons of Agent Orange on Vietnam. In some emergency situations, the gas had been dumped near military bases. In 1989, each soldier who had sued the government was awarded about $12,000.

There are other scattered cases. The Soviets have been accused of using chemicals in Afghanistan and Laos, not against plants but against people (Douglass 1998). They deny the allegations. For using poison gas to quell an uprising by the Kurds, Saddam Hussein was sentenced to death. Images of his victims had gone a long way toward gaining U.S. support for Gulf War II.

THE PRODUCTION OF THESE AGENTS. The justification for producing biological and chemical agents was the same that the West and the Soviet Union used to give for producing nuclear weapons. The Pentagon would tell Congress: "The Soviet Union has achieved a dangerous advantage over the United States." Congress would then fund a new program to "catch up." At one point, the Pentagon reported that we were behind in **binary chemical weapons.** These are shells or bombs in which two benign chemicals are kept in separate chambers. When the weapon is detonated, the chemicals mix, releasing a lethal agent. We caught up, of course. And, of course, the Soviet Union then had to rush to catch up to us again, producing even more destructive agents. This, in turn, forced us to move into even higher gear—and so the weapons race was given push after push.

THE TREATY WITH A HUGE FLAW. Because the Pentagon does not have money of its own, it has to go to Congress to finance its weapons. In true Orwellian fashion, the Pentagon once told Congress that chemical weapons could help bring about peace. If we develop more powerful chemical weapons, they said, this might force the Soviets to agree to "a complete and verifiable ban on the development, production, and stockpiling of chemical weapons by dangling the threat of retaliation over the heads of the Soviets" (*Wall Street Journal,* February 9, 1982). Apparently, the irony of producing chemical weapons in order to stop the production of chemical weapons was lost on Congress, the Pentagon, and the Politburo.

The United States, Russia, and other nations have signed a Chemical Weapons Convention. In this treaty, they agreed not to produce, stockpile, or use chemical weapons. By 2012, the nations are supposed to have destroyed their total supply of chemical weapons. The flaw? Biological weapons are not covered by the treaty.

CONTINUED RESEARCH AND PRODUCTION. After the Cold War ended, the United States and Russia continued to develop even more lethal biological weapons. Russia announced that it has genetically engineered an anthrax microbe that attacks blood cells, making vaccines useless (Broad and Miller 1998). Supposedly, Russia has armed some of its ICBMs with warheads loaded with plague, anthrax, and smallpox (Douglass 1998). If so, we can assume that the United States has done the same. If Russia and the United States continue their budding alliance, and with Russia now a part of NATO and WTO, it is likely that this race toward mutual biological destruction will stop.

Even if the major nations have begun to scale back, the possibility that terrorists will get their hands on some of these weapons poses a major threat. Let's consider this possibility.

Terrorism

How times change. When I wrote this section for the first edition of this book over twenty years ago, terrorism was only a theoretical topic. There had been no terrorist acts in the United States, although they were taking place elsewhere. What I wrote back then seemed, at the time, so distant and remote from everyday life.

Now, in contrast, terrorism has become part of today's nightmare. With 9/11, the world changed, and U.S. officials—and those throughout the West—are concerned that terrorists lurk around the corner. They view our nuclear plants as vulnerable and are concerned that terrorists could be targeting stadiums filled with spectators. Boarding a plane used to be a simple matter, but no longer. Armed security agents scrutinize our baggage and person, while screening devices do the same. Billions of dollars have been spent to fortify our embassies around the world, and yet they remain vulnerable.

POLITICAL TERRORISM. Political terrorism is similar to warfare. Although it is not war between nations, **political terrorism** is the use of the means of war—intimidation, coercion, threats, and violence—to achieve political objectives (Boston et al. 1977). Political terrorists use violence to sow fear. They do not recognize civilians as "noncombatants." On the contrary, they often target civilians because they are easier to reach, and the apparent randomness of the attack sows fear. The three types of political terrorism are revolutionary, repressive, and state-sponsored. Criminal terrorism, a fourth type, can be part of each of these. Let's look at each.

REVOLUTIONARY TERRORISM. In the *first* type, **revolutionary terrorism,** enemies of the state use terrorism to try to overthrow the government. Walter Laqueur (1977), a political scientist, identified these background factors in revolutionary terrorism:

1. Existence of a segregated, ethnic, cultural, or religious minority
2. Perceptions of being deprived or oppressed
3. Higher-than-average unemployment or inflation
4. External encouragement (often from an ethnic, cultural, or religious counterpart living elsewhere)
5. A historical "them" (a group they blame for their oppressed condition)
6. Frustrated elites who provide leadership and justify ideological violence

Goals of Revolutionary Terrorism ■ Revolutionary terrorism doesn't appear overnight out of nowhere, as though it spontaneously sprang into existence in a social vacuum. The group that has chosen terrorism has usually tried official channels to change its situation. Finding the authorities unresponsive to their grievances, the group members choose targets designed to

1. Publicize the group and its grievances
2. Demonstrate the government's vulnerability
3. Force political and social change

Because terrorists often want publicity for their "cause," terrorism is sometimes called "political theater." As political scientist Brian Jenkins (1987) put it: "Terrorists want a lot of people watching, not a lot of people dead." Consequently, terrorists choose targets that will attract the media. In light of 9/11 and the Madrid train bombings, I would modify Jenkins' observation. Some political terrorists do want a lot of people dead. It depends on their message. Suleiman Abu Ghaith, a spokesman for al-Qaeda, has said that al-Qaeda's goal is to kill 4 million Americans. After that, the rest can convert to Islam (Simon 2004).

Some terrorists have a fourth purpose which we explore in the Global Glimpse box on the next page. During the Russian revolution of 1917, communist terrorists believed that "false consciousness" deluded the masses, blinding them to their oppression. What Trotsky called the "theater of terrorism" was designed to provoke the capitalist rulers to overreact. Terrorist acts were designed to provoke harshness and brutality, which, revealing how repressive the political system was, would arouse the masses (Rubenstein 1987). Al-Qaeda, too, tries to entice a brutal reaction from the West to expose what they see as the true nature of Western civilization. If, in response to al-Qaeda's attacks, the West oppresses Arabs in its midst or invades Arab countries, the Arab masses will

In Uganda, revolutionary soldiers kidnapped children from their villages. They trained the boys to use guns, and forced them to kill. They used the girls as sex slaves and cooks. How do you compute the costs of war, in terms of quality of life, in this case lost childhoods, brutalized consciences, nightmares?

How can we make sense of 9/11, the bombings in Madrid or London, and whatever attacks are still to come? Certainly, we know that we need to look beyond those particular events to try to see what underlies them. To do this, let's begin by sketching a broad historical context:

1. In earlier centuries, the Arabs were a powerful political force. They led an advanced civilization and were world leaders in agriculture, architecture, astronomy, mathematics, medicine, and metallurgy. They ruled an empire that extended into Europe. The terraced fields developed by the Arabs are still a distinctive feature of southern Spain.

2. In the late 1400s, Queen Isabella and King Ferdinand married, uniting two major provinces of what is now Spain. They turned their united armies against their neighbors, including the Arabs, who ruled vast parts of this region.

3. In addition to motives of gaining territory and treasure, this was a religious war. The goal was to drive out all non-Catholics from the Iberian peninsula (Spain). The pope blessed the armies, wanting the infidels out of Europe. The Jews, who were not a political force, were given three choices: to convert to Christianity, to leave the area, or to die by the sword.

4. After a series of battles, with heavy losses on both sides, the Christian armies defeated the Islamic armies. The Arabs retreated back to Africa, although they continued to control other parts of Europe for another hundred years. Their political and economic power declined, as well as their leadership in the academics and arts.

5. As the Europeans developed strong economies and political power, they conquered peoples around the globe, from the Americas to Africa. The sands of Arab lands, many of them under the control of the Ottoman Empire, were of little interest to them, but the British (and the French) conquered the Arabs to extend their global empire.

6. When vast pools of oil were discovered beneath those sands, that interest changed. The global dominance of the British depended on uninterrupted supplies of oil, which were not present in the British Isles. They needed oil for their economic machinery, and for their warships, which they changed to burn oil instead of coal.

7. In the 1920s, after the defeat of the Ottoman Empire in World War I, the British, to help maintain their rule over the Arabs and to help settle squabbles among them, divided the land into countries. To do so, they drew lines on maps, declaring that those lines marked one country from another. They also set up Arab rulers in those territories. Until this time, the Arabs were loose confederations of tribes and did not think in terms of countries, but of kin.

8. The Americans possessed vast sources of oil in their own country. As they grew more powerful and populous and their need for oil increased, they looked beyond their borders for additional sources of this essential commodity. As British power weakened and they began to lose control over Arab lands, the United States stepped in.

9. The American public did not like their armies to be in foreign lands, and U.S. politicians were careful to use them only for limited excursions. To control access to oil, they supported cooperative Arab leaders, keeping them submissive by giving them military aid in return for oil. Following the British model, at times the Americans even set up puppets to head a country, as with the Shah of Iran, who was deposed by revolutionaries in 1979.

10. Kept alive in the collective memory, that is, in the Arab cultures, were remembrances of a golden Arab past—the times of grandeur and wealth, of power and prestige. Those

recognize the true hostility that the West harbors against Islam and will join in the *jihad* that will bring about Islamic world dominance. The Global Glimpse box above explores this issue in more detail.

The Oklahoma City Bombing ■ Although the truck filled with fertilizer and fuel oil that exploded in Oklahoma City in 1995 was not the first act of terrorism on U.S. soil, it was the most destructive to that time. The resulting destruction of a federal building and the deaths of almost 200 people, including 19 children in a day care center, opened the eyes of Americans to a new form of warfare. Up to that time, they assumed that terrorism only happened "someplace over there."

September 11 ■ As recounted in this chapter's opening vignette, an even more lethal act of terrorism followed, the destruction of the World Trade Center in New York City memories always stood in sharp contrast to the shame of the present—domination by the West and, despite vast oil wealth, most of the population living in poverty.

Having sketched this historical background, let's move to the present. Following a primary principle of symbolic interactionism, the need to take the role of the other, we will try to understand how al-Qaeda and similar groups see things.

11. An independence movement needs ideology to spur people to action, especially to sacrifice. It must be built around ideas of something greater than the individual. Islam serves this purpose. Images of the Great Infidel polluting a holy land strike that responsive chord. So do images of the Evil One plundering resources and holding the people captive through their puppet leaders. It also helps that this Great Satan supports Israel, the Arab archenemy, which came into existence after World War II when the Western nations again drew map lines on Arab lands.

12. Killing the Infidel, then, becomes an act of service to Allah. Losing one's life in that service becomes a sacrifice to God. The loss of the individual life is nothing in comparison with this noble cause.

13. The Infidel possesses great military power—soldiers, planes, ships, missiles, and bombs. The Great Satan also equips its puppets, as long as they remain loyal, with military weapons. Because only a few are enlightened, the movement to depose the Infidel is small. With such one-sidedness in political power, their military cannot be defeated in open battle.

14. The answer to this dilemma is to attack where the Infidel has the fewest defenses, back in the Infidel's homeland. This requires long-range planning, coordination, patience, and people so dedicated that they will give their lives to the holy cause. Suicide attacks are effective because it is difficult for the Infidel to know where or when they are coming.

15. There are no civilians. The entire culture of the Wicked One is evil, and all its members eagerly receive benefits from the dominance and exploitation of Arab lands.

16. The goal of suicide attacks is not to destroy the Infidel, but, rather, to strike fear and create outrage, especially to provoke large-scale violent retaliation. When the Infidel kills Arabs—instead of working behind the scenes to manipulate Arab leaders—it can arouse those who focus on their personal affairs and ignore the broader cause to join the movement for independence. If the Great Satan can be provoked to send an invading army into the sacred lands, so much the better.

17. The goal is pan-Arab unity, which surpasses the artificial boundaries drawn on maps by Western powers. It will not be Iraqis, Iranians, Saudi Arabians, or any such group, but united Arabs, who will defeat the foreign conquerors and depose their Arab puppets. In control of Arab resources, Arabs will take their rightful place of prestige at the world's political table. Once again, Arab glory will be resplendent.

18. Because the West will not easily give up its dominance over Arab oil, the struggle will last for decades.

FOR YOUR CONSIDERATION

Placed within this context, the activities of al-Qaeda—and the many groups destined to grow around this independence movement—take on a different light. Suicide attacks are viewed as only a current manifestation of long-term historical events. Why does this analysis seem so different from what we usually hear from our politicians? Why is sociological analysis sometimes so different from the common interpretation of events? If this analysis is correct, what can we expect in the future?

on September 11, 2001. This attack, accompanied by the attack on the Pentagon in Washington, caused several thousand deaths. These two targets were not random choices. The leaders of al-Qaeda chose the World Trade Center because it symbolized the U.S. dominance of global capitalism. They targeted the Pentagon because it symbolized the U.S. military. To strike at the heart of two of its major symbols exposed the vulnerability of the United States. Al-Qaeda was right, and the attack struck widespread fear in Americans. They realized that nothing was safe.

September 11 also served as theater, in precisely the way that analysts had indicated. The timing—a Tuesday morning—meant that a huge audience would gather immediately. The act went beyond the terrorists' dream, of course, for none could have anticipated the dramatic collapse of the Twin Towers. Yet they did collapse and, in even more dramatic fashion, took with them over 300 firefighters. The message could not have been clearer, nor a worldwide audience as quickly summoned.

A Sense of Morality ■ The terrorists' acts of bloodshed are immoral to outsiders and victims, but to their perpetrators they are righteous acts. Using a neutralization technique we reviewed in Chapter 6, terrorists appeal to a higher morality to justify their killings. It does not matter to them that almost everyone else in the world views their actions as evil—the terrorists are convinced of their moral superiority. As they see it, their "cause" justifies mass, indiscriminate killing of civilians, for these deaths can help usher in their apocalyptic vision of Islamic society.

It is this conviction (the cause, seeming so righteous, justifies any act, no matter how heinous) that makes revolutionary terrorists such formidable opponents of the established order. Some revolutionaries become as dedicated to "the cause" as any monk to his god. Listen to Karari Mjama, a Mau Mau insurgent (the Mau Mau were a militant group whose goal was to liberate Kenya from British rule):

> No one can serve two masters. In order to become a strong faithful warrior who would persevere to the last minute, one had to renounce all worldly wealth, including his family. . . . In fact, I had said to my wife . . . not to expect any sort of help from me for at least ten years' time. I had instructed her to take care of herself and our beloved daughter. I had trained myself to think of the fight, and the African Government; and nothing of the country's progress before independence. I had learned to forget all pleasures and imagination of the past. I confined my thoughts (to) the fight only—the end of which would open my thoughts to the normal world. (Schreiber 1978:32)

Japanese Subways ▪ Japan had prided itself on being a "community nation" insulated from the "profane" social problems of the West. Its soothing, self-serving myth was shattered by a religious leader who launched a poison gas attack on Tokyo subways. Twelve people died, and 5,000 were injured (Miller and Broad 1999). The gas, sarin, can be manufactured from chemicals used in pesticides that you can buy at your local hardware store. Other frightening recipes for poisons have turned up on the Internet—a sort of Betty Crocker cookbook on how to poison the world (Greenberger and Bishop 1995).

REPRESSIVE TERRORISM. A second type of terrorism is **repressive terrorism,** terrorism waged by a government against its own citizens. For example:

> Diana, a dedicated Christian, worked among the poor in Buenos Aires. One midnight, soldiers broke down her door, rushed in, and knocked her to the floor. They blindfolded her and beat her across the head. They then threw her into a car and drove to a building with an underground chamber. Here she was threatened, tortured, and interrogated for six straight hours about church leaders, the Vatican Council, and the Jews.
>
> Beaten beyond all tears, she suddenly blurted, "Good God, aren't you Christians?"
>
> Abrupt silence followed. One of the soldiers grabbed her hand and pressed her fingers to a metal cross on his chest. Afterward, they seemed to give up on her. "I'm convinced that small incident saved my life," she says. "The man apparently wanted to be recognized as a person rather than a torturer. He couldn't have that recognition without making me a person, too, rather than an object to be disposed of."
>
> Diana was later taken back to her apartment and held there for two more days by four officers who took turns raping her. The police then released her. (Cornell 1981)

The massive brutality and killing in Argentina was typical of repressive terrorism: The generals who headed the military dictatorship of Argentina felt vulnerable. Fearful of their government's collapse, they became afraid even of ideas. They arrested tens of thousands of people like Diana between 1976 and 1983. Thousands were tortured and executed. Some bodies were dumped in public places, a mute warning to others. Some captives were dropped alive from airplanes into the ocean. Thousands of parents never knew what happened to their children.

The Khmer Rouge ▪ Pol Pot, the dictator of Cambodia, directed perhaps the most ruinous terrorism that any government has ever inflicted on its people. The extent of his regime's devastation is mind-boggling. For almost four years, from April 1975 to January

At Tuol Sleng Prison outside of Phnom Penh, Cambodia, the Khmer Rouge tortured and killed thousands of people during its bloody reign from 1975 to 1979. The prison is now a museum and tourist attraction.

1979, Cambodia was Pol Pot's private slaughterhouse. On an average day, the Khmer Rouge killed 1,500 Cambodians. In just forty-five months, the government killed about 2 million Cambodians (Wain 1981). Death often came by rubber hoses and bamboo sticks. Some victims were tortured for weeks before their death. Others were killed on the spot.

The Khmer Rouge targeted *all* intellectuals for death, for they represented an elite, and the Pol Pot government was supposedly ushering in a classless society (Miles 1980). Being able to speak a foreign language was enough to merit execution. In one area of Cambodia, members of the Khmer Rouge could count only to ten. Anyone who could count higher was an "intellectual." To ferret them out, the Khmer Rouge would have someone count other people—they executed those who counted to twenty, instead of counting two groups of ten. Only 50 of Cambodia's 800 doctors survived.

On a visit to the killing fields of Cambodia, I saw one of Pol Pot's slaughterhouses. Today, on the outskirts of Phnom Penh, the capital of Cambodia, the buildings are maintained as a sort of museum, so the people won't forget. I could see the metal cots on which the prisoners had been chained, the torture devices used to break the men, women, and children before they were executed. Emblazoned on my mind is the cabinet of skulls—the larger ones of adults and the smaller ones of children—each cracked where someone had struck that living person. So, too, is the huge vat that once had a wooden bar above it. The vat was filled with water, and the victims, hung upside down, were lowered slowly head first into the water. They could be immersed as many times as the torturers wanted, until they finally were forced to drink their death.

Russia ■ To dictators, who hold power uneasily and have few checks on what they can do, repressive terrorism is a way to silence criticism and suppress ideas they don't like. Soviet officials were sensitive to criticism of any sort, and they even persecuted poets and artists who dared to express "incorrect" political thought. They also felt threatened by religion, with party leaders referring to the Church as "the enemy within" (Ra'anan et al. 1986). Authorities felt so threatened by alternative views that they arrested Christians who witnessed to Christ, beating them to death (Wurmbrand 1970). Andrei Sakharov (1977), a dissenter who drew attention to "the persecution of Baptists, of the True Orthodox church, of Pentecostals, and uniates, and others" said,

> It is a common practice of the Russian government to take children away from parents who are evangelical; that is, they believe that Jesus of Nazareth is God incarnate or the Savior who should be placed ahead of the State. Pastors of underground churches are regularly arrested, beaten, tortured, and killed.

STATE-SPONSORED TERRORISM. In the *third* type, **state-sponsored terrorism,** a government finances, trains, and arms terrorists. Colonel Moammar Gadhafi of Libya, who viewed terrorism as a legitimate extension of the state, bankrolled terrorists and provided training camps for them. After the U.S. Air Force tried to kill him by bombing his palace, Gadhafi became more clandestine in his support of terrorism. Then after years of economic sanctions that worsened conditions in his country, Gadhafi renounced his support of terrorism and invited international inspectors to verify that he had dismantled his efforts to produce nuclear weapons.

CRIMINAL TERRORISM. Beyond political terrorism but often affiliated with it is **criminal terrorism.** In this type, criminals use terrorism to attain their objectives. The most well-known example today is the Russian Mafia. To maintain their sources of wealth, these gangsters intimidate and kill anyone who opposes them. They terrorize both the public and government into submission. The Russian Mafia guns down bankers who won't launder money for them; and, as the executions of reporters, prosecutors, judges, and other government officials attest, death awaits anyone who dares to investigate or prosecute them.

Narcoterrorism is a form of criminal terrorism that centers on drugs. Some narcoterrorists have political goals, and they use drug dealing to finance their ambitions. Mehemet Ali Agca, for example, sold drugs to finance his attempted assassination of Pope John Paul II (Oakley 1985; Ehrenfeld 1990). For other narcoterrorists, money is the primary objective; terrorism is simply a way to protect their drug operations. In Colombia, international drug dealers hired thugs to assassinate the justices of the Colombian supreme court. They also terrorized the Colombian government to cancel its extradition treaty with the United States.

NUCLEAR AND BIOLOGICAL TERRORISM. Nuclear and biological weapons could be used by any type of terrorist, but since they are so extreme, we will treat them as a class by themselves. Let's look at each.

Nuclear Terrorism ▪ Because plutonium can be used to manufacture nuclear weapons, you would think it would be guarded carefully. This will sound as though I am making it up, but about 5,000 pounds—two and a half tons—of plutonium are missing from U.S. nuclear facilities. A former security agent reported that protective measures at the Rocky Flats weapons factory near Denver were so lax that it was "like having a window in a bank vault" (Hosenball 1999). When the missing plutonium was made public, officials took a cavalier attitude. "What's to worry?" they asked. The plutonium "probably got stuck in pipes and manufacturing tools." The solution? Simple. They suspended the individual who revealed that the plutonium was missing.

In light of 9/11, you might think that such a cavalier approach to nuclear materials, if it ever existed, would be a thing of the past. Unfortunately, even now, safeguards are sometimes inadequate. Some nuclear materials in Russia are said to be secured only by a chain-link fence and a night watchman (Bunn and Weir 2005). The situation in Russia has rung alarm bells. When the breakup of the Soviet empire brought a void of legitimate power, the Russian Mafia stepped into it. These gangsters stole plutonium and uranium and offered them for sale to Iraq and other dictatorships ("The Wild Wild East" 1995). Part of the difficulty in making Russia's nuclear material secure is that the Soviet Union produced 1,300 tons of enriched uranium and 220 tons of plutonium, and stored them in forty to fifty different places (Gordon 1996). With the cooperation of and financing by the West, about half of this nuclear material has been destroyed (Bunn and Weir 2005).

Some enriched uranium has been smuggled out of nuclear plants and naval facilities, however. One worker simply hid nuclear material in his protective gloves and walked out the gate (Zaitseva and Hand 2003).

As mentioned, the West's nightmare scenario has a dictator developing nuclear-tipped missiles and, unrestrained by the checks and balances built into democracies, terrorizing an entire region—and, with advanced delivery systems, perhaps the world. These concerns are not unrealistic. The "father of the Pakistani bomb," Abdul Qadeer Khan, who headed Pakistan's nuclear program, sold blueprints and parts for making nuclear bombs (Rubin 2004). Among his customers were Iran and North Korea.

Because the potential destruction is enormous, at some point nuclear terrorists could hold major governments captive, including that of the United States. To do so, they don't need advanced delivery systems; they could simply smuggle a "dirty bomb" or some other nuclear weapons into the country. Few of the tens of thousands of containers arriving each day at U.S. ports are searched. What would U.S. officials do if terrorists threatened to detonate a nuclear weapon in the heart of New York City or Atlanta or Los Angeles? The thought of nuclear weapons in the hands of a ruthless, hell-bent-for-destruction dictator or terrorists sends chills down the spine of the industrialized nations.

Biological Terrorism ▪ Perhaps an even greater threat is biological terrorism. The components for weapons such as anthrax, smallpox, and the plague are cheaper to obtain, and they can be transported in tiny containers. Terrorists could infiltrate the United States or any other country and simultaneously release anthrax or other killer germs in several cities. If this were to occur in the United States, the deaths could be numbered in the millions. That this is not so unlikely is underscored by the sending of anthrax through the U.S. mails in 2001. As I write this, the person who mailed the envelopes remains unknown. The fingerprint of the anthrax should have revealed the laboratory in which it was produced; and, from there, telltale clues should have pointed to the killer. But after years of frustrating search, the FBI has continued to come up short.

We explore other aspects of biological terrorism in the Technology and Social Problems box on the next page.

Social Policy

Let's look at social policies on the two major problems we have reviewed in this chapter, political terrorism and nuclear war.

Political Terrorism

THE OVERARCHING PRINCIPLE IN SOCIAL POLICY. The first principle for dealing with terrorists is, Don't give in to their demands, for this encourages terrorism. This principle is very difficult to put into practice because not meeting their demands can bring high immediate costs: property damage, injuries, and deaths. Although giving in to terrorists might relieve the immediate situation, it also encourages further terrorism—because the tactic worked. In short, giving in to terrorists' demands is a recipe for escalating incidents of terrorism.

TEN BASIC POLICIES. Legal and government experts suggest the following as effective social policies (Bremer 1988; Ehrenfeld 1990; FBI 1998; "National Strategy . . ." 2006):

1. Promise anything during negotiations. Promises made under threat are not valid.
2. Make no distinction between terrorists and their state sponsors. Even though they hide behind the scenes, states that sponsor terrorists are not neutral and should not be treated as neutrals. This principle allows both retaliatory and preemptive acts.

Technology and Social Problems
OUR FUTURE: BIOLOGICAL TERRORISM IN THE TWENTY-FIRST CENTURY

Consider this scenario:

Over a period of years, agents of a nation whose leader hates the United States and has a score to settle quietly infiltrate the United States. Most gain admission as students at universities around the country. All have been trained by their country's secret police. On a predetermined day, at a specified hour, they release anthrax and smallpox into the air of twenty major cities. Within days, a third of Americans are dead.

Scenarios like this haunt U.S. officials. Few safeguards exist to protect against such an attack. There will be no warning, no attempt to hold the United States hostage in order to extort billions of dollars. The motive will be revenge for humiliations suffered at U.S. hands. The goal will be not money, but the annihilation of the United States itself.

How seriously officials are taking this threat and other threats by terrorists is indicated by the federal budget: Thirty-nine billion dollars are spent by the Department of Homeland Security each year (*Statistical Abstract* 2006:Table 516). Officials have stockpiled vaccines around the country, and emergency medical teams have been trained in major cities. All military personnel, active and reserve, are being vaccinated against anthrax, as well as all civilian employees of the Department of Defense

who are designated essential workers ("Anthrax Vaccination . . . " 2004).

If a biological attack occurs, U.S. officials have a plan. It is not to evacuate populations, but to try to prevent the disease from spreading by blocking roads and stopping people, at gunpoint, from fleeing cities. Plans also include a military takeover of state and local governments to fight the chaos that would result from such an attack (Miller and Broad 1999). For at least a while after a biological attack, the Pentagon would have direct control over the United States.

An ancient Chinese proverb says: "May you live in exciting times." This simple saying is actually a curse, for it expresses the hope that an enemy's life will be chaotic. We live in exciting times. Let's hope that the curse with which we live— weapons of mass destruction, hatreds engendered by foreign domination, and retaliatory action by terrorists—does not mean our destruction.

3. Use economic and political sanctions to break the connection between terrorists and the states that provide them weapons, financing, safe houses, training areas, and identity documents in return for terrorism done on their behalf.
4. Treat terrorists as war criminals. Track them, arrest them, and punish them. Bomb them, if that is what it takes.
5. Discourage media coverage because publicity is a prime goal of terrorists. Make it illegal for the media to pay terrorists for interviews.
6. Establish international extradition and prosecution agreements: Terrorists need to know that if they are caught anywhere, they will be extradited or tried.
7. Develop an international organization to combat terrorism. This organization would coordinate worldwide intelligence and advise nations. It would also direct international teams to respond to specific events—such as freeing hostages or locating evidence to identify sponsors of terrorists.
8. Offer large rewards for information leading to the disabling of known terrorists. Just as in the old West, rewards can be paid on a "dead-or-alive" basis. With rewards of $50,000, or $1 million, or $5 million, terrorists will never know whether associates

9/11 has had far-reaching effects on the United States. Whether the country ever returns to its more easygoing ways based on feelings of internal security remains to be seen. The anti-terrorism laws passed after 9/11 give the police more authority than they have had since the Civil War.

can be trusted. Informants should also be guaranteed safe passage and offered new identities.

9. Cut the funding of terrorist organizations. For travel, weapons, training, and other activities, they need money, so disrupt their remittance systems.

10. Infiltrate terrorist organizations.

APPLICATION OF THE POLICIES. Some of these policies, such as the last three, are being put into effect. Consistent implementation of the second and third ones was the primary reason that Libya's dictator, Moammar Gadhafi, renounced terrorism, paid large settlements to the families of those killed in one of his state-sponsored attacks on an airliner, and opened Libya to inspections from the West. Some of these policies are controversial—and disturbing. Gulf War II, for example, is an example of the policy of preemptive strikes. Because Hussein supposedly possessed weapons of mass destruction and was intending to use them against the West, the United States (with troops from a few other nations) struck first. At least this was the reason given prior to the invasion.

Targeted Killings ▪ Targeted killings, an application of the fourth policy, are also disturbing. When the CIA determines that a certain individual is responsible for a terrorist attack or is planning such an act, he is put on a "hit list" and marked for assassination (Risen and Johnston 2002). Lest you think that I am exaggerating—since trials and evidence, prosecution and defense, and judges and juries are an essential part of our legal heritage—the CIA has already done this. Launching a Predator, an unmanned plane, the CIA tracked suspected terrorists traveling by car in Djibouti. CIA agents in Yemen then fired a Hellfire missile, which struck their automobile, killing all six (Hersh 2002).

How often this occurs is anyone's guess; but since targeted killings are effective, although lacking legal sanction, and the CIA dislikes publicity, I suspect that this policy is implemented regularly by the CIA and perhaps by other U.S. government agencies. This is also a policy of the KGB (now FSB) of Russia and the Mossad of Israel.

Nuclear Warfare and the Elusive Path to Peace

MUTUAL DETERRENCE. The primary policy that the United States and the former Soviet Union pursued after World War II was **mutual deterrence**—using threats and the fear of mutual destruction to prevent the other from striking first. Each was afraid to use its nuclear arsenal, because each had developed doomsday safeguards—that is, if a country were attacked and destroyed, even out of the ashes missiles would be launched that would destroy the other. Because neither country would survive, there was no benefit to attacking the other. The resulting balance of power was called Mutual Assured Destruction (MAD).

A Strange Path to Peace ■ The path to peace, then, has been a MAD one. Each superpower armed itself to the teeth, stockpiled weapons of mass destruction—nuclear, chemical, and biological—and signaled to its counterpart that it was willing to unleash those weapons. Thus the superpowers struck a balance of power—or terror—that kept them from attacking each other. Sociologist Nicholas Timasheff (1965:291) explained how it worked:

> Each party may consider that it has a fair chance to win, but each party also knows that the cost of victory would be prohibitive; physical destruction of 90–95 percent of the total population, almost complete destruction of industrial equipment, transformation of almost the total territory into an uninhabitable area because of radiation, contamination of air, water, plants and animals and other natural resources. Under these circumstances victory can be worse than the most crucial defeat before this atomic age. Each of the parties to the possible conflict has full reason to refrain from attack.

THE BALANCE OF POWER. G8, the association of the world's eight most powerful nations, is working out a new balance of power—sometimes called the New World Order. The balance, however, is precarious. Of its many sources of disequilibrium, perhaps the most disturbing is the proliferation of nuclear weapons. Poor nations may not be able to make it to G8's bargaining table, but if they join the nuclear club, G8 will listen to them. The proliferation of nuclear weapons to desperately poor nations like Pakistan and North Korea makes this balance of power even more precarious. Also entering this picture is India, which has developed a missile system that can be fired from mobile launchers. Not only can India's missiles hit targets in Pakistan, its neighbor and historical enemy, but they can also reach Beijing and Shanghai (Norris and Kristensen 2005). Look again at the Social Map on pages 536–537.

Even local conflicts, ordinarily of little interest to G8, can upset its balance of power. Local conflicts can heat up, dragging in other nations and spreading beyond the local area. Because of this, NATO (North Atlantic Treaty Organization) took quick action against Serbia. Bombs speak louder than words, as the president of Serbia, Slobodan Milosevic, discovered. If a minor, hostile power comes close to possessing nuclear weapons or, as in the case of Hussein's Iraq, is suspected of doing so, the United States, accompanied by larger or smaller numbers of followers, acts—preferring to bomb now and ask questions later, updating the slogan of the old Western movies. Serving to restrain the United States and G8, though, are fears of Iran unleashing terrorists, the million soldiers that North Korea can unleash on South Korea, and uncertainty regarding China's reaction if G8 bombs North Korea.

Few of us realize how fragile our current balance of power is. It appears so solid. But threats can come from unexpected directions, even incompetence at a low level. Consider this event from the 1970s:

> For nearly four years, the public library of the Los Alamos Scientific Laboratory in New Mexico had on its shelves a report that provided precise details of the devices that trigger hydrogen bombs (Mintz 1979). Only a few pages of the report were supposed to have been declassified, but through a "clerical error" the entire report was made available to the public, both Americans and foreigners, for inspection and copying. A nuclear expert, Dimitri

Rotow, who copied this report, was quoted as saying: "It was easier than getting something out of the Library of Congress. At the Library of Congress, they at least check your briefcase." (*Associated Press*, May 25, 1979)

Apparently, this event did not teach U.S. officials to safeguard information on how to make nuclear weapons. In March 2005, federal officials took their incompetence one step further, making sure that someone who might be interested in atomic secrets didn't have to make the trip all the way to New Mexico. They simply posted on the Web what critics called "a guide" on how to make atomic bombs. When someone suggested that these instructions might be inappropriate, they quickly yanked the information off the Web (Broad 2006b).

THREE POTENTIAL POLICIES. Assuming such obvious policies as keeping manuals on "how to make your own bomb" off Web sites, social policies that can help ensure peace include disarmament, interlocking networks of mutual interests, and international law. Let's look at each.

Disarmament ◼ Proponents of disarmament are of two types. Some propose **bilateral disarmament;** that is, both sides agree to disarm simultaneously. Others favor **unilateral disarmament:** One nation would announce its intention to disarm and begin to dismantle some weapons system. When its antagonist sees that it has made itself more vulnerable, it supposedly would begin to disarm, too. Just as each step of armament led to the escalation and proliferation of weapons systems, so each step of disarmament would reduce and ultimately eliminate that stockpile.

Another group argues that only a strong military and the will to use it can make a nation secure. Those who favor this position oppose disarmament. Although full military preparedness may indeed prevent war, extremists have carried this argument to logical absurdities. They argue that because nuclear weapons kept the superpowers from attacking one another, it will do the same for other nations. The nuclear powers, then, should help other nations build nuclear weapons (Sagan 1994). The more the merrier!

Russia and the United States have signed treaties to reduce their stockpiles of nuclear weapons, and the nations in G8 that possess nuclear weapons have stopped testing them, as has China. This is not disarmament, however, as none of these nations intends to rid itself of nuclear weapons. The testing of nuclear weapons by a nation that does not now have them could stimulate the United States and other countries to develop a new generation of nuclear weapons (Wirtz 2006).

Developing Interlocking Networks of Mutual Interest ◼ Some feel that the key to peace is to develop interlocking networks of mutual interest. It is thought that the more a nation depends on another for its own well-being, the less likely it will be to destroy that nation. The principle is sound, but the route to such dependence may come as a surprise, for it could be global capitalism. The expansion of capitalism has produced a **global economy,** one that links the world's nations to one another. As a nation's trading partners increase, its affairs become more interlinked with those of the other nations. To develop further interlocking interests, then, we should encourage trade among the world's nations. To stimulate peace, we also would encourage communication, including travel and scientific and cultural exchanges.

International Law. ◼ International law is essential for world peace. If each nation is a law unto itself and feels free to wage war when its goals are frustrated, we can never have peace. The major obstacle to implementing international law is the unwillingness of nations to yield sovereignty to an international organization. The rule of law, as represented by the United Nations, was dealt a severe blow when NATO bombed Kosovo. Despite the official reason given for the bombing, with which most of us can agree—to prevent further ethnic slaughter—NATO placed itself above international law by attacking without the approval of the United Nations. International law was dealt a further blow by the refusal of the United States to submit to the International Criminal Court.

Officials of the United States fear that its officials could be charged with war crimes (Sewall and Kaysen 2000). This is not so far-fetched, for "one person's freedom fighter is another person's terrorist."

SURVIVAL AS A MUTUAL BENEFIT. In the end, perhaps it will be the desire for self-preservation that will prevent the nuclear annihilation of humanity. Leaders don't want themselves, their families, or their own country destroyed. Unfortunately, there are exceptions—madmen who want to dominate the world and, failing to do so, want to destroy it. As Albert Speer (1970), one of Hitler's close associates, noted, Hitler held on to the illusion of victory until the end. When he saw that the war was lost, he blamed failure on the Germans' lack of will, and he wanted to destroy his country. If Hitler had had nuclear bombs, the history of the world might have been written with a different hand.

IN SUM The best social policies would be those that remove weapons of mass destruction from humanity. I foresee no social policies, however, that will eliminate these weapons, whether nuclear, biological, or chemical. The knowledge of how to produce weapons of mass destruction has proliferated, and the best we can hope for are social policies that limit that knowledge and prevent the use of these weapons.

The Future of the Problem

ARMS SALES AND WAR. There certainly is no indication that war will disappear. On the contrary, it appears that wars will continue indefinitely. Some of these wars will be fueled by the merchants of death, which are listed in Table 15-4. As you can see, the United States takes an easy lead in this questionable category, selling twice as many weapons as its nearest competitor. With dictators needing to prop up their sagging regimes and with borders in jeopardy, there is no end to eager buyers. It seems that when profit knocks on the door, morality flies out the window.

Recall the earlier materials on the military-industrial complex (page 533). The U.S. factories that produce the weapons for the U.S. military have a production capacity in excess of what the U.S. military needs. The recipient nations listed in the second part of Table 15-4 provide an excellent outlet for this excess capacity. It is unlikely that this profitable merchandising in death will diminish—regardless of the destruction of human life that ensues.

Look again at the nations that spend the most for weapons of war. As you can see, some poor nations pay huge amounts for arms. Some of the buyers are dirt poor. Egypt, India, Malaysia, and Pakistan are using money they desperately need to feed, house, and educate their people. Then why do they spend so much? The potential of aggression by neighboring countries encourages this reckless spending, to be sure, but the most direct answer is that the elite of these nations are insecure politically. The weapons undergird their power.

POLITICAL TERRORISM. It is likely that political terrorism will not only continue but increase. The unshackling of the central dictatorship in the former Soviet Union unleashed ethnic antagonisms that have been nourished by centuries of animosity. This uncorking released prejudices and hatreds among groups that we had never heard of. In the former Yugoslavia, for example, Serbs, Croats, Muslims, and Albanians rushed at each other's throats and tried to eliminate each other. Kurds and Turks find themselves at an uneasy stalemate, their mutual desire to kill one another barely held in check. Groups in India and Pakistan fight one

TABLE 15-4 The Global Arms Trade: Buying and Selling the Weapons of Death

THE TOP 10 SELLERS

RANK	SUPPLIER	1998–2005
1	United States	97,100
2	Russia	41,600
3	France	30,000
4	Germany	17,000
5	United Kingdom	14,900
6	China	9,100
7	Israel	7,900
8	Sweden	6,800
9	Spain	5,700
10	Italy	5,600

THE TOP 10 BUYERS

RANK	RECIPIENT	1998–2005
1	Saudi Arabia	50,100
2	China	14,300
3	Taiwan	13,900
4	United Arab Emirates	11,400
5	Egypt	10,300
6	India	9,500
7	Israel	9,200
8	South Korea	7,600
9	Pakistan	4,400
10	Malaysia	3,400

Source: By the author. Based on Grimmett 2006:Tables 8C, 2I.

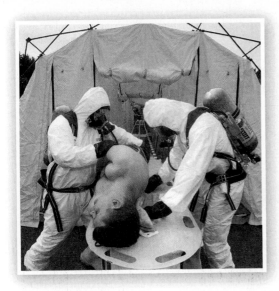

Authorities around the world are holding their collective breath, awaiting the next terrorist attack in some unexpected way at some unanticipated location. To test how prepared we are for such an attack, this man is being prepared for decontamination.

another—both killing and dying over the same sliver of disputed land. Groups in Africa do the same.

Revolutionary Terrorism ■ Some revolutionary terrorists are motivated by hatred every bit as bitter as the antagonisms just mentioned. Others simply want political change. It seems almost inevitable that as time goes on, revolutionary terrorists, such as those who bombed the World Trade Center in New York in 2001, will acquire more sophisticated weapons. Supposedly available on the black market are shoulder-fired, precision-guided surface-to-air missiles that can bring down jumbo jets. If terrorists acquire systems that can target cars in a motorcade several miles away, more political leaders will be in jeopardy. That we will one day face weapons of mass destruction—nuclear, chemical, and biological—is also likely. With advances in genetic engineering, the potential of using biological weapons haunts officials.

Repressive Terrorism ■ Despite democratic crosscurrents, repressive terrorism will continue, particularly in China, Central and South America, Africa, and the Middle East. Demands for more democratic government will typically be met with heavy-handed repression. In some cases, this repression will be extreme, with the population cowering in fear of its own government. Political repression, in turn, will stimulate resistance—and the bloody struggles will continue.

State-Sponsored Terrorism ■ It is likely that state-sponsored terrorism will decrease. We won't see a decrease in the number of rulers in weaker countries who would *like* to sponsor terrorists and send them against their enemies. Rather, investigative techniques have become more powerful, enabling state-sponsored sources to be more easily tracked—and vengeance taken. The desire for self-preservation will deter leaders from this route.

Russia ■ Russia holds fascinating prospects. After seven decades of persecution, its people gained freedom of speech, press, politics, education, religion, and the arts. Increased trade and cultural exchanges with the West reduced suspicions and hostilities on both sides. Russia's acceptance into NATO, albeit as a junior partner at first, also allows us to visualize a better future. Nothing about Russia is certain, however. At any time, its leaders may slap their repressive hats firmly on their heads. The nation's arduous experiment with democracy may prove too threatening—inflation, poverty, the Russian Mafia, and criticism and even defiance of leaders. On one side are the hard-liners, straining to seize power and make repression state policy. They are restrained only with difficulty. On the other side is the potential for the state to fail and the nation to fall into anarchy. With an arsenal of nuclear weapons hanging in the balance, either the rise of the hard-liners or a descent into anarchy threatens world peace.

I expect that in the end we will muddle through. A muddle-through future, while not exciting to contemplate, is certainly preferable to some of those sketched earlier.

SUMMARY AND REVIEW

1. The three essential conditions of war are a cultural tradition for *war,* an antagonistic situation, and a "spark" that sets off the war. Wars have occurred throughout history, but today's wars are much more destructive.

2. Symbolic interactionists analyze how symbols (perceptions) underlie war. The West and the Soviets saw each other as mortal enemies arming for deadly combat. Each felt obliged to arm itself, setting off a nuclear arms race. In this view, nuclear weapons are not intended to be used, but to symbolize a country's capacity to destroy an enemy.

3. Functionalists identify these functions of war: the extension of political boundaries, social integration, economic gain, social change, ideology, vengeance, military security, and credibility. The dysfunctions of war are defeat, dependence, and destruction. Apply these functions to the U.S. war on terrorism. How about the dysfunctions?

4. Conflict theorists identify four causes of war: competition for resources, a conflict of interests, a surplus of capital, and the dominance of a military machine.

5. Humans are no more peaceful today than in earlier times. The following do *not* diminish the chances of warfare: the type of government, the group's religion, prosperity, a common language or religion, shared political boundaries, or level of education.

6. Modern weapons are expensive and come at the cost of alternative expenditures. A major cost of war is *dehumanization.*

7. Both the military and business gain from producing, selling, and using weapons. The *military-industrial complex* is a powerful force in promoting war.

8. One of the more serious threats facing humanity is weapons of mass destruction: biological, chemical, and nuclear. Unless effective international controls are put into place, these weapons will proliferate, one day leading to vast destruction. Today's nations are vulnerable to these forms of terrorism.

9. *Political terrorism*—that is, the use of war to achieve political objectives—is of three types: *revolutionary terrorism,* waged by groups (or in rare cases, individuals) against the state; *repressive terrorism,* waged by the state against its own people; and *state-sponsored terrorism,* waged by one state against another. *Criminal terrorism* cuts across these types.

10. Disarmament, international law, and growing interlocking interests among the nations of the world could increase the chances for peace.

11. The future holds more terrorism and war. All-out nuclear war is unlikely because it means mutual destruction. Revolutionary terrorism will continue. This, in turn, will stimulate repressive terrorism. The ethnic antagonisms unleashed in the former Soviet Union will lead to more terrorism. Al-Qaeda and its supporters are likely to remain agents of terrorism. The Russian Mafia is likely to be brought under control, but political instabilities may bring hard-liners back into power.

KEY TERMS

Arms race, 517
Bilateral disarmament, 551
Binary chemical weapons, 540
Cold War, 517
Criminal terrorism, 546
Dehumanization, 530

Global economy, 551
Imperialism, 525
Megaton, 534
Military-industrial complex, 533
Mutual deterrence, 550
Political terrorism, 541

Repressive terrorism, 544
Revolutionary terrorism, 541
State-sponsored terrorism, 546
Total war, 530
Unilateral disarmament, 551
War, 519

1. Sociologist Nicholas Timasheff identified three essential conditions of war and seven "sparks" that can ignite these conditions into war (pages 519–520). Analyze a war that the United States has participated in. In this war, what were the essential conditions and the sparks?
2. Which of the three perspectives (symbolic interactionism, functionalism, or conflict theory) do you think best explains why countries go to war? Explain.
3. The functions of war are summarized on pages 523–525. Apply these functions to the U.S. war on terrorism. How about the dysfunctions?
4. Do you think that the United States would ever be able to trust the other nuclear countries of the world if a worldwide treaty to destroy all nuclear weapons were signed? How would we be able to protect ourselves if just one country decided to secretly retain their weapons?
5. Do you think that the United States has the right to intervene in another country to protect our economic or political interests? Under what conditions is intervention justified? Explain.
6. Do you think that other countries have the right to intervene in the United States to protect their economic or political interest? Under what conditions is intervention justified? Explain.
7. Do you think that nuclear war is more or less likely now than it was during the Cold War? Explain.

Acid rain Rain with heavy concentrations of sulfuric and nitric acids.

Addiction Dependence on a substance to make it through the day.

Ageism Discrimination against people on the basis of their age; this concept is not limited to older people.

Alcoholic A person with severe alcohol-related problems.

Amotivational syndrome The tendency for people who smoke marijuana extensively to become apathetic, lose their concentration, and become unable to carry out long-range plans.

Anglo-conformity Requiring or expecting everyone in the United States to adopt the dominant culture, the customs inherited from English settlers.

Anomie The feeling of being estranged, uprooted, unanchored, normless—not knowing what rules to apply to the situations one faces.

Apartheid (ah-par′-tate) The enforced segregation of people on the basis of their perceived race or ethnicity.

Arms race The attempt by nations to match one another's war capabilities, usually referring to the buildup of weapons during Cold War standoff between the Soviet Union and the West.

Assimilation The absorption of a minority group into the mainstream culture.

Attention deficit-hyperactivity disorder A term used to refer to a supposed medical condition that causes children not to pay attention and to disrupt classroom activities. Also known as hyperactivity, attention deficit disorder, and hyperkinesis.

Bilateral disarmament Two or more nations disarming simultaneously.

Binary chemical weapons Shells or bombs in which two benign chemicals are kept in separate chambers in the weapon. Upon detonation, they mix, forming a lethal agent.

Biodegradable Capable of disintegrating in outdoor weather.

Biological poverty Material deprivation so severe that it affects someone's health (biological functioning).

Black market The underground channeling of illegitimate goods or services.

Bureaucracy A highly structured hierarchy with specialized personnel.

Capital punishment The death penalty.

Capitalism An economic system that is based on the private ownership of property and investing capital to make a profit.

Capitalist economy An economy based on the private ownership of the means of production, the pursuit of profit, and market competition. See *Socialist economy*.

Capitalists Owners of the means of production (land, factories, tools) who buy the labor of workers.

Carcinogen A cancer-causing substance.

Case study A type of research design that focuses on a single case. The case or subject of the study can be an individual, an event, or an organization such as a church, hospital, or abortion clinic.

Chicago school of sociology An approach to research that originated with the Department of Sociology at the University of Chicago in the 1920s. It emphasized participant observation, symbolic interactionism, and seeing things from an insider's point of view.

City Place of residence of a large number of people who live there permanently and do not produce their own food.

Civil disobedience Deliberately but peacefully disobeying laws that are considered unjust.

Cogeneration Production of electricity as a by-product of one's ordinary operations.

Cohabitation Situation in which a couple live together in a sexual relationship outside marriage.

Cold War A period of hostilities after World War II between the former Soviet Union and nations of the West.

Collective violence Another term for *group violence*.

Commodity riot Collective violence that involves extensive looting.

Common sense The ideas common to a society or to some group within a society that people use to make sense out of their experiences.

Communal riot Collective violence between the residents of two areas for control of a contested area.

Community People identifying with an area and with one another, sensing that they belong and that others care about what happens to them.

Compartmentalize To keep separate in one's mind feelings, attitudes, and behaviors that are incompatible with one another or that threaten the self-concept.

Concentric zone theory A theory developed by Ernest Burgess suggesting that cities develop outward from their center, resulting in areas, or zones, that have specialized functions. The area closest to the central business district—the zone in transition—has the most severe urban problems.

Condominium in-filling An urban policy in which condominiums for older people are built in vacant areas of their neighborhood, and the larger homes they vacate are taken over by younger families.

Conflict theory A sociological theory that views society as a system in competition and conflict. Each group in society attempts to further its own interests, even at the expense of others. Those who gain power power exploit people and resources for their own benefit. Social problems stem from exploitation and resistance to exploitation.

Containment theory A functionalist theory that focuses on the pushes and pulls thought to cause people to commit criminal acts. Whether one commits a violent act depends on the relative strength of inner containment (controls within the individual) and on outer containment (controls outside the individual).

Control group The group in an experiment that is not exposed to an experience (or independent variable).

Control theory Another term for *containment theory*.

Corporate crime See *White-collar crime*.

Corporate welfare Handouts given to corporations, usually in the form of tax breaks; may also be reductions in rent or bargain-priced real estate.

Correlation Two or more things occurring together.

Cosa nostra The term by which East Coast mobsters refer to the Mafia. See *Mafia*.

Craving An intense desire for a drug.

Crime Any act prohibited by law. What constitutes crime varies from one social group to another.

Crime rates The number of crimes per some unit of population, most commonly the number of crimes per 100,000 people.

Criminal justice system The agencies that respond to crime, including the police, courts, jails, and prisons.

Criminal sexual assault A legal term that refers to sexual attacks, especially to attempted rape and forcible rape.

Criminal terrorism People in organized crime using terrorism to achieve their objectives.

Cultural goal A goal held out as legitimate for the members of a society.

Cultural means The approved ways of reaching cultural goals.

Culture of poverty Characteristics of the poor—such as family violence, alcoholism, and low self-esteem—that help the poor stay poor.

Culture of wealth Characteristics of the wealthy—such as social connections—that help keep them from falling down the social-class ladder.

Defensive medicine Medical procedures performed by physicians to protect themselves in case they are sued for malpractice.

Dehumanization Viewing and treating a person as an object not deserving the treatment ordinarily accorded humans.

Deinstitutionalization A policy developed in the 1960s of discharging patients from state and county mental hospitals into the community, where they were supposed to receive community-based services.

Delinquent subculture A subculture whose members are oriented toward illegal acts.

Demographic transition A four-stage process of population growth. The first is high birth rates and high death rates. The second is high birth rates and low death rates. The third is low birth rates and low death rates. The fourth stage, which has just emerged is birth rates so low that a population shrinks.

Demography The study of the size, composition, growth, and distribution of human populations.

Dependency ratio The number of workers compared with the number of Social Security recipients.

Depersonalization Treating patients as things, rather than as people with personal needs.

Deterrence The attempt to prevent crime by producing fear.

Differential association A symbolic interactionist theory that stresses how criminal behavior is learned. Applied to violence, it assumes that people learn to be violent in the same way that people learn to be cooperative.

Dirty work The tasks in society that few people want.

Discrimination The act of singling people out for unfair treatment.

Disengagement theory The view that society prevents disruption by having the elderly disengage from (or give up) their positions of responsibility so that the younger generation can step into their shoes.

Disinvestment A policy of withholding investments from an area.

Diversion A response to crime that diverts offenders away from courts and jails to keep them out of the criminal justice system.

Division of labor People performing different sets of specialized tasks.

Documents Written sources or records used as a source of information.

Dominant group The group that has more power, privilege, and social status and that discriminates against minority groups.

Drug A substance taken to change bodily functions, behavior, emotions, thinking, or consciousness.

Drug abuse Using drugs in such a way that they harm one's health, impair one's physical or mental functioning, or interfere with one's social life.

Drug addiction Dependence on the regular consumption of a drug in order to make it through the day. Also known as *drug dependence.*

Drug therapy The use of drugs such as tranquilizers and antidepressants to treat emotional problems.

Dual labor market A pool of workers divided into two main segments, regularly employed and better-paid workers and low-paid temporary workers.

Dysfunction When some part of a social system interferes with the functioning of another part or disrupts the stability (or equilibrium) of the system, it is a dysfunction.

Ecology The study of the relationship between living things and their environment.

Economic colonialism One nation exploiting another nation's resources.

Economy A society's system of producing and distributing goods and services.

Ecosystem The interconnection of life on the planet's outer surface; the web made up of organisms and their environment.

Electroconvulsive therapy (ECT) A treatment for emotional problems in which a low-voltage electric current is passed through the brain. Also known as electroshock therapy.

Enterprise zones An urban policy that attempts to encourage private enterprise (investment) in a designated area by reducing taxes and government regulations.

Environmental injustice Location of polluting industries (and other forms of pollution, such as dumping) in places inhabited primarily by the poor and minorities.

Ethnic group A group of people who identify with one another on the basis of their ancestry and cultural heritage. Also called a *racial-ethnic group.*

Ethnocentrism A strong identity with one's own group, often accompanied by thinking of other groups as inferior.

Euthanasia Mercy killing.

Experiment A research design that divides a group into an *experimental group* (those who are exposed to some experience) and a *control group* (those who are not exposed to the experience). Measurements are taken before and after to determine the effects of the experience.

Experimental group The group in an experiment that is exposed to an experience (or independent variable).

Exponential growth curve As growth doubles during approximately equal intervals, it accelerates in the latter stages.

Extended family A family in which other relatives, such as the "older generation" or unmarried aunts and uncles, live with the parents and their children.

False class consciousness Karl Marx's term for the workers' illusion that they are not oppressed; for example, workers thinking of themselves as entrepreneurs or investors.

Family of orientation The family into which people are born and from which they receive their basic orientations to life.

Family of procreation The family that is formed by marriage and that generally results in procreation, or the birth of children.

Feminization of poverty Poverty clustered among women and children.

Fetal alcohol syndrome A cluster of congenital problems caused by the alcohol consumption of the newborn's mother.

Fetal narcotic syndrome A cluster of congenital problems caused by the narcotic use of the newborn's mother.

Field study (or *Participant observation*) A method of gathering information through direct observation of some setting.

Food pollution (also called *food contamination*) The transmission of disease during food processing or the addition of chemicals to food to help process it, lengthen its shelf life, or enhance its appearance or taste. *Genetically modified foods* might be a form of food pollution.

Forcible rape Nonconsensual or forced sexual relations.

Frustration-aggression A psychological theory that stresses that aggression is likely when a goal is blocked.

Function The contribution of a part to its system; or people's actions that contribute to the equilibrium of a social system.

Functionalism (also called *functional analysis, functional theory,* and the *functional perspective*) A sociological theory that views society as a system of interconnected parts, each part contributing in some way to the equilibrium or stability of the system. The contribution of each part is called its function; hence the term *functionalism.* Functionalists view social problems as the failure of some part of the system to function correctly.

Future shock The confusion or disorientation that accompanies rapid social change.

Gemeinschaft A group of people characterized by bonds of intimacy combined with a sense of tradition and belonging. See also *Gesellschaft.*

Gender How we express our "maleness" or "femaleness." Refers to socialization or culture. Commonly called femininity or masculinity. See also *Sex.*

Gender roles The behaviors and attitudes expected of males and females.

Generalize To apply to other people the findings that were learned from one setting, group, or sample.

Generalized other Basically, the community or groups in general that people take into account as they consider a course of action.

Genetically modified foods (GMF) Foods, either plant or animal, that contain genetic materials from another species or whose genes have been modified in a way that does not occur in nature.

Genocide Killing or attempting to kill an entire people.

Gentrification A process in which the relatively affluent displace the poor and renovate their homes.

Gesellschaft A group of people characterized by impersonality and the pursuit of self-interest. See also *Gemeinschaft.*

Global economy The economic interdependence of the nations of the world; economic events that occur in one place are no longer isolated but have far-reaching ramifications for other nations.

Global warming An increase in the earth's temperature because of the *greenhouse effect.*

Green revolution The world's rapidly expanded food production during the 1950s and 1960s as the result of new fertilizers and high-yield strains of wheat and rice.

Greenhouse effect The concentration of gases in the atmosphere that serve as a blanket around the earth, allowing sunlight to enter but inhibiting the release of heat.

Group therapy A treatment for emotional problems in which members of the group talk about how they interact with others and help each other to cope with their problems.

Group violence A number of people attacking others or destroying their property.

Hate crimes Crimes that are motivated by hostility based on race–ethnicity, religion, disability, national origin, or sexual orientation.

Health maintenance organization (HMO) A comprehensive prepaid health care organization designed to reduce costs by minimizing unnecessary medical services.

Heterosexuality The sexual preference for people of the opposite sex.

Home health care Organized health services for people who are living at home with chronic or disabling diseases.

Homosexual behavior Sexual relations between people of the same sex, regardless of their sexual preference.

Homosexuality The sexual preference for people of one's own sex.

Housing unit A place of residence normally occupied by a family, individual, or group of people. Examples are a detached house, a mobile home, an apartment, and a condominium.

Iatrogenesis Illnesses or other health problems caused by medical care.

Illegitimate opportunity structure The opportunity, built into one's environment, to learn and participate in illegal activities.

Imperialism The pursuit of unlimited geographic expansion.

Incapacitation A response to crime that focuses on removing offenders from circulation.

Incest Forbidden sexual relations between relatives, such as brothers and sisters or parents and their children.

Individual discrimination Discrimination by one person against another.

Individual psychotherapy Treatment for emotional problems. A therapist listens and tries to guide the client toward a resolution of his or her problems.

Individual violence One person attacking another.

Infanticide Killing infants shortly after birth, usually as a form of population control.

Institutional discrimination Discrimination that is built into the social system.

Institutionalized group violence Group violence that is carried out under the direction of legally constituted officials.

Interest groups Groups organized around different interests (from the dairy industry to animal rights).

Interview A method of gathering information whereby the researcher asks questions. In a *structured* interview, specific questions are asked, whereas in an *unstructured* interview, people are simply encouraged to talk about their experiences, with the researcher making certain that they cover specific areas.

Invasion-succession cycle One group moving into an area that is inhabited by a group that has different characteristics. Moving in represents the invasion; dominating the area, the succession.

Job deconcentration An urban policy that moves jobs to specified areas adjacent to a city.

Juvenile delinquency Illegal acts committed by minors.

Labeling Stereotyping, or putting a tag on someone, and treating him or her accordingly.

Labor force participation rate The proportion of the population 16 years and older that is in the labor force.

Latent dysfunctions The *unintended* consequences of people's actions that *disrupt* the equilibrium or stability of a system or the adjustment of its parts.

Latent functions The *unintended* consequences of people's actions that contribute to the equilibrium or stability of a social system or the functioning of its parts.

Laterization The tendency of certain tropical soils to become laterite, a rocklike material, when they are exposed to the air.

Lay referral network Friends, relatives, and acquaintances from whom sick people get suggestions about what to do about their illnesses. See also *Professional referral network.*

Lesbian A female homosexual.

Life chances What one may expect to get out of life (because of the conditions of the group into which one is born).

Looking-glass self Our self-images are dependent on what we think others think of us. We see ourselves, in other words, as a reflection in the eyes of others; hence the term *looking-glass self.*

Machine See *Political machine.*

Mafia An organized crime group. The Sicilian-American version is bureaucratized with specialized personnel and departmentalization.

Manifest function The consequences of people's actions that are *intended* to contribute to the adaptation, adjustment, or equilibrium of a system or its parts.

Masochists People who receive sexual gratification by having pain inflicted on themselves.

Mass murder Killing four or more people at one time in one location.

Mass poverty Poverty so widespread that most people are poor.

Master trait A trait considered so important that it overrides an individual's other characteristics. One's sex is an example.

Matriarchy A society in which women-as-a-group dominate men as a group.

Medicalization of human problems To define problems of daily life as a matter of sickness and therefore properly handled by the medical profession.

Megalopolis Urban areas spilling onto one another, making them an interconnected region.

Megaton The explosive power of 1 million tons of TNT.

Melting pot The expectation that the European immigrants to the United States would "melt" or blend together—that is, interact, intermarry, and form a cultural and biological blend.

Methadone maintenance A program for heroin addicts in which the narcotic methadone is substituted for the narcotic heroin.

Methods (Research methods or Methodology) Ways of doing research.

Militancy Seeking to dominate society (in Wirth's terminology).

Military-industrial complex The merged interests of the military and business to pressure politicians to produce armaments. The military-industrial complex has become a potent political force in the contemporary world.

Minority group A group of people who, on the basis of physical or cultural characteristics, are singled out for unequal treatment and who regard themselves as objects of discrimination.

Modeling Copying another's behavior.

Moral entrepreneur A crusading reformer who wages battle to enforce his or her ideas of morality.

Multiculturalism Another term for *pluralism.*

Mutual deterrence Preventing a first strike by making the enemy fear that a massive retaliation would follow, which would also destroy them.

National debt The total amount that a nation owes; computed by adding its annual deficits and subtracting its annual surpluses.

Neutralization See *Techniques of neutralization.*

Normal violence The amount of violence that a group usually has.

Normalization (of deviance) To think of one's norm violations as normal; a second meaning is *mainstreaming*, when acts previously defined as deviant or criminal become accepted.

Nuclear family A family that consists of a husband, wife, and their children.

Objective condition A condition of society that can be measured or experienced. See also *Subjective concern.*

Observation A means of gathering information whereby the researcher directly observes what is occurring in a setting. In the *overt* form, people know they are being studied; in the *covert* form, they do not.

Official poverty The level of income that a government recognizes as constituting poverty.

Organized crime Organizations devoted to criminal activities.

Organized group violence Violence that a group plans and carries out, although the group is not authorized to do so.

Ozone shield A layer of the earth's upper stratosphere that screens out much of the sun's ultraviolet rays.

Pan-Indianism Moving beyond tribal identification to work for the welfare of all Native Americans.

Participant observation (or *Field study*) A method of gathering information through direct observation of some setting.

Patriarchy A society in which men-as-a-group dominate women as a group.

Personal trouble An individual's own experience of a social problem.

Personal violence Another term for *individual violence.*

Plea bargaining Pleading guilty to a lesser crime in exchange for a reduced sentence.

Pluralism Different racial-ethnic groups living peacefully with one another, while maintaining their distinctiveness and tolerating differences in others.

Police discretion The decisions that the police make about whether to overlook or to enforce a law.

Political crime Illegal acts that are intended to alter or to maintain a political system.

Political machine A political organization that distributes government jobs or favors. Essential to its operation is an informal, behind-the-scenes working arrangement that circumvents the official ways of handling a city's business.

Political process A power struggle between interest groups and ideologies.

Political terrorism Using the means of war to try to achieve political objectives. It is of four types: revolutionary terrorism, repressive terrorism, state-sponsored terrorism, and criminal terrorism.

Pollution The presence of substances that interfere with socially desired uses of the air, water, land, or food.

Population In research the group that one wishes to study.

Population pyramid A graphic representation of a population, showing its age levels by sex (see Figure 13-7 on page 447).

Population shrinkage A country's population shrinking because its birth rate and immigration are too low to replace the people who die or emigrate.

Population transfer A minority relocating within a society or leaving the society altogether. In *direct* transfer, the minority is moved forcibly; in *indirect* transfer, the dominant group makes life so miserable for the members of a minority group that they "choose" to leave.

Pornography Writings, pictures, or objects of a sexual nature that are considered filthy.

Poverty line The official measure of poverty; originally calculated in the 1930s as three times a low-cost food budget and since then adjusted for inflation.

Power The ability to get one's way despite obstacles.

Power elite A small group of wealthy, powerful people who are said to make the major economic and political decisions in the United States.

Precipitating incident An incident that triggers a riot.

Prejudice An attitude whereby one prejudges others, usually negatively.

Primary prevention Measures that keep a disease from occurring, such as vaccinations. See also *Secondary prevention, Tertiary prevention.*

Professional criminals People who earn their living from crime.

Progressive tax Tax rates that increase with income.

Pronatalist policies Social policies that encourage women to bear children.

Property crime Obtaining or destroying property illegally: burglary, theft, robbery, vandalism, arson, and fencing.

Prostitution The renting of one's body for sexual purposes.

Psychoanalysis A treatment for emotional problems created by Sigmund Freud; the goal is to uncover subconscious motives, fantasies, and fears by having patients speak about whatever comes to mind.

Psychological dependence The craving for a drug even though there no longer is a physical dependence on that drug.

Questionnaire The use of written questions to gather information. *Closed-ended* questions provide specific choices, while *open-ended* questions allow people to answer in their own words.

Race Inherited physical characteristics that distinguish a group of people.

Racial-ethnic group A group of people who identify with one another on the basis of their ancestry and cultural heritage. Also called an ethnic group.

Racial-ethnic stratification Society divided along racial-ethnic lines; the unequal distribution of resources on the basis of race-ethnicity.

Random sample A sample that gives everyone in the group being studied an equal chance of being included in the research.

Rate of violence The number of violent acts per some unit of measurement of population, usually per 100,000 people.

Real income Income in constant dollars, that is, adjusted for inflation.

Recidivism rate The percentage of people released from prison who are rearrested.

Redlining The refusal to service a designated area, such as a bank not offering mortgages or an insurance company not writing insurance.

Regional restratification A shift in the population and relative wealth and power of the regions that make up a country. The current shift in the United States is toward the sunbelt.

Rehabilitation A response to crime that is designed to resocialize or reform offenders, so that they can become law-abiding citizens.

Relative poverty Deprivation as measured by the standards of one's society and culture. On a personal level, people think of themselves as poor or not poor on the basis of their reference groups.

Repressive terrorism Terrorism directed by a government against its own citizens.

Research design The methods that sociologists use to study social life. For social problems, these are *case studies, experiments, field studies,* and *surveys.*

Reserve labor force The unemployed, who can be put to work during periods of labor strife or economic expansion and laid off when these conditions change. Also called reserve labor army.

Residual poverty Pockets of poverty in an otherwise affluent society.

Restitution A form of retribution by which offenders compensate their victims.

Retribution A response to crime based on upholding moral values and restoring the moral balance upset by a criminal act. Making thieves repay what they stole is an example.

Revolutionary terrorism Terrorism used in the attempt to bring about change in the political structure.

Riot Violent crowd behavior aimed against people and property.

Rising expectations The belief that better conditions will come soon. Rising expectations develop when institutional barriers begin to fall; if conditions do not change immediately, frustration builds, sometimes resulting in group violence.

Role ambivalence Feeling indecisive, or both positive and negative, about one's role.

Sadists People who receive sexual gratification by inflicting pain on others.

Safety valve theory (of pornography) The view that pornography protects people by providing a private release of sexual fantasies.

Sample A relatively small number of people who are intended to represent the larger group from which it is selected.

Secession A minority withdrawing from a society to establish its own nation.

Secondary prevention Early detection and precautions that keep a disease from getting worse.

Segregation Confining an activity to specified geographical areas.

Selective perception Seeing only certain things, while being blind to others.

Self-fulfilling prophecy A prediction or expectation about how things will be that brings about the situation that was predicted or expected.

Serial murder Killing several victims in three or more separate events.

Sex The physical identity of a person as male or female. Refers to biology. See also *Gender.*

Sexism The belief that one sex is innately superior to the other and the discrimination that supports such a belief.

Sex-typing Associating something with one sex or the other. "Men's work" and "women's work" are examples of sex-typing of occupations.

Sexual harassment The use of one's position to make unwanted sexual advances.

Short-term directive therapy A treatment for emotional problems in which a therapist actively tries to solve the client's problems.

Situational group violence Spontaneous group violence, such as a brawl among hockey players.

Situational homosexual behavior Homosexual behavior by someone who has a heterosexual identity; often occurs in same-sex settings such as prisons or boarding schools.

Social class A group of people who are on about the same rung of the economic ladder; they have similar education, types of work, and income.

Social inequality The unequal distribution of wealth, income, power, and other opportunities.

Social problem Some aspect of society that large numbers of people are concerned about and would like changed.

Socialist economy An economy based on the public ownership of the means of production, central planning, and the distribution of goods without a profit motive. See *Capitalist economy.*

Sociological imagination (or **sociological perspective**) A framework of thought that looks at the broad, social context that shapes people's experiences. This perspective helps people transcend personal values and emotions in order to see the larger picture that affects their situation.

Sociological perspective Another term for *Sociological imagination.*

Sociology The overarching social science in which the emphasis is on how groups affect human behavior.

Split-labor market Workers who are split along lines of race-ethnicity or gender.

State-sponsored terrorism A country supporting terrorism against another nation.

Status crimes Acts that are crimes when committed by people of a designated status (such as juveniles) but not when committed by others (such as adults). Examples are curfew violations, underage drinking, and running away from home.

Statutory rape Consensual sexual relations in which one person is under the legal age of consent.

Steady-state society A society in which the economy does not grow or shrink.

Stereotype A belief that consists of unfounded generalizations of what people are like.

Strain theory A functionalist theory that stresses how people adapt when their access to the cultural means to reach cultural goals is blocked.

Structural inequality Inequality that is built into social institutions.

Structure The interrelations between the parts or subunits of society or some other social system.

Structured interview Interviews that use closed-ended questions.

Subcultural theory A symbolic interactionist theory that stresses a group's orientations: its distinctive norms, attitudes, values, beliefs, and behaviors. Applied to violence, people who grow up or associate with groups that have an orientation to violence will learn violent ways of handling life's problems.

Subjective concern The concern or distress that people feel about some aspect of society.

Suburban sprawl The disappearance of open areas as a suburb expands into the countryside.

Surplus value of labor If an item sells for more than it cost to produce, that profit (or extra amount, or surplus value) is said to exist because of the value of the labor that went into producing the item.

Survey Research that focuses on a sample of respondents from a target population. The sample is intended to represent the larger group from which it is selected.

Symbiosis A mutually beneficial relationship.

Symbol Items of social life to which we give meaning and that we then use to communicate with one another. Symbols include signs, gestures, words, and even our posture and appearance.

Symbolic interactionism A sociological theory that views society as consisting of the patterns common to a group of people. Social problems are not considered objective conditions but, rather, the issues that people have decided to call social problems.

Synergistic (literally, "working together") Applied to chemicals, it refers to their interactions.

Taking the role of the other Putting yourself in someone else's shoes to try to see things as that person sees them.

Talk therapy Treatments of emotional problems that are based on "talking" (psychotherapy, group therapy, etc.).

Techniques of neutralization Ways that people justify their norm-breaking activities, making their behaviors more acceptable to themselves and others.

Temple prostitution Prostitution that takes place in a temple, as a type of worship.

Tertiary prevention Medical care of an existing disease aimed at preventing further damage.

(The) social construction of reality The attempt to make sense of life by giving meaning to one's experiences.

(The) sociological question of violence What is it about a society that increases or decreases the likelihood of violence?

Theory An explanation of how two or more concepts, such as age and suicide, are related to one another.

Thermal inversion A layer of cold air sealing in a lower layer of warm air.

Total war No-holds-barred warfare.

Trigger theory (of pornography) The view that pornography triggers sexual offenses by stimulating people's sexual appetite.

Two-tier system of medical care A medical delivery system in which the poor receive one type of medical care and the affluent another.

Underclass Alienated people who live primarily in the inner cities; they have little education and high rates of unemployment, female-headed families, welfare dependency, violent crimes, drug abuse, disease, births to single women, and murder.

Uniform sentencing Giving the same sentence to everyone who is convicted of the same crime.

Unilateral disarmament One nation disarming itself. When used to refer to a social policy, it generally refers to one nation taking some dramatic step in disarmament in order to encourage a similar step by the enemy.

Unstructured interview Interviews that use open-ended questions.

Urban crisis The interrelated problems of governing and financing our cities, including their poverty, violence, crime, and deterioration of services.

Urban homesteading An urban policy whereby a city sells at a token price tax-foreclosed property to an individual who agrees to bring it into compliance with city codes and to live in it for a designated period of time.

Urban sprawl The expansion of a city onto adjacent farmland.

Victimless crime An illegal act to which the participants consent.

Violence The use of physical force to injure people or to destroy their property.

Violent crimes A classification used by the FBI and other police to refer to murder, forcible rape, robbery, and aggravated assault.

War Violent armed conflict between countries.

Wealth Savings, property, investments, income, and other economic assets.

Welfare wall The disincentive to work when the income from working is not much more than the income from welfare

White-collar crime Crime committed either against a business, agency, or corporation (such as embezzlement and fraud) or on behalf of the corporation (such as price fixing, fraudulent advertising, antitrust violations, and corporate tax evasion).

Withdrawal The distress that people feel when they don't take a drug to which they are addicted.

Zero population growth Women bearing only enough children to replace those who die.

BIBLIOGRAPHY

All new references are printed in blue.

"AA Fact File." Alcoholics Anonymous. Online, 2004.

Acharyya, Suddhasatta, and Heping Zhang. "Assessing Sex Differences on Treatment Effectiveness from the Drug Abuse Treatment Outcome Study." *American Journal of Drug and Alcohol Abuse,* May 2003.

Achenbaum, W. Andrew. *Old Age in the New Land: The American Experience Since 1970.* Baltimore: Johns Hopkins University Press, 1978.

"Acid Rain Called Peril to Ontario Lakes." *New York Times,* November 10, 2006.

Aizenman, N. C. "Opium Trade Not Easily Uprooted, Afghanistan Finds." *Washington Post,* July 15, 2005.

Alihan, Milla A. *Social Ecology.* New York: Columbia University Press, 1938.

Allen, Charlotte Low. "Anti-Abortion Movement's Anti-Establishment Face." *Wall Street Journal,* December 8, 1988:A14.

Allen, Frank Edward. "Environment." *Wall Street Journal,* May 28, 1991.

Allman, William F., " A Laboratory of Human Conflict." *U.S. News & World Report,* April 11, 1988:57–58.

Allport, Gordon. *The Nature of Prejudice.* Reading, Mass.: Addison-Wesley, 1954.

American Lung Association. "Search Lung USA." November 2003.

American Savings Education Council. "Personal Savings Rate, 1929–1998." Online, 1999.

Amott, Teresa, and Julie Matthaei. *Race, Gender, and Work: A Multicultural Economic History of Women in the United States.* Boston: South End, 1991.

Andersen, Margaret L. *Thinking About Women: Sociological Perspectives on Sex and Gender.* New York: Macmillan, 1988.

Anderson, Elijah. *A Place on the Corner.* Chicago: University of Chicago Press, 1978.

Anderson, Elijah. "Streetwise." In *Society: Readings to Accompany Sociology: A Down-to-Earth Approach, Core Concepts,* James M. Henslin, ed. Boston: Allyn & Bacon, 2006:54–63.

Anderson, Elijah. *Streetwise: Race, Class, and Change in an Urban Community.* Chicago: University of Chicago Press, 1990.

Anderson, Jack. "Chicago's Public Housing Official Tries to Thwart Gangs." *Alton Telegraph,* March 24, 1995:A6.

Anderson, Jack, and Jan Moller. "Gorton Under Republican Fire for Indian Wars." January 1998.

Anderson, Robert T. "From Mafia to Cosa Nostra." *American Journal of Sociology, 71,* November 1965:302–310.

Anslinger, Harry J., and Courtney Ryley Cooper. "Marijuana: Assassin of Youth." *American Magazine,* July 1937.

Anthrax Vaccination Immunization Program. Online, November 14, 2004.

Aposporos, Demetra. "Hunting for Glory with the Barabaig of Tanzania." *National Geographic,* July 2004.

Arías, Jesús. "La Junta rehabilita en Grenada casas que deberá tirar por ruina." *El Pais,* January 2, 1993:1.

Aries, Philippe. *Centuries of Childhood: A Social History of Family Life.* Robert Baldick, trans. New York: Vintage, 1962.

Arlacchi, P. *Mafia, Peasants and Great Estates: Society in Traditional Calabria.* Cambridge: Cambridge University Press, 1980.

Armitage, Richard L. "Red Army Retreat Doesn't Signal End of U.S. Obligation." *Wall Street Journal,* February 7, 1989:A20.

Arnason, Vilhjalmur, Devin Bartley, Serge Garcia, Robert H. Haraldsson, Dagfinnur Sveinbjornsson, and Hiromoto Watanabe. *Ethical Issues in Fisheries.* Rome: Food and Agriculture Organization of the United Nations, 2005.

Ashley, Richard. *Cocaine: Its History, Uses, and Effects.* New York: St. Martin's, 1975.

Ashley, Steven. "Divide and Vitrify." *Scientific American, 286,* 6, June 2002.

Ashworth, William. "The Great and Fragile Lakes." *Sierra,* November–December 1987:42–50.

Associated Press. "Father's Persistence Pays Off." February 12, 1995.

Aston, G., and V. Foubister. "MD and Physician Extender Turf War." *The American Medical News, 41,* 1998:27, 9–10.

Atchley, Robert C. "Dimensions of Widowhood in Later Life." *The Gerontologist, 15,* April 1975:176–178.

Athens, Lonnie H. *Violent Criminal Acts and Actors: A Symbolic Interactionist Study.* Boston: Routledge, 1980.

Auerbach, Judith D. "Employer-Supported Child Care as a Women-Responsive Policy." *Journal of Family Issues, 11,* 4, December 1990:384–400.

Bagne, Paul. "High-Tech Breeding." In *Marriage and Family in a Changing Society,* 4th ed., James M. Henslin, ed. New York: Free Press, 1992:226–234.

Bai, Matt. "Anatomy of a Massacre." *Newsweek,* May 3, 1999:25–31.

Bailey, Jeff. "Economics of Trash Shift as Cities Learn Dumps Aren't So Full." *Wall Street Journal,* June 2, 1992:A1, A7.

Bain, Brandon. "Ways GPS Technology Can Aid Police Officers." *Newsday,* March 31, 2006.

Ball, Deborah, and Vanessa O'Connell. "As Young Women Drink More, Alcohol Sales, Concerns Rise." *New York Times,* February 15, 2006.

Ball, Jeffrey. "Auto Makers Race to Sell Cars Powered by Fuel Cells." *Wall Street Journal,* March 15, 1999.

Bandura, Albert, and Richard H. Walters. *Social Learning and Personality Development.* New York: Holt, 1963.

Bansal, R., S. John, and P. M. Ling. "Cigarette Advertising in Mumbai, India: Targeting Different Socioeconomic Groups, Women, and Youth." *Tobacco Control, 14,* 2005:201–206.

Barber, James Allen, Jr. "The Military-Industrial Complex." In *The Military and American Society: Essays and Readings,* Stephen E. Ambrose and James A. Barber, Jr., eds. New York: Free Press, 1972.

Bardwick, Judith M. *Psychology of Women: A Study of Bio-Cultural Conflicts.* New York: Harper & Row, 1971.

Barnes, Edward, and William Shebar. "Quitting the Mafia." *Life,* December 1987:108–112.

Baron, Larry. "Immoral, Inviolate or Inconclusive?" *Society,* July/August 1987:6–12.

Barringer, Felicity. "Growth Stirs a Battle to Draw More Water from the Great Lakes." *New York Times,* August 12, 2005.

Bart, Pauline B., and Patricia H. O'Brien. "How the Women Stopped Their Rapes." *Signs, 10,* 1984.

Bart, Pauline B., and Patricia H. O'Brien. *Stopping Rape: Successful Survival Strategies.* New York: Pergamon, 1985.

Bartlett, Donald L., and James B. Steele. "Paying a Price for Polluters." *Time,* November 23, 1998:72–80.

Bartoi, Marla Green, and Bill N. Kinder. "Effects of Child and Adult Sexual Abuse on Adult Sexuality." *Journal of Sex & Marital Therapy, 24,* 1998:75–90.

Basler, Barbara. "Where Wall-to-Wall Means People." *New York Times,* October 3, 1988:A4.

Batalova, Jeanne A., and Philip N. Cohen. "Premarital Cohabitation and Housework: Couples in Cross-National Perspective." *Journal of Marriage and Family, 64,* August 2002:743–755.

Baumann, Mary. U.S. Senate Historical Office. Personal communication, September 14, 2006.

Bayles, Fred. "Mass. to Allow Gay Marriage Monday." *USA Today,* May 17, 2004.

Beals, Ralph L., and Harry Hoijer. *An Introduction to Anthropology,* 3rd ed. New York: Macmillan, 1965.

Beasley, Berrin, and Tracy Collins Standley. "Shirts vs. Skins: Clothing as an Indicator of Gender Role Stereotyping in Video Games." *Mass Communication and Society, 5,* 3, 2002:279–293.

Becker, Howard S. "Editor's Introduction." In *Social Problems: A Modern Approach.* Howard S. Becker, ed. New York: Wiley, 1966:1–31.

Becker, Howard S. "History, Culture, and Subjective Experience: An Exploration of the Social Bases of Drug Induced Experiences." *Journal of Health and Social Behavior, 7,* June 1967:163–176.

Beckett, Katherine. "Choosing Cesarean: Feminism and the Politics of Childbirth in the United States." *Feminist Theory, 6,* 3, 2005: 251–275.

Beddoe, Christine, C., Michael Hall, and Chris Ryan. *The Incidence of Sexual Exploitation of Children in Tourism.* Madrid: World Tourism Organization, 2001.

Beech, Hannah. "Unhappy Returns." *Time,* July 26–August 2, 2004.

Beeghley, Leonard. *The Structure of Social Stratification in the United States,* 4th ed. Boston: Allyn & Bacon, 2005.

Bell, Alan P., Martin S. Weinberg, and Sue Kiefer Hammersmith. *Sexual Preference: Its Development in Men and Women.* Bloomington: Indiana University Press, 1981.

Bell, Daniel. *The End of Ideology.* New York: Free Press, 1960.

Bell, David A. "An American Success Story: The Triumph of Asian-Americans." In *Sociological Footprints: Introductory Readings in Sociology,* 5th ed., Leonard Cargan and Jeanne H. Ballantine, eds. Belmont, Calif.: Wadsworth, 1991:308–316.

Bell, Julie. "Aspirin May Help Women Cut Heart Attack Risk, Study Says." *Sun-Sentinel,* March 22, 2006.

Belluck, Pam. "First-Ever Criminal Conviction Levied in Food Poisoning Case." *New York Times,* July 24, 1998a.

Belluck, Pam. "Forget Prisons: Americans Cry Out for the Pillory." *New York Times,* October 4, 1998b.

Bengtson, Vern L., Carolyn Rosenthal, and Linda Burton. "Families and Aging: Diversity and Heterogeneity." In *Handbook of Aging and the Social Sciences,* 3rd ed., Robert H. Binstock and Linda K. George, eds. San Diego: Academic Press, 1990:263–287.

Bengtson, Vern L., Gerardo Marti, and Robert E. L. Roberts. "Age-Group Relationships: Generational Equity and Inequity." In *Parent-Child Relations Throughout Life,* Karl Pillemer and Kathleen McCartney, eds. Hillsdale, N.J.: Erlbaum, 1991:253–278.

Bennice, Jennifer A., and Patricia A. Resick. "Marital Rape: History, Research, and Practice." *Trauma, Violence, and Abuse, 4,* 3, July 2003:228–246.

Benson, Michael L. "Denying the Guilty Mind: Accounting for Involvement in White-Collar Crime." *Criminology, 23,* November 1985:585–607.

Bergström, Hans. "Pressures Behind the Swedish Health Reforms." *Viewpoint Sweden, 12,* July 1992:1–5.

Bernard, Jessie. *Women and the Public Interest: An Essay on Policy and Protest.* Chicago: Aldine-Atherton, 1971.

Bernard, Viola W., Perry Ottenberg, and Fritz Redl. "Dehumanization: A Composite Psychological Defense in Relation to Modern War." In *The Triple Revolution Emerging: Social Problems in Depth,* Robert Perucci and Marc Pilisuk, eds. Boston: Little, Brown, 1971:17–34.

Bernhardt, Eva M., and Frances K. Goldscheider. "Men, Resources, and Family Living: The Determination of Union and Parental Status in the United States and Sweden." *Journal of Marriage and the Family, 63,* 3, August 2001:793–803.

Bernstein, Elizabeth. "The Meaning of the Purchase: Desire, Demand, and the Commerce of Sex." *Ethnography, 2,* 3, 2001: 389–420.

Bhattacharya, Shaoni. "Multi-Drug-Resistant HIV Strain Raises Alarm." NewScientist.com, February 14, 2005.

Bianchi, Suzanne M., Melissa A. Milkie, Liana C. Sayer, and John P. Robinson. "Is Anyone Doing the Housework? Trends in the Gender Division of Household Labor." *Social Forces, 79,* 1, September 2000:191–228.

Biddle, RiShawn. "The Ghost of Energy Crisis Past." *Reason,* April 1, 2001.

Biello, David. "Vegetable Compounds Combat Cancer." *Scientific American Online,* April 5, 2006.

Bilmes, Linda, and Joseph E. Stiglitz. "The Economic Costs of the Iraq War: An Appraisal Three Years After the Beginning of the Conflict." Paper presented at the ASSA meetings, January 2006.

"Births, Marriages, and Divorce." National Center for Health Statistics. *National Vital Statistics, 52,* 3, February 13, 2004:Table A.

Bishop, Jerry E., and Ken Wells. "Two Scientists Claim Breakthrough in Quest for Fusion Energy." *Wall Street Journal,* March 24, 1989:A1, A5.

Blackstone, Sir William. *Commentaries on the Laws of England,* 4th ed., Thomas M. Cooley, ed. Chicago: Callaghan and Co., 1899.

Blanchard, Ray, James M. Cantor, Anthony F. Bogaert, S. Marc Breedlover, and Lee Ellis. "Interaction of Fraternal Birth Order and Handedness in the Development of Male Homosexuality." *Hormones and Behavior, 49,* 2006:405–414.

Blau, Francine D. "Women in the Labor Force: An Overview." In *Women: A Feminist Perspective,* Jo Freeman, ed. Palo Alto, Calif.: Mayfield, 1975:211–226.

Block, Richard, and Wesley G. Skogan. "Resistance and Outcome in Robbery and Rape: Nonfatal, Stranger to Stranger Violence." *Mimeo,* 1982.

Blok, Anton. *The Mafia of a Sicilian Village: A Study of Violent Peasant Entrepreneurs.* New York: Harper Torchbooks, 1974.

Blum, Richard H., and Associates. *Drugs I, Society and Drugs: Social and Cultural Observations.* San Francisco: Jossey-Bass, 1969.

Blum, Richard H., Eva Blum, and E. Garfield. *Drug Education: Results and Recommendations.* Lexington, Mass.: Heath, 1976.

Blumberg, Abraham S. "The Practice of Law as Confidence Game: Organizational Cooptation of a Profession." *Law and Social Review, 1,* 1967:15–39.

Blumemthal, Ralph. "Polluted Midwest Rain Is Killing New York Lakes." *Alton Telegraph,* June 8, 1981.

Blumstein, Alfred, et al. *Criminal Careers and "Career Criminals." 1.* Washington, D.C.: National Academy Press, 1988.

Bogo, Jennifer. "Consider the Source: How Clean Is Your Bottled Water?" *E/The Environmental Magazine,* March 1, 2001.

Boot, Max. "Your Money or Your Life? That Depends." *Wall Street Journal,* March 4, 1998:A18.

Booth, Alan, and James M. Dabbs, Jr. "Testosterone and Men's Marriages." *Social Forces, 72,* 2, December 1993:463–477.

Boston, Guy D., Kevin O'Brien, and Joanne Palumbo, *Terrorism: A Selected Bibliography,* 2nd ed. Washington, D. C.: National Institute of Law Enforcement and Criminal Justice, March 1977.

Bottcher, Jean, and Michael E. Ezell. "Examining the Effectiveness of Boot Camps: A Randomized Experiment with a Long-Term Follow Up." *Journal of Research in Crime and Delinquency, 42,* 3, August 2005:309–332.

Bowen, Crosswell. "Donora, Pennsylvania." In *Society and Environment: The Coming Collision,* Rex R. Campbell and Jerry L. Wade, eds. Boston: Allyn and Bacon, 1972:163–168.

Brace, Charles Loring. *The Dangerous Classes of New York and Twenty Years' Work Among Them,* 3rd ed. New York: Wynkoop and Hallenbeck, 1880.

Bramlett, M. D., and W. D. Mosher. "Cohabitation, Marriage, Divorce, and Remarriage in the United States." Hyattsville, Md.: National Center for Health Statistics, *Vital Health Statistics,* Series 23, Number 22, July 2002.

Brannigan, Augustine. "Is Obscenity Criminogenic?" *Society,* July/August 1987:12–19.

Brecher, Edward M., and the Editors of Consumer Reports. *Licit and Illicit Drugs.* Boston: Little, Brown, 1972.

Bremer, L. Paul III. "Terrorism: Myths and Reality." *Department of State Bulletin,* May 1988:63.

Brewer, Devon D., John J. Potterat, Sharon B. Garrett, Stephen Q. Muth, John M. Roberts, Danuta Kasprzyk, Daniel E. Montano, and William W. Darrow. "Prostitution and the Sex Discrepancy in Reported Number of Sex Partners." *Proceedings of the National Academy of Sciences,* 97, 22, October 24, 2000: 12385–12388.

Bridges, George S., and Sara Steen. "Racial Disparities in Official Assessments of Juvenile Offenders: Attributional Stereotypes as Mediating Mechanisms." *American Sociological Review, 63,* August 1998:554–570.

Broad, William J. "In Ancient Fossils, Seeds of a New Debate on Warming." *New York Times,* November 7, 2006a.

Broad, William J. "U.S. Web Site Is Said to Reveal a Nuclear Primer." *New York Times,* November 3, 2006b.

Broad, William J., and Judith Miller. "Rocky Start for U.S. Plan to Stockpile Vaccines to Fight Germ Warfare." *New York Times,* August 7, 1998.

Brockerhoff, Martin P. "An Urbanizing World." *Population Bulletin, 55,* 3, September 2000:1–44.

Brockman, Joshua. "Child Sex as Internet Fare, Through Eyes of a Victim." *New York Times,* April 5, 2006.

Broder, M. S., D. E. Kanouse, B. S. Mittman, and S. J. Bernstein. "The Appropriateness of Recommendations for Hysterectomy." *Obstetrics and Gynecology, 95,* February 2000:199–205.

Brody, Elaine M. "The Aging of the Family." *Annals of the American Academy of Political and Social Science, 438,* July 1978:13–27.

Brody, Jane E. "1,100 Tested in Michigan for Effects of Toxin That Poisoned Food in '73." *New York Times,* November 5, 1976.

Broff, Nancy. Statements supplied to the author from NARAL, January 1989.

Brooke, James. "Deep Desert Grave Awaits First Load of Nuclear Waste." *New York Times,* March 26, 1999.

Brooks, Jack. *FDA Continues to Permit the Illegal Marketing of Carcinogenic Additives.* Twenty-fifth Report of the Committee on Government Operations. Washington, D.C.: U.S. Government Printing Office, 1987.

Brooks, Jack. *HHS' Failure to Enforce the Food, Drug, and Cosmetic Act: The Case of Cancer-Causing Color Additives.* Eleventh Report of the Committee on Government Operations. Washington, D.C.: U.S. Government Printing Office, 1985.

Brown, Donald A. "The Ethical Dimensions of Global Environmental Issues." *Daedalus, 130,* 4, Fall 2001:59–69.

Brown, Janet Welsh. Environmental Defense Fund Letter. New York, n.d.

Brown, Lester R. "Food Growth Slowdown: Danger Signal for the Future." In *Food Policy: Integrating Supply, Distribution, and Consumption,* J. Price Gittinger, Joanne Leslie, and Caroline Hoisington, eds. Baltimore: Johns Hopkins University Press, 1987:89–102.

Brown, Lester R. "'Human Element,' Not Drought, Causes Famine." *U.S. News & World Report,* February 25, 1985:71–72.

Brown, Michael H. "Love Canal and the Poisoning of America." *Atlantic Monthly, 235,* December 1979:33–47.

Brown, Richard Maxwell. "Historical Patterns of Violence in America." In *Violence in America: Historical and Comparative Perspectives.* Hugh Davis Graham and Ted Robert Gurr, eds. New York: Bantam, 1969.

Brownfield, David, and Ann Marie Sorenson. "Self-Control and Juvenile Delinquency: Theoretical Issues and an Empirical Assessment of Selected Elements of a General Theory of Crime." *Deviant Behavior, 14,* July–September 1993:243–264.

Brownmiller, Susan. *Against Our Will: Men, Women, and Rape.* New York: Simon & Schuster, 1975.

Buck, K. J. "Recent Progress Toward the Identification of Genes Related to Risk for Alcoholism." *Mamm Genome, 12,* December 9, 1998:927–928.

Budiansky, Stephen A. "The Trees Fell—And So Did the People." *U.S. News & World Report,* February 9, 1987:75.

Buff, Stephen A. "Lois Lee Takes Back Children from the Night." *ASA Footnotes, 15,* 5, May, 1987:1, 2.

Bulkeley, William M. "Untested Treatments, Cures Find Stronghold on On-Line Services." *Wall Street Journal,* February 27, 1995:A1, A7.

Bunn, Matthew, and Anthony Weir. "Preventing a Nuclear 9/11." *Washington Post,* September 12, 2004.

Burch, William R., Jr. *Daydreams and Nightmares: A Sociological Essay on the American Environment.* New York: Harper & Row, 1971.

Burgess, Ann Wolbert, and Lynda Lytle Holmstrom. "Rape Trauma Syndrome." *American Journal of Psychiatry, 131,* 1974:981–986.

Burgess, Ernest W. "The Growth of the City: An Introduction to a Research Project." In *The City,* Robert E. Park, Ernest W. Burgess, and Roderick D. McKenzie, eds. Chicago: University of Chicago Press, 1925 (pages 47–62 in the 1967 edition).

Burns, John F. "Bangladesh, Still Poor, Cuts Birth Rate Sharply." *New York Times,* September 13, 1994:A10.

Burros, Marian. "Experts Worry About the Return of a Deadly Germ in Cold Cuts." *New York Times,* March 14, 1999.

Burroughs, William. "Excerpts from 'Deposition: Testimony Concerning a Sickness.'" In *Drugs in American Life,* Morrow Wilson and Suzanne Wilson, eds. New York: Wilson, 1975:133–158.

Burton, Velmer S., Jr., Francis T. Cullen, T. David Evans, Leanne Fiftal Alarid, and R. Gregory Dunaway. "Gender, Self-Control, and Crime." *Journal of Research in Crime and Delinquency, 35,* 2, May 1998:123–147.

Butler, Robert N., et al. *Ageism in America.* New York: Open Society Institute, 2006.

Butterfield, Fox. "Indians' Wish List: Big-City Sites for Casinos." *New York Times,* April 8, 2005.

Butterfield, Fox. "Prison Population Increases as Release of Inmates Slows." *New York Times,* January 11, 1999.

Calle, Eugenia E., Carmen Rodriguez, Kimberly Walker-Thurmond, and Michael J. Thun. "Overweight, Obesity, and Mortality from Cancer in a Prospectively Studied Cohort of U.S. Adults." *New England Journal of Medicine, 348,* 17, April 24, 2003.

Campbell, Duncan. "Electronic Tagging May be Used for Prisoners Released on Parole." *Guardian,* August 12, 1995.

Campbell, John L. "The State and the Nuclear Waste Crisis: An Institutional Analysis of Policy Constraints." *Social Problems, 34,* 1, February 1987:18–33.

Campo-Flores, Arian. "A Crackdown on Call Girls." *Newsweek,* September 2, 2002.

"Canada Tries to Bar Pro-Nazi View on the Internet." *New York Times,* August 2, 1998.

Caplan, Bryan. "The Economics of Szasz: Preferences, Constraints, and Mental Illness." *Rationality and Society, 18,* 3, 2006: 333–366.

Caplow, Theodore, et al. *Middletown Families: Fifty Years of Change and Continuity.* Minneapolis: University of Minnesota Press, 1982.

Carey, Benedict. "In the Hospital, a Degrading Shift from Person to Patient." *New York Times,* August 16, 2005.

Carlson, Kenneth, and Jan Chaiken. "White Collar Crime." Special Report of the Bureau of Justice Statistics. Washington, D.C.: U.S. Department of Justice, September 1987.

Carlson, Lewis H., and George A. Colburn. *In Their Place: White America Defines Her Minorities, 1850–1950.* New York: Wiley, 1972.

Carlson, Rick J. *The End of Medicine.* New York: Wiley, 1975.

Carnevale, Anthony P., and Stephen J. Rose. *Socioeconomic Status, Race/Ethnicity, and Selective College Admissions.* New York: The Century Foundation, March 2003.

Carnevale, Mary Lu. "New Jolt for Nynex: Bawdy 'Conventions' of Buyers, Suppliers." *Wall Street Journal,* July 12, 1990:A1, A6.

Carroll, Charles R. *Drugs in Modern Society,* 5th ed. New York: McGraw-Hill, 2000.

Carton, Barbara. "At Jenny Craig, Men Are Ones Who Claim Sex Discrimination." *Wall Street Journal,* November 29, 1994:A1, A7.

Cass, Vivienne C. "Homosexual Identity Formation: A Theoretical Model." *Journal of Homosexuality, 4,* Spring 1979:219–235.

Castaneda, Carlos. *A Separate Reality: Further Conversations with Don Juan.* New York: Simon & Schuster, 1971.

Castaneda, Carlos. *Tales of Power.* New York: Simon & Schuster, 1974.

Castaneda, Carlos. *The Teachings of Don Juan: A Yaqui Way of Knowledge.* New York: Ballantine, 1968.

Castells, Manuel. *The City and the Grass Roots.* Berkeley: University of California Press, 1983.

Castells, Manuel. *The Informational City.* Oxford, England: Blackwell, 1989.

Castells, Manuel. *The Urban Question: A Marxist Approach.* Alan Sheridan, trans. Cambridge, Mass.: MIT Press, 1977.

Catanzaro, Raimondo. *Men of Respect: A Social History of the Mafia.* New York: Free Press, 1992.

Cates, Jim A., and Jeffrey Markley. "Demographic, Clinical, and Personality Variables Associated with Male Prostitution By Choice." *Adolescence, 27,* 107, Fall 1992:695–706.

Centers for Disease Control and Prevention. *Deaths, Percent of Total Deaths, and Death Rates for the Leading Causes of Death: United States and Each State, 2003.* 2006a.

Centers for Disease Control and Prevention. *HIV/AIDS Surveillance Report, 2004. 16, 2005.*

Centers for Disease Control and Prevention. *Leading Causes of Death, 1900–1998.* 2006b.

Chafetz, Janet Saltzman. *Gender Equity: An Integrated Theory of Stability and Change.* Newbury Park, Calif.: Sage, 1990.

Chagnon, Napoleon A. "Life Histories, Blood Revenge, and Warfare in a Tribal Population." *Science,* February 26, 1988:985–992.

Chalkey, Kate. "Female Genital Mutilation: New Laws, Programs Try to End Practice." *Population Today, 25,* 10, October 1997:4–5.

Chambliss, William J. "The Saints and the Roughnecks." In *Down-to-Earth Sociology: Introductory Readings,* 14th ed., James M. Henslin, ed. New York: Free Press, 2007.

Chang, Iris. *The Rape of Nanking: The Forgotten Holocaust of World War II.* New York: Basic Books, 1997.

Chase, Marilyn. "Defying Treatment, a New, Virulent Bug Sparks Health Fears." *Wall Street Journal,* January 20, 2006.

Chen, Michelle. "Tex Court Overturns Conviction Under 'Fetal Rights' Law." *The New Standard,* April 4, 2006.

Cheng, V. "328 Useful Drugs Are Said to Lie Hidden in Tropical Forests." *New York Times,* June 27, 1995:C4.

Cherlin, Andrew J. "A 'Quieting' of Change." *Contexts, 1,* 1, Spring 2002:67–68.

Chernoff, Nina W., and Rita J. Simon. "Women and Crime the World Over." *Gender Issues, 18,* 3, Summer 2000:5–20.

Chilman, Catherine S. "Public Policies and Families." In *Mental Illness, Delinquency, Addictions, and Neglect,* Elam W. Nunnally, Catherine S. Chilman, and Fred M. Cox, eds. Newbury Park, Calif.: Sage, 1988:189–197.

Cho, Eunyoung, et al. "Dairy Foods, Calcium, and Colorectal Cancer: A Pooled Analysis of 10 Cohort Studies." *Journal of the National Cancer Institute, 96,* 13, July 7, 2004:1015–1022.

Choo, R. E., M. A. Huestis, J. R. Schroeder, A. S. Shin, and H. E. Jones. "Neonatal Abstinence Syndrome in Methadone-Exposed Infants Is Altered by Level of Prenatal Tobacco Exposure." *Drug and Alcohol Dependence, 75,* 3, 2004:253–260.

Churchill, Ward, and Jim Vander Wall. *Agents of Repression: The FBI's Secret Wars Against the Black Panther Party and the American Indian Movement.* Boston: South End Press, 1990.

Clarke, Steve. "Earnings of Men and Women in the EU: The Gap Narrowing But Only Slowly." *Eurostat: Statistics in Focus: Population and Social Conditions,* 2001.

Clausing, Jeri. "Senate Adds Internet Proposals to Spending Bill." *New York Times Bulletin,* July 22, 1998.

Cleaver, Eldridge. *Soul on Ice.* New York: McGraw-Hill, 1968.

Clinard, Marshall B. *Corporate Corruption: The Abuse of Power.* New York: Praeger, 1990.

Clinard, Marshall B., Peter C. Yeager, Jeanne Brisette, David Petrashek, and Elizabeth harries. *Illegal Corporate Behavior.* Washington, D.C.: U.S. Department of Justice, 1979.

Clines, Francis X. "Soviets Now Admit '57 Nuclear Blast." *New York Times,* June 18, 1998.

Clinton, Hillary Rodham. *It Takes a Village: And Other Lessons Children Teach Us.* New York: Touchstone Books, 1997.

Cloward, Richard A., and Lloyd E. Ohlin. *Delinquency and Opportunity: A Theory of Delinquent Gangs.* New York: Free Press, 1960.

Cockerham, William C. "The Social Determinants of the Decline of Life Expectancy in Russia and Eastern Europe: A Lifestyle Explanation." *Journal of Health and Social Behavior, 38,* June 1997: 117–130.

Cockerham, William C. *This Aging Society.* Englewood Cliffs, N.J.: Prentice Hall, 1991.

Cohen, Albert K. *Delinquent Boys: The Culture of the Gang.* New York: Free Press, 1955.

Cohen, Elizabeth. "Shrinks Aplenty Online, But Are They Credible?" *New York Times,* January 17, 1997.

Cohen, Jacqueline. "The Incapacitative Effect of Imprisonment: A Critical Review of the Literature." In *Deterrence and Incapacitation: Estimating the Effects of Criminal Sanctions on Crime Rates,* Alfred Blumstein, Jacqueline Cohen, and Daniel Nagin, eds. Washington, D.C.: National Academy of Sciences, 1978.

Cohen, Morris R. "Moral Aspects of the Criminal Law." *Yale Law Journal, 49,* April 1940:1009–1026.

Cohen, Murray, Theoharis Seghorn, and Wilfred Calamas. "Sociometric Study of the Sex Offender." *Journal of Abnormal Psychology, 74,* April 1969:249–255.

Coleman, James William. *The Criminal Elite: The Sociology of White Collar Crime.* New York: St. Martin's, 1989.

Coleman, James William. "Politics and the Abuse of Power." In *Down-to-Earth Sociology: Introductory Readings,* 8th ed., James M. Henslin, ed. New York: Free Press, 1995:442–450.

"Colombia." U.S. Department of State, Bureau of Western Hemisphere Affairs, October 2006.

Coltrane, Scott, and Melinda Messineo. "The Perpetuation of Subtle Prejudice: Race and Gender Imagery in 1990s Television Advertising." *Sex Roles: A Journal of Research,* 2000.

Comer, James P. "Education for Community." In *Common Decency: Domestic Policies After Reagan,* Alvin L. Schorr, ed. New Haven, Conn.: Yale University Press, 1986:186–209.

Conahan, Frank C. Statement of Frank C. Conahan, Assistant Comptroller General, National Security and International

Affairs Division, US General Accounting Office, before the Committee on the Budget: Cost of Operation Desert Shield and Desert Storm and Allied Contributions, 15 May 1991, GAO/T-NSIAD-91-34.

"Congress Looks to Fund Efforts to Beat Back Fetal Alcohol Syndrome." *The Nation's Health, 24,* 3, March 1994:5.

Conley, Dalton. "Capital for College: Parental Assets and Postsecondary Schooling." *Sociology of Education, 74,* 1, January 2001: 59–68.

Conner, Roger L. "Demographic Doomsayers: Five Myths About Population." *Current,* February 1990:21–25.

Conrad, Peter. "Learning to Doctor: Reflections on Medical School." In *Down-to-Earth Sociology: Introductory Readings,* 8th ed., James M. Henslin, ed. New York: Free Press, 1995:420–430.

Conti, Massimo. "The Famine Controversy." *World Press Review, 27,* January 1980:56.

Cookson, Peter W., Jr., and Caroline Hodges Persell. "Preparing for Power: Cultural Capital and Elite Boarding Schools." In *Life in Society: Readings to Accompany Sociology: A Down-to-Earth Approach,* 7th ed., James M. Henslin, ed. Boston: Allyn & Bacon 2005:175–185.

Cooper, P. F. "Historical Aspects of Wastewater Treatment." In *Decentralized Sanitation and Reuse: Concepts, Systems and Implementation,* P. Lens, G. Zeeman, and G. Lettinga, eds. London: IWA, 2002:11–38.

Corcoran, Mary, Greg J. Duncan, Gerald Gurin, and Patricia Gurin. "Myth and Reality: The Causes and Persistence of Poverty." *Journal of Policy Analysis and Management, 4,* 4, 1985:516–536.

Cornell, George W. "Modern Persecutions Mirror Those of Jesus." Associated Press, April 13, 1981.

Corzine, Jay, and Richard Kirby. "Cruising the Truckers: Sexual Encounters in a Highway Rest Area." *Urban Life, 6,* July 1977: 171–192.

Cose, Ellis. "The Good News About Black America." *Newsweek,* June 7, 1999:29–40.

Coser, Lewis A. *The Functions of Social Conflict.* New York: Free Press, 1956.

Coser, Lewis A. *Masters of Sociological Thought: Ideas in Historical and Social Context.* New York: Harcourt, 1977.

Cowley, Geoffrey. "The Life of a Virus Hunter." *Newsweek,* May 15, 2006.

Cowley, Joyce. *Pioneers of Women's Liberation.* New York: Merit, 1969.

Cressey, Donald R. *Other People's Money.* New York: Free Press, 1953.

Cressey, Donald R. *Theft of the Nation: The Structure and Operations of Organized Crime in America.* New York: Harper & Row, 1969.

Crider, Raquel. "Phencyclidine: Changing Abuse Patterns." In *Phencyclidine: An Update,* Doris H. Clouet, ed. Rockville, Md.: National Institute on Drug Abuse, 1986:163–173.

Critchfield, Richard. "China's Agricultural Success Story." *Wall Street Journal,* January 13, 1986:25.

"Cross National Comparison of Rape Rates: Problems and Issues." Working Paper #18. Statistical Commission and UN Economic Commission for Europe, October 28, 2004.

Cuffel, B., W. Goldman, and H. Schlesinger. "Does Managing Behavioral Health Care Services Increase the Cost of Providing Medical Care?" *Journal of Behavioral Health Services and Research 26,* 4, 1999:372–380.

Cumming, Elaine, and William E. Henry. *Growing Old: The Process of Disengagement.* New York: Basic Books, 1961.

Currie, Elliott. *Confronting Crime: An American Challenge.* New York: Pantheon, 1985.

Cushman, John H. "Industries Press Plan for Credits in Emissions Control." *New York Times,* January 3, 1999.

Dabbs, James M., Jr., and Robin Morris. "Testosterone, Social Class, and Antisocial Behavior in a Sample of 4,462 Men." *Psychological Science, 1,* 3, May 1990:209–211.

Dahl, Robert A. *Who Governs?* New Haven, Conn.: Yale University Press, 1961.

Dahrendorf, Ralf. *Class and Class Conflict in Industrial Society.* Stanford, Calif.: Stanford University Press, 1959.

Dahrendorf, Ralf. "Toward a Theory of Social Conflict." In *Social Change: Sources, Patterns, and Consequences,* Amitai Etzioni and Eva Etzioni, eds. New York: Basic Books, 1973.

Daly, Martin, and Margo Wilson. *Homicide.* New York: Aldine de Gruyter, 1988.

Daniels, Roger. *The Decision to Relocate the Japanese Americans.* Philadelphia: Lippincott, 1975.

Dao, James. "U.S. Government Joins Oneida Indians' Suit Against New York State." *New York Times,* January 13, 1999.

Dash, Leon. "When Children Want Children." *Society, 27,* 5, July–August 1990:17–19.

Davey, Monica. "Missourians Back Ban on Same-Sex Marriage." *New York Times,* August 4, 2004.

Davies, J. Clarence III, and Barbara S. Davies. *The Politics of Pollution,* 2nd ed. Indianapolis, Ind.: Bobbs-Merrill, 1975.

Davis, Angela. *Angela Davis: An Autobiography.* New York: Random House, 1974.

Davis, Kingsley. "Sexual Behavior." In *Contemporary Social Problems,* 2nd ed., Robert Merton and Robert Nisbet, eds. New York: Harcourt, 1966.

Davis, Kingsley. "The Sociology of Prostitution." *American Sociological Review, 2,* October 1937:744–755.

Davis, Kingsley, and Wilbert E. Moore. "Some Principles of Stratification." *American Sociological Review, 10,* 1945:242–249.

Davis, Nancy J., and Robert V. Robinson. "Class Identification of Men and Women in the 1970s and 1980s." *American Sociological Review, 53,* February 1988:103–112.

Davis, Nanette J. "Prostitution: Identity, Career, and Legal-Economic Enterprise." In *The Sociology of Sex: An Introductory Reader,* James M. Henslin and Edward Sagarin, eds. New York: Schocken, 1978:297–322.

Daws, Gavin. *Prisoners of the Japanese: POWs of World War II in the Pacific.* New York: Morrow, 1994.

Day, Charles R., Jr. "Tear Up the Tracks." *Industry Week, 239,* 5, March 5, 1990:5.

De Beauvoir, Simone. *The Second Sex.* New York: Knopf, 1953.

De Mott, Benjamin. "The Pro-Incest Lobby." *Psychology Today, 13,* March 1980:11–12, 15–16.

de Silva, Rex. 1980. "Developing the Third World." *World Press Review,* May 1980:48.

Delph, Edward William. *The Silent Community: Public Homosexual Encounters.* Beverly Hills, Calif.: Sage, 1978.

Denes, Magda. *In Necessity and Sorrow: Life and Death in an Abortion Hospital.* New York: Basic Books, 1976.

Denzin, Norman K. "The Suicide Machine." *Society,* July–August 1992:7–10.

DeOilos, Ione Y., and Carolyn A. Kapinus. "Aging Childless Individuals and Couples: Suggestions for New Directions in Research." *Sociological Inquiry, 72,* 1, Winter 2002:72–80.

DeRios, Marlene Dobkin, and David E. Smith. "Drug Use and Abuse in Cross-Cultural Perspective." *Human Organization, 36,* 1977:14–21.

Deschner, Amy, and Susan A. Cohen. "Contraceptive Use Is Key to Reducing Abortion Worldwide." *The Guttmacher Report on Public Policy 6,* 4, October 2003.

DeSouza, Eros, and A. Gigi Fansler. "Contrapower Sexual Harassment: A Survey of Students and Faculty Members." *Sex Roles, 48,* 11/12, June 2003:529–542.

Devine, Michael A. "A Fresh Look at Cogeneration." *Energy User News, 29,* 1, September 2004:13–15.

Diamond, Milton, and Ayako Uchiyama. "Pornography, Rape, and Sex Crimes in Japan." *International Journal of Law and Psychiatry, 22,* 1, 1999:1–22.

DiChiara, Albert, and Russell Chabot. "Gangs and the Contemporary Urban Struggle: An Unappreciated Aspect of Change." In *Gangs and Society: Alternative Perspectives,* Louis Kontos, David Brotherton, and Luis Barrios, eds. New York: Columbia University Press, 2003:77–94.

Dickey, Christopher, and Adam Rogers. "Smoke and Mirrors." *Newsweek,* February 25, 2002.

Dickman, Amanda B., and Sarah K. Murnen. "Learning to Be Little Women and Little Men: The Inequitable Gender Equality of Nonsexist Children's Literature." *Sex Roles, 50,* 5, March 2004.

Dickson, Donald T. "Bureaucracy and Morality: An Organizational Perspective on a Moral Crusade." *Social Problems, 16,* Fall 1968: 143–156.

DiEugenio, James. "The Posthumous Assassination of JFK, Part II." *Probe, 5,* 1, November–December, 1997.

Digest of Education Statistics. Washington, D.C.: U.S. Department of Education, November 2005.

Dingell, John D. *Sulfites: Hearing Before the Subcommittee on Oversight and Investigations of the Committee on Energy and Commerce, House of Representatives.* Washington, D.C.: U.S. Government Printing Office, March 27, 1985.

"Dispute Between EU and U.S. Over Beef Now Before WTO." *The Food Institute Report,* November 2004.

Dobyns, Henry F. *Their Numbers Became Thinned: Native American Population Dynamics in Eastern North America.* Knoxville: University of Tennessee Press, 1983.

Doerner, William G. "The Index of Southernness Revisited: The Influence of Wherefrom upon Whodunnit." *Criminology, 16,* May 1978:47–56.

Dollard, John, Neal E. Miller, Leonard W. Doob, O. H. Mowrer, and Robert R. Sears. *Frustration and Aggression.* New Haven, Conn.: Yale University Press, 1961 (originally published in 1939).

Domhoff, G. William. *The Bohemian Grove and Other Retreats: A Study in Ruling-Class Cohesiveness.* New York: Harper & Row, 1974.

Domhoff, G. William. *The Power Elite and the State: How Policy Is Made in America.* New York: Aldine de Gruyter, 1990.

Domhoff, G. William. *The Powers That Be.* New York: Random House, 1978a.

Domhoff, G. William. *Who Really Rules?* New Brunswick, N.J.: Transaction, 1978b.

Domhoff, G. William. *Who Rules America? Power and Politics,* 4th ed. Mountain View, Calif.: Mayfield, 2001.

Domhoff, G. William. *Who Rules America? Power and Politics in the Year 2000,* 3rd ed. Mountain View, Calif.: Mayfield, 1998.

Donaldson, Samuel. "World News Tonight." May 25, 1992.

Doran, Bob. "How Green Is My Plastic?" *North Coast Journal,* August 24, 2006.

Douglass, Joseph D. "A Biological Weapons Threat Worse Than Saddam." *Wall Street Journal,* March 10, 1998:A22.

Douvan, Elizabeth. "Is the American Family Obsolete?" University of California, University Extension, Courses by News-paper, San Diego, 1980.

Dove, Adrian. "Soul Folk 'Chitling' Test or the Dove Counterbalance Intelligence Test." Mimeo, n.d.

Dowie, Mark. 1979. "The Corporate Crime of the Century." *Mother Jones, 4,* November 1979:23–25, 37.

Dowie, Mark. "Pinto Madness." *Mother Jones, 2,* September–October 1977:18–32.

Downing, Bob. "Coalition Sees Damage to Great Lakes Growing." *Akron Beacon Journal,* September 23, 2006.

Draper, R. "The History of Advertising in America." *New York Review of Books 33,* June 26, 1986:14–18.

Drug Dependence in Pregnancy: Clinical Management of Mother and Child. Rockville, Md.: U.S. Department of Health, Education, and Welfare, 1979.

Dubar, Helen. "American Discovers Child Pornography." In *Human Sexuality 80/81,* James R. Barbour, ed. Guilford, Conn.: Dushkin, 1980.

Dufay, Joanne. "Ten Years After Chernobyl: A Witness to the Devastation." Greenpeace online, n.d.

Durkheim, Emile. *The Division of Labor in Society,* George Simpson, trans. New York: Free Press, 1964 (originally published in 1893).

Durkheim, Emile. *The Rules of Sociological Method,* Sir George E. G. Catlin, ed. New York: Macmillan, 1938 (originally published in 1904; 8th ed. 1950)

Durkheim, Emile. *Suicide,* John A. Spaulding and George Simpson, trans. New York: Free Press, 1951 (originally published in 1897).

Durning, Alan. "Cradles of Life." In *Social Problems 90/91,* Leroy W. Barnes, ed. Guilford, Conn.: Dushkin, 1990:231–241.

Duskin, Edgar W. "Environment Continues to Get Better." *Southwest Farm Press,* August 7, 2003.

Duster, Troy. "From Structural Analysis to Public Policy." *Contemporary Sociology, 17,* 3, May 1988:287–290.

Duster, Troy. *The Legalization of Morality: Law, Drugs, and Moral Judgment.* New York: Free Press, 1970.

Dye, Lee. "Tiny Firm Sees Process as Big Answer to Waste." *Los Angeles Times,* March 1, 1999.

Eberstadt, Nick. *The Poverty of Communism.* New Brunswick, N.J.: Transaction, 1988.

Ebomoyi, Ehigie. "The Prevalence of Female Circumcision in Two Nigerian Communities." *Sex Roles, 17,* 3/4, 1987:139–151.

Eder, Donna. *School Talk: Gender and Adolescent Culture.* New Brunswick, N.J.: Rutgers University Press, 1995.

Egan, Timothy, and Adam Liptak. "Fraught Issue, But Narrow Ruling in Oregon Suicide Case." *New York Times,* January 18, 2006.

Ehrenfeld, Rachel. *Narcoterrorism.* New York: Basic Books, 1990.

Ehrenreich, Barbara, and Deirdre English. *Witches, Midwives, and Nurses: A History of Women Healers.* Old Westbury, N.Y.: Feminist Press, 1973.

Ehrlich, Paul R., and Anne H. Ehrlich. *Extinction: The Causes and Consequences of the Disappearance of Species.* New York: Random House, 1981.

Ehrlich, Paul R., and Anne H. Ehrlich. *Population, Resources, and Environment: Issues in Human Ecology,* 2nd ed. San Francisco: Freeman, 1972.

Eichenwald, Kurt. "Through His Webcam, a Boy Joins a Sordid Online World." *New York Times,* December 19, 2005.

Eisenhart, R. Wayne. "You Can't Hack It, Little Girl: A Discussion of the Covert Psychological Agenda of Modern Combat Training." *Journal of Social Issues, 31,* Fall 1975:13–23.

Eisenhower, Dwight D. "From 'Farewell Address to the Nation,' January 17, 1961." In *The Military and American Society: Essays and Readings,* Stephen E. Ambrose and James A. Barber, Jr., eds. New York: Free Press, 1972:61–63.

Eisinger, Peter K. *The Politics of Displacement: Racial and Ethnic Transition in Three American Cities.* Campbell Calif.: Academic Press, 1980.

Elias, Paul. "Molecular Pharmers' Hope to Raise Human Proteins in Crop Plants." *St. Louis Post-Dispatch,* October 28, 2001:F7.

Ellis, Havelock. "Mescal: A New Artificial Paradise." *Annual Report of the Smithsonian Institution, 52,* 1897:547–548.

Ellis, Havelock. "Mescal: A Study of a Divine Plant." *Popular Science Monthly, 61,* 1902:52–71.

Elwood, William N., Kathryn Greene, and Karen K. Carter. "Gentlemen Don't Speak: Communication Norms and Condom Use in Bath Houses." *Journal of Applied Communication Research, 31,* 4, November 2003:277–297.

Engelmayer, Paul A. "Violence by Students, from Rape to Racism, Raises College Worries." *Wall Street Journal,* November 21, 1983:1, 18.

Englund, Will, and Gary Cohn. "A Third World Dump for America's Ships?" *Baltimore Sun,* December 9, 1997.

Environmental Protection Agency. "The Great Lakes: Report to Congress on the Great Lakes Ecosystem." February 1994.

Environmental Protection Agency. "Reduction of Toxic Loadings to the Niagara River From Hazardous Waste Sites in the United States." November 1998.

Epstein, Cynthia Fuchs. *Deceptive Distinctions: Sex, Gender, and the Social Order.* New Haven, Conn.: Yale University Press, 1988.

Epstein, Cynthia Fuchs. "Inevitabilities of Prejudice." *Society,* September–October 1986:7–13.

Epstein, Cynthia Fuchs. Letter to the author, January 26, 1989.

Erik, John. "China's Policy on Births." *New York Times,* January 3, 1982:IV, 19.

Escalante, Jaime, and Jack Dirmann. "The Jaime Escalante Math Program." *Journal of Negro Education, 59,* 3, Summer 1990: 407–423.

Espenshade, Thomas J. "A Short History of U.S. Policy toward Illegal Immigration." *Population Today,* February 1990:6–9.

Etzioni, Amitai. "Letter to the Editor: Porn Filters Are a Net Benefit." *Wall Street Journal,* November 3, 1998:A23.

"Facts About Sexual Harassment." U.S. Equal Employment Opportunity Commission, Online, 2006.

Faison, Seth, Jr. "Friend Says Girl Killed on Train Resisted Robbery of Other Girls." *New York Times,* September 22, 1991:34.

"Fall Colors: 2003–04 Prime Time Diversity Report." Oakland, Calif.: Children Now, 2004.

Farah, Judy. "Crime and Creative Punishment." *Wall Street Journal,* March 15, 1995:A15.

Faris, R. E. L., and W. W. Dunham. *Mental Disorders in Urban Areas.* Chicago: University of Chicago Press, 1939.

Farney, Dennis. "On the Great Plains, Life Becomes a Fight for Water and Survival." *Wall Street Journal,* August 16, 1989:A1, A12.

Faunce, William A. *Problems of an Industrial Society,* 2nd ed. New York: McGraw-Hill, 1981.

Faupel, Charles E., and Carl B. Klockars. "Drugs-Crime Connections: Elaborations from the Life Histories of Hard-Core Addicts." *Social Problems, 34,* 1, February 1987:54–68.

FBI Uniform Crime Reports. Washington, D.C.: U.S. Government Printing Office, annual.

Federal Bureau of Investigation. *Terrorism in the United States, 1997.* Washington, D.C.: U.S. Department of Justice, 1998.

Feinsilber, Mike. "Agent Orange May Have Fallen Near U.S. Bases." Associated Press, September 24, 1981.

Feldman, Harvey M. "Background and Purpose of the Ethnographers' Policymakers' Symposium." In *Ethnography: A Research Tool for Policymakers in the Drug and Alcohol Fields,* Karl Akins and George Beschner, eds. Rockville, Md.: Department of Health and Human Services, 1985.

Felsenthal, Edward. "Justices' Ruling Further Defines Sex Harassment." *Wall Street Journal,* March 5, 1998:B1, B2.

Ferguson, Ronald E. "Community Revitalization, Jobs, and the Well-Being of the Inner-City Poor." In *Understanding Poverty,* Sheldon H. Danziger and Robert H. Haveman, eds. New York: Russell Sage, 2001:417–443.

Fergusson, David M., L. John Horwood, and Annette L. Beutrais. "Cannabis and Educational Attainment." *Addiction,* 2003: 1681–1692.

Fernandez, Fabian G., Kristofer D. Johnson, Richard E. Terry, Sheldon Nelson, and David Webster. "Soil Resources of the Ancient Maya at Piedras Negras, Guatemala." *American Journal of the Soil Science Society, 696,* October 27, 2005:2020–2032.

Feshbach, Murray. "Russia's Farms, Too Poisoned for the Plow." *Wall Street Journal,* May 14, 1992:A14.

Fialka, John J. "Pentagon Outlines Plans to Use Troops to Join Border 'War' Against Drugs." *Wall Street Journal,* February 23, 1988:A10.

Fialka, John J. "Position Available: Indestructible Bugs To Eat Nuclear Waste." *Wall Street Journal,* November 16, 2004:A1.

Field, Mark G. "The Health Crisis in the Former Soviet Union: A Report from the 'Post-War' Zone. In *Readings in Medical Sociology,* William C. Cockerham, Michael Glasser, and Linda S. Heuser, eds. Upper Saddle River, New Jersey, N.J.: Prentice Hall, 1998: 506–519.

Fields, George. "Racism Is Accepted Practice in Japan." *Wall Street Journal,* November 10, 1986:19.

Finckenauer, James O. *Scared Straight and the Panacea Phenomenon.* Englewood Cliffs, N.J.: Prentice Hall, 1982.

Finkelhor, David, and Kersti Yllo. *License to Rape: Sexual Abuse of Wives.* New York: Holt, 1985.

Finkelhor, David, and Kersti Yllo. "Marital Rape: The Myth versus the Reality." In *Marriage and Family in a Changing Society,* James M. Henslin, ed. New York: Free Press, 1989:382–391.

Finsterbusch, Kurt, and H. C. Greisman. "The Unprofitability of Warfare in the Twentieth Century." *Social Problems, 22,* February 1975:450–463.

Firestone, Shulamith. *The Dialectic of Sex: The Case for Feminist Revolution.* New York: Morrow, 1970.

"First Death Sentence Under New Drug Law." *New York Times,* May 15, 1991:A24.

Fischer, Claude S. *The Urban Experience.* New York: Harcourt, 1976.

Fish, Jefferson M. "Mixed Blood." *Psychology Today, 28,* 6, November–December 1995:55–58, 60, 61, 76, 80.

Fisher, Gordon M. "Setting American Standards of Poverty: A Look Back." *Focus, 19,* 2, Spring 1988:47–52.

Fisher, Sue. *In the Patient's Best Interest: Women and the Politics of Medical Decisions.* New Brunswick, N.J.: Rutgers University Press, 1986.

Fisse, Brent, and John Braithwaite. "The Impact of Publicity on Corporate Offenders: Ford Motor Company and the Pinto Papers." In *Corporate and Governmental Deviance: Problems of Organizational Behavior in Contemporary Society,* 3rd ed., M. David Ermann and Richard J. Lundman, eds. New York: Oxford University Press, 1987:244–262.

Flavin, Christopher. "Reassessing Nuclear Power." In *State of the World,* Lester R. Brown, ed. New York: Norton, 1987:57–80.

Foley, Douglas E. "The Great American Football Ritual." In *Society: Readings to Accompany Core Concepts,* James M. Henslin, ed. Boston: Allyn & Bacon, 2006:64–76 (originally published 1990).

Food and Drug Administration. "Food Allergies—Rare But Risky." *FDA Consumer,* May 1994.

Ford, Clellan S., and Frank A. Beach. *Patterns of Sexual Behavior.* New York: Harper Colophon, 1972.

Forero, Juan. "Bolivia's Knot: No to Cocaine, But Yes to Coca." *New York Times,* February 12, 2006.

Forney, Mary Ann, James A. Inciardi, and Dorothy Lockwood. "Exchanging Sex for Crack-Cocaine: A Comparison of Women from Rural and Urban Communities." *Journal of Community Health, 17,* 2, April 1992:73–85.

Forward, Susan, and Craig Buck. *Betrayal of Innocence: Incest and Its Devastation.* New York: Penguin, 1978.

Fouts, Gregory, and Kimberley Burggraf. "Television Situation Comedies: Female Body Images and Verbal Reinforcements." *Sex Roles: A Journal of Research,* March 1999.

Fox, James Alan, and Jack Levin. *Extreme Killing: Understanding Serial and Mass Murder.* Thousand Oaks, Calif.: Sage, 2005.

Fox, John W. "Social Class, Mental Illness, and Social Mobility: The Social Selection-Drift Hypothesis for Serious Mental Illness." *Journal of Health and Social Behavior, 31,* 4, December 1990: 344–353.

Frankenberg, Erica, and Chungmei Lee. "Rapidly Resegregating School Districts." The Civil Rights Project. Cambridge, Mass.: Harvard University, August 2002.

Frazier, Steve, and Brenton R. Schlender. "Huge Area in Midwest Relying on Irrigation Is Depleting Its Water." *Wall Street Journal,* August 6, 1980:1.

Freed, Anne O. "How Japanese Families Cope with Fragile Elderly." In *Perspectives in Social Gerontology,* Robert B. Enright, Jr., ed. Boston: Allyn & Bacon, 1994:76–86.

Freedman, Alix M. "How a Tobacco Giant Doctors Snuff Brands to Boost Their 'Kick.'" *Wall Street Journal,* October 26, 1994:A1, A6.

Freidson, Eliot. *Patient's Views of Medical Practice.* New York: Russell Sage, 1961.

"Frequent Tobacco Use Among U.S. Youth Declines." *Smokers' Advocate,* February 1992.

Freund, Matthew, Nancy Lee, and Terri Leonard. *Journal of Sex Research, 28,* 4, November 1991:579–591.

Friedan, Betty. *The Feminine Mystique.* New York: Norton, 1963.

Friedl, Ernestine. "Society and Sex Roles." In *Conformity and Conflict: Readings in Cultural Anthropology.* James P. Spradley and David W. McCurdy, eds. Glenview Ill.: Scott, Foresman, 1990:229–238.

Friends of the Earth. Press release, online 2004.

Friess, Steve. "Betting on the Studs." *Newsweek,* December 12, 2005.

Froman, Ingmarie. "Sweden for Women." *Current Sweden, 407,* November 1994:1–4.

Fromm, Erich. *The Anatomy of Human Destructiveness.* New York: Holt, 1973.

Fuller, Rex, and Richard Schoenberger. "The Gender Salary Gap: Do Academic Achievement, Internship Experience, and College Major Make a Difference?" *Social Science Quarterly, 72,* 4, December 1991:715–726.

Galbraith, John Kenneth. *The Nature of Mass Poverty.* Cambridge, Mass.: Harvard University Press, 1979.

Gale, Richard P. "From Sit-In to Hike-In: A Comparison of the Civil Rights and Environmental Movements." In *Social Behavior, Natural Resources, and the Environment,* William R. Burch, Jr., Neil H. Cheek, Jr., and Lee Taylor, eds. New York: Harper & Row, 1972:280–305.

Gall, Carlotta. "Despite Afghan Strictures, the Poppy Flourishes." *New York Times,* February 17, 2006.

Galliher, John R., and Allyn Walker. "The Puzzle of the Social Origins of the Marihuana Tax Act of 1937." *Social Problems, 24,* February 1977:367–376.

Ganahl, Dennis J., Thomas J. Prinsen, and Sara Baker Netzley. "A Content Analysis of Prime Time Commercials: A Contextual Framework of Gender Representation." *Sex Roles, 49,* 9/10, November 2003:545–551.

Gans, Herbert J. *People and Plans: Essays on Urban Problems and Solutions.* New York: Basic Books, 1968.

Gans, Herbert J. "The Uses of Poverty: The Poor Pay All." In *Down-to-Earth Sociology: Introductory Readings,* 14th ed., James M. Henslin, ed. New York: Free Press, 2007.

Gans, Herbert J. "The Uses of Poverty: The Poor Pay All." In *Down-to-Earth Sociology: Introductory Readings,* 13th ed., James M. Henslin, ed. New York: The Free Press, 2005 (originally appeared in *Social Policy,* July/August 1971:20–24).

Gans, Herbert J. "The Way We'll Live Soon." *Washington Post,* September 1, 1991:BW3.

Gans, Herbert J. *The Urban Villagers.* New York: Free Press, 1962.

"GAO Delineates State Use of Tobacco Funds." *Alcoholism and Drug Abuse Weekly, 15,* 10, March 10, 2003:3.

Garbarino, Merwin S. *American Indian Heritage.* Boston: Little, Brown, 1976.

Gardner, Sandra. "Coping with a Daughter's Murder." *New York Times,* January 5, 1992:NJ3.

Garelik, Glenn. "Russia's Legacy of Death." *National Wildlife,* June–July 1996.

Garreau, Joel. *Edge City: Life on the New Frontier.* New York: Doubleday, 1991.

Garrett, Laurie. "Global Warning." *Los Angeles Times,* March 1, 1999.

Gartner, Michael. "A Dream of Peace, the Reality of Never-Ending Wars." *Wall Street Journal,* December 22, 1988:A13.

Gattari, P., L. Spizzichino, C. Valenzi, M. Zaccarelli, and G. Rezza. "Behavioural Patterns and HIV Infection Among Drug Using Transvestites Practising Prostitution in Rome." *AIDS Care, 4,* 1, 1992:83–87.

Gaufberg, Slava V. "Russia." *E-Medicine,* March 11, 2004.

Gay, Jill. "The 'Patriotic' Prostitute." *The Progressive,* February 1985:34–36.

Gaylin, Willard. *Partial Justice: A Study of Bias in Sentencing.* New York: Knopf, 1974.

Gelles, Richard I. "The Myth of Battered Husbands and New Facts About Family Violence." In *Social Problems 80–81,* Robert L. David, ed. Guilford, Conn.: Dushkin, 1980.

Gellhorn, Martha. *The Face of War.* New York: Simon & Schuster, 1959.

Gemme, Robert. "Prostitution: A Legal, Criminological, and Sexological Perspective." *Canadian Journal of Human Sexuality, 2,* 4, Winter 1993:227–237.

George, David T., Monte J. Phillips, Linda Doty, John C. Umhau, and Robert R. Rawlings. "A Model Linking Biology, Behavior, and Psychiatric Diagnoses in Perpetrators of Domestic Violence." *Medical Hypotheses,* 2006.

Gerbner, George. "The 1998 Screen Actors Guild Report: Casting the American Scene." Online. December 1998.

Gerlin, Andrea. "Quirky Sentences Make Bad Guys Squirm." *Wall Street Journal,* August 4, 1994:B1, B2.

Gerstl-Pepin, Cynthia I. "The Paradox of Poverty Narratives: Educators Struggling with Children Left Behind." *Educational Policy, 20,* 1, March 2006:143–162.

Gerth, Jeff. "Two Companies Pay Penalties for Improving China Rockets." *New York Times,* March 3, 2003.

Gessen, Masha. "The Nuclear Wasteland." *U.S. News & World Report,* February 26, 2001.

Gest, Ted. "Teaching Convicts Real Street Smarts." *U.S. News & World Report,* May 18, 1987:72.

Getter, Lisa. "Cancer Risk From Air Pollution Still High, Study Says." *Los Angeles Times,* March 1, 1999.

"Getting the Message." Children Now. Online, 1997.

Gibbs, Nancy. "In Sorrow and Disbelief." *Time,* May 3, 1999:25–36.

Gibbs, Nancy, and Amanda Bower. "Q: What Scares Doctors? A: Being the Patient." *Time,* May 1, 2006.

Giddens, Anthony. "Georg Simmel." In *The Founding Fathers of Social Science,* Timothy Raison, ed. Baltimore: Penguin, 1969: 165–173.

Giele, Janet Zollinger. *Women and the Future: Changing Sex Roles in Modern America.* New York: Free Press, 1978.

Gilham, Steven A. "The Marines Build Men: Resocialization in Recruit Training." In *The Sociological Outlook: A Text with Readings,* 2nd ed., Reid Luhman, ed. San Diego, Calif.: Collegiate Press, 1989:232–244.

Gilmore, David G. *Manhood in the Making: Cultural Concepts of Masculinity.* New Haven, Conn.: Yale University Press, 1990.

Glascock, Jack. "Gender Roles on Prime-Time Network Television: Demographics and Behaviors." *Journal of Broadcasting and Electronics Media, 45,* Fall 2001:656–669.

Glaser, Daniel. *Crime in Our Changing Society.* New York: Holt, 1978.

Goering, Laurie. "Paranoia Pervasive in Amazon." *Seattle Times,* August 28, 1998.

Goetting, Ann. *Getting Out: Life Stories of Women Who Left Abusive Men.* New York: Columbia University Press, 2001.

Goldberg, Carey, and Sophia Kishkovsky. "Russia's Doctors Are Beggars at Work, Paupers at Home." *New York Times,* December 16, 2000.

Goldberg, Steven. *The Inevitability of Patriarchy,* rev. ed. New York: Morrow, 1974.

Goldberg, Steven. Letter to the Author. January 18, 1989.

Goldberg, Steven. "Reaffirming the Obvious." *Society,* September–October 1986:4–7.

Goldberg, Susan, and Michael, Lewis. "Play Behavior in the Year-Old Infant: Early Sex Differences." *Child Development, 40,* March 1969:21–31.

Goleman, Daniel. "Girls and Math: Is Biology Really Destiny?" *New York Times,* August 2, 1987:42–44, 46.

Goode, Erich. *Drugs in American Society,* 3rd ed. New York: Knopf, 1989.

Gooden, Angela M., and Mark A. Gooden. "Gender Representation in Notable Children's Picture Books: 1995–1999." *Sex Roles, 45,* 1/2, July 2001:89–101.

Gordon, Michael R. "Russia Struggles in Long Race to Prevent an Atomic Theft." *New York Times,* April 20, 1996.

Gordon, Milton. *Assimilation in American Life.* New York: Oxford University Press, 1964.

Gorman, Steve. "Hollywood Madam to Open Nevada 'Stud Farm.'" *New York Times,* November 18, 2005.

Gosch, Martin A., and Richard Hammer. *The Last Testament of Lucky Luciano.* New York: Dell, 1975.

Gottfredson, Michael, and Travis Hirschi. *A General Theory of Crime.* Stanford, Calif.: Stanford University Press, 1990.

"GPS Creates Global Jail." Online, April 8, 1998.

"Granddaddy of All Ghettos Faces Wrecking Ball." Associated Press, October 8, 2006.

Graven, Kathryn. "Sex Harassment at the Office Stirs Up Japan." *Wall Street Journal,* March 21, 1990:B1, B7.

Green, Gary S. "White-Collar Crime and the Study of Embezzlement." *Annals of the American Academy of Political and Social Sciences, 525,* January 1993:95–106.

Greenall, Robert. "Russia Turns Spotlight on Abortion." BBC News Online, September 16, 2003.

Greenberg, David F. "The Incapacitative Effect of Imprisonment: Some Estimates." *Law and Society Review, 9,* Summer 1975: 541–579.

Greenberger, Robert S. "U.S., Russia Agree to Faster Timetable for Destruction of Nuclear Arsenals." *Wall Street Journal,* September 29, 1994:A22.

Greenberger, Robert S. "U.S., Russia Will Explore Joint System for Early Warning of Missile Attacks." *Wall Street Journal,* February 19,1992:A7.

Greenberger, Robert S., and Jerry E. Bishop. "Suspected Toxic Agent in Attack Is Made of Chemicals Easily Available in U.S." *Wall Street Journal,* March 21, 1995:A12.

Greenhouse, Steven. "Doctors, Under Pressure from H.M.O.'s, Are Ready Union Recruits." *New York Times,* February 4, 1999.

Greer, Germaine. *The Female Eunuch.* New York: Bantam, 1972.

Grimmett, Richard F. "Conventional Arms Transfers to Developing Nations, 1998–2005." Washington, D.C.: CRS Report for Congress, October 23, 2006.

"Guardian of Brazil Indians Faces Many Foes." Reuters online, June 10, 1997.

Gudkov, Yuri. "The 'Respectable' Mafia." *World Press Review, 27,* January 1980:51.

Gurvich, Tatyana, and Janet A. Cunningham. "Appropriate Use of Psychotropic Drugs in Nursing Homes." *American Family Physician, 6,* 2000:1437–1446.

Gusfield, Joseph R. *Symbolic Crusade: Status Politics and the American Temperance Movement.* Urbana: University of Illinois Press, 1963.

Haas, Jack, and William Shaffir. "The Cloak of Competence." In *Down-to-Earth Sociology: Introductory Readings,* 7th ed., James M. Henslin, ed. New York: Free Press, 1993.

Hacker, Helen Mayer. "Women as a Minority Group." *Social Forces, 30,* October 1951:60–69.

Hackett, George. "Kids: Deadly Force." *Newsweek,* January 11, 1988: 18–19.

Hadden, Jeffrey K., and Josef J. Barton. "An Image That Will Not Die: Thoughts on the History of Anti-Urban Ideology." In *The Urbanization of the Suburbs,* Louis H. Masoti and Jeffrey K. Hadden, eds. Beverly Hills, Calif.: Sage, 1973:79–116.

Hage, Dave. *Reforming Welfare by Rewarding Work.* Minneapolis: University of Minnesota Press, 2004.

Hagedorn, John M. "The Global Impact of Gangs." *Journal of Contemporary Criminal Justice, 21,* 2, May 2005:153–169.

Hale, Marion. "In Courts, Defendant's Color Counts." *Fort Lauderdale News,* October 3, 1980.

Hall, Susan. *Gentleman of Leisure: A Year in the Life of a Pimp.* New York: New American Library, 1972.

Hamer, Dean H., Stella Hu, Victoria L. Magnuson, Nan Hu, and Angela M. L. Pattatucci. "A Linkage Between DNA Markers on the X Chromosome and Male Sexual Orientation." *Science, 261,* July 16, 1993:321–327.

Hampson, Rick. "Studies: Gentrification a Boost for Everyone." *USA Today,* April 19, 2005.

Hanson, David J. *Preventing Alcohol Abuse: Alcohol, Culture, and Control.* Westport, Conn.: Praeger, 1995.

Hanssen, M. *The New Additive Code Breaker.* Port Melbourne, Australia: Lothian Books, 1997.

Hardin, Garrett. "The Tragedy of the Commons." *Science, 162,* December 1968:1243–1248.

Harlan, Christi. "Come Out with Your Hands Up and No Funny Stuff with the Peas." *Wall Street Journal,* November 4, 1988:B1.

Harrington, Michael. *The Other America.* New York: Macmillan, 1962.

Harrington, Michael. *The Vast Majority: A Journey to the World's Poor.* New York: Simon & Schuster, 1977.

Harris, Chauncy, and Edward Ullman. "The Nature of Cities." *Annals of the American Academy of Political and Social Science, 242,* November 1945:7–17.

Harris, Diana K., and Michael L. Benson. *Maltreatment of Patients in Nursing Homes: There Is No Safe Place.* New York: Haworth Pastoral Press, 2006.

Harris, Gardiner. "Panel Advises Disclosure of Drugs' Psychotic Effects." *New York Times,* March 23, 2006.

Harris, Marvin. "Why Men Dominate Women." *New York Times Magazine,* November 13, 1977:46, 115, 117, 123.

Harris, Sheldon H. *Factories of Death.* New York: Routledge, 1994.

Harrison, Paige M., and Allen J. Beck. "Prison and Jail Inmates at Midyear 2005." *Bureau of Justice Statistics Bulletin,* May 2005.

Hart, C. W. M., and Arnold R. Pilling. *The Tiwi of North Australia,* Fieldwork Edition. New York: Holt, Rinehart and Winston, 1979.

Hart, Hornell. "Acceleration in Social Change." In *Technology and Social Change,* Francis R. Allen, Hornell Hart, Delbert C. Miller, William F. Ogburn, and Meyer F. Nimkoff, eds. New York: Appleton, 1957.

Haskins, Ron. "The Welfare Check." *Wall Street Journal,* July 30, 2006.

Haub, Carl, and Diana Cornelius. "1999 World Population Data Sheet." Washington, D.C.: Population Reference Bureau, 1999.

Haub, Carl, and Diana Cornelius. "World Population Data Sheet." Population Reference Bureau, 2004.

Haub, Carl. "2005 World Population Data Sheet." Washington, D.C.: Population Reference Bureau, 2005.

Hauser, Philip, and Leo Schnore, eds. *The Study of Urbanization.* New York: Wiley, 1965.

Haveman, Robert H., and John Karl Scholz. "The Clinton Welfare Reform Plan: Will It End Poverty as We Know It?" *Focus, 16,* 2, Winter 1994–95:1–11.

Hayden, F. Gregory, Kellee R. Wood, and Asuman Kaya. "The Use of Power Blocs of Integrated Corporate Directorships to Articulate a Power Structure: Case Study and Research Recommendations." *Journal of Economic Issues, 36,* 3, September 2002: 671–706.

Hayes, Arthur S. "How the Courts Define Harassment." *Wall Street Journal,* October 11, 1991:B1, B3.

Health Grades. "The Eighth Annual Health Grades Hospital Quality in America Study." October 17, 2005.

Healy, Patrick. "Hoisting Rainbow Flags, Wearing Campaign Buttons." *New York Times,* June 28, 2004.

Heins, Marjorie. "The War on Nudity, Continued." *Playboy,* November 1991:53.

Hellinger, Daniel, and Dennis R. Judd. *The Democratic Facade.* Pacific Grove, Calif.: Brooks/Cole, 1991.

"Hello Kitty Robot Receptionist Debuts in Japan." Reuters, January 26, 2006.

Helmer, J. *Drugs and Minority Oppression.* New York: Seabury, 1975.

Hench, David. "Jail Sends TB Patient to Hospital in Boston." *Portland Press Herald,* September 28, 2006.

Hendin, Herbert. "Euthanasia and Physician-Assisted Suicide in the Netherlands." *New England Journal of Medicine, 336,* 19, May 8, 1997:1385–1387.

Hendin, Herbert. "Suicide, Assisted Suicide, and Mental Illness." *Harvard Mental Health Letter, 16,* 7, January 2000:4–7.

Henriques, Fernando. *Prostitution and Society.* New York: Grove, 1966.

Henslin, James M. "Guilt and Guilt Neutralization: Response and Adjustment to Suicide." In *Deviance and Respectability: The Social Construction of Moral Meanings,* Jack D. Douglas, ed. New York: Basic Books, 1970.

Henslin, James M. "On Becoming Male: Reflections of a Sociologist on Childhood and Early Socialization." In *Down-to-Earth Sociology: Introductory Readings,* 14th ed., James M. Henslin, ed. New York: Free Press, 2007a.

Henslin, James M. *Sociology: A Down-to-Earth Approach,* 8th edition. Boston: Allyn & Bacon, 2007b.

Henslin, James M., and Mae A. Biggs. "Behavior in Pubic Places: The Sociology of the Vaginal Examination." In *Down-to-Earth Sociology: Introductory Readings,* 14th ed., James M. Henslin, ed. New York: Free Press, 2007.

Herbert, Bob. "Don't Flunk the Future." *New York Times,* August 13, 1998.

Herbert, Bob. "The Hate Virus." *New York Times,* August 10, 1988.

Herper, Matthew. "The Best-Selling Drugs in America." *Forbes,* February 27, 2006.

Hersh, Seymour. "Manhunt." *New Yorker,* December 23, 2002.

Hertsgaard, Mark. "Bhopal's Legacy." *The Nation,* May 24, 2004.

Heyl, Barbara Sherman. *The Madam as Entrepreneur: Career Management in House Prostitution.* New Brunswick, N.J.: Transaction, 1979.

Hibbert, Christopher. *The Roots of Evil: A Social History of Crime and Punishment.* New York: Minerva, 1963.

Hill, Catherine, and Elena Silva. "Drawing the Line. Sexual Harassment on Campus." Washington, D.C.: American Association of University Women Educational Foundation, 2005.

Hilliard, Asa, III. "Do We Have the Will to Educate All Children?" *Educational Leadership, 49,* September 1991:31–36.

Hills, Stuart L., ed. *Corporate Violence: Injury and Death for Profit.* Totowa, N.J.: Rowman & Littlefield, 1987.

Hills, Stuart L. *Demystifying Social Deviance.* New York: McGraw-Hill, 1980.

Hiltz, Starr Roxanne. "Widowhood." In *Marriage and Family in a Changing Society,* James M. Henslin, ed. New York: Free Press, 1989:521–531.

Himmelhoch, Jerome, and Sylvia Fleis Fava (eds.). *Sexual Behavior in American Society: An Appraisal of the First Two Kinsey Reports.* New York: Norton, 1955.

Hindelang, Michael J. "Race and Involvement in Common Personal Crimes." *American Sociological Review, 43,* February 1978:93–109.

Hirschi, Travis. *Causes of Delinquency.* Berkeley: University of California Press, 1969.

Historical Statistics of the United States: From Colonial Times to the Present. New York: Basic Books, 1976.

Hochschild, Arlie, and Anne Machung. "Men Who Share the 'Second Shift.'" In *Down-to-Earth Sociology: Introductory Readings,* 11th ed., James M. Henslin, ed. New York: Free Press, 2001: 395–409.

Hodgson, James F. *Games Pimps Play: Pimps, Players and Wives-In-Law.* Toronto: Canadian Scholars' Press, 1997.

Hoffman, Albert. "Psychotomimetic Agents." In *Drugs Affecting the Central Nervous System* (vol. 2). New York: Marcel Dekker, 1968.

Hoffman, Stanley. "The Foreign Policy the U.S. Needs." *New York Review of Books, 53,* 13, August 10, 2006.

Hogan, Bill. "The Wages of Synfuels." *Mother Jones,* September 1, 2001.

Holdren, John P., and Paul R. Ehrlich. "Human Population and the Global Environment." *American Scientist, 62,* May–June 1974: 282–292.

Holman, Richard L. "World Wire." *Wall Street Journal,* July 28, 1994:A10.

Holmstrom, Lynda Lytle, and Ann Wolbert Burgess. "Rape and Everyday Life." In *Deviance in American Life,* James M. Henslin, ed. New Brunswick, N.J.: Transaction, 1989:349–371.

Holtzman, Abraham. *The Townsend Movement: A Political Study.* New York: Bookman, 1963.

Homblin, Dora Jane. *The First Cities.* Boston: Little, Brown, Time-Life Books, 1973.

Hooker, Evelyn. "The Adjustment of the Male Overt Homosexual." *Journal of Projective Techniques, 21,* March 1957:18–31.

Hooton, Earnest A. *Crime and the Man.* Cambridge, Mass.: Harvard University Press, 1939.

Hope, Christine A., and Ronald G. Stover. "Gender Status, Monotheism, and Social Complexity." *Social Forces, 65,* 1987:1132–1138.

Hornblower, Margot. "The Skin Trade." *Time,* June 21, 1993:45–51.

Horowitz, Ruth. *Honor and the American Dream: Culture and Identity in a Chicano Community.* New Brunswick, N.J.: Rutgers University Press, 1983.

Hosenball, Mark. "A Plutonium Mystery." *Newsweek,* May 3, 1999: 62–64.

Hotchkiss, Sandy. "The Realities of Rape." *Human Behavior, 12,* December 1978:18–23.

Hotz, Robert Lee. "Early Humans' Fire Use Linked to Extinctions." *Los Angeles Times,* January 8, 1999.

Howard, Jan, and Anselm Strauss (eds.). *Humanizing Health Care.* New York: Wiley, 1975.

Howell, Karen K., Mary Ellen Lynch, Kathleen A. Platzman, G. Harold Smith, and Claire D. Coles. "Prenatal Alcohol Exposure and Ability, Academic Achievement, and School Functioning in Adolescence: A Longitudinal Follow-Up." *Journal of Pediatric Psychology, 31,* 1, 2006:116–126.

Hsu, Francis L. K. *The Challenge of the American Dream: The Chinese in the United States.* Belmont, Calif.: Wadsworth, 1971.

Huber, Joan. "Micro-Macro Links in Gender Stratification." *American Sociological Review, 55,* February 1990:1–10.

Huddle, Donald. "The Net National Cost of Immigration." Washington, D.C.: Carrying Capacity Network, 1993.

Hudson, Robert B. "The 'Graying' of the Federal Budget and Its Consequences for Old-Age Policy." *The Gerontologist, 18,* October 1978:428–440.

Huff-Corzine, Lin, Jay Corzine, and David C. Moore. "Deadly Connections: Culture, Poverty, and the Direction of Lethal Violence." *Social Forces, 69,* 3, March 1991:715–732.

Huff-Corzine, Lin, Jay Corzine, and David C. Moore. "Southern Exposure: Deciphering the South's Influence on Homicide Rates." *Social Forces, 64,* 1986:906–924.

Huggins, Martha K. "Lost Childhood: Assassinations of Youth in Democratizing Brazil." Paper presented at the annual meetings of the American Sociological Association, 1993.

Huggins, Martha K., Mika Haritos-Fatouros, and Philip G. Zimbardo. *Violence Workers: Police Torturers and Murderers Reconstruct Brazilian Atrocities.* Berkeley: University of California Press, 2002.

Hull, Jon D. "Life and Death with the Gangs." *Time,* August 24, 1987:21–22.

Humphreys, Laud. *Tearoom Trade.* Chicago: Aldine, 1970. (Expanded version, Chicago: Aldine-Atherton, 1975.)

Humphries, Drew, John Dawson, Valerie Cronin, Phyllis Keating, Christ Wisniewski, and Jennine Eichfeld. "Mothers and Children, Drugs and Crack: Reactions to Maternal Drug Dependency." *Women and Criminal Justice, 3,* 2, 1992:81–99.

Huxley, Aldous. *The Doors of Perception.* New York: Harper & Row, 1954.

"Hybrid Car Market Revs Up." *USA Today,* May 3, 2004.

Ilminen, Gary R. "New Strategies Ramping Up Quality in Wisconsin Medicaid Managed Care." *Home Health Care Management & Practice, 18,* 3, April 2006:235–238.

"Implementation of Measures to Prevent Sexual Harassment of National Civil Servants." *Woman in Japan Today,* January 2000.

Inciardi, James A. *The War on Drugs: Heroin, Cocaine, Crime, and Public Policy.* Mountain View, Calif.: Mayfield, 1986.

Inciardi, James A., and Anne E. Pottieger. "Crack-Cocaine Use and Street Crime." *Journal of Drug Issues, 24,* 2, Winter 1994: 273–292.

Ingersoll, Bruce. "Faster Slaughter Lines Are Contaminating Much U.S. Poultry." *Wall Street Journal,* November 16, 1990:A1, A6.

Ingersoll, Bruce. "FDA Is Proposing Limits on Sulfites in Range of Foods." *Wall Street Journal,* December 20, 1988:C21.

Iovine, Nicole M., and Martin J. Blaser. "Antibiotics in Animal Feed and Spread of Resistant Campylobacter from Poultry to Humans." *Emerging Infectious Diseases,* June 2004. Online. "Iran Test Fires Longer Range Missile as Part of New Maneuvers." *International Herald Tribune,* November 9, 2006.

Isbell, Harris. "Historical Development of Attitudes Toward Opiate Addiction in the United States." In *Man and Civilization: Conflict, and Creativity,* Seymour M. Farber and Roger H. L. Wilson, eds. New York: McGraw-Hill, 1969:154–170.

Izaak Walton League of America. "Conservation Policies," 2000.

Izumi, Lance T. "Cutting Through the Smoke: Facts on Cigarette Tax." November 18, 1997.

Jacobs, Jane. *Dark Age Ahead.* New York: Random House, 2004.

Jaffe, Jerome H. "Drug Addiction and Drug Abuse." In *The Pharmacological Basis of Therapeutics,* Louis S. Goodman and Alfred Gilmann, eds. New York: Macmillan, 1965:285–311.

Jain, Sonu. "It's Official: Asbestos Is Crippling Alang Workers." *Indian Express,* September 6, 2006.

James, Jennifer, and J. Meyerding. "Early Sexual Experiences in Prostitution." *Archives of Sexual Behavior, 7,* 1977:31–42.

James, Jennifer, and Nanette J. Davis. "Contingencies in Female Sexual Role Deviance: The Case of Prostitution." *Human Organization, 41,* 4, Winter 1982: 345–350.

Janowitz, Morris. "The Twentieth-Century Race Riot, Commodity Type: The Summer of 1967." In *American Violence,* Richard Maxwell, ed. Englewood Cliffs, N.J.: Prentice Hall, 1970a: 147–155.

Janowitz, Morris. "The Twentieth-Century Race Riot, Communal Type: Chicago, 1919." In *American Violence,* Richard Maxwell, ed. Englewood Cliffs, N.J.: Prentice Hall, 1970b: 126–136.

Jefferson, Thomas. *Notes on the State of Virginia,* Bernard Wishy and William C. Leuchtenburg, eds. New York: Harper & Row, 1977 (originally published 1784)

Jekielek, Susan M. "Parental Conflict, Marital Disruption and Children's Emotional Well-Being." *Social Forces, 76,* 3, March 1998: 905–935.

Jenkins, Brian Michael. "The Future Course of Terrorism." *The Futurist,* July–August 1987:8.

Jenkins, Brian Michael. "Future Trends in International Terrorism." Symposium on International Terrorism. Washington, D.C.: Defense Intelligence Agency, December 2–3, 1985.

Joffe, Carole. "What Haven? For Whom?" *Social Policy, 9,* May–June 1978:58–60.

Johnson, Bruce D., Kevin Anderson, and Eric D. Wish. "A Day in the Life of 105 Drug Addicts and Abusers: Crimes Committed and How the Money Was Spent." *Sociology and Social Research, 72,* 3, April 1988:185–191.

Johnson, Bruce D., Paul J. Goldstein, Edward Preble, James Schmeidler, Douglas S. Lipton, Barry Spunt, and Thomas Miller. *Taking Care of Business: The Economics of Crime by Heroin Abusers.* Lexington, Mass.: Lexington Books, 1985.

Johnson, Danny R. "Tobacco Stains: Cigarette Firms Buy into African-American Groups." *The Progressive, 56,* 12, December 1992:26–28.

Johnson, Dirk. "Murder Charges Are Met by Cries of Compassion." *New York Times,* August 8, 1988:A14.

Johnson, Terry R., Randall J. Pozdena, and Gary Steiger. *The Impact of Alternative Negative Income Tax Programs on Non-Durable Consumption.* Menlo Park, Calif.: SRI International, October 1979.

Johnston, Lloyd D., Patrick M. O'Malley, Jerald G. Bachman, and John E. Schulenberg. *Monitoring the Future: National Results on Adolescent Drug Use.* Washington, D.C.: U.S. Department of Health and Human Services, 2006.

Johnston, Lloyd D., John E. Schulenberg, and Jerald G. Bachman. *Monitoring the Future: National Survey Results on Drug Use, 1975–2004,* Volume 1: *Secondary Students.* Washington, D.C.: U.S. Department of Health and Human Services, 2005.

Jordan, Jan. "Worlds Apart? Women, Rape and the Police Reporting Process." *British Journal of Criminology, 41,* 2001:679–706.

Josephy, Alvin M., Jr. "Indians in History." *Atlantic Monthly,* June 1970:67–72.

Julien, Robert M. *A Primer of Drug Action.* New York: Worth Publishers, 2001.

Kahn, Joseph. "Sane Chinese Put in Asylum, Doctors Find." *New York Times,* March 17, 2006.

Kalb, Claudia. "Drugged-Out Toddlers." *Newsweek,* March 6, 2000.

Kane, Emily. "'No Way My Boys Are Going to Be Like That!' Parents' Responses to Children's Gender Nonconformity." *Gender and Society, 20,* 2, April 2006:149–176.

Kanin, Eugene J. "Date Rapists: Differential Sexual Socialization and Relative Deprivation." In *Violence and Society: A Reader,* Matthew Silberman, ed. Upper Saddle River, N.J.: Prentice Hall, 2003:207–225.

Kantor, Glenda Kaufman, and Murray A. Straus. "The 'Drunken Bum' Theory of Wife Beating." *Social Problems, 34,* 3, June 1987:213–230.

Kaplan, Carl. S. "Anti-Porn Law Enters Court; Delay Soon Follows." *New York Times,* November 20, 1998.

Kaplan, Sidney. "Historical Efforts to Encourage White-Indian Intermarriage in the United States and Canada." *International Social Science Review, 65,* 3, Summer, 1990:126–132.

Karlen, Arno. "Homosexuality: The Scene and Its Students." In *The Sociology of Sex: An Introductory Reader,* rev. ed., James M. Henslin and Edward Sagarin, eds. New York: Schocken, 1978:223–248.

Karlen, Neal, and Barbara Burgower. "Dumping the Mentally Ill." *Newsweek, 105,* January 7, 1985:17.

Karmen, Andrew. "The Narcotics Problem: Views from the Left." In *Is America Possible? Social Problems from Conservative, Liberal, and Socialist Perspectives,* 2nd ed., Henry Etzkowitz, ed. St. Paul, Minn.: West, 1980:171–180.

Karp, David A., Gregory P. Stone, and William C. Yoels. *Being Urban: A Sociology of City Life,* 2nd ed. New York: Praeger, 1991.

Karp, David A., and William C. Yoels. "Sport and Urban Life." *Journal of Sport and Social Issues, 14,* 2, 1990:77–102.

Katz, Michael B. *The Undeserving Poor: From the War on Poverty to the War on Welfare.* New York: Pantheon, 1989.

Keans, Carl. "Socioenvironmental Determinants of Community Formation." *Environment and Behavior, 23,* 1, January 1991:27–46.

Kelley, Kitty. "The Dark Side of Camelot." *People,* February 28, 1988:107–114.

Kemp, Jack. "Tackling Poverty: Market-Based Policies to Empower the Poor." *Policy Review, 51,* Winter 1990:2–5.

Kemper, Peter, Harriet L. Komisar, and Lisa Alexich. "Long-Term Care over an Uncertain Future: What Can Current Retirees Expect?" *Inquiry, 42,* 4, 2006:335–350.

Kerner, Otto. Report of the National Advisory Commission on Civil Disorders. Washington, D.C.: U.S. Government Printing Office, 1968.

Kettl, Donald F. "The Savings-and-Loan Bailout: The Mismatch Between the Headlines and the Issues." *PS, 24,* 3, September 1991:441–447.

Keyes, Ken, Jr. *The Hundredth Monkey.* St. Mary, Ky.: Vision Books, n.d.

"Kids Count Data Sheet." Baltimore, Md.: Annie E. Casey Foundation, 2004.

Kilborn, Peter T. "Reality of H.M.O. System Does Not Live Up to Hopes for Health Care." *New York Times,* October 5, 1998.

Kilman, Scott. "Seed Firms Bolster Crops Using Traits of Distant Relatives." *Wall Street Journal,* October 31, 2006.

King, Martin Luther, Jr. *Stride Toward Freedom: The Montgomery Story.* New York: Harper, 1958.

King, Storm A., and Stephan T. Poulos. "Ethical Guidelines for Online Therapy." In *How to Use Computers and Cyberspace in the Clinical Practice of Psychotherapy,* Jeri Fink, ed. Lanham, Md.: Jason Aronson, 1999:121–132.

King, Wayne, "Violent Klan Group Gaining Members." *New York Times,* March 15, 1979.

Kinkade, Ward. "Population Trends: Russia." Washington, D.C.: U.S. Department of Commerce, February 1997.

Kinsey, Alfred C., Wardell B. Pomeroy, and Clyde E. Martin. *Sexual Behavior in the Human Male.* Philadelphia: Saunders, 1948.

Kinsey, Alfred C., Wardell B. Pomeroy, Clyde E. Mantin, and Paul H. Gebhard. *Sexual Behavior in the Human Female.* New York: Saunders, 1953.

Kirkham, George L. "Homosexuality in Prison." In *Studies in the Sociology of Sex,* James M. Henslin, ed. New York: Appleton, 1971: 325–349.

Kirkpatrick, Melanie. "On the Abortion Barricades." *Wall Street Journal,* April 23, 1992:A14.

Kirkpatrick, Terry. "A New Breed of Pioneers Are Homesteading America's Cities." *Alton Telegraph,* June 26, 1981.

Kitano, Harry H. L. *Race Relations.* Englewood Cliffs N.J.: Prentice Hall, 1974.

"Kitty Genovese." A Picture History of Kew Gardens, NY. Online. April 15, 2005.

Kleck, Gary, and Susan Sayles. "Rape and Resistance." *Social Problems, 37,* 2, May 1990:149–162.

Klein, Stephen, Joan Petersilia, and Susan Turner. "Race and Imprisonment Decisions in California." *Science, 247,* 4944, February 16, 1990:812–816.

Kleinman, Paul H., Eric D. Wish, Shreey Deren, Gregory Rainone, and Ellen Morehouse. "Daily Marijuana Use and Problem Behaviors Among Adolescents." *International Journal of the Addictions, 22,* 12, 1987.

Kluger, Jeffrey. "Polar Ice Caps Are Melting Faster Than Ever . . ." *Time,* April 3, 2006.

Knights, Roger. "Electronic Tagging in Practice." *Teleconnect,* January 22, 1999.

Kocieniewski, David, and John Sullivan. "In Newark, a Ward Boss with Influence to Spare." *New York Times,* January 16, 2006.

Kohn, Alfie. "Make Love, Not War." *Psychology Today,* June 1988: 35–38.

Komisar, Lucy. "The Image of Woman in Advertising." In *Woman in Sexist Society: Studies in Power and Powerlessness.* Vivian Gornick and Barbara K. Moran, eds. New York: Basic Books, 1971: 207–217.

Korda, Michael. *Male Chauvinism: How It Works.* New York: Random House, 1973.

Kornhauser, William. "'Power Elite' or 'Veto Groups'?" In *Culture and Social Character,* Seymour Martin Lipset and Leo Lowenthal, eds. Glencoe, Ill.: Free Press, 1961:252–267.

Kozel, Nicholas J. *Epidemiologic Trends in Drug Abuse.* Community Epidemiology Work Group. Bethesda, Maryland: National Institutes of Health, June, 1996.

Kozol, Jonathan. "Savage Inequalities." In *Down-to-Earth Sociology: Introductory Readings,* 10th ed., James M. Henslin, ed. New York: Free Press, 1999:343–351.

Krieger, Lisa. "Abortion Foes, Proponents Intensify Battle." *American Medical News, 28,* June 7, 1985:2–3.

Kristoff, Nicholas D. "Interview with a Humanoid." *New York Times,* July 23, 2002.

Kruk, Joanna, and Hassan Y. Aboul-Enein. "Environmental Exposure, and Other Risk Factors in Breast Cancer." *Current Cancer Therapy Reviews, 2,* 1, February 2006:3–21.

Kumanyika, Shiriki. "Obesity, Health Disparities, and Prevention Paradigms: Hard Questions and Hard Choices." *Preventing Chronic Disease, 2,* 4, October 2005.

Kurth, James R. "American Military Policy and Advanced Weapons." In *Social Problems and Public Policy: Inequality and Justice,* Lee Rainwater, ed. Chicago: Aldine, 1974:336–352.

Kusum. "The Use of Pre-Natal Diagnostic Techniques for Sex Selection: The Indian Scene." *Bioethics, 7,* 2–3, April 1993: 149–165.

Kutchinsky, Berl. "The Effects of Easy Availability of Pornography on the Incidence of Sex Crimes in Copenhagen: The Danish Experience." *Journal of Social Issues, 29,* 1973:163–181.

La Barre, Weston. *The Human Animal.* Chicago: University of Chicago Press, 1954.

LaBastille, Anne. "The Deadly Toll of Acid Rain: All of Nature Is Suffering." *Science Digest, 86,* October 1979:61–66.

Lacayo, Richard. "Crusading Against the Pro-Choice Movement." *Time,* October 21, 1991.

Lacey, Marc. "African Activists Urge End to Female Mutilation." *International Herald Tribune,* February 7, 2003:10.

LaFree, Gary D. "The Effect of Sexual Stratification by Race on Official Reactions to Rape." *American Sociological Review, 45,* October 1980:842–854.

La Gory, Mark, Russell Ward, and Thomas Juravich. "The Age Segregation Process." *Urban Affairs Quarterly, 16,* 1980:59–80.

Lalumiere, Martin L., Grant T. Harris, Vernon L. Quinsey, and Marnie E. Rice. *The Causes of Rape: Understanding Individual Differences in Male Propensity for Sexual Aggression.* Washington, D.C.: American Psychological Association, 2005.

Lamar, Jacob V., Jr. "An Inmate and a Gentleman." *Time,* August 11, 1986:17.

Lamptey, Peter R., Jami L. Johnson, and Marya Khan. "The Global Challenge of HIV and AIDS." *Population Bulletin, 61,* 1, March 2006.

Landes, David S. *The Wealth and Poverty of Nations: Why Some Are Rich and Some So Poor.* New York: W.W. Norton, 1998.

Lang, Kurt, and Gladys Lang. "Racial Disturbances as Collective Protest." In *Riots and Rebellion: Civil Violence in the Urban Community,* Louis H. Masotti, and Don R. Bowen, eds. Beverly Hills, Calif.: Sage, 1968:121–130.

Lang, Robert E. *Edgeless Cities: Exploring the Elusive Metropolis.* Washington, D.C.: Brookings Institution Press, 2003.

Langan, Patrick A., and David J. Levin. "Recidivism of Prisoners Released in 1994." Bureau of Justice, Special Report. June 2002.

Langan, Patrick A., and Mark A. Cunniff. "Recidivism of Felons on Probation, 1986–1989." Bureau of Justice Statistics Special Report, Washington, D.C., February, 1992.

Laqueur, Walter. *Terrorism.* Boston: Little, Brown, 1977.

Larned, Deborah. "The Epidemic in Unnecessary Hysterectomies." In *Seizing Our Bodies: The Politics of Women's Health,* Claudia Dreyfus, ed. New York: Random House, 1977.

Larson, Mary Strom. "Interactions, Activities and Gender in Children's Television Commercials: A Content Analysis." *Journal of Broadcasting and Electronic Media, 45,* Winter 2001:41–51.

Larsson, Susanna C., Leif Bergkvist, and Alicja Wolk. "Milk and Lactose Intakes and Ovarian Cancer Risk in the Swedish Mammography Cohort." *American Journal of Clinical Nutrition, 80,* 5, November 2004:1353–1357.

Lasch, Christopher. *Haven in a Heartless World: The Family Besieged.* New York: Basic Books, 1977.

Laslett, Barbara. "Family, Social Change Can Often Spell Trouble." University of California, University Extension, Course by Newspaper, San Diego, 1980.

Laumann, Edward O., John H. Gagnon, Robert T. Michael, and Stuart Michaels. *The Social Organization of Sexuality: Sexual Practices in the United States.* Chicago: University of Chicago Press, 1994.

"Law Enacted to Protect Ainu Culture, Tradition." Foreign Press Center of Japan, June 19, 1997.

Leaf, Clifton. "Enough Is Enough." In *Sociology,* 33rd ed., Kurt Finsterbusch, ed. New York: McGraw-Hill/ Dushkin, 2004:52–59.

LeBlanc, Steve. "Mass. Lawmakers Advance Proposed Gay Marriage Ban." *Associated Press,* January 2, 2007.

Lee, Dorothy. *Freedom and Culture.* Englewood Cliffs, N.J.: Prentice Hall, 1959.

Lee, Rex E. *A Lawyer Looks at the Equal Rights Amendment.* Provo, Utah: Brigham Young University Press, 1980.

Lee, Sharon M. "Asian Americans: Diverse and Growing." *Population Bulletin, 53,* 2, June 1998:1–39.

Leighty, Keith E. "Germ Testing by Japanese Killed POWs." Associated Press, October 31, 1981.

Leinwand, Donna. "Judges Write Creative Sentences." *USA Today,* February 24, 2004.

Leland, John. "A New Harlem Gentry in Search of Its Latte." *New York Times,* August 7, 2003.

Lender, Mark Edward, and James Kirby Martin. *Drinking in America: A History.* New York: Free Press, 1982.

Lenz-Romeiss, Felizitas. *The City: New Town or Home Town?* Edith Kustner and J. A. Underwood, trans. New York: Praeger, 1973.

Leonard, Rebecca, and Don C. Locke. "Communication Stereotypes: Is Interracial Communication Possible?" *Journal of Black Studies, 23,* 3, March 1993:332–343.

Lerner, Gerda. *The Creation of Patriarchy.* New York: Oxford University Press, 1986.

Lerner, Robert, Althea K. Nagai, and Stanley Rothman. "Abortion and Social Change in America." *Society, 2,* 27, January–February 1990:8–15.

Lesser, Alexander. "War and the State." *In War: The Anthropology of Armed Conflict and Aggression,* Morton Fried, Marvin Harris, and Robert Murphy, eds. Garden City, N.Y.: Natural History, 1968.

Lester, David. "Incest." *Journal of Sex Research, 8,* November 1972: 268–285.

Leuchtag, Alice. "Human Rights, Sex Trafficking, and Prostitution." In *Social Problems,* 32nd ed., Kurt Pinsterbusch, ed. New York: McGraw-Hill/Dushkin, 2004:88–93.

LeVay, Simon. *The Sexual Brain.* Cambridge, Mass.: MIT Press, 1993.

Levine, Art. "Drug Education Gets an F." *U.S. News & World Report,* October 13, 1986:63–64.

Levine, Joseph W. "National Educators Meet to Discuss Success of Small Public School in New York's *El Barrio.*" *Siempre,* December 16, 2004.

Levine, Samantha. "Who'll Stop the Mercury Rain?" *U.S. News & World Report,* April 5, 2004.

Lewin, Tamar. "1 in 8 Boys of High-School Age Has Been Abused, Survey Says." *New York Times,* June 26, 1998.

Lewis, David L. "Bias in Drug Sentences." *National Law Journal,* February 5, 1996.

Lewis, Jack. "The Ogallala Aquifer: An Underground Sea." *EPA Journal, 16,* 6, November 1990:42–44.

Lewis, Karen J. "Abortion: Judicial Control." Washington, D.C.: Congressional Research Service, American Law Division. Mimeo. September 13, 1988.

Lewis, Oscar. "The Culture of Poverty." *Scientific American, 115,* October 1966:19–25.

Lewis, Oscar. *Five Families.* New York: Basic Books, 1959.

Lewis, Peter W., and Kenneth D. Peoples. *The Supreme Court and the Criminal Process: Cases and Comments.* Philadelphia: Saunders, 1978.

Liazos, Alex. "Corporate Crime and Capitalism." Paper presented at the annual meeting of the Society for the Study of Social Problems, 1981.

Light, Donald W., Jr. "Perestroika for Russian Health Care." *Footnotes, 20,* 3, March 1992:7, 9.

Light, Donald W., Jr. "Treating Suicide: The Illusions of a Professional Movement." *International Social Science Journal, 25,* 1973:473–488.

Lightfoot-Klein, H. "Rites of Purification and Their Effects: Some Psychological Aspects of Female Genital Circumcision and Infibulation (Pharaonic Circumcision) in an Afro-Arab Society (Sudan)." *Journal of Psychological Human Sexuality, 2,* 1989: 61–78.

Linden, Eugene. "Lost Tribes, Lost Knowledge." *Time,* September 23, 1991:46, 48, 50, 52, 54, 56.

Lindner, Katharina. "Images of Women in General Interest and Fashion Magazine Advertisements from 1955 to 2002." *Sex Roles, 51,* 7/8, October 2004:409–421.

Linton, Ralph. *The Study of Man.* New York: Appleton, 1936.

Linz, Daniel, Edward Donnerstein, and Steven Penrod. "The Findings and Recommendations of the Attorney General's Commission on Pornography: Do the Psychological 'Facts' Fit the Political Fury?" *American Psychologist,* October 1987: 946–953.

Liptak, Adam. "Ex-Inmate's Suit Offers View into Sexual Slavery in Prisons." *New York Times,* October 16, 2004.

Liptak, Adam. "Kansas Law on Gay Sex by Teenagers Overturned." *New York Times,* October 22, 2005.

Little, Peter D., and Michael M. Horowitz (eds.). *Lands at Risk in the Third World: Local-Level Perspectives.* Boulder, Colo.: Westview, 1987.

Littleton, Heather, and Carmen Radecki Breitkopf. "Coping with the Experience of Rape." *Psychology of Women Quarterly, 30,* 2006: 106–116.

Liu, Yuanli. "China's Public Health-Care System: Facing the Challenges." *Bulletin of the World Health Organization, 82,* 7, July 2004:532–538.

Livernash, Robert, and Eric Rodenburg. "Population Change, Resources, and the Environment." *Population Bulletin, 53,* 1, March, 1998:1–40.

Lloyd, Jane. "The Link Between Environment and Disease." *UN Chronicle,* 1, 2006.

Locy, Toni, and Joan Biskupic. "Anti-Porn Filters in Libraries Upheld." *USA Today,* June 23, 2003.

Lohn, Martiga. "Minnesota May Expand Meth Boot Camp Program." Associated Press, February 17, 2005.

Lombroso, Cesare. *Crime: Its Causes and Remedies,* H. P. Horton, trans. Boston: Little, Brown, 1911.

Lopez, Adalberto, ed. *The Puerto Ricans: Their History, Culture, and Society.* Cambridge, Mass.: Schenkman, 1980.

Lorber, Judith. "Beyond Equality of the Sexes: The Question of Children." In *Marriage and Family in a Changing Society,* James M. Henslin, ed. New York: Free Press, 1980:522–533.

Lorenz, Konrad. *On Aggression.* New York: Harcourt, 1966.

Loven, Jennifer. "Religious Charities Get More Money." Associated Press, March 9, 2006.

Lowenstein, Sophie Freud. "Understanding Lesbian Women." *Social Casework, 61,* January 1980:29–38.

Lowi, Theodore J. "Machine Politics—Old and New." In *City Scenes: Problems and Prospects,* J. John Palen, ed. Boston: Little, Brown, 1977.

Lucas, Ann M. "The Work of Sex Work: Elite Prostitutes' Vocational Orientations and Experiences." *Deviant Behavior, 26,* 2005: 513–546.

Luckenbill, David F. "Deviant Career Mobility: The Case of Male Prostitutes." *Social Problems 33,* 4, April 1986:283–296.

Luker, Kristen. *Taking Chances: Abortion and the Decision Not to Contracept.* Berkeley: University of California Press, 1975.

Lundberg, Ollie. "Causal Explanations for Class Inequality in Health: An Empirical Analysis." *Social Science and Medicine, 32,* 4, 1991:385–393.

Lutz, Harold J. *Aboriginal Man and White Man as Historical Causes of Fires in the Boreal Forest, with Particular Reference to Alaska.* New Haven, Conn.: Yale University School of Forestry. No. 65, 1959 [as referenced in Burch 1971].

Luy, Mary Lynn M. "Rape: Not a Sex Act—A Violent Crime, An Interview with Dr. Dorothy J. Hicks." *Modern Medicine.* February 15, 1977:36–41.

Lynch, Mitchell C. "Old Ice Indicates Acid Was Present in Rain Long Ago." *Wall Street Journal,* September 18, 1980:13.

Lynd, Robert S., and Helen M. Lynd. *Middletown.* New York: Harcourt, 1929.

Lynd, Robert S., and Helen M Lynd. *Middletown in Transition.* New York: Harcourt, 1937.

Mackellar, Landis, and David Horlacher. "Population Ageing in Japan: A Brief Survey." *The European Journal of Social Sciences, 13,* 4, December 2000.

MacKenzie, Doris Layton, and Claire Souryal. "Inmate Attitude Change During Incarceration: A Comparison of Boot Camp With Traditional Prison." *Justice Quarterly, 12,* 2 1995.

MacKinnon, Catharine A. *Sexual Harassment of Working Women: A Case of Sex Discrimination.* New Haven, Conn.: Yale University Press, 1979.

MacNamara, Donal E. J., and Edward Sagarin. *Sex, Crime, and the Law.* New York: Free Press. 1977.

Madigan, Lee, and Nancy Gamble. *The Second Rape: Society's Continued Betrayal of the Victim.* New York: Free Press, 1991.

Magee, Elizabeth A., Laurie M. Edmond, Shiona M. Tasker, San Choon Kong, Richard Curno, and John H. Cummings. "Associations Between Diet and Disease Activity in Ulcerative Colitis." *Nutrition Journal, 4,* 7, February 10, 2005.

Mahran, M. "Medical Dangers of Female Circumcision." *International Planned Parenthood Federation Medical Bulletin, 2,* 1981:1–2.

Mahran, M. Proceedings of the Third International Congress of Medical Sexology. Littleton, Mass.: PSG, 1978.

Malamuth, Neil M., Tamara Addison, and Mary Koss. "Pornography and Sexual Aggression: Are There Reliable Effects and Can We Understand Them?" *Annual Review of Sex Research, 11,* 2000: 26–91.

Malthus, Thomas Robert. *First Essay on Population.* London: Macmillan, 1926 (originally published in 1798).

Mamdani, Mahmood. *The Myth of Population Control: Family, Caste, and Class in an Indian Village.* New York: Monthly Review, 1973 [as contained in Simon 1981].

Mandel-Campbell, Andrea. "A Breath of Fresh(er) Air." *U.S. News & World Report,* June 25, 2001.

Manpower Report to the President. Washington, D.C.: U.S. Department of Labor, Manpower Administration, April 1971.

Manski, Charles F. "Income and Higher Education." *Focus, 14,* 3, Winter 1992–93:14–19.

Marger, Martin N. *Elites and Masses: An Introduction to Political Sociology,* 2nd ed. Belmont, Calif.: Wadsworth, 1987.

Martin, Paul Schultz. "Prehistoric Overkill." In *Pleistocene Extinctions: The Search for a Cause,* Paul Schultz Martin and H. E. Wright, Jr., eds. New Haven, Conn.: Yale University Press, 1967.

Martin, Philip, and Elizabeth Midgley. "Immigration to the United States." *Population Bulletin, 54,* 2, June 1999:1–43.

Martinez, Juan Francisco Esteva. "Urban Street Activists: Gang and Community Efforts to Bring Peace and Justice to Los Angeles Neighborhoods." In *Gangs and Society: Alternative Perspectives,* Louis Kontos, David Brotherton, and Luis Barrios, eds. New York: Columbia University Press, 2003:95–115.

Marx, Karl, and Friedrich Engels. *Capital: A Critique of Political Economy,* E. Aveling, trans. Chicago: Charles Kerr, 1906.

Marx, Karl, and Friedrich Engels. *The Communist Manifesto,* S. Moore, trans. New York: Washington Square, 1964 (originally published in 1848).

Marx, Karl. *Das Kapital.* New York: International, 1967 (originally published in 1867–1895).

Massey, Douglas S. As quoted in *Footnotes,* September/October 2001:6.

Masters, William, and Virginia Johnson. *Homosexuality in Perspective.* Boston: Little, Brown, 1979.

Mauer, Marc. "Race, Class, and the Development of Criminal Justice Policy." *Review of Policy Research, 21,* 1, 2004:79–92.

Maynard, Douglas W. *Inside Plea Bargaining: The Language of Negotiation.* New York: Plenum, 1984.

Mayne, Susan Taylor, Dwight T. Janerich, Peter Greenwald, Sherry Chorost, Cathy Tucci, Muhammad B. Zaman, Myron R. Melamed, Maureen Kiely, and Martin F. McKneally. "Dietary Beta Carotene and Lung Cancer Risk in U.S. Nonsmokers." *Journal of the National Cancer Institute, 86,* 1, January 5, 1995: 33–38.

McCain, Chiree. "The Pros of Preventing Cons." *Business First of Columbus,* June 25, 2004.

McCarthy, Bill, and John Hagan. "Mean Streets: The Theoretical Significance of Situational Delinquency Among Homeless Youths." *American Journal of Sociology, 98,* 3, November 1992:597–627.

McCool, Craig. "More Contamination Found at Bay Harbor." *Traverse City Record Eagle,* April 29, 2006.

McCormick, John. "Change Has Taken Place." *Newsweek,* June 7, 1999:34.

McCurley, Carl, and Howard N. Snyder. "Risk, Protection, and Family Structure." *Juvenile Justice Bulletin,* forthcoming.

McDonald, Peter. "Low Fertility Not Politically Sustainable." *Population Today,* August–September 2001:3, 8.

McDowell, Bart. "Mexico City: An Alarming Giant." *National Geographic, 166,* 1984:139–174.

McFarling, Usha Lee. "Climate is Warming at Steep Rate, Study Says." *Los Angeles Times,* February 23, 2000.

McGarigle, Bill. "Satellite Tracking for House Arrest." *Geo Info,* May 1997.

McGinley, Laurie. "Health-Care Debate Heats Up Over Control of Medical Decisions." *Wall Street Journal,* February 18, 1999.

McGinty, Jo Craven. "New York Killers, and Those Killed, by Numbers." *New York Times, April 28, 2006.*

McIntyre, Jennie, Thelma Myint, and Lynn Curtis. "Sexual Assault Outcomes: Completed and Attempted Rapes." Paper presented at the annual meeting of the American Sociological Association. Boston, 1979.

McKeown, Thomas. *The Modern Rise of Population.* New York: Academic Press, 1977.

McKeown, Thomas. *The Role of Medicine: Dream, Mirage, or Nemesis?* Princeton, N.J.: Princeton University Press, 1980.

McKinley, James C., Jr. "Mexico: Grisly Message from Drug Gang." *New York Times,* October 30, 2006a.

McKinley, James C., Jr., "With Beheadings and Attacks, Drug Gangs Terrorize Mexico." *New York Times,* October 26, 2006b.

McKinley, James C., Jr., and Marc Lacey. "Mexico's Drug War Brings New Brutality." *New York Times,* October 25, 2006.

McManus, Michael J. "Introduction." In *Final Report of the Attorney General's Commission on Pornography.* Nashville, Tenn.: Rutledge Hill, 1986:ix–l.

McNeely, R. L., and Carl E. Pope. "Socioeconomic and Racial Issues in the Measurement of Criminal Involvement." In *Race, Crime, and Criminal Justice,* R. L. McNeely and Carl E. Pope, eds. Beverly Hills, Calif.: Sage, 1981:31–47.

Meese Commission. *Final Report of the Attorney General's Commission on Pornography.* Washington, D.C.: U.S. Department of Justice, 1986.

Meier, Barry. "As Food Imports Rise, Consumers Face Peril from Use of Pesticides," *Wall Street Journal,* March 26, 1987.

Melloan, George. "Europe Struggles with the Burdens of Old Age." *Wall Street Journal,* December 12, 1994:A15.

Melman, Seymour. *Pentagon Capitalism.* New York: McGraw-Hill, 1970.

Melody, G. F. "Chronic Pelvic Congestion in Prostitutes." *Medical Aspects of Human Sexuality, 3,* November 1969:103–104.

Mendels, Pamela. "Judge Rules Against Filters at Library." *New York Times,* November 23, 1998.

Merton, Robert K. *Social Theory and Social Structure,* enlarged ed. New York: Free Press, 1968.

Merton, Robert K., and Robert Nisbet (eds.). *Contemporary Social Problems,* 4th ed. New York: Harcourt, 1976.

Merwine, Maynard H. "How Africa Understands Female Circumcision." *New York Times,* November 24, 1993.

Messner, Michael A., Margaret Carlisle Duncan, and Cheryl Cooky. "Silence, Sports Bras, and Wrestling Porn." *Journal of Sport and Social Issues, 27,* 1, February 2003:38–51.

Meyer, H. *Old English Coffee Houses.* Emmaus, Pa.: Rodale, 1954.

Miall, Charlene E. "The Stigma of Involuntary Childlessness." *Social Problems, 33,* 4, April 1986:268–282.

Michelman, Kate. As quoted in "NARAL," pamphlet published by the National Abortion Rights Action League, 1988:1.

Milbank, Dana. "In His Solitude, A Finnish Thinker Posits Cataclysms." *Wall Street Journal,* May 20, 1994:A1, A8.

Miles, Steven. "Intellectualism Meant Death in Cambodia." *St. Louis Post-Dispatch,* April 8, 1980:D3.

Miller, Judith. "U.S. and Uzbeks Agree on Chemical Arms Plant Cleanup." *New York Times,* May 25, 1999.

Miller, Judith, and William J. Broad. "Clinton Describes Terrorism Threat for 21st Century." *New York Times,* January 22, 1999.

Miller, Laura L. "Women in the Military." In *Down-to-Earth Sociology: Introductory Readings,* 14th ed., James M. Henslin, ed. New York: Free Press, 2007.

Miller, Michael W. "Quality Stuff: Firm Is Peddling Cocaine, and Deals Are Legit." *Wall Street Journal,* October 27, 1994:A1, A8.

Miller, Walter B. "Lower-Class Culture as a Generating Milieu of Gang Delinquency." *Journal of Social Issues, 14,* 1958:5–19.

Millett, Kate. *The Prostitution Papers: A Candid Dialogue.* New York: Avon, 1973.

Millett, Kate. *Sexual Politics.* Garden City, N.Y.: Doubleday, 1970.

Mills, C. Wright. *The Causes of World War Three.* New York: Simon & Schuster, 1958.

Mills, C. Wright. *The Power Elite.* New York: Oxford University Press, 1959a.

Mills, C. Wright. *The Sociological Imagination.* New York: Oxford University Press, 1959b.

Mills, Karen M., and Thomas J. Palumbo. *A Statistical Portrait of Women in the United States: 1978.* Washington, D.C.: U.S. Government Printing Office, 1980.

Milner, Christina, and Richard Milner. *Black Players.* Boston: Little Brown, 1972.

Milvy, Paul. "Cancer from the Radiation." *New York Times,* April 12, 1979:19.

Mintz, Morton. "Error Placed H-Bomb Secrets on Library Shelf." *St. Louis Globe-Democrat,* May 18, 1979:5a.

Moffitt, Robert A. "The Idea of a Negative Income Tax: Past, Present, and Future." *Focus, 23,* 2, Summer 2004.

Mokdad A. H., J. S. Marks, D. F. Stroup, and J. L. Gerberding. "Actual Causes of Death in the United States." *Journal of the American Medical Association, 291,* 2004:1238–1245.

Mokhiber, Russell, and Leonard Shen. "Love Canal." In *Who's Poisoning America: Corporate Polluters and Their Victims in the Chemical Age,* Ralph Nader, Ronald Brownstein, and John Richard, eds. San Francisco: Sierra Club Books, 1981:268–310.

Montagu, M. F. Ashley. *The Concept of Race.* New York: Free Press, 1964.

Monto, Martin A. "Female Prostitution, Customers, and Violence." *Violence Against Women, 10,* 2, February 2004:160–188.

Moore, Brent A., Erik M. Augustson, Richard P. Moser, and Alan J. Budney. "Respiratory Effects of Marijuana and Tobacco Use in a U.S. Sample." *Journal of General Internal Medicine, 20,* 2004: 33–37.

Moore, Gwen. "The Structure of a National Elite Network." *American Sociological Review, 44,* October 1979:673–691.

Moore, Joan W. *Homeboys: Gangs, Drugs, and Prison in the Barrios of Los Angeles.* Philadelphia: Temple University Press, 1978.

Morash, Merry A., and Etta A. Anderson. "Liberal Thinking on Rehabilitation: A Work-Able Solution to Crime." *Social Problems, 25,* June 1978:556–563.

Morash, Merry, and Lila Rucker. "A Critical Look at the Idea of Boot Camp as a Correctional Reform." *Crime and Delinquency, 36,* 2, April 1990:204–222.

Morgan, Patricia A. "The Legislation of Drug Law: Economic Crisis and Social Control." *Journal of Drug Issues, 8,* Winter 1978: 54–62.

Morrison, Denton E., Kenneth E. Hornback, and W. Keith Warner. "The Environmental Movement: Some Preliminary Observations and Predictions." In *Social Behavior, Natural Resources, and the Environment,* William R. Burch, Jr., Neil H. Cheek, Jr., and Lee Taylor, eds. New York: Harper & Row, 1972:259–279.

Mosher, Steven W. "Why Are Baby Girls Being Killed in China?" *Wall Street Journal,* July 25, 1983:9.

Mukamal, Kenneth J., Hyoju Chung, Nancy S. Jenny, Lewis H. Kuller, W. T. Longstreth, Jr., Murray A. Mittleman, Gregory L. Burke, Mary Cushman, Bruce M. Psaty, and David S. Siscovick. "Alcohol Consumption and Risk of Coronary Heart Disease in Older Adults: The Cardiovascular Health Study." *Journal of the American Geriatrics Society, 54,* 2006:30–37.

Mulvihill, Donald J., Melvin M. Tumin, and Lynn A. Curtis. *Crimes of Violence: A Staff Report to the National Commission on the Causes and Prevention of Violence.* Washington, D.C.: U.S. Government Printing Office, 1969.

Murphy, Kim. "Last Stand of an Aging Aryan." *Los Angeles Times,* January 10, 1999.

Murphy, Tom. "Hybrids, FCVs, Oddities Abound." *Ward's Auto World,* December 1, 2003.

Murray, Charles. "A Plan to Replace the Welfare State." *Focus, 24,* 2, Spring–Summer 2006:1–4.

Murray, Christopher J. L., Sabdeep C. Kulkarni, and Majid Ezzati. "Eight Americas: Investigating Mortality Disparities Across Races and Counties in the United States." *PLoS Medicine,* September 2006.

Murray, Rosie. "First Death, Then Shag." *Business Telegraph.* February 1, 2004.

Mydans, Seth. "Bullets and Crayons: Children Learn Lessons of the 90s." *New York Times,* June 16, 1991:14.

Myers, Martha A., and Susette M. Talarico. "The Social Contexts of Racial Discrimination in Sentencing." *Social Problems, 33,* 3, February 1986:236–251.

Myrdal, Gunnar. *An American Dilemma.* New York: Harper, 1944.

Naj, Amal Kumar. "Kuwait Oil-Well Fires Did Little Damage to the Global Environment, Study Says." *Wall Street Journal,* May 15, 1992:B5.

Nash, Gary B. *The Urban Crucible.* Cambridge, Mass.: Harvard University Press, 1979.

National Conference of State Legislatures. Women's Legislative Network of NCSL. www.ncsl.org.

"National Strategy for Combatting Terrorism." Washington, D.C.: The White House, September 2006.

National Women's Political Caucus. "News & Opinions: 1998 Election Results." November 5, 1998.

Neergaard, Lauran. "Strong Tainted Food Warnings Urged." Associated Press, December 31, 1998.

Nelan, Bruce W. "Sudan: Why Is This Happening Again?" *Time,* July 27, 1998:29–32.

Nettler, Gwynn. "Embezzlement Without Problems." *British Journal of Criminology, 14,* January 1974:70–77.

Nettler, Gwynn. *Social Concerns.* New York: McGraw-Hill, 1976.

Newdorf, David. "Bailout Agencies Like to Do it in Secret." *Washington Journalism Review, 13,* 4, May 1991:15–16.

Newman, Donald J. *Conviction: The Determination of Guilt or Innocence Without Trial.* Boston: Little, Brown, 1966.

Newman, Dorothy K., Nancy J. Amidei, Barbara L. Cater, Dawn Day, William J. Kruvant, and Jack S. Russell. *Protest, Politics, and Prosperity: Black Americans and White Institutions, 1940–1975.* New York: Pantheon, 1978.

1969 Handbook on Women Workers. Washington, D.C.: U.S. Department of Labor, Woman's Bureau, 1969.

Nishio, Harry Kaneharu. "Japan's Welfare Vision: Dealing with a Rapidly Increasing Elderly Population." In *The Graying of the World: Who Will Care for the Frail Elderly?* New York: Haworth, 1994:233–260.

NOAA. "Has Prince William Sound Recovered from the Spill?" National Ocean Service, Office of Response and Restoration, October 2006.

Norris, Robert S., and Hans M. Kristensen. "India's Nuclear Forces, 2005." *Bulletin of the Atomic Scientists, 61,* 5, September/ October 2005:73–75.

North, Andrew. "Following the Afghan Drugs Trail." BBC News, November 18, 2004.

Nucleus: A Report to Union of Concerned Scientists Sponsors, 3, Spring–Summer 1981.

Nuland, Sherwin. "The Debate over Dying." *USA Weekend,* February 3–5, 1995:4–6.

Nurge, Dana. "Liberating Yet Limiting: The Paradox of Female Gang Membership." In *Gangs and Society: Alternative Perspectives,* Louis Kontos, David Brotherton, and Luis Barrios, eds. New York: Columbia University Press, 2003:161–182.

Oakley, Robert B. "Combating International Terrorism." *Department of State Bulletin,* June 1985:73–78.

O'Connell, Pamela Licalzi. "Web Erotica Aims for New Female Customers." *New York Times,* August 13, 1998.

"Of Birds and Bacteria." *Consumer Reports,* January 2003.

O'Hare, William P. "America's Minorities: The Demographics of Diversity." *Population Bulletin, 47,* 4, December 1992:1–47.

Oliver, Melvin L., and Thomas M. Shapiro. *Black Wealth/White Wealth: A New Perspective on Racial Inequality.* New York: Routledge, 1995.

Olivo, Antonio. "Doctor Shortage Severe in Poor Areas." *Los Angeles Times,* April 19, 1999.

Olshansky, S. Jay, Douglas J. Passar, Ronald C. Hershow, et al. "A Potential Decline in Life Expectancy in the United States in the 21st Century." *New England Journal of Medicine, 352,* 11, March 17, 2005:1138–1145.

Olson, James S., Mark Baxter, Jason M. Tetzloff, and Darren Pierson. *Encyclopedia of American Indian Civil Rights.* Westport, Conn.: Greenwood Press, 1997.

Olson, Walter K. "Give It Back to the Indians?" *City Journal,* Autumn 2002.

Onion, Amanda. "Getting Better . . . Virtually." ABC News online, July 7, 2004.

Organized Crime: Report of the Task Force on Organized Crime. Washington, D.C.: National Advisory Committee on Criminal Justice Standards and Goals, 1976.

Osborne, Lawrence. "Got Silk?" *New York Times Magazine,* June 15, 2002.

Oster, Shai, and Jane Spencer. "A Poison Spreads amid China's Boom." *New York Times,* September 30, 2006.

Otten, Alan L. "People Patterns." *Wall Street Journal,* January 27, 1995:B1.

Ozturk, M., H. Ozcelik, S. Sakcali, and A. Guvensen. "Land Degradation Problems in the Euphrates Basin, Turkey." *International Society of Environmental Botanists, 10,* July 2004:1–5.

Paddock, Richard C. "Patient Deaths Point to Depth of Russian Crisis." *Los Angeles Times,* March 13, 1999.

Pagelow, Mildred Daley. "Protecting the Fetus From Its Mom: A New Form of Social Control." Paper presented at the annual meeting of the Society for the Study of Social Problems, 1992.

Palen, J. John. *The Urban World,* 7th ed. New York: McGraw-Hill, 2005.

Pamuck, Elsie. A study for the National Centre for Health Statistics, as reported in America Online, "Rich Get Richer, Poor Get Sicker in U.S." July 30, 1998.

Park, Robert E. "The Social Function of War." *American Journal of Sociology, 46,* January 1941:551–570.

Parmesan, Camille, and Gary Yohe. "A Globally Coherent Fingerprint of Climate Change Impacts Across Natural Systems." *Nature,* January 2003:37–42.

Partington, Donald H. "The Incidence of the Death Penalty for Rape in Virginia." *Washington and Lee Law Review, 22,* 1965:43–75.

Passel, Jeffrey S. "Unauthorized Migrants: Numbers and Characteristics." Washington, D.C.: Pew Hispanic Center, June 14, 2005.

Passell, Peter. "Race, Mortgages and Statistics." *New York Times,* May 10, 1996:D1, D4.

Pattis, Norm. "A Plea on Plea Bargains: Don't Tie Hands of Justice." *Connecticut Law Tribune,* October 17, 2005.

Paul, Bill. "Cogeneration Is Rapidly Coming of Age." *Wall Street Journal,* March 2, 1987:6.

Paul, Pamela. *Pornified: How Pornography Is Transforming Our Lives, Our Relationships, and Our Families.* New York: Henry Holt, 2005.

Pearse, Peter H. "The Environment Revisited." *Au Courant, 7,* Winter 1987:7.

Peele, Stanton. "The Addiction Experience." In *Social Problems: A Critical Thinking Approach,* Paul J. Baker and Louis E. Anderson, eds. Belmont, Calif.: Wadsworth, 1987:210–218.

Penn, Stanley. "How Public Defenders Deal with the Pressure of the Crowded Courts." *Wall Street Journal,* July 5, 1985:1, 22.

Penn, Stanley. "Organized Crime Finds Rich Pickings in Rise of Union Health Plans." *Wall Street Journal,* October 5, 1982:1, 26.

Peplau, Letitia Anne, and Hortensia Amaro. "Understanding Lesbian Relationships." In *Homosexuality: Social, Psychological and Biological Issues,* William Paul, James D. Weinrich, John C. Gonsiorek, and Mary E. Hotvedt, eds. Beverly Hills, Calif.: Sage, 1982:233–247.

Pereira, Joseph. "Toys 'R' Us Decides to Pull Night Trap from Store Shelves." *Wall Street Journal,* December 17, 1993:A9A.

Pereira, Luiz Alberto Amador, Conceição de Sousa, Margarete Gleice, and Alfesio L. F. Braga. "Cardiovascular Effects of Air Pollution in Adults in Cubatao, Sao Paulo, Brazil." *Epidemiology, 15,* 4, July 2004:S21.

Persell, Caroline Hodges, and Peter W. Cookson, Jr. "Where the Power Starts." *Signature,* August 1985:51–57.

Persell, Caroline Hodges, Sophia Catsambis, and Peter W. Cookson, Jr. "Family Background, School Type, and College Attendance: A Conjoint System of Cultural Capital Transmission." *Journal of Research on Adolescence, 2,* 1, 1992:1–23.

Pestka, Elizabeth L. "Genetic Counseling for Mental Health Disorders." *Journal of the American Psychiatric Nurses Association, 11,* 6, 2006:338–343.

Petersilia, Joan. *Racial Disparities in the Criminal Justice System.* Santa Monica, Calif.: Rand, June 1983.

Peterson, Iver. "1993 Deal for Indian Casino Is Called a Model to Avoid." *New York Times,* June 30, 2003.

Pettigrew, Thomas. "How the People Really Feel." *The Center Magazine, 9,* January–February 1976:35.

Phelps, Orme Wheelock. *The Legislative Background of the Fair Labor Standards Act: A Study of the Growth of National Sentiment in Favor of Government Regulation of Wages, Hours, and Child Labor.* Chicago: University of Chicago Press, 1939.

"Physicians and Surgeons." *Occupational Outlook Handbook.* U.S. Department of Labor, Bureau of Labor Statistics, 2006.

Piliavin, Irving, and Scott Briar. "Police Encounters with Juveniles." *American Journal of Sociology, 70,* September 1964:206–214.

Pillemer, Karl, and David W. Moore. "Abuse of Patients in Nursing Homes: Findings from a Survey of Staff." *The Gerontologist, 29,* 3, 1989:314–320.

Piotrow, Phylis Tilson. *World Population Crisis: The United States' Response.* New York: Praeger, 1973.

Pittman, David J. "The Male House of Prostitution." *Transaction, 8,* March–April 1971:21–27.

Piven, Frances Fox, and Richard A. Cloward. *The Breaking of the American Social Compact.* New York: New Press, 1997.

Piven, Frances Fox, and Richard A. Cloward. *The New Class War: Reagan's Attack on the Welfare State and Its Consequences.* New York: Pantheon, 1982.

Piven, Frances Fox, and Richard A. Cloward. *Poor People's Movements: Why They Succeed, How They Fail.* New York: Pantheon, 1977.

Piven, Frances Fox, and Richard A. Cloward. *Regulating the Poor.* New York: Vintage, 1971.

Piven, Frances Fox, and Richard A. Cloward. *Why Americans Don't Vote.* New York: Random House, 1989.

Platt, Anthony M. *The Child Savers.* Chicago: University of Chicago Press, 1979.

Polgreen, Lydia, and Marlise Simons. "Global Sludge Ends in Tragedy for Ivory Coast." *New York Times,* October 2, 2006.

Pollack, Andrew. "U.N. Unit Sees Great Promise in Biotech Research on Crops." *New York Times,* May 18, 2004.

Pollay, Richard W. "Hacks, Flacks, and Counter-Attacks: Cigarette Advertising, Sponsored Research, and Controversy." *Journal of Social Issues, 53,* 1, 1997:43–74.

Pope, Carl E. "The Family, Delinquency, and Crime." In *Mental Illness, Delinquency, Addictions, and Neglect,* Elam W. Nunnally, Catherine S. Chilman, and Fred M. Cox, eds. Newbury Park, Calif.: Sage, 1988:108–127.

Potterat, John J., Donald E. Woodhouse, John B. Muth, and Stephen Q. Muth. "Estimating the Prevalence and Career Longevity of Prostitute Women." *Journal of Sex Research, 27,* 2, May 1990: 233–243.

Pozdena, Randall J., and Terry R. Johnson. *Income Maintenance and Asset Demand.* Menlo Park, Calif.: SRI International, March, 1979.

Preidt, Robert. "Smoking Claimed 5 Million Lives in 2000." *HealthDay,* September 11, 2003a.

Preidt, Robert. "Tobacco Companies Target Women in Developing Countries." *HealthDay,* August 7, 2003b.

Prescott, Carol A. *Alcoholism: Clinical and Experimental Research,* January 2004.

Price, Daniel O., ed. *The 99th Hour.* Chapel Hill: University of North Carolina Press, 1967 [as contained in Simon 1981].

"The Price of Success." *Economist, 371,* 8371, April 17, 2004.

Pridemore, William Alex, and Joshua D. Freilich. "A Test of Recent Subcultural Explanations of White Violence in the United States." *Journal of Criminal Justice, 34,* 2006:1–16.

Pruitt, Dean G., and Richard C. Snyder. "Motives and Perceptions Underlying Entry into War." In *Theory and Research on the Causes of War,* Dean G. Pruitt and Richard C. Synder, eds. Englewood Cliffs, N.J.: Prentice Hall, 1969.

Prus, Robert, and Styllianoss Irini. *Hookers, Rounders, and Desk Clerks: The Social Organization of the Hotel Community.* Salem, Wis.: Sheffield, 1988.

Public Health, Seattle and King County. "Gay, Lesbian, Bisexual and Transgender Health." February 1, 2002.

Ra'anan, Uri, Robert L. Pfaltzgraff, Jr., Richard H. Shultz, Ernst Halperin, and Igor Lukes, eds. *Hydra of Carnage: The International Linkages of Terrorism and Other Low-Intensity Operations, The Witnesses Speak.* Lexington, Ky.: Lexington Books, 1986.

Rabinovitz, Jonathan. "For Sale: Used Nuclear Reactor." *New York Times,* July 7, 1998.

Rabinowitz, Dorothy. *No Crueler Tyrannies: Accusation, False Witness, and Other Terrors of Our Times.* New York: Simon & Schuster, 2004.

Raghunathan, V. K. "Millions of Baby Girls Killed in India." *The Straits Times,* February 8, 2003.

Rahman, Qazi. "The Neurodevelopment of Human Sexual Orientation." *Neuroscience and Biobehavioral Reviews, 29,* 2005: 1057–1066.

Rakow, Lana F. "'Don't Hate Me Because I'm Beautiful': Feminist Resistance to Advertising's Irresistible Meanings." *Southern Communication Journal, 57,* 2, Winter 1992:132–142.

Raloff, Janet. "The Colloid Threat." *Science News, 137,* 11, March 17, 1990:169–170.

Ramaekers, J. G., G. Berghaus, M. van Laar, and O. H. Drummer. "Dose Related Risk of Motor Vehicle Crashes After Cannabis Use." *Drug and Alcohol Dependence, 73,* 2004:109–119.

Ramo, Alan. "The Environmental Justice Clinic at the Golden Gate University School of Law." *Human Rights, 30,* 4, Fall 2003:6.

"Rates of Cesarean Delivery Among Puerto Rican Women—Puerto Rico and the U.S. Mainland, 1992–2002." *Journal of the American Medical Association, 295,* 2006:1369–1371.

Ray, Oakley S. *Drugs, Society, and Human Behavior,* 8th ed. New York: McGraw-Hill, 1998.

Ray, Oakley, and Charles J. Ksir. *Drugs, Society, and Human Behavior,* 10th ed. New York: McGraw-Hill, 2004.

Reasons, Charles E., ed. *The Criminologist: Crime and the Criminal.* Pacific Palisades, Calif.: Goodyear, 1974.

Reay, Diane, Jacqueline Davies, Miriam David, and Stephen J. Ball. "Choice of Degrees or Degrees of Choice? Class, 'Race,' and the Higher Education Choice Process." *Sociology, 35,* 4, November 2001:855–876.

Reckless, Walter C. *The Crime Problem,* 5th ed. New York: Appleton, 1973.

Redlich, Fritz, and Stephen R. Kellert. "Trends in American Mental Health." *American Journal of Psychiatry, 135,* January 1978: 22–28.

Reed, Terry, and John Cummings. *Compromised: Clinton, Bush, and the CIA.* Kew Gardens, New York: Clandestine Publishing, 1994.

Reeves, Terrance, and Claudette Bennett. "The Asian and Pacific Islander Population in the United States: March 2002." *Current Population Reports,* 2003.

Regaldo, Antonio. "When a Plant Emerges From Melting Glacier, Is It Global Warming?" *Wall Street Journal,* October 22, 2004:B1.

Rehm, Jurgen, Gerhard Gmel, Christopher T. Sempos, and Maurizio Trevisan. "Alcohol-Related Morbidity and Mortality." *Alcohol Research and Health, 27,* 1, 2003:39–51.

Reich, Michael. "The Economic Impact in the Postwar Period." In *Impacts of Racism on White Americans,* Benjamin P. Bowser and Raymond G. Hunt, eds. Beverly Hills, Calif.: Sage, 1981: 165–176.

Reich, Michael. "The Economics of Racism." In *The Capitalist System,* Richard C. Edwards, Michael Reich, and Thomas E. Weiskopf, eds. Englewood Cliffs, N.J.: Prentice Hall, 1972: 313–326.

Reichert, Loren D., and James H. Frey. "The Organization of Bell Desk Prostitution." *Sociology and Social Research, 69,* 4, July 1985:516–526.

Reiss, Albert J. "The Sociological Integration of Queers and Peers." *Social Problems, 9,* Fall 1961:102–120.

Revzin, Philip. "U.S. Claims Progress at Global Meeting Discussing Ban on Chemical Weapons." *Wall Street Journal,* January 9, 1989:A3.

Reynolds, Janice. "The Medical Institution: The Death and Disease-producing Appendage." In *American Society: A Critical Analysis,* Larry T. Reynolds and James M. Henslin, eds. New York: McKay, 1973:198–224.

Reynolds, Janice. "Rape as Social Control." In *Social Problems in American Society,* 2nd ed., James M. Henslin and Larry T. Reynolds, eds. Boston: Holbrook, 1976:79–86.

Richardson, Lewis F. *Statistics of Deadly Quarrels.* Chicago: Quadrangle, 1960.

Riesel, Victor. "Crackdown on Mobsters." Syndicated column, January 16, 1982a.

Riesel, Victor. "Racketeers Infest New Jersey Construction Trade." Syndicated column, January 25, 1982b.

Riesman, David, Nathan Glazer, and Reuel Denney. *The Lonely Crowd: A Study of the Changing American Character.* New Haven, Conn.: Yale University Press, 1951.

Riley, K. Jack. "Crack, Powder Cocaine, and Heroin. Drug Purchase and Use Patterns in Six U.S. Cities." National Institute of Justice, online, December 12, 1998.

Risen, James, and David Johnston. "Bush Has Widened Authority of C.I.A. to Kill Terrorists." *New York Times,* December 15, 2002.

Roach, John. "Rain Forest Plan Blends Drug Research, Conservation." *National Geographic News,* October 7, 2003.

Roberts, Sam. "It's Official: To Be Married Means to Be Outnumbered." *New York Times,* October 15, 2006.

Rockett, Ian R. H. "Population and Health: An Introduction to Epidemiology." *Population Bulletin, 49,* 3, November 1994:1–47.

Rockwell, Don. "Social Problems: Alcohol and Marijuana." *Journal of Psychedelic Drugs, 5,* Fall 1972:49–55.

Roe, Kathleen M. "Private Troubles and Public Issues: Providing Abortion Amid Competing Definitions." *Social Science and Medicine, 29,* 10, 1989:1191–1198.

Roffman, Roger, and Roger S. Stephens, eds. *Cannabis Dependence: Its Nature, Consequences, and Treatment.* Cambridge: Cambridge University Press, 2006.

Rolo, Mark Anthony. "Marked Media." *The Circle.* Online, n.d.

Rosaldo, Michelle Zimbalist. "Women, Culture, and Society: A Theoretical Overview." In *Women, Culture, and Society,* Michelle Zimbalist Rosaldo and Louise Lamphere, eds. Stanford, Calif.: Stanford University Press, 1974.

Rosen, Lawrence, Leonard Savitz, Michael Lalli, and Stanley Turner. "Early Delinquency, High School Graduation, and Adult Criminality." *Sociological Viewpoints, 7,* Fall 1991:37–60.

Rosen, Yereth. "Exxon Valdez Oil Spill of 1989 Crippled Sound, Alaskans Say." Reuters, March 14, 1999.

Rosenberg, Charles E. *The Care of Strangers: The Rise of America's Hospital System.* New York: Basic Books, 1987.

Rosenfeld, Rachel A., and Arne L. Kalleberg. "A Cross-National Comparison of the Gender Gap in Income." *American Journal of Sociology, 96,* 1, July 1990:69–106.

Rosenthal, Elisabeth. "'Virtually Untreatable' TB Raises Fears." *International Herald Tribune,* September 6, 2006.

Rosett, Claudia. "Big Oil-Pipeline Spill in Russia May Be a Sign of Things to Come." *Wall Street Journal,* October 27, 1994:A14.

Rothman, David J. *The Discovery of the Asylum.* Boston: Little, Brown, 1971.

Rothman, David J., and Sheila M. Rothman. *On Their Own.* Reading, Mass.: Addison-Wesley, 1972.

Royko, Mike. *Boss: Richard J. Daly of Chicago.* New York: Dutton, 1971.

Rubenstein, Richard E. *Alchemists of Revolution: Terrorism in the Modern World.* London: I. B. Tauris, 1987.

Rubin, Trudy. "Nuclear 'Supermarket' Another Concern for U.S." *Philadelphia Inquirer,* February 8, 2004.

Ruethling, Gretchen. "27 Charged in International Online Pornography Ring." *New York Times,* March 16, 2006.

Ruggles, Patricia. *Drawing the Line: Alternative Poverty Measures and Their Implication for Public Policy.* Washington, D.C.: Urban Institute, 1990.

Ruggles, Patricia. "Measuring Poverty." *Focus, 14,* 1, Spring 1992: 1–5.

Ruggles, Patricia. *Short and Long Term Poverty in the United States: Measuring the American "Underclass."* Washington, D.C.: Urban Institute, June 1989.

Rumbaut, Ruben G., and John R. Weeks. "Unraveling a Public Health Enigma: Why Do Immigrants Experience Superior Perinatal Health Outcomes?" Paper presented at the annual meeting of the American Public Health Association, 1994.

Russell, Diana E. H. "Rape in Marriage: A Case Against Legalized Crime." Paper presented at the annual meeting of the American Society of Criminology, 1980.

Russell, Diana E. H. *The Secret Trauma: Incest in the Lives of Girls and Women.* New York: Basic Books, 1986.

Sagan, Scott D. "The Perils of Proliferation: Organization Theory, Deterrence Theory, and the Spread of Nuclear Weapons." *International Security, 18,* 4, Spring 1994:66–107.

Sager, Ira, Ben Elgin, Peter Elstrom, Faith Keenan, and Pallavi Gogoi. "The Under Ground Web." *Business Week,* September 2, 2002.

Saguy, Abigail. "Are We Eating Ourselves to Death?" *Contexts,* Spring 2006:11–13.

Sakharov, Andrei. "Text of Sakharov Letter to Carter on Human Rights." *New York Times,* January 29, 1977.

Sanchez Taylor, Jacqueline. "Dollars Are a Girl's Best Friend: Female Tourists' Sexual Behavior in the Caribbean." *Sociology, 35,* 2001: 749–764.

Savitch, H. V., and Ronald K. Vogel. "Suburbs Without a City: Power and City-County Consolidation." *Urban Affairs Review, 39,* 6, July 2004:758–790.

Sawhill, Isabel V. "Poverty in the U.S.: Why Is It So Persistent?" *Journal of Economic Literature, 26,* 3, September 1988: 1073–1119.

Schaefer, Richard T. *Racial and Ethnic Groups,* 9th ed. Upper Saddle River, N.J.: Prentice Hall, 2004.

Scherer, Michael. "The Return of the Poppy Fields." *Mother Jones,* May 19, 2003.

Schlafly, Phyllis. *The Phyllis Schlafly Report, 13,* November 1979.

Schmidt, Gunter, and Volkmar Sigusch. "Sex Differences in Response to Psychosexual Stimulation by Films and Slides." *Journal of Sex Research, 6,* November, 268–283.

Schmitt, Richard B. "Some Towns Jail Indigents Illegally and Get Free Labor." *Wall Street Journal,* February 2, 1982:1, 16.

Schneider, Keith. "Burning Trash for Energy: Is It an Endangered Industry?" *New York Times,* October 11, 1994:A18.

Schneider, Keith. "Nuclear Disarmament Raises Fear on Storage of 'Triggers.'" *New York Times,* February 26, 1992:A1.

Schoenfeld, A. Clay, Robert F. Meier, and Robert J. Griffin. "Constructing a Social Problem: The Press and the Environment." *Social Problems, 27,* October 1979:38–61.

Schoepfer, Andrea, and Alex R. Piquero. "Self-Control, Moral Beliefs, and Criminal Activity." *Deviant Behavior, 27,* 2006: 51–71.

Schottland, Charles I. *The Social Security Plan in the U.S.* New York: Appleton, 1963.

Schreiber, Jan. *The Ultimate Weapon: Terrorists and the World Order.* New York: Morrow, 1978.

Schrieke, Bertram J. *Alien Americans.* New York: Viking, 1936.

Schumpeter, Joseph A. *The Sociology of Imperialism.* New York: Meridian, 1955 (first published in 1919).

Schuster, Lynda. "Industrialization of Brazilian Village Brings Jobs at Cost of Heavy Pollution and Even Death." *Wall Street Journal,* April 15, 1985:28.

Schwidrowski, Klaus. "Italy's Mafia Blight." *World Press Review, 17,* March 1980:56.

Scott, Gregg. "'It's a Sucker's Outfit:' How Urban Gangs Enable and Impede the Reintegration of Ex-Convicts." *Ethnography, 51,* 1, 2004:107–140.

Scott, Janny. "White Flight: This Time Toward Harlem." *New York Times,* February 25, 2001.

Scott, Monster Kody. *Monster: The Autobiography of an L.A. Gang Member.* New York: Penguin Books, 1994.

Scully, Diana. "Negotiating to Do Surgery." In *Dominant Issues in Medical Sociology,* 3rd ed. Howard D. Schwartz, ed. New York: McGraw-Hill, 1994:146–152.

Scully, Diana. *Understanding Sexual Violence: A Study of Convicted Rapists.* Boston: Unwin Hyman, 1990.

Scully, Diana, and Joseph Marolla. "'Riding the Bull at Gilley's': Convicted Rapists Describe the Rewards of Rape." In *Down-to-Earth Sociology: Introductory Readings,* 13th ed., James M. Henslin, ed. New York: Free Press, 2005:48–62. Originally appeared in *Social Problems, 32,* 3, February 1985:251–263.

Seib, Gerald F. "U.S. Aides Say Toxins on a Cambodian Leaf Hint at Chemical War." *Wall Street Journal,* September 15, 1981:22.

Seligmann, Jean. "The Date Who Rapes." *Newsweek,* April 9, 1984:91–92.

Sellin, Thorsten. "The Negro Criminal: A Statistical Note." *Annals of the American Academy of Political and Social Sciences, 140,* Part II, November 1928:52–64.

"Serum Results Study Update." *Love Canal Health News.* Troy, New York: Center for Environmental Health, Spring 2006.

Seventh Special Report to the U.S. Congress on Alcohol and Health. Rockville, Md.: U.S. Department of Health and Human Services, 1990.

Sewall, Sarah B., and Carl Kaysen, eds. *The United States and the International Criminal Court: National Security and International Law.* Lanham, Md.: Rowman and Littlefield, 2000.

Shaffer, Harry G. "$1,000,000,000,000." *Republic,* May 1986:24.

Shafir, Gershon, and Yoav Peled. "Citizenship and Stratification in an Ethnic Democracy." *Ethnic and Racial Studies, 21,* 3, May 1998: 408–427.

Shapiro, Joseph P. "Euthanasia's Home: What the Dutch Experience Can Teach Americans about Assisted Suicide." *U.S. News* online, January 17, 1997.

Shaw, Sue. "Wretched of the Earth." *New Statesman, 20,* March 1987:19–20.

Sheehy, Gail. *Hustling: Prostitution in Our Wide-Open Society.* New York: Dell, 1973.

Shellenbarger, Sue. "Companies Help Solve Day-Care Problems." *Wall Street Journal,* July 22, 1994:B1.

Shellenbarger, Sue. "Sales Offers Women Fairer Pay, but Bias Lingers." *Wall Street Journal,* January 24, 1995:B1, B14.

Sheppard, Nathaniel, Jr. "Chicago Project Dwellers Live Under Siege." *New York Times,* August 6, 1980:A14.

Shibutani, Tamotsu. "On the Personification of Adversaries." In *Human Nature and Collective Behavior,* Tamotsu Shibutani, ed. Englewood Cliffs, N.J.: Prentice Hall, 1970:223–233.

Shilts, Randy. *And the Band Played On: People, Politics and the AIDS Epidemic.* New York: St. Martin's, 1987.

Shim, Kelly H., and Marshall DeBerry. *Criminal Victimization in the United States, 1986.* Washington, D.C.: U.S. Department of Justice, Bureau of Justice Statistics, August 1988.

Shinnar, Revel, and Shlomo Shinnar. "The Effects of the Criminal Justice System on the Control of Crime: A Quantitative Approach." *Law and Society Review, 9,* Summer 1975:581–611.

Shishkin, Philip, and David Crawford. "In Afghanistan, Heroin Trade Soars Despite U.S. Aid." *Wall Street Journal,* January 18, 2006.

Shively, JoEllen. "Cowboys and Indians." In *Down-to-Earth Sociology: Introductory Readings,* 10th ed., James M. Henslin, ed. New York: Free Press, 1999:104–116.

Shribman, David. "Even After 10 Years, Victims of Love Canal Can't Quite Escape It." *Wall Street Journal,* March 9, 1989:A1, A8.

Silver, Jonathan M. "Medical Terms—A Two-Way Block?" *Colloquy: The Journal of Physician-Patient Communications,* November 1979:4–10.

Silverman, Deidre. "Sexual Harassment: The Working Women's Dilemma." *Building Feminist Theory: Essays from Quest.* New York: Longman, 1981:84–93.

Simmel, Georg. "The Sociology of Conflict." *American Journal of Sociology, 9,* January 1904:490–525; March 1904:672–689; and May 1904:798–811.

Simon, David R. "The Political Economy of Crime." In *Political Economy: A Critique of American Society,* Scott G. McNall, ed. Glenview, Ill.: Scott Foresman, 1981:347–366.

Simon, Judit, Anita Patel, and Michelle Sleed. "The Costs of Alcoholism." *Journal of Mental Health, 14,* 4, August 2005:321–330.

Simon, Julian L. "The Case for Greatly Increased Immigration." *The Public Interest, 102,* Winter 1991:89–103.

Simon, Julian L. Conversation with the author. March 23, 1982.

Simon, Julian L. *The Economics of Population Growth.* Princeton, N.J.: Princeton University Press, 1977.

Simon, Julian L. "Global Confusion, 1980: A Hard Look at the Global 2000 Report." *Public Interest, 62,* Winter 1980:3–20.

Simon, Julian L. *Theory of Population and Economic Growth.* New York: Blackwell, 1986.

Simon, Julian L. *The Ultimate Resource.* Princeton, N.J.: Princeton University Press, 1981.

Simon, Steven. "The New Terrorism: Securing the Nation Against a Messianic Foe." In *Sociology,* 33rd ed., Kurt Finsterbusch, ed., New York: McGraw-Hill/Dushkin, 2004:215–220.

Simons, Marlise. "Social Change and Amazon Indians." In *Life in Society: Readings to Accompany Sociology: A Down-to-Earth Approach,* 7th ed. James M. Henslin, ed. Boston: Allyn & Bacon, 2005: 158–165.

Simpson, George Eaton, and J. Milton Yinger. *Racial and Cultural Minorities: An Analysis of Prejudice and Discrimination,* 4th ed. New York: Harper & Row, 1972.

Sindler, Allan P. *Bakke, De Funis, and Minority Admissions: The Quest for Equal Opportunity.* New York: Longman, 1978.

Sitomer, Curtis J. "Fencing Out Pornography Without Fencing in Free Speech." *Christian Science Monitor,* March 13, 1986:23.

Skinner, B. F. *Beyond Freedom and Dignity.* New York: Knopf, 1971.

Skinner, B. F. *Science and Human Behavior.* New York: Macmillan, 1953.

Skinner, B. F. *Walden Two.* New York: Macmillan, 1948.

Skinner, Jonathan, James N. Weinstein, Scott M. Sporer, and John E. Wennberg. "Racial, Ethnic, and Geographic Disparities in Rates of Knee Arthroplasty Among Medicare Patients." *New England Journal of Medicine, 349,* 14, October 2, 2003: 1350–1359.

Slikker, William, Jr. "Behavioral, Neurochemical, and Neurohistological Effects of Chronic Marijuana Smoke Exposure in the Nonhuman Primate." In *Marijuana Cannabinoids Neurobiology and Neurophysiology,* Laura Murphy and Andrzej Bartke, eds. Boca Raton, Florida: CRC Press, 1992.

Smedley, Brian D., Adrienne Y. Stith, and Alan R. Nelson, eds. *Unequal Treatment: Confronting Racial and Ethnic Disparities in Health Care.* Washington, D.C.: The National Academies Press, 2003.

Smith, Barbara Ellen. *Digging Our Own Graves: Coal Miners and the Struggle over Black Lung Disease.* Philadelphia: Temple University Press, 1987.

Smith, Clark. "Oral History as 'Therapy': Combatants' Accounts of Vietnam War." In *Strangers at Home: Vietnam Veterans Since the War,* Charles R. Figley and Seymore Leventman (eds.). New York: Praeger, 1980:9–34.

Smith, Douglas A., and Christy A. Visher. "Street-Level Justice: Situational Determinants of Police Arrest Decisions." *Social Problems, 29,* December 1981:167–177.

Smith, Harold, "A Colossal Cover-Up." *Christianity Today,* December 1986:16–17.

Smith, James P., and Barry Edmonston, eds. *The New American: Economic, Demographic, and Fiscal Effects of Immigration.* Washington, D.C.: National Academy Press, 1997.

Smith, Kristen F., and Vern L. Bengtson. "Positive Consequences of Institutionalization: Solidarity Between Elderly Parents and Their Middle-Aged Children." *The Gerontologist, 19,* October 1979:438–447.

Smith, Wesley J. "Dependence or Death? Oregonians Make a Chilling Choice." *Wall Street Journal,* February 25, 1999.

Snipp, C. Matthew, and Alan L. Sorkin, "American Indian Housing: An Overview of Conditions and Public Policy." In *Race, Ethnicity, and Minority Housing in the United States,* Jamshid A. Momeni, ed. New York: Greenwood, 1986:147–175.

Snow, Ronald W., and Orville R. Cunningham. "Age, Machismo, and the Drinking Locations of Drunken Drivers: A Research Note." *Deviant Behavior, 6,* 1985:57–66.

Snyder, Howard. *Court Careers of Juvenile Offenders.* Washington, D.C.: Office of Juvenile Justice and Delinquency Prevention, 1988.

"Social Darwinism in Sweden." *Report* (Alberta Edition), *28,* 14, July 9, 2001:4.

Solomon, Deborah. "Shift in Federal Bench Spurs Governors, Legislators to Battle Roe." *Wall Street Journal,* March 9, 2006.

Solomon, Jeanne, and Dan Rather. "The Kyshtym Disaster." A segment of *60 Minutes,* November 9, 1980 (Jean Solomon, producer, and Dan Rather, interviewer).

Solomon, Jolie. "Companies Try Measuring Cost Savings from New Types of Corporate Benefits." *Wall Street Journal,* December 29, 1988:B1.

"Some Facts About Members of New Congress," Associated Press, January 3, 2007.

Sorensen, Jesper B. "Perceptions of Women's Opportunity in Five Industrialized Nations." *European Sociological Review, 6,* 2, September 1990:151–164.

Sorokin, Pitrim A. *Social and Cultural Dynamics,* 4 vols. New York: American Book, 1937, 1941.

Sourcebook of Criminal Justice Statistics. Washington, D.C.: U.S. Government Printing Office, annual.

Spaeth, Anthony. "Court Settlement Stuns Bhopal Survivors." *Wall Street Journal,* February 22, 1989:A10.

Specter, Michael. "Plunging Life Expectancy Puzzles Russians." *New York Times,* August 1, 1995:A1, A6.

Specter, Michael. "Population Implosion Worries a Graying Europe." *New York Times,* July 10, 1998.

Specter, Michael. "TB Carriers See Clash of Liberty and Health." *New York Times,* October 14, 1992:A1, A20.

Speer, Albert. *Inside the Third Reich,* Richard and Clara Winston, trans. New York: Avon, 1970.

Spivak, Jonathan. "Israel's Discrimination Problem." *Wall Street Journal,* December 3, 1980:28.

Spunt, Barry. "The Current New York City Heroin Scene." *Substance Use and Misuse, 38,* 10, 2003:1539–1549.

Squires, Gregory D. "Racial Profiling, Insurance Style: Insurance Redlining and the Uneven Development of Metropolitan Areas." *Journal of Urban Affairs, 25,* 4, 2003:391–410.

Srole, Leo, et al. *Mental Health in the Metropolis: The Midtown Manhattan Study.* New York: New York University Press, 1978.

Stafford, Linda, Sonya R. Kennedy, JoAnne E. Lehman, and Gail Arnold. "Wealth in America." *ISR Newsletter,* Winter 1986–87.

"Stakeholders and Radiological Protection: Lessons from Chernobyl 20 Years After." Committee on Radiation Protection and Public Health. Nuclear Energy Agency, 2006.

Stalenheim, Peter, Damien Fruchart, Wuyi Omitoogun, and Catalina Perdomo. "Military Expenditures." *Stockholm International Peace Research Institute Yearbook,* 2006:15–16.

Stanford, Sally. "Madamhood as a Vocation." In *In Their Own Behalf: Voices from the Margin,* Charles H. McCaghy, James K. Skipper, Jr., and Mark Lefton, eds. New York: Appleton, 1968:204–207.

Starfield, Barbara, Judy Robertson, and Anne W. Riley. "Social Class Gradients and Health in Childhood." *Ambulatory Pediatrics,* July–August 2002.

Starr, Mark. "Violence on the Right." *Newsweek,* March 4, 1985:23, 25–26.

Starr, Mark, and Frank Maier. "Chicago's Gang Warfare." *Newsweek,* January 28, 1985:32.

"State of Food Insecurity in the World 2005." Food and Agriculture Organization of the United Nations, 2005.

Statistical Abstract of the United States. Washington, D.C.: U.S. Bureau of the Census, annual.

Stein, Peter J. "The Diverse World of Single Adults." In *Marriage and Family in a Changing Society,* 4th ed., James M. Henslin, ed. New York: Free Press, 1992:93–103.

Steinhauer, Jennifer. "Angry at Managed Care, Doctors Start Fighting Back." *New York Times,* January 10, 1999a.

Steinhauer, Jennifer. "For Women in Medicine, a Road to Compromise, Not Perks." *New York Times,* March 1, 1999b.

Steinhauer, Jennifer. "So, the Tumor Is on the Left, Right?" *New York Times,* April 1, 2001.

Steinhauer, Jennifer, and Ford Fessenden. "Medical Retreads: Doctors Punished by State But Prized at the Hospitals." *New York Times,* March 27, 2001.

Steinhoff, Patricia G., and Milton Diamond. *Abortion Politics: The Hawaii Experience.* Honolulu: University Press of Hawaii, 1977.

Steinmetz, Suzanne K. *Duty Bound: Elder Abuse and Family Care.* Newbury Park, Calif.: Sage, 1988.

Steinmetz, Suzanne K., and Murray A. Straus (eds.). *Violence in the Family.* New York: Dodd Mead, 1974.

Stevens, Amy. "Sensible Victims Will Be Hoping Their Burglar Drives Up in a Rolls." *Wall Street Journal,* April 8, 1992:B1.

Stevens, Charles W. "Advance in Hydrogen Storage May Make Use of Abundant Element More Practical." *Wall Street Journal,* March 8, 1989:B4.

Stevens, Charles W. "Integration Is Elusive Despite Recent Gains; Social Barriers Remain." *Wall Street Journal,* September 29, 1980:1.

Stevens, William K. "Great Plains or Great Desert?" *New York Times,* May 28, 1996.

Stevens, William K. "Science Academy Disputes Attack on Global Warming." *New York Times,* April 22, 1998.

Stockard, Jean, and Miriam M. Johnson. *Sex Roles: Sex Inequality and Sex Role Development.* Englewood Cliffs, N.J.: Prentice Hall, 1980.

Stolberg, Sheryl Gay. "AIDS Is Becoming an Epidemic of Silence Among Blacks." *New York Times,* June 29, 1998.

Stolberg, Sheryl Gay. "Blacks Found on Short End of Heart Attack Procedure." *New York Times,* May 10, 2001.

Stolz, Martin, and Matthew L. Wald. "Interior Department Rejects Interim Plan for Nuclear Waste." *New York Times,* September 9, 2006.

Stouffer, Samuel A., Arthur A. Lumsdaine, Marion Harper Lumsdaine, Robin M. Williams, Jr., M. Brewster Smith, Irving L. Janis, Shirley A. Star, and Leonard S. Cottrell, Jr. *The American Soldier: Combat and Its Aftermath,* vol. 2. New York: Wiley, 1949.

Straus, Murray A. "Explaining Family Violence." *Marriage and Family in a Changing Society,* 4th ed., James M. Henslin, ed. New York: Free Press, 1992:344–356.

Straus, Murray A. "Victims and Aggressors in Marital Violence." *American Behavioral Scientist, 23,* May–June 1980:681–704.

Straus, Murray A., and Richard J. Gelles. "Violence in American Families: How Much Is There and Why Does It Occur?" In *Troubled Relationships,* Elam W. Nunnally, Catherine S. Chilman, and Fred M. Cox, eds. Newbury Park, Calif.: Sage, 1988:141–162.

Straus, Murray A., Richard J. Gelles, and Suzanne K. Steinmetz. *Behind Closed Doors: Violence in the American Family.* New York: Anchor/Doubleday, 1980.

Strobel, Lee. *Reckless Homicide: Ford's Pinto Trial.* South Bend, Ind.: And Books, 1980.

Strohschein, Lisa A. "Parental Divorce and Child Mental Health Trajectories." *Journal of Marriage and Family, 67,* 2005: 1286–1300.

Strom, Stephanie. "A Charity's Enviable Problem: Race to Spend Buffett Billions." *New York Times,* August 13, 2006.

Stroud, Joseph S. "Ogallala Aquifer Starting to Run on Empty." *Express-News,* August 16, 2006.

Struck, Doug. "Canada in Quandary over Gas Emissions." *Washington Post,* October 5, 2006.

"Suicide Rates." United Nations: World Health Organization, 2004.

"Suit Settled by Neil Bush." *New York Times,* March 29, 1992:A43.

Surgeon General of the United States. "Surgeon General's Report." Washington, D.C.: Centers for Disease Control and Prevention, 2005.

Sutherland, Edwin H. *Principles of Criminology,* 4th ed. Philadelphia: Lippincott, 1947.

Sutherland, Edwin H. *The Professional Thief.* Chicago: University of Chicago Press, 1937.

Sutherland, Edwin H. *White Collar Crime.* New York: Dryden, 1949.

Suttles, Gerald D. *The Social Order of the Slum: Ethnicity and Territory in the Inner City.* Chicago: University of Chicago Press, 1968.

Suzuki, Bob H. "Asian-American Families." In *Marriage and Family in a Changing Society,* 2nd ed., James M. Henslin, ed. New York: Free Press, 1985:104–119.

"Swedish Health Care in the 1990s." Stockholm: Federation of Swedish County Councils, July 2002.

Swedish Institute. "Fact Sheets on Sweden." February 1992.

Sykes, Gresham M. *Criminology.* New York: Harcourt, 1978.

Sykes, Gresham M., and David Matza. "Techniques of Neutralization: A Theory of Delinquency." *American Sociological Review, 22,* December 1957:664–670.

Szasz, Thomas. *Ceremonial Chemistry: The Ritual Persecution of Drugs, Addicts, and Pushers.* Garden City, N.Y.: Anchor, 1975.

Szasz, Thomas. *The Myth of Mental Illness.* Harper & Row, 1961.

Taslitz, Andrew E. "Willfully Blinded: On Date Rape and Self-Deception." *Harvard Journal of Law & Gender,* 2005:381–446.

Tavernise, Sabrina, and Donald G. McNeil, Jr. "Iraqi Dead May Total 600,000, Study Says." *New York Times,* October 10, 2006.

Tax Foundation. "America Celebrates Tax Freedom Day." Online, September 5, 2006.

Taylor, Monique M. *Harlem: Between Heaven and Hell.* Minneapolis: University of Minnesota, Press, 2002.

Teaford, John. *The Twentieth Century American City.* Baltimore: Johns Hopkins University Press, 1986.

Teller, Edward. "The Energy Crisis: No Contingency Plan." San Diego, Calif.: World Research, 1980.

Teresa, Vincent, with Thomas C. Renner. *My Life in the Mafia.* Greenwich, Conn.: Fawcett, 1973.

Tetreault, Steve. "Judge Dismisses Suit, But State is Happy." *Las Vegas Review-Journal,* September 28, 2006.

Thayer, Frederick C. "The Holy War on Surplus Americans: Soviet Dogma, Old-time Religion and Classical Economics." *Social Policy, 28,* 1, Fall 1997:8–18.

Thio, Alex. *Deviant Behavior.* Boston: Houghton Mifflin, 1978.

Thomas, Paulette. "Boston Fed Finds Racial Discrimination in Mortgage Lending Is Still Widespread." *Wall Street Journal,* October 9, 1992:A3.

Thornburgh, Nathan. "Inside the Life of the Migrants Next Door." *Time,* February 6, 2006:35–42.

Thorsheim, Peter. "Interpreting the London Fog Disaster of 1952." In *Smoke and Mirrors: The Politics and Culture of Air Pollution,* E. Malanie DuPuis, ed. New York: New York University Press, 2004:154–169.

Thrasher, Frederic M. *The Gang.* Chicago: University of Chicago Press, 1927.

Tierney, John. "Betting on the Planet." *New York Times,* December 2, 1990.

Tierney, John. "The Population Crisis Revisited." *Wall Street Journal,* January 20, 1986:16.

Tiger, Lionel, and Robin Fox. *The Imperial Animal.* New York: Holt, 1971.

Tilove, Jonathan. "Election Finds Secure Place in Annals of Black Politics." Newhouse News Service Online, November 9, 2006.

Timasheff, Nicholas S. *War and Revolution.* Joseph F. Scheuer, ed. New York: Sheed & Ward, 1965.

Tinker, John N. "Ethnic Bias in California Courts: A Case Study of Chicano and Anglo Felony Defendants." Paper presented at the annual meeting of the Society for the Study of Social Problems," 1981.

Toffler, Alvin. *Future Shock.* New York: Bantam, 1971.

Tolchin, Martin. "Fund Established to Help Pay Legal Fees for President's Son." *New York Times,* June 9, 1991b:1–31.

Tolchin, Martin. "Mildest Possible Penalty Is Imposed on Neil Bush." *New York Times,* April 19, 1991a:D2.

Tönnies, Ferdinand. *Community and Society.* East Lansing: Michigan State University, 1957 (originally published in 1887).

"To Restore and Protect the Great Lakes." Great Lakes Regional Collaboration Survey, December 2005.

Toth, Mike. "According to Professor Ehrlich, Shouldn't the World Be Over By Now?" *Stanford Review,* March 10, 1998.

Trebach, Arnold S. *The Great Drug War: And Radical Proposals That Could Make America Safe Again.* New York: Macmillan, 1987.

Trust, Cathy. "Presidential Panel Says 4 Major Unions Have Connections to Organized Crime." *Wall Street Journal,* January 15, 1986:48.

Tsuda, S., M. Murakami, N. Matsusaka, K. Kano, K. Taniguchi, Y. F. Sasaki. "DNA Damage Induced by Red Food Dyes Orally Administered to Pregnant and Male Mice." *Toxicological Sciences, 61,* 1, May 2001:92–99.

Turner, Jonathan H. *The Structure of Sociological Theory.* Homewood, Ill.: Dorsey, 1978.

Uchitelle, Louis. "How to Define Poverty? Let Us Count the Ways." *New York Times,* May 28, 2001.

Ullman, Sarah E. "Does Offender Violence Escalate When Rape Victims Fight Back?" *Journal of Interpersonal Violence, 13,* 2, April 1998:179–192.

Umberger, Alison. "The Transatlantic Dispute over Genetically Modified Organisms" Culture, Politics and Economics." *International Affairs Review, 14,* 1, Spring 2005.

UNICEF. "Female Genital Mutilation/Cutting: A Statistical Exploration." New York: United Nations, November 2005.

United Nations. "Fact Sheet: Sub-Saharan Africa." 2002.

United Nations Schoolbus. "Habitat at Unit 1." Online data, October 2006.

United Nations Surveys of Crime Trends and Operations of Criminal Justice Systems. New York: United Nations Office of Drugs and Crime, 2004.

United States Department of State. "Environmental Diplomacy: The Environment and U.S. Foreign Policy," April 22, 1997.

Useem, Michael. *The Inner Circle: Large Corporations and the Rise of Business Political Activity in the U.S. and U.K.* New York: Oxford University Press, 1984.

Useem, Michael. "The Social Organization of the American Business Elite." *American Sociological Review, 44,* August 1979:553–572.

U.S. Census Bureau. Estimates of Metro and Non-Metro Populations by State, 2005. FSCPE Population Estimates Program, 2006a.

U.S. Census Bureau. International Data Base, 2006b.

"U.S. Greenhouse Gas Inventory." Washington: Environmental Protection Agency, October 2006.

"U.S. Pesticide Exports and the Circle of Poison." Committee on Foreign Affairs, Subcommittee on Economic Policy, Trade and Environment, House of Representatives, January 26, 1994.

Valocchi, Steve. "The Racial Basis of Capitalism and the State, and the Impact of the New Deal on African Americans." *Social Problems, 41,* 3, August 1994:347–362.

van den Haag, Ernest. *Punishing Criminals: Concerning a Very Old and Painful Question.* New York: Basic Books, 1975.

van den Haag, Ernest, and John P. Conrad. *The Death Penalty: A Debate.* New York: Plenum, 1983.

Vatz, Richard E. "Attention Deficit Delirium." *Wall Street Journal,* July 27, 1994:A14.

Veevers, Jean E. *Childless by Choice.* Toronto: Butterworths, 1980.

Veevers, Jean E. "Voluntarily Childless Wives." *Sociology and Social Research, 57,* April 1973:356–366.

Vidal, David. "Bilingual Education Is Thriving but Criticized." *New York Times,* January 30, 1977.

Vigil, James Diego. *A Rainbow of Gangs: Street Cultures in the Mega-City.* Austin: University of Texas Press, 2002.

Waddington, Conrad H. *The Man-Made Future.* New York: St. Martin's, 1978.

Wagley, Charles, and Marvin Harris. *Minorities in the New World.* New York: Columbia University Press, 1958.

Wagman, Robert. "Is Japanese Mafia Threat to U.S.?" Syndicated column, November 27, 1981.

Wain, Barry. "Cambodia: What Remains of the Killing Ground." *Wall Street Journal,* January 29, 1981:24.

Waitzkin, Howard, and Barbara Waterman. *The Exploitation of Illness in Capitalist Society.* New York: Bobbs-Merrill, 1974.

Wald, Patricia M. "Making Sense Out of 12 Rights of Youth." *Human Rights, 4,* Fall 1974:13–29.

Walker, Alice, and Pratibha Parmar. *Warrior Marks: Female Genital Mutilation and the Sexual Binding of Women.* New York: Harcourt Brace, 1993.

Wallace, James N. "Green Revolution Hits Double Trouble." *U.S. News & World Report,* July 28, 1980:37, 40.

Wallace, L. J. David, Alice D. Calhoun, Kenneth E. Powell, Joann O'Neil, and Stephen P. James. *Homicide and Suicide Among Native Americans, 1979–1992.* Atlanta, Ga.: National Center for Injury Prevention and Control, 1996.

Walsh, Edward, and Amy Goldstein. "Supreme Court Upholds Two Key Abortion Rights." *Washington Post,* June 29, 2000.

Walsh, Mark. "Supreme Court Refuses to Weigh Race-Based College Admissions." Education Week on the WEB, July 1, 1996.

Ward, L. Monique, Edwina Hansbrough, and Eboni Walker. "Contributions of Music Video Exposure to Black Adolescents' Gender and Sexual Schemas." *Journal of Adolescent Research, 20,* 2, March 2005:143–166.

Ward, Russell A. "Patient-Provider Ties and Satisfaction with Health Care." *Research in the Sociology of Health Care, 9,* 1991: 169–190.

Watanabe, Teresa. "The Green Movement Is Getting Religion." *Los Angeles Times,* December 25, 1998.

Wax, Murray L. *Indian Americans: Unity and Diversity.* Englewood Cliffs, N.J.: Prentice Hall, 1971.

Wax, Murray L., and Rosalie H. Wax. "Cultural Deprivation as an Educational Ideology." *Journal of American Indian Education, 3,* January 15–18, 1964.

Wax, Murray L., and Rosalie H. Wax. "Indian Education for What?" *Midcontinent American Studies Journal, 6,* Fall 1965:164–170.

Wax, Rosalie H. "The Warrior Dropouts." *Trans-Action, 4,* May 1967:40–46.

Webber, Melvin M. "Urbanization and Communications." In *Communications Technology and Social Policy; Understanding the New Cultural Revolution.* George Gerbner, Larry P. Gross, and William H. Melody, eds. New York: John Wiley, 1973.

Weinberg, S. Kirson, and Henry Arond. "The Occupational Culture of the Boxer." *American Journal of Sociology, 57,* March 1953: 460–469.

Weitz, Rose. *Life with AIDS.* New Brunswick, N.J.: Rutgers University Press, 1991.

Weitzman, Lenore J., Deborah Eifler, Elizabeth Hokada, and Catherine Ross. "Sex Role Socialization in Picture Books for Pre-School Children." *American Journal of Sociology, 77,* May 1972: 1125–1150.

Weitzstein, Cheryl. "Gays Poised to Wed Legally." *Washington Times,* May 16, 2004.

Wells, John Warren. *Tricks of the Trade.* New York: New American Library, 1970.

Wells, Ken. "Hazelwood is Acquitted of Most Charges." *Wall Street Journal,* March 23, 1990:A3, A4.

Wells, Ken, and Charles McCoy. "Exxon Says Fast Containment of Oil Spill in Alaska Could Have Caused Explosion." *Wall Street Journal,* April 5, 1989:A3.

West, Richard W., and Gary Steiger. *The Effects of the Seattle and Denver Income Management Experiments on Alternative Measures of Labor Supply.* Menlo Park, Calif.: SRI International Research Memorandum, 72, May 1980.

Whitaker, Mark. "'It Was Like Breathing Fire . . .'" *Newsweek,* December 17, 1984:26–32.

White, Helene Raskin. "Marijuana Use and Delinquency: A Test of the 'Independent Cause' Hypothesis." *Journal of Drug Issues, 21,* 2, Spring 1991:231–256.

Whitehurst, Carol A. *Women in America: The Oppressed Majority.* Santa Monica, Calif.: Goodyear, 1977.

"WHO/Europe: Highlights on Health, Russian Federation 2005." World Health Organization, October 9, 2006.

Whyte, William Foote. "Street Corner Society." In *Down-to-Earth Sociology: Introductory Readings,* 8th ed., James M. Henslin, ed. New York: Free Press, 1995:59–67.

Whyte, William Foote. *Street Corner Society.* Chicago: University of Chicago Press, 1943.

Widdowson, Marc-Alain, Alana Sulk, Sandra N. Bulens, R. Suzanne Beard, et al. "Norovirus and Foodborne Disease, United States, 1991–2000." *Emerging Infectious Diseases, 11,* 1, January 2005.

Wilcox, Ansley II. 1957. Letter from Hooker Electro-chemical Company to the President of the Niagara Falls Board of Education, November 21, 1957.

"The Wild Wild East." CNN, March 12, 1995.

Willhelm, Sidney M. "Can Marxism Explain America's Racism?" *Social Problems, 28,* December 1980:98–112.

Williams, Robert C. "Three Mile Island as History." *Washington University Magazine, 50,* October 1980:56, 58–59, 61–63.

Williams, Terry M., and William Kornblum. *Growing Up Poor.* Lexington, Mass.: Lexington Books, 1985.

Williamson, Celia, and Terry Cluse-Tolar. "Pimp-Controlled Prostitution." *Violence Against Women, 8,* 9, September 2002: 1074–1092.

Williamson, John B., Judith A. Shindul, and Linda Evans. *Aging and Social Policy: Social Control or Social Justice?* Springfield, Ill.: Charles C. Thomas, 1985.

Willing, Richard. "U.S. Prisons to End Boot Camp Program." *USA Today,* February 4, 2005.

Wilson, James Q. "Lock 'Em Up and Other Thoughts on Crime." *New York Times Magazine,* March 9, 1975:11, 44–48.

Wilson, William Julius. *The Declining Significance of Race: Blacks and Changing American Institutions.* Chicago: University of Chicago Press, 1978.

Wilson, William Julius. Scholar in Residence Lecture at Southern Illinois University, Edwardsville, June 14, 1992.

Wilson, William Julius. *The Truly Disadvantaged: The Inner City, the Underclass, and Public Policy.* Chicago: University of Chicago Press, 1987.

Winick, Charles. "Physician Narcotic Addicts." *Social Problems, 9,* Fall 1961:174–186.

Winick, Charles, and Paul M. Kinsie. *The Lively Commerce: Prostitution in the United States.* Chicago: Quadrangle, 1971.

Wirth, Louis. "The Problem of Minority Groups." In *The Science of Man in the World Crisis,* Ralph Linton, ed. New York: Columbia University Press, 1945.

Wirth, Louis. "Urbanism as a Way of Life." *American Journal of Sociology, 44,* July 1938:1–24.

Wirtz, James J. "Do U.S. Nuclear Weapons Have a Future?" *Strategic Insights, 5,* 3, March 2006.

Wolf, Deborah Goleman. *The Lesbian Community.* Berkeley: University of California Press, 1979.

Wolfensohn, James D., and Kathryn S. Fuller. "Making Common Cause: Seeing the Forest for the Trees." *International Herald Tribune,* May 27, 1998:11.

Wolfgang, Marvin E. *Patterns in Criminal Homicide.* Philadelphia: University of Pennsylvania Press, 1958.

Wolfgang, Marvin, E., and Marc Reidel. "Rape, Race, and the Death Penalty." *American Journal of Orthopsychiatry, 45,* July 1975: 658–668.

"Women in the Riksdag." Swedish Parliament Factsheet. Online. November 2006.

"The World of the Child 6 Billion." Population Reference Bureau, 2000.

World Population Profile. Washington, D.C.: Bureau of the Census, U.S. Department of Commerce, various years.

Worm, Boris, et al. "Impacts of Biodiversity Loss on Ocean Ecosystem Services. *Science, 314,* 5800, November 3, 2006:787–790.

Wren, Christopher S. "Methadone Use Emerged in City Where It Is Now Challenged." *New York Times,* October 3, 1998.

Wright, Erik Olin. *Classes.* London: Verso, 1985.

Wright, Erik Olin. *Class Structure and Income Determination.* New York: Academic Press, 1979.

Wright, Quincy. *A Study of War,* 2 vols. Chicago: University of Chicago Press, 1942.

Wu, Qi. "China Cools Down Coal Liquefication." *China Business,* October 4, 2006.

Wurmbrand, Richard. *Torturado Por Cristo: La Iglesia Martir de Hoy.* Cuernavaca, Mexico: 1970.

Wyatt-Brown, Bertram. "Anatomy of a Wife-Killing." In *Violence and Society: A Reader,* Matthew Silberman, ed. Upper Saddle River, N.J.: Prentice Hall, 2003:182–189.

Yablonsky, Judy. "Survey Finds World Trend Toward More Liberal Abortion Laws." Associated Press, May 20, 1981.

Yonas, Michael A., Patricia O'Campo, Jessica G. Burke, and Andrea C. Gielen. "Neighborhood-Level Factors and Youth Violence: Giving Voice to the Perception of Prominent Neighborhood Individuals." *Health, Education, and Behavior OnlineFirst,* July 21, 2006.

Yuan, D. Y. "Voluntary Segregation: A Study of New York Chinatown." *Phylon, 24,* Fall 1963:255–265.

Zaitseva, Lyudmila, and Kevin Hand. "Nuclear Smuggling Chains: Suppliers, Intermediaries, and End-Users." *American Behavioral Scientist, 46,* 6, February 2003:822–844.

Zawitz, Marianne W., ed. *Report to the Nation on Crime and Justice,* 2nd ed. Washington, D.C.: U.S. Department of Justice, Bureau of Justice Statistics, July 1988.

Zernike, Kate. "Hospitals Say Meth Cases Are Rising, and Hurt Care." *New York Times,* January 18, 2006.

Zhou, Ming, and Yang Sao Xiong. "The Multifaceted American Experiences of the Children of Asian Immigrants: Lessons for Segmented Assimilation." *Ethnic and Racial Studies, 26,* 6, November 2005:119–1152.

Zibechi, Raul. "Brazilian Military Getting Ready for Vietnam-Style US Invasion." *Brazzil Magazine,* July 22, 2005.

Zielbauer, Paul. "Study Finds Pequot Businesses Lift Economy." *New York Times,* November 29, 2000.

Zimbardo, Philip G. "The Pathology of Imprisonment." In *Down-to-Earth Sociology: Introductory Readings,* 14th ed., James M. Henslin, ed. New York: Free Press, 2007.

Zimbardo, Philip G. "The Pathology of Imprisonment." *Society, 9,* 6, April 1972:4–8.

Zimmerman, Ann. "As Shoplifters Use High-Tech Scams, Retail Losses Rise." *Wall Street Journal,* October 25, 2006.

Zinn, Maxine Baca, and D. Stanley Eitzen. *Diversity in Families,* 2nd ed. New York: HarperCollins, 1990.

Zoucha-Jensen, Janice M., and Ann Coyne. "The Effects of Resistance Strategies on Rape." *American Journal of Public Health, 83,* 11, November 1993:1633–1634.

Zundel, Ernst. *Setting the Record Straight: Letters from Cell #7.* New York: Soaring Eagles Gallery, 2004.